£68·00

BUTTERWORTHS BANKING LAW HANDBOOK

BUTTERWORTHS
BANKING LAW
HANDBOOK

Third Edition

Consultant Editor
Graham S McBain   MA(Cantab), LLB(Cantab), LLM(Harv)
Solicitor

Materials prepared by Butterworths Editorial Staff

BUTTERWORTHS
LONDON, DUBLIN, EDINBURGH
1995

United Kingdom	Butterworths a Division of Reed Elsevier (UK) Ltd, Halsbury House, 35 Chancery Lane, LONDON WC2A 1EL and 4 Hill Street, EDINBURGH EH2 3JZ
Australia	Butterworths, SYDNEY, MELBOURNE, BRISBANE, ADELAIDE, PERTH, CANBERRA and HOBART
CANADA	BUTTERWORTHS CANADA LTD, TORONTO and VANCOUVER
Ireland	Butterworth (Ireland) Ltd, DUBLIN
Malaysia	Malayan Law Journal Sdn Bhd, KUALA LUMPUR
New Zealand	Butterworths of New Zealand Ltd, WELLINGTON and AUCKLAND
Puerto Rico	Butterworths of Puerto Rico, Inc, SAN JUAN
South Africa	Butterworths Publishers (Pty) Ltd, DURBAN
Singapore	Reed Elsevier (Singapore) Pte, Ltd, SINGAPORE
USA	Michie, CHARLOTTESVILLE, Virginia

A CIP catalogue record for this book is available from the British Library.

ISBN 0 406 08095 X

Typeset by Phoenix Photosetting, Chatham, Kent
Printed and bound in Great Britain by Clays Ltd, St Ives plc

PO 001146

PREFACE

Banking law has begun to assume an increasingly European complexion, as the common market develops. The changes wrought by the advent of further EC Directives has necessitated a third edition of the Banking Law Handbook. As before, every effort has been made to include not only primary legislation but also the secondary materials which supplement it and direct its operation, in particular Bank of England Notices. The Banking Law Handbook is intended to provide busy practitioners and persons working in the banking industry with a useful compilation of those materials to which they are often obliged to make reference. The Handbook is divided into four sections:

I   Banking and banking related statutes
II   Banking statutory instruments
III Bank of England Notices
IV EC Directives on banking

The contents of the Handbook take into account materials available as at 1 October 1995. Legislation which applies to Scotland or Northern Ireland only is omitted. Legislation included applies to Northern Ireland where indicated.

The Bank of England Notices are reproduced by kind permission of the Bank of England.

I am grateful to the staff at Butterworths for their help. My thanks also to Nick Martin-Smith, Patrick O'Connor and Nicola Stanhope of Clifford Chance for their suggestions and comments.

Graham McBain
October 1995

CONTENTS

PART II   STATUTORY INSTRUMENTS

PART III   BANK OF ENGLAND NOTICES

PART IV EC DIRECTIVES

PART I
STATUTES

BANKING

BANKERS' BOOKS EVIDENCE ACT 1879
(42 & 43 Vict c 11)

ARRANGEMENT OF SECTIONS

An Act to amend the Law of Evidence with respect to Bankers' Books
[23 May 1879]

1 Short title

This Act may be cited as the Bankers' Books Evidence Act 1879.   **[1]**

2 (*Repealed by the Statute Law Revision Act 1894.*)

3 Mode of proof of entries in bankers' books

Subject to the provisions of this Act, a copy of any entry in a banker's book shall in all legal proceedings be received as prima facie evidence of such entry, and of the matters, transactions, and accounts therein recorded.   **[2]**

4 Proof that book is a banker's book

A copy of an entry in a banker's book shall not be received in evidence under this Act unless it be first proved that the book was at the time of the making of the entry one of the ordinary books of the bank, and that the entry was made in the usual and ordinary course of business, and that the book is in the custody or control of the bank.

Such proof may be given by a partner or officer of the bank, and may be given orally or by an affidavit sworn before any commissioner or person authorised to take affidavits.   **[3]**

5 Verification of copy

A copy of an entry in a banker's book shall not be received in evidence under this Act unless it be further proved that the copy has been examined with the original entry and is correct.

Such proof shall be given by some person who has examined the copy with the original entry, and may be given either orally or by an affidavit sworn before any commissioner or person authorised to take affidavits.   **[4]**

6 Case in which banker, etc, not compellable to produce book, etc

A banker or officer of a bank shall not, in any legal proceeding to which the bank is not a party, be compellable to produce any banker's book the contents of which can be proved under this Act [or under the Civil Evidence (Scotland) Act 1988] [or Schedule 3 to the Prisoners and Criminal Proceedings (Scotland) Act 1993], or to appear as a witness to prove the matters, transactions, and accounts therein recorded, unless by order of a judge made for special cause. **[5]**

NOTE
Words in first pair of square brackets inserted by the Civil Evidence (Scotland) Act 1988, s 7(3) and words in second pair of square brackets inserted by the Prisoners and Criminal Proceedings (Scotland) Act 1993, s 29, Sch 3, para 7(3).

7 Court or judge may order inspection, etc

On the application of any party to a legal proceeding a court or judge may order that such party be at liberty to inspect and take copies of any entries in a banker's book for any of the purposes of such proceedings. An order under this section may be made either with or without summoning the bank or any other party, and shall be served on the bank three clear days before the same is to be obeyed, unless the court or judge otherwise directs. **[6]**

8 Costs

The costs of any application to a court or judge under or for the purposes of this Act, and the costs of anything done or to be done under an order of a court or judge made under or for the purposes of this Act shall be in the discretion of the court or judge, who may order the same or any part thereof to be paid to any party by the bank where the same have been occasioned by any default or delay on the part of the bank. Any such order against a bank may be enforced as if the bank was a party to the proceeding. **[7]**

[9 Interpretation of "bank", "banker", and "bankers' books"

(1) In this Act the expressions "bank" and "banker" mean—

[(a)　an institution authorised under the Banking Act 1987 or a municipal bank within the meaning of that Act;]

[(aa)　a building society (within the meaning of the Building Societies Act 1986);]

(b)　. . .

(c)　the National Savings Bank; and

(d)　the Post Office, in the exercise of its powers to provide banking services.

(2) Expressions in this Act relating to "bankers' books" include ledgers, day books, cash books, account books and other records used in the ordinary business of the bank, whether those records are in written form or are kept on microfilm, magnetic tape or any other form of mechanical or electronic data retrieval mechanism.] **[8]**

NOTES
This section substituted, with savings, by the Banking Act 1979, s 51(1), Sch 6, Pt I, para 1, Pt II, para 13.

Sub-s (1): sub-s (1)(a) substituted, with savings, by the Banking Act 1987, s 108(1), Sch 6, para 1; sub-s (1)(aa) inserted by the Building Societies Act 1986, s 120(1), Sch 18, Pt I, para 1; sub-s (1)(b) repealed by the Trustee Savings Banks Act 1985, ss 4(3), 7(3), Sch 4.

Modifications: by virtue of the Banking Coordination (Second Council Directive) Regulations 1992, SI 1992/3218, reg 82(1), Sch 10, Pt I, para 2, sub-s (1) of this section has effect as if the reference to an institution authorised under the Banking Act included a reference to a European deposit-taker.

10 Interpretation of "legal proceeding," "court," "judge"

In this Act—

The expression "legal proceeding" means any civil or criminal proceed-

ing or inquiry in which evidence is or may be given, and includes an
arbitration [and an application to, or an inquiry or other proceeding
before, the Solicitors Disciplinary Tribunal or any body exercising
functions in relation to solicitors in Scotland or Northern Ireland
corresponding to the functions of that Tribunal];

The expression "the court" means the court, judge, arbitrator, persons
or person before whom a legal proceeding is held or taken;

The expression "a judge" means with respect to England a judge of the
High Court . . ., and with respect to Scotland a lord ordinary of the
Outer House of the Court of Session, and with respect to Ireland a
judge of the High Court . . . in Ireland;

The judge of a county court may with respect to any action in such court
exercise the powers of a judge under this Act.   **[9]**

NOTES
Words in square brackets inserted by the Solicitors Act 1974, s 86.
Words omitted repealed by the Statute Law Revision Act 1898.

11 Computation of time

Sunday, Christmas Day, Good Friday, and any bank holiday shall be excluded
from the computation of time under this Act.   **[10]**

BANKING AND FINANCIAL DEALINGS ACT 1971
(1971 c 80)

ARRANGEMENT OF SECTIONS

*An Act to make new provision in place of the Bank Holidays Act 1871, to confer
power to suspend financial and other dealings on bank holidays or other
days, and to amend the law relating to bills of exchange and promissory
notes with reference to the maturity of bills and notes and other matters
affected by the closing of banks on Saturdays, and for purposes connected
therewith*   [16 December 1971]

1 Bank holidays

(1) Subject to subsection (2) below, the days specified in Schedule 1 to this
Act shall be bank holidays in England and Wales, in Scotland and in Northern
Ireland as indicated in the Schedule.

(2) If it appears to Her Majesty that, in the special circumstances of any
year, it is inexpedient that a day specified in Schedule 1 to this Act should be a
bank holiday, Her Majesty may by proclamation declare that that day shall not
in that year be a bank holiday and appoint another day in place of it; and the
day appointed by the proclamation shall, in that year, be a bank holiday under
this Act instead of the day specified in Schedule 1.

(3) Her Majesty may from time to time by proclamation appoint a special day to be, either throughout the United Kingdom or in any place or locality in the United Kingdom, a bank holiday under this Act.

(4) No person shall be compellable to make any payment or to do any act on a bank holiday under this Act which he would not be compellable to make or do on Christmas Day or Good Friday; and where a person would, apart from this subsection, be compellable to make any payment or to do any act on a bank holiday under this Act, his obligation to make the payment or to do the act shall be deemed to be complied with if he makes or does it on the next following day on which he is compellable to make or do it.

(5) The powers conferred on Her Majesty by subsections (2) and (3) above may, as respects Northern Ireland, be exercised by the Governor of Northern Ireland.

(6) The provision made by this section for January 2nd or 3rd to be a bank holiday in Scotland shall have effect for the year 1973 and subsequent years.

[11]

NOTES

Sub-s (5): the office of Governor of Northern Ireland was abolished by the Northern Ireland Constitution Act 1973, s 32(1), and any reference to the Governor is now to be construed as a reference to the Secretary of State for Northern Ireland; see s 40(1) of, and Sch 5, para 4(1) to, the 1973 Act.

2 Power to suspend financial dealings

(1) If it appears to the Treasury necessary or expedient so to do in the national interest, they may by order (made by statutory instrument, which shall be laid before Parliament after being made) give, with respect to a day specified in the order, all or any of the following directions, namely:—

    (a) a direction that, subject to any exceptions for which provision may be made by the order, no person carrying on the business of a banker shall, except with permission granted by or on behalf of the Treasury, effect on that day, in the course of that business, any transaction or, according as may be specified in the order, a transaction of such kind as may be so specified;

    (b) a direction that, subject as aforesaid, [no person] shall, on that day, except with permission so granted, deal in any foreign currency or, according as may be specified in the order, foreign currency of such kind as may be so specified;

    (c) a direction that, subject as aforesaid, [no person] shall on that day, except with permission so granted, deal in any gold [or, according as may be specified in the order, gold of such kind as may be so specified];

    (d) a direction that, subject as aforesaid, no person shall on that day, except with permission so granted, deal in silver bullion;

    (e) a direction that, subject as aforesaid, no member of any commodity exchange or, as the case may be, of any such commodity exchange as may be specified in the order, shall, on that day, except with permission so granted, deal thereon in futures in any commodity or, according as may be so specified, in futures in a commodity of such kind as may be so specified;

    (f) a direction that the Post Office shall, on that day, suspend the operation of any banking service provided by it in exercise of the power conferred on it by section 7(1)(b) of the Post Office Act 1969; and

(g) a direction that no member of a stock exchange in the United Kingdom shall, on that day, effect any transaction on that exchange [; and

(h) a direction that, subject as aforesaid, no building society shall, on that day, except with permission so granted, effect in the course of its business any transaction or, according as may be specified in the order, a transaction of such kind as may be so specified.]

(2) Subsection (1)(a) above shall not authorise the giving of directions to a person carrying on the business of a savings bank in respect of that business, nor to the Post Office in respect of any business carried on in exercise of the power conferred on it by section 7(1)(b) of the Post Office Act 1969.

(3) An obligation on a person to do a thing on a day on which he is prevented from doing it by an order under this section, or is unable to do it by reason of any such order, shall be deemed to be complied with if he does it so soon as practicable thereafter.

(4) A person who knowingly or recklessly contravenes a direction given by an order under subsection (1) of this section shall be guilty of an offence and liable—

(a) on summary conviction, to a fine of not more than [the prescribed sum];

(b) on conviction on indictment, to imprisonment for not more than two years or to a fine or to both.

(5) Where an offence under this section which has been committed by a body corporate is proved to have been committed with the consent or connivance of, or to be attributable to any neglect on the part of, a director, manager, secretary or other similar officer of the body corporate, or any person who was purporting to act in any such capacity he, as well as the body corporate, shall be guilty of that offence and shall be liable to be proceeded against accordingly.

Where the affairs of a body corporate are managed by its members, this subsection shall apply in relation to the acts and defaults of a member in connection with his functions of management as if he were a director of the body corporate.

(6) In this section—

["building society" means a building society within the meaning of the Building Societies Act 1986]

"commodity exchange" means an association established in the United Kingdom for the purpose of facilitating dealings by the members thereof in a commodity;

["foreign currency" means any currency other than sterling and any units of account defined by reference to more than one currency (whether or not including sterling); and

"gold" includes gold coin, gold bullion and gold wafers.]   **[12]**

NOTES

Sub-s (1): words in square brackets in sub-s (1)(b) and words in first pair of square brackets in sub-s (1)(c) substituted by the Finance Act 1981, s 136(2); words in second pair of square brackets in sub-s (1)(c) added by the Finance Act 1987, s 69(a); sub-s (1)(h) and the preceding word "and" added by the Building Societies Act 1986, s 120(1), Sch 18, Pt I, para 8(2).

Sub-s (4): words in square brackets in sub-s (4)(a) substituted by virtue of the Magistrates' Courts Act 1980, s 32(2).

Sub-s (6): definitions omitted repealed by the Finance Act 1981, s 139(6), Sch 19, Pt XI; definition of "building society" inserted by the Building Societies Act 1986, s 120(1), Sch 18, Pt I, para 8(3); definitions of "foreign currency" and "gold" substituted by the Finance Act 1987, s 69(b).

3 (*Amends the Bills of Exchange Act 1882, s 92(a), and substitutes s 14(1) thereof.*)

4 Consequential and supplementary

(1) Except as otherwise provided by this Act, in any enactment or instrument passed or made before the coming into force of this section (including an enactment of the Parliament of Northern Ireland or instrument having effect under such an enactment) any reference to a bank holiday under the Bank Holidays Act 1871 or a holiday under the Holidays Extension Act 1875 shall have effect as a reference to a bank holiday under this Act.

(2) . . .

(3) An order under section 2 above may be made with respect to a bank holiday or other day which is a non-business day for the purposes of the enactments relating to bills of exchange and promissory notes or with respect to a business day; but if a day specified under section 2(1) is otherwise a business day for those purposes, the order may declare it a non-business day.

(4), (5) . . .   **[13]**

NOTES
Sub-s (2): repealed by the Employment Act 1989, s 29(4), Sch 7, Pt II.
Sub-s (4): amends the Bills of Exchange Act 1882, s 92.
Sub-s (5): introduces Sch 2 to this Act (enactments repealed).

5 Short title and extent

(1) This Act may be cited as the Banking and Financial Dealings Act 1971.

(2) It is hereby declared that this Act . . . extends to Northern Ireland; . . .
                                                                                 [14]

NOTE
Sub-s (2): words omitted in first place repealed by the Employment Act 1989, s 29(4), Sch 7, Pt II; words omitted in second place repealed by the Northern Ireland Constitution Act 1973, s 41(1), Sch 6, Pt I.

SCHEDULES

SCHEDULE 1

Section 1

BANK HOLIDAYS

1. The following are to be bank holidays in England and Wales:—

Easter Monday.
The last Monday in May.
The last Monday in August.
26th December, if it be not a Sunday.
27th December in a year in which 25th or 26th December is a Sunday.

2. The following are to be bank holidays in Scotland:—

New Year's Day, if it be not a Sunday or, if it be a Sunday, 3rd January.
2nd January, if it be not a Sunday or, if it be a Sunday, 3rd January.
Good Friday.
The first Monday in May.
The first Monday in August.
Christmas Day, if it be not a Sunday or, if it be a Sunday, 26th December.

3. The following are to be bank holidays in Northern Ireland:—

17th March, if it be not a Sunday or, if it be a Sunday, 18th March.
Easter Monday.
The last Monday in May.
The last Monday in August.
26th December, if it be not a Sunday.
27th December in a year in which 25th or 26th December is a Sunday. **[15]**

(Sch 2 specifies enactments repealed by s 4(5).)

BANKING ACT 1979
(1979 c 37)

An Act to regulate the acceptance of deposits in the course of a business; to confer functions on the Bank of England with respect to the control of institutions carrying on deposit-taking businesses; to give further protection to persons who are depositors with such institutions; to make provision with respect to advertisements inviting the making of deposits; to restrict the use of names and descriptions associated with banks and banking; to prohibit fraudulent inducement to make a deposit; to amend the Consumer Credit Act 1974 and the law with respect to instruments to which section 4 of the Cheques Act 1957 applies; to repeal certain enactments relating to banks and banking; and for purposes connected therewith [4 April 1979]

1–37 *(Repealed by the Banking Act 1987, s 108(2), Sch 7, Pt I.)*

PART IV
MISCELLANEOUS AND GENERAL

38–46 *(S 38 amends the Consumer Credit Act 1974, ss 74, 114, 185(2); ss 39–46 repealed by the Banking Act 1987, s 108(2), Sch 7, Pt I.)*

47 Defence of contributory negligence

In any circumstances in which proof of absence of negligence on the part of a banker would be a defence in proceedings by reason of section 4 of the Cheques Act 1957, a defence of contributory negligence shall also be available to the banker notwithstanding the provisions of section 11(1) of the Torts (Interference with Goods) Act 1977. **[16]**

48–51 *(Ss 48–50 repealed by the Banking Act 1987, s 108(2), Sch 7, Pt I; s 51 introduces Schs 6, 7 to this Act (consequential amendments and repeals).)*

52 Short title, commencement and extent

(1) This Act may be cited as the Banking Act 1979.

(2) This Act extends to Northern Ireland.

(3) This Act shall come into operation on such day as the Treasury may appoint by order made by statutory instrument; and different days may be so appointed for different provisions of this Act and for such different purposes of the same provision as may be specified in the order.

(4) Any reference in any provision of this Act to "the appointed day" shall be construed as a reference to the day appointed for the purposes of that provision; and any reference in this Act to the day appointed for the purposes of any provision of this Act—

(a) shall be construed as a reference to the day appointed under this section for the coming into operation of that provision; and
(b) where different days are appointed for different purposes of that provision, shall be construed, unless an order under this section otherwise provides, as a reference to the first day so appointed. **[17]**

(Schs 1–5 repealed by the Banking Act 1987, s 108(2), Sch 7, Pt I; Sch 6, in so far as unrepealed, specifies consequential amendments made by s 51; Sch 7 repealed by the Banking Act 1987, s 108(2), Sch 7, Pt I.)

BANKING ACT 1987
(1987 c 22)

ARRANGEMENT OF SECTIONS

PART I

REGULATION OF DEPOSIT-TAKING BUSINESS

The Bank of England and the Board of Banking Supervision

PART II

THE DEPOSIT PROTECTION SCHEME

PART III

BANKING NAMES AND DESCRIPTIONS

PART IV

OVERSEAS INSTITUTIONS WITH REPRESENTATIVE OFFICES

PART V
RESTRICTION ON DISCLOSURE OF INFORMATION

PART VI
MISCELLANEOUS AND SUPPLEMENTARY

SCHEDULES

An Act to make new provision for regulating the acceptance of deposits in the course of a business, for protecting depositors and for regulating the use of banking names and descriptions; to amend section 187 of the Consumer Credit Act 1974 in relation to arrangements for the electronic transfer of funds; to clarify the powers conferred by section 183 of the Financial Services Act 1986; and for purposes connected with those matters

[15 May 1987]

PART I
REGULATION OF DEPOSIT-TAKING BUSINESS

The Bank of England and the Board of Banking Supervision

1 Functions and duties of the Bank of England

(1) The Bank of England (in this Act referred to as "the Bank") shall have the powers conferred on it by this Act and the duty generally to supervise the institutions authorised by it in the exercise of those powers.

(2) It shall also be the duty of the Bank to keep under review the operation of this Act and developments in the field of banking which appear to it to be relevant to the exercise of its powers and the discharge of its duties.

(3) The Bank shall, as soon as practicable after the end of each of its financial years, make to the Chancellor of the Exchequer and publish in such manner as it thinks appropriate a report on its activities under this Act in that year; and the Chancellor of the Exchequer shall lay copies of every such report before Parliament.

(4) Neither the Bank nor any person who is a member of its Court of Directors or who is, or is acting as, an officer or servant of the Bank shall be liable in damages for anything done or omitted in the discharge or purported discharge of the functions of the Bank under this Act unless it is shown that the act or omission was in bad faith. **[18]**

NOTES

Transitional provision: see s 107, Sch 5, para 1.

Modifications: as to modifications to this section, see the Banking Coordination (Second Council Directive) Regulations 1992, SI 1992/3218, reg 47, Sch 8, para 2; see **[693]**.

2 The Board of Banking Supervision

(1) As soon as practicable after the coming into force of this section the Bank shall establish a committee to be known as the Board of Banking Supervision.

(2) The Board shall consist of—

(a) three ex officio members, namely, the Governor of the Bank for the time being, who shall be the chairman of the Board, the Deputy Governor of the Bank for the time being and the executive director of the Bank for the time being responsible for the supervision of institutions authorised under this Act; and

(b) six independent members, that is to say, members appointed jointly by the Chancellor of the Exchequer and the Governor, being persons having no executive responsibility in the Bank.

(3) It shall be the duty of the independent members to give such advice as they think fit to the ex officio members—

(a) on the exercise by the Bank of its functions under this Act, either generally or in any particular respect or in relation to a particular institution or institutions; and

(b) on any matter relating to or arising out of the exercise of those functions.

(4) The Bank shall make regular reports to the Board on matters which the Bank considers relevant to the discharge by the independent members of their duty under subsection (3) above and shall provide them with such other information as they may reasonably require.

(5) The ex officio members shall give written notice to the Chancellor of the Exchequer in any case in which it is decided that the advice of the independent members should not be followed and the independent members shall be entitled to place before the Chancellor the reasons for their advice.

(6) The Board shall prepare an annual report on its activities and that report shall be included in the report made by the Bank under section 1(3) above for the financial year in question.

(7) Section 1(4) above shall apply to an act or omission by a member of the Board in the discharge or purported discharge of his functions under this section as it applies to an act or omission of a person there mentioned in the discharge or purported discharge of the functions of the Bank.

(8) Schedule 1 to this Act shall have effect with respect to the Board. **[19]**

NOTE
Modifications: as to modifications to this section, see the Banking Coordination (Second Council Directive) Regulations 1992, SI 1992/3218, reg 47, Sch 8, para 3; see **[693]**.

Restriction on acceptance of deposits

3 Restriction on acceptance of deposits

(1) Subject to section 4 below, no person shall in the United Kingdom accept a deposit in the course of carrying on (whether there or elsewhere) a business which for the purposes of this Act is a deposit-taking business unless that person is an institution for the time being authorised by the Bank under the following provisions of this Part of this Act.

(2) Any person who contravenes this section shall be guilty of an offence and liable—

(a) on conviction on indictment, to imprisonment for a term not exceeding two years or to a fine or to both;

(b) on summary conviction, to imprisonment for a term not exceeding six months or to a fine not exceeding the statutory maximum or to both.

(3) The fact that a deposit has been taken in contravention of this section shall not affect any civil liability in respect of the deposit or the money deposited.   **[20]**

NOTE
Transitional provisions: see s 107, Sch 5, paras 2–5, 7(3).

4 Exempted persons and exempted transactions

(1) Section 3 above shall not apply to the acceptance of a deposit by the Bank or by a person for the time being specified in Schedule 2 to this Act.

(2) The exemption of a person specified in that Schedule shall be subject to any restriction there specified in the case of that person.

(3) The Treasury may after consultation with the Bank by order amend that Schedule—

(a) by adding any person or relaxing any restriction; or

(b) by removing any person for the time being specified in it or imposing or extending any restriction.

(4) Section 3 above shall apply to any transaction prescribed for the purposes of this subsection by regulations made by the Treasury.

(5) Regulations under subsection (4) above may prescribe transactions by reference to any factors appearing to the Treasury to be appropriate and, in particular, by reference to all or any of the following—

(a) the amount of the deposit;

(b) the total liability of the person accepting the deposit to his depositors or to any other creditors;

(c) the circumstances in which or the purpose for which the deposit is made;

(d) the identity of the person by whom the deposit is made or accepted, including his membership of a class whose membership is determined otherwise than by the Treasury;

(e) the number of, or the amount involved in, transactions of any particular description carried out by the person accepting the deposit or the frequency with which he carries out transactions of any particular description.

(6) Regulations under subsection (4) above may make any exemption for which they provide subject to compliance with specified conditions of requirements.

(7) Any order under subsection (3)(a) above and any regulations under subsection (4) above shall be subject to annulment in pursuance of a resolution of either House of Parliament, and no order shall be made under subsection (3)(b) above unless a draft of it has been laid before and approved by a resolution of each House of Parliament. **[21]**

NOTE
Regulations and orders: the Banking Act 1987 (Exempt Transactions) Regulations 1988, SI 1988/646, as amended by SI 1989/465, SI 1990/20, SI 1990/1018, SI 1990/1529, SI 1991/29, SI 1991/2168, SI 1994/2567, and as modified by the Solicitors' Incorporated Practices Order 1991, SI 1991/2684, the Registered Foreign Lawyers Order 1991, SI 1991/2831, the Banking Coordination (Second Council Directive) Regulations 1992, SI 1992/3218; the Banking Act 1987 (Exempt Persons) Order 1989, SI 1989/125; the Banking Act 1987 (Exempt Persons) Order 1991, SI 1991/66; the Banking Act 1987 (Exempt Persons) Order 1991, SI 1991/2734; the Banking Act 1987 (Exempt Persons) Order 1993, SI 1993/953.

5 Meaning of "deposit"

(1) Subject to the provisions of this section, in this Act "deposit" means a sum of money [(whether denominated in a currency or in ecus)] paid on terms—

(a) under which it will be repaid, with or without interest or a premium, and either on demand or at a time or in circumstances agreed by or on behalf of the person making the payment and the person receiving it; and

(b) which are not referable to the provision of property or services or the giving of security;

and references in this Act to money deposited and to the making of a deposit shall be construed accordingly.

[(1A) In subsection (1) above 'ecu' means—

(a) the European currency unit as defined in Article 1 of Council Regulation No. 3320/94/EC

(b) any other unit of account which is defined by reference to the European currency unit as so defined.]

(2) For the purposes of subsection (1)(b) above, money is paid on terms which are referable to the provision of property or services or to the giving of security if, and only if—

(a) it is paid by way of advance or part payment under a contract for the sale, hire or other provision of property or services, and is repayable only in the event that the property or services is not or are not in fact sold, hired or otherwise provided;

(b) it is paid by way of security for the performance of a contract or by way of security in respect of loss which may result from the non-performance of a contract; or

(c) without prejudice to paragraph (b) above, it is paid by way of security for the delivery up or return of any property, whether in a particular state of repair or otherwise.

(3) Except so far as any provision of this Act otherwise provides, in this Act "deposit" does not include—

(a) a sum paid by the Bank or an authorised institution;

(b) a sum paid by a person for the time being specified in Schedule 2 to this Act;

(c) a sum paid by a person, other than a person within paragraph (a) or (b) above, in the course of carrying on a business consisting wholly or mainly of lending money;

(d) a sum which is paid by one company to another at a time when one is a subsidiary of the other or both are subsidiaries of another company or the same individual is a majority or principal shareholder controller of both of them; or

(e) a sum which is paid by a person who, at the time when it is paid, is a close relative of the person receiving it or who is, or is a close relative of, a director, controller or manager of that person.

(4) In the application of paragraph (e) of subsection (3) above to a sum paid by a partnership that paragraph shall have effect as if for the reference to the person paying the sum there were substituted a reference to each of the partners.

(5) In subsection (3)(e) above "close relative", in relation to any person, means—

(a) his spouse;

(b) his children and step-children, his parents and step-parents, his brothers and sisters and step-brothers and step-sisters; and

(c) the spouse of any person within paragraph (b) above.   **[22]**

NOTES

Commencement: 1 October 1987 (sub-ss (1), (2)–(5)) (SI 1987/1664); 1 July 1995 (sub-s (1A)) (SI 1995/1442).

Sub-ss (1), (1A): words in square brackets in sub-s (1), and sub-s (1A), inserted by the Credit Institutions (Protection of Depositors) Regulations 1995, SI 1995/1442, reg 45.

Modifications: as to modifications to this section, see the Banking Coordination (Second Council Directive) Regulations 1992, SI 1992/3218, reg 47, Sch 8, para 4; see **[693]**.

6 Meaning of "deposit-taking business"

(1) Subject to the provisions of this section, a business is a deposit-taking business for the purposes of this Act if—

(a) in the course of the business money received by way of deposit is lent to others; or

(b) any other activity of the business is financed, wholly or to any material extent, out of the capital of or the interest on money received by way of deposit.

(2) Notwithstanding that paragraph (a) or (b) of subsection (1) above applies to a business, it is not a deposit-taking business for the purposes of this Act if—

(a) the person carrying it on does not hold himself out as accepting deposits on a day to day basis; and

(b) any deposits which are accepted are accepted only on particular occasions, whether or not involving the issue of debentures or other securities.

(3) For the purposes of subsection (1) above all the activities which a person carries on by way of business shall be regarded as a single business carried on by him.

(4) In determining for the purposes of subsection (2)(b) above whether deposits are accepted only on particular occasions regard shall be had to the frequency of those occasions and to any characteristics distinguishing them from each other.

(5) For the purposes of subsection (2) above there shall be disregarded any deposit in respect of the acceptance of which the person in question is exempt from the prohibition in section 3 above and any money received by way of deposit which is not used in the manner described in subsection (1) above. **[23]**

7 Power to amend definitions

(1) The Treasury may after consultation with the Bank by order amend the meaning of deposit or deposit-taking business for the purposes of all or any provisions of this Act.

(2) Without prejudice to the generality of the power conferred by subsection (1) above, an order under that subsection amending the meaning of deposit-taking business may provide for taking into account as activities of an institution the activities of any person who is connected with it in such manner as is specified in the order.

(3) Any order under this section shall be subject to annulment in pursuance of a resolution of either House of Parliament.

(4) An order under this section may contain such transitional provisions as the Treasury think necessary or expedient and may exclude or modify the effect of the order on any other enactment which is expressed to have effect in relation to a deposit or a deposit-taking business within the meaning of this Act. **[24]**

NOTE

Order: the Banking Act 1987 (Meaning of Deposit) Order 1991, SI 1991/1776.

Authorisations

8 Applications for authorisation

(1) Any institution may make an application for authorisation to the Bank [other than—

(a) a credit institution incorporated in or formed under the law of any part of the United Kingdom whose principal place of business is outside the United Kingdom; and

(b) a credit institution incorporated in or formed under the law of another member State].

(2) Any such application—

(a) shall be made in such manner as the Bank may direct; and

(b) shall be accompanied by—

(i) a statement setting out the nature and scale of the deposit-taking business which the applicant intends to carry on, any plans of the applicant for the future development of *[26]* ness and particulars of the applicant's arrangements management of that business; and

(ii) such other information or documents as the Bank may re ably require for the purpose of determining the applicatio

(3) At any time after receiving an application and before determining it t. Bank may by written notice require the applicant or any person who is or is to be a director, controller or manager of the applicant to provide additional information or documents.

(4) The directions and requirements given or imposed under subsections (2) and (3) above may differ as between different applications.

(5) Any information or statement to be provided to the Bank under this section shall be in such form as the Bank may specify; and the Bank may by written notice require the applicant or any such person as is mentioned in subsection (3) above to provide a report by an accountant or other qualified person approved by the Bank on such aspects of that information as may be specified by the Bank.

(6) An application may be withdrawn by written notice to the Bank at any time before it is granted or refused. **[25]**

NOTE
Sub-s (1): words in square brackets added by the Banking Coordination (Second Council Directive) Regulations 1992, SI 1992/3218, reg 25.

9 Grant and refusal of authorisation

(1) The Bank may, on an application duly made in accordance with section 8 above and after being provided with all such information, documents and reports as it may require under that section, grant or refuse the application.

(2) The Bank shall not grant an application unless satisfied that the criteria specified in Schedule 3 to this Act are fulfilled with respect to the applicant.

(3) In the case of an application by an applicant whose principal place of business is in a country or territory outside the United Kingdom the Bank may regard itself as satisfied that the criteria specified in paragraphs 1, 4 and 5 of that Schedule are fulfilled if—

(a) the relevant supervisory authority in that country or territory informs the Bank that it is satisfied with respect to the prudent management and overall financial soundness of the applicant; and

(b) the Bank is satisfied as to the nature and scope of the supervision exercised by that authority.

(4) In determining whether to grant or refuse an application the Bank may take into account any matters relating—

(a) to any person who is or will be employed by or associated with the applicant for the purposes of the applicant's deposit-taking business; and

(b) if the applicant is a body corporate, to any other body corporate in the same group or to any director or controller of any such other body.

(5) No authorisation shall be granted to a partnership or unincorporated association if the whole of the assets available to it are owned by a single individual.

An authorisation granted to a partnership shall be granted in the partnership name and, without prejudice to sections 11 and 12 below, shall not be affected by any change in the partners.

[(7) Before granting an authorisation to a credit institution incorporated in or formed under the law of any part of the United Kingdom which is—

    (a) a subsidiary undertaking;
    (b) a subsidiary undertaking of the parent undertaking; or
    (c) controlled by the parent controller,

of a credit institution which is for the time being authorised to act as such an institution by the relevant supervisory authority in another member State, the Bank shall consult that authority.] **[26]**

NOTES

Commencement: 1 October 1987 (sub-ss (1)–(6)) (SI 1987/1664); 1 January 1993 (sub-s (7)) (SI 1992/3218).

Sub-s (7): added by the Banking Coordination (Second Council Directive) Regulations 1992, SI 1992/3218, reg 26.

10 Notice of grant or refusal

(1) Where the Bank grants an application for authorisation it shall give written notice of that fact to the applicant.

(2) Where the Bank proposes to refuse an application for authorisation it shall give the applicant written notice of its intention to do so, stating the grounds on which it proposes to act and giving particulars of the applicant's rights under subsection (4) below.

(3) Where the ground or a ground for the proposed refusal is that the Bank is not satisfied that the criterion in paragraph 1 of Schedule 3 to this Act is fulfilled in the case of any such person as is there mentioned, the Bank shall give that person a copy of the notice mentioned in subsection (2) above, together with a statement of his rights under subsection (4) below.

(4) An applicant who is given a notice under subsection (2) above and a person who is given a copy of it under subsection (3) above may within such period (not being less than twenty-eight days) as is specified in the notice make written representations to the Bank; and where such representations are made the Bank shall take them into account before reaching a decision on the application.

(5) Where the Bank refuses an application it shall give written notice of that fact to the applicant and to any such person as is mentioned in subsection (3) above, stating the reasons for the refusal and [(except in the case of a refusal in pursuance of a direction under section 26A below)] giving particulars of the rights conferred by section 27 below.

(6) Any notice under subsection (5) above shall be given before the end of the period of six months beginning with the day on which the application was received by the Bank or, where the Bank has under section 8 above required additional information or documents in connection with the application, before the end of whichever of the following first expires—

    (a) the period of six months beginning with the day on which the additional information or documents are provided;
    (b) the period of twelve months beginning with the day on which the application was received.

(7) The Bank may omit from the copy given to a person under subsection (3) above and from a notice given to him under subsection (5) above any matter which does not relate to him.   **[27]**

NOTE
Sub-s (5): words in square brackets inserted by the Banking Coordination (Second Council Directive) Regulations 1992, SI 1992/3218, reg 32(2)(a).

11 Revocation of authorisation

(1) The Bank may revoke the authorisation of an institution if it appears to the Bank that—

- (a) any of the criteria specified in Schedule 3 to this Act is not or has not been fulfilled, or may not be or may not have been fulfilled, in respect of the institution;
- (b) the institution has failed to comply with any obligation imposed on it by or under this Act;
- (c) a person has become a controller of the institution in contravention of section 21 below or has become or remains a controller after being given a notice of objection under section 22, 23 or 24 below;
- (d) the Bank has been provided with false, misleading or inaccurate information by or on behalf of the institution or, in connection with an application for authorisation, by or on behalf of a person who is or is to be a director, controller or manager of the institution; or
- (e) the interests of depositors or potential depositors of the institution are in any other way threatened, whether by the manner in which the institution is conducting or proposes to conduct its affairs or for any other reason.

[(1A) The Bank may revoke the authorisation of a credit institution incorporated in or formed under the law of any part of the United Kingdom if—

- (a) it appears to the Bank that the institution's principal place of business is or may be outside the United Kingdom;
- (b) it appears to the Bank that the institution has carried on in the United Kingdom or elsewhere a listed activity (other than the acceptance of deposits from the public) without having given prior notice to the Bank of its intention to do so;
- (c) the Bank is informed by The Securities and Investments Board, or a connected UK authority having regulatory functions in relation to the provision of financial services, that the institution—
  - (i) has contravened any provision of the Financial Services Act 1986 or any rules or regulations made under it;
  - (ii) in purported compliance with any such provision, has furnished that Board or authority with false, misleading or inaccurate information;
  - (iii) has contravened any prohibition or requirement imposed under that Act; or
  - (iv) has failed to comply with any statement of principle issued under that Act;
- (d) the Bank is informed by the Director General of Fair Trading that the institution, or any of the institution's employees, agents or associates (whether past or present) or, where the institution is a body corporate, any controller of the institution or an associate of any such controller, has done any of the things specified in paragraphs (a) to (d) of section 25(2) of the Consumer Credit Act 1974;

(e) it appears to the Bank that the institution has failed to comply with any obligation imposed on it by the Banking Coordination (Second Council Directive) Regulations 1992 [or the Credit Institutions (Protection of Depositors) Regulations 1995]; or

(f) the Bank is informed by a supervisory authority in another member State that the institution has failed to comply with any obligation imposed on it by or under any rule of law in force in that State for purposes connected with the implementation of the Second Council Directive [or Directive 94/19/EC on deposit-guarantee schemes].]

(2) The Bank may revoke the authorisation of an institution if it appears to the Bank that the institution—

(a) has not accepted a deposit in the United Kingdom in the course of carrying on a deposit-taking business (whether there or elsewhere) within the period of twelve months beginning with the day on which it was authorised; or

(b) having accepted a deposit or deposits as aforesaid, has subsequently not done so for any period of more than six months.

(3) If in the case of an authorised institution whose principal place of business is in a country or territory outside the United Kingdom it appears to the Bank that the relevant supervisory authority in that country or territory has withdrawn from the institution an authorisation corresponding to that conferred by the Bank under this Part of this Act, the Bank may revoke the authorisation and shall do so if that country or territory is a member State.

[(3A) In relation to a credit institution incorporated in or formed under the law of any part of the United Kingdom, subsection (3) above shall have effect as if the words "and shall do so if that country or territory is a member State" were omitted.]

(4) In the case of an authorised institution which is an authorised person under the Financial Services Act 1986 or holds a consumer credit licence under the Consumer Credit Act 1974 the Bank may revoke the authorisation if it appears to the Bank that the institution has ceased to be an authorised person under the said Act of 1986 (otherwise than at the request or with the consent of the institution) that the licence under the said Act of 1974 has been revoked.

(5) The Treasury may after consultation with the Bank by order make provision corresponding to subsection (4) above in relation to any authorisation or licence granted under such other enactments as may appear to the Treasury to be appropriate; but any such order shall be subject to annulment in pursuance of a resolution of either House of Parliament.

(6) If in the case of an authorised institution wherever incorporated it appears to the Bank that—

(a) a winding-up order has been made against it in the United Kingdom; or

(b) a resolution for its voluntary winding up in the United Kingdom has been passed,

the Bank shall revoke the authorisation; and the Bank may revoke the authorisation of any authorised institution incorporated outside the United Kingdom if it appears to the Bank that an event has occurred in respect of it outside the United Kingdom which corresponds as nearly as may be to either of those mentioned in paragraphs (a) and (b) above.

(7) The Bank may revoke the authorisation of an authorised institution incorporated in the United Kingdom if it appears to the Bank that—

(a) a composition or arrangement with creditors has been made in respect of the institution;

(b) a receiver or manager of the institution's undertaking has been appointed; or

(c) possession has been taken, by or on behalf of the holders of any debenture secured by a charge, of any property of the institution comprised in or subject to the charge;

or, in the case of an authorised institution incorporated elsewhere, that an event has occurred in respect of it which corresponds as nearly as may be to any of those mentioned in paragraphs (a), (b) and (c) above.

(8) The Bank may revoke the authorisation of an authorised institution if it appears to the Bank that an administration order has been made in relation to the institution under section 8 of the Insolvency Act 1986 [or under Article 21 of the Insolvency (Northern Ireland) Order 1989].

(9) The Bank shall revoke the authorisation of an unincorporated institution if it appears to the Bank that a winding-up order has been made against it in the United Kingdom and may revoke the authorisation of such an institution if it appears to the Bank that—

(a) the institution has been dissolved; or

(b) a bankruptcy order, an award of sequestration, an order of adjudication of bankruptcy or a composition or arrangement with creditors has been made or a trust deed for creditors granted in respect of that institution or any of its members; or

(c) any event corresponding as nearly as may be to any of those mentioned in paragraph (b) above or in subsection (6)(a) or (b) or (7)(b) or (c) above has occurred in respect of that institution or any of its members; or

(d) the whole of the assets available to the institution have passed into the ownership of a single individual.

[(10) The rules and prohibitions referred to in subsection (1A)(c) above include the rules of any recognised self-regulating organisation of which the institution is a member and any prohibition imposed by virtue of those rules; and in subsection (1A)(d) above—

"associate" has the same meaning as in section 25(2) of the Consumer Credit Act 1974;

"controller" has the meaning given by section 189(1) of that Act.] **[28]**

NOTES

Commencement: 1 October 1987 (sub-ss (1), (2), (3), (4)–(9)) (SI 1987/1664); 1 January 1993 (sub-ss (1A), (3A), (10)) (SI 1992/3218).

Transitional provision: see s 107, Sch 5, para 2(2).

Sub-s (1A): inserted by the Banking Coordination (Second Council Directive) Regulations 1992, SI 1992/3218, reg 28(1). For transitional provisions, see reg 83, Sch 11, Pt II, para 5; see **[694]**. Words in square brackets inserted by the Credit Institutions (Protection of Depositors) Regulations 1995, SI 1995/1442, reg 49(1).

Sub-s (3A): inserted by the Banking Coordination (Second Council Directive) Regulations 1992, SI 1992/3218, reg 28(2).

Sub-s (8): words in square brackets added by the Insolvency (Northern Ireland) Order 1989, SI 1989/2405 (NI 19), art 381(2), Sch 9, Pt II, para 49.

Sub-s (10): added by the Banking Coordination (Second Council Directive) Regulations 1992, SI 1992/3218, reg 28(3).

12 Restriction of authorisation

(1) Where it appears to the Bank—

(a) that there are grounds on which the Bank's power to revoke an institution's authorisation are exercisable; but
(b) that the circumstances are not such as to justify revocation,

the Bank may restrict the authorisation instead of revoking it.

(2) An authorisation may be restricted—

(a) by imposing such limit on its duration as the Bank thinks fit;
(b) by imposing such conditions as it thinks desirable for the protection of the institution's depositors or potential depositors; or
(c) by the imposition both of such a limit and of such conditions.

(3) A limit on the duration of an authorisation shall not be such as to allow the authorisation to continue in force for more than three years from the date on which it is imposed; and such a limit may, in particular, be imposed in a case in which the Bank considers that an institution should be allowed time to repay its depositors in an orderly manner.

(4) The conditions imposed under this section may in particular—

(a) require the institution to take certain steps or to refrain from adopting or pursuing a particular course of action or to restrict the scope of its business in a particular way;
(b) impose limitations on the acceptance of deposits, the granting of credit or the making of investments;
(c) prohibit the institution from soliciting deposits, either generally or from persons who are not already depositors;
(d) prohibit it from entering into any other transaction or class of transactions;
(e) require the removal of any director, controller or manager;
(f) specify requirements to be fulfilled otherwise than by action taken by the institution.

(5) Any condition imposed under this section may be varied or withdrawn by the Bank; and any limit imposed under this section on the duration of an authorisation may be varied but not so as to allow the authorisation to continue in force for longer than the period mentioned in subsection (3) above from the date on which the limit was first imposed.

(6) An institution which fails to comply with any requirement or contravenes any prohibition imposed on it by a condition under this section shall be guilty of an offence and liable—

(a) on conviction on indictment, to a fine;
(b) on summary conviction, to a fine not exceeding the statutory maximum.

(7) The fact that a condition imposed under this section has not been complied with (whether or not constituting an offence under subsection (6) above) shall be a ground for the revocation of the authorisation in question but shall not invalidate any transaction.

(8) An institution whose authorisation is restricted by the imposition of a limit on its duration may apply under section 8 above for a new authorisation and, if that authorisation is granted, the restricted authorisation shall cease to have effect. **[29]**

NOTES
Transitional provision: see s 107, Sch 5, para 3.
Modifications: as to modifications to this section, see the Credit Institutions (Protection of Depositors) Regulations 1995, SI 1995/1442, reg 49(2), at **[711K]**.

[12A Revocation or restriction on information from supervisory authority

(1) This section applies where, in the case of an authorised institution which is a credit institution incorporated in or formed under the law of any part of the United Kingdom, the Bank is informed by a supervisory authority in another member State that the institution is failing to comply with an obligation imposed by or under any rule of law in force in that State for purposes connected with the implementation of the Second Council Directive.

(2) The Bank shall as soon as practicable send a copy of the information received by it to every other authority which it knows is a connected UK authority.

(3) The Bank shall also—

(a) consider whether to exercise its powers under section 11 or 12 above; and

(b) notify its decision, and any action which it has taken or intends to take, to the supervisory authority and to every other authority which it knows is a connected UK authority.] [30]

NOTES
Commencement: 1 January 1993 (SI 1992/3218).
This section inserted by the Banking Coordination (Second Council Directive) Regulations 1992, SI 1992/3218, reg 29.

13 Notice of revocation or restriction

(1) Subject to section 14 below where the Bank proposes—

(a) to revoke an authorisation; or
(b) to restrict an authorisation; or
(c) to vary the restrictions imposed on an authorisation otherwise than with the agreement of the institution concerned,

the Bank shall give to the institution concerned written notice of its intention to do so.

(2) If the proposed action is within paragraph (b) or (c) of subsection (1) above the notice under that subsection shall specify the proposed restrictions or, as the case may be, the proposed variation.

(3) A notice under subsection (1) above shall state the grounds on which the Bank proposes to act and give particulars of the institution's rights under subsection (5) below.

[(3A) Where the Bank gives a notice under subsection (1) above to a credit institution incorporated in or formed under the law of any part of the United Kingdom, it shall give a copy of that notice to every other authority which the Bank knows is—

(a) a connected UK authority; or
(b) a supervisory authority in another member State in which the institution is carrying on a listed activity.]

(4) Where—

(a) the ground or a ground for a proposed revocation or for a proposal to impose or vary a restriction is that it appears to the Bank that the criterion in paragraph 1 of Schedule 3 to this Act is not or has not been fulfilled, or may not be or may not have been fulfilled, in the case of any person; or

(b) a proposed restriction consists of or includes a condition requiring the removal of any person as director, controller or manager,

the Bank shall give that person a copy of the notice mentioned in subsection (1) above, together with a statement of his rights under subsection (5) below.

(5) An institution which is given a notice under subsection (1) above and a person who is given a copy of it under subsection (4) above may within the period of fourteen days beginning with the day on which the notice was given make representations to the Bank.

(6) After giving a notice under subsection (1) above and taking into account any representations made under subsection (5) above the Bank shall decide whether—

(a) to proceed with the action proposed in the notice;
(b) to take no further action;
(c) if the proposed action was to revoke the institution's authorisation, to restrict its authorisation instead;
(d) if the proposed action was to restrict the institution's authorisation or to vary the restrictions on an authorisation, to restrict it or to vary the restrictions in a different manner.

(7) The Bank shall give the institution and any such person as is mentioned in subsection (4) above written notice of its decision and, except where the decision is to take no further action, the notice shall state the reasons for the decision and give particulars of the rights conferred by subsection (9) and section 27 below;

(8) A notice under subsection (7) above of a decision to revoke or restrict an authorisation or to vary the restrictions on an authorisation shall, subject to section 27(4) below, have the effect of revoking the authorisation or, as the case may be, restricting the authorisation or varying the restrictions in the manner specified in the notice.

(9) Where the decision notified under subsection (7) above is to restrict the authorisation or to vary the restrictions on an authorisation otherwise than as stated in the notice given under subsection (1) above the institution may within the period of seven days beginning with the day on which the notice was given under subsection (7) above make written representations to the Bank with respect to the restrictions and the Bank may, after taking those representations into account, alter the restrictions.

(10) A notice under subsection (7) above shall be given within the period of twenty-eight days beginning with the day on which the notice under subsection (1) above was given; and if no notice under subsection (7) is given within that period the Bank shall be treated as having at the end of that period given a notice under that subsection to the effect that no further action is to be taken.

(11) Where the Bank varies a restriction on an institution's authorisation with its agreement or withdraws a restriction consisting of a condition the variation or withdrawal shall be effected by written notice to the institution.

(12) The Bank may omit from the copy given to a person under subsection (4) above and from a notice given to him under subsection (7) above any matter which does not relate to him.   [31]

NOTES

Commencement: 1 October 1987 (sub-ss (1)–(3), (4)–(12)) (SI 1987/1664); 1 January 1993 (sub-s (3A)) (SI 1992/3218).

Sub-s (3A): inserted by the Banking Coordination (Second Council Directive) Regulations 1992, SI 1992/3218, reg 30(1).

14 Mandatory revocation and restriction in cases of urgency

(1) No notice need be given under section 13 above in respect of—

    (a) the revocation of an institution's authorisation in any case in which revocation is mandatory under section 11 above; or

    (b) the imposition or variation of a restriction on an institution's authorisation in any case in which the Bank considers that the restriction should be imposed or varied as a matter of urgency.

(2) In any such case the Bank may by written notice to the institution revoke the authorisation or impose or vary the restriction.

(3) Any such notice shall state the reasons for which the Bank has acted and, in the case of a notice imposing or varying a restriction, particulars of the rights conferred by subsection (5) and by section 27 below.

(4) Subsection (4) of section 13 above shall apply to a notice under subsection (2) above imposing or varying a restriction as it applies to a notice under subsection (1) of that section in respect of a proposal to impose or vary a restriction; but the Bank may omit from a copy given to a person by virtue of this subsection any matter which does not relate to him.

(5) An institution to which a notice is given under this section of the imposition or variation of a restriction and a person who is given a copy of it by virtue of subsection (4) above may within the period of fourteen days beginning with the day on which the notice was given make representations to the Bank.

(6) After giving a notice under subsection (2) above imposing or varying a restriction and taking into account any representations made in accordance with subsection (5) above the Bank shall decide whether—

    (a) to confirm or rescind its original decision; or

    (b) to impose a different restriction or to vary the restriction in a different manner.

(7) The Bank shall within the period of twenty-eight days beginning with the day on which the notice was given under subsection (2) above give the institution concerned written notice of its decision under subsection (6) above and, except where the decision is to rescind the original decision, the notice shall state the reasons for the decision.

(8) Where the notice under subsection (7) above is of a decision to take the action specified in subsection (6)(b) above the notice under subsection (7) shall have the effect of imposing the restriction or making the variation specified in the notice and with effect from the date on which it is given.

(9) Where a notice of the proposed revocation of an institution's authorisation under section 13 above is followed by a notice revoking its authorisation under this section the latter notice shall have the effect of terminating any right to make representations in respect of the proposed revocation and any pending appeal proceedings in respect of a decision implementing that proposal. **[32]**

15 Surrender of authorisation

(1) An authorised institution may surrender its authorisation by written notice to the Bank.

(2) A surrender shall take effect on the giving of the notice or, if a later date is specified in it, on that date; and where a later date is specified in the notice the institution may by a further written notice to the Bank substitute an earlier date, not being earlier than that on which the first notice was given.

(3) The surrender of an authorisation shall be irrevocable unless it is expressed to take effect on a later date and before that date the Bank by notice in writing to the institution allows it to be withdrawn.

[(4) Where the Bank receives a notice of surrender under subsection (1) above from a credit institution incorporated in or formed under the law of any part of the United Kingdom, it shall give a copy of that notice to every other authority which the Bank knows is—

    (a) a connected UK authority; or

    (b) a supervisory authority in another member State in which the institution is carrying on a listed activity.] **[33]**

NOTES

Commencement: 1 October 1987 (sub-ss (1)–(3)) (SI 1987/1664); 1 January 1993 (sub-s (4)) (SI 1992/3218).

Sub-s (4): added by the Banking Coordination (Second Council Directive) Regulations 1992, SI 1992/3218, reg 30(2).

16 Statement of principles

(1) The Bank shall, as soon as practicable after the coming into force of this section, publish in such manner as it thinks appropriate a statement of the principles in accordance with which it is acting or proposing to act—

    (a) in interpreting the criteria specified in Schedule 3 to this Act and the grounds for revocation specified in section 11 above; and

    (b) in exercising its power to grant, revoke or restrict an authorisation.

(2) If in the course of a financial year of the Bank it makes a material change in the principles in accordance with which it is acting or proposing to act as mentioned in subsection (1) above it shall include a statement of the change in the report made by it for that year under section 1(3) above; and the Bank may, at any time, publish in such manner as it thinks appropriate a statement of the principles in accordance with which it is acting or proposing to act as mentioned in that subsection. **[34]**

17 Information as to authorised institutions

(1) Every report made by the Bank under section 1(3) above shall contain a list of the institutions which are authorised under this Act at the end of the financial year to which the report relates.

(2) The Bank shall make available to any person on request and on payment of such fee, if any, as the Bank may reasonably require a list of the institutions which are authorised either at the date of the request or at such earlier date, being not more than one month earlier, as may be specified in the list.

(3) The Bank may give public notice of the fact that an institution has ceased to be authorised. **[35]**

NOTE

Modifications: as to modifications to this section, see the Banking Coordination (Second Council Directive) Regulations 1992, SI 1992/3218, reg 47, Sch 8, para 5; see **[693]**.

18 False statements as to authorised status

(1) No person other than an authorised institution shall—

    (a) describe himself as an authorised institution; or

    (b) so hold himself out as to indicate or to be reasonably understood to indicate that he is an authorised institution.

(2) No person shall falsely state, or do anything which falsely indicates, that he is entitled although not an authorised institution to accept a deposit in the course of carrying on a business which for the purposes of this Act is a deposit-taking business.

(3) Any person who contravenes this section shall be guilty of an offence and liable—

    (a) on conviction on indictment, to imprisonment for a term not exceeding two years or to a fine or to both;

    (b) on summary conviction, to imprisonment for a term not exceeding six months or to a fine not exceeding the statutory maximum or to both.   **[36]**

NOTE

Modifications: as to modifications to this section, see the Banking Coordination (Second Council Directive) Regulations 1992, SI 1992/3218, reg 47, Sch 8, para 6; see **[693]**.

Directions

19 Directions to institutions

(1) The Bank may give an institution directions under this section—

    (a) when giving it notice that the Bank proposes to revoke its authorisation;

    (b) at any time after such a notice has been given to the institution (whether before or after its authorisation is revoked);

    (c) when giving the institution a notice of revocation under section 14(2) above by virtue of section 11(6)(b) above in the case of a members' voluntary winding up;

    (d) at any time after the institution has served a notice surrendering its authorisation, whether with immediate effect or with effect from a later date specified in the notice;

    (e) at or at any time after the expiry (otherwise than by virtue of section 12(8) above) of a restricted authorisation of the institution;

    (f) at any time after a disqualification notice has been served on the institution under section 183 of the Financial Services Act 1986.

(2) Directions under this section shall be such as appear to the Bank to be desirable in the interests of the institution's depositors or potential depositors, whether for the purpose of safeguarding its assets or otherwise, and may in particular—

    (a) require the institution to take certain steps or to refrain from adopting or pursuing a particular course of action or to restrict the scope of its business in a particular way;

    (b) impose limitations on the acceptance of deposits, the granting of credit or the making of investments;

    (c) prohibit the institution from soliciting deposits either generally or from persons who are not already depositors;

(d) prohibit it from entering into any other transaction or class of transactions;

(e) require the removal of any director, controller or manager.

(3) No direction shall be given by virtue of paragraph (a) or (b) of subsection (1) above, and any direction given by virtue of either of those paragraphs shall cease to have effect, if the Bank gives the institution notice that it is not proposing to take any further action pursuant to the notice mentioned in that paragraph or if the Bank's decision to revoke the institution's authorisation is reversed on appeal.

(4) No direction shall be given by virtue of paragraph (d) of subsection (1) above, and any direction given by virtue of that paragraph shall cease to have effect, if the Bank allows the institution to withdraw the surrender of its authorisation.

(5) No direction shall be given to an institution under this section after it has ceased to have any liability in respect of deposits for which it had a liability at a time when it was authorised; and any such direction which is in force with respect to an institution shall cease to have effect when the institution ceases to have any such liability.

(6) An institution which fails to comply with any requirement or contravenes any prohibition imposed on it by a direction under this section shall be guilty of an offence and liable—

(a) on conviction on indictment, to a fine;

(b) on summary conviction, to a fine not exceeding the statutory maximum.

(7) A contravention of a prohibition imposed under this section shall not invalidate any transaction.   [37]

NOTE

Transitional provision: see s 107, Sch 5, para 6.

20 Notification and confirmation of directions

(1) A direction under section 19 above shall be given by notice in writing and may be varied by a further direction; and a direction may be revoked by the Bank by a notice in writing to the institution concerned.

(2) A direction under that section, except one varying a previous direction with the agreement of the institution concerned—

(a) shall state the reasons for which it is given and give particulars of the institution's rights under subsection (4) and section 27 below; and

(b) without prejudice to section 19(3), (4) and (5) above, shall cease to have effect at the end of the period of twenty-eight days beginning with the day in which it is given unless before the end of that period it is confirmed by a further written notice given by the Bank to the institution concerned.

(3) Where a direction requires the removal of a person as director, controller or manager of an institution the Bank shall give that person a copy of the direction (together with a statement of his rights under subsection (4) below) and, if the direction is confirmed, a copy of the notice mentioned in subsection (2)(b) above.

(4) An institution to which a direction is given which requires confirmation under subsection (2) above and a person who is given a copy of it under

subsection (3) above may, within the period of fourteen days beginning with the day on which the direction is given, make written representations to the Bank; and the Bank shall take any such representations into account in deciding whether to confirm the direction.

(5) The Bank may omit from the copies given to a person under subsection (3) above any matter which does not relate to him.   **[38]**

Objections to controllers

21 Notification of new or increased control

(1) [No person shall become a minority, 10 per cent., 20 per cent., 33 per cent., majority or principal shareholder controller, a parent controller or an indirect controller of an authorised institution unless]—

  (a) he has served on the Bank a written notice stating that he intends to become such a controller of the institution; and
  (b) either the Bank has, before the end of the period of three months beginning with the date of service of that notice, notified him in writing that there is no objection to his becoming such a controller of the institution or that period has elapsed without the Bank having served on him under section 22 or 23 below a written notice of objection to his becoming such a controller of the institution.

(2) Subsection (1) above applies also in relation to a person becoming a partner in an authorised institution which is a partnership formed under the law of any part of the United Kingdom.

(3) A notice under paragraph (a) of subsection (1) above shall contain such information as the Bank may direct and the Bank may, after receiving such a notice from any person, by notice in writing require him to provide such additional information or documents as the Bank may reasonably require for deciding whether to serve a notice of objection.

(4) Where additional information or documents are required from any person by a notice under subsection (3) above the time between the giving of the notice and the receipt of the information or documents shall be added to the period mentioned in subsection (1)(b) above.

(5) A notice served by a person under paragraph (a) of subsection (1) above shall not be regarded as a compliance with that paragraph except as respects his becoming a controller of the institution in question within the period of one year beginning—

  (a) in a case where the Bank has notified him that there is no objection to his becoming such a controller, with the date of that notification;
  (b) in a case where the period mentioned in paragraph (b) of that subsection has elapsed without any such notification and without his having been served with a written notice of objection, with the expiration of that period;
  (c) in a case in which he has been served with a notice of objection which has been quashed on appeal, with the date on which it is quashed.
                                                                          [39]

NOTE
  Sub-s (1): words in square brackets substituted for the words "No person shall become a minority, majority or principal shareholder controller or an indirect controller of an authorised institution incorporated in the United Kingdom unless—" by the Banking Coordination (Second Council Directive) Regulations 1992, SI 1992/3218, reg 31(1), subject to reg 46(a); see **[684]**.

22 Objection to new or increased control

(1) The Bank may serve a notice of objection under this section on a person who has given a notice under section 21 above unless it is satisfied—

    (a) that the person concerned is a fit and proper person to become a controller of the description in question of the institution;

    (b) that the interests of depositors and potential depositors of the institution would not be in any other manner threatened by that person becoming a controller of that description of the institution; and

    (c) without prejudice to paragraphs (a) and (b) above, that, having regard to that person's likely influence on the institution as a controller of the description in question the criteria in Schedule 3 to this Act would continue to be fulfilled in the case of the institution or, if any of those criteria is not fulfilled, that that person is likely to undertake adequate remedial action.

[(1A) Before deciding whether or not to serve a notice of objection under this section in any case where—

    (a) the person concerned is, or is a parent controller of, a credit institution which is for the time being authorised to act as such an institution by the relevant supervisory authority in another member State; and

    (b) the notice under section 21 above stated an intention to become a parent controller,

the Bank shall consult that authority.]

(2) Before serving a notice of objection under this section the Bank shall serve the person concerned with a preliminary written notice stating that the Bank is considering the service on that person of a notice of objection; and that notice—

    (a) shall specify which of the matters mentioned in subsection (1) above the Bank is not satisfied about and, subject to subsection (5) below, the reasons for which it is not satisfied; and

    (b) shall give particulars of the rights conferred by subsection (3) below,

(3) A person served with a notice under subsection (2) above may, within the period of one month beginning with the day on which the notice is served, make written representations to the Bank; and where such representations are made the Bank shall take them into account in deciding whether to serve a notice of objection.

(4) A notice of objection under this section shall—

    (a) specify which of the matters mentioned in subsection (1) above the Bank is not satisfied about and, subject to subsection (5) below, the reasons for which it is not satisfied; and

    (b) give particulars of the rights conferred by section 27 below.

(5) Subsections (2)(a) and (4)(a) above shall not require the Bank to specify any reason which would in its opinion involve the disclosure of confidential information the disclosure of which would be prejudicial to a third party.

(6) Where a person required to give a notice under section 21 above in relation to his becoming a controller of any description becomes a controller of that description without having given the notice the Bank may serve him with a notice of objection under this section at any time within three months after becoming aware of his having done so and may, for the purpose of deciding

whether to serve him with such a notice, require him by notice in writing to provide such information or documents as the Bank may reasonably require.

(7) The period mentioned in section 21(1)(b) above (with any extension under subsection (4) of that section) and the period mentioned in subsection (6) above shall not expire, if it would otherwise do so, until fourteen days after the end of the period within which representations can be made under subsection (3) above. **[40]**

NOTES
Commencement: 1 October 1987 (sub-ss (1), (2)–(7)) (SI 1987/1664); 1 January 1993 (sub-s (1A)) (SI 1992/3218).
Sub-s (1A): inserted by the Banking Coordination (Second Council Directive) Regulations 1992, SI 1992/3218, reg 31(2).

23 Objection by direction of the Treasury

(1) The Treasury may direct the Bank to serve a notice of objection under this section on a person—

> (a) who has given notice under section 21 above of his intention to become a shareholder controller of any description of an institution [which is not a credit institution]; or
> (b) who has become such a controller without giving the required notice under that section,

if it appears to the Treasury that, in the event of his becoming or, as the case may be, as a result of his having become, such a controller, a notice could be served on the institution by the Treasury under section 183 of the Financial Services Act 1986 (disqualification or restriction of persons connected with overseas countries which do not afford reciprocal facilities for financial business).

(2) No direction shall be given in a case within subsection (1)(b) above more than three months after the Treasury becomes aware of the fact that the person concerned has become a controller of the relevant description.

(3) Any notice of objection served by virtue of a direction under this section shall state the grounds on which it is served. **[41]**

NOTE
Sub-s (1): words in square brackets in sub-s (1)(a) inserted by the Banking Coordination (Second Council Directive) Regulations 1992, SI 1992/3218, reg 32(2)(b).

24 Objection to existing shareholder controller

(1) Where it appears to the Bank that a person who is a shareholder controller of any description of an authorised institution incorporated in the United Kingdom is not or is no longer a fit and proper person to be such a controller of the institution it may serve him with a written notice of objection to his being such a controller of the institution.

(2) Before serving a notice of objection under this section the Bank shall serve the person concerned with a preliminary written notice stating that the Bank is considering the service on that person of a notice of objection; and that notice shall—

> (a) subject to subsection (5) below, specify the reasons for which it appears to the Bank that the person in question is not or is no longer a fit and proper person as mentioned in subsection (1) above; and
> (b) give particulars of the rights conferred by subsection (3) below.

(3) A person served with a notice under subsection (2) above may, within the period of one month beginning with the day on which the notice is served, make written representations to the Bank; and where such representations are made the Bank shall take them into account in deciding whether to serve a notice of objection.

(4) A notice of objection under this section shall—

(a) subject to subsection (5) below, specify the reasons for which it appears to the Bank that the person in question is not or is no longer a fit and proper person as mentioned in subsection (1) above; and
(b) give particulars of the rights conferred by section 27 below.

(5) Subsections (2)(a) and (4)(a) above shall not require the Bank to specify any reason which would in its opinion involve the disclosure of confidential information the disclosure of which would be prejudicial to a third party. **[42]**

25 Contraventions by controller

(1) Subject to subsection (2) below, any person who contravenes section 21 above by—

(a) failing to give the notice required by paragraph (a) of subsection (1) of that section; or
(b) becoming a controller of any description to which that section applies before the end of the period mentioned in paragraph (b) of that subsection in a case where the Bank has not served him with the preliminary notice under section 22(2) above,

shall be guilty of an offence.

(2) A person shall not be guilty of an offence under subsection (1) above if he shows that he did not know of the acts or circumstances by virtue of which he became a controller of the relevant description; but where any person becomes a controller of any such description without such knowledge and subsequently becomes aware of the fact that he has become such a controller he shall be guilty of an offence unless he gives the Bank written notice of the fact that he has become such a controller within fourteen days of becoming aware of that fact.

(3) Any person who—

(a) before the end of the period mentioned in paragraph (b) of subsection (1) of section 21 above becomes a controller of any description to which that subsection applies after being served with a preliminary notice under section 22(2) above;
(b) contravenes section 21 above by becoming a controller of any description after being served with a notice of objection to his becoming a controller of that description; or
(c) having become a controller of any description in contravention of that section (whether before or after being served with such a notice of objection) continues to be such a controller after such a notice has been served on him,

shall be guilty of an offence.

(4) A person guilty of an offence under subsection (1) or (2) above shall be liable on summary conviction to a fine not exceeding the fifth level on the standard scale.

(5) A person guilty of an offence under subsection (3) above shall be liable—

(a) on conviction on indictment, to imprisonment for a term not exceeding two years or to a fine or to both;

(b) on summary conviction, to a fine not exceeding the statutory maximum and, in respect of an offence under paragraph (c) of that subsection, to a fine not exceeding one tenth of the statutory maximum for each day on which the offence has continued.   **[43]**

26 Restrictions on and sale of shares

(1) The powers conferred by this section shall be exercisable where a person—

(a) has contravened section 21 above by becoming a shareholder controller of any description after being served with a notice of objection to his becoming a controller of that description; or

(b) having become a shareholder controller of any description in contravention of that section continues to be one after such a notice has been served on him; or

(c) continues to be a shareholder controller of any description after being served under section 24 above with a notice of objection to his being a controller of that description.

(2) The Bank may by notice in writing served on the person concerned direct that any specified shares to which this section applies shall, until further notice, be subject to one or more of the following restrictions—

(a) any transfer of, or agreement to transfer, those shares or, in the case of unissued shares, any transfer of or agreement to transfer the right to be issued with them shall be void;

(b) no voting rights shall be exercisable in respect of the shares;

(c) no further shares shall be issued in right of them or in pursuance of any offer made to their holder;

(d) except in a liquidation, no payment shall be made of any sums due from the institution on the shares, whether in respect of capital or otherwise.

(3) The court may, on the application of the Bank, order the sale of any specified shares to which this section applies and, if they are for the time being subject to any restrictions under subsection (2) above, that they shall cease to be subject to those restrictions.

(4) No order shall be made under subsection (3) above in a case where the notice of objection was served under section 22 or 24 above—

(a) until the end of the period within which an appeal can be brought against the notice of objection; and

(b) if such an appeal is brought, until it has been determined or withdrawn.

(5) Where an order has been made under subsection (3) above the court may, on the application of the Bank, make such further order relating to the sale or transfer of the shares as it thinks fit.

(6) Where shares are sold in pursuance of an order under this section the proceeds of sale, less the costs of the sale, shall be paid into court for the benefit of the persons beneficially interested in them; and any such person may apply to the court for the whole or part of the proceeds to be paid to him.

(7) This section applies—

(a) to all the shares in the institution of which the person in question is a controller of the relevant description which are held by him or any associate of his and were not so held immediately before he became such a controller of the institution; and

(b) where the person in question became a controller of the relevant description of an institution as a result of the acquisition by him or any associate of his of shares in another company to all the shares in that company which are held by him or any associate of his and were not so held before he became such a controller of that institution.

(8) A copy of the notice served on the person concerned under subsection (2) above shall be served on the institution or company to whose shares it relates and, if it relates to shares held by an associate of that person, on that associate.

(9) The jurisdiction conferred by this section shall be exercisable by the High Court and the Court of Session.   **[44]**

[Implementation of certain EC decisions

26A Treasury directions for implementing decisions

(1) In this section "relevant decision" means any decision of the Council or Commission of the Communities under article 9(4) of the Second Council Directive (relations with third countries: limitation or suspension of decisions regarding applications for authorisations).

(2) For the purpose of implementing a relevant decision, the Treasury may direct the Bank—

(a) to refuse an application for authorisation made by a credit institution incorporated in or formed under the law of any part of the United Kingdom;

(b) to defer its decision on such an application either indefinitely or for such period as may be specified in the direction; or

(c) to serve a notice of objection on a person—

(i) who has given notice under section 21 above of his intention to become a parent controller of any description of such an institution; or

(ii) who has become such a controller without giving the required notice under that section.

(3) A direction to the Bank may relate to a particular institution or a class of institution and may be given before the application in question or, as the case may be, any notice under section 21 above is received.

(4) Any notice of objection served by virtue of a direction falling within subsection (2)(c) above shall state the grounds on which it is served.

(5) A direction under this section may be revoked at any time by the Treasury, but such revocation shall not affect anything done in accordance with the direction before it was revoked.]   **[45]**

NOTES

Commencement: 1 January 1993 (SI 1992/3218).

This section and the preceding heading inserted by the Banking Coordination (Second Council Directive) Regulations 1992, SI 1992/3218, reg 32(1).

Appeals

27 Rights of appeal

(1) An institution which is aggrieved by a decision of the Bank—

(a) to refuse an application by the institution for authorisation [otherwise than in a case in which the refusal is in pursuance of a direction under section 26A above];

(b) to revoke its authorisation otherwise than in a case in which revocation is mandatory under section 11 above;

(c) to restrict its authorisation, to restrict it in a particular manner or to vary any restrictions of its authorisation; or

(d) to give it a direction under section 19 above or to vary a direction given to it under that section,

may appeal against the decision to a tribunal constituted in accordance with section 28 below.

(2) Where—

(a) the ground or a ground for a decision within paragraph (a), (b) or (c) of subsection (1) above is that mentioned in section 10(3) or 13(4)(a) above; or

(b) the effect of a decision within paragraph (c) or (d) of that subsection is to require the removal of a person as director, controller or manager of an institution,

the person to whom the ground relates or whose removal is required may appeal to a tribunal constituted as aforesaid against the finding that there is such a ground for the decision or, as the case may be, against the decision to require his removal.

(3) Any person on whom a notice of objection is served under section 22 or 24 above may appeal to a tribunal constituted as aforesaid against the decision of the Bank to serve the notice; but this subsection does not apply to a person in any case in which he has failed to give a notice or become or continued to be a controller in circumstances in which his doing so constitutes an offence under section 25(1), (2) or (3) above.

(4) The revocation of an institution's authorisation pursuant to a decision against which there is a right of appeal under this section shall not have effect—

(a) until the end of the period within which an appeal can be brought; and

(b) if such an appeal is brought, until it is determined or withdrawn.

(5) The Tribunal may suspend the operation of a restriction or direction or a variation of a restriction or direction pending the determination of an appeal in respect of the decision imposing or varying the restriction or giving or varying the direction. **[46]**

NOTES
Sub-s (1): words in square brackets in sub-s (1)(a) added by the Banking Coordination (Second Council Directive) Regulations 1992, SI 1992/3218, reg 32(2)(c).
Modifications: as to modifications to this section, see the Banking Coordination (Second Council Directive) Regulations 1992, SI 1992/3218, regs 9(7), 22(6), 23(7), Sch 3, para 4(1), Sch 6, para 8(1), Sch 7, para 4; see **[690]**, **[691]**, **[692]**.

28 Constitution of tribunals

(1) Where an appeal is brought under section 27 above a tribunal to determine the appeal shall be constituted in accordance with subsection (2) below.

(2) The tribunal shall consist of—

(a) a chairman appointed by the Lord Chancellor or, in a case where the institution concerned is a company registered in Scotland or has its principal or prospective principal place of business in the United Kingdom in Scotland, by the Lord Chancellor in consultation with the Lord Advocate; and

(b) two other members appointed by the Chancellor of the Exchequer.

(3) The chairman shall be

[(a) a person who has a 7 year general qualification, within the meaning of section 71 of the Courts and Legal Services Act 1990;

(b) an advocate or solicitor in Scotland of at least 7 years' standing; or

(c) a member of the Bar of Northern Ireland or solicitor of the Supreme Court of Northern Ireland of at least 7 years' standing]

and the other two members shall be persons appearing to the Chancellor of the Exchequer to have respectively experience of accountancy and experience of banking.

[(3A) A person shall not be appointed after the day on which he attains the age of 70 to be the chairman of a tribunal under this section.]

(4) The Treasury may out of money provided by Parliament pay to the persons appointed as members of a tribunal under this section such fees and allowances in respect of expenses as the Treasury may determine and may also out of such money defray any other expenses of a tribunal. **[47]**

NOTES
Commencement: 1 October 1987 (sub-ss (1)–(3), (4)) (SI 1987/1664); 31 March 1995 (sub-s (3A)) (SI 1995/631).
Sub-s (3): words in square brackets substituted by the Courts and Legal Services Act 1990, s 71(2), Sch 10, para 69.
Sub-s (3A): inserted by the Judicial Pensions and Retirement Act 1993, s 26(10), Sch 6, para 65, subject to ss 26(11), 27 of and Sch 7 to that Act.

29 Determination of appeals

(1) On an appeal under section 27(1) or (3) above the question for the determination of the tribunal shall be whether, for the reasons adduced by the appellant, the decision was unlawful or not justified by the evidence on which it was based.

(2) On any such appeal the tribunal may confirm or reverse the decision which is the subject of the appeal but shall not have power to vary it except that—

(a) where the decision was to revoke an authorisation the tribunal may direct the Bank to restrict it instead;

(b) where the decision was to impose or vary any restrictions the tribunal may direct the Bank to impose different restrictions or to vary them in a different way; or

(c) where the decision was to give or vary a direction the tribunal may direct the Bank to give a different direction or to vary it in a different way.

(3) Where the tribunal gives a direction to the Bank under subsection (2)(a), (b) or (c) above it shall be for the Bank to decide what restrictions should be imposed or how they should be varied or, as the case may be, what direction should be given or how a direction should be varied; and—

(a) the Bank shall by notice in writing to the institution concerned impose the restrictions, give the direction or make the variation on which it has decided;

(b) the institution may appeal to the tribunal against the Bank's decision,

and on any such appeal the tribunal may confirm the decision or give a further direction under paragraph (b) or (c) of subsection (2) above and, if it gives such a further direction, this subsection shall continue to apply until the Bank's decision is confirmed by the tribunal or accepted by the institution.

(4) Where the tribunal reverses a decision of the Bank to refuse an application for authorisation it shall direct the Bank to grant it.

(5) On an appeal under section 27(2)(a) above the question for the determination of the tribunal shall be whether, for the reasons adduced by the appellant the finding of the Bank was not justified by the evidence on which it was based; and on an appeal under section 27(2)(b) above the question for the determination of the tribunal shall be whether, for the reasons adduced by the appellant, the decision requiring the appellant's removal was unlawful or not justified by the evidence on which it was based.

(6) A decision by the tribunal on an appeal under section 27(2)(a) above that a finding in respect of the appellant was not justified shall not affect any refusal, revocation or restriction wholly or partly based on that finding; but on an appeal under section 27(2)(b) above the tribunal may confirm or reverse the decision to require the removal of the appellant.

(7) Notice of a tribunal's determination, together with a statement of its reasons, shall be given to the appellant and to the Bank; and, unless the tribunal otherwise directs, the determination shall come into operation when the notice is given to the appellant and to the Bank.

(8) Notice of a tribunal's determination of an appeal under section 27(2) above shall also be given to the institution concerned and, where the determination is to reverse a decision to require the removal of the appellant as director, controller or manager of an institution, the determination shall not come into operation until notice of the determination has been given to that institution.

[48]

NOTE
  Modifications: as to modifications to this section, see the Banking Coordination (Second Council Directive) Regulations 1992, SI 1992/3218, regs 9(7), 22(6), Sch 3, para 4(2), (3), Sch 6, para 8(2); see **[690]**, **[691]**.

30 Costs, procedure and evidence

(1) A tribunal may give such directions as it thinks fit for the payment of costs or expenses by any party to the appeal.

(2) On an appeal under section 27(2) above the institution concerned shall be entitled to be heard.

(3) Subject to subsection (4) below, the Treasury may, . . . make regulations with respect to appeals under this Part of this Act; and those regulations may in particular make provision—

(a) as to the period within which and the manner in which such appeals are to be brought;

(b) as to the manner in which such appeals are to be conducted, including provision for any hearing to be held in private, as to the persons entitled to appear on behalf of the parties and for enabling appeals to be heard notwithstanding the absence of a member of the tribunal other than the chairman;

(c) as to the procedure to be adopted where appeals are brought both by an institution and a person who is or is to be a director, controller or manager of the institution, including the provision for hearing the appeals together and for the mutual disclosure of information;

(d) for requiring an appellant or the Bank to disclose or allow the inspection of documents in his or its custody or under his or its control;

(e) for requiring any person, on tender of the necessary expenses of his attendance, to attend and give evidence or produce documents in his custody or under his control and for authorising the administration of oaths to witnesses;

(f) for enabling an appellant to withdraw an appeal or the Bank to withdraw its opposition to an appeal and for the consequences of any such withdrawal;

(g) for taxing or otherwise settling any costs or expenses which the tribunal directs to be paid and for the enforcement of any such direction;

(h) for enabling any preliminary or incidental functions in relation to an appeal to be discharged by the chairman of a tribunal; and

(j) as to any other matter connected with such appeals.

(4) Regulations under this section with respect to appeals where the institution concerned—

(a) is a company registered in Scotland; or

(b) has its principal or prospective principal place of business in the United Kingdom in Scotland,

shall be made by the Lord Advocate . . . .

(5) A person who, having been required in accordance with regulations under this section to attend and give evidence, fails without reasonable excuse to attend or give evidence, shall be liable on summary conviction to a fine not exceeding the fifth level on the standard scale.

(6) A person who without reasonable excuse alters, suppresses, conceals, destroys or refuses to produce any document which he has been required to produce in accordance with regulations under this section, or which he is liable to be so required to produce, shall be guilty of an offence and liable—

(a) on conviction on indictment, to imprisonment for a term not exceeding two years or to a fine or to both;

(b) on summary conviction, to a fine not exceeding the statutory maximum.

(7) Any regulations made under this section shall be subject to annulment in pursuance of a resolution of either House of Parliament.   [49]

NOTES

Sub-ss (3), (4): words omitted repealed by the Tribunals and Inquiries Act 1992, s 18(2), Sch 4, Pt I.

Regulations: the Banking Appeal Tribunal Regulations 1987, SI 1987/1299, as amended by SI 1993/982.

31 Further appeals on points of law

(1) An institution or other person who has appealed to a tribunal may appeal to the court on any question of law arising from the decision of the appeal by the tribunal and an appeal on any such question shall also lie at the instance of the Bank; and if the court is of opinion that the decision was erroneous in point of law, it shall remit the matter to the tribunal for re-hearing and determination by it.

(2) In subsection (1) above "the court" means the High Court, the Court of Session or the High Court in Northern Ireland according to whether—

(a) if the institution concerned is a company registered in the United Kingdom, it is registered in England and Wales, Scotland or Northern Ireland;

(b) in the case of any other institution, its principal or prospective principal place of business in the United Kingdom is situated in England and Wales, Scotland or Northern Ireland.

(3) No appeal to the Court of Appeal or to the Court of Appeal in Northern Ireland shall be brought from a decision under subsection (1) above except with the leave of that court or of the court or judge from whose decision the appeal is brought.

(4) . . . [50]

NOTE
Sub-s (4): applies to Scotland only.

Invitations to make deposits

32 Advertisement regulations

(1) The Treasury may after consultation with the Bank and the Building Societies Commission make regulations for regulating the issue, form and content of deposit advertisements.

(2) Regulations under this section may make different provision for different cases and, without prejudice to the generality of subsection (1) above, may in particular—

(a) prohibit the issue of advertisements of any description (whether by reference to their contents, to the persons by whom they are issued or otherwise);

(b) make provision with respect to matters which must be, as well as matters which may not be, included in advertisements;

(c) provide for exemptions from any prohibition or requirement imposed by the regulations, including exemptions by reference to a person's membership of a class whose membership is determined otherwise than by the Treasury.

(3) Subject to subsection (4) below, any person who issues or causes to be issued in the United Kingdom an advertisement the issue of which is prohibited by regulations under this section or which does not comply with any requirements imposed by those regulations shall be guilty of an offence and liable—

(a) on conviction on indictment, to imprisonment for a term not exceeding two years or to a fine or to both;

(b) on summary conviction, to imprisonment for a term not exceeding six months or to a fine not exceeding the statutory maximum or to both.

(4) A person whose business it is to publish or arrange for the publication of advertisements shall not be guilty of an offence under this section if he proves that he received the advertisement for publication in the ordinary course of his business, that the matters contained in the advertisement were not (wholly or in part) devised or selected by him or by any person under his direction or control and that he did not know and had no reason for believing that publication of the advertisement would constitute an offence.

(5) In this section "a deposit advertisement" means any advertisement containing—

  (a) an invitation to make a deposit; or
  (b) information which is intended or might reasonably be presumed to be intended to lead directly or indirectly to the making of a deposit;

and for the purposes of this section an advertisement includes any means of bringing such an invitation or such information to the notice of the person or persons to whom it is addressed and references to the issue of an advertisement shall be construed accordingly.

(6) For the purposes of this section—

  (a) an advertisement issued or caused to be issued by any person by way of display or exhibition in a public place shall be treated as issued or caused to be issued by him on every day on which he causes or permits it to be displayed or exhibited;
  (b) an advertisement inviting deposits with a person specified in the advertisement shall be presumed, unless the contrary is proved, to have been issued to the order of that person.

(7) For the purposes of this section an advertisement issued outside the United Kingdom shall be treated as issued in the United Kingdom if it is directed to persons in the United Kingdom or is made available to them otherwise than in a newspaper, journal, magazine or other periodical publication published and circulating principally outside the United Kingdom or in a sound or television broadcast transmitted principally for reception outside the United Kingdom.

(8) Regulations under this section shall be subject to annulment in pursuance of a resolution of either House of Parliament.   [51]

NOTES

Regulations: the Banking Act 1987 (Advertisements) Regulations 1988, SI 1988/645, as modified by the Banking Coordination (Second Council Directive) Regulations 1992, SI 1992/3218, and the Insurance Companies (Third Insurance Directives) Regulations 1994, SI 1994/1696.

Modifications: as to modifications to this section, see the Credit Institutions (Protection of Depositors) Regulations 1995, SI 1995/1442, reg 48(7), at **[711K]**.

33 Advertisement directions

(1) If the Bank considers that any deposit advertisement issued or proposed to be issued by or on behalf of an authorised institution is misleading, the Bank may by notice in writing give the institution a direction under this section.

(2) A direction under this section may contain all or any of the following prohibitions or requirements—

  (a) a prohibition on the issue of advertisements of a specified kind;
  (b) a requirement that advertisements of a particular description shall be modified in a specified manner;
  (c) a prohibition on the issue of any advertisements which are, wholly or substantially, repetitions of an advertisement which has been issued and which is identified in the direction;
  (d) a requirement to take all practical steps to withdraw from display in any place any advertisements or any advertisements of a particular description specified in the direction.

(3) Not less than seven days before giving a direction under this section the Bank shall give the institution concerned notice in writing of its intention to

give the direction stating the reasons for the proposed direction and giving particulars of the rights conferred by subsection (4) below.

(4) An institution to which a notice is given under subsection (3) above may within the period of seven days beginning with the day on which the notice was given make written representations to the Bank; and the Bank shall take any such representation into account in deciding whether to give the direction.

(5) A direction under this section may be varied by a further direction; and a direction may be revoked by the Bank by a notice in writing to the institution concerned.

(6) Any person who issues or causes to be issued an advertisement the issue of which is prohibited by a direction under this section or which does not comply with any requirements imposed by such a direction shall be guilty of an offence and liable—

   (a) on conviction on indictment, to imprisonment for a term not exceeding two years or to a fine or to both;
   (b) on summary conviction, to imprisonment for a term not exceeding six months or to a fine not exceeding the statutory maximum or to both.

(7) In this section "deposit advertisement" has the same meaning as in section 32 above and subsections (4) and (6) of that section shall apply also for the purposes of this section.   **[52]**

NOTE
   Modifications: as to modifications to this section, see the Banking Coordination (Second Council Directive) Regulations 1992, SI 1992/3218, reg 47, Sch 8, para 7; see **[693]**.

34 Unsolicited calls

(1) The Treasury may after consultation with the Bank and the Building Societies Commission make regulations for regulating the making of unsolicited calls—

   (a) on persons in the United Kingdom; or
   (b) from the United Kingdom on persons elsewhere,

with a view to procuring the making of deposits.

(2) Regulations under this section may make different provision for different cases and, without prejudice to the generality of subsection (1) above, may in particular—

   (a) prohibit the soliciting of deposits from, and the making of agreements with a view to the acceptance of deposits from, persons on whom unsolicited calls are made and prohibit the procuring of such persons to make deposits or to enter into such agreements;
   (b) specify persons by whom or circumstances in which unsolicited calls may be made;
   (c) require specified information to be disclosed to persons on whom unsolicited calls are made.

(3) Any person who contravenes regulations made under this section shall be guilty of an offence and liable—

   (a) on conviction on indictment, to imprisonment for a term not exceeding two years or to a fine or to both;
   (b) on summary conviction, to imprisonment for a term not exceeding six months or to a fine not exceeding the statutory maximum or to both.

(4) In this section "unsolicited call" means a personal visit or oral communication made without express invitation.

(5) Regulations under this section shall be subject to annulment in pursuance of a resolution of either House of Parliament.   **[53]**

35 Fraudulent inducement to make a deposit

(1) Any person who—

(a) makes a statement, promise or forecast which he knows to be misleading, false or deceptive, or dishonestly conceals any material facts; or

(b) recklessly makes (dishonestly or otherwise) a statement, promise or forecast which is misleading, false or deceptive,

is guilty of an offence if he makes the statement, promise or forecast or conceals the facts for the purpose of inducing, or is reckless as to whether it may induce, another person (whether or not the person to whom the statement, promise or forecast is made or from whom the facts are concealed)—

(i) to make, or refrain from making, a deposit with him or any other person; or

(ii) to enter, or refrain from entering, into an agreement for the purpose of making such a deposit.

(2) This section does not apply unless—

(a) the statement, promise or forecast is made in or from, or the facts are concealed in or from, the United Kingdom or arrangements are made in or from the United Kingdom for the statement, promise or forecast to be made or the facts to be concealed;

(b) the person on whom the inducement is intended to or may have effect is in the United Kingdom; or

(c) the deposit is or would be made, or the agreement is or would be entered into, in the United Kingdom.

(3) A person guilty of an offence under this section shall be liable—

(a) on conviction on indictment, to imprisonment for a term not exceeding seven years or to a fine or to both;

(b) on summary conviction, to imprisonment for a term not exceeding six months or to a fine not exceeding the statutory maximum or to both.

(4) For the purposes of this section the definition of deposit in section 5 above shall be treated as including any sum that would be otherwise excluded by subsection (3) of that section.   **[54]**

NOTE

Transitional provision: see s 107, Sch 5, para 7(3).

Information

36 Notification of change of director, controller or manager

(1) Subject to subsection (3) below, an authorised institution shall give written notice to the Bank of the fact that any person has become or ceased to be a director, controller or manager of the institution.

(2) A notice required to be given under subsection (1) above shall be given before the end of the period of fourteen days beginning with the day on which the institution becomes aware of the relevant facts.

(3) The Bank may by a notice in writing wholly or partly dispense from the obligation imposed by subsection (1) above any authorised institution whose principal place of business is outside the United Kingdom.

(4) An institution which fails to give a notice required by this section shall be guilty of an offence and liable on summary conviction to a fine not exceeding the fifth level on the standard scale.   **[55]**

[36A Annual notification of shareholder controllers

(1) An authorised institution which is a credit institution incorporated in or formed under the law of any part of the United Kingdom shall at least once in each year give to the Bank written notice of the name of each person who, to the institution's knowledge, is a shareholder controller of the institution at the date of the notice.   .

(2) A notice under subsection (1) above shall also, in relation to each such person, state to best of the institution's knowledge—

    (a) whether he is a minority, 10 per cent., 20 per cent., 33 per cent. or 50 per cent. shareholder controller;

    (b) what percentage of the shares of the institution he holds either alone or with any associate or associates; and

    (c) what percentage of the voting power at a general meeting of the institution he is entitled to exercise, or control the exercise of, either alone or with any associate or associates;

and in this subsection "share" has the same meaning as in Part VII of the Companies Act 1985 or Part VIII of the Companies (Northern Ireland) Order 1986.

(3) An institution which fails to give a notice required by this section shall be guilty of an offence and liable on summary conviction to a fine not exceeding the fifth level on the standard scale.]   **[56]**

NOTES
  Commencement: 1 January 1993 (SI 1992/3218).
  This section inserted by the Banking Coordination (Second Council Directive) Regulations 1992, SI 1992/3218, reg 33.

37 Notification of acquisition of significant shareholding

(1) A person who becomes a significant shareholder in relation to an authorised institution incorporated in the United Kingdom shall within seven days give written notice of that fact to the Bank.

[(2) For the purposes of this section "a significant shareholder", in relation to an institution, means a person who is not a shareholder controller but who, either alone or with any associate or associates—

    (a) holds 5 per cent. or more of the shares in the institution or another institution of which it is a subsidiary undertaking; or

    (b) is entitled to exercise, or control the exercise of, 5 per cent. or more of the voting power at any general meeting of the institution or of another institution of which it is such an undertaking;

and in this subsection "share" has the same meaning as in Part VII of the Companies Act 1985 or Part VIII of the Companies (Northern Ireland) Order 1986.]

(3) Subject to subsection (4) below, any person who contravenes subsection (1) above shall be guilty of an offence.

(4) A person shall not be guilty of an offence under subsection (3) above if he shows that he did not know of the acts or circumstances by virtue of which he became a significant shareholder in relation to the institution; but where any person becomes such a shareholder without such knowledge and subsequently becomes aware of the fact that he has become such a shareholder he shall be guilty of an offence unless he gives the Bank written notice of the fact that he has become such a shareholder within fourteen days of becoming aware of that fact.

(5) A person guilty of an offence under this section shall be liable on summary conviction to a fine not exceeding the fifth level on the standard scale.

[57]

NOTES

Commencement: 1 October 1987 (SI 1987/1664); 1 January 1993 (sub-s (2), as substituted) (SI 1992/3218).

Sub-s (2): substituted by the Banking Coordination (Second Council Directive) Regulations 1992, SI 1992/3218, reg 34, subject to reg 46(a); see **[684]**.

The original sub-s (2) read—

(2) For the purposes of this section "a significant shareholder", in relation to an institution, means a person who, either alone or with any associate or associates, is entitled to exercise, or control the exercise of, 5 per cent or more but less than 15 per cent of the voting power at any general meeting of the institution or of another institution of which it is a subsidiary.

[37A Prior notification of ceasing to be a relevant controller

(1) A person shall not cease to be a minority, 10 per cent., 20 per cent., 33 per cent. or 50 per cent. shareholder controller or a parent controller of an authorised institution which is a credit institution incorporated in or formed under the law of any part of the United Kingdom unless he has first given to the Bank written notice of his intention to cease to be such a controller of the institution.

(2) If, after ceasing to be such a controller of such an institution, a person will, either alone or with any associate or associates—

(a) still hold 10 per cent. or more of the shares in the institution or another institution of which it is a subsidiary undertaking;
(b) still be entitled to exercise or control the exercise of 10 per cent. or more of the voting power at any general meeting of the institution or of another institution of which it is such an undertaking; or
(c) still be able to exercise a significant influence over the management of the institution or another institution of which it is such an undertaking by virtue of—

(i) a holding of shares in; or
(ii) an entitlement to exercise, or control the exercise of, the voting power at any general meeting of,

the institution or, as the case may be, the other institution concerned,

his notice under subsection (1) above shall state the percentage of the shares or voting power which he will (alone or with any associate or associates) hold or be entitled to exercise or control; and in this subsection "share" has the same meaning as in Part VII of the Companies Act 1985 or Part VIII of the Companies (Northern Ireland) Order 1986.

(3) Subject to subsection (4) below, any person who contravenes subsection (1) or (2) above shall be guilty of an offence.

(4) Subject to subsection (5) below, a person shall not be guilty of an offence under subsection (3) above if he shows that he did not know of the acts or

circumstances by virtue of which he ceased to be a controller of the relevant description in sufficient time to enable him to comply with subsection (1) above.

(5) Notwithstanding anything in subsection (4) above, a person who ceases to be a controller of a relevant description without having complied with subsection (1) above shall be guilty of an offence if, within fourteen days of becoming aware of the fact that he has ceased to be such a controller—

(a) he fails to give the Bank written notice of that fact; or
(b) he gives the Bank such a notice but the notice fails to comply with subsection (2) above.

(6) A person guilty of an offence under this section shall be liable on summary conviction to a fine not exceeding the fifth level on the standard scale.]   **[58]**

NOTES

Commencement: 1 January 1993 (SI 1992/3218).
This section inserted by the Banking Coordination (Second Council Directive) Regulations 1992, SI 1992/3218, reg 35.

38 Reports of large exposures

(1) An authorised institution, other than one whose principal place of business is outside the United Kingdom, shall make a report to the Bank if—

(a) it has entered into a transaction or transactions relating to any one person as a result of which it is exposed to the risk of incurring losses in excess of 10 per cent. of its available capital resources; or
(b) it proposes to enter into a transaction or transactions relating to any one person which, either alone or together with a previous transaction or previous transactions entered into by it in relation to that person, would result in its being exposed to the risk of incurring losses in excess of 25 per cent. of those resources.

(2) Subsection (1) above applies also where the transaction or transactions relate to different persons if they are connected in such a way that the financial soundness of any of them may affect the financial soundness of the other or others or the same factors may affect the financial soundness of both or all of them.

(3) If an authorised institution to which subsection (1) above applies has one or more subsidiaries which are not authorised institutions the Bank may by notice in writing to that institution direct that that subsection shall apply to it as if the transactions and available capital resources of the subsidiary or subsidiaries, or such of them as are specified in the notice, were included in those of the institution.

(4) The reports required to be made by an institution under subsection (1) above shall be made, in a case within paragraph (a) of that subsection, in respect of such period or periods and, in a case within paragraph (b) of that subsection, at such time before the transaction or transactions are entered into, as may be specified by notice in writing given to the institution by the Bank; and those reports shall be in such form and contain such particulars as the Bank may reasonably require.

(5) For the purposes of this section a transaction entered into by an institution relates to a person if it is—

(a) a transaction under which that person incurs an obligation to the institution or as a result of which he may incur such an obligation;

(b) a transaction under which the institution will incur, or as a result of which it may incur, an obligation in the event of that person defaulting on an obligation to a third party; or

(c) a transaction under which the institution acquires or incurs an obligation to acquire, or as a result of which it may incur an obligation to acquire, an asset the value of which depends wholly or mainly on that person performing his obligations or otherwise on his financial soundness;

and the risk of loss attributable to a transaction is, in a case within paragraph (a) or (b) above, the risk of the person concerned defaulting on the obligation there mentioned and, in a case within paragraph (c) above, the risk of the person concerned defaulting on the obligations there mentioned or of a deterioration in his financial soundness.

(6) Any question whether an institution is or would be exposed to risk as mentioned in subsection (1) above (or in that subsection as extended by subsection (2)) shall be determined in accordance with principles published by the Bank or notified by it to the institution concerned; and those principles may in particular make provision for determining the amount at risk in particular circumstances or the extent to which any such amount is to be taken into account for the purposes of this section.

(7) For the purposes of this section the available capital resources of an institution (or, in a case within subsection (3) above, of an institution and its relevant subsidiary or subsidiaries) and the value of those resources at any time shall be determined by the Bank and notified by it to the institution by notice in writing; and any such determination, which may be varied from time to time, shall be made by the Bank after consultation with the institution concerned and in accordance with principles published by the Bank.

(8) The principles referred to in subsections (6) and (7) above may make different provision for different cases and those referred to in subsection (6) may, in particular, exclude from consideration, either wholly or in part, risks resulting from transactions of a particular description or entered into in particular circumstances or with persons of particular descriptions.

(9) An institution which fails to make a report as required by this section shall be guilty of an offence; but where an institution shows that at the time when the report was required to be made it did not know that the facts were such as to require the making of the report it shall not be guilty of an offence by reason of its failure to make a report at that time but shall be guilty of an offence unless it makes the report within seven days of becoming aware of those facts.

(10) An institution guilty of an offence under this section shall be liable on summary conviction to a fine not exceeding the fifth level on the standard scale.

(11) The Treasury may after consultation with the Bank by order—

(a) amend subsection (1) above so as to substitute for either of the percentages for the time being specified in that subsection such other percentage as may be specified in the order;

(b) make provision, whether by amending subsection (5) above or otherwise, with respect to the transactions and risks to be taken into account for the purposes of this section,

but any such order shall be subject to annulment in pursuance of a resolution of either House of Parliament.

(12) For the avoidance of doubt it is hereby declared that references in this section to "one person" include references to a partnership. **[59]**

39 Power to obtain information and require production of documents

(1) The Bank may by notice in writing served on an authorised institution—

    (a) require the institution to provide the Bank, at such time or times or at such intervals or in respect of such period or periods as may be specified in the notice, with such information as the Bank may reasonably require for the performance of its functions under this Act;

    (b) require the institution to provide the Bank with a report by an accountant or other person with relevant professional skill on, or on any aspect of, any matter about which the Bank has required or could require the institution to provide information under paragraph (a) above.

(2) The accountant or other person appointed by an institution to make any report required under subsection (1)(b) above shall be a person nominated or approved by the Bank; and the Bank may require his report to be in such form as is specified in the notice.

(3) The Bank may—

    (a) by notice in writing served on an authorised institution require it to produce, within such time and at such place as may be specified in the notice, such document or documents of such description as may be so specified;

    (b) authorise an officer, servant or agent of the Bank, on producing evidence of his authority, to require any such institution to provide him forthwith with such information, or to produce to him forthwith such documents, as may specify,

being such information or documents as the Bank may reasonably require for the performance of its functions under this Act.

(4) Where, by virtue of subsection (3) above, the Bank or any officer, servant or agent of the Bank has power to require the production of any documents from an authorised institution, the Bank or that officer, servant or agent shall have the like power to require the production of those documents from any person who appears to be in possession of them; but where any person from whom such production is required claims a lien on documents produced by him, the production shall be without prejudice to the lien.

(5) The power under this section to require an institution or other person to produce any documents includes power—

    (a) if the documents are produced, to take copies of them or extracts from them and to require that institution or person, or any other person who is a present or past director, controller or manager of, or is or was at any time employed by or acting as an employee of, the institution in question, to provide in explanation of any of them; and

    (b) if the documents are not produced, to require the person who was required to produce them to state, to the best of his knowledge and belief, where they are.

[(6) If it appears to the Bank to be desirable in the interests of the depositors or potential depositors of an authorised institution to do so, it may also exercise the powers conferred by subsections (1) and (3) above in relation to any undertaking which is or has at any relevant time been—

(a) a parent undertaking, subsidiary undertaking or related company of that institution;

(b) a subsidiary undertaking of a parent undertaking of that institution;

(c) a parent undertaking of a subsidiary undertaking of that institution; or

(d) an undertaking in the case of which a shareholder controller of that institution, either alone or with any associate or associates, holds 50 per cent. or more of the shares or is entitled to exercise, or control the exercise of, more than 50 per cent. of the voting power at a general meeting;

or in relation to any partnership of which that institution is or has at any relevant time been a member.

(7) If it appears to the Bank to be desirable to do so in the interests of the depositors or potential depositors of an authorised institution which is a partnership ("the authorised partnership"), it may also exercise the powers conferred by subsections (1) and (3) above in relation to—

(a) any other partnership having a member in common with the authorised partnership;

(b) any undertaking which is or has at any time been a member of the authorised partnership;

(c) any undertaking in the case of which the partners in the authorised partnership, either alone or with any associate or associates, hold 20 per cent. or more of the shares or are entitled to exercise, or control the exercise of, more than 50 per cent. of the voting power at a general meeting; or

(d) any subsidiary undertaking or parent undertaking of any such undertaking as is mentioned in paragraph (b) or (c) above or any parent undertaking of any such subsidiary undertaking.

(7A) In subsections (6) and (7) above "share" has the same meaning as in Part VII of the Companies Act 1985 or Part VIII of the Companies (Northern Ireland) Order 1986.]

(8) The foregoing provisions of this section shall apply to a former authorised institution as they apply to an authorised institution.

(9) The Bank may by notice in writing served on any person who is or is to be a director, controller or manager of an authorised institution require him to provide the Bank, within such time as may be specified in the notice, with such information or documents as the Bank may reasonably require for determining whether he is a fit and proper person to hold the particular position which he holds or is to hold.

(10) The Bank may exercise the powers conferred by subsections (1) and (3) above in relation to any person who is a significant shareholder of an authorised institution within the meaning of section 37 above if the Bank considers that the exercise of those powers is desirable in the interests of the depositors or potential depositors of that institution.

(11) Any person who without reasonable excuse fails to comply with a requirement imposed on him under this section shall be guilty of an offence and liable on summary conviction to imprisonment for a term not exceeding six months or to a fine not exceeding the fifth level on the standard scale or to both.

(12) A statement made by a person in compliance with a requirement imposed by virtue of this section may be used in evidence against him.

(13) Nothing in this section shall compel the production by a barrister, advocate or solicitor of a document containing a privileged communication made by him or to him in that capacity. **[60]**

NOTES

Commencement: 1 October 1987 (SI 1987/1664); 1 January 1993 (sub-ss (6), (7), (7A) as substituted) (SI 1992/3218).

Sub-ss (6), (7), (7A): substituted for the original sub-ss (6), (7) by the Banking Coordination (Second Council Directive) Regulations 1992, SI 1992/3218, reg 36, subject to reg 46(a); see **[684]**. The original sub-ss (6), (7) read—

(6) If it appears to the Bank to be desirable in the interests of the depositors or potential depositors of an authorised institution to do so, it may also exercise the powers conferred by subsections (1) and (3) above in relation to any body corporate which is or has at any relevant time been—

    (a) a holding company, subsidiary or related company of that institution;
    (b) a subsidiary of a holding company of that institution;
    (c) a holding company of a subsidiary of that institution; or
    (d) a body corporate in the case of which a shareholder controller of that institution, either alone or with any associate or associates, is entitled to exercise, or control the exercise of, more than 50 per cent of the voting power at a general meeting;

or in relation to any partnership of which that institution is or has at any relevant time been a member.

(7) If it appears to the Bank to be desirable to do so in the interests of the depositors or potential depositors or an authorised institution which is a partnership ("the authorised partnership") it may also exercise the powers conferred by subsections (1) and (3) above in relation to—

    (a) any other partnership having a member in common with the authorised partnership;
    (b) any body corporate which is or has at any relevant time been a member of the authorised partnership;
    (c) any body corporate in the case of which the partners in the authorised partnership hold more than 20 per cent of the shares or any partner in the authorised partnership, either alone or with any associate or associates, is entitled to exercise, or control the exercise of, more than 50 per cent of the voting power at a general meeting; or
    (d) any subsidiary or holding company of any such body corporate as is mentioned in paragraph (b) or (c) above or any holding company of any such subsidiary.

Modifications: as to modifications to this section, see the Banking Coordination (Second Council Directive) Regulations 1992, SI 1992/3218, reg 47, Sch 8, para 8(1), (2); see **[693]**. For transitional provisions, see reg 83, Sch 11, Pt II, para 7; see **[694]**.

40 Right of entry to obtain information and documents

(1) Any officer, servant or agent of the Bank may, on producing if required evidence of his authority, enter any premises occupied by a person on whom a notice has been served under section 39 above for the purpose of obtaining there the information or documents required by that notice and of exercising the powers conferred by subsection (5) of that section.

(2) Any officer, servant or agent of the Bank may, on producing if required evidence of his authority, enter any premises occupied by any person on whom a notice could be served under section 39 above for the purpose of obtaining there such information or documents as are specified in the authority, being information or documents that could have been required by such a notice; but the Bank shall not authorise any person to act under this subsection unless it has reasonable cause to believe that if such a notice were served it would not be complied with or that any documents to which it would relate would be removed, tampered with or destroyed.

(3) Any person who intentionally obstructs a person exercising rights conferred by this section shall be guilty of an offence and liable on summary conviction to imprisonment for a term not exceeding six months or to a fine not exceeding the fifth level on the standard scale or to both. **[61]**

NOTE

Modifications: as to modifications to this section, see the Banking Coordination (Second Council Directive) Regulations 1992, SI 1992/3218, reg 47, Sch 8, para 9(1); see **[693]**.

Investigations

41 Investigations on behalf of the Bank

(1) If it appears to the Bank desirable to do so in the interests of the depositors or potential depositors of an authorised institution the Bank may appoint one or more competent persons to investigate and report to the Bank on—

(a) the nature, conduct or state of the institution's business or any particular aspect of it; or

(b) the ownership or control of the institution;

and the Bank shall give written notice of any such appointment to the institution concerned.

[(2) If a person appointed under subsection (1) above thinks it necessary for the purposes of his investigation, he may also investigate the business of any undertaking which is or has at any relevant time been—

(a) a parent undertaking, subsidiary undertaking or related company of the institution under investigation;

(b) a subsidiary undertaking or related company of a parent undertaking of that institution;

(c) a parent undertaking of a subsidiary undertaking of that institution; or

(d) an undertaking in the case of which a shareholder controller of that institution, either alone or with any associate or associates, holds 20 per cent. or more of the shares or is entitled to exercise, or control the exercise of, more than 20 per cent. of the voting power at a general meeting;

or the business of any partnership of which that institution is or has at any relevant time been a member.

(3) If a person appointed under subsection (1) above thinks it necessary for the purposes of his investigation in the case of an authorised institution which is a partnership ("the authorised partnership"), he may also investigate the business of—

(a) any other partnership having a member in common with the authorised partnership;

(b) any undertaking which is or has at any time been a member of the authorised partnership;

(c) any undertaking in the case of which the partners in the authorised partnership, either alone or with any associate or associates, hold 20 per cent. or more of the shares or are entitled to exercise, or control the exercise of, more than 20 per cent. of the voting power at a general meeting; or

(d) any subsidiary undertaking, related company or parent undertaking of any such undertaking as is mentioned in paragraph (b) or (c) above or any parent undertaking of any such subsidiary undertaking.

(3A) In subsections (2) and (3) above "share" has the same meaning as in Part VII of the Companies Act 1985 or Part VIII of the Companies (Northern Ireland) Order 1986.]

(4) Where a person appointed under subsection (1) above decides to investigate the business of any body by virtue of subsection (2) or (3) above he shall give it written notice to that effect.

(5) It shall be the duty of every person who is or was a director, controller, manager, employee, agent, banker, auditor or solicitor of a body which is under investigation (whether by virtue of subsection (1), (2) or (3) above), any person appointed to make a report in respect of that body under section 8(5) or 39(1)(b) above and anyone who is a significant shareholder in relation to that body within the meaning of section 37 above—

(a) to produce to the persons appointed under subsection (1) above, within such time and at such place as they may require, all documents relating to the body concerned which are in his custody or power;
(b) to attend before the persons so appointed at such time and place as they may require; and
(c) otherwise to give those persons all assistance in connection with the investigation which he is reasonably able to give;

and those persons may take copies of or extracts from any documents produced to them under paragraph (a) above.

(6) The foregoing provisions of this section shall apply to a former authorised institution as they apply to an authorised institution.

(7) For the purpose of exercising his powers under this section a person appointed under subsection (1) above may enter any premises occupied by a body which is being investigated by him under this section; but he shall not do so without prior notice in writing unless he has reasonable cause to believe that if such a notice were given any documents whose production could be required under this section would be removed, tampered with or destroyed.

(8) A person exercising powers by virtue of an appointment under this section shall, if so required, produce evidence of his authority.

(9) Any person who—

(a) without reasonable excuse fails to produce any documents which it is his duty to produce under subsection (5) above;
(b) without reasonable excuse fails to attend before the persons appointed under subsection (1) above when required to do so;
(c) without reasonable excuse fails to answer any question which is put to him by persons so appointed with respect to an institution which is under investigation or a body which is being investigated by virtue of subsection (2) or (3) above; or
(d) intentionally obstructs a person in the exercise of the rights conferred by subsection (7) above,

shall be guilty of an offence and liable on summary conviction to imprisonment for a term not exceeding six months or to a fine not exceeding the fifth level on the standard scale or to both.

(10) A statement made by a person in compliance with a requirement imposed by virtue of this section may be used in evidence against him.

(11) Nothing in this section shall compel the production by a barrister, advocate or solicitor of a document containing a privileged communication made by him or to him in that capacity.   **[62]**

NOTES

Commencement: 1 October 1987 (SI 1987/1664); 1 January 1993 (sub-ss (2), (3), (3A) as substituted) (SI 1992/3218).

Sub-ss (2), (3), (3A): substituted for the original sub-ss (2), (3) by the Banking Coordination (Second Council Directive) Regulations 1992, SI 1992/3218, reg 37, subject to reg 46(a); see **[684]**. The original sub-ss (2), (3) read—

(2) If a person appointed under subsection (1) above thinks it necessary for the purposes of his investigation, he may also investigate the business of any body corporate which is or has at any relevant time been—

    (a)   a holding company, subsidiary or related company of the institution under investigation;

    (b)   a subsidiary or related company of a holding company of that institution;

    (c)   a holding company of a subsidiary of that institution; or

    (d)   a body corporate in the case of which a shareholder controller of that institution, either alone or with any associate or associates, is entitled to exercise, or control the exercise of, more than 20 per cent of the voting power at a general meeting;

or the business of any partnership of which that institution is or has at any relevant time been a member.

(3) If a person appointed under subsection (1) above thinks it necessary for the purposes of his investigation in the case of an authorised institution which is a partnership ("the authorised partnership") he may also investigate the business of—

    (a)   any other partnership having a member in common with the authorised partnership;

    (b)   any body corporate which is or has at any relevant time been a member of the authorised partnership;

    (c)   any body corporate in the case of which the partners in the authorised partnership hold more than 20 per cent of the shares or any partner in the authorised partnership, either alone or with any associate or associates, is entitled to exercise, or control the exercise of, more than 20 per cent of the voting power at a general meeting; or

    (d)   any subsidiary, related company or holding company of any such body corporate as is mentioned in paragraph (b) or (c) above or any holding company of any such subsidiary.

Modifications: as to modifications to this section, see the Banking Coordination (Second Council Directive) Regulations 1992, SI 1992/3218, reg 47, Sch 8, para 10(1), (2); see **[693]**. For transitional provisions, see reg 83, Sch 11, Pt II, para 7; see **[694]**.

42 Investigation of suspected contraventions

(1) Where the Bank has reasonable grounds for suspecting that a person is guilty of contravening section 3 or 35 above the Bank or any duly authorised officer, servant or agent of the Bank may by notice in writing require that or any other person—

    (a)   to provide, at such place as may be specified in the notice and either forthwith or at such time as may be so specified, such information as the Bank may reasonably require for the purpose of investigating the suspected contravention;

    (b)   to produce, at such place as may be specified in the notice and either forthwith or at such time as may be so specified, such documents, or documents of such description, as may be specified, being documents the production of which may be reasonably required by the Bank for that purpose;

    (c)   to attend at such place and time as may be specified in the notice and answer questions relevant for determining whether such a contravention has occurred.

(2) The Bank or a duly authorised officer, servant or agent of the Bank may take copies of or extracts from any documents produced under this section.

(3) Any officer, servant or agent of the Bank may, on producing if required evidence of his authority, enter any premises occupied by a person on whom a notice has been served under subsection (1) above for the purpose of obtaining

there the information or documents required by the notice, putting the questions referred to in paragraph (c) of that subsection or exercising the powers conferred by subsection (2) above.

(4) Any person who without reasonable excuse fails to comply with a requirement imposed on him under this section or intentionally obstructs a person in the exercise of the rights conferred by subsection (3) above shall be guilty of an offence and liable on summary conviction to imprisonment for a term not exceeding six months or to a fine not exceeding the fifth level on the standard scale or to both.

(5) A statement made by a person in compliance with a requirement imposed by virtue of this section may be used in evidence against him.

(6) Nothing in this section shall compel the production by a barrister, advocate or solicitor of a document containing a privileged communication made by him or to him in that capacity.   **[63]**

NOTE

Transitional provision: see s 107, Sch 5, para 7(3).

43 Powers of entry in cases of suspected contraventions

(1) A justice of the peace may issue a warrant under this section if satisfied on information on oath laid by an officer or servant of the Bank or laid under the Bank's authority that there are reasonable grounds for suspecting that a person is guilty of such a contravention as is mentioned in section 42 above and—

    (a) that that person has failed to comply with a notice served on him under that section; or

    (b) that there are reasonable grounds for suspecting the completeness of any information provided or documents produced by him in response to such a notice; or

    (c) that there are reasonable grounds for suspecting that if a notice were served on him under that section it would not be complied with or that any documents to which it would relate would be removed, tampered with or destroyed.

(2) A warrant under this section shall authorise any constable, together with any other person named in the warrant and any other constables—

    (a) to enter any premises occupied by the person mentioned in subsection (1) above which are specified in the warrant, using such force as is reasonably necessary for the purpose;

    (b) to search the premises and take possession of any documents appearing to be such documents as are mentioned in subsection (1)(c) above or to take, in relation to any such documents, any other steps which may appear to be necessary for preserving them or preventing interference with them;

    (c) to take copies of or extracts from any such documents;

    (d) to require any person named in the warrant to answer questions relevant for determining whether that person is guilty of any such contravention as is mentioned in section 42 above.

(3) A warrant under this section shall continue in force until the end of the period of one month beginning with the day on which it is issued.

(4) Any documents of which possession is taken under this section may be retained—

(a) for a period of three months; or
(b) if within that period proceedings to which the documents are relevant are commenced against any person for any such contravention as is mentioned in section 42 above, until the conclusion of those proceedings.

(5) Any person who intentionally obstructs the exercise of any right conferred by a warrant issued under this section or fails without reasonable excuse to comply with any requirement imposed in accordance with subsection (2)(d) above shall be guilty of an offence and liable—

(a) on conviction on indictment, to imprisonment for a term not exceeding two years or to a fine or to both;
(b) on summary conviction, to imprisonment for a term not exceeding six months or to a fine not exceeding the statutory maximum or to both.

(6) A statement made by a person in compliance with a requirement imposed by virtue of this section may be used in evidence against him.

(7) . . .   [64]

NOTES
Transitional provision: see s 107, Sch 5, para 7(3).
Sub-s (7): applies to Scotland only.

44 Obstruction of investigations

(1) A person who knows or suspects that an investigation is being or is likely to be carried out—

(a) under section 41 above; or
(b) into a suspected contravention of section 3 or 35 above,

shall be guilty of an offence if he falsifies, conceals, destroys or otherwise disposes of, or causes or permits the falsification, concealment, destruction or disposal of, documents which he knows or suspects are or would be relevant to such an investigation unless he proves that he had no intention of concealing facts disclosed by the documents from persons carrying out such an investigation.

(2) A person guilty of an offence under this section shall be liable—

(a) on conviction on indictment, to imprisonment for a term not exceeding two years or to a fine or to both;
(b) on summary conviction, to imprisonment for a term not exceeding six months or to a fine not exceeding the statutory maximum or to both.   [65]

NOTE
Transitional provision: see s 107, Sch 5, para 7(3).

Accounts and auditors

45 Audited accounts to be open to inspection

(1) An authorised institution shall at each of its offices in the United Kingdom at which it holds itself out as accepting deposits—

(a) keep a copy of its most recent audited accounts; and
(b) during normal business hours make that copy available for inspection by any person on request.

(2) An institution which fails to comply with paragraph (a) of subsection (1) above or with any request made in accordance with paragraph (b) of that subsection shall be guilty of an offence and liable on summary conviction to a fine not exceeding the fifth level on the standard scale.

(3) In the case of an institution incorporated in the United Kingdom the accounts referred to in subsection (1) above include the auditors' report on the accounts and, in the case of any other institution whose accounts are audited, the report of the auditors.   **[66]**

NOTE

Modifications: as to modifications to this section, see the Banking Coordination (Second Council Directive) Regulations 1992, SI 1992/3218, reg 47, Sch 8, para 11; see **[693]**.

46 Notification in respect of auditors

(1) An authorised institution incorporated in the United Kingdom shall forthwith give written notice to the Bank if the institution—

   (a) proposes to give special notice to its shareholders of an ordinary resolution removing an auditor before the expiration of his term of office; or

   (b) gives notice to its shareholders of an ordinary resolution replacing an auditor at the expiration of his term of office with a different auditor,

or if a person ceases to be an auditor of the institution otherwise than in consequence of such a resolution.

(2) An auditor of an authorised institution [appointed under Chapter V of Part XI] of the Companies Act 1985 shall forthwith give written notice to the Bank if he—

   (a) resigns before the expiration of his term of office;

   (b) does not seek to be re-appointed; or

   (c) decides to include in his report on the institution's accounts any qualification as to a matter mentioned in [section 235(2)] or any statement pursuant to [section 235(3) or section 237] of that Act.

(3) The foregoing provisions of this section shall apply to a former authorised institution as they apply to an authorised institution.

(4) In the application of subsection (2) above to Northern Ireland for the references to [Chapter V of Part XI and sections] [235(2) and 235(3) and 237] of the Companies Act 1985 there shall be substituted references to [Chapter V of Part XII and Articles] [243(2), 243(3) and 245] of the Companies (Northern Ireland) Order 1986.

(5) An institution or auditor who fails to comply with this section shall be guilty of an offence and liable on summary conviction to a fine not exceeding the fifth level on the standard scale.   **[67]**

NOTES

Sub-s (2): words in first pair of square brackets substituted by the Companies Act 1989, s 119(3); words in square brackets in sub-s (2)(c) substituted by the Companies Act 1989, s 23, Sch 10, Pt II, para 37(1),(2).

Sub-s (4): words in first pair of square brackets substituted by the Companies Act 1989, s 119(3); words in second pair of square brackets substituted by the Companies Act 1989, s 23, Sch 10, Pt II, para 37(1),(2); words in third pair of square brackets substituted by the Companies (No 2) (Northern Ireland) Order 1990, SI 1990/1504 (NI 10), art 54(3), subject to transitional and savings provisions set out in the Companies (1990 No 2 Order) (Commencement No 1) Order (Northern Ireland) 1991, SR 1991/26, art 4, Schedule, para 3, with regard to auditors; words in fourth pair of square brackets substituted by the Companies (Northern Ireland) Order 1990, SI 1990/593 (NI 5), art 25, Sch 10, Pt II, para 29.

47 Communication by auditor etc with the Bank

(1) No duty to which—

(a) an auditor of an authorised institution; or

(b) a person appointed to make a report under section 8(5) or 39(1)(b) above,

may be subject shall be regarded as contravened by reason of his communicating in good faith to the Bank, whether or not in response to a request made by it, any information or opinion on a matter to which this section applies and which is relevant to any function of the Bank under this Act.

(2) In relation to an auditor of an authorised institution this section applies to any matter of which he becomes aware in his capacity as auditor and which relates to the business or affairs of the institution or any associated body.

(3) In relation to a person appointed to make a report under section 8(5) or 39(1)(b) above this section applies to any matter of which he becomes aware in his capacity as the person making the report and which—

(a) relates to the business of affairs of the institution in relation to which his report is made or any associated body of that institution; or

(b) if by virtue of section 39(6) or (7) above the report relates to an associated body of an institution, to the business or affairs of that body.

(4) In this section "associated body", in relation to an institution, means any such body as is mentioned in section 39(6) or (7) above.

(5) If it appears to the Treasury that any accountants or class of accountants who are persons to whom subsection (1) above applies are not subject to satisfactory rules made or guidance issued by a professional body specifying circumstances in which matters are to be communicated to the Bank as mentioned in that subsection the Treasury may, after consultation with the Bank and such bodies as appear to the Treasury to represent the interests of accountants and authorised institutions, make regulations applying to those accountants and specifying such circumstances; and it shall be the duty of an accountant to whom the regulations apply to communicate a matter to the Bank in the circumstances specified by the regulations.

(6) Regulations under this section may make different provision for different cases and no such regulations shall be made unless a draft of them has been laid before and approved by a resolution of each House of Parliament.

(7) This section applies to the auditor of a former authorised institution as it applies to the auditor of an authorised institution. **[68]**

NOTES

Modifications: as to modifications to this section, see the Banking Coordination (Second Council Directive) Regulations 1992, SI 1992/3218, reg 47, Sch 8, para 12; see **[693]**.

Regulations: the Accountants (Banking Act 1987) Regulations 1994, SI 1994/524.

Unauthorised acceptance of deposits

48 Repayment of unauthorised deposits

(1) If on the application of the Bank it appears to the court that a person has accepted deposits in contravention of section 3 above the court may—

(a) order him and any other person who appears to the court to have been knowingly concerned in the contravention to repay the deposits forthwith or at such time as the court may direct; or

(b) except in Scotland, appoint a receiver to recover those deposits;

but in deciding whether and, if so, on what terms to make an order under this section the court shall have regard to the effect that repayment in accordance with the order would have on the solvency of the person concerned or otherwise on his ability to carry on his business in a manner satisfactory to his creditors.

(2) The jurisdiction conferred by this section shall be exercisable by the High Court and the Court of Session.   **[69]**

49 Profits from unauthorised deposits

(1) If on the application of the Bank the court is satisfied that profits have accrued to a person as a result of deposits having been accepted in contravention of section 3 above the court may order him to pay into court or, except in Scotland, appoint a receiver to recover from him, such sum as appears to the court to be just having regard to the profits appearing to the court to have accrued to him.

(2) In deciding whether, and if so, on what terms to make an order under this section the court shall have regard to the effect that payment in accordance with the order would have on the solvency of the person concerned or otherwise on his ability to carry on his business in a manner satisfactory to his creditors.

(3) Any amount paid into court or recovered from a person in pursuance of an order under this section shall be paid out to such person or distributed among such persons as the court may direct, being a person or persons appearing to the court to have made the deposits as a result of which the profits mentioned in subsection (1) above have accrued or such other person or persons as the court thinks just.

(4) On an application under this section the court may require the person concerned to furnish it with such accounts or other information as it may require for determining whether any and if so, what profits have accrued to him as mentioned in subsection (1) above and for determining how any amounts are to be paid or distributed under subsection (3) above; and the court may require any such accounts or other information to be verified in such manner as it may direct.

(5) The jurisdiction conferred by this section shall be exercisable by the High Court and the Court of Session.   **[70]**

PART II
THE DEPOSIT PROTECTION SCHEME

The Board and the Fund

50 The Deposit Protection Board

(1) The body corporate known as the Deposit Protection Board and the Fund known as the Deposit Protection Fund established by section 21 of the Banking Act 1979 shall continue to exist.

(2) The Deposit Protection Board (in this Part of this Act referred to as "the Board") shall—

 (a) hold, manage and apply the Fund in accordance with the provisions of this Part of this Act;

(b) levy contributions for the Fund, in accordance with those provisions, from [contributory institutions]; and

(c) have such other functions as are conferred on the Board by those provisions.

(3) Schedule 4 to this Act shall have effect with respect to the Board. **[71]**

NOTES

Sub-s (2): words in square brackets substituted by the Credit Institutions (Protection of Depositors) Regulations 1995, SI 1995/1442, reg 25, subject to transitional provisions and savings in reg 53 at **[711M]**.

Transitory modification: see the Credit Institutions (Protection of Depositors) Regulations 1995, SI 1995/1442, reg 54, at **[711N]**.

51 The Deposit Protection Fund

(1) The Fund shall consist of—

(a) any money which forms part of the Fund when this section comes into force;

(b) initial, further and special contributions levied by the Board under this Part of this Act;

(c) money borrowed by the Board under this Part of this Act; and

(d) any other money required by any provision of this Part of this Act to be credited to the Fund or received by the Board and directed by it to be so credited.

(2) The money constituting the Fund shall be placed by the Board in an account with the Bank.

(3) As far as possible, the Bank shall invest money placed with it under subsection (2) above in Treasury bills; and any income from money so invested shall be credited to the Fund.

[(3A) In subsection (3) above, the reference to Treasury bills includes a reference to bills and other short-term instruments issued by the government of another EEA State and appearing to the Bank to correspond as nearly as may be to Treasury bills.]

(4) There shall be chargeable to the Fund—

(a) repayments of special contributions under section 55(2) below;

(b) payments under section 58 below;

(c) money required for the repayment of, and the payment of interest on, money borrowed by the Board; and

(d) the administrative and other necessary or incidental expenses incurred by the Board. **[72]**

NOTES

Commencement: 1 October 1987 (sub-ss (1), (2), (3), (4)) (SI 1987/1664); 1 July 1995 (sub-s (3A)) (SI 1995/1442).

Sub-s (3A): inserted by the Credit Institutions (Protection of Depositors) Regulations 1995, SI 1995/1442, reg 26, subject to transitional provisions and savings in reg 53 at **[711M]**.

Transitory modification: see the Credit Institutions (Protection of Depositors) Regulations 1995, SI 1995/1442, reg 54, at **[711N]**.

Contributions to the Fund

52 Contributory institutions and general provisions as to contributions

[(1) All UK institutions and participating institutions shall be liable to contribute to the Fund and are in this Part of this Act referred to as "contributory institutions".]

(2) Contributions to the Fund shall be levied on a contributory institution by the Board by the service on the institution of a notice specifying the amount due, which shall be paid by the institution not later than twenty-one days after the date on which the notice is served.

[(2A) Where—

    (a) a notice under subsection (2) above is served on a contributory institution; and

    (b) the amount specified in the notice remains unpaid after the period of twenty-one days mentioned in that subsection,

the Board shall as soon as practicable give written notice of that fact to the Bank.]

(3) Subject to section 56 below, on each occasion on which contributions are to be levied from contributory institutions (other than the occasion of the levy of an initial contribution from a particular institution under section 53 below)—

    (a) a contribution shall be levied from each of the contributory institutions; and

    (b) the amount of the contribution of each institution shall be ascertained by applying to the institution's deposit base the percentage determined by the Board for the purpose of the contribution levied on that occasion.

[(4) Subject to subsection (4B) and section 57 below, the deposit base of an institution in relation to any contribution is the amount which the Board determines as representing the average, over such period preceding the levying of the contribution as appears to the Board to be appropriate, of deposits in EEA currencies with the United Kingdom offices of that institution other than—

    (a) secured deposits;

    (b) deposits which are own funds within the meaning given by Article 2 of Directive 89/229/EEC;

    (c) deposits which fall within item 1 or 2 of Annex I to Directive 94/19/EC; and

    (d) deposits in respect of which the institution has in the United Kingdom issued a certificate of deposit in an EEA currency.

(4A) In its application to UK institutions, subsection (4) above shall have effect as if the reference to United Kingdom offices included a reference to offices in other EEA States.

(4B) In the case of a participating EEA institution, the amount determined under subsection (4) above shall be reduced by the amount given by the formula—

$$PA \times \frac{HS}{UK}$$

where—

    PA = so much of the amount so determined as is attributable to deposits which are protected by the institution's home State scheme;

    HS = the level of protection (expressed in ecus) afforded by that scheme at the time when the determination is made, or the level of protection mentioned below, whichever is the less;

    UK = the level of protection (so expressed) afforded by this Part of this Act at that time.]

(5) In its application to this section, section 5(3) above shall have effect with the omission of paragraphs (b) and (c).

[(6) In this Part of this Act—

"the 1995 Regulations" means the Credit Institutions (Protection of Depositors) Regulations 1995;

"administrator", in relation to an institution, means an administrator of the institution under Part II of the Insolvency Act 1986 or Part III of the Insolvency (Northern Ireland) Order 1989;

"building society" means a building society incorporated (or deemed to be incorporated) under the Building Societies Act 1986;

"the deposit protection scheme" means the scheme for the protection of depositors continued in force by this Part of this Act;

"ecu" means—

(a) the European currency unit as defined in Article 1 of Council Regulation No. 3320/94/EC; or

(b) except in section 60(1) below, any other unit of account which is defined by reference to the European currency unit as so defined;

"EEA currency" means the currency of an EEA State or ecus;

"EEA State" means a State which is a Contracting Party to the Agreement on the European Economic Area signed at Oporto on 2nd May 1992 as adjusted by the Protocol signed at Brussels on 17th March 1993;

"former authorised institution" does not include any institution which is a former UK institution or a former participating institution;

"former participating institution" means an institution which was formerly a participating institution and continues to have a liability in respect of any deposit for which it had a liability at a time when it was a participating institution, and "former participating EEA institution" and "former participating non-EEA institution" shall be construed accordingly;

"former UK institution" means an institution which was formerly a UK institution and continues to have a liability in respect of any deposit for which it had a liability at a time when it was a UK institution;

"home State scheme" has the same meaning as in the 1995 Regulation;

"participating EEA institution" means a European authorised institution which, in accordance with Chapter I of Part II of the 1995 Regulations, is participating in the deposit protection scheme;

"participating institution" means a participating EEA institution or a participating non-EEA institution;

"participating non-EEA institution" means an authorised institution which is incorporated in or formed under the law of a country or territory outside the European Economic Area, not being one—

(a) which has, in accordance with Chapter III of Part II of the 1995 Regulations, elected not to participate in the deposit protection scheme; and

(b) whose election under that Chapter is still in force;

"UK institution" means an authorised institution which is incorporated in or formed under the law of any part of the United Kingdom.

(7) In its application to this Part, section 5(3) above shall have effect as if—

(a) the references in paragraph (a) to an authorised institution included references to a building society and to any credit institution which is incorporated in or formed under the law of a country or territory outside the United Kingdom; and

(b) in Schedule 2 to this Act, paragraph 5 (building societies) were omitted.] **[73]**

NOTES
Commencement: 1 October 1987 (sub-ss (2), (3), (5)) (SI 1987/1664); 1 July 1995 (sub-ss (1), (2A), (4), (4A), (4B), (6), (7)) (SI 1995/1442).
Sub-ss (1), (2A), (4), (4A), (4B), (6), (7): sub-ss (1), (4), (4A), (4B) substituted, and sub-ss (2A), (6), (7) inserted, by the Credit Institutions (Protection of Depositors) Regulations 1995, SI 1995/1442, reg 27, subject to transitional provisions and savings in reg 53 at **[711M]**.
Transitory modification: see the Credit Institutions (Protection of Depositors) Regulations 1995, SI 1995/1442, reg 54, at **[711N]**.

53 Initial contributions

(1) Subject to subsection (4) below, where an institution becomes a contributory institution after the coming into force of this Part of this Act the Board shall levy from it, on or as soon as possible after the day on which it becomes a contributory institution, an initial contribution of an amount determined in accordance with subsection (2) or (3) below.

(2) Where the institution concerned has a deposit base, then, subject to section 56(1) below, the amount of an initial contribution levied under this section shall be such percentage of the deposit base as the Board considers appropriate to put the institution on a basis of equality with the other contributory institutions, having regard to—

(a) the initial contributions previously levied under this section or under section 24(1) of the Banking Act 1979; and

(b) so far as they are attributable to an increase in the size of the Fund resulting from an order under subsection (2) of section 54 below or subsection (2) of section 25 of that Act, further contributions levied under either of those sections.

[(2A) In its application to participating EEA institutions, subsection (2) above shall have effect as if the reference to a basis of equality were a reference to a basis of parity.]

(3) Where the institution concerned has no deposit base the amount of an initial contribution levied under this section shall be the minimum amount for the time being provided for in section 56(1) below.

(4) The Board may waive an initial contribution under this section if it appears to it that the institution concerned is to carry on substantially the same business as that previously carried on by one or more institutions which are or were contributory institutions. **[74]**

NOTES
Commencement: 1 October 1987 (sub-ss (1), (2), (3), (4)) (SI 1987/1664); 1 July 1995 (sub-s (2A)) (SI 1995/1442).
Sub-s (2A): inserted by the Credit Institutions (Protection of Depositors) Regulations 1995, SI 1995/1442, reg 28, subject to transitional provisions and savings in reg 53 at **[711M]**.
Transitional provision: see s 107, Sch 5, para 9.
Transitory modification: see the Credit Institutions (Protection of Depositors) Regulations 1995, SI 1995/1442, reg 54, at **[711N]**.

54 Further contributions

(1) If at the end of any financial year of the Board the amount standing to the

credit of the Fund is less than £3 million the Board may, with the approval of the Treasury, levy further contributions from contributory institutions so as to restore the amount standing to the credit of the Fund to a minimum of £5 million and a maximum of £6 million.

(2) If at any time it appears to the Treasury to be desirable in the interests of depositors to increase the size of the Fund, the Treasury may, after consultation with the Board, by order amend subsection (1) above so as to substitute for the sums for the time being specified in that subsection such larger sums as may be specified in the order; but no such order shall be made unless a draft of it has been laid before and approved by a resolution of each House of Parliament.

(3) An order under subsection (2) above may authorise the Board forthwith to levy further contributions from contributory institutions so as to raise the amount standing to the credit of the Fund to a figure between the new minimum and maximum amounts provided for by the order. [75]

NOTE
Transitory modification: see the Credit Institutions (Protection of Depositors) Regulations 1995, SI 1995/1442, reg 54, at **[711N]**.

55 Special contributions

(1) If it appears to the Board that payments under section 58 below are likely to exhaust the Fund, the Board may, with the approval of the Treasury, levy special contributions from contributory institutions to meet the Fund's commitments under that section.

(2) Where at the end of any financial year of the Board there is money in the Fund which represents special contributions and will not in the opinion of the Board be required for making payments under section 58 below in consequence of institutions having become insolvent or subject to administration orders before repayments are made under this subsection the Board—

  (a) shall repay to the institutions from which it was levied so much (if any) of that money as can be repaid without reducing the amount standing to the credit of the Fund below the maximum amount for the time being specified in subsection (1) of section 54 above; and
  (b) may repay to those institutions so much (if any) of that money as can be repaid without reducing the amount standing to the credit of the Fund below the minimum amount for the time being specified in that subsection.

(3) Repayments to institutions under this section shall be made pro rata according to the amount of the special contribution made by each of them but the Board may withhold the whole or part of any repayment due to an institution that has become insolvent and, in the case of an institution that has ceased to be a contributory institution, may either withhold its repayment or make it to any other contributory institution which, in the opinion of the Board, is its successor. [76]

NOTE
Transitory modification: see the Credit Institutions (Protection of Depositors) Regulations 1995, SI 1995/1442, reg 54, at **[711N]**.

56 Maximum and minimum contributions

(1) The amount of the initial contribution levied from a contributory institution shall be not less than £10,000.

(2) The amount of the initial contribution or any further contribution levied from a contributory institution shall not exceed £300,000.

(3) No contributory institution shall be required to pay a further or special contribution if, or to the extent that, the amount of that contribution, together with previous initial, further and special contributions made by the institution after allowing for any repayments made to it under section 55(2) above or section 63 below, amounts to more than 0.3 per cent. of the institution's deposit base as ascertained for the purpose of the contribution in question.

(4) Nothing in subsection (3) above—

(a) shall entitle an institution to repayment of any contribution previously made; or
(b) shall prevent the Board from proceeding to levy contributions from other contributory institutions in whose case the limit in that subsection has not been reached.

(5) The Treasury may from time to time after consultation with the Board by order—

(a) amend subsection (1) or (2) above so as to substitute for the sum for the time being specified in that subsection such other sum as may be specified in the order; or
(b) amend subsection (3) above so as to substitute for the percentage for the time being specified in that subsection such other percentage as may be specified in the order.

(6) No order shall be made under subsection (5) above unless a draft of it has been laid before and approved by a resolution of each House of Parliament.

[77]

NOTES

Transitional provision: see s 107, Sch 5, para 10.
Transitory modification: see the Credit Institutions (Protection of Depositors) Regulations 1995, SI 1995/1442, reg 54, at **[711N]**.

57 Deposit base of transferee institutions

(1) This section applies where the liabilities in respect of deposits of a person specified in Schedule 2 to this Act (an "exempted person") are transferred to an institution which is not such a person (a "transferee institution").

(2) If the transferee institution becomes a contributory institution on the occasion of the transfer or immediately thereafter it shall be treated for the purposes of section 53 above as having such deposit base as it would have if—

(a) [deposits in EEA currencies] with the United Kingdom offices of the exempted person at any time had at that time been [deposits in EEA currencies] with the United Kingdom offices of the transferee institution; and
(b) [certificates of deposit in EEA currencies] issued by the exempted person had been issued by the transferee institution.

(3) If the transferee institution is already a contributory institution at the time of the transfer, the Board shall levy from it, as soon as possible after the transfer, a further initial contribution of an amount equal to the initial contribution which it would have been liable to make if—

(a) it had become a contributory institution on the date of the transfer;
(b) its deposit base were calculated by reference (and by reference only)

to the [deposits in EEA currencies] with the United Kingdom offices
of the exempted person, taking [certificates of deposit in EEA
currencies] issued by the exempted person as having been issued by
the transferee institution; and

(c) the amount specified in section 56(2) above were reduced by the
amount of any initial contribution which the transferee institution
has already made.

(4) Whether or not the transferee institution is already a contributory institution at the time of the transfer it shall be treated for the purposes of the
levying from it of any further or special contribution as having such deposit
base as it would have if the [deposits in EEA currencies] with its United
Kingdom offices and the [certificates of deposit in EEA currencies] issued by it
included respectively [deposits in EEA currencies] with the United Kingdom
offices of the exempted person and [certificates of deposit in EEA currencies]
issued by that person.

[(4A) In their application to UK institutions, subsections (2) to (4) above
shall have effect as if references to United Kingdom offices included references
to offices in other EEA States.]

(5) In its application to this section, section 5(3) above shall have effect with
the omission of paragraphs (b) and (c).   **[78]**

NOTES
Commencement: 1 October 1987 (sub-ss (1)–(4), (5)) (SI 1987/1664); 1 July 1995 (sub-s (4A))
(SI 1995/1442).
Sub-ss (2), (3), (4), (4A): words in square brackets in sub-ss (2), (3), (4) substituted, and sub-s
(4A) inserted, by the Credit Institutions (Protection of Depositors) Regulations 1995, SI 1995/1442,
reg 29, subject to transitional provisions and savings in reg 53 at **[711M]**.
Transitory modifications: see the Credit Institutions (Protection of Depositors) Regulations
1995, SI 1995/1442, reg 54, at **[711N]**.

Payments out of the Fund

58 Compensation payments to depositors

[(1) Subject to the provisions of this section, if at any time an institution to
which this subsection applies becomes insolvent, the Board—

(a) shall as soon as practicable pay out of the Fund to depositors who have
protected deposits with that institution which are due and payable
amounts equal to nine-tenths of their protected deposits; and

(b) shall in any event secure that, before the end of the relevant period,
it is in a position to make those payments as soon as they fall to be
made.

(2) Subsection (1) above applies to an institution which—

(a) is a UK institution or participating institution;
(b) is a former UK institution or a former participating institution; or
(c) is a former authorised institution (not being a recognised bank or
licensed institution excluded by an order under section 23(2) of the
Banking Act 1979);

and if at any time such an institution ceases to be insolvent, subsection (1)
above shall cease to apply in relation to that institution.

(2A) In subsection (1) above "the relevant period" means—

(a) the period of three months beginning with the time when the institution becomes insolvent; or

(b) that period and such additional period or periods, being not more than three and of not more than three months each, as the Bank may in exceptional circumstances allow.

(2B) A person claiming to be entitled to a payment under subsection (1) above in respect of a protected deposit with a participating institution shall make his claim in such form, with such evidence proving it, and within such period, as the Board directs.

(2C) The amount of any payment which falls to be made under subsection (1) above in respect of a protected deposit made with an office of a UK institution in another EEA State shall not exceed such amount as the Board may determine is or would be payable, in respect of an equivalent deposit made with an institution authorised in that State, under any corresponding scheme for the protection of depositors or investors which is in force in that State.

(2D) Where, in the case of a participating EEA institution, the Board is satisfied that a depositor has received or is entitled to receive a payment in respect of his protected deposit under any home State scheme, the Board shall deduct an amount equal to that payment from the payment that would otherwise be made to the depositor under subsection (1) above.]

(3) [Where, in the case of a UK institution or participating non-EEA institution, the Board is satisfied that a depositor has received or will receive a payment] in respect of his protected deposit under any scheme for protecting depositors or investors which is comparable to that for which provision is made by this Part of this Act or under a guarantee given by a government or other authority the Board may—

(a) deduct an amount equal to the whole or part of that payment from the payment that would otherwise be made to him under subsection (1) . . . above; or
(b) in pursuance of an agreement made by the Board with the authority responsible for the scheme or by which the guarantee was given, make in full the payment required by that subsection and recoup from that authority such contribution to it as may be specified in or determined under the agreement.

(4) Where the Board makes such a deduction as is mentioned in paragraph (a) of subsection (3) above it may agree with the authority responsible for the scheme or by which the guarantee was given to reimburse that authority to the extent of the deduction or any lesser amount.

(5) The Board may decline to make any payment under subsection (1) . . . above to a person who, in the opinion of the Board, has any responsibility for, or may have profited directly or indirectly from, the circumstances giving rise to the institution's financial difficulties.

[(6) There shall be deducted from any payment to be made by the Board under subsection (1) above in respect of a deposit any payment already made in respect of that deposit by a liquidator or administrator of the institution; and in this subsection, in relation to an institution formed under the law of a country or territory outside the United Kingdom, the reference to a liquidator or administrator includes a reference to a person whose functions appear to the Board to correspond as nearly as may be to those of a liquidator or administrator.]

(7) The Treasury may, after consultation with the Board, by order amend [subsection (1)] above so as to substitute for the fraction for the time being

specified in [that subsection] such other fraction as may be specified in the order; but no such order shall be made unless a draft of it has been laid before and approved by a resolution of each House of Parliament.

(8) Notwithstanding that the Board may not yet have made or become liable to make a payment under subsection (1) above in relation to an institution falling within that subsection—

    (a) the Board shall at all times be entitled to receive any notice or other document [required to be sent to a creditor of the institution under Part II of the Insolvency Act 1986 or under Part III of the Insolvency (Northern Ireland) Order 1989, or] required to be sent to a creditor of the institution whose debt has been proved; and

    (b) a duly authorised representative of the Board shall be entitled—

        (i) to attend any meeting of creditors of the institution and to make representations as to any matter for decision at that meeting;

       (ii) to be a member of any committee established under [section 26 or 301] of the Insolvency Act 1986;

      (iii) to be a commissioner under section 30 of the Bankruptcy (Scotland) Act 1985; and

      (iv) to be a member of a committee established for the purposes of Part IV or V of the Insolvency Act 1986 under section 101 of that Act or under section 141 or 142 of that Act . . . .

      [(v) to be a member of any committee established under [Article 38 or 274] of the Insolvency (Northern Ireland) Order 1989; and

      (vi) to be a member of a committee established for the purposes of Part V or VI of the Insolvency (Northern Ireland) Order 1989 under Article 87 of that Order or under Article 120 of that Order.]

(9) Where a representative of the Board exercises his right to be a member of such a committee as is mentioned in paragraph (b)(ii) or (iv) of subsection (8) above or to be a commissioner by virtue of paragraph (b)(iii) of that subsection he may not be removed except with the consent of the Board and his appointment under that subsection shall be disregarded for the purposes of any provision made by or under any enactment which specifies a minimum or maximum number of members of such a committee or commission.

[(10) References in this section and sections 59 and 60 below to a former authorised institution include references to an institution which—

    (a) was formerly a European authorised institution which accepted deposits in the United Kingdom; and

    (b) continues to have a liability in respect of any deposit for which it had a liability when it was such an institution;

and references in section 60 below to ceasing to be an authorised institution include references to ceasing to be a European authorised institution which accepted deposits in the United Kingdom.]   [79]

NOTES
    Commencement: 1 October 1987 (sub-ss (3)–(5), (7)–(9)) (SI 1987/1664); 1 July 1995 (sub-ss (1), (2), (2A)–(2D), (6), (10)) (SI 1995/1442).
    Sub-ss (1), (2), (2A)–(2D): substituted for sub-ss (1), (2) by the Credit Institutions (Protection of Depositors) Regulations 1995, SI 1995/1442, reg 30(1), subject to transitional provisions and savings in reg 53, at **[711M]**.
    Sub-ss (3), (5), (7): words in square brackets substituted, and words omitted repealed, by the Credit Institutions (Protection of Depositors) Regulations 1995, SI 1995/1442, reg 30(2), (3), (5), subject to transitional provisions and savings in reg 53, at **[711M]**.
    Sub-ss (6), (10): substituted by the Credit Institutions (Protection of Depositors) Regulations 1995, SI 1995/1442, reg 30(4), (7), subject to transitional provisions and savings in reg 53, at **[711M]**.

Sub-s (8): words in square brackets in sub-s (8)(a), (b)(ii) inserted and substituted respectively by the Credit Institutions (Protection of Depositors) Regulations 1995, SI 1995/1442, reg 30(6), subject to transitional provisions and savings in reg 53, at **[711M]**; words omitted in sub-s (8)(b)(iv) repealed by the Insolvency (Northern Ireland) Order 1989, SI 1989/2405 (NI 19), art 381(2), Sch 9, Pt II, para 50(b)(i); sub-s (8)(b)(v), (vi) added by the Insolvency (Northern Ireland) Order 1989, SI 1989/2405 (NI 19), art 381(2), Sch 9, Pt II, para 50(b)(ii); words in square brackets in sub-s (8)(b)(v) substituted by the Credit Institutions (Protection of Depositors) Regulations 1995, SI 1995/1442, reg 30(6), subject to transitional provisions and savings in reg 53, at **[711M]**.

Modifications: as to modifications to this section, see the Credit Institutions (Protection of Depositors) Regulations 1995, SI 1995/1442, reg 18, at **[711A]**.

Transitory modification: see the Credit Institutions (Protection of Depositors) Regulations 1995, SI 1995/1442, reg 54, at **[711N]**.

[59 Meaning of insolvency

(1) For the purposes of this Part of this Act, a UK institution or participating non-EEA institution becomes insolvent—

    (a) on the making by the Bank of a determination that, for reasons which directly relate to the institution's financial circumstances, the institution—

        (i) is unable to repay deposits which are due and payable; and
        (ii) has no current prospect of being able to do so;

    (b) on the making by a court in any part of the United Kingdom, or in another EEA State, or a judicial ruling which—

        (i) directly relates to the institution's financial circumstances; and
        (ii) has the effect of suspending the ability of depositors to make claims against the institution; or

    (c) in the case of a participating non-EEA institution, on the making by a court in any country or territory outside the European Economic Area of a judicial ruling which appears to the Board to correspond as nearly as may be to such a judicial ruling as is mentioned in paragraph (b) above,

but only if deposits made with the institution have become due and payable and have not been repaid.

(2) For the purposes, a participating EEA institution becomes insolvent—

    (a) on the making by the supervisory authority in the institution's home State of a declaration that deposits held by the institution are no longer available; or

    (b) on the making by a court in any part of the United Kingdom, or in an EEA State other than the institution's home State, of a judicial ruling which—

        (i) directly relates to the institution's financial circumstances; and
        (ii) has the effect of suspending the ability of depositors to make claims against the institution,

but only if, in a case falling within paragraph (b) above, deposits made with the institution have become due and payable and have not been repaid.

(3) For those purposes—

    (a) an institution which has become insolvent by virtue of such a determination or declaration as is mentioned in subsection (1)(a) or (2)(a) above ceases to be insolvent on any withdrawal of the determination or declaration; and

(b) an institution which has become insolvent by virtue of such a judicial ruling as is mentioned in subsection (1)(b) or (c) or (2)(b) above ceases to be insolvent on any reversal of the ruling (whether on appeal or otherwise).

(4) In relation to a UK institution or participating non-EEA institution, it shall be the duty of the Bank—

(a) to make such a determination as is mentioned in subsection (1)(a) above within 21 days of its being satisfied as there mentioned; and
(b) to withdraw such a determination within 21 days of its ceasing to be so satisfied.

(5) In this section—

(a) any reference to a UK institution includes references to a former UK institution, and to a former authorised institution which is incorporated in or formed under the law of any part of the United Kingdom;
(b) any reference to a participating EEA institution includes references to a former participating EEA institution, and to a former authorised institution which is incorporated in or formed under the law of an EEA State other than the United Kingdom; and
(c) any reference to a participating non-EEA institution includes references to a former participating non-EEA institution, and to a former authorised institution which is incorporated in or formed under the law of a country or territory which is outside the European Economic Area.]   [80]

NOTES
Commencement: 1 July 1995 (SI 1995/1442).
This section substituted by the Credit Institutions (Protection of Depositors) Regulations 1995, SI 1995/1442, reg 31, subject to transitional provisions and savings in reg 53 at [711M] (and see in particular reg 53(3)).
Sub-s (1)(b): it is thought that "or a judicial ruling" should read "of a judicial ruling".
Transitory modification: see the Credit Institutions (Protection of Depositors) Regulations 1995, SI 1995/1442, reg 54, at [711N].

60 Protected deposits

[(1) Subject to the provisions of this section, in relation to an institution in respect of which a payment falls to be made under section 58(1) above, any reference in this Act to a depositor's protected deposit is a reference to the liability of the institution to him in respect of—

(a) the principal amount of each deposit in an EEA currency which was made by him with a United Kingdom office of the institution before the time when the institution became insolvent and has become due and payable; and
(b) accrued interest on any such deposit up to the time when it became due and payable,

but so that the total liability of the institution to him in respect of such deposits does not exceed £20,000, or the sterling equivalent of 22,222 ecus immediately before the time when the institution became insolvent, whichever is the greater.

(2) In calculating a depositor's protected deposit for the purposes of subsection (1) above, the amount to be taken into account as regards any deposit made in another EEA currency shall be its sterling equivalent immediately before the time when the institution became insolvent, or the time when the deposit became due and payable, whichever is the later.

(2A) In its application to UK institutions, subsection (1) above shall have effect as if any reference to United Kingdom offices included a reference to offices in other EEA States.

(3) For the purposes of subsection (1) above no account shall be taken of any liability unless—

(a) proof of the debt, or a claim for repayment of the deposit, which gives rise to the liability has been lodged with a liquidator or administrator of the institution; or

(b) the depositor has provided the Board with all such written authorities, information and documents as, in the event of a liquidator or administrator being appointed, the Board will need for the purpose of lodging and pursuing, on the depositor's behalf, a proof of the debt, or a claim for the repayment of the deposit, which gives rise to the liability.

(4) In subsection (3) above, in relation to an institution incorporated in or formed under the law of a country or territory outside the United Kingdom—

(a) references to a liquidator or administrator include references to a person whose functions appear to the Board to correspond as nearly as may be to those of a liquidator or administrator; and

(b) references to the lodging, or the lodging and pursuing, of a proof of the debt, or a claim for the repayment of the deposit, which gives rise to the liability include references to the doing of an act or acts which appear to the Board to correspond as nearly as may be to the lodging, or the lodging and pursuing, of such a proof or claim.]

(5) The Treasury may, after consultation with the Board, by order amend [subsection (1)] above so as to substitute for the sum for the time being specified in those subsections such larger sum as may be specified in the order; but no such order shall be made unless a draft of it has been laid before and approved by a resolution of each House of Parliament.

[(6) In determining the liability or total liability of an institution to a depositor for the purposes of subsection (1) above, no account shall be taken of any liability in respect of a deposit if—

(a) it is a secured deposit; or

(b) it is a deposit which is own funds within the meaning given by Article 2 of Directive 89/299/EEC; or

(c) it is a deposit which the Board is satisfied was made in the course of a money-laundering transaction; or

(d) it is a deposit by a person mentioned in item 1 or 2 of Annex I to Directive 94/19/EC which was made otherwise than as trustee for a person not so mentioned; or

(e) the institution is a former UK institution or former authorised institution and the deposit was made after it ceased to be a UK institution or authorised institution unless, at the time the deposit was made, the depositor did not know, and could not reasonably be expected to have known, that it had ceased to be a UK institution or authorised institution; or

(f) the institution is a former participating EEA institution and the deposit was made after it ceased to be a participating EEA institution; or

(g) the institution is a former participating non-EEA institution and the deposit was made after it ceased to be a participating non-EEA institution unless the Board is satisfied—

      (i) that the depositor is entitled under the institution's home State scheme to a payment in respect of the deposit; and

      (ii) that he has not received, and has no prospect of receiving, that payment;

and references in paragraph (e) above to an institution ceasing to be an authorised institution include references an institution ceasing to be a recognised bank or licensed institution under the Banking Act 1979.

(6A) A transaction in connection with which an offence has been committed under—

    (a) any enactment specified in regulation 2(3) of the Money Laundering Regulations 1993; or

    (b) any enactment in force in another EEA State, or in a country or territory outside the European Economic Area, which has effect for the purpose of prohibiting money laundering within the meaning of Article 1 of Directive 91/308/EEC,

is a money-laundering transaction for the purposes of subsection (6)(c) above at any time if, at that time, a person stands convicted of the offence or has been charged with the offence and has not been tried.]

(7) Unless the Board otherwise directs in any particular case, in determining the total liability of an institution to a depositor for the purposes of subsection (1) . . . above there shall be deducted the amount of any liability of the depositor to the institution—

    (a) in respect of which a right of set-off existed immediately before the institution became insolvent [against any such deposit in an EEA currency] as is referred to in subsection (1) . . . above; or

    (b) in respect of which such right would then have existed if the deposit in question had been repayable on demand and the liability in question had fallen due.

(8) . . .

(9) For the purposes of this section and sections 61 and 62 below the definition of deposit in section 5 above—

    (a) shall be treated as including—

      (i) any sum that would otherwise be excluded by paragraph (a), (d) or (e) of subsection (3) of that section if the sum is paid as trustee for a person not falling within any of those paragraphs;

      (ii) any sum that would otherwise be excluded by paragraph (b) or (c) of that subsection;

    (b) subject to subsections (10) and (11) below, shall be treated as excluding any sum paid by a trustee for a person falling within paragraph (e) of subsection (3) of that section; and

    (c) shall be treated as including any sum the right to repayment of which is evidenced by a transferable certificate of deposit or other transferable instrument and which would be a deposit within the meaning of section 5 as extended by paragraph (a) and restricted by paragraph (b) above if it had been paid by the person who is entitled to it at the time when the institution in question becomes insolvent.

(10) Where the trustee referred to in paragraph (b) of subsection (9) above is not a bare trustee and there are two or more beneficiaries that paragraph applies only if all the beneficiaries fall within section 5(3)(e) above.

(11) . . .   **[81]**

NOTES

Commencement: 1 October 1987 (sub-ss (5), (7), (9), (10)) (SI 1987/1664); 1 July 1995 (sub-ss (1), (2), (2A), (3), (4), (6), (6A)) (SI 1995/1442).

Sub-ss (1), (2), (2A), (3), (4), (6), (6A): substituted (for sub-ss (1)–(4) and (6)) by the Credit Institutions (Protection of Depositors) Regulations 1995, SI 1995/1442, reg 32(1), (3), subject to transitional provisions and savings in reg 53 at **[711M]**.

Sub-ss (5), (7), (8): words in square brackets in sub-ss (5), (7) substituted, and words omitted from sub-s (7), and whole of sub-s (8), repealed, by the Credit Institutions (Protection of Depositors) Regulations 1995, SI 1995/1442, reg 32(2), (4), (5), subject to transitional provisions and savings in reg 53 at **[711M]**.

Sub-s (11): applies to Scotland only.

Transitory modification: see the Credit Institutions (Protection of Depositors) Regulations 1995, SI 1995/1442, reg 54, at **[711N]**.

61 Trustee deposits, joint deposits etc

(1) In the cases to which this section applies sections 58 and 60 above shall have effect with the following modifications.

(2) Subject to the provisions of this section, where any persons are entitled to a deposit as trustees they shall be treated as a single and continuing body of persons distinct from the persons who may from time to time be the trustees, and if the same persons are entitled as trustees to different deposits under different trusts they shall be treated as a separate and distinct body with respect to each of those trusts.

(3) Where a deposit is held for any person or for two or more persons jointly by a bare trustee, that person or, as the case may be, those persons jointly shall be treated as entitled to the deposit without the intervention of any trust.

(4) . . .

(5) A deposit to which two or more persons are entitled as members of a partnership (whether or not in equal shares) shall be treated as a single deposit.

(6) Subject to subsection (5) above, where two or more persons are jointly entitled to a deposit and subsection (2) above does not apply each of them shall be treated as having a separate deposit of an amount produced by dividing the amount of the deposit to which they are jointly entitled by the number of persons who are so entitled.

(7) Where a person is entitled (whether as trustee or otherwise) to a deposit made out of a clients' or other similar account containing money to which one or more other persons are entitled, that other person or, as the case may be, each of those other persons shall be treated (to the exclusion of the first-mentioned person) as entitled to so much of the deposit as corresponds to the proportion of the money in the account to which he is entitled.

(8) Where an authorised institution is entitled as trustee to a sum which would be a deposit apart from section 5(3)(a) above and represents deposits made with the institution, each of the persons who made those deposits shall be treated as having made a deposit equal to so much of that sum as represents the deposit made by him.

(9) The Board may decline to make any payment under section 58 above in respect of a deposit until the person claiming to be entitled to it informs the Board of the capacity in which he is entitled to the deposit and provides sufficient information to enable the Board to determine what payment (if any) should be made under that section and to whom.

(10) In this section "jointly entitled" means—

    (a) in England and Wales and in Northern Ireland, beneficially entitled
        as joint tenants, tenants in common or coparceners;
    (b) . . .

[(11) In the application of this section in relation to deposits made with an
office of a UK institution in another EEA State, references to persons entitled
in any of the following capacities, namely—

    (a) as trustees;
    (b) as bare trustees;
    (c) as members of a partnership; or
    (d) as persons jointly entitled,

shall be construed as references to persons entitled under the law of that State
in a capacity appearing to the Board to correspond as nearly as may be to that
capacity.]   [82]

NOTES

Commencement: 1 October 1987 (sub-ss (1)–(10)) (SI 1987/1664); 1 July 1995 (sub-s (11)) (SI
1995/1442).

Sub-ss (4), (10)(b): apply to Scotland only.

Sub-s (11): inserted by the Credit Institutions (Protection of Depositors) Regulations 1995, SI
1995/1442, reg 33, subject to transitional provisions and savings in reg 53 at **[711M]**.

Transitory modification: see the Credit Institutions (Protection of Depositors) Regulations
1995, SI 1995/1442, reg 54, at **[711N]**.

62 Liability of institution in respect of compensation payments

(1) This section applies where—

    (a) an institution becomes insolvent . . .; and
    (b) the Board has made, or is under a liability to make, a payment under
        section 58 above by virtue of the institution becoming insolvent . . .;

and in the following provisions of this section a payment falling within paragraph (b) above, less any amount which the Board is entitled to recoup by
virtue of any such agreement as is mentioned in subsection (3)(b) of that
section, is referred to as "a compensation payment" and the person to whom
such a payment has been or is to be made is referred to as "the depositor".

(2) Where this section applies in respect of an institution [that is being
wound up]—

    (a) the institution shall become liable to the Board, as in respect of a
        contractual debt incurred immediately before the institution [began
        to be wound up], for an amount equal to the compensation payment;
    (b) the liability of the institution to the depositor in respect of any
        deposit or deposits of his ("the liability to the depositor") shall be
        reduced by an amount equal to the compensation payment made or
        to be made to him by the Board; and
    (c) the duty of the liquidator of the insolvent institution to make
        payments to the Board on account of the liability referred to in
        paragraph (a) above ("the liability to the Board") and to the depos-
        itor on account of the liability to him (after taking account of
        paragraph (b) above) shall be varied in accordance with subsection
        (3) below.

(3) The variation referred to in subsection (2)(c) above is as follows—

(a) in the first instance the liquidator shall pay to the Board instead of to the depositor any amount which, apart from this section, would be payable on account of the liability to the depositor except in so far as that liability relates to any such deposit as is mentioned in section 60(6) above; and

(b) if at any time the total amount paid to the Board by virtue of paragraph (a) above and in respect of the liability to the Board equals the amount of the compensation payment made to the depositor, the liquidator shall thereafter pay to the depositor instead of to the Board any amount which, apart from this paragraph, would be payable to the Board in respect of the liability to the Board.

(4) Where this section applies in respect of an institution [that is not being wound up]—

(a) the institution shall, at the time when the compensation payment in respect of a deposit falls to be made by the Board, become liable to the Board for an amount equal to that payment; and

(b) the liability of the institution to the depositor in respect of that deposit shall be reduced by an amount equal to that payment.

(5) Where an institution [is wound up after it has become insolvent] subsections (2) and (3) above shall not apply to any compensation payment to the extent to which the Board has received a payment in respect of it by virtue of subsection (4)(a) above.

(6) Where by virtue of section 61 above the compensation payment is or is to be made by the Board to a person other than the person to whom the institution is liable in respect of the deposit any reference in the foregoing provisions of this section to the liability to the depositor shall be construed as a reference to the liability of the institution to the person to whom that payment would fall to be made by the Board apart from that section.

(7) Where the Board makes a payment under section 58(4) above in respect of an amount deducted from a payment due to a depositor this section shall have effect as if the amount had been paid to the depositor.

(8) Rules may be made—

(a) for England and Wales, under sections 411 and 412 of the Insolvency Act 1986;

(b) . . .

(c) for Northern Ireland, under [Article 359 of the Insolvency (Northern Ireland) Order 1989] and section 65 of the Judicature (Northern Ireland) Act 1978,

for the purpose of integrating the procedure provided for in this section into the general procedure on a winding-up, bankruptcy or sequestration or under Part II of the Insolvency Act 1986 [or Part III of the Insolvency (Northern Ireland) Order 1989].   **[83]**

NOTES

Sub-ss (1), (2), (4), (5): words omitted from sub-s (1) repealed, and words in square brackets in sub-ss (2), (4), (5) substituted, by the Credit Institutions (Protection of Depositors) Regulations 1995, SI 1995/1442, reg 34, subject to transitional provisions and savings in reg 53 at **[711M]**.

Sub-s (8): sub-s (8)(b) applies to Scotland only; words in square brackets in sub-s (8)(c) substituted, and words in square brackets at the end of sub-s (8) added, by the Insolvency (Northern Ireland) Order 1989, SI 1989/2405 (NI 19), art 381(2), Sch 9, Pt II, para 52(a), (b).

Modifications: as to modifications to this section, see the Credit Institutions (Protection of Depositors) Regulations 1995, SI 1995/1442, reg 14, at **[708]**.

Transitory modification: see the Credit Institutions (Protection of Depositors) Regulations 1995, SI 1995/1442, reg 54, at **[711N]**.

Repayments in respect of contributions

63 Repayments in respect of contributions

(1) Any money received by the Board under section 62 above ("recovered money") shall not form part of the Fund but, for the remainder of the financial year of the Board in which it is received, shall be placed by the Board in an account with the Bank which shall as far as possible invest the money in Treasury bills; and any income arising from the money so invested during the remainder of the year shall be credited to the Fund.

(2) The Board shall prepare a scheme for the making out of recovered money of repayments to institutions in respect of—

(a) special contributions; and
(b) so far as they are not attributable to an increase in the size of the Fund resulting from an order under subsection (2) of section 54 above, further contributions levied under that section,

which have been made in the financial year of the Board in which the money was received or in any previous such financial year.

(3) A scheme under subsection (2) above—

(a) shall provide for the making of repayments first in respect of special contributions and then, if those contributions can be repaid in full (taking into account any previous repayments under this section and under section 55(2) above) in respect of further contributions;
(b) may make provision for repayments in respect of contributions made by an institution which has ceased to be a contributory institution to be made to a contributory institution which, in the opinion of the Board, is its successor; and
(c) subject to paragraph (b) above, may exclude from the scheme further contributions levied from institutions which have ceased to be contributory institutions.

(4) Except where special or further contributions can be repaid in full, repayments to institutions under this section shall be made pro rata according to the amount of the special or further contribution made by each of them.

(5) If at the end of a financial year of the Board in which recovered money is received by it—

(a) that money; and
(b) the amount standing to the credit of the Fund, after any repayments made under section 55 above,

exceeds the maximum amount for the time being specified in section 54(1) above the Board shall as soon as practicable make out of the recovered money, up to an amount not greater than the excess, the repayments required by the scheme under subsection (2) above and may out of the recovered money make such further repayments required by the scheme as will not reduce the amounts mentioned in paragraphs (a) and (b) above below the minimum amount for the time being specified in section 54(1) above.

(6) If in any financial year of the Board—

(a) any of the recovered money is not applied in making payments in accordance with subsection (5) above; or
(b) the payments made in accordance with that subsection are sufficient to provide for the repayment in full of all the contributions to which the scheme relates,

any balance of that money shall be credited to the Fund.   **[84]**

NOTES

  Transitional provision: see s 107, Sch 5, para 11.
  Transitory modification: see the Credit Institutions (Protection of Depositors) Regulations 1995, SI 1995/1442, reg 54, at **[711N]**.

Supplementary provisions

64 Borrowing powers

  (1) If in the course of operating the Fund it appears to the Board desirable to do so, the Board may borrow up to a total outstanding at any time of £10 million or such larger sum as, after consultation with the Board, the Treasury may from time to time by order prescribe.

  (2) An order under subsection (1) above shall be subject to annulment in pursuance of a resolution of either House of Parliament.

  (3) Any amount borrowed by virtue of this section shall be disregarded in ascertaining the amount standing to the credit of the Fund for the purposes of sections 54(1), 55(2) and 63(5) above.   **[85]**

NOTES

  Transitional provision: see s 107, Sch 5, para 12.
  Transitory modification: see the Credit Institutions (Protection of Depositors) Regulations 1995, SI 1995/1442, reg 54, at **[711N]**.
  Order: the Deposit Protection Board (Increase of Borrowing Limit) Order 1991, SI 1991/1684.

65 Power to obtain information

  (1) If required to do so by a request in writing made by the Board, the Bank may by notice in writing served on a contributory institution require the institution, within such time and at such place as may be specified in the notice, to provide the Board with such information and to produce to it such documents, or documents of such a description, as the Board may reasonably require for the purpose of determining the contributions of the institution under this Part of this Act.

  [(2) Subsections (4), (5), (11) and (13) of section 39 above shall have effect in relation to any requirement imposed under subsection (1) above on a UK institution or participating non-EEA institution as they have effect in relation to a requirement imposed under this section.]

  (3) The Board may by notice in writing served on [an insolvent institution or, where a person has been appointed as liquidator or administrator of such an institution, on that person, require the institution or person], at such time or times and at such place as may be specified in the notice—

  (a) to provide the Board with such information; and
  (b) to produce to the Board such documents specified in the notice,

as the Board may reasonably require to enable it to carry out its functions under this Part of this Act.

  (4) Where, as a result of an institution [being wound up], any documents have come into the possession of the Official Receiver or, in Northern Ireland, [the Official Receiver for Northern Ireland], he shall permit any person duly authorised by the Board to inspect the documents for the purpose of establishing—

(a) the identity of those of the institution's depositors to whom the Board are liable to make a payment under section 58 above; and

(b) the amount of the protected deposit held by each of the depositors.

[86]

NOTES

Commencement: 1 October 1987 (sub-ss (1), (3), (4)) (SI 1987/1664); 1 July 1995 (sub-s (2)) (SI 1995/1442).

Sub-ss (2), (3), (4): sub-s (2), and words in square brackets in sub-ss (3), (4), substituted by the Credit Institutions (Protection of Depositors) Regulations 1995, SI 1995/1442, reg 35, subject to transitional provisions and savings in reg 53, at **[711M]**.

Modifications: as to modifications to this section, see the Credit Institutions (Protection of Depositors) Regulations 1995, SI 1995/1442, reg 18, at **[711A]**.

Transitory modification: see the Credit Institutions (Protection of Depositors) Regulations 1995, SI 1995/1442, reg 54, at **[711N]**.

66 Tax treatment of contributions and repayments

In computing for the purposes of the Tax Acts the profits or gains arising from the trade carried on by a contributory institution—

(a) to the extent that it would not be deductible apart from this section, any sum expended by the institution in paying a contribution to the Fund may be deducted as an allowable expense;

(b) any payment which is made to the institution by the Board under section 55(2) above or pursuant to a scheme under section 63(2) above shall be treated as a trading receipt. **[87]**

NOTE

Transitory modification: see the Credit Institutions (Protection of Depositors) Regulations 1995, SI 1995/1442, reg 54, at **[711N]**.

PART III
BANKING NAMES AND DESCRIPTIONS

67 Restriction on use of banking names

(1) Subject to section 68 below, no person carrying on any business in the United Kingdom shall use any name which indicates or may reasonably be understood to indicate (whether in English or any other language) that he is a bank or banker or is carrying on a banking business unless he is an authorised institution to which this section applies.

(2) This section applies to an authorised institution which—

(a) is a company incorporated in the United Kingdom which has—

(i) an issued share capital in respect of which the amount paid up is not less than £5 million (or an amount of equivalent value denominated wholly or partly otherwise than in sterling); or

(ii) undistributable reserves falling within paragraph (a), (b) or (d) of section 264(3) of the Companies Act 1985 or Article 272(3)(a), (b) or (d) of the Companies (Northern Ireland) Order 1986 of not less than that sum (or such an equivalent amount); or

(iii) such undistributable reserves of an amount which together with the amount paid up in respect of its issued share capital equals not less than that sum (or such an equivalent amount); or

(b) is a partnership formed under the law of any part of the United Kingdom in respect of which one or more designated fixed capital accounts are maintained to which there has been credited not less than £5 million (or such an equivalent amount).

(3) For the purposes of subsection (2)(a) above "share capital" does not include share capital which under the terms on which it is issued is to be, or may at the option of the shareholder be, redeemed by the company.

(4) For the purposes of subsection (2)(b) above "designated fixed capital account", in relation to a partnership, means an account—

(a) which is prepared and designated as such under the terms of the partnership agreement;
(b) which shows capital contributed by the partners; and
(c) from which under the terms of that agreement an amount representing capital may only be withdrawn by a partner if—

(i) he ceases to be a partner and an equal amount is transferred to a designated fixed capital account by his former partners or any person replacing him as their partner; or
(ii) the partnership is otherwise dissolved or wound up.

(5) An authorised institution to which subsection (2) above applies whose issued share capital, undistributable reserves or designated fixed capital account is denominated wholly or partly otherwise than in sterling shall not be regarded as ceasing to be such an institution by reason only of a fluctuation in the rate of exchange of sterling unless and until it has ceased to satisfy any of the conditions in that subsection for a continuous period of three months.

(6) The Treasury may from time to time after consultation with the Bank by order amend subsection (2)(a) and (b) above so as to substitute for the sum for the time being specified in that subsection such other sum as may be specified in the order; but an order under this subsection shall be subject to annulment in pursuance of a resolution of either House of Parliament.   **[88]**

NOTE
Transitional provision: see s 107, Sch 5, para 13.

68 Exemptions from s 67

(1) Section 67 above does not prohibit the use of a name by a relevant savings bank, a municipal bank or a school bank if the name contains an indication that the bank or body is a savings bank, municipal bank or, as the case may be, a school bank.

(2) In subsection (1) above—

"relevant savings bank" means—

(i) the National Savings Bank; and
(ii) any penny savings bank;

"school bank" means a body of persons certified as a school bank by the National Savings Bank or an authorised institution.

(3) Section 67 above does not prohibit the use by an authorised institution which is a company incorporated under the law of a country or territory outside the United Kingdom or is formed under the law of a member State other than the United Kingdom of a name under which it carries on business in that country or territory or State (or an approximate translation in English of that name).

(4) Section 67 above does not prohibit the use by—

(a) an authorised institution which is a wholly-owned subsidiary of an authorised institution to which that section or subsection (3) above applies; or

(b) a company which has a wholly-owned subsidiary which is an authorised institution to which that section or subsection applies,

of a name which includes the name of the authorised institution to which that section or subsection applies for the purpose of indicating the connection between the two companies.

(5) Section 67 above does not prohibit the use by an overseas institution (within the meaning of Part IV of this Act) which has its principal place of business in a country or territory outside the United Kingdom and a representative office in the United Kingdom of the name under which it carries on business in that country or territory (or an approximate translation in English of that name) if—

(a) the name is used in immediate conjunction with the description "representative office"; and

(b) where the name appears in writing, that description is at least as prominent as the name;

and in this subsection "representative office" has the same meaning as in Part IV of this Act.

(6) Section 67 above does not apply to—

(a) the Bank;
(b) the central bank of a member State other than the United Kingdom;
(c) the European Investment Bank;
(d) the International Bank for Reconstruction and Development;
(e) the African Development Bank;
(f) the Asian Development Bank;
(g) the Caribbean Development Bank;
(h) the Inter-American Development Bank.

(7) The Treasury may, after consultation with the Bank, by order provide—

(a) that the prohibition in section 67 above shall not apply to any person or class of persons; or

(b) that that prohibition shall apply to a person mentioned in any of paragraphs (c) to (h) of subsection (6) above or a person previously exempted from it by virtue of an order under paragraph (a) above.

(8) An order under paragraph (a) of subsection (7) above shall be subject to annulment in pursuance of a resolution of either House of Parliament; and no order shall be made under paragraph (b) of that subsection unless a draft of it has been laid before and approved by a resolution of each House of Parliament.

(9) Nothing in section 67 above shall prevent an institution which ceases to be an authorised institution to which that section or subsection (4) above applies or ceases to be exempted from the prohibition in that section by virtue of subsection (1) above from continuing to use any name it was previously permitted to use by virtue of that provision during the period of six months beginning with the day when it ceases to be such an institution. **[89]**

NOTES

Modifications: as to modifications to this section, see the Banking Coordination (Second Council Directive) Regulations 1992, SI 1992/3218, reg 47, Sch 8, para 17; see **[693]**.

Order: the Banking Act 1987 (Exempt Persons) Order 1991, SI 1991/66.

69 Restriction on use of banking descriptions

(1) No person carrying on any business in the United Kingdom shall so describe himself or hold himself out as to indicate or reasonably be understood to indicate (whether in English or in any other language) that he is a bank or banker or is carrying on a banking business unless he is an authorised institution or is exempted from the requirements of this subsection under the following provisions of this section.

(2) Subsection (1) above shall not be taken to authorise the use by an authorised institution to which the prohibition in section 67 above applies of any description of itself as a bank or a banker or as carrying on a banking business which is in such immediate conjunction with the name of the institution that the description might reasonably be thought to be part of it.

(3) Subsection (1) above does not prohibit the use by a building society authorised under the Building Societies Act 1986 of any description of itself as providing banking services unless the description is in such immediate conjunction with its name that it might reasonably be thought to be part of it.

(4) Subsection (1) above does not prohibit a person from using the expression "bank" or "banker" (or a similar expression) where it is necessary for him to do so in order to be able to assert that he is complying with, or entitled to take advantage of, any enactment, any instrument made under an enactment, any international agreement, any rule of law or any commercial usage or practice which applies to a person by virtue of his being a bank or banker.

(5) Subsection (1) above does not prohibit the use of a description by a relevant savings bank, a municipal bank or a school bank if the description is accompanied by a statement that the bank or body is a savings bank, a municipal bank or, as the case may be, a school bank; and for the purposes of this subsection "relevant savings bank" and "school bank" have the same meanings as in section 68 above.

(6) Subsection (1) above does not apply to—

    (a) the Bank;
    (b) the central bank of a member State other than the United Kingdom;
    (c) the European Investment Bank;
    (d) the International Bank for Reconstruction and Development;
    (e) the International Finance Corporation;
    (f) the African Development Bank;
    (g) the Asian Development Bank;
    (h) the Caribbean Development Bank;
    (i) the Inter-American Development Bank.

(7) The Treasury may, after consultation with the Bank, by order provide—

    (a) that the prohibition in subsection (1) above shall not apply to any person or class of persons; or
    (b) that that prohibition shall apply to a person mentioned in any of paragraphs (c) to (i) of subsection (6) above or a person previously exempted from it by an order under paragraph (a) above.

(8) An order under paragraph (a) of subsection (7) above shall be subject to annulment in pursuance of a resolution of either House of Parliament; and no order shall be made under paragraph (b) of that subsection unless a draft of it has been laid before and approved by a resolution of each House of Parliament.

NOTES
Modifications: as to modifications to this section, see the Banking Coordination (Second Council Directive) Regulations 1992, SI 1992/3218, reg 47, Sch 8, para 18; see **[693]**.
Order: the Banking Act 1987 (Exempt Persons) Order 1991, SI 1991/66.

70 Power to object to institution's names

(1) Where an institution applies for authorisation under this Act it shall give notice to the Bank of any name it is using or proposes to use for the purposes of or in connection with any business carried on by it and the Bank may give the institution notice in writing—

(a) that it objects to the notified name; or

(b) in the case of an institution which is or will be obliged to disclose any name in connection with any business carried on by it by virtue of section 4 of the Business Names Act 1985 or Article 6 of the Business Names (Northern Ireland) Order 1986, that it objects to that name.

(2) Where an authorised institution proposes to change any name it uses for the purposes of or in connection with any business carried on by it or, in the case of such an institution as is mentioned in subsection (1)(b) above, any such name as is there mentioned, it shall give notice to the Bank of the proposed name and the Bank may within the period of two months beginning with the day on which it receives the notification give notice to the institution in writing that it objects to the proposed name.

(3) The Bank shall not give notice objecting to a name under subsection (1) or (2) above unless it considers that the name is misleading to the public or otherwise undesirable and, in the case of the use of a name by an authorised institution to which section 67 above applies—

(a) the whole of the name shall be taken into account in considering whether it is misleading or undesirable; but

(b) no objection may be made to so much of the name as it is entitled to use by virtue of that section.

(4) Where as a result of a material change in circumstances since the time when notice was given to the Bank under subsection (1) or (2) above or as a result of further information becoming available to the Bank since that time, it appears to the Bank that a name to which it might have objected under that subsection gives so misleading an indication of the nature of the institution's activities as to be likely to cause harm to the public, the Bank may give notice in writing to the institution objecting to the name.

(5) Any notice to be given by an institution under this section shall be given in such manner and form as the Bank may specify and shall be accompanied by such information or documents as the Bank may reasonably require.   **[91]**

NOTES
Transitional provision: see s 107, Sch 5, para 2(3).
Modifications: as to modifications to this section, see the Banking Coordination (Second Council Directive) Regulations 1992, SI 1992/3218, reg 47, Sch 8, para 19; see **[693]**.

71 Effect of notices under s 70 and appeals

(1) Where the Bank has given notice to an authorised institution under section 70 above the institution shall not use the name to which the Bank has objected for the purposes of or in connection with any business carried on in the United Kingdom after the objection has taken effect; and for the purposes of this subsection the disclosure of a name in connection with such a business by

virtue of section 4 of the Business Names Act 1985 or Article 6 of the Business Names (Northern Ireland) Order 1986 shall be treated (if it would not otherwise be) as for the purposes of that business.

(2) For the purposes of this section an objection under section 70(1) or (2) above takes effect when the institution receives the notice of objection.

(3) An institution to which a notice of objection is given under section 70(1) or (2) above may within the period of three weeks beginning with the day on which it receives the notice apply to the court to set aside the objection and on such an application the court may set it aside or confirm it (but without prejudice to its operation before that time).

(4) For the purposes of this section an objection under section 70(4) above takes effect—

    (a) in a case where no application is made under subsection (5) below, at the expiry of the period of two months beginning with the day on which the institution receives the notice of objection or such longer period as the notice may specify; or

    (b) where an application is made under subsection (5) below and the court confirms the objection, after such period as the court may specify.

(5) An institution to which a notice of objection is given under section 70(4) above may within the period of three weeks beginning with the day on which it receives the notice apply to the court to set aside the objection.

(6) In this section "the court" means the High Court, the Court of Session or the High Court in Northern Ireland according to whether—

    (a) if the institution concerned is a company registered in the United Kingdom, it is registered in England and Wales, Scotland or Northern Ireland; and

    (b) in the case of any other institution, its principal or prospective principal place of business in the United Kingdom is situated in England and Wales, Scotland or Northern Ireland. [92]

NOTE

Modifications: as to modifications to this section, see the Banking Coordination (Second Council Directive) Regulations 1992, SI 1992/3218, reg 47, Sch 8, para 20; see **[693]**.

72 Registration of substitute corporate name by oversea company

(1) Where the Bank gives notice under section 70 above objecting to the corporate name of a company incorporated outside the United Kingdom, subsection (4) of section 694 of the Companies Act 1985 or, in Northern Ireland, paragraph (4) of Article 644 of the Companies (Northern Ireland) Order 1986 shall apply, subject to subsection (2) below, as it applies where a notice is served on a company under subsection (1) or (2) of that section or, as the case may be, paragraph (1) or (2) of that Article.

(2) No statement or further statement may be delivered under subsection (4) of section 694 or paragraph (4) of Article 644 by virtue of subsection (1) above unless the Bank has signified that it does not object to the name specified in the statement.

(3) Section 70(2) above shall not apply to a proposed change of a name which has been registered under section 694(4) of the Companies Act 1985 or Article 644(4) of the Companies (Northern Ireland) Order 1986 by virtue of subsection (1) above. [93]

73 Offences under Part III

A person who contravenes any provision in this Part of this Act shall be guilty of an offence and liable on summary conviction to imprisonment for a term not exceeding six months or to a fine not exceeding the fifth level on the standard scale or to both and, where the contravention involves a public display or exhibition of any name or description, there shall be a fresh contravention on each day on which the person causes or permits the display or exhibition to continue. **[94]**

PART IV

OVERSEAS INSTITUTIONS WITH REPRESENTATIVE OFFICES

74 Meaning of "overseas institution" and "representative office"

(1) In this Part of this Act "overseas institution" means a person (other than an authorised institution or any person for the time being specified in Schedule 2 to this Act) who—

(a) is a body corporate incorporated in a country or territory outside the United Kingdom or a partnership or other unincorporated association formed under the law of such a country or territory; or
(b) has his principal place of business in such a country or territory,

being, in either case, a person who satisfies one of the conditions mentioned in subsection (2) below.

(2) The conditions referred to in subsection (1) above are—

(a) that the person's principal place of business is outside the United Kingdom and the person is authorised by the relevant supervisory authority in a country or territory outside the United Kingdom;
(b) that the person describes himself or holds himself out as being authorised by such an authority in a country or territory outside the United Kingdom;
(c) that the person uses any name or in any other way so describes himself or holds himself out as to indicate or reasonably be understood to indicate (whether in English or any other language), that he is a bank or banker or is carrying on a banking business (whether in the United Kingdom or elsewhere).

(3) In this Part of this Act "representative office", in relation to any overseas institution, means premises from which the deposit-taking, lending or other financial or banking activities of the overseas institution are promoted or assisted in any way; and "establishment", in relation to such an office, includes the making of any arrangements by virtue of which such activities are promoted or assisted from it. **[95]**

NOTE
Modifications: as to modifications to this section, see the Banking Coordination (Second Council Directive) Regulations 1992, SI 1992/3218, reg 47, Sch 8, para 21; see **[693]**.

75 Notice of establishment of representative office

(1) An overseas institution shall not establish a representative office in the United Kingdom unless it has given not less than two months' notice to the Bank that it proposes to establish such an office and a notice under this subsection shall specify—

(a) any name the institution proposes to use in relation to activities conducted by it in the United Kingdom after the establishment of that office; and

(b) in the case of an institution which will be obliged to disclose any name in connection with those activities by virtue of section 4 of the Business Names Act 1985 or Article 6 of the Business Names (Northern Ireland) Order 1986, that name.

(2) Where an overseas institution has established a representative office in the United Kingdom before the date on which this Part of this Act comes into force and has not given notice of that fact to the Bank under section 40 of the Banking Act 1979 it shall give notice in writing to the Bank of the continued existence of that office within the period of two months beginning with that date; and the obligation of an overseas institution to give notice under this subsection in respect of the establishment of an office established within the period of one month ending with that date shall supersede any obligation to give notice in respect of that matter under that subsection.

(3) A notice under this section shall be given in such manner and form as the Bank may specify. **[96]**

76 Power to object to names of overseas institutions

(1) An overseas institution which has established a representative office in the United Kingdom shall not change any name used by it in relation to activities conducted by it in the United Kingdom or, in the case of an institution which is obliged to disclose any name in connection with those activities as mentioned in section 75(1) above, that name unless it has given not less than two months' notice to the Bank of the proposed name.

(2) Where notice of a name is given to the Bank by an overseas institution under section 75(1) or subsection (1) above and it appears to the Bank that the name is misleading to the public or otherwise undesirable it may, within the period of two months beginning with the day on which that notice was given, give notice in writing to the institution that it objects to that name.

(3) Where it appears to the Bank that an overseas institution which has established a representative office in the United Kingdom before the date on which this Part of this Act comes into force is using a name in relation to activities conducted by it in the United Kingdom which is misleading to the public or otherwise undesirable, the Bank may give notice in writing to the institution that it objects to the name—

(a) in a case where the Bank was notified of the establishment of the representative office before that date, within the period of six months beginning with that date; and

(b) otherwise, within the period of six months beginning with the date on which the establishment of the representative office comes to the Bank's knowledge.

(4) Where, as a result of a material change in circumstances since the time when notice of a name was given to the Bank under section 75(1) or subsection (1) above or as a result of further information becoming available to the Bank since that time, it appears to the Bank that the name is so misleading as to be likely to cause harm to the public, the Bank may give notice in writing to the overseas institution in question that it objects to the name. **[97]**

77 Effect of notices under s 76 and appeals

(1) Where the Bank has given notice under section 76 above to an overseas institution the institution shall not use the name to which the Bank has objected in relation to activities conducted by it in the United Kingdom after the objection has taken effect; and for the purposes of this subsection the disclosure of a name in connection with those activities as mentioned in section 75(1)(b) above shall be treated (if it would not otherwise be) as use of that name in relation to those activities.

(2) For the purposes of this section an objection under section 76(2) above takes effect when the institution receives the notice of objection.

(3) An institution to which a notice of objection is given under section 76(2) above may within the period of three weeks beginning with the day on which it receives the notice apply to the court to set aside the objection and on such an application the court may set it aside or confirm it (but without prejudice to its operation before that time).

(4) For the purposes of this section an objection under section 76(3) or (4) above takes effect—

   (a) in a case where no application is made under subsection (5) below, at the expiry of the period of two months beginning with the day on which the institution receives the notice of objection or such longer period as the notice may specify; or
   (b) where an application is made under subsection (5) below and the court confirms the objection, after such period as the court may specify.

(5) An institution to which a notice of objection is given under section 76(3) or (4) above may within the period of three weeks beginning with the day on which it receives the notice apply to the court to set aside the objection.

(6) In this section "the court" means the High Court, the Court of Session or the High Court in Northern Ireland according to whether the representative office of the institution in question is situated in England and Wales, Scotland or Northern Ireland.   **[98]**

78 Registration of substitute corporate name by overseas institution

(1) Where the Bank gives notice under section 76 above objecting to the corporate name of an overseas institution, subsection (4) of section 694 of the Companies Act 1985 or, in Northern Ireland, paragraph (4) of Article 644 of the Companies (Northern Ireland) Order 1986 shall apply, subject to subsection (2) below, as it applies where a notice is served on a company under subsection (1) or (2) of that section or, as the case may be, paragraph (1) or (2) of that Article.

(2) No statement or further statement may be delivered under subsection (4) of section 694 or paragraph (4) of Article 644 by virtue of subsection (1) above unless the Bank has signified that it does not object to the name specified in the statement.

(3) Section 76(1) above shall not apply to a change of a name which has been registered under section 694(4) of the Companies Act 1985 or Article 644(4) of the Companies (Northern Ireland) Order 1986 by virtue of subsection (1) above.   **[99]**

79 Duty to provide information and documents

(1) The Bank may by notice in writing require any overseas institution which has established a representative office in the United Kingdom or has given notice to the Bank under section 75(1) above of its intention to establish such an office to provide the Bank with such information or documents as the Bank may reasonably require.

(2) Without prejudice to the generality of subsection (1) above, the Bank may by notice in writing require such an overseas institution to deliver to the Bank—

(a) in the case of an overseas institution which is a company incorporated in the United Kingdom, copies of the documents which the company is required to send to the registrar of companies under section 10 of the Companies Act 1985 or Article 21 of the Companies (Northern Ireland) Order 1986;

[(aa) in the case of an overseas institution to which section 690A of that Act applies, copies of the documents which it is required to deliver for registration in accordance with paragraph 1(1) or (2) of Schedule 21A of that Act;]

(b) in the case of an overseas institution to which section 691(1) of that Act or Article 641(1) of that Order applies, copies of the document which it is required to deliver for registration in accordance with that section or Article;

(c) in the case of any other overseas institution (other than an individual), information corresponding to that which would be contained in the documents which it would be required to deliver as mentioned in paragraph (b) above if it were a company to which section 691(1) applied;

(d) in the case of an overseas institution which is authorised to take deposits or conduct banking business in a country or territory outside the United Kingdom by the relevant supervisory authority in that country or territory, a certified copy of any certificate from that authority conferring such authorisation on it.

(3) An overseas institution to which a notice is given under subsection (1) or (2) above shall comply with the notice—

(a) in the case of an institution which has established a representative office in the United Kingdom, before the end of such period as is specified in the notice; and

(b) in the case of an institution which has given notice under section 75(1) above of its intention to establish such an office, before it establishes the office.

(4) If at any time an overseas institution which has been required to deliver information or documents to the Bank under subsection (2) above is required to deliver any document or give notice to the registrar of companies under section 18 or 288(2) of the said Act of 1985 or Article 29 or 296(2) of the said Order of 1986, it shall no later than the time by which it must have complied with that requirement deliver a copy of that document or give notice to the Bank.

(5) If at any time an overseas institution is required to furnish any document or give notice to the registrar of companies under [section 692, 695A(3) or 696 of, or paragraph 7 or 8 of Schedule 21A to,] the said Act of 1985 or Article 642 or 646 of the said Order of 1986 (or would be so required if it were a company to

which [that section, paragraph or Article applied)], it shall no later than the time by which it must have complied with that requirement deliver a copy of that document to the Bank.

(6) If at any time a certificate of authorisation of which a copy was required to be delivered to the Bank under subsection (2)(d) above is amended or the authorisation is withdrawn, the overseas institution shall no later than one month after the amendment or withdrawal deliver a copy of the amended certificate or, as the case may be, a notice stating that the authorisation has been withdrawn to the Bank.

(7) The Treasury may after consultation with the Bank by order provide that sections 39 and 40 above shall apply in relation to overseas institutions as they apply in relation to authorised institutions; but no order shall be made under this section unless a draft of it has been laid before and approved by a resolution of each House of Parliament. **[100]**

NOTES

Sub-s (2): sub-s (2)(aa) inserted in relation to Great Britain by the Oversea Companies and Credit and Financial Institutions (Branch Disclosure) Regulations 1992, SI 1992/3179, reg 4, Sch 3, para 10(1), (2).

Sub-s (5): words in square brackets substituted in relation to Great Britain by the Oversea Companies and Credit and Financial Institutions (Branch Disclosure) Regulations 1992, SI 1992/3179, reg 4, Sch 3, para 10(1), (3).

80 Regulations imposing requirements on overseas-based banks

(1) The Treasury may, after consultation with the Bank, by regulations impose on overseas institutions which have established or propose to establish representative offices in the United Kingdom such requirements as the Treasury consider appropriate in connection with those offices and the activities conducted from them.

(2) Regulations under this section may in particular require the establishment or continued existence of a representative office to be authorised by the Bank and such regulations may make provision for—

(a) the granting and revocation of such authorisations;
(b) the imposition of conditions in connection with the grant or retention of such authorisations; and
(c) appeals against the refusal or withdrawal of such authorisations or the imposition of such conditions.

(3) No regulations shall be made under this section unless a draft of the regulations has been laid before and approved by a resolution of each House of Parliament. **[101]**

81 Offences under Part IV

A person who contravenes any provision in this Part of this Act or any requirement imposed under it shall be guilty of an offence and liable on summary conviction to imprisonment for a term not exceeding six months or to a fine not exceeding the fifth level on the standard scale or to both and, where the contravention involves a public display or exhibition of any name or description, there shall be a fresh contravention on each day on which the person causes or permits the display or exhibition to continue. **[102]**

PART V

RESTRICTION ON DISCLOSURE OF INFORMATION

82 Restricted information

(1) Except as provided by the subsequent provisions of this Part of this Act—

> (a) no person who under or for the purposes of this Act receives information relating to the business or other affairs of any person; and
>
> (b) no person who obtains any such information directly or indirectly from a person who has received it as aforesaid,

shall disclose the information without the consent of the person to whom it relates and (if different) the person from whom it was received as aforesaid.

(2) This section does not apply to information which at the time of the disclosure is or has already been made available to the public from other sources or to information in the form of a summary or collection of information so framed as not to enable information relating to any particular person to be ascertained from it.

(3) Any person who discloses information in contravention of this section shall be guilty of an offence and liable—

> (a) on conviction on indictment, to imprisonment for a term not exceeding two years or to a fine or to both;
>
> (b) on summary conviction, to imprisonment for a term not exceeding three months or to a fine not exceeding the statutory maximum or to both.   **[103]**

NOTES

Transitional provision: see s 107, Sch 5, para 14.

Modifications: as to modifications to this section, see the Banking Coordination (Second Council Directive) Regulations 1992, SI 1992/3218, reg 47, Sch 8, para 22; see **[693]**.

83 Disclosure for facilitating discharge of functions by the Bank

(1) Section 82 above does not preclude the disclosure of information in any case in which disclosure is for the purpose of enabling or assisting the Bank to discharge

> [(a) its functions under this Act;
>
> (b) its functions as a monetary authority; or
>
> (c) its functions as a supervisor of money market and gilt market institutions].

(2) Without prejudice to the generality of subsection (1) above, that section does not preclude the disclosure of information by the Bank to the auditor of an authorised institution or former authorised institution if it appears to the Bank that disclosing the information would enable or assist the Bank to discharge the functions mentioned in that subsection or would otherwise be in the interests of depositors.

(3) If, in order to enable or assist the Bank properly to discharge any of its functions under this Act, the Bank considers it necessary to seek advice from any qualified person on any matter of law, accountancy, valuation or other matter requiring the exercise of professional skill, section 82 above does not preclude the disclosure by the Bank to that person of such information as

appears to the Bank to be necessary to ensure that he is properly informed with respect to the matters on which his advice is sought.   **[104]**

NOTES
Sub-s (1): words in square brackets substituted for the words "its functions under this Act" by the Banking Coordination (Second Council Directive) Regulations 1992, SI 1992/3218, reg 38, subject to reg 46(b); see **[684]**.
Modifications: as to modifications to this section, see the Banking Coordination (Second Council Directive) Regulations 1992, SI 1992/3218, reg 47, Sch 8, para 23; see **[693]**.

84 Disclosure for facilitating discharge of functions by other supervisory authorities

(1) Section 82 above does not preclude the disclosure by the Bank of information to any person specified in the first column of the following Table if the Bank considers that the disclosure would enable or assist that person to discharge the functions specified in relation to him in the second column of that Table.

TABLE

Person	*Functions*
[1] The Secretary of State.	Functions under the Insurance Companies Act 1982, Part XIV of the Companies Act 1985, Part XIII of the Insolvency Act 1986 [, the Financial Services Act 1986 or Part II, III or VII of the Companies Act 1989].
[[2] The Treasury.	Functions under the Financial Services Act 1986 or under Part III or VII of the Companies Act 1989.]
[[3] An inspector appointed under Part XIV of the Companies Act 1985 or section 94 or 177 of the Financial Services Act 1986.	Functions under that Part or that section.]
[[4] [A person authorised to exercise powers under section 43A or 44 of the Insurance Companies Act 1982], section 447 of the Companies Act 1985, section 106 of the Financial Services Act 1986 or section 84 of the Companies Act 1989.	Functions under that section.]
[5] The Chief Registrar of friendly societies, . . . and the Assistant Registrar of Friendly Societies for Scotland.	Functions under the enactments relating to friendly societies . . .
[The Friendly Societies Commission.	Functions under the enactments relating to friendly societies or under the Financial Services Act 1986.]

TABLE—*continued*

Person	*Functions*
[6] The Industrial Assurance Commissioner and the Industrial Assistance Commissioner for Northern Ireland.	Functions under the enactments relating to industrial assurance.
[7] The Building Societies Commission.	Functions under the Building Societies Act 1986 and protecting the interests of the shareholders and depositors of building societies.
[8] The Director General of Fair Trading.	Functions under the Consumer Credit Act 1974.
[[9] A designated agency (within the meaning of the Financial Services Act 1986).	Functions under the Financial Services Act 1986 or Part VII of the Companies Act 1989.
[10] A transferee body or the competent authority (within the meaning of the Financial Services Act 1986).	Functions under the Financial Services Act 1986.]
[11] A recognised self-regulating organisation, recognised professional body, recognised investment exchange, recognised clearing house or recognised self-regulating organisation for friendly societies (within the meaning of the Financial Services Act 1986).	Functions in its capacity as an organisation, body, exchange or clearing house recognised under the Financial Services Act 1986.
. . . . .	
[12] A recognised professional body (within the meaning of section 391 of the Insolvency Act 1986).	Functions in its capacity as such a body under the Insolvency Act 1986.
[13] The Department of Economic Development in Northern Ireland.	Functions under Part XV of the Companies (Northern Ireland) Order 1986 [or Part XII of the Insolvency (Northern Ireland) Order 1989] [or Part III of the Companies (Northern Ireland) Order 1990 or Part II or V of the Companies (No 2) (Northern Ireland) Order 1990].
[[14] An inspector appointed under Part XV of the Companies (Northern Ireland) Order 1986 . . .	Functions under that Part . . .
[15] A person authorised to exercise powers under Article 440 of the Companies (Northern Ireland) Order 1986 or section 84 of the Companies Act 1989.	Functions under that Article or section.]

TABLE—*continued*

Person	Functions
[16] The Official Receiver or, in Northern Ireland, the Official [Receiver for Northern Ireland].	Investigating the cause of the failure of an authorised institution or former authorised institution in respect of which a winding-up order [or bankruptcy order] has been made.
[[17] The Panel on Take-overs and Mergers.	All its functions.]
[[18] A person included in the list maintained by the Bank for the purposes of section 171 of the Companies Act 1989.	Functions under settlement arrangements to which regulations under that section relate.]
[[19] A recognised professional body (within the meaning of Article 350 of the Insolvency (Northern Ireland) Order 1989).	Functions in its capacity as such a body under the Insolvency (Northern Ireland) Order 1989.]

(2) The Treasury may after consultation with the Bank by order amend the Table in subsection (1) above by—

(a) adding any person exercising regulatory functions and specifying functions in relation to that person;

(b) removing any person for the time being specified in the Table; or

(c) altering the functions for the time being specified in the Table in relation to any person;

and the Treasury may also after consultation with the Bank by order restrict the circumstances in which, or impose conditions subject to which, disclosure is permitted in the case of any person for the time being specified in the Table.

(3) An order under subsection (2) above shall be subject to annulment in pursuance of a resolution of either House of Parliament.

(4) Section 82 above does not preclude the disclosure by any person specified in the first column of the Table in subsection (1) above of information obtained by him by virtue of that subsection if he makes the disclosure with the consent of the Bank and for the purpose of enabling or assisting him to discharge any functions specified in relation to him in the second column of that Table; and before deciding whether to give its consent to such a disclosure by any person the Bank shall take account of such representations made by him as to the desirability of or the necessity for the disclosure.

[(5) Section 82 above does not preclude the disclosure by the Bank of information to the Treasury if disclosure appears to the Bank to be—

(a) desirable or expedient in the interests of depositors; or

(b) in the public interest,

and (in either case) in accordance with article 12(7) of the First Council Directive.

(5A) Section 82 above does not preclude the disclosure by the Bank of information to the Secretary of State for purposes other than those specified in relation to him in subsection (1) above if the disclosure is made with the consent of the Treasury and—

  (a) the information relates to an authorised institution or former authorised institution and does not enable the financial affairs of any other identifiable person to be ascertained and disclosure appears to the Bank to be necessary in the interests of depositors or in the public interest; or
  (b) in any other case, disclosure appears to the Bank to be necessary in the interests of depositors;

and (in either case) disclosure appears to the Bank to be in accordance with article 12(7) of the First Council Directive.]

  (6) Section 82 above does not preclude the disclosure of information for the purpose of enabling or assisting an authority in a country or territory outside the United Kingdom to exercise—

  (a) functions corresponding to those of—
      (i) the Bank under this Act [or the Banking Coordination (Second Council Directive) Regulations 1992];
      (ii) the Secretary of State [or the Treasury] under the Insurance Companies Act 1982, Part XIII of the Insolvency Act 1986 or the Financial Services Act 1986; or
      (iii) the competent authority under Part IV of the Financial Services Act 1986;
  (b) functions in connection with rules of law corresponding to any of the provisions of [Part V of the Criminal Justice Act 1993 (insider dealing)] or Part VII of the Financial Services Act 1986; or
  (c) supervisory functions in respect of bodies carrying on business corresponding to that of building societies.

  [(7) Subsection (6) above does not apply in relation to disclosures to an authority which is not a supervisory authority in another member State unless the Bank is satisfied that the authority is subject to restrictions on further disclosures at least equivalent to those imposed by this Part of this Act.

  (8) Information which is disclosed to a person in pursuance of subsection (1), (4) or (6) above shall not be used otherwise than for the purpose mentioned in that subsection.

  (9) Any person who uses information in contravention of subsection (8) above shall be liable on summary conviction to imprisonment for a term not exceeding three months or to a fine not exceeding the fifth level on the standard scale or to both.

  (10) Any reference in this section to enabling or assisting any person to discharge or exercise any functions is a reference to enabling or assisting that person to discharge or exercise those functions in relation to—

  (a) a financial market; or
  (b) persons carrying on the business of banking or insurance, Consumer Credit Act businesses or the business of providing other financial services;

and in this subsection "Consumer Credit Act business" has the same meaning as in the Banking Coordination (Second Council Directive) Regulations 1992.]

NOTES

Commencement: 15 July 1987 (sub-ss (1)–(4), (6)) (SI 1987/1189); 1 January 1993 (sub-ss (5), (5A) as substituted, (7)–(10)) (SI 1992/3218).

Sub-s (1): the entries in this Table were numbered 1 to 19 by the Banking Coordination (Second Council Directive) Regulations 1992, SI 1992/3218, reg 39(1). The entry 'The Friendly Societies Commission' is unnumbered because it was prospectively inserted and was not in force on 1 January 1993 when SI 1992/3218 came into force. It appears that there is no authority for numbering this entry.

Words in square brackets in entry 1 substituted by the Companies Act 1989, s 81(1), (2); entry 2 inserted by the Transfer of Functions (Financial Services) Order 1992, SI 1992/1315, art 10(1), Sch 4, para 11(1); entry 3 substituted by the Companies Act 1989, s 81(1), (3); entry 4 substituted by the Companies Act 1989, s 81(1), (4) and words in square brackets in that entry substituted, subject to transitional provisions, by the Insurance Companies (Amendment) Regulations 1994, SI 1994/3132, regs 11, 13–15 (superseding an amendment by the Insurance Companies (Third Insurance Directives) Regulations 1994, SI 1994/1696, reg 68(1), Sch 8, Pt I, para 14(1)); words omitted from entry 5 repealed by the Friendly Societies Act 1992, s 120(2), Sch 22, Pt I; entry following entry 5 inserted by the Friendly Societies Act 1992, s 120(1), Sch 21, Pt I, para 9; entries 9, 10 substituted by the Companies Act 1989, s 81(1), (5); entry relating to persons appointed under section 94, 106 or 177 of the Financial Services Act 1986 which followed entry 11 repealed by the Companies Act 1989, s 212, Sch 24; words in first pair of square brackets in entry 13 inserted by the Insolvency (Northern Ireland) Order 1989, SI 1989/2405 (NI 19), art 381(2), Sch 9, Pt II, para 54(a); words in second pair of square brackets in entry 13 added by the Companies (No 2) (Northern Ireland) Order 1990, SI 1990/1504 (NI 10), art 25(1), (2); entries 14, 15 substituted by the Companies (No 2) (Northern Ireland) Order 1990, SI 1990/1504 (NI 10), art 25(1), (3) and words omitted from entry 14 repealed by the Criminal Justice Act 1993, s 79(14), Sch 6, Pt I; words in square brackets in entry 16 substituted by the Insolvency (Northern Ireland) Order 1989, SI 1989/2405 (NI 19), art 381(2), Sch 9, Pt II, para 54(b); entry 17 added by the Banking Act 1987 (Disclosure of Information) (Specified Persons) Order 1987, SI 1987/1292, art 2; entry 18 prospectively added by the Companies Act 1989, s 171(7); entry 19 added by the Insolvency (Northern Ireland) Order 1989, SI 1989/2405 (NI 19), art 381(2), Sch 9, Pt II, para 54(c).

In the Table, an entry relating to the Operator as defined in the Uncertificated Securities Regulations 1992, SI 1992/225, was added by SI 1993/491, which order was revoked by SI 1993/836 following the cancellation of TAURUS.

Sub-ss (5), (5A): substituted for original sub-s (5) by the Banking Coordination (Second Council Directive) Regulations 1992, SI 1992/3218, reg 39(2), subject to reg 46(b); see **[684]**.

The original sub-s (5) read—

(5) Section 82 above does not preclude the disclosure by the Bank of information to the Treasury if disclosure appears to the Bank to be desirable or expedient in the interests of depositors or in the public interest; and that section does not preclude the disclosure by the Bank of information to the Secretary of State for purposes other than those specified in relation to him in subsection (1) above if the disclosure is made with the consent of the Treasury and—

(a) the information relates to an authorised institution or former authorised institution and does not enable the financial affairs of any other identifiable person to be ascertained and disclosure appears to the Bank to be necessary in the interests of depositors or in the public interest; or

(b) in any other case, disclosure appears to the Bank to be necessary in the interests of depositors.

Sub-s (6): words in square brackets in sub-s (6)(a)(i) added by the Banking Coordination (Second Council Directive) Regulations 1992, SI 1992/3218, reg 39(3), subject to reg 46(b); see **[684]**; words in square brackets in sub-s (6)(a)(ii) inserted by the Transfer of Functions (Financial Services) Order 1992, SI 1992/1315, art 10(1), Sch 4, para 11; words in square brackets in sub-s (6)(b) substituted by the Criminal Justice Act 1993, s 79(13), Sch 5, Pt I, para 13.

Sub-ss (7)–(10): added by the Banking Coordination (Second Council Directive) Regulations 1992, SI 1992/3218, reg 39(4), subject to reg 46(b); see **[684]**.

Modifications: as to modifications to this section, see the Banking Coordination (Second Council Directive) Regulations 1992, SI 1992/3218, reg 47, Sch 8, para 24; see **[693]**; as to Northern Ireland, see the Companies Act 1989, s 88(3).

Orders: the Banking Act 1987 (Disclosure of Information) (Specified Persons) Order 1987, SI 1987/1292; the Banking Act 1987 (Disclosure of Information) (Specified Persons) Order 1993, SI 1993/491, revoked by SI 1993/836.

85 Other permitted disclosures

(1) Section 82 above does not preclude the disclosure of information—

(a) for the purpose of enabling or assisting the Board of Banking Supervision or the Deposit Protection Board or any other person to discharge its or his functions under this Act;

(b) for the purpose of enabling or assisting a person to do anything which he is required to do in pursuance of a requirement imposed under section 39(1)(b) above;

(c) with a view to the institution of, or otherwise for the purposes of, any criminal proceedings, whether under this Act or otherwise;

(d) in connection with any other proceedings arising out of this Act;

(e) with a view to the institution of, or otherwise for the purposes of, proceedings under section 7 or 8 of the Company Directors Disqualification Act 1986 [or Article 10 or 11 of the Companies (Northern Ireland) Order 1989] in respect of a director or former director of an authorised institution or former authorised institution;

(f) in connection with any proceedings in respect of an authorised institution or former authorised institution under the Bankruptcy (Scotland) Act 1985 or Parts I to VII or IX to XI of the Insolvency Act 1986 [or Parts II to VII or IX and X of the Insolvency (Northern Ireland) Order 1989] which the Bank has instituted or in which it has a right to be heard;

(g) . . .

(h) in pursuance of a Community obligation.

[(1A) The disclosures permitted by subsection (1)(f) above do not include the disclosure of information relating to a person who (not being a director, controller or manager of the institution) is or has been, to the knowledge of the person making the disclosure, involved in an attempt to secure the survival of the institution as a going concern.]

(2) Section 82 above does not preclude the disclosure by the Bank to the Director of Public Prosecutions, the Director of Public Prosecutions for Northern Ireland, the Lord Advocate, a procurator fiscal or a constable of information obtained by virtue of section 41, 42 or 43 above or of information in the possession of the Bank as to any suspected contravention in relation to which the powers conferred by those sections are exercisable.

(3) Section 82 above does not preclude the disclosure of information by the Deposit Protection Board to any person or body responsible for a scheme for protecting depositors or investors (whether in the United Kingdom or elsewhere) similar to that for which provision is made by Part II of this Act if it appears to the Board that disclosing the information would enable or assist the recipient of the information or the Board to discharge his or its functions.

[106]

NOTES

Commencement: 15 July 1987 (sub-ss (1), (2), (3)) (SI 1987/1189); 1 January 1993 (sub-s (1A)) (SI 1992/3218).

Sub-s (1): words in square brackets in sub-s (1)(e) inserted by the Companies (Northern Ireland) Order 1989, SI 1989/2404 (NI 18), art 25(2), Sch 4, Pt I, para 5; words in square brackets in sub-s (1)(f) inserted by the Insolvency (Northern Ireland) Order 1989, SI 1989/2405 (NI 19), art 381(2), Sch 9, Pt II, para 55; sub-s (1)(g) repealed by the Banking Coordination (Second Council Directive) Regulations 1992, SI 1992/3218, reg 40(1), subject to reg 46(b); see **[684]**. The original para (g) read "with a view to the institution of, or otherwise for the purposes of, any disciplinary proceedings relating to the exercise of his professional duties by an auditor of an authorised institution or former authorised institution or an accountant or other person nominated or approved for the purposes of section 39(1)(b) above or appointed under section 41 above".

Sub-s (1A): inserted by the Banking Coordination (Second Council Directive) Regulations 1992, SI 1992/3218, reg 40(2), subject to reg 46(b); see **[684]**.

[86 Information supplied to Bank by relevant overseas authority etc

(1) Section 82 above applies also to information which—

(a) has been supplied to the Bank for the purposes of any relevant functions by the relevant supervisory authority in a country or territory outside the United Kingdom; or

(b) has been obtained for those purposes by the Bank, or by a person acting on its behalf, in another member State.

(2) Subject to subsections (3) and (4) below, information supplied or obtained as mentioned in subsection (1)(a) or (b) above shall not be disclosed except as provided by section 82 above or—

(a) for the purpose of enabling or assisting the Bank to discharge any relevant functions; or

(b) with a view to the institution of, or otherwise for the purposes of, criminal proceedings, whether under this Act or otherwise.

(3) Information supplied to the Bank for the purposes of any relevant functions by the relevant supervisory authority in another member State may be disclosed—

(a) to a relevant recipient, if the authority consents to its disclosure and the case is one in which information to which section 82 above applies could be so disclosed by virtue of section 84(1) or (2) above; or

(b) to the Treasury or the Secretary of State, if the authority consents to its disclosure and the case is one in which information to which section 82 above applies could be so disclosed by virtue of section 84(5) or (5A) above.

(4) Information obtained as mentioned in subsection (1)(b) above may be disclosed—

(a) to a relevant recipient, if the relevant supervisory authority in the member State concerned consents to its disclosure and the case is one in which information to which section 82 above applies could be so disclosed by virtue of section 84(1) or (2) above; or

(b) to the Treasury or the Secretary of State, if that authority consents to its disclosure and the case is one in which information to which section 82 above applies could be so disclosed by virtue of section 84(5) or (5A) above.

(5) In this section—

"relevant functions", in relation to the Bank, means its functions under this Act, its functions as a monetary authority and its functions as a supervisor of money market and gilt market institutions;

"relevant recipient" means a person specified in any of entries 1 to 8, 13 to 15 and 17 in the Table in section 84(1) above.] **[107]**

NOTES

Commencement: 1 January 1993 (SI 1992/3218).

This section substituted by the Banking Coordination (Second Council Directive) Regulations 1992, SI 1992/3218, reg 41, subject to reg 46(b); see **[684]**. The original s 86 read—

86. Information supplied to Bank by relevant overseas authority

Section 82 above applies also to information which has been supplied to the Bank for the purposes of its functions under this Act by a relevant supervisory authority in a country or territory outside the United Kingdom but no such information shall be disclosed except as provided in that section or for the purpose of enabling or assisting the Bank to discharge those functions or with a view to the institution of, or otherwise for the purposes of, criminal proceedings, whether under this Act or otherwise.

Modifications: as to modifications to this section, see the Banking Coordination (Second Council Directive) Regulations 1992, SI 1992/3218, reg 47, Sch 8, para 25; see **[693]**.

87 Disclosure of information obtained under other Acts

(1) . . .

(2) Information disclosed to the Bank under subsection (1) of section 449 of the Companies Act 1985 for the purpose of enabling or assisting it to discharge its functions under this Act or in its capacity as a competent authority under subsection (3) of that section may be disclosed—

  (a) with the consent of the Secretary of State, in any case in which information to which section 82 applies could be disclosed by virtue of section 84(1) or (2) above; and
  (b) in any case in which information to which section 82 above applies could be disclosed by virtue of any of the other provisions of this Part of this Act.

(3) Information disclosed to the Bank under paragraph (1) of Article 442 of the Companies (Northern Ireland) Order 1986 for the purpose of enabling or assisting it to discharge its functions under this Act or in its capacity as a competent authority under paragraph (3) of that Article may be disclosed—

  (a) with the consent of the [Department of Economic Development in Northern Ireland], in any case in which information to which section 82 above applies could be disclosed by virtue of section 84(1) or (2) above; and
  (b) in any case in which information to which section 82 above applies could be disclosed by virtue of any of the other provisions of this Part of this Act.

[(3A) Information disclosed by the Building Societies Commission to the Bank for the purpose of enabling or assisting it to discharge any relevant functions may be disclosed—

  (a) to a relevant recipient, if the Commission consents to its disclosure and the case is one in which information to which section 82 above applies could be so disclosed by virtue of section 84(1) or (2) above; or
  (b) to the Treasury or the Secretary of State, if the Commission consents to its disclosure and the case is one in which information to which section 82 above applies could be so disclosed by virtue of section 84(5)(a) or (5A) above;

and in this subsection "relevant functions" has the same meaning as in section 86 above and "relevant recipient" means a person specified in any of entries 1 to 8, 13 to 15 and 17 in the Table in section 84(1) above.]

(4) Any information which has been lawfully disclosed to the Bank may be disclosed by it to the Board of Banking Supervision so far as necessary for enabling or assisting the Board to discharge its functions under this Act. **[108]**

NOTES
  Commencement: 15 July 1987 (sub-ss (1)–(3), (4)) (SI 1987/1189); 1 January 1993 (sub-s (3A)) (SI 1992/3218).
  Sub-s (1): inserts the Consumer Credit Act 1974, s 174(3A).
  Sub-s (3): words in square brackets in sub-s (3)(a) substituted by the Companies (Northern Ireland) Order 1989, SI 1989/2404 (NI 18), art 36(2), Sch 4, Pt II, para 13.
  Sub-s (3A): inserted by the Banking Coordination (Second Council Directive) Regulations 1992, SI 1992/3218, reg 42, subject to reg 46(b); see **[684]**.

Modifications: as to modifications to this section, see the Banking Coordination (Second Council Directive) Regulations 1992, SI 1992/3218, reg 47, Sch 8, para 26; see **[693]**.

PART VI
MISCELLANEOUS AND SUPPLEMENTARY

88 (*Amends the Consumer Credit Act 1974, ss 16(1), (3), 189(1).*)

89 (*Inserts the Consumer Credit Act 1974, s 187(3A).*)

90 (*Sub-s (1) superseded and repealed by the Companies Act 1989, s 212, Sch 24, as from a day to be appointed; sub-s (2) repealed by the Companies (Northern Ireland) Order 1990, SI 1990/593 (NI 5), art 26, Sch 15, Pt I.*)

91 Powers for securing reciprocal facilities for banking and other financial business

For the avoidance of doubt it is hereby declared that a notice under section 183 of the Financial Services Act 1986 (disqualification or restriction of persons connected with overseas countries which do not afford reciprocal facilities for financial business) may be served on any person connected with the country in question who is carrying on or appears to the Secretary of State or the Treasury to intend to carry on in, or in relation to, the United Kingdom business of any of the descriptions specified in subsection (1) of that section whether or not it is of the same description as that affected by the less favourable terms which are the occasion for the service of the notice.   **[109]**

92 Winding up on petition from the Bank

(1) On a petition presented by the Bank by virtue of this section the court having jurisdiction under the Insolvency Act 1986 may wind up an authorised institution or former authorised institution if—

    (a) the institution is unable to pay its debts within the meaning of section 123 or, as the case may be, section 221 of that Act; or

    (b) the court is of the opinion that it is just and equitable that the institution should be wound up;

and for the purposes of such a petition an institution which defaults in an obligation to pay any sum due and payable in respect of a deposit shall be deemed to be unable to pay its debts as mentioned in paragraph (a) above.

(2) Where a petition is presented under subsection (1) above for the winding up of a partnership on the ground mentioned in paragraph (b) of that subsection or, in Scotland, on the ground mentioned in paragraph (a) or (b) of that subsection, the court shall have jurisdiction and the Insolvency Act 1986 shall have effect as if the partnership were an unregistered company within the meaning of section 220 of that Act.

(3) On a petition presented by the Bank by virtue of this section the High Court in Northern Ireland may wind up an authorised institution if—

    (a) the institution is unable to pay its debts within the meaning of [Article 103 or, as the case may be, Article 185 of the Insolvency (Northern Ireland) Order 1989]; or

    (b) the court is of the opinion that it is just and equitable that the institution should be wound up;

and for the purposes of such a petition an institution which defaults in an obligation to pay any sum due and payable in respect of a deposit shall be deemed to be unable to pay its debts as mentioned in paragraph (a) above.

(4) Where a petition is presented under subsection (3) above for the winding up of a partnership on the ground mentioned in paragraph (b) of that subsection, the court shall have jurisdiction and the said Order of [1989] shall have effect as if the partnership were an unregistered company within the meaning of [Article 184] of that Order.

(5) For the purposes of this section the definition of deposit in section 5 above shall be treated as including any sum that would otherwise be excluded by subsection (3)(a), (b) or (c) of that section.

(6) This section applies to a company or partnership which has contravened section 3 above as it applies to an authorised institution.   **[110]**

NOTE
Sub-ss (3), (4): words in square brackets in sub-ss (3)(a), (4) substituted by the Insolvency (Northern Ireland) Order 1989, SI 1989/2405 (NI 19), art 381(2), Sch 9, Pt II, para 56.

93 Injunctions

(1) If on the application of the Bank, the Director of Public Prosecutions, the Lord Advocate or the Director of Public Prosecutions for Northern Ireland the court is satisfied—

    (a) that there is a reasonable likelihood that a person will contravene section 3, 18, 35, 67, 69, 71, or 77 above, a direction under section 19 above or regulations under section 32, 34, or 80 above; or

    (b) that any person has been guilty of any such contravention and that there is a reasonable likelihood that the contravention will continue or be repeated,

the court may grant an injunction restraining, or in Scotland an interdict prohibiting, the contravention.

(2) If on the application of the Bank, the Director of Public Prosecutions, the Lord Advocate or the Director of Public Prosecutions for Northern Ireland it appears to the court that a person may have been guilty of such a contravention as is mentioned in subsection (1) above the court may grant an injunction restraining, or in Scotland an interdict prohibiting, him from disposing of or otherwise dealing with any of his assets while the suspected contravention is investigated.

(3) The jurisdiction conferred by this section shall be exercisable by the High Court and the Court of Session.   **[111]**

NOTE
Modifications: as to modifications to this section, see the Banking Coordination (Second Council Directive) Regulations 1992, SI 1992/3218, reg 47, Sch 8, para 27; see **[693]**.

94 False and misleading information

(1) Any person who knowingly or recklessly provides the Bank or any other person with information which is false or misleading in a material particular shall be guilty of an offence if the information is provided—

    (a) in purported compliance with a requirement imposed by or under this Act; or

    (b) otherwise than as mentioned in paragraph (a) above but in circumstances in which the person providing the information intends, or could reasonably be expected to know, that the information would be used by the Bank for the purposes of exercising its functions under this Act.

(2) Any person who knowingly or recklessly provides the Bank or any other person with information which is false or misleading in a material particular shall be guilty of an offence if the information is provided in connection with an application for authorisation under this Act.

(3) An authorised institution or former authorised institution shall be guilty of an offence if it fails to provide the Bank with any information in its possession knowing or having reasonable cause to believe—

(a) that the information is relevant to the exercise by the Bank of its functions under this Act in relation to the institution; and
(b) that the withholding of the information is likely to result in the Bank being misled as to any matter which is relevant to and of material significance for the exercise of those functions in relation to the institution.

(4) Any person who knowingly or recklessly provides any person appointed under section 41 above with information which is false or misleading in a material particular shall be guilty of an offence.

(5) Any person guilty of an offence under this section shall be liable—

(a) on conviction on indictment, to imprisonment for a term not exceeding two years or to a fine or to both;
(b) on summary conviction, to imprisonment for a term not exceeding six months or to a fine not exceeding the statutory maximum or to both. **[112]**

NOTE
Modifications: as to modifications to this section, see the Banking Coordination (Second Council Directive) Regulations 1992, SI 1992/3218, reg 47, Sch 8, para 28; see **[693]**.

95 Restriction of Rehabilitation of Offenders Act 1974

(1) The Rehabilitation of Offenders Act 1974 shall have effect subject to the provisions of this section in cases where the spent conviction is for—

(a) an offence involving fraud or other dishonesty; or
(b) an offence under legislation (whether or not of the United Kingdom) relating to companies (including insider dealing), building societies, industrial and provident societies, credit unions, friendly societies, insurance, banking or other financial services, insolvency, consumer credit or consumer protection.

(2) Nothing in section 4(1) (restriction on evidence as to spent convictions in proceedings) shall prevent the determination in any proceeding arising out of any such decision of the Bank as is mentioned in section 27(1) or (3) above (including proceedings on appeal to any court) of any issue, or prevent the admission or requirement in any such such proceedings of any evidence, relating to a person's previous convictions for any such offence as is mentioned in subsection(1) above or the circumstances ancillary thereto.

(3) A conviction for such an offence as is mentioned in subsection (1) above shall not be regarded as spent for the purposes of section 4(2) (questions relating to an individual's previous convictions) if—

(a) the question is put by or on behalf of the Bank and the individual is a person who is or is seeking to become a director, controller or manager of an authorised institution, a former authorised institution or an institution which has made an application for authorisation which has not been disposed of; or

(b) the question is put by or on behalf of any such institution and the individual is or is seeking to become a director, controller or manager of that institution,

and the person questioned is informed that by virtue of this section convictions for any such offence are to be disclosed.

(4) Section 4(3)(b) (spent conviction not to be ground for excluding person from office, occupation etc.) shall not—

(a) prevent the Bank from refusing to grant or revoking an authorisation on the ground that an individual is not a fit and proper person to be a director, controller or manager of the institution in question or from imposing a restriction or giving a direction requiring the removal of an individual as director, controller or manager of an institution,

(b) prevent an authorised institution, a former authorised institution or an institution which has made an application for authorisation which has not yet been disposed of from dismissing or excluding an individual from being a director, controller or manager of the institution,

by reason, or partly by reason, of a spent conviction of that individual for such an offence as is mentioned in subsection (1) above or any circumstances ancillary to such a conviction or of a failure (whether or not by that individual) to disclose such a conviction or any such circumstances.

(5) For the purposes of subsections (3) and (4) above an application by an institution is not disposed of until the decision of the Bank on the application is communicated to the institution.

(6) This section shall apply to Northern Ireland with the substitution for the references to the said Act of 1974 and section 4(1), (2) and (3)(b) of that Act of references to the Rehabilitation of Offenders (Northern Ireland) Order 1978 and Article 5(1), (2) and (3)(b) of that Order.   **[113]**

NOTE
Modifications: as to modifications to this section, see the Banking Coordination (Second Council Directive) Regulations 1992, SI 1992/3218, reg 47, Sch 8, para 29; see **[693]**.

96 Offences

(1) Where an offence under this Act committed by a body corporate is proved to have been committed with the consent or connivance of, or to be attributable to any neglect on the part of any director, manager, secretary or other similar officer of the body corporate, or any person who was purporting to act in any such capacity, he, as well as the body corporate, shall be guilty of that offence and be liable to be proceeded against and punished accordingly.

(2) Where the affairs of a body corporate are managed by its members, subsection (1) above shall apply in relation to the acts and defaults of a member in connection with his functions of management as if he were a director of the body corporate.

(3) In the case of a person who by virtue of subsection (1) or (2) above or section 98(6) or (7) below is guilty of an offence under section 12(6) or 19(6) above the penalty that can be imposed on conviction on indictment shall be imprisonment for a term not exceeding two years or a fine or both.

(4) In any proceedings for an offence under this Act it shall be a defence for the person charged to prove that he took all reasonable precautions and exercised all due diligence to avoid the commission of such an offence by himself or any person under his control.

(5) No proceedings for an offence under this Act shall be instituted—

(a) in England and Wales, except by or with the consent of the Director of Public Prosecutions or the Bank; or
(b) in Northern Ireland, except by or with the consent of the Director of Public Prosecutions for Northern Ireland or the Bank.

(6) In relation to proceedings against a building society incorporated (or deemed to be incorporated) under the Building Societies Act 1986 subsection (5) above shall have effect with the substitution for references to the Bank of references to the Building Societies Commission.

(7) In relation to proceedings against a friendly society within the meaning of section 7(1)(a) of the Friendly Societies Act 1974 the reference in paragraph (a) of subsection (5) above to the Bank shall include a reference to the Chief Registrar of friendly societies; . . .   **[114]**

NOTE

Sub-s (7): words omitted repealed by the Friendly Societies Act 1992, s 120(2), Sch 22, Pt I.

97 Summary proceedings

(1) Summary proceedings for any offence under this Act may, without prejudice to any jurisdiction exercisable apart from this subsection, be taken against an institution, including an unincorporated institution, at any place at which it has a place of business, and against an individual at any place at which he is for the time being.

(2) Notwithstanding anything in section 127(1) of the Magistrates' Courts Act 1980, any information relating to an offence under this Act which is triable by a magistrates' court in England and Wales may be so tried if it is laid at any time within three years after the commission of the offence and within six months after the relevant date.

(3) (*Applies to Scotland only.*)

(4) Notwithstanding anything in Article 19(1) of the Magistrates' Courts (Northern Ireland) Order 1981, a complaint relating to such an offence which is triable by a court of summary jurisdiction in Northern Ireland may be so tried if it is made at any time within three years after the commission of the offence and within six months after the relevant date.

(5) In this section—

"the relevant date" means the date on which evidence sufficient in the opinion of the prosecuting authority to justify proceedings comes to its knowledge; and
"the prosecuting authority" means the authority by or with whose consent the proceedings are instituted in accordance with section 96 above or, in Scotland, the Lord Advocate.

(6) For the purposes of subsection (5) above, a certificate of any prosecuting authority as to the date on which such evidence as is there mentioned came to its knowledge shall be conclusive evidence of that fact.   **[115]**

98 Offences committed by unincorporated associations

(1) Proceedings for an offence alleged to have been committed under this Act by an unincorporated association shall be brought in the name of that association (and not in that of any of its members) and, for the purposes of any such proceedings, any rules of court relating to the service of documents shall have effect as if the association were a corporation.

(2) A fine imposed on an unincorporated association on its conviction of an offence under this Act shall be paid out of the funds of the association.

(3) Section 33 of the Criminal Justice Act 1925 and Schedule 3 to the Magistrates' Courts Act 1980 (procedure on charge of offence against a corporation) shall have effect in a case in which an unincorporated association is charged in England or Wales with an offence under this Act in like manner as they have effect in the case of a corporation so charged.

(4) (*Applies to Scotland only.*)

(5) Section 18 of the Criminal Justice Act (Northern Ireland) 1945 and Schedule 4 to the Magistrates' Courts (Northern Ireland) Order 1981 (procedure on charge of offence against a corporation) shall have effect in a case in which an unincorporated association) shall have effect in a case in which an unincorporated association is charged in Northern Ireland with an offence under this Act in like manner as they have effect in the case of a corporation so charged.

(6) Where a partnership is guilty of an offence under this Act, every partner, other than a partner who is proved to have been ignorant of, or to have attempted to prevent the commission of the offence, shall also be guilty of that offence and be liable to be proceeded against and punished accordingly.

(7) Where any other unincorporated association is guilty of an offence under this Act, every officer of the association who is bound to fulfil any duty whereof the offence is a breach, or if there is no such officer then every member of the committee or other similar governing body, other than a member who is proved to have been ignorant of, or to have attempted to prevent the commission of the offence, shall also be guilty of that offence and be liable to be proceeded against and punished accordingly.   **[116]**

99 Service of notices on the Bank

(1) No notice required by this Act to be given to or served on the Bank shall be regarded as given or served until it is received.

(2) Subject to subsection (1) above, any such notice may be given or served by telex or other similar means which produce a document containing the text of the communication.   **[117]**

NOTE
Modifications: as to modifications to this section, see the Banking Coordination (Second Council Directive) Regulations 1992, SI 1992/3218, reg 47, Sch 8, para 30; see **[693]**.

100 Service of other notices

(1) This section has effect in relation to any notice, direction or other document required or authorised by or under this Act to be given to or served on any person other than the Bank.

(2) Any such document may be given to or served on the person in question—

    (a) by delivering it to him; or
    (b) by leaving it at his proper address; or
    (c) by sending it by post to him at that address; or
    (d) by sending it to him at that address by telex or other similar means which produce a document containing the text of the communication.

(3) Any such document may—

    (a) in the case of a body corporate, be given to or served on the secretary or clerk of that body; and
    (b) in the case of any other description of institution, be given to or served on a controller of the institution.

(4) For the purposes of this section and section 7 of the Interpretation Act 1978 (service of documents by post) in its application to this section, the proper address of any person to or on whom a document is to be given or served shall be his last known address, except that—

    (a) in the case of a body corporate or its secretary or its secretary or clerk, it shall be the address of the registered or principal office of that body in the United Kingdom; and
    (b) in the case of any other description of institution or a person having control or management of its business, it shall be that of the principal office of the institution in the United Kingdom.

(5) If the person to or on whom any document mentioned in subsection (1) above is to be given or served has notified the Bank of an address within the United Kingdom, other than his proper address within the meaning of subsection (4) above, as the one at which he or someone on his behalf will accept documents of the same description as that document, that address shall also be treated for the purposes of this section and section 7 of the Interpretation Act 1978 as his proper address. **[118]**

NOTE

Modifications: as to modifications to this section, see the Banking Coordination (Second Council Directive) Regulations 1992, SI 1992/3218, reg 47, Sch 8, para 31; see **[693]**.

101 Evidence

(1) In any proceedings, a certificate purporting to be signed on behalf of the Bank and certifying—

    (a) that a particular person is or is not an authorised institution or was or was not such an institution at a particular time;
    (b) the date on which a particular institution became or ceased to be authorised;
    (c) whether or not a particular institution's authorisation is or was restricted;
    (d) the date on which a restricted authorisation expires; or
    (e) the date on which a particular institution became or ceased to be a recognised bank or licensed institution under the Banking Act 1979,

shall be admissible in evidence and, in Scotland, shall be sufficient evidence of the facts stated in the certificate.

(2) A certificate purporting to be signed as mentioned in subsection (1) above shall be deemed to have been duly signed unless the contrary is shown. **[119]**

NOTE
  Modifications: as to modifications to this section, see the Banking Coordination (Second Council Directive) Regulations 1992, SI 1992/3218, reg 47, Sch 8, para 32; see **[693]**.

102 Orders and regulations

Any power of the Treasury to make orders or regulations under this Act shall be exercisable by statutory instrument. **[120]**

103 Municipal banks

(1) References in this Act to a municipal bank are to a company within the meaning of the Companies Act 1985 which—

    (a) carries on a deposit-taking business,
    (b) is connected with a local authority as mentioned in subsection (2) below, and
    (c) has its deposits guaranteed by that local authority in accordance with subsection (5) below.

(2) The connection referred to in paragraph (b) of subsection (1) above between a company and a local authority is that—

    (a) the company's articles of association provide that the shares in the company are to be held only by members of the local authority; and
    (b) substantially all the funds lent by the company are lent to the local authority.

(3) Where on 9th November 1978 a company or its predecessor—

    (a) was carrying on a deposit-taking business, and
    (b) was connected with a local authority as mentioned in subsection (2) above,

that local authority or its successor may for the purposes of this Act resolve to guarantee deposits with the company.

(4) A resolution passed by a local authority under subsection (3) above may not be rescinded.

(5) Where a local authority has passed a resolution under subsection (3) above or under section 48(3) of the Banking Act 1979, that local authority and any local authority which is its successor shall be liable, if the company concerned defaults in payment, to make good to a depositor the principal and interest owing in respect of any deposit with the company, whether made before or after the passing of the resolution.

(6) For the purposes of this section—

    (a) one company is the predecessor of another if that other succeeds to its obligations in respect of its deposit-taking business; and
    (b) one local authority is the successor of another if, as a result of or in connection with, an order under Part IV of the Local Government Act 1972 [or Part II of the Local Government Act 1992 or under Part II] of the Local Government (Scotland) Act 1973 (change of local government area), it becomes connected as mentioned in subsection (2) above with a company formerly so connected with that other local authority. **[121]**

NOTE
  Sub-s (6): words in square brackets in sub-s (6)(b) substituted by the Local Government Act 1992, s 27(1), Sch 3, para 22.

104 (*Applies to Scotland only.*)

105 Meaning of "director", "controller", "manager", and "associate"

(1) In the provisions of this Act other than section 96 "director", "controller", "manager" and "associate" shall be construed in accordance with the provisions of this section.

(2) "Director", in relation to an institution, includes—

(a) any person who occupies the position of a director, by whatever name called; and

(b) in the case of an institution established in a country or territory outside the United Kingdom, any person, including a member of a managing board, who occupies a position appearing to the Bank to be analogous to that of a director of a company registered under the Companies Act 1985;

and in the case of a partnership "director", where it is used in subsections (6) and (7) below, includes a partner.

(3) "Controller", in relation to an institution, means—

(a) a managing director of the institution or of another institution of which it is a subsidiary or, in the case of an institution which is a partnership, a partner;

(b) a chief executive of the institution or of another institution of which it is a subsidiary;

(c) a person who, [satisfies the requirements of this paragraph];

(d) a person in accordance with whose directions or instructions the directors of the institution or of another institution of which it is a subsidiary or persons who are controllers of the institution by virtue of paragraph (c) above (or any of them) are accustomed to act; [and

(e) a person who is, or would be if he were an undertaking, a parent undertaking of the institution.]

[(3A) A person satisfies the requirements of subsection (3)(c) above in relation to an institution if, either alone or with any associate or associates—

(a) he holds 10 per cent. or more of the shares in the institution or another institution of which it is a subsidiary undertaking;

(b) he is entitled to exercise, or control the exercise of, 10 per cent. or more of the voting power at any general meeting of the institution or another institution of which it is such an undertaking; or

(c) he is able to exercise a significant influence over the management of the institution or another institution of which it is such an undertaking by virtue of—

(i) a holding of shares in; or

(ii) an entitlement to exercise, or control the exercise of, the voting power at any general meeting of,

the institution or, as the case may be, the other institution concerned;

and in this subsection "share" has the same meaning as in Part VII of the Companies Act 1985 or Part VIII of the Companies (Northern Ireland) Order 1986.

(4) A person who is a controller of an institution by virtue of subsection (3)(c) above is in this Act referred to as a "shareholder controller" of the institution; and in this Act—

(a) a "minority shareholder controller" means a shareholder controller not falling within paragraph (a) or (b) of subsection (3A) above;

(b) a "10 per cent. shareholder controller" means a shareholder controller in whose case the percentage referred to in the relevant paragraph is 10 or more but less than 20;

(c) a "20 per cent. shareholder controller" means a shareholder controller in whose case that percentage is 20 or more but less than 33;

(d) a "33 per cent. shareholder controller" means a shareholder controller in whose case that percentage is 33 or more but less than 50;

(e) a "50 per cent. shareholder controller" means a shareholder controller in whose case that percentage is 50 or more;

(f) a "majority shareholder controller" means a shareholder controller in whose case that percentage is 50 or more but less than 75; and

(g) a "principal shareholder controller" means a shareholder in whose case that percentage is 75 or more;

and in this subsection "the relevant paragraph", in relation to a shareholder controller, means whichever one of paragraphs (a) and (b) of subsection (3A) above gives the greater percentage in his case.]

(5) A person who is a controller of an institution by virtue of subsection (3)(d) above is in this Act referred to as "an indirect controller" of the institution.

[(5A) A person who is a controller of an institution by virtue of subsection (3)(e) above is in this Act referred to as a "parent controller" of the institution.]

(6) "Manager", in relation to an institution, means a person (other than a chief executive) who, under the immediate authority of a director or chief executive of the institution—

(a) exercises managerial functions; or

(b) is responsible for maintaining accounts or other records of the institution.

(7) In this section "chief executive", in relation to an institution, means a person who, either alone or jointly with one or more other persons, is responsible under the immediate authority of the directors for the conduct of the business of the institution.

(8) Without prejudice to subsection (7) above, in relation to an institution whose principal place of business is in a country or territory outside the United Kingdom, "chief executive" also includes a person who, either alone or jointly with one or more other persons, is responsible for the conduct of its business in the United Kingdom.

[(9) In this Act "associate", in relation to a person entitled to exercise or control the exercise of voting power in relation to, or holding shares in, an undertaking, means—

(a) the wife or husband or son or daughter of that person;

(b) the trustees of any settlement under which that person has a life interest in possession or, in Scotland, a life interest;

(c) any company of which that person is a director;

(d) any person who is an employee or partner of that person;

(e) if that person is a company—

(i) any director of that company;

(ii) any subsidiary undertaking of that company; and

(iii) any director or employee of any such subsidiary undertaking; and

(f) if that person has with any other person an agreement or arrangement with respect to the acquisition, holding or disposal of shares or other interests in that undertaking or body corporate or under which they undertake to act together in exercising their voting power in relation to it, that other person.

(10) For the purposes of subsection (9) above—

"son" includes stepson and "daughter" includes stepdaughter; "settlement" includes any disposition or arrangement under which property is held in trust.] **[122]**

NOTES

Commencement: 1 October 1987 (sub-ss (1)–(3), (5), (6)–(8)) (SI 1987/1664); 1 January 1993 (sub-ss (3A), (4), (5A), (9), (10)) (SI 1992/3218).

Sub-s (3): words in square brackets in sub-s (3)(c) substituted for the words "either alone or with any associate or associates, is entitled to exercise, or control the exercise of, 15 per cent or more of the voting power at any general meeting of the institution or of another institution of which it is a subsidiary; and", and sub-s (3)(e) and the word "and" preceding it added, by the Banking Coordination (Second Council Directive) Regulations 1992, SI 1992/3218, reg 43(1), subject to reg 46(a); see **[684]**.

Sub-ss (3A), (4): substituted for the original sub-s (4) by the Banking Coordination (Second Council Directive) Regulations 1992, SI 1992/3218, reg 43(2), subject to reg 46(a); see **[684]**. The original sub-s (4) read—

(4) A person who is a controller of an institution by virtue of paragraph (c) of subsection (3) above is in this Act referred to as a "shareholder controller" of the institution; and in this Act—

(a) a "minority shareholder controller" means a shareholder controller in whose case the percentage referred to in that paragraph does not exceed 50;

(b) a "majority shareholder controller" means a shareholder controller in whose case that percentage exceeds 50 but not 75; and

(c) a "principal shareholder controller" means a shareholder controller in whose case that percentage exceeds 75.

Sub-s (5A): inserted by the Banking Coordination (Second Council Directive) Regulations 1992, SI 1992/3218, reg 43(3), subject to reg 46(a); see **[684]**.

Sub-ss (9), (10): substituted by the Banking Coordination (Second Council Directive) Regulations 1992, SI 1992/3218, reg 43(4), subject to reg 46(a); see **[684]**. The original sub-ss (9), (10) read—

(9) In this Act "associate", in relation to a person entitled to exercise or control the exercise of voting power in relation to, or holding shares in, a body corporate, means—

(a) the wife or husband or son or daughter of that person;

(b) any company of which that person is a director;

(c) any person who is an employee or partner of that person;

(d) if that person is a company—

(i) any director of that company;

(ii) any subsidiary of that company; and

(iii) any director or employee of any such subsidiary; and

(e) if that person has with any other person an agreement or arrangement with respect to the acquisition, holding or disposal of shares or other interests in that body corporate or under which they undertake to act together in exercising their voting power in relation to it, that other person.

(10) For the purposes of subsection (9) above "son" includes stepson and "daughter" includes step-daughter.

[105A Meaning of "related company"

[(1) In this Act a "related company", in relation to an institution or the parent undertaking of an institution, means a body corporate (other than a subsidiary undertaking) in which the institution or parent undertaking holds a qualifying capital interest.]

(2) A qualifying capital interest means an interest in relevant shares of the body corporate which the institution or [parent undertaking] holds on a long-

term basis for the purpose of securing a contribution to its own activities by the exercise of control or influence arising from that interest.

(3) Relevant shares means shares comprised in the equity share capital of the body corporate of a class carrying rights to vote in all circumstances at general meetings of the body.

(4) A holding of 20 per cent. or more of the nominal value of the relevant shares of a body corporate shall be presumed to be a qualifying capital interest unless the contrary is shown.

(5) In this paragraph "equity share capital" has the same meaning as in the Companies Act 1985 and the Companies (Northern Ireland) Order 1986.] **[123]**

NOTES

Commencement: 1 April 1990 (sub-ss (2)–(5)) (SI 1990/355); 1 January 1993 (sub-s (1)) (SI 1992/3218).

This section inserted by the Companies Act 1989, s 23, Sch 10, Pt II, para 37(1), (3).

Sub-s (1): substituted by the Banking Coordination (Second Council Directive) Regulations 1992, SI 1992/3218, reg 44(1), subject to reg 46(a); see **[684]**.

The original sub-s (1) read—

(1) In this Act a "related company", in relation to an institution or the holding company of an institution, means a body corporate (other than a subsidiary) in which the institution or holding company holds a qualifying capital interest.

Sub-s (2): words in square brackets substituted for the words "holding company" by the Banking Coordination (Second Council Directive) Regulations 1992, SI 1992/3218, reg 44(2), subject to reg 46(a); see **[684]**.

106 Interpretation

(1) In this Act—

"associate" has the meaning given in section 105(9) above;

"authorisation" means authorisation granted by the Bank under this Act and "authorised" shall be construed accordingly;

"the Bank" means the Bank of England;

"bare trustee", in relation to a deposit, means a person holding the deposit on trust for another person who has the exclusive right to direct how it shall be dealt with subject only to satisfying any outstanding charge, lien or other right of the trustee to resort to it for the payment of duty, taxes, costs or other outgoings;

"controller" has the meaning given in section 105(3) above;

"director" has the meaning given in section 105(2) above;

"debenture" has the same meaning as in the Companies Act 1985;

"deposit" and "deposit-taking business" have the meaning given in sections 5 and 6 above but subject to any order under section 7 above;

"documents" includes information recorded in any form and, in relation to information recorded otherwise than in legible form, references to its production include references to producing a copy of the information in legible form;

"former authorised institution" means an institution which was formerly an authorised institution or a recognised bank or licensed institution under the Banking Act 1979 and continues to have a liability in respect of any deposit for which it had a liability at a time when it was an authorised institution, recognised bank or licensed institution;

"group", in relation to a body corporate, means that body corporate, any other body corporate which is its holding company or subsidiary and any other body corporate which is a subsidiary of that holding company;

"indirect controller" has the meaning given in section 105(5) above;
"institution", except in the expression "overseas institution" means—

(a)   a body corporate wherever incorporated;
(b)   a partnership formed under the law of any part of the United Kingdom;
(c)   a partnership or other unincorporated association of two or more persons formed under the law of a member State other than the United Kingdom; or
(d)   a savings bank to which section 104 above applies;

. . . . .

"local authority" means—

(a)   in England and Wales, a local authority within the meaning of the Local Government Act 1972, the Common Council of the City of London or the Council of the Isles of Scilly;
(b)   . . . ; and
(c)   in Northern Ireland, a district council within the meaning of the Local Government Act (Northern Ireland) 1972;

"manager" has the meaning given in section 105(6) above;
"municipal bank" has the meaning given in section 103 above;
["parent controller" has the meaning given in section 105(5A) above;]
"penny savings bank" has the meaning as in the National Savings Bank Act 1971;
["related company" has the meaning given by section 105A above;]
["relevant supervisory authority"—

(a)   in relation to another member State, has the meaning given in regulation 2 of the Banking Coordination (Second Council Directive) Regulations 1992;
(b)   in relation to any other country or territory outside the United Kingdom, means the authority discharging in that country or territory functions corresponding to those of the Bank under this Act;]

["shareholder controller", "minority shareholder controller", "10 per cent. shareholder controller", "20 per cent. shareholder controller", "33 per cent. shareholder controller", "50 per cent. shareholder controller", "majority shareholder controller" and "principal shareholder controller" have the meanings given in section 105(4) above].

(2) Section 736 of the Companies Act 1985 (meaning of subsidiary and holding company) shall apply for the purposes of this Act.

[(2A) In this Act the following expressions, namely—

another member State;
connected UK authority;
credit institution;
European authorised institution;
the First Council Directive;
home State;
listed activity;
parent undertaking;
recognised self-regulating organisation;
relevant supervisory authority;

the Second Council Directive;
subsidiary undertaking;
supervisory authority;
undertaking,

have the same meanings as in the Banking Coordination (Second Council Directive) Regulations 1992.]

(3) Any reference in this Act to any provision of Northern Ireland legislation within the meaning of section 24 of the Interpretation Act 1978 includes a reference to any subsequent provision of that legislation which, with or without modification, re-enacts the provision referred to in this Act.   **[124]**

NOTES

Commencement: 15 July 1987 (sub-ss (1), (2), (3)) (SI 1987/1189); 1 January 1993 (sub-s (2A)) (SI 1992/3218).

Sub-s (1): words omitted apply to Scotland only; definition "parent controller" inserted by the Banking Coordination (Second Council Directive) Regulations 1992, SI 1992/3218, reg 45(1)(a), subject to reg 46(a); see **[684]**; definition "related company" substituted by the Companies Act 1989, s 23, Sch 10, Pt II, para 37(1), (4); definition "relevant supervisory authority" substituted by the Banking Coordination (Second Council Directive) Regulations 1992, SI 1992/3218, reg 45(1)(b), subject to reg 46(a); see **[684]**.

The original definition read—

"relevant supervisory authority", in relation to a country or territory outside the United
Kingdom, means the authority discharging in that country or territory functions corresponding to those of the Bank under this Act;

Definition "shareholder controller" and related definitions substituted by the Banking Coordination (Second Council Directive) Regulations 1992, SI 1992/3218, reg 45(1)(c), subject to reg 46(a); see **[684]**.

The original definitions read—

"shareholder controller", "minority shareholder controller", "majority shareholder controller"
and "principal shareholder controller" have the meaning given in section 105(4) above.

Sub-s (2A): inserted by the Banking Coordination (Second Council Directive) Regulations 1992, SI 1992/3218, reg 45(2), subject to reg 46(a); see **[684]**.

Modifications: as to modifications to this section, see the Banking Coordination (Second Council Directive) Regulations 1992, SI 1992/3218, reg 47, Sch 8, para 33; see **[693]**.

107 Transitional provisions

Schedule 5 to this Act shall have effect with respect to the transitional matters there mentioned.

                                                                          [125]

108 (*Introduces Schs 6, 7 to this Act (minor and consequential amendments, repeals and revocations).*)

109 Northern Ireland

(1) This Act extends to Northern Ireland.

(2) Subject to any Order made after the passing of this Act by virtue of subsection (1)(a) of section 3 of the Northern Ireland Constitution Act 1973, the regulation of banking shall not be a transferred matter for the purposes of that Act but shall for the purposes of subsection (2) of that section be treated as specified in Schedule 3 to that Act.   **[126]**

110 Short title and commencement

(1) This Act may be cited as the Banking Act 1987.

(2) Section 91 above shall come into force on the passing of this Act and the other provisions of this Act shall come into force on such day as the Treasury may by order appoint; and different days may be appointed for different provisions or different purposes.   **[127]**

NOTE
  Orders: SI 1987/1189; SI 1987/1664; SI 1988/502; SI 1988/644.

SCHEDULES

SCHEDULE 1

Section 2

THE BOARD OF BANKING SUPERVISION

Terms of office

1.—(1) The independent members of the Board shall hold office for five years except that some of those first appointed may be appointed to hold office for shorter and different periods so as to secure that all the members do not retire simultaneously.

(2) An independent member may resign his office by written notice to the Bank and the Chancellor of the Exchequer.

(3) A person shall vacate his office as an independent member if he takes up a post with executive responsibility in the Bank.

(4) Subject to sub-paragraph (3) above, a person who has ceased to be an independent member of the Board shall be eligible for re-appointment.

Removal from office

2. An independent member may be removed by the Bank with the consent of the Chancellor of the Exchequer if it is satisfied—

(a) that he has been absent from meetings of the Board for more than three months without the permission of the Board;
(b) that he has become bankrupt, that his estate has been sequestrated or that he has made an arrangement with or granted a trust deed for his creditors;
(c) that he is incapacitated by physical or mental illness; or
(d) that he is otherwise unable or unfit to discharge his functions as a member of the Board.

Increase in number of members

3.—(1) The Treasury may, after consultation with the Bank, by order increase or, subject to section 2(2) of this Act, reduce the number of ex officio or independent members of the Board, provided always that there shall be a majority of independent members on the Board.

(2) Any order under this paragraph shall be subject to annulment in pursuance of a resolution of either House of Parliament.

Proceedings

4.—(1) The quorum for a meeting of the Board shall be one ex officio member and three independent members.

(2) Subject to sub-paragraph (1) above, the Board shall determine its own procedure.

Facilities, remuneration and allowances

5. The Bank shall make such provision as it thinks necessary for providing the Board with facilities for the exercise of its functions and for providing remuneration, allowances or other benefits for or in respect of the independent members.   **[128]**

SCHEDULE 2

Section 4(1)

EXEMPTED PERSONS

1. The central bank of a member State other than the United Kingdom.

2. The National Savings Bank.

3. A penny savings bank.

4. A municipal bank.

5. A building society incorporated (or deemed to be incorporated) under the Building Societies Act 1986.

6.—(1) A friendly society within the meaning of section 7(1)(a) of the Friendly Societies Act 1974 . . .

(2) This paragraph applies only to the acceptance of deposits in the course of carrying on the authorised insurance business.

7. A society registered under either of the Acts mentioned in paragraph 6 above other than such a society as is there mentioned.

8.—(1) Any institution which is for the time being authorised under section 3 or 4 of the Insurance Companies Act 1982 to carry on insurance business of a class specified in Schedule 1 or 2 to that Act.

(2) This paragraph applies only to the acceptance of deposits in the course of carrying on the authorised insurance business.

9. A loan society whose rules are certified, deposited and enrolled in accordance with the Loan Societies Act 1840.

10. A credit union within the meaning of the Credit Unions Act 1979 or the Credit Unions (Northern Ireland) Order 1985.

[10A.—(1) Keesler Federal Credit Union.

(2) This paragraph applies only to the acceptance of deposits made by members, or dependants of members, of a visiting force of the United States of America, or by members, or dependants of members, of a civilian component of such a force, where "member", "dependant", "visiting force" and "member of a civilian component" have the meanings given to them by the Visiting Forces Act 1952.]

11. A body of persons certified as a school bank by the National Savings Bank or an authorised institution.

12. A local authority.

13. Any other body which by virtue of any enactment has power to issue a precept to a local authority in England or Wales or a requisition to a local authority in Scotland.

14. The Crown Agents for Overseas Governments and Administrations.

[14A. Crown Agents Financial Services Limited.]

15. The European Atomic Energy Community.

16. The European Coal and Steel Community.

17. The European Economic Community.

18. The European Investment Bank.

19. The International Bank for Reconstruction and Development.

20. The International Finance Corporation.

21. The International Monetary Fund.

22. The African Development Bank.

23. The Asian Development Bank.

24. The Caribbean Development Bank.

25. The Inter-American Development Bank.

[26. The European Bank for Reconstruction and Development.]

[27. The Council of Europe Resettlement Fund.] **[129]**

NOTES
Commencement: 28 March 1991 (para 26) (SI 1991/66); 23 April 1993 (para 27) (SI 1993/953); 26 December 1991 (para 10A) (SI 1991/2734); 1 April 1989 (para 14A) (SI 1989/125); 1 October 1987 (remainder) (SI 1987/1664).
Para 6: words omitted in para 6(1) repealed by the Friendly Societies Act 1992, s 120(2), Sch 22, Pt I.
Para 10A: inserted by the Banking Act 1987 (Exempt Persons) Order 1991, SI 1991/2734, art 2.
Para 14A: inserted by the Banking Act 1987 (Exempt Persons) Order 1989, SI 1989/125, art 2.
Para 26: added by the Banking Act 1987 (Exempt Persons) Order 1991, SI 1991/66, art 3.
Para 27: added by the Banking Act 1987 (Exempt Persons) Order 1993, SI 1993/953, art 2.
Modifications: para 8 of this Schedule has effect as if the reference to an institution which is for the time being authorised under s 3 or 4 of the Insurance Companies Act 1982 to carry on insurance business of a class specified in Sch 1 or 2 to that Act included a reference to an EC company which is lawfully carrying on insurance business, or providing insurance, in the United Kingdom; see the Insurance Companies (Third Insurance Directives) Regulations 1994, SI 1994/1696, reg 68(1), Sch 8, Pt I, para 14(2).

SCHEDULE 3
Sections 9, 11, 13(4), 16(1), 22
MINIMUM CRITERIA FOR AUTHORISATION

Directors etc. to be fit and proper persons

1.—(1) Every person who is, or is to be, a director, controller or manager of the institution is a fit and proper person to hold the particular position which he holds or is to hold.

(2) In determining whether a person is a fit and proper person to hold any particular position, regard shall be had to his probity, to his competence and soundness of judgment for fulfilling the responsibilities of that position, to the diligence with which he is fulfilling or likely to fulfil those responsibilities and to whether the interests of depositors or potential depositors of the institution are, or are likely to be, in any way threatened by his holding that position.

(3) Without prejudice to the generality of the foregoing provisions, regard may be had to the previous conduct and activities in business or financial matters of the person in question and, in particular, to any evidence that he has—

(a) committed an offence involving fraud or other dishonesty or violence;
(b) contravened any provision made by or under any enactment appearing to the Bank to be designed for protecting members of the public against financial loss due to dishonesty, incompetence or malpractice by persons concerned in the provision of banking, insurance, investment or other financial services or the management of companies or against financial loss due to the conduct of discharged or undischarged bankrupts;
(c) engaged in any business practices appearing to the Bank to be deceitful or oppressive or otherwise improper (whether unlawful or not) or which otherwise reflect discredit on his method of conducting business;
(d) engaged in or been associated with any other business practices or otherwise conducted himself in such a way as to cast doubt on his competence and soundness of judgement.

Business to be directed by at least two individuals

2. At least two individuals effectively direct the business of the institution.

Composition of board of directors

3. In the case of an institution incorporated in the United Kingdom the directors include such number (if any) of directors without executive responsibility for the management of its business as the Bank considers appropriate having regard to the circumstances of the institution and the nature and scale of its operations.

Business to be conducted in prudent manner

4.—(1) The institution conducts, or, in the case of an institution which is not yet carrying on a deposit-taking business, will conduct its business in a prudent manner.

(2) An institution shall not be regarded as conducting its business in a prudent manner unless it maintains or, as the case may be, will maintain [own funds] which, together with other financial resources available to the institution of such nature and amount as are considered appropriate by the Bank, are—

(a) of an amount which is commensurate with the nature and scale of the institution's operations; and
(b) of an amount and nature sufficient to safeguard the interests of its depositors and potential depositors, having regard to the particular factors mentioned in sub-paragraph (3) below and any other factors appearing to the Bank to be relevant.

[(3) The particular factors referred to above are—

(a) the nature and scale of the institution's operations; and
(b) the risks inherent in those operations and in the operations of any other undertaking in the same group so far as capable of affecting the institution.

(3A) An institution shall not be regarded as conducting its business in a prudent manner unless it maintains or, as the case may be, will maintain own funds which amount to not less than ecu 5 million (or an amount of equal value denominated wholly or partly in another unit of account).]

(4) An institution shall not be regarded as conducting its business in a prudent manner unless it maintains or, as the case may be, will maintain adequate liquidity, having regard to the relationship between its liquid assets and its actual and contingent liabilities, to the times at which those liabilities will or may fall due and its assets mature, to the factors mentioned in sub-paragraph (3) above and to any other factors appearing to the Bank to be relevant.

(5) For the purposes of sub-paragraph (4) above the Bank may, to such extent as it thinks appropriate, take into account as liquid assets, assets of the institution and facilities available to it which are capable of providing liquidity within a reasonable period.

(6) An institution shall not be regarded as conducting its business in a prudent manner unless it makes or, as the case may be, will make adequate provision for depreciation or diminution in the value of its assets (including provision for bad or doubtful debts), for liabilities which will or may fall to be discharged by it and for losses which it will or may incur.

(7) An institution shall not be regarded as conducting its business in a prudent manner unless it maintains or, as the case may be, will maintain adequate accounting and other records of business and adequate systems of control of its business and records.

(8) Those records and systems shall not be regarded as adequate unless they are such as to enable the business of the institution to be prudently managed and the institution to comply with the duties imposed on it by or under this Act and in determining whether those systems are adequate the Bank shall have regard to the functions and responsibilities in respect of them of any such directors of the institution as are mentioned in paragraph 3 above.

(9) Sub-paragraphs (2) to (7) above are without prejudice to the generality of sub-paragraph (1) above.

[(10) In this paragraph "ecu" and "own funds" have the same meanings as in the Banking Coordination (Second Council Directive) Regulations 1992.]

Integrity and skill

5. The business of the institution is or, in the case of an institution which is not yet carrying on a deposit-taking business, will be carried on with integrity and the professional skills appropriate to the nature and scale of its activities.

Minimum net assets

[6.—(1) The institution will at the time when authorisation is granted to it have initial capital amounting to not less than ecu 5 million (or an amount of equal value denominated wholly or partly in another unit of account).

(2) In this paragraph "ecu" and "initial capital" have the same meanings as in the Banking Coordination (Second Council Directive) Regulations 1992.] **[130]**

NOTES

Commencement: 1 October 1987 (paras 1–3, 4(1), (2), (4)–(9), 5) (SI 1987/1664); 1 January 1993 (paras 4(3), (3A), (10), 6) (SI 1992/3218).

Transitional provision: see, in relation to para 6(1), s 107, Sch 5, para 3(2).

Para 4: words in square brackets in para 4(2) substituted for the words "net assets" by the Banking Coordination (Second Council Directive) Regulations 1992, SI 1992/3218, reg 27(1), subject to reg 46(a); see **[684]**; paras 4(3), (3A) substituted for the original para 4(3), subject to transitional provisions, by the Banking Coordination (Second Council Directive) Regulations 1992, SI 1992/3218, regs 27(2), 83, Sch 11, Pt II, para 4, subject to reg 46(a); see **[694]**, **[684]**. The original para 4(3) read—

    (3) The particular factors referred to above are—

        (a)   the nature and scale of the institution's operations; and
        (b)   the risks inherent in those operations and, if the institution is a body corporate, in the operations of any other body corporate in the same group so far as capable of affecting the institution.

Para 4(10) substituted by the Banking Coordination (Second Council Directive) Regulations 1992, SI 1992/3218, reg 27(3), subject to reg 46(a); see **[684]**. The original para 4(10) read—

    (10) For the purposes of this paragraph "net assets", in relation to a body corporate, means paid-up capital and reserves.

Para 6: substituted by the Banking Coordination (Second Council Directive) Regulations 1992, SI 1992/3218, reg 27(4), subject to reg 46(a); see **[684]**. The original para 6 read—

    6.—(1) The institution will at the time when authorisation is granted to it have net assets amounting to not less than £1 million (or an amount of equivalent value denominated wholly or partly otherwise than in sterling).

    (2) In this paragraph "net assets", in relation to a body corporate, means paid-up capital and reserves.

    (3) The Treasury may, after consultation with the Bank, by order vary the sum specified in sub-paragraph (1) above.

    (4) Any order under sub-paragraph (3) above shall be subject to annulment in pursuance of a resolution of either House of Parliament.

Modifications: as to modifications to this Schedule, see the Banking Coordination (Second Council Directive) Regulations 1992, SI 1992/3218, regs 23(3), 83, Sch 11, Pt II, para 4(2); see **[694]**.

SCHEDULE 4

Section 50

THE DEPOSIT PROTECTION BOARD

Constitution

1.—(1) The Board shall consist of three ex officio members, namely—

    (a)   the Governor of the Bank for the time being, who shall be the chairman of the Board;
    (b)   the Deputy Governor of the Bank for the time being; and
    (c)   the Chief Cashier of the Bank for the time being;

and such ordinary members as shall from time to time be appointed under sub-paragraph (2) below.

(2) The Governor of the Bank shall appoint as ordinary members of the Board—

    (a)   three persons who are directors, controllers or managers of contributory institutions; and
    (b)   persons who are officers or employees of the Bank.

(3) Each ex officio member of the Board may appoint an alternate member, being an officer or employee of the Bank, to perform his duties as a member in his absence.

(4) Each ordinary member of the Board may appoint an appropriately qualified person as an alternate member to perform his duties as a member in his absence; and for this purpose a person is appropriately qualified for appointment as an alternate—

    (a) by a member appointed under paragraph (a) of sub-paragraph (2) above, if he is a director, controller or manager of a contributory institution; and

    (b) by a member appointed under paragraph (b) of that sub-paragraph, if he is either an officer or an employee of the Bank.

(5) Ordinary and alternate members of the Board shall hold and vacate office in accordance with the terms of their appointment.

Expenses

2. The Board may pay to its members such allowances in respect of expenses as the Board may determine.

Proceedings

3.—(1) The Board shall determine its own procedure, including the quorum necessary for its meetings.

(2) The validity of any proceedings of the Board shall not be affected by any vacancy among the ex officio members of the Board or by any defect in the appointment of any ordinary or alternate member.

4.—(1) The fixing of the common seal of the Board shall be authenticated by the signature of the chairman of the Board or some other person authorised by the Board to act for that purpose.

(2) A document purporting to be duly executed under the seal of the Board shall be received in evidence and deemed to be so executed unless the contrary is proved.

Accounts, audit and annual report

5.—(1) The Board may determine its own financial year.

(2) It shall be the duty of the Board—

    (a) to keep proper accounts and proper records in relation to the accounts; and

    (b) to prepare in respect of each of its financial years a statement of accounts showing the state of affairs and income and expenditure of the Board.

(3) A statement of accounts prepared in accordance with sub-paragraph (2)(b) above shall be audited by auditors appointed by the Board and the auditors shall report to the Board stating whether in their opinion the provisions of sub-paragraph (2) above have been complied with.

[(4) A person shall not be appointed as auditor by the Board under sub-paragraph (3) above unless he is eligible for appointment as a company auditor under section 25 of the Companies Act 1989.]

(5) It shall be the duty of the Board, as soon as practicable after the end of each of its financial years, to prepare a report on the performance of its functions during that year.

(6) It shall be the duty of the Board to publish, in such manner as it thinks appropriate, every statement of account prepared in accordance with with sub-paragraph (2)(b) above and every report prepared in accordance with sub-paragraph (5) above.   **[131]**

NOTES

Commencement: 1 October 1987 (paras 1–4, 5(1)–(3), (5), (6)) (SI 1987/1664); 1 October 1991 (para 5(4)) (SI 1991/1997).

Transitional provision: see s 107, Sch 5, para 8.

Para 5: para 5(4) substituted by the Companies Act 1989 (Eligibility for Appointment as Company Auditor) (Consequential Amendments) Regulations 1991, SI 1991/1997, reg 2, Schedule, para 67. For transitional provisions as to termination and resignation of appointments, see reg 4 of those regulations.

SCHEDULE 5

TRANSITIONAL PROVISIONS

First report by Bank of England

1. If this Act comes into force in the course of a financial year of the Bank of England its first report under section 1 of this Act shall include a report on its activities during that year under the Banking Act 1979 (in this Schedule to as "the former Act").

Existing recognised banks and licensed institutions

2.—(1) Any institution (within the meaning of this Act) which at the coming into force of section 3 of this Act or by virtue of paragraph 4 or 5 below is—

(a) a recognised bank; or
(b) a licensed institution,

under the former Act shall be deemed to have been granted an authorisation under this Act.

(2) In relation to any such institution the reference in paragraph (a) of section 11(2) of this Act to the day on which it was authorised shall be construed as a reference to the day on which it was recognised or licensed under the former Act; and in relation to an institution recognised under the former Act by virtue of Part II of Schedule 3 to that Act that paragraph shall have effect with the omission of the words "in the United Kingdom".

(3) In relation to any such institution the reference to in section 70(4) of this Act to the time when notice was given to the Bank under subsection (1) shall be construed as a reference to the day on which it first applied for recognition or a licence under the former Act.

Conditional licences

3.—(1) Any conditional licence in force under the former Act when section 3 of this Act comes into force or granted by virtue of paragraph 4 or 5 below shall be treated as an authorisation granted under this Act subject to restrictions (as to duration and conditions) corresponding to those applying to the conditional licence; but no institution shall be guilty of an offence under section 12 of this Act by reason only of a contravention of or failure to comply with a condition which is treated as a restriction of such an authorisation except so far as the condition is attributable to a variation under this Act.

(2) In relation to an application for authorisation made by an institution holding a conditional licence which by virtue of this paragraph is treated as a restricted authorisation, paragraph 6(1) of Schedule 3 to this Act shall have effect with the substitution for the reference to £1 million of a reference to £250,000.

Applications subject to appeal

4.—(1) Where an application for recognition or a licence under the former Act has been refused by the Bank and at the coming into force of section 3 of this Act—

(a) an appeal is pending against that refusal; or
(b) the time for appealing against that refusal has not expired,

the repeal of the former Act shall not preclude the determination, or the bringing and determin-ation, of the appeal and the grant or refusal of recognition or a licence as a result of that determination.

(2) Sub-paragraph (1) above does not apply to an appeal by a licensed institution against a refusal to grant it recognition.

Revocation

5.—(1) Where the Bank has given an institution a notice under section 7(3) or (4) of the former Act and the proceedings pursuant to that notice under the provisions of Schedule 4 to that Act have not been concluded at the coming into force of section 3 of this Act the repeal of that Act shall not affect the operation of those provisions in relation to that notice.

(2) Paragraph 2 above does not apply to an institution which is a recognised bank or licensed institution at the coming into force of section 3 of this Act if its recognition or licence is subsequently revoked by virtue of this paragraph.

Directions

6.—(1) The repeal of the former Act shall not affect the continued operation of any direction under section 8 of that Act which has been confirmed in accordance with section 9 before the repeal and any such direction may be varied or revoked as if given under section 19 of this Act.

(2) A direction may be given under section 19 of this Act to an institution which was a recognised bank or licensed institution under the former Act if—

(a) its recognition or licence under that Act was revoked or surrendered; or
(b) a disqualification notice has been served on it under section 183 of the Financial Services Act 1986;

but subsection (5) of section 19 shall apply to it as it applies to an authorised institution, taking references to the time when it was authorised as references to the time when it was recognised or licensed under the former Act.

Information and investigations

7.—(1) The repeal of the former Act shall not affect the operation of any requirement imposed under section 16 of that Act before the repeal or any powers exercisable under that section in relation to any such requirement.

(2) The repeal of the former Act shall not affect the operation of section 17 of that Act in any case in which a person or persons to carry out an investigation under that section have been appointed before the repeal.

(3) Sections 42, 43 and 44 of this Act shall have effect in relation to a contravention of section 1 or 39 of the former act as they have effect in relation to a contravention of section 3 or 35 of this Act.

Members of Deposit Protection Board

8. Any person who is an ordinary member or alternate member of the Deposit Protection Board at the coming into force of Part II of this Act shall be treated as having been appointed under Schedule 4 to this Act.

Initial contributions by excluded institutions

9.—(1) On or as soon as possible after the coming into force of Part II of this Act the Deposit Protection Board shall levy an initial contribution from each authorised institution which by virtue of an order under section 23(2) of the former Act did not have such a contribution levied from it under section 24 of that Act.

(2) The amount of the initial contribution to be levied from an institution under this paragraph shall be the amount of the initial contribution that would have been levied from it under that section if it has not been exempted from levy by virtue of the order.

Maximum contributions

10. For the purposes of section 56(3) of this Act there shall be taken into account any contribution or repayment made under any provision of the former Act which corresponds to any provision of this Act.

Insolvencies before commencement of Part II

11. This Act does not affect the operation of sections 28 to 31 of the former Act in relation to any insolvency occurring before the coming into force of Part II of this Act; but section 63 of this Act shall apply (instead of section 32 of that Act) to any money received by the Board under section 31.

Borrowing

12. Any sum borrowed by virtue of section 26(3) of the said Act of 1979 shall, so far as outstanding at the coming into force of Part II of this Act, be treated as having been borrowed under section 64 of this Act.

Use of banking names

13.—(1) Subject to sub-paragraph (2) below, section 67 of this Act does not prohibit the use by an institution which is incorporated in or is a partnership formed under the law of any part of the United Kingdom and is deemed to be an authorised institution by virtue of paragraph 2 above of a name which was its registered business or company name immediately before the coming into force of Part III of this Act or of section 36 of the former Act.

(2) Sub-paragraph (1) above shall cease to apply—

(a) in the case of an incorporated institution, if the total value in sterling of its issued share capital and undistributable reserves falls below their total value at the coming into force of Part III of this Act; or

(b) in the case of a partnership in respect of which one or more designated fixed capital accounts are maintained, if the total value in sterling of those accounts falls below their value at that time.

(3) Section 67 of this Act does not prohibit the use by—

(a) an authorised institution which is a wholly-owned subsidiary of an institution to which sub-paragraph (1) above applies; or

(b) a company which has a wholly-owned subsidiary which is an institution to which that sub-paragraph applies,

of a name which includes the name of the institution to which that sub-paragraph applies for the purpose of indicating the connection between the two companies.

(4) In sub-paragraph (2) above "share capital" and "designated fixed capital account" have the same meaning as in subsection (2) of section 67 of this Act and "undistributable reserves" means such reserves as mentioned in paragraph (a)(ii) of that subsection.

Restriction on disclosure of information

14. In section 82(1) of this Act the reference to information received under or for the purposes of this Act includes a reference to information received under or for the purposes of the former Act.

[132]

(Sch 6, in so far as unrepealed, specifies minor and consequential amendments; Sch 7 specifies certain enactments and instruments repealed or revoked.)

BILLS OF EXCHANGE

STAMP ACT 1853
(16 & 17 Vict c 59)

An Act . . . to amend the Laws relating to Stamp Duties, and to make perpetual certain Stamp Duties in Ireland [4 August 1853]

NOTE
  Words omitted from long title repealed by the Statute Law Revision Act 1892.

1–18 (*Ss 1–7, 9–16 and 18 repealed by the Inland Revenue Repeal Act 1870, s 2, Schedule; s 8 (repealed) applied to Scotland only; s 17 repealed by the Inland Revenue Regulation Act 1890, s 40, Schedule.*)

19 Drafts on bankers payable to order on demand, and endorsed by payees, shall be sufficient authority for payment, etc

Provided always, that any draft or order drawn upon a banker for a sum of money payable to order on demand, which shall, when presented for payment, purport to be endorsed by the person to whom the same shall be drawn payable, shall be a sufficient authority to such banker to pay the amount of such draft or order to the bearer thereof; and it shall not be incumbent on such banker to prove that such endorsement, or any subsequent endorsement, was made by or under the direction or authority of the person to whom the said draft or order was or is made payable either by the drawer or any endorser thereof. **[133]**

NOTE
  By virtue of the Bills of Exchange Act (1882) Amendment Act 1932, s 1 (repealed), the Bills of Exchange Act 1882, ss 76–81, as amended, relating to crossed cheques, applied also to a banker's draft. The 1932 Act was repealed by the Cheques Act 1957, s 6(3) and Schedule (itself repealed by the Statute Law (Repeals) Act 1974) and its presently relevant provisions are re-enacted by ss 4 and 5 of the 1957 Act; see **[239]**, **[240]**. Therefore a banker's draft can now be crossed as if it were a cheque.

20 (*Repealed by the Statute Law (Repeals) Act 1978.*)

(*Schedule repealed by the Inland Revenue Repeal Act 1870.*)

COMMON LAW PROCEDURE ACT 1854
(17 & 18 Vict c 125)

An Act for the further Amendment of the Process, Practice, and Mode of Pleading in and enlarging the Jurisdiction of the Superior Courts of Common Law at Westminster, and of the Superior Courts of Common Law of the Counties Palatine of Lancaster and Durham . . . [12 August 1854]

NOTE
  Part of long title repealed by the Statute Law Revision and Civil Procedure Act 1883, s 3, Schedule, and the Statute Law Revision Act 1892. Repeals by those Acts were, however, subject to savings of jurisdiction established by the repealed enactments and savings of the application of the repealed enactments to local courts.

1–86 (*Ss 1, 2, 18, 19, 31–58, 60–86 repealed by the Statute Law Revision and Civil Procedure Act 1883, s 3, Schedule and ss 21–27, 30 repealed by the Statute Law Revision Act 1892, all subject to the savings mentioned in the Introductory Note to this Act; ss 3–17 repealed by the Arbitration Act 1889, s 26, Sch 2; s 20 repealed by the Oaths Act 1888, s 6, Schedule; ss 28, 29 repealed by the Inland Revenue Repeal Act 1870, s 2, Schedule; s 59 repealed by the Courts Act 1971, s 56, Sch 11, Pt I.*)

87 Actions on lost negotiable instruments

In case of any action founded upon a . . . negotiable instrument, it shall be lawful for the court or a judge to order that the loss of such instrument shall not be set up, provided an indemnity is given, to the satisfaction of the court or judge, or a master, against the claims of any other person upon such negotiable instrument.   **[134]**

NOTE
  Words omitted, which related to bills of exchange, were repealed by the Statute Law Revision Act 1892.

88–98 (*S 88 repealed by the Common Law Procedure Act 1860, s 35; s 89 repealed by the Statute Law Revision Act 1892 and ss 90–96 repealed by the Statute Law Revision and Civil Procedure Act 1883, s 3, Schedule, subject to the savings mentioned in the Introductory Note to this Act; ss 97, 98 repealed by the Supreme Court of Judicature (Officers) Act 1879, s 29, Sch 2.*)

99 Interpretation of terms

In the construction of this Act the word "court" shall be understood to mean any one of the Superior Courts of Common Law at Westminster: and the word "judge" shall be understood to mean a judge or baron of any of the said courts; and the word "master" shall be understood to mean a master of any of the said courts; and the word "action" shall be understood to mean any personal action in any of the said courts.   **[135]**

NOTES
  This section repealed by the Statute Law Revision and Civil Procedure Act 1883, s 3, Schedule, subject to the savings mentioned in the Introductory Note to this Act.
  Superior Courts of Common Law: the jurisdiction of the former Courts of Common Law was vested in the High Court by the Supreme Court of Judicature (Consolidation) Act 1925, ss 18, 224 (repealed); see now the Supreme Court Act 1981, s 19, Sch 4, para 1.

100–105 (*Ss 100–102, 104, 105 repealed by the Statute Law Revision and Civil Procedure Act 1883, s 3, Schedule, and s 103 repealed by the Statute Law Revision Act 1892, subject to the savings mentioned in the Introductory Note to this Act.*)

106 Short title of Act

In citing this Act in any instrument, document, or proceeding, it shall be sufficient to use the expression, "The Common Law Procedure Act 1854."   **[136]**

107 Act not to extend to Ireland or Scotland

Nothing in this Act shall extend to Ireland or Scotland . . .   **[137]**

NOTE
  Words omitted repealed by the Statute Law Revision Act 1875.

BILLS OF EXCHANGE ACT 1882
(45 & 46 Vict c 61)

ARRANGEMENT OF SECTIONS
PART I
PRELIMINARY

PART II
BILLS OF EXCHANGE

Form and interpretation

Capacity and authority of parties

The consideration for a bill

Negotiation of bills

PART III
CHEQUES ON A BANKER

PART IV

PROMISSORY NOTES

PART V

SUPPLEMENTARY

SCHEDULES

An Act to codify the law relating to Bills of Exchange, Cheques, and Promissory Notes   [18 August 1882]

NOTE
By the Bills of Exchange (Time of Noting) Act 1917, s 2, the Bills of Exchange Act 1882 and the 1917 Act may be cited by the collective title of the Bills of Exchange Acts 1882 to 1917.

PART I

PRELIMINARY

1 Short title

This Act may be cited as the Bills of Exchange Act, 1882.   **[138]**

2 Interpretation of terms

In this Act, unless the context otherwise requires,—

"Acceptance" means an acceptance completed by delivery or notification.

"Action" includes counter claim and set off.

"Banker" includes a body of persons whether incorporated or not who carry on the business of banking.

"Bankrupt" includes any person whose estate is vested in a trustee or assignee under the law for the time being in force relating to bankruptcy.

"Bearer" means the person in possession of a bill or note which is payable to bearer.

"Bill" means bill of exchange, and "note" means promissory note.

"Delivery" means transfer of possession, actual or constructive, from one person to another.

"Holder" means the payee or indorsee of a bill or note who is in possession of it, or the bearer thereof.

"Indorsement" means an indorsement completed by delivery.

"Issue" means the first delivery of a bill or note, complete in form to a person who takes it as a holder.

"Person" includes a body of persons whether incorporated or not.

"Value" means valuable consideration.

"Written" includes printed, and "writing" includes print.   **[139]**

PART II
BILLS OF EXCHANGE

Form and interpretation

3 Bill of exchange defined

(1) A bill of exchange is an unconditional order in writing, addressed by one person to another, signed by the person giving it, requiring the person to whom it is addressed to pay on demand or at a fixed or determinable future time a sum certain in money to or to the order of a specified person, or to bearer.

(2) An instrument which does not comply with these conditions, or which orders any act to be done in addition to the payment of money, is not a bill of exchange.

(3) An order to pay out of a particular fund is not unconditional within the meaning of this section; but an unqualified order to pay, coupled with (a) an indication of a particular fund out of which the drawee is to re-imburse himself or a particular account to be debited with the amount, or (b) a statement of the transaction which gives rise to the bill, is unconditional.

(4) A bill is not invalid by reason—

(a) That it is not dated;
(b) That it does not specify the value given, or that any value has been given therefor;
(c) That it does not specify the place where it is drawn or the place where it is payable.   **[140]**

NOTE
Bill of exchange: a bill of exchange drawn on or after 15 February 1971 is invalid if the sum payable is an amount of money wholly or partly in shillings or pence; see the Decimal Currency Act 1969, s 2(1).

4 Inland and foreign bills

(1) An inland bill is a bill which is or on the face of it purports to be (a) both drawn and payable within the British Islands, or (b) drawn within the British Islands upon some person resident therein. Any other bill is a foreign bill.

For the purposes of this Act "British Islands" mean any part of the United Kingdom of Great Britain and Ireland, the islands of Man, Guernsey, Jersey, Alderney, and Sark, and the islands adjacent to any of them being part of the dominions of Her Majesty.

(2) Unless the contrary appear on the face of the bill the holder may treat it as an inland bill. **[141]**

NOTE

British Islands: in this context "British Islands" is construed as exclusive of Eire; see Irish Free State (Consequential Adaptation of Enactments) Order 1923, SR & O 1923/405.

5 Effect where different parties to bill are the same person

(1) A bill may be drawn payable to, or to the order of, the drawer; or it may be drawn payable to, or to the order of, the drawee.

(2) Where in a bill drawer and drawee are the same person, or where the drawee is a fictitious person or a person not having capacity to contract, the holder may treat the instrument, at his option, either as a bill of exchange or as a promissory note. **[142]**

6 Address to drawee

(1) The drawee must be named or otherwise indicated in a bill with reasonable certainty.

(2) A bill may be addressed to two or more drawees whether they are partners or not, but an order addressed to two drawees in the alternative or to two or more drawees in succession is not a bill of exchange. **[143]**

7 Certainty required as to payee

(1) Where a bill is not payable to bearer, the payee must be named or otherwise indicated therein with reasonable certainty.

(2) A bill may be made payable to two or more payees jointly, or it may be made payable in the alternative to one of two, or one or some of several payees. A bill may also be made payable to the holder of an office for the time being.

(3) Where the payee is a fictitious or non-existing person the bill may be treated as payable to bearer. **[144]**

8 What bills are negotiable

(1) When a bill contains words prohibiting transfer, or indicating an intention that it should not be transferable, it is valid as between the parties thereto, but is not negotiable.

(2) A negotiable bill may be payable either to order or to bearer.

(3) A bill is payable to bearer which is expressed to be so payable, or on which the only or last indorsement is an indorsement in blank.

(4) A bill is payable to order which is expressed to be so payable, or which is expressed to be payable to a particular person, and does not contain words prohibiting transfer or indicating an intention that it should not be transferable.

(5) Where a bill, either originally or by indorsement, is expressed to be payable to the order of a specified person, and not to him or his order, it is nevertheless payable to him or his order at his option. **[145]**

9 Sum payable

(1) The sum payable by a bill is a sum certain within the meaning of this Act, although it was required to be paid—

    (a) With interest.

    (b) By stated instalments.

    (c) By stated instalments, with a provision that upon default in payment of any instalment the whole shall become due.

    (d) According to an indicated rate of exchange or according to a rate of exchange to be ascertained as directed by the bill.

(2) Where the sum payable is expressed in words and also in figures, and there is a discrepancy between the two, the sum denoted by the words is the amount payable.

(3) Where a bill is expressed to be payable with interest, unless the instrument otherwise provides, interest runs from the date of the bill, and if the bill is undated from the issue thereof.   **[146]**

10 Bill payable on demand

(1) A bill is payable on demand—

    (a) Which is expressed to be payable on demand, or at sight, or on presentation; or

    (b) In which no time for payment was expressed.

(2) Where a bill is accepted or indorsed when it is overdue, it shall, as regards the acceptor who so accepts, or any indorser who so indorses it, be deemed a bill payable on demand.   **[147]**

11 Bill payable at a future time

A bill is payable at a determinable future time within the meaning of this Act which is expressed to be payable—

    (1) At a fixed period after date or sight.

    (2) On or at a fixed period after the occurrence of a specified event which is certain to happen, though the time of happening may be uncertain.

An instrument expressed to be payable on a contingency is not a bill, and the happening of the event does not cure the defect.   **[148]**

12 Omission of date in bill payable after date

Where a bill expressed to be payable at a fixed period after date is issued undated, or where the acceptance of a bill payable at a fixed period after sight is undated, any holder may insert therein the true date of issue or acceptance, and the bill shall be payable accordingly.

Provided that (1) where the holder in good faith and by mistake inserts a wrong date, and (2) in every case where a wrong date is inserted, if the bill subsequently comes into the hands of a holder in due course the bill shall not be avoided thereby, but shall operate and be payable as if the date so inserted had been the true date.   **[149]**

13 Ante-dating and post-dating

(1) Where a bill or an acceptance or any indorsement on a bill is dated, the

date shall, unless the contrary be proved, be deemed to be the true date of the drawing, acceptance, or indorsement, as the case may be.

(2) A bill is not invalid by reason only that it is ante-dated or post-dated, or that it bears date on a Sunday.   **[150]**

14 Computation of time of payment

Where a bill is not payable on demand the day on which it falls due is determined as follows:

[(1) The bill is due and payable in all cases on the last day of the time of payment as fixed by the bill or, if that is a non-business day, on the succeeding business day.]

(2) Where a bill is payable at a fixed period after date, after sight, or after the happening of a specified event, the time of payment is determined by excluding the day from which the time is to begin to run and by including the day of payment.

(3) Where a bill is payable at a fixed period after sight, the time begins to run from the date of the acceptance if the bill be accepted, and from the date of noting or protest if the bill be noted or protested for non-acceptance, or for non-delivery.

(4) The term "month" in a bill means calendar month.   **[151]**

NOTE
Sub-s (1): substituted by the Banking and Financial Dealings Act 1971, s 3(2).

15 Case of need

The drawer of a bill and any indorser may insert therein the name of a person to whom the holder may resort in case of need, that is to say, in case the bill is dishonoured by non-acceptance or non-payment. Such person is called the referee in case of need. It is in the option of the holder to resort to the referee in case of need or not as he may think fit.   **[152]**

16 Optional stipulations by drawer or indorser

The drawer of a bill, and any indorser, may insert therein an express stipulation—

(1) Negativing or limiting his own liability to the holder.

(2) Waiving as regards himself some or all of the holder's duties. **[153]**

17 Definition and requisites of acceptance

(1) The acceptance of a bill is the signification by the drawee of his assent to the order of the drawer.

(2) An acceptance is invalid unless it complies with the following conditions, namely:

(a) It must be written on the bill and be signed by the drawee. The mere signature of the drawee without additional words is sufficient.

(b) It must not express that the drawee will perform his promise by any other means than the payment of money.   **[154]**

18 Time for acceptance

A bill may be accepted—

(1) Before it has been signed by the drawer, or while otherwise incomplete:

(2) When it is overdue, or after it has been dishonoured by a previous refusal to accept, or by non-payment:

(3) When a bill payable after sight is dishonoured by non-acceptance, and the drawee subsequently accepts it, the holder, in the absence of any different agreement, is entitled to have the bill accepted as of the date of first presentment to the drawee for acceptance.   **[155]**

19 General and qualified acceptances

(1) An acceptance is either (a) general or (b) qualified.

(2) A general acceptance assents without qualification to the order of the drawer. A qualified acceptance in expressed terms varies the effect of the bill as drawn.

In particular an acceptance is qualified which is—

  (a) conditional, that is to say, which makes payment by the acceptor dependent on the fulfilment of a condition therein stated:
  (b) partial, that is to say, an acceptance to pay part only of the amount for which the bill is drawn:
  (c) local, that is to say, an acceptance to pay only at a particular specified place:

      An acceptance to pay at a particular place is a general acceptance, unless it expressly states that the bill is to be paid there only and not elsewhere:

  (d) qualified as to time:
  (e) the acceptance of some one or more of the drawees, but not of all.
        [156]

20 Inchoate instruments

(1) Where a simple signature on a blank . . . paper is delivered by the signer in order that it may be converted into a bill, it operates as a primâ facie authority to fill it up as a complete bill for any amount . . ., using the signature for that of the drawer, or the acceptor, or an indorser; and, in like manner, when a bill is wanting in any material particular, the person in possession of it has a primâ facie authority to fill up the omission in any way he thinks fit.

(2) In order that any such instrument when completed may be enforceable against any person who became a party thereto prior to its completion, it must be filled up within a reasonable time, and strictly in accordance with the authority given. Reasonable time for this purpose is a question of fact.

Provided that if any such instrument after completion is negotiated to a holder in due course it shall be valid and effectual for all purposes in his hands, and he may enforce it as if it had been filled up within a reasonable time and strictly in accordance with the authority given.   **[157]**

NOTE
Sub-s (1): words omitted repealed, except as to Northern Ireland, by the Finance Act 1970, s 36(8), Sch 8, Pt V, in consequence of the abolition of stamp duties on bills of exchange and promissory notes. As to Northern Ireland, amended by the Finance Act (Northern Ireland) 1970, s 19, Sch 3, Pt III.

21 Delivery

(1) Every contract on a bill, whether it be the drawer's, the acceptor's, or an indorser's, is incomplete and revocable, until delivery of the instrument in order to give effect thereto.

Provided that where an acceptance is written on a bill, and the drawee gives notice to or according to the directions of the person entitled to the bill that he has accepted it, the acceptance then becomes complete and irrevocable.

(2) As between immediate parties, and as regards a remote party other than a holder in due course, the delivery—

(a) in order to be effectual must be made either by or under the authority of the party drawing, accepting, or indorsing, as the case may be:
(b) may be shown to have been conditional or for a special purpose only, and not for the purpose of transferring the property in the bill.

But if the bill be in the hands of a holder in due course a valid delivery of the bill by all parties prior to him so as to make them liable to him is conclusively presumed.

(3) Where a bill is no longer in the possession of a party who has signed it as drawer, acceptor, or indorser, a valid and unconditional delivery by him is presumed until the contrary is proved.   **[158]**

Capacity and authority of parties

22 Capacity of parties

(1) Capacity to incur liability as a party to a bill is co-extensive with capacity to contract.

Provided that nothing in this section shall enable a corporation to make itself liable as drawer, acceptor, or indorser of a bill unless it is competent to it so to do under the law for the time being in force relating to corporations.

(2) Where a bill is drawn or indorsed by an infant, minor, or corporation having no capacity or power to incur liability on a bill, the drawing or indorsement entitles the holder to receive payment of the bill, and to enforce it against any other party thereto.   **[159]**

23 Signature essential to liability

No person is liable as drawer, indorser, or acceptor of a bill who has not signed it as such: Provided that

(1) Where a person signs a bill in a trade or assumed name, he is liable thereon as if he had signed it in his own name:
(2) The signature of the name of a firm is equivalent to the signature by the person so signing of the names of all persons liable as partners in that firm.   **[160]**

24 Forged or unauthorised signature

Subject to the provisions of this Act, where a signature on a bill is forged or placed thereon without the authority of the person whose signature it purports to be, the forged or unauthorised signature is wholly inoperative, and no right to retain the bill or to give a discharge therefor or to enforce payment thereof against any party thereto can be acquired through or under that signature, unless the party against whom it is sought to retain or enforce payment of the bill is precluded from setting up the forgery or want of authority.

Provided that nothing in this section shall affect the ratification of an unauthorised signature not amounting to a forgery.   **[161]**

25 Procuration signatures

A signature by procuration operates as notice that the agent has but a limited authority to sign, and the principal is only bound by such signature if the agent in so signing was acting within the actual limits of his authority.   **[162]**

26 Person signing as agent or in representative capacity

(1) Where a person signs a bill as drawer, indorser, or acceptor, and adds words to his signature, indicating that he signs for or on behalf of a principal, or in a representative character, he is not personally liable thereon; but the mere addition to his signature of words describing him as an agent, or as filling a representative character, does not exempt him from personal liability.

(2) In determining whether a signature on a bill is that of the principal or that of the agent by whose hand it is written, the construction most favourable to the validity of the instrument shall be adopted.   **[163]**

The consideration for a bill

27 Value and holder for value

(1) Valuable consideration for a bill may be constituted by,—

    (a) Any consideration sufficient to support a simple contract;
    (b) An antecedent debt or liability. Such a debt or liability is deemed valuable consideration whether the bill is payable on demand or at a future time.

(2) Where value has at any time been given for a bill the holder is deemed to be a holder for value as regards the acceptor and all parties to the bill who became parties prior to such time.

(3) Where the holder of a bill has a lien on it arising either from contract or by implication of law, he is deemed to be a holder for value to the extent of the sum for which he has a lien.   **[164]**

28 Accommodation bill or party

(1) An accommodation party to a bill is a person who has signed a bill as drawer, acceptor, or indorser, without receiving value therefor, and for the purpose of lending his name to some other person.

(2) An accommodation party is liable on the bill to a holder for value; and it is immaterial whether, when such holder took the bill, he knew such party to be an accommodation party or not.   **[165]**

29 Holder in due course

(1) A holder in due course is a holder who has taken a bill, complete and regular on the face of it, under the following conditions; namely,

    (a) That he became the holder of it before it was overdue, and without notice that it had been previously dishonoured, if such was the fact:

(b) That he took the bill in good faith and for value, and that at the time the bill was negotiated to him he had no notice of any defect in the title of the person who negotiated it.

(2) In particular the title of a person who negotiates a bill is defective within the meaning of this Act when he obtained the bill, or the acceptance thereof, by fraud, duress, or force and fear, or other unlawful means, or an illegal consideration, or when he negotiates it in breach of faith, or under such circumstances as amount to a fraud.

(3) A holder (whether for value or not), who derives his title to a bill through a holder in due course, and who is not himself a party to any fraud or illegality affecting it, has all the rights of that holder in due course as regards the acceptor and all parties to the bill prior to that holder.   **[166]**

30 Presumption of value and good faith

(1) Every party whose signature appears on a bill is primâ facie deemed to have become a party thereto for value.

(2) Every holder of a bill is primâ facie deemed to be a holder in due course; but if in an action on a bill it is admitted or proved that the acceptance, issue, or subsequent negotiation of the bill is affected with fraud, duress, or force and fear, or illegality, the burden of proof is shifted, unless and until the holder proves that, subsequent to the alleged fraud or illegality, value has in good faith been given for the bill.   **[167]**

Negotiation of bills

31 Negotiation of bill

(1) A bill is negotiated when it is transferred from one person to another in such a manner as to constitute the transferee the holder of the bill.

(2) A bill payable to bearer is negotiated by delivery.

(3) A bill payable to order is negotiated by the indorsement of the holder completed by delivery.

(4) Where the holder of a bill payable to his order transfers it for value without indorsing it, the transfer gives the transferee such title as the transferor had in the bill, and the transferee in addition acquires the right to have the indorsement of the transferor.

(5) Where any person is under obligation to indorse a bill in a representative capacity, he may indorse the bill in such terms as to negative personal liability.
                    [168]

32 Requisites of a valid indorsement

An indorsement in order to operate as a negotiation must comply with the following conditions, namely,—

(1) It must be written on the bill itself and be signed by the indorser. The simple signature of the indorser on the bill, without additional words, is sufficient.

An indorsement written on an allonge, or on a "copy" of a bill issued or negotiated in a country where "copies" are recognised, is deemed to be written on the bill itself.

(2) It must be an indorsement of the entire bill. A partial indorsement, that is to say, an indorsement which purports to transfer to the indorsee a part only of the amount payable, or which purports to transfer the bill to two or more indorsees severally, does not operate as a negotiation of the bill.

(3) Where a bill is payable to the order of two or more payees or indorsees who are not partners all must indorse, unless the one indorsing has authority to indorse for the others.

(4) Where, in a bill payable to order, the payee or indorsee is wrongly designated, or his name is mis-spelt, he may indorse the bill as therein described, adding, if he think fit, his proper signature.

(5) Where there are two or more indorsements on a bill, each indorsement is deemed to have been made in the order in which it appears on the bill, until the contrary is proved.

(6) An indorsement may be made in blank or special. It may also contain terms making it restrictive.   **[169]**

33 Conditional indorsement

Where a bill purports to be indorsed conditionally the condition may be disregarded by the payer, and payment to the indorsee is valid whether the condition has been fulfilled or not.   **[170]**

34 Indorsement in blank and special indorsement

(1) An indorsement in blank specifies no indorsee, and a bill so indorsed becomes payable to bearer.

(2) A special indorsement specifies the person to whom, or to whose order, the bill is to be payable.

(3) The provisions of this Act relating to a payee apply with the necessary modifications to an indorsee under a special indorsement.

(4) When a bill has been indorsed in blank, any holder may convert the blank indorsement into a special indorsement by writing above the indorser's signature a direction to pay the bill to or to the order of himself or some other person.   **[171]**

35 Restrictive indorsement

(1) An indorsement is restrictive which prohibits the further negotiation of the bill or which expresses that it is a mere authority to deal with the bill as thereby directed and not a transfer of the ownership thereof, as, for example, if a bill be indorsed "Pay D. only," or "Pay D. for the account of X.," or "Pay D. or order for collection."

(2) A restrictive indorsement gives the indorsee the right to receive payment of the bill and to sue any party thereto that his indorser could have sued, but gives him no power to transfer his rights as indorsee unless it expressly authorise him to do so.

(3) Where a restrictive indorsement authorises further transfer, all subsequent indorsees take the bill with the same rights and subject to the same liabilities as the first indorsee under the restrictive indorsement.   **[172]**

36 Negotiation of overdue or dishonoured bill

(1) Where a bill is negotiable in its origin it continues to be negotiable until it has been (a) restrictively indorsed or (b) discharged by payment or otherwise.

(2) Where an overdue bill is negotiated, it can only be negotiated subject to any defect of title affecting it at its maturity, and thenceforward no person who takes it can acquire or give a better title than that which the person from whom he took it had.

(3) A bill payable on demand is deemed to be overdue within the meaning and for the purposes of this section, when it appears on the face of it to have been in circulation for an unreasonable length of time. What is an unreasonable length of time for this purpose is a question of fact.

(4) Except where an indorsement bears date after the maturity of the bill, every negotiation is primâ facie deemed to have been effected before the bill was overdue.

(5) Where a bill which is not overdue has been dishonoured any person who takes it with notice of the dishonour takes it subject to any defect of title attaching thereto at the time of dishonour, but nothing in this sub-section shall affect the rights of a holder in due course.   **[173]**

37 Negotiation of bill to party already liable thereon

Where a bill is negotiated back to the drawer, or to a prior indorser or to the acceptor, such party may, subject to the provisions of this Act, re-issue and further negotiate the bill, but he is not entitled to enforce payment of the bill against any intervening party to whom he was previously liable.   **[174]**

38 Rights of the holder

The rights and powers of the holder of a bill are as follows:

(1) He may sue on the bill in his own name:

(2) Where he is a holder in due course, he holds the bill free from any defect of title of prior parties, as well as from mere personal defences available to prior parties among themselves, and may enforce payment against all parties liable on the bill:

(3) Where his title is defective (a) if he negotiates the bill to a holder in due course, that holder obtains a good and complete title to the bill, and (b) if he obtains payment of the bill the person who pays him in due course gets a valid discharge for the bill.   **[175]**

General duties of the holder

39 When presentment for acceptance is necessary

(1) Where a bill is payable after sight, presentment for acceptance is necessary in order to fix the maturity of the instrument.

(2) Where a bill expressly stipulates that it shall be presented for acceptance, or where a bill is drawn payable elsewhere than at the residence or place of business of the drawee, it must be presented for acceptance before it can be presented for payment.

(3) In no other case is presentment for acceptance necessary in order to render liable any party to the bill.

(4) Where the holder of a bill, drawn payable elsewhere than at the place of business or residence of the drawee, has not time, with the exercise of reasonable diligence, to present the bill for acceptance before presenting it for payment on the day that it falls due, the delay caused by presenting the bill for acceptance before presenting it for payment is excused, and does not discharge the drawer and indorsers.   **[176]**

40 Time for presenting bill payable after sight

(1) Subject to the provisions of this Act, when a bill payable after sight is negotiated, the holder must either present it for acceptance or negotiate it within a reasonable time.

(2) If he do not do so, the drawer and all indorsers prior to that holder are discharged.

(3) In determining what is a reasonable time within the meaning of this section, regard shall be had to the nature of the bill, the usage of trade with respect to similar bills, and the facts of the particular case. **[177]**

41 Rules as to presentment for acceptance, and excuses for non-presentment

(1) A bill is duly presented for acceptance which is presented in accordance with the following rules:

- (a) The presentment must be made by or on behalf of the holder to the drawee or to some person authorised to accept or refuse acceptance on his behalf at a reasonable hour on a business day and before the bill is overdue:
- (b) Where a bill is addressed to two or more drawees, who are not partners, presentment must be made to them all, unless one has authority to accept for all, then presentment may be made to him only:
- (c) Where the drawee is dead presentment may be made to his personal representative:
- (d) Where the drawee is bankrupt, presentment may be made to him or to his trustee:
- (e) Where authorised by agreement or usage, a presentment through the post office is sufficient.

(2) Presentment in accordance with these rules is excused, and a bill may be treated as dishonoured by non-acceptance—

- (a) Where the drawee is dead or bankrupt, or is a fictitious person or a person not having capacity to contract by bill:
- (b) Where, after the exercise of reasonable diligence, such presentment cannot be effected:
- (c) Where, although the presentment has been irregular, acceptance has been refused on some other ground.

(3) The fact that the holder has reason to believe that the bill, on presentment, will be dishonoured does not excuse presentment. **[178]**

42 Non-acceptance

When a bill is duly presented for acceptance and is not accepted within the customary time, the person presenting it must treat it as dishonoured by non-acceptance. If he do not, the holder shall lose his right of recourse against the drawer and indorsers. **[179]**

43 Dishonour by non-acceptance and its consequences

(1) A bill is dishonoured by non-acceptance—

- (a) when it is duly presented for acceptance, and such an acceptance as is prescribed by this Act is refused or cannot be obtained; or
- (b) when presentment for acceptance is excused and the bill is not accepted.

(2) Subject to the provisions of this Act when a bill is dishonoured by non-acceptance, an immediate right of recourse against the drawer and indorsers accrues to the holder, and no presentment for payment is necessary.
                                                                    [180]

44 Duties as to qualified acceptances

(1) The holder of a bill may refuse to take a qualified acceptance, and if he does not obtain an unqualified acceptance may treat the bill as dishonoured by non-acceptance.

(2) Where a qualified acceptance is taken, and the drawer or an indorser has not expressly or impliedly authorised the holder to take a qualified acceptance, or does not subsequently assent thereto, such drawer or indorser is discharged from his liability on the bill.

The provisions of this subsection do not apply to a partial acceptance, whereof due notice has been given. Where a foreign bill has been accepted as to part, it must be protested as to the balance.

(3) When the drawer or indorser of a bill receives notice of a qualified acceptance, and does not within a reasonable time express his dissent to the holder he shall be deemed to have assented thereto.   **[181]**

45 Rules as to presentment for payment

Subject to the provisions of this Act a bill must be duly presented for payment. If it be not so presented the drawer and indorsers shall be discharged.

A bill is duly presented for payment which is presented in accordance with the following rules:—

(1) Where the bill is not payable on demand, presentment must be made on the day it falls due.

(2) Where the bill is payable on demand, then, subject to the provisions of this Act, presentment must be made within a reasonable time after its issue in order to render the drawer liable, and within a reasonable time after its indorsement, in order to render the indorser liable.

In determining what is a reasonable time, regard shall be had to the nature of the bill, the usage of trade with regard to similar bills, and the facts of the particular case.

(3) Presentment must be made by the holder or by some person authorised to receive payment on his behalf at a reasonable hour on a business day, at the proper place as herein-after defined, either to the person designated by the bill as payer, or to some person authorised to pay or refuse payment on his behalf if with the exercise of reasonable diligence such person can there be found.

(4) A bill is presented at the proper place:—

(a) Where a place of payment is specified in the bill and the bill is there presented.

(b) Where no place of payment is specified, but the address of the drawee or acceptor is given in the bill, and the bill is there presented.

(c) Where no place of payment is specified and no address given, and the bill is presented at the drawee's or acceptor's place of business if known, and if not, at his ordinary residence if known.

(d) In any other case if presented to the drawee or acceptor wherever he can be found, or if presented at his last known place of business or residence.

(5) Where a bill is presented at the proper place, and after the exercise of reasonable diligence no person authorised to pay or refuse payment can be found there, no further presentment to the drawee or acceptor is required.

(6) Where a bill is drawn upon, or accepted by two or more persons who are not partners, and no place of payment is specified, presentment must be made to them all.

(7) Where the drawee or acceptor of a bill is dead, and no place of payment is specified, presentment must be made to a personal representative, if such there be, and with the exercise of reasonable diligence he can be found.

(8) Where authorised by agreement or usage a presentment through the post office is sufficient. [182]

46 Excuses for delay or non-presentment for payment

(1) Delay in making presentment for payment is excused when the delay is caused by circumstances beyond the control of the holder, and not imputable to his default, misconduct, or negligence. When the cause of delay ceases to operate presentment must be made with reasonable diligence.

(2) Presentment for payment is dispensed with,—

(a) Where, after the exercise of reasonable diligence presentment, as required by this Act, cannot be effected.
The fact that the holder has reason to believe that the bill will, on presentment, be dishonoured, does not dispense with the necessity for presentment.

(b) Where the drawee is a fictitious person.

(c) As regards the drawer where the drawee or acceptor is not bound as between himself and the drawer, to accept or pay the bill, and the drawer has no reason to believe that the bill would be paid if presented.

(d) As regards an indorser, where the bill was accepted or made for the accommodation of that indorser, and he has no reason to expect that the bill would be paid if presented.

(e) By waiver of presentment, express or implied. [183]

47 Dishonour by non-payment

(1) A bill is dishonoured by non-payment (a) when it is duly presented for payment and payment is refused or cannot be obtained, or (b) when presentment is excused and the bill is overdue and unpaid.

(2) Subject to the provisions of this Act, when a bill is dishonoured by non-payment, an immediate right of recourse against the drawer and indorsers accrues to the holder. [184]

48 Notice of dishonour and effect of non-notice

Subject to the provisions of this Act, when a bill has been dishonoured by non-acceptance or by non-payment, notice of dishonour must be given to the drawer and each indorser, and any drawer or indorser to whom such notice is not given is discharged: Provided that—

(1) Where a bill is dishonoured by non-acceptance, and notice of dishonour is not given, the rights of a holder in due course, subsequent to the omission, shall not be prejudiced by the omission.

(2) Where a bill is dishonoured by non-acceptance, and due notice of dishonour is given, it shall not be necessary to give notice of a subsequent dishonour by non-payment unless the bill shall in the meantime have been accepted.   **[185]**

49 Rules as to notice of dishonour

Notice of dishonour in order to be valid and effectual must be given in accordance with the following rules:—

(1)   The notice must be given by or on behalf of the holder, or by or on behalf of an indorser who, at the time of giving it, is himself liable on the bill.

(2)   Notice of dishonour may be given by an agent either in his own name, or in the name of any party entitled to give notice whether that party be his principal or not.

(3)   Where the notice is given by or on behalf of the holder, it enures for the benefit of all subsequent holders and all prior indorsers who have a right of recourse against the party to whom it is given.

(4)   Where notice is given by or on behalf of an indorser entitled to give notice as herein-before provided, it enures for the benefit of the holder and all indorsers subsequent to the party to whom notice is given.

(5)   The notice may be given in writing or by personal communication, and may be given in any terms which sufficiently identify the bill, and intimate that the bill has been dishonoured by non-acceptance or non-payment.

(6)   The return of a dishonoured bill to the drawer or an indorser is, in point of form, deemed a sufficient notice of dishonour.

(7)   A written notice need not be signed, and an insufficient written notice may be supplemented and validated by verbal communication. A misdescription of the bill shall not vitiate the notice unless the party to whom the notice is given is in fact misled thereby.

(8)   Where notice of dishonour is required to be given to any person, it may be given either to the party himself, or to his agent in that behalf.

(9)   Where the drawer or indorser is dead, and the party giving notice knows it, the notice must be given to a personal representative if such there be, and with the exercise of reasonable diligence he can be found.

(10) Where the drawer or indorser is bankrupt, notice may be given either to the party himself or to the trustee.

(11) Where there are two or more drawers or indorsers who are not partners, notice must be given to each of them, unless one of them has authority to receive such notice for the others.

(12) The notice may be given as soon as the bill is dishonoured and must be given within a reasonable time thereafter.

In the absence of special circumstances notice is not deemed to have been given within a reasonable time, unless—

(a)   where the person giving and the person to receive notice reside in the same place, the notice is given or sent off in time to reach the latter on the day after the dishonour of the bill.

(b) where the person giving and the person to receive notice reside in different places, the notice is sent off on the day after the dishonour of the bill, if there be a post at a convenient hour on that day, and if there be no post on that day then by the next post thereafter.

(13) Where a bill when dishonoured is in the hands of an agent, he may either himself give notice to the parties liable on the bill, or he may give notice to his principal. If he give notice to his principal, he must do so within the same time as if he were the holder, and the principal upon receipt of such notice has himself the same time for giving notice as if the agent had been an independent holder.

(14) Where a party to a bill receives due notice of dishonour, he has after the receipt of such notice the same period of time for giving notice to antecedent parties that the holder has after the dishonour.

(15) Where a notice of dishonour is duly addressed and posted, the sender is deemed to have given due notice of dishonour, notwithstanding any miscarriage by the post office.   **[186]**

50 Excuses for non-notice and delay

(1) Delay in giving notice of dishonour is excused where the delay is caused by circumstances beyond the control of the party giving notice, and not imputable to his default, misconduct, or negligence. When the cause of delay ceases to operate the notice must be given with reasonable diligence.

(2) Notice of dishonour is dispensed with—

(a) When, after the exercise of reasonable diligence, notice as required by this Act cannot be given to or does not reach the drawer or indorser sought to be charged:

(b) By waiver express or implied. Notice of dishonour may be waived before the time of giving notice has arrived, or after the omission to give due notice:

(c) As regards the drawer in the following cases, namely, (1) where drawer and drawee are the same person, (2) where the drawee is a fictitious person or a person not having capacity to contract, (3) where the drawer is the person to whom the bill is presented for payment, (4) where the drawee or acceptor is as between himself and the drawer under no obligation to accept or pay the bill, (5) where the drawer has countermanded payment:

(d) As regards the indorser in the following cases, namely, (1) where the drawee is a fictitious person or a person not having capacity to contract, and the indorser was aware of the fact at the time he indorsed the bill, (2) where the indorser is the person to whom the bill is presented for payment, (3) where the bill was accepted or made for his accommodation.   **[187]**

51 Noting or protest of bill

(1) Where an inland bill has been dishonoured it may, if the holder think fit, be noted for non-acceptance or non-payment, as the case may be; but it shall not be necessary to note or protest any such bill in order to preserve the recourse against the drawer or indorser.

(2) Where a foreign bill, appearing on the face of it to be such, has been dishonoured by non-acceptance it must be duly protested for non-acceptance, and where such a bill, which has not been previously dishonoured by non-

acceptance, is dishonoured by non-payment it must be duly protested for non-payment. If it be not so protested the drawer and indorsers are discharged. Where a bill does not appear on the face of it to be a foreign bill, protest thereof in case of dishonour is unnecessary.

(3) A bill which has been protested for non-acceptance may be subsequently protested for non-payment.

(4) Subject to the provisions of this Act, when a bill is noted or protested, [it may be noted on the day of its dishonour and must be noted not later than the next succeeding business day]. When a bill has been duly noted, the protest may be subsequently extended as of the date of the noting.

(5) Where the acceptor of a bill becomes bankrupt or insolvent or suspends payment before it matures, the holder may cause the bill to be protested for better security against the drawer and indorsers.

(6) A bill must be protested at the place where it is dishonoured: Provided that—

(a) When a bill is presented through the post office, and returned by post dishonoured, it may be protested at the place to which it is returned and on the day of its return if received during business hours, and if not received during business hours, then not later than the next business day:
(b) When a bill drawn payable at the place of business or residence of some person other than the drawee has been dishonoured by non-acceptance, it must be protested for non-payment at the place where it is expressed to be payable, and no further presentment for payment to, or demand on, the drawee is necessary.

(7) A protest must contain a copy of the bill, and must be signed by the notary making it, and must specify—

(a) The person at whose request the bill is protested:
(b) The place and date of protest, the cause or reason for protesting the bill, the demand made, and the answer given, if any, or the fact that the drawee or acceptor could not be found.

(8) Where a bill is lost or destroyed, or is wrongly detained from the person entitled to hold it, protest may be made on a copy or written particulars thereof.

(9) Protest is dispensed with by any circumstance which would dispense with notice of dishonour. Delay in noting or protesting is excused when the delay is caused by circumstances beyond the control of the holder, and not imputable to his default, misconduct, or negligence. When the cause of delay ceases to operate the bill must be noted or protested with reasonable diligence.   **[188]**

NOTE

Sub-s (4): words in square brackets substituted by the Bills of Exchange (Time of Noting) Act 1917, s 1.

52 Duties of holder as regards drawee or acceptor

(1) When a bill is accepted generally presentment for payment is not necessary in order to render the acceptor liable.

(2) When by the terms of a qualified acceptance presentment for payment is required, the acceptor, in the absence of an express stipulation to that effect, is not discharged by the omission to present the bill for payment on the day that it matures.

(3) In order to render the acceptor of a bill liable it is not necessary to protest it, or that notice of dishonour should be given to him.

(4) Where the holder of a bill presents it for payment, he shall exhibit the bill to the person from whom he demands payment, and when a bill is paid the holder shall forthwith deliver it up to the party paying it. **[189]**

Liabilities of parties

53 Funds in hands of drawee

(1) A bill, of itself, does not operate as an assignment of funds in the hands of the drawee available for the payment thereof, and the drawee of a bill who does not accept as required by this Act is not liable on the instrument. This sub-section shall not extend to Scotland.

(2) (*Applies to Scotland only.*) **[190]**

54 Liability of acceptor

The acceptor of a bill, by accepting it—

(1) Engages that he will pay it according to the tenor of his acceptance:

(2) Is precluded from denying to a holder in due course:

    (a) The existence of the drawer, the genuineness of his signature, and his capacity and authority to draw the bill;

    (b) In the case of a bill payable to drawer's order, the then capacity of the drawer to indorse, but not the genuineness or validity of his indorsement;

    (c) In the case of a bill payable to the order of a third person, the existence of the payee and his then capacity to indorse, but not the genuineness or validity of his indorsement. **[191]**

55 Liability of drawer or indorser

(1) The drawer of a bill by drawing it—

    (a) Engages that on due presentment it shall be accepted and paid according to its tenor, and that if it be dishonoured he will compensate the holder or any indorser who is compelled to pay it, provided that the requisite proceedings on dishonour be duly taken;

    (b) Is precluded from denying to a holder in due course the existence of the payee and his then capacity to indorse.

(2) The indorser of a bill by indorsing it—

    (a) Engages that on due presentment it shall be accepted and paid according to its tenor, and that if it be dishonoured he will compensate the holder or a subsequent indorser who is compelled to pay it, provided that the requisite proceedings on dishonour be duly taken;

    (b) Is precluded from denying to a holder in due course the genuineness and regularity in all respects of the drawer's signature and all previous indorsements;

    (c) Is precluded from denying to his immediate or a subsequent indorsee that the bill was at the time of his indorsement a valid and subsisting bill, and that he had then a good title thereto. **[192]**

56 Stranger signing bill liable as indorser

Where a person signs a bill otherwise than as drawer or acceptor, he thereby incurs the liabilities of an indorser to a holder in due course.   **[193]**

57 Measure of damages against parties to dishonoured bill

Where a bill is dishonoured, the measure of damages, which shall be deemed to be liquidated damages, shall be as follows:

(1) The holder may recover from any party liable on the bill, and the drawer who has been compelled to pay the bill may recover from the acceptor, and an indorser who has been compelled to pay the bill may recover from the acceptor or from the drawer, or from a prior indorser—

    (a) The amount of the bill:

    (b) Interest thereon from the time of presentment for payment if the bill is payable on demand, and from the maturity of the bill in any other case:

    (c) The expenses of noting, or, when protest is necessary, and the protest has been extended, the expenses of protest.

(2) . . .

(3) Where by this Act interest may be recovered as damages, such interest may, if justice require it, be withheld wholly or in part, and where a bill is expressed to be payable with interest at a given rate, interest as damages may or may not be given at the same rate as interest proper.   **[194]**

NOTE

  Sub-s (2): repealed by the Administration of Justice Act 1977, ss 4, 32(4), Sch 5, Pt I, except in relation to bills drawn before 29 August 1977.

58 Transferor by delivery and transferee

(1) Where the holder of a bill payable to bearer negotiates it by delivery without indorsing it he is called a "transferor by delivery."

(2) A transferor by delivery is not liable on the instrument.

(3) A transferor by delivery who negotiates a bill thereby warrants to his immediate transferee being a holder for value that the bill is what it purports to be, that he has a right to transfer it, and that at the time of transfer he is not aware of any fact which renders it valueless.   **[195]**

Discharge of bill

59 Payment in due course

(1) A bill is discharged by payment in due course by or on behalf of the drawee or acceptor.

"Payment in due course" means payment made at or after the maturity of the bill to the holder thereof in good faith and without notice that his title to the bill is defective.

(2) Subject to the provisions herein-after contained, when a bill is paid by the drawer or an indorser it is not discharged; but

    (a) Where a bill payable to, or to the order of, a third party is paid by the drawer, the drawer may enforce payment thereof against the acceptor, but may not re-issue the bill.

(b) Where a bill is paid by an indorser, or where a bill payable to drawer's order is paid by the drawer, the party paying it is remitted to his former rights as regards the acceptor or antecedent parties, and he may, if he thinks fit, strike out his own subsequent indorsements, and again negotiate the bill.

(3) Where an accommodation bill is paid in due course by the party accommodated the bill is discharged. **[196]**

NOTE
Sub-s (2): the word "and" would appear to be needed between "own" and "subsequent", but does not appear in the Queen's Printer's copy of the Act.

60 Banker paying demand draft whereon indorsement is forged

When a bill payable to order on demand is drawn on a banker, and the banker on whom it is drawn pays the bill in good faith and in the ordinary course of business, it is not incumbent on the banker to show that the indorsement of the payee or any subsequent indorsement was made by or under the authority of the person whose indorsement it purports to be, and the banker is deemed to have paid the bill in due course, although such indorsement has been forged or made without authority. **[197]**

61 Acceptor the holder at maturity

When the acceptor of a bill is or becomes the holder of it at or after its maturity, in his own right, the bill is discharged. **[198]**

62 Express waiver

(1) When the holder of a bill at or after its maturity absolutely and unconditionally renounces his rights against the acceptor the bill is discharged.

The renunciation must be in writing, unless the bill is delivered up to the acceptor.

(2) The liabilities of any party to a bill may in like manner be renounced by the holder before, at, or after its maturity; but nothing in this section shall affect the rights of a holder in due course without notice of the renunciation. **[199]**

63 Cancellation

(1) Where a bill is intentionally cancelled by the holder or his agent, and the cancellation is apparent thereon, the bill is discharged.

(2) In like manner any party liable on a bill may be discharged by the intentional cancellation of his signature by the holder or his agent. In such case any indorser who would have had a right of recourse against the party whose signature is cancelled is also discharged.

(3) A cancellation made unintentionally, or under a mistake, or without the authority of the holder is inoperative; but where a bill or any signature thereon appears to have been cancelled the burden of proof lies on the party who alleges that the cancellation was made unintentionally, or under a mistake, or without authority. **[200]**

64 Alteration of bill

(1) Where a bill or acceptance is materially altered without the assent of all parties liable on the bill, the bill is avoided except as against a party who has

himself made, authorised, or assented to the alteration, and subsequent indorsers.

Provided that,

> Where a bill has been materially altered, but the alteration is not apparent, and the bill is in the hands of a holder in due course, such holder may avail himself of the bill as if it had not been altered, and may enforce payment of it according to its original tenour.

(2) In particular the following alterations are material, namely, any alteration of the date, the sum payable, the time of payment, the place of payment, and, where a bill has been accepted generally, the addition of a place of payment without the acceptor's assent.   **[201]**

Acceptance and payment for honour

65 Acceptance for honour suprà protest

(1) Where a bill of exchange has been protested for dishonour by non-acceptance, or protested for better security, and is not overdue, any person, not being a party already liable thereon, may, with the consent of the holder, intervene and accept the bill suprà protest, for the honour of any party liable thereon, or for the honour of the person for whose account the bill is drawn.

(2) A bill may be accepted for honour for part only of the sum for which it is drawn.

(3) An acceptance for honour suprà protest in order to be valid must—

(a) be written on the bill, and indicate that it is an acceptance for honour:

(b) be signed by the acceptor for honour.

(4) Where an acceptance for honour does not expressly state for whose honour it is made, it is deemed to be an acceptance for the honour of the drawer.

(5) Where a bill payable after sight is accepted for honour, its maturity is calculated from the date of the noting for non-acceptance, and not from the date of the acceptance for honour.   **[202]**

66 Liability of acceptor for honour

(1) The acceptor for honour of a bill by accepting it engages that he will, on due presentment, pay the bill according to the tenor of his acceptance, if it is not paid by the drawee, provided it has been duly presented for payment, and protested for non-payment, and that he receives notice of these facts.

(2) The acceptor for honour is liable to the holder and to all parties to the bill subsequent to the party for whose honour he has accepted.   **[203]**

67 Presentment to acceptor for honour

(1) Where a dishonoured bill has been accepted for honour suprà protest, or contains a reference in case of need, it must be protested for non-payment before it is presented for payment to the acceptor for honour, or referee in case of need.

(2) Where the address of the acceptor for honour is in the same place where the bill is protested for non-payment, the bill must be presented to him not later than the day following its maturity; and where the address of the acceptor for

honour is in some place other than the place where it was protested for non-payment, the bill must be forwarded not later than the day following its maturity for presentment to him.

(3) Delay in presentment or non-presentment is excused by any circumstance which would excuse delay in presentment for payment or non-presentment for payment.

(4) When a bill of exchange is dishonoured by the acceptor for honour it must be protested for non-payment by him.   **[204]**

68 Payment for honour suprà protest

(1) Where a bill has been protested for non-payment, any person may intervene and pay it suprà protest for the honour of any party liable thereon, or for the honour of the person for whose account the bill is drawn.

(2) Where two or more persons offer to pay a bill for the honour of different parties, the person whose payment will discharge most parties to the bill shall have the preference.

(3) Payment for honour suprà protest, in order to operate as such and not as a mere voluntary payment, must be attested by a notarial act of honour which may be appended to the protest or form an extension of it.

(4) The notarial act of honour must be founded on a declaration made by the payer for honour, or his agent in that behalf, declaring his intention to pay the bill for honour, and for whose honour he pays.

(5) Where a bill has been paid for honour, all parties subsequent to the party for whose honour it is paid are discharged, but the payer for honour is subrogated for, and succeeds to both the rights and duties of, the holder as regards the party for whose honour he pays, and all parties liable to that party.

(6) The payer for honour on paying to the holder the amount of the bill and the notarial expenses incidental to its dishonour is entitled to receive both the bill itself and the protest. If the holder do not on demand deliver them up he shall be liable to the payer for honour in damages.

(7) Where the holder of a bill refuses to receive payment suprà protest he shall lose his right of recourse against any party who would have been discharged by such payment.   **[205]**

Lost instruments

69 Holder's right to duplicate of lost bill

Where a bill has been lost before it is overdue the person who was the holder of it may apply to the drawer to give him another bill of the same tenor, giving security to the drawer if required to indemnify him against all persons whatever in case the bill alleged to have been lost shall be found again.

If the drawer on request as aforesaid refuses to give such duplicate bill he may be compelled to do so.   **[206]**

70 Action on lost bill

In any action or proceeding upon a bill, the court or a judge may order that the loss of the instrument shall not be set up, provided an indemnity be given to the satisfaction of the court or judge against the claims of any other person upon the instrument in question.   **[207]**

NOTE
 This section repealed as it applies to Northern Ireland by the Judicature (Northern Ireland) Act 1978, s 122, Sch 7, Pt I.

Bill in a set

71 Rules as to sets

(1) Where a bill is drawn in a set, each part of the set being numbered, and containing a reference to the other parts the whole of the parts constitute one bill.

(2) Where the holder of a set indorses two or more parts to different persons, he is liable on every such part, and every indorser subsequent to him is liable on the part he has himself indorsed as if the said parts were separate bills.

(3) Where two or more parts of a set are negotiated to different holders in due course, the holder whose title first accrues is as between such holders deemed the true owner of the bill; but nothing in this sub-section shall affect the rights of a person who in due course accepts or pays the part first presented to him.

(4) The acceptance may be written on any part, and it must be written on one part only.

If the drawee accepts more than one part, and such accepted parts get into the hands of different holders in due course, he is liable on every such part as if it were a separate bill.

(5) When the acceptor of a bill drawn in a set pays it without requiring the part bearing his acceptance to be delivered up to him, and that part at maturity is outstanding in the hands of a holder in due course, he is liable to the holder thereof.

(6) Subject to the preceding rules, where any one part of a bill drawn in a set is discharged by payment or otherwise, the whole bill is discharged.   **[208]**

Conflict of laws

72 Rules where laws conflict

Where a bill drawn in one country is negotiated, accepted, or payable in another, the rights, duties, and liabilities of the parties thereto are determined as follows:

   (1) The validity of a bill as regards requisites in form is determined by the law of the place of issue, and the validity as regards requisites in form of the supervening contracts, such as acceptance, or indorsement, or acceptance suprà protest, is determined by the law of the place where such contract was made.
      Provided that—

   (a) Where a bill is issued out of the United Kingdom it is not invalid by reason only that it is not stamped in accordance with the law of the place of issue:

   (b) Where a bill, issued out of the United Kingdom, conforms, as regards requisites in form, to the law of the United Kingdom, it may, for the purpose of enforcing payment thereof, be treated as valid as between all persons who negotiate, hold, or become parties to it in the United Kingdom.

(2) Subject to the provisions of this Act, the interpretation of the drawing, indorsement, acceptance, or acceptance suprà protest of a bill, is determined by the law of the place where such contract is made.

Provided that where an inland bill is indorsed in a foreign country the indorsement shall as regards the payer be interpreted according to the law of the United Kingdom.

(3) The duties of the holder with respect to presentment for acceptance or payment and the necessity for or sufficiency of a protest or notice of dishonour, or otherwise, are determined by the law of the place where the act is done or the bill is dishonoured.

(4) . . .

(5) Where a bill is drawn in one country and is payable in another, the due date thereof is determined according to the law of the place where it is payable. **[209]**

NOTE

Sub-s (4): repealed by the Administration of Justice Act 1977, ss 4, 32(4), Sch 5, Pt I, except in relation to bills drawn before 29 August 1977.

PART III
CHEQUES ON A BANKER

73 Cheque defined

A cheque is a bill of exchange drawn on a banker payable on demand.

Except as otherwise provided in this Part, the provisions of this Act applicable to a bill of exchange payable on demand apply to a cheque. **[210]**

NOTE

Cheque: certain Bank of England or Bank of Ireland warrants are deemed cheques by virtue of the National Loans Act 1968, s 14(7).

74 Presentment of cheque for payment

Subject to the provisions of this Act—

(1) Where a cheque is not presented for payment within a reasonable time of its issue, and the drawer or the person on whose account it is drawn had the right at the time of such presentment as between him and the banker to have the cheque paid and suffers actual damage through the delay, he is discharged to the extent of such damage, that is to say, to the extent to which such drawer or person is a creditor of such banker to a larger amount than he would have been had such cheque been paid.

(2) In determining what is a reasonable time regard shall be had to the nature of the instrument, the usage of trade and of bankers, and the facts of the particular case.

(3) The holder of such cheque as to which such drawer or person is discharged shall be a creditor, in lieu of such drawer or person, of such banker to the extent of such discharge, and entitled to recover the amount from him. **[211]**

75 Revocation of banker's authority

The duty and authority of a banker to pay a cheque drawn on him by his customer are determined by—

(1) Countermand of payment:

(2) Notice of the customer's death. **[212]**

75A (*Inserted, in relation to Scotland only, by the Law Reform (Miscellaneous Provisions) (Scotland) Act 1985, s 11(b).*)

Crossed cheques

76 General and special crossings defined

(1) Where a cheque bears across its face an addition of—

 (a) The words "and company" or any abbreviation thereof between two parallel transverse lines, either with or without the words "not negotiable"; or

 (b) Two parallel transverse lines simply, either with or without the words "not negotiable";

that addition constitutes a crossing, and the cheque is crossed generally.

(2) Where a cheque bears across its face an addition of the name of a banker, either with or without the words "not negotiable," that addition constitutes a crossing, and the cheque is crossed specially and to that banker. **[213]**

NOTE

Applications: this section, ss 77(1), (3), (4), (5), and (so far as it relates to crossed cheques) (6), 78–81 are applied by the Savings Bank Annuity Regulations 1969, SI 1969/1336, reg 3(4); the Savings Contracts Regulations 1969, SI 1969/1342, reg 6(2); the Premium Savings Bonds Regulations 1972, SI 1972/765, reg 8(2), as amended by SI 1976/1543, SI 1980/767; the Savings Certificates (Yearly Plan) Regulations 1984, SI 1984/779, reg 7(2); the Savings Certificates Regulations 1991, SI 1991/1031, reg 7(2); and the Savings Certificates (Children's Bonus Bonds) Regulations 1991, SI 1991/1407, reg 7(2).

77 Crossing by drawer or after issue

(1) A cheque may be crossed generally or specially by the drawer.

(2) Where a cheque is uncrossed, the holder may cross it generally or specially.

(3) Where a cheque is crossed generally the holder may cross it specially.

(4) Where a cheque is crossed generally or specially, the holder may add the words "not negotiable."

(5) Where a cheque is crossed specially, the banker to whom it is crossed may again cross it specially to another banker for collection.

(6) Where an uncrossed cheque, or a cheque crossed generally, is sent to a banker for collection, he may cross it specially to himself. **[214]**

78 Crossing a material part of cheque

A crossing authorised by this Act is a material part of the cheque; it shall not be lawful for any person to obliterate or, except as authorised by this Act, to add to or alter the crossing. **[215]**

79 Duties of banker as to crossed cheques

(1) Where a cheque is crossed specially to more than one banker except when crossed to an agent for collection being a banker, the banker on whom it is drawn shall refuse payment thereof.

(2) Where the banker on whom a cheque is drawn which is so crossed nevertheless pays the same, or pays a cheque crossed generally otherwise than to a banker, or if crossed specially otherwise than to the banker to whom it is crossed, or his agent for collection being a banker, he is liable to the true owner of the cheque for any loss he may sustain owing to the cheque having been so paid.

Provided that where a cheque is presented for payment which does not at the time of presentment appear to be crossed, or to have had a crossing which has been obliterated, or to have been added to or altered otherwise than as authorised by this Act, the banker paying the cheque in good faith and without negligence shall not be responsible or incur any liability, nor shall the payment be questioned by reason of the cheque having been crossed, or of the crossing having been obliterated or having been added to or altered otherwise than as authorised by this Act, and of payment having been made otherwise than to a banker or to the banker to whom the cheque is or was crossed, or to his agent for collection being a banker, as the case may be. **[216]**

80 Protection to banker and drawer where cheque is crossed

Where the banker, on whom a crossed cheque [(including a cheque which under section 81A below or otherwise is not transferable)] is drawn, in good faith and without negligence pays it, if crossed generally, to a banker, and if crossed specially, to the banker to whom it is crossed, or his agent for collection being a banker, the banker paying the cheque, and, if the cheque has come into the hands of the payee, the drawer, shall respectively be entitled to the same rights and be placed in the same position as if payment of the cheque had been made to the true owner thereof. **[217]**

NOTE
 Words in square brackets inserted by the Cheques Act 1992, s 2.

81 Effect of crossing on holder

Where a person takes a crossed cheque which bears on it the words "not negotiable," he shall not have and shall not be capable of giving a better title to the cheque than that which the person from whom he took it had. **[218]**

[81A Non-transferable cheques

(1) Where a cheque is crossed and bears across its face the words "account payee" or "a/c payee", either with or without the word "only", the cheque shall not be transferable, but shall only be valid as between the parties thereto.

(2) A banker is not to be treated for the purposes of section 80 above as having been negligent by reason only of his failure to concern himself with any purported indorsement of a cheque which under subsection (1) above or otherwise is not transferable.] **[219]**

NOTE
 This section inserted by the Cheques Act 1992, s 1.

82 (*Repealed by the Cheques Act 1957, s 6(3), Schedule; see now s 4 of that Act; see* **[239]**.)

PART IV
PROMISSORY NOTES

83 Promissory note defined

(1) A promissory note is an unconditional promise in writing made by one person to another signed by the maker, engaging to pay, on demand or at a fixed or determinable future time, a sum certain in money, to, or to the order of, a specified person or to bearer.

(2) An instrument in the form of a note payable to maker's order is not a note within the meaning of this section unless and until it is indorsed by the maker.

(3) A note is not invalid by reason only that it contains also a pledge of collateral security with authority to sell or dispose thereof.

(4) A note which is, or on the face of it purports to be, both made and payable within the British Islands is an inland note. Any other note is a foreign note. **[220]**

84 Delivery necessary

A promissory note is inchoate and incomplete until delivery thereof to the payee or bearer. **[221]**

85 Joint and several notes

(1) A promissory note may be made by two or more makers, and they may be liable thereon jointly, or jointly and severally according to its tenour.

(2) Where a note runs "I promise to pay" and is signed by two or more persons it is deemed to be their joint and several note. **[222]**

86 Note payable on demand

(1) Where a note payable on demand has been indorsed, it must be presented for payment within a reasonable time of the indorsement. If it be not so presented the indorser is discharged.

(2) In determining what is reasonable time, regard shall be had to the nature of the instrument, the usage of trade, and the facts of the particular case.

(3) Where a note payable on demand is negotiated, it is not deemed to be overdue, for the purpose of affecting the holder with defects of title of which he had no notice, by reason that it appears that a reasonable time for presenting it for payment has elapsed since its issue. **[223]**

87 Presentment of note for payment

(1) Where a promissory note is in the body of it made payable at a particular place, it must be presented for payment at that place in order to render the maker liable. In any other case, presentment for payment is not necessary in order to render the maker liable.

(2) Presentment for payment is necessary in order to render the indorser of a note liable.

(3) Where a note is in the body of it made payable at a particular place, presentment at that place is necessary in order to render an indorser liable; but when a place of payment is indicated by way of memorandum only,

presentment at that place is sufficient to render the indorser liable, but a presentment to the maker elsewhere, if sufficient in other respects, shall also suffice. **[224]**

88 Liability of maker

The maker of a promissory note by making it—

(1) Engages that he will pay it according to its tenour;
(2) Is precluded from denying to a holder in due course the existence of the payee and his then capacity to indorse. **[225]**

89 Application of Part II to notes

(1) Subject to the provisions in this part, and except as by this section provided, the provisions of this Act relating to bills of exchange apply, with the necessary modifications, to promissory notes.

(2) In applying those provisions the maker of a note shall be deemed to correspond with the acceptor of a bill, and the first indorser of a note shall be deemed to correspond with the drawer of an accepted bill payable to drawer's order.

(3) The following provisions as to bills do not apply to notes; namely, provisions relating to—

(a) Presentment for acceptance;
(b) Acceptance;
(c) Acceptance suprà protest;
(d) Bills in a set.

(4) Where a foreign note is dishonoured, protest thereof is unnecessary.
[226]

PART V
SUPPLEMENTARY

90 Good faith

A thing is deemed to be done in good faith, within the meaning of this Act, where it is in fact done honestly, whether it is done negligently or not. **[227]**

91 Signature

(1) Where, by this Act, any instrument or writing is required to be signed by any person it is not necessary that he should sign it with his own hand, but it is sufficient if his signature is written thereon by some other person by or under his authority.

(2) In the case of a corporation, where, by this Act, any instrument or writing is required to be signed, it is sufficient if the instrument or writing be sealed with the corporate seal.

But nothing in this section shall be construed as requiring the bill or note of a corporation to be under seal. **[228]**

92 Computation of time

Where, by this Act, the time limited for doing any act or thing is less than three days, in reckoning time, non-business days are excluded.

"Non-business days" for the purposes of this Act mean—

(a) [Saturday] Sunday, Good Friday, Christmas Day:
(b) A bank holiday under [the Banking and Financial Dealings Act 1971]:
(c) A day appointed by Royal proclamation as a public fast or thanksgiving day.
[(d) a day declared by an order under section 2 of the Banking and Financial Dealings Act 1971 to be a non-business day].

Any other day is a business day. **[229]**

NOTE
Paras (a), (b), (d): words in square brackets in para (a) inserted by the Banking and Financial Dealings Act 1971, s 3(1), (3); words in square brackets in para (b) substituted by the Banking and Financial Dealings Act 1971, s 4(4); para (d) added by the Banking and Financial Dealings Act 1971, s 4(4).

93 When noting equivalent to protest

For the purposes of this Act, where a bill or note is required to be protested within a specified time or before some further proceeding is taken, it is sufficient that the bill has been noted for protest before the expiration of the specified time or the taking of the proceeding; and the formal protest may be extended at any time thereafter as of the date of the noting. **[230]**

94 Protest when notary not accessible

Where a dishonoured bill or note is authorised or required to be protested, and the services of a notary cannot be obtained at the place where the bill is dishonoured, any householder or substantial resident of the place may, in the presence of two witnesses, give a certificate, signed by them, attesting the dishonour of the bill, and the certificate shall in all respects operate as if it were a formal protest of the bill.

The form given in Schedule 1 to this Act may be used with necessary modifications, and if used shall be sufficient. **[231]**

95 Dividend warrants may be crossed

The provisions of this Act as to crossed cheques shall apply to a warrant for payment of dividend. **[232]**

96 (*Repealed by the Statute Law Revision Act 1898.*)

97 Savings

(1) The rules in bankruptcy relating to bills of exchange, promissory notes, and cheques, shall continue to apply thereto notwithstanding anything in this Act contained.

(2) The rules of common law including the law merchant, save in so far as they are inconsistent with the express provisions of this Act, shall continue to apply to bills of exchange, promissory notes, and cheques.

(3) Nothing in this Act or in any repeal effected thereby shall affect—

(a) . . . any law or enactment for the time being in force relating to the revenue:
(b) The provisions of the Companies Act, 1862, or Acts amending it, or any Act relating to joint stock banks or companies:

(c) The provisions of any Act relating to or confirming the privileges of the Bank of England or the Bank of Ireland respectively:

(d) The validity of any usage relating to dividend warrants, or the indorsements thereof.   **[233]**

NOTE
Sub-s (3): words omitted in sub-s (3)(a) repealed by the Statute Law Revision Act 1898.

98 (*Applies to Scotland only.*)

99 Construction with other Acts, etc

Where any Act or document refers to any enactment repealed by this Act, the Act or document shall be construed, and shall operate, as if it referred to the corresponding provisions of this Act.   **[234]**

100 (*Applies to Scotland only.*)

SCHEDULES

Section 94

FIRST SCHEDULE

Form of protest which may be used when the services of a notary cannot be obtained.

Know all men that I, *A.B.* [householder], of   in the county of   in the United Kingdom, at the request of *C.D.*, there being no notary public available, did on the   day of   188   at   demand payment [*or* acceptance] of the bill of exchange hereunder written, from *E.F.*, to which demand he made answer [state answer, if any] wherefore I now, in the presence of *G.H.* and *J.K.* do protest the said bill of exchange.

        (Signed) *A.B.*
              G.H.}
              J.K. } Witnesses.

N.B.—The bill itself should be annexed, or a copy of the bill and all that is written thereon should be underwritten.   **[235]**

(*Sch 2 repealed by the Statute Law Revision Act 1898.*)

CHEQUES ACT 1957
(5 & 6 Eliz 2 c 36)

ARRANGEMENT OF SECTIONS

An Act to amend the law relating to cheques and certain other instruments
                         [17 July 1957]

1 Protection of bankers paying unindorsed or irregularly indorsed cheques, etc

(1) Where a banker in good faith and in the ordinary course of business pays a cheque drawn on him which is not indorsed or is irregularly indorsed, he does not, in doing so, incur any liability by reason only of the absence of, or irregularity in, indorsement, and he is deemed to have paid it in due course.

(2) Where a banker in good faith and in the ordinary course of business pays any such instrument as the following, namely,—

   (a) a document issued by a customer of his which, though not a bill of exchange, is intended to enable a person to obtain payment from him of the sum mentioned in the document;
   (b) a draft payable on demand drawn by him upon himself, whether payable at the head office or some other office of his bank;

he does not, in doing so, incur any liability by reason only of the absence of, or irregularity in, indorsement, and the payment discharges the instrument.

[236]

2 Rights of bankers collecting cheques not indorsed by holders

A banker who gives value for, or has a lien on, a cheque payable to order which the holder delivers to him for collection without indorsing it, has such (if any) rights as he would have had if, upon delivery, the holder had indorsed it in blank.   [237]

3 Unindorsed cheques as evidence of payment

An unindorsed cheque which appears to have been paid by the banker on whom it is drawn is evidence of the receipt by the payee of the sum payable by the cheque.   [238]

4 Protection of bankers collecting payment of cheques, etc

(1) Where a banker, in good faith and without negligence,—

   (a) receives payment for a customer of an instrument to which this section applies; or
   (b) having credited a customer's account with the amount of such an instrument, receives payment thereof for himself;

and the customer has no title, or a defective title, to the instrument, the banker does not incur any liability to the true owner of the instrument by reason only of having received payment thereof.

(2) This section applies to the following instruments, namely,—

   (a) cheques [(including cheques which under section 81A(1) of the Bills of Exchange Act 1882 or otherwise are not transferable)];
   (b) any document issued by a customer of a banker which, though not a bill of exchange, is intended to enable a person to obtain payment from that banker of the sum mentioned in the document;
   (c) any document issued by a public officer which is intended to enable a person to obtain payment from the Paymaster General or the Queen's and Lord Treasurer's Remembrancer of the sum mentioned in the document but is not a bill of exchange;

(d) any draft payable on demand drawn by a banker upon himself, whether payable at the head office or some other office of his bank.

(3) A banker is not to be treated for the purposes of this section as having been negligent by reason only of his failure to concern himself with absence of, or irregularity in, indorsement of an instrument.   **[239]**

NOTES
Sub-s (2): words in square brackets in sub-s (2)(a) inserted by the Cheques Act 1992, s 3.
Applications: this section and s 3 are applied to certain warrants issued by the Director of Savings by the Premium Savings Bonds Regulations 1972, SI 1972/765 (see reg 8(2), as amended by SI 1976/1543, SI 1980/767), the National Savings Stock Register Regulations 1976, SI 1976/2012 (see reg 22(2)), the Savings Certificates (Yearly Plan) Regulations 1984, SI 1984/779 (see reg 7(2)), the Savings Certificates Regulations 1991, SI 1991/1031 (see reg 7(2)) and the Savings Certificates (Children's Bonus Bonds) Regulations 1991, SI 1991/1407 (see reg 7(2)).

5 Application of certain provisions of Bills of Exchange Act, 1882, to instruments not being bills of exchange

The provisions of the Bills of Exchange Act, 1882, relating to crossed cheques shall, so far as applicable, have effect in relation to instruments (other than cheques) to which the last foregoing section applies as they have effect in relation to cheques.   **[240]**

6 Construction, saving and repeal

(1) This Act shall be construed as one with the Bills of Exchange Act, 1882.

(2) The foregoing provisions of this Act do not make negotiable any instrument which, apart from them, is not negotiable.

(3) . . .   **[241]**

NOTE
Sub-s (3): repealed by the Statute Law (Repeals) Act 1974.

7 Provisions as to Northern Ireland

This Act extends to Northern Ireland, . . .   **[242]**

NOTE
Words omitted repealed by the Northern Ireland Constitution Act 1973, s 41(1), Sch 6, Pt I.

8 Short title and commencement

(1) This Act may be cited as the Cheques Act 1957.

(2) This Act shall come into operation at the expiration of a period of three months beginning with the day on which it is passed.   **[243]**

NOTE
This Act was passed, ie received the Royal Assent, on 17 July 1957 and accordingly came into force on 17 October 1957.

(Schedule repealed by the Statutes Law (Repeals) Act 1974.)

BILLS OF SALE

BILLS OF SALE ACT 1878
(41 & 42 Vict c 31)

ARRANGEMENT OF SECTIONS

An Act to consolidate and amend the Law for preventing Frauds upon Creditors by secret Bills of Sale of Personal Chattels   [22 July 1878]

NOTE
 Bills of Sale Acts 1878 and 1882: by the Bills of Sale Act (1878) Amendment Act 1882, s 1, that Act and this Act may be cited together as the Bills of Sale Acts 1878 and 1882; see **[269]**.

1 Short title

This Act may be cited for all purposes as the Bills of Sale Act 1878.   **[244]**

2 Commencement

. . . the first day of January one thousand eight hundred and seventy-nine, . . . is in this Act referred to as the commencement of this Act.   **[245]**

NOTE
 Words omitted repealed by the Statute Law Revision Act 1894.

3 Application

This Act shall apply to every bill of sale executed on or after the first day of

January one thousand eight hundred and seventy-nine (whether the same be absolute, or subject or not subject to any trust) whereby the holder or grantee has power, either with or without notice, and either immediately or at any future time, to seize or take possession of any personal chattels comprised in or made subject to such bill of sale.   **[246]**

NOTE

   Application, construction and partial repeal of this Act: this Act remains in force so far as it relates to absolute bills of sale executed after its commencement; as to bills of sale given as security for the payment of money it is to be construed as one with the Bills of Sale Act (1878) Amendment Act 1882 (by virtue of s 3 of the 1882 Act), but as to such bills of sale only, this Act is repealed as far as it is inconsistent with the 1882 Act (by virtue of s 15 of the 1882 Act); see **[271]**, **[284]** respectively.

4 Interpretation of terms

In this Act the following words and expressions shall have the meanings in this section assigned to them respectively, unless there be something in the subject or context repugnant to such construction; (that is to say),

> The expression "bill of sale" shall include bills of sale, assignments, transfers, declarations of trust without transfer, inventories of goods with receipt thereto attached, or receipts for purchase moneys of goods, and other assurances of personal chattels, and also powers of attorney, authorities, or licenses to take possession of personal chattels as security for any debt, and also any agreement, whether intended or not to be followed by the execution of any other instrument, by which a right in equity to any personal chattels, or to any charge or security thereon, shall be conferred, but shall not include the following documents; that is to say, assignments for the benefit of the creditors of the person making or giving the same, marriage settlements, transfers or assignments of any ship or vessel or any share thereof, transfers of goods in the ordinary course of business of any trade or calling, bills of sale of goods in foreign parts or at sea, bills of lading, India warrants, warehouse-keepers' certificates, warrants or orders for the delivery of goods, or any other documents used in the ordinary course of business as proof of the possession or control of goods, or authorising or purporting to authorise, either by indorsement or by delivery, the possessor of such document to transfer or receive goods thereby represented:
>
> The expression "personal chattels" shall mean goods, furniture, and other articles capable of complete transfer by delivery, and (when separately assigned or charged) fixtures and growing crops, but shall not include chattel interests in real estate, nor fixtures (except trade machinery as herein-after defined), when assigned together with a freehold or leasehold interest in any land or building to which they are affixed, nor growing crops when assigned together with any interest in the land on which they grow, nor shares or interests in the stock, funds, or securities of any government, or in the capital or property of incorporated or joint stock companies, nor choses in action, nor any stock or produce upon any farm or lands which by virtue of any covenant or agreement or of the custom of the country ought not to be removed from any farm where the same are at the time of making or giving of such bill of sale:
>
> Personal chattels shall be deemed to be in the "apparent possession" of the person making or giving a bill of sale, so long as they remain or are in or upon any house, mill, warehouse, building, works, yard, land, or other premises occupied by him, or are used and enjoyed by

him in any place whatsoever, notwithstanding that formal possession thereof may have been taken by or given to any other person:
"Prescribed" means prescribed by rules made under the provisions of
this Act.   **[247]**

5 Application of Act to trade machinery

From and after the commencement of this Act trade machinery shall, for the
purposes of this Act, be deemed to be personal chattels, and any mode of
disposition of trade machinery by the owner thereof which would be a bill of
sale as to any other personal chattels shall be deemed to be a bill of sale within
the meaning of this Act.

For the purposes of this Act—

"Trade machinery" means the machinery used in or attached to any
factory or workshop;

1st   Exclusive of the fixed motive-powers, such as the water-wheels
and steam-engines, and the steam-boilers, donkey-engines,
and other fixed appurtenances of the said motive-powers; and,
2nd   Exclusive of the fixed power machinery, such as the shafts,
wheels, drums, and their fixed appurtenances, which transmit
the action of the motive-powers to the other machinery, fixed
and loose; and,
3rd   Exclusive of the pipes for steam gas and water in the factory or
workshop.

The machinery or effects excluded by this section from the
definition of trade machinery shall not be deemed to be personal
chattels within the meaning of this Act.

"Factory or workshop" means any premises on which any manual labour
is exercised by way of trade, or for purposes of gain, in or incidental
to the following purposes or any of them; that is to say,

(a)   In or incidental to the making any article or part of an article; or
(b)   In or incidental to the altering, repairing, ornamenting, finishing, of any article; or
(c)   In or incidental to the adapting for sale any article.   **[248]**

6 Certain instruments giving powers of distress to be subject to this Act

Every attornment instrument or agreement, not being a mining lease, whereby a
power of distress is given or agreed to be given by any person to any other person
by way of security for any present future or contingent debt or advance, and
whereby any rent is reserved or made payable as a mode of providing for the
payment of interest on such debt or advance, or otherwise for the purpose of such
security only, shall be deemed to be a bill of sale, within the meaning of this Act, of
any personal chattels which may be seized or taken under such power of distress.

Provided, that nothing in this section shall extend to any mortgage of any
estate or interest in any land tenement or hereditament which the mortgagee,
being in possession, shall have demised to the mortgagor as his tenant at a fair
and reasonable rent.   **[249]**

7 Fixtures or growing crops not to be deemed separately assigned when the land passes by the same instrument

No fixtures or growing crops shall be deemed, under this Act, to be separately
assigned or charged by reason only that they are assigned by separate words, or

that power is given to sever them from the land or building to which they are affixed, or from the land on which they grow, without otherwise taking possession of or dealing with such land or building, or land, if by the same instrument any freehold or leasehold interest in the land or building to which such fixtures are affixed, or in the land on which such crops grow, is also conveyed or assigned to the same persons or person.

The same rule of construction shall be applied to all deeds or instruments, including fixtures or growing crops, executed before the commencement of this Act, and then subsisting and in force, in all questions arising under any bankruptcy liquidation assignment for the benefit of creditors, or execution of any process of any court, which shall take place or be issued after the commencement of this Act. **[250]**

8 Avoidance of unregistered bill of sale in certain cases

Every bill of sale to which this Act applies shall be duly attested and shall be registered under this Act, within seven days after the making or giving thereof, and shall set forth the consideration for which such bill of sale was given, otherwise such bill of sale, as against all trustees or assignees of the estate of the person whose chattels, or any of them, are comprised in such bill of sale under the law relating to bankruptcy or liquidation, or under any assignment for the benefit of the creditors of such person, and also as against all sheriffs officers and other persons seizing any chattels comprised in such bill of sale, in the execution of any process of any court authorising the seizure of the chattels of the person by whom or of whose chattels such bill has been made, and also as against every person on whose behalf such process shall have been issued, shall be deemed fraudulent and void so far as regards the property in or right to the possession of any chattels comprised in such bill of sale which, at or after the time of filing the petition for bankruptcy or liquidation, or of the execution of such assignment, or of executing such process (as the case may be), and after the expiration of such seven days are in the possession or apparent possession of the person making such bill of sale (or of any person against whom the process has issued under or in the execution of which such bill has been made or given, as the case may be). **[251]**

NOTE
This section is in terms repealed by the Bills of Sale Act (1878) Amendment Act 1882, s 15, but, notwithstanding that, the effect of the Bills of Sale Act (1878) Amendment Act 1882, s 3, is that the repeal applies only to bills of sale to which the later Act applies, so that this section remains in force so far as regards bills of sale not given as a security for money (ie absolute bills of sale).

9 Avoidance of certain duplicate bills of sale

Where a subsequent bill of sale is executed within or on the expiration of seven days after the execution of a prior unregistered bill of sale, and comprises all or any part of the personal chattels comprised in such prior bill of sale, then, if such subsequent bill of sale is given as a security for the same debt as is secured by the prior bill of sale, or for any part of such debt, it shall, to the extent to which it is a security for the same debt or part thereof, and so far as respects the personal chattels or part thereof comprised in the prior bill, be absolutely void, unless it is proved to the satisfaction of the court having cognizance of the case that the subsequent bill of sale was bonâ fide given for the purpose of correcting some material error in the prior bill of sale, and not for the purpose of evading this Act. **[252]**

10 Mode of registering bills of sale

A bill of sale shall be attested and registered under this Act in the following manner:

(1) The execution of every bill of sale shall be attested by a solicitor of the Supreme Court, and the attestation shall state that before the execution of the bill of sale the effect thereof has been explained to the grantor by the attesting solicitor:

(2) Such bill, with every schedule or inventory thereto annexed or therein referred to, and also a true copy of such bill and of every such schedule or inventory, and of every attestation of the execution of such bill of sale, together with an affidavit of the time of such bill of sale being made or given, and of its due execution and attestation, and a description of the residence and occupation of the person making or giving the same (or in case the same is made or given by any person under or in the execution of any process, then a description of the residence and occupation of the person against whom such process issued), and of every attesting witness to such bill of sale, shall be presented to and the said copy and affidavit shall be filed with the registrar within seven clear days after the making or giving of such bill of sale, in like manner as a warrant of attorney in any personal action given by a trader is now by law required to be filed:

(3) If the bill of sale is made or given subject to any defeasance or condition, or declaration of trust not contained in the body thereof, such defeasance, condition, or declaration shall be deemed to be part of the bill, and shall be written on the same paper or parchment therewith before the registration, and shall be truly set forth in the copy filed under this Act therewith and as part thereof, otherwise the registration shall be void.

In case two or more bills of sale are given, comprising in whole or in part any of the same chattels, they shall have priority in the order of the date of their registration respectively as regards such chattels.

A transfer or assignment of a registered bill of sale need not be registered.

[253]

NOTES

Sub-s (1): as regards absolute bills of sale the requirements of sub-s (1) must still be observed, for, although repealed by the Bills of Sale Act (1878) Amendment Act 1882, s 10, it remains in force so far as absolute bills are concerned by virtue of s 3 of that Act; see **[271]**.

Local registration: see the Bills of Sale Act (1878) Amendment Act 1882, s 11, and the Bills of Sale (Local Registration) Rules 1960, SI 1960/2326, as to local registration in the county court; see **[280]**, **[775]** respectively.

11 Renewal of registration

The registration of a bill of sale, whether executed before or after the commencement of this Act, must be renewed once at least every five years, and if a period of five years elapses from the registration or renewed registration of a bill of sale without a renewal or further renewal (as the case may be), the registration shall become void.

The renewal of a registration shall be effected by filing with the registrar an affidavit stating the date of the bill of sale and of the last registration thereof, and the names, residences, and occupations of the parties thereto as stated therein, and that the bill of sale is still a subsisting security.

Every such affidavit may be in the form set forth in the schedule (A.) to this Act annexed.

A renewal of registration shall not become necessary by reason only of a transfer or assignment of a bill of sale. **[254]**

12 Form of register

The registrar shall keep a book (in this Act called "the register") for the purposes of this Act, and shall, upon the filing of any bill of sale or copy under this Act, enter therein in the form set forth in the second schedule (B.) to this Act annexed, or in any other prescribed form, the name, residence and occupation of the person by whom the bill was made or given (or in case the same was made or given by any person under or in the execution of process, then the name residence and occupation of the person against whom such process was issued, and also the name of the person or persons to whom or in whose favour the bill was given), and the other particulars shown in the said schedule or to be prescribed under this Act, and shall number all such bills registered in each year consecutively, according to the respective dates of their registration.

Upon the registration of any affidavit of renewal the like entry shall be made, with the addition of the date and number of the last previous entry relating to the same bill, and the bill of sale or copy originally filed shall be thereupon marked with the number affixed to such affidavit of renewal.

The registrar shall also keep an index of the names of the grantors of registered bills of sale with reference to entries in the register of the bills of sale given by each such grantor.

Such index shall be arranged in divisions corresponding with the letters of the alphabet, so that all grantors whose surnames begin with the same letter (and no others) shall be comprised in one division, but the arrangement within each such division need not be strictly alphabetical. **[255]**

13 The registrar

The masters of the Supreme Court of Judicature attached to the Queen's Bench Division of the High Court of Justice, or such other officers as may for the time being be assigned for this purpose under the provisions of the Supreme Court of Judicature Acts, 1873 and 1875, shall be the registrar for the purposes of this Act, and any one of the said masters may perform all or any of the duties of the registrar. **[256]**

NOTE

Supreme Court of Judicature Acts 1873 and 1875: these Acts repealed by the Supreme Court of Judicature (Consolidation) Act 1925, s 226, Sch 6 (repealed).

14 Rectification of register

Any judge of the High Court of Justice on being satisfied that the omission to register a bill of sale or an affidavit or renewal thereof within the time prescribed by this Act, or the omission or mis-statement of the name residence or occupation of any person, was accidental or due to inadvertence, may in his discretion order such omission or mis-statement to be rectified by the insertion in the register of the true name residence or occupation, or by extending the time for such registration on such terms and conditions (if any) as to security, notice by advertisement or otherwise, or as to any other matter, as he thinks fit to direct. **[257]**

15 Entry of satisfaction

Subject to and in accordance with any rules to be made under and for the purposes of this Act, the registrar may order a memorandum of satisfaction to be written upon any registered copy of a bill of sale, upon the prescribed evidence being given that the debt (if any) for which such bill of sale was made or given has been satisfied or discharged. **[258]**

16 Copies may be taken, etc

Any person shall be entitled to have an office copy or extract of any registered bill of sale, and affidavit of execution filed therewith, or copy thereof, and of any affidavit filed therewith, if any, or registered affidavit of renewal, upon paying for the same at the like rate as for office copies of judgments of the High Court of Justice, and any copy of a registered bill of sale, and affidavit purporting to be an office copy thereof, shall in all courts and before all arbitrators or other persons, be admitted as primâ facie evidence thereof, and of the fact and date of registration as shown thereon . . . **[259]**

NOTE
Words omitted repealed by the Bills of Sale Act (1878) Amendment Act 1882, s 16.

17 Affidavits

Every affidavit required by or for the purposes of this Act may be sworn before a master of any division of the High Court of Justice, or before any commissioner empowered to take affidavits in the Supreme Court of Judicature. . . . **[260]**

NOTE
Words omitted repealed by the Perjury Act 1911, s 17 (repealed); see now s 2(2) of that Act.

18 (*Repealed by the Statute Law Revision Act 1950.*)

19 Collection of fees under 38 & 39 Vict c 77 s 26

Section twenty-six of the Supreme Court of Judicature Act 1875, and any enactments for the time being in force amending or substituted for that section, shall apply to fees under this Act, and an order under that section may, if need be, be made in relation to such fees accordingly. **[261]**

NOTE
Supreme Court of Judicature 1875, s 26: repealed by the Supreme Court of Judicature (Consolidation) Act 1925, s 226, Sch 6 (repealed). See now the Supreme Court Act 1981, s 130, and the Supreme Court Fees Order 1980, SI 1980/821, Schedule, Fees Nos 21, 22.

20 Order and disposition

Chattels comprised in a bill of sale which has been and continues to be duly registered under this Act shall not be deemed to be in the possession, order, or disposition of the grantor of the bill of sale within the meaning of the Bankruptcy Act 1869. **[262]**

NOTES
The provisions of this section are not affected, so far as regards absolute bills of sale, by the repeal of the section by the Bills of Sale Act (1878) Amendment Act 1882, s 15, the effect of s 3 of the 1882 Act being that the repeal only applies to bills which are within the latter Act (ie bills given as security for the payment of money).
Bankruptcy Act 1869: repealed by the Bankruptcy Act 1883, s 169, Sch 5 (repealed). See now the Insolvency Act 1986, s 283, and cf ss 307–309, 338 of that Act.

21 Rules

Rules for the purposes of this Act may be made and altered from time to time by the like persons and in the like manner in which rules and regulations may be made under and for the purposes of the Supreme Court of Judicature Acts 1873 and 1875.   **[263]**

NOTES

Supreme Court of Judicature Acts 1873 and 1875: repealed as to the relevant provisions for the purposes of this section by the Supreme Court of Judicature (Consolidation) Act 1925, s 226, Sch 6 (repealed). See now the Supreme Court Act 1981, ss 84, 85, 87(1), (3), 127(1).

Rules: RSC Ord 95. See also the Bills of Sale (Local Registration) Rules 1960, SI 1960/2326, made by virtue of the Bills of Sale Act (1878) Amendment Act 1882, s 3.

22 Time for registration

When the time for registering a bill of sale expires on a Sunday, or other day on which the registrar's office is closed, the registration shall be valid if made on the next following day on which the office is open.   **[264]**

23 As to bills of sale and under repealed Acts

. . . Except as is herein expressly mentioned with respect to construction and with respect to renewal of registration, nothing in this Act shall affect any bill of sale executed before the commencement of this Act, and as regards bills of sale so executed the Acts hereby repealed shall continue in force.

Any renewal after the commencement of this Act of the registration of a bill of sale executed before the commencement of this Act, and registered under the Acts hereby repealed, shall be made under this Act in the same manner as the renewal of a registration made under this Act.   **[265]**

NOTE

Words omitted repealed the Bills of Sale Act 1854 and the Bills of Sale Act 1866 and were themselves repealed by the Statute Law Revision Act 1894.

24 Extent of Act

This Act shall not extend to Scotland or to Ireland.   **[266]**

SCHEDULES

Section 11

SCHEDULE A

I [*A.B.*]   of   do swear that a bill of sale, bearing date the day of   18   [*insert the date of the bill*], and made between [*insert the names and descriptions of the parties in the original bill of sale*] and which said bill of sale [*or*, and a copy of which said bill of sale, *as the case may be*] was registered on the   day of 18   [*insert date of registration*], is still a subsisting security.

Sworn, &*c*.   **[267]**

Section 12

SCHEDULE B

Satisfaction entered	No	By whom given (or against whom process issued)			To whom given	Nature of Instrument	Date	Date of Registration	Date of Registration of affidavit of renewal
		Name	Residence	Occupation					

[268]

BILLS OF SALE ACT (1878) AMENDMENT ACT 1882
(45 & 46 Vict c 43)

ARRANGEMENT OF SECTIONS

An Act to amend the Bills of Sale Act 1878   [18 August 1882]

1 Short title

This Act may be cited for all purposes as the Bills of Sale Act (1878) Amendment Act 1882; and this Act and the Bills of Sale Act 1878 may be cited together as the Bills of Sale Acts 1878 and 1882. **[269]**

2 Commencement of Act

This Act shall come into operation on the first day of November one thousand eight hundred and eighty-two, which date is herein-after referred to as the commencement of this Act. **[270]**

3 Construction of Act

The Bills of Sale Act 1878 is herein-after referred to as "the principal Act," and this Act shall, so far as is consistent with the tenor thereof, be construed as one with the principal Act; but unless the context otherwise requires shall not apply to any bill of sale duly registered before the commencement of this Act so long as the registration thereof is not avoided by non-renewal or otherwise.

The expression "bill of sale," and other expressions in this Act, have the same meaning as in the principal Act, except as to bills of sale or other documents mentioned in section four of the principal Act, which may be given otherwise than by way of security for the payment of money, to which last-mentioned bills of sale and other documents this Act shall not apply. **[271]**

4 Bill of sale to have schedule of property attached thereto

Every bill of sale shall have annexed thereto or written thereon a schedule containing an inventory of the personal chattels comprised in the bill of sale; and such bill of sale, save as herein-after mentioned, shall have effect only in respect of the personal chattels specifically described in the said schedule; and shall be void, except as against the grantor, in respect of any personal chattels not so specifically described. **[272]**

5 Bill of sale not to affect after acquired property

Save as herein-after mentioned, a bill of sale shall be void, except as against the grantor, in respect of any personal chattels specifically described in the schedule thereto of which the grantor was not the true owner at the time of the execution of the bill of sale. **[273]**

6 Exception as to certain things

Nothing contained in the foregoing sections of this Act shall render a bill of sale void in respect of any of the following things; (that is to say,)

(1) Any growing crops separately assigned or charged where such crops were actually growing at the time when the bill of sale was executed.

(2) Any fixtures separately assigned or charged, and any plant, or trade machinery where such fixtures, plant, or trade machinery are used in, attached to, or brought upon any land, farm, factory, workshop, shop, house, warehouse, or other place in substitution for any of the like fixtures, plant, or trade machinery specifically described in the schedule to such bill of sale. **[274]**

7 Bill of sale with power to seize except in certain events to be void

Personal chattels assigned under a bill of sale shall not be liable to be seized or taken possession of by the grantee for any other than the following causes:—

(1) If the grantor shall make default in payment of the sum or sums of money thereby secured at the time therein provided for payment, or in the performance of any covenant or agreement contained in the bill of sale and necessary for maintaining the security;

(2) If the grantor shall become a bankrupt, or suffer the said goods or any of them to be distrained for rent, rates, or taxes;

(3) If the grantor shall fraudulently either remove or suffer the said goods, or any of them, to be removed from the premises;

(4) If the grantor shall not, without reasonable excuse, upon demand in writing by the grantee, produce to him his last receipts for rent, rates, and taxes;

(5) If execution shall have been levied against the goods of the grantor under any judgment at law:

Provided that the grantor may within five days from the seizure or taking possession of any chattels on account of any of the above-mentioned causes, apply to the High Court, or to a judge thereof in chambers, and such court or judge, if satisfied that by payment of money or otherwise the said cause of seizure no longer exists, may restrain the grantee from removing or selling the said chattels, or may make such other order as may seem just.   **[275]**

[7A Defaults under consumer credit agreements

(1) Paragraph (1) of section 7 of this Act does not apply to a default relating to a bill of sale given by way of security for the payment of money under a regulated agreement to which section 87(1) of the Consumer Credit Act 1974 applies—

(a) unless the restriction imposed by section 88(2) of that Act has ceased to apply to the bill of sale; or

(b) if, by virtue of section 89 of that Act, the default is to be treated as not having occurred.

(2) Where paragraph (1) of section 7 of this Act does apply in relation to a bill of sale such as is mentioned in subsection (1) of this section, the proviso to that section shall have effect with the substitution of "county court" for "High Court".]   **[276]**

NOTE
This section inserted by the Consumer Credit Act 1974, s 192(3)(a), Sch 4, para 1.

8 Bill of sale to be void unless attested and registered

Every bill of sale shall be duly attested, and shall be registered under the principal Act within seven clear days after the execution thereof, or if it is executed in any place out of England then within seven clear days after the time at which it would in the ordinary course of post arrive in England if posted immediately after the execution thereof; and shall truly set forth the consideration for which it was given; otherwise such bill of sale shall be void in respect of the personal chattels comprised therein.   **[277]**

NOTE
Principal Act: ie the Bills of Sale Act 1878.

9 Form of bill of sale

A bill of sale made or given by way of security for the payment of money by the grantor thereof shall be void unless made in accordance with the form in the schedule to this Act annexed.   **[278]**

10 Attestation

The execution of every bill of sale by the grantor shall be attested by one or more credible witness or witnesses, not being a party or parties thereto. . . .

[279]

NOTE
Words omitted repealed by the Statute Law Revision Act 1898.

11 Local registration of contents of bills of sale

Where the affidavit (which under section ten of the principal Act is required to accompany a bill of sale when presented for registration) describes the residence of the person making or giving the same or of the person against whom the process is issued to be in some place outside [the London insolvency district] or where the bill of sale describes the chattels enumerated therein as being in some place outside [the London insolvency district], the registrar under the principal Act shall forthwith and within three clear days after registration in the principal registry, and in accordance with the prescribed directions, transmit an abstract in the prescribed form of the contents of such bill of sale to the county court registrar in whose district such places are situate, and if such places are in the districts of different registrars to each such registrar.

Every abstract so transmitted shall be filed, kept, and indexed by the registrar of the county court in the prescribed manner, and any person may search, inspect, make extracts from, and obtain copies of the abstract so registered in the like manner, and upon the like terms as to payment or otherwise as near as may be as in the case of bills of sale registered by the registrar under the principal Act. **[280]**

NOTES
Words in square brackets substituted by the Insolvency Act 1985, s 235(1), Sch 8, para 1. For savings, see the Insolvency Act 1986, s 437, Sch 11, Pt II, para 10.
Registration: the Bills of Sale (Local Registration) Rules 1960, SI 1960/2326, regulate the local registration of bills of sale.
Principal Act: ie the Bills of Sale Act 1878.

12 Bill of sale under £30 to be void

Every bill of sale made or given in consideration of any sum under thirty pounds shall be void. **[281]**

13 Chattels not to be removed or sold

All personal chattels seized or of which possession is taken . . . under or by virtue of any bill of sale (whether registered before or after the commencement of this Act), shall remain on the premises where they were so seized or so taken possession of, and shall not be removed or sold until after the expiration of five clear days from the day they were so seized or so taken possession of. **[282]**

NOTE
Words omitted repealed by the Statute Law Revision Act 1898.

14 Bill of sale not to protect chattels against poor and parochial rates

A bill of sale to which this Act applies shall be no protection in respect of personal chattels included in such bill of sale which but for such bill of sale would have been liable to distress under a warrant for the recovery of taxes and poor and other parochial rates. **[283]**

15 Repeal of part of Bills of Sale Act 1878

. . . all . . . enactments contained in the principal Act which are inconsistent with this Act are repealed. . . .   **[284]**

NOTES
  Words omitted repealed by the Statute Law Revision Act 1898.
  Principal Act: ie the Bills of Sale Act 1878.

16 Inspection of registered bills of sale

. . . any person shall be entitled at all reasonable times to search the register, on payment of a fee of one shilling, or such other fee as may be prescribed, and subject to such regulations as may be prescribed, and shall be entitled at all reasonable times to inspect, examine, and make extracts from any and every registered bill of sale without being required to make a written application, or to specify any particulars in reference thereto, upon payment of one shilling for each bill of sale inspected, and such payment shall be made by a judicature stamp: Provided that the said extracts shall be limited to the dates of execution, registration, renewal of registration, and satisfaction, to the names, addresses, and occupations of the parties, to the amount of the consideration, and to any further prescribed particulars.   **[285]**

NOTE
  Words omitted repealed by the Statute Law Revision Act 1898.

17 Debentures to which Act not to apply

Nothing in this Act shall apply to any debentures issued by any mortgage, loan, or other incorporated company, and secured upon the capital stock or goods, chattels, and effects of such company.   **[286]**

18 Extent of Act

This Act shall not extend to Scotland or Ireland.   **[287]**

SCHEDULE

Section 9

FORM OF BILL OF SALE

This Indenture made the   day of   , between *A.B.* of   of the one part, and *C.D.* of   of the other part, witnesseth that in consideration of the sum of £   now paid to *A.B.* by *C.D.*, the receipt of which the said *A.B.* hereby acknowledges [*or whatever else the consideration may be*], he the said *A.B.* doth hereby assign unto *C.D.*, his executors, administrators, and assigns, all and singular the several chattels and things specifically described in the schedule hereto annexed by way of security for the payment of the sum of £   , and interest thereon at the rate of   per cent. per annum [*or whatever else may be the rate*]. And the said *A.B.* doth further agree and declare that he will duly pay to the said *C.D.* the principal sum aforesaid, together with the interest then due, by equal   payments of £   on the   day of   [*or whatever else may be the stipulated times or time of payment*]. And the said *A.B.* doth also agree with the said *C.D.* that he will [*here insert terms as to insurance, payment of rent, or otherwise, which the parties may agree to for the maintenance or defeasance of the security*].

Provided always, that the chattels hereby assigned shall not be liable to seizure or to be taken possession of by the said *C.D.* for any cause other than those specified in section seven of the Bills of Sale Act (1878) Amendment Act 1882.

In Witness, &c.

Signed and sealed by the said *A.B.* in the presence of me *E.F.* [*add witness' name, address, and description*].   **[288]**

BILLS OF SALE ACT 1890
(53 & 54 Vict c 53)

An Act to exempt certain letters of hypothecation from the operation of the Bills of Sale Act 1882   [10 August 1890]

1 Exemption of letters of hypothecation of imported goods from 41 & 42 Vict c 31, and 45 & 46 Vict c 43, s 9

[An instrument charging or creating any security on or declaring trusts of imported goods given or executed at any time prior to their deposit in a warehouse, factory, or store, or to their being reshipped for export, or delivered to a purchaser not being the person giving or executing such instrument, shall not be deemed a bill of sale within the meaning of the Bills of Sale Acts 1878 and 1882.]   **[289]**

NOTE
  This section substituted by the Bills of Sale Act 1891, s 1.

2 Savings of 46 & 47 Vict c 52, s 44

Nothing in this Act shall affect the operation of section forty-four of the Bankruptcy Act 1883 in respect of any goods comprised in any such instrument as is herein-before described, if such goods would but for this Act be goods within the meaning of sub-section three of that section.   **[290]**

NOTE
  Bankruptcy Act 1883, s 44: repealed by the Bankruptcy Act 1914, s 168, Sch 6 (repealed). See now the Insolvency Act 1986, s 283, and cf ss 307-309, 338 of that Act.

3 Short title

This Act may be cited as the Bills of Sale Act 1890.   **[291]**

ADMINISTRATION OF JUSTICE ACT 1925
(15 & 16 Geo 5 c 28)

An Act to amend the law with respect to the jurisdiction and business of the Supreme Court in England and with respect to the judges, officers and offices thereof and otherwise with respect to the administration of justice
                                                              [7 May 1925]

1–21 *(Ss 1–18, 21 repealed by the Supreme Court of Judicature (Consolidation) Act 1925, s 226(1), Sch 6; s 19 repealed by the Courts Act 1971, s 56(4), Sch 11, Pt IV; s 20 repealed by the County Courts Act 1934, s 193, Sch 5.)*

Miscellaneous

22 *(Relates to deeds of arrangement.)*

23 Local registration of bills of sale under Bills of Sale Acts 1878 and 1882

(1) Section eleven of the Bills of Sale Act (1878) Amendment Act 1882 (which makes provision for the local registration of the contents of bills of sale), shall have effect as if it required the registrar of bills of sale to transmit to county court registrars copies of the bills instead of abstracts of the contents of

the bills, and references in that section to the abstract transmitted and the abstract registered shall be construed accordingly.

(2) Section ten of the Bills of Sale Act 1878 shall have effect as though it required the presentation to the registrar on the registration of a bill of sale, in addition to the copy of the bill of sale mentioned in paragraph (2) of that section, of such number of copies of the bill and every schedule and inventory annexed thereto as the registrar may deem to be necessary for the purpose of carrying out the requirements of the said section eleven as amended by this section.   **[292]**

24–28 (*Ss 24–26 repealed by the Supreme Court of Judicature (Consolidation) Act 1925, s 226(1), Sch 6; s 27 repealed by the Statute Law Revision Act 1950; s 28 spent.*)

29 Short title, interpretation and extent

(1) This Act may be cited as the Administration of Justice Act 1925.

(2) . . .

(3) This Act shall not extend to Scotland or Northern Ireland.

(4), (5) . . .   **[293]**

NOTES
Sub-s (2): repealed by the Statute Law (Repeals) Act 1973.
Sub-ss (4), (5): repealed by the Statute Law Revision Act 1950.

(*Schs 1–3 repealed by the Supreme Court of Judicature (Consolidation) Act 1925, s 226(1), Sch 6; Schs 4, 5 repealed by the Statute Law Revision Act 1950.*)

CONTRACTS

STATUTE OF FRAUDS (1677)
(29 Car 2 c 3)

An Act for prevention of Frauds and Perjuryes

NOTE
   The short title was given to this Act by the Short Titles Act 1896.

1–3 (*Repealed by the Law of Property Act 1925, s 207, Sch 7.*)

4 No action against executors, etc, upon a special promise, or upon any agreement, or contract for sale of lands, etc, unless agreement, etc, be in writing, and signed

. . . noe action shall be brought . . . whereby to charge the defendant upon any speciall promise to answere for the debt default or miscarriages of another person . . . unlesse the agreement upon which such action shall be brought or some memorandum or note thereof shall be in writeing and signed by the partie to be charged therewith or some other person thereunto by him lawfully authorized.   **[294]**

NOTE
   Words omitted in first place repealed by the Statute Law Revision Act 1883 and the Statute Law Revision Act 1948; words omitted in second place repealed by the Law Reform (Enforcement of Contracts) Act 1954, s 1; words omitted in third place repealed by the Law of Property Act 1925, s 207, Sch 7, and the Law Reform (Enforcement of Contracts) Act 1954, s 1.

5–24 (*Ss 5, 6, 12, 18–21, 22 repealed by the Wills Act 1837, s 2; ss 7–9 repealed by the Law of Property Act 1925, s 207, Sch 7; ss 10, 11, 23 repealed by the Administration of Estates Act 1925, s 56, Sch 2; ss 13, 14 repealed by the Civil Procedure Acts Repeal Act 1879, s 2, Schedule, Pt I; ss 15, 16 repealed by the Sale of Goods Act 1893, s 60, Schedule; s 17 repealed by the Statute Law Revision and Civil Procedure Act 1881; s 24 repealed by the Law of Property Act 1925, s 207, Sch 7 and by the Administration of Estates Act 1925, s 56, Sch 2.*)

STATUTE OF FRAUDS AMENDMENT ACT 1828
(9 Geo 4 c 14)

An Act for rendering a written Memorandum necessary to the Validity of certain Promises and Engagements   **[9 May 1828]**

NOTE
   The short title was given to this Act by the Short Titles Act 1896. It is also known as Lord Tenterden's Act.

1–5 (*Ss 1, 3, 4 repealed by the Limitation Act 1939, s 34, Schedule, and the Statute of Limitations Act (Northern Ireland) 1958, s 75, Schedule; s 2 repealed by the Statute Law Revision Act 1890; s 5 repealed by the Statute Law Revision Act 1875.*)

6 Action not maintainable on representations of character, etc, unless they be in writing signed by the party chargeable

No action shall be brought whereby to charge any person upon or by reason of any representation or assurance made or given concerning or relating to the character, conduct, credit, ability, trade, or dealings of any other person, to the intent or purpose that such other person may obtain credit, money, or goods upon, unless such representation or assurance be made in writing, signed by the party to be charged therewith. **[295]**

7, 8 (*S 7 repealed by the Sale of Goods Act 1893, s 60, Schedule; s 8 repealed by the Limitation Act 1939, s 34, Schedule, and the Statute of Limitations Act (Northern Ireland) 1958, s 75, Schedule.*)

9 Act not to extend to Scotland

Nothing in this Act contained shall extend to Scotland. **[296]**

10 (*Repealed by the Statute Law Revision Act 1873.*)

MERCANTILE LAW AMENDMENT ACT 1856
(19 & 20 Vict c 97)

An Act to amend the Laws of England and Ireland affecting Trade and Commerce
[29 July 1856]

1, 2 (*Repealed by the Sale of Goods Act 1893, s 60, Schedule.*)

3 Written guarantee not to be invalid by reason that the consideration does not appear in writing

No special promise to be made by any person . . . to answer for the debt, default, or miscarriage of another person, being in writing, and signed by the party to be charged therewith, or some other person by him thereunto lawfully authorised, shall be deemed invalid to support an action, suit, or other proceeding to charge the person by whom such promise shall have been made, by reason only that the consideration for such promise does not appear in writing, or by necessary inference from a written document. **[297]**

NOTE
Words omitted repealed by the Statute Law Revision Act 1892.

4 (*Repealed by the Partnership Act 1890, s 48, Schedule.*)

5 Surety who discharges the liability to be entitled to assignment of all securities held by the creditor, and to stand in the place of the creditor

Every person who, being surety for the debt or duty of another, or being liable with another for any debt or duty, shall pay such debt or perform such duty, shall be entitled to have assigned to him, or to a trustee for him, every judgment, specialty, or other security which shall be held by the creditor in respect of such debt or duty, whether such judgment, specialty, or other security shall or shall not be deemed at law to have been satisfied by the payment of the debt or performance of the duty, and such person shall be entitled to stand in the place of the creditor, and to use all the remedies, and, if need be, and upon a proper indemnity, to use the name of the creditor, in any action or other proceeding, at law or in equity, in order to obtain from the principal debtor, or any co-surety, co-contractor, or co-debtor, as the case may be, indemnification for the advances made and loss sustained by the person who shall have so paid such debt or performed such duty, and such payment or performance so made by such surety shall not be pleadable in bar of any such action or other proceeding by him: Provided always, that no co-surety, co-contractor, or co-debtor shall be entitled to recover from any other co-surety, co-contractor, or co-debtor, by the means aforesaid, more than the just proportion to which, as between those parties themselves, such last-mentioned person shall be justly liable.   **[298]**

6–15 (*Ss 6, 7 repealed by the Bills of Exchange Act 1882, s 96, Sch 2; s 8 (definition of home port) is outside the scope of this work; ss 9–14 repealed by the Limitation Act 1939, s 34, Schedule, and the Statute of Limitations Act (Northern Ireland) 1958, s 75, Schedule; s 15 repealed by the Statute Law Revision Act 1894.*)

16 Short title

In citing this Act, it shall be sufficient to use the expression "The Mercantile Law Amendment Act 1856."   **[299]**

17 Extent

Nothing in this Act shall extend to Scotland.   **[300]**

LAW REFORM (FRUSTRATED CONTRACTS) ACT 1943
(6 & 7 Geo 6 c 40)

An Act to amend the law relating to the frustration of contracts
[5 August 1943]

1 Adjustment of rights and liabilities of parties to frustrated contracts

(1) Where a contract governed by English law has become impossible of performance or been otherwise frustrated, and the parties thereto have for that reason been discharged from the further performance of the contract, the following provisions of this section shall, subject to the provisions of section two of this Act, have effect in relation thereto.

(2) All sums paid or payable to any party in pursuance of the contract before the time when the parties were so discharged (in this Act referred to as "the time of discharge") shall, in the case of sums so paid, be recoverable from him as money received by him for the use of the party by whom the sums were paid, and, in the case of sums so payable, cease to be so payable:

Provided that, if the party to whom the sums were so paid or payable incurred expenses before the time of discharge in, or for the purpose of, the performance of the contract, the court may, if it considers it just to do so having regard to all the circumstances of the case, allow him to retain or, as the case may be, recover the whole or any part of the sums so paid or payable, not being an amount in excess of the expenses so incurred.

(3) Where any party to the contract has, by reason of anything done by any other party thereto in, or for the purpose of, the performance of the contract, obtained a valuable benefit (other than a payment of money to which the last foregoing subsection applies) before the time of discharge, there shall be recoverable from him by the said other party such sum (if any), not exceeding the value of the said benefit to the party obtaining it, as the court considers just, having regard to all the circumstances of the case and, in particular,—

    (a) the amount of any expenses incurred before the time of discharge by the benefited party in, or for the purpose of, the performance of the contract, including any sums paid or payable by him to any other party in pursuance of the contract and retained or recoverable by that party under the last foregoing subsection, and

    (b) the effect, in relation to the said benefit, of the circumstances giving rise to the frustration of the contract.

(4) In estimating, for the purposes of the foregoing provisions of this section, the amount of any expenses incurred by any party to the contract, the court may, without prejudice to the generality of the said provisions, include such sum as appears to be reasonable in respect of overhead expenses and in respect of any work or services performed personally by the said party.

(5) In considering whether any sum ought to be recovered or retained under the foregoing provisions of this section by any party to the contract, the court shall not take into account any sums which have, by reason of the circumstances giving rise to the frustration of the contract, become payable to that party under any contract of insurance unless there was an obligation to insure imposed by an express term of the frustrated contract or by or under any enactment.

(6) Where any person has assumed obligations under the contract in consideration of the conferring of a benefit by any other party to the contract upon any other person, whether a party to the contract or not, the court may, if in all the circumstances of the case it considers it just to do so, treat for the purposes of subsection (3) of this section any benefit so conferred as a benefit obtained by the person who has assumed the obligations as aforesaid.   **[301]**

2 Provision as to application of this Act

(1) This Act shall apply to contracts, whether made before or after the commencement of this Act, as respects which the time of discharge is on or after the first day of July, nineteen hundred and forty-three, but not to contracts as respects which the time of discharge is before the said date.

(2) This Act shall apply to contracts to which the Crown is a party in like manner as to contracts between subjects.

(3) Where any contract to which this Act applies contains any provision which, upon the true construction of the contract, is intended to have effect in the event of circumstances arising which operate, or would but for the said provision operate, to frustrate the contract, or is intended to have effect whether such circumstances arise or not, the court shall give effect to the said provision and shall only give effect to the foregoing section of this Act to such extent, if any, as appears to the court to be consistent with the said provision.

(4) Where it appears to the court that a part of any contract to which this Act applies can properly be severed from the remainder of the contract, being a part wholly performed before the time of discharge, or so performed except for the payment in respect of that part of the contract of sums which are or can be

ascertained under the contract, the court shall treat that part of the contract as if it were a separate contract and had not been frustrated and shall treat the foregoing section of this Act as only applicable to the remainder of that contract.

(5) This Act shall not apply—

   (a) to any charterparty, except a time charterparty or a charterparty by way of demise, or to any contract (other than a charterparty) for the carriage of goods by sea; or

   (b) to any contract of insurance, save as is provided by subsection (5) of the foregoing section; or

   (c) to any contract to which [section 7 of the Sale of Goods Act 1979] (which avoids contracts for the sale of specific goods which perish before the risk has passed to the buyer) applies, or to any other contract for the sale, or for the sale and delivery, of specific goods, where the contract is frustrated by reason of the fact that the goods have perished. **[302]**

NOTE
  Sub-s (5): words in square brackets in sub-s (5)(c) substituted by the Sale of Goods Act 1979, s 63, Sch 2, para 2.

3 Short title and interpretation

(1) This Act may be cited as the Law Reform (Frustrated Contracts) Act 1943.

(2) In this Act the expression "court" means, in relation to any matter, the court or arbitrator by or before whom the matter falls to be determined. **[303]**

CORPORATE BODIES' CONTRACTS ACT 1960
(8 & 9 Eliz 2 c 46)

An Act to amend the law governing the making of contracts by or on behalf of bodies corporate; and for connected purposes   [29 July 1960]

1 Cases where contracts need not be under seal

(1) Contracts may be made on behalf of any body corporate, wherever incorporated, as follows:—

   (a) a contract which if made between private persons would be by law required to be in writing, signed by the parties to be charged therewith, may be made on behalf of the body corporate in writing signed by any person acting under its authority, express or implied, and

   (b) a contract which if made between private persons would by law be valid although made by parol only, and not reduced into writing, may be made by parol on behalf of the body corporate by any person acting under its authority, express or implied.

(2) A contract made according to this section shall be effectual in law, and shall bind the body corporate and its successors and all other parties thereto.

(3) A contract made according to this section may be varied or discharged in the same manner in which it is authorised by this section to be made.

(4) Nothing in this section shall be taken as preventing a contract under seal from being made by or on behalf of a body corporate.

(5) This section shall not apply to the making, variation or discharge of a contract before the commencement of this Act but shall apply whether the body corporate gave its authority before or after the commencement of this Act. **[304]**

2 Exclusion of companies under Companies Acts

This Act shall not apply to any company formed and registered under the [Companies Act 1985] or an existing company as defined in that Act. **[305]**

NOTE
Words in square brackets substituted by the Companies Consolidation (Consequential Provisions) Act 1985, s 30, Sch 2.

3 (*Repealed by the Northern Ireland Constitution Act 1973, s 41, Sch 6, Pt I.*)

4 Short title, repeal and extent

(1) This Act may be cited as the Corporate Bodies' Contracts Act 1960.

(2) . . .

(3) This Act shall not affect the law of Scotland or . . . of Northern Ireland.
[306]

NOTES
Sub-s (2): repealed by the Statute Law (Repeals) Act 1974.
Sub-s (3): words omitted repealed by the Northern Ireland Constitution Act 1973, s 41(1), Sch 6, Pt I.

(*Schedule repealed by the Statute Law (Repeals) Act 1974.*)

MISREPRESENTATION ACT 1967
(1967 c 7)

An Act to amend the law relating to innocent misrepresentations and to amend sections 11 and 35 of the Sale of Goods Act 1893 [22 March 1967]

1 Removal of certain bars to rescission for innocent misrepresentation

Where a person has entered into a contract after a misrepresentation has been made to him, and—

(a) the misrepresentation has become a term of the contract; or
(b) the contract has been performed;

or both, then, if otherwise he would be entitled to rescind the contract without alleging fraud, he shall be so entitled, subject to the provisions of this Act, notwithstanding the matters mentioned in paragraphs (a) and (b) of this section. **[307]**

2 Damages for misrepresentation

(1) Where a person has entered into a contract after a misrepresentation has been made to him by another party thereto and as a result thereof he has suffered loss, then, if the person making the misrepresentation would be liable to damages in respect thereof had the misrepresentation been made fraudulently, that person shall be so liable notwithstanding that the misrepresentation was not made fraudulently, unless he proves that he had reasonable ground to

believe and did believe up to the time the contract was made that the facts represented were true.

(2) Where a person has entered into a contract after a misrepresentation has been made to him otherwise than fraudulently, and he would be entitled, by reason of the misrepresentation, to rescind the contract, then, if it is claimed, in any proceedings arising out of the contract, that the contract ought to be or has been rescinded, the court or arbitrator may declare the contract subsisting and award damages in lieu of rescission, if of opinion that it would be equitable to do so, having regard to the nature of the misrepresentation and the loss that would be caused by it if the contract were upheld, as well as to the loss that rescission would cause to the other party.

(3) Damages may be awarded against a person under subsection (2) of this section whether or not he is liable to damages under subsection (1) thereof, but where he is so liable any award under the said subsection (2) shall be taken into account in assessing his liability under the said subsection (1).   **[308]**

[3 Avoidance of provision excluding liability for misrepresentation

If a contract contains a term which would exclude or restrict—

(a) any liability to which a party to a contract may be subject by reason of any misrepresentation made by him before the contract was made; or

(b) any remedy available to another party to the contract by reason of such a misrepresentation,

that term shall be of no effect except in so far as it satisfies the requirement of reasonableness as stated in section 11(1) of the Unfair Contract Terms Act 1977; and it is for those claiming that the term satisfies that requirement to show that it does.]   **[309]**

NOTE
This section substituted by the Unfair Contract Terms Act 1977, s 8(1).

4 (*Repealed by the Sale of Goods Act 1979, s 63(2), Sch 3.*)

5 Saving for past transactions

Nothing in this Act shall apply in relation to any misrepresentation or contract of sale which is made before the commencement of this Act.   **[310]**

6 Short title, commencement and extent

(1) This Act may be cited as the Misrepresentation Act 1967.

(2) This Act shall come into operation at the expiration of the period of one month beginning with the date on which it is passed.

(3) (*Applies to Scotland only.*)

(4) This Act does not extend to Northern Ireland.   **[311]**

UNFAIR CONTRACT TERMS ACT 1977
(1977 c 50)

ARRANGEMENT OF SECTIONS

PART I
AMENDMENT OF LAW FOR ENGLAND AND WALES AND NORTHERN IRELAND

Introductory

PART III
PROVISIONS APPLYING TO WHOLE OF UNITED KINGDOM

Miscellaneous

An Act to impose further limits on the extent to which under the law of England and Wales and Northern Ireland civil liability for breach of contract, or for negligence or other breach of duty, can be avoided by means of contract terms and otherwise, and under the law of Scotland civil liability can be avoided by means of contract terms   [26 October 1977]

PART I
AMENDMENT OF LAW FOR ENGLAND AND WALES AND NORTHERN IRELAND

Introductory

1 Scope of Part I

(1) For the purposes of this Part of this Act, "negligence" means the breach—

    (a) of any obligation, arising from the express or implied terms of a contract, to take reasonable care or exercise reasonable skill in the performance of the contract;

    (b) of any common law duty to take reasonable care or exercise reasonable skill (but not any stricter duty);

    (c) of the common duty of care imposed by the Occupiers' Liability Act 1957 or the Occupiers' Liability Act (Northern Ireland) 1957.

(2) This Part of this Act is subject to Part III; and in relation to contracts, the operation of sections 2 to 4 and 7 is subject to the exceptions made by Schedule 1.

(3) In the case of both contract and tort, sections 2 to 7 apply (except where the contrary is stated in section 6(4)) only to business liability, that is liability for breach of obligations or duties arising—

    (a) from things done or to be done by a person in the course of a business (whether his own business or another's); or

    (b) from the occupation of premises used for business purposes of the occupier;

and references to liability are to be read accordingly [but liability of an occupier of premises for breach of an obligation or duty towards a person obtaining access to the premises for recreational or educational purposes, being liability for loss or damage suffered by reason of the dangerous state of the premises, is not a business liability of the occupier unless granting that person such access for the purposes concerned falls within the business purposes of the occupier].

(4) In relation to any breach of duty or obligation, it is immaterial for any purpose of this Part of this Act whether the breach was inadvertent or intentional, or whether liability for it arises directly or vicariously. **[312]**

NOTE
Sub-s (3): words in square brackets added by the Occupiers' Liability Act 1984, s 2.

Avoidance of liability for negligence, breach of contract, etc

2 Negligence liability

(1) A person cannot by reference to any contract term or to a notice given to persons generally or to particular persons exclude or restrict his liability for death or personal injury resulting from negligence.

(2) In the case of other loss or damage, a person cannot so exclude or restrict his liability for negligence except in so far as the term or notice satisfies the requirement of reasonableness.

(3) Where a contract term or notice purports to exclude or restrict liability for negligence a person's agreement to or awareness of it is not of itself to be taken as indicating his voluntary acceptance of any risk. **[313]**

3 Liability arising in contract

(1) This section applies as between contracting parties where one of them deals as consumer or on the other's written standard terms of business.

(2) As against that party, the other cannot by reference to any contract term—

    (a) when himself in breach of contract, exclude or restrict any liability of his in respect of the breach; or

    (b) claim to be entitled—

        (i) to render a contractual performance substantially different from that which was reasonably expected of him, or

        (ii) in respect of the whole or any part of his contractual obligation, to render no performance at all,

except in so far as (in any of the cases mentioned above in this subsection) the contract term satisfies the requirement of reasonableness.   **[314]**

4 Unreasonable indemnity clauses

(1) A person dealing as consumer cannot by reference to any contract term be made to indemnify another person (whether a party to the contract or not) in respect of liability that may be incurred by the other for negligence or breach of contract, except in so far as the contract term satisfies the requirement of reasonableness.

(2) This section applies whether the liability in question—

    (a) is directly that of the person to be indemnified or is incurred by him vicariously;

    (b) is to the person dealing as consumer or to someone else.   **[315]**

Liability arising from sale or supply of goods

5 "Guarantee" of consumer goods

(1) In the case of goods of a type ordinarily supplied for private use or consumption, where loss or damage—

    (a) arises from the goods proving defective while in consumer use; and

    (b) results from the negligence of a person concerned in the manufacture or distribution of the goods,

liability for the loss or damage cannot be excluded or restricted by reference to any contract term or notice contained in or operating by reference to a guarantee of the goods.

(2) For these purposes—

    (a) goods are to be regarded as "in consumer use" when a person is using them, or has them in his possession for use, otherwise than exclusively for the purposes of a business; and

    (b) anything in writing is a guarantee if it contains or purports to contain some promise or assurance (however worded or presented) that defects will be made good by complete or partial replacement, or by repair, monetary compensation or otherwise.

(3) This section does not apply as between the parties to a contract under or in pursuance of which possession or ownership of the goods passed.   **[316]**

6 Sale and hire-purchase

(1) Liability for breach of the obligations arising from—

> (a) [section 12 of the Sale of Goods Act 1979] (seller's implied undertakings as to title, etc.);
> (b) section 8 of the Supply of Goods (Implied Terms) Act 1973 (the corresponding thing in relation to hire-purchase),

cannot be excluded or restricted by reference to any contract term.

(2) As against a person dealing as consumer, liability for breach of the obligations arising from—

> (a) [section 13, 14 or 15 of the 1979 Act] (seller's implied undertakings as to conformity of goods with description or sample, or as to their quality or fitness for a particular purpose);
> (b) section 9, 10 or 11 of the 1973 Act (the corresponding things in relation to hire-purchase),

cannot be excluded or restricted by reference to any contract term.

(3) As against a person dealing otherwise than as consumer, the liability specified in subsection (2) above can be excluded or restricted by reference to a contract term, but only in so far as the term satisfies the requirement of reasonableness.

(4) The liabilities referred to in this section are not only the business liabilities defined by section 1(3), but include those arising under any contract of sale of goods or hire-purchase agreement.   **[317]**

NOTE
Sub-ss (1), (2): words in square brackets in sub-ss (1)(a) and (2)(a) substituted by the Sale of Goods Act 1979, s 63, Sch 2, para 19.

7 Miscellaneous contracts under which goods pass

(1) Where the possession or ownership of goods passes under or in pursuance of a contract not governed by the law of sale of goods or hire-purchase, subsections (2) to (4) below apply as regards the effect (if any) to be given to contract terms excluding or restricting liability for breach of obligation arising by implication of law from the nature of the contract.

(2) As against a person dealing as consumer, liability in respect of the goods' correspondence with description or sample, or their quality or fitness for any particular purpose, cannot be excluded or restricted by reference to any such term.

(3) As against a person dealing otherwise than as consumer, that liability can be excluded or restricted by reference to such a term, but only in so far as the term satisfies the requirement of reasonableness.

[(3A) Liability for breach of the obligations arising under section 2 of the Supply of Goods and Services Act 1982 (implied terms about title etc in certain contracts for the transfer of the property in goods) cannot be excluded or restricted by references to any such term.]

(4) Liability in respect of—

(a) the right to transfer ownership of the goods, or give possession; or
(b) the assurance of quiet possession to a person taking goods in pursuance of the contract,

cannot [(in a case to which subsection (3A) above does not apply)] be excluded or restricted by reference to any such term except in so far as the term satisfies the requirement of reasonableness.

(5) This section does not apply in the case of goods passing on a redemption of trading stamps within the Trading Stamps Act 1964 or the Trading Stamps Act (Northern Ireland) 1965. **[318]**

NOTES
Sub-s (3A): inserted by the Supply of Goods and Services Act 1982, s 17(2).
Sub-s (4): words in square brackets inserted by the Supply of Goods and Services Act 1982, s 17(3).

Other provisions about contracts

8 (*Substitutes the Misrepresentation Act 1967, s 3, and the Misrepresentation Act (Northern Ireland) 1967, s 3.*)

9 Effect of breach

(1) Where for reliance upon it a contract term has to satisfy the requirement of reasonableness, it may be found to do so and be given effect accordingly notwithstanding that the contract has been terminated either by breach or by a party electing to treat it as repudiated.

(2) Where on a breach the contract is nevertheless affirmed by a party entitled to treat it as repudiated, this does not of itself exclude the requirement of reasonableness in relation to any contract term. **[319]**

10 Evasion by means of secondary contract

A person is not bound by any contract term prejudicing or taking away rights of his which arise under, or in connection with the performance of, another contract, so far as those rights extend to the enforcement of another's liability which this Part of this Act prevents that other from excluding or restricting.
[320]

Explanatory provisions

11 The "reasonableness" test

(1) In relation to a contract term, the requirement of reasonableness for the purposes of this Part of this Act, section 3 of the Misrepresentation Act 1967 and section 3 of the Misrepresentation Act (Northern Ireland) 1967 is that the term shall have been a fair and reasonable one to be included having regard to the circumstances which were, or ought reasonably to have been, known to or in the contemplation of the parties when the contract was made.

(2) In determining for the purposes of section 6 or 7 above whether a contract term satisfies the requirement of reasonableness, regard shall be had in particular to the matters specified in Schedule 2 to this Act; but this subsection does not prevent the court or arbitrator from holding, in accordance with any rule of law, that a term which purports to exclude or restrict any relevant liability is not a term of the contract.

(3) In relation to a notice (not being a notice having contractual effect), the requirement of reasonableness under this Act is that it should be fair and

reasonable to allow reliance on it, having regard to all the circumstances obtaining when the liability arose or (but for the notice) would have arisen.

(4) Where by reference to a contract term or notice a person seeks to restrict liability to a specified sum of money, and the question arises (under this or any other Act) whether the term or notice satisfies the requirement of reasonableness, regard shall be had in particular (but without prejudice to subsection (2) above in the case of contract terms) to—

(a) the resources which he could expect to be available to him for the purpose of meeting the liability should it arise; and

(b) how far it was open to him to cover himself by insurance.

(5) It is for those claiming that a contract term or notice satisfies the requirement of reasonableness to show that it does. **[321]**

12 "Dealing as consumer"

(1) A party to a contract "deals as consumer" in relation to another party if—

(a) he neither makes the contract in the course of a business nor holds himself out as doing so; and

(b) the other party does make the contract in the course of a business; and

(c) in the case of a contract governed by the law of sale of goods or hire-purchase, or by section 7 of this Act, the goods passing under or in pursuance of the contract are of a type ordinarily supplied for private use or consumption.

(2) But on a sale by auction or by competitive tender the buyer is not in any circumstances to be regarded as dealing as consumer.

(3) Subject to this, it is for those claiming that a party does not deal as consumer to show that he does not. **[322]**

13 Varieties of exemption clause

(1) To the extent that this Part of this Act prevents the exclusion or restriction of any liability it also prevents—

(a) making the liability or its enforcement subject to restrictive or onerous conditions;

(b) excluding or restricting any right or remedy in respect of the liability, or subjecting a person to any prejudice in consequence of his pursuing any such right or remedy;

(c) excluding or restricting rules of evidence or procedure;

and (to that extent) sections 2 and 5 to 7 also prevent excluding or restricting liability by reference to terms and notices which exclude or restrict the relevant obligation or duty.

(2) But an agreement in writing to submit present or future differences to arbitration is not to be treated under this Part of this Act as excluding or restricting any liability. **[323]**

14 Interpretation of Part I

In this Part of this Act—

"business" includes a profession and the activities of any government
      department or local or public authority;

"goods" has the same meaning as in [the Sale of Goods Act 1979]:

"hire-purchase agreement" has the same meaning as in the Consumer
      Credit Act 1974;

"negligence" has the meaning given by section 1(1);

"notice" includes an announcement, whether or not in writing, and any
      other communication or pretended communication; and

"personal injury" includes any disease and any impairment of physical or
      mental condition.   [324]

NOTE
Words in square brackets in definition "goods" substituted by the Sale of Goods Act 1979, s 63,
Sch 2, para 20.

15–25 ((*Pt II*) *Applies to Scotland only.*)

PART III

PROVISIONS APPLYING TO WHOLE OF UNITED KINGDOM

Miscellaneous

26 International supply contracts

(1) The limits imposed by this Act on the extent to which a person may
exclude or restrict liability by reference to a contract term do not apply to
liability arising under such a contract as is described in subsection (3) below.

(2) The terms of such a contract are not subject to any requirement of
reasonableness under section 3 or 4 . . .

(3) Subject to subsection (4), that description of contract is one whose
characteristics are the following—

(a) either it is a contract of sale of goods or it is one under or in pursuance
      of which the possession or ownership of goods passes; and

(b) it is made by parties whose places of business (or, if they have none,
      habitual residences) are in the territories of different States (the
      Channel Islands and the Isle of Man being treated for this purpose as
      different States from the United Kingdom).

(4) A contract falls within subsection (3) above only if either—

(a) the goods in question are, at the time of the conclusion of the
      contract, in the course of carriage, or will be carried, from the
      territory of one State to the territory of another; or

(b) the acts constituting the offer and acceptance have been done in the
      territories of different States; or

(c) the contract provides for the goods to be delivered to the territory of
      a State other than that within whose territory those acts were done.
                                                                           [325]

NOTE
Sub-s (2): words omitted apply to Scotland only.

27 Choice of law clauses

(1) Where the [law applicable to] a contract is the law of any part of the
United Kingdom only by choice of the parties (and apart from that choice

would be the law of some country outside the United Kingdom) sections 2 to 7 and 16 to 21 of this Act do not operate as part [of the law applicable to the contract].

(2) This Act has effect notwithstanding any contract term which applies or purports to apply the law of some country outside the United Kingdom, where (either or both)—

    (a) the term appears to the court, or arbitrator or arbiter to have been imposed wholly or mainly for the purpose of enabling the party imposing it to evade the operation of this Act; or

    (b) in the making of the contract one of the parties dealt as consumer, and he was then habitually resident in the United Kingdom, and the essential steps necessary for the making of the contract were taken there, whether by him or by others on his behalf.

(3) (*Applies to Scotland only.*)   **[326]**

NOTE

Sub-s (1): words in square brackets substituted by the Contracts (Applicable Law) Act 1990, s 5, Sch 4, para 4.

28 Temporary provision for sea carriage of passengers

(1) This section applies to a contract for carriage by sea of a passenger or of a passenger and his luggage where the provisions of the Athens Convention (with or without modification) do not have, in relation to the contract, the force of law in the United Kingdom.

(2) In a case where—

    (a) the contract is not made in the United Kingdom, and

    (b) neither the place of departure nor the place of destination under it is in the United Kingdom,

a person is not precluded by this Act from excluding or restricting liability for loss or damage, being loss or damage for which the provisions of the Convention would, if they had the force of law in relation to the contract, impose liability on him.

(3) In any other case, a person is not precluded by this Act from excluding or restricting liability for that loss or damage—

    (a) in so far as the exclusion or restriction would have been effective in that case had the provisions of the Convention had the force of law in relation to the contract; or

    (b) in such circumstances and to such extent as may be prescribed, by reference to a prescribed term of the contract.

(4) For the purposes of subsection (3)(a), the values which shall be taken to be the official values in the United Kingdom of the amounts (expressed in gold francs) by reference to which liability under the provisions of the Convention is limited shall be such amounts in sterling as the Secretary of State may from time to time by order made by statutory instrument specify.

(5) In this section,—

    (a) the references to excluding or restricting liability include doing any of those things in relation to the liability which are mentioned in section 13 or section 25(3) and (5); and

    (b) "the Athens Convention" means the Athens Convention relating to the Carriage of Passengers and their Luggage by Sea, 1974; and

    (c) "prescribed" means prescribed by the Secretary of State by regula-
        tions made by statutory instrument;

and a statutory instrument containing the regulations shall be subject to annulment in pursuance of a resolution of either House of Parliament.   **[327]**

NOTES
    The Athens Convention: Cmnd 6326; set out in the Merchant Shipping Act 1979, Sch 3 and given
the force of law by s 14 of that Act (as from 1 January 1996, replaced by the Merchant Shipping Act
1995, Sch 6 and s 183 respectively); brought fully into force on 30 April 1987 by the Merchant
Shipping Act 1979 (Commencement No 11) Order 1987, SI 1987/635.
    Modifications: the Merchant Shipping Act 1995, s 184(2), provides that Orders in Council made
under s 184(1) of that Act may modify this section as the Secretary of State considers appropriate.
By the Carriage of Passengers and their Luggage by Sea (Interim Provisions) Order 1980,
SI 1980/1092 (made under s 16(1), (2), (5) of the 1979 Act and now having effect under s 184 of the
1995 Act), this section ceased to apply to any contract to which that Order applies on 1 January
1981, but continues to apply to any contract made before that date. Contracts made after 30 April
1987 are governed by the Athens Convention, subject, in the case of contracts for domestic
carriage, to modifications contained in the Carriage of Passengers and their Luggage by Sea
(Domestic Carriage) Order 1987, SI 1987/670.
    Orders: as a result of the coming into force of the 1976 Protocol to the Athens Convention which
replaced the references to gold francs in the Convention with references to special drawing rights,
no equivalents for gold francs are now provided for by order under this section.

29 Saving for other relevant legislation

    (1) Nothing in this Act removes or restricts the effect of, or prevents reliance
upon, any contractual provision which—

    (a) is authorised or required by the express terms or necessary impli-
        cation of an enactment; or
    (b) being made with a view to compliance with an international agree-
        ment to which the United Kingdom is a party, does not operate more
        restrictively than is contemplated by the agreement.

    (2) A contract term is to be taken—

    (a) for the purposes of Part I of this Act, as satisfying the requirement of
        reasonableness; and
    (b) *(applies to Scotland only)*,

if it is incorporated or approved by, or incorporated pursuant to a decision or
ruling of, a competent authority acting in the exercise of any statutory jurisdiction or function and is not a term in a contract to which the competent authority
is itself a party.

    (3) In this section—

    "competent authority" means any court, arbitrator or arbiter,
        government department or public authority;
    "enactment" means any legislation (including subordinate legislation) of
        the United Kingdom or Northern Ireland and any instrument
        having effect by virtue of such legislation; and
    "statutory" means conferred by an enactment.   **[328]**

30 *(Repealed by the Consumer Safety Act 1978, s 10(1), Sch 3.)*

General

31 Commencement; amendments; repeals

    (1) This Act comes into force on 1st February 1978.

(2) Nothing in this Act applies to contracts made before the date on which it comes into force; but subject to this, it applies to liability for any loss or damage which is suffered on or after that date.

(3) The enactments specified in Schedule 3 to this Act are amended as there shown.

(4) The enactments specified in Schedule 4 to this Act are repealed to the extent specified in column 3 of that Schedule.   **[329]**

32 Citation and extent

(1) This Act may be cited as the Unfair Contract Terms Act 1977.

(2) Part I of this Act extends to England and Wales and to Northern Ireland; but it does not extend to Scotland.

(3) (*Applies to Scotland only.*)

(4) This Part of this Act extends to the whole of the United Kingdom. **[330]**

NOTE
Commencement: 1 February 1978 (s 31(1)).

SCHEDULES

SCHEDULE 1

Section 1(2)

SCOPE OF SECTIONS 2 TO 4 AND 7

1. Sections 2 to 4 of this Act do not extend to—

   (a) any contract of insurance (including a contract to pay an annuity on human life);
   (b) any contract so far as it relates to the creation or transfer of an interest in land, or to the termination of such an interest, whether by extinction, merger, surrender, forfeiture or otherwise;
   (c) any contract so far as it relates to the creation or transfer of a right or interest in any patent, trade mark, copyright [or design right], registered design, technical or commercial information or other intellectual property, or relates to the termination of any such right or interest;
   (d) any contract so far as it relates—

      (i) to the formation or dissolution of a company (which means any body corporate or unincorporated association and includes a partnership), or
      (ii) to its constitution or the rights or obligations of its corporators or members;

   (e) any contract so far as it relates to the creation or transfer of securities or of any right or interest in securities.

2. Section 2(1) extends to—

   (a) any contract of marine salvage or towage;
   (b) any charterparty of a ship or hovercraft; and
   (c) any contract for the carriage of goods by ship or hovercraft;

but subject to this sections 2 to 4 and 7 do not extend to any such contract except in favour of a person dealing as consumer.

3. Where goods are carried by ship or hovercraft in pursuance of a contract which either—

   (a) specifies that as the means of carriage over part of the journey to be covered, or
   (b) makes no provision as to the means of carriage and does not exclude that means,

then sections 2 (2), 3 and 4 do not, except in favour of a person dealing as consumer, extend to the contract as it operates for and in relation to the carriage of the goods by that means.

4. Section 2(1) and (2) do not extend to a contract of employment, except in favour of the employee.

5. Section 2(1) does not affect the validity of any discharge and indemnity given by a person, on or in connection with an award to him of compensation for pneumoconiosis attributable to employment in the coal industry, in respect of any further claim arising from his contracting that disease.   **[331]**

NOTE
    Para 1: words in square brackets in para 1(c) inserted by the Copyright, Designs and Patents Act 1988, s 303(1), Sch 7, para 24.

SCHEDULE 2
Sections 11(2), 24(2)
"GUIDELINES" FOR APPLICATION OF REASONABLENESS TEST

The matters to which regard is to be had in particular for the purposes of sections 6(3), 7(3) and (4), 20 and 21 are any of the following which appear to be relevant—

(a) the strength of the bargaining positions of the parties relative to each other, taking into account (among other things) alternative means by which the customer's requirements could have been met;

(b) whether the customer received an inducement to agree to the term, or in accepting it had an opportunity of entering into a similar contract with other persons, but without having to accept a similar term;

(c) whether the customer knew or ought reasonably to have known of the existence and extent of the term (having regard, among other things, to any custom of the trade and any previous course of dealing between the parties);

(d) where the term excludes or restricts any relevant liability if some condition is not complied with, whether it was reasonable at the time of the contract to expect that compliance with that condition would be practicable;

(e) whether the goods were manufactured, processed or adapted to the special order of the customer.   **[332]**

(Sch 3, in so far as unrepealed, specifies amendments of the Supply of Goods (Implied Terms) Act 1973, ss 14, 15 (as originally enacted and as substituted by the Consumer Credit Act 1974); Sch 4 specifies certain enactments repealed by s 31(4).)

MINORS' CONTRACTS ACT 1987
(1987 c 13)

An Act to amend the law relating to minors' contracts   [9 April 1987]

1 Disapplication of Infants Relief Act 1874 etc

The following enactments shall not apply to any contract made by a minor after the commencement of this Act—

(a) the Infants Relief Act 1874 (which invalidates certain contracts made by minors and prohibits actions to enforce contracts ratified after majority); and

(b) section 5 of the Betting and Loans (Infants) Act 1892 (which invalidates contracts to repay loans advanced during minority).   **[333]**

NOTE
    Minor: ie a person under the age of 18; see the Family Law Reform Act 1969, s 1(1), (2).

2 Guarantees

Where—

   (a) a guarantee is given in respect of an obligation of a party to a contract made after the commencement of this Act, and
   (b) the obligation is unenforceable against him (or he repudiates the contract) because he was a minor when the contract was made,

the guarantee shall not for that reason alone be unenforceable against the guarantor.   **[334]**

3 Restitution

   (1) Where—

   (a) a person ("the plaintiff") has after the commencement of this Act entered into a contract with another ("the defendant"), and
   (b) the contract is unenforceable against the defendant (or he repudiates it) because he was a minor when the contract was made,

the court may, if it is just and equitable to do so, require the defendant to transfer to the plaintiff any property acquired by the defendant under the contract, or any property representing it.

   (2) Nothing in this section shall be taken to prejudice any other remedy available to the plaintiff.   **[335]**

4 (*Sub-s (1) amends the Consumer Credit Act 1974, s 113(7); sub-s (2) repeals the Infants Relief Act 1874 and the Betting and Loans (Infants) Act 1892 (in accordance with s 1).*)

5 Short title, commencement and extent

   (1) This Act may be cited as the Minors' Contracts Act 1987.

   (2) This Act shall come into force at the end of the period of two months beginning with the date on which it is passed.

   (3) This Act extends to England and Wales only.   **[336]**

LAW OF PROPERTY (MISCELLANEOUS PROVISIONS)
ACT 1989
(1989 c 34)

An Act to make new provision with respect to deeds and their execution and contracts for the sale or other disposition of interests in land; and to abolish the rule of law known as the rule in Bain v Fothergill   [27 July 1989]

1 Deeds and their execution

   (1) Any rule of law which—

   (a) restricts the substances on which a deed may be written;
   (b) requires a seal for the valid execution of an instrument as a deed by an individual; or
   (c) requires authority by one person to another to deliver an instrument as a deed on his behalf to be given by deed,

is abolished.

(2) An instrument shall not be a deed unless—

(a) it makes it clear on its face that it is intended to be a deed by the person making it or, as the case may be, by the parties to it (whether by describing itself as a deed or expressing itself to be executed or signed as a deed or otherwise); and

(b) it is validly executed as a deed by that person or, as the case may be, one or more of those parties.

(3) An instrument is validly executed as a deed by an individual if, and only if—

(a) it is signed—

(i) by him in the presence of a witness who attests the signature; or

(ii) at his direction and in his presence and the presence of two witnesses who each attest the signature; and

(b) it is delivered as a deed by him or a person authorised to do so on his behalf.

(4) In subsections (2) and (3) above "sign", in relation to an instrument, includes making one's mark on the instrument and "signature" is to be construed accordingly.

(5) Where a solicitor [, duly certificated notary public] or licensed conveyancer, or an agent or employee of a solicitor [, duly certificated notary public] or licensed conveyancer, in the course of or in connection with a transaction involving the disposition or creation of an interest in land, purports to deliver an instrument as a deed on behalf of a party to the instrument, it shall be conclusively presumed in favour of a purchaser that he is authorised so to deliver the instrument.

(6) In subsection (5) above—

"disposition" and "purchaser" have the same meanings as in the Law of Property Act 1925;

["duly certificated notary public" has the same meaning as it has in the Solicitors Act 1974 by virtue of section 87 of that Act;] and

"interest in land" means any estate, interest or charge in or over land or in or over the proceeds of sale of land.

(7) Where an instrument under seal that constitutes a deed is required for the purposes of an Act passed before this section comes into force, this section shall have effect as to signing, sealing or delivery of an instrument by an individual in place of any provision of that Act as to signing, sealing or delivery.

(8) The enactments mentioned in Schedule 1 to this Act (which in consequence of this section require amendments other than those provided by subsection (7) above) shall have effect with the amendments specified in that Schedule.

(9) Nothing in subsection (1)(b), (2), (3), (7) or (8) above applies in relation to deeds required or authorised to be made under—

(a) the seal of the county palatine of Lancaster;

(b) the seal of the Duchy of Lancaster; or

(c) the seal of the Duchy of Cornwall.

(10) The references in this section to the execution of a deed by an individual do not include execution by a corporation sole and the reference in subsection (7) above to signing, sealing or delivery by an individual does not include signing, sealing or delivery by such a corporation.

(11) Nothing in this section applies in relation to instruments delivered as deeds before this section comes into force.   **[337]**

NOTE
Sub-ss (5), (6): words in square brackets inserted by the Courts and Legal Services Act 1990, s 125(2), Sch 17, para 20.

2 Contracts for sale etc of land to be made by signed writing

(1) A contract for the sale or other disposition of an interest in land can only be made in writing and only by incorporating all the terms which the parties have expressly agreed in one document or, where contracts are exchanged, in each.

(2) The terms may be incorporated in a document either by being set out in it or by reference to some other document.

(3) The document incorporating the terms or, where contracts are exchanged, one of the documents incorporating them (but not necessarily the same one) must be signed by or on behalf of each party to the contract.

(4) Where a contract for the sale or other disposition of an interest in land satisfies the conditions of this section by reason only of the rectification of one or more documents in pursuance of an order of a court, the contract shall come into being, or be deemed to have come into being, at such time as may be specified in the order.

(5) This section does not apply in relation to—

   (a) a contract to grant such a lease as is mentioned in section 54(2) of the Law Property Act 1925 (short leases);
   (b) a contract made in the course of a public auction; or
   (c) a contract regulated under the Financial Services Act 1986;

and nothing in this section affects the creation or operation of resulting, implied or constructive trusts.

(6) In this section—

   "disposition" has the same meaning as in the Law of Property Act 1925;
   "interest in land" means any estate, interest or charge in or over land or in or over the proceeds of sale of land.

(7) Nothing in this section shall apply in relation to contracts made before this section comes into force.

(8) Section 40 of the Law of Property Act 1925 (which is superseded by this section) shall cease to have effect.   **[338]**

3 Abolition of rule in Bain v Fothergill

The rule of law known as the rule in Bain v Fothergill is abolished in relation to contracts made after this section comes into force.   **[339]**

4 (*Introduces Sch 2 to this Act (repeals).*)

5 Commencement

(1) The provisions of this Act to which this subsection applies shall come into force on such day as the Lord Chancellor may by order made by statutory instrument appoint.

(2) The provisions to which subsection (1) above applies are—

(a) section 1 above; and

(b) section 4 above, except so far as it relates to section 40 of the Law of Property Act 1925.

(3) The provisions of this Act to which this subsection applies shall come into force at the end of the period of two months beginning with the day on which this Act is passed.

(4) The provisions of this Act to which subsection (3) above applies are—

(a) sections 2 and 3 above; and

(b) section 4 above, so far as it relates to section 40 of the Law of Property Act 1925.   **[340]**

NOTE
    Order: Law of Property (Miscellaneous Provisions) Act 1989 (Commencement) Order 1990, SI 1990/1175, bringing s 1 and s 4 (except insofar as it relates to the Law of Property Act 1925, s 40) into force on 31 July 1990.

6 Citation

(1) This Act may be cited as the Law of Property (Miscellaneous Provisions) Act 1989.

(2) This Act extends to England and Wales only.   **[341]**

(Sch 1 specifies certain enactments amended by s 1(8) (consequential amendments relating to deeds); Sch 2 specifies certain enactments repealed by s 4.)

CONTRACTS (APPLICABLE LAW) ACT 1990
(1990 c 36)

ARRANGEMENT OF SECTIONS

An Act to make provision as to the law applicable to contractual obligations in the case of conflict of laws   [26 July 1990]

1 Meaning of "the Conventions"

In this Act—

(a) "the Rome Convention" means the Convention on the law applicable to contractual obligations opened for signature in Rome on

19th June 1980 and signed by the United Kingdom on 7th December 1981;

(b) "the Luxembourg Convention" means the Convention on the accession of the Hellenic Republic to the Rome Convention signed by the United Kingdom in Luxembourg on 10th April 1984; and

(c) "the Brussels Protocol" means the first Protocol on the interpretation of the Rome Convention by the European Court signed by the United Kingdom in Brussels on 19th December 1988;

[(d) "the Funchal Convention" means the Convention on the accession of the Kingdom of Spain and the Portuguese Republic to the Rome Convention and the Brussels Protocol, with adjustments made to the Rome Convention by the Luxembourg Convention, signed by the United Kingdom in Funchal on 18th May 1992;]

and [these Conventions and this Protocol] are together referred to as "the Conventions".   **[342]**

NOTES

Commencement: 1 April 1991 (SI 1991/707).

Sub-s 1(d) added and words in square brackets substituted by the Contracts (Applicable Law) Act 1990 (Amendment) Order 1994, SI 1994/1900, arts 3, 4, with effect from 1 September 1994 in accordance with art 1 thereof.

2 Conventions to have force of law

(1) Subject to subsections (2) and (3) below, the Conventions shall have the force of law in the United Kingdom.

[(1A) The internal law for the purposes of Article 1(3) of the Rome Convention is whichever of the following are applicable, namely—

(a) the provisions of Schedule 3A to the Insurance Companies Act 1982 (law applicable to certain contracts of insurance with insurance companies), and

(b) the provisions of Schedule 20 to the Friendly Societies Act 1992 as applied by subsections (1)(a) and (2)(a) of section 101 of that Act (law applicable to certain contracts of insurance with friendly societies).]

(2) Articles 7(1) and 10(1)(e) of the Rome Convention shall not have the force of law in the United Kingdom.

(3) Notwithstanding Article 19(2) of the Rome Convention, the Conventions shall apply in the case of conflicts between the laws of 'different parts of the United Kingdom.

(4) For ease of reference there are set out in [Schedules 1, 2, 3 and 3A] to this Act respectively the English texts of—

(a) the Rome Convention;

(b) the Luxembourg Convention; . . .

(c) the Brussels Protocol[; and

(d) the Funchal Conventions.]   **[343]**

NOTES

Commencement: 1 April 1991 (sub-s (1) (in so far as relates to the Rome Convention and the Luxembourg Convention), sub-ss (2)–(4)) (SI 1991/707); 1 January 1994 (sub-s (1A)); remainder not yet in force.

Sub-s (1A): inserted by the Insurance Companies (Amendment) Regulations 1993, SI 1993/174, reg 9 and substituted by the Friendly Societies (Amendment) Regulations 1993, SI 1993/2519, reg 6(5).

Sub-s (4): first words in square brackets substituted, word omitted repealed and second words in square brackets added by the Contracts (Applicable Law) Act 1990 (Amendment) Order 1994, SI 1994/1900, arts 5, 6 with effect from 1 September 1994, in accordance with art 1 thereof.

3 Interpretation of Conventions

(1) Any question as to the meaning or effect of any provision of the Conventions shall, if not referred to the European Court in accordance with the Brussels Protocol, be determined in accordance with the principles laid down by, and any relevant decision of, the European Court.

(2) Judicial notice shall be taken of any decision of, or expression of opinion by, the European Court on any such question.

(3) Without prejudice to any practice of the courts as to the matters which may be considered apart from this subsection—

> (a) the report on the Rome Convention by Professor Mario Giuliano and Professor Paul Lagarde which is reproduced in the Official Journal of the Communities of 31st October 1980 may be considered in ascertaining the meaning or effect of any provision of that Convention; and
> (b) any report on the Brussels Protocol which is reproduced in the Official Journal of the Communities may be considered in ascertaining the meaning or effect of any provision of that Protocol. **[344]**

NOTE

Commencement: 1 April 1991 (sub-s (3)(a)) (SI 1991/707); remainder not yet in force.

4 Revision of Conventions etc

(1) If at any time it appears to Her Majesty in Council that Her Majesty's Government in the United Kingdom—

> (a) have agreed to a revision of any of the Conventions (including, in particular, any revision connected with the accession to the Rome Convention of any state); or
> (b) have given notification in accordance with Article 22(3) of the Rome Convention that either or both of the provisions mentioned in section 2(2) above shall have the force of law in the United Kingdom,

Her Majesty may by Order in Council make such consequential modifications of this Act or any other statutory provision, whenever passed or made, as Her Majesty considers appropriate.

(2) An Order in Council under subsection (1) above shall not be made unless a draft of the Order has been laid before Parliament and approved by a resolution of each House.

(3) In subsection (1) above—

> "modifications" includes additions, omissions and alterations;
> "revision" means an omission from, addition to or alteration of any of the Conventions and includes replacement of any of the Conventions to any extent by another convention, protocol or other description of international agreement; and
> "statutory provision" means any provision contained in an Act, or in any Northern Ireland legislation, or in—
>
> > (a) subordinate legislation (as defined in section 21(1) of the Interpretation Act 1978); or

(b)   any instrument of a legislative character made under any
Northern Ireland legislation.   **[345]**

NOTES
Commencement: 1 April 1991 (SI 1991/707).
Order in Council: Contracts (Applicable Law) Act 1990 (Amendment) Order 1994, SI 1994/
1900, with effect from 1 September 1994, in accordance with art 1 thereof.

5 (*Introduces Sch 4 (consequential amendments).*)

6 Application to Crown
This Act binds the Crown.   **[346]**

NOTE
Commencement: 1 April 1991 (SI 1991/707).

7 Commencement
This Act shall come into force on such day as the Lord Chancellor and the Lord
Advocate may by order made by statutory instrument appoint; and different
days may be appointed for different provisions or different purposes.   **[347]**

NOTES
Commencement: 1 April 1991 (SI 1991/707).
Order: Contracts (Applicable Law) Act 1990 (Commencement No 1) Order 1991, SI 1991/707.

8 Extent
(1) This Act extends to Northern Ireland.

(2) Her Majesty may by Order in Council direct that all or any of the
provisions of this Act shall extend to any of the following territories, namely—

(a)   the Isle of Man;
(b)   any of the Channel Islands;
(c)   Gibraltar;
(d)   the Sovereign Base Areas of Akrotiri and Dhekelia (that is to say,
the areas mentioned in section 2(1) of the Cyprus Act 1960).

(3) An Order in Council under subsection (2) above may modify this Act in
its application to any of the territories mentioned in that subsection and may
contain such supplementary provisions as Her Majesty considers appropriate;
and in this subsection "modify" shall be construed in accordance with section 4
above.   **[348]**

NOTE
Commencement: 1 April 1991 (SI 1991/707).

9 Short title
This Act may be cited as the Contracts (Applicable Law) Act 1990.   **[349]**

NOTE
Commencement: 1 April 1991 (SI 1991/707).

SCHEDULES

SCHEDULE 1

Section 2

THE ROME CONVENTION

The High Contracting Parties to the Treaty establishing the European Economic Community,

Anxious to continue in the field of private international law the work of unification of law which has already been done within the Community, in particular in the field of jurisdiction and enforcement of judgments,

Wishing to establish uniform rules concerning the law applicable to contractual obligations,

Have agreed as follows:

TITLE I

SCOPE OF THE CONVENTION

ARTICLE 1

Scope of the Convention

1. The rules of this Convention shall apply to contractual obligations in any situation involving a choice between the laws of different countries.

2. They shall not apply to:

(a) questions involving the status or legal capacity of natural persons, without prejudice to Article 11;

(b) contractual obligations relating to:

—wills and succession,
—rights in property arising out of a matrimonial relationship,
—rights and duties arising out of a family relationship, parentage, marriage or affinity, including maintenance obligations in respect of children who are not legitimate;

(c) obligations arising under bills of exchange, cheques and promissory notes and other negotiable instruments to the extent that the obligations under such other negotiable instruments arise out of their negotiable character;

(d) arbitration agreements and agreements on the choice of court;

(e) questions governed by the law of companies and other bodies corporate or unincorporate such as the creation, by registration or otherwise, legal capacity, internal organisation or winding up of companies and other bodies corporate or unincorporate and the personal liability of officers and members as such for the obligations of the company or body;

(f) the question whether an agent is able to bind a principal, or an organ to bind a company or body corporate or unincorporate, to a third party;

(g) the constitution of trusts and the relationship between settlors, trustees and beneficiaries;

(h) evidence and procedure, without prejudice to Article 14.

3. The rules of this Convention do not apply to contracts of insurance which cover risks situated in the territories of the Member States of the European Economic Community. In order to determine whether a risk is situated in these territories the court shall apply its internal law.

4. The preceding paragraph does not apply to contracts of re-insurance.

ARTICLE 2

Application of law of non-contracting States

Any law specified by this Convention shall be applied whether or not it is the law of a Contracting State.

TITLE II
UNIFORM RULES
ARTICLE 3
Freedom of choice

1. A contract shall be governed by the law chosen by the parties. The choice must be express or demonstrated with reasonable certainty by the terms of the contract or the circumstances of the case. By their choice the parties can select the law applicable to the whole or a part only of the contract.

2. The parties may at any time agree to subject the contract to a law other than that which previously governed it, whether as a result of an earlier choice under this Article or of other provisions of this Convention. Any variation by the parties of the law to be applied made after the conclusion of the contract shall not prejudice its formal validity under Article 9 or adversely affect the rights of third parties.

3. The fact that the parties have chosen a foreign law, whether or not accompanied by the choice of a foreign tribunal, shall not, where all the other elements relevant to the situation at the time of the choice are connected with one country only, prejudice the application of rules of the law of that country which cannot be derogated from by contract, hereinafter called "mandatory rules".

4. The existence and validity of the consent of the parties as to the choice of the applicable law shall be determined in accordance with the provisions of Articles 8, 9 and 11.

ARTICLE 4
Applicable law in the absence of choice

1. To the extent that the law applicable to the contract has not been chosen in accordance with Article 3, the contract shall be governed by the law of the country with which it is most closely connected. Nevertheless, a severable part of the contract which has a closer connection with another country may by way of exception be governed by the law of that other country.

2. Subject to the provisions of paragraph 5 of this Article, it shall be presumed that the contract is most closely connected with the country where the party who is to effect the performance which is characteristic of the contract has, at the time of conclusion of the contract, his habitual residence, or, in the case of a body corporate or unincorporate, its central administration. However, if the contract is entered into in the course of that party's trade or profession, that country shall be the country in which the principal place of business is situated or, where under the terms of the contract the performance is to be effected through a place of business other than the principal place of business, the country in which that other place of business is situated.

3. Notwithstanding the provisions of paragraph 2 of this Article, to the extent that the subject matter of the contract is a right in immovable property or a right to use immovable property it shall be presumed that the contract is most closely connected with the country where the immovable property is situated.

4. A contract for the carriage of goods shall not be subject to the presumption in paragraph 2. In such a contract if the country in which, at the time the contract is concluded, the carrier has his principal place of business is also the country in which the place of loading or the place of discharge or the principal place of business of the consignor is situated, it shall be presumed that the contract is most closely connected with that country. In applying this paragraph single voyage charter-parties and other contracts the main purpose of which is the carriage of goods shall be treated as contracts for the carriage of goods.

5. Paragraph 2 shall not apply if the characteristic performance cannot be determined, and the presumptions in paragraphs 2, 3 and 4 shall be disregarded if it appears from the circumstances as a whole that the contract is more closely connected with another country.

ARTICLE 5
Certain consumer contracts

1. This Article applies to a contract the object of which is the supply of goods or services to a person ("the consumer") for a purpose which can be regarded as being outside his trade or profession, or a contract for the provision of credit for that object.

2. Notwithstanding the provisions of Article 3, a choice of law made by the parties shall not have the result of depriving the consumer of the protection afforded to him by the mandatory rules of the law of the country in which he has his habitual residence:

—if in that country the conclusion of the contract was preceded by a specific invitation addressed to him or by advertising, and he had taken in that country all the steps necessary on his part for the conclusion of the contract, or

—if the other party or his agent received the consumer's order in that country, or

—if the contract is for the sale of goods and the consumer travelled from that country to another country and there gave his order, provided that the consumer's journey was arranged by the seller for the purpose of inducing the consumer to buy.

3. Notwithstanding the provisions of Article 4, a contract to which this Article applies shall, in the absence of choice in accordance with Article 3, be governed by the law of the country in which the consumer has his habitual residence if it is entered into in the circumstances described in paragraph 2 of this Article.

4. This Article shall not apply to:

(a) a contract of carriage;

(b) a contract for the supply of services where the services are to be supplied to the consumer exclusively in a country other than that in which he has his habitual residence.

5. Notwithstanding the provisions of paragraph 4, this Article shall apply to a contract which, for an inclusive price, provides for a combination of travel and accommodation.

ARTICLE 6

Individual employment contracts

1. Notwithstanding the provisions of Article 3, in a contract of employment a choice of law made by the parties shall not have the result of depriving the employee of the protection afforded to him by the mandatory rules of the law which would be applicable under paragraph 2 in the absence of choice.

2. Notwithstanding the provisions of Article 4, a contract of employment shall, in the absence of choice in accordance with Article 3, be governed:

(a) by the law of the country in which the employee habitually carries out his work in performance of the contract, even if he is temporarily employed in another country; or

(b) if the employee does not habitually carry out his work in any one country, by the law of the country in which the place of business through which he was engaged is situated;

unless it appears from the circumstances as a whole that the contract is more closely connected with another country, in which case the contract shall be governed by the law of that country.

ARTICLE 7

Mandatory rules

1. When applying under this Convention the law of a country, effect may be given to the mandatory rules of the law of another country with which the situation has a close connection, if and in so far as, under the law of the latter country, those rules must be applied whatever the law applicable to the contract. In considering whether to give effect to these mandatory rules, regard shall be had to their nature and purpose and to the consequences of their application or non-application.

2. Nothing in this Convention shall restrict the application of the rules of the law of the forum in a situation where they are mandatory irrespective of the law otherwise applicable to the contract.

ARTICLE 8

Material validity

1. The existence and validity of a contract, or of any term of a contract, shall be determined by the law which would govern it under this Convention if the contract or term were valid.

2. Nevertheless a party may rely upon the law of the country in which he has his habitual residence to establish that he did not consent if it appears from the circumstances that it would not be reasonable to determine the effect of his conduct in accordance with the law specified in the preceding paragraph.

ARTICLE 9

Formal validity

1. A contract concluded between persons who are in the same country is formally valid if it satisfies the formal requirements of the law which governs it under this Convention or of the law of the country where it is concluded.

2. A contract concluded between persons who are in different countries is formally valid if it satisfies the formal requirements of the law which governs it under this Convention or of the law of one of those countries.

3. Where a contract is concluded by an agent, the country in which the agent acts is the relevant country for the purposes of paragraphs 1 and 2.

4. An act intended to have legal effect relating to an existing or contemplated contract is formally valid if it satisfies the formal requirements of the law which under this Convention governs or would govern the contract or of the law of the country where the act was done.

5. The provisions of the preceding paragraphs shall not apply to a contract to which Article 5 applies, concluded in the circumstances described in paragraph 2 of Article 5. The formal validity of such a contract is governed by the law of the country in which the consumer has his habitual residence.

6. Notwithstanding paragraphs 1 to 4 of this Article, a contract the subject matter of which is a right in immovable property or a right to use immovable property shall be subject to the mandatory requirements of form of the law of the country where the property is situated if by that law those requirements are imposed irrespective of the country where the contract is concluded and irrespective of the law governing the contract.

ARTICLE 10

Scope of the applicable law

1. The law applicable to a contract by virtue of Articles 3 to 6 and 12 of this Convention shall govern in particular:

   (a) interpretation;
   (b) performance;
   (c) within the limits of the powers conferred on the court by its procedural law, the consequences of breach, including the assessment of damages in so far as it is governed by rules of law;
   (d) the various ways of extinguishing obligations, and prescription and limitation of actions;
   (e) the consequences of nullity of the contract.

2. In relation to the manner of performance and the steps to be taken in the event of defective performance regard shall be had to the law of the country in which performance takes place.

ARTICLE 11

Incapacity

In a contract concluded between persons who are in the same country, a natural person who would have capacity under the law of that country may invoke his incapacity resulting from another law only if the other party to the contract was aware of this incapacity at the time of the conclusion of the contract or was not aware thereof as a result of negligence.

ARTICLE 12

Voluntary assignment

1. The mutual obligations of assignor and assignee under a voluntary assignment of a right against another person ("the debtor") shall be governed by the law which under this Convention applies to the contract between the assignor and assignee.

2. The law governing the right to which the assignment relates shall determine its assignability, the relationship between the assignee and the debtor, the conditions under which the assignment can be invoked against the debtor and any question whether the debtor's obligations have been discharged.

ARTICLE 13

Subrogation

1. Where a person ("the creditor") has a contractual claim upon another ("the debtor"), and a third person has a duty to satisfy the creditor, or has in fact satisfied the creditor in discharge of that duty, the law which governs the third person's duty to satisfy the creditor shall determine whether the third person is entitled to exercise against the debtor the rights which the creditor had against the debtor under the law governing their relationship and, if so, whether he may do so in full or only to a limited extent.

2. The same rule applies where several persons are subject to the same contractual claim and one of them has satisfied the creditor.

ARTICLE 14

Burden of proof, etc.

1. The law governing the contract under this Convention applies to the extent that it contains, in the law of contract, rules which raise presumptions of law or determine the burden of proof.

2. A contract or an act intended to have legal effect may be proved by any mode of proof recognised by the law of the forum or by any of the laws referred to in Article 9 under which that contract or act is formally valid, provided that such mode of proof can be administered by the forum.

ARTICLE 15

Exclusion of renvoi

The application of the law of any country specified by this Convention means the application of the rules of law in force in that country other than its rules of private international law.

ARTICLE 16

"Ordre public"

The application of a rule of the law of any country specified by this Convention may be refused only if such application is manifestly incompatible with the public policy ("ordre public") of the forum.

ARTICLE 17

No retrospective effect

This Convention shall apply in a Contracting State to contracts made after the date on which this Convention has entered into force with respect to that State.

ARTICLE 18

Uniform interpretation

In the interpretation and application of the preceding uniform rules, regard shall be had to their international character and to the desirability of achieving uniformity in their interpretation and application.

ARTICLE 19

States with more than one legal system

1. Where a State comprises several territorial units each of which has its own rules of law in respect of contractual obligations, each territorial unit shall be considered as a country for the purposes of identifying the law applicable under this Convention.

2. A State within which different territorial units have their own rules of law in respect of contractual obligations shall not be bound to apply this Convention to conflicts solely between the laws of such units.

ARTICLE 20

Precedence of Community Law

This Convention shall not affect the application of provisions which, in relation to particular matters, lay down choice of law rules relating to contractual obligations and which are or will be contained in acts of the institutions of the European Communities or in national laws harmonised in implementation of such acts.

ARTICLE 21

Relationship with other conventions

This Convention shall not prejudice the application of international conventions to which a Contracting State is, or becomes, a party.

ARTICLE 22

Reservations

1. Any Contracting State may, at the time of signature, ratification, acceptance or approval, reserve the right not to apply:

    (a) the provisions of Article 7(1);
    (b) the provisions of Article 10(1)(e).

2. . . .

3. Any Contracting State may at any time withdraw a reservation which it has made; the reservation shall cease to have effect on the first day of the third calendar month after notification of the withdrawal.

TITLE III

FINAL PROVISIONS

ARTICLE 23

1. If, after the date on which this Convention has entered into force for a Contracting State, that State wishes to adopt any new choice of law rule in regard to any particular category of contract within the scope of this Convention, it shall communicate its intention to the other signatory States through the Secretary-General of the Council of the European Communities.

2. Any signatory State may, within six months from the date of the communication made to the Secretary-General, request him to arrange consultations between signatory States in order to reach agreement.

3. If no signatory State has requested consultations within this period or if within two years following the communication made to the Secretary-General no agreement is reached in the course of consultations, the Contracting State concerned may amend its law in the manner indicated. The measures taken by that State shall be brought to the knowledge of the other signatory States through the Secretary-General of the Council of the European Communities.

ARTICLE 24

1. If, after the date on which this Convention has entered into force with respect to a Contracting State, that State wishes to become a party to a multilateral convention whose principal aim or one of whose principal aims is to lay down rules of private international law concerning any of the matters governed by this Convention, the procedure set out in Article 23 shall apply. However, the period of two years, referred to in paragraph 3 of that Article, shall be reduced to one year.

2. The procedure referred to in the preceding paragraph need not be followed if a Contracting State or one of the European Communities is already a party to the multilateral convention, or if its

object is to revise a convention to which the State concerned is already a party, or if it is a convention concluded within the framework of the Treaties establishing the European Communities.

ARTICLE 25

If a Contracting State considers that the unification achieved by this Convention is prejudiced by the conclusion of agreements not covered by Article 24(1), that State may request the Secretary-General of the Council of the European Communities to arrange consultations between the signatory States of this Convention.

ARTICLE 26

Any Contracting State may request the revision of this Convention. In this event a revision conference shall be convened by the President of the Council of the European Communities.

ARTICLE 27

ARTICLE 28

1. This Convention shall be open from 19 June 1980 for signature by the States party to the Treaty establishing the European Economic Community.

2. This Convention shall be subject to ratification, acceptance or approval by the signatory States. The instruments of ratification, acceptance or approval shall be deposited with the Secretary-General of the Council of the European Communities.

ARTICLE 29

1. This Convention shall enter into force on the first day of the third month following the deposit of the seventh instrument of ratification, acceptance or approval.

2. This Convention shall enter into force for each signatory State ratifying, accepting or approving at a later date on the first day of the third month following the deposit of its instrument of ratification, acceptance or approval.

ARTICLE 30

1. This Convention shall remain in force for 10 years from the date of its entry into force in accordance with Article 29(1), even for States for which it enters into force at a later date.

2. If there has been no denunciation it shall be renewed tacitly every five years.

3. A Contracting State which wishes to denounce shall, not less than six months before the expiration of the period of 10 or five years, as the case may be, give notice to the Secretary-General of the Council of the European Communities. . . .

4. The denunciation shall have effect only in relation to the State which has notified it. The Convention will remain in force as between all other Contracting States.

ARTICLE 31

The Secretary-General of the Council of the European Communities shall notify the States party to the Treaty establishing the European Economic Community of:

    (a) the signatures;
    (b) the deposit of each instrument of ratification, acceptance or approval;
    (c) the date of entry into force of this Convention;
    [(d)communications made in pursuance of Articles 23, 24, 25, 26 and 30;]
    (e) the reservations and withdrawals of reservations referred to in Article 22.

ARTICLE 32

The Protocol annexed to this Convention shall form an integral part thereof.

ARTICLE 33

This Convention, drawn up in a single original in the Danish, Dutch, English, French, German, Irish and Italian languages, these texts being equally authentic, shall be deposited in the archives of the Secretariat of the Council of the European Communities. The Secretary-General shall transmit a certified copy thereof to the Government of each signatory State.

PROTOCOL

The High Contracting Parties have agreed upon the following provision which shall be annexed to the Convention:

Notwithstanding the provisions of the Convention, Denmark may retain the rules contained in Søloven (Statute on Maritime Law) paragraph 169 concerning the applicable law in matters relating to carriage of goods by sea and may revise these rules without following the procedure prescribed in Article 23 of the Convention.   **[350]**

NOTES
  Commencement: 1 April 1991 (SI 1991/707).
  Articles 22.2, 27, and the second sentence in Article 30.3 repealed and Article 31(d) substituted by the Contracts (Applicable Law) Act 1990 (Amendment) Order 1994, SI 1994/1900, arts 7, 8, with effect from 1 September 1994, in accordance with art 1 thereof.

SCHEDULE 2

Section 2

THE LUXEMBOURG CONVENTION

The High Contracting Parties to the Treaty establishing the European Economic Community,

Considering that the Hellenic Republic, in becoming a Member of the Community, undertook to accede to the Convention on the law applicable to contractual obligations, opened for signature in Rome on 19 June 1980,

Have decided to conclude this Convention, and to this end have designated as their plenipotentiaries:

(Designation of plenipotentiaries)

Who, meeting within the Council, having exchanged their full powers, found in good and due form,

Have agreed as follows:

ARTICLE 1

The Hellenic Republic hereby accedes to the Convention on the law applicable to contractual obligations, opened for signature in Rome on 19 June 1980.

ARTICLE 2

The Secretary-General of the Council of the European Communities shall transmit a certified copy of the Convention on the law applicable to contractual obligations in the Danish, Dutch, English, French, German, Irish and Italian languages to the Government of the Hellenic Republic.

The text of the Convention on the law applicable to contractual obligations in the Greek language is annexed hereto. The text in the Greek language shall be authentic under the same conditions as the other texts of the Convention on the law applicable to contractual obligations.

ARTICLE 3

This Convention shall be ratified by the Signatory States. The instruments of ratification shall be deposited with the Secretary-General of the Council of the European Communities.

ARTICLE 4

This Convention shall enter into force, as between the States which have ratified it, on the first day of the third month following the deposit of the last instrument of ratification by the Hellenic

Republic and seven States which have ratified the Convention on the law applicable to contractual obligations.

This Convention shall enter into force for each Contracting State which subsequently ratifies it on the first day of the third month following the deposit of its instrument of ratification.

ARTICLE 5

The Secretary-General of the Council of the European Communities shall notify the Signatory States of:

    (a) the deposit of each instrument of ratification;

    (b) the dates of entry into force of this Convention for the Contracting States.

ARTICLE 6

This Convention, drawn up in a single original in the Danish, Dutch, English, French, German, Greek, Irish and Italian languages, all eight texts being equally authentic, shall be deposited in the archives of the General Secretariat of the Council of the European Communities. The Secretary-General shall transmit a certified copy to the Government of each Signatory State.　　　**[351]**

NOTE
    Commencement: 1 April 1991 (SI 1991/707).

SCHEDULE 3

Section 2

THE BRUSSELS PROTOCOL

    The High Contracting Parties to the Treaty establishing the European Economic Community,

    Having regard to the Joint Declaration annexed to the Convention on the law applicable to contractual obligations, opened for signature in Rome on 19 June 1980,

    Have decided to conclude a Protocol conferring jurisdiction on the Court of Justice of the European Communities to interpret that Convention, and to this end have designated as their Plenipotentiaries:

    (Designation of plenipotentiaries)

    Who, meeting within the Council of the European Communities, having exchanged their full powers, found in good and due form,

    Have agreed as follows:

ARTICLE 1

The Court of Justice of the European Communities shall have jurisdiction to give rulings on the interpretation of—

    (a) the Convention on the law applicable to contractual obligations, opened for signature in Rome on 19 June 1980, hereinafter referred to as "the Rome Convention";

    (b) the Convention on accession to the Rome Convention by the States which have become Members of the European Communities since the date on which it was opened for signature;

    (c) this Protocol.

ARTICLE 2

Any of the courts referred to below may request the Court of Justice to give a preliminary ruling on a question raised in a case pending before it and concerning interpretation of the provisions contained in the instruments referred to in Article 1 if that court considers that a decision on the question is necessary to enable it to give judgment:

    (a) —in Belgium:

        la Cour de cassation (het Hof van Cassatie) and le Conseil d'Etat (de Raad van State),

—in Denmark:
    Højesteret,
—in the Federal Republic of Germany:
    die obersten Gerichtschöfe des Bundes,
—in Greece:
    τα ανώτατα Αικαστήρια,
—in Spain:
    el Tribunal Supremo,
—in France:
    la Cour de cassation and le Conseil d'Etat,
—in Ireland:
    the Supreme Court,
—in Italy:
    la Corte suprema di cassazione and il Consiglio di Stato,
—in Luxembourg:
    la Cour Supérieure de Justice, when sitting as Cour de cassation,
—in the Netherlands:
    de Hoge Raad,
—in Portugal:
    o Supremo Tribunal de Justiça and o Supremo Tribunal Administrativo,
—in the United Kingdom:
    the House of Lords and other courts from which no further appeal is possible;
  (b) the courts of the Contracting States when acting as appeal courts.

ARTICLE 3

1. The competent authority of a Contracting State may request the Court of Justice to give a ruling on a question of interpretation of the provisions contained in the instruments referred to in Article 1 if judgments given by courts of that State conflict with the interpretation given either by the Court of Justice or in a judgment of one of the courts of another Contracting State referred to in Article 2. The provisions of this paragraph shall apply only to judgments which have become *res judicata*.

2. The interpretation given by the Court of Justice in response to such a request shall not affect the judgments which gave rise to the request for interpretation.

3. The Procurators-General of the Supreme Courts of Appeal of the Contracting States, or any other authority designated by a Contracting State, shall be entitled to request the Court of Justice for a ruling on interpretation in accordance with paragraph 1.

4. The Registrar of the Court of Justice shall give notice of the request to the Contracting States, to the Commission and to the Council of the European Communities; they shall then be entitled within two months of the notification to submit statements of case or written observations to the Court.

5. No fees shall be levied or any costs or expenses awarded in respect of the proceedings provided for in this Article.

ARTICLE 4

1. Except where this Protocol otherwise provides, the provisions of the Treaty establishing the European Economic Community and those of the Protocol on the Statute of the Court of Justice annexed thereto, which are applicable when the Court is requested to give a preliminary ruling, shall also apply to any proceedings for the interpretation of the instruments referred to in Article 1.

2. The Rules of Procedure of the Court of Justice shall, if necessary, be adjusted and supplemented in accordance with Article 188 of the Treaty establishing the European Economic Community.

ARTICLE 5

This Protocol shall be subject to ratification by the Signatory States. The instruments of ratification shall be deposited with the Secretary-General of the Council of the European Communities.

ARTICLE 6

1. To enter into force, this Protocol must be ratified by seven States in respect of which the Rome Convention is in force. This Protocol shall enter into force on the first day of the third month

following the deposit of the instrument of ratification by the last such State to take this step. If, however, the Second Protocol conferring on the Court of Justice of the European Communities certain powers to interpret the Convention on the law applicable to contractual obligations, opened for signature in Rome on 19 June 1980, concluded in Brussels on 19 December 1988, enters into force on a later date, this Protocol shall enter into force on the date of entry into force of the Second Protocol.

2. Any ratification subsequent to the entry into force of this Protocol shall take effect on the first day of the third month following the deposit of the instrument of ratification provided that the ratification, acceptance or approval of the Rome Convention by the State in question has become effective.

ARTICLE 7

The Secretary-General of the Council of the European Communities shall notify the Signatory States of:

    (a) the deposit of each instrument of ratification;
    (b) the date of entry into force of this Protocol;
    (c) any designation communicated pursuant to Article 3(3);
    (d) any communication made pursuant to Article 8.

ARTICLE 8

The Contracting States shall communicate to the Secretary-General of the Council of the European Communities the texts of any provisions of their laws which necessitate an amendment to the list of courts in Article 2(a).

ARTICLE 9

This Protocol shall have effect for as long as the Rome Convention remains in force under the conditions laid down in Article 30 of that Convention.

ARTICLE 10

Any Contracting State may request the revision of this Protocol. In this event, a revision conference shall be convened by the President of the Council of the European Communities.

ARTICLE 11

This Protocol, drawn up in a single original in the Danish, Dutch, English, French, German, Greek, Irish, Italian, Portuguese and Spanish languages, all 10 texts being equally authentic, shall be deposited in the archives of the General Secretariat of the Council of the European Communities. The Secretary-General shall transmit a certified copy to the Government of each Signatory State.   **[352]**

NOTE
Commencement: 1 April 1991 (SI 1991/707).

Section 2

[SCHEDULE 3A

THE FUNCHAL CONVENTION

The High Contracting Parties to the Treaty establishing the European Economic Community.

Considering that the Kingdom of Spain and the Portuguese Republic, in becoming Members of the Community, undertook to accede to the Convention on the law applicable to contractual obligations, opened for signature in Rome on 19th June 1980.

Have decided to conclude this Convention, and to this end have designated as their plenipotentiaries:
(Designation of plenipotentiaries).

Who, meeting within the Council, having exchanged their full powers, found in good and due form. Have agreed as follows:

ARTICLE 1

The Kingdom of Spain and the Portuguese Republic hereby accede to the Convention on the law applicable to contractual obligations, opened for signature in Rome on 19th June 1980.

ARTICLE 2

The Convention on the law applicable to contractual obligations is hereby amended as follows:

    (1) Article 22(2), Article 27 and the second sentence of Article 30(3) shall be deleted;
    (2) The reference to Article 27 in Article 31(d) shall be deleted.

ARTICLE 3

The Secretary-General of the Council of the European Communities shall transmit a certified copy of the Convention on the law applicable to contractual obligations in the Danish, Dutch, English, French, German, Greek, Irish and Italian languages to the Governments of the Kingdom of Spain and the Portuguese Republic.

ARTICLE 4

This Convention shall be ratified by the Signatory States. The instruments of ratification shall be deposited with the Secretary-General of the Council of the European Communities.

ARTICLE 5

This Convention shall enter into force, as between the States which have ratified it, on the first day of the third month following deposit of the last instrument of ratification by the Kingdom of Spain or the Portuguese Republic and by one State which has ratified the Convention on the law applicable to contractual obligations.

This Convention shall enter into force for each Contracting State which subsequently ratifies it on the first day of the third month following that of deposit of its instrument of ratification.

ARTICLE 6

The Secretary-General of the Council of the European Communities shall notify the Signatory States of:

    (a) the deposit of each instrument of ratification;
    (b) the dates of entry into force of this Convention for the Contracting States.

ARTICLE 7

This Convention, drawn up in a single original in the Danish, Dutch, English, French, German, Greek, Irish, Italian, Portuguese and Spanish languages, all ten texts being equally authentic, shall be deposited in the archives of the General Secretariat of the Council of the European Communities. The Secretary-General shall transmit a certified copy to the Government of each Signatory State.]

[352A]

NOTES
    Commencement: 1 September 1994 (SI 1994/1900).
    Schedule inserted by the Contracts (Applicable Law) Act 1990 (Amendment) Order 1994, SI 1994/1900, art 9, Schedule, with effect from 1 September 1994 in accordance with art 1 thereof.

(Sch 4 sets out amendments of certain enactments (consequential amendments).)

AGENCY

FACTORS ACT 1889
(52 & 53 Vict c 45)

ARRANGEMENT OF SECTIONS

Preliminary

An Act to amend and consolidate the Factors Acts   [26 August 1889]

Preliminary

1 Definitions

For the purposes of this Act—

(1) The expression "mercantile agent" shall mean a mercantile agent having in the customary course of his business as such agent authority either to sell goods, or to consign goods for the purpose of sale, or to buy goods, or to raise money on the security of goods:

(2) A person shall be deemed to be in possession of goods or of the documents of title to goods, where the goods or documents are in his actual custody or are held by any other person subject to his control or for him or on his behalf:

(3) The expression "goods" shall include wares and merchandise:

(4) The expression "document of title" shall include any bill of lading, dock warrant, warehouse-keeper's certificate, and warrant or order for the delivery of goods, and any other document used in the ordinary course of business as proof of the possession or control of goods, or authorising or purporting to authorise, either by endorsement or by delivery, the possessor of the document to transfer or receive goods thereby represented:

(5) The expression "pledge" shall include any contract pledging, or giving a lien or security on, goods, whether in consideration of an

original advance or of any further or continuing advance or of any pecuniary liability:

(6) The expression "person" shall include any body of persons corporate or unincorporate.   **[353]**

Dispositions by mercantile agents

2 Powers of mercantile agent with respect to disposition of goods

(1) Where a mercantile agent is, with the consent of the owner, in possession of goods or of the documents of title to goods, any sale, pledge, or other disposition of the goods, made by him when acting in the ordinary course of business of a mercantile agent, shall, subject to the provisions of this Act, be as valid as if he were expressly authorised by the owner of the goods to make the same; provided that the person taking under the disposition acts in good faith, and has not at the time of the disposition notice that the person making the disposition has not authority to make the same.

(2) Where a mercantile agent has, with the consent of the owner, been in possession of goods or of the documents of title to goods, any sale, pledge, or other disposition, which would have been valid if the consent had continued, shall be valid notwithstanding the determination of the consent: provided that the person taking under the disposition has not at the time thereof notice that the consent has been determined.

(3) Where a mercantile agent has obtained possession of any documents of title to goods by reason of his being or having been, with the consent of the owner, in possession of the goods represented thereby, or of any other documents of title to the goods, his possession of the first-mentioned documents shall, for the purposes of this Act, be deemed to be with the consent of the owner.

(4) For the purposes of this Act the consent of the owner shall be presumed in the absence of evidence to the contrary.   **[354]**

3 Effect of pledges of documents of title

A pledge of the documents of title to goods shall be deemed to be a pledge of the goods.   **[355]**

4 Pledge for antecedent debt

Where a mercantile agent pledges goods as security for a debt or liability due from the pledgor to the pledgee before the time of the pledge, the pledgee shall acquire no further right to the goods than could have been enforced by the pledgor at the time of the pledge.   **[356]**

5 Rights acquired by exchange of goods or documents

The consideration necessary for the validity of a sale, pledge, or other disposition, of goods, in pursuance of this Act, may be either a payment in cash, or the delivery or transfer of other goods, or of a document of title to goods, or of a negotiable security, or any other valuable consideration; but where goods are pledged by a mercantile agent in consideration of the delivery or transfer of other goods, or of a document of title to goods, or of a negotiable security, the pledgee shall acquire no right or interest in the goods so pledged in excess of the value of the goods, documents, or security when so delivered or transferred in exchange.   **[357]**

6 Agreements through clerks, etc

For the purposes of this Act an agreement made with a mercantile agent through a clerk or other person authorised in the ordinary course of business to make contracts of sale or pledge on his behalf shall be deemed to be an agreement with the agent.   **[358]**

7 Provisions as to consignors and consignees

(1) Where the owner of goods has given possession of the goods to another person for the purpose of consignment or sale, or has shipped the goods in the name of another person, and the consignee of the goods has not had notice that such person is not the owner of the goods, the consignee shall, in respect of advances made to or for the use of such person, have the same lien on the goods as if such person were the owner of the goods, and may transfer any such lien to another person.

(2) Nothing in this section shall limit or effect the validity of any sale, pledge, or disposition, by a mercantile agent.   **[359]**

Dispositions by sellers and buyers of goods

8 Disposition by seller remaining in possession

Where a person, having sold goods, continues, or is, in possession of the goods or of the documents of title to the goods, the delivery or transfer by that person, or by a mercantile agent acting for him, of the goods or documents of title under any sale, pledge, or other disposition thereof, or under any agreement for sale, pledge, or other disposition thereof, to any person receiving the same in good faith and without notice of the previous sale, shall have the same effect as if the person making the delivery or transfer were expressly authorised by the owner of the goods to make the same.   **[360]**

9 Disposition by buyer obtaining possession

Where a person, having bought or agreed to buy goods, obtains with the consent of the seller possession of the goods or the documents of title to the goods, the delivery or transfer, by that person or by a mercantile agent acting for him, of the goods or documents of title, under any sale, pledge, or other disposition thereof, or under any agreement for sale, pledge, or other disposition thereof, to any person receiving the same in good faith and without notice of any lien or other right of the original seller in respect of the goods, shall have the same effect as if the person making the delivery or transfer were a mercantile agent in possession of the goods or documents of title with the consent of the owner.

[For the purposes of this section—

- (i) the buyer under a conditional sale agreement shall be deemed not to be a person who has bought or agreed to buy goods, and
- (ii) "conditional sale agreement" means an agreement for the sale of goods which is a consumer credit agreement within the meaning of the Consumer Credit Act 1974 under which the purchase price or part of it is payable by instalments, and the property in the goods is to remain in the seller (notwithstanding that the buyer is to be in possession of the goods) until such conditions as to the payment of instalments or otherwise as may be specified in the agreement are fulfilled.]   **[361]**

10 Effect of transfer of documents on vendor's lien or right of stoppage in transitu

Where a document of title to goods has been lawfully transferred to a person as a buyer or owner of the goods, and that person transfers the document to a person who takes the document in good faith and for valuable consideration, the last-mentioned transfer shall have the same effect for defeating any vendor's lien or right of stoppage in transitu as the transfer of a bill of lading has for defeating the right of stoppage in transitu.   **[362]**

Supplemental

11 Mode of transferring documents

For the purposes of this Act, the transfer of a document may be by endorsement, or, where the document is by custom or by its express terms transferable by delivery, or makes the goods deliverable to the bearer, then by delivery.
                                                                                [363]

12 Saving for rights of true owner

(1) Nothing in this Act shall authorise an agent to exceed or depart from his authority as between himself and his principal, or exempt him from any liability, civil or criminal, for so doing.

(2) Nothing in this Act shall prevent the owner of goods from recovering the goods from an agent or his trustee in bankruptcy at any time before the sale or pledge thereof, or shall prevent the owner of goods pledged by an agent from having the right to redeem the goods at any time before the sale thereof, on satisfying the claim for which the goods were pledged, and paying to the agent, if by him required, any money in respect of which the agent would by law be entitled to retain the goods or the documents of title thereto, or any of them, by way of lien as against the owner, or from recovering from any person with whom the goods have been pledged any balance of money remaining in his hands as the produce of the sale of the goods after deducting the amount of his lien.

(3) Nothing in this Act shall prevent the owner of goods sold by an agent from recovering from the buyer the price agreed to be paid for the same, or any part of that price, subject to any right of set off on the part of the buyer against the agent.   **[364]**

13 Saving for common law powers of agent

The provisions of this Act shall be construed in amplification and not in derogation of the powers exercisable by an agent independently of this Act.
                                                                                [365]

14, 15 (*Repealed by the Statute Law Revision Act 1908.*)

16 Extent of Act

This Act shall not extend to Scotland.   **[366]**

17 Short title

This Act may be cited as the Factors Act 1889.   **[367]**

(*Schedule repealed by virtue of the Statute Law Revision Act 1908.*)

POWERS OF ATTORNEY ACT 1971
(1971 c 27)
ARRANGEMENT OF SECTIONS

An Act to make new provision in relation to powers of attorney and the delegation by trustees of their trusts, powers and discretions   [12 May 1971]

1 Execution of powers of attorney

(1) An instrument creating a power of attorney shall be [executed as a deed by] the donor of the power.

(2) . . .

(3) This section is without prejudice to any requirement in, or having effect under, any other Act as to the witnessing of instruments creating powers of attorney and does not affect the rules relating to the execution of instruments by bodies corporate.   **[368]**

NOTE
Sub-ss (1), (2): words in square brackets substituted, and sub-s (2) repealed, by the Law of Property (Miscellaneous Provisions) Act 1989, ss 1(8), 4, Sch 1, para 6, Sch 2.

2 (*Repealed by the Supreme Court Act 1981, s 152(4), Sch 7.*)

3 Proof of instruments creating powers of attorney

(1) The contents of an instrument creating a power of attorney may be proved by means of a copy which—

   (a) is a reproduction of the original made with a photographic or other device for reproducing documents in facsimile; and
   (b) contains the following certificate or certificates signed by the donor of the power or by a solicitor [duly certificated notary public] or stockbroker, that is to say—

      (i) a certificate at the end to the effect that the copy is a true and complete copy of the original; and

      (ii) if the original consists of two or more pages, a certificate at the end of each page of the copy to the effect that it is a true and complete copy of the corresponding page of the original.

(2) Where a copy of an instrument creating a power of attorney has been made which complies with subsection (1) of this section, the contents of the instrument may also be proved by means of a copy of that copy if the further copy itself complies with that subsection, taking references in it to the original as references to the copy from which the further copy is made.

(3) In this section ["duly certified notary public" has the same meaning as it has in the Solicitors Act 1974 by virtue of section 87(1) of that Act and] "stockbroker" means a member of any stock exchange within the meaning of the Stock Transfer Act 1963 or the Stock Transfer Act (Northern Ireland) 1963.

(4) This section is without prejudice to section 4 of the Evidence and Powers of Attorney Act 1940 (proof of deposited instruments by office copy) and to any other method of proof authorised by law.

(5) For the avoidance of doubt, in relation to an instrument made in Scotland the references to a power of attorney in this section and in section 4 of the Evidence and Powers of Attorney Act 1940 include references to a factory and commission.   **[369]**

NOTES

Sub-ss (1), (3): words in square brackets inserted by the Courts and Legal Services Act 1990, s 125(2), Sch 17, para 4.

Solicitors' incorporated practices: the provisions of sub-s (1)(b) of this section are applied, with modifications, in relation to a "recognised body" under the Administration of Justice Act 1985, s 9, by the Solicitors' Incorporated Practices Order 1991, SI 1991/2684, arts 2–5, Sch 1.

4 Powers of attorney given as security

(1) Where a power of attorney is expressed to be irrevocable and is given to secure—

    (a) a proprietary interest of the donee of the power; or
    (b) the performance of an obligation owed to the donee,

then, so long as the donee has that interest or the obligation remains undischarged, the power shall not be revoked—

    (i) by the donor without the consent of the donee; or
    (ii) by the death, incapacity or bankruptcy of the donor or, if the donor is a body corporate, by its winding up or dissolution.

(2) A power of attorney given to secure a proprietary interest may be given to the person entitled to the interest and persons deriving title under him to that interest, and those persons shall be duly constituted donees of the power for all purposes of the power but without prejudice to any right to appoint substitutes given by the power.

(3) This section applies to powers of attorney whenever created.   **[370]**

5 Protection of donee and third persons where power of attorney is revoked

(1) A donee of a power of attorney who acts in pursuance of the power at a time when it has been revoked shall not, by reason of the revocation, incur any liability (either to the donor or to any other person) if at that time he did not know that the power had been revoked.

(2) Where a power of attorney has been revoked and a person, without knowledge of the revocation, deals with the donee of the power, the transaction between them shall, in favour of that person, be as valid as if the power had then been in existence.

(3) Where the power is expressed in the instrument creating it to be irrevocable and to be given by way of security then, unless the person dealing with the donee knows that it was not in fact given by way of security, he shall be entitled to assume that the power is incapable of revocation except by the donor acting with the consent of the donee and shall accordingly be treated for the purposes of subsection (2) of this section as having knowledge of the revocation only if he knows that it has been revoked in that manner.

(4) Where the interest of a purchaser depends on whether a transaction between the donee of a power of attorney and another person was valid by virtue of subsection (2) of this section, it shall be conclusively presumed in favour of the purchaser that that person did not at the material time know of the revocation of the power if—

   (a) the transaction between that person and the donee was completed within twelve months of the date on which the power came into operation; or
   (b) that person makes a statutory declaration, before or within three months after the completion of the purchase, that he did not at the material time know of the revocation of the power.

(5) Without prejudice to subsection (3) of this section, for the purposes of this section knowledge of the revocation of a power of attorney includes knowledge of the occurrence of any event (such as the death of the donor) which has the effect of revoking the power.

(6) In this section "purchaser" and "purchase" have the meanings specified in section 205(1) of the Law of Property Act 1925.

(7) This section applies whenever the power of attorney was created but only to acts and transactions after the commencement of this Act.   **[371]**

6 Additional protection for transferees under stock exchange transactions

(1) Without prejudice to section 5 of this Act, where—

   (a) the donee of a power of attorney executes, as transferor, an instrument transferring registered securities; and
   (b) the instrument is executed for the purposes of a stock exchange transaction,

it shall be conclusively presumed in favour of the transferee that the power had not been revoked at the date of the instrument if a statutory declaration to that effect is made by the donee of the power on or within three months after that date.

(2) In this section "registered securities" and "stock exchange transaction" have the same meanings as in the Stock Transfer Act 1963.   **[372]**

7 Execution of instruments etc by donee of power of attorney

[(1) If the donee of a power of attorney is an individual, he may, if he thinks fit—

   (a) execute any instrument with his own signature, and]

(b) do any other thing in his own name,

by the authority of the donor of the power; and any document executed or thing done in that manner shall be as effective as if executed or done by the donee with the signature . . ., or, as the case may be, in the name, of the donor of the power.

(2) For the avoidance of doubt it is hereby declared that an instrument to which subsection (3) . . . of section 74 of the Law of Property Act 1925 applies may be executed either as provided in [that subsection] or as provided in this section.

(3) This section is without prejudice to any statutory direction requiring an instrument to be executed in the name of an estate owner within the meaning of the said Act of 1925.

(4) This section applies whenever the power of attorney was created. [373]

NOTE

Sub-ss (1), (2): words in square brackets substituted, and words omitted repealed, by the Law of Property (Miscellaneous Provisions) Act 1989, ss 1(8), 4, Sch 1, para 7, Sch 2.

8, 9 (*S 8 repeals the Law of Property Act 1925, s 129; s 9 amends the Trustee Act 1925, s 25.*)

10 Effect of general power of attorney in specified form

(1) Subject to subsection (2) of this section, a general power of attorney in the form set out in Schedule 1 to this Act, or in a form to the like effect but expressed to be made under this Act, shall operate to confer—

(a) on the donee of the power; or
(b) if there is more than one donee, on the donees acting jointly or acting jointly or severally, as the case may be,

authority to do on behalf of the donor anything which he can lawfully do by an attorney.

(2) This section does not apply to functions which the donor has as a trustee or personal representative or as a tenant for life or statutory owner within the meaning of the Settled Land Act 1925.   **[374]**

11 Short title, repeals, consequential amendments, commencement and extent

(1) This Act may be cited as the Powers of Attorney Act 1971.

(2), (3) . . .

(4) This Act shall come into force on 1st October 1971.

(5) Section 3 of this Act extends to Scotland and Northern Ireland but, save as aforesaid, this Act extends to England and Wales only.   **[375]**

NOTES

Sub-s (2): introduces Sch 2 to this Act (repeals).

Sub-s (3): in part amends the Law of Property Act 1925, s 125(2); remainder repealed by the Supreme Court Act 1981, s 152(4), Sch 7.

SCHEDULE 1
Section 10

FORM OF GENERAL POWER OF ATTORNEY FOR PURPOSES OF SECTION 10

THIS GENERAL POWER OF ATTORNEY is made this   day of
      19 by AB of
 I appoint CD of
[*or* CD of   and
EF of   jointly *or* jointly
and severally] to be my attorney[s] in accordance with section 10 of the Powers of Attorney Act 1971.

IN WITNESS etc.,   **[376]**

(Sch 2 specifies certain enactments repealed by s 11(2).)

MORTGAGES AND CHARGES

AGRICULTURAL CREDITS ACT 1928
(18 & 19 Geo 5 c 43)

ARRANGEMENT OF SECTIONS

PART II
AGRICULTURAL SHORT-TERM CREDITS

PART III
GENERAL

An Act to secure, by means of the formation of a company and the assistance
thereof out of public funds, the making of loans for agricultural purposes on
favourable terms, and to facilitate the borrowing of money on the security of
farming stock and other agricultural assets, and for purposes connected
therewith   [3 August 1928]

1–4 (*Ss 1, 2, 4, repealed by the Agriculture and Forestry (Financial Provisions)*
Act 1991, s 1(1), (2), Schedule, Pt I; s 3 repealed by the Trustee Investments Act
1961, s 16(2), Sch 5.)

PART II

AGRICULTURAL SHORT-TERM CREDITS

5 Agricultural charges on farming stock and assets

(1) It shall be lawful for a farmer as defined by this Act by instrument in writing to create in favour of a bank as so defined a charge (hereinafter referred to as an agricultural charge) on all or any of the farming stock and other agricultural assets belonging to him as security for sums advanced or to be advanced to him or paid or to be paid on his behalf under any guarantee by the bank and interest, commission and charges thereon.

(2) An agricultural charge may be either a fixed charge, or a floating charge, or both a fixed and a floating charge.

(3) The property affected by a fixed charge shall be such property forming part of the farming stock and other agricultural assets belonging to the farmer at the date of the charge as may be specified in the charge, but may include—

(a) in the case of live stock, any progeny thereof which may be born after the date of the charge; and

(b) in the case of agricultural plant, any plant which may whilst the charge is in force be substituted for the plant specified in the charge.

(4) The property affected by a floating charge shall be the farming stock and other agricultural assets from time to time belonging to the farmer, or such part thereof as is mentioned in the charge.

(5) The principal sum secured by an agricultural charge may be either a specified amount, or a fluctuating amount advanced on current account not exceeding at any one time such amount (if any) as may be specified in the charge, and in the latter case the charge shall not be deemed to be redeemed by reason only of the current account having ceased to be in debit.

(6) An agricultural charge may be in such form and made upon such conditions as the parties thereto may agree, and sureties may be made parties thereto.

(7) For the purposes of this Part of this Act—

"Farmer" means any person (not being an incorporated company or society) who, as tenant or owner of an agricultural holding, cultivates the holding for profit; and "agriculture" and "cultivation" shall be deemed to include horticulture, and the use of land for any purpose of husbandry, inclusive of the keeping or breeding of live stock, poultry, or bees, and the growth of fruit, vegetables, and the like;

["Bank" means the Bank of England, [an institution authorised under the Banking Act 1987], . . . or the Post Office, in the exercise of its powers to provide banking services];

"Farming stock" means crops or horticultural produce, whether growing or severed from the land, and after severance whether subjected to any treatment or process of manufacture or not; live stock, including poultry and bees, and the produce and progeny thereof; any other agricultural or horticultural produce whether subjected to any treatment or process of manufacture or not; seeds and manures; agricultural vehicles, machinery, and other plant; agricultural tenant's fixtures and other agricultural fixtures which a tenant is by law authorised to remove;

"Other agricultural assets" means a tenant's right to compensation under the [Agricultural Holdings Act 1986, except under section 60(2)(b) or 62] for improvements, damage by game, disturbance or otherwise [a tenant's right to compensation under section 16 of the Agricultural Tenancies Act 1995,] and any other tenant right. [377]

NOTES

Sub-s (7): definition "Bank" substituted, with savings, by the Banking Act 1979, s 51(1), Sch 6, paras 2, 14; words in square brackets in that definition substituted, with savings, by the Banking Act 1987, s 108(1), Sch 6, para 2; words omitted in that definition repealed, subject to transitional provisions, by the Trustee Savings Banks Act 1985, ss 4(3), (5), 7(3), Sch 4; first words in square brackets in definition "Other agricultural assets" substituted, subject to transitional provisions and savings, by the Agricultural Holdings Act 1986, ss 98–100, Schs 12, 13, Sch 14, para 16; second words in square brackets in that definition inserted by the Agricultural Tenancies Act 1995, s 40, Schedule, para 7.

Modifications: by virtue of the Banking Coordination (Second Council Directive) Regulations 1992, SI 1992/3218, reg 82(1), Sch 10, Pt I, para 3, sub-s (7) of this section has effect as if the reference to an institution authorised under the Banking Act included a reference to a European deposit-taker.

6 Effect of fixed charge

(1) A fixed charge shall, so long as the charge continues in force, confer on the bank the following rights and impose upon the bank the following obligations, that is to say:—

    (a) a right, upon the happening of any event specified in the charge as being an event authorising the seizure of property subject to the charge, to take possession of any property so subject;

    (b) where possession of any property has been so taken, a right, after an interval of five clear days or such less time as may be allowed by the charge, to sell the property either by auction or, if the charge so provides, by private treaty, and either for a lump sum payment or payment by instalments;

    (c) an obligation, in the event of such power of sale being exercised, to apply the proceeds of sale in or towards the discharge of the moneys and liabilities secured by the charge, and the cost of seizure and sale, and to pay the surplus (if any) of the proceeds to the farmer.

(2) A fixed charge shall, so long as the charge continues in force, impose on the farmer the following obligations:—

    (a) an obligation whenever he sells any of the property, or receives any money in respect of other agricultural assets comprised in the charge, forthwith to pay to the bank the amount of the proceeds of the sale or the money so received, except to such extent as the charge otherwise provides or the bank otherwise allows; the sums so paid to be applied, except so far as otherwise agreed, by the bank in or towards the discharge of moneys and liabilities secured by the charge;

    (b) an obligation in the event of the farmer receiving any money under any policy of insurance on any of the property comprised in the charge, or any money paid by way of compensation under the Diseases of Animals Acts 1894 to 1927 in respect of the destruction of any live stock comprised in the charge, or by way of compensation under the Destructive Insects and Pests Acts 1877 to 1927 in respect of the destruction of any crops comprised in the charge, forthwith to pay the amount of the sums so received to the bank, except to such extent as the charge otherwise provides or the bank otherwise allows; the sums so paid to be applied, except so far as otherwise agreed by the bank, in or towards the discharge of the moneys and liabilities secured by the charge.

(3) Subject to compliance with the obligations so imposed, a fixed charge shall not prevent the farmer selling any of the property subject to the charge, and neither the purchaser, nor, in the case of a sale by auction, the auctioneer, shall be concerned to see that such obligations are complied with notwithstanding that he may be aware of the existence of the charge.

(4) Where any proceeds of sale which in pursuance of such obligation as aforesaid ought to be paid to the bank are paid to some other person, nothing in this Act shall confer on the bank a right to recover such proceeds from that other person unless the bank proves that such other person knew that the proceeds were paid to him in breach of such obligation as aforesaid, but such other person shall not be deemed to have such knowledge by reason only that he has notice of the charge.   **[378]**

NOTES

Diseases of Animals Acts 1894 to 1927: see now the Animal Health Act 1981.
Destructive Insects and Pests Acts 1877 to 1927: see now the Plant Health Act 1967.

7 Effect of floating charge

(1) An agricultural charge creating a floating charge shall have the like effect as if the charge had been created by a duly registered debenture issued by a company:

Provided that—

(a) the charge shall become a fixed charge upon the property comprised in the charge as existing at the date of its becoming a fixed charge—

(i) upon a [bankruptcy order] being made against the farmer;
(ii) upon the death of the farmer;
(iii) upon the dissolution of partnership in the case where the property charged is partnership property;
(iv) upon notice in writing to that effect being given by the bank on the happening of any event which by virtue of the charge confers on the bank the right to give such a notice;

(b) the farmer, whilst the charge remains a floating charge, shall be subject to the like obligation as in the case of a fixed charge to pay over to the bank the amount received by him by way of proceeds of sale, in respect of other agricultural assets, under policies of insurance, or by way of compensation, and the last foregoing section shall apply accordingly: Provided that it shall not be necessary for a farmer to comply with such obligation if and so far as the amount so received is expended by him in the purchase of farming stock which on purchase becomes subject to the charge.   **[379]**

NOTES

Sub-s (1): words in square brackets in sub-s (1)(a)(i) substituted by the Insolvency Act 1985, s 235(1), Sch 8, para 6. For savings, see the Insolvency Act 1986, s 437, Sch 11, Pt II.
There is no sub-s (2) in the King's Printer's copy of this Act.

8 Supplemental provisions as to agricultural charges

(1) An agricultural charge shall have effect notwithstanding anything in the Bills of Sale Acts 1878 and 1882 and shall not be deemed to be a bill of sale within the meaning of those Acts.

(2) Agricultural charges shall in relation to one another have priority in accordance with the times at which they are respectively registered under this Part of this Act.

(3) Where an agricultural charge creating a floating charge has been made, an agricultural charge purporting to create a fixed charge on, or a bill of sale comprising any of the property comprised in the floating charge shall, as respects the property subject to the floating charge, be void so long as the floating charge remains in force.

(4) . . .

(5) Where a farmer who is adjudged bankrupt has created in favour of a bank an agricultural charge on any of the farming stock or other agricultural assets belonging to him, and the charge was created within three months of the date of the presentation of the bankruptcy petition and operated to secure any sum owing to the bank immediately prior to the giving of the charge, then, unless it is proved that the farmer immediately after the execution of the charge was solvent, the amount which but for this provision would have been secured by the charge shall be reduced by the amount of the sum so owing to the bank immediately prior to the giving of the charge, but without prejudice to the

bank's right to enforce any other security for that sum or to claim payment thereof as an unsecured debt.

(6) Where after the passing of this Act the farmer has mortgaged his interest in the land comprised in the holding, then, if growing crops are included in an agricultural charge, the rights of the bank under the charge in respect of the crops shall have priority to those of the mortgagee, whether in possession or not, and irrespective of the dates of the mortgage and charge.

(7) An agricultural charge shall be no protection in respect of property included in the charge which but for the charge would have been liable to distress for rent, taxes, or rates.

(8) An instrument creating an agricultural charge shall be exempt from stamp duty. **[380]**

NOTE
Sub-s (4): repealed by the Insolvency Act 1985, s 235(3), Sch 10, Pt III. For transitional provisions and savings, see the Insolvency Act 1986, s 437, Sch 11, Pt II.

9 Registration of agricultural charges

(1) Every agricultural charge shall be registered under this Act within seven clear days after the execution thereof, and, if not so registered, shall be void as against any person other than the farmer:

Provided that the High Court on proof that omission to register within such time as aforesaid was accidental or due to inadvertence may extend the time for registration on such terms as the Court thinks fit.

(2) The Land Registrar shall keep at the Land Registry a register of agricultural charges in such form and containing such particulars as may be prescribed.

(3) Registration of an agricultural charge shall be effected by sending by post to the Land Registrar at the Land Registry a memorandum of the instrument creating the charge and such particulars of the charge as may be prescribed, together with the prescribed fee; and the Land Registrar shall enter the particulars in the register and shall file the memorandum.

(4) The register kept and the memoranda filed under this section shall at all reasonable times be open to inspection by any person on payment (except where the inspection is made by or on behalf of a bank) of the prescribed fee, and any person inspecting the register or any such filed memorandum on payment (except as aforesaid) of the prescribed fee may make copies or extracts therefrom.

(5) Any person may on payment of the prescribed fee require to be furnished with a copy of any entry in the register or of any filed memorandum or any part thereof certified to be a true copy by the Land Registrar.

(6) Registration of an agricultural charge may be proved by the production of a certified copy of the entry in the register relating to the charge, and a copy of any entry purporting to be certified as a true copy by the Land Registrar shall in all legal proceedings be evidence of the matters stated therein without proof of the signature or authority of the person signing it.

[(7) The Schedule to this Act shall have effect in relation to official searches in the register of agricultural charges.]

(8) Registration of an agricultural charge under this section shall be deemed to constitute actual notice of the charge, and of the fact of such registration, to

all persons and for all purposes connected with the property comprised in the charge, as from the date of registration or other prescribed date, and so long as the registration continues in force:

Provided that, where an agricultural charge created in favour of a bank is expressly made for securing a current account or other further advances, the bank, in relation to the making of further advances under the charge, shall not be deemed to have notice of another agricultural charge by reason only that it is so registered if it was not so registered at the time when the first-mentioned charge was created or when the last search (if any) by or on behalf of the bank was made, whichever last happened.

(9) The Lord Chancellor may make regulations prescribing anything which under this section is to be prescribed, subject as respects fees to the approval of the Treasury, and generally as to the keeping of the register and the filing of memoranda, the removal of entries from the register on proof of discharge, and the rectification of the register. **[381]**

NOTES
Sub-s (7): substituted by the Land Charges Act 1972, s 18(1), Sch 3, para 7.
Regulations and order: the Agricultural Credits Regulations 1928, SR & O 1928/667; the Agricultural Credits Fees Order 1985, SI 1985/372.

10 Restriction on publication of agricultural charges

(1) It shall not be lawful to print for publication or publish any list of agricultural charges or of the names of farmers who have created agricultural charges.

(2) If any person acts in contravention of this section, he shall in respect of each offence be liable on summary conviction to a fine not exceeding [level 2 on the standard scale]:

Provided that no person other than a proprietor, editor, master printer, or publisher, shall be liable to be convicted under this section.

(3) No prosecution for an offence under this section shall be commenced without the consent of the Attorney-General.

(4) For the purpose of this section, "publication" means the issue of copies to the public, and "publish" has a corresponding meaning, and without prejudice to the generality of the foregoing definition the confidential notification by an association representative of a particular trade to its members trading or carrying on business in the district in which property subject to an agricultural charge is situate of the creation of the charge shall not be deemed to be publication for the purposes of this section. **[382]**

NOTE
Sub-s (2): words in square brackets substituted by virtue of the Criminal Law Act 1977, s 31(5), (6), and the Criminal Justice Act 1982, ss 37, 46.

11 Frauds by farmers

(1) If, with intent to defraud, a farmer who has created an agricultural charge—

    (a) fails to comply with the obligations imposed by this Act as to the payment over to the bank of any sums received by him by way of proceeds of sale, or in respect of other agricultural assets, or under a policy of insurance or by way of compensation; or

(b) removes or suffers to be removed from his holding any property subject to the charge;

he shall be guilty of a misdemeanour and liable on conviction on indictment to penal servitude for a term not exceeding three years.

(2) . . . **[383]**

NOTE

Sub-s (2): repealed by the Magistrates' Courts Act 1952, s 132, Sch 6.

12 (*Repealed by the Statute Law Revision Act 1950.*)

13 Rights of tenants

Any farmer being the tenant of an agricultural holding shall have the right to create an agricultural charge notwithstanding any provision in his contract of tenancy to the contrary. **[384]**

14 Provisions as to agricultural societies

(1) A debenture issued by a society registered under the Industrial and Provident Societies Acts 1893 to 1928, creating in favour of a bank a floating charge on property which is farming stock within the meaning of this Part of this Act, may be registered in like manner as an agricultural charge, and section nine of this Act shall apply to such a charge in like manner as it applies to an agricultural charge, and the charge if so registered shall as respects such property be valid notwithstanding anything in the Bills of Sale Acts 1878 and 1882, and shall not be deemed to be a bill of sale within the meaning of those Acts:

Provided that, where any such charge is so registered, notice thereof signed by the secretary of the society shall be sent to the central office established under the Friendly Societies Act 1896 and registered there.

(2) Any such debenture may create a floating charge on any farming stock the property in which is vested in the society. **[385]**

NOTES

Industrial and Provident Societies Acts 1893 to 1928: repealed and replaced by the Industrial and Provident Societies Act 1965.

Friendly Societies Act 1896: repealed and replaced by the Friendly Societies Act 1974; see now also the Friendly Societies Act 1992.

PART III
GENERAL

15 Short title, commencement and extent

(1) This Act may be cited as the Agricultural Credits Act 1928.

(2) . . .

(3) This Act shall not (except as otherwise expressly provided) extend to Scotland or Northern Ireland. **[386]**

NOTE

Sub-s (2): repealed by the Statute Law Revision Act 1950.

[SCHEDULE
OFFICIAL SEARCHES IN THE REGISTER OF AGRICULTURAL CHARGES

1. Where any person requires search to be made at the Land Registry for entries of agricultural charges, he may on payment of a prescribed fee lodge at the Land Registry a requisition in that behalf.

2. The reference to the Land Registry in paragraph 1 above shall, if the Land Registrar so directs, be read as a reference to such office of Her Majesty's Land Registry (whether in London or elsewhere) as may be specified in the direction.

3. The Land Registrar shall make the search required, and shall issue a certificate setting forth the result of the search.

4. In favour of a purchaser or an intending purchaser, as against persons interested under or in respect of an agricultural charge, the certificate, according to its tenor, shall be conclusive, affirmatively or negatively, as the case may be.

5. Every requisition under this Schedule shall be in writing, signed by the person making it, specifying the name against which he desires search to be made, or in relation to which he requires a certificate of result of search, and other sufficient particulars.

6. If any officer, clerk or person employed in the Land Registry commits, or is party or privy to, any act of fraud or collusion, or is wilfully negligent, in the making of or otherwise in relation to any certificate under this Schedule, he shall be guilty of an offence and shall be liable on conviction on indictment to imprisonment for a term not exceeding two years, or on summary conviction to imprisonment for a term not exceeding three months or to a fine not exceeding [the prescribed sum], or to both such imprisonment and fine.

7. A solicitor, or a trustee, personal representative, agent, or other person in a fiduciary position, shall not be answerable for any loss that may arise from error in a certificate under this Schedule obtained by him.]

[387]

NOTES
This Schedule added by the Land Charges Act 1972, s 18(1), Sch 3, para 7.
Para 6: words in square brackets substituted by virtue of the Magistrates' Courts Act 1980, s 32(2).
Solicitors' incorporated practices: the provisions of para 7 of this Schedule are applied, with modifications, in relation to a "recognised body" under the Administration of Justice Act 1985, s 9, by the Solicitors' Incorporated Practices Order 1991, SI 1991/2684, arts 2–5, Sch 1.

COMPANIES ACT 1985
(1985 c 6)

ARRANGEMENT OF SECTIONS

PART XII
REGISTRATION OF CHARGES

CHAPTER I
REGISTRATION OF CHARGES (ENGLAND AND WALES)

PART XXVII

FINAL PROVISIONS

An Act to consolidate the greater part of the Companies Acts
[11 March 1985]

NOTE

Prospective amendment: ss 395–420 (new provisions relating to registration of charges with respect to companies registered in Great Britain) prospectively inserted in place of ss 395–408, 410–423, by the Companies Act 1989, ss 92–104, as follows (the words omitted from s 396(2)(d)(i), as substituted, repealed by the Trade Marks Act 1994, s 106(2), Sch 5, and the reference in that sub-para to a trade mark is to be construed as a reference to a trade mark within the meaning of the 1994 Act, by virtue of s 106(1) of, and Sch 4, para 1 to, that Act)—

Registration in the company charges register

395 Introductory provisions

(1) The purpose of this Part is to secure the registration of charges on a company's property.

(2) In this Part—

"charge" means any form of security interest (fixed or floating) over property, other than an interest arising by operation of law; and

"property", in the context of what is the subject of a charge, includes future property.

(3) It is immaterial for the purposes of this Part where the property subject to a charge is situated.

(4) References in this Part to "the registrar" are—

(a) in relation to a company registered in England and Wales, to the registrar of companies for England and Wales, and

(b) in relation to a company registered in Scotland, to the registrar of companies for Scotland;

and references to registration, in relation to a charge, are to registration in the register kept by him under this Part.

396 Charges requiring registration

(1) The charges requiring registration under this Part are—

(a) a charge on land or any interest in land, other than—

(i) in England and Wales, a charge for rent or any other periodical sum issuing out of the land,

(ii) in Scotland, a charge for any rent, ground annual or other periodical sum payable in respect of the land;

(b) a charge on goods or any interest in goods, other than a charge under which the chargee is entitled to possession either of the goods or of a document of title to them;

(c) a charge on intangible movable property (in Scotland, incorporeal moveable property) of any of the following descriptions—

(i) goodwill,

(ii) intellectual property,

(iii) book debts (whether book debts of the company or assigned to the company),

(iv) uncalled share capital of the company or calls made but not paid;

(d) a charge for securing an issue of debentures; or
(e) a floating charge on the whole or part of the company's property.

(2) The descriptions of charge mentioned in subsection (1) shall be construed as follows—

(a) a charge on a debenture forming part of an issue or series shall not be treated as falling within paragraph (a) or (b) by reason of the fact that the debenture is secured by a charge on land or goods (or on an interest in land or goods);
(b) in paragraph (b) "goods" means any tangible movable property (in Scotland, corporeal moveable property) other than money;
(c) a charge is not excluded from paragraph (b) because the chargee is entitled to take possession in case of default or on the occurrence of some other event;
(d) in paragraph (c)(ii) "intellectual property" means—

(i) any patent, trade mark, . . . registered design, copyright or design right, or
(ii) any licence under or in respect of any such right;

(e) a debenture which is part of an issue or series shall not be treated as a book debt for the purposes of paragraph (c)(iii);
(f) the deposit by way of security of a negotiable instrument given to secure the payment of book debts shall not be treated for the purposes of paragraph (c)(iii) as a charge on book debts;
(g) a shipowner's lien on subfreights shall not be treated as a charge on book debts for the purposes of paragraph (c)(iii) or as a floating charge for the purposes of paragraph (e).

(3) Whether a charge is one requiring registration under this Part shall be determined—

(a) in the case of a charge created by a company, as at the date the charge is created, and
(b) in the case of a charge over property acquired by a company, as at the date of the acquisition.

(4) The Secretary of State may by regulations amend subsections (1) and (2) so as to add any description of charge to, or remove any description of charge from, the charges requiring registration under this Part.

(5) Regulations under this section shall be made by statutory instrument which shall be subject to annulment in pursuance of a resolution of either House of Parliament.

(6) In the following provisions of this Part references to a charge are, unless the context otherwise requires, to a charge requiring registration under this Part.

Where a charge not otherwise requiring registration relates to property by virtue of which it requires to be registered and to other property, the references are to the charge so far as it relates to property of the former description.

397 The companies charges register

(1) The registrar shall keep for each company a register, in such form as he thinks fit, of charges on property of the company.

(2) The register shall consist of a file containing with respect to each charge the particulars and other information delivered to the registrar under the provisions of this Part.

(3) Any person may require the registrar to provide a certificate stating the date on which any specified particulars of, or other information relating to, a charge were delivered to him.

(4) The certificate shall be signed by the registrar or authenticated by his official seal.

(5) The certificate shall be conclusive evidence that the specified particulars or other information were delivered to the registrar no later than the date stated in the certificate; and it shall be presumed unless the contrary is proved that they were not delivered earlier than that date.

398 Company's duty to deliver particulars of charge for registration

(1) It is the duty of a company which creates a charge, or acquires property subject to a charge—

(a) to deliver the prescribed particulars of the charge, in the prescribed form, to the registrar for registration, and
(b) to do so within 21 days after the date of the charge's creation or, as the case may be, the date of the acquisition;

but particulars of a charge may be delivered for registration by any person interested in the charge.

(2) Where the particulars are delivered for registration by a person other than the company concerned, that person is entitled to recover from the company the amount of any fees paid by him to the registrar in connection with the registration.

(3) If a company fails to comply with subsection (1), then, unless particulars of the charge have

been delivered for registration by another person, the company and every officer of it who is in default is liable to a fine.

(4) Where prescribed particulars in the prescribed form are delivered to the registrar for registration, he shall file the particulars in the register and shall note, in such form as he thinks fit, the date on which they were delivered to him.

(5) The registrar shall send to the company and any person appearing from the particulars to be the chargee, and if the particulars were delivered by another person interested in the charge to that person, a copy of the particulars filed by him and of the note made by him as to the date on which they were delivered.

399 Effect of failure to deliver particulars for registration

(1) Where a charge is created by a company and no prescribed particulars in the prescribed form are delivered for registration within the period of 21 days after the date of the charge's creation, the charge is void against—

(a) an administrator or liquidator of the company, and
(b) any person who for value acquires an interest in or right over property subject to the charge,

where the relevant event occurs after the creation of the charge, whether before or after the end of the 21 day period.

This is subject to section 400 (late delivery of particulars).

(2) In this Part "the relevant event" means—

(a) in relation to the voidness of a charge as against an administrator or liquidator, the beginning of the insolvency proceedings, and
(b) in relation to the voidness of a charge as against a person acquiring an interest in or right over property subject to a charge, the acquisition of that interest or right;

and references to "a relevant event" shall be construed accordingly.

(3) Where a relevant event occurs on the same day as the charge is created, it shall be presumed to have occurred after the charge is created unless the contrary is proved.

400 Late delivery of particulars

(1) Where prescribed particulars of a charge created by a company, in the prescribed form, are delivered for registration more than 21 days after the date of the charge's creation, section 399(1) does not apply in relation to relevant events occurring after the particulars are delivered.

(2) However, where in such a case—

(a) the company is at the date of delivery of the particulars unable to pay its debts, or subsequently becomes unable to pay its debts in consequence of the transaction under which the charge is created, and
(b) insolvency proceedings begin before the end of the relevant period beginning with the date of delivery of the particulars,

the charge is void as against the administrator or liquidator.

(3) For this purpose—

(a) the company is "unable to pay its debts" in the circumstances specified in section 123 of the Insolvency Act 1986; and
(b) the "relevant period" is—

(i) two years in the case of a floating charge created in favour of a person connected with the company (within the meaning of section 249 of that Act),
(ii) one year in the case of a floating charge created in favour of a person not so connected, and
(iii) six months in any other case.

(4) Where a relevant event occurs on the same day as the particulars are delivered, it shall be presumed to have occurred before the particulars are delivered unless the contrary is proved.

401 Delivery of further particulars

(1) Further particulars of a charge, supplementing or varying the registered particulars, may be delivered to the registrar for registration at any time.

(2) Further particulars must be in the prescribed form signed by or on behalf of both the company and the chargee.

(3) Where further particulars are delivered to the registrar for registration and appear to him to be duly signed, he shall file the particulars in the register and shall note, in such form as he thinks fit, the date on which they were delivered to him.

(4) The registrar shall send to the company and any person appearing from the particulars to be the chargee, and if the particulars were delivered by another person interested in the charge to that other person, a copy of the further particulars filed by him and of the note made by him as to the date on which they were delivered.

402 Effect of omissions and errors in registered particulars

(1) Where the registered particulars of a charge created by a company are not complete and accurate, the charge is void, as mentioned below, to the extent that rights are not disclosed by the registered particulars which would be disclosed if they were complete and accurate.

(2) The charge is void to that extent, unless the court on the application of the chargee orders otherwise, as against—

    (a) an administrator or liquidator of the company, and
    (b) any person who for value acquires an interest in or right over property subject to the charge,

where the relevant event occurs at a time when the particulars are incomplete or inaccurate in a relevant respect.

(3) Where a relevant event occurs on the same day as particulars or further particulars are delivered, it shall be presumed to have occurred before those particulars are delivered unless the contrary is proved.

(4) The court may order that the charge is effective as against an administrator or liquidator of the company if it is satisfied—

    (a) that the omission or error is not likely to have misled materially to his prejudice any unsecured creditor of the company, or
    (b) that no person became an unsecured creditor of the company at a time when the registered particulars of the charge were incomplete or inaccurate in a relevant respect.

(5) The court may order that the charge is effective as against a person acquiring an interest in or right over property subject to the charge if it is satisfied that he did not rely, in connection with the acquisition, on registered particulars which were incomplete or inaccurate in a relevant respect.

(6) For the purposes of this section an omission or inaccuracy with respect to the name of the chargee shall not be regarded as a failure to disclose the rights of the chargee.

403 Memorandum of charge ceasing to affect company's property

(1) Where a charge of which particulars have been delivered ceases to affect the company's property, a memorandum to that effect may be delivered to the registrar for registration.

(2) The memorandum must be in the prescribed form signed by or on behalf of both the company and the chargee.

(3) Where a memorandum is delivered to the registrar for registration and appears to him to be duly signed, he shall file it in the register, and shall note, in such form as he thinks fit, the date on which it was delivered to him.

(4) The registrar shall send to the company and any person appearing from the memorandum to be the chargee, and if the memorandum was delivered by another person interested in the charge to that person, a copy of the memorandum filed by him and of the note made by him as to the date on which it was delivered.

(5) If a duly signed memorandum is delivered in a case where the charge in fact continues to affect the company's property, the charge is void as against—

    (a) an administrator or liquidator of the company, and
    (b) any person who for value acquires an interest in or right over property subject to the charge,

where the relevant event occurs after the delivery of the memorandum.

(6) Where a relevant event occurs on the same day as the memorandum is delivered, it shall be presumed to have occurred before the memorandum is delivered unless the contrary is proved.

Further provisions with respect to voidness of charges

404 Exclusion of voidness as against unregistered charges

(1) A charge is not void by virtue of this Part as against a subsequent charge unless some or all of the relevant particulars of that charge are duly delivered for registration—

(a) within 21 days after the date of its creation, or
(b) before complete and accurate relevant particulars of the earlier charge are duly delivered for registration.

(2) Where relevant particulars of the subsequent charge so delivered are incomplete or inaccurate, the earlier charge is void as against that charge only to the extent that rights are disclosed by registered particulars of the subsequent charge duly delivered for registration before the corresponding relevant particulars of the earlier charge.

(3) The relevant particulars of a charge for the purposes of this section are those prescribed particulars relating to rights inconsistent with those conferred by or in relation to the other charge.

405 Restrictions on voidness by virtue of this Part

(1) A charge is not void by virtue of this Part as against a person acquiring an interest in or right over property where the acquisition is expressly subject to the charge.

(2) Nor is a charge void by virtue of this Part in relation to any property by reason of a relevant event occurring after the company which created the charge has disposed of the whole of its interest in that property.

406 Effect of exercise of power of sale

(1) A chargee exercising a power of sale may dispose of property to a purchaser freed from any interest or right arising from the charge having become void to any extent by virtue of this Part—

(a) against an administrator or liquidator of the company, or
(b) against a person acquiring a security interest over property subject to the charge;

and a purchaser is not concerned to see or inquire whether the charge has become so void.

(2) The proceeds of the sale shall be held by the chargee in trust to be applied—

First, in discharge of any sum effectively secured by prior incumbrances to which the sale is not made subject;
Second, in payment of all costs, charges and expenses properly incurred by him in connection with the sale, or any previous attempted sale, of the property;
Third, in discharge of any sum effectively secured by the charge and incumbrances ranking *pari passu* with the charge;
Fourth, in discharge of any sum effectively secured by incumbrances ranking after the charge;

and any residue is payable to the company or to a person authorised to give a receipt for the proceeds of the sale of the property.

(3) For the purposes of subsection (2)—

(a) prior incumbrances include any incumbrance to the extent that the charge is void as against it by virtue of this Part; and
(b) no sum is effectively secured by a charge to the extent that it is void as against an administrator or liquidator of the company.

(4) In this section—

(a) references to things done by a chargee include things done by a receiver appointed by him, whether or not the receiver acts as his agent;
(b) "power of sale" includes any power to dispose of, or grant an interest out of, property for the purpose of enforcing a charge (but in relation to Scotland does not include the power to grant a lease), and references to "sale" shall be construed accordingly; and
(c) "purchaser" means a person who in good faith and for valuable consideration acquires an interest in property.

(5) The provisions of this section as to the order of application of the proceeds of sale have effect subject to any other statutory provision (in Scotland, any other statutory provision or rule of law) applicable in any case.

(6) Where a chargee exercising a power of sale purports to dispose of property freed from any such interest or right as is mentioned in subsection (1) to a person other than a purchaser, the above provisions apply, with any necessary modifications, in relation to a disposition to a purchaser by that person or any successor in title of his.

(7) In Scotland, subsections (2) and (7) of section 27 of the Conveyancing and Feudal Reform (Scotland) Act 1970 apply to a chargee unable to obtain a discharge for any payment which he is required to make under subsection (2) above as they apply to a creditor in the circumstances mentioned in those subsections.

407 Effect of voidness on obligation secured

(1) Where a charge becomes void to any extent by virtue of this Part, the whole of the sum secured by the charge is payable forthwith on demand; and this applies notwithstanding that the sum secured by the charge is also the subject of other security.

(2) Where the charge is to secure the repayment of money, the references in subsection (1) to the sum secured include any interest payable.

Additional information to be registered

408 Particulars of taking up of issue of debentures

(1) Where particulars of a charge for securing an issue of debentures have been delivered for registration, it is the duty of the company—

    (a) to deliver to the registrar for registration particulars in the prescribed form of the date on which any debentures of the issue are taken up, and of the amount taken up, and

    (b) to do so before the end of the period of 21 days after the date on which they are taken up.

(2) Where particulars in the prescribed form are delivered to the registrar for registration under this section, he shall file them in the register.

(3) If a company fails to comply with subsection (1), the company and every officer of it who is in default is liable to a fine.

409 Notice of appointment of receiver or manager, &c

(1) If a person obtains an order for the appointment of a receiver or manager of a company's property, or appoints such a receiver or manager under powers contained in an instrument, he shall within seven days of the order or of the appointment under those powers, give notice of that fact in the prescribed form to the registrar for registration.

(2) Where a person appointed receiver or manager of a company's property under powers contained in an instrument ceases to act as such receiver or manager, he shall, on so ceasing, give notice of that fact in the prescribed form to the registrar for registration.

(3) Where a notice under this section in the prescribed form is delivered to the registrar for registration, he shall file it in the register.

(4) If a person makes default in complying with the requirements of subsection (1) or (2), he is liable to a fine.

(5) This section does not apply in relation to companies registered in Scotland (for which corresponding provision is made by sections 53, 54 and 62 of the Insolvency Act 1986).

410 Notice of crystallisation of floating charge, &c

(1) The Secretary of State may by regulations require notice in the prescribed form to be given to the registrar of—

    (a) the occurrence of such events as may be prescribed affecting the nature of the security under a floating charge of which particulars have been delivered for registration, and

    (b) the taking of such action in exercise of powers conferred by a fixed or floating charge of which particulars have been delivered for registration, or conferred in relation to such a charge by an order of the court, as may be prescribed.

(2) The regulations may make provision as to—

    (a) the persons by whom notice is required to be, or may be, given, and the period within which notice is required to be given;

    (b) the filing in the register of the particulars contained in the notice and the noting of the date on which the notice was given; and

    (c) the consequences of failure to give notice.

(3) As regards the consequences of failure to give notice of an event causing a floating charge to crystallise, the regulations may include provision to the effect that the crystallisation—

    (a) shall be treated as ineffective until the prescribed particulars are delivered, and

    (b) if the prescribed particulars are delivered after the expiry of the prescribed period, shall continue to be ineffective against such persons as may be prescribed,

subject to the exercise of such powers as may be conferred by the regulations on the court.

(4) The regulations may provide that if there is a failure to comply with such of the requirements of the regulations as may be prescribed, such persons as may be prescribed are liable to a fine.

(5) Regulations under this section shall be made by statutory instrument which shall be subject to annulment in pursuance of a resolution of either House of Parliament.

(6) Regulations under this section shall not apply in relation to a floating charge created under the law of Scotland by a company registered in Scotland.

Copies of instruments and register to be kept by company

411 Duty to keep copies of instruments and register

(1) Every company shall keep at its registered office a copy of every instrument creating or evidencing a charge over the company's property.

In the case of a series of uniform debentures, a copy of one debenture of the series is sufficient.

(2) Every company shall also keep at its registered office a register of all such charges, containing entries for each charge giving a short description of the property charged, the amount of the charge and (except in the case of securities to bearer) the names of the persons entitled to it.

(3) This section applies to any charge, whether or not particulars are required to be delivered to the registrar for registration.

(4) If a company fails to comply with any requirement of this section, the company and every officer of it who is in default is liable to a fine.

412 Inspection of copies of register

(1) The copies and the register referred to in section 411 shall be open to the inspection of any creditor or member of the company without fee; and to the inspection of any other person on payment of such fee as may be prescribed.

(2) Any person may request the company to provide him with a copy of—

    (a) any instrument creating or evidencing a charge over the company's property, or
    (b) any entry in the register of charges kept by the company, on payment of such fee as may be prescribed.

This subsection applies to any charge, whether or not particulars are required to be delivered to the registrar for registration.

(3) The company shall send the copy to him not later than ten days after the day on which the request is received or, if later, on which payment is received.

(4) If inspection of the copies or register is refused, or a copy requested is not sent within the time specified above—

    (a) the company and every officer of it who is in default is liable to a fine, and
    (b) the court may by order compel an immediate inspection of the copies or register or, as the case may be, direct that the copy be sent immediately.

Supplementary provisions

413 Power to make further provision by regulations

(1) The Secretary of State may by regulations make further provision as to the application of the provisions of this Part in relation to charges of any description specified in the regulations.

Nothing in the following provisions shall be construed as restricting the generality of that power.

(2) The regulations may require that where the charge is contained in or evidenced or varied by a written instrument there shall be delivered to the registrar for registration, instead of particulars or further particulars of the charge, the instrument itself or a certified copy of it together with such particulars as may be prescribed.

(3) The regulations may provide that a memorandum of a charge ceasing to affect property of the company shall not be accepted by the registrar unless supported by such evidence as may be prescribed, and that a memorandum not so supported shall be treated as not having been delivered.

(4) The regulations may also provide that where the instrument creating the charge is delivered to the registrar in support of such a memorandum, the registrar may mark the instrument as cancelled before returning it and shall send copies of the instrument cancelled to such persons as may be prescribed.

(5) The regulations may exclude or modify, in such circumstances and to such extent as may be prescribed, the operation of the provisions of this Part relating to the voidness of a charge.

(6) The regulations may require, in connection with the delivery of particulars, further particulars or a memorandum of the charge's ceasing to affect property of the company, the delivery of such supplementary information as may be prescribed, and may—

    (a) apply in relation to such supplementary information any provisions of this Part relating to particulars, further particulars or such a memorandum, and

(b) provide that the particulars, further particulars or memorandum shall be treated as not having been delivered until the required supplementary information is delivered.

(7) Regulations under this section shall be made by statutory instrument which shall be subject to annulment in pursuance of a resolution of either House of Parliament.

414 Date of creation of charge

(1) References in this Part to the date of creation of a charge by a company shall be construed as follows.

(2) A charge created under the law of England and Wales shall be taken to be created—

(a) in the case of a charge created by an instrument in writing, when the instrument is executed by the company or, if its execution by the company is conditional, upon the conditions being fulfilled, and

(b) in any other case, when an enforceable agreement is entered into by the company conferring a security interest intended to take effect forthwith or upon the company acquiring an interest in property subject to the charge.

(3) A charge created under the law of Scotland shall be taken to be created—

(a) in the case of a floating charge, when the instrument creating the floating charge is executed by the company, and

(b) in any other case, when the right of the person entitled to the benefit of the charge is constituted as a real right.

(4) Where a charge is created in the United Kingdom but comprises property outside the United Kingdom, any further proceedings necessary to make the charge valid or effectual under the law of the country where the property is situated shall be disregarded in ascertaining the date on which the charge is to be taken to be created.

415 Prescribed particulars and related expressions

(1) References in this Part to the prescribed particulars of a charge are to such particulars of, or relating to, the charge as may be prescribed.

(2) The prescribed particulars may, without prejudice to the generality of subsection (1), include—

(a) whether the company has undertaken not to create other charges ranking in priority to or *pari passu* with the charge, and

(b) whether the charge is a market charge within the meaning of Part VII of the Companies Act 1989 or a charge to which the provisions of that Part apply as they apply to a market charge.

(3) References in this Part to the registered particulars of a charge at any time are to such particulars and further particulars of the charge as have at that time been duly delivered for registration.

(4) References in this Part to the registered particulars of a charge being complete and accurate at any time are to their including all the prescribed particulars which would be required to be delivered if the charge were then newly created.

416 Notice of matters disclosed on register

(1) A person taking a charge over a company's property shall be taken to have notice of any matter requiring registration and disclosed on the register at the time the charge is created.

(2) Otherwise, a person shall not be taken to have notice of any matter by reason of its being disclosed on the register or by reason of his having failed to search the register in the course of making such inquiries as ought reasonably to have been made.

(3) The above provisions have effect subject to any other statutory provision as to whether a person is to be taken to have notice of any matter disclosed on the register.

417 Power of court to dispense with signature

(1) Where it is proposed to deliver further particulars of a charge, or to deliver a memorandum of a charge ceasing to affect the company's property, and—

(a) the chargee refuses to sign or authorise a person to sign on his behalf, or cannot be found, or

(b) the company refuses to authorise a person to sign on its behalf,

the court may on the application of the company or the chargee, or of any other person having a sufficient interest in the matter, authorise the delivery of the particulars or memorandum without that signature.

(2) The order may be made on such terms as appear to the court to be appropriate.

(3) Where particulars or a memorandum are delivered to the registrar for registration in reliance on an order under this section, they must be accompanied by an office copy of the order.

In such a case the references in sections 401 and 403 to the particulars or memorandum being duly signed are to their being otherwise duly signed.

(4) The registrar shall file the office copy of the court order along with the particulars or memorandum.

418 Regulations

Regulations under any provision of this Part, or prescribing anything for the purposes of any such provision—

    (a) may make different provision for different cases, and
    (b) may contain such supplementary, incidental and transitional provisions as appear to the Secretary of State to be appropriate.

419 Minor definitions

(1) In this Part—

    "chargee" means the person for the time being entitled to exercise the security rights conferred by the charge;
    "issue of debentures" means a group of debentures, or an amount of debenture stock, secured by the same charge; and
    "series of debentures" means a group of debentures each containing or giving by reference to another instrument a charge to the benefit of which the holders of debentures of the series are entitled *pari passu*.

(2) References in this Part to the creation of a charge include the variation of a charge which is not registrable so as to include property by virtue of which it becomes registrable.

The provisions of section 414 (construction of references to date of creation of charge) apply in such a case with any necessary modifications.

(3) References in this Part to the date of acquisition of property by a company are—

    (a) in England and Wales, to the date on which the acquisition is completed, and
    (b) in Scotland, to the date on which the transaction is settled.

(4) In the application of this Part to a floating charge created under the law of Scotland, references to crystallisation shall be construed as references to the attachment of the charge.

(5) References in this Part to the beginning of insolvency proceedings are to—

    (a) the presentation of a petition on which an administration order or winding-up order is made, or
    (b) the passing of a resolution for voluntary winding up.

420 Index of defined expressions

The following Table shows the provisions of this Part defining or otherwise explaining expressions used in this Part (other than expressions used only in the same section)—

charge	sections 395(2) and 396(6)
charge requiring registration	section 396
chargee	section 419(1)
complete and accurate (in relation to registered particulars)	section 415(4)
creation of charge	section 419(2)
crystallisation (in relation to Scottish floating charge)	section 419(4)
date of acquisition (of property by a company)	section 419(3)
date of creation of charge	section 414
further particulars	section 401
insolvency proceedings, beginning of	section 419(5)
issue of debentures	section 419(1)
memorandum of charge ceasing to affect company's property	section 403
prescribed particulars	section 415(1) and (2)
property	section 395(2)
registered particulars	section 415(3)
registrar and registration in relation to a charge	section 395(4)
relevant event	section 399(2)
series of debentures	section 419(1).

NOTE
   Prospective amendment: Chapter III of Pt XXIII (ss 703A–703N) (new provisions relating to
registration of charges with respect to oversea companies) prospectively inserted in place of ss 409,
424, by the Companies Act 1989, ss 92(b), 105, Sch 15, as follows (words in square brackets inserted
or substituted by the Oversea Companies and Credit and Financial Institutions (Branch Disclosure)
Regulations 1992, SI 1992/3179, reg 4, Sch 3, paras 11–15)—

CHAPTER III
REGISTRATION OF CHARGES

703A Introductory provisions

(1) The provisions of this Chapter have effect for securing the registration in Great Britain of
charges on the property of a registered oversea company.

(2) Section 395(2) and (3) (meaning of "charge" and "property") have effect for the purposes of
this Chapter.

(3) A "registered oversea company", in relation to England and Wales or Scotland, means an
oversea company which

[(a) has duly delivered documents under paragraph 1 of Schedule 21A to the registrar for
that part of Great Britain and has not subsequently given notice to him under section
695A(3) that it has closed the branch in respect of which the documents were registered,
or
(b)] has duly delivered documents to the registrar for that part of Great Britain under section
691 and has not subsequently given notice to him under section 696(4) that it has ceased
to have an established place of business in that part.

(4) References in this Chapter to the registrar shall be construed in accordance with section
703E below and references to registration, in relation to a charge, are to registration in the register
kept by him under this Chapter.

703B Charges requiring registration

(1) The charges requiring registration under this Chapter are those which if created by a
company registered in Great Britain would require registration under Part XII of this Act.

(2) Whether a charge is one requiring registration under this Chapter shall be determined—

[(a) in the case of a charge over property of a company at the date when it becomes a
registered oversea company, as at that date,]
(b) in the case of a charge created by a registered oversea company, as at the date the charge
is created, and
(c) in the case of a charge over property acquired by a registered oversea company, as at the
date of the acquisition.

(3) In the following provisions of this Chapter references to a charge are, unless the context
otherwise requires, to a charge requiring registration under this Chapter.

Where a charge not otherwise requiring registration relates to property by virtue of which it
requires to be registered and to other property, the references are to the charge so far as it relates to
property of the former description.

703C The register

(1) The registrar shall keep for each registered oversea company a register, in such form as he
thinks fit, of charges on property of the company.

(2) The register shall consist of a file containing with respect to each such charge the particulars
and other information delivered to the registrar under or by virtue of the following provisions of
this Chapter.

(3) Section 397(3) to (5) (registrar's certificate as to date of delivery of particulars) applies in
relation to the delivery of any particulars or other information under this Chapter.

703D Company's duty to deliver particulars of charges for registration

(1) If when an oversea company

[(a) delivers documents for registration under paragraph 1 of Schedule 21A—

(i)   in respect of a branch in England and Wales, or
(ii) in respect of a branch in Scotland,

for the first time since becoming a company to which section 690A applies, or
   (b) delivers documents for registration under section 691,]

any of its property is situated in Great Britain and subject to a charge, it is the company's duty at the same time to deliver the prescribed particulars of the charge, in the prescribed form, to the registrar for registration.

  [(1A) Subsection (1) above does not apply in relation to a charge if—

   (a) the particulars of it required to be delivered under that subsection have already been so delivered to the registrar to whom the documents mentioned in subsection (1) above are delivered, and
   (b) the company has at all times since they were so delivered to him been a registered oversea company in relation to the part of Great Britain for which he is registrar.]

  (2) Where a registered oversea company—

   (a) creates a charge on property situated in Great Britain, or
   (b) acquires property which is situated in Great Britain and subject to a charge,

it is the company's duty to deliver the prescribed particulars of the charge, in the prescribed form, to the registrar for registration within 21 days after the date of the charge's creation or, as the case may be, the date of the acquisition.

This subsection does not apply if the property subject to the charge is at the end of that period no longer situated in Great Britain.

  (3) Where the preceding subsections do not apply and property of a registered oversea company is for a continuous period of four months situated in Great Britain and subject to a charge, it is the company's duty before the end of that period to deliver the prescribed particulars of the charge, in the prescribed form, to the registrar for registration.

  (4) Particulars of a charge required to be delivered under subsections (1), (2) or (3) may be delivered for registration by any person interested in the charge.

  (5) If a company fails to comply with subsection (1), (2) or (3), then, unless particulars of the charge have been delivered for registration by another person, the company and every officer of it who is in default is liable to a fine.

  (6) Section 398(2), (4) and (5) (recovery of fees paid in connection with registration, filing of particulars in register and sending of copy of particulars filed and note as to date) apply in relation to particulars delivered under this Chapter.

703E Registrar to whom particulars, &c to be delivered

  (1) The particulars required to be delivered by section 703D(1) (charges over property of oversea company becoming registered in a part of Great Britain) shall be delivered to the registrar to whom the documents are delivered under [paragraph 1 of Schedule 21A or, as the case may be,] section 691.

  (2) The particulars required to be delivered by section 703D(2) or (3) (charges over property of registered oversea company) shall be delivered—

   [(a) where the company is a company to which section 690A applies—

     (i) if it has registered a branch in one part of Great Britain but has not registered a branch in the other, to the registrar for the part in which it has registered a branch,
    (ii) if it has registered a branch in both parts of Great Britain but the property subject to the charge is situated in one part of Great Britain only, to the registrar for that part, and
   (iii) in any other case, to the registrars for both parts of Great Britain; and

   (b) where the company is a company to which section 691 applies—

     (i) if it is registered in one part of Great Britain and not in the other, to the registrar for the part in which it is registered,
    (ii) if it is registered in both parts of Great Britain but the property subject to the charge is situated in one part of Great Britain only, to the registrar for that part, and
   (iii) in any other case, to the registrar for both parts of Great Britain.]

  (3) Other documents required or authorised by virtue of this Chapter to be delivered to the registrar shall be delivered to the registrar or registrars to whom particulars of the charge to which they relate have been, or ought to have been, delivered.

  (4) [If a company ceases to be a registered oversea company in relation to either part of Great Britain, charges over property of the company shall cease to be subject to the provisions of this Chapter, as regards registration in that part of Great Britain, as from the date on which the notice under section 695A(3) or, as the case may be, 696(3) is given.]

This is without prejudice to rights arising by reason of events occurring before that date.

703F Effect of failure to deliver particulars, late delivery and effect of errors and omissions

(1) The following provisions of Part XII—

    (a) section 399 (effect of failure to deliver particulars),
    (b) section 400 (late delivery of particulars), and
    (c) section 402 (effect of errors and omissions in particulars delivered),

apply, with the following modifications, in relation to a charge created by a registered oversea company of which particulars are required to be delivered under this Chapter.

(2) Those provisions do not apply to a charge of which particulars are required to be delivered under section 703D(1) (charges existing when company delivers documents under section 691).

(3) In relation to a charge of which particulars are required to be delivered under section 703D(3) (charges registrable by virtue of property being within Great Britain for requisite period), the references to the period of 21 days after the charge's creation shall be construed as references to the period of four months referred to in that subsection.

703G Delivery of further particulars or memorandum

Sections 401 and 403 (delivery of further particulars and memorandum of charge ceasing to affect company's property) apply in relation to a charge of which particulars have been delivered under this Chapter.

703H Further provisions with respect to voidness of charges

(1) The following provisions of Part XII apply in relation to the voidness of a charge by virtue of this Chapter—

    (a) section 404 (exclusion of voidness as against unregistered charges),
    (b) section 405 (restrictions on cases in which charge is void),
    (c) section 406 (effect of exercise of power of sale), and
    (d) section 407 (effect of voidness on obligation secured).

(2) In relation to a charge of which particulars are required to be delivered under section 703D(3) (charges registrable by virtue of property being within Great Britain for requisite period), the reference in section 404 to the period of 21 days after the charge's creation shall be construed as a reference to the period of four months referred to in that subsection.

703I Additional information to be registered

(1) Section 408 (particulars of taking up of issue of debentures) applies in relation to a charge of which particulars have been delivered under this Chapter.

(2) Section 409 (notice of appointment of receiver or manager) applies in relation to the appointment of a receiver or manager of property of a registered oversea company.

(3) Regulations under section 410 (notice of crystallisation of floating charge, &c.) may apply in relation to a charge of which particulars have been delivered under this Chapter; but subject to such exceptions, adaptations and modifications as may be specified in the regulations.

703J Copies of instruments and register to be kept by company

(1) Sections 411 and 412 (copies of instruments and register to be kept by company) apply in relation to a registered oversea company and any charge over property of the company situated in Great Britain.

(2) They apply to any charge, whether or not particulars are required to be delivered to the registrar.

(3) In relation to such a company the references to the company's registered office shall be construed as references to its principal place of business in Great Britain.

703K Power to make further provision by regulations

(1) The Secretary of State may by regulations make further provision as to the application of the provisions of this Chapter, or the provisions of Part XII applied by this Chapter, in relation to charges of any description specified in the regulations.

(2) The regulations may apply any provisions of regulations made under section 413 (power to make further provision with respect to application of Part XII) or make any provision which may be made under that section with respect to the application of provisions of Part XII.

703L Provisions as to situation of property

(1) The following provisions apply for determining for the purposes of this Chapter whether a vehicle which is the property of an oversea company is situated in Great Britain—

(a) a ship, aircraft or hovercraft shall be regarded as situated in Great Britain if, and only if, it is registered in Great Britain;

(b) any other description of vehicle shall be regarded as situated in Great Britain on a day if, and only if, at any time on that day the management of the vehicle is directed from a place of business of the company in Great Britain;

and for the purposes of this Chapter a vehicle shall not be regarded as situated in one part of Great Britain only.

(2) For the purposes of this Chapter as it applies to a charge on future property, the subject-matter of the charge shall be treated as situated in Great Britain unless it relates exclusively to property of a kind which cannot, after being acquired or coming into existence, be situated in Great Britain; and references to property situated in a part of Great Britain shall be similarly construed.

703M Other supplementary provisions

The following provisions of Part XII apply for the purposes of this Chapter—

(a) section 414 (construction of references to date of creation of charge),

(b) section 415 (prescribed particulars and related expressions),

(c) section 416 (notice of matters disclosed on the register),

(d) section 417 (power of court to dispense with signature),

(e) section 418 (regulations) and

(f) section 419 (minor definitions).

703N Index of defined expressions

The following Table shows the provisions of this Chapter and Part XII defining or otherwise explaining expressions used in this Chapter (other than expressions used only in the same section)—

charge	sections 703A(2), 703B(3) and 395(2)
charge requiring registration	sections 703B(1) and 396
creation of charge	sections 703M(f) and 419(2)
date of acquisition (of property by a company)	sections 703M(f) and 419(3)
date of creation of charge	sections 703M(a) and 414
property	sections 703A(2) and 395(2)
registered oversea company	section 703A(3)
registrar and registration in relation to a charge	sections 703A(4) and 703E
situated in Great Britain	in relation to vehicles section 703L(1)
in relation to future property	section 703L(2)

1–394 (*Ss 1–394 are outside the scope of this work.*)

PART XII
REGISTRATION OF CHARGES

NOTES

Prospective amendments: see notes at pp 229, 238.

CHAPTER I
REGISTRATION OF CHARGES (ENGLAND AND WALES)

395 Certain charges void if not registered

(1) Subject to the provisions of this Chapter, a charge created by a company registered in England and Wales and being a charge to which this section applies

is, so far as any security on the company's property or undertaking is conferred by the charge, void against the liquidator [or administrator] and any creditor of the company, unless the prescribed particulars of the charge together with the instrument (if any) by which the charge is created or evidenced, are delivered to or received by the registrar of companies for registration in the manner required by this Chapter within 21 days after the date of the charge's creation.

(2) Subsection (1) is without prejudice to any contract or obligation for repayment of the money secured by the charge; and when a charge becomes void under this section, the money secured by it immediately becomes payable. **[388]**

NOTES
Sub-s (1): words in square brackets inserted by the Insolvency Act 1985, s 109(1), Sch 6, para 10.
Prospective replacement: see the introductory note to this Part.
Prescribed particulars: for prescribed particulars, see Form 395 in the Companies (Forms) Regulations 1985, SI 1985/854.

396 Charges which have to be registered

(1) Section 395 applies to the following charges—

(a) a charge for the purpose of securing any issue of debentures,
(b) a charge on uncalled share capital of the company,
(c) a charge created or evidenced by an instrument which, if executed by an individual, would require registration as a bill of sale,
(d) a charge on land (wherever situated) or any interest in it, but not including a charge for any rent or other periodical sum issuing out of the land,
(e) a charge on book debts of the company,
(f) a floating charge on the company's undertaking or property,
(g) a charge on calls made but not paid,
(h) a charge on a ship or aircraft, or any share in a ship,
(j) a charge on goodwill, [or on any intellectual property].

(2) Where a negotiable instrument has been given to secure the payment of any book debts of a company, the deposit of the instrument for the purpose of securing an advance to the company is not, for purposes of section 395, to be treated as a charge on those book debts.

(3) The holding of debentures entitling the holder to a charge on land is not for purposes of this section deemed to be an interest in land.

[(3A) The following are "intellectual property" for the purposes of this section—

(a) any patent, trade mark, . . . registered design, copyright or design right;
(b) any licence under or in respect of any such right.]

(4) In this Chapter, "charge" includes mortgage. **[389]**

NOTES
Sub-ss (1), (3A): words in square brackets in sub-s (1)(j) substituted, and sub-s (3A) inserted, by the Copyright, Designs and Patents Act 1988, s 303(1), Sch 7, para 31(1), (2); words omitted from sub-s (3A)(a) repealed by the Trade Marks Act 1994, s 106(2), Sch 5; reference in sub-s (3A)(a) to a trade mark to be construed as a reference to a trade mark within the meaning of the 1994 Act, by virtue of s 106(1) of, and Sch 4, para 1 to, that Act.
Prospective replacement: see the introductory note to this Part.

397 Formalities of registration (debentures)

(1) Where a series of debentures containing, or giving by reference to another instrument, any charge to the benefit of which the debenture holders of that series

are entitled *pari passu* is created by a company, it is for purposes of section 395 sufficient if there are delivered to or received by the registrar, within 21 days after the execution of the deed containing the charge (or, if there is no such deed, after the execution of any debentures of the series), the following particulars in the prescribed form—

    (a) the total amount secured by the whole series, and

    (b) the dates of the resolutions authorising the issue of the series and the date of the covering deed (if any) by which the security is created or defined, and

    (c) a general description of the property charged, and

    (d) the names of the trustees (if any) for the debenture holders,

together with the deed containing the charge or, if there is no such deed, one of the debentures of the series:

Provided that there shall be sent to the registrar of companies, for entry in the register, particulars in the prescribed form of the date and amount of each issue of debentures of the series, but any omission to do this does not affect the validity of any of those debentures.

(2) Where any commission, allowance or discount has been paid or made either directly or indirectly by a company to a person in consideration of his—

    (a) subscribing or agreeing to subscribe, whether absolutely or conditionally, for debentures of the company, or

    (b) procuring or agreeing to procure subscriptions, whether absolute or conditional, for such debentures,

the particulars required to be sent for registration under section 395 shall include particulars as to the amount or rate per cent. of the commission, discount or allowance so paid or made, but omission to do this does not affect the validity of the debentures issued.

(3) The deposit of debentures as security for a debt of the company is not, for the purposes of subsection (2), treated as the issue of the debentures at a discount.

[390]

NOTES

Prospective replacement: see the introductory note to this Part.

Particulars in the prescribed form: for particulars prescribed, see Forms 397, 397a in the Companies (Forms) Regulations 1985, SI 1985/854.

398 Verification of charge on property outside United Kingdom

(1) In the case of a charge created out of the United Kingdom comprising property situated outside the United Kingdom, the delivery to and the receipt by the registrar of companies of a copy (verified in the prescribed manner) of the instrument by which the charge is created or evidenced has the same effect for purposes of sections 395 to 398 as the delivery and receipt of the instrument itself.

(2) In that case, 21 days after the date on which the instrument or copy could, in due course of post (and if despatched with due diligence), have been received in the United Kingdom are substituted for the 21 days mentioned in section 395(1) (or as the case may be, section 397(1)) as the time within which the particulars and instrument or copy are to be delivered to the registrar.

(3) Where a charge is created in the United Kingdom but comprises property outside the United Kingdom, the instrument creating or purporting to create the charge may be sent for registration under section 395 notwithstanding that

further proceedings may be necessary to make the charge valid or effectual according to the law of the country in which the property is situated.

(4) Where a charge comprises property situated in Scotland or Northern Ireland and registration in the country where the property is situated is necessary to make the charge valid or effectual according to the law of that country, the delivery to and receipt by the registrar of a copy (verified in the prescribed manner) of the instrument by which the charge is created or evidenced, together with a certificate in the prescribed form stating that the charge was presented for registration in Scotland or Northern Ireland (as the case may be) on the date on which it was so presented has, for purposes of sections 395 to 398, the same effect as the delivery and receipt of the instrument itself. **[391]**

NOTES
  Prospective replacement: see the introductory note to this Part.
  Copy (verified in the prescribed manner): see the Companies (Forms) Regulations 1985, SI 1985/854, reg 7(1), (3), as amended by SI 1986/2097.
  Certificate in the prescribed form: for particulars prescribed, see Form 398 in the Companies (Forms) Regulations 1985, SI 1985/854.

399 Company's duty to register charges it creates

(1) It is a company's duty to send to the registrar of companies for registration the particulars of every charge created by the company and of the issues of debentures of a series requiring registration under sections 395 to 398; but registration of any such charge may be effected on the application of any person interested in it.

(2) Where registration is effected on the application of some person other than the company, that person is entitled to recover from the company the amount of any fees properly paid by him to the registrar on the registration.

(3) If a company fails to comply with subsection (1), then, unless the registration has been effected on the application of some other person, the company and every officer of it who is in default is liable to a fine and, for continued contravention, to a daily default fine. **[392]**

NOTE
  Prospective replacement: see the introductory note to this Part.

400 Charges existing on property acquired

(1) This section applies where a company registered in England and Wales acquires property which is subject to a charge of any such kind as would, if it had been created by the company after the acquisition of the property, have been required to be registered under this Chapter.

(2) The company shall cause the prescribed particulars of the charge, together with a copy (certified in the prescribed manner to be a correct copy) of the instrument (if any) by which the charge was created or is evidenced, to be delivered to the registrar of companies for registration in manner required by this Chapter within 21 days after the date on which the acquisition is completed.

(3) However, if the property is situated and the charge was created outside Great Britain, 21 days after the date on which the copy of the instrument could in due course of post, and if despatched with due diligence, have been received in the United Kingdom is substituted for the 21 days above-mentioned as the time within which the particulars and copy of the instrument are to be delivered to the registrar.

(4) If default is made in complying with this section, the company and every officer of it who is in default is liable to a fine and, for continued contravention, to a daily default fine.   **[393]**

NOTES
Prospective replacement: see the introductory note to this Part.
Prescribed particulars: for prescribed particulars, see Form 400 in the Companies (Forms) Regulations 1985, SI 1985/854, as amended by SI 1987/752.
Copy (certified in the prescribed manner . . .): for prescribed manner, see the Companies (Forms) Regulations 1985, SI 1985/854, reg 7(1), (3), as amended by SI 1986/2097.

401 Register of charges to be kept by registrar of companies

(1) The registrar of companies shall keep, with respect to each company, a register in the prescribed form of all the charges requiring registration under this Chapter; and he shall enter in the register with respect to such charges the following particulars—

(a) in the case of a charge to the benefit of which the holders of a series of debentures are entitled, the particulars specified in section 397(1),

(b) in the case of any other charge—

(i) if it is a charge created by the company, the date of its creation, and if it is a charge which was existing on property acquired by the company, the date of the acquisition of the property, and

(ii) the amount secured by the charge, and

(iii) short particulars of the property charged, and

(iv) the persons entitled to the charge.

(2) The registrar shall give a certificate of the registration of any charge registered in pursuance of this Chapter, stating the amount secured by the charge.

The certificate—

(a) shall be either signed by the registrar, or authenticated by his official seal, and

(b) is conclusive evidence that the requirements of this Chapter as to registration have been satisfied.

(3) The register kept in pursuance of this section shall be open to inspection by any person.   **[394]**

NOTES
Prospective replacement: see the introductory note to this Part.
Prescribed form: for form of register, see Form 401 in the Companies (Forms) Regulations 1985, SI 1985/854.

402 Endorsement of certificate on debentures

(1) The company shall cause a copy of every certificate of registration given under section 401 to be endorsed on every debenture or certificate of debenture stock which is issued by the company, and the payment of which is secured by the charge so registered.

(2) But this does not require a company to cause a certificate of registration of any charge so given to be endorsed on any debenture or certificate of debenture stock issued by the company before the charge was created.

(3) If a person knowingly and wilfully authorises or permits the delivery of a debenture or certificate of debenture stock which under this section is required to

*have endorsed on it a copy of a certificate of registration, without the copy being
so endorsed upon it, he is liable (without prejudice to any other liability) to a fine.*

[395]

NOTE
Prospective replacement: see the introductory note to this Part.

403 Entries of satisfaction and release

*(1) The registrar of companies, on receipt of a statutory declaration in the
prescribed form verifying, with respect to a registered charge,—*

  *(a) that the debt for which the charge was given has been paid or satisfied
        in whole or in part, or*
  *(b) that part of the property or undertaking charged has been released
        from the charge or has ceased to form part of the company's property
        or undertaking,*

*may enter on the register a memorandum of satisfaction in whole or in part, or of
the fact that part of the property or undertaking has been released from the charge
or has ceased to form part of the company's property or undertaking (as the case
may be).*

*(2) Where the registrar enters a memorandum of satisfaction in whole, he
shall if required furnish the company with a copy of it.*   **[396]**

NOTES
Prospective replacement: see the introductory note to this Part.
Prescribed form: for prescribed forms, see Forms 403a, 403b in the Companies (Forms) Regulations 1985, SI 1985/854, as amended by SI 1987/752.

404 Rectification of register of charges

*(1) The following applies if the court is satisfied that the omission to register a
charge within the time required by this Chapter or that the omission or mis-
statement of any particular with respect to any such charge or in a memorandum
of satisfaction was accidental, or due to inadvertence or to some other sufficient
cause, or is not of a nature to prejudice the position of creditors or shareholders
of the company, or that on other grounds it is just and equitable to grant relief.*

*(2) The court may, on the application of the company or a person interested,
and on such terms and conditions as seem to the court just and expedient, order
that the time for registration shall be extended or, as the case may be, that the
omission or mis-statement shall be rectified.*   **[397]**

NOTE
Prospective replacement: see the introductory note to this Part.

405 Registration of enforcement of security

*(1) If a person obtains an order for the appointment of a receiver or manager
of a company's property, or appoints such a receiver or manager under powers
contained in an instrument, he shall within 7 days of the order or of the
appointment under those powers, give notice of the fact to the registrar of
companies; and the registrar shall enter the fact in the register of charges.*

*(2) Where a person appointed receiver or manager of a company's property
under powers contained in an instrument ceases to act as such receiver or
manager, he shall, on so ceasing, give the registrar notice to that effect, and the
registrar shall enter the fact in the register of charges.*

(3) A notice under this section shall be in the prescribed form.

(4) If a person makes default in complying with the requirements of this section, he is liable to a fine and, for continued contravention, to a daily default fine.   **[398]**

NOTES
Prospective replacement: see the introductory note to this Part.
Give notice of the fact: for form of notice to be given, see Form 405(1) in the Companies (Forms) Regulations 1985, SI 1985/854.
Give . . . notice to that effect: for form of notice to be given, see Form 405(2) in the Companies (Forms) Regulations 1985, SI 1985/854.

406 Companies to keep copies of instruments creating charges

(1) Every company shall cause a copy of every instrument creating a charge requiring registration under this Chapter to be kept at its registered office.

(2) In the case of a series of uniform debentures, a copy of one debenture of the series is sufficient.   **[399]**

NOTE
Prospective replacement: see the introductory note to this Part.

407 Company's register of charges

(1) Every limited company shall keep at its registered office a register of charges and enter in it all charges specifically affecting property of the company and all floating charges on the company's undertaking or any of its property.

(2) The entry shall in each case give a short description of the property charged, the amount of the charge and, except in the case of securities to bearer, the names of the persons entitled to it.

(3) If an officer of the company knowingly and wilfully authorises or permits the omission of an entry required to be made in pursuance of this section, he is liable to a fine.   **[400]**

NOTE
Prospective replacement: see the introductory note to this Part.

408 Right to inspect instruments which create charges, etc

(1) The copies of instruments creating any charge requiring registration under this Chapter with the registrar of companies, and the register of charges kept in pursuance of section 407, shall be open during business hours (but subject to such reasonable restrictions as the company in general meeting may impose, so that not less than 2 hours in each day be allowed for inspection) to the inspection of any creditor or member of the company without fee.

(2) The register of charges shall also be open to the inspection of any other person on payment of such fee, not exceeding 5 pence, for each inspection, as the company may prescribe.

(3) If inspection of the copies referred to, or of the register, is refused, every officer of the company who is in default is liable to a fine and, for continued contravention, to a daily default fine.

(4) If such a refusal occurs in relation to a company registered in England and Wales, the court may by order compel an immediate inspection of the copies or register.   **[401]**

NOTE
Prospective replacement: see the introductory note to this Part.

409 Charges on property in England and Wales created by oversea company

(1) This Chapter extends to charges on property in England and Wales which are created, and to charges on property in England and Wales which is acquired, by a company (whether a company within the meaning of this Act or not) incorporated outside Great Britain which has an established place of business in England and Wales.

(2) In relation to such a company, sections 406 and 407 apply with the substitution, for the reference to the company's registered office, of a reference to its principal place of business in England and Wales. **[402]**

NOTE
Prospective replacement: see the introductory note to this Part.

410–744A *((Ss 410–424 Chapter II) apply to Scotland only; see further the introductory note to this Part; ss 425–744A are outside the scope of this work.)*

PART XXVII
FINAL PROVISIONS

745 Northern Ireland

(1) Except where otherwise expressly provided, nothing in this Act (except provisions relating expressly to companies registered or incorporated in Northern Ireland or outside Great Britain) applies to or in relation to companies so registered or incorporated.

(2) Subject to any such provision, and to any express provision as to extent, this Act does not extend to Northern Ireland. **[403]**

746 Commencement

. . . this Act comes into force on 1st July 1985. **[404]**

NOTE
Words omitted repealed by the Companies Act 1989, s 212, Sch 24.

747 Citation

This Act may be cited as the Companies Act 1985. **[405]**

(Schs 1–25 are outside the scope of this work.)

MERCHANT SHIPPING ACT 1995
(1995 c 21)

An Act to consolidate the Merchant Shipping Acts 1894 to 1994 and other enactments relating to merchant shipping [19 July 1995]

1–7 *((Part I): these sections are outside the scope of this work.)*

PART II
REGISTRATION

8–15 *(These sections are outside the scope of this work.)*

16 Private law provisions for registered ships and liability as owner

(1) Schedule 1 (which makes provision relating to the title to, and the registration of mortgages over, ships) shall have effect.

(2) Schedule 1 does not apply in relation to ships which are excluded from its application by registration regulations under section 10(4)(a).

(3) Where any person is beneficially interested, otherwise than as mortgagee, in any ship or share in a ship registered in the name of some other person as owner, the person so interested shall, as well as the registered owner, be liable to any pecuniary penalties imposed by or under this Act or any other Act on the owners of registered ships.

(4) Where the registration of any ship terminates by virtue of any provision of registration regulations, the termination of that registration shall not affect any entry made in the register so far as relating to any undischarged registered mortgage of that ship or of any share in it.

(5) In subsection (4) above "registered mortgage" has the same meaning as in that Schedule.

(6) In this Part "the private law provisions for registered ships" means the provisions of Schedule 1 and registration regulations made for the purposes of that Schedule or the provisions of registration regulations made under section 10(4)(a). **[406]**

NOTES

Commencement: 1 January 1996.

This section replaces the Merchant Shipping (Registration, etc) Act 1993, s 6.

17–291 *(These section are outside the scope of this work.)*

PART XIII
SUPPLEMENTAL

292–312 *(These section are outside the scope of this work.)*

Final provisions

313, 314 *(S 313 contains definitions; s 314 introduces Schs 12, 13, 14 (repeals, consequential amendments and transitional provisions).)*

315 Extent and application

(1) Except for sections 18 and 193(5), this Act extends to England and Wales, Scotland and Northern Ireland.

(2) Her Majesty may by Order in Council direct that any provision of this Act and instruments made under this Act shall, with such exceptions, adaptations and modifications (if any) as may be specified in the Order, extend to any relevant British possession.

(3) Her Majesty may, in relation to any relevant British possession, by Order in Council direct that, with such exceptions, adaptations and modifications (if any) as may be specified in the Order, any of the provisions of this Act shall have effect as if references in them to the United Kingdom included a reference to that possession.

(4) An Order in Council under subsection (2) above may make such transitional, incidental or supplementary provision as appears to Her Majesty to be necessary or expedient.

(5) Without prejudice to the generality of subsection (4) above, an Order in Council under this section may, in its application to any relevant British possession, provide for such authority in that possession as is specified in the Order to furnish the Secretary of State or the registrar with such information with respect to the registration of ships in that possession under its law as is specified in the Order or as the Secretary of State may from time to time require, and for any such information to be so furnished at such time or times and in such manner as is or are so specified or (as the case may be) as the Secretary of State may so require.   **[407]**

316 Short title and commencement

(1) This Act may be cited as the Merchant Shipping Act 1995.

(2) This Act shall come into force on 1st January 1996.   **[407A]**

SCHEDULE 1

Section 16

PRIVATE LAW PROVISIONS FOR REGISTERED SHIPS

General

1.—(1) Subject to any rights and powers appearing from the register to be vested in any other person, the registered owner of a ship or of a share in a ship shall have power absolutely to dispose of it provided the disposal is made in accordance with this Schedule and registration regulations.

(2) Sub-paragraph (1) above does not imply that interests arising under contract or other equitable interests cannot subsist in relation to a ship or a share in a ship; and such interests may be enforced by or against owners and mortgagees of ships in respect of their interest in the ship or share in the same manner as in respect of any other personal property.

(3) The registered owner of a ship or of a share in a ship shall have power to give effectual receipts for any money paid or advanced by way of consideration on any disposal of the ship or share.

Transfers etc of registered ships

2.–6. . . .

Mortgages of registered ships

7.—(1) A registered ship, or share in a registered ship, may be made a security for the repayment of a loan or the discharge of any other obligation.

(2) The instrument creating any such security (referred to in the following provisions of this Schedule as a "mortgage") shall be in the form prescribed by or approved under registration regulations.

(3) Where a mortgage executed in accordance with sub-paragraph (2) above is produced to the registrar, he shall register the mortgage in the prescribed manner.

(4) Mortgages shall be registered in the order in which they are produced to the registrar for the purposes of registration.

Priority of registered mortgages

8.—(1) Where two or more mortgages are registered in respect of the same ship or share, the priority of the mortgagees between themselves shall, subject to sub-paragraph (2) below, be determined by the order in which the mortgages were registered (and not by reference to any other matter).

(2) Registration regulations may provide for the giving to the registrar by intending mortgagees of "priority notices" in a form prescribed by or approved under the regulations which, when recorded in the register, determine the priority of the interest to which the notice relates.

Registered mortgagee's power of sale

9.—(1) Subject to sub-paragraph (2) below, every registered mortgagee shall have power, if the mortgage money or any part of it is due, to sell the ship or share in respect of which he is registered, and to give effectual receipts for the purchase money.

(2) Where two or more mortgagees are registered in respect of the same ship or share, a subsequent mortgagee shall not, except under an order of a court of competent jurisdiction, sell the ship or share without the concurrence of every prior mortgagee.

Protection of registered mortgagees

10. Where a ship or share is subject to a registered mortgage then—

    (a) except so far as may be necessary for making the ship or share available as a security for the mortgage debt, the mortgagee shall not by reason of the mortgage be treated as owner of the ship or share; and

    (b) the mortgagor shall be treated as not having ceased to be owner of the ship or share.

Transfer of registered mortgage

11.—(1) A registered mortgage may be transferred by an instrument made in the form prescribed by or approved under registration regulations.

(2) Where any such instrument is produced to the registrar, the registrar shall register the transferee in the prescribed manner.

Transmission of registered mortgage by operation of law

12. Where the interest of a mortgagee in a registered mortgage is transmitted to any person by any lawful means other than by a transfer under paragraph 11 above, the registrar shall, on production of the prescribed evidence, cause the name of that person to be entered in the register as mortgagee of the ship or share in question.

Discharge of registered mortgage

13. Where a registered mortgage has been discharged, the registrar shall, on production of the mortgage deed and such evidence of the discharge of the mortgage as may be prescribed, cause an entry to be made in the register to the effect that the mortgage has been discharged.

Definitions

14. In this Schedule—

    "mortgage" shall be construed in accordance with paragraph 7(2) above;
    "prescribed" means prescribed in registration regulations; and
    "registered mortgage" means a mortgage registered under paragraph 7(3) above.

[408]–[413]

NOTES

Commencement: 1 January 1996.

This Schedule replaces the Merchant Shipping (Registration, etc) Act 1993, Sch 1.

Paras 2–6 are outside the scope of this work.

Prescribed: see the Merchant Shipping (Registration of Ships) Regulations 1993, SI 1993/3138, as amended by SI 1994/541.

(Schs 2–14 are outside the scope of this work.)

FOREIGN CORPORATIONS

FOREIGN CORPORATIONS ACT 1991
(1991 c 44)

An Act to make provision about the status in the United Kingdom of bodies incorporated or formerly incorporated under the laws of certain territories outside the United Kingdom [25 July 1991]

1 Recognition of corporate status of certain foreign corporations

(1) If at any time—

    (a) any question arises whether a body which purports to have or, as the case may be, which appears to have lost corporate status under the laws of a territory which is not at that time a recognised State should or should not be regarded as having legal personality as a body corporate under the law of any part of the United Kingdom, and

    (b) it appears that the laws of that territory are at that time applied by a settled court system in that territory,

that question and any other material question relating to the body shall be determined (and account shall be taken of those laws) as if that territory were a recognised State.

(2) For the purposes of subsection (1) above—

    (a) "a recognised State" is a territory which is recognised by Her Majesty's Government in the United Kingdom as a State;

    (b) the laws of a territory which is so recognised shall be taken to include the laws of any part of the territory which are acknowledged by the federal or other central government of the territory as a whole; and

    (c) a material question is a question (whether as to capacity, constitution or otherwise) which, in the case of a body corporate, falls to be determined by reference to the laws of the territory under which the body is incorporated.

(3) Any registration or other thing done at a time before the coming into force of this section shall be regarded as valid if it would have been valid at that time, had subsections (1) and (2) above then been in force.   **[414]**

NOTE
Commencement: 25 September 1991 (s 2(3)).

2 Citation, extent and commencement

(1) This Act may be cited as the Foreign Corporations Act 1991.

(2) This Act extends to Northern Ireland.

(3) This Act shall come into force at the end of the period of two months beginning with the day on which it is passed.   **[415]**

INTERNATIONAL FINANCIAL ORGANISATIONS

INTERNATIONAL ORGANISATIONS ACT 1968
(1968 c 48)

ARRANGEMENT OF SECTIONS

An Act to make new provision (in substitution for the International Organis-ations (Immunities and Privileges) Act 1950 and the European Coal and Steel Community Act 1955) as to privileges, immunities and facilities to be accorded in respect of certain international organisations and in respect of persons connected with such organisations and other persons; and for purposes connected with the matters aforesaid   [26 July 1968]

NOTE

By the International Organisations Act 1981, s 6(1), this Act and the 1981 Act may be cited together by the collective title of the International Organisations Acts 1968 and 1981.

1 Organisations of which United Kingdom is a member

(1) This section shall apply to any organisation declared by Order in Council to be an organisation of which—

    (a) the United Kingdom, or Her Majesty's Government in the United Kingdom, and

    [(b) any other sovereign Power or the Government of any other sover-eign Power,]

are members.

(2) Subject to subsection (6) of this section, Her Majesty may by Order in Council made under this subsection specify an organisation to which this section applies and make any one or more of the following provisions in respect of the organisation so specified (in the following provisions of this section referred to as "the organisation"), that is to say—

    (a) confer on the organisation the legal capacities of a body corporate;

    (b) provide that the organisation shall, to such extent as may be specified in the Order, have the privileges and immunities set out in Part I of Schedule 1 to this Act;

(c) confer the privileges and immunities set out in Part II of Schedule 1 to this Act, to such extent as may be specified in the Order, on persons of any such class as is mentioned in the next following subsection;

(d) confer the privileges and immunities set out in Part III of Schedule 1 to this Act, to such extent as may be specified in the Order, on such classes of officers and servants of the organisation (not being classes mentioned in the next following subsection) as may be so specified.

(3) The classes of persons referred to in subsection (2)(c) of this section are—

(a) persons who (whether they represent Governments or not) are representatives to the organisation or representatives on, or members of, any organ, committee or other subordinate body of the organisation (including any sub-committee or other subordinate body of a subordinate body of the organisation);

(b) such number of officers of the organisation as may be specified in the Order, being the holders (whether permanent, temporary or acting) of such high offices in the organisation as may be so specified; and

(c) persons employed by or serving under the organisation as experts or as persons engaged on missions for the organisation.

(4) Where an Order in Council is made under subsection (2) of this section, the provisions of Part IV of Schedule 1 to this Act shall have effect by virtue of that Order (in those provisions, as they so have effect, referred to as "the relevant Order"), except in so far as that Order otherwise provides.

(5) Where an Order in Council is made under subsection (2) of this section, then for the purpose of giving effect to any agreement made in that behalf between the United Kingdom or Her Majesty's Government in the United Kingdom and the organisation Her Majesty may by the same or any subsequent Order in Council make either or both of the following provisions, that is to say—

(a) confer the exemptions set out in paragraph 13 of Schedule 1 of this Act, to such extent as may be specified in the Order, in respect of officers and servants of the organisation of any class specified in the Order in accordance with subsection (2)(d) of this section and in respect of members of the family of any such officer or servant who form part of his household;

(b) confer the exemptions set out in Part V of that Schedule in respect of—

(i) members of the staff of the organisation recognised by Her Majesty's Government in the United Kingdom as holding a rank equivalent to that of a diplomatic agent, and

(ii) members of the family of any such member of the staff of the organisation who form part of his household.

(6) Any Order in Council made under subsection (2) or subsection (5) of this section shall be so framed as to secure—

(a) that the privileges and immunities conferred by the Order are not greater in extent than those which, at the time when the Order takes effect, are required to be conferred in accordance with any agreement to which the United Kingdom or Her Majesty's Government in the United Kingdom is then a party (whether made with [any other sovereign Power or Government] or made with one or more organisations such as are mentioned in subsection (1) of this section), and

(b) that no privilege or immunity is conferred on any person as the representative of the United Kingdom, or of Her Majesty's Government in the United Kingdom, or as a member of the staff of such a representative. **[416]**

NOTES

Sub-ss (1), (6): sub-s (1)(b) and words in square brackets in sub-s (6) substituted by the International Organisations Act 1981, s 1(1).

Orders in Council: the table below lists the organisations in respect of which Privileges and Immunities Orders have been made under this section.

Organisation	Order in Council
African Development Bank	1983/142
African Development Fund	1973/958, as amended by 1975/1209
Asian Development Bank	1974/1251, as amended by 1975/1209
Caribbean Development Bank	1972/113, as amended by 1975/1209
Central Treaty Organisation	1974/1252, as amended by 1975/1209
Commission for the Conservation of Antarctic Marine Living Resources*	1981/1108
Common Fund for Commodities	1981/1802
Commonwealth Agricultural Bureaux*	1982/1071
Commonwealth Foundation*	1983/143
Commonwealth Telecommunications Organisation	1983/144
Customs Co-operation Council	1974/1253, as amended by 1975/1209
European Bank for Reconstruction and Development	1991/757
European Centre for Medium-range Weather Forecasts	1975/158, as amended by 1975/1209, 1976/216 and 1981/1109
European Molecular Biology Laboratory	1994/1890
European Organisation for the Exploitation of Meteorological Satellites (EUMETSAT)	1988/1298
European Organisation for Nuclear Research	1972/115
European Organisation for the Safety of Air Navigation (Eurocontrol)*	1970/1940, as amended by 1975/1209, 1980/1076 and 1984/127
European Patent Organisation	1978/179, as amended by 1980/1096
European Space Agency	1978/1105, as amended by 1980/1096
European Telecommunications Satellite Organisation (EUTELSAT)	1988/1299
Financial Support Fund of the OECD	1976/224, as amended by 1980/1096
Food and Agriculture Organisation	1974/1260, as amended by 1975/1209, 1985/451* and 1985/753
Inter-American Development Bank	1976/222, as amended by 1980/1096 and 1984/1981
Inter-Governmental Maritime Consultative Organisation	1986/1862, as amended by 1972/118, 1975/1209 and 1982/709
Interim Commission for the International Trade Organisation	1972/699
International Atomic Energy Agency	1974/1256, as amended by 1975/1209
International Civil Aviation Organisation	1974/1260, as amended by 1975/1209, 1985/451* and 1985/753
International Cocoa Organisation	1975/411, as amended by 1975/1209
International Coffee Organisation	1969/733, as amended by 1975/1209
International Court of Justice	1974/1261, as amended by 1975/1209
International Fund for Agricultural Development	1977/824, as amended by 1980/1096
International Fund for Ireland	1986/2017
International Hydrographic Organisation	1972/119
International Institute for the Management of Technology Organisation	1972/670
International Jute Organisation	1983/1111
International Labour Organisation	1974/1260, as amended by 1975/1209, 1985/451* and 1985/753
International Lead and Zinc Study Group	1978/1893, as amended by 1984/1982
International Maritime and Satellite Organisation (INMARSAT)	1980/187
International Monetary Fund	1977/825

Organisation	Order in Council
International Natural Rubber Organisation*	1981/1804
International Oil Pollution Compensation Fund	1979/912
International Rubber Study Group	1978/181, as amended by 1980/1096
International Sugar Organisation	1969/734, as amended by 1975/1209
International Telecommunications Satellite Organisation (INTELSAT)	1979/911
International Telecommunication Union	1974/1260, as amended by 1975/1209, 1985/451* and 1985/753
International Tin Council	1972/120, as amended by 1975/1209
International Tropical Timber Organisation (Legal Capacities)*	1984/1152
International Trust Fund for Tuvalu*	1988/245
International Union for the Protection of New Varieties of Plants (Legal Capacities)	1985/446
International Whaling Commission	1975/1210
International Wheat Council (and Food Aid Committee)	1968/1863, as amended by 1975/1209
North Atlantic Treaty Organisation	1974/1257, as amended by 1975/1209
Organisation for Economic Co-operation and Development	1974/1258, as amended by 1975/1209
Oslo and Paris Commissions	1979/914
South East Asia Treaty Organisation	1974/1259, as amended by 1975/1209
United Nations	1974/1261, as amended by 1975/1209
United Nations Educational, Scientific and Cultural Organisation	1974/1260, as amended by 1975/1209, 1985/451* and 1985/753
United Nations Industrial Development Organisation*	1982/1074
Universal Postal Union	1974/1260, as amended by 1975/1209, 1985/451* and 1985/753
World Health Organisation	1974/1260, as amended by 1975/1209, 1985/451* and 1985/753
World Intellectual Property Organisation	1974/1260, as amended by 1975/1209, 1985/451* and 1985/753
World Meteorological Organisation	1974/1260, as amended by 1975/1209, 1985/451* and 1985/753
World Trade Organisation	1995/266

The Orders indicated by asterisks will come into force on a day to be notified in the London Gazette.

An Order in Council under this section may confer immunities on representatives of the United Kingdom to the Assembly of Western European Union or the Consultative Assembly of the Council of Europe, notwithstanding the provisions of sub-s (6) above (see the International Organisations Act 1981, s 4) or on representatives to any conference convened in the United Kingdom (see s 5A of this Act).

For further provisions as to Orders in Council, see s 10 at **[426]**. For similar Orders in Council made under the Foreign Organisations (Immunities and Privileges) Act 1950 which remain in force by virtue of s 12(5) of this Act, see s 12 at **[428]**.

2 Specialised agencies of United Nations

(1) Where an Order in Council under section 1(2) of this Act is made in respect of an organisation which is a specialised agency of the United Nations having its headquarters or principal office in the United Kingdom, then for the purpose of giving effect to any agreement between the United Kingdom or Her Majesty's Government in the United Kingdom and that organisation Her Majesty may by the same or any other Order in Council confer the exemptions, privileges and reliefs specified in the next following subsection, to such extent as may be specified in the Order, on officers of the organisation who are recognised by Her Majesty's Government in the United Kingdom as holding a rank equivalent to that of a diplomatic agent.

(2) The exemptions, privileges and reliefs referred to in the preceding subsection are—

    (a) the like exemption or relief from income tax, capital gains tax and rates as, in accordance with Article 34 of the 1961 Convention Articles, is accorded to a diplomatic agent, and

[(aa) the like exemption or relief from being [liable to pay anything in respect of council tax], as in accordance with that Article is accorded to a diplomatic agent, and]

    (b) the exemptions, privileges and reliefs specified in paragraphs 10 to 12 of Schedule 1 to this Act [and the exemption comprised in paragraph 9 of that Schedule from vehicle excise duty . . .].

(3) Where by virtue of subsection (1) of this section any of the exemptions, privileges and reliefs referred to in subsection (2)(b) of this section are conferred on persons as being officers of the organisation, Her Majesty may by the same or any other Order in Council confer the like exemptions, privileges and reliefs on persons who are members of the families of those persons and form part of their households.

(4) The powers conferred by the preceding provisions of this section shall be exercisable in addition to any power exercisable by virtue of subsection (2) or subsection (5) of section 1 of this Act; and any exercise of the powers conferred by those provisions shall have effect without prejudice to the operation of subsection (4) of that section.

(5) Subsection (6) of section 1 of this Act shall have effect in relation to the preceding provisions of this section as it has effect in relation to subsections (2) and (5) of that section.

(6) In this section "specialised agency" has the meaning assigned to it by Article 57 of the Charter of the United Nations.   **[417]**

NOTES

Sub-s (2): sub-s (2)(aa) inserted by the Local Government Finance Act 1988, s 137, Sch 12, Pt III, para 40; words in square brackets in sub-s (2)(aa) substituted by the Local Government Finance Act 1992, s 117(1), Sch 13, para 27; words in square brackets in sub-s (2)(b) added by the Diplomatic and other Privileges Act 1971, s 3 and words omitted therefrom repealed by the Vehicle Excise and Registration Act 1994, s 65, Sch 5, Pt I.

    Order in Council: the Inter-Governmental Maritime Consultative Organisation (Immunities and Privileges) Order 1968, SI 1968/1862, as amended by SI 1972/118, is made partly under this section.

    See also notes to s 1.

3 *(Repealed by the European Communities Act 1972, s 4, Sch 3, Pt IV.)*

4 Other organisations of which United Kingdom is not a member

Where an organisation . . . of which two or more . . . sovereign Powers, or the Governments of two or more such Powers, are members but of which neither the United Kingdom nor Her Majesty's Government in the United Kingdom is a member, maintains or proposes to maintain an establishment in the United Kingdom, then for the purpose of giving effect to any agreement made in that behalf between the United Kingdom or Her Majesty's Government in the United Kingdom and that organisation, Her Majesty may by Order in Council specifying the organisation make either or both of the following provisions in respect of the organisation, that is to say—

    (a) confer on the organisation the legal capacities of a body corporate, and

(b) provide that the organisation shall, to such extent as may be specified in the Order, be entitled to the like exemption or relief from taxes on income and capital gains as is accorded to a foreign sovereign Power.   **[418]**

NOTES
   Words omitted in first place repealed by the European Communities Act 1972, s 4, Sch 3, Pt IV; words omitted in second place repealed by the International Organisations Act 1981, ss 1(2), 6(4), Schedule.
   Order in Council: the African Development Bank (Privileges) Order 1983, SI 1983/142.
   See also notes to s 1.

[4A International commodity organisations

(1) In this section, "international commodity organisation" means any such organisation as is mentioned in section 4 of this Act (international organisations of which the United Kingdom is not a member) which appears to Her Majesty to satisfy each of the following conditions—

(a) that the members of the organisation are States or the Governments of States in which a particular commodity is produced or consumed;
(b) that the exports or imports of that commodity from or to those States account (when taken together) for a significant volume of the total exports or imports of that commodity throughout the world; and
(c) that the purpose or principal purpose of the organisation is—

   (i) to regulate trade in that commodity (whether as an import or an export or both) or to promote or study that trade; or
   (ii) to promote research into that commodity or its uses or further development.

(2) Subject to the following provisions of this section, an Order made under section 4 of this Act with respect to an international commodity organisation may, for the purpose there mentioned and to such extent as may be specified in the Order—

(a) provide that the organisation shall have the privileges and immunities set out in paragraphs 2, 3, 4, 6 and 7 of Schedule 1 to this Act;
(b) confer on persons of any such class as is mentioned in subsection (3) of this section the privileges and immunities set out in paragraphs 11 and 14 of that Schedule;
(c) provide that the official papers of such persons shall be inviolable; and
(d) confer on officers and servants of the organisation of any such class as may be specified in the Order the privileges and immunities set out in paragraphs 13, 15 and 16 of that Schedule.

(3) The classes of persons referred to in subsection (2)(b) of this section are—

(a) persons who (whether they represent Governments or not) are representatives to the organisation or representatives on, or members of, any organ, committee or other subordinate body of the organisation (including any sub-committee or other subordinate body of a subordinate body of the organisation);
(b) persons who are members of the staff of any such representative and who are recognised by Her Majesty's Government in the United Kingdom as holding a rank equivalent to that of a diplomatic agent.

(4) An Order in Council made under section 4 of this Act shall not confer on any person of such class as is mentioned in subsection (3) of this section any

immunity in respect of a civil action arising out of an accident caused by a motor vehicle or other means of transport belonging to or driven by such a person, or in respect of a traffic offence involving such a vehicle and committed by such a person.

(5) In this section "commodity" means any produce of agriculture, forestry or fisheries or any mineral, either in its natural state or having undergone only such processes as are necessary or customary to prepare the produce or mineral for the international market.]   **[419]**

NOTE

This section inserted by the International Organisations Act 1981, s 2.

5 International judicial and other proceedings

(1) Her Majesty may by Order in Council confer on any class of persons to whom this section applies such privileges, immunities and facilities as in the opinion of Her Majesty in Council are or will be required for giving effect—

    (a) to any agreement to which, at the time when the Order takes effect, the United Kingdom or Her Majesty's Government in the United Kingdom is or will be a party, or

    (b) to any resolution of the General Assembly of the United Nations.

(2) This section applies to any persons who are for the time being—

    (a) judges or members of any international tribunal, or persons exercising or performing, or appointed (whether permanently or temporarily) to exercise or perform, any jurisdiction or functions of such a tribunal;

    (b) registrars or other officers of any international tribunal;

    (c) parties to any proceedings before any international tribunal;

    (d) agents, advisers or advocates (by whatever name called) for any such parties;

    (e) witnesses in, or assessors for the purposes of, any proceedings before any international tribunal.

(3) For the purposes of this section any petition, complaint or other communication which, with a view to action to be taken by or before an international tribunal,—

    (a) is made to the tribunal, or

    (b) is made to a person through whom, in accordance with the constitution, rules or practice of the tribunal, such a communication can be received by the tribunal,

shall be deemed to be proceedings before the tribunal, and the person making any such communication shall be deemed to be a party to such proceedings.

(4) Without prejudice to subsection (3) of this section, any reference in this section to a party to proceedings before an international tribunal shall be construed as including a reference to—

    (a) any person who, for the purposes of any such proceedings, acts as next friend, guardian or other representative (by whatever name called) of a party to the proceedings, and

    (b) any person who (not being a person to whom this section applies apart from this paragraph) is entitled or permitted, in accordance with the constitution, rules or practice of an international tribunal, to participate in proceedings before the tribunal by way of advising or assisting the tribunal in the proceedings.

(5) In this section "international tribunal" means any court (including the International Court of Justice), tribunal, commission or other body which, in pursuance of any such agreement or resolution as is mentioned in subsection (1) of this section,—

    (a) exercises, or is appointed (whether permanently or temporarily) for the purpose of exercising, any jurisdiction, or

    (b) performs, or is appointed (whether permanently or temporarily) for the purpose of performing, any functions of a judicial nature or by way of arbitration, conciliation or inquiry,

and includes any individual who, in pursuance of any such agreement or resolution, exercises or performs, or is appointed (whether permanently or temporarily) for the purpose of exercising or performing, any jurisdiction or any such functions. **[420]**

NOTES

    Orders in Council: The European Commission and the Court of Human Rights (Immunities and Privileges) Order 1970, SI 1970/1941, as amended by SI 1990/2290; the Organisation for Economic Co-operation and Development (Immunities and Privileges) Order 1974, SI 1974/1258, as amended by 1975/1209; the United Nations and International Court of Justice (Immunities and Privileges) Order 1974, SI 1974/1261, as amended by SI 1975/1209; the INTELSAT (Immunities and Privileges) Order 1979, SI 1979/911; the European Committee for the Prevention of Torture and Inhuman or Degrading Treatment or Punishment (Immunities and Privileges) Order 1988, SI 1988/926.

    See also notes to s 1.

[5A Orders under ss 1 and 4 extending to UK conferences

(1) An Order in Council made under section 1 of this Act in respect of any organisation, or section 4 of this Act in respect of an international commodity organisation, may to such extent as may be specified in the Order, and subject to the following provisions of this section,—

    (a) confer on persons of any such class as may be specified in the Order, being persons who are or are to be representatives (whether of Governments or not) at any conference which the organisation may convene in the United Kingdom—

        (i) in the case of an Order under section 1, the privileges and immunities set out in Part II of Schedule 1 to this Act;

        (ii) in the case of an Order under section 4, the privileges and immunities set out in paragraphs 11 and 14 of that Schedule; and

    (b) in the case of an Order under section 4, provide that the official papers of such persons shall be inviolable.

(2) Where in the exercise of the power conferred by subsection (1)(a) of this section an Order confers privileges and immunities on persons of any such class as is mentioned in that paragraph, the provisions of paragraphs 19 to 22 of Schedule 1 to this Act shall have effect in relation to the members of the official staffs of such persons as if in paragraph 19 of that Schedule "representative" were defined as a person of such a class.

(3) The powers exercisable by virtue of this section may be exercised notwithstanding the provisions of any such agreement as is mentioned in section 1(6)(a) of this Act, but no privilege or immunity may thereby be conferred on any such representative, or member of his staff, as is mentioned in section 1(6)(b) of this Act.

(4) In this section "international commodity organisation" has the meaning given by section 4A(1) of this Act.

(5) This section is without prejudice to section 6 of this Act.]   **[421]**

NOTE
This section inserted by the International Organisations Act 1981, s 3.

6 Representatives at international conferences in United Kingdom

(1) This section applies to any conference which is, or is to be, held in the United Kingdom and is, or is to be, attended by representatives—

(a) of the United Kingdom, or of Her Majesty's Government in the United Kingdom, and

[(b) of any other sovereign Power or the Government of any other sovereign Power.]

(2) Her Majesty may by Order in Council specify one or more classes of persons who are, or are to be, representatives of [a sovereign power (other than the United Kingdom)], or of the Government of such a Power, at a conference to which this section applies, and confer on persons of the class or classes in question, to such extent as may be specified in the Order, the privileges and immunities set out in Part II of Schedule 1 to this Act.

(3) Where an Order in Council is made under subsection (2) of this section in relation to a particular conference, then, except in so far as that Order otherwise provides, the provisions of paragraphs 19 to 22 of Schedule 1 to this Act shall have effect in relation to members of the official staffs of persons of a class specified in the Order in accordance with that subsection as if in paragraph 19 of that Schedule "representative" were defined as a person of a class so specified in the Order.   **[422]**

NOTES
Sub-ss (1), (2): sub-s (1)(b) and the words in square brackets in sub-s (2) substituted by the International Organisations Act 1981, s 1(3).
Orders in Council: the CSCE Information Forum (Immunities and Privileges) Order 1989, SI 1989/480.
See also notes to s 1.

7 Priority of telecommunications

So far as may be necessary for the purpose of giving effect to the International Telecommunication Convention done at Montreux on 12th November 1965 or any subsequent treaty or agreement whereby that Convention is amended or superseded, priority shall, wherever practicable, be given to messages from, and to replies to messages from, any of the following, that is to say—

(a) the Secretary General of the United Nations;

(b) the heads of principal organs of the United Nations; and

(c) the International Court of Justice.   **[423]**

NOTE
International Telecommunication Convention: Cmd 3054.

8 Evidence

If in any proceedings a question arises whether a person is or is not entitled to any privilege or immunity by virtue of this Act or any Order in Council made thereunder, a certificate issued by or under the authority of the Secretary of State stating any fact relating to that question shall be conclusive evidence of that fact.   **[424]**

9 Financial provisions

Any amount refunded under any arrangements made in accordance with any provisions of Schedule 1 to this Act relating to refund of [duty] [value added tax or car tax]—

(a) if the arrangements were made by the Secretary of State, shall be paid out of moneys provided by Parliament, or

(b) if the arrangements were made by the Commissioners of Customs and Excise, shall be paid out of the moneys standing to the credit of the General Account of those Commissioners.   **[425]**

NOTES
 Word in first pair of square brackets substituted by the Customs and Excise Management Act 1979, s 177(1), Sch 4, para 12, Table, Pt I; words in second pair of square brackets substituted by the Finance Act 1972, ss 55(5), (7).

10 Orders in Council

(1) No recommendation shall be made to Her Majesty in Council to make an Order under any provision (other than section 6) of this Act unless a draft of the Order has been laid before Parliament and approved by a resolution of each House of Parliament.

(2) Any Order in Council made under section 6 of this Act shall be subject to annulment in pursuance of a resolution of either House of Parliament.

(3) Any power conferred by any provision of this Act to make an Order in Council shall include power to revoke or vary the Order by a subsequent Order in Council made under that provision.   **[426]**

11 Interpretation

(1) In this Act "the 1961 Convention Articles" means the Articles (being certain Articles of the Vienna Convention on Diplomatic Relations signed in 1961) which are set out in Schedule 1 to the Diplomatic Privileges Act 1964, and "the International Court of Justice" means the court set up by that name under the Charter of the United Nations.

(2) Expressions used in this Act to which a meaning is assigned by Article 1 of the 1961 Convention Articles, and other expressions which are used both in this Act and in those Articles, shall, except in so far as the context otherwise requires, be construed as having the same meanings in this Act as in those Articles.

(3) For the purpose of giving effect to any arrangements made in that behalf between Her Majesty's Government in the United Kingdom and any organisation, premises which are not premises of the organisation but are recognised by that Government as being temporarily occupied by the organisation for its official purposes shall, in respect of such period as may be determined in accordance with the arrangements, be treated for the purposes of this Act as if they were premises of the organisation.

(4) Except in so far as the context otherwise requires, any reference in this Act to an enactment is a reference to that enactment as amended or extended by or under any other enactment.   **[427]**

12 Consequential amendments, repeals and transitional provisions

(1), (2) . . .

(3) References in any enactment to the powers conferred by the International Organisations (Immunities and Privileges) Act 1950 shall be construed as including references to the powers conferred by this Act.

(4) . . .

(5) Any Order in Council which has been made, or has effect as if made, under an enactment repealed by subsection (4) of this section and is in force immediately before the passing of this Act shall continue to have effect notwithstanding the repeal of that enactment and, while any such Order in Council continues to have effect in relation to an organisation,—

(a) the enactment in question shall continue to have effect in relation to that organisation as if that enactment had not been repealed, and

(b) section 8 of this Act shall have effect as if in that section any reference to this Act or an Order in Council made thereunder included a reference to that enactment or that Order in Council.

(6) Any such Order in Council as is mentioned in subsection (5) of this section—

(a) if made, or having effect as if made, under section 1 of the International Organisations (Immunities and Privileges) Act 1950, may be revoked or varied as if it had been made under section 1 of this Act:

(b) if made, or having effect as if made, under section 3 of that Act, may be revoked or varied as if it had been made under section 5 of this Act.

(7) . . .   **[428]**

NOTES

Sub-s (1): repealed by the Civil Aviation Act 1982, s 109, Sch 16; see now Sch 4, para 1(2) to that Act.

Sub-s (2): amends the Consular Relations Act 1968, s 1(3).

Sub-s (4): introduces Sch 2 (enactments repealed).

Sub-s (7): repealed by the Statute Law (Repeals) Act 1993, s 1(1), Sch 1, Pt XI.

Sub-s (5): the following Orders in Council are saved by sub-s (5): the International Organisations (Immunities and Privileges of the Commission for Technical Co-operation in Africa South of the Sahara) Order 1955, SI 1955/1208; the International Organisations (Immunities and Privileges of Western European Union) Order 1955, SI 1955/1209, as amended by SI 1976/221; the Council of Europe (Immunities and Privileges) Order 1960, SI 1960/442; the Western European Union (Immunities and Privileges) Order 1960, SI 1960/444; the World Intellectual Property Organisation (Immunities and Privileges) Order 1968, SI 1968/890 (revoked and replaced by the Specialised Agencies of the United Nations (Immunities and Privileges) (Amendment) Order 1985, SI 1985/451, as from a date to be notified in the London Gazette).

International Organisations (Immunities and Privileges) Act 1950: repealed by sub-s (4) above and Sch 2 to this Act.

13 Short title

This Act may be cited as the International Organisations Act 1968.   **[429]**

SCHEDULES

SCHEDULE 1

Sections 1, 2, 3, 6

PRIVILEGES AND IMMUNITIES

PART I

PRIVILEGES AND IMMUNITIES OF THE ORGANISATION

1. Immunity from suit and legal process.

2. The like inviolability of official archives and premises of the organisation as, in accordance with the 1961 Convention Articles, is accorded in respect of the official archives and premises of a diplomatic mission.

3.—(1) Exemption or relief from taxes, other than [duties (whether of customs or excise)] and taxes on the importation of goods.

(2) The like relief from rates as in accordance with Article 23 of the 1961 Convention Articles is accorded in respect of the premises of a diplomatic mission.

4. Exemption from [duties (whether of customs or excise)] and taxes on the importation of goods imported by or on behalf of the organisation for its official use in the United Kingdom, or on the importation of any publications of the organisation imported by it or on its behalf, such exemption to be subject to compliance with such conditions as the Commissioners of Customs and Excise may prescribe for the protection of the Revenue.

5. Exemption from prohibitions and restrictions on importation or exportation in the case of goods imported or exported by the organisation for its official use and in the case of any publications of the organisation imported or exported by it.

6. Relief, under arrangements made either by the Secretary of State or by the Commissioners of Customs and Excise, by way of refund of [duty (whether of customs or excise) paid on imported hydrocarbon oil (within the meaning of the Hydrocarbon Oil Duties Act 1979) or value added tax paid on the importation of such oil which is] bought in the United Kingdom and used for the official purposes of the organisation, such relief to be subject to compliance with such conditions as may be imposed in accordance with the arrangements.

7. Relief, under arrangements made by the Secretary of State, by way of refund of [car tax paid on any vehicles and value added tax paid on the supply of any goods or services] which are used for the official purposes of the organisation, such relief to be subject to compliance with such conditions as may be imposed in accordance with the arrangements.

NOTES
Paras 3, 4, 6: words in square brackets substituted by the Customs and Excise Management Act 1979, s 177(1), Sch 4, para 12, Table, Pt I.
Para 7: words in square brackets substituted by the Finance Act 1972, s 55(5), (7).

PART II

PRIVILEGES AND IMMUNITIES OF REPRESENTATIVES, MEMBERS OF SUBORDINATE BODIES, HIGH OFFICERS, EXPERTS, AND PERSONS ON MISSIONS

8. For the purpose of conferring on any person any such exemption, privilege or relief as is mentioned in any of the following paragraphs of this Part of this Schedule, any reference in that paragraph to the representative or officer shall be construed as a reference to that person.

9. The like immunity from suit and legal process, the like inviolability of residence, and the like exemption or relief from taxes and rates, other than [duties (whether of customs or excise)] and taxes on the importation of goods, as are accorded to or in respect of the head of a diplomatic mission.

[9A. The like inviolability of official premises as is accorded in respect of the premises of a diplomatic mission.]

[9B. The like exemption or relief from being [liable to pay anything in respect of council tax], as is accorded to or in respect of the head of a diplomatic mission.]

10. The like exemption from [duties (whether of customs or excise)] and taxes on the importation of articles imported for the personal use of the representative or officer or of members of his family forming part of his household, including articles intended for his establishment [and the like privilege as to the importation of such articles], as in accordance with paragraph 1 of Article 36 of the 1961 Convention Articles is accorded to a diplomatic agent.

11. The like exemption and privileges in respect of the personal baggage of the representative or officer as in accordance with paragraph 2 of Article 36 of those Articles are accorded to a diplomatic

agent, as if in that paragraph the reference to paragraph 1 of that Article were a reference to paragraph 10 of this Schedule.

12. Relief, under arrangements made either by the Secretary of State or by the Commissioners of Customs and Excise, by way of refund of [duty (whether of customs or excise) paid on imported hydrocarbon oil (within the meaning of Hydrocarbon Oil Duties Act 1979) or value added tax paid on the importation of such oil which is] bought in the United Kingdom by or on behalf of the representative or officer, such relief to be subject to compliance with such conditions as may be imposed in accordance with the arrangements.

13. Exemptions whereby, [for the purposes of the enactments relating to . . . social security, including enactments in force in Northern Ireland—

> (a) services rendered for the organisation by the representative or officer shall be deemed to be excepted from any class of employment in respect of which contributions *or premiums* under those enactments are payable, but]
> (b) no person shall be rendered liable to pay any contribution [or premium] which he would not be required to pay if those services were not deemed to be so excepted.

NOTES
Para 9: words in square brackets substituted by the Customs and Excise Management Act 1979, s 177(1), Sch 4, para 12, Table, Pt I.
Para 9A: inserted by the International Organisations Act 1981, s 5(1).
Para 9B: inserted by the Local Government and Housing Act 1989, s 194(1), Sch 11, para 14; words in square brackets substituted by the Local Government Finance Act 1992, s 117(1), Sch 13, para 28.
Para 10: words in first pair of square brackets substituted by the Customs and Excise Management Act 1979, s 177(1), Sch 4, para 12, Table, Pt I; words in second pair of square brackets inserted by the International Organisations Act 1981, s 5(2).
Para 12: words in square brackets substituted by the Customs and Excise Management Act 1979, s 177(1), Sch 4, para 12, Table, Pt I.
Para 13: words in the first pair of square brackets substituted by the Social Security Act 1973, ss 100, 101, Sch 27, para 80(a) except that the words "or premiums" in italics are not in force; words omitted repealed by the Social Security (Consequential Provisions) Act 1975, ss 1(2), 5, Sch 1, Pt I; words in square brackets in sub-para (b) prospectively inserted by the Social Security Act 1973, ss 100, 101, Sch 27, para 80(b).

PART III

PRIVILEGES AND IMMUNITIES OF OTHER OFFICERS OR SERVANTS

14. Immunity from suit and legal process in respect of things done or omitted to be done in the course of the performance of official duties.

15. Exemption from income tax in respect of emoluments received as an officer or servant of the organisation.

16. The like exemption from [duties (whether of customs or excise)] and taxes on the importation of articles which—

> (a) at or about the time when an officer or servant of the organisation first enters the United Kingdom as such an officer or servant are imported for his personal use or that of members of his family forming part of his household, including articles intended for his establishment, and
> (b) are articles which were in his ownership or possession or that of such a member of his family, or which he or such a member of his family was under contract to purchase, immediately before he so entered the United Kingdom,

[and the like privilege as to the importation of such articles] as in accordance with paragraph 1 of Article 36 of the 1961 Convention Articles is accorded to a diplomatic agent.

17. Exemption from [duties (whether of customs or excise)] and taxes on the importation of any motor vehicle imported by way of replacement of a motor vehicle in respect of which the conditions specified in sub-paragraphs (a) and (b) of paragraph 16 of this Schedule were fulfilled, such exemption to be subject to compliance with such conditions as the Commissioners of Customs and Excise may prescribe for the protection of the Revenue.

18. The like exemption and privileges in respect of the personal baggage of an officer or servant of the organisation as in accordance with paragraph 2 of Article 36 of the 1961 Convention Articles are accorded to a diplomatic agent, as if in that paragraph the reference to paragraph 1 of that Article were a reference to paragraph 16 of this Schedule.

NOTES
Para 16: words in first pair of square brackets substituted by the Customs and Excise Management Act 1979, s 177(1), Sch 4, para 12, Table, Pt I; words in second pair of square brackets inserted by the International Organisations Act 1981, s 5(3).
Para 17: words in square brackets substituted by the Customs and Excise Management Act 1979, s 177(1), Sch 4, para 12, Table, Pt I.

PART IV

PRIVILEGES AND IMMUNITIES OF OFFICIAL STAFFS AND OF FAMILIES OF
REPRESENTATIVES, HIGH OFFICERS AND OFFICIAL STAFFS

19. In this Part of this Schedule—

(a) "representative" means a person who is such a representative to the organisation specified in the relevant Order or such a representative on, or member of, an organ, committee or other subordinate body of that organisation as is mentioned in section 1(3)(a) of this Act;

(b) "member of the official staff" means a person who accompanies a representative as part of his official staff in his capacity as a representative.

[(c) references to importation, in relation to value added tax, shall include references to anything charged with tax in accordance with section [10 or 15 of the Value Added Tax Act 1994] (acquisitions from other member States and importations from outside the European Community), and "imported" shall be construed accordingly.]

20. A member of the official staff who is recognised by Her Majesty's Government in the United Kingdom as holding a rank equivalent to that of a diplomatic agent shall be entitled to the privileges and immunities set out in Part II of this Schedule to the like extent as, by virtue of the relevant Order, the representative whom he accompanies is entitled to them.

21.—(1) Subject to sub-paragraph (2) of this paragraph, a member of the official staff who is not so recognised, and who is employed in the administrative or technical service of the representative whom he accompanies, shall be entitled to the privileges and immunities set out in paragraphs 9 and 13 of this Schedule to the like extent as, by virtue of the relevant Order, that representative is entitled to them.

(2) Such a member of the official staff shall not by virtue of the preceding sub-paragraph be entitled to immunity from any civil proceedings in respect of any cause of action arising otherwise than in the course of his official duties.

(3) Such a member of the official staff shall also be entitled to the exemption set out in paragraph 16 of this Schedule as if he were an officer of the organisation specified in the relevant Order.

22. A member of the official staff who is employed in the domestic service of the representative whom he accompanies shall be entitled to the following privileges and immunities, that is to say—

(a) immunity from suit and legal process in respect of things done or omitted to be done in the course of the performance of official duties, and

(b) the exemptions set out in paragraph 13 of this Schedule,

to the like extent as, by virtue of the relevant Order, that representative is entitled to them, and shall be entitled to exemption from taxes on his emoluments in respect of that employment to the like extent as, by virtue of the relevant Order, that representative is entitled to exemption from taxes on his emoluments as a representative.

23.—(1) Persons who are members of the family of a representative and form part of his household shall be entitled to the privileges and immunities set out in Part II of this Schedule to the like extent as, by virtue of the relevant Order, that representative is entitled to them.

(2) Persons who are members of the family and form part of the household of an officer of the organisation specified in the relevant Order, where that officer is the holder (whether permanent,

temporary or acting) of an office specified in that Order in accordance with section 1(3)(b) of this Act, shall be entitled to the privileges and immunities set out in Part II of this Schedule to the like extent as, by virtue of the relevant Order, that officer is entitled to them.

(3) Persons who are members of the family and form part of the household of such a member of the official staff as is mentioned in paragraph 20 of this Schedule shall be entitled to the privileges and immunities set out in Part II of this Schedule to the like extent as, by virtue of that paragraph, that member of the official staff is entitled to them.

(4) Persons who are members of the family and form part of the household of such a member of the official staff as is mentioned in paragraph 21 of this Schedule shall be entitled to the privileges and immunities set out in paragraphs 9 and 13 of this Schedule to the like extent as, by virtue of paragraph 21 of this Schedule, that member of the official staff is entitled to them.

NOTE

Para 19: para 19(c) inserted by the Finance (No 2) Act 1992, s 14, Sch 3, Pt III, para 90 and words in square brackets therein substituted by the Value Added Tax Act 1994, s 100(1), Sch 14, para 4.

PART V

ESTATE DUTY AND CAPITAL GAINS TAX ON DEATH

24. In the event of the death of the person in respect of whom the exemptions under this paragraph are conferred, exemptions from—

(a) estate duty leviable on his death under the law of any part of the United Kingdom in respect of movable property which is in the United Kingdom immediately before his death and whose presence in the United Kingdom at that time is due solely to his presence there in the capacity by reference to which the exemptions are conferred, and

(b) . . .   **[430]**

NOTE

Sub-para(b): repealed by the Taxation of Chargeable Gains Act 1992, s 290(3), Sch 12.

(Sch 2 specifies certain enactments repealed by s 12.)

INTERNATIONAL MONETARY FUND ACT 1979
(1979 c 29)

ARRANGEMENT OF SECTIONS

An Act to consolidate the enactments relating to the International Monetary Fund and to repeal, as obsolete, the European Monetary Agreement Act 1959 and the entries relating to it in Schedule 2 to the National Loans Act 1968   [4 April 1979]

1 Payments to International Monetary Fund

(1) All sums which the Government of the United Kingdom requires for the purpose of paying to the International Monetary Fund in accordance with the Fund's Articles of Agreement—

(a) subscriptions of such amounts as may from time to time be authorised by order of the Treasury in the event of proposals being made for increases in the United Kingdom's quota under section 3(a) of Article III;

(b) any sums payable under section 11 of Article V (maintenance of value of assets);

(c) any sums required for implementing the guarantee required by section 3 of Article XIII (guarantee against loss resulting from failure or default of designated depository); and

(d) any compensation required to be paid to the Fund or any member of it under Schedule J or K (withdrawal of members and liquidation),

shall be paid out of the National Loans Fund.

(2) The power of the Treasury to make orders under subsection (1)(a) above shall be exercisable by statutory instrument; and no such order shall be made until a draft of it has been laid before and approved by a resolution of the House of Commons.

(3) All sums which the Government of the United Kingdom requires for the purpose of paying any charges payable to the International Monetary Fund under section 8 of Article V of the Fund's Articles of Agreement shall be paid out of the Exchange Equalisation Account. **[431]**

NOTES
International Monetary Fund; Articles of Agreement: the International Monetary Fund was established by an Agreement drawn up at the United Nations Monetary and Financial Conference held at Bretton Woods, New Hampshire, USA, in July 1944. The original Articles of Agreement were published as Treaty Series No 21 (1946), Cmd 6885; the first Amendment was published as Treaty Series No 44 (1978), Cmnd 7205; and the second Amendment was published as Treaty Series No 83 (1978), Cmnd 7331. The second Amendment contains the full text of the Articles of Agreement as amended; it does not set out the actual amendments made at that time.
Subscriptions . . . as may . . . be authorised: the International Monetary Fund (Increase in Subscription) Order 1990, SI 1990/2352, authorises payment of a further subscription to the Fund of 1,220,600,000 Special Drawing Rights.
Order: the International Monetary Fund (Increase in Subscription) Order 1990, SI 1990/2352.

2 Loans to Fund

[(1) The Treasury may make loans to the International Monetary Fund in accordance with the Fund's borrowing arrangements; but the aggregate amount outstanding in respect of the principal of loans under this section shall not exceed 1,700 million special drawing rights.

(1A) For the purposes of subsection (1) above, a loan under this section, or repayment of such a loan, in any currency shall be treated as a loan or, as the case may be, repayment of the amount of special drawing rights which for the purposes of those arrangements is the value of the loan or repayment.]

(2) The Treasury may by order raise or further raise the limit on lending imposed by subsection (1) above.

(3) The power of the Treasury to make orders under subsection (2) above shall be exercisable by statutory instrument; and no such order shall be made until a draft of it has been laid before and approved by a resolution of the House of Commons.

(4) Sums to be lent under this section shall be issued out of the National Loans Fund.

(5) In this section "the Fund's borrowing arrangements" means arrangements made by the International Monetary Fund for enabling it to borrow the currency of any member of the Fund taking part in the arrangements.	**[432]**

NOTE
Sub-ss (1), (1A): substituted for original sub-s (1) by the International Monetary Arrangements Act 1983, s 1.

3 Receipts from Fund

Sums received by the Government of the United Kingdom from the International Monetary Fund (other than sums received by reason of the operation of the Exchange Equalisation Account) shall be paid into the National Loans Fund.	**[433]**

4 Power of Treasury to create and issue notes and other obligations to Fund

(1) The Treasury may, if they think fit so to do, create and issue to the International Monetary Fund, in such form as they think fit, any such non-interest- bearing and non-negotiable notes or other obligations as are provided for by section 4 of Article III of the Fund's Articles of Agreement.

(2) The sums payable under any such notes or other obligations shall be charged on the National Loans Fund with recourse to the Consolidated Fund.	**[434]**

5 Immunities and privileges etc

(1) Without prejudice to the powers conferred by the International Organisations Act 1968 or any other Act, Her Majesty may by Order in Council make such provision as She may consider reasonably necessary for carrying into effect any of the provisions of the Articles of Agreement of the International Monetary Fund relating to the status, immunities and privileges of the Fund and its governors, executive directors, alternates, officers and employees, or as to the unenforceability of exchange contracts.

(2) Subject to subsection (3) below, Orders in Council made under this section may be so made as to extend to any of the Channel Islands, the Isle of Man, any colony and, to the extent that Her Majesty has jurisdiction there, to any country outside Her Majesty's dominions in which Her Majesty has jurisdiction in right of the Government of the United Kingdom.

(3) If, whether before or after the coming into force of this Act, effect is given by or under the law of any part of Her Majesty's dominions or other territory to the provisions of the Articles of Agreement of the International Monetary Fund specified in subsection (1) above, no Order in Council made under this section shall extend to that part of Her Majesty's dominions or other territory as respects any period as respects which effect is so given to those provisions.	**[435]**

NOTE
Orders in Council: by virtue of s 6(2), the Bretton Woods Agreements Order in Council 1946, SR & O 1946/36, as amended by SI 1976/221 and SI 1977/825, and the International Monetary Fund (Immunities and Privileges) Order 1977, SI 1977/825, have effect as if made under this section.

6 Repeals and saving

(1) . . .

(2) Without prejudice to sections 14 and 17(2) of the Interpretation Act 1978 (implied powers to revoke, amend and re-enact subordinate legislation

and savings for such legislation where enactments are repealed and re-
enacted), any Order in Council made under section 3 of the Bretton Woods
Agreements Act 1945 and in force immediately before this Act comes into
force shall have effect, so far as it applies to the International Monetary Fund,
as if made under section 5 above and may accordingly, so far as it so applies, be
amended or revoked by an Order in Council under that section.   **[436]**

NOTES
   Sub-s (1): introduces the Schedule to this Act (enactments repealed).
   Bretton Woods Agreement Act 1945, s 3: s 3 of the 1945 Act was repealed in part by s 6(1) of and
the Schedule to this Act. The whole of the 1945 Act was repealed by the Overseas Development
and Co-operation Act 1980, s 18(1), Sch 2, Pt I.

7 Short title and commencement

   (1) This Act may be cited as the International Monetary Fund Act 1979.

   (2) This Act shall come into force on the expiration of the period of one
month from the date on which it is passed.   **[437]**

(Schedule specifies certain enactments repealed by s 6.)

OVERSEAS DEVELOPMENT AND CO-OPERATION ACT 1980
(1980 c 63)

ARRANGEMENT OF SECTIONS

PART II

INTERNATIONAL FINANCIAL INSTITUTIONS

General

PART V

SUPPLEMENTARY

*An Act to consolidate certain enactments relating to overseas development and
   co-operation and to repeal, as unnecessary, section 16(1) and (2) of the West
   Indies Act 1967*   [13 November 1980]

1–3 *(Relate to assistance to overseas countries etc; not printed in this work.)*

PART II

INTERNATIONAL FINANCIAL INSTITUTIONS

General

4 International development banks

(1) If the Government of the United Kingdom has become bound before the coming into force of this Act, or thereafter becomes bound, by an international agreement for the establishment and operation of an international development bank which provides for the making by members of the bank of an initial subscription or other initial contribution to the capital stock of the bank or becomes bound by any arrangements for the making by the members of any further payment to any such bank, the Secretary of State may with the approval of the Treasury by order made by statutory instrument make provision—

　　(a) for the payment out of money provided by Parliament of sums required by the Secretary of State for the making on behalf of the Government of the United Kingdom in accordance with the agreement or arrangements a payment of any such initial contribution or further payment, including a payment to maintain the value of any such contribution or further payment which has already been paid; and

　　(b) for the payment out of such money of sums required to enable the Secretary of State to redeem any non-interest-bearing and non-negotiable notes or other obligations which may be issued or created by him and accepted by the bank in accordance with the agreement or arrangements; and

　　(c) for the payment into the Consolidated Fund of sums received by the Government of the United Kingdom in pursuance of the agreement or arrangements.

(2) In this section "international development bank" means an international financial institution (whether or not mentioned in section 5, 6 or 7 below) having as one of its objects economic development either generally or in any region of the world.

(3) An order under this section shall not be made unless a draft of the order has been laid before and approved by the House of Commons.　　**[438]**

NOTES

Orders: the following orders have been made under this section: the International Fund for Agricultural Development (First Replenishment) Order 1982, SI 1982/1288; the African Development Fund (Third Replenishment) Order 1982, SI 1982/1798; the Asian Development Bank (Third Replenishment of the Asian Development Fund) Order 1983, SI 1983/697; the African Development Bank (Subscription to Capital Stock) Order 1983, SI 1983/816; the International Bank for Reconstruction and Development (1979 General Capital Increase) Order 1983, SI 1983/1297; the International Bank for Reconstruction and Development (1979 Additional Increase in Capital Stock) Order 1983, SI 1983/1298; the Asian Development Bank (Further Payments to Capital Stock) Order 1983, SI 1983/1952; the Inter-American Development Bank (Sixth General Increase) Order 1984, SI 1984/30; the International Bank for Reconstruction and Development (1984 Selective Capital Increase) Order 1985, SI 1985/79; the Caribbean Development Bank (Further Payments) Order 1985, SI 1985/592; the African Development Fund (Fourth Replenishment) Order 1985, SI 1985/1289; the International Finance Corporation (1985 General Capital Increase) Order 1986, SI 1986/1587; the International Fund for Agricultural Development (Second Replenishment) Order 1986, SI 1986/2328; the Asian Development Bank (Fourth Replenishment of the Asian Development Fund) Order 1987, SI 1987/1252; the Caribbean Development Bank (Further Payments) Order 1988, SI 1988/906; the International Bank for Reconstruction and Development (1988 General Capital Increase) Order 1988, SI 1988/1486; the African Development Bank (Further Subscription to Capital Stock) Order 1989, SI 1989/538; the African Development Fund (Fifth Replenishment) Order 1989, SI 1989/539; the Inter-American Development Bank (Seventh General Increase) Order 1990, SI 1990/1042; the International Fund for Agricultural Development (Third Replenishment) Order 1991, SI 1991/150; the Caribbean Development Bank (Further Payments) Order 1991, SI

1991/717; the European Bank for Reconstruction and Development (Subscription to Capital Stock) Order 1991, SI 1991/1144; the African Development Fund (Sixth Replenishment) Order 1992, SI 1992/398; the Caribbean Development Bank (Further Payments) Order 1992, SI 1992/399; the International Finance Corporation (1991 General Capital Increase) Order 1993, SI 1993/1059; the Asian Development Bank (Fifth Replenishment of the Asian Development Fund and Second Regularised Replenishment of the Technical Assistance Special Fund) Order 1993, SI 1993/1060.

In addition, by virtue of the Interpretation Act 1978, s 17(2)(b), the following orders have effect hereunder: the Caribbean Development Bank (Subscription to Shares of the Capital Stock) Order 1970, SI 1970/437; the Asian Development Bank (Additional Contributions) Order 1972, SI 1972/2066; the African Development Fund (Initial Subscription) Order 1973, SI 1973/1446; the Caribbean Development Bank (Additional Contributions) Order 1975, SI 1975/480; the Inter-American Development Bank (Subscription to Shares of the Additional Capital Stock) Order 1976, SI 1976/1121; the International Fund for Agricultural Development (Initial Contribution) Order 1977, SI 1977/1381; the African Development Fund (Further Payments to Capital Stock) Order 1977, SI 1977/1590; the Asian Development Bank (Further Payments to Capital Stock) Order 1978, SI 1978/154; the International Finance Corporation (Further Payments to Capital Stock) Order 1978, SI 1978/1152; the Caribbean Development Bank (Further Payments) Order 1979, SI 1979/1160; the Asian Development Bank (Second Replenishment of the Asian Development Fund) Order 1979, SI 1979/1225; the African Development Fund (Further Payments to Capital Stock) Order 1980, SI 1980/781; the Inter-American Development Bank (Further Payments) Order 1980, SI 1980/1381.

Particular international development banks

5 The International Bank for Reconstruction and Development and the International Finance Corporation

(1) There shall be paid out of money provided by Parliament—

(a) the subscriptions payable to the International Bank for Reconstruction and Development (in this Act referred to as "the International Bank") under paragraph (a) of section 3 of Article II of the International Bank's Articles of Agreement, including any increase in those sums not exceeding the equivalent of 1,300,000,000 United States dollars; and

(b) any sums payable under section 9 of that Article (falls in the par or foreign exchange value of currencies of members).

(2) The Treasury may, if they think fit so to do, create and issue to the International Bank, as they think fit, any such non-interest-bearing and non-negotiable notes or other obligations as are provided for by section 12 of Article V of the International Bank's Articles of Agreement.

(3) Sums payable under any such notes or other obligations shall be charged on the National Loans Fund with recourse to the Consolidated Fund.

(4) There shall be paid into the Consolidated Fund—

(a) sums received by the Government of the United Kingdom from the International Bank (other than sums received by reason of the operation of the Exchange Equalisation Account); and

(b) sums received by the Government of the United Kingdom from the International Finance Corporation in pursuance of the agreement for the establishment and operation of that body. **[439]**

NOTES

International Bank for Reconstruction and Development; Articles of Agreement: the International Bank for Reconstruction and Development was established by an Agreement drawn up at the United Nations Monetary and Financial Conference held at Bretton Woods, New Hampshire, USA, in July 1944. The original Articles of Agreement were published as Treaty Series No 21 (1946), Cmd 6885.

International Finance Corporation: the International Finance Corporation was established pursuant to an international agreement for the establishment and operation of a body affiliated to the International Bank for Reconstruction and Development (Cmd 9502). The text of the Articles of Agreement of the Corporation is published as Treaty Series No 37 (1961), Cmnd 1377.

6 The International Development Association

(1) The Secretary of State shall pay out of money provided by Parliament any sums required—

    (a) for making on behalf of the Government of the United Kingdom—

        (i) contributions in accordance with any resolution of the Board of Governors of the International Development Association adopted before the coming into force of this Act; or

        (ii) payments in respect of any such contributions under paragraph (a) of section 2 of Article IV of the Articles of Agreement of that Association (falls in the par or foreign exchange value of currencies of members) as applied by any such resolution; and

    (b) for redeeming any such non-interest-bearing and non-negotiable notes or other obligations as may be issued or created by the Secretary of State and accepted by the Association in accordance with paragraph (e) of section 2 of Article II of the Articles of Agreement as applied by any such resolution.

(2) If the Government of the United Kingdom becomes bound by arrangements for the making of additional payments to the Association, the Secretary of State may with the approval of the Treasury by order may be statutory instrument provide for the payment out of money provided by Parliament of any sums required—

    (a) for making on behalf of the Government of the United Kingdom additional payments to the Association in accordance with the arrangements or under paragraph (a) of section 2 of Article IV of the Articles of Agreement, as applied by the arrangments; and

    (b) for redeeming any non-interest-bearing and non-negotiable notes or other obligations which may be issued or created by the Secretary of State and accepted by the Association in accordance with the arrangements or any provision of the Articles of Agreement as applied by the arrangements,

and may provide for payment into the Consolidated Fund of sums received by the Government of the United Kingdom in pursuance of the Articles of Agreement as so applied.

(3) An order under subsection (2) above shall not be made unless a draft of the order has been laid before and approved by the House of Commons. **[440]**

NOTES

International Development Association; Articles of Agreement: the International Development Association was established pursuant to an international agreement for the establishment and operation of a body affiliated to the International Bank for Reconstruction and Development (Cmnd 965). The text of the Articles of Agreement of the Association is published as Treaty Series No 1 (1961), Cmnd 1244.

Orders: the International Development Association (Sixth Replenishment: Interim Payments) Order 1981, SI 1981/517; the International Development Association (Sixth Replenishment) Order 1981, SI 1981/1504; the International Development Association (Special Contributions) Order 1983, SI 1983/1299; the International Development Association (Seventh Replenishment) Order 1985, SI 1985/80; the International Development Association (Eighth Replenishment) Order 1988, SI 1988/750; the International Development Association (Ninth Replenishment) Order 1991, SI 1991/462; the International Development Association (Tenth Replenishment) Order 1993, SI 1993/2046.

In addition, by virtue of the Interpretation Act 1978, s 17(2)(b), the following orders have effect under sub-s (2) above: the International Development Association (Additional Payments) Order 1969, SI 1969/429; the International Development Association (Third Replenishment: Interim Payments) Order 1971, SI 1971/1773; the International Development Association (Third

Replenishment) Order 1972, SI 1972/1576; the International Development Association (Fourth Replenishment: Interim Payments) Order 1974, SI 1974/1881; the International Development Association (Fourth Replenishment) Order 1975, SI 1975/1088; the International Development Association (Fifth Replenishment: Interim Payments) Order 1977, SI 1977/1839; the International Development Association (Fifth Replenishment) Order 1978, SI 1978/472.

7 The Asian Development Bank

(1) Subject to subsection (2) below, the Secretary of State shall pay out of money provided by Parliament any sum which may be required to make payments—

    (a) in fulfilment of any undertaking given by the Government of the United Kingdom in pursuance of paragraph 3 of Article 3 of the Agreement for the establishment and operation of the Asian Development Bank (undertaking to be responsible for obligations of another member for whose external relations the United Kingdom is responsible); or

    (b) under paragraph 1 of Article 25 of the Agreement (falls in the par or foreign exchange value of currencies of members).

(2) The aggregate amount of the sums which may be paid under subsection (1)(a) above shall not exceed £90,000,000 or such greater sum as may from time to time be specified in an order made by statutory instrument by the Secretary of State with the approval of the Treasury.

(3) An order under this section shall not be made unless a draft of the order has been laid before and approved by the House of Commons.

(4) Section 14 of the Interpretation Act 1978 (implied power to revoke, amend and re-enact subordinate legislation) does not apply to an order under this section.

(5) Any sums—

    (a) received by the Secretary of State on behalf of the Government of the United Kingdom from the Asian Development Bank in pursuance of the Agreement, or

    (b) paid to the Government of the United Kingdom in repayment of any payment mentioned in subsection (1)(a) above,

shall be paid into the Consolidated Fund. **[441]**

NOTES

    Agreement for the establishment and operation of the Asian Development Bank: this agreement was signed on behalf of the United Kingdom on 4 December 1965. The text of the Articles of Agreement establishing the Bank is published as Treaty Series No 53 (1968), Cmnd 3762.

    Order: the Asian Development Bank (Extension of Time Limit on Guarantees) Order 1986, SI 1986/286.

Miscellaneous

8 Guarantees of International Bank's loans to colonial territories

(1) The Treasury may, subject to the provisions of this section, guarantee in such manner and on such conditions as they think fit the repayment of the principal of [the payment of interest on and the discharge of any other financial obligation in connection with] any loan made by the International Bank—

    (a) to the Government of a colonial territory, or

    (b) to any Government constituted for two or more colonial territories, or

(c) to any authority established for the purpose of providing or administering services which are common to, or relate to matters of common
interest to, two or more territories of which at least one is a colonial
territory.

(2) The amount of the principal of the loans to be guaranteed under this
section shall not in the aggregate exceed the equivalent of £150 million.

(3) For the purposes of subsection (2) above, the sterling equivalent of the
principal of any loan made in a currency other than sterling shall be calculated
as at the time when the guarantee is given at such rate of exchange as the
Treasury may determine to be the proper rate at that time.

(4) No loan shall be guaranteed under this section unless the purpose of the
loan is approved by the Secretary of State with the concurrence of the Treasury, as likely to promote the development of the resources of the territory or
of all or any of the territories concerned.

(5) A guarantee shall not be given under this section until the Government
or authority to which the loan is to be made has provided to the satisfaction of
the Treasury and the Secretary of State—

(a) for appropriating and duly applying the loan for the purpose
approved under subsection (4) above;
(b) for ensuring that any part of the loan which cannot be applied for
that purpose will be applied only for such purposes as may be
approved by the Secretary of State with the concurrence of the
Treasury;
(c) for the establishment, subject to subsection (6) below, of one or
more sinking funds for the purpose of repayment of the principal of
the loan or any instalment of it, and for the regulation of any sinking
fund so established;
(d) for charging on the general revenues and assets of the territory
concerned, or of all or any of the territories concerned, or on any
other revenues or assets which may be made available for the
purpose—

(i) the principal of and interest on, and other [payments in
discharge of financial obligations in connection with], the loan
and the payments to be made to any sinking funds to be
established under paragraph (c) above; and
(ii) the repayment to the Treasury of any sum issued in pursuance
of this section on account of the guarantee under this section,
with interest on that sum at such rate as the Treasury may fix;
and

(e) for raising, or securing the raising of, sufficient money to meet the
above charges.

(6) Subsection (5)(c) above does not apply in a case where the Treasury and
the Secretary of State are satisfied that the arrangements for the repayment of
the principal of the loan, and for the payment of interest on and [the discharge
of any other financial obligation in connection with] the loan, are such as not to
require the establishment of a sinking fund.

(7) Sums required by the Treasury for fulfilling any guarantees given under
this section shall be charged on and issued out of the Consolidated Fund and
any sums received by way of repayment of any sums so issued shall be paid into
that Fund.

(8) Immediately after any guarantee is given under this section, the Treasury shall lay a statement of the guarantee before each House of Parliament.

(9) Where any sum is issued for fulfilling such a guarantee the Treasury shall, as soon as possible after the end of each financial year beginning with that in which the sum is issued and ending with that in which all liability in respect of the principal of the sum and in respect of interest on it is finally discharged, lay before each House of Parliament a statement relating to that sum.

(10) In this section "colonial territory" means any territory which at the date of the making of the loan in question is, or is part of—

(a) a colony; or
(b) an associated state; or
(c) a British protectorate or protected state; or
(d) a territory for the time being administered by the Government of the United Kingdom under the Trusteeship System of the United Nations.   **[442]**

NOTES
Sub-ss (1), (5), (6): words in square brackets in sub-ss (1), (5)(d)(i), (6) substituted by the Miscellaneous Financial Provisions Act 1983, s 4(4).
Trusteeship System of the United Nations: the Trusteeship System of the United Nations was established in accordance with arts 75 and 77 of the United Nations Charter (Cmd 7015), signed at San Francisco on 26 June 1945.

9 Immunities and privileges of international financial institutions

(1) Without prejudice to the powers conferred by the International Organisations Act 1968 or any other Act, Her Majesty may by Order in Council make such provision as She may consider reasonably necessary for carrying into effect any of those of the provisions of the Agreement establishing an institution to which this section applies which relate to the status, immunities and privileges of the institution and of its governors, directors or executive directors, alternates, officers and employees.

(2) The institutions to which this section applies are—

(a) the International Bank;
(b) the International Finance Corporation; and
(c) the International Development Association.

(3) Subject to subsection (4) below, Orders in Council made under this section may be so made as to extend to any of the Channel Islands, the Isle of Man, any colony and, to the extent that Her Majesty has jurisdiction there, to any country outside Her Majesty's dominions in which Her Majesty has jurisdiction in right of the Government of the United Kingdom.

(4) If, whether before or after the coming into force of this Act, effect is given by or under the law of any part of Her Majesty's dominions or other territory to any provisions specified in subsection (1) above, no Order in Council made under this section and giving effect to those provisions shall extend to that part of Her Majesty's dominions or other territory as respects any period as respects which effect is given to them by or under that law.

(5) No recommendation shall be made to Her Majesty in Council to make an Order under this section relating to the International Finance Corporation or the International Development Association unless a draft of the Order has been laid before Parliament and approved by resolution of each House of Parliament.

(6) Without prejudice to sections 14 and 17(2) of the Interpretation Act 1978 (implied power to revoke, amend and re-enact subordinate legislation and savings for such legislation where enactments are repealed and re-enacted)—

(a) an Order in Council under the Bretton Woods Agreements Act 1945, so far as it applies to the International Bank;

(b) an Order in Council under the International Finance Corporation Act 1955; or

(c) an Order in Council under the International Development Association Act 1960;

shall have effect as if made under this section and may accordingly be amended or revoked by an Order in Council under this section. **[443]**

NOTES

Sub-s (6): the Bretton Woods Agreement 1945, the International Finance Corporation Act 1955 and the International Development Association Act 1960 were repealed by s 18 of, and Sch 2, Pt I to, this Act.

Orders in Council: Up to 1 September 1995, no Order in Council had been made under this section but by virtue of the sub-s (6) the Bretton Woods Agreements Order in Council 1946, SR & O 1946/36, as amended by SI 1976/221 (so far as it applies to the International Bank), the International Finance Corporation Order 1955, SI 1955/1954, as amended by SI 1976/221, and the International Development Association Order 1960, SI 1960/1383, as amended by SI 1976/221, have effect as if made hereunder.

10–17 *(Ss 10–13 relate to overseas service (not printed in this work (s 11 repealed)); (ss 14–17; relate to education (not printed in this work).)*

PART V
SUPPLEMENTARY

18 *(Introduces Sch 2 (enactments repealed and orders revoked) and makes repeals and savings.)*

19 Short title, commencement and extent

(1) This Act may be cited as the Overseas Development and Co-operation Act 1980.

(2) This Act shall come into force on the expiration of the period of one month from the date on which it is passed.

(3) It is hereby declared that this Act extends to Northern Ireland. **[444]**

(Sch 1 is introduced by s 2; not printed in this work; Sch 2 relates to repeals; not printed in this work.)

INTERNATIONAL ORGANISATIONS ACT 1981
(1981 c 9)

An Act to make further provision as to the privileges and immunities to be accorded in respect of certain international organisations and in respect of persons connected wth such organisations and other persons; and for the purposes connected therewith [15 April 1981]

1–3 (*S 1 amends the International Organisations Act 1968, ss 1, 4, 6; s 2 inserts s 4A in the 1968 Act; s 3 inserts s 5A in the 1968 Act.*)

4 Immunities for UK representatives to certain Assemblies

Notwithstanding section 1(6)(b) of the 1968 Act (Orders under section 1 not to confer privileges or immunities on representatives of the United Kingdom, etc), an Order in Council made under section 1 of that Act may confer immunities on representatives of the United Kingdom to the Assembly of Western European Union or to the Consultative Assembly of the Council of Europe.   **[445]**

NOTES
Western European Union: the Western European Union was created in 1954 by the Protocols signed at Paris on 23 October 1954 (Treaty Series No 39 (1955), Cmd 9498) to the Treaty of Economic Social and Cultural Collaboration and Collective Self-Defence, signed at Brussels on 17 March 1948 (Treaty Series No 1 (1949), Cmd 7599). These were supplemented by the Agreement signed at Paris on 14 December 1958 (Treaty Series No 37 (1962), Cmnd 1712) in implementation of Art V of Protocol No 11 of the Brussels Treaty of 17 March 1948 as modified by the Protocols signed at Paris on 23 October 1954.

Council of Europe: the Council of Europe was created in 1949 by the Statute of the Council of Europe signed at London on 5 May 1949 (Treaty Series No 51 (1949), Cmd 7778) . The Consultative Assembly is one of the main organs of the Council and, by virtue of art 40 of the Statute of the Council of Europe, all representatives are to have immunity from arrest and all legal proceedings in the territories of all member States in respect of words spoken and votes cast in debates of the Assembly or its committees or commissions.

Orders in Council: up to 1 September 1995 no Order in Council had been made under the International Organisations Act 1968, s 1 by virtue of the present section. The existing Orders in Council under that section relating to the organisations mentioned in this section are the Council of Europe (Immunities and Privileges) Order 1960, SI 1960/442 and the International Organisations (Immunities and Privileges of Western European Union) Order 1955, SI 1955/1209, as amended by SI 1976/221, and the Western European Union (Immunities and Privileges) Order 1960, SI 1960/444, which prospectively revokes and replaces SI 1955/1209, but had not been brought into force up to 1 September 1995.

5 (*Inserts Sch 1, para 9A in the International Organisations Act 1968 and amends paras 10, 16 of that Schedule.*)

6 Citation, interpretation, extent and repeals

(1) This Act may be cited as the International Organisations Act 1981; and this Act and the 1968 Act may be cited together as the International Organisations Acts 1968 and 1980.

(2) In this Act "the 1968 Act" means the International Organisations Act 1968.

(3) It is hereby declared that this Act extends to Northern Ireland.

(4) ...   **[446]**

NOTE
Sub-s (4): introduces the Schedule to this Act (enactments repealed).

(*Schedule specifies certain enactments repealed by s 6.*)

MULTILATERAL INVESTMENT GUARANTEE AGENCY ACT 1988
(1988 c 8)

ARRANGEMENT OF SECTIONS
Preliminary

*An Act to enable the United Kingdom to give effect to the Convention estab-
lishing the Multilateral Investment Guarantee Agency*   [24 March 1988]

Preliminary

1 The Convention establishing the Agency

(1) In this Act "the Convention" means the Convention establishing the
Multilateral Investment Guarantee Agency which was signed on behalf of the
United Kingdom on 9th April 1986 and presented to Parliament as Command
Paper No. Cm. 150 on 25th June 1987.

(2) The provisions of the Convention referred to in sections 2 to 7 below,
together with certain related provisions, are set out in the Schedule to this Act.
[447]

Payments to and from the Agency

2 Payments to and from the Agency

(1) The Secretary of State may with the consent of the Treasury make out of
money provided by Parliament—

(a) any payment in cash required to be made by the United Kingdom
     under Article 7(i) of the Convention;
(b) any payment required to be made by the United Kingdom for
     redeeming such notes or obligations as are there mentioned; and
(c) any payment required to be made by the United Kingdom under
     Article 7(ii) of the Convention.

(2) The Secretary of State may with the consent of the Treasury by order make provision—

    (a) for the payment out of money provided by Parliament of any sums required by the Secretary of State for making any other payments by the United Kingdom under the Convention; and

    (b) for the payment into the Consolidated Fund of any sums received by the United Kingdom in pursuance of the Convention.

(3) The power to make an order under subsection (2) above shall be exercisable by statutory instrument; and no such order shall be made unless a draft of it has been laid before and approved by the House of Commons.   **[448]**

Status, privileges and immunities of the Agency

3 Status, privileges and immunities of the Agency

(1) The Articles of the Convention specified in subsection (2) below shall have the force of law in the United Kingdom.

(2) The Articles referred to in subsection (1) above are Articles 1(b), 44, 45, 46(a), 47, 48(i) and 50.

(3) Nothing in Article 47(a) shall be construed—

    (a) as entitling the Agency to import goods free of duty or tax without restriction on their subsequent sale in the country to which they were imported;

    (b) except as provided in subsection (4) below, as conferring on the Agency any exemption from duties or taxes which form part of the price of goods sold; or

    (c) as conferring on the Agency any exemption from duties or taxes which are no more than charges for services rendered.

(4) The Secretary of State shall make arrangements for refunding to the Agency, subject to compliance with such conditions as may be imposed in accordance with the arrangements, car tax paid on new vehicles, and value added tax paid on the supply of goods or services, which are necessary for the exercise of the official activities of the Agency.

(5) If in any proceedings any question arises whether a person is or is not entitled to any privilege or immunity by virtue of this section, a certificate issued by or under the authority of the Secretary of State stating any fact relevant to that question shall be conclusive evidence of that fact.   **[449]**

Arbitration proceedings under the Convention

4 Registration and enforcement of arbitration awards

(1) A party to a dispute which is the subject of an award rendered pursuant to Article 4 of Annex II to the Convention shall be entitled to have the award registered in the High Court subject to proof of such matters as are prescribed by rules of court and to the other provisions of this section.

(2) In addition to any sum payable under the award, the award shall be registered for the reasonable costs of and incidental to registration.

(3) If at the date of the application for registration any sum payable under the award has been partly paid, the award shall be registered only in respect of the balance and accordingly if that sum has then been wholly paid the award shall not be registered.

(4) An award registered under this section shall be of the same force and effect for the purpose of execution as if it had been a judgment of the High Court given when the award was rendered as mentioned in subsection (1) above and entered on the date of registration under this section and—

(a) proceedings may be taken on the award;
(b) any sum for which the award is registered shall carry interest; and
(c) the High Court shall have the same control over the execution of the award,

as if the award has been such a judgment of the High Court.

(5) This section shall bind the Crown but not so as to make an award enforceable against the Crown in a manner in which a judgment would not be enforceable against the Crown; and an award shall not be enforceable against a State to which the provisions of Part I of the State Immunity Act 1978 apply except in accordance with those provisions.

(6) In this section "award" includes any decision interpreting an award; and for the purposes of this section an award shall be deemed to have been rendered pursuant to Article 4 of Annex II when a copy of it is transmitted to each party as provided in paragraph (h) of that Article.   **[450]**

5 Rules of court

The power to make rules under section 84 of the Supreme Court Act 1981 shall include the power—

(a) to prescribe the procedure for applying for registration under section 4 above and to require an applicant to give prior notice of his intention to other parties;
(b) to prescribe the matters to be proved on the application and the manner of proof;
(c) to provide for the service of notice of registration of the award by the applicant on other parties; and
(d) to make provision requiring the court on proof of such matters as may be prescribed by the rules to stay execution of an award registered under section 4 above in cases where enforcement of the award has been stayed pursuant to Article 4 of Annex II to the Convention.
    [451]

6 Application of Arbitration Act

(1) The Lord Chancellor may by order made by statutory instrument direct that any of the provisions of section 12 of the Arbitration Act 1950 (attendance of witnesses, production of documents etc.) shall apply, with such modifications or exceptions as are specified in the order, to such arbitration proceedings pursuant to Annex II to the Convention as are specified in the order.

(2) Subject to subsection (1) above, no provision of the said Act of 1950 other than section 4 (stay of proceedings where there is a submission to arbitration) shall apply to any such proceedings as are mentioned in subsection (1) above.   **[452]**

7 (*Applies to Scotland only.*)

8 Northern Ireland

(1) Sections 5 and 6 above shall apply to Northern Ireland with the following modifications.

(2) In section 5 for the reference to section 84 of the Supreme Court Act 1981 there shall be substituted a reference to section 55 of the Judicature (Northern Ireland) Act 1978.

(3) In section 6—

(a) for the reference in subsection (1) to section 12 of the Arbitration Act 1950 there shall be substituted a reference to any corresponding enactments forming part of the law of Northern Ireland;

(b) for the references in subsection (2) to the said Act of 1950 and section 4 of that Act there shall be substituted references to the Arbitration Act (Northern Ireland) 1937 and section 4 of that Act.
[453]

Supplemental

9 Short title, commencement and extent

(1) This Act may be cited as the Multilateral Investment Guarantee Agency Act 1988.

(2) This Act shall come into force on such date as the Secretary of State may appoint by an order made by statutory instrument.

(3) This Act extends to Northern Ireland.

(4) Her Majesty may by Order in Council make provision for extending the provisions of sections 3, 4, 5 and 6 above, with such modifications and exceptions as may be specified in the Order, to any of the Channel Islands, the Isle of Man or any colony.   **[454]**

NOTES

Order under sub-s (2): the Multilateral Investment Guarantee Agency Act 1988 (Commencement) Order 1988, SI 1988/715, bringing the whole Act into force on 12 April 1988.

Order in Council under sub-s (4): the Multilateral Investment Guarantee Agency (Overseas Territories) Order 1988, SI 1988/791, as amended by SI 1988/1300.

SCHEDULE

Section 1(2)

PROVISIONS OF THE CONVENTION ESTABLISHING THE MULTILATERAL INVESTMENT GUARANTEE AGENCY

CHAPTER I

Article 1. Establishment and Status of the Agency

(a) There is hereby established the Multilateral Investment Guarantee Agency (hereinafter called the Agency).

(b) The Agency shall possess full juridical personality and, in particular, the capacity to:

(i) contract;

(ii) acquire and dispose of movable and immovable property; and

(iii) institute legal proceedings.

CHAPTER II

Article 7. Division and Calls of Subscribed Capital

The initial subscription of each member shall be paid as follows—

(i) Within ninety days from the date on which this Convention enters into force with respect to such member, ten per cent. of the price of each share shall be paid in cash as stipulated in Section (a) of Article 8 and an additional ten per cent. in the form of non-negotiable, non-interest-bearing promissory notes or similar obligations to be encashed pursuant to a decision of the Board in order to meet the Agency's obligations.

(ii) The remainder shall be subject to call by the Agency when required to meet its obligations.

Article 8. Payment of Subscription of Shares

(a) Payments of subscriptions shall be made in freely usable currencies except that payments by developing member countries may be made in their own currencies up to twenty-five per cent. of the paid-in cash portion of their subscriptions payable under Article 7(i).

(b) Calls on any portion of unpaid subscriptions shall be uniform on all shares.

(c) If the amount received by the Agency on a call shall be insufficient to meet the obligations which have necessitated the call, the Agency may make further successive calls on unpaid subscriptions until the aggregate amount received by it shall be sufficient to meet such obligations.

(d) Liability on shares shall be limited to the unpaid portion of the issue price.

CHAPTER V

Article 30. Structure of the Agency

The Agency shall have a Council of Governors, a Board of Directors, a President and staff to perform such duties as the Agency may determine.

Article 31. The Council

(b) The Council shall be composed of one Governor and one Alternate appointed by each member in such manner as it may determine. The Council shall select one of the Governors as Chairman.

Article 32. The Board

(b) Each Director may appoint an Alternate with full power to act for him in case of the Director's absence or inability to act.

CHAPTER VII

Article 44. Legal Process

Actions other than those within the scope of Articles 57 and 58 may be brought against the Agency only in a court of competent jurisdiction in the territories of a member in which the Agency has an office or has appointed an agent for the purpose of accepting service or notice of process. No such action against the Agency shall be brought (i) by members or persons acting for or deriving claims from members or (ii) in respect of personnel matters. The property and assets of the Agency shall, wherever located and by whomsoever held, be immune from all forms of seizure, attachment or execution before the delivery of the final judgment or award against the Agency.

Article 45. Assets

(a) The property and assets of the Agency, wherever located and by whomsoever held, shall be immune from search, requisition, confiscation, expropriation or any other form of seizure by executive or legislative action.

(b) To the extent necessary to carry out its operations under this Convention, all property and assets of the Agency shall be free from restrictions, regulations, controls and moratoria of any nature; provided that property and assets acquired by the Agency as successor to or subrogee of a holder of a guarantee, a reinsured entity or an investor insured by a reinsured entity shall be free from applicable foreign exchange restrictions, regulations and controls in force in the territories of the member concerned to the extent that the holder, entity or investor to whom the Agency was subrogated was entitled to such treatment.

(c) For purposes of this Chapter, the term "assets" shall include the assets of the Sponsorship Trust Fund referred to in Annex I to this Convention and other assets administered by the Agency in furtherance of its objective.

Article 46. Archives and Communications

(a) The archives of the Agency shall be inviolable, wherever they may be.

Article 47. Taxes

(a) The Agency, its assets, property and income, and its operations and transactions authorised by this Convention, shall be immune from all taxes and customs duties. The Agency shall also be immune from liability for the collection or payment of any tax or duty.

(b) Except in the case of local nationals, no tax shall be levied on or in respect of expense allowances paid by the Agency to Governors and their Alternates or on or in respect of salaries, expense allowances or other emoluments paid by the Agency to the Chairman of the Board, Directors, their Alternates, the President or staff of the Agency.

(c) No taxation of any kind shall be levied on any investment guaranteed or reinsured by the Agency (including any earnings therefrom) or any insurance policies reinsured by the Agency (including any premiums and other revenues therefrom) by whomsoever held: (i) which discriminates against such investment or insurance policy solely because it is guaranteed or reinsured by the Agency; or (ii) if the sole jurisdictional basis for such taxation is the location of any office or place of business maintained by the Agency.

Article 48. Officials of the Agency

All Governors, Directors, Alternates, the President and staff of the Agency:

(i) shall be immune from legal process with respect to acts performed by them in their official capacity;

Article 50. Waiver

The immunities, exemptions and privileges provided in this Chapter are granted in the interests of the Agency and may be waived, to such extent and upon such conditions as the Agency may determine, in cases where such a waiver would not prejudice its interests. The Agency shall waive the immunity of any of its staff in cases where, in its opinion, the immunity would impede the course of justice and can be waived without prejudice to the interests of the Agency.

CHAPTER IX

Article 56. Interpretation and Application of the Convention

(a) Any question of interpretation or application of the provisions of this Convention arising between any member of the Agency and the Agency or among members of the Agency shall be submitted to the Board for its decision. Any member which is particularly affected by the question and which is not otherwise represented by a national in the Board may send a representative to attend any meeting of the Board at which such question is considered.

(b) In any case where the Board has given a decision under Section (a) above, any member may require that the question be referred to the Council, whose decision shall be final. Pending the result of the referral to the Council, the Agency may, so far as it deems necessary, act on the basis of the decision of the Board.

Article 57. Disputes between the Agency and Members

(a) Without prejudice to the provisions of Article 56 and of Section (b) of this Article, any dispute between the Agency and a member or an agency thereof and any dispute between the Agency and a country (or agency thereof) which has ceased to be a member, shall be settled in accordance with the procedure set out in Annex II to this Convention.

(b) Disputes concerning claims of the Agency acting as subrogee of an investor shall be settled in accordance with either (i) the procedure set out in Annex II to this Convention, or (ii) an agreement to be entered into between the Agency and the member concerned on an alternative method or methods for the settlement of such disputes. In the latter case, Annex II to this Convention shall serve as a basis for such an agreement which shall, in each case, be approved by the Board by special majority prior to the undertaking by the Agency of operations in the territories of the member concerned.

Article 58. Disputes Involving Holders of a Guarantee or Reinsurance

Any dispute arising under a contract of guarantee or reinsurance between the parties thereto shall be submitted to arbitration for final determination in accordance with such rules as shall be provided for or referred to in the contract of guarantee or reinsurance.

ANNEX I

Article 2. Sponsorship Trust Fund

    (a) Premiums and other revenues attributable to guarantees of sponsored investments, including returns on the investment of such premiums and revenues, shall be held in a separate account which shall be called the Sponsorship Trust Fund.

    (b) All administrative expenses and payments on claims attributable to guarantees issued under this Annex shall be paid out of the Sponsorship Trust Fund.

    (c) The assets of the Sponsorship Trust Fund shall be held and administered for the joint account of sponsoring members and shall be kept separate and apart from the assets of the Agency.

ANNEX II

Article 1. Application of the Annex

All disputes within the scope of Article 57 of this Convention shall be settled in accordance with the procedure set out in this Annex, except in the cases where the Agency has entered into an agreement with a member pursuant to Section (b)(ii) of Article 57.

Article 4. Arbitration

    (a) Arbitration proceedings shall be instituted by means of a notice by the party seeking arbitration (the claimant) addressed to the other party or parties to the dispute (the respondent). The notice shall specify the nature of the dispute, the relief sought and the name of the arbitrator appointed by the claimant. The respondent shall, within thirty days after the date of receipt of the notice, notify the claimant of the name of the arbitrator appointed by it. The two parties shall, within a period of thirty days from the date of appointment of the second arbitrator, select a third arbitrator, who shall act as President of the Arbitral Tribunal (the Tribunal).

    (b) If the Tribunal shall not have been constituted within sixty days from the date of the notice, the arbitrator not yet appointed or the President not yet selected shall be appointed, at the joint request of the parties, by the Secretary-General of ICSID (the International Centre for Settlement of Investment Disputes). If there is no such joint request, or if the Secretary-General shall fail to make the appointment within thirty days of the request, either party may request the President of the International Court of Justice to make the appointment.

    (c) No party shall have the right to change the arbitrator appointed by it once the hearing of the dispute has commenced. In case any arbitrator (including the President of the Tribunal) shall resign, die, or become incapacitated, a successor shall be appointed in the manner followed in the appointment of his predecessor and such successor shall have the same powers and duties of the arbitrator he succeeds.

    (d) The Tribunal shall convene first at such time and place as shall be determined by the President. Thereafter, the Tribunal shall determine the place and dates of its meetings.

    (e) Unless otherwise provided in this Annex or agreed upon by the parties, the Tribunal shall determine its procedure and shall be guided in this regard by the arbitration rules adopted pursuant to the Convention on the Settlement of Investment Disputes between States and Nationals of Other States.

    (f) The Tribunal shall be the judge of its own competence except that, if an objection is raised before the Tribunal to the effect that the dispute falls within the jurisdiction of the Board or the Council under Article 56 or within the jurisdiction of a judicial or arbitral body designated in an agreement under Article 1 of this Annex and the Tribunal is satisfied that the objection is genuine, the objection shall be referred by the Tribunal to the Board or the Council or the designated body, as the case may be, and the arbitration proceedings shall be stayed until a decision has been reached on the matter, which shall be binding upon the Tribunal.

    (g) The Tribunal shall, in any dispute within the scope of this Annex, apply the provisions of this Convention, any relevant agreement between the parties to the dispute, the Agency's by-laws and regulations, the applicable rules of international law, the domestic law of the member concerned as well as the applicable provisions of the investment contract, if any. Without prejudice to the provisions of this Convention, the Tribunal may decide a dispute *ex aequo et bono* if the Agency and the member concerned so agree. The Tribunal may not bring a finding of *non liquet* on the ground of silence or obscurity of the law.

(h) The Tribunal shall afford a fair hearing to all the parties. All decisions of the Tribunal shall be taken by a majority vote and shall state the reasons on which they are based. The award of the Tribunal shall be in writing, and shall be signed by at least two arbitrators and a copy thereof shall be transmitted to each party. The award shall be final and binding upon the parties and shall not be subject to appeal, annulment or revision.

(i) If any dispute shall arise between the parties as to the meaning or scope of an award, either party may, within sixty days after the award was rendered, request interpretation of the award by an application in writing to the President of the Tribunal which rendered the award. The President shall, if possible, submit the request to the Tribunal which rendered the award and shall convene such Tribunal within sixty days after receipt of the application. If this shall not be possible, a new Tribunal shall be constituted in accordance with the provisions of Sections (a) to (d) above. The Tribunal may stay enforcement of the award pending its decision on the requested interpretation.

(j) Each member shall recognize an award rendered pursuant to this Article as binding and enforceable within its territories as if it were a final judgment of a court in that member. Execution of the award shall be governed by the laws concerning the execution of judgments in force in the State in whose territories such execution is sought and shall not derogate from the law in force relating to immunity from execution.

(k) Unless the parties shall agree otherwise, the fees and remuneration payable to the arbitrators shall be determined on the basis of the rates applicable to ICSID arbitration. Each party shall defray its own costs associated with the arbitration proceedings. The costs of the Tribunal shall be borne by the parties in equal proportion unless the Tribunal decides otherwise. Any question concerning the division of the costs of the Tribunal or the procedure for payment of such costs shall be decided by the Tribunal.   **[455]**

SOVEREIGN IMMUNITY AND PROTECTION OF TRADING INTERESTS

STATE IMMUNITY ACT 1978
(1978 c 33)

ARRANGEMENT OF SECTIONS

PART I
PROCEEDINGS IN UNITED KINGDOM BY OR AGAINST OTHER STATES

PART II
JUDGMENTS AGAINST UNITED KINGDOM IN CONVENTION STATES

PART III
MISCELLANEOUS AND SUPPLEMENTARY

An Act to make new provision with respect to proceedings in the United Kingdom by or against other States; to provide for the effect of judgments given against the United Kingdom in the courts of States parties to the European Convention on State Immunity; to make new provision with respect to the immunities and privileges of heads of State; and for connected purposes [20 July 1978]

PART I

PROCEEDINGS IN UNITED KINGDOM BY OR AGAINST OTHER STATES

Immunity from jurisdiction

1 General immunity from jurisdiction

(1) A State is immune from the jurisdiction of the courts of the United Kingdom except as provided in the following provisions of this Part of this Act.

(2) A court shall give effect to the immunity conferred by this section even though the State does not appear in the proceedings in question. **[456]**

Exceptions from immunity

2 Submission to jurisdiction

(1) A State is not immune as respects proceedings in respect of which it has submitted to the jurisdiction of the courts of the United Kingdom.

(2) A State may submit after the dispute giving rise to the proceedings has arisen or by a prior written agreement; but a provision in any agreement that it is to be governed by the law of the United Kingdom is not to be regarded as a submission.

(3) A State is deemed to have submitted—

(a) if it has instituted the proceedings; or
(b) subject to subsections (4) and (5) below, if it has intervened or taken any step in the proceedings.

(4) Subsection (3)(b) above does not apply to intervention or any step taken for the purpose only of—

(a) claiming immunity; or
(b) asserting an interest in property in circumstances such that the State would have been entitled to immunity if the proceedings had been brought against it.

(5) Subsection (3)(b) above does not apply to any step taken by the State in ignorance of facts entitling it to immunity if those facts could not reasonably have been ascertained and immunity is claimed as soon as reasonably practicable.

(6) A submission in respect of any proceedings extends to any appeal but not to any counter-claim unless it arises out of the same legal relationship or facts as the claim.

(7) The head of a State's diplomatic mission in the United Kingdom, or the person for the time being performing his functions, shall be deemed to have authority to submit on behalf of the State in respect of any proceedings; and any person who has entered into a contract on behalf of and with the authority of a State shall be deemed to have authority to submit on its behalf in respect of proceedings arising out of the contract. **[457]**

3 Commercial transactions and contracts to be performed in United Kingdom

(1) A State is not immune as respects proceedings relating to—

(a) a commercial transaction entered into by the State; or

(b) an obligation of the State which by virtue of a contract (whether a commercial transaction or not) falls to be performed wholly or partly in the United Kingdom.

(2) This section does not apply if the parties to the dispute are States or have otherwise agreed in writing; and subsection (1)(b) above does not apply if the contract (not being a commercial transaction) was made in the territory of the State concerned and the obligation in question is governed by its administrative law.

(3) In this section "commercial transaction" means—

(a) any contract for the supply of goods or services;
(b) any loan or other transaction for the provision of finance and any guarantee or indemnity in respect of any such transaction or of any other financial obligation; and
(c) any other transaction or activity (whether of a commercial, industrial, financial, professional or other similar character) into which a State enters or in which it engages otherwise than in the exercise of sovereign authority;

but neither paragraph of subsection (1) above applies to a contract of employment between a State and an individual.   **[458]**

4 Contracts of employment

(1) A State is not immune as respects proceedings relating to a contract of employment between the State and an individual where the contract was made in the United Kingdom or the work is to be wholly or partly performed there.

(2) Subject to subsections (3) and (4) below, this section does not apply if—

(a) at the time when the proceedings are brought the individual is a national of the State concerned; or
(b) at the time when the contract was made the individual was neither a national of the United Kingdom nor habitually resident there; or
(c) the parties to the contract have otherwise agreed in writing.

(3) Where the work is for an office, agency or establishment maintained by the State in the United Kingdom for commercial purposes, subsection (2) (a) and (b) above do not exclude the application of this section unless the individual was, at the time when the contract was made, habitually resident in that State.

(4) Subsection (2)(c) above does not exclude the application of this section where the law of the United Kingdom requires the proceedings to be brought before a court of the United Kingdom.

(5) In subsection (2)(b) above "national of the United Kingdom" [means—

(a) a British citizen, a British Dependent Territories citizen [, a British National (Overseas)] or a British Overseas citizen; or
(b) a person who under the British Nationality Act 1981 is a British subject; or
(c) a British protected person (within the meaning of that Act)].

(6) In this section "proceedings relating to a contract of employment" includes proceedings between the parties to such a contract in respect of any statutory rights or duties to which they are entitled or subject as employer or employee.   **[459]**

NOTE
   Sub-s (5): words in first (outer) pair of square brackets substituted by the British Nationality Act 1981, s 52(6), Sch 7; words in second (inner) pair of square brackets inserted by the Hong Kong (British Nationality) Order 1986, SI 1986/948, art 8, Schedule.

5 Personal injuries and damage to property

A State is not immune as respects proceedings in respect of—

> (a) death or personal injury; or
> (b) damage to or loss of tangible property,

caused by an act or omission in the United Kingdom.   [460]

6 Ownership, possession and use of property

(1) A State is not immune as respects proceedings relating to—

> (a) any interest of the State in, or its possession or use of, immovable property in the United Kingdom; or
> (b) any obligation of the State arising out of its interest in, or its possession or use of, any such property.

(2) A State is not immune as respects proceedings relating to any interest of the State in movable or immovable property, being an interest arising by way of succession, gift or bona vacantia.

(3) The fact that a State has or claims an interest in any property shall not preclude any court from exercising in respect of it any jurisdiction relating to the estates of deceased persons or persons of unsound mind or to insolvency, the winding up of companies or the administration of trusts.

(4) A court may entertain proceedings against a person other than a State notwithstanding that the proceedings relate to property—

> (a) which is in the possession or control of a State; or
> (b) in which a State claims an interest,

if the State would not have been immune had the proceedings been brought against it or, in a case within paragraph (b) above, if the claim is neither admitted nor supported by prima facie evidence.   [461]

7 Patents, trade-marks etc

A State is not immune as respects proceedings relating to— .

> (a) any patent, trade-mark, design or plant breeders' rights belonging to the State and registered or protected in the United Kingdom or for which the State has applied in the United Kingdom;
> (b) an alleged infringement by the State in the United Kingdom of any patent, trade-mark, design, plant breeders' rights or copyright; or
> (c) the right to use a trade or business name in the United Kingdom.
>   [462]

NOTE
   Trade-mark: the references to a trade mark in paras (a), (b) are to be construed as references to a trade mark within the meaning of the Trade Marks Act 1994, by virtue of s 106(1) of, and Sch 4, para 1 to, that Act.

8 Membership of bodies corporate etc

(1) A State is not immune as respects proceedings relating to its membership of a body corporate, an unincorporated body or a partnership which—

    (a) has members other than States; and

    (b) is incorporated or constituted under the law of the United Kingdom or is controlled from or has its principal place of business in the United Kingdom,

being proceedings arising between the State and the body or its other members or, as the case may be, between the State and the other partners.

(2) This section does not apply if provision to the contrary has been made by an agreement in writing between the parties to the dispute or by the constitution or other instrument establishing or regulating the body or partnership in question. **[463]**

9 Arbitrations

(1) Where a State has agreed in writing to submit a dispute which has arisen, or may arise, to arbitration, the State is not immune as respects proceedings in the courts of the United Kingdom which relate to the arbitration.

(2) This section has effect subject to any contrary provision in the arbitration agreement and does not apply to any arbitration agreement between States. **[464]**

10 Ships used for commercial purposes

(1) This section applies to—

    (a) Admiralty proceedings; and

    (b) proceedings on any claim which could be made the subject of Admiralty proceedings.

(2) A State is not immune as respects—

    (a) an action in rem against a ship belonging to that State; or

    (b) an action in personam for enforcing a claim in connection with such a ship,

if, at the time when the cause of action arose, the ship was in use or intended for use for commercial purposes.

(3) Where an action in rem is brought against a ship belonging to a State for enforcing a claim in connection with another ship belonging to that State, subsection (2)(a) above does not apply as respects the first-mentioned ship unless, at the time when the cause of action relating to the other ship arose, both ships were in use or intended for use for commercial purposes.

(4) A State is not immune as respects—

    (a) an action in rem against a cargo belonging to that State if both the cargo and the ship carrying it were, at the time when the cause of action arose, in use or intended for use for commercial purposes; or

    (b) an action in personam for enforcing a claim in connection with such a cargo if the ship carrying it was then in use or intended for use as aforesaid.

(5) In the foregoing provisions references to a ship or cargo belonging to a State include references to a ship or cargo in its possession or control or in which it claims an interest; and, subject to subsection (4) above, subsection (2) above applies to property other than a ship as it applies to a ship.

(6) Sections 3 to 5 above do not apply to proceedings of the kind described in subsection (1) above if the State in question is a party to the Brussels Con-

vention and the claim relates to the operation of a ship owned or operated by that State, the carriage of cargo or passengers on any such ship or the carriage of cargo owned by that State on any other ship.   **[465]**

11 Value added tax, customs duties etc

A State is not immune as respects proceedings relating to its liability for—

    (a) value added tax, any duty of customs or excise or any agricultural levy; or

    (b) rates in respect of premises occupied by it for commercial purposes.
                                                                     [466]

Procedure

12 Service of process and judgments in default of appearance

(1) Any writ or other document required to be served for instituting proceedings against a State shall be served by being transmitted through the Foreign and Commonwealth Office to the Ministry of Foreign Affairs of the State and service shall be deemed to have been effected when the writ or document is received at the Ministry.

(2) Any time for entering an appearance (whether prescribed by rules of court or otherwise) shall begin to run two months after the date on which the writ or document is received as aforesaid.

(3) A State which appears in proceedings cannot thereafter object that subsection (1) above has not been complied with in the case of those proceedings.

(4) No judgment in default of appearance shall be given against a State except on proof that subsection (1) above has been complied with and that the time for entering an appearance as extended by subsection (2) above has expired.

(5) A copy of any judgment given against a State in default of appearance shall be transmitted through the Foreign and Commonwealth Office to the Ministry of Foreign Affairs of that State and any time for applying to have the judgment set aside (whether prescribed by rules of court or otherwise) shall begin to run two months after the date on which the copy of the judgment is received at the Ministry.

(6) Subsection (1) above does not prevent the service of a writ or other document in any manner to which the State has agreed and subsections (2) and (4) above do not apply where service is effected in any such manner.

(7) This section shall not be construed as applying to proceedings against a State by way of counter-claim or to an action in rem; and subsection (1) above shall not be construed as affecting any rules of court whereby leave is required for the service of process outside the jurisdiction.   **[467]**

13 Other procedural privileges

(1) No penalty by way of committal or fine shall be imposed in respect of any failure or refusal by or on behalf of a State to disclose or produce any document or other information for the purposes of proceedings to which it is a party.

(2) Subject to subsections (3) and (4) below—

    (a) relief shall not be given against a State by way of injunction or order for specific performance or for the recovery of land or other property; and

    (b) the property of a State shall not be subject to any process for the enforcement of a judgment or arbitration award or, in an action in rem, for its arrest, detention or sale.

(3) Subsection (2) above does not prevent the giving of any relief or the issue of any process with the written consent of the State concerned; and any such consent (which may be contained in a prior agreement) may be expressed so as to apply to a limited extent or generally; but a provision merely submitting to the jurisdiction of the courts is not to be regarded as a consent for the purposes of this subsection.

(4) Subsection (2)(b) above does not prevent the issue of any process in respect of property which is for the time being in use or intended for use for commercial purposes; but, in a case not falling within section 10 above, this subsection applies to property of a State party to the European Convention on State Immunity only if—

    (a) the process is for enforcing a judgment which is final within the meaning of section 18(1)(b) below and the State has made a declaration under Article 24 of the Convention; or

    (b) the process is for enforcing an arbitration award.

(5) The head of a State's diplomatic mission in the United Kingdom, or the person for the time being performing his functions, shall be deemed to have authority to give on behalf of the State any such consent as is mentioned in subsection (3) above and, for the purposes of subsection (4) above, his certificate to the effect that any property is not in use or intended for use by or on behalf of the State for commercial purposes shall be accepted as sufficient evidence of that fact unless the contrary is proved.

(6) (*Applies to Scotland only.*)　　　　　　　　　　　　　　**[468]**

NOTE
    Ships and cargoes of (former) USSR: the State Immunity (Merchant Shipping) (Union of Soviet Socialist Republics) Order 1978, SI 1978/1524, made under s 15(1), provides that notwithstanding sub-s (4) above:

    (i) no application shall be made for the issue of a warrant of arrest in an action in rem against a ship owned by the Union of Soviet Socialist Republics or cargo aboard it until notice has been served on a consular officer of that State in London or in the port at which it is intended to cause the ship to be arrested; and

    (ii) no ship or cargo owned by the Union of Soviet Socialist Republics shall be subject to any process for the enforcement of a judgment or for the enforcement of terms of settlement filed with and taking effect as a court order.

The Order gives effect to Arts 2 and 3 of the Protocol to the Treaty on Merchant Navigation between the United Kingdom and the Soviet Union signed at London on 3 April 1968.

Supplementary provisions

14 States entitled to immunities and privileges

(1) The immunities and privileges conferred by this Part of this Act apply to any foreign or commonwealth State other than the United Kingdom; and references to a State include references to—

    (a) the sovereign or other head of that State in his public capacity;

    (b) the government of that State; and

    (c) any department of that government,

but not to any entity (hereafter referred to as a "separate entity") which is distinct from the executive organs of the government of the State and capable of suing or being sued.

(2) A separate entity is immune from the jurisdiction of the courts of the United Kingdom if, and only if—

   (a) the proceedings relate to anything done by it in the exercise of sovereign authority; and
   (b) the circumstances are such that a State (or, in the case of proceedings to which section 10 above applies, a State which is not a party to the Brussels Convention) would have been so immune.

(3) If a separate entity (not being a State's central bank or other monetary authority) submits to the jurisdiction in respect of proceedings in the case of which it is entitled to immunity by virtue of subsection (2) above, subsections (1) to (4) of section 13 above shall apply to it in respect of those proceedings as if references to a State were references to that entity.

(4) Property of a State's central bank or other monetary authority shall not be regarded for the purposes of subsection (4) of section 13 above as in use or intended for use for commercial purposes; and where any such bank or authority is a separate entity subsections (1) to (3) of that section shall apply to it as if references to a State were references to the bank or authority.

(5) Section 12 above applies to proceedings against the constituent territories of a federal State; and Her Majesty may by Order in Council provide for the other provisions of this Part of this Act to apply to any such constituent territory specified in the Order as they apply to a State.

(6) Where the provisions of this Part of this Act do not apply to a constituent territory by virtue of any such Order subsections (2) and (3) above shall apply to it as if it were a separate entity.   [469]

NOTE
   Orders in Council: the State Immunity (Federal States) Order 1979, SI 1979/457; the State Immunity (Federal States) Order 1993, SI 1993/2809.

15 Restriction and extension of immunities and privileges

(1) If it appears to Her Majesty that the immunities and privileges conferred by this Part of this Act in relation to any State—

   (a) exceed those accorded by the law of that State in relation to the United Kingdom; or
   (b) are less than those required by any treaty, convention or other international agreement to which that State and the United Kingdom are parties,

Her Majesty may by Order in Council provide for restricting or, as the case may be, extending those immunities and privileges to such extent as appears to Her Majesty to be appropriate.

(2) Any statutory instrument containing an Order under this section shall be subject to annulment in pursuance of a resolution of either House of Parliament.   [470]

NOTE
   Order in Council: the State Immunity (Merchant Shipping) (Union of Soviet Socialist Republics) Order 1978, SI 1978/1524 (as to which, see the note "Ships and cargoes of (former) USSR" to s 13).

16 Excluded matters

(1) This Part of this Act does not affect any immunity or privilege conferred by the Diplomatic Privileges Act 1964 or the Consular Relations Act 1968; and—

    (a) section 4 above does not apply to proceedings concerning the employment of the members of a mission within the meaning of the Convention scheduled to the said Act of 1964 or of the members of a consular post within the meaning of the Convention scheduled to the said Act of 1968;

    (b) section 6(1) above does not apply to proceedings concerning a State's title to or its possession of property used for the purposes of a diplomatic mission.

(2) This Part of this Act does not apply to proceedings relating to anything done by or in relation to the armed forces of a State while present in the United Kingdom and, in particular, has effect subject to the Visiting Forces Act 1952.

(3) This Part of this Act does not apply to proceedings to which section 17(6) of the Nuclear Installations Act 1965 applies.

(4) This Part of this Act does not apply to criminal proceedings.

(5) This Part of this Act does not apply to any proceedings relating to taxation other than those mentioned in section 11 above. **[471]**

17 Interpretation of Part I

(1) In this Part of this Act—

"the Brussels Convention" means the International Convention for the Unification of Certain Rules Concerning the Immunity of State-owned Ships signed in Brussels on 10th April 1926;
"commercial purposes" means purposes of such transactions or activities as are mentioned in section 3(3) above;
"ship" includes hovercraft.

(2) In sections 2(2) and 13(3) above references to an agreement include references to a treaty, convention or other international agreement.

(3) For the purposes of sections 3 to 8 above the territory of the United Kingdom shall be deemed to include any dependent territory in respect of which the United Kingdom is a party to the European Convention on State Immunity.

(4) In sections 3(1), 4(1), 5 and 16(2) above references to the United Kingdom include references to its territorial waters and any area designated under section 1(7) of the Continental Shelf Act 1964.

(5) (*Applies to Scotland only.*) **[472]**

NOTE

Brussels Convention: the text of the Brussels Convention is set out in Cmd 5672.

PART II

JUDGMENTS AGAINST UNITED KINGDOM IN CONVENTION STATES

18 Recognition of judgments against United Kingdom

(1) This section applies to any judgment given against the United Kingdom by a court in another State party to the European Convention on State Immunity, being a judgment—

(a) given in proceedings in which the United Kingdom was not entitled to immunity by virtue of provisions corresponding to those of sections 2 to 11 above; and

(b) which is final, that is to say, which is not or is no longer subject to appeal or, if given in default of appearance, liable to be set aside.

(2) Subject to section 19 below, a judgment to which this section applies shall be recognised in any court in the United Kingdom as conclusive between the parties thereto in all proceedings founded on the same cause of action and may be relied on by way of defence or counter-claim in such proceedings.

(3) Subsection (2) above (but not section 19 below) shall have effect also in relation to any settlement entered into by the United Kingdom before a court in another State party to the Convention which under the law of that State is treated as equivalent to a judgment.

(4) In this section references to a court in a State party to the Convention include references to a court in any territory in respect of which it is a party.

[473]

19 Exceptions to recognition

(1) A court need not give effect to section 18 above in the case of a judgment—

(a) if to do so would be manifestly contrary to public policy or if any party to the proceedings in which the judgment was given had no adequate opportunity to present his case; or

(b) if the judgment was given without provisions corresponding to those of section 12 above having been complied with and the United Kingdom has not entered an appearance or applied to have the judgment set aside.

(2) A court need not give effect to section 18 above in the case of a judgment—

(a) if proceedings between the same parties, based on the same facts and having the same purpose—

  (i) are pending before a court in the United Kingdom and were the first to be instituted; or

  (ii) are pending before a court in another State party to the Convention, were the first to be instituted and may result in a judgment to which that section will apply; or

(b) if the result of the judgment is inconsistent with the result of another judgment given in proceedings between the same parties and—

  (i) the other judgment is by a court in the United Kingdom and either those proceedings were the first to be instituted or the judgment of that court was given before the first-mentioned judgment became final within the meaning of subsection (1)(b) of section 18 above; or

  (ii) the other judgment is by a court in another State party to the Convention and that section has already become applicable to it.

(3) Where the judgment was given against the United Kingdom in proceedings in respect of which the United Kingdom was not entitled to immunity by virtue of a provision corresponding to section 6(2) above, a court need not give

effect to section 18 above in respect of the judgment if the court that gave the judgment—

   (a) would not have had jurisdiction in the matter if it had applied rules of jurisdiction corresponding to those applicable to such matters in the United Kingdom; or
   (b) applied a law other than that indicated by the United Kingdom rules of private international law and would have reached a different conclusion if it had applied the law so indicated.

(4) In subsection (2) above references to a court in the United Kingdom include references to a court in any dependent territory in respect of which the United Kingdom is a party to the Convention, and references to a court in another State party to the Convention include references to a court in any territory in respect of which it is a party.   **[474]**

PART III
MISCELLANEOUS AND SUPPLEMENTARY

20 Heads of State

(1) Subject to the provisions of this section and to any necessary modifications, the Diplomatic Privileges Act 1964 shall apply to—

   (a) a sovereign or other head of State;
   (b) members of his family forming part of his household; and
   (c) his private servants,

as it applies to the head of a diplomatic mission, to members of his family forming part of his household and to his private servants.

(2) The immunities and privileges conferred by virtue of subsection (1)(a) and (b) above shall not be subject to the restrictions by reference to nationality or residence mentioned in Article 37(1) or 38 in Schedule 1 to the said Act of 1964.

(3) Subject to any direction to the contrary by the Secretary of State, a person on whom immunities and privileges are conferred by virtue of subsection (1) above shall be entitled to the exemption conferred by section 8 (3) of the Immigration Act 1971.

(4) Except as respects value added tax and duties of customs or excise, this section does not affect any question whether a person is exempt from, or immune as respects proceedings relating to, taxation.

(5) This section applies to the sovereign or other head of any State on which immunities and privileges are conferred by Part I of this Act and is without prejudice to the application of that Part to any such sovereign or head of State in his public capacity.   **[475]**

21 Evidence by certificate

A certificate by or on behalf of the Secretary of State shall be conclusive evidence on any question—

   (a) whether any country is a State for the purposes of Part I of this Act, whether any territory is a constituent territory of a federal State for those purposes or as to the person or persons to be regarded for those purposes as the head or government of a State;

(b) whether a State is a party to the Brussels Convention mentioned in Part I of this Act.

(c) whether a State is a party to the European Convention on State Immunity, whether it has made a declaration under Article 24 of that Convention or as to the territories in respect of which the United Kingdom or any other State is a party;

(d) whether, and if so when, a document has been served or received as mentioned in section 12(1) or (5) above.   **[476]**

NOTE

Brussels Convention: see the note to s 17.

22 General interpretation

(1) In this Act "court" includes any tribunal or body exercising judicial functions; and references to the courts or law of the United Kingdom include references to the courts or law of any part of the United Kingdom.

(2) In this Act references to entry of appearance and judgments in default of appearance include references to any corresponding procedures.

(3) In this Act "the European Convention on State Immunity" means the Convention of that name signed in Basle on 16th May 1972.

(4) In this Act "dependent territory" means—

(a) any of the Channel Islands;

(b) the Isle of Man;

(c) any colony other than one for whose external relations a country other than the United Kingdom is responsible; or

(d) any country or territory outside Her Majesty's dominions in which Her Majesty has jurisdiction in right of the government of the United Kingdom.

(5) Any power conferred by this Act to make an Order in Council includes power to vary or revoke a previous Order.   **[477]**

NOTE

European Convention on State Immunity: the text of this Convention is set out in Cmnd 5081.

23 Short title, repeals, commencement and extent

(1) This Act may be cited as the State Immunity Act 1978.

(2) . . .

(3) Subject to subsection (4) below, Parts I and II of this Act do not apply to proceedings in respect of matters that occurred before the date of the coming into force of this Act and, in particular—

(a) sections 2(2) and 13(3) do not apply to any prior agreement, and

(b) sections 3, 4 and 9 do not apply to any transaction, contract or arbitration agreement,

entered into before that date.

(4) Section 12 above applies to any proceedings instituted after the coming into force of this Act.

(5) This Act shall come into force on such date as may be specified by an order made by the Lord Chancellor by statutory instrument.

(6) This Act extends to Northern Ireland.

(7) Her Majesty may by Order in Council extend any of the provisions of this Act, with or without modification, to any dependent territory.   **[478]**

NOTES

Sub-s (2): repeals the Administration of Justice (Miscellaneous Provisions) Act 1938, s 13, and the Law Reform (Miscellaneous Provisions) (Scotland) Act 1940, s 7.

Orders: the State Immunity Act 1978 (Commencement) Order 1978, SI 1978/1572, bringing the whole Act into force on 22 November 1978.

Orders in Council: the State Immunity (Overseas Territories) Order 1979, SI 1979/458, extending the provisions of this Act, with modifications, to the following dependent territories:

> Belize
> British Antarctic Territory
> British Virgin Islands
> Cayman Islands
> Falkland Islands and Dependencies
> Gilbert Islands
> Hong Kong
> Montserrat
> Pitcairn, Henderson, Ducie and Oeno Islands
> Sovereign Base Areas of Akrotiri and Dhekelia
> Turks and Caicos Islands;

the State Immunity (Guernsey) Order 1980, SI 1980/871, extending the provisions of this Act, with exceptions, adaptations and modifications, to the Bailiwick of Guernsey; the State Immunity (Isle of Man) Order 1981, SI 1981/1112, extending the provisions of this Act, with modifications, to the Isle of Man; the State Immunity (Jersey) Order 1985, SI 1985/1642, extending the provisions of this Act, with modifications, to the Bailiwick of Jersey.

PROTECTION OF TRADING INTERESTS ACT 1980
(1980 c 11)

ARRANGEMENT OF SECTIONS

An Act to provide protection from requirements, prohibitions and judgments imposed or given under the laws of countries outside the United Kingdom and affecting the trading or other interests of persons in the United Kingdom
[20 March 1980]

1 Overseas measures affecting United Kingdom trading interests

(1) If it appears to the Secretary of State—

     (a) that measures have been or are proposed to be taken by or under the law of any overseas country for regulating or controlling international trade; and

     (b) that those measures, in so far as they apply or would apply to things done or to be done outside the territorial jurisdiction of that country by persons carrying on business in the United Kingdom, are damaging or threaten to damage the trading interests of the United Kingdom, the Secretary of State may by order direct that this section shall apply to those measures either generally or in their application to such cases as may be specified in the order.

(2) The Secretary of State may by order make provision for requiring, or enabling the Secretary of State to require, a person in the United Kingdom who carries on business there to give notice to the Secretary of State of any requirement or prohibition imposed or threatened to be imposed on that person pursuant to any measures in so far as this section applies to them by virtue of an order under subsection (1) above.

(3) The Secretary of State may give to any person in the United Kingdom who carries on business there such directions for prohibiting compliance with any such requirement or prohibition as aforesaid as he considers appropriate for avoiding damage to the trading interests of the United Kingdom.

(4) The power of the Secretary of State to make orders under subsection (1) or (2) above shall be exercisable by statutory instrument subject to annulment in pursuance of a resolution of either House of Parliament.

(5) Directions under subsection (3) above may be either general or special and may prohibit compliance with any requirement or prohibition either absolutely or in such cases or subject to such conditions as to consent or otherwise as may be specified in the directions; and general directions under that subsection shall be published in such manner as appears to the Secretary of State to be appropriate.

(6) In this section "trade" includes any activity carried on in the course of a business of any description and "trading interests" shall be construed accordingly. **[479]**

NOTE
Orders: the Protection of Trading Interests (US Re-export Control) Order 1982, SI 1982/885; the Protection of Trading Interests (US Antitrust Measures) Order 1983, SI 1983/900; the Protection of Trading Interests (US Cuban Assets Control Regulations) Order 1992, SI 1992/2449.

2 Documents and information required by overseas courts and authorities

(1) If it appears to the Secretary of State—

   (a) that a requirement has been or may be imposed on a person or persons in the United Kingdom to produce to any court, tribunal or authority of an overseas country any commercial document which is not within the territorial jurisdiction of that country or to furnish any commercial information to any such court, tribunal or authority; or

   (b) that any such authority has imposed or may impose a requirement on a person or persons in the United Kingdom to publish any such document or information,

the Secretary of State may, if it appears to him that the requirement is inadmissible by virtue of subsection (2) or (3) below, give directions for prohibiting compliance with the requirement.

(2) A requirement such as is mentioned in subsection (1)(a) or (b) above is inadmissible—

   (a) if it infringes the jurisdiction of the United Kingdom or is otherwise prejudicial to the sovereignty of the United Kingdom; or

   (b) if compliance with the requirement would be prejudicial to the security of the United Kingdom or to the relations of the government of the United Kingdom with the government of any other country.

(3) A requirement such as is mentioned in subsection (1)(a) above is also inadmissible—

(a) if it is made otherwise than for the purposes of civil or criminal proceedings which have been instituted in the overseas country; or

(b) if it requires a person to state what documents relevant to any such proceedings are or have been in his possession, custody or power or to produce for the purposes of any such proceedings any documents other than particular documents specified in the requirement.

(4) Directions under subsection (1) above may be either general or special and may prohibit compliance with any requirement either absolutely or in such cases or subject to such conditions as to consent or otherwise as may be specified in the directions; and general directions under that subsection shall be published in such manner as appears to the Secretary of State to be appropriate.

(5) For the purposes of this section the making of a request or demand shall be treated as the imposition of a requirement if it is made in circumstances in which a requirement to the same effect could be or could have been imposed; and

(a) any request or demand for the supply of a document or information which, pursuant to the requirement of any court, tribunal or authority of an overseas country, is addressed to a person in the United Kingdom; or

(b) any requirement imposed by such a court, tribunal or authority to produce or furnish any document or information to a person specified in the requirement,

shall be treated as a requirement to produce or furnish that document or information to that court, tribunal or authority.

(6) In this section "commercial document" and "commercial information" mean respectively a document or information relating to a business of any description and "document" includes any record or device by means of which material is recorded or stored.   **[480]**

3 Offences under ss 1 and 2

(1) Subject to subsection (2) below, any person who without reasonable excuse fails to comply with any requirement imposed under subsection (2) of section 1 above or knowingly contravenes any directions given under subsection (3) of that section or section 2(1) above shall be guilty of an offence and liable—

(a) on conviction on indictment, to a fine;

(b) on summary conviction, to a fine not exceeding the statutory maximum.

(2) A person who is neither a citizen of the United Kingdom and Colonies nor a body corporate incorporated in the United Kingdom shall not be guilty of an offence under subsection (1) above by reason of anything done or omitted outside the United Kingdom in contravention of directions under section 1(3) or 2(1) above.

(3) No proceedings for an offence under subsection (1) above shall be instituted in England, Wales or Northern Ireland except by the Secretary of

State or with the consent of the Attorney General or, as the case may be, the Attorney General for Northern Ireland.

(4) Proceedings against any person for an offence under this section may be taken before the appropriate court in the United Kingdom having jurisdiction in the place where that person is for the time being.

(5) . . .   [481]

NOTE

Sub-s (5): repealed by the Statute Law (Repeals) Act 1993, s 1(1), Sch 1, Pt XIV.

4 Restriction of Evidence (Proceedings in Other Jurisdictions) Act 1975

A court in the United Kingdom shall not make an order under section 2 of the Evidence (Proceedings in Other Jurisdictions) Act 1975 for giving effect to a request issued by or on behalf of a court or tribunal of an overseas country if it is shown that the request infringes the jurisdiction of the United Kingdom or is otherwise prejudicial to the sovereignty of the United Kingdom; and a certificate signed by or on behalf of the Secretary of State to the effect that it infringes that jurisdiction or is so prejudicial shall be conclusive evidence of that fact.   [482]

5 Restriction on enforcement of certain overseas judgments

(1) A judgment to which this section applies shall not be registered under Part II of the Administration of Justice Act 1920 or Part I of the Foreign Judgments (Reciprocal Enforcement) Act 1933 and no court in the United Kingdom shall entertain proceedings at common law for the recovery of any sum payable under such a judgment.

(2) This section applies to any judgment given by a court of an overseas country, being—

    (a) a judgment for multiple damages within the meaning of subsection (3) below;

    (b) a judgment based on a provision or rule of law specified or described in an order under subsection (4) below and given after the coming into force of the order; or

    (c) a judgment on a claim for contribution in respect of damages awarded by a judgment falling within paragraph (a) or (b) above.

(3) In subsection (2)(a) above a judgment for multiple damages means a judgment for an amount arrived at by doubling, trebling or otherwise multiplying a sum assessed as compensation for the loss or damage sustained by the person in whose favour the judgment is given.

(4) The Secretary of State may for the purposes of subsection (2)(b) above make an order in respect of any provision or rule of law which appears to him to be concerned with the prohibition or regulation of agreements, arrangements or practices designed to restrain, distort or restrict competition in the carrying on of business of any description or to be otherwise concerned with the promotion of such competition as aforesaid.

(5) The power of the Secretary of State to make orders under subsection (4) above shall be exercisable by statutory instrument subject to annulment in pursuance of a resolution of either House of Parliament.

(6) Subsection (2)(a) above applies to a judgment given before the date of the passing of this Act as well as to a judgment given on or after that date but

this section does not affect any judgment which has been registered before that date under the provisions mentioned in subsection (1) above or in respect of which such proceedings as are there mentioned have been finally determined before that date.   **[483]**

NOTE

Orders: the Protection of Trading Interests (Australian Trade Practices) Order 1988, SI 1988/569.

6 Recovery of awards of multiple damages

(1) This section applies where a court of an overseas country has given a judgment for multiple damages with the meaning of section 5(3) above against—

    (a) a citizen of the United Kingdom and Colonies; or

    (b) a body corporate incorporated in the United Kingdom or in a territory outside the United Kingdom for whose international relations Her Majesty's Government in the United Kingdom are responsible; or

    (c) a person carrying on business in the United Kingdom,

(in this section referred to as a "qualifying defendant") and an amount on account of the damages has been paid by the qualifying defendant either to the party in whose favour the judgment was given or to another party who is entitled as against the qualifying defendant to contribution in respect of the damages.

(2) Subject to subsections (3) and (4) below, the qualifying defendant shall be entitled to recover from the party in whose favour the judgment was given so much of the amount referred to in subsection (1) above as exceeds the part attributable to compensation; and that part shall be taken to be such part of the amount as bears to the whole of it the same proportion as the sum assessed by the court that gave the judgment as compensation for the loss or damage sustained by that party bears to the whole of the damages awarded to that party.

(3) Subsection (2) above does not apply where the qualifying defendant is an individual who was ordinarily resident in the overseas country at the time when the proceedings in which the judgment was given were instituted or a body corporate which had its principal place of business there at that time.

(4) Subsection (2) above does not apply where the qualifying defendant carried on business in the overseas country and the proceedings in which the judgment was given were concerned with activities exclusively carried on in that country.

(5) A court in the United Kingdom may entertain proceedings on a claim under this section notwithstanding that the person against whom the proceedings are brought is not within the jurisdiction of the court.

(6) The reference in subsection (1) above to an amount paid by the qualifying defendant includes a reference to an amount obtained by execution against his property or against the property of a company which (directly or indirectly) is wholly owned by him; and references in that subsection and subsection (2) above to the party in whose favour the judgment was given or to a party entitled to contribution include references to any person in whom the rights of any such party have become vested by succession or assignment or otherwise.

(7) This section shall, with the necessary modifications, apply also in relation to any order which is made by a tribunal or authority of an overseas country and would, if that tribunal or authority were a court, be a judgment for multiple damages within the meaning of section 5(3) above.

(8) This section does not apply to any judgment given or order made before the passing of this Act.   **[484]**

7 Enforcement of overseas judgment under provision corresponding to s 6

(1) If it appears to Her Majesty that the law of an overseas country provides or will provide for the enforcement in that country of judgments given under section 6 above, Her Majesty may by Order in Council provide for the enforcement in the United Kingdom of [judgments of any description specified in the Order which are given under any provision of the law of that country relating to the recovery of sums paid or obtained pursuant to a judgment for multiple damages within the meaning of section 5(3) above, whether or not that provision corresponds to section 6 above].

[(1A) Such an Order in Council may, as respects judgments to which it relates—

    (a) make different provisions for different descriptions of judgment; and

    (b) impose conditions or restrictions on the enforcement of judgments of any description.]

(2) An Order under this section may apply, with or without modification, any of the provisions of the Foreign Judgments (Reciprocal Enforcement) Act 1933.   **[485]**

NOTES

    Sub-ss (1), (1A): words in square brackets in sub-s (1) substituted, and sub-s (1A) inserted, by the Civil Jurisdiction and Judgments Act 1982, s 38.

    Order in Council: the Reciprocal Enforcement of Foreign Judgments (Australia) Order 1994, SI 1994/1901, with effect in accordance with art 1 thereof.

8 Short title, interpretation, repeals and extent

(1) This Act may be cited as the Protection of Trading Interests Act 1980.

(2) In this Act "overseas country" means any country or territory outside the United Kingdom other than one for whose international relations Her Majesty's Government in the United Kingdom are responsible.

(3) References in this Act to the law or a court, tribunal or authority of an overseas country include, in the case of a federal state, references to the law or a court, tribunal or authority of any constituent part of that country.

(4) References in this Act to a claim for, or to entitlement to, contribution are references to a claim or entitlement based on an enactment or rule of law.

(5), (6) . . .

(7) This Act extends to Northern Ireland.

(8) Her Majesty may by Order in Council direct that this Act shall extend with such exceptions, adaptations and modifications, if any, as may be specified in the Order to any territory outside the United Kingdom, being a territory for the international relations of which Her Majesty's Government in the United Kingdom are responsible.   **[486]**

NOTES

Sub-ss (5), (6): sub-s (5) repealed in part by the Magistrates' Courts Act 1980, s 154(3), Sch 9; remainder of sub-s (5), and sub-s (6), repeal the Shipping Contracts and Commercial Documents Act 1964, save in relation to any direction given under that Act before 20 March 1980.

Orders in Council: the Protection of Trading Interests Act 1980 (Jersey) Order 1983, SI 1983/607, as amended by SI 1983/1700, extending this Act, with exceptions, adaptations and modifications, to the Bailiwick of Jersey; the Protection of Trading Interests Act 1980 (Guernsey) Order 1983, SI 1983/1703, extending this Act, with exceptions, adaptations and modifications, to the Bailiwick of Guernsey; the Protection of Trading Interests Act 1980 (Isle of Man) Order 1983, SI 1983/1704, extending this Act, with exceptions, adaptations and modifications, to the Isle of Man; the Protection of Trading Interests Act 1980 (Hong Kong) Order, SI 1990/2291, extending this Act, with exceptions, adaptations and modifications, to Hong Kong.

EXPORTS

EXPORT AND INVESTMENT GUARANTEES ACT 1991
(1991 c 67)

ARRANGEMENT OF SECTIONS

PART I
POWERS OF ECGD

An Act to make new provision as to the functions exercisable by the Secretary of State through the Export Credits Guarantee Department; and make provision as to the delegation of any such functions and the transfer of property, rights and liabilities attributable to the exercise of any such functions
[22 October 1991]

PART I
POWERS OF ECGD

1 Assistance in connection with exports of goods and services

(1) The Secretary of State may make arrangements under this section with a view to facilitating, directly or indirectly, supplies by persons carrying on business in the United Kingdom of goods or services to persons carrying on business outside the United Kingdom.

(2) The Secretary of State may make arrangements under this section for the purpose of rendering economic assistance to countries outside the United Kingdom.

(3) The Secretary of State may make arrangements under this section with a view to facilitating—

  (a) the performance of obligations created or arising, directly or indirectly, in connection with matters as to which he has exercised his powers under this section or section 2 of this Act, or

  (b) the reduction or avoidance of losses arising in connection with any failure to perform such obligations.

(4) The arrangements that may be made under this section are arrangements for providing financial facilities or assistance for, or for the benefit of, persons carrying on business; and the facilities or assistance may be provided in any form, including guarantees, insurance, grants or loans.   **[487]**

NOTE
  Commencement: 23 October 1991 (SI 1991/2430).

2 Insurance in connection with overseas investment

(1) The Secretary of State may make arrangements for insuring any person carrying on business in the United Kingdom against risks of losses arising—

  (a) in connection with any investment of resources by the insured in enterprises carried on outside the United Kingdom, or

  (b) in connection with guarantees given by the insured in respect of any investment of resources by others in such enterprises, being enterprises in which the insured has any interest,

being losses resulting directly or indirectly from war, expropriation, restrictions on remittances and other similar events.

(2) The Secretary of State may make arrangements for insuring persons providing such insurance.

(3) References in subsection (1) above to a person carrying on business in the United Kingdom and to the insured include any company controlled directly or indirectly by him.   **[488]**

NOTE
  Commencement: 23 October 1991 (SI 1991/2430).

3 Financial management

(1) The Secretary of State may make any arrangements which, in his opinion, are in the interests of the proper financial management of the ECGD portfolio, or any part of it.

(2) In pursuance of arrangements under this section the Secretary of State may enter into any form of transaction, including—

  (a) lending, and
  (b) providing and taking out insurance and guarantees.

(3) The Secretary of State may not, in pursuance of such arrangements, enter into any transaction for the purpose of borrowing money but, subject to that, he is not precluded from entering into any transaction by reason of its involving borrowing.

(4) In pursuance of such arrangements the Secretary of State may—

  (a) alter any arrangements made under section 1 or 2 of this Act or the old law or make new arrangements in place of arrangements so made, or

(b) make further arrangements in connection with arrangements so made.

(5) Arrangements under this section may be made in anticipation of further rights being acquired or liabilities being incurred by the Secretary of State.

(6) In this section the "ECGD portfolio" means the rights and liabilities to which the Secretary of State is entitled or subject by virtue of the exercise of his powers under this Act or the old law or in consequence of arrangements made in the exercise of those powers.

(7) The Secretary of State may certify that any transaction he has entered into or is entering into has been or, as the case may be, is entered into in the exercise of the powers conferred by this section and such a certificate shall be conclusive evidence of the matters stated in it.   **[489]**

NOTE
Commencement: 23 October 1991 (SI 1991/2430).

4 Provisions supplementary to sections 1 to 3

(1) Transactions entered into in pursuance of arrangements made under sections 1 to 3 of this Act may be on such terms and conditions as the Secretary of State considers appropriate.

(2) The powers of the Secretary of State under those sections are exercisable only with the consent of the Treasury and such consent may be given in relation to particular cases or in relation to such descriptions of cases as may be specified in the consent.

(3) In those sections—
    (a) "business" includes a profession,
    (b) "guarantee" includes indemnity,
    (c) references to persons carrying on business, in relation to things done outside the United Kingdom, include persons carrying on any other activities, and
    (d) references to things done in or outside the United Kingdom are to things done wholly or partly in or, as the case may be, outside the United Kingdom.

(4) References in this and those sections to the United Kingdom include the Isle of Man and the Channel Islands.   **[490]**

NOTE
Commencement: 23 October 1991 (SI 1991/2430).

5 Provision of services and information

(1) The Secretary of State may provide to any person—
    (a) information relating to credit or investment insurance,
    (b) services ancillary to the provision by that person of credit or investment insurance, and
    (c) such other goods or services as may be specified in an order under this section,

and may make such charges for doing so as he may determine.

(2) The power to make an order under this section is exercisable only with the consent of the Treasury.   **[491]**

NOTE
Commencement: 23 October 1991 (SI 1991/2430).

6 Commitment limits

(1) The aggregate amount of the Secretary of State's commitments at any time under arrangements relating to exports and insurance shall not exceed—

    (a) in the case of commitments in sterling, £35,000 million, and

    (b) in the case of commitments in foreign currency, 15,000 million special drawing rights.

(2) In subsection (1) above, "arrangements relating to exports and insurance" means—

    (a) arrangements under section 1 or 2 of this Act, other than arrangements for giving grants or arrangements under section 1(3), and

    (b) arrangements under the old law, other than arrangements for giving grants.

(3) The aggregate amount of the Secretary of State's commitments at any time under section 3 of this Act shall not exceed—

    (a) in the case of commitments in sterling, £15,000 million, and

    (b) in the case of commitments in foreign currency, 10,000 million special drawing rights.

(4) The Secretary of State may by order increase or further increase—

    (a) either of the limits in subsection (1) above by a sum specified in the order not exceeding £5,000 million or, as the case may be, 5,000 million special drawing rights,

    (b) either of the limits in subsection (3) above by a sum specified in the order not exceeding £3,000 million or, as the case may be, 2,000 million special drawing rights,

but the Secretary of State shall not in respect of any limit exercise the power on more than three occasions.

(5) For the purposes of this section and section 7 of this Act—

    (a) the commitments of the Secretary of State under any arrangements are his rights and liabilities relating to the arrangements,

    (b) the amount of any commitments shall be ascertained in accordance with principles determined from time to time by the Secretary of State with the consent of the Treasury,

    (c) "foreign currency" means any currency other than sterling, including special drawing rights and any other units of account defined by reference to more than one currency,

    (d) whether any commitments are in sterling or foreign currency is to be determined by reference to the currency in which the amount of the commitments is measured (rather than the currency of payment) but, if the commitments are expressed to be subject to a sterling or foreign currency limit, the commitments are to be taken to be in sterling or, as the case may be, foreign currency, and

    (e) the equivalent in special drawing rights of the amount of any commitments in foreign currency shall be ascertained at intervals determined from time to time by the Secretary of State with the consent of the Treasury and in accordance with principles so determined.

(6) A determination under subsection (5)(e) above may provide for leaving out of account for the purposes of the limit in subsection (1)(b) or (3)(b) above any amount by which the limit would otherwise be exceeded to the extent that the amount is attributable to—

(a) a revaluation of commitments under subsection (5)(e) above, or
(b) the fulfilment of an undertaking which, had it been fulfilled when given, would not have caused the limit to be exceeded.

(7) Any power to make an order under this section is exercisable only with the consent of the Treasury.   **[492]**

NOTE
Commencement: 23 October 1991 (SI 1991/2430).

7 Reports and returns

(1) The Secretary of State shall prepare an annual report on the discharge of his functions under sections 1 to 5 of this Act.

(2) The Secretary of State shall prepare, as soon as practicable after 31st March in each year, a return showing separately the aggregate amounts of the commitments in sterling and in foreign currency on that date for the purposes of the limits in section 6(1) and (3) of this Act.

(3) Any return under this section may also give such further information as to the amounts of his commitments for the purposes of those limits as the Secretary of State may determine for that return.

(4) The first return under this section shall be prepared as soon as practicable after 31st March 1991.

(5) Reports and returns prepared under this section shall be laid before Parliament.   **[493]**

NOTE
Commencement: 23 October 1991 (SI 1991/2430).

PART II

TRANSFER OR DELEGATION OF ECGD FUNCTIONS

8 Scheme of transfer

(1) The Secretary of State may make a scheme or schemes for the transfer to any person or persons of such property, rights and liabilities as are specified in or determined in accordance with the scheme, being property, rights or liabilities—

(a) to which the Secretary of State (or, in the case of copyright, Her Majesty) is entitled or subject immediately before the day on which the scheme providing for the transfer comes into force, and
(b) which then subsisted for the purposes of or in connection with or are otherwise attributable (wholly or partly) to the exercise of functions under Part I of this Act or the old law.

(2) Without prejudice to the generality of subsection (1)(b) above, any property, rights or liabilities shall be taken to fall within that subsection if the Secretary of State issues a certificate to that effect.

(3) A scheme under this section may apply—

    (a) to property wherever situated, and
    (b) to property, rights and liabilities whether or not otherwise capable
        of being transferred or assigned by the Secretary of State or, as the
        case may be, Her Majesty.

(4) A scheme under this section shall come into force on such day as may be specified in, or determined in accordance with, the scheme; and on that day the property, rights and liabilities to which the scheme applies shall be transferred and vest in accordance with the scheme.

(5) A scheme under this section may contain such supplementary, incidental, consequential or transitional provisions as appear to the Secretary of State to be necessary or expedient.

(6) The Schedule to this Act (scheme of transfer: supplementary provisions) shall have effect.

(7) References below in this Act to a transferee are to any person to whom anything is transferred by virtue of a scheme under this section.   **[494]**

NOTE
Commencement: 23 October 1991 (SI 1991/2430).

9 Transferred staff

(1) No scheme under section 8 of this Act shall provide for the transfer of any rights or liabilities relating to a person's employment, but the Transfer of Undertakings (Protection of Employment) Regulations 1981 shall apply to the transfer of property, rights or liabilities by virtue of such a scheme whether or not the transfer would, apart from this subsection, be a relevant transfer for the purposes of those regulations.

(2) Where, by reason of the operation of those regulations in relation to a transfer of property, rights or liabilities by virtue of such a scheme, a person ceases to be employed in the civil service of the State and becomes employed by a transferee—

    (a) he shall not, on so ceasing, be treated for the purposes of any scheme
        under section 1 of the Superannuation Act 1972 as having retired on
        redundancy, and
    (b) his ceasing to be employed in that service shall not be regarded as an
        occasion of redundancy for the purposes of the agreed redundancy
        procedures applicable to persons employed in that service.   **[495]**

NOTE
Commencement: 23 October 1991 (SI 1991/2430).

10 Vehicle companies

(1) In this section "vehicle company" means a company formed or acquired for the purpose of—

    (a) becoming a transferee, or
    (b) holding shares in a company formed or acquired for that purpose.

(2) Subject to subsections (3) and (4) below, the Secretary of State may—

    (a) subscribe for or otherwise acquire shares in or securities of a vehicle
        company, or acquire rights to subscribe for such shares or securities,
    (b) by a direction given to a company formed or acquired for the
        purpose of becoming a transferee require it, in consequence of the

transfer by virtue of a scheme under section 8 of this Act of property, rights or liabilities, to issue to him, or to such other person as may be specified in the direction, such shares or securities as may be so specified,

(c) from time to time by a direction given to a vehicle company require it to issue to him, or to such other person as may be specified in the direction, such shares or securities as may be so specified, or

(d) make loans to a vehicle company on such terms and conditions as he may determine.

(3) A direction under subsection (2)(b) or (c) above may require any shares to which it relates to be issued as fully or partly paid up.

(4) The Secretary of State shall not—

(a) subscribe for or otherwise acquire shares in or securities of a vehicle company, or acquire rights to subscribe for such shares or securities, unless all the relevant shares are to be held by or on behalf of the Crown, or

(b) at any time give a direction or make a loan to a vehicle company unless all the relevant shares are then held by or on behalf of the Crown.

(5) For the purposes of subsection (4) above—

(a) shares are held by or on behalf of the Crown where the Crown or any person acting on behalf of the Crown has a legal interest in them; and

(b) "relevant shares", in relation to a vehicle company, means the issued shares of that company or, if it is a subsidiary of another vehicle company, the issued shares of that other company.

(6) A scheme under section 8 of this Act may, as between any vehicle companies or as between a vehicle company and the Secretary of State, confer or impose rights and liabilities in connection with any of the matters as to which the Secretary of State may exercise his powers under this Act.

(7) The Secretary of State shall not exercise any of the powers conferred by the preceding provisions of this section or dispose of any shares in or securities of a vehicle company without the consent of the Treasury.   **[496]**

NOTE
Commencement: 23 October 1991 (SI 1991/2430).

11 Reinsurance

(1) The Secretary of State may make arrangements with any transferee under which the transferee insures the Secretary of State against risks of losses arising in consequence of arrangements made, before the day on which any scheme under section 8 of this Act comes into force, under Part I of this Act or the old law.

(2) The Secretary of State shall from time to time determine, in relation to such classes of risk determined by him as might be insured by him under section 1 of this Act, whether it is expedient in the national interest for him to exercise his powers under that section to make arrangements for reinsuring persons providing insurance for risks of that class.

(3) This section is without prejudice to any power of the Secretary of State under Part I of this Act.   **[497]**

NOTE
Commencement: 23 October 1991 (SI 1991/2430).

12 Delegation of assistance function

(1) The Secretary of State may make arrangements for any of the functions to which this section applies to be exercised on his behalf by any transferee or any other person, instead of through the Export Credits Guarantee Department, on such terms and conditions as he may determine.

(2) This section applies to the power of the Secretary of State to make arrangements under section 1 of this Act and to any functions of his under arrangements so made, or arrangements under the old law, including, so far as relating to any such arrangements, arrangements made by virtue of section 3(4) of this Act.

(3) This section does not affect any requirement for the consent of the Treasury. **[498]**

NOTE
Commencement: 23 October 1991 (SI 1991/2430).

PART III
GENERAL

13 The Export Credits Guarantee Department and the Export Guarantees Advisory Council

(1) All the functions of the Secretary of State under Part I of this Act, except the power to make orders under section 5 or 6 of this Act, shall be exercised and performed through the Export Credits Guarantee Department, which shall continue to be a Department of the Secretary of State.

(2) There shall continue to be an Export Guarantees Advisory Council.

(3) The function of the Council shall be to give advice to the Secretary of State, at his request, in respect of any matter relating to the exercise of his functions under this Act.

(4) In exercising his duty under section 11(2) of this Act, the Secretary of State shall consult the Export Guarantees Advisory Council.˙ **[499]**

NOTE
Commencement: 23 October 1991 (SI 1991/2430).

14 Expenses

(1) Any sums required by the Secretary of State for making payments or for defraying his administrative expenses under this Act shall be paid out of money provided by Parliament and any sums received by the Secretary of State by virtue of this Act shall be paid into the Consolidated Fund.

(2) If any sum required by the Secretary of State for fulfilling his liabilities under this Act is not paid out of money provided by Parliament, it shall be charged on and paid out of the Consolidated Fund. **[500]**

NOTE
Commencement: 23 October 1991 (SI 1991/2430).

15 Short title, interpretation, commencement, etc

(1) This Act may be cited as the Export and Investment Guarantees Act 1991.

(2) In this Act "the old law" means the Export Guarantees and Overseas Investment Act 1978 and any earlier enactment from which any provision of that Act was derived.

(3) Any power to make an order under section 5 or 6 of this Act shall be exercisable by statutory instrument and no such order shall be made unless a draft of it has been laid before and approved by resolution of the House of Commons.

(4) . . .

(5) Subsection (4) above does not affect any power exercisable by the Secretary of State in respect of arrangements made under the old law.

(6) This Act shall come into force on such day as the Secretary of State may by order made by statutory instrument appoint and different days may be appointed for different provisions and for different purposes.   **[501]**

NOTES
Commencement: 23 October 1991 (SI 1991/2430).
Sub-s (4): repeals the Export Guarantees and Overseas Investment Act 1978.
Order: the Export and Investment Guarantees Act 1991 (Commencement) Order 1991, SI 1991/2430, bringing this Act into force on 23 October 1991.

SCHEDULE

Section 8

SCHEME OF TRANSFER: SUPPLEMENTARY PROVISIONS

Certificate of vesting

1. A certificate by the Secretary of State that anything specified in the certificate has vested on any day in any person by virtue of a scheme under section 8 of this Act shall be conclusive evidence for all purposes of that fact.

Construction of agreements etc

2.—(1) This paragraph applies to any agreement made, transaction effected or other thing (not contained in an enactment) which—

    (a) has been made, effected or done by, to or in relation to the Secretary of State,

    (b) relates to any property, right or liability transferred from the Secretary of State in accordance with the scheme, and

    (c) is in force or effective immediately before the day on which the scheme comes into force.

(2) The agreement, transaction or other thing shall have effect on and after that day as if made, effected or done by, to or in relation to the transferee.

(3) Accordingly, references to the Secretary of State which relate to or affect any property, right or liability of the Secretary of State vesting by virtue of the scheme in the transferee and which are contained—

    (a) in any agreement (whether or not in writing), deed, bond or instrument,

    (b) in any process or other document issued, prepared or employed for the purpose of any proceeding before a court or other tribunal or authority, or

(c) in any other document whatever (other than an enactment) relating to or affecting any property, right or liability of the Secretary of State which vests by virtue of the scheme in the transferee,

shall be taken on and after that day to refer to the transferee.   **[502]–[600]**

NOTE

Commencement: 23 October 1991 (SI 1991/2430).

PART II
STATUTORY INSTRUMENTS

BANKING ACT 1987

BANKING APPEAL TRIBUNAL REGULATIONS 1987

(SI 1987/1299)

NOTES

Made: 23 July 1987.
Authority: Banking Act 1987, s 30(3).
Commencement: 1 October 1987.

1 Citation and commencement

(1) These Regulations may be cited as the Banking Appeal Tribunal Regulations 1987.

(2) These Regulations shall come into force on 1st October 1987.   **[601]**

2 Interpretation

(1) In these Regulations, unless the context otherwise requires—

"the Act" means the Banking Act 1987;
"appeal" means an appeal to which these Regulations apply in accordance with regulation 3;
"appellant" means a person who under the Act is entitled to appeal or has appealed, as the case may be, to the Tribunal against a decision of the Bank or against a finding on which such a decision is based;
"the Bank" means the Bank of England;
["the Banking Coordination Regulations" means the Banking Coordination (Second Council Directive) Regulations 1992;]
"the chairman" means the chairman of the Tribunal appointed in accordance with section 28 of the Act;
"preliminary hearing" means a hearing held pursuant to regulation 10;
"the secretary" means the person appointed by the Treasury to act as secretary to the Tribunal.

(2) Unless the context otherwise requires any reference in these Regulations to a numbered regulation is a reference to the regulation bearing that number in these Regulations and any reference in a regulation to a numbered paragraph is a reference to the paragraph bearing that number in that regulation.   **[602]**

NOTE

Para (1): definition "the Banking Coordination Regulations" inserted by SI 1993/982, reg 2(a).

3 Application of Regulations

These Regulations apply to appeals under Part I of the Act, other than appeals where the institution concerned (a) is a company registered in Scotland or (b) has its principal or prospective principal place of business in the United Kingdom in Scotland.   **[603]**

4 Time for and manner of bringing appeals

[An appeal shall be brought by sending a notice of appeal to the secretary of the Banking Appeal Tribunal, 15–19 Bedford Avenue, London WC1B 3AS not later than—

(a) in the case of an appeal against the decision of the Bank (or any finding relating thereto) to revoke authorisation, 10 days from the date on which the Bank serves notice in writing on the appellant of its decision, or

(b) in the case of an appeal against the decision of the Bank to impose or vary a restriction on an institution's authorisation as a matter of urgency, 28 days from the date on which the Bank imposes or varies the restriction by written notice to the institution under section 14(2) of the Act or 10 days from the date on which the Bank gives written notice to the institution under section 14(7) of the Act of its decision under section 14(6) of the Act, whichever is the later, or

(c) in the case of an appeal against the decision of the Bank to give a direction to an institution, 28 days from the date on which the Bank gives the direction by notice in writing under section 20(1) of the Act or 10 days from the date on which the Bank gives written notice to the institution under section 20(2)(b) of the Act confirming its decision, whichever is the later, on

(d) in any other case, 28 days from the date on which the Bank serves notice in writing on the appellant of its decision.]   **[604]**

NOTES
Commencement: 30 April 1993.
Substituted by SI 1993/982, reg 2(b).

5 Notice of appeal

(1) The notice of appeal shall be signed by or on behalf of the appellant and shall contain the following particulars:—

(a) the appellant's name;

[(b) his address or where the appellant is an institution—
  (i) which has its registered or principal office in the United Kingdom, the address of that office, or
  (ii) which has its principal place of business in another member State, the address of that place of business;

(c) the address, if different from that referred to in sub-paragrah (b) to which applications, notices and other documents in connection with the appeal should be sent to the appellant—
  (i) within the United Kingdom, or
  (ii) within the member State where the appellant has its principal place of business.]

(d) the name and address of any person appointed by the appellant to represent him or it in connection with the appeal;

(e) a statement of the decision or finding of the Bank against which the appeal is made.

(2) The appellant shall, upon sending notice of appeal to the secretary send forthwith a copy of the notice to the Bank, to any person to whom a copy of the notice or refusal, revocation, restriction or direction was sent under section 10(5), 13(7) or 20(3) of the Act, and, in the case of an appeal under section 27(2) of the Act, to the institution concerned.   **[605]**

NOTE
Para (1): paras (b), (c) substituted by SI 1993/982, reg 2(c).

6 Establishment of the Tribunal

On receipt of a notice of appeal the secretary shall forthwith request the Lord

Chancellor and the Chancellor of the Exchequer to appoint respectively the Chairman and other members of the Tribunal to hear the appeal.   **[606]**

7 Respondent

On every appeal the Bank shall be the respondent.   **[607]**

8 Grounds of appeal

(1) The appellant shall send to the secretary a notice setting out the grounds of appeal, which in the case of [an appeal other than an appeal under section 27(2)(a)] shall contain sufficient particulars to show why the appellant considers the decision appealed against was unlawful or was not justified by the evidence on which it was based or in the case of an appeal under section 27(2)(a) shall contain sufficient particulars to show why the appellant considers the finding appealed against was not justified by the evidence on which it was based—

    (a) within 28 days from the date on which the Bank served notice in writing on the appellant of its decision, in the case of an appeal against the decision of the Bank (or any finding relating thereto) to revoke authorisation, and

    (b) within 14 days of serving the notice of appeal, in any other case.

(2) The appellant shall upon sending the notice of grounds of appeal referred to in paragraph (1), send a copy of the notice to the persons to whom a copy of the notice of appeal was sent pursuant to regulation 5(2).

(3) In the case of an appeal under section 27(1) of the Act the appellant may omit any information from the notice of grounds of appeal referred to in paragraph (1) on the ground that it is confidential or commercially sensitive, in which event it shall include such information in a notice of supplementary grounds of appeal, which it shall send to the secretary and the Bank, with an explanation in writing of the reasons for the omission, at the same time as it sends the notice of grounds of appeal under paragraph (1).   **[608]**

NOTE

Para (1): words in square brackets substituted by SI 1993/982, reg 2(d).

---

9 Supply of documents by the Bank

(1) Within 14 days of receiving the copy of the notice of appeal under regulation 5, the Bank shall send to the secretary four copies of the documents listed in the Schedule to these Regulations and shall send to the appellant and, in the case of an appeal under section 27(2) of the Act, to the institution concerned, a list of those documents together with a copy of any of those documents which the Bank has not already supplied to the appellant or, in the case of an appeal under section 27(2) of the Act, to the institution concerned (as the case may be).

(2) Where the Bank—

    (a) gave a copy of a notice to a person under section 10(3) of the Act, or gave a notice to a person under section 10(5) of the Act, and under section 10(7) of the Act omitted any matter which did not relate to him, or

(b) gave a copy of a notice to a person under section 13(4) of the Act, or gave a notice to a person under section 13(7) of the Act, and under section 13(12) of the Act omitted any matter which did not relate to him, or

(c) gave a copy of a notice to a person under section 20(3) of the Act and under section 20(5) of the Act omitted any matter which did not relate to him,

the Bank may omit that matter from any copy of that document supplied to that person under paragraph (1). **[609]**

10 Preliminary hearing

(1) Subject to paragraph (2) the secretary shall send to the appellant, the Bank and, in the case of an appeal under section 27(2) of the Act, to the institution concerned, a notice informing them of the time and place of the preliminary hearing which, unless the appellant and the Bank otherwise agree, shall be—

[(a) not earlier than 5 days after the date on which the notice is sent; and

(b) not earlier than 21 days and not later than 35 days after the date of receipt by the secretary of the notice of appeal unless the chairman otherwise directs on the ground that he considers that the preliminary hearing should be held as a matter of urgency.]

(2) There shall be no preliminary hearing of an appeal under section 29(3) of the Act unless the chairman otherwise directs.

(3) The preliminary hearing shall be in private and shall be heard by the chairman.

(4) The appellant and the Bank and, in the case of an appeal under section 27(2) of the Act, the institution concerned may appear at the preliminary hearing and may be represented by counsel or solicitor or by any other person.

(5) The chairman shall give such directions as he considers necessary or desirable for the conduct of the appeal and shall fix the time and place of the hearing at the preliminary hearing or, if there is no preliminary hearing, by notice to the parties and, in the case of an appeal under section 27(2) of the Act, to the institution concerned.

(6) Without prejudice to the generality of paragraph (5) and subject to regulations 22(2), the chairman shall consider whether any matters contained in a notice of supplementary grounds of appeal submitted under regulation 8(3) should be disclosed to any other person and may direct accordingly.

(7) Notwithstanding that the preliminary hearing shall be in private, the other members of the Tribunal may attend and a member of the Council on Tribunals may attend in his capacity as such. **[610]**

NOTE
Para (1): paras (a), (b) substituted for the original paras (i), (ii) by SI 1993/982, reg 2(e).

11 Interim relief

(1) [On an application for the suspension under section 27(5) of the Act] of the operation of any restriction or direction or any variation of a restriction or direction which is the subject of an appeal, the Tribunal may determine it on the basis of written representations if the parties and, in the case of an appeal under section 27(2) of the Act, the institution concerned so agree in writing or

may direct the parties and, in the case of an appeal under section 27(2) of the Act, the institution concerned to appear before it.

(2) The Tribunal shall notify its determination and the reasons for it to the Bank and to the party who made the application for interim relief and may do so to any other party to the appeal or to any person to whom notice of the appeal has been given under regulation 5(2).   **[611]**

NOTE
Para (1): words in square brackets substituted by SI 1993/982, reg 2(f).

12 Amendment of grounds of appeal

(1) An appellant may amend a notice of grounds of appeal or supplementary grounds of appeal at any time before the preliminary hearing and shall forthwith notify the Bank and the secretary in writing of the amendment.

(2) An appellant may amend a notice of grounds of appeal or supplementary grounds of appeal in the course of the preliminary hearing with the leave of the chairman or at any time thereafter with the leave of the Tribunal.

(3) The chairman or the Tribunal shall not give such leave unless he or it has afforded the Bank an opportunity of making representations on the proposed amendment.

(4) Leave may be granted on such terms (if any), including terms as to costs or expenses, as the chairman or the Tribunal (as the case may be) thinks fit.

(5) Where a notice of grounds of appeal is amended the appellant shall forthwith notify any person to whom a copy of the notice was sent pursuant to regulation 8(2) and where a notice of supplementary grounds of appeal is amended the chairman shall consider whether any matters contained therein should be disclosed to any other person and may direct accordingly.   **[612]**

13 Evidence and procedure

(1) For the purposes of the appeal the chairman may, on the application of a party to the appeal or on his own motion, by direction given at the preliminary hearing or by notice in writing require the appellant, the Bank or any other person, at a time and place stated in the notice, to attend and give evidence or produce any document in that person's custody or under his control which relates to any matter in question at the hearing; provided that—

   (a) no person other than the appellant or the Bank shall be required, in obedience to such direction or notice, to attend and give evidence or to produce any such document unless the necessary expenses of his attendance are paid or tendered to him; and

   (b) no person shall be compelled to give any evidence or produce any document which he could not be compelled to give or produce if the hearing were a proceeding in a court of law in that part of the United Kingdom where the appeal is to be determined; and

   (c) in exercising the power conferred by this paragraph the chairman shall take into account, in particular, the need to protect [information which relates to a person who is not a party to the appeal and which is commercially sensitive or was communicated or obtained in confidence.]

(2) Except where the chairman otherwise directs, a witness shall not be obliged to attend and give evidence or produce any document in obedience to a direction or notice issued by the chairman unless that direction or notice has

been served on him not less than 5 days before the day appointed for the hearing.

(3) The chairman may set aside any direction or notice under this regulation on the application of the person to whom the direction or notice was addressed but shall not do so without first notifying any person who applied for the direction or notice and considering any representations made by that person.

(4) The secretary shall supply a copy of any document obtained under this regulation to any party to the appeal if that party does not already have a copy of the document and it shall be a condition of such supply that the information so supplied shall be used only for the purposes of the appeal.

(5) The hearing shall be in private unless, at a preliminary hearing or at any other time, the chairman directs that the hearing or any part of it shall be in public, but nothing in this paragraph shall prevent a member of the Council on Tribunals from attending the hearing, and (with the consent of the parties to the appeal) any deliberations of the Tribunal, in his capacity as such.

(6) The appellant and the Bank may appear at the hearing and may be represented by counsel or solicitor or by any other person.

(7) At the hearing the appellant and the Bank shall each be entitled to make an opening statement, to call witnesses to give evidence, to cross examine witnesses called by the other party and to make a final statement.

(8) In the case of an appeal under section 27(2) of the Act, the institution concerned shall be entitled to be heard, notwithstanding that the hearing is in private, and may be represented by counsel or solicitor or by any other person.

(9) The Tribunal may require any witness to give evidence on oath or affirmation which may be administered for that purpose by the chairman.

(10) Subject to paragraph (1), evidence may be admitted by the Tribunal whether or not it would be admissible in a court of law.

(11) If the appellant or the Bank or, in the case of an appeal under section 27(2) of the Act, the institution concerned shall fail to appear or be represented at the time and place fixed for the hearing, the Tribunal may proceed with the hearing or adjourn it to a later date; and if it proceeds with the hearing, it shall take into consideration any written representations which may have been submitted by either party and, in the case of an appeal under section 27(2) of the Act, the institution concerned whether in accordance with any provision contained in these Regulations or otherwise.

(12) The Tribunal may from time to time adjourn the hearing and, if the date, time and place of the adjourned hearing are announced before the adjournment, no further notice shall be required.　　　　　　　　**[613]**

NOTE

Para (1): words in square brackets in para (c) substituted by SI 1993/982, reg 2(g).

14 Membership of the Tribunal

Notwithstanding the provisions of regulation 6, an appeal may with the consent of the parties continue to be heard in the absence of any one member of the Tribunal other than the chairman, and in that event the Tribunal shall be deemed to be properly constituted.　　　　　　　　**[614]**

15 Procedure after hearing

(1) The Tribunal shall after the close of the hearing notify its determination and its reasons therefor in accordance with section 29(7) and (8) of the Act (which provide for the giving of notice of a Tribunal's determination, together with a statement of its reasons, to the appellant and to the Bank and, in the case of an appeal under section 27(2) of the Act, for the giving of notice of the Tribunal's determination to the institution concerned).

(2) The Tribunal may, after hearing representations from the parties, make arrangements for the publication of its determination and its reasons therefor but in doing so shall have regard to the desirability of safeguarding commercially sensitive information or information given to the appellant or the Bank in confidence and the interests of depositors and potential depositors and for that purpose may make any necessary amendments to the text of the decision to conceal the identity of the appellant or the source of any such information.

[615]

16 Withdrawal of appeal

(1) The appellant may withdraw the appeal at any time before the hearing by giving notice in writing to the Bank and to the secretary.

(2) The appellant may at the hearing give notice to the Tribunal that he or it desires to withdraw the appeal and thereupon the Tribunal shall bring the hearing to a close.

(3) The Bank may at any time withdraw its opposition to an appeal by giving notice to the appellant and the Tribunal.

(4) If an appeal is withdrawn, it shall be deemed to be dismissed and the Tribunal shall accordingly formally notify the persons whom it would have notified under regulation 15(1) if it had determined the appeal.

(5) . . .   **[616]**

NOTE
Para (5): revoked by SI 1993/982, reg 2(h).

17 Costs

(1) Any costs or expenses directed to be paid under section 30(1) of the Act (which provides that the Tribunal may give such directions as it thinks fit for the payment of costs or expenses by any party to the appeal) and required to be taxed shall be taxed by a taxing master of the Supreme Court.

(2) A direction under section 30(1) of the Act in respect of the payment of costs by a party to the appeal shall, on application being made to the High Court by the party to whom costs have been directed to be paid, be enforceable as if he had obtained a judgment of that Court in his favour.   **[617]**

18 Time and miscellaneous powers

(1) Where the time prescribed by or under these Regulations for doing any act expires on a Saturday, Sunday or public holiday and by reason thereof the act cannot be done on that day, the act shall be in time if done on the next working day.

(2) The periods referred to in regulations 8, 9 and 10 may be extended by the chairman on such terms (if any) as the chairman after consulting the parties thinks fit and any application for such extension may be granted although it is not made until after the expiration of the period.

(3) The chairman may, after consulting the parties—

(a) postpone the date fixed for the hearing of an appeal; or
(b) alter the place appointed for any hearing;

and, if he exercises either of the above powers, the secretary shall notify each party, any witnesses concerned and, in the case of an appeal under section 27(2) of the Act, the institution concerned of the revised arrangements. **[618]**

19 Tribunal's power to determine its own procedure

Subject to the provisions of the Act and of these Regulations, the Tribunal shall have power to determine its own procedure. **[619]**

20 Service of notices etc

(1) Any notice or other document to be sent, served or given to any person for the purposes of the appeal may be delivered or may be sent by first class recorded delivery service or registered letter—

(a) in the case of a document directed to the Tribunal, to the address set out in regulation 4;
(b) in the case of a document directed to the appellant or his representative, to the address provided in the notice of appeal in accordance with regulation 5 or such other address as may subsequently be notified to the Tribunal and the Bank;
(c) in the case of a document directed to the Bank, to the Head of Banking Supervision [Division], Bank of England, Threadneedle Street, London EC2R 8AH;
(d) in any other case, to the last known address of the person to whom the document is directed;

and documents falling within (b) or (d) above, if sent, served or given to the authorised representative of any person, shall be deemed to be sent, served or given to that person.

(2) Any such notice or other document may be sent, served or given by telex or other similar means which produce a document containing the text of the communication. **[620]**

NOTE
Para (1): word in square brackets in para (c) inserted by SI 1993/982, reg 2(i).

21 Irregularities

(1) Any irregularity resulting from failure to comply with any provision of these Regulations before the Tribunal has reached its decision shall not of itself render the proceedings void.

(2) Where any such irregularity comes to the attention of the Tribunal before it has reached its decision, the Tribunal may, and shall if it considers that any person may have been prejudiced, take such steps as it thinks fit before reaching its decision to cure the irregularity.

(3) Clerical mistakes in any document recording a decision of the chairman or Tribunal, or errors arising in such a document from an accidental slip or omission, may be corrected by the chairman under his hand. **[621]**

22 Consolidation of appeals

[(1) Where in making its decision the Bank made a finding that a person is not a fit and proper person to hold the particular position in the institution which he holds or is to hold or imposed a requirement that a person be removed as a director, controller or manager of the institution and both the institution and the person concerned appeal against the decision, or where the institution appeals against the decision and the person concerned appeals against the finding, the chairman may at the preliminary hearing or at some other time direct that the appeals shall be consolidated:

Provided that the chairman shall not make such a direction without giving all parties concerned an opportunity to show cause to why such a direction should not be made.]

(2) If the chairman directs that the appeals shall be consolidated the secretary shall send to the person concerned a copy of any notice of supplementary grounds of appeal submitted by the institution under regulation 8(3) unless all of the matters contained in the notice have been disclosed to the person concerned under regulations 10(6) or 12(5) or unless the institution when showing cause why such a direction should not be made under paragraph (1) represented that it did not wish the notice of supplementary grounds of appeal to be disclosed to the person concerned and the person concerned consented to the notice not being disclosed to him.   **[622]**

NOTES
   Commencement: 1 October 1987 (para (2)); 30 April 1993 (para (1)).
   Para (1): substituted by SI 1993/982, reg 2(j).

SCHEDULE

Regulation 9

DOCUMENTS TO BE SENT TO THE TRIBUNAL BY THE BANK

1. In the case of an appeal against a decision of the Bank (or any finding relating thereto) to refuse to grant authorisation—

    (a) a copy of the application for authorisation submitted under section 8 of the Act, together with a copy of the statement required by section 8(2)(b)(i) thereof to accompany the application and copies of any information and documents required by the Bank under section 8(2)(b)(ii) thereof,

    (b) a copy of any information and documents submitted under section 8(3) thereof,

    (c) a copy of any report provided under section 8(5) thereof,

    (d) a copy of any notice served by the Bank under section 10(2) or 10(3) thereof,

    (e) a copy of any written representations made in accordance with section 10(4) thereof, and

    (f) a copy of any notice served under section 10(5) thereof.

2. In the case of an appeal against a decision of the Bank (or any finding relating thereto) to revoke an authorisation, to restrict an authorisation or to vary the restrictions imposed on an authorisation—

    (a) a copy of any notice served under section 13(1) or 13(4) of the Act,

    (b) a copy of any written representations made in accordance with section 13(5) thereof,

    (c) a copy of any notice served under section 13(7) thereof, and

    (d) a copy of any written representations made in accordance with section 13(9) thereof.

3. In the case of an appeal against a decision of the Bank to give a direction—

    (a) a copy of any notice served under section 20(1) or 20(3) of the Act,

    (b) a copy of any written representations made in accordance with section 20(4) thereof, and

    (c) a copy of any notice served under section 20(2)(b) thereof.

4. In the case of an appeal against a decision of the Bank to object to a person who wishes to become a shareholder controller or indirect controller of any description of an authorised institution—

   (a) a copy of any notice served under section 21(1), 21(3), 22(1) and (2) or 22(6) of the Act, together with a copy of any information and documents required by a notice under section 21(3) thereof, and
   (b) a copy of any written representations made under section 22(3) of the Act.

5. In the case of an appeal against a decision of the Bank to object to an existing shareholder controller of an authorised institution—

   (a) a copy of the notices served under section 24(1) and (2) of the Act, and
   (b) a copy of any written representations made under section 24(3) of the Act.

[6. In the case of an appeal against a decision of the Bank to impose a prohibition or a restriction under regulation 9 or 10 of the Banking Coordination Regulations and pursuant to Schedule 3 to the Regulations—

   (a) a copy of any notice served under paragraph 2(2) of Schedule 3 thereof,
   (b) a copy of any written representations made in accordance with paragraph 2(5) of Schedule 3 thereof,
   (c) a copy of any notice served under paragraph 2(7) of Schedule 3 thereof, and
   (d) a copy of any written representations made in accordance with paragraph 2(11) of Schedule 3 thereof.

7. In the case of an appeal against a refusal by the Bank to give a notice as required under regulation 22 of the Banking Coordination Regulations and under paragraph 3(1) or (2) or paragraph 6(1) of Schedule 6 to the Regulations, a copy of any notification of refusal to give such a notice under paragraph 4(6)(b) or paragraph 6(5)(b) of Schedule 6 therefore respectively.

8. In the case of an appeal against a decision of the Bank to impose a restriction under regulation 23 of the Banking Coordination Regulations and pursuant to Schedule 7 to the Regulations—

   (a) a copy of any notice served under paragraph 2(1) of Schedule 7 thereof,
   (b) a copy of any written representations made in accordance with paragraph 2(4) of Schedule 7 thereof,
   (c) a copy of any notice served under paragraph 2(6) of Schedule 7 thereof, and
   (d) a copy of any written representations made in accordance with paragraph 2(10) of Schedule 7 thereof.]   **[623]**

NOTES
   Commencement: 1 October 1987 (paras 1–5); 30 April 1993 (paras 6–8).
   Paras 6–8 added by SI 1993/982, reg 2(k).

BANKING ACT 1987 (ADVERTISEMENTS) REGULATIONS 1988

(SI 1988/645)

NOTES
   Made: 29 March 1988.
   Authority: Banking Act 1987, s 32(1), (2).
   Commencement: 29 April 1988.

1 Citation, commencement and interpretation

(1) These Regulations may be cited as the Banking Act 1987 (Advertisements) Regulations 1988.

(2) These Regulations shall come into force on 29th April 1988.

(3) In these Regulations, unless the context otherwise requires—

"controlled advertisement" means a deposit advertisement to which, in accordance with regulation 2 below, these Regulations apply;

"deposit-taker" means the person with whom the deposits which are invited by a deposit advertisement are to be made;

"full name" in respect of any person means the name under which that person carries on business and, if different and if that person is a body corporate, its corporate name;

"liabilities" includes provisions where such provisions have not been deducted from the value of assets;

(4) A reference in these Regulations to the payment of interest in respect of a deposit includes a reference to the payment of any premium in respect of a deposit, and to the crediting of interest to the deposit so as to constitute an accretion to the principal.

(5) For the purposes of these Regulations a deposit advertisement which contains information which is intended or might reasonably be presumed to be intended to lead directly or indirectly to the making of a deposit shall be treated as if it contained an invitation to make such deposit, and references to an invitation to make a deposit shall be construed accordingly.   **[624]**

2 Application of Regulations

(1) Subject to paragraphs (2) to (5) of this regulation these Regulations apply to a deposit advertisement unless it contains an invitation to make deposits only with offices of the deposit-taker in the United Kingdom or another member State.

(2) These Regulations do not apply to a deposit advertisement which does not indicate the offices with which the deposits are invited to be made if the deposit-taker carries on a deposit-taking business in the United Kingdom or another member State.

(3) These Regulations do not apply to a deposit advertisement which invites the making of deposits with an institution or unincorporated institution which is a body for the time being authorised under section 3 or 4 of the Insurance Companies Act 1982 to carry on insurance business of a class specified in Schedule 1 or 2 to that Act.

(4) These Regulations do not apply—

(a) in relation to any issue of a prospectus [a prospectus to which regulation 8 of the Public Offers of Securities Regulations 1995 applies, or would apply but for regulation 7 of those regulations where—

 (i) the prospectus is issued to existing members or debenture holders of a company; and

 (ii) the prospectus relates to shares in or debentures of the company,

 whether an applicant for shares or debentures will or will not have the right to renounce in favour of other persons];

(b) in relation to any issue of [a prospectus to which regulation 8 of the Public Offers of Securities Regulations 1995 applies, or would apply but for regulation 7 of those regulations where—

 (i) the prospectus is issued to existing members or debenture holders of a company; and

 (ii) the prospectus relates to shares in or debentures of the company,

 whether an applicant for shares or debentures will or will not have the right to renounce in favour of other persons] or by section 76 of that Act;

(c) in relation to any issue of a form of application for shares in, or debentures of, a company, [together with a prospectus to which regulation 8 of the Public Offers of Securities Regulations 1995 applies, or would apply but for regulation 7 of those regulations where—

   (i) the prospectus is issued to existing members or debenture holders of a company; and

  (ii) the prospectus relates to shares in or debentures of the company,

whether an applicant for shares or debentures will or will not have the right to renounce in favour of other persons];

(d) in relation to any issue of a form of application for shares in, or debentures of, a company where the form of application was issued either—

   (i) in connection with a bona fide invitation to a person to enter into an underwriting agreement with respect to the shares or debentures; or

  (ii) in relation to shares or debentures which were not offered to the public;

(e) in relation to any issue of a form of application for any securities, if such form is issued with a document which either sets out the approved listing particulars for the purposes of any listing rules made pursuant to section 142(6) of the Financial Services Act 1986 or indicates where such particulars can be obtained or inspected;

(f) in relation to any issue of documents to which the corresponding Northern Ireland legislation applies (or would apply if not excluded by that legislation).

(5) These Regulations do not apply to a deposit advertisement which invites the making of deposits on terms involving the issue by the deposit-taker of debt securities which have been admitted to official listing within a member State other than the United Kingdom.

(6) These Regulations do not apply to a deposit advertisement which is an investment business advertisement regulated by rules (made by the appropriate authority or a recognised organisation) of the kind described in section 48(2)(e) of the Financial Services Act 1986 (rules as to the form and content of advertisements in respect of investment business).

(7) For the purposes of this regulation—

(a) "company" means—

   (i) any company which is a company within the meaning of section 735(1) of the Companies Act 1985,

  (ii) any body corporate to which the prospectus and allotment provisions of that Act are applied by regulations made under section 718 of that Act,

  (iii) any company of a kind described in section 72 of that Act, or

  (iv) any company or body corporate in respect of which the corresponding Northern Ireland legislation has effect;

(b) "investment business advertisement" means an advertisement—

   (i) which is issued or caused to be issued by or on behalf of a person authorised under Chapter III of Part I of the Financial Services Act 1986 or an appointed representative within the meaning of section 44 of that Act,

  (ii) which contains an invitation to make a deposit which will be accepted by the deposit-taker in the course of or for the purpose of engaging in any permitted dealing activity with or on behalf of the person by whom or on whose behalf the deposit is made or in any permitted service activity on behalf of that person, and

(iii) which contains no other invitation to make a deposit;

(c) "dealing activity" means an activity falling within paragraph 12 of Schedule 1 to the Financial Services Act 1986 construed without reference to Parts III and IV of that Schedule;

(d) "service activity" means an activity falling within paragraph 13, 14 or 16 of Schedule 1 to the Financial Services Act 1986 construed without reference to Parts III and IV of that Schedule;

(e) "permitted" in relation to a dealing activity or a service activity means an activity in which the deposit-taker may engage without any contravention occurring of—

(i) any rules (made by the appropriate authority or a recognised organisation) of the kind described in section 48(2)(a) and (b) of that Act (rules as to the type of business carried on or the persons in relation to whom business is carried on), or

(ii) any prohibition of the kind described in section 65 of that Act;

(f) "appropriate authority" means the Secretary of State, a designated agency within the meaning of section 114(3) of the Financial Services Act 1986, the Chief Registrar of friendly societies, the Registrar of Friendly Societies for Northern Ireland or a transferee body within the meaning of paragraph 28(4) of Schedule 11 to that Act; and

(g) "recognised organisation" means a body which is a recognised professional body, a recognised self-regulating organisation or a recognised self-regulating organisation for friendly societies within the meaning of section 207(1) of the Financial Services Act 1986.

(8) In this regulation references to rules made by a recognised organisation include rules (whether or not laid down by the organisation itself) which the organisation has power to enforce.

(9) In this regulation "the corresponding Northern Ireland legislation" means those provisions of the Companies (Northern Ireland) Order 1986 which correspond to any of the provisions of the Companies Act 1985 specified in this regulation. **[625]**

NOTE

Para (4): words in square brackets substituted by the Public Offers of Securities Regulations 1995, SI 1995/1537, reg 24, Sch 5, para 1.

Modifications: by virtue of the Banking Coordination (Second Council Directive) Regulations 1992, SI 1992/3218, reg 82(1), Sch 10, para 45, this regulation has effect as if the reference in para (7) to a person authorised under Chapter III of Part I of the Financial Services Act included a reference to a European institution carrying on home-regulated investment business in the United Kingdom. By virtue of the Insurance Companies (Third Insurance Directives) Regulations 1994, SI 1994/1696, this regulation has effect as if the reference in para (3) to a body authorised under the Insurance Companies Act 1982, s 3 or 4 to carry on insurance business of a class specified in Sch 1 or 2 to that Act included a reference to an EC company which is lawfully carrying on insurance business, or providing insurance, in the United Kingdom.

3 Control of advertisements

No controlled advertisement shall be issued unless it complies with the following provisions of these Regulations. **[626]**

4 General requirements for advertisements

Every controlled advertisement shall state—

    (a) the full name of the deposit-taker,
    (b) the country or territory in which the deposit-taker's principal place of business is situated, described as such, and
    (c) if the deposit-taker is a body corporate, the country or territory in which it is incorporated, described as such, unless this is the same as the country or territory referred to in sub-paragraph (b).   **[627]**

5 Assets and liabilities

(1) Every controlled advertisement shall state the amount of the paid-up capital and reserves, described as such, of the deposit-taker (if a body corporate) or the amount of the total assets less liabilities, described as such, of the deposit-taker (if a person other than a body corporate).

(2) Where a controlled advertisement contains any reference to the amount of the assets of the deposit-taker it shall state with equal prominence the amount of the deposit-taker's liabilities, described as such.

(3) Paragraphs (1) and (2) of this regulation shall be treated as complied with if the advertisement states that the amount of any assets or paid-up capital and reserves required to be stated exceeds an amount specified in the advertisement or that the amount of any liabilities required to be stated does not exceed an amount so specified.

(4) A controlled advertisement shall not contain any reference to the assets or liabilities of any person other than the deposit-taker.   **[628]–[629]**

6 (*Revoked by the Credit Institutions (Protection of Depositors) Regulations 1995, SI 1995/1442, reg 52(2).*)

7 Interest

(1) This regulation applies to a controlled advertisement which specifies the rate at which interest will be payable in respect of the deposits which are invited.

(2) Every advertisement to which this regulation applies shall state—

    (a) the minimum amount, if any, which must be deposited to earn that rate of interest,
    (b) the period of time, if any, during which no interest will be payable,
    (c) the minimum period of time, if any, during which a deposit must be retained by the deposit-taker in order to earn that rate of interest,
    (d) the minimum period of notice, if any, which must be given before repayment may be required of a deposit earning that rate of interest, and
    (e) the intervals at which the interest will be paid.

(3) If the rate of interest which is specified is not an annual rate of simple interest, the advertisement shall state the basis on which the rate will be calculated.

(4) If the rate of interest which is specified may be varied during the period for which the deposit will be held this shall be stated in the advertisement.

(5) If interest will or may not be paid in full at the rate which is specified, this shall be stated in the advertisement, and the advertisement shall state the nature and the amount of or rate of any deductions which will or may be made from the interest before payment.

(6) If the rate of interest which is specified is or may not be the rate at which interest will be payable in respect of the deposits on the date on which the advertisement is issued this shall be stated in the advertisement, and the advertisement shall state the date on which interest was payable at the rate

which is specified, such date being as close as reasonably practicable to the date on which the advertisement is issued.

(7) If an advertisement specifies more than one rate of interest payable in respect of deposits of a particular amount the advertisement shall contain the information required by any of the foregoing paragraphs of this regulation in relation to each such rate.

(8) Where different rates of interest apply to deposits of different amounts, the advertisement shall contain the information required by any of the forego-ing paragraphs of this regulation in relation to each such rate.   **[630]**

8 Currency

Every controlled advertisement shall state the currency in which the deposits are to be made.   **[631]**

9 Supplementary provisions

(1) Subject to paragraph (2) of this regulation, the matters required by these Regulations to be included in an advertisement shall be shown clearly and legibly or, in the case of an advertisement by way of sound broadcasting, spoken clearly.

(2) In the case of an advertisement by way of television or exhibition or cinematographic film, the matters required by these Regulations to be included shall be shown clearly and legibly or spoken clearly.   **[632]–[633]**

10 (*Revokes SI 1985/220 and SI 1987/64.*)

BANKING ACT 1987 (EXEMPT TRANSACTIONS) REGULATIONS 1988

(SI 1988/646)

NOTES
Made: 29 March 1988.
Authority: Banking Act 1987, s 4(4), (5).
Commencement: 29 April 1988.

1 Citation, commencement and interpretation

(1) These Regulations may be cited as the Banking Act 1987 (Exempt Transactions) Regulations 1988, and shall come into force on 29th April 1988.

[(2) In these Regulations, unless the context otherwise requires—

"the Act" means the Banking Act 1987;
"commercial paper" means a debt security which may not be redeemed in whole or in part until after seven days beginning with the date of issue but which must be redeemed within one year beginning with the date of issue;
"company" means a body corporate, including a body corporate consti-tuted under the law of a country or territory outside the United Kingdom;
"the corresponding Northern Ireland legislation" means, in relation to any of the provisions of the Companies Act 1985 specified in these

Regulations, the corresponding provisions of the Companies (Northern Ireland) Order 1986;

. . . . .

"debt security" includes bonds, notes, debentures and debenture stock;

"deposit", except in the expressions "pre-contract deposit" and "deposit fund", shall be construed in accordance with section 5 of the Act;

"exempt transactions" shall be construed in accordance with regulation 2 of these Regulations;

"financial year" has the meaning ascribed to it by section 742 of the Companies Act 1985;

"industrial and provident society" means a society registered or deemed to be registered under the Industrial and Provident Societies Act 1965 or under the Industrial and Provident Societies Act (Northern Ireland) 1969 but does not include a credit union within the meaning of the Credit Unions Act 1979 or the Credit Unions (Northern Ireland) Order 1985;

"the listing rules" means any rules made pursuant to section 142(6) of the Financial Services Act 1986;

"medium term note" means a debt security which may not be redeemed in whole or in part until after one year beginning with the date of issue but which must be redeemed within five years beginning with date of issue;

"net assets" has the meaning ascribed to it by section 264(2) of the Companies Act 1985;

"the Official List" means the Official List of The Stock Exchange;

"Recognised Overseas Exchange" means an exchange, market place or association for the time being included in the list published by the Council for the purposes of rule 535.4 of the Rules of The Stock Exchange (permitted dealings in foreign securities) (or any rule of The Stock Exchange having substantially the same effect);

"redemption value", in relation to any debt security, means the amount of the principal which is payable upon redemption of that security;

"relevant debt security" means a debt security which is commercial paper or a medium term note;

"The Stock Exchange" means The International Stock Exchange of the United Kingdom and Republic of Ireland Limited;

"subsidiary" and "wholly-owned subsidiary" shall be construed in accordance with section 736 of the Companies Act 1985;

"successor", in relation to a body, means any company in which property, rights and liabilities of the body shall have become vested by virtue of an Act;

"the Unlisted Securities Market" means the Unlisted Securities Market of The Stock Exchange.]   **[634]**

NOTE

Para (2): substituted by SI 1990/20, reg 3(a); definition "the Council" revoked by SI 1991/2168, reg 2.

2 Exempt transactions

The transactions referred to in the following regulations are prescribed for the purposes of section 4(4) of the Act as transactions to which the prohibition in section 3 of the Act on the acceptance of a deposit does not apply. Such transactions are referred to in these Regulations as "exempt transactions".

[635]

NOTE

The Act: Banking Act 1987.

3 Charities

(1) The acceptance by a charity of a deposit is an exempt transaction if—

  (a) the deposit is made by another charity, or
  (b) there is payable in respect of the deposit neither interest nor a premium.

(2) In this regulation "charity" means any institution, trust or undertaking, whether corporate or not, which is established solely for charitable purposes, and in the application of this regulation to Scotland "charitable" shall be construed in the same way as in the Income Tax Acts.   **[636]**

4 Church deposit funds

(1) The acceptance by the Central Board of Finance of the Church of England of a deposit in the course of administering a deposit fund within the meaning of paragraph 1 of the scheme contained in the Schedule to the Church Funds Investment Measure 1958 is an exempt transaction.

(2) The acceptance by the Central Finance Board of the Methodist Church of a deposit in the course of administering a deposit fund within the meaning of paragraph 1 of the scheme contained in the First Schedule to the Methodist Church Funds Act 1960 is an exempt transaction.   **[637]**

5 Industrial and provident societies

The acceptance by an industrial and provident society of a deposit in the form of a withdrawable share capital is an exempt transaction.   **[638]**

6 Agricultural, forestry and fisheries associations

(1) Without prejudice to regulation 5, the acceptance by an association to which section 33 of the Restrictive Trade Practices Act 1976 applies of a deposit by a member of that association is an exempt transaction.

(2) The reference in paragraph (1) of this regulation to a member of an association to which section 33 of the Restrictive Trade Practices Act 1976 applies includes a reference to—

  (a) a member of any such association which is a member of that association, and
  (b) a prospective member, provided that the deposit is made in order to qualify him for membership of the association.   **[639]**

7 Retail and other co-operative societies

(1) Without prejudice to regulation 5, the acceptance by a co-operative society of a deposit is an exempt transaction if the society fulfils the requirements of paragraph (2) of this regulation and the deposit is not taken in breach of the society's obligations under the Scheme.

(2) The requirements of this paragraph are—

  (a) that the society is an industrial and provident society,
  (b) that . . . —

    (i) the principal business of the society is the sale by retail of goods for the domestic or personal use of individuals dealing with the society, or the provision of services for such individuals, or
    (ii) at least seventy-five per cent. of the votes which may be cast to determine the conduct of the society's affairs and at least ninety

per cent. of its shares by reference to their nominal value are held by qualifying shareholders, [or]

[(iii) the principal business of the society is the sale of goods or the provision of services to societies fulfilling the requirements of paragraph (i) above, and]

(c) the society participates in the Scheme and accordingly is a Participating Society within the meaning of clause 2(4) thereof.

(3) In this regulation—

(a) references to the Scheme are to the Scheme constituted by deed dated the 29th February 1980 between the Co-operative Union Limited of the one part and the Co-operative Bank Limited of the other part [(as amended by qualifying resolutions of Participating Societies (as therein defined) dated 29th May 1989)] the provisions of which are set out in Schedule 1 to these Regulations, and such references do not include references to the Scheme as [subsequently] amended or varied;

(b) the reference to qualifying shareholders is to industrial and provident societies which have the principal business described in paragraph 2(b)(i) of this regulation and societies which are registered within the meaning of the Friendly Societies Act 1974 or are registered or deemed to be registered under the Friendly Societies Act (Northern Ireland) 1970.   **[640]**

NOTES

Para (2): word omitted in sub-para (b) revoked, and words in square brackets therein substituted or added, by SI 1990/1018, reg 2.

Para (3): words in square brackets in sub-para (a) inserted by SI 1990/20, reg 3(b).

8 Solicitors

(1) The acceptance by a practising solicitor in the course of his profession of a deposit is an exempt transaction.

(2) In this regulation "practising solicitor" means a solicitor who is qualified to act as such under section 1 of the Solicitors Act 1974, article 4 of the Solicitors (Northern Ireland) Order 1976 or section 4 of the Solicitors (Scotland) Act 1980, and in Scotland includes a firm of practising solicitors. **[641]**

NOTES

Modifications: reference in para (1) to a practising solicitor in the course of his profession to include a recognised body in the course of providing professional services such as are provided by individuals practising as solicitors or by multi-national partnerships as defined in the Courts and Legal Services Act 1990, s 89 and in para (2) the definition "practising solicitor" also includes a recognised body, but the words "a firm practising solicitors" has no reference to a recognised body or recognised bodies: Solicitors' Incorporated Practices Order 1991, SI 1991/2684, arts 4, 5, Sch 2.

Reference in para (1) to a practising solicitor modified to include, so far as it relates to a solicitor who is qualified to act as such under the Solicitors Act 1974, s 1, a registered foreign lawyer in the course of providing professional services as a member of a multi-national partnership, by the Registered Foreign Lawyers Order 1991, SI 1991/2831, reg 3.

9 Deposits accepted in the course of estate agency work

(1) The acceptance in the course of estate agency work of a deposit which is a pre-contract deposit is an exempt transaction.

(2) In this regulation "estate agency work" has the meaning assigned to it by section 1(1) of the Estate Agents Act 1979, and "pre-contract deposit" has the meaning assigned to it by section 12(3) of that Act.   **[642]**

10 Certain public undertakings

(1) Subject to paragraph (2) of this regulation, the acceptance by a body listed in Schedule 2 to these Regulations of a deposit made by another such body is an exempt transaction.

(2) Paragraph (1) shall apply to a successor . . . only so long as each of its issued shares is held by, or by a nominee of, the Treasury or the Secretary of State.   **[643]**

[10A Student Loans Company Limited

(1) The acceptance by Student Loans Company Limited of a deposit made by a government department is an exempt transaction if the deposit is accepted in furtherance of arrangements made by the Secretary of State under the Education (Student Loans) Act 1990, or by the Department of Education for Northern Ireland under the Education (Student Loans) (Northern Ireland) Order 1990, for enabling eligible students to receive loans towards their maintenance.

(2) In this regulation "eligible students" has the meaning ascribed to it by section 1(2) of the Education (Student Loans) Act 1990, or as the case may be, Article 3(2) of the Education (Student Loans) (Northern Ireland) Order 1990.]
                                                                                   [644]

11 The National Children's Charities Fund

The acceptance by The National Children's Charities Fund of a deposit is an exempt transaction if the deposit is accepted on terms that no interest or premium shall be payable in respect thereof unless the total amount of deposits by that person with The National Children's Charities Fund exceeds £10,000.
                                                                             [645]–[646]

12 (*Revoked by SI 1990/20.*)

[13 Relevant debt securities

The acceptance of a deposit by a person [(not being a body to which regulation 10(1) of these Regulations applies)] on terms involving the issue of any relevant debt security is an exempt transaction if

  (a) the person accepting the deposit is—
    (i) a company whose shares or debt securities have been admitted to the Official List (and are not the subject of a notice issued by [The Stock Exchange] cancelling or suspending the listing or suspending dealings) or are dealt in on the Unlisted Securities Market (and are not the subject of a notice issued by [The Stock Exchange] cancelling or suspending dealings); or
    (ii) a company not falling within sub-paragraph (a)(i) above which is incorporated in the United Kingdom or whose shares or debt securities have been admitted to listing on a Recognised Overseas Exchange (and are not the subject of official action taken in accordance with the rules of the Recognised Overseas Exchange cancelling or suspending the listing or suspending

dealings), which has complied with the requirements of Schedule 3 to these Regulations; or

(iii) the government of any country or territory, or a public authority, outside the United Kingdom the debt securities of which are admitted to trading on the Stock Exchange or on a Recognised Overseas Exchange (and are not the subject of a notice issued by [The Stock Exchange] or official action taken in accordance with the rules of the Recognised Overseas Exchange (as the case may be) cancelling or suspending the admission to trading or suspending dealings); or

(iv) a person who does not fall within sub-paragraphs (a)(i) to (iii) above, if either a company which falls within sub-paragraph (a)(i) or an authorised institution has guaranteed to the holder of the relevant debt security the repayment of the principal and the payment of any interest or premium in connection therewith;

(b) in the case of a company falling within sub-paragraph (a)(i) or (ii) above, its net assets, or, in the case of a person falling within sub-paragraph (a)(iv) above where the guarantor is not an authorised institution, the guarantor's net assets, were shown in its last audited individual or group accounts (as the case may be) to be not less than £25 million (or an amount of equivalent value denominated wholly or partly otherwise than in sterling);

(c) in consideration of the deposit a single debt security is issued, in the form of a relevant debt security, which has a redemption value of not less than £100,000 (or an amount of equivalent value denominated wholly or partly otherwise than in sterling), the whole or part of which may be transferred only if the redemption value of each relevant debt security being transferred is not less than £100,000 (or an amount of equivalent value denominated wholly or partly otherwise than in sterling); and

(d) the relevant debt security—

(i) if commercial paper, bears the rubric

"commercial paper issued in accordance with regulations made under section 4 of the Banking Act 1987";

(ii) if a medium term note, bears the rubric

"medium term note issued in accordance with regulations made under section 4 of the Banking Act 1987";

(iii) states the name of the issuer and that the issuer is not an authorised institution and either states that repayment of the principal and the payment of any interest or premium in connection with the relevant debt security have not been guaranteed, or, if they have been guaranteed, states that this is the case, the name of the guarantor and whether or not the guarantor is an authorised institution; and

(iv) if it is issued by a company falling within sub-paragraph (a)(i) or (ii) above, or where it is not issued by such a company but is guaranteed by a company falling within sub-paragraph (a)(i) above, and is not offered by a prospectus to which [regulation 8 of the Public Offers of Securities Regulations 1995] applies, includes a statement made by the company accepting the deposit or the guarantor (as the case may be) that the relevant company has complied with its obligations under the relevant rules and that, since the last publication in compliance with the relevant rules of information about the relevant company, the relevant company, having made all reasonable enquiries, has not become aware of any change in circumstances which could reasonably be regarded as significantly and adversely affecting its ability to meet its obligations in respect of the relevant debt security as they fall due. In this paragraph "the relevant rules" means—

(aa)   in the case of a company whose shares or debt securities have been admitted to the Official List, the listing rules, or

(bb)   in the case of a company whose shares or debt securities are dealt in on the Unlisted Securities Market, the terms and conditions of entry to the Unlisted Securities Market, or

(cc)   in the case of a company not falling within sub-paragraph (aa) or (bb) above, Schedule 3 to these Regulations.]

[647]

NOTES

Commencement: 1 February 1990.

This regulation substituted by SI 1990/20, reg 3(d).

Words in first pair of square brackets substituted by SI 1991/29, reg 2; words in square brackets in para (a) substituted by SI 1991/2168, reg 2; words in square brackets in para (d)(iv) substituted by the Public Offers of Securities Regulations 1995, SI 1995/1537, reg 24, Sch 5, para 2.

Modification: by virtue of the Banking Coordination (Second Council Directive) Regulations 1992, SI 1992/3218, reg 82(1), Sch 10, para 46(1), this regulation has effect as if the reference to an authorised institution within the meaning of the Banking Act included a reference to a European deposit-taker.

14 Authorised and exempted persons under the Financial Services Act 1986

(1)   Subject to paragraphs (2) and (3) below, the acceptance of a deposit by a person who is an authorised person or an exempted person under the Financial Services Act 1986 (in this regulation called "an authorised person" and "an exempted person" respectively) is an exempt transaction if the deposit is accepted in the course of or for the purpose of engaging in any dealing activity with or on behalf of the person by whom or on whose behalf the deposit is made or any service activity on behalf of that person.

(2)   Paragraph (1) applies to an authorised person only if the activity is one in which he may engage without contravening any rules (made by the appropriate authority or a recognised organisation) of the kind described in section 48(2)(a) and (b) of the Financial Services Act 1986 (rules as to the type of business carried on or the persons in relation to whom business is carried on) or any prohibition of the kind described in section 65 of that Act.

(3)   Paragraph (1) applies to an exempted person only if the activity is one in respect of which he is exempt under the Financial Services Act 1986.

(4)   In this regulation—

(a)   "appropriate authority" means the Secretary of State or a designated agency within the meaning of section 114(3) of the Financial Services Act 1986;

(b)   "dealing activity" means an activity falling within paragraph 12 of Schedule 1 to that Act, construed without reference to Parts III and IV of that Schedule;

(c)   "recognised organisation" means a body which is a recognised professional body or a recognised self-regulating organisation within the meaning of section 207(1) of that Act and references to rules made by a recognised organisation include rules (whether or not laid down by the organisation itself) which the organisation has power to enforce; and

(d) "service activity" means an activity falling within paragraph 13, 14 or 16 of Schedule 1 to that Act, construed without reference to Parts III and IV of that Schedule. **[648]–[649]**

NOTE
Modification: by virtue of the Banking Coordination (Second Council Directive) Regulations 1992, SI 1992/3218, reg 82(1), Sch 10, para 46(2), this regulation has effect as if the reference in para (1) to a person who is an authorised person under the Financial Services Act included a reference to a European institution carrying on home-regulated investment business in the United Kingdom and the reference in para (2) to such an authorised person included a reference to a European institution.

15 (*This regulation revokes SI 1986/1712 and SI 1987/65.*)

[SCHEDULE 1

Regulation 7

DEED ESTABLISHING THE CO-OPERATIVE DEPOSIT PROTECTION SCHEME

(As amended by qualifying resolutions of Participating Societies dated 29th May 1989 which also continued the Scheme in force for a further period of ten years after the initial period)

THIS DEED is made the 29th day of February 1980 between CO-OPERATIVE UNION LIMITED of Holyoake House Hanover Street Manchester (hereinafter called "the Union") of the one part and CO-OPERATIVE BANK LIMITED of New Century House Corporation Street Manchester (hereinafter called "the Bank") of the other part

WHEREAS:

(a) It is the purpose of this Deed to set up a scheme to grant certain protection on the terms and conditions and subject to the limitations hereinafter contained to persons who have deposited money with or who have withdrawable shares in a co-operative society in membership of the Union against the consequences of the insolvency of that society;

(b) The Treasury is empowered by Section 4(4) of the Banking Act 1987 to make regulations prescribing for the purpose of that Section certain transactions;

(c) It is intended that a co-operative society so in membership which has elected to join the Scheme established by this Deed shall be able to have its taking of deposits so prescribed by the Treasury and that its withdrawable share capital shall be included within the definition of "Deposit" for the purposes of the Scheme.

NOW THIS DEED WITNESSETH AND IT IS HEREBY DECLARED as follows:

1. This Scheme hereby constituted shall be known as the "Co-operative Deposit Protection Scheme".

2.—(1) Subject to sub-paragraphs (2) and (3) below, in this Deed "Deposit" shall mean withdrawable share capital and loan capital of a co-operative society and a sum of money paid on terms

(i) under which it will be repaid in full, with or without interest or a premium, and either on demand or at a time or in circumstances agreed by or on behalf of the person making the payment and the person receiving it; and

(ii) which are not referable to the provision of property or services or the giving of security;

(2) "Deposit" shall not however include:

(a) interest unless compounded and added to capital; or

(b) deposits whether or not secured, having an original term to maturity of more than 5 years; or

(c) any sum paid to a co-operative society so in membership by a person who at the time it is paid is a director, controller or manager of the society or the wife, husband, son or daughter of such a person;

(3) For the purpose of sub-paragraph 2(1)(ii) above money is paid on terms which are referable to the provision of property or services or to the giving of security if, and only if:

(i) it is paid by way of advance or part payment for the sale, hire or other provision of property or services of any kind and is repayable only in the event that the property or services is or are not in fact sold, hired or otherwise provided; or

(ii) it is paid by way of security for payment for the provision of property or services of any kind provided or to be provided by the person by whom or on whose behalf the money is accepted; or

(iii) it is paid by way of security for the delivery up or return of any property whether in a particular state of repair or otherwise.

(4) In this Deed "a Participating Society" shall mean a co-operative society which (a) has joined the Scheme by (i) resolution of its governing body adopting and agreeing to the Scheme established by this Deed (ii) paying a joining contribution in accordance with clause 5(2) hereof and (iii) executing and delivering to the Union a Deed of Participation in the Scheme to which Deed the Bank and the Union are parties in the form set out in the Schedule to this Scheme; and (*b*) has not ceased in accordance with clause 10(1) hereof to be a Participating Society.

(5) In this Deed "Founding Date" shall mean 1st April 1980.

(6) In this Deed—

"director" shall mean any person who occupies the position of a director by whatever named called;

"controller" shall mean a managing director chief executive or a person in accordance with whose directions or instructions the directors of the co-operative society are accustomed to act; and

"manager" shall mean a person other than the chief executive, employed by a co-operative society who, under the immediate authority of a director or chief executive of the co-operative society, exercises managerial functions or is responsible for maintaining accounts or other records of the co-operative society.

"depositor" shall mean a person who has deposited money with or who is the holder of withdrawable share capital in a co-operative society.

3.—(1) The Union and the Bank hereby agree and declare that, subject as is by this Deed provided, they will hold manage and apply in accordance with the provisions of this Deed the Fund as hereinafter defined (hereinafter called "the Fund");

(2) The Fund and any investments money or other assets for the time being comprised therein may in the absolute discretion of the Union and the Bank be held in the sole name of the Bank;

(3) Any real property for the time being forming part of the Fund shall be held upon trust for sale;

(4) The Union and the Bank delegate to the Union the duty of administering the Scheme in accordance with the provisions of this Deed;

(5) The Union and the Bank delegate to the Bank the investment of the Fund;

(6) The banking administrative and management expenses of the Union and/or the Bank shall be defrayed out of the Fund.

4.—(1) The Fund shall consist of:

(a) joining and supplementary contributions as hereafter mentioned;
(b) monies borrowed for the purposes of the Fund;
(c) interest and dividends from investments;
(d) dividends recovered in any liquidation;
(e) the investments, property and other assets representing from time to time the above or any of them.

(2) There shall be chargeable to the Fund:

(a) payments to meet the banking administrative and management expenses of the Union and/or the Bank in accordance with sub clause 3(6) above and clause 14 hereof;
(b) refunds to Participating Societies as hereinafter provided;
(c) moneys required for the repayment of borrowings and any interest thereon;
(d) payments to depositors in respect of protected deposits as hereinafter provided.

5.—(1) Societies which are or are seeking to be Participating Societies shall make 2 classes of contribution, namely

(i) joining contributions, and
(ii) supplementary contributions.

(2) At the Founding Date or on joining the Scheme Societies shall make a joining contribution of an amount prescribed by the Union being (a) 0.5 per cent of the deposit base of the Society at

that time, such deposit base being the aggregate amount of the deposits recorded in the then most recent annual return of the Society made to the Union provided that (i) such annual return shall not be in respect of a period ending earlier than 2 years before the Founding Date or joining the Scheme as the case may be and (ii) such percentage joining contribution shall be not less than £300 nor greater than £23,000, or, if the amount under (a) above is not calculable or not readily calculable, (b) such amount as the Union shall determine, being an amount (so far as the Union can estimate) equal to or greater than such percentage joining contribution would have been.

(3) The Union shall maintain the net assets of the Fund at such an amount, not being less than £500,000 at any time, as the Union and the Bank shall in their absolute discretion consider to be not less than reasonable so as to afford protection to Deposits to the extent provided for in this Scheme and for this purpose the Union may at any time (including on the Founding Date and on joining the Scheme) require Participating Societies to make supplementary contributions of such an amount and on such occasions and in such manner as the Union may determine, it being the intention that the Union (whilst not being required or bound so to do) should exercise its power to require supplementary contributions by fixing the amount of such contributions in proportion to the deposit base (calculated in such manner as the Union shall in its discretion consider reasonable) for each of the Participating Societies subject to a minimum and maximum payment.

6.—(1) A Participating Society shall for the purpose of this Deed and the Scheme hereby constituted become insolvent

(i) on the making of a winding up order against it; or

(ii) on the passing of a resolution for a creditors' voluntary winding up.

(2) Subject to the provisions of this Deed, if at any time a Participating Society becomes insolvent or is to be treated as insolvent by virtue of Clauses 10(1) and 12(2) hereof the Union shall as soon as practicable pay out of the Fund to a depositor who has a protected Deposit with that Society an amount equal to three-quarters of the protected Deposit, but so that such amount shall in no case exceed £15,000;

(3) Subject to the provisions of this Deed, a reference to a depositor's protected Deposit is a reference to the total liability of the Participating Society to him, but limited in any event to a maximum of £20,000, in respect of the principal amounts of Deposits made to the Participating Society

PROVIDED THAT

(i) any such Deposit was not made after such society had ceased to be a Participating Society;

(ii) the principal amounts of Deposits shall only include any interest or premium which has been credited to the Deposit in question if such interest or premium has been so credited at the time such Society becomes insolvent so as to constitute an accretion to the principal;

(iii) in determining the total liability of such Society to a depositor for the purposes of this and the previous sub-clause, there shall be deducted the amount of any liability of the depositor to such Society—

(a) in respect of which a right of set-off or counter-claim against the Deposit (including in Scotland a right of retention or compensation) existed immediately before such Society became insolvent; or

(b) in respect of which such a right would then have existed if the Deposit in question had been repayable on demand and the liability in question had fallen due; and

(iv) the Union may in its absolute discretion decline to make any payment under this Scheme in respect of a Deposit to a person who, in the opinion of the Union, had any responsibility for, or may have profited directly or indirectly from, the circumstances, or some of the circumstances, giving rise to the financial difficulties of the Participating Society which had become insolvent.

7.—(1) For the purposes of clauses 6 and 8 hereof where any persons are entitled to a Deposit as trustees, then, unless the Deposit is held on trust for a person absolutely entitled to it as against the trustees, the trustees shall be treated as a single and continuing body of persons distinct from the persons who may from time to time be the trustees, and if the same persons are entitled as trustees to different deposits under different trusts or, in Scotland, trust purposes, they shall be treated as a separate and distinct body with respect to each of those trusts or, in Scotland, trust purposes.

(2) For the purposes of this clause a Deposit is held on trust for a person absolutely entitled to it as against the trustees where the person has the exclusive right (subject only to satisfying any

outstanding charge, lien or other right of the trustees to resort to the Deposit for payment of duty, taxes, costs or other outgoings) to direct how the Deposit shall be dealt with.

(3) Any reference in sub-clauses (1) and (2) above to a person absolutely entitled to a Deposit as against the trustees includes a reference to two or more persons who are so entitled jointly; and in the application of sub-clause (2) above to Scotland the words in parenthesis from "subject" to "outgoings" shall be omitted.

(4) For the purposes of Clause 6 above and the following provisions of this clause, where a Deposit is held on trust for any person absolutely entitled to it or, as the case may be, for two or more persons so entitled jointly, that person or, as the case may be, those persons jointly shall be treated as entitled to the Deposit without the intervention of any trust.

(5) For the purpose of Clause 6 above where two or more persons are jointly entitled to a Deposit and sub-clause 7(1) above does not apply, each of them shall be treated as having a separate Deposit of an amount produced by dividing the amount of the Deposit to which they are jointly entitled by the number of persons who are so entitled.

(6) The Union may decline to make any payment under clause 6 above in respect of a Deposit until the person claiming to be entitled to it informs the Union of the capacity in which he is entitled to the Deposit; and if it appears to the Union

(a) that the persons entitled to a Deposit are so entitled as trustees, or
(b) that sub-clause 7(4) above applies to a Deposit, or
(c) that two or more persons are jointly entitled to a Deposit otherwise than as trustees,

the Union may decline to make any payment in respect of the Deposit until the Union is satisfied that it has sufficient information to enable it to determine what payment (if any) should be made and to whom.

(7) In this clause "jointly entitled" means—

(a) In England and Wales and Northern Ireland, beneficially entitled as joint tenants, tenants in common or as coparceners; and
(b) in Scotland, beneficially entitled as joint owners or owners in common.

8.—(1) Where a Society has become insolvent or is by virtue of clauses 10(1) or 12(2) hereof to be treated as insolvent and any payment is or should be made under this Scheme in respect of a Deposit, the Bank (on behalf of itself and the Union) shall seek to recover all dividends compositions or payments made or to be made in respect of the Deposit (not limited to three quarters thereof or otherwise howsoever) and as between the Bank and the depositor the Bank (without prejudice to additional rights arising by virtue by subrogation) shall be entitled to all dividends, compositions and payments up to the amount of the payment made or to be made by the Union under this Scheme and the depositor shall not be entitled to any of such dividends compositions or payments until the whole of the payment made or to be made by the Union under this Scheme shall first have been equalled.

(2) Where a Society has become insolvent or is by virtue of clauses 10(1) or 12(2) hereof to be treated as insolvent, then if and whenever requested by the Bank, the depositor shall by an assignment or in Scotland, an assignation, in writing assign to the Bank his rights and/or execute a declaration of trust in favour of the Bank in respect of his rights to all or any of such dividends compositions and payments and the Bank shall hold the rights so assigned or in respect of which a declaration of trust has been executed first in trust to pay to itself such dividends compositions and payments as it shall be entitled to under the previous sub-clause, and second in trust for the depositor or as he may direct, and the Bank may as attorney for and on behalf of the depositor execute any such assignment assignation or declaration of trust as aforesaid.

(3) Without prejudice to the generality of its rights hereunder the Union and/or the Bank may stipulate as a pre-condition of any payment in respect of a Deposit under the Scheme that an assignment or, in Scotland, an assignation, to it and/or a declaration of trust should be made as aforesaid.

(4) Where a Society has become insolvent or is by virtue of clauses 10(1) or 12(2) hereof to be treated as insolvent it shall be the duty of the Bank and also of the depositor to inform the Liquidator, or where it is treated as insolvent the Society, of the Bank's rights hereunder as soon as possible with a view to the preservation for the Bank of all such dividends compositions and payments and the depositor shall authorise the Liquidator, or where it is treated as insolvent the Society, to provide on request all relevant information to the Bank.

(5) The Union and/or the Bank shall be entitled for the purposes of the Scheme to have access to and copy such of the books records files and other documents of, and to obtain such information from, any body corporate which is or has been a Participating Society as the Union and/or the Bank (as the case may be) shall in their or its discretion consider necessary or helpful in order to carry the provision of the Scheme into effect.

9. It is the duty of the Union to maintain the net assets of the Fund at such an amount, not being less than £500,000 at any time, as the Union and the Bank shall in their absolute discretion consider to be not less than reasonable so as to afford protection to Deposits to the extent provided for in this Scheme, but subject as aforesaid the Union and the Bank may during the continuance of this Scheme make such refunds out of the Fund to Participating Societies as they shall consider proper, and such refunds shall be made to such Participating Societies and calculated in such manner as the Union shall in its absolute discretion determine.

10.—(1) Any Participating Society may apply to leave the Scheme by sending written notice to that effect to the Union, and shall, save under the protection of Part II of the Banking Act 1987 cease to accept new Deposits (with the exception of withdrawable share capital) and shall within the period of 9 months from the receipt by the Union of such written notice either (i) repay all Deposits (with the exception of withdrawable share capital) held by it or (ii) secure protection for those Deposits (with the exception of withdrawable share capital) under Part II of the Banking Act 1987. Upon the due performance of (i) or (ii) above the Society shall cease to be a Participating Society, and upon such due performance as above within the said period of 9 months there shall be repaid to such Society out of the Fund such sum (if any) as the Union shall in its absolute discretion consider appropriate. Without prejudice to the application of clause 6 hereof (and the provisions of clauses 7 and 8) in the case of a Participating Society which becomes insolvent during the said period of 9 months, if such Society shall not have duly performed (i) or (ii) above within the said period of 9 months, clause 6 hereof (and the provisions of clauses 7 and 8 so far as applicable) shall apply to the depositors of such Society who have not had their Deposits (with the exception of withdrawable share capital) so repaid or secured as if that Society had become insolvent, but so that any payment thereunder shall be made within 6 months after the end of the said 9 months' period.

(2) Without prejudice to the generality of the foregoing, the following shall rank among the circumstances to be considered by the Union in respect of any such repayment to a society—

(a) The amount of the Fund;
(b) The income generated by the Fund since its inception;
(c) The expenses borne by the Fund since its inception; and
(d) Payments out of the Fund in respect of Deposits.

11.—(1) The Scheme shall continue in force, unless earlier terminated, for an initial period of 10 years. (NOTE: By a qualifying resolution of Participating Societies dated 29th May 1989 the Scheme is continued in force for a further period of ten years after the initial period.)

(2) Subject to sub-clause (3) below, the Scheme may be

(a) terminated during such initial period, or
(b) continued in force after the initial period or
(c) altered at any time

by a qualifying resolution or resolutions (as hereinafter provided).

(3) The perpetuity period applicable in respect of the Scheme shall be the period of eighty years commencing on the Founding Date, and the Scheme shall not be capable of being continued, or of being altered so as to be continued, beyond that period.

(4) A qualifying resolution may be moved by—

(a) the Union; or
(b) the Bank; or
(c) any Participating Society,

and it shall be moved by giving at least 28 days' clear notice to the Union, the Bank and all Participating Societies of (a) the business to be transacted and (b) the date time and place of the meeting.

(5) Such notice shall be given in writing and sent by post to the last known address of the person or body so to be notified, but the accidental omission to give one or more notices shall not invalidate the meeting or any resolution passed thereat.

(6) A qualifying resolution shall be duly passed and valid if adopted by Participating Societies at such meeting holding between them 75% of the Deposits held at the date of the resolution by Participating Societies and afforded protection by this Scheme (and so that such percentage shall be calculated by reference to the full amount of such Deposits).

12.—(1) Upon termination of the Scheme and in any event at the expiration of the period of 78 years less 1 day from the Founding Date (from which time no new Deposits (with the exception of withdrawable share capital) shall, save under the protection of Part II of the Banking Act 1987, be accepted by Participating Societies), all the then Participating Societies shall within the period of 9 months thereafter either

(i) repay all their Deposits (with the exception of withdrawable share capital); or
(ii) secure protection for those Deposits (with the exception of withdrawable share capital) under Part II of the Banking Act 1987.

(2) If any Participating Society (hereinafter called "a Defaulting Society") shall not in respect of the Deposits (with the exception of withdrawable share capital) taken by it have either

(i) repaid them, or
(ii) secured protection for them under Part II of the Banking Act 1987, within the period of 9 months from

(a) such termination or
(b) the expiration of the said period of 78 years less 1 day whichever is the sooner,

clause 6 hereof (and the provisions of clauses 7 and 8 hereof so far as applicable) shall apply to the depositors of that Defaulting Society who have not had their Deposits (with the exception of withdrawable share capital) so repaid or secured as if that Defaulting Society had become insolvent but so that any payment thereunder shall be made within 6 months after the end of the said 9 months period.

(3) Subject to any payments required to be made under this Scheme (including under sub-clause (2) above) and subject to the payment or provision of all proper charges for banking and of all the expenses of administering, managing and winding up this Scheme, the Union shall within 15 months after the expiration of the 9 months' period referred to in the preceding sub-clause (2) distribute the Fund among the Participating Societies other than Defaulting Societies in such amounts and in such manner as it shall in its absolute discretion determine but with a view to making repayments in proportion to their respective contributions.

(4) Clause 6 hereof (and the provisions of clauses 7 and 8) shall apply in the case of a Participating Society which becomes insolvent during the said period of 9 months referred to in sub-clause (2) of this clause. Any payment under the said clause 6 whether made under the present sub-clause or otherwise shall be made not later than 6 months after the end of the said 9 months' period.

(5) If by reason of an amalgamation or transfer of engagements (hereinafter called "a merger") a co-operative society (hereinafter called "the Merged Society") becomes possessed of or entitled to Deposits some of which are protected under this Scheme and some of which are not so protected the following provisions shall apply:

(a) Forthwith upon the merger's becoming effective the Merged Society shall marshall its Deposits into two classes namely

(i) the Protected Class, being Deposits taken in circumstances such that they were protected by the Scheme; and
(ii) the Unprotected Class, being Deposits not so protected.

(b) To the Protected Class the Scheme shall continue to give protection subject to its terms and conditions for which purpose the Merged Society shall be treated as a Participating Society.
(c) The Merged Society shall within a period of three months from the Merger's becoming effective by joining the Scheme arrange protection under the Scheme for the Unprotected Class.
(d) If the Merged Society shall have failed within the said period by joining the Scheme to obtain protection for all of the Unprotected Class it shall be deemed to have given notice under clause 10(1) hereof as at the expiration of the said period of 3 months.

(6) If by reason of a merger a Merged Society becomes entitled to or possessed of Deposits all of which were taken in the circumstances such that they were protected under the Scheme the Merged Society shall forthwith upon the merger's becoming effective join the Scheme under clause 2(4)(a)

but shall be relieved of a joining contribution, and if it shall fail to join the Scheme within the period of 3 months from the merger's becoming effective it shall be deemed to have given notice under clause 10(1) hereof.

13.—(1) All monies in the Fund shall be paid by the Bank and unless and until otherwise invested the Bank shall pay to the Fund interest thereon at the published rate for 7 day deposits.

(2) The Fund may be invested in any one or more of the following:—

    (i) monies held by or deposited with the Bank at interest as aforesaid;
    (ii) Treasury bills payable not more than 91 days from the date of issue;
    (iii) Deposits with or withdrawable share capital of a building society authorised under the Building Societies Act 1986;
    (iv) Deposits with the National Savings Bank and National Girobank;
    (v) Deposits with an authorised institution within the remaining of the Banking Act 1987.

14.—(1) The Bank may act as bankers to this Scheme and to the Fund and may make advances or loans to the Fund upon the usual terms as to interest and charges in the ordinary course of the Bank's business and share stockbroker's commission and generally act as a banker may in relation to his customer and without accounting for any profit so made, and without prejudice to the generality of the foregoing the Bank shall be entitled to charge and recover from the Fund all proper charges for banking, administration and management (including investment management) provided to the Fund or in respect of this Scheme.

(2) The Union shall be entitled to charge and recover from the Fund all proper charges for administration and management provided to the Fund or in respect of this Scheme.

IN WITNESS whereof this Deed has been executed by the parties the day and year first before written

    SEALED by Co-operative Union Limited

in the presence of:

    J.H. Perrow, Chairman
    D.L. Wilkinson, General Secretary

    SEALED by Co-operative Bank Limited

in the presence of:

    L.Lee, Director
    G.J. Melmoth, Secretary

THE SCHEDULE BEFORE REFERRED TO

This Deed is made the   day of   19   BETWEEN CO-OPERATIVE UNION LIMITED of Holyoake House Hanover Street Manchester (hereinafter called "the Union") of the first part CO-OPERATIVE BANK LIMITED of New Century House Corporation Street Manchester (hereinafter called "the Bank") of the second part and   LIMITED of   (hereinafter called "the Society") of the third part

WHEREAS

    A. This Deed is supplemental to a Deed dated and made between the Union and the Bank establishing a Scheme (hereinafter called "the Scheme") which is called the Co-operative Deposit Protection Scheme.
    B. The purpose of the Scheme is to provide certain protection to Deposits (as defined in the said Deed) with Participating Societies.
    C. The Society is an Industrial and Provident Society and is a member of the Union.
    D. The Society has by resolution of its governing body elected to participate in the Scheme and has by such resolution undertaken to adopt and agree to the Scheme.
    E. The Society has paid a joining contribution in accordance with clause 5(2) of the said Deed
    F. The Union has approved the admission of the Society to the Scheme as a Participating Society.

NOW THIS DEED WITNESSETH that the Society hereby adopts and agrees to the provisions of the Scheme to the intent that it may become a Participating Society as defined in the Scheme and be bound thereby and undertakes to procure that the Scheme's provisions are incorporated in documents issued by the Society securing Deposits and bind the holders of those Deposits.

IN WITNESS whereof the parties have executed this Deed

THE COMMON SEAL OF CO-OPERATIVE UNION LIMITED was hereunto affixed in the presence of:—

Chairman
General Secretary

THE COMMON SEAL OF CO-OPERATIVE BANK LIMITED was hereunto affixed in the presence of:—

Director
Secretary

THE COMMON SEAL OF   SOCIETY LIMITED was hereunto affixed in the presence of:—

Director
Secretary]   **[650]**

NOTES
   Commencement: 1 February 1990.
   Substituted by SI 1990/20, reg 3(e), Sch 1.

SCHEDULE 2

Regulation 10

BODIES REFERRED TO IN REGULATION 10

An Area Board within the meaning of section 1(3) of the Electricity Act 1947.
[Any successor to such an Area Board.]
The British Broadcasting Corporation.
. . .
The British Railways Board.
British Shipbuilders.
. . .
The British Waterways Board.
The Central Electricity Generating Board.
[Any successor to the Central Electricity Generating Board.]
The Civil Aviation Authority.
The Commission for the New Towns.
A development corporation established for the purposes of a new town by an order made, or having effect as if made, under 3(1) of the New Towns Act 1981, or section 2(1) of the New Towns (Scotland) Act 1968.
The Electricity Council.
The Housing Corporation.
[London Regional Transport.]
The National Bus Company.
The North of Scotland Hydro-Electric Board.
[Any successor to the North of Scotland Hydro-Electric Board.]
[Northern Ireland Electricity.]
The Northern Ireland Housing Executive.
The Northern Ireland Transport Holding Company.
[The Post Office.]
The Scottish Transport Group.
The South of Scotland Electricity Board.
[Any successor to the South of Scotland Electricity Board.]   **[651]**

NOTE
   First words omitted revoked by SI 1994/2567, art 2, Schedule; other words omitted revoked, fifth words in square brackets substituted and other words in square brackets added by SI 1989/465, reg 3(d).

[SCHEDULE 3

Regulation 13

REQUIREMENTS TO BE COMPLIED WITH BY CERTAIN ISSUERS OF RELEVANT DEBT SECURITIES

Interpretation

1. In this Schedule—

"the issuer" means a company accepting a relevant deposit;

"the relevant date" means the date on which the information set out in paragraph 2 below was first provided by the issuer to The Stock Exchange in accordance with paragraph 4 below; and

"a relevant deposit" means a deposit accepted on terms involving the issue of any relevant debt security.

Information to have been notified to The Stock Exchange

2. Not less than fourteen days prior to the acceptance of its first relevant deposit the issuer shall have provided the following information to The Stock Exchange:

The issuer

(a) the name of the issuer and, if the relevant debt security was guaranteed, the name of the guarantor;

(b) the country or territory of incorporation of the issuer and, if applicable, the guarantor;

(c) the address of the registered office of the issuer (if it has one) and, if it has no registered office or if its principal place of business was not at its registered office, the address of its principal place of business;

(d) the date on which the issuer was incorporated and, if it has a limited life, the length of its life;

(e) the legislation under which the issuer is incorporated and the legal form which it has adopted under that legislation;

(f) the place of registration of the issuer, if different to the country or territory of incorporation, and the number with which it is registered;

(g) the names and addresses of the issuer's principal bankers;

(h) details of any legal or arbitration proceedings pending or threatened against the issuer or, if it is a member of a group, any member of the group, which might have, or might have had during the twelve months prior to the relevant date, a significant effect on the financial position of the issuer or the group (as the case may be) or, if there were no such proceedings, a statement to that effect;

(i) the address in the City of London where copies of the documents referred to in paragraph 6 of this Schedule were available for inspection;

(j) if the relevant debt security was guaranteed by a company falling within regulation 13(a)(i) of these Regulations, an address in the City of London where information about that company was available for inspection in accordance with the listing rules or the terms and conditions of entry to the Unlisted Securities Market (as the case may be);

(k) a description of the principal activities of the issuer, stating the main categories of products sold or services performed, together with, in a case where two or more activities were carried on which were material in terms of profits or losses, such figures and explanations as were necessary to determine the relative importance of each activity;

(l) details of any patent, licence, new manufacturing process or industrial, commercial or financial contract on which the business or profitability of the issuer or its group depended to a material extent;

(m) if the issuer is a member of a group, a brief description of the group and of the issuer's position within it and, if the issuer is a subsidiary, the name of each holding company of the issuer;

Financial information

(n) the amount of the authorised and issued share capital of the issuer, the amount of any share capital agreed to be issued and the number and classes of the shares of which it was composed with details of their principal characteristics; if any part of the issued share capital was still to be paid up, an indication of the number, or total nominal value, and the type of the securities not then fully paid up, broken down, where applicable, according to the extent to which they had been paid up;

(o) information with respect to the profits and losses, assets and liabilities and financial record and position of the issuer and, if it is a member of a group, of the group, set out as a comparative table for each of the latest five financial years of the issuer for which such information was available, together with copies of individual and (if applicable) group accounts for each of the latest two such financial years, including, in the case of a company incorporated in the United Kingdom, all notes, reports or other information required by the Companies Act 1985 or the Companies (Northern Ireland) Order 1986;

(p) if more than nine months had elapsed since the end of the financial year to which the last published annual accounts related, an interim financial statement covering at least the first six months of the then current financial year and if such an interim financial statement had not been audited, a statement to this effect;

(q) the names, addresses and qualifications of the auditors who have audited the issuer's annual accounts for the preceding two financial years and in the case of a company incorporated outside the United Kingdom a statement as to whether or not those accounts conformed to United Kingdom or generally accepted international accounting standards;

(r) if during the two financial years of the issuer preceding the relevant date the issuer's auditors had refused to sign an auditor's report on the annual accounts of the issuer, or had qualified any such report in any way, a copy of the refusal (if in writing) or of the qualification together with details of any reasons given by the auditors for such action;

(s) details as at the most recent practicable date (which shall have been stated) prior to the relevant date of the following, which, if the issuer is a member of a group, shall also have been provided on a consolidated basis:

  (i) the total amount of any loan capital outstanding in any member of the group, and loan capital created but unissued, and term loans, distinguishing between loans guaranteed and unguaranteed, and those secured (whether the security is provided by the issuer or by third parties) and unsecured;

  (ii) the total amount of all other borrowings and indebtedness in the nature of borrowing of the issuer or the group (as the case may be), distinguishing between guaranteed and unguaranteed and secured and unsecured borrowings and debts, including bank overdrafts and liabilities under acceptances (other than normal trade bills) or acceptance credits or hire purchase commitments;

  (iii) all mortgages and charges of the issuer or the group (as the case may be); and

  (iv) the total amount of any contingent liabilities and guarantees of the issuer or the group (as the case may be);

  if the issuer or the group (as the case may be) had no such loan capital, borrowings, indebtedness or contingent liabilities, this shall have been stated;

  no account should have been taken of liabilities between undertakings within the same group, a statement to that effect having been made if necessary;

Directors

(t) the names, home or business addresses and functions within the issuer or its group (if applicable) of the directors of the issuer and an indication of the principal activities performed by them outside the issuer or the group (as the case may be) where these were significant with respect to the issuer or the group (as the case may be);

Recent developments

(u) general information on the trend of the business of the issuer or its group (if applicable) since the end of the financial year to which the last published annual accounts related, in particular:

  (i) the most significant recent trends in production, sales and stocks and the state of the order book; and

  (ii) recent trends in costs and selling prices;

Overseas companies

(v) where information was being provided by a company whose shares or debt securities have been admitted to listing on a Recognised Overseas Exchange, the name of the Recognised Overseas Exchange and the type of securities listed;

The relevant debt securities

(w) the total amount which the issuer intended to raise by the issue of commercial paper and medium term notes respectively and details of the intended application of the proceeds raised;

(x) the name and address of any issuing and paying agent for the relevant debt securities and the name and address of any managing agent, if different;

(y) the period after which entitlement to interest or repayment of capital would lapse, or if there was no period after which such entitlement would lapse, a statement to that effect; and

(z) details of the procedures for the delivery of the relevant debt securities to holders (including any applicable time limits) and whether temporary documents of title would be issued.

3. Prior to the acceptance by the issuer of a further relevant deposit the issuer shall either have complied with paragraph 2 above as if such further deposit were its first relevant deposit or—

(a) the issuer shall have provided to The Stock Exchange details of all material changes to the information provided under paragraph 2 above (other than the information provided under sub-paragraphs (n) to (s) (financial information)) as soon as practicable after each such change occurred;

(b) if no information was required to be provided under sub-paragraph 2(p) above, but the nine months' period referred to in that sub-paragraph has since elapsed, the issuer shall have provided the information specified in that sub-paragraph to The Stock Exchange; and

(c) if more than twelve months has elapsed since the relevant date, the issuer shall have provided to The Stock Exchange an updated version of all the information required by paragraph 2 above at intervals of not more than twelve months.

4. The information set out in paragraphs 2 and 3 above shall have been provided in English and in good faith to the Quotations Department of The Stock Exchange in the form of three copies of a document which, in the case of information provided under paragraphs 2 or 3(c) above, shall have been annotated to indicate where each item set out in paragraph 2 above had been met and (in those cases) shall have been accompanied by a declaration by the directors of the issuer in the following form—

"The Directors of the Company accept responsibility for the information provided. To the best of the knowledge and belief of the Directors (who have taken all reasonable care to ensure that such is the case) the information is in accordance with the facts and does not omit anything likely to affect the import of such information."

5. The issuer shall have made arrangements with The Stock Exchange for The Stock Exchange to make available to the public all information provided to The Stock Exchange by the issuer under this Schedule and at the date of acceptance of the relevant deposit such arrangements are in force.

Information to be available for public inspection

6. The issuer shall have made available at an address in the City of London copies of the following documents during normal business hours for a period beginning on the relevant date and continuing at least until the acceptance of its first relevant deposit:

(i) the memorandum and articles of association or equivalent documents of the issuer;

(ii) any trust deed or other document constituting debt securities of the issuer;

(iii) any contract directly relating to the issue of the relevant debt securities and any existing or proposed service contract between a director of the issuer and the issuer or any member of its group;

(iv) any report, letter, valuation, statement, balance sheet or other document any part of which is extracted or referred to in any other document provided to The Stock Exchange under this Schedule; and

    (v) the audited accounts of the issuer and, if it is a member of a group, the consolidated audited accounts of the group, for each of the two latest financial years preceding the relevant date for which such accounts are available together with, in the case of a company incorporated in the United Kingdom, all notes, reports or other information required by the Companies Act 1985 or the Companies (Northern Ireland) Order 1986 to be attached thereto;

any reference in this paragraph 6 to a document which is not in English shall be taken to include in addition a reference to a translation of that document which is either certified to be correct by a notary public or which has been made by a person certified by a practising solicitor within the meaning of regulation 8 of these Regulations to be in his opinion competent to make such a translation.

    7. Prior to the acceptance by the issuer of a further relevant deposit the issuer shall either have complied with paragraph 6 above as if such further deposit were its first relevant deposit or shall have continued to make available at the address for the time being provided to The Stock Exchange under sub-paragraph 2(i) above up-to-date copies of the documents referred to in that paragraph as soon as practicable after they became available.

Information to have been notified to the Bank of England

    8. If the relevant deposit is accepted as part of a programme for the issue of relevant debt securities, the issuer, before it accepted the first deposit relating to the programme, shall have notified to the Bank of England the total amount to be raised under the programme, the maturity period of the relevant debt securities to be issued under the programme (if known) and a detailed description of the purposes for which the proceeds of the programme would be used, distinguishing in each case where possible between commercial paper and medium term notes and between issues denominated in sterling and issues not so denominated (in the latter case specifying the currency of payment), and the name of any guarantor; and if the issuer subsequently extended the programme, shall also have notified details of the increased amount to be raised and any other material changes to the information initially provided.

    9. If the issuer has provided information to the Bank of England under paragraph 8 in relation to a relevant deposit, it shall also have reported to the Bank of England within one week after the end of each calendar month following the month in which such information was so provided the amount of relevant debt securities issued by it outstanding at the end of that calendar month and (in the case of a second or subsequent report) the amounts of relevant debt securities issued and redeemed by it since the date of the previous report, distinguishing in each case between commercial paper and medium term notes, between relevant debt securities guaranteed by an authorised institution and relevant debt securities not so guaranteed and between issues denominated in sterling and issues not so denominated (specifying in the latter case the currency of payment).]   **[652]**

NOTES
Commencement: 1 February 1990.
Added by SI 1989/465, reg 3(e); substituted by SI 1990/20, reg 3(e), Sch 2.
Modification: by virtue of the Banking Coordination (Second Council Directive) Regulations 1992, SI 1992/3218, reg 82(1), Sch 10, para 46(1), this Schedule has effect as if the reference to an authorised institution within the meaning of the Banking Act included a reference to a European deposit-taker.

BANKING ACT 1987 (MEANING OF DEPOSIT) ORDER 1991

(SI 1991/1776)

NOTES
Made: 30 July 1991.
Authority: Banking Act 1987, s 7.
Commencement: 31 July 1991.

1 Citation and commencement

This Order may be cited as the Banking Act 1987 (Meaning of Deposit) Order 1991 and shall come into force on 31st July 1991.   **[653]**

2 Amendment of meaning of "deposit"

(1) For the purposes of sections 60, 61 and 62 of the Banking Act 1987 the definition of deposit in section 5 of that Act shall be treated as excluding any sum to which a person becomes entitled (otherwise than by operation of law), or comes to be treated as entitled for the purposes of sections 58 and 60 of that Act, after a petition is presented for the winding up of the institution, or, in the case of an institution in respect of which such a petition has been presented before the date on which this Order comes into force, 30th July 1991.

(2) Paragraph (1) above does not apply in respect of a payment falling to be made under section 58(2) of the Banking Act 1987. **[654]**

3 Interpretation

For the purposes of this Order, references to the presentation of a petition for the winding up of an institution shall be taken to mean—

    (a) where the institution becomes insolvent within the meaning of section 59 of the Banking Act 1987 on the making of an order or award, the presentation of a petition that the order or award be made;

    (b) where the institution becomes so insolvent on the passing of a resolution for a voluntary winding-up in the circumstances described in section 59(1)(b) of that Act, the summoning of a meeting at which such a resolution is to be proposed;

    (c) where the institution becomes so insolvent on the holding of a creditors' meeting, the summoning of such meeting;

    (d) where the institution becomes so insolvent on the occurrence of an event which appears to the Deposit Protection Board to correspond as nearly as may be to any of those mentioned in section 59(1)(a), (b) or (c) or 59(2)(a), (b) or (c) of that Act, the event which appears to the Board to correspond as nearly as may be to that mentioned in paragraph (a), (b) or (c) of this article (as the case may be). **[655]**

ACCOUNTANTS (BANKING ACT 1987) REGULATIONS 1994

(SI 1994/524)

NOTES
Made: 3 March 1994.
Authority: Banking Act 1987, s 47(5).
Commencement: 1 May 1994.

1 Citation and commencement

These Regulations may be cited as the Accountants (Banking Act 1987) Regulations 1994 and shall come into force on 1st May 1994. **[655A]**

2 Interpretation

In these Regulations—

    "the Act" means the Banking Act 1987;

    "auditor" means an auditor of an authorised institution who is an accountant;

    "authorised institution" includes a former authorised institution;

    "the Bank" means the Bank of England;

"matters" means any matter to which section 47 of the Act applies;
"the Regulations" means the Banking Coordination (Second Council Directive) Regulations 1992; and
"reporting accountant" means a person appointed to make a report under section 8(5) or 39(1)(b) of the Act who is an accountant.

[655B]

3 Matters to be communicated to the Bank

(1) Matters are to be communicated to the Bank by an auditor or reporting accountant in the circumstances specified in paragraph (2) below.

(2) The circumstances referred to in paragraph (1) above are circumstances in which the matters are such as to give an auditor or reporting accountant reasonable cause to believe—

(a) that any of the criteria specified in Schedule 3 to the Act is not or has not been fulfilled, or may not be or may not have been fulfilled, in respect of the authorised institution in relation to which his reporting accountant's report is made, as the case may be; and

(b) that the matters are likely to be of material significance for the exercise, in relation to such an institution or authorised institution, of the Bank's functions under the Act or under the Regulations.

[655C]

NOTES
The Act: Banking Act 1987.
The Regulations: Banking Coordination (Second Council Directive) Regulations 1992, SI 1992/3218 at **[665]**.

EUROPEAN COMMUNITIES ACT 1972

BANK ACCOUNTS DIRECTIVE (MISCELLANEOUS BANKS) REGULATIONS 1991

(SI 1991/2704)

NOTES
Made: 1 December 1991.
Authority: European Communities Act 1972, s 2(2).
Commencement: 2 December 1991.

1 Citation, commencement and extent

These Regulations, which extend to Great Britain, may be cited as the Bank Accounts Directive (Miscellaneous Banks) Regulations 1991 and shall come into force on the day after the day on which they are made.   **[656]**

2 Interpretation

In these Regulations—

"the 1985 Act" means the Companies Act 1985;
"accounts" means the annual accounts, the directors' report and the auditors' report required by Regulation 4(1);
"director" includes, in the case of a body which is not a company, any corresponding officer of that body;
"enactment" includes any subordinate legislation within the meaning of section 21(1) of the Interpretation Act 1978, other than these Regulations;
"financial year", in relation to a body to which these Regulations apply, means any period in respect of which a profit and loss account of the undertaking is required to be made up by its constitution or by any enactment (whether that period is a year or not) or, failing any such requirement, a period of 12 months beginning on 1st April;

and other expressions shall have the meanings ascribed to them by the 1985 Act.   **[657]**

3 Scope of application

These Regulations apply to any body of persons, whether incorporated or unincorporated, which:—

(a) is incorporated or formed by or established under any public general Act of Parliament passed before the year 1837;
(b) has a principal place of business within Great Britain;
(c) is an authorised institution within the meaning of the Banking Act 1987; and
(d) is not required by any enactment to prepare accounts under Part VII of the 1985 Act.   **[658]**

NOTE
1985 Act: Companies Act 1985.

4 Preparation of accounts

(1) The directors of a body of persons to which these Regulations apply shall in respect of each financial year of the body prepare such annual accounts and

directors' report, and cause to be prepared such auditors' report, as would be required under Part VII of the 1985 Act if the body were a banking company formed and registered under that Act, subject to the provisions of the Schedule to these Regulations.

(2) The accounts required by paragraph (1) shall be prepared within a period of 7 months beginning immediately after the end of the body's financial year. **[659]**

NOTE

1985 Act: Companies Act 1985.

5 Publication of accounts

(1) A body of persons to which these Regulations apply shall make available the latest accounts prepared under Regulation 4 for inspection by any person, without charge and during business hours, at the body's principal place of business within Great Britain.

(2) The body shall supply to any person upon request a copy of those accounts (or such part of those accounts as may be requested) at a price not exceeding the administrative cost of making the copy.

(3) Paragraph (2) applies whether the request for a copy is made orally during inspection under paragraph (1) above, by post or otherwise.

(4) The annual accounts prepared under Regulation 4 shall be the body's accounts for the purposes of section 45 of the Banking Act 1987 (Audited accounts to be open to inspection) and the auditors' report prepared under that Regulation shall be the auditors' report on the accounts or report of the auditors for the purposes of that section. **[660]**

6 Penalties for non-compliance

(1) If the directors of a body of persons to which these Regulations apply fail to prepare, or (in the case of the auditors' report), fail to cause to be prepared, the accounts required by Regulation 4(1) within the period referred to in Regulation 4(2), every person who, immediately before the end of the period referred to in Regulation 4(2), was a director of the body is guilty of an offence and liable on summary conviction to a fine not exceeding the statutory maximum.

(2) If any annual accounts or a directors' report are made available for inspection under Regulation 5 which do not comply with the requirements of Regulation 4(1) as to the matters to be included therein, every person who, at the time the annual accounts or report were first made available for inspection, was a director of the body is guilty of an offence and liable on summary conviction to a fine not exceeding the statutory maximum.

(3) In proceedings against a person for an offence under this Regulation, it is a defence for him to prove that he took all reasonable steps for securing compliance with the requirements in question. **[661]**

7 Penalties for non-compliance

(1) If a body of persons to which these Regulations apply fails to comply with Regulation 5 it is guilty of an offence and liable on summary conviction to a fine not exceeding the statutory maximum.

(2) Sections 733(2) and (3) and 734(1) to (4) and (6) of the 1985 Act shall apply to an offence under paragraph (1) as they do to an offence under section 394A(1) of that Act. **[662]**

NOTE
1985 Act: Companies Act 1985.

8 Transitional provisions

(1) The directors of a body of persons to which these Regulations apply need not prepare accounts in accordance with Regulation 4 with respect to a financial year of the body commencing on a date prior to 23rd December 1992.

(2) Where advantage is taken of paragraph (1), Regulation 5 shall not apply.
[663]

SCHEDULE

Regulation 4

MODIFICATIONS AND ADAPTATIONS OF PART VII
OF THE 1985 ACT

1. Where a body of persons subject to these Regulations is unincorporated, the accounts shall comply with the requirements of Part VII of the 1985 Act (Accounts and Audit) subject to any necessary modifications to take account of that fact; in particular the accounts shall comply with Part VII of the 1985 Act subject to the provisions of section 259(2) and (3) of that Act.

2. Accounts prepared under these Regulations shall state they are so prepared.

3. Accounts prepared under these Regulations shall comply with the provisions of Schedule 4A to the 1985 Act (as modified by Part II of Schedule 9 to that Act) as if paragraphs 13(3) to (5), 14 and 15 were omitted and paragraph 13(6) only required a statement of any adjustments to consolidated reserves.

4. Accounts prepared under these Regulations shall comply with the provisions of Schedule 5 to the 1985 Act (as modified by Part III of Schedule 9 to that Act) as if paragraphs 4, 5, 10, 18, 19 and 29 were omitted.

5. Accounts prepared under these Regulations shall comply with the provisions of Schedule 6 to the 1985 Act (as modified by Part IV of Schedule 9 to that Act) as if paragraphs 2 to 6, 8 and 9 were omitted.

6.—(1) Accounts prepared under these Regulations shall comply with paragraph 6 of Schedule 7 to the 1985 Act, but otherwise that Schedule shall not apply to such a body.

(2) Where a body subject to these Regulations has a share capital and may lawfully acquire its own shares, the directors' report of that body shall, in addition to the matters referred to in sub-paragraph (1), state:

   (a) the reasons for any acquisition of such shares during the financial year;
   (b) the number and nominal value of any such shares acquired during the financial year and the number and nominal value of any such shares disposed of during the financial year, together, in each case, with the percentage of the total issued share capital of the body that they represent;
   (c) the value and nature of any consideration given for the acquisition of such shares and the value and nature of any consideration received for the disposal of such shares during the financial year; and
   (d) the number and nominal value of all such shares held by the body at the end of the financial year, together with the percentage they represent of the total issued share capital of the body.

7. Accounts prepared under these Regulations shall comply with the provisions of Part I of Schedule 9 to the 1985 Act subject to the following modifications:—

   (a) in Section B of Chapter I of that Part, the profit and loss account formats there prescribed shall apply as if item 15 of format 1 and Charges item 9 and Income item 8 of format 2 were omitted; and

(b) in Chapter III of that Part, paragraphs 49, 54, 56, 57, 66(1)(b), 68(1)(b) and (2), 73(2), 74 and 75 shall not apply.

8. For the purposes of the provisions of Part VII of the 1985 Act as applied by these Regulations, these Regulations shall be regarded as part of the requirements of that Act.

9. Paragraphs 3 to 7 of this Schedule shall not be construed as affecting the requirement to give a true and fair view under sections 226 and 227 of the 1985 Act, as applied by these Regulations.

[664]

NOTE
1985 Act: Companies Act 1985.

BANKING COORDINATION (SECOND COUNCIL DIRECTIVE) REGULATIONS 1992
(SI 1992/3218)

ARRANGEMENT OF REGULATIONS

NOTES
Made: 16 December 1992.
Authority: European Communities Act 1972, s 2(2).
Commencement: 1 January 1993.
The regulations printed in italics are not reproduced.

PART I

GENERAL

PART II

RECOGNITION IN UK OF EUROPEAN INSTITUTIONS

Preliminary

Effect of recognition

Effect of non-recognition

Functions of Bank

PART I

GENERAL

1 Citation and commencement

(1) These Regulations may be cited as the Banking Coordination (Second Council Directive) Regulations 1992.

(2) These Regulations shall come into force on 1st January 1993.   **[665]**

2 Interpretation: general

(1) In these Regulations—

"the Banking Act" means the Banking Act 1987;
"the Building Societies Act" means the Building Societies Act 1986;
"the Consumer Credit Act" means the Consumer Credit Act 1974;
"the Financial Services Act" means the Financial Services Act 1986;
"the Insurance Companies Act" means the Insurance Companies Act 1982;
"another member State" means a member State other than the United Kingdom;

"appointed representative" has the same meaning as in the Financial
Services Act;

"authorised or permitted", in relation to the carrying on of a listed
activity, shall be construed in accordance with regulation 4 or, as the
case may be, regulation 21 below;

"the Bank" means the Bank of England;

"the Board" means The Securities and Investments Board;

"branch" means one or more places of business established or proposed
to be established in the same member State for the purpose of
carrying on home-regulated activities;

"the commencement date" means 1st January 1993 [except in relation to
the application of these Regulations as they have effect by virtue of
section 2(1) of the European Economic Area Act 1993 to the
carrying on by credit institutions and financial institutions incorporated in or formed under the law of a member State of the
Communities of listed activities in a relevant EFTA State and to the
carrying on by credit institutions and financial institutions incorporated in or formed under the law of a relevant EFTA State of
listed activities in the European Economic Area, where it means 1st
January 1994] [in relation to a relevant EFTA State other than
Liechtenstein and 1st June 1995 in relation to Liechtenstein;]

"the Commission" means the Building Societies Commission;

"connected UK authority", in relation to a credit or financial institution
carrying on or proposing to carry on a listed activity in the United
Kingdom, means an authority in the United Kingdom which has
regulatory functions in relation to that activity;

"constituent instrument", in relation to an institution, includes any
memorandum or articles of the institution;

"Consumer Credit Act business" means consumer credit business, consumer hire business or ancillary credit business;

"consumer credit business", "consumer hire business" and "ancillary
credit business" have the same meanings as in the Consumer Credit
Act;

"credit institution" means a credit institution as defined in article 1 of the
First Council Directive, that is to say, an undertaking whose business is to receive deposits or other repayable funds from the public
and to grant credits for its own account;

"delegation order" and "designated agency" have the same meanings as
in the Financial Services Act;

"deposit" has the same meaning as in the Banking Act;

"the Director" means the Director General of Fair Trading;

"ecu" means the European currency unit as defined in Article 1 of
Council Regulation No 3180/78/EEC;

"establish", in relation to a branch, means establish the place of business
or, as the case may be, the first place of business which constitutes
the branch;

"the European Commission" means the Commission of the
Communities;

"European institution", "European authorised institution" and
"European subsidiary" have the meanings given by regulation 3
below;

"financial institution" means a financial institution as defined in article 1
of the Second Council Directive, that is to say, an undertaking other
than a credit institution the principal activity of which is to acquire
holdings or to carry on one or more of the activities listed in points 2

to 12 in the Annex (the text of which is set out in Schedule 1 to these Regulations);
"the First Council Directive" means the First Council Directive on the coordination of laws, regulations and administrative provisions relating to the taking up and pursuit of the business of credit institutions (No 77/780/EEC);
"home-regulated activity" shall be construed in accordance with regulation 3(7) or, as the case may be, regulation 20(6) below;
"home-regulated investment business", in relation to a European institution or quasi-European authorised institution, means investment business which consists in carrying on one or more listed activities—

(a) in relation to which a supervisory authority in its home State has regulatory functions; and
(b) which, in the case of a European subsidiary, it is carrying on its home State;

"home State", in relation to an institution incorporated in or formed under the law of another member State, means that State;
"initial capital" means capital as defined in points 1 and 2 of article 2(1) of the Council Directive on the own funds of credit institutions (No 89/299/EEC);
"investment business" has the same meaning as in the Financial Services Act;
"listed activity" means an activity listed in the Annex to the Second Council Directive (list of activities subject to mutual recognition), the text of which is set out in Schedule 1 to these Regulations;
"member" and "rules", in relation to a recognised self-regulating organisation, have the same meanings as in the Financial Services Act;
["member State" means a member State of the Communities or a relevant EFTA State;]
"own funds" means own funds as defined in the Council Directive on the own funds of credit institutions (No 89/299/EEC);
"principal", in relation to an appointed representative, has the same meaning as in the Financial Services Act;
"quasi-European institution", "quasi-European authorised institution" and "quasi-European subsidiary" have the meanings given by regulation 3(4) below;
"recognised self-regulating organisation" has the same meaning as in the Financial Services Act;
["relevant EFTA State" means any of Austria, Finland, Iceland [Liechtenstein], Norway and Sweden;]
"the relevant supervisory authority", in relation to another member State, means the authority in that State which has regulatory functions in relation to the acceptance of deposits from the public, whether or not it also has such functions in relation to one or more other listed activities;
"requisite details", in relation to a branch in the United Kingdom or another member State (whether established or proposed to be established), means—

(a) particulars of the programme of operations of the business to be carried on from the branch, including a description of the particular home-regulated activities to be carried on and of the structural organisation of the branch;
(b) the name under which the business is to be carried on and the

address in the member State from which information about the business may be obtained; and

(c) the names of the managers of the business;

"the Second Council Directive" means the Second Council Directive on the coordination of laws, regulations and administrative provisions relating to the taking up and pursuit of the business of credit institutions and amending the First Council Directive (No 89/646/ EEC);

"the Solvency Ratio Directive" means the Council Directive on a solvency ratio for credit institutions (No 89/647/EEC);

"supervisory authority", in relation to another member State, means an authority in that State which has regulatory functions in relation to one or more listed activities;

"the UK authority", "UK institution", "UK authorised institution" and "UK subsidiary" have the meanings given by regulation 20 below;

"voting rights", in relation to an undertaking, shall be construed in accordance with paragraph 2 of Schedule 10A to the Companies Act 1985 or paragraph 2 of Schedule 10A to the Companies (Northern Ireland) Order 1986.

(2) In these Regulations "parent undertaking", "share", "subsidiary undertaking" and "undertaking" have the same meanings as in Part VII of the Companies Act 1985 or Part VIII of the Companies (Northern Ireland) Order 1986 except that—

(a) "subsidiary undertaking" also includes, in relation to an institution incorporated in or formed under the law of another member State, any undertaking which is a subsidiary undertaking within the meaning of any rule of law in force in that State for purposes connected with the implementation of the Seventh Company Law Directive based on article 54(3)(g) of the Treaty on consolidated accounts (No 83/349/EEC); and

(b) "parent undertaking" shall be construed accordingly.

(3) For the purposes of these Regulations a subsidiary undertaking of an institution is a 90 per cent subsidiary undertaking of the institution if the institution holds 90 per cent. or more of the voting rights in the subsidiary undertaking.

(4) Any reference in these Regulations to the carrying on of home-regulated investment business in the United Kingdom—

(a) is a reference to the carrying on of such business in reliance on regulation 5(1)(b) below; and

(b) shall be construed in accordance with section 1(3) of the Financial Services Act. [666]

NOTE

Para (1): words in first pair of square brackets in definition "the commencement date", and definitions "member State" and "relevant EFTA State" inserted by SI 1993/3225, reg 2(a)–(c); words in second pair of square brackets in definition "the commencement date" and word in square brackets in definition "relevant EFTA State" inserted by SI 1995/1217, reg 2.

[2A Iceland

(1) For the period commencing with 1st January 1994 and ending on the implementation date and subject to paragraph (2) below, wherever the expressions "another member State", "member State" and "relevant EFTA State"

are used in these Regulations they have effect for the purposes of these Regulations as if they did not include a reference to Iceland.

(2) Paragraph (1) above does not apply to—

(a) the definition of "the commencement date" in regulation 2(1) above where it has effect in relation to the provisions described in sub-paragraph (e) below;

(b) regulation 22(1), (2) and (3) below;

(c) regulation 24(1) and (3) below;

(d) paragraphs 1 to 7 of Schedule 6 to these Regulations;

(e) paragraphs 2 and 3 of Schedule 11 to these Regulations;

(f) the definitions of "another member State", "relevant supervisory authority" and "supervisory authority" in section 106 of the Banking Act as inserted by regulation 45 below in so far as those definitions are used in the following provisions of the Banking Act—

(i) section 9(7) as inserted by regulation 26 below;

(ii) section 11(1A)(f) as inserted by regulation 28(1) below;

(iii) section 12A(1) and (3)(b) as inserted by regulation 29 below;

(iv) section 13(3A) as inserted by regulation 30(1) below;

(v) section 15(4) as inserted by regulation 30(2) below;

(vi) section 22(1A) as inserted by regulation 31(2) below; and

(vii) section 86(1)(b), (3) and (4) as substituted by regulation 41 below;

(g) the definitions of "another member State", "relevant supervisory authority" and "supervisory authority" in section 119(2A) of the Building Societies Act as inserted by regulation 81 below in so far as those definitions are used in the following provisions of the Building Societies Act—

(i) section 43(1A)(f) as inserted by regulation 71(1) below;

(ii) section 45A(1) and (3)(b) as inserted by regulation 74 below;

(iii) section 54(3B) as inserted by regulation 77(1) below; and

(iv) section 54(6) as inserted by regulation 77(2) below.

(3) In relation to a credit institution incorporated in or formed under the law of Iceland, any reference to the commencement date in paragraphs 1, 6 and 7 of Schedule 11 to these Regulations is construed as a reference to the implementation date.

(4) In this regulation "the implementation date" means the date, to be notified in the London, Edinburgh and Belfast Gazettes, on which the EFTA Surveillance Authority to be established under Article 108 of the Agreement on the European Economic Area is notified by Iceland that it has implemented the Second Council Directive, or 1st January 1995, which is the sooner.] **[666A]**

NOTES
Commencement: 1 January 1994.
Inserted by SI 1993/3225, reg 2(d).

PART II

RECOGNITION IN UK OF EUROPEAN INSTITUTIONS

Preliminary

3 European institutions

(1) In these Regulations "European institution" means a European authorised institution or a European subsidiary.

(2) A credit institution is a European authorised institution for the purposes of these Regulations if—

(a) it is incorporated in or formed under the law of another member State;

(b) its principal place of business is in that State;

(c) it is for the time being authorised to act as a credit institution by the relevant supervisory authority in that State; and

(d) the requirements of paragraph 1 of Schedule 2 to these Regulations have been complied with in relation to its carrying on of an activity or its establishment of a branch.

(3) A financial institution is a European subsidiary for the purposes of these Regulations if—

(a) it is incorporated in or formed under the law of another member State;

(b) it is a 90 per cent subsidiary undertaking of a credit institution which—

(i) is incorporated in or formed under the law of that State; and

(ii) is a European authorised institution or a quasi-European authorised institution;

(c) the conditions mentioned in paragraph (6) below are fulfilled in relation to it; and ˙

(d) the requirements of paragraph 1 of Schedule 2 to these Regulations have been (and continue to be) complied with in relation to its carrying on of an activity or its establishment of a branch.

(4) In these Regulations "quasi-European institution" means an institution—

(a) which is not a European institution; but

(b) which would be such an institution if the requirements of paragraph 1 of Schedule 2 to these Regulations had been (and continued to be) complied with in relation to its carrying on of an activity or its establishment of a branch;

and "quasi-European authorised institution" and "quasi-European subsidiary" shall be construed accordingly.

(5) For the purposes of paragraph (3)(b) above, any two or more European authorised institutions or quasi-European authorised institutions which—

(a) are incorporated in or formed under the law of the same member State; and

(b) hold voting rights in the same undertaking,

shall be regarded as a single institution; and in these Regulations "parent undertaking", in relation to an institution which is a European subsidiary or quasi-European subsidiary by virtue of this paragraph, shall be construed accordingly.

(6) The conditions referred to in paragraph (3)(c) above are—

(a) that each home-regulated activity stated in the institution's recognition notice is carried on by it in its home State;

(b) that the constituent instrument of the institution permits it to carry on each such activity;

(c) that the consolidated supervision of the institution's parent undertaking or, if more than one, any of them effectively includes supervision of the institution; and

(d) that the institution's parent undertaking has guaranteed or, if more than one, they have jointly and severally guaranteed, with the consent of the relevant supervisory authority in its or their home State, the institution's obligations;

and in this paragraph "recognition notice", in relation to an institution, means a notice given by it in accordance with paragraph 2 of Schedule 2 to these Regulations.

(7) In these Regulations "home-regulated activity", in relation to a European institution or quasi-European authorised institution, means any listed activity—

(a) in relation to which a supervisory authority in its home State has regulatory functions; and

(b) which, in the case of a European subsidiary, it is carrying on in its home State.

(8) Schedule 2 to these Regulations (which contains requirements to be complied with by or in relation to European institutions) shall have effect. **[667]**

4 Authorised and permitted activities

(1) For the purposes of these Regulations a European authorised institution is authorised to carry on in its home State any listed activity which its authorisation as a credit institution authorises it to carry on.

(2) For the purposes of these Regulations a European subsidiary is permitted to carry on in its home State any listed activity which it is lawful for it to carry on, and it is carrying on, in that State. **[668]**

Effect of recognition

5 Authorisations and licences not required

(1) Subject to [paragraphs (2) and (3)] below, nothing in the following enactments, namely—

(a) section 3 of the Banking Act (restriction on acceptance of deposits);

(b) sections 3 and 4 of the Financial Services Act (restrictions on carrying on investment business);

(c) sections 21, 39(1) and 147(1) of the Consumer Credit Act (Consumer Credit Act businesses needing a licence); and

(d) section 2 of the Insurance Companies Act (restriction on carrying on insurance business),

shall prevent a European institution from carrying on in the United Kingdom any listed activity which it is authorised or permitted to carry on in its home State.

(2) In relation to a European institution in respect of which a prohibition under these Regulations is in force—

(a) paragraph (1)(a) above shall not apply if the prohibition is under regulation 9 below;

(b) paragraph (1)(b) above shall not apply if the prohibition is under regulation 15 below; and

(c) paragraph (1)(c) above shall not apply if the prohibition is under regulation 18 below.

[(3) Paragraph (1)(a) above shall not apply in relation to a European institution in respect of which a determination under regulation 13A below is in force.] **[669]**

NOTES
Commencement: 1 January 1993 (paras (1), (2)); 1 January 1994 (para (3)).
Para (1): words in square brackets substituted by SI 1993/3225, reg 2(e).
Para (3): added by SI 1993/3225, reg 2(f).

6 Procedural requirements for carrying on listed activities

(1) A European institution shall not—

    (a) carry on in the United Kingdom by the provision of services any home-regulated activity; or

    (b) establish a branch in the United Kingdom for the purpose of carrying on such an activity,

unless the requirements of paragraph 1 of Schedule 2 to these Regulations have been (and, in the case of a European subsidiary, continue to be) complied with in relation to its carrying on of the activity or, as the case may be, its establishment of the branch.

(2) A European institution shall not change the requisite details of a branch established by it in the United Kingdom unless the requirements of paragraph 4 of Schedule 2 to these Regulations have been complied with in relation to its making of the change.

(3) An institution which contravenes paragraph (1) or (2) above shall be guilty of an offence and liable on summary conviction to a fine not exceeding level 5 on the standard scale; but such a contravention shall not invalidate any transaction.

(4) In proceedings brought against an institution for an offence under paragraph (3) above it shall be a defence for the institution to show that it took all reasonable precautions and exercised all due diligence to avoid the commission of the offence. **[670]**

Effect of non-recognition

7 Prohibition on carrying on certain listed activities

(1) A quasi-European authorised institution shall not—

    (a) carry on in the United Kingdom by the provision of services any home-regulated activity; or

    (b) establish a branch in the United Kingdom for the purpose of carrying on such an activity.

(2) An institution which contravenes paragraph (1) above shall be guilty of an offence and liable on summary conviction to a fine not exceeding level 5 on the standard scale; but such a contravention shall not invalidate any transaction.

(3) In proceedings brought against an institution for an offence under paragraph (2) above it shall be a defence for the institution to show that it took all reasonable precautions and exercised all due diligence to avoid the commission of the offence. **[671]**

Functions of Bank

8 Duty to prepare for supervision

(1) In any case where—

(a) the Bank receives from the relevant supervisory authority in an institution's home State a notice given in accordance with paragraph 3 of Schedule 2 to these Regulations; and

(b) the notice states that the institution intends to establish a branch in the United Kingdom,

the Bank shall, before the expiry of the period of two months beginning with the day on which it received the notice, draw to the attention of the institution such provisions of these Regulations, the relevant Acts or regulations or rules made under those Acts as, having regard to the activities mentioned in the notice, the Bank considers appropriate.

(2) In any case where the Bank receives from the relevant supervisory authority in an institution's home State such a notice as is mentioned in paragraph (1) above—

(a) the Bank shall also, before the expiry of the said period of two months, consider whether the situation as respects the institution is such that the powers conferred by paragraph (2) of regulation 9 below are likely to become exercisable; and

(b) if it considers that the situation is such as is mentioned in subparagraph (a) above, the Bank may impose, as soon as the requirements of paragraph 1 of Schedule 2 to these Regulations have been complied with in relation to the institution, such restriction under regulation 10 below as appears to it desirable.

(3) In any case where the Bank receives from an institution a notice given in accordance with paragraph 4 of Schedule 2 to these Regulations, the Bank shall, before the expiry of the period of one month beginning with the day on which it received the notice, draw to the attention of the institution such provisions of these Regulations, the relevant Acts or regulations or rules made under those Acts as, having regard to the proposed change mentioned in the notice, the Bank considers appropriate.

(4) Nothing in this regulation shall require the Bank to draw to the attention of an institution any provision which, in connection with the same notice, has been or will be drawn to its attention under regulation 14 below.

(5) In this regulation and regulation 9 below "the relevant Acts" means the Banking Act, the Financial Services Act, the Consumer Credit Act and the Insurance Companies Act.   **[672]**

9 Power to prohibit the acceptance of deposits

(1) In this regulation "prohibition" means a prohibition on accepting deposits in the United Kingdom.

(2) Subject to paragraph (3) and regulation 11 below, the Bank may impose a prohibition on a European institution if—

(a) the institution is a European authorised institution which has established a branch in the United Kingdom and it appears to the Bank that the branch is not or may not be maintaining or, as the case may be, will not or may not maintain adequate liquidity;

(b) the Bank is informed by the relevant supervisory authority in the institution's home State that it has failed to take any or sufficient steps to cover risks arising from its open positions on financial markets in the United Kingdom;

(c) it appears to the Bank that the institution has failed to comply with any obligation imposed on it

[(i) by these Regulations or by or under any of the relevant Acts; or

(ii) by the Credit Institutions (Protection of Depositors) Regulations 1995;]

(d) the Bank is informed by a supervisory authority in the institution's home State that it has failed to comply with any obligation imposed on it by or under any rule of law in force in that State for purposes connected with

[(i) the implementation of the Second Council Directive; or

(ii) the implementation of Directive 94/19/EC on deposit-guarantee schemes;]

(e) it appears to the Bank that it has been provided with false, misleading or inaccurate information by or on behalf of the institution or by or on behalf of a person who is or is to be a director, controller or manager of the institution; or

(f) it appears to the Bank that the situation as respects the institution is such that, if it were authorised by the Bank under the Banking Act, the Bank could revoke the authorisation.

(3) The Bank may not impose a prohibition on a European institution on the ground mentioned in paragraph (2)(f) above unless—

(a) the Bank has requested the relevant supervisory authority in the institution's home State to take all appropriate measures for the purpose of securing that the institution remedies the situation; and

(b) the Bank is satisfied either—

(i) that that authority has failed or refused to take measures for that purpose; or

(ii) that the measures taken by that authority have proved inadequate for that purpose.

(4) Any prohibition imposed under this regulation may be withdrawn by written notice served by the Bank on the institution concerned; and any such notice shall take effect on such date as is specified in the notice.

(5) In the case of a European institution which is a member of a self-regulating organisation, the reference in paragraph (2)(c) above to any obligation imposed by or under the relevant Acts shall be taken to include a reference to any obligation imposed by the rules of that organisation.

(6) In this regulation "controller", "director" and "manager" have the same meanings as in the Banking Act.

(7) Schedule 3 to these Regulations (which makes supplemental provision with respect to prohibitions imposed under this regulation and restrictions imposed under regulation 10 below) shall have effect. **[673]**

NOTE

Para (2): words in square brackets substituted by the Credit Institutions (Protection of Depositors) Regulations 1995, SI 1995/1442, reg 50.

10 Power to restrict listed activities

(1) In this regulation "restriction" means a direction that a European institution or former European institution—

    (a) may not carry on in the United Kingdom any home-regulated activity (other than the acceptance of deposits) which is specified in the direction; or

    (b) may not carry on in the United Kingdom, otherwise than in accordance with such condition or conditions as may be specified in the direction, any home-regulated activity which is so specified.

(2) Where it appears to the Bank that the situation as respects a European institution is such that the powers conferred by paragraph (2) of regulation 9 above are exercisable, the Bank may, instead of or as well as imposing a prohibition, impose such restriction as appears to it desirable.

(3) Where it appears to the Bank that the situation as respects a former European authorised institution is such that the powers conferred by paragraph (2) of regulation 9 above would be exercisable if the institution were still a European authorised institution, the Bank may impose such restriction as appears to it desirable.

(4) Subsection (4) of section 12 of the Banking Act (examples of conditions that may be imposed) applies for the purposes of this regulation as it applies for the purposes of that section.

(5) Any restriction imposed under this regulation—

    (a) may be withdrawn; or

    (b) may be varied with the agreement of the institution concerned,

by written notice served by the Bank on the institution; and any such notice shall take effect on such date as is specified in the notice.

(6) An institution which fails to comply with a restriction shall be guilty of an offence and liable—

    (a) on conviction on indictment, to a fine;

    (b) on summary conviction, to a fine not exceeding the statutory maximum.

(7) The fact that a restriction has not been complied with (whether or not constituting an offence under paragraph (6) above) shall not invalidate any transaction but, in the case of a European institution, shall be a ground for the imposition of a prohibition under regulation 9 above.

(8) In this regulation "former European authorised institution" means an institution which was formerly a European authorised institution and continues to have a liability in respect of any deposit for which it had a liability when it was a European authorised institution.   **[674]**

11 Limitations on Bank's powers

(1) This regulation applies where it appears to the Bank that the situation as respects a European institution is such that the Bank's power—

    (a) to impose a prohibition or restriction on the institution; or

    (b) to vary otherwise than with the agreement of the institution any restriction imposed on the institution,

is exercisable by virtue of regulation 9(2)(a) above, or by virtue of any failure to comply with a requirement imposed under section 39 of the Banking Act (information and production of documents) for statistical purposes.

(2) The Bank shall require the institution in writing to remedy the situation.

(3) If the institution fails to comply with the requirement under paragraph (2) above within a reasonable time, the Bank shall give a notice to that effect to the relevant supervisory authority in the institution's home State requesting that authority—

(a) to take all appropriate measures for the purpose of ensuring that the institution remedies the situation; and

(b) to inform the Bank of the measures it proposes to take or has taken or the reasons for not taking any such measures.

(4) Subject to paragraph (5) below, the Bank shall not take any steps to impose a prohibition or restriction on a European institution, or to vary otherwise than with the agreement of a European institution any restriction imposed on the institution, unless it is satisfied—

(a) that the relevant supervisory authority has failed or refused to take measures for the purpose mentioned in sub-paragraph (a) of paragraph (3) above; or

(b) that the measures taken by that authority have proved inadequate for that purpose.

(5) Where the Bank considers that the prohibition, restriction or variation should be imposed as a matter of urgency, it may take steps to impose the prohibition, restriction or variation—

(a) before complying with paragraphs (2) and (3) above; or

(b) where it has complied with those paragraphs, without being satisfied as mentioned in paragraph (4) above;

but in such a case the Bank shall, at the earliest opportunity, inform the relevant supervisory authority in the institution's home State and the European Commission of the steps taken.

(6) In any case where—

(a) by virtue of paragraph (5) above, the Bank has imposed a prohibition or restriction on a European institution, or varied a restriction imposed on such an institution, before complying with paragraphs (2) and (3) above or, as the case may be, before it is satisfied as mentioned in paragraph (4) above; and

(b) the European Commission decides under the Second Council Directive that the Bank must withdraw or vary the prohibition, restriction or variation,

the Bank shall in accordance with the decision withdraw or vary the prohibition, restriction or variation.

(7) In any case where—

(a) the Bank has given notice to a European institution under paragraph 2 of Schedule 3 to these Regulations of a proposal to impose a prohibition or restriction or vary a restriction;

(b) the prohibition, restriction or variation has not taken effect; and

(c) the European Commission decides under the Second Council Directive that the Bank must withdraw or vary the notice,

the Bank shall in accordance with the decision withdraw or vary the notice.

(8) This regulation shall not apply—

(a) as respects the imposition of a restriction in pursuance of regulation 8(2) above; or
(b) in any case where regulation 12 below applies. [675]

12 Prohibition or restriction on information from supervisory authority

(1) This regulation applies where in the case of a European institution—

(a) the Bank is informed by the relevant supervisory authority in the institution's home State that it has failed to take any or sufficient steps to cover risks arising from its open positions on financial markets in the United Kingdom; or
(b) the Bank is informed by a supervisory authority in that State that the institution is failing to comply with an obligation imposed by or under any rule of law in force in that State for purposes connected with the implementation of the Second Council Directive.

(2) The Bank shall as soon as practicable send a copy of the information received by it to every other authority which it knows is a connected UK authority.

(3) The Bank shall also—

(a) consider whether to exercise its powers under regulation 9 or 10 above; and
(b) notify its decision, and any action which it has taken or intends to take, to the supervisory authority and to every other authority which it knows is a connected UK authority. [676]

13 Obligation of Bank where institution ceases to be a European institution etc

Where the Bank is informed that—

(a) an institution has ceased to be a European institution; or
(b) a European institution has ceased to carry on any particular home-regulated activity in the United Kingdom,

the Bank shall inform every other authority which it knows is a connected UK authority of that fact. [677]

[13A Treasury determinations for implementing decisions

(1) For the purpose of implementing a relevant decision within the meaning of section 26A(1) of the Banking Act the Treasury may following consultation with the Bank make a determination in respect of a credit institution if—

(a) it is incorporated in or formed under the law of a relevant EFTA State;
(b) it is the subsidiary undertaking of a parent undertaking governed by the laws of a third country whose treatment of credit institutions from the European Economic Area or any part of it gave rise to the relevant decision; and
(c) it conforms to regulation 3(2)(b) and (c) above but not to regulation 3(2)(d).

(2) A determination made under paragraph (1) shall prohibit a credit institution in respect of which it is made from thereafter carrying on in the United Kingdom by the provision of services any home-regulated activity or establishing a branch in the United Kingdom for the purpose of carrying on such an

activity notwithstanding that the requirements of paragraph 1 of Schedule 2 to these Regulations are at any time complied with in relation to its carrying on of the activity or, as the case may be, its establishment of the branch.

(3) A determination made under paragraph (1) above may relate to a particular institution or class of institution.

(4) A determination made under paragraph (1) above may be withdrawn at any time by the Treasury, but such withdrawal shall not affect anything done in accordance with the determination before it was withdrawn.

(5) Notice of a determination made under paragraph (1) above in respect of a particular institution or of the withdrawal of such a determination shall be given in writing by the Treasury to that institution and notice of any determination made under paragraph (1) or of the withdrawal of any determination shall be published in the London, Edinburgh and Belfast Gazettes on the date of the determination or, as the case may be, on the date of the withdrawal, or as soon as practicable thereafter.

(6) A credit institution which fails to comply with a determination made under paragraph (1) shall be guilty of an offence and liable on summary conviction to a fine not exceeding level 5 on the standard scale; but such a contravention shall not invalidate any transaction.

(7) In proceedings brought against a credit institution for an offence under paragraph (6) above it shall be a defence for the institution to show that it took all reasonable precautions and exercised all due diligence to avoid the commission of the offence.]   [677A]

NOTES
Commencement: 1 January 1994.
Inserted by SI 1993/3225, reg 2(g).

Functions of Board

14 Duty to prepare for supervision

(1) In any case where—

   (a) the Board receives from the Bank under paragraph 3 of Schedule 2 to these Regulations a copy of a notice given in accordance with that paragraph; and
   (b) the notice states that the institution concerned intends to establish a branch in the United Kingdom for the purpose of carrying on a home-regulated activity appearing to the Board to constitute investment business,

the Board shall, before the expiry of the period of two months beginning with the day on which the Bank received the notice, draw to the attention of the institution such provisions of these Regulations, the Financial Services Act or rules or regulations made under that Act as, having regard to the activities mentioned in the notice, it considers appropriate.

(2) In any case where—

   (a) the Board receives from the Bank under paragraph 4 of Schedule 2 to these Regulations a copy of a notice given in accordance with that paragraph; and
   (b) the institution concerned is, or as a result of the proposed change mentioned in the notice will be, carrying on in the United Kingdom a home-regulated activity appearing to the Board to constitute investment business,

the Board shall, before the expiry of the period of one month beginning with the day on which the Bank received the notice, draw to the attention of the institution such provisions of these Regulations, the Financial Services Act or rules or regulations made under that Act as, having regard to the proposed change mentioned in the notice, it considers appropriate. **[678]**

15–19 (*Not printed (ss 15–17 relate to the Financial Services Act 1986 and ss 18, 19 relate to the Consumer Credit Act 1974.*)

PART III
RECOGNITION IN OTHER MEMBER STATES OF UK INSTITUTIONS

Preliminary
20 UK institutions etc

(1) In these Regulations "UK institution" means a UK authorised institution or a UK subsidiary.

(2) A credit institution is a UK authorised institution for the purposes of these Regulations if—

    (a) it is incorporated in or formed under the law of any part of the United Kingdom;

    (b) its principal place of business is in the United Kingdom; and

    (c) it is for the time being authorised by the Bank under the Banking Act or by the Commission under the Building Societies Act.

(3) A financial institution is a UK subsidiary for the purposes of these Regulations if—

    (a) it is incorporated in or formed under the law of any part of the United Kingdom;

    (b) it is a 90 per cent subsidiary undertaking of a UK authorised institution; and

    (c) the conditions mentioned in paragraph (5) below are fulfilled in relation to it.

(4) For the purposes of paragraph (3)(b) above, any two or more UK authorised institutions which hold voting rights in the same undertaking shall be regarded as a single institution; and in these Regulations "parent undertaking", in relation to an institution which is a UK subsidiary by virtue of this paragraph, shall be construed accordingly.

(5) The conditions referred to in paragraph (3)(c) above are—

    (a) that each listed activity stated in the institution's recognition notice is carried on by it in the United Kingdom;

    (b) that the constituent instrument of the institution permits it to carry on each such activity;

    (c) that the consolidated supervision of the institution's parent undertaking or, if more than one, any of them effectively includes supervision of the institution; and

    (d) that the institution's parent undertaking has guaranteed or, if more than one, they have each jointly and severally guaranteed, with the consent of the UK authority, the institution's obligations;

and in this paragraph and regulation 23(1) below "recognition notice", in relation to an institution, means a notice given by it in accordance with paragraph 2 of Schedule 6 to these Regulations.

(6) In these Regulations "home-regulated activity"—

   (a) in relation to a UK authorised institution, means any listed activity;
   (b) in relation to a UK subsidiary, means any listed activity which it is carrying on in the United Kingdom.

(7) In these Regulations "the UK authority"—

   (a) in relation to a UK authorised institution which is authorised by the Bank under the Banking Act or a UK subsidiary whose parent undertaking (or each of whose parent undertakings) is so authorised, means the Bank;
   (b) in relation to a UK authorised institution which is authorised by the Commission under the Building Societies Act or a UK subsidiary whose parent undertaking (or each of whose parent undertakings) is so authorised, means the Commission;
   (c) in relation to a UK subsidiary of whose parent undertakings one is authorised by the Bank under the Banking Act and another is authorised by the Commission under the Building Societies Act, means such one of the Bank and the Commission as may be agreed between them.

(8) An agreement made for the purposes of sub-paragraph (c) of paragraph (7) above—

   (a) may relate to particular UK subsidiaries or to UK subsidiaries of particular descriptions; and
   (b) shall provide that the UK authority in relation to any UK subsidiary falling within that sub-paragraph shall keep the other party informed of anything done by it in relation to that subsidiary.

(9) In the case of a UK authorised institution which is authorised by the Commission under the Building Societies Act, the power conferred by section 18(1)(b) of that Act to guarantee the discharge of the liabilities of the bodies corporate there mentioned includes power, with the consent of the Commission, to guarantee their obligations for the purposes of this regulation. **[679]**

21 Authorised and permitted activities

(1) For the purposes of these Regulations a UK authorised institution is authorised to carry on in the United Kingdom any listed activity which it is lawful for it to carry on in the United Kingdom.

(2) For the purposes of these Regulations a UK subsidiary is permitted to carry on in the United Kingdom any listed activity which it is lawful for it to carry on, and it is carrying on, in the United Kingdom. **[680]**

Procedural requirements

22 Procedural requirements for carrying on certain listed activities

(1) Subject to paragraph (2) below, a UK institution shall not—

   (a) carry on in another member State by the provision of services any listed activity which it is authorised or permitted to carry on in the United Kingdom; or

(b) establish a branch in another member State for the purpose of carrying on such an activity,

unless the requirements of paragraph 1 of Schedule 6 to these Regulations have been (and, in the case of a UK subsidiary, continue to be) complied with in relation to its carrying on of the activity or, as the case may be, its establishment of the branch.

(2) Paragraph (1) above shall not apply in relation to a UK subsidiary if—

(a) there has been no compliance with the requirements of paragraph 1 of Schedule 6 to these Regulations in relation to its carrying on of an activity or its establishment of a branch; or

(b) each such compliance has ceased to have effect.

(3) A UK institution shall not change the requisite details of a branch established by it in another member State unless the requirements of paragraph 5 of Schedule 6 to these Regulations have been complied with in relation to its making of the change.

(4) An institution which contravenes paragraph (1) or (3) above shall be guilty of an offence and liable on summary conviction to a fine not exceeding level 5 on the standard scale.

(5) In proceedings brought against an institution for an offence under paragraph (4) above it shall be a defence for the institution to show that it took all reasonable precautions and exercised all due diligence to avoid the commission of the offence.

(6) Schedule 6 to these Regulations (which contains requirements to be complied with by or in relation to UK institutions) shall have effect.   **[681]**

Regulation of UK subsidiaries for recognition purposes

23 Restriction on activities of UK subsidiaries

(1) In this regulation "restriction" means a direction that a UK subsidiary to which section 22(1) above applies—

(a) may not carry on in the United Kingdom any listed activity stated in its recognition notice which is specified in the direction; or

(b) may not carry on in the United Kingdom, otherwise than in accordance with such condition or conditions as may be specified in the direction, any such activity which is so specified.

(2) Where it appears to the UK authority that the situation as respects a UK subsidiary is such that, if it were authorised by the Bank under the Banking Act, the Bank could revoke its authorisation on the ground specified in section 11(1)(a) of that Act, the UK authority may impose on the institution such restriction as appears to it desirable.

(3) Subsection (4) of section 12 of the Banking Act (examples of conditions that may be imposed) applies for the purposes of this regulation as it applies for the purposes of that section; and Schedule 3 to that Act (minimum criteria for authorisation) as applied by this regulation shall have effect as if—

(a) paragraph 6 (minimum initial capital) were omitted; and

(b) where the Commission is the UK authority, the reference to that Act in paragraph 4(8) were a reference to the Building Societies Act.

(4) Any restriction imposed under this regulation—

(a) may be withdrawn; or

(b) may be varied with the agreement of the institution concerned,

by written notice served by the UK authority on the institution; and any such notice shall take effect on such date as is specified in the notice.

(5) An institution which contravenes or fails to comply with a restriction shall be guilty of an offence and liable—

(a) on conviction on indictment, to a fine;

(b) on summary conviction, to a fine not exceeding the statutory maximum.

(6) The fact that a restriction has not been complied with (whether or not constituting an offence under paragraph (5) above) shall not invalidate any transaction.

(7) Schedule 7 to these Regulations (which makes supplemental provision with respect to restrictions imposed under this regulation) shall have effect.

[682]

24 Restriction on information from supervisory authority

(1) This regulation applies where in the case of a UK subsidiary the UK authority is informed by a supervisory authority in another member State that the institution is failing to comply with an obligation imposed by or under any rule of law in force in that State for purposes connected with the implementation of the Second Council Directive.

(2) The UK authority shall as soon as practicable send a copy of the information received by it to every other authority which it knows is a connected UK authority.

(3) The UK authority shall also—

(a) consider whether to exercise its powers under regulation 23 above; and

(b) notify its decision, and any action which it has taken or intends to take, to the supervisory authority and to every other authority which it knows is a connected UK authority. **[683]**

PART IV
AMENDMENTS OF BANKING ACT

25–45 (*Amend the Banking Act 1987.*)

Miscellaneous

46 Savings for certain institutions

The Banking Act shall have effect—

(a) in relation to institutions which are not credit institutions incorporated in or formed under the law of a part of the United Kingdom, without the amendments made by regulations 27, 31(1), 34, 36, 37 and 43 to 45 above; and

(b) in relation to information relating to the business or other affairs of institutions which are authorised institutions within the meaning of that Act but are not credit institutions, without the amendments made by regulations 38, 39(2) to (4) and 40 to 42 above. **[684]**

47 Other amendments of Banking Act

The provisions of the Banking Act which are mentioned in Schedule 8 to these Regulations shall have effect subject to the amendments there specified. **[685]**

PART V
AMENDMENTS OF FINANCIAL SERVICES ACT

48–56 (*Amend the Financial Services Act 1986.*)

PART VI
AMENDMENTS OF CONSUMER CREDIT ACT

57–63 (*Amend the Consumer Credit Act 1974.*)

PART VII
AMENDMENTS OF INSURANCE COMPANIES ACT

64–66 (*Amend the Insurance Companies Act 1982.*)

PART VIII
AMENDMENTS OF BUILDING SOCIETIES ACT

67–81 (*Amend the Building Societies Act 1986.*)

PART IX
SUPPLEMENTAL

82 Minor and consequential amendments

(1) The provisions mentioned in Schedule 10 to these Regulations shall have effect subject to the amendments there specified, being minor amendments or amendments consequential on the provisions of these Regulations.

(2) Any deed, contract or other instrument made before the commencement date shall have effect, unless the context otherwise requires, as if any reference to an institution authorised by the Bank under the Banking Act (however expressed) included a reference to a European deposit-taker.

(3) In this regulation and Schedule 10 to these Regulations "European deposit-taker" means a European authorised institution which has lawfully established a branch in the United Kingdom for the purpose of accepting deposits. **[686]**

83 Transitional provisions and savings

Schedule 11 to these Regulations shall have effect with respect to the transitional and other matters there mentioned. **[687]**

SCHEDULE 1

Regulation 2(1)

ANNEX TO THE SECOND COUNCIL DIRECTIVE

"ANNEX

LIST OF ACTIVITIES SUBJECT TO MUTUAL RECOGNITION

1   Acceptance of deposits and other repayable funds from the public.
2   Lending (1).
3   Financial leasing.
4   Money transmission services.
5   Issuing and administering means of payment (eg credit cards, travellers' cheques and bankers' drafts).
6   Guarantees and commitments.
7   Trading for own account or for account of customers in:
    (a) money market instruments (cheques, bills, CDs, etc);
    (b) foreign exchange;
    (c) financial futures and options;
    (d) exchange and interest rate instruments;
    (e) transferable securities.
8   Participation in securities issues and the provision of services relating to such issues.
9   Advice to undertakings on capital structure, industrial strategy and related questions and advice and services relating to mergers and the purchase of undertakings.
10 Money broking.
11 Portfolio management and advice.
12 Safekeeping and administration of securities.
13 Credit reference services.
14 Safe custody services.
(1) Including inter alia:
    –consumer credit,
    –mortgage credit,
    –factoring, with or without recourse,
    –financing of commercial transactions (including forfaiting)."   **[688]**

SCHEDULE 2

Regulation 3(8)

REQUIREMENTS AS RESPECTS EUROPEAN INSTITUTIONS

Requirements for carrying on activities etc

1.—(1) In relation to the carrying on of a home-regulated activity by the provision of services, the requirements of this paragraph are that the institution has given to the relevant supervisory authority in its home State a notice in accordance with paragraph 2 below.

(2) In relation to the establishment of a branch, the requirements of this paragraph are—

(a) that the institution has given to the relevant supervisory authority in its home State a notice in accordance with paragraph 2 below;
(b) that the Bank has received from that authority a notice in accordance with paragraph 3 below; and
(c) that either—

(i)   the Bank has informed the institution that it may establish the branch; or
(ii) the period of two months beginning with the day on which the Bank received the notice mentioned in paragraph (b) above has elapsed.

2. A notice given by an institution to the relevant supervisory authority in its home State is given in accordance with this paragraph if it states—

(a) the United Kingdom to be a member State in which the institution proposes to carry on home-regulated activities;

(b) whether the institution intends to establish a branch in the United Kingdom;

(c) if the notice states that the institution does not intend to establish such a branch, the home-regulated activities in relation to which the notice is given; and

(d) if the notice states that the institution intends to establish such a branch, the requisite details of the branch.

3.—(1) A notice given in respect of a European authorised institution or quasi-European authorised institution by the relevant supervisory authority in its home State is in accordance with this paragraph if it—

(a) certifies that the institution is a credit institution which is for the time being authorised to act as such an institution by the authority;

(b) contains the information stated in the institution's notice; and

(c) if the institution intends to establish a branch in the United Kingdom, contains—

   (i) a statement of the amount of the institution's own funds and the solvency ratio of the institution (calculated in accordance with the Solvency Ratio Directive); and

   (ii) details of any deposit guarantee scheme which is intended to secure the protection of depositors in the branch.

(2) A notice given in respect of a European subsidiary or quasi-European subsidiary by the relevant supervisory authority in its home State is in accordance with this paragraph if it—

(a) certifies that the institution is a financial institution which is a 90 per cent subsidiary undertaking of a European institution incorporated in or formed under the law of that State;

(b) certifies that the conditions mentioned in regulation 3(6) of these Regulations are fulfilled in relation to the institution;

(c) certifies that the institution's business is being conducted in a prudent manner;

(d) contains the information stated in the institution's notice; and

(e) if the institution intends to establish a branch in the United Kingdom, contains a statement of the amount of the institution's own funds and the consolidated solvency ratio of the institution's parent undertaking (calculated in accordance with the Solvency Ratio Directive).

(3) The Bank shall as soon as practicable send a copy of any notice received by it in accordance with this paragraph, and a note of the date of its receipt, to every other authority which it knows is a connected UK authority.

Requirements for changing requisite details of branch

4.—(1) Subject to sub-paragraph (2) below, the requirements of this paragraph are—

(a) that the institution has given a notice to the Bank, and to the relevant supervisory authority in its home State, stating the details of the proposed change;

(b) that the Bank has received from that authority a notice stating those details; and

(c) that either the Bank has informed the institution that it may make the change, or the period of one month beginning with the day on which it gave the Bank the notice mentioned in paragraph (a) above has elapsed.

(2) In the case of a change occasioned by circumstances beyond the institution's control, the requirements of this paragraph are that the institution has, as soon as practicable (whether before or after the change), given a notice to the Bank, and to the relevant supervisory authority in its home State, stating the details of the change.

(3) The Bank shall as soon as practicable send a copy of any notice received by it in accordance with this paragraph, and a note of the date of its receipt, to every other authority which it knows is a connected UK authority.

Cancellation of compliance with certain requirements

5.—(1) The Bank may, on an application by a European subsidiary, direct that any compliance with the requirements of paragraph 1 above in relation to—

(a) its carrying on of any activity; or

(b) its establishment of a branch,

shall cease to have effect as from such date as may be specified in the direction.

(2) The Bank shall not give a direction under this paragraph unless—

    (a) the applicant has given notice of the application to the relevant supervisory authority in its home State; and

    (b) the Bank has agreed with that authority that the direction should be given.

(3) The date specified in a direction under this paragraph—

    (a) shall not be earlier than the date requested in the application; but

    (b) subject to that, shall be such date as may be agreed between the Bank and the relevant supervisory authority.

(4) The Bank shall as soon as practicable send a copy of any direction given under this paragraph to the applicant, to the relevant supervisory authority and to every other authority which it knows is a connected UK authority. **[689]**

SCHEDULE 3

Regulation 9(7)

PROHIBITIONS AND RESTRICTIONS BY THE BANK

Preliminary

1. In this Schedule—

    "prohibition" means a prohibition under regulation 9 of these Regulations;

    "restriction" means a restriction under regulation 10 of these Regulations.

Notice of prohibition or restriction in non-urgent cases

2.—(1) Subject to paragraph 3 below, where the Bank proposes, in relation to a European institution—

    (a) to impose a prohibition;

    (b) to impose a restriction; or

    (c) to vary a restriction otherwise than with the agreement of the institution,

the Bank shall give notice of its proposal to the institution and to every other authority which it knows is a connected UK authority.

(2) If the proposed action is within paragraph (b) or (c) of sub-paragraph (1) above, the notice under that sub-paragraph shall specify the proposed restriction or, as the case may be, the proposed variation.

(3) A notice under sub-paragraph (1) above shall state the grounds on which the Bank proposes to act and give particulars of the institution's rights under sub-paragraph (5) below.

(4) Where a proposed restriction consists of or includes a condition requiring the removal of any person as director, controller or manager, the Bank shall give that person a copy of the notice mentioned in sub-paragraph (1) above, together with a statement of his rights under sub-paragraph (5) below.

(5) An institution which is given a notice under sub-paragraph (1) above and a person who is given a copy under sub-paragraph (4) above may, within the period of 14 days beginning with the day on which the notice was given, make representations to the Bank.

(6) After giving a notice under sub-paragraph (1) above and taking into account any representations made under sub-paragraph (5) above, the Bank shall decide whether—

    (a) to proceed with the action proposed in the notice;

    (b) to take no further action;

    (c) if the proposed action was the imposition of a prohibition, to impose a restriction instead of or in addition to the prohibition; or

    (d) if the proposed action was the imposition or variation of a restriction, to impose a different restriction or make a different variation.

(7) The Bank shall give—

(a) the institution;

(b) any such person as is mentioned in sub-paragraph (4) above; and

(c) the relevant supervisory authority in the institution's home State,

written notice of its decision and, except where the decision is to take no further action, the notice shall state the reasons for the decision and give particulars of the rights conferred by sub-paragraph (11) below and section 27 of the Banking Act.

(8) A notice under sub-paragraph (7) above shall be given—

(a) within the period of 28 days beginning with the day on which the notice under sub-paragraph (1) above was given; or

(b) where a reply of the relevant supervisory authority to a notice under regulation 11(3) of these Regulations was received during the second half of that period, within the period of 14 days beginning with the day on which that reply was so received;

and where such a reply was so received, the Bank shall give notice of that fact to the institution and to any such person as is mentioned in sub-paragraph (4) above.

(9) If no notice under sub-paragraph (7) above is given within the period mentioned in sub-paragraph (8) above, the Bank shall be treated as having at the end of that period given a notice under that sub-paragraph to the effect that no further action is to be taken.

(10) A notice under sub-paragraph (7) above imposing a prohibition or a restriction on an institution or varying a restriction shall, subject to section 27(4) of the Banking Act, have the effect of prohibiting the institution from accepting deposits in the United Kingdom or restricting its activities or varying the restriction in the manner specified in the notice.

(11) Where the decision notified under sub-paragraph (7) above is to impose or vary a restriction otherwise than as stated in the notice given under sub-paragraph (1) above—

(a) the institution concerned; and

(b) in the case of a European institution, the relevant supervisory authority,

may, within the period of seven days beginning with the day on which the notice was given under sub-paragraph (7) above, make written representations to the Bank with respect to the restriction or variation and the Bank may, after taking those representations into account, alter the restriction.

(12) The Bank may omit from the copy given to a person under sub-paragraph (4) above and from a notice given to him under sub-paragraph (7) above any matter which does not relate to him.

Notice of prohibition or restriction in urgent cases

3.—(1) No notice need be given in accordance with paragraph 2 above in respect of—

(a) the imposition of a prohibition;

(b) the imposition of a restriction; or

(c) the variation of a restriction otherwise than with the agreement of the institution concerned,

in any case in which the Bank considers that the prohibition or restriction should be imposed, or the variation should be made, as a matter of urgency.

(2) In any such case the Bank may by written notice to the institution impose the prohibition or restriction or make the variation.

(3) Any such notice shall state the reasons for which the Bank has acted and particulars of the rights conferred by sub-paragraph (5) below and by section 27 of the Banking Act.

(4) Where a restriction consists of or includes a condition requiring the removal of any person as director, controller or manager, the Bank shall give that person a copy of the notice mentioned in sub-paragraph (2) above, together with a statement of his rights under sub-paragraph (5) below.

(5) An institution to which a notice is given under this paragraph and a person who is given a copy of it by virtue of sub-paragraph (4) above may within the period of 14 days beginning with the day on which the notice was given make representations to the Bank.

(6) After giving a notice under sub-paragraph (2) above and taking into account any representations made in accordance with sub-paragraph (5) above, the Bank shall decide whether—

(a) to confirm or rescind its original decision; or

(b) to impose a different restriction or to vary the restriction in a different manner.

(7) The Bank shall, within the period of 28 days beginning with the day on which the notice was given under sub-paragraph (2) above, give—

(a) the institution; and

(b) the relevant supervisory authority in the institution's home State,

written notice of its decision under sub-paragraph (6) above and, except where the decision is to rescind the original decision, the notice shall state the reasons for the decision.

(8) Where the notice under sub-paragraph (7) above is of a decision to take the action specified in sub-paragraph (6)(b) above, the notice under sub-paragraph (7) shall have the effect of imposing the prohibition or restriction, or making the variation specified in the notice, with effect from the date on which it is given.

Appeals

4.—(1) Section 27 of the Banking Act (rights of appeal) shall have effect as if—

(a) the decisions mentioned in subsection (1) included a decision of the Bank to impose a prohibition or impose or vary a restriction; and

(b) the reference in subsection (4) to the revocation of an institution's authorisation included a reference to the imposition of a prohibition on the institution.

(2) Section 29 of that Act (determination of appeals) shall have effect as if in subsection (2)(a)—

(a) the reference to revoking an authorisation included a reference to imposing a prohibition; and

(b) the reference to restricting an authorisation instead included a reference to imposing instead a restriction.

(3) That section shall also have effect as if it included provision that, in the case of any appeal by a European institution, notice of the tribunal's determination, together with a statement of its reasons, shall be given to the relevant supervisory authority in the institution's home State.

Statement of principles

5.—(1) The Bank shall, as soon as practicable after the coming into force of these Regulations, publish in such manner as it thinks appropriate a statement of the principles in accordance with which it is acting or proposing to act in exercising its power to impose a prohibition on or to restrict the listed activities of a European institution.

(2) Subsection (2) of section 16 of the Banking Act (statement of principles) shall apply for the purposes of sub-paragraph (1) above as it applies for the purpose of subsection (1) of that section.

[690]

SCHEDULE 4
PROHIBITIONS BY THE BOARD

(*Not printed; relates to the Financial Services Act 1986.*)

SCHEDULE 5
PROHIBITIONS AND RESTRICTIONS BY THE DIRECTOR

(*Not printed; relates to the Consumer Credit Act 1974.*)

SCHEDULE 6

Regulation 22(6)

REQUIREMENTS AS RESPECTS UK INSTITUTIONS

Requirements for carrying on activities etc

1.—(1) In relation to the carrying on of a home-regulated activity by the provision of services, the requirements of this paragraph are that the institution has given to the UK authority a notice in accordance with paragraph 2 below.

(2) In relation to the establishment of a branch, the requirements of this paragraph are—

(a) that the institution has given to the UK authority a notice in accordance with paragraph 2 below;

(b) that the UK authority has given to the relevant supervisory authority in the member State concerned the notice which, subject to paragraph 4 below, it is required by paragraph 3(1) or (2) below to give; and

(c) that either—

(i) the relevant supervisory authority has informed the institution that it may establish the branch; or

(ii) the period of two months beginning with the day on which the UK authority gave the relevant supervisory authority the notice mentioned in paragraph (b) above has elapsed.

2. A notice given by an institution to the UK authority is given in accordance with this paragraph if it states—

(a) the member State in which the institution proposes to carry on home-regulated activities;

(b) whether the institution intends to establish a branch in that member State;

(c) if the notice states that the institution does not intend to establish such a branch, the home-regulated activities in relation to which the notice is given; and

(d) if the notice states that the institution intends to establish such a branch, the requisite details of the branch.

3.—(1) The notice which, subject to paragraph 4 below, the UK authority is required to give in respect of a UK authorised institution is a notice which is addressed to the relevant supervisory authority in the member State identified in the institution's notice under paragraph 2 above and which—

(a) certifies that the institution is a credit institution which is for the time being authorised by the UK authority under the Banking Act or, as the case may be, the Building Societies Act;

(b) contains the information stated in the institution's notice; and

(c) if the institution intends to establish a branch in the member State, contains—

(i) a statement of the amount of the institution's own funds and the solvency ratio of the institution (calculated in accordance with the Solvency Ratio Directive); and

(ii) details of any deposit guarantee scheme which is intended to secure the protection of depositors in the branch.

(2) The notice which, subject to paragraph 4 below, the UK authority is required to give in respect of a UK subsidiary is a notice which is addressed to the relevant supervisory authority in the member State identified in the institution's notice under paragraph 2 above and which—

(a) certifies that the institution is a financial institution which is a 90 per cent subsidiary undertaking of a UK authorised institution;

(b) certifies that the conditions mentioned in regulation 20(5) of these Regulations are fulfilled in relation to the institution;

(c) certifies that the institution's business is being conducted in a prudent manner;

(d) contains the information stated in the institution's notice; and

(e) if the institution intends to establish a branch in the member State, contains a statement of the amount of the institution's own funds and the consolidated solvency ratio of the institution's parent undertaking (calculated in accordance with the Solvency Ratio Directive).

4.—(1) Where the institution's notice under paragraph 2 above states that the institution does not intend to establish a branch in the member State, the notice referred to in paragraph 3(1) or (2) above shall be given within the period of one month beginning with the date on which the institution's notice was received by the UK authority.

(2) Where the institution's notice under paragraph 2 above states that the institution intends to establish a branch in the member State, the UK authority shall, within the period of three months beginning with the date on which the institution's notice was received—

(a) give the notice referred to in paragraph 3(1) or (2) above; or

(b) refuse to give such a notice.

(3) The UK authority may not refuse to give such a notice unless, having regard to the home-regulated activities proposed to be carried on, the UK authority doubts the adequacy of the administrative structure or the financial situation of the institution.

(4) Before determining to give or to refuse to give such a notice, the UK authority—

(a) shall seek and take into account the views of every other authority which it knows is a connected UK authority in relation to any of the home-regulated activities proposed to be carried on; and

(b) may regard itself as satisfied in relation to any matter relating to those activities which is relevant to the decision if any such authority informs the UK authority that it is so satisfied.

(5) In reaching a determination as to the adequacy of the administrative structure, the UK authority may have regard to the adequacy of management, systems and controls and the presence of relevant skills needed for the activities proposed to be carried on.

(6) Where the institution's notice under paragraph 2 above states that the institution proposes to establish a branch, the UK authority shall, within the period of three months referred to in sub-paragraph (2) above, notify the institution—

(a) that it has given the notice referred to in paragraph 3(1) or (2) above, stating the date on which it did so; or

(b) that it has refused to give the notice, stating the reasons for the refusal and giving particulars of the rights conferred by section 27 of the Banking Act or, as the case may be, section 46 of the Building Societies Act.

Requirements for changing requisite details of branch

5.—(1) Subject to sub-paragraph (2) below, the requirements of this paragraph are—

(a) that the institution has given a notice to the UK authority, and to the relevant supervisory authority in the member State in which it has established the branch, stating the details of the proposed change;

(b) that that authority has received from the UK authority a notice under paragraph 6(1) below; and

(c) that either that authority has informed the institution that it may make the change, or the period of one month beginning with the day on which it gave that authority the notice mentioned in paragraph (a) above has elapsed.

(2) In the case of a change occasioned by circumstances beyond the institution's control, the requirements of this paragraph are that the institution has, as soon as practicable (whether before or after the change), given a notice to the UK authority, and to the relevant supervisory authority in the member State in which it has established the branch, stating the details of the change.

6.—(1) The UK authority shall, within the period of one month beginning with the date on which the notice under paragraph 5(1) above was received—

(a) give a notice to the relevant supervisory authority informing it of the details of the proposed change; or

(b) refuse to give such a notice.

(2) The UK authority may not refuse to give a notice under sub-paragraph (1) above unless, having regard to the changes and to the home-regulated activities proposed to be carried on, the UK authority doubts the adequacy of the administrative structure or the financial situation of the institution.

(3) Before determining to give or to refuse to give such a notice, the UK authority—

(a) shall seek and take into account the views of any connected UK authority in relation to any changes to the home-regulated activities proposed to be carried on; and

(b) may regard itself as satisfied in relation to any matter relating to those activities which is relevant to the decision if any such authority informs the UK authority that it is so satisfied.

(4) In reaching a determination as to the adequacy of the administrative structure, the UK authority may have regard to the adequacy of management, systems and controls and the presence of relevant skills needed for the activities proposed to be carried on.

(5) The UK authority shall, within the period of one month referred to in sub-paragraph (1) above, notify the institution—

(a) that it has given the notice referred to in that sub-paragraph, stating the date on which it did so; or

(b) that it refused to give the notice, stating the reasons for the refusal and giving particulars of the rights conferred by section 27 of the Banking Act or, as the case may be, section 46 of the Building Societies Act.

Cancellation of compliance with certain requirements

7.—(1) The UK authority may, on an application by a UK subsidiary, direct that any compliance with the requirements of paragraph 1 above in relation to—

(a) its carrying on of any activity in another member State; or

(b) its establishment of a branch in another member State,

shall cease to have effect as from such date as may be specified in the direction.

(2) The UK authority shall not give a direction under this paragraph unless—

(a) the applicant has given notice of the application to the relevant supervisory authority in the member State concerned; and

(b) the UK authority has agreed with the relevant supervisory authority that the direction should be given.

(3) The date specified in a direction under this paragraph—

(a) shall not be earlier than the date requested in the application; but

(b) subject to that, shall be such date as may be agreed between the UK authority and the relevant supervisory authority.

(4) The UK authority shall as soon as practicable send a copy of any direction given under this paragraph to the applicant, to the relevant supervisory authority and to every other authority which it knows is a connected UK authority.

Appeals

8.—(1) Section 27 of the Banking Act (rights of appeal) shall have effect as if the decisions mentioned in subsection (1) included a decision of the Bank to refuse to give a notice under paragraph 3(1) or (2) or 6(1) above.

(2) Section 29 of the Banking Act (determination of appeals) shall have effect as if it included provision that, where the tribunal reverses a decision of the Bank to refuse to give a notice under paragraph 3(1) or (2) or 6(1) above, the tribunal shall direct the Bank to give the notice.

9. (*Modifies the Building Societies Act 1986, ss 46, 47.*)   **[691]**

SCHEDULE 7

Regulation 23(7)

RESTRICTIONS BY THE UK AUTHORITY

Preliminary

1. In this Schedule "restriction" means a restriction under regulation 23 of these Regulations.

Notice of restriction in non-urgent cases

2.—(1) Subject to paragraph 3 below, where the UK authority proposes, in relation to a UK subsidiary—

(a) to impose a restriction; or

(b) to vary a restriction otherwise than with the agreement of the institution,

the UK authority shall give notice of its proposal to the institution and to every other authority which it knows is a connected UK authority.

(2) A notice under sub-paragraph (1) above shall—

(a) specify the proposed restriction or, as the case may be, the proposed variation; and

(b) state the grounds on which the UK authority proposes to act and give particulars of the institution's rights under sub-paragraph (4) below.

(3) Where—

(a) a proposed restriction consists of or includes a condition requiring the removal of any person as director, controller or manager; or

(b) the ground or a ground for a proposal to impose or vary a restriction is that it appears to the UK authority that the criterion in paragraph 1 of Schedule 3 to the Banking Act is not or has not been fulfilled, or may not or may not have been fulfilled, in the case of any person,

the UK authority shall give that person a copy of the notice mentioned in sub-paragraph (1) above, together with a statement of his rights under sub-paragraph (4) below.

(4) An institution which is given a notice under sub-paragraph (1) above and a person who is given a copy under sub-paragraph (3) above may, within the period of 14 days beginning with the day on which the notice was given, make representations to the UK authority.

(5) After giving a notice under sub-paragraph (1) above and taking into account any representations made under sub-paragraph (4) above, the UK authority shall decide whether—

(a) to proceed with the action proposed in the notice;

(b) to take no further action; or

(c) to impose a different restriction or, as the case may be, make a different variation.

(6) The UK authority shall give—

(a) the institution; and

(b) any such person as is mentioned in sub-paragraph (4) above,

written notice of its decision and, except where the decision is to take no further action, the notice shall state the reasons for the decision and give particulars of the rights conferred by sub-paragraph (10) below and section 27 of the Banking Act or, as the case may be, section 46 of the Building Societies Act.

(7) A notice under sub-paragraph (6) above shall be given within the period of 28 days beginning with the day on which the notice under sub-paragraph (1) above was given.

(8) If no notice under sub-paragraph (6) above is given within the period mentioned in sub-paragraph (7) above, the UK authority shall be treated as having at the end of that period given a notice under that sub-paragraph to the effect that no further action is to be taken.

(9) A notice under sub-paragraph (6) above imposing a restriction on an institution or varying a restriction shall have the effect of restricting the institution's activities or varying the restriction in the manner specified in the notice.

(10) Where the decision notified under sub-paragraph (6) above is to impose or vary a restriction otherwise than as stated in the notice given under sub-paragraph (1) above—

(a) the institution concerned may, within the period of seven days beginning with the day on which the notice was given under sub-paragraph (6) above, make written representations to the UK authority with respect to the restriction or variation; and

(b) the UK authority may, after taking those representations into account, alter the restriction.

(11) The UK authority may omit from the copy given to a person under sub-paragraph (4) above and from a notice given to him under sub-paragraph (6) above any matter which does not relate to him.

Notice of restriction in urgent cases

3.—(1) No notice need be given in accordance with paragraph 2 above in respect of—

(a) the imposition of a restriction; or

(b) the variation of a restriction otherwise than with the agreement of the institution concerned,

in any case in which the UK authority considers that the restriction should be imposed, or the variation should be made, as a matter of urgency.

(2) In any such case the UK authority may by written notice to the institution impose the restriction or make the variation.

(3) Any such notice shall state the reasons for which the UK authority has acted and particulars of the rights conferred by sub-paragraph (5) below and by section 27 of the Banking Act or, as the case may be, section 46 of the Building Societies Act.

(4) Where—

(a) a restriction consists of or includes a condition requiring the removal of any person as director, controller or manager; or

(b) the ground or a ground for a restriction or variation of a restriction is that it appears to the UK authority that the criterion in paragraph 1 of Schedule 3 to the Banking Act is not or has not been fulfilled, or may not or may not have been fulfilled, in the case of any person,

the UK authority shall give that person a copy of the notice mentioned in sub-paragraph (2) above, together with a statement of his rights under sub-paragraph (5) below.

(5) An institution to which a notice is given under this paragraph and a person who is given a copy of it by virtue of sub-paragraph (4) above may within the period of 14 days beginning with the day on which the notice was given make representations to the UK authority.

(6) After giving a notice under sub-paragraph (2) above and taking into account any representations made in accordance with sub-paragraph (5) above, the UK authority shall decide whether—

(a) to confirm or rescind its original decision; or

(b) to impose a different restriction or to vary the restriction in a different manner.

(7) The UK authority shall, within the period of 28 days beginning with the day on which the notice was given under sub-paragraph (2) above, give the institution written notice of its decision under sub-paragraph (6) above and, except where the decision is to rescind the original decision, the notice shall state the reasons for the decision.

(8) Where the notice under sub-paragraph (7) above is of a decision to take the action specified in sub-paragraph (6)(b) above, the notice under sub-paragraph (7) shall have the effect of imposing the restriction, or making the variation specified in the notice, with effect from the date on which it is given.

Appeals

4. Section 27 of the Banking Act (rights of appeal) shall have effect as if the decisions mentioned in subsection (1) included a decision of the Bank to impose or vary a restriction.

5. (*Modifies the Building Societies Act 1986, ss 46, 47.*)

Statement of principles

6.—(1) The Bank shall, as soon as practicable after the coming into force of these Regulations, publish in such manner as it thinks appropriate a statement of the principles in accordance with which it is acting or proposing to act in exercising its power to restrict the listed activities of a UK subsidiary.

(2) Subsection (2) of section 16 of the Banking Act (statement of principles) shall apply for the purposes of sub-paragraph (1) above as it applies for the purpose of subsection (1) of that section.

SCHEDULE 8

Regulation 47

AMENDMENTS OF BANKING ACT

Preliminary

1. In this Schedule—

"the Act" means the Banking Act;

"former European institution" means an institution which was formerly a European institution and continues to have a liability in respect of any deposit for which it had a liability when it was a European institution, and "former European authorised institution" shall be construed accordingly;

"former UK subsidiary" means an institution which was formerly a UK subsidiary and continues to have a liability in respect of any deposit for which it had a liability when it was a UK subsidiary.

The Bank and the Board of Banking Supervision

2. Section 1 of the Act (functions and duties of the Bank) shall have effect as if—

(a) the reference in subsection (3) to the Bank's activities under the Act included a reference to its activities under these Regulations; and

(b) the reference in subsection (4) to the Bank's functions under the Act included a reference to its functions under these Regulations.

3. Section 2 of the Act (the Board of Banking Supervision) shall have effect as if references in subsection (3) to the Bank's functions under the Act included references to its functions under these Regulations.

Meaning of "deposit"

4. Section 5 of the Act (meaning of "deposit") shall have effect as if the reference in subsection (3) to an authorised institution included a reference to a European authorised institution which has lawfully established a branch in the United Kingdom for the purpose of accepting deposits.

Authorisations

5.—(1) Section 17 of the Act (information as to authorised institutions) shall have effect as if—

(a) references in subsections (1) and (2) to the institutions which are authorised under the Act included references to European authorised institutions in respect of which the Bank has received a notice given in accordance with paragraph 3 of Schedule 2 to these Regulations; and

(b) the reference in subsection (3) to the fact that an institution has ceased to be so authorised included a reference to the fact that an institution has ceased to be a European authorised institution.

(2) That section shall also have effect as if it included provision that any such list as is mentioned in subsection (1) shall indicate the European authorised institutions as respects which the Bank is satisfied that they are entitled to accept deposits in the United Kingdom in the course of carrying on a deposit-taking business (within the meaning of the Act).

6.—(1) Section 18 of the Act (false statements as to authorised status) shall have effect as if subsection (1) also precluded any person other than a European institution from—

(a) describing himself as a European institution; or

(b) so holding himself out as to indicate or be reasonably understood to indicate that he is a European institution.

(2) That section shall also have effect as if any reference in subsection (2) to an authorised institution included a reference to a European institution.

Invitations to make deposits

7. Section 33 of the Act (advertisement directions) shall have effect as if the reference in subsection (1) to an authorised institution included a reference to a European authorised institution.

Information

8.—(1) Section 39 of the Act (power to obtain information and require production of documents) shall have effect as if—

  (a) references to an authorised institution included references to a European institution, a quasi-European authorised institution or a UK subsidiary;

  (b) references to the Bank's functions under the Act included references to its functions under these Regulations;

  (c) references to an officer, servant or agent of the Bank included references to an officer, servant or agent of the relevant supervisory authority in a European institution's or quasi-European authorised institution's home State;

  (d) references to such information or documents as the Bank may reasonably require for the performance of its functions under the Act included references to such information or documents as such an authority may reasonably require for the performance of any of its functions corresponding to those of the Bank under the Act or these Regulations or those of a connected UK authority; and

  (e) the reference to a former authorised institution included a reference to a former European institution.

(2) That section shall also have effect as if it included provision empowering the Bank to exercise the powers conferred by that section for the purpose of assisting a supervisory authority in a European institution's home State in the performance of any functions corresponding to those of the Bank under the Act or these Regulations or to those of a connected UK authority.

(3) . . .

9.—(1) Section 40 of the Act (right of entry to obtain information and documents) shall have effect as if the reference in subsection (2) to any officer, servant or agent of the Bank included a reference to any officer, servant or agent of a supervisory authority in a European institution's or quasi-European authorised institution's home State.

(2) . . .

Investigations

10.—(1) Section 41 of the Act (investigations on behalf of the Bank) shall have effect as if—

  (a) references to an authorised institution included references to a European institution or a quasi-European authorised institution; and

  (b) the reference to a former authorised institution included a reference to a former European institution.

(2) That section shall also have effect as if it included provision empowering the Bank to exercise the powers conferred by that section for the purpose of assisting a supervisory authority in a European institution's home State in the performance of any functions corresponding to those of the Bank under the Act or these Regulations or those of a connected UK authority.

(3) . . .

Accounts and auditors

11. Section 45 of the Act (audited accounts to be open for inspection) shall have effect as if the reference in subsection (1) to an authorised institution included a reference to a European authorised institution.

12. Section 47 of the Act (communications by auditor etc with the Bank) shall have effect as if—

  (a) references to authorised institutions included references to European institutions and UK subsidiaries;

  (b) the reference in subsection (1) to any function of the Bank under the Act included a reference to any function of the Bank under these Regulations; and

  (c) the reference in subsection (7) to a former authorised institution included a reference to a former European institution.

13.–16. . . .

Banking names and descriptions

17. Section 68 of the Act (exemptions from section 67) shall have effect as if the reference in subsection (3) to an authorised institution included a reference to a European authorised institution.

18. Section 69 of the Act (restriction on use of banking descriptions) shall have effect as if the reference in subsection (1) to an authorised institution included a reference to a European authorised institution.

19.—(1) Section 70 of the Act (power to object to institution's names) shall have effect as if—

    (a) subsection (1) included provision enabling the Bank to give notice in writing to a European institution or quasi-European institution whose recognition notice stated an intention to establish a branch in the United Kingdom that it objects to the name stated in that notice as one of the requisite details of the branch;

    (b) the reference in subsection (1) to an institution applying for an authorisation under the Act included a reference to a European institution or quasi-European institution whose recognition notice stated no such intention;

    (c) the reference in subsection (2) to an authorised institution included a reference to a European institution;

    (d) the reference in subsection (3) to an authorised institution to which section 67 of the Act applies included a reference to a European authorised institution; and

    (e) the reference in paragraph (b) of that subsection to the said section 67 included a reference to section 68(3) of the Act.

(2) In this paragraph "recognition notice", in relation to a European institution or quasi-European institution, means a notice given by it in accordance with paragraph 2 of Schedule 2 to these Regulations.

20. Section 71 of the Act (effect of notices under section 70 and appeals) shall have effect as if the reference in subsection (1) to an authorised institution included a reference to a European institution.

Overseas institutions

21. Section 74 of the Act (meaning of "overseas institution" and "representative office") shall have effect as if the reference in subsection (1) to an authorised institution included a reference to a European institution.

Disclosure of information

22. Section 82 of the Act (restrictions on disclosure) shall have effect as if the reference to the Bank's functions under the Act included a reference to its functions under these Regulations.

23. Section 83 of the Act (disclosure for facilitating discharge of functions by Bank) shall have effect as if—

    (a) the reference to the Bank's functions under the Act included a reference to its functions under these Regulations;

    (b) references to an authorised institution included references to a European institution or UK subsidiary; and

    (c) the reference to a former authorised institution included a reference to a former European institution or former UK subsidiary.

24. Section 84 of the Act (disclosure for facilitating discharge of functions by other supervisory authorities) shall have effect as if the reference in subsection (5A)(a) to an authorised institution or former authorised institution included a reference to a European institution or former European institution.

25. Section 86 of the Act (information supplied to Bank by overseas authority etc) shall have effect as if the references in subsections (1) to (3) to the Bank's functions under the Act included a reference to its functions under these Regulations.

26. Section 87 of the Act (disclosure of information obtained under other Acts) shall have effect as if the reference in subsection (3A) to the Bank's functions under the Act included a reference to its functions under these Regulations.

Miscellaneous and supplementary

27. Section 93 of the Act (injunctions) shall have effect as if the reference in subsection (1) to a direction under section 19 of the Act included a reference to a restriction under regulation 10 or 23 of these Regulations.

28. Section 94 of the Act (false and misleading information) of that Act shall have effect as if—

(a) the reference in subsection (1) to a requirement imposed by or under the Act included a reference to a requirement imposed by or under these Regulations;

(b) references in subsections (1) and (3) to the Bank's functions under the Act included references to its functions under these Regulations;

(c) the reference in subsection (3) to an authorised institution included a reference to a European institution or UK subsidiary; and

(d) the reference in that subsection to a former authorised institution included a reference to a former European institution or former UK subsidiary.

29. Section 95 of the Act (restriction of Rehabilitation of Offenders Act 1974) shall have effect as if in subsection (4)—

(a) the reference to imposing a restriction included a reference to imposing a restriction under regulation 10 or 23 of these Regulations;

(b) the reference to an authorised institution included a reference to a European institution or UK subsidiary; and

(c) the reference to a former authorised institution included a reference to a former European institution or former UK subsidiary.

30. Section 99 of the Act (service of notices on Bank) shall have effect as if the reference in subsection (1) to a notice required by that Act to be given to or served on the Bank included a reference to a notice required by these Regulations to be so given or served.

31. Section 100 of the Act (service of other notices) shall have effect in relation to a European institution which has not established a branch in the United Kingdom as if in subsection (4) the words from "except that" to the end were omitted.

32.—(1) Section 101 of the Act (evidence) shall have effect as if in subsection (1)—

(a) the reference to an authorised institution included a reference to a European institution or UK subsidiary;

(b) the reference to the date on which a particular institution became or ceased to be authorised included a reference to the date on which a particular institution became or ceased to be a European institution or UK subsidiary; and

(c) the reference to whether or not a particular institution's authorisation is or was restricted included a reference to whether or not a restriction under regulation 10 or 23 of these Regulations has or had been imposed on a particular European institution or UK subsidiary.

(2) In giving a certificate under subsection (1) of that section in relation to a European institution, the Bank may rely on any information supplied to it by the relevant supervisory authority in the institution's home State.

33. Section 106 of the Act (interpretation) shall have effect as if the reference in the definition of "former authorised institution" in subsection (1) to an institution which was formerly an authorised institution did not include a reference to a European authorised institution.   **[693]**

NOTES

Paras 8(3), 9(2), 10(3): revoked by the Criminal Justice Act 1993, ss 70(1), 79(14), Sch 6, Pt II.

Paras 13–16: revoked by the Credit Institutions (Protection of Depositors) Regulations 1995, SI 1995/1442, reg 52(4).

(Sch 9 modifies the Financial Services Act 1986; Sch 10 modifies various Acts and statutory instruments which are not printed here. However, the Acts and statutory instruments referred to in this work which are modified by Sch 10 comprise: Bankers' Books Evidence Act 1879, s 9(1); see **[8]**, *Agricultural Credits Act 1928, s 5(7); see* **[385]**, *Banking Act 1987 (Advertisements) Regulations*

1988, SI 1988/645, reg 2; see **[625]** *and the Banking Act 1987 (Exempt Transactions) Regulations 1988, SI 1988/646, regs 13, 14; see* **[647]**, **[648]**.

SCHEDULE 11

Regulation 83

TRANSITIONAL PROVISIONS AND SAVINGS

PART I

RECOGNITION OF INSTITUTIONS

European authorised institutions

1.—(1) This paragraph applies to a credit institution incorporated in or formed under the law of
another member State which immediately before the commencement date is authorised to act as a
credit institution by the relevant supervisory authority in that State.

(2) If an institution to which this paragraph applies—

   (a) is immediately before the commencement date carrying on in the United Kingdom by
        the provision of services any home-regulated activity; or
   (b) has established in the United Kingdom for the purpose of carrying on such an activity a
        branch which immediately before that date is in existence,

it shall be treated for all purposes of these Regulations as if the requirements of paragraph 1 of
Schedule 2 to these Regulations had been complied with in relation to its carrying on of the activity
or, as the case may be, its establishment of the branch.

UK authorised institutions

2.—(1) This paragraph applies to a credit institution incorporated in or formed under the law of
any part of the United Kingdom which immediately before the commencement date is authorised
by the Bank under the Banking Act or by the Commission under the Building Societies Act.

(2) If an institution to which this paragraph applies—

   (a) is immediately before the commencement date carrying on in another member State by
        the provision of services any listed activity; or
   (b) has established in another member State for the purpose of carrying on such an activity a
        branch which immediately before that date is in existence,

it shall be treated for all purposes of these Regulations as if the requirements of paragraph 1 of
Schedule 6 to these Regulations had been complied with in relation to its carrying on of the activity
or, as the case may be, its establishment of the branch.

3.—(1) An institution which by virtue of paragraph 2 above is treated as if the requirements of
paragraph 1 of Schedule 6 to these Regulations had been complied with in relation to its carrying on of
one or more listed activities shall, before the end of the period of three months beginning with the
commencement date, give to the UK authority a notice stating the activity or activities in question.

(2) An institution which by virtue of paragraph 2 above is treated as if the requirements of
paragraph 1 of Schedule 6 to these Regulations had been complied with in relation to its establishment of a branch shall, before the end of the period of three months beginning with the
commencement date, give to the UK authority a notice stating the requisite details of the branch.

(3) . . .

PART II

AMENDMENTS OF BANKING ACT

Requirement as to minimum initial capital

4.—(1) This paragraph applies to a credit institution incorporated in or formed under the law of any part of the United Kingdom which immediately before the commencement date is authorised by the Bank under the Banking Act.

(2) Paragraph 4(3A) of Schedule 3 to the Banking Act (institution to have own funds amounting to ecu 5 million or equivalent) shall have effect in relation to an institution to which this paragraph applies as if the reference to ecu 5 million were a reference to the relevant amount.

(3) Subject to sub-paragraphs (4) to (7) below, the relevant amount is the amount of own funds which the institution has on the commencement date.

(4) If, at any time after 22nd December 1989, the institution had or has own funds of a greater amount than the amount of its own funds on the commencement date, the relevant amount is that greater amount, or ecu 5 million, whichever is the less.

(5) Subject to sub-paragraph (6) below if, at any time after the commencement date, there is any change in the person who is the parent controller of the institution (not being a parent controller which is a subsidiary undertaking of another parent controller of the institution) the relevant amount is ecu 5 million.

(6) If—

    (a) the institution merges with another institution which is also an institution to which this paragraph applies; and

    (b) the Bank is satisfied that in the circumstances the merged institution need not have own funds amounting to not less than ecu 5 million,

then, subject to sub-paragraph (7) below, the relevant amount in relation to the merged institution is the aggregate own funds of the merging institutions on the date of the change, or ecu 5 million, whichever is the less.

(7) If, at any time after the commencement date, the merged institution has own funds of ecu 5 million or more, the relevant amount is ecu 5 million.

(8) Any reference in this paragraph to ecu 5 million includes a reference to an amount of equal value denominated wholly or partly in a different unit of account.

Revocation of authorisation

5.—(1) This paragraph applies to a credit institution incorporated in or formed under the law of any part of the United Kingdom which immediately before the commencement date is authorised by the Bank under the Banking Act.

(2) If an institution to which this paragraph applies is immediately before the commencement date carrying on in the United Kingdom or elsewhere a listed activity (other than the acceptance of deposits from the public), it shall be treated for the purposes of subsection (1A)(b) of section 11 of the Banking Act (revocation of authorisation) as if it had given prior notice to the Bank of its intention to carry on that activity.

Restriction of authorisation

6.—(1) This paragraph applies to a credit institution incorporated in or formed under the law of another member State which immediately before the commencement date—

    (a) is authorised to act as a credit institution by the relevant supervisory authority in that State; and

    (b) is authorised by the Bank under the Banking Act.

(2) Subject to sub-paragraph (3) below, if immediately before the commencement date the authorisation of an institution to which this paragraph applies is subject to a restriction under section 12 of the Banking Act (restriction of authorisation), the restriction shall, if and to the extent that it is capable after that date of being imposed under regulation 10 of these Regulations, have effect as if it had been so imposed.

(3) If the restriction under that section imposes a limit on the duration of the authorisation, the restriction shall, at the time when (but for these Regulations) the authorisation would have expired, have effect as if it were a prohibition imposed on the institution under regulation 9 of these Regulations.

(4) The Bank shall, as soon as practicable after the commencement date, give written notice of every restriction under that section having effect as mentioned in sub-paragraph (2) or (3) above—

(a) to the institution;
(b) to the relevant supervisory authority in the institution's home State; and
(c) to every other authority which the Bank knows is a connected UK authority.

Information and documents

7. Where a notice served on an institution to which paragraph 6 above applies under—

(a) section 39 of the Banking Act (power to obtain information and require production of documents); or
(b) section 41 of that Act (investigations on behalf of Bank),

is in force immediately before the commencement date, the notice shall have effect on and after that date as if it had been served under that section as extended by paragraph 8 or, as the case may be, paragraph 10 of Schedule 8 to these Regulations.

PART III

AMENDMENTS OF FINANCIAL SERVICES ACT

8.–17. (*Amend the Financial Services Act 1986.*)

PART IV

AMENDMENTS OF BUILDING SOCIETIES ACT

18., 19. (*Amend the Building Societies Act 1986.*) **[694]**

NOTE
   Para 3: sub-para (3) revoked by SI 1993/3225, reg 2(h).

UNFAIR TERMS IN CONSUMER CONTRACTS REGULATIONS 1994

(SI 1994/3159)

NOTES
   Made: 8 December 1994.
   Authority: European Communities Act 1972, s 2(2).
   Commencement: 1 July 1995.

ARRANGEMENT OF REGULATIONS

1 Citation and commencement

These Regulations may be cited as the Unfair Terms in Consumer Contracts Regulations 1994 and shall come into force on 1st July 1995.   **[694A]**

NOTE
Commencement: 1 July 1995.

2 Interpretation

(1) In these Regulations—

"business" includes a trade or profession and the activities of any government department or local or public authority;

"the Community" means the European Economic Community and the other States in the European Economic Area;

"consumer" means a natural person who, in making a contract to which these Regulations apply, is acting for purposes which are outside his business;

"court" in relation to England and Wales and Northern Ireland means the High Court, and in relation to Scotland, the Court of Session;

"Director" means the Director General of Fair Trading;

"EEA Agreement" means the Agreement on the European Economic Area signed at Oporto on 2 May 1992 as adjusted by the protocol signed at Brussels on 17 March 1993;

"member State" shall mean a State which is a contracting party to the EEA Agreement but until the EEA Agreement comes into force in relation to Liechtenstein does not include the State of Liechtenstein;

"seller" means a person who sells goods and who, in making a contract to which these Regulations apply, is acting for purposes relating to his business; and

"supplier" means a person who supplies goods or services and who, in making a contract to which these Regulations apply, is acting for purposes relating to his business.

(2) *(Applies to Scotland only.)*   **[694B]**

NOTE
Commencement: 1 July 1995.

3 Terms to which these Regulations apply

(1) Subject to the provisions of Schedule 1, these Regulations apply to any term in a contract concluded between a seller or supplier and a consumer where the said term has not been individually negotiated.

(2) In so far as it is in plain, intelligible language, no assessment shall be made of the fairness of any term which—

(a) defines the main subject matter of the contract, or
(b) concerns the adequacy of the price or remuneration, as against the goods or services sold or supplied.

(3) For the purposes of these Regulations, a term shall always be regarded as not having been individually negotiated where it has been drafted in advance and the consumer has not been able to influence the substance of the term.

(4) Notwithstanding that a specific term or certain aspects of it in a contract has been individually negotiated, these Regulations shall apply to the rest of a contract if an overall assessment of the contract indicates that it is a pre-formulated standard contract.

(5) It shall be for any seller or supplier who claims that a term was individually negotiated to show that it was. **[694C]**

NOTE
Commencement: 1 July 1995.

4 Unfair terms

(1) In these Regulations, subject to paragraphs (2) and (3) below, "unfair term" means any term which contrary to the requirement of good faith causes a significant imbalance in the parties' rights and obligations under the contract to the detriment of the consumer.

(2) An assessment of the unfair nature of a term shall be made taking into account the nature of the goods or services for which the contract was concluded and referring, as at the time of the conclusion of the contract, to all circumstances attending the conclusion of the contract and to all the other terms of the contract or of another contract on which it is dependent.

(3) In determining whether a term satisfies the requirement of good faith, regard shall be had in particular to the matters specified in Schedule 2 to these Regulations.

(4) Schedule 3 to these Regulations contains an indicative and non-exhaustive list of the terms which may be regarded as unfair. **[694D]**

NOTE
Commencement: 1 July 1995.

5 Consequence of inclusion of unfair terms in contracts

(1) An unfair term in a contract concluded with a consumer by a seller of supplier shall not be binding on the consumer.

(2) The contract shall continue to bind the parties if it is capable of continuing in existence without the unfair term. **[694E]**

NOTE
Commencement: 1 July 1995.

6 Construction of written contracts

A seller or supplier shall ensure that any written term of a contract is expressed in plain, intelligible language, and if there is doubt about the meaning of a written term, the interpretation most favourable to the consumer shall prevail. **[694F]**

NOTE
Commencement: 1 July 1995.

7 Choice of law clauses

These Regulations shall apply notwithstanding any contract term which applies or purports to apply the law of a non member State, if the contract has a close connection with the territory of the member States. **[694G]**

NOTE
Commencement: 1 July 1995.

8   Prevention of continued use of unfair terms

(1) It shall be the duty of the Director to consider any complaint made to him that any contract term drawn up for general use is unfair, unless the complaint appears to the Director to be frivolous or vexatious.

(2) If having considered a complaint about any contract term pursuant to paragraph (1) above the Director considers that the contract term is unfair he may, if he considers it appropriate to do so, bring proceedings for an injunction (in which proceedings he may also apply for an interlocutory injunction) against any person appearing to him to be using or recommending use of such a term in contracts concluded with consumers.

(3) The Director may, if he considers it appropriate to do so, have regard to any undertakings given to him by or on behalf of any person as to the continued use of such a term in contracts concluded with consumers.

(4) The Director shall give reasons for his decision to apply or not to apply, as the case may be, for an injunction in relation to any complaint which these Regulations require him to consider.

(5) The court on an application by the Director may grant an injunction on such terms as it thinks fit.

(6) An injunction may relate not only to use of a particular contract term drawn up for general use but to any similar term, or a term having like effect, used or recommended for use by any party to the proceedings.

(7) The Director may arrange for the dissemination in such form and manner as he considers appropriate of such information and advice concerning the operation of these Regulations as may appear to him to be expedient to give to the public and to all persons likely to be affected by these Regulations. **[694H]**

NOTE
Commencement: 1 July 1995.

SCHEDULE 1

Regulation 3(1)

CONTRACTS AND PARTICULAR TERMS EXCLUDED FROM THE SCOPE OF THESE REGULATIONS

These Regulations do not apply to–

    (a) any contract relating to employment;
    (b) any contract relating to succession rights;
    (c) any contract relating to rights under family law;
    (d) any contract relating to the incorporation and organisation of companies or partnerships; and
    (e) any term incorporated in order to comply with or which reflects–

        (i) statutory or regulatory provisions of the United Kingdom; or
        (ii) the provisions or principles of international conventions to which the member States or the Community are party.   **[694I]**

NOTE
Commencement: 1 July 1995.

SCHEDULE 2

Regulation 4(3)

ASSESSMENT OF GOOD FAITH

In making an assessment of good faith, regard shall be had in particular to–

- (a) the strength of the bargaining positions of the parties;
- (b) whether the consumer had an inducement to agree to the term;
- (c) whether the goods or services were sold or supplied to the special order of the consumer, and
- (d) the extent to which the seller or supplier has dealt fairly and equitably with the consumer.   **[694J]**

NOTE
  Commencement: 1 July 1995.

SCHEDULE 3

Regulation 4(4)

INDICATIVE AND ILLUSTRATIVE LIST OF TERMS WHICH MAY BE REGARDED AS UNFAIR

1. Terms which have the object or effect of—

- (a) excluding or limiting the legal liability of a seller or supplier in the event of the death of a consumer or personal injury to the latter resulting from an act or omission of that seller or supplier;
- (b) inappropriately excluding or limiting the legal rights of the consumer vis-à-vis the seller or supplier or another party in the event of total or partial non-performance or inadequate performance by the seller or supplier of any of the contractual obligations, including the option of offsetting a debt owed to the seller or supplier against any claim which the consumer may have against him;
- (c) making an agreement binding on the consumer whereas provision of services by the seller or supplier is subject to a condition whose realisation depends on his own will alone;
- (d) permitting the seller or supplier to retain sums paid by the consumer where the latter decides not to conclude or perform the contract, without providing for the consumer to receive compensation of an equivalent amount from the seller or supplier where the latter is the party cancelling the contract;
- (e) requiring any consumer who fails to fulfil his obligation to pay a disproportionately high sum in compensation;
- (f) authorising the seller or supplier to dissolve the contract on a discretionary basis where the same facility is not granted to the consumer, or permitting the seller or supplier to retain the sums paid for services not yet supplied by him where it is the seller or supplier himself who dissolves the contract;
- (g) enabling the seller or supplier to terminate a contract of indeterminate duration without reasonable notice except where there are serious grounds for doing so;
- (h) automatically extending a contract of fixed duration where the consumer does not indicate otherwise, when the deadline fixed for the consumer to express this desire not to extend the contract is unreasonably early;
- (i) irrevocably binding the consumer to terms with which he had no real opportunity of becoming acquainted before the conclusion of the contract;
- (j) enabling the seller or supplier to alter the terms of the contract unilaterally without a valid reason which is specified in the contract;
- (k) enabling the seller or supplier to alter unilaterally without a valid reason any characteristics of the product or service to be provided;
- (l) providing for the price of goods to be determined at the time of delivery or allowing a seller of goods or supplier of services to increase their price without in both cases giving the consumer the corresponding right to cancel the contract if the final price is too high in relation to the price agreed when the contract was concluded;

(m) giving the seller or supplier the right to determine whether the goods or services supplied are in conformity with the contract, or giving him the exclusive right to interpret any term of the contract;

(n) limiting the seller's or supplier's obligation to respect commitments undertaken by his agents or making his commitments subject to compliance with a particular formality;

(o) obliging the consumer to fulfil all his obligations where the seller or supplier does not perform his;

(p) giving the seller or supplier the possibility of transferring his rights and obligations under the contract, where this may serve to reduce the guarantees for the consumer, without the latter's agreement;

(q) excluding or hindering the consumer's right to take legal action or exercise any other legal remedy, particularly by requiring the consumer to take disputes exclusively to arbitration not covered by legal provisions, unduly restricting the evidence available to him or imposing on him a burden of proof which, according to the applicable law, should lie with another party to the contract.

2. Scope of subparagraphs 1(g), (j) and (l)

(a) Subparagraph 1(g) is without hindrance to terms by which a supplier of financial services reserves the right to terminate unilaterally a contract of indeterminate duration without notice where there is a valid reason, provided that the supplier is required to inform the other contracting party or parties thereof immediately.

(b) Subparagraph 1(j) is without hindrance to terms under which a supplier of financial services reserves the right to alter the rate of interest payable by the consumer or due to the latter, or the amount of other charges for financial services without notice where there is a valid reason, provided that the supplier is required to inform the other contracting party or parties thereof at the earliest opportunity and that the latter are free to dissolve the contract immediately.

Subparagraph 1(j) is also without hindrance to terms under which a seller or supplier reserves the right to alter unilaterally the conditions of a contract of indeterminate duration, provided that he is required to inform the consumer with reasonable notice and that the consumer is free to dissolve the contract.

(c) Subparagraphs 1(g), (j) and (l) do not apply to:

– transactions in transferable securities, financial instruments and other products or services where the price is linked to fluctuations in a stock exchange quotation or index or a financial market rate that the seller or supplier does not control;

– contracts for the purchase or sale of foreign currency, traveller's cheques or international money orders denominated in foreign currency;

(d) Subparagraph 1(l) is without hindrance to price indexation clauses, where lawful, provided that the method by which prices vary is explicitly described. **[694K]**

NOTE

Commencement: 1 July 1995.

CREDIT INSTITUTIONS (PROTECTION OF DEPOSITORS) REGULATIONS 1995

(SI 1995/1442)

ARRANGEMENT OF REGULATIONS

NOTES

Made: 6 June 1995.
Authority: European Communities Act 1972, s 2(2).
Commencement: 1 July 1995.
The regulations printed in italics are not reproduced.

PART I

GENERAL

PART II

PARTICIPATION IN HOST STATE SCHEMES

CHAPTER I

PARTICIPATION IN UK SCHEME BY EEA INSTITUTION

Main provisions

Supplementary provisions

CHAPTER II

PARTICIPATION IN EEA SCHEME BY UK INSTITUTION OR BUILDING SOCIETY

CHAPTER III

NON-PARTICIPATION IN DEPOSIT PROTECTION SCHEME BY NON-EEA INSTITUTION

Main provisions

Supplementary provisions

PART III

AMENDMENTS OF PART II OF 1987 ACT

PART IV
AMENDMENT OF PART IV OF 1986 ACT

PART V
MISCELLANEOUS AND SUPPLEMENTAL

Miscellaneous

Supplemental

PART I
GENERAL

1 Citation, commencement and extent

(1) These Regulations may be cited as the Credit Institutions (Protection of Depositors) Regulations 1995.

(2) These Regulations shall come into force on 1st July 1995.

(3) These Regulations extend to Northern Ireland.   **[695]**

2 Interpretation

(1) In these Regulations—

"the 1986 Act" means the Building Societies Act 1986;
"the 1987 Act" means the Banking Act 1987;
"the 1992 Regulations" means the Banking Coordination (Second Council Directive) Regulations 1992;

"the Bank" means the Bank of England;

"building society" means a building society incorporated (or deemed to be incorporated) under the 1986 Act;

"the commencement date" means 1st July 1995;

"the Commission" means the Building Societies Commission;

"the Deposit Protection Board" means the Deposit Protection Board continued in existence by Part II of the 1987 Act;

"the deposit protection scheme" means the scheme for the protection of depositors continued in force by that Part;

"EEA institution" means a European authorised institution (within the meaning of the 1992 Regulation);

"EEA State" means a State which is a Contracting Party of the Agreement on the European Economic Area signed at Oporto on 2nd May 1992 as adjusted by the Protocol signed at Brussels on 17th March 1993;

"home State", in relation to an EEA institution or a non-EEA institution, means the EEA State, or the country or territory, in which it is incorporated or under the law of which it is formed;

"home State scheme"—

(a) in relation to an EEA institution, means a scheme for the protection of depositors which is in force in the institution's home State and in which the institution participates;

(b) in relation to a non-EEA institution, means a scheme or other arrangement for the protection of depositors which is in force in the institution's home State and in which the institution participates;

"host State scheme", in relation to a UK institution or building society, means a scheme for the protection of depositors which is in force in an EEA State other than the United Kingdom and in which the institution or society participates;

"investment", in relation to a building society or an Irish building society which, in accordance with Chapter I or Part II of these Regulations, is participating in the investor protection scheme, means a deposit with or a share in the society;

"the Investor Protection Board" means the Building Societies Investor Protection Board established by Part IV of the 1986 Act;

"the investor protection scheme" means the scheme for the protection of investors established by that Part;

"Irish building society" means an EEA institution which is incorporated in or formed under the law of the Republic of Ireland and whose characteristics correspond as nearly as may be to those of a building society;

"non-EEA institution" means an authorised institution (within the meaning of the 1987 Act) which is incorporated in or formed under the law of a country or territory outside the European Economic Area;

"supervisory authority", in relation to an EEA State other than the United Kingdom or a country or territory outside the European Economic Area, means an authority in that State, country or territory which has regulatory functions in relation to the acceptance of deposits;

"UK institution" means an authorised institution (within the meaning of the 1987 Act) which is incorporated in or formed under the law of any part of the United Kingdom;

"UK scheme" means the deposit protection scheme or the investor protection scheme.

(2) In these Regulations, unless the context otherwise requires, references to deposits include references to investments, and references to depositors or intending depositors shall be construed accordingly.   **[696]**

NOTES
It is thought that in the definition of "investment", "Chapter I or Part II" should read "Chapter I of Part II".
Banking Coordination (Second Council Directive) Regulations 1992: SI 1992/3218 at **[665]** et seq.
Agreement on the European Economic Area signed at Oporto on 2 May 1992 as adjusted by the Protocol signed at Brussels on 17 March 1993: Cm 2073 and Cm 2183.

PART II
PARTICIPATION IN HOST STATE SCHEMES

CHAPTER I
PARTICIPATION IN UK SCHEME BY EEA INSTITUTION

Main provisions

3 Eligibility to participate in scheme

(1) An EEA institution which accepts or proposes to accept deposits through offices in the United Kingdom shall be eligible to participate in a UK scheme if the Deposit Protection Board ("the Board") determines under this regulation, on an application made by the institution, that it is so eligible; and an application under this paragraph may state a preference for one or other of the UK schemes.

(2) The Board shall not make a determination under this regulation unless, after consultation with such of the relevant authorities (if any) as it considers appropriate, it is satisfied that—

(a) the scope of the protection afforded to depositors by the institution's home State scheme; or

(b) the level of the protection so afforded,

is less than that afforded to depositors by the UK scheme specified in the determination.

(3) Whether or not the Board is satisfied as mentioned in paragraph (2) above, it shall decide which of the UK schemes appears to be the more appropriate for the institution, having regard to whether the institution's characteristics correspond more closely to those of a UK institution or to those of a building society.

(4) The Board shall not under paragraph (3) above—

(a) decide in favour of the investor protection scheme except with the consent of the Investor Protection Board; or

(b) decide in favour of the deposit protection scheme, in a case where the application stated a preference for the investor protection scheme, except after consulting with that Board.

(5) Written notice of a decision of the Board under paragraph (2) or (3) above, stating the reasons for it, shall be given to the institution—

(a) within 90 days after the day on which the institution's application is received by the Board; or

(b) within that period and such additional period, not exceeding 30 days, as the Bank may in exceptional circumstances allow.

(6) In this regulation and regulation 6 below "the relevant authorities" means—

(a) the Bank, the Commission and the supervisory authority in the institution's home State; and

(b) the Investor Protection Board and the authority responsible for the institution's home State scheme. **[697]**

4 Participation in scheme

(1) An EEA institution which is eligible to participate in the deposit protection scheme by virtue of a determination under regulation 3 above shall cease to be so eligible unless, within two months after the date of the determination—

(a) it commences its participation in that scheme by paying to the Deposit Protection Board the amount which is specified in the determination in accordance with paragraph (2) below; or

(b) in the case of an institution which was participating in that scheme immediately before the commencement date and whose application under paragraph (1) of that regulation was made within six months of that date, it resumes its participation in that scheme by giving notice to that Board of its decision to do so.

(2) Where—

(a) a determination under regulation 3 above specifies the deposit protection scheme; and

(b) the institution is not such an institution as is mentioned in paragraph (1)(b) above,

the determination shall also specify the amount which the Deposit Protection Board considers would be determined in accordance with subsection (2) or (3) of section 53 of the 1987 Act (initial contributions) if the institution participated in the scheme.

(3) An EEA institution which is eligible to participate in the investor protection scheme by virtue of a determination under regulation 3 above shall cease to be so eligible unless, within two months after date of the determination, it commences its participation in that scheme by giving to the Investor Protection Board notice of its decision to do so.

(4) No initial contribution shall be levied under section 53 of the 1987 Act from an EEA institution which commences or resumes its participation in the deposit protection scheme in accordance with paragraph (1) above.

(5) The amount payable under sub-paragraph (a) of paragraph (1) above by an EEA institution which has withdrawn under regulation 5 below, or has been excluded under regulation 6 below, from participation in the deposit protection scheme shall be reduced by the aggregate of—

(a) any amount previously paid by the institution under that sub-paragraph;

(b) so much of any further contribution levied on the institution under section 54 of the 1987 Act as was attributable to an order under subsection (2) of that section; and

(c) if any previous participation in that scheme was resumed in accordance with sub-paragraph (b) of that paragraph, the amount of the initial contribution levied on the institution under section 53 of that Act. **[698]**

NOTE
1987 Act: Banking Act 1987.

5 Withdrawal from scheme

(1) An EEA institution which is participating in a UK scheme may withdraw from participation in that scheme by giving to the relevant Board not less than six months notice of its intention to do so.

(2) In this regulation and regulation 7 below "the relevant Board"—

(a) in relation to the deposit protection scheme, means the Deposit Protection Board; and

(b) in relation to the investor protection scheme, means the Investor Protection Board.   **[699]**

6 Exclusion where institution no longer eligible

(1) An EEA institution which is participating in a UK scheme shall be excluded from participation in that scheme if the Deposit Protection Board ("the Board") determines under this regulation that it is no longer eligible to participate in that scheme.

(2) The Board shall not make a determination under this regulation unless, after consultation with such of the relevant authorities (if any) as it considers appropriate, it is satisfied that—

(a) the scope of the protection afforded to depositors by the institution's home State scheme; and

(b) the level of the protection so afforded,

are each not less than that afforded to depositors by the UK scheme in which the institution is participating.

(3) Written notice of a decision of the Board under paragraph (2) above, stating the reasons for it, shall be given to the institution.

(4) An exclusion under this regulation shall not have effect—

(a) until the time for appealing under regulation 8 below against the Board's decision under paragraph (2) above has expired; or

(b) if an appeal is made under that regulation, unless and until that decision is confirmed by the Chancellor of the Exchequer.   **[700]**

7 Exclusion where institution in default

(1) This regulation applies where an EEA institution which is participating in a UK scheme ("the scheme") is in default by reason of—

(a) any failure to pay in whole or in part any contribution due from it under the scheme; or

(b) any failure to produce any documents or provide any information to the relevant Board which it is required to produce or provide under section 65 of the 1987 Act or, as the case may be, section 29A of the 1986 Act.

(2) Where this regulation applies the relevant Board shall give notice of the default to the supervisory authority in the institution's home State ("the supervisory authority") requesting that authority—

(a) to take all appropriate measures for the purpose of ensuring that the default is remedied; and

(b) to inform the Board of the measures which it proposes to take or has taken or of the reasons for not taking any such measures.

(3) If the relevant Board is satisfied either—

(a) that the supervisory authority has failed or refused to take measures for the purpose mentioned in paragraph (2)(a) above; or

(b) that the measures taken by the authority have proved inadequate for that purpose,

it may give notice to the institution that if the default is not remedied before the end of the period of 12 months beginning with the date of the notice, the institution may be excluded from participation in the scheme.

(4) If the default has not been remedied before the end of the period of 12 months referred to in paragraph (3) above the relevant Board may, with the consent of the supervisory authority, by notice to the institution exclude the institution from participation in the scheme.

(5) Nothing in paragraph (4) above shall prohibit recovery by the relevant Board of any unpaid amount.   **[701]**

NOTES
1987 Act: Banking Act 1987.
1986 Act: Building Societies Act 1986.

8 Appeals against decisions of Board

(1) An EEA institution which is aggrieved by a decision under regulation 3(2) or (3), 6(2) or 7(3) above may, within 28 days after the day on which it received notice of the decision, appeal against the decision to the Chancellor of the Exchequer.

(2) An appeal under this regulation shall be made by sending to the Chancellor of the Exchequer (with copies to the relevant Board)—

(a) a notice of appeal, including a statement of the grounds of appeal;
(b) written representations in support of those grounds; and
(c) any documents that may be relevant for the purposes of the appeal;

and the procedure for determining such an appeal shall be as the Chancellor of the Exchequer may direct.

(3) On such an appeal the Chancellor of the Exchequer may confirm or vary the decision which is the subject of the appeal.

(4) Written notice of the Chancellor of the Exchequer's decision, stating the reasons for it, shall be given to the appellant and to the relevant Board; and, unless the Chancellor of the Exchequer otherwise directs, the decision shall take effect when the notice is so given.

(5) In this regulation "the relevant Board"—

(a) in relation to a decision under regulation 3(2) or 6(2) above, means the Deposit Protection Board;
(b) in relation to a decision under regulation 3(3) above, means the Deposit Protection Board and the Investor Protection board; and
(c) in relation to a decision under regulation 7(3) above, has the same meaning as in that regulation.   **[702]**

Supplementary provisions

9 Duty of institution to notify withdrawal or exclusion

(1) Where an EEA institution withdraws or is excluded from participation in a UK scheme, it shall as soon as practicable take all such steps as may be necessary to bring the withdrawal or exclusion to the notice of depositors whose deposits were made with United Kingdom offices of the institution.

(2) Where it appears to the Bank that an EEA institution has failed to comply with paragraph (1) above, the Bank shall require the institution by

notice in writing to take all such steps as appear to it necessary to comply with that paragraph and are specified in the notice.

(3) If an EEA institution fails to comply with a requirement under paragraph (2) above within a reasonable time, the Bank shall give notice to that effect to the supervisory authority in the institution's home State requesting that authority—

(a) to take all appropriate measures for the purpose of ensuring that the institution complies with that requirement; and

(b) to inform the Bank of the measures which it proposes to take or has taken or of the reasons for not taking any such measures.   **[703]**

10 Duty of Board to consult with home State authority

(1) As soon as practicable after an EEA institution commences or resumes its participation in a UK scheme, the relevant Board shall, if it has not already done so in connection with another such institution's participation in the UK scheme—

(a) consult with the authority having responsibility for the institution's home State scheme; and

(b) come to an agreement with that authority as to the rules and procedures to be adopted for determining, in the event of such institutions becoming insolvent (within the meaning of the relevant Part), the respective amounts of compensation which, after any deductions by way of set-off, would be payable under that scheme and the UK scheme.

(2) As soon as practicable after an EEA institution which is participating in a UK scheme becomes insolvent (within the meaning of the relevant Part), the relevant Board shall—

(a) consult with the authority having responsibility for the institution's home State scheme; and

(b) come to an agreement with that authority as to the respective amounts of compensation which, after any deductions by way of set-off, are payable under that scheme and the UK scheme.

(3) In this regulation "the relevant Board" and "the relevant Part" mean respectively—

(a) in relation to the deposit protection scheme, the Deposit Protection Board and Part II of the 1987 Act;

(b) in relation to the investor protection scheme, the Investor Protection Board and Part IV of the 1986 Act.

(4) Any reference in this regulation to an EEA institution includes a reference to an institution which was formerly an EEA institution and continues to have a liability in respect of any deposit for which it had a liability at a time when it was an EEA institution.   **[704]**

NOTES
1987 Act: Banking Act 1987.
1986 Act: Building Societies Act 1986.

11 Power of Board to make agency and information agreements

(1) Where an EEA institution commences or resumes its participation in a UK scheme, the relevant Board may enter into an agency or information agreement with the authority responsible for the institution's home State scheme.

(2) In this regulation—

"agency agreement" means an agreement between the relevant Board and the authority responsible for the institution's home State scheme under which either agrees, whether or not for a consideration, to make on the other's behalf any payments falling to be made under the scheme for which the other is responsible;

"information agreement" means an agreement between the relevant Board and the authority responsible for the institution's home State scheme under which either agrees, whether or not for a consideration, to disclose to the other any information in its possession which would or might assist the other to discharge its functions;

"the relevant Board" has the same meaning as in regulation 10 above.

[705]

12 Duty of Board to maintain list of participating EEA institutions

The Deposit Protection Board and the Investor Protection Board shall each compile and maintain a list of the EEA institutions which are participating in the UK scheme for which it is the responsible authority. [706]

CHAPTER II
PARTICIPATION IN EEA SCHEME BY UK INSTITUTION OR BUILDING SOCIETY

13 Duty of institution or society to notify withdrawal or exclusion

Where a UK institution or building society withdraws or is excluded from a scheme for the protection of depositors which is in force in an EEA State other than the United Kingdom, it shall as soon as practicable take all such steps as may be necessary to bring the withdrawal or exclusion to the notice of depositors whose deposits were made with offices of the institution or society in that State. [707]

14 Liability of institution or society in respect of payments under host State scheme

(1) Where a UK institution or building society which is participating in a host State scheme becomes insolvent (within the meaning of the relevant Part), the relevant enactment shall have effect as if—

(a) any reference to the relevant Board included a reference to the authority responsible for the host State scheme; and

(b) any reference to the making of a payment under any provision of the relevant Part included a reference to the making of a payment under that scheme.

(2) In this regulation "the relevant Board", "the relevant enactment" and "the relevant Part" mean respectively—

(a) in relation to a UK institution, the Deposit Protection Board, section 62 of the 1987 Act and Part II of that Act;

(b) in relation to a building society, the Investor Protection Board, section 28 of the 1986 Act and Part IV of that Act.

(3) Any reference in this regulation to a UK institution includes a reference to an institution which was formerly a UK institution and continues to have a liability in respect of any deposit for which it had a liability at a time when it was a UK institution. [708]

NOTES
1987 Act: Banking Act 1987.
1986 Act: Building Societies Act 1986.

15 Duty of Board to consult with host State authority

(1) As soon as practicable after a UK institution or building society commences or resumes its participation in a host State scheme, the relevant Board shall, if it has not already done so in connection with another such institution's or society's participation in that scheme—

(a) consult with the authority having responsibility for that scheme; and
(b) come to an agreement with that authority as to the rules and procedures to be adopted for determining, in the event of such institutions or societies becoming insolvent (with the meaning of the relevant Part), the respective amounts of compensation which, after any deductions by way of set-off, would be payable under that scheme and the relevant UK scheme.

(2) As soon as practicable after a UK institution or building society which is participating in a host State scheme becomes insolvent (within the meaning of the relevant Part), the relevant Board shall—

(a) consult with the authority having responsibility for that scheme; and
(b) come to an agreement with that authority as to the respective amounts of compensation which, after any deductions by way of set-off, are payable under that scheme and the relevant UK scheme.

(3) In this regulation "the relevant Board", "the relevant Part" and "the relevant UK scheme" mean respectively—

(a) in relation to a UK institution, the Deposit Protection Board, Part II of the 1987 Act and the deposit protection scheme;
(b) in relation to a building society, the Investor Protection Board, Part IV of the 1986 Act and the investor protection scheme.

(4) Any reference in this regulation to a UK institution includes a reference to an institution which was formerly a UK institution and continues to have a liability in respect of any deposit for which it had a liability at a time when it was a UK institution.   **[709]**

NOTES
1987 Act: Banking Act 1987.
1986 Act: Building Societies Act 1986.

16 Power of Board to make agency and information agreements

(1) Where a UK institution or building society commences or resumes its participation in a host State scheme, the relevant Board may enter into an agency or information agreement with the authority responsible for that scheme.

(2) In this regulation—

"agency agreement" means an agreement between the relevant Board and the authority responsible for the host State scheme under which either one agrees, whether or not for a consideration, to make on the other's behalf any payments falling to be made under the scheme for which the other is responsible;

"information agreement" means an agreement between the relevant Board and the authority responsible for the host State scheme under which either agrees, whether or not for a consideration, to disclose to the other any information in its possession which would or might assist the other to discharge its functions;

"the relevant Board" has the same meaning as in regulation 15 above.
        [710]

17 Duty of Bank or Commission to declare that deposits are no longer available

(1) Where a UK institution or building society which is or has been a participating institution has become insolvent, it shall be the duty of the relevant authority—

(a) to make a declaration that deposits held by the institution or society are no longer available; and

(b) to send a copy of the declaration to the authority responsible for each scheme which is or has been a host State scheme in relation to the institution or society.

(2) Where a UK institution or building society which is or has been a participating institution has ceased to be insolvent, it shall be the duty of the relevant authority—

(a) to withdraw the declaration made by it under paragraph (1) above; and

(b) to notify the withdrawal to each authority to which it has sent a copy of that declaration.

(3) In this regulation—

(a) references to a participating institution are references to an institution which is participating in a host State scheme; and

(b) references to becoming or ceasing to be insolvent shall be construed in accordance with the relevant enactment.

(4) In this regulation "the relevant authority" and "the relevant enactment" mean respectively—

(a) in relation to a UK institution, the Bank and section 59 of the 1987 Act;

(b) in relation to a building society, the Commission and section 25A of the 1986 Act. **[711]**

NOTES
1987 Act: Banking Act 1987.
1986 Act: Building Societies Act 1986.

18 Powers of authority responsible for host State scheme

(1) Where a UK institution or building society which is participating in a host State scheme becomes insolvent (within the meaning of the relevant Part), the relevant enactments (which enable the relevant Board to obtain information) shall have effect as if—

(a) any reference to the relevant Board included a reference to the authority having responsibility for the host State scheme;

(b) any reference to the relevant Part included a reference to the corresponding provision of the law of the EEA State in which the host State scheme is in force; and

(c) any reference (however expressed) to a deposit protected by, or to a payment under, the relevant UK scheme included a reference to a deposit protected by, or to a payment under, the host State scheme.

(2) In this regulation "the relevant Board", "the relevant enactments", "the relevant Part" and "the relevant UK scheme" mean respectively—

(a) in relation to a UK institution, the Deposit Protection Board, section 58(8) and (9) and section 65(3) and (4) of the 1987 Act, Part II of that Act and the deposit protection scheme;

    (b) in relation to a building society, the Investor Protection Board, section 29A(3) and (4) of the 1986 Act, Part IV of that Act and the investor protection scheme.

    (3) Any reference in this regulation to a UK institution includes a reference to an institution which was formerly a UK institution and continues to have a liability in respect of any deposit for which it had a liability at a time when it was a UK institution.

    (4) Nothing in section 65(3) of the 1987 Act (as modified by this regulation), or section 29A(3) of the 1986 Act (as so modified), shall entitle an authority having responsibility for a host State scheme to require information to be provided or furnished, or documents, books or papers to be produced, at a place outside the United Kingdom.   **[711A]**

NOTES
1987 Act: Banking Act 1987.
1986 Act: Building Societies Act 1986.

CHAPTER III
NON-PARTICIPATION IN DEPOSIT PROTECTION SCHEME BY NON-EEA INSTITUTION

Main provisions

19 Eligibility not to participate in scheme

    (1) A non-EEA institution shall be eligible not to participate in the deposit protection scheme ("the scheme") if the Deposit Protection Board ("the Board") determines under this regulation, on an application made by the institution, that it is so eligible.

    (2) The Board shall not make such a determination under this regulation unless after consultation with such of the relevant authorities (if any) as it considers appropriate, it is satisfied that—

        (a) the scope of the protection afforded by the institution's home State scheme to depositors with United Kingdom offices; and
        (b) the level of the protection so afforded,

are each not less than that afforded to such depositors by the scheme.

    (3) Written notice of the Board's decision under paragraph (2) above, stating the reasons for it, shall be given to the institution—

        (a) within 90 days after the day on which the institution's application is received by the Board; or
        (b) within that period and such additional period, not exceeding 30 days, as the Bank may in exceptional circumstances allow.

    (4) In this regulation and regulation 21 below "the relevant authorities" means—

        (a) the Bank and the supervisory authority in the institution's home State; and
        (b) the authority responsible for the institution's home State scheme.
                                              [711B]

20 Election not to participate in scheme

A non-EEA institution which is eligible not to participate in the deposit protection scheme by virtue of a determination under regulation 19 above shall cease to be so eligible unless, within two months after the date of the determination, it elects not to participate in that scheme by giving notice of its election to the Deposit Protection Board. **[711C]**

21 Election to cease to have effect where institution no longer eligible

(1) An election by a non-EEA institution not to participate in the deposit protection scheme ("the scheme") shall cease to have effect if the deposit Protection Board ("the Board") determines under this regulation that it is no longer eligible not to participate in the scheme.

(2) The Board shall not make a determination under this regulation unless, after consultation with such of the relevant authorities (if any) as it considers appropriate, it is satisfied that—

(a) the scope of the protection afforded to depositors by the institution's home State scheme; or

(b) the level of the protection so afforded,

is less than that afforded to depositors by the scheme.

(3) Written notice of a decision of the Board under paragraph (2) above, stating the reasons for it, shall be given to the institution.

(4) An election shall not cease to have effect by virtue of this regulation—

(a) until the time for appealing under regulation 22 below against the Board's decision under paragraph (2) above has expired; or

(b) if an appeal is made under that regulation, unless and until that decision is confirmed by the Chancellor of the Exchequer.

(5) Where an election ceases to have effect by virtue of this regulation, the amount of the initial contribution levied on the institution under section 53 of the 1987 Act shall be reduced by the aggregate of—

(a) the amount of any previous initial contribution levied on the institution under that section; and

(b) so much of any further contribution levied on the institution under section 54 of that Act as was attributable to an order under subsection (2) of that section. **[711D]**

NOTE
1987 Act: Banking Act 1987.

22 Appeals against decisions of Board

(1) A non-EEA institution which is aggrieved by a decision under regulation 19(2) or 21(2) above may, within 28 days after the day on which it received notice of the decision, appeal against the decision to the Chancellor of the Exchequer.

(2) An appeal under this regulation shall be made by sending to the Chancellor of the Exchequer (with copies to the Deposit Protection Board)—

(a) a notice of appeal, including a statement of the grounds of appeal;
(b) written representations in support of those grounds; and
(c) any documents that may be relevant for the purposes of the appeal;

and the procedure for determining such an appeal shall be as the Chancellor of the Exchequer may direct.

(3) On such an appeal the Chancellor of the Exchequer may confirm or vary the decision which is the subject of the appeal.

(4) Written notice of the Chancellor of the Exchequer's decision, stating the reasons for it, shall be given to the appellant and to the Deposit Protection Board; and, unless the Chancellor of the Exchequer otherwise directs, the decision shall take effect when the notice is so given.   **[711E]**

Supplementary provisions

23 Duty of institution to notify election not to participate

Where a non-EEA institution elects not to participate in the deposit protection scheme, it shall as soon as practicable take all such steps as may be necessary to bring the election to the notice of depositors whose deposits were made with United Kingdom offices of the institution.   **[711F]**

24 Duty of institution to notify election not to participate

The Deposit Protection Board shall compile and maintain a list of the non-EEA institutions which are participating in the deposit protection scheme.
                                                                                                [711G]

PART III
AMENDMENTS OF PART II OF 1987 ACT

25–35 (*Amend the Banking Act 1987.*)

PART IV
AMENDMENTS OF PART IV OF 1986 ACT

36–44 (*Amend the Building Societies Act 1986.*)

PART V
MISCELLANEOUS AND SUPPLEMENTAL

Miscellaneous

45 (*Amends the Banking Act 1987, s 5(1) and inserts s 5(1A).*)

46 Information to be supplied on request

(1) Each of the following, namely, a UK institution, a building society, an EEA institution and a non-EEA institution, shall secure that the information required by paragraph (4) below is supplied to any depositor or intending depositor who requests it—

    (a) immediately in a case of a request made at a United Kingdom office of the institution; and

    (b) as soon as practicable in any other case.

(2) In its application to UK institutions or building societies which accept deposits at offices in EEA States other than the United Kingdom, paragraph (1) above shall have effect as if the reference to a United Kingdom office included a reference to an office in such a State.

(3) Any information supplied in pursuance of paragraph (1) above shall be supplied in English except that, where the request is made at an office in an EEA State other than the United Kingdom, it shall be supplied instead in an official language of that State.

(4) The information required by this paragraph is as follows—

(a) in the case of a UK institution or building society—

(i) a summary of the provisions of the relevant UK scheme; and
(ii) where the institution or society participates in a relevant host State scheme, details of the level and scope of the supplementary protection afforded by that scheme;

(b) in the case of an EEA institution—

(i) a summary of the provisions of its home State scheme; and
(ii) where the institution participates in a UK scheme, details of the level and scope of the supplementary protection afforded by that scheme;

(c) in the case of a non-EEA institution which is participating in the deposit protection scheme, a summary of the provisions of that scheme;

(d) in the case of a non-EEA institution which is not so participating, a summary of the provisions of its home State scheme.

(5) Any reference in paragraph (4) above to a summary of the provisions of a scheme is a reference to a summary of those provisions which includes (but is not limited to) details of the level and scope of the protection afforded by the Scheme.

(6) Any reference in paragraph (4) above—

(a) to a summary of the provisions of a scheme; or
(b) to details of the level and scope of the supplementary protection afforded by a scheme,

includes a reference to a summary of any conditions that must be fulfilled, and any procedural steps that must be taken, before payments may be made in pursuance of the scheme.

(7) A host State scheme is a relevant host State scheme for the purposes of paragraph (4) above if the request is made at or is communicated to an office in the EEA State in which that scheme is in force.

(8) If the relevant authority is satisfied that it is necessary to do so—

(a) for the purpose of enabling a UK institution or building society which is participating in a host State scheme to comply both—

(i) with the provisions of this regulation; and
(ii) with the corresponding provisions of the law of the EEA State in which that scheme is in force; or

(b) for the purpose of enabling an EEA institution to comply both—

(i) with the provision of this regulation; and
(ii) with the corresponding provisions of the law of its home State,

the relevant authority may, on the application or with the consent of the institution or society, by order direct that any of the provisions of this regulation shall apply in relation to the institution or society with such modifications as may be specified in the order.

(9) In this regulation—

"the relevant authority"—

    (a) in relation to a UK institution or EEA institution, means the Bank;

    (b) in relation to a building society, means the Commission;

"the relevant UK scheme"—

    (a) in relation to a UK institution, means the deposit protection scheme;

    (b) in relation to a building society, means the investor protection scheme.

(10) For the purposes of this regulation and regulations 47 and 48 below—

    (a) any reference to an EEA institution's home State scheme includes a reference to any alternative permitted system or arrangement for the protection of depositors which is in force in the institution's home State and in which the institution participates;

    (b) any reference to an EEA institution participating in a UK scheme is a reference to it doing so in accordance with Chapter I of Part II of these Regulations;

    (c) any reference to a non-EEA institution participating in the deposit protection scheme is a reference to it not being one—

        (i) which has, in accordance with Chapter III of Part II of these Regulations, elected not to participate in that scheme; and

        (ii) whose election under that Chapter is still in force; and

    (d) any reference to a non-EEA institution not so participating shall be construed accordingly.   **[711H]**

47 Information in explanatory literature

(1) Each of the following, namely, a UK institution, a building society, an EEA institution and a non-EEA institution, shall secure that either the information required by regulation 46(4) above or the information required by paragraphs (2) and (3) below is included in any explanatory literature which—

    (a) relates to the making of deposits; and

    (b) is supplied to depositors or intending depositors by the institution or society in the ordinary course of business.

(2) The information required by this paragraph is as follows—

    (a) in the case of a UK institution or a building society, a statement to the effect—

        (i) that most relevant deposits with the institution or society are protected by the relevant UK scheme; and

        (ii) where the institution or society participates in a relevant host State scheme, that supplemental protection is afforded to such deposits by that scheme;

    (b) in the case of an EEA institution, a statement to the effect—

        (i) that most relevant deposits with the institution are protected by its home State scheme; and

        (ii) where the institution participates in a UK scheme, that supplemental protection is afforded to such deposits by that scheme;

    (c) in the case of a non-EEA institution which is participating in the deposit protection scheme, a statement to the effect that most relevant deposits with the institution are protected by that scheme;

    (d) in the case of a non-EEA institution which is not participating in the deposit protection scheme, a statement to the effect that most relevant deposits with the institution are protected by its home State scheme.

(3) The information required by this paragraph is as follows—

    (a) a statement as to the level of the protection afforded by the scheme or, as the case may be, each of the schemes as respects which a statement is required by paragraph (2) above; and

    (b) a statement to the effect that additional information about that scheme or each of those schemes may, in accordance with regulation 46 above, be obtained by any depositor or intending depositor who requests it.

(4) A host State scheme is a relevant host State scheme for the purposes of paragraph (2) above if the explanatory literature is sent from an office in the EEA State in which that scheme is in force.

(5) Paragraph (8) of regulation 46 above applies for the purposes of this regulation as it applies for the purposes of that regulation.

(6) In this regulation—

"ecu" means—

    (a) the European currency unit as defined in Article 1 of Council Regulation No 3320/94/EC; or

    (b) any other unit of account which is defined by reference to the European currency unit as so defined;

"EEA currency" means the currency of an EEA State or ecus;
"relevant deposit", in relation to a UK institution, a building society, an EEA institution or a non-EEA institution, means a deposit in an EEA currency—

    (a) made with a United Kingdom office of the institution or society; or

    (b) in the case of a UK institution or building society, made with an office of the institution or society in another EEA State;

"the relevant UK scheme" has the same meaning as in regulation 46 above. **[711I]**

48 Information in advertisements

(1) In this regulation "deposit advertisement" means any advertisement containing—

    (a) an invitation to make a deposit; or

    (b) information which is intended or might reasonably be presumed to be intended to lead directly or indirectly to the making of a deposit,

and for the purposes of this regulation an advertisement includes any means of bringing such an invitation or such information to the notice of the person or persons to whom it is addressed and any reference to the issue of an advertisement shall be construed accordingly.

(2) Subject to the provisions of this regulation, no deposit advertisement which is issued in the United Kingdom and relates to any of the following, namely, a UK institution, a building society, an EEA institution and a non-EEA institution, shall include any information about—

(a) the protection available to its depositors under the relevant UK scheme; or

(b) the protection so available under any host State scheme or home State scheme.

(3) A deposit advertisement may include—

(a) if it relates to a UK institution or a building society, a statement to the effect—

    (i) that most relevant deposits with the institution or society are protected by the relevant UK scheme; and

    (ii) where the institution or society participates in a host State scheme, that supplemental protection is afforded to such deposits by that scheme;

(b) if it relates to an EEA institution, a statement to the effect—

    (i) that most relevant deposits with the institution are protected by its home State scheme; and

    (ii) where the institution participates in a UK scheme, that supplemental protection is afforded to such deposits by that scheme;

(c) if it relates to a non-EEA institution which is participating in the deposit protection scheme, a statement to the effect that most relevant deposits with the institution are protected by that scheme;

(d) if it relates to a non-EEA institution which is not participating in the deposit protection scheme, a statement to the effect that most relevant deposits with the institution are protected by its home State scheme.

(4) A deposit advertisement which includes a statement authorised by paragraph (3) above may also include—

(a) a statement as to the level of the protection afforded by the scheme or, as the case may be, each of the schemes referred to in the statement so authorised; and

(b) a statement to the effect that additional information about that scheme or each of those schemes may, in accordance with regulation 46 above, be obtained by any depositor or intending depositor who requests it.

(5) Nothing in this regulation shall be taken to prohibit the inclusion, in any explanatory literature which relates to the making of deposits and is supplied to depositors or intending depositors in the ordinary course of business, of any information required by regulation 46(4) above.

(6) In this regulation—

"relevant deposit" has the same meaning as in regulation 47 above;
"the relevant UK scheme"—

(a) in relation to a UK institution, means the deposit protection scheme;

(b) in relation to a building society, means the investor protection scheme;

(c) in relation to a participating EEA institution, means the UK scheme in which it is participating.

(7) Subsections (6) and (7) of section 32 of the 1987 Act (advertisement regulations) shall apply for the purposes of this regulation as they apply for the purposes of that section; and in subsection (6) of that section as it so applies the reference to deposits shall be construed in accordance with regulation 2(2) above.   **[711J]**

NOTE
1987 Act: Banking Act 1987.

Supplemental

49 Enforcement: UK and non-EEA institutions

(1) . . .

(2) In its application to a UK institution or participating non-EEA institution, subsection (2) of section 12 of the 1987 Act (restriction of authorisation) shall have effect as if the reference in paragraph (b) to the protection of the institution's depositors or potential depositors included references to—

(a) securing the payment by the institution of unpaid contributions; and
(b) in the case of a UK institution, securing that the institution complies with any obligation imposed by or under the law of another EEA State in connection with its participation in a scheme for the protection of depositors or investors which is in force in that State.

(3) Where the Bank—

(a) is informed by the Deposit Protection Board of an unpaid contribution of a UK institution or participating non-EEA institution; or
(b) is informed by a supervisory authority in another EEA State that a UK institution is failing to comply with such an obligation as is mentioned in paragraph (2)(b) above,

the Bank shall, after such consultation with that Board or supervisory authority as it considers appropriate, consider whether to exercise its powers under section 11 or 12 of the 1987 Act.

(4) In this regulation "unpaid contribution", in relation to an institution, means any amount specified in a notice served on the institution under subsection (2) of section 52 of the 1987 Act which remains unpaid after the period of 21 days mentioned in that subsection.   **[711K]**

NOTES
Sub-s (1): amends the Banking Act 1987, s 11(1A).
1987 Act: Banking Act 1987.

50 (*Amends SI 1992/3218, reg 9(2)*.)

51 Enforcement: building societies

(1) In relation to any building society, subsection (1) of section 42 of the 1986 Act (imposition of conditions on authorisation) shall have effect as if the reference to protecting the investments of the society's shareholders or depositors included references to—

(a) securing the payment by the society of unpaid contributions; and
(b) securing that the society complies with any obligation imposed by or

under the law of another EEA State in connection with its participation in a scheme for the protection of depositors or investors which is in force in that State.

(2) . . .

(3) Where the Commission—

(a) is informed by the Investor Protection Board of an unpaid contribution of a building society; or

(b) is informed by a supervisory authority in another EEA State that a building society is failing to comply with such an obligation as is mentioned in paragraph (1)(b) above,

the Commission shall, after such consultation with that Board or supervisory authority as it considers appropriate, consider whether to exercise its powers under section 42 or 43 of the 1986 Act.

(4) In this regulation "unpaid contribution", in relation to a building society, means any amount specified in a notice served on the institution under subsection (8) of section 26 of the 1986 Act which remains unpaid after the period of 21 days mentioned in that subsection.   **[711L]**

NOTES
Para (2): amends the Building Societies Act 1986, s 43(1A).
1986 Act: the Building Societies Act 1986.

52 (*Amends the Building Societies Act 1986, s 119(2A) and revokes SI 1988/645, reg 6, the Insolvency (Northern Ireland) Order 1989, SI 1989/2405, Sch 9, paras 42, 43(a), 50(a), (c), 51 and SI 1992/3218, Sch 8, paras 13–16.*)

53 Transitional provisions and savings

(1) The provisions of Part III of these Regulations shall not apply in any case where—

(a) an institution becomes insolvent (within the meaning of Part II of the 1987 Act) at any time before the commencement date and at that time—

(i) it is an authorised institution; or

(ii) it is a former authorised institution (not being a recognised bank or licensed institution excluded by an order under section 23(2) of the Banking Act 1979; or

(b) an administration order is made in relation to an institution under section 8 of the Insolvency Act 1986 or under Article 21 of the Insolvency (Northern Ireland) Order 1989 at any time before the commencement date and at that time it is such an institution as is mentioned in sub-paragraph (a)(i) or (ii) above.

(2) The provisions of Part IV of these Regulations shall not apply in any case where a building society becomes insolvent (within the meaning of Part IV of the 1986 Act) at any time before the commencement date.

(3) Where, as regards a UK institution or non-EEA institution, the Bank is satisfied before the commencement date that, for reasons which directly relate to the institution's financial circumstances, the institution—

(a) is unable to repay protected deposits which are due and payable; and

(b) has no current prospect of being able to do so,

the 21 days mentioned in subsection (4)(a) of section 59 of the 1987 Act shall begin to run on that date.

(4) Where, as regards a building society, the Commission is satisfied before the commencement date that, for reasons which directly relate to the society's financial circumstances, the society—

(a) is unable to repay investments which are due and payable; and
(b) has no current prospect of being able to do so,

the 21 days mentioned in subsection (4)(a) of section 25A of the 1986 Act shall begin to run on that date.

(5) In this regulation "authorised institution" and "former authorised institution" have the same meanings as in the 1987 Act. **[711M]**

NOTES

1987 Act: the Banking Act 1987.
1986 Act: the Building Societies Act 1986.

54 Transitory provisions

(1) This regulation applies to any institution which—

(a) is authorised to act as a credit institution by a supervisory authority in Spain or Greece;
(b) is listed in Annex III to Directive 94/19/EC on deposit-guarantee schemes; and
(c) accepts or proposes to accept deposits in the United Kingdom.

(2) In relation to any time before 1st January 2000, these Regulations, Part II of the 1987 Act and Part IV of the 1986 Act shall each have effect in relation to an institution to which this regulation applies as if—

(a) the institution were an authorised institution (within the meaning of the 1987 Act); and
(b) Spain or, as the case may require, Greece were not an EEA State.
[711N]

NOTES

1987 Act: the Banking Act 1987.
1986 Act: the Building Societies Act 1986.

CIVIL AVIATION ACT 1982

MORTGAGING OF AIRCRAFT ORDER 1972
(SI 1972/1268)

NOTES .
  Made: 14 August 1972.
  Authority: Civil Aviation Act 1968, s 16 (now repealed); takes effect as if made under the Civil
Aviation Act 1982, s 86.
  Commencement: 1 October 1972.

Citation and Commencement

1   This Order may be cited as the Mortgaging of Aircraft Order 1972 and shall
come into operation on 1st October 1972.   **[712]**

Interpretation

2—(1) The Interpretation Act 1889 applies for the interpretation of this Order
as it applies for the interpretation of an Act of Parliament.

   (2) In this Order:

   "appropriate charge" means the charge payable under section 9 of the
        Civil Aviation Act 1971;
   "the Authority" means the Civil Aviation Authority;
   "mortgage of an aircraft" includes a mortgage which extends to any store
        of spare parts for that aircraft but does not otherwise include a
        mortgage created as a floating charge;
   "owner" means the person shown as the owner of a mortgaged aircraft
        on the form of application for registration of that aircraft in the
        United Kingdom nationality register;
   "United Kingdom nationality register" means the register of aircraft
        maintained by the Authority in pursuance of an Order in Council
        under section 8 of the Civil Aviation Act 1949.   **[713]**

Mortgage of aircraft

3   An aircraft registered in the United Kingdom nationality register or such an
aircraft together with any store of spare parts for that aircraft may be made
security for a loan or other valuable consideration.   **[714]**

Registration of Aircraft Mortgages

4—(1) Any mortgage of an aircraft registered in the United Kingdom nationality register may be entered in the Register of Aircraft Mortgages kept by the
Authority.

   (2) Applications to enter a mortgage in the Register shall be made to the
Authority by or on behalf of the mortgagee in the form set out in Part I of
Schedule 1 hereto, and shall be accompanied by a copy of the mortgage, which
the applicant shall certify to be a true copy, and the appropriate charge. **[715]**

5—(1) A notice of intention to make an application to enter a contemplated
mortgage of an aircraft in the Register (hereinafter referred to as "a priority
notice") may also be entered in the Register.

   (2) Applications to enter a priority notice in the Register shall be made to
the Authority by or on behalf of the prospective mortgagee in the form set out

in Part II of Schedule 1 hereto, and shall be accompanied by the appropriate charge. **[716]**

6—(1) Where two or more aircraft are the subject of one mortgage or where the same aircraft is the subject of two or more mortgages, separate applications shall be made in respect of each aircraft or of each mortgage, as the case may be.

(2) Where a mortgage is in a language other than English, the application to enter that mortgage in the Register shall be accompanied not only by a copy of that mortgage but also by a translation thereof, which the applicant shall certify as being, to the best of his knowledge and belief, a true translation. **[717]**

7—(1) When an application to enter a mortgage or priority notice in the Register is duly made, the Authority shall enter the mortgage or the priority notice, as the case may be, in the Register by placing the application form therein and by noting on it the date and the time of the entry.

(2) Applications duly made shall be entered in the Register in order of their receipt by the Authority.

(3) The Authority shall by notice in its Official Record specify the days on which the hours during which its office is open for registering mortgages and priority notices. Any application delivered when the office is closed for that purpose shall be treated as having bean received immediately after the office is next opened.

(4) The Authority shall notify the applicant of the date and time of the entry of the mortgage or the priority notice, as the case may be, in the Register and of the register number of the entry and shall send a copy of the notification to the mortgagor and the owner. **[718]**

Amendment of entries in the Register

8—(1) Any change in the person appearing in the Register as mortgagee or as mortgagor or in the name or address of such person or in the description of the mortgaged property shall be notified to the Authority by or on behalf of the mortgagee, in the form set out in Part III of Schedule 1 hereto.

(2) On receipt of the said form, duly completed and signed by or on behalf of the mortgagor and the mortgagee and on payment of the appropriate charge, the Authority shall enter the notification in the Register and shall notify the mortgagor, the mortgagee and the owner that it has done so. **[719]**

Discharge of Mortgages

[**9** On receipt of the form set out in Part IV of Schedule 1 hereto duly completed and signed by or on behalf of the mortgagee and of a copy of the document of discharge or receipt for the mortgage money, or of any other document which shows, to the satisfaction of the Authority, that the mortgage has been discharged and on payment of the appropriate charge, the Authority shall enter the said form in the Register and mark the relevant entries in the Register "Discharged", and shall notify the mortgagee, mortgagor and the owner that it has done so.] **[720]**

NOTES

Commencement: 1 May 1981.
Substituted by SI 1981/611.

Rectification of the Register

10 Any of the following courts, that is to say the High Court of Justice in England, the Court of Session in Scotland and the High Court of Justice in Northern Ireland may order such amendments to be made to the Register as may appear to the court to be necessary or expedient for correcting any error therein. On being served with the order the Authority shall make the necessary amendment to the Register.   **[721]**

Inspection of Register and copies of entries

11—(1) On such days and during such hours as the Authority may specify in its Official Record, any person may, on application to the Authority and on payment to it of the appropriate charge inspect any entry in the Register specified in the application.

(2) The Authority shall, on the application of any person and on payment by him of the appropriate charge, supply to the applicant a copy, certified as a true copy, of the entries in the Register specified in the application.

(3) The Authority shall, on the application of any person and on payment by him of the appropriate charge, notify the applicant whether or not there are any entries in the Register relating to any aircraft specified in the application by reference to its nationality and registration marks.

(4) A document purporting to be a copy of an entry in the Register shall be admissible as evidence of that entry if it purports to be certified as a true copy by the Authority.

(5) Nothing done in pursuance of paragraph (2) or (3) of this Article shall affect the priority of any mortgage.   **[722]**

Removal of aircraft from the United Kingdom Nationality Register

12 The removal of an aircraft from the United Kingdom nationality register shall not affect the rights of any mortgagee under any registered mortgage and entries shall continue to be made in the Register in relation to the mortgage as if the aircraft had not been removed from the United Kingdom nationality register.   **[723]**

Register as notice of facts appearing in it

13 All persons shall at all times be taken to have express notice of all facts appearing in the Register, but the registration of a mortgage shall not be evidence of its validity.   **[724]**

Priority of Mortgages

14—(1) Subject to the following provisions of this article, a mortgage of an aircraft entered in the Register shall have priority over any other mortgage of or charge on that aircraft, other than another mortgage entered in the Register: provided that mortgages made before 1st October 1972, whether entered in the Register or not, shall up to and including 31st December 1972 have the same priority as they would have had if this Order had not been made.

(2) Subject to the following provisions of this article, where two or more mortgages of an aircraft are entered in the Register, those mortgages shall as between themselves have priority according to the times at which they were respectively entered in the Register:

Provided that:

> (i) mortgages of an aircraft made before 1st October 1972 which are entered in the Register before 31st December 1972 shall have priority over any mortgages of that aircraft made on or after 1st October 1972 and shall as between themselves have the same priority as they would have had if this Order had not been made;
>
> (ii) without prejudice to proviso (i), where a priority notice has been entered in the Register and the contemplated mortgage referred to therein is made and entered in the Register within 14 days thereafter that mortgage shall be deemed to have priority from the time when the priority notice was registered.

(3) In reckoning the period of 14 days under the preceding paragraph of this article, there shall be excluded any day which the Authority has by notice in its Official Record specified as a day on which its office is not open for registration of mortgages.

(4) The priorities provided for by the preceding provisions of this article shall have effect notwithstanding any express, implied or constructive notice affecting the mortgagee.

(5) Nothing in this article shall be construed as giving a registered mortgage any priority over any possessory lien in respect of work done on the aircraft (whether before or after the creation or registration of the mortgage) on the express or implied authority of any persons lawfully entitled to possession of the aircraft or over any right to detain the aircraft under any Act of Parliament.

[725]

15 (*Revoked by SI 1986/2001.*)

Application of Bills of Sale Acts and registration provisions of the Companies Act

16—(1) The provisions of the Bills of Sale Acts 1878 and 1882 and the Bills of Sale (Ireland) Acts 1879 and 1883 insofar as they relate to bills of sale and other documents given by way of security for the payment of money shall not apply to any mortgage of an aircraft registered in the United Kingdom nationality register, which is made on or after 1st October 1972.

(2) Section 95(2)(h) of the Companies Act 1948, section 106A(2)(d) of that Act as set out in the Companies (Floating Charges) (Scotland) Act 1961 or any re-enactment thereof and section 93(2)(h) of the Companies Act (Northern Ireland) 1960 shall have effect as if after the word "ship" where it first occurs in each case there were inserted the words "or aircraft":

Provided that nothing in this paragraph shall render invalid as against the liquidator or creditor of the company, any mortgage or charge created by a company before the date on which this Order comes into force which would not have been invalid against the liquidator or such a creditor if this Order had not been made.

[726]

False Statement and Forgery

17—(1) If, in furnishing any information for the purpose of this Order, any person makes any statement which he knows to be false in a material particular, or recklessly makes any statement which is false in a material particular, he shall be guilty of an offence.

(2) Any person guilty of an offence under paragraph (1) of this article shall:—

    (a) on summary conviction be liable to a fine not exceeding [the statutory maximum];

    (b) on conviction on indictment be liable to a fine of such amount as the court think fit or to imprisonment for a term not exceeding 2 years or to both such a fine and such imprisonment.

(3) Without prejudice to any rule of the law of Scotland relating to forging and uttering, the Forgery Act 1913 shall apply in relation to documents forwarded to the Authority in pursuance of this Order as if such documents were included in the list of documents in section 3(3) of that Act.   **[727]**

NOTE

Para (2): reference to the statutory maximum substituted by virtue of the Criminal Justice Act 1988, s 51.

Indemnity

18—(1) Subject to paragraph (2) of this article, any person who suffers loss by reason of any error or omission in the Register or of any inaccuracy in a copy of an entry in the Register supplied pursuant to Article 11(2) of this Order or in a notification made pursuant to Article 11(3) of this Order shall be indemnified by the Authority.

(2) No indemnity shall be payable under this article:

    (a) where the person who has suffered loss has himself caused or substantially contributed to the loss by his fraud or has derived title from a person so committing fraud;

    (b) on account of costs or expenses incurred in taking or defending any legal proceedings without the consent of the Authority.   **[728]**

19 (*Applies to Scotland only.*)

SCHEDULE 1
FORMS
PART I
REGISTER OF AIRCRAFT MORTGAGES

Article 4(2)

Entry of Aircraft Mortgage

To be completed by Applicant:—

I hereby apply for the mortgage, particulars of which are given below, to be entered in the Register of Aircraft Mortgages.

    1. Date of mortgage.

    2. Description of the mortgaged aircraft (including its type, nationality and registration marks and aircraft serial number) and of any store of spare parts for that aircraft to which the mortgage extends.
(The description of the store of spare parts must include an indication of their character and approximate number and the place or places where they are stored must be given *1).

    3. The sum secured by the mortgage *2.

    4. Does the mortgage require the mortgagee to make further advances? If so, of what amount?

    5. Name and address and, where applicable, company registration number of the mortgagor.

    6. Register number of priority notice, if any.

    *1 The description of the mortgaged property may, if necessary, be continued on a separate sheet, which shall be signed by the applicant.

    *2 Where the sum secured is of a fluctuating amount this should be stated and the upper and lower limits, if any, should be set out.

    *3 Delete where inapplicable.

Signed ....

Name in block capitals ....

On behalf of *3 ....

(insert name and, where applicable, company registration number of mortgagee)

of ....

(insert address of mortgagee)

PART II

REGISTER OF AIRCRAFT MORTGAGES

Article 5(2)

Entry of Priority Notice

To be completed by Applicant:—

I hereby give notice that I am contemplating entering into a mortgage, particulars of which are given below, and that if I do enter into the said mortgage I shall apply for it to be entered in the Register of Aircraft Mortgages. I hereby apply for this notice to be entered in the said Register.

1. Description of the aircraft which is the subject of the contemplated mortgage (including its type, nationality and registration marks and aircraft serial number) and of any store of spare parts for that aircraft to which it is contemplated that the mortgage will extend. *1.

2. The sum to be secured by the contemplated mortgage. *2.

3. Is it contemplated that the mortgage will require the mortgagee to make further advances? If so, of what amount?

4. Name and address and, where applicable, company registration number of the prospective mortgagor.

*1 The description of the property which is the subject of the contemplated mortgage may, if necessary, be continued on a separate sheet which shall be signed by the applicant.

*2 Where the sum to be secured is of a fluctuating amount, this should be stated and the upper and lower limits, if any, should be set out.

*3 Delete where inapplicable.

Signed ....

Name in block capitals ....

On behalf of *3 ....

(insert name and, where applicable, company registration number of mortgagee)

of ....

(insert address of mortgagee)

PART III
REGISTER OF AIRCRAFT MORTGAGES
Article 8(1)

Change in Particulars

We hereby give notice that the particulars show on the Register of Aircraft Mortgages under Register number .... should be amended as follows:—

(*a*) Signed ....
    Name in block capitals ....
    on behalf of *1 ....
    (insert name of mortgagee)

(*b*) Signed ....
    Name in block capitals ....
    on behalf of *1 ....
    (insert name of person shown in the
    Register as the mortgagee)*2

(*c*) Signed ....
    Name in block capitals ....
    on behalf of *1 ....
    (insert name of mortgagor)

*1 Delete where inapplicable
*2 Applicable only where the change in particulars is a change in the person appearing in the Register as mortgagee.

[PART IV
REGISTER OF AIRCRAFT MORTGAGES]
Article 9

Discharge of registered mortgage

I hereby confirm that the mortgage entered in the Register of Aircraft Mortgages under register number .... has been discharged.

Signed ....
Name in block capitals ....
On behalf of * ....
(insert name of mortgagee)

* Delete where inapplicable]

[729]

NOTE
  Part IV: substituted by SI 1981/611.

(Sch 2 applies to Scotland only.)

MERCHANT SHIPPING ACT 1995

MERCHANT SHIPPING (REGISTRATION OF SHIPS) REGULATIONS 1993
(SI 1993/3138)

NOTES
Made: 14 December 1993.
Authority: Merchant Shipping (Registration, etc) Act 1993, ss 2, 3, 5(2), 7(5), 9(5), Sch 1 (repealed as from 1 January 1996); take effect from that date as if made under the Merchant Shipping Act 1995, ss 9, 10, 15(2), 17(5), Sch 1.
Commencement: 21 March 1994.

PART I
GENERAL

1 Citation, commencement and interpretation

(1) These Regulations may be cited as the Merchant Shipping (Registration of Ships) Regulations 1993 and shall come into force on 21st March 1994.

(2) In these Regulations unless the context otherwise requires:—

"the Act" means the Merchant Shipping (Registration, etc) Act 1993;

"application for registration" includes, except where otherwise stated, application for registration of a ship or share in a ship; application for registration of a small ship; application for re-registration of the same; and application for the registration of a transfer or transmission of a ship or a share in a ship; but not application for the renewal of registration;

. . .

"certificate of registry" means a certificate of registration which is issued to a ship which is registered under the Act and includes a certificate of bareboat charter unless the context otherwise requires;

"certificate of bareboat charter" means a certificate of registration issued to a ship which is registered under section 7 of the Act;

. . .

"fishing vessel" means a vessel within the meaning of paragraph 2(1)(c) of Schedule 4 to the Act;

. . .

"the Register" means the Register of British ships established under section 1 of the Act;

"the Registrar" means the person described as "the registrar" in section 9(2) of the Act;

"representation" means probate, administration, confirmation, or other instrument constituting a person the executor, administrator or other legal representative of a deceased person, including a certificate of confirmation relating to a vessel;

. . .

"ship" includes a fishing vessel but does not include a small ship or a bareboat charter ship except for the purposes of Part XII (Miscellaneous) and Part XIII (Offences);

"small ship" means a ship which is less than 24 metres in overall length and is, or is applying to be, registered under Part XI;

[729A]

. . .

2–56 *((Pts II–VI); these regulations are outside the scope of this work.)*

PART VII

MORTGAGES

57 Form of mortgage

 (a) A mortgage produced for registration under Schedule 1 to the Act,
   and
 (b) a transfer of a registered mortgage, and
 (c) a discharge of a registered mortgage,

shall be in a form approved by [the Secretary of State], in each case with
appropriate attestation.   **[729B]**

NOTES
 Words in square brackets substituted by SI 1994/541, reg 8.
 The Act: Merchant Shipping (Registration, etc) Act 1993; repealed and replaced by the
Merchant Shipping Act 1995 as from 1 January 1996.

58 Registration of mortgage

Where a mortgage executed in accordance with regulation 57 (Form of
mortgage) is produced to the Registrar for registration, he shall:—

 (a) register the mortgage, and
 (b) endorse on it the date and time it was registered.   **[729C]**

59 Notices by intending mortgagees: priority notices

 (1) Where any person who is an intending mortgagee under a proposed
mortgage of:—

 (a) a registered ship, or
 (b) a share in a registered ship,

notifies the Registrar of the interest which it is intended that he should have
under the proposed mortgage, the Registrar shall record that interest.

 (2) For the purpose of paragraph (1) the notice to the Registrar shall be in a
form approved by the Secretary of State and shall contain the name and official
number of the ship, the name address and signature of the intending mortgagor, the number of shares to be mortgaged, and the name and address of the
intending mortgagee.

 (3) Where any person who is an intending mortgagee under a proposed
mortgage of:—

 (a) a ship which is not for the time being registered, or
 (b) a share in any such ship,

notifies the Registrar in writing of the interest which it is intended that he
should have under the proposed mortgage, the Registrar:—

 (i) shall record that interest in the Register, and
 (ii) if the ship is subsequently registered, shall register the ship subject

to that interest or, if the mortgage has by then been executed in accordance with regulation 57 and produced to the Registrar, subject to that mortgage.

(4) For the purposes of paragraph (3) the notice shall be in a form approved by the Secretary of State and contain the following information:—

(a) the present name of the ship;
(b) the intended name of the ship;
(c) the approximate length of the ship;
(d) where the ship is registered outside the United Kingdom, a copy of its certificate of registry or other document evidencing its registration and giving its port of registration;
(e) where the ship is a new ship, the builder's certificate or if that is not available, the name and address of the builder and the ship's yard number;
(f) where the ship is neither a new ship nor a registered ship, details of any permanent marks on the ship which enable it to be clearly identified;
(g) the name, address and signature of the intending mortgagor, the number of shares to be mortgaged, and the name and address of the intending mortgagee.

(5) In a case where:—

(a) paragraph 8 of Schedule 1 to the Act operates to determine the priority between two or more mortgagees, and
(b) any of those mortgages gave notification under paragraph (1) or (3) above with respect to his mortgage,

paragraph 8 of the said Schedule shall have effect in relation to that mortgage as if it had been registered at the time when the relevant entry was made in the Register under the said paragraphs (1) or (3).

(6) Any notification given by a person under paragraphs (1) or (3) (and anything done as a result of it) shall cease to have effect:—

(a) if the notification is withdrawn, or
(b) at the end of the period of 30 days beginning with the date of the notification, unless the notification is renewed in accordance with paragraph (7).

(7) The person by whom any such notification is given may renew or further renew the notification on each occasion for a period of 30 days, by notice in writing given to the Registrar:—

(a) before the end of the period mentioned in paragraph (6)(b), or
(b) before the end of a period of renewal,

as the case may be.

(8) Any notice given under this regulation shall be in a form approved by the Secretary of State. **[729D]**

NOTE
The Act: Merchant Shipping (Registration, etc) Act 1993; repealed and replaced by the Merchant Shipping Act 1995 as from 1 January 1996.

[60 Evidence of transmission of mortgage

On the application for registration of a transmission of a registered mortgage as mentioned in paragraph 12 of Schedule 1 to the Act the evidence to be produced to the Registrar shall be:—

    (a) a declaration of transmission of mortgage in a form approved by the Secretary of State; and

    (b)   (i) if the transmission was consequent on death, the grant of representation or an office copy thereof or of an extract therefrom;

        (ii) if the transmission was consequent on bankruptcy such evidence as is for the time being receivable in courts of justice as proof of title of persons claiming under bankruptcy;

        (iii) if the transmission was consequent on an order of a court, a copy of the order of that court.]   **[729E]**

NOTES

  This regulation was substituted by SI 1994/541, reg 9.

  The Act: Merchant Shipping (Registration, etc) Act 1993; repealed and replaced by the Merchant Shipping Act 1995 as from 1 January 1996.

61 Transfer or transmission of registered mortgage

[Where a transfer of a registered mortgage or evidence of a transmission is produced to the Registrar, he shall:—

    (a) enter the name of the transferee, or the name of the person to whom the mortgage has been transmitted, in the Register as mortgagee of the ship or share in question;

    (b) in respect of a transfer, endorse on the instrument of transfer the date and time the entry was made.]   **[729F]**

NOTE

  This regulation was substituted by SI 1994/541, reg 10.

62 Discharge of mortgages

(1) Where a registered mortgage has been discharged, the Registrar shall, on production of the mortgage deed and with such evidence of the discharge as satisfies him that the mortgage has been discharged, record in the Register that the mortgage has been discharged.

(2) If for good reason the registered mortgage cannot be produced to the Registrar, he may, on being satisfied that the mortgage has been properly discharged, record in the Register that the mortgage has been discharged.

63 Effect of termination of registration on registered mortgage

Where the registration of a ship terminates by virtue of any of these Regulations, that termination shall not affect any entry in the Register of any undischarged registered mortgage of that ship or any share in it.   **[729H]**

64–122 *((Pts VIII–XV); these regulations are outside the scope of this work.)*

(Schs 1–5 are outside the scope of this work.)

INTERNATIONAL MONETARY FUND ACT 1979

INTERNATIONAL MONETARY FUND (IMMUNITIES AND PRIVILEGES) ORDER 1977
(SI 1977/825)

NOTES

Made: 11 May 1977.

Authority: Bretton Woods Agreement Act 1945, s 3(3) (now repealed) and International Organisations Act 1968, s 1; in so far as made under the 1945 Act, s 3(3), now takes effect as if made under the International Monetary Fund Act 1979, s 5.

Commencement: 1 April 1978 (save for provisions relating to Council representatives, which come into operation when that Council is established).

1—(1) This Order may be cited as the International Monetary Fund (Immunities and Privileges) Order 1977.

   (2) (a) Articles 1 to 6 of this Order shall come into operation on the date on which the Second Amendment to the Articles of Agreement of the International Monetary Fund enters into force. This date shall be notified in the London, Edinburgh and Belfast Gazettes.

      (b) Article 7 of this Order shall come into operation on the date on which a Council is established under Article XII, Section 1 of the Articles of Agreement of the International Monetary Fund as amended (hereinafter referred to as the Fund Agreement). This date shall be notified in the London, Edinburgh and Belfast Gazettes. **[730]**

2 The Interpretation Act 1889 shall apply for the interpretation of this Order as it applies for the interpretation of an Act of Parliament. **[731]**

3 (*Revokes section 8 of Art IX of the Fund Agreement in Pt I of the Schedule to S R & O 1946/36.*)

4 The International Monetary Fund (hereinafter referred to as the Fund) is an organisation of which the United Kingdom and foreign sovereign Powers are members. **[732]**

Representatives

5—(1) All Governors, Executive Directors, Alternates, members of committees, and representatives of Member States appointed to attend a meeting of the Executive Board under Article XII, Section 3(j) of the Fund Agreement shall enjoy immunity from suit and legal process with respect to acts performed by them in their official capacity except when the Fund waives this immunity.

   (2) Part IV of Schedule I to the Act shall not operate so as to confer any immunity on the families of persons to whom this Article applies.

   (3) Part IV of Schedule I to the Act shall not operate so as to confer any immunity on the official staff, other than advisers, of persons to whom this Article applies.

   (4) This Article shall not operate so as to confer any immunity on any person as the representative of Her Majesty's Government in the United Kingdom or as a member of the staff of such a representative. **[733]**

Officers

6 All officers and employees of the Fund shall enjoy immunity from suit and legal process with respect to acts performed by them in their official capacity except when the Fund waives this immunity.   **[734]**

Representatives to the Council

7—(1) All Councillors, their Alternates and Associates shall enjoy immunity from suit and legal process with respect to acts performed by them in their official capacity except when the Fund waives this immunity.

(2) Part IV of Schedule I to the Act shall not operate so as to confer any immunity on the families of persons to whom this Article applies.

(3) Part IV of Schedule I to the Act shall not operate so as to confer any immunity on the official staff, other than advisers, of persons to whom this Article applies.

(4) This Article shall not operate so as to confer any immunity on any person as the representative of Her Majesty's Government in the United Kingdom or as a member of the staff of such a representative.   **[735]**

INTERNATIONAL ORGANISATIONS ACT 1968

EUROPEAN BANK FOR RECONSTRUCTION AND DEVELOPMENT (IMMUNITIES AND PRIVILEGES) ORDER 1991
(SI 1991/757)

NOTES
Made: 20 March 1991.
Authority: International Organisations Act 1968, s 1.
Commencement: 15 April 1991.

PART I
GENERAL

1 Citation, Entry into Force and Revocation

(1) This Order may be cited as the European Bank for Reconstruction and Development (Immunities and Privileges) Order 1991 and shall come into force on the date on which the Headquarters Agreement between the Government of the United Kingdom of Great Britain and Northern Ireland and the European Bank for Reconstruction and Development enters into force. That date will be notified in the London, Edinburgh and Belfast Gazettes.

(2) (*Revokes SI 1990/2142.*)   [736]

2 Interpretation

In this Order:

(a) "the 1961 Convention Articles" means the Articles (being certain Articles of the Vienna Convention on Diplomatic Relations signed in 1961) which are set out in Schedule 1 to the Diplomatic Privileges Act 1964;

(b) "Agreement Establishing the Bank" means the Agreement Establishing the European Bank for Reconstruction and Development signed in Paris on 29th May 1990, and any amendments thereto;

(c) "Bank" means the European Bank for Reconstruction and Development;

(d) the terms "Member", "President", "Vice-President", "Governor", "Alternate Governor", "Temporary Alternate Governor", "Board of Governors", "Director", "Alternate Director" and "Temporary Alternate Director", "Board of Directors", have the same meaning as in the Agreement Establishing the Bank, its By-laws or Rules of Procedure;

(e) "Premises of the Bank" means the land, buildings and parts of buildings, including access facilities, used for the Official Activities of the Bank;

(f) "Representatives of Members" means heads of delegations of Members participating in meetings convened by the Bank other than meetings of the Board of Governors or the Board of Directors;

(g) "Members of Delegation" means alternates, advisers, technical experts and secretaries of delegations of Representatives of Members;

(h) "Officers" means the President, the Vice-President and other persons appointed by the President to be Officers of the Bank;

(i) "Employees of the Bank" means the staff of the Bank excluding those staff both recruited locally and assigned to hourly rates of pay;

(j) "Archives of the Bank" includes all records, correspondence, documents, manuscripts, still and moving pictures and films, sound recordings, computer programmes and written materials, video tapes or discs, and discs or tapes containing data belonging to, or held by, the Bank;

(k) "Official Activities of the Bank" includes all activities undertaken pursuant to the Agreement Establishing the Bank, and all activities appropriate to fulfil its purpose and functions under Articles 1 and 2 of that Agreement, or undertaken in exercise of its powers under Article 20 of that Agreement including its administrative activities; and

(l) "Persons Connected with the Bank" means Governors, Alternate Governors, Temporary Alternate Governors, Representatives of Members, Members of Delegations, Directors, Alternate Directors, Temporary Alternate Directors, the President, the Vice-Presidents, Officers and Employees of the Bank, and experts performing missions for the Bank.   **[737]**

PART II

THE BANK

3 The Bank is an organisation of which the United Kingdom and other sovereign Powers are members.   **[738]**

4 The Bank shall have the legal capacities of a body corporate.   **[739]**

5—(1) Except to the extent that the Board of Directors of the Bank shall have waived immunity, the Bank shall have immunity from suit and legal process—

(a) where the Bank has no office in the United Kingdom, nor has appointed an agent in the United Kingdom for the purpose of accepting service or notice of process, nor has issued or guaranteed securities in the United Kingdom; or

(b) where actions are brought by any member of the Bank or by any person acting for or deriving claims from any member of the Bank; or

(c) in respect of any form of seizure of, or restraint, attachment or execution on, the property or assets of the Bank, wheresoever located or by whomsoever held, before the delivery of final judgment against the Bank; or

(d) in respect of the search, requisition, confiscation or expropriation of, or any other form of interference with, or taking of or foreclosure on, the property or assets of the Bank, wheresoever located and by whomsoever held.

(2) Without prejudice to paragraph (1), the Bank shall, within the scope of its Official Activities, have immunity from suit and legal process, except that the immunity of the Bank shall not apply—

(a) to the extent that the Bank shall have expressly waived any such immunity in any particular case or in any written document;

   (b) in respect of a civil action arising out of the exercise of its powers to borrow money, to guarantee obligations and to buy or sell or underwrite the sale of any securities;

   (c) in respect of a civil action by a third party for damage arising from a road traffic accident caused by an Officer or an Employee of the Bank acting on behalf of the Bank;

   (d) in respect of a civil action relating to death or personal injury caused by an act or omission in the United Kingdom;

   (e) in respect of the enforcement of an arbitration award made against the Bank as a result of an express submission to arbitration by or on behalf of the Bank; or

   (f) in respect of any counter-claim directly connected with court proceedings initiated by the Bank.   **[740]**

6—(1) The Premises of the Bank and the Archives of the Bank shall have the like inviolability as, in accordance with the 1961 Convention Articles, is accorded in respect of the official archives and premises of a diplomatic mission, except that the Premises of the Bank may be entered with the consent of and under conditions approved by the President; such consent may be assumed in the case of fire or other disasters requiring prompt action.

(2) The Premises of the Bank may be entered in connection with fire prevention, sanitary regulations or emergencies without the prior consent of the Bank in such circumstances and in such a manner as may have been determined by any agreement for that purpose entered into between the Government and the Bank.   **[741]**

7 Within the scope of its Official Activities the Bank, its property, assets, income and profits shall have exemption from income tax, capital gains tax and corporation tax.   **[742]**

8 The Bank shall have the like relief from rates on the Premises of the Bank as in accordance with Article 23 of the 1961 Convention Articles is accorded in respect of the premises of a diplomatic mission.   **[743]**

9 The Bank shall have exemption from duties (whether of customs or excise) and taxes on the importation by it or on its behalf of goods necessary for the exercise of the Official Activities of the Bank and on the importation of any publications of the Bank imported by it or on its behalf, such exemption to be subject to compliance with such conditions as the Commissioners of Customs and Excise may prescribe for the protection of the Revenue.   **[744]**

10 The Bank shall have exemption from prohibitions and restrictions on importation or exportation in the case of goods imported or exported by the Bank and necessary for the exercise of its Official Activities and in the case of any publications of the Bank imported or exported by it.   **[745]**

11 The Bank shall have relief, under arrangements made by the Commissioners of Customs and Excise, by way of refund of duty (whether of customs or excise) paid on imported hydrocarbon oil (within the meaning of the Hydrocarbon Oil Duties Act 1979) or value added tax paid on the importation of such oil which is bought in the United Kingdom and is necessary for the exercise of its Official Activities, such relief to be subject to compliance with such conditions as may be imposed in accordance with the arrangements.   **[746]**

12 The Bank shall have relief, under arrangements made by Secretary of State, by way of refund of car tax and value added tax paid on any official vehicle and value added tax paid on the supply of any goods or services which are supplied for the Official Activities of the Bank, such relief to be subject to compliance with such conditions as may be imposed in accordance with the arrangements.

[747]

PART III

PERSONS CONNECTED WITH THE BANK

13—(1) A Person Connected with the Bank shall enjoy—

(a) immunity from suit and legal process, even after the termination of his mission or service, in respect of acts performed by him in his official capacity including words written or spoken by him, except in respect of civil liability in the case of damage arising from a road traffic accident caused by him;

(b) such immunity from suit and legal process as is necessary to ensure that all their official papers and documents have the like inviolability as, in accordance with the 1961 Convention Articles, is accorded in respect of official archives of a diplomatic mission.

(2) In addition to the immunities set out in paragraph (1), Directors, Alternate Directors, Officers and Employees, and experts performing missions for the Bank under contract longer than 18 months shall, at the time of first taking up their post in the United Kingdom, be exempt from duties (whether of customs or excise) and taxes on the importation of articles (except payments for services) in respect of import of their furniture and personal effects (including one motor car each), and the furniture and personal effects of members of their family forming part of their household, which are in their ownership or possession or already ordered by them and intended for their personal use or for their establishment.

(3) In addition to the privileges and immunities set out in paragraph (1), Governors, Alternate Governors, and Representatives of Members shall enjoy—

(i) the like exemption from duties (whether of customs or excise) and taxes on the importation of their personal baggage, and the like privilege as to the importation of such articles, as in accordance with paragraph 1 of Article 36 of the 1961 Convention Articles is accorded to a diplomatic agent;

(ii) the like exemption and privileges in respect of their personal baggage as in accordance with paragraph 2 of Article 36 of the 1961 Convention Articles are accorded to a diplomatic agent;

(iii) such immunity from suit and legal process as is necessary to ensure that their personal baggage cannot be seized;

(iv) immunity from arrest or detention.

(4) In addition to the immunities set out in paragraph (1), the President and five Vice-Presidents, as nominated by the President, shall enjoy—

(a) the like immunity from suit and legal process, the like inviolability of residence and the like exemption or relief from taxes (other than income tax in respect of their emoluments and duties and taxes on the importation of goods) as are accorded to or in respect of a diplomatic agent;

(b) the like exemption or relief from being subject to a community charge, or being liable to pay anything in respect of a community charge or anything by way of contribution in respect of a collective community charge, as is accorded to or in respect of a diplomatic agent;

(c) the like exemption from duties and taxes on the importation of articles imported for their personal use, including articles intended for their establishment, as in accordance with paragraph 1 of Article 36 of the 1961 Convention Articles is accorded to a diplomatic agent;

(d) the like exemption and privileges in respect of their personal baggage as in accordance with paragraph 2 of Article 36 of the 1961 Convention Articles are accorded to a diplomatic agent;

(e) relief, under arrangements made by the Commissioners of Customs and Excise, by way of refund of duty (whether of customs or excise) or value added tax paid on any hydrocarbon oil (within the meaning of the Hydrocarbon Oil Duties Act 1979) which is bought in the United Kingdom by them or on their behalf and which is for the personal use or for that of members of their family forming part of their household, such relief to be subject to compliance with such conditions as may be imposed in accordance with the arrangements.

(5) Paragraphs (2), (3) and (4) of this Article shall not apply to any person who is a British citizen, a British Dependent Territories citizen, a British Overseas citizen, or a British National (Overseas), or who is a permanent resident of the United Kingdom.

(6) Part IV of Schedule 1 to the Act shall not operate so as to confer any privilege or immunity on the official staff of representatives other than Members of Delegations, nor so as to confer any privilege or immunity on the family of any person to whom this Article applies.

(7) Neither the provisions of the preceding paragraphs of this Article, nor those of Part IV of Schedule 1 to the Act, shall operate so as to confer any privilege or immunity on any persons as the representative of the United Kingdom or as a member of the delegation of such a representative.

(8) Any privilege or immunity conferred by the preceding paragraphs of this Article may be waived as follows:—

(i) in the case of any privilege or immunity conferred on any officer or employee of the Bank (other than the President or a Vice-President), or on an expert performing a mission for the Bank, by the President;

(ii) in the case of any privilege or immunity conferred on the President or a Vice-President, by the Board of Directors;

(iii) in the case of any privilege or immunity conferred on a Representative of a Member or a member of his delegation, by the Member concerned. **[748]**

NOTE
The Act: International Organisations Act 1968.

14—(1) As from the date on which an internal effective tax for the benefit of the Bank on the salaries and emoluments paid to him by the Bank is applied, any Director, Alternate, Officer and Employee of the Bank shall enjoy exemption from income tax in respect of such salaries and emoluments, provided that nothing in this paragraph shall be interpreted as precluding such salaries and emoluments from being taken into account for the purpose of assessing the amount of taxation to be applied to income from other sources.

(2) Paragraph (1) of this Article shall not apply to pensions or annuities paid by the Bank. **[749]**

15 As from the date on which the Bank establishes or joins a social security scheme, the Directors, Alternate Directors, Officers and Employees of the Bank shall enjoy exemptions whereby for the purposes of the enactments relating to social security, including enactments in force in Northern Ireland—

    (i) services rendered for the Bank by them shall be deemed to be excepted from any class of employment in respect of which contributions or premiums under those enactments are payable, but

    (ii) no person shall be rendered liable to pay any contribution or premium which he would not be required to pay if those services were not deemed to be so excepted. **[750]**

OVERSEAS DEVELOPMENT AND CO-OPERATION ACT 1980

BRETTON WOODS AGREEMENTS ORDER
IN COUNCIL 1946
(SR&O 1946/36)

NOTES

Made: 10 January 1946.

Authority: Bretton Woods Agreements Act 1945, s 3 (now repealed); now takes effect, so far as applies to the International Monetary Fund, under the International Monetary Fund Act 1979, s 5, and so far as applies to the International Bank, under the Overseas Development and Co-operation Act 1980, s 9.

Commencement: 10 January 1946.

1 This Order may be cited as "The Bretton Woods Agreements Order in Council 1946."   [751]

2—(1) In this Order, the expressions "the Fund Agreement" and "the Bank Agreement" mean, respectively, the Agreement for the establishment and operation of an international body to be called the International Monetary Fund and the Agreement for the establishment and operation of an international body to be called the International Bank for Reconstruction and Development, which were signed on behalf of His Majesty's Government in the United Kingdom on the twenty-seventh day of December, nineteen hundred and forty-five, and the expressions "the Fund" and "the Bank" mean the bodies established under these Agreements respectively.

(2) The Interpretation Act 1889, shall apply to the interpretation of this Order as it applies to the interpretation of an Act of Parliament.   [752]

3 To enable the Fund and the Bank to fulfil the functions with which they are respectively entrusted, the provisions of the Fund Agreement and the Bank Agreement set out in the Schedule to this Order shall have the force of law:

Provided that nothing in Section 9 of Article IX of the Fund Agreement or in Section 9 of Article VII of the Bank Agreement shall be construed as—

(a) entitling the Fund or the Bank to import goods free of customs duty without any restriction on their subsequent sale in the country to which they were imported; or

(b) conferring on the Fund or the Bank any exemption from duties or taxes which form part of the price of goods sold [, except that the Fund and the Bank shall have relief, under arrangements made by the Secretary of State, by way of refund of car tax paid on any vehicles and value added tax paid on the supply of any goods and services which are necessary for the exercise of the official activities of the Fund or the Bank, such relief to be subject to compliance with such conditions as may be imposed in accordance with the arrangements]; or

(c) conferring on the Fund or the Bank any exemption from taxes or duties which are in fact no more than charges for services rendered.
                                                                           [753]

NOTE

Words in square brackets inserted by the International Organisations (Immunities and Privileges) Miscellaneous Provisions Order 1976, SI 1976/221, art 3.

4 This Order shall extend to all parts of His Majesty's dominions (other than Dominions within the meaning of the Statute of Westminster 1931, territories administered by the Government of any such Dominion and British India) and, to the extent that His Majesty has jurisdiction therein, to all other territories in which His Majesty has from time to time jurisdiction (other than territories in respect of which a mandate from the League of Nations is being exercised by, or which are being administered by, the Government of such a Dominion as aforesaid and territories in India):

Provided that, if, whether before or after the passing of the Bretton Woods Agreements Act 1945, or the making of this Order, effect is given by or under the law of any part of His Majesty's dominions or other territory to any provisions of the said Agreements set out in the Schedule to this Order, this Order, so far as it gives effect to that provision, shall not extend to that part of His Majesty's dominions or other territory as respects any period as respects which effect is given as aforesaid to that provision. **[754]**

SCHEDULE
PROVISIONS OF AGREEMENT WHICH ARE TO HAVE FORCE OF LAW

PART I
FUND AGREEMENT

Article VIII, Section 2 (b)

Exchange contracts which involve the currency of any Member and which are contrary to the exchange control regulations of that member maintained or imposed consistently with this Agreement shall be unenforceable in the territories of any member . . .

ARTICLE IX
STATUS, IMMUNITIES AND PRIVILEGES

* * * * *

Section 2. Status of the Fund.

The Fund shall possess full juridical personality, and, in particular, the capacity:

    (i) to contract;
    (ii) to acquire and dispose of immovable and movable property;
    (iii) to institute legal proceedings.

Section 3. Immunity from judicial process.

The Fund, its property and its assets, wherever located and by whomsoever held, shall enjoy immunity from every form of judicial process except to the extent that it expressly waives its immunity for the purpose of any proceedings or by the terms of any contract.

Section 4. Immunity from other action.

Property and assets of the Fund, wherever located and by whomsoever held, shall be immune from search, requisition, confiscation, expropriation or any other form of seizure by executive or legislative action.

Section 5. Immunity of archives.

The archives of the Fund shall be inviolable.

Section 6. Freedom of assets from restrictions.

To the extent necessary to carry out the operations provided for in this Agreement, all property and assets of the Fund shall be free from restrictions, regulations, controls and moratoria of any nature.

* * * * * *

(*Section 8 revoked by SI 1977/825.*)

Section 9. Immunities from taxation.

(*a*) The Fund, its assets, property, income and its operations and transactions authorised by this Agreement, shall be immune from all taxation and from all customs duties. The Fund shall also be immune from liability for the collection or payment of any tax or duty.

(*b*) No tax shall be levied on or in respect of salaries and emoluments paid by the Fund to executive directors, alternates, officers or employees of the Fund who are not local citizens, local subjects, or other local nationals.

(*c*) No taxation of any kind shall be levied on any obligation or security issued by the Fund, including any dividend or interest thereon, by whomsoever held

   (i) which discriminates against such obligation or security solely because of its origin; or
   (ii) if the sole jurisdictional basis for such taxation is the place of currency in which it is issued, made payable or paid, or the location of any office or place of business maintained by the Fund. [755]

PART II

BANK AGREEMENT

ARTICLE VII

STATUS, IMMUNITIES AND PRIVILEGES

* * * * *

Section 2. Status of the Bank.

The Bank shall possess full juridical personality, and, in particular, the capacity:

   (i) to contract;
   (ii) to acquire and dispose of immovable and movable property;
   (iii) to institute legal proceedings.

Section 3. Position of the Bank with regard to judicial process.

Actions may be brought against the Bank only in a court of competent jurisdiction in the territories of a member in which the Bank has an office, has appointed an agent for the purpose of accepting service or notice of process, or has issued or guaranteed securities. No actions shall, however, be brought by members or persons acting for or deriving claims from members. The property and assets of the Bank shall, wheresoever located and by whomsoever held, be immune from all forms of seizure, attachment or execution before the delivery of final judgment against the Bank.

Section 4. Immunity of assets from seizure.

Property and assets of the Bank, wherever located and by whomsoever held, shall be immune from search, requisition, confiscation, expropriation or any other form of seizure by executive or legislative action.

Section 5. Immunity of archives.

The archives of the Bank shall be inviolable.

Section 6. Freedom of assets from restrictions.

To the extent necessary to carry out the operations provided for in this Agreement and subject to the provisions of this Agreement, all property and assets of the Bank shall be free from restrictions, regulations, controls and moratoria of any nature.

* * * * *

Section 8. Immunities and privileges of officers and employees.

All governors, executive directors, alternates, officers and employees of the Bank

    (i)   shall be immune from legal process with respect to acts performed by them in their official capacity except when the Bank waives this immunity.

Section 9. Immunities from taxation.

    (a)   The Bank, its assets, property, income and its operations and transactions authorised by this Agreement, shall be immune from all taxation and from all customs duties. The Bank shall also be immune from liability for the collection or payment of any tax or duty.

    (b)   No tax shall be levied on or in respect of salaries and emoluments paid by the Bank to executive directors, alternates, officials or employees of the Bank who are not local citizens, local subjects, or other local nationals.

    (c)   No taxation of any kind shall be levied on any obligation or security issued by the Bank (including any dividend or interest thereon) by whomsoever held—

        (i)   which discriminates against such obligation or security solely because it is issued by the Bank; or

        (ii)   if the sole jurisdictional basis for such taxation is the place or currency in which it is issued, made payable or paid, or the location of any office or place of business maintained by the Bank.

    (d)   No taxation of any kind shall be levied on any obligation or security guaranteed by the Bank (including any dividend or interest thereon) by whomsoever held—

        (i)   which discriminates against such obligation or security solely because it is guaranteed by the Bank; or

        (ii)   if the sole jurisdictional basis for such taxation is the location of any office or place of business maintained by the Bank.   **[756]**

INTERNATIONAL FINANCE CORPORATION ORDER 1955
(SI 1955/1954)

NOTES
Made: 22 December 1955.
Authority: International Finance Corporation Act 1955, s 3 (now repealed); now takes effect under the Overseas Development and Co-operation Act 1980, s 9.
Commencement: 20 July 1956.

1—(1) This Order may be cited as the International Finance Corporation Order 1955.

(2) This Order shall come into operation on the date on which her Majesty's Government in the United Kingdom becomes a member of the Corporation, which date shall be notified in the London Gazette.   **[757]**

2—(1) In this Order, "the Agreement" means the Agreement for the establishment and operation of an International Finance Corporation signed on behalf of her Majesty's Government in the United Kingdom on the twenty-fifth day of October, 1955, in pursuance of the Articles referred to in section one of the said Act; and "the Corporation" means the body established under the Agreement.

(2) The Interpretation Act 1889 shall apply to the interpretation of this Order as it applies to the interpretation of an Act of Parliament.   **[758]**

3 The provisions of the Agreement set out in the Schedule to this Order shall have the force of law:

Provided that nothing in Section 9 of Article VI of the Agreement shall be construed as—

  (a) entitling the Corporation to import goods free of customs duty without any restriction on their subsequent sale in the country to which they were imported; or

  (b) conferring on the Corporation any exemption from duties or taxes which form part of the price of goods sold [,except that it shall have relief, under arrangements made by the Secretary of State, by way of refund of car tax paid on any vehicles and value added tax paid on the supply of any goods and services which are necessary for the exercise of its official activities, such relief to be subject to compliance with such conditions as may be imposed in accordance with the arrangements]; or

  (c) conferring on the Corporation any exemption from duties or taxes which are in fact no more than charges for services rendered. **[759]**

NOTE
  Para (b): words in square brackets substituted by the International Organisations (Immunities and Privileges) Miscellaneous Provisions Order 1976, SI 1976/221, art 4.

4 This Order shall extend to all parts of Her Majesty's dominions (other than Canada, Australia, New Zealand, the Union of South Africa, Pakistan and Ceylon, and any territory administered by the Government of any of those countries) and, to the extent that Her Majesty has jurisdiction therein, to all other territories for whose foreign relations Her Majesty's Government in the United Kingdom is responsible:

Provided that if, whether before or after the passing of the International Finance Corporation Act 1955, and whether before or after the coming into force of this Order, effect is given by or under the law of any such part of Her Majesty's dominions or other territory to any provision of the Agreement set out in the Schedule to this Order, this Order, so far as it gives effect to that provision, shall not extend to that part of Her Majesty's dominions or other territory in respect of any period for which effect is so given to that provision.
[760]

SCHEDULE
PROVISIONS OF THE AGREEMENT AS TO STATUS, IMMUNITIES AND PRIVILEGES

ARTICLE III
OPERATIONS

* * * * *

Section 5. Applicability of certain foreign exchange restrictions

Funds received by or payable to the Corporation in respect of an investment of the Corporation made in any member's territories pursuant to Section 1 of this Article shall not be free, solely by reason of any provision of this Agreement, from generally applicable foreign exchange restrictions, regulations and controls in force in the territories of that member.

ARTICLE VI
STATUS, IMMUNITIES AND PRIVILEGES
* * * * *

Section 2. Status of the Corporation

The Corporation shall possess full juridical personality and, in particular, the capacity:

  (i) to contract;
  (ii) to acquire and dispose of immovable and movable property;
  (iii) to institute legal proceedings.

Section 3. Position of the Corporation with regard to judicial process

Actions may be brought against the Corporation only in a court of competent jurisdiction in the territories of a member in which the Corporation has an office, has appointed an agent for the purpose of accepting service or notice of process, or has issued or guaranteed securities. No actions shall, however, be brought by members of persons acting for or deriving claims from members. The property and assets of the Corporation shall, wheresoever located and by whomsoever held, be immune from all forms of seizure, attachment or execution before the delivery of final judgment against the Corporation.

Section 4. Immunity of assets from seizure

Property and assets of the Corporation, wherever located and by whomsoever held, shall be immune from search, requisition, confiscation, expropriation or any other form of seizure by executive or legislative action.

Section 5. Immunity of archives

The archives of the Corporation shall be inviolable.

Section 6. Freedom of assets from restrictions

To the extent necessary to carry out the operations provided for in this Agreement and subject to the provisions of Article III, Section 5, and the other provisions of this Agreement, all property and assets of the Corporation shall be free from restrictions, regulations, controls and moratoria of any nature.

* * * * *

Section 8. Immunities and privileges of officers and employees

All Governors, Directors, Alternates, officers and employees of the Corporation:

  (i) shall be immune from legal process with respect to acts performed by them in their official capacity. . . .

Section 9. Immunities from taxation

  (a) The Corporation, its assets, property, income and its operations and transactions authorised by this Agreement, shall be immune from all taxation and from all customs duties. The Corporation shall also be immune from liability for the collection or payment of any tax or duty.
  (b) No tax shall be levied on or in respect of salaries and emoluments paid by the Corporation to Directors, Alternates, officials or employees of the Corporation who are not local citizens, local subjects, or other local nationals.
  (c) No taxation of any kind shall be levied on any obligation or security issued by the Corporation (including any dividend or interest thereon) by whomsoever held:
    (i) which discriminates against such obligation or security solely because it is issued by the Corporation; or
    (ii) if the sole jurisdictional basis for such taxation is the place or currency in which it is issued, made payable or paid, or the location of any office or place of business maintained by the Corporation.
  (d) No taxation of any kind shall be levied on any obligation or security guaranteed by the Corporation (including any dividend or interest thereon) by whomsoever held

(i) which discriminates against such obligation or security solely because it is guaranteed by the Corporation; or

(ii) if the sole jurisdictional basis for such taxation is the location of any office or place of business maintained by the Corporation.

* * * * *

Section 11. Waiver

The Corporation in its discretion may waive any of the privileges and immunities conferred under this Article to such extent and upon such conditions as it may determine. **[761]**

INTERNATIONAL DEVELOPMENT ASSOCIATION ORDER 1960
(SI 1960/1383)

NOTES
  Made: 3 August 1960.
  Authority: International Development Association Act 1960, s 3 (now repealed); now takes effect under the Overseas Development and Co-operation Act 1980, s 9.
  Commencement: 24 September 1960.

1—(1) This Order may be cited as the International Development Association Order 1960.

(2) This Order shall come into operation on the date on which Her Majesty's Government in the United Kingdom becomes a member of the Association, which date shall be notified in the London Gazette. **[762]**

2—(1) In this Order "the Agreement" and "the Association" have the same meanings respectively as in the International Development Association Act 1960.

(2) The Interpretation Act 1889 shall apply to the interpretation of this Order as it applies to the interpretation of an Act of Parliament. **[763]**

3 The provisions of the Agreement set out in the Schedule to this Order shall have the force of law:

Provided that nothing in Section 9 of Article VIII of the Agreement shall be construed as—

(a) entitling the Association to import goods free of customs duty without any restriction on their subsequent sale in the country to which they were imported; or

(b) conferring on the Association any exemption from duties or taxes which form part of the price of goods sold [, except that it shall have relief, under arrangements made by the Secretary of State, by way of refund of car tax paid on any vehicles and value added tax paid on the supply of any goods and services which are necessary for the exercise of its official activities, such relief to be subject to compliance with such conditions as may be imposed in accordance with the arrangements]; or

(c) conferring on the Association any exemption from duties or taxes which are in fact no more than charges for services rendered. **[764]**

NOTE
  Para (b): words in square brackets inserted by the International Organisations (Immunities and Privileges) Miscellaneous Provisions Order 1976, SI 1976/221, art 4.

4 This Order shall extend to all parts of Her Majesty's dominions (other than Canada, Australia, New Zealand, the Union of South Africa and Ceylon, and any territory administered by the Government of any of those countries) and, to the extent that Her Majesty has jurisdiction therein, to all other territories for whose foreign relations Her Majesty's Government in the United Kingdom is responsible:

Provided that if, whether before or after the passing of the International Development Association Act 1960, and whether before or after the coming into operation of this Order, effect is given by or under the law of any such part of Her Majesty's dominions or other territory to any provision of the Agreement set out in the Schedule to this Order, this Order, so far as it gives effect to that provision, shall not extend to that part of Her Majesty's dominions or other territory in respect of any period for which effect is so given to that provision. **[765]**

SCHEDULE

PROVISIONS OF THE AGREEMENT AS TO STATUS, IMMUNITIES AND PRIVILEGES

ARTICLE VIII

STATUS, IMMUNITIES AND PRIVILEGES

* * * * *

Section 2. Status of the Association

The Association shall possess full judicial personality and, in particular, the capacity:

    (i) to contract;
   (ii) to acquire and dispose of immovable and movable property;
  (iii) to institute legal proceedings.

Section 3. Position of the Association with Regard to Judicial Process

Actions may be brought against the Association only in a court of competent jurisdiction in the territories of a member in which the Association has an office, has appointed an agent for the purpose of accepting service or notice of process, or has issued or guaranteed securities. No actions shall, however, be brought by members or persons acting for or deriving claims from members. The property and assets of the Association shall, wheresoever located and by whomsoever held, be immune from all forms of seizure, attachment or execution before the delivery of final judgment against the Association.

Section 4. Immunity of Assets from Seizure

Property and assets of the Association, wherever located and by whomsoever held, shall be immune from search, requisition, confiscation, expropriation or any other form of seizure by executive or legislative action.

Section 5. Immunity of Archives

The archives of the Association shall be inviolable.

Section 6. Freedom of Assets from Restrictions

To the extent necessary to carry out the operations provided for in this Agreement and subject to the provisions of this Agreement, all property and assets of the Association shall be free from restrictions, regulations, controls and moratoria of any nature.

* * * * *

Section 8. Immunities and Privileges of Officers and Employees

All Governors, Executive Directors, Alternates, officers and employees of the Association:

   (i)   shall be immune from legal process with respect to acts performed by them in their official capacity except when the Association waives this immunity . . .

Section 9. Immunities from Taxation

   (a)   The Association, its assets, property, income and its operations and transactions authorized by this Agreement, shall be immune from all taxation and from all customs duties. The Association shall also be immune from liability for the collection or payment of any tax or duty.

   (b)   No tax shall be levied on or in respect of salaries and emoluments paid by the Association to Executive Directors, Alternates, officials or employees of the Association who are not local citizens, local subjects, or other local nationals.

   (c)   No taxation of any kind shall be levied on any obligation or security issued by the Association (including any dividend or interest thereon) by whomsoever held

   (i)   which discriminates against such obligation or security solely because it is issued by the Association; or

   (ii)   if the sole jurisdictional basis for such taxation is the place or currency in which it is issued, made payable or paid, or the location of any office or place of business maintained by the Association.

   (d)   No taxation of any kind shall be levied on any obligation or security guaranteed by the Association (including any dividend or interest thereon) by whomsoever held

   (i)   which discriminates against such obligation or security solely because it is guaranteed by the Association; or

   (ii)   if the sole jurisdictional basis for such taxation is the location of any office or place of business maintained by the Association.   **[766]**

PROTECTION OF TRADING INTERESTS ACT 1980

PROTECTION OF TRADING INTERESTS (US RE-EXPORT CONTROL) ORDER 1982
(SI 1982/885)

NOTES
Made: 30 June 1982.
Authority: Protection of Trading Interests Act 1980, s 1(1).
Commencement: 1 July 1982.

1 This Order may be cited as the Protection of Trading Interests (US Reexport Control) Order 1982 and shall come into operation on 1st July 1982.   **[767]**

2 The Secretary of State hereby directs that section 1 of the 1980 Act shall apply to the measures referred to in the following Article.   **[768]**

3 The measures to which this Order relates are those provisions of parts 374, 376, 379, 385 and 399 of the Export Administration Regulations, as amended, made by the United States Secretary of Commerce under the powers conferred on him by the United States Export Administration Act 1979 which affect the re-export or export of goods from the United Kingdom.   **[769]**

NOTES
Export Administration Regulations: US Code of Federal Regulations, Title 15, Chapter III, sub-chapter C.
US Export Administration Act 1979: US Public Law 96–72.

PROTECTION OF TRADING INTERESTS (US ANTITRUST MEASURES) ORDER 1983
(SI 1983/900)

NOTES
Made: 23 June 1983.
Authority: Protection of Trading Interests Act 1980, s 1(1).
Commencement: 27 June 1983.

1—(1) This Order may be cited as the Protection of Trading Interests (US Antitrust Measures) Order 1983 and shall come into operation on 27th June 1983.

(2) In this Order—

"the Bermuda 2 Agreement" means the Agreement between the Government of the United Kingdom of Great Britain and Northern Ireland and the Government of the United States signed at Bermuda on 23rd July 1977, concerning air services;

"air service" and "tariff" shall be construed in accordance with the Bermuda 2 Agreement;

"UK designated airline" means a British airline (within the meaning of section 4(2) of the Civil Aviation Act 1982 designated by the Government of the United Kingdom under the Bermuda 2 Agreement.   **[770]**

2—(1) The Secretary of State hereby directs that section 1 of the 1980 Act shall apply to sections 1 and 2 of the United States' Sherman Act and sections 4 and 4A of the United States' Clayton Act in their application to the cases described in the following paragraph.

(2) The cases mentioned in paragraph (1) of this Article are:

(i) an agreement or arrangement (whether legally enforceable or not) to which a UK designated airline is a party,

(ii) a discussion or communication to which a UK designated airline is a party,

(iii) any act done by a UK designated airline,

which, in respect of each case, concerns the tariffs charged or to be charged by any such airline or otherwise relates to the operation by it of an air service authorised pursuant to the Bermuda 2 Agreement.   **[771]–[774]**

BILLS OF SALE ACT 1878

BILLS OF SALE (LOCAL REGISTRATION) RULES 1960
(SI 1960/2326)

NOTES
Made: 12 December 1960.
Authority: Bills of Sale Act 1878, s 21.
Commencement: 2 January 1961.

1 These Rules may be cited as the Bills of Sale (Local Registration) Rules 1960 and shall come into operation on the second day of January, 1961.   **[775]**

2—(1) The Interpretation Act 1889 shall apply to the interpretation of these Rules as it applies to the interpretation of an Act of Parliament.

(2) In these Rules—

"affidavit of renewal" means an affidavit made for the purpose of renewing the registration of a bill of sale pursuant to section 11 of the Bills of Sale Act 1878;

"registrar of bills of sale" means the registrar for the purposes of the said Act of 1878;

"section 11 of the Act of 1882" means section 11 of the Bills of Sale Act (1878) Amendment Act 1882, as amended by section 23 of the Administration of Justice Act 1925.   **[776]**

3 Every copy of a bill of sale or of an affidavit of renewal which is transmitted to a county court registrar under section 11 of the Act of 1882 shall bear a certificate by the registrar of bills of sale showing the date on which the registration or, as the case may be, the renewal of registration, of the bill of sale was effected and the date on which the copy of the bill of sale or affidavit is transmitted to the county court registrar.   **[777]**

NOTES
The Act of 1882: Bills of Sale Act (1878) Amendment Act 1882.
Modification: reference to county court registrar to be construed as reference to district judge, by virtue of the Courts and Legal Services Act 1990, s 74.

4 Where a memorandum of satisfaction has been written on a registered copy of a bill of sale, the registrar of bills of sale shall transmit a notice of satisfaction in the form set out in the Schedule to these Rules to every county court registrar to whom a copy of the bill of sale was transmitted under section 11 of the Act of 1882.   **[778]**

NOTES
The Act of 1882: Bills of Sale Act (1878) Amendment Act 1882.
Modification: modified as noted to r 3.

5 Every county court registrar shall number consecutively the copies of bills of sale and of affidavits of renewal transmitted to him under section 11 of the Act of 1882 and shall file and keep them in the court office.   **[779]**

NOTES
The Act of 1882: Bills of Sale Act (1878) Amendment Act 1882.
Modification: modified as noted to r 3.

6 Every county court registrar shall keep an alphabetical index of the copies of bills of sale and of affidavits of renewal transmitted to him under section 11 of the Act of 1882 and shall enter in the index under the first letter of the surname of the grantor of every bill the grantor's full name, address and description and the number of the copy of the bill of sale or affidavit.   **[780]**

NOTES
   The Act of 1882: Bills of Sale Act (1878) Amendment Act 1882.
   Modification: modified as noted to r 3.

7 A county court registrar to whom a notice of satisfaction is transmitted shall annex the notice to the copy of the bill of sale to which it relates and shall add to the entry in the index relating to the bill of sale a note that it has been satisfied.
                                                                          [781]

NOTE
   Modification: modified as noted to r 3.

8 (*Revokes RSC dated 28 December 1883 relating to the Bills of Sale Acts, 1878 and 1882.*)

SCHEDULE
Rule 4

NOTICE OF SATISFACTION

Filing and Record Department,
Central Office,
Royal Courts of Justice
London W.C.2

   In the Matter of a Bill of Sale
granted by
to
and dated the   day of   19   .
   TAKE NOTICE that a memorandum of satisfaction of the above bill of sale, a copy [of an affidavit of renewal] of which was sent to you on the day of   , 19   , has been entered this day.
   Dated this   day of   , 19
To the Registrar of the   County Court.

                                                                          [781A]

AGRICULTURAL CREDITS ACT 1928

AGRICULTURAL CREDITS REGULATIONS 1928
(SR&O 1928/667)

NOTES
Made: 24 September 1928.
Authority: Agricultural Credits Act 1928 (see s 9(9) thereof).
Commencement: 1 October 1928.

1 Form and particulars in Register

The register directed by the Act to be kept at H.M. Land Registry shall contain the following particulars:—

(1) The date of the instrument creating the charge;

(2) The Surname and Christian names of the farmer or farmers or name of the society whose farming stock and other agricultural assets are affected;

(3) The amount of the loan;

(4) Whether the charge is a fixed or floating charge or both;

(5) The name and address of the Bank in whose favour the charge is made;

and shall be in such form and may contain such additional or alternative particulars (if any) as the Land Registrar may from time to time determine.

[782]

2 Form of Applications

(1) Applications for registration, searches (official and otherwise), official certificates, certified copies of or extracts from the register or such memoranda filed thereunder as are open to public inspection, shall be made on and shall furnish the particulars set forth in the several forms for these purposes given in the Schedule hereto, or on such other forms as the Registrar shall from time to time determine.

(2) Applications shall not, unless the Registrar otherwise directs, be accompanied by the original instruments in respect of which they are made.

[783]

3 Cancellation of registration

(1) Applications for the cancellation of a registration on discharge of the charge shall be made on and shall furnish the particulars set forth in the form given in the Schedule hereto, or on such other form as the Registrar shall from time to time prescribe.

(2) Such evidence in respect thereof as the Registrar shall think necessary shall also be furnished if required.   **[784]**

4 Rectifications of the register

On rectification of any entry in the register, such particulars, explanation and evidence in respect thereof as the Registrar shall think necessary, shall be furnished.   **[785]**

5 Posting of Applications

Applications accompanied by the prescribed fee must be sent by prepaid post addressed to the Agricultural Credits Superintendent, H.M. Land Registry, Lincoln's Inn Fields, London, W.C.2.   **[786]**

NOTE
Address: now the Agricultural Credits Department, Burrington Way, Plymouth PL5 3LP.

6 Priority of Applications for registration

(1) Application for registration delivered by post or under cover during the hours in which the office is open for registration shall be treated as having been made or given at the same time and immediately before the closing of the office for that day and shall be numbered accordingly.

(2) Application for registration delivered by post or under cover between the hours of closing and of the next opening of the office for registration shall be treated as having been made or given at the same time and immediately after such opening and shall be numbered accordingly.

(3) In reckoning the number of days under section 9(1) of the Act in which registration shall be affected, Sundays and other days when the Registry is not open to the public shall be excluded.   **[787]**

7 Responsibility for accuracy, etc of applications

Save in the case of applications for the modification or cancellation of a registration on discharge of the charge, the Registrar shall not be concerned to inquire into or otherwise verify the accuracy, validity or sufficiency of any matter or thing stated or appearing in any notice given or application made to him.   **[788]**

8 Official Searches

(1) Applications for an official search shall be prepared on the prescribed form and forwarded to the Registry in duplicate.

(2) An official certificate of the result of searches shall extend to registrations effected during the day of the date of the certificate, and shall be issued only after the office is closed for registration on that date.   **[789]**

9 Certified copies

For the purposes of subsections (5) and (6) of section 9 of the Act the official stamp of H.M. Land Registry shall be a sufficient authentication on behalf of the Land Registrar of the certified copy of entries in the register.   **[790]**

10 Sale of Forms

(1) All forms except such as may from time to time be issued by direction of the Registrar free of charge shall be sold under arrangements to be made by H.M. Stationery Office, or otherwise as the Registrar may from time to time approve.

(2) No forms other than those so issued, sold or approved shall be accepted for registration.   **[791]**

11 Interpretation

In these Regulations "the Act" means the "Agricultural Credits Act 1928" and words or expressions, defined in the Act, have the same meaning in these Regulations as in the Act.   **[792]**

12 Short title and commencement

These Regulations may be cited as the Agricultural Credits Regulations, 1928, and shall come into operation on the first day of October, 1928.   **[793]–[800]**

THE SCHEDULE

NOTES

The Schedule sets out the forms referred to in regs 2, 3.

The forms are not printed here, but the following is a list of the forms prescribed:

Form AC1 Application for registration of memorandum of an agricultural charge: registration in farmer's name.

Form AC2 Application for registration under s 14 of the Agricultural Credits Act 1928 of a memorandum of a debenture of an agricultural society: registration in the name of an agricultural society.

Form AC3 Application for cancellation of an entry in the register on proof of discharge.

Form AC4 Application for certificate that a registration has been cancelled.

Form AC5 Application for a certified copy of the memorandum filed in the registry under the Act.

Form AC6 Application for an official search.

Form AC7 Application for the rectification of an entry in the register.

Form AC8 Application for personal search.

PART III
BANK OF ENGLAND NOTICES

FOREIGN CURRENCY EXPOSURE

A Introduction

1 This paper sets out the basis on which the Bank will measure, monitor and discuss with banks and licensed deposit-taking institutions (both groups hereafter referred to collectively as 'banks') their exposure to movements in exchange rates.[1] These arrangements will form part of the regular process of supervision and be included within the scope of prudential interviews.

2 The arrangements set out in this paper will apply to those banks for which the Bank of England has supervisory responsibility under the Banking Act. Banks in the Channel Islands and the Isle of Man are, therefore, not included. There are different arrangements for UK-incorporated banks and for branches of foreign banks, although both will participate in the same reporting system. These arrangements are covered in detail in Section C.

3 The primary responsibility for the control of exposures arising from foreign currency operations, as for any other aspect of a bank's business, must rest with a bank's own management. However, in the discharge of its supervisory responsibilities, the Bank needs to know the methods by which bank managements control such exposures, the extent of each bank's exposure, and its relation to other risks and to its capital.

4 Foreign currency operations give rise to risks which, although not unique, are probably more pronounced than in other markets. Satisfactory internal control procedures are essential. A number of the more important aspects of such controls were described in the Bank's circular of December 1974, an extract of which is attached as an annex to this paper. The Bank will wish to be informed about the general arrangements within each bank for controlling its foreign currency trading.

5 Exposure to movements in exchange rates is only one of the many categories of risk to which banks are subject in the conduct of their foreign currency operations. The broad range of risks is considered in the risk assets ratio, set out in the Bank's paper *The measurement of capital*[2] in which the aggregate foreign currency position is included. However, the nature of foreign currency operations and the short time scale in which significant exposures to loss can be incurred as a result of them present particular problems and, in the Bank's view, justify special arrangements.

---

[1] The paper reflects the outcome of consultations with the banking community on the discussion paper on the same subject issued in December 1979, following the Governor's letter to banks of 23 October 1979, and is reproduced here with the permission of the Bank of England.
[2] Issued by the Bank in September 1980. See now BSD/1990/2 and BSD/1990/3.

B Elements to be measured

Positions

6 The Bank is concerned with exposures arising out of any uncovered foreign currency position in any currency. Furthermore, each bank's exposure needs to be considered both in terms of its net position in any one currency and its overall position, ie the aggregate net position in all currencies.

7 Net currency positions will include the position held against sterling (more easily measured as the net position in sterling) because the risk of loss arising from a net open position in sterling is no different from that arising from a position in any other currency. The net position in sterling will, therefore, be monitored separately and included in the assessment of each bank's overall exposure.

8 Transactions in precious metals which result in positions have similar characteristics to those in currency. All references in this paper to currency should be taken to include gold; for a few specialist banks, the Bank will also take positions in silver into account.

Accruals and future flows of income and expense

9 Anticipated flows of income and expense not yet received can give rise to an exposure which, if determinable, should in principle be measured. Those which have been

accrued will have been included by the bank as an asset or a liability in the measurement of its overall exposure. Those which have not been accrued (including known future flows) need not be included, unless the bank wishes to do so because it has already covered them.

Dealing and structural positions

10 Banks often find it convenient to identify and distinguish foreign currency exposures which arise from their daily or 'normal' banking operations (henceforth referred to as 'dealing' positions) from those exposures which are intended to be of a longer-term nature (henceforth referred to as 'structural' positions). The Bank believes this is a valid distinction and that structural positions may conveniently be considered separately from dealing positions. It will, therefore, be prepared to exclude structural positions from the guidelines agreed with each bank. This distinction does not mean that the Bank considers structural exposures are without risk, and the aggregate foreign currency position included in the risk assets ratio set out in the Bank's paper *The measurement of capital*[1] encompasses dealing and structural positions.

11 Each bank will have its own views on the categorisation of exposures as dealing or structural. The dividing line will not always be clear cut and will depend on the particular circumstances of that bank. The Bank will wish to ensure, however, that the make-up of a structural position does not undermine the application of the guidelines for the dealing position. Therefore the Bank will wish to be consulted on whether any part of a position in any currency should be treated as structural. The Bank would normally accept, as structural, exposures arising from banks' fixed and long-term assets and liabilities, including such items as loan capital, premises, and investments in subsidiaries and associates. It might also be appropriate to treat, as structural, positions which banks are obliged to maintain as a result of laws or market conditions to which their overseas affiliates are subject, and positions which arise as a result of reserves or provisions being maintained in currencies appropriate to the banking risks against which they are being held.

[1] See now BSD/1990/2 and BSD/1990/3.

C Reporting and monitoring

UK-incorporated banks

12 The Bank will not set any formal limits on the size of a bank's foreign currency positions, but will agree dealing position guidelines with each institution individually. These will take account of the institution's particular circumstances and expertise.

13 The guidelines will be expressed in terms of a relationship between the dealing position and the bank's capital, because it is ultimately from this source that any loss arising from the position has to be made good. As a general rule, for banks which are experienced in foreign exchange the Bank will expect to agree the following guidelines:

(i) Net open dealing position in any one currency: not more than 10% of the adjusted capital base, as defined in the Bank's paper *The measurement of capital*[1] for the risk assets measure.

(ii) Net short open dealing positions of all currencies taken together: not more than 15% of the adjusted capital base.

The Bank would expect banks inexperienced in foreign exchange to operate within more conservative guidelines. Since exposure to a movement in any exchange rate is represented by both a long position in one currency and an equal but opposite short position in another currency (or several currencies combined), a bank's aggregate exposure can be measured as the sum of either its long or short positions. For purposes of calculating (ii) above, each bank's overall exposure will be measured as the sum of its net short open positions, spot and forward taken together.

[1] See now BSD/1990/2 and BSD/1990/3.

Overseas branches of UK banks

14 For banks incorporated in the United Kingdom, the arrangements described above will apply to the operations of all their branches, both in the United Kingdom and overseas. The Bank appreciates that some banks are still developing their internal reporting systems for overseas branches and will be prepared to discuss with individual banks any problems arising from this proposal.

Subsidiaries of UK banks

15 The Bank will wish eventually to include in its consolidated assessment of capital adequacy foreign currency exposures of UK banks' subsidiaries, both domestic and overseas. This will be the subject of further consultation with the banking community in due course.

UK branches of foreign banks

16 The Bank of England has supervisory responsibility under the Banking Act for UK branches of foreign banks, although, in fulfilling such responsibility, it is enabled, under the Act, to place substantial reliance on the supervisory authorities in the country of origin. In order to carry out its responsibility under the Act and to see that foreign exchange markets in the United Kingdom are conducted in an orderly manner, the Bank wil require returns to be made by UK branches of foreign banks.

17 The Bank appreciates that the operations of UK branches of foreign banks are frequently closely integrated with those of their parents and that it would be inappropriate to supervise such branches in isolation. Furthermore, these branches do not have a separate capital base against which positions can be measured. In monitoring the foreign currency operations of foreign branches, the Bank will take account of a branch's own internal controls, those exercised by its head office, and the monitoring arrangements of its own supervisory authority. Where it considers these are sastisfactory the Bank will not apply separate guidelines. Where they are not satisfactory, the Bank will agree appropriate absolute levels of exposure to serve as guidelines.

Frequency and method of reporting

18 In order to monitor banks' positions, the Bank will require returns to be made on a monthly basis. The returns will give, in contracted currency amounts, the net spot long or short position and the net forward long or short position in each currency at the close of business on the reporting day. The sum of these positions will give the overall net position in each currency, in currency terms.

19 Where it has been agreed that part of a bank's position in a particular currency should be regarded as structural, this part will be deducted from the overall net position in that currency to give the dealing position.

20 The Bank will expect apparent positions arising from covered transactions, such as swaps, to be excluded from dealing positions. In a swap, one exchange transaction is linked to another at a later date and exchange differences create an apparent open position in one of the currencies comprising the swap. In most cases such positions would be eliminated by including in dealing positions appropriate amounts drawn from the internal accounts or records associated with swap transactions.

21 Dealing positions once established should be translated into sterling at current spot exchange rates. The use of forward exchange rates within the structure of the reporting arrangements described above would be inappropriate, as it would draw into the exercise exposure to movements in interest rates. The valuation of positions arising from spot and forward transactions in each currency at a single rate will also be simpler.

22 The overall net position in sterling need not be independently calculated. It should be reported as that balancing amount which ensures that the sum of all the overall net long positions equals the sum of all the overall net short positions.

23 The return made at the end of each period should also contain a report of each occasion on which the net open dealing position in each currency or the aggregate net

short open position has exceeded the guidelines agreed between the Bank and the reporting institution.

Other arrangements

24 These reporting requirements will not change the existing informal arrangements whereby the Gold and Foreign Exchange Office of the Bank may from time to time discuss dealing positions directly with dealers.

Bank of England
April 1981

Annex   Control of foreign exchange dealing[1]

Reports of the losses suffered this year by banks in a number of countries, as a result of operations in foreign exchange markets, will undoubtedly have caused many banks to undertake a rigorous review of their internal regulations governing procedures for foreign exchange dealings by, and dealing and overnight and forward credit limits imposed on, individual branches and wholly-owned subsidiaries at home and abroad. Any banks which have not yet done so are urged to undertake such a review as soon as possible and to ensure in particular that authorities to deal are specific and are confined to strictly selected staff and branches.

The list that follows is not intended as an exhaustive check for conducting such a review; it merely covers points which have arisen from the Bank's discussions in a number of centres about the losses:

1 Some general managements seem to have placed their dealers in an exposed position by looking well beyond the service element of the dealing function and imposing ambitious profit targets upon them.

2 In some overseas offices, managements do not appear to have paid sufficient attention to the relations between dealers and brokers in London; the Foreign Exchange and Currency Deposit Brokers' Association has exercised a beneficial influence in this area.

3 Dealers should never write their own outgoing confirmations or receive incoming confirmations.

4 Forward deals should always be confirmed at once; in particular, confirmations should not be delayed until instructions are passed just prior to maturity.

5 There should be snap checks of dealing activities between regular internal audits or inspections.

6 Central management should from time to time, on a random basis, seek from correspondent banks independent second confirmations of outstanding forward contracts.

7 A bank should check with its correspondent's head or main dealing office if it notices that a branch of that bank has suddenly or appreciably expanded its operations in the forward market.   **[801]**

[1] Extract from the Bank of England circular of December 1974.

THE MEASUREMENT OF LIQUIDITY[1]

Introduction

1 In a paper 'The Liquidity of Banks' published in March 1981, the Bank set out the main principles of its intended approach to the prudential supervision of banks' liquidity. A further paper, entitled The Measurement of Liquidity, was circulated as a consultative document in the summer of 1981. That paper developed the principles of the earlier paper and proposed a common framework for measuring the liquidity of banks based on the expected cash flows arising from their assets and liabilities. The present final version is intended to provide the basis for assessing the adequacy of liquidity of all deposit-taking companies for the purpose of the Bank's continuing supervision under the Banking Act.

¹ In this paper the word 'bank' is to be read to include institutions licensed to take deposits under the Banking Act 1979.

Objectives

2 Banks must be capable of meeting their obligations when they fall due. Such obligations mainly comprise deposits at sight or short notice, term deposits and commitments to lend, including unutilised overdraft facilities. The mix of these obligations and their incidence in any period of time will vary between different banks but the maintenance of an assured capacity to meet them is an essential principle of banking which is common to all. This capacity may be provided in the following ways:

> (i) by holding sufficient immediately available cash or liquefiable assets, subject to the qualification that marketable assets vary in quality in terms of the prices at which they are capable of being sold;
> (ii) by securing an appropriately matching future profile of cash flows from maturing assets, subject to the qualification that there may be shortfalls in practice if borrowers are unable to repay;
> (iii) by maintaining an adequately diversified deposit base in terms both of maturities and range of counterparties (bank and non-bank) which, depending importantly on the individual bank's standing in the market and on the general liquidity situation in the system at the time, may provide the ability to raise fresh deposits without undue cost.

3 The Bank's supervisory objective is to ensure that banks' management policies apply a prudent mix of these different forms of liquidity appropriate to the circumstances of the bank and that these policies are sustained at all times. The Bank regards a prudent mix as one which offers security of access to liquidity without undue exposure to suddenly rising costs from liquefying assets or bidding for deposits.

4 The responsibility for ensuring the liquidity of a bank rests with its own management. The Bank does not seek to impose across-the-board liquidity ratio norms, just as it does not seek across-the-board capital adequacy ratio norms, and thereby to supplant the exercise of judgment by bank management. Instead, in determining what is a prudent policy for a bank, the Bank will take full account of its particular characteristics and situation within the banking system. As part of its regular discussions with senior management, the Bank will require to be fully satisfied that banks have both prudent policies and adequate management systems to ensure that policies are followed; and it will continue to monitor banks' liquidity management during the normal course of its supervision. The Bank will wish to examine the extent to which potentially immediate obligations (deposits at sight and short notice and commitments to lend) should be supported by cash and immediately maturing or liquefiable assets and their appropriate quality; and the extent to which banks have planned ahead to meet the maturing of deposits with fixed maturity dates.

5 With these principles in mind, this paper establishes a framework for measuring liquidity applicable to banks generally, that will serve as a first step towards a qualitative assessment of the adequacy of the liquidity of individual banks taking account of their particular circumstances.

6 Measures of liquidity which have been employed hitherto have generally involved a comparison of deposit liabilities (in part or in total) with the available stock of certain assets classed as 'liquid'. This approach has the virtue of simplicity but does not take account of the development of liability or asset management techniques for controlling liquidity through cash flows. It also involves an over-sharp distinction between 'liquid' assets and other assets, many of which will be capable of generating cash in particular circumstances.

7 In measuring liquidity a distinction has often been made between the position in sterling-denominated business and that in other currencies, although the positions in different foreign currencies have not normally been separately identified. Such distinctions may be appropriate because of the particular circumstances of a bank or its internal management policies. When this is the case, the Bank would expect to take account of these same divisions as a basis for its own monitoring. The Bank, however, also wishes

to assess the liquidity of a bank's total business, undifferentiated as to currency denomination, since in principle, through the foreign exchange markets, obligations in one currency may be met by the availability of liquid funds in another.

The basis of measurement

8 The measurement described below is based on a cash flow approach, normally taking liabilities and assets in all currencies together, although it can also be applied to liabilities and assets in one or a group of currencies. In this approach, liabilities and assets are inserted in a 'maturity ladder', with the net positions in each time period being accumulated. In the first maturity bands on the ladder this measure, by comparing sight and near sight liabilities with cash and assets capable of generating cash immediately, is similar to a customary liquid assets ratio. Marketable assets are placed at the start of the maturity ladder, rather than according to their maturity date, but account needs to be taken of limitations on their marketability and their susceptibility to price fluctuations. Commitments are recognised by being included as liabilities or as agreed in specific cases. The measure is thus a series of accumulating net mismatch positions in successive time bands. This will provide the framework for discussion with individual banks about their policies for managing liquidity and for establishing and subsequently monitoring the particular guidelines of liquidity adequacy that come to be agreed.

9 The measurement incorporates the following particular features:

(a) *Liabilities*

   (i) Deposits of all types are included according to earliest maturity.[1] The volatility of deposits, particularly call or notice deposits taken in aggregate, may in practice tend to be more closely related to a bank's credit-worthiness as perceived by depositors and to its position in the system or to current economic or financial conditions rather than to the precise terms of the deposits. It is recognised that for some banks distinctions can be drawn between different types of deposit, for example, between retail and wholesale deposits. This stability and diversification of the deposit base will be taken into account in discussion of appropriate guidelines.

   (ii) Known firm commitments to make funds available on a particular date are included in the appropriate time band at their full value.

   (iii) Commitments which are not due to be met on a particular date, for example, undrawn overdraft and other facilities, are unlikely to have to be met in full and cannot be treated precisely. The extent to which undrawn facilities should be included as a liability will vary with their nature. This imprecision will be reflected by the inclusion of only a proportion of outstanding commitments in the first maturity band, the remainder being excluded. The appropriate proportion for each bank will be determined having regard to its past and prospective draw-down experience.

   (iv) Contingent liabilities are not included in the measurement, unless there is a reasonable likelihood that the conditions necessary to trigger them might be fulfilled.

(b) *Assets*

   (i) Assets are measured by reference to their maturity, unless, as in the case of overdrafts, they are repayable on demand in practice only nominally, or unless they are marketable, or are known to be of doubtful value.

   (ii) Lending repayable on demand only nominally may yield some regular cash flow but this cannot be measured at all precisely. The Bank will wish to agree appropriate treatment with each bank. Possibilities which might be appropriate to normal circumstances would be to treat some proportion of the total as generating an immediate cash flow or to treat it as repayable in instalments over a period.

   (iii) The treatment of marketable assets takes account of the extent to which they can be sold for cash quickly (or used as security for borrowing), incurring little or no cost penalty; and of any credit or investment risks which may make their potential value less predictable. It is important that the market for the asset should be sufficiently deep to ensure a stable demand for it. An important factor in this is the willingness of the central bank to use the asset in its normal market operations. These considerations are recognised in the measurement by applying varying discounts normally against the market value of marketable assets, all of which, as indicated earlier, are included at the start of the maturity ladder. Discounts for the majority of sterling assets are set out in Annex 1 to this paper. Similar discounts will obtain on comparable foreign currency assets. Assets not covered in Annex 1 will be a matter for agreement, on a common basis, arising out of discussion with individual banks.

(iv) Assets known to be of doubtful value are excluded from the measurement, or treated on a case-by-case basis.

(v) Contractual standby facilities made available to the banks by other banks provide support which should be recognised, and they are therefore included as equivalent to a sight asset. Due regard, however, will be paid to their remaining term and the possibility that they may not be renewed. Standby facilities provided by a bank to other banks are treated in the same way as commitments to lend at some uncertain future date.

(c) *Other items*

(i) Where items in course of transmission or collection are material, credits in course of transmission are deducted from debits in course of collection and the balance added to assets at the start of the maturity ladder.

(ii) Items in suspense are normally treated on a gross basis.

10 How far into the future it is desirable to measure liquidity profiles depends very much on the circumstances of each bank. The point of maximum excess of liabilities over assets normally occurs within the first six months, although it can be later and it is therefore proposed that the profile should be measured up to 12 months. The Bank recognises, however, that in analysis and discussion it may be appropriate to concentrate more on the earlier maturities.

11 As a separate matter, the Bank will also wish to continue to monitor the overall maturity transformation undertaken: for the further ahead a bank's assets mature, the more difficult it is to estimate confidently the credit and other risks which will attach to them until they mature, or to forecast the circumstances in which the bank will then be trading.

12 The system of measurement is illustrated in Annex 2.

---

[1] It may, however, be appropriate for certain special categories of deposit, for example those where it is agreed that set-off should apply, to be netted off against specific assets and excluded from the calculation. The Bank would expect to agree such treatment with individual banks.

Application

13 The Bank's aim is to relate its measurement to the realities of the circumstances of each bank, and to achieve this discussions with each bank are needed. For example, the proper treatment of parental responsibilities for the liquidity of affiliates (ie subsidiaries and participations) needs to be considered. If these operate mainly in the UK, it may be right to seek additional information from individual banks in order to monitor on a consolidated basis. This may be less appropriate if the affiliates (or indeed branches) operate abroad for, even if the UK parent bank has ultimate responsibility, local conditions and regulatory requirements may mean that the liquidity needs of the parent and the operation abroad are so different that consolidation of the two would be unhelpful. In these cases, the Bank needs to satisfy its prudential objectives in some other way: for example, by examination of the internal arrangements of the parent bank for monitoring and controlling its worldwide liquidity needs.

14 Hitherto, the Bank has not closely monitored the overall liquidity of UK branches of foreign banks, although it has taken steps to ascertain that this is done by the head office of these banks. The Bank will wish to do so more actively in future, taking account of the relationship between the branch and its head office, and will have particular regard to the position in sterling.

Statistical returns

15 In principle, the measurement takes in all assets and liabilities and not just those at present analysed in the two principal maturity analyses (Q6 and S5) completed by many banks. Thus, liabilities should include any significant non-deposit liabilities which mature within the time span of the measurement: for example, tax liabilities. Similarly assets should include non-financial assets which are marketable within the time span of the measurement. The present returns, however, provide a sufficient basis for the proposed measurement for the time being. But some modification and extension of the present maturity analyses will be sought using the normal procedures in order to implement the proposed measurement in full.

Bank of England
July 1982

Annex 1

NIL DISCOUNT	Treasury, eligible local authority and eligible bank bills. Government and Government guaranteed marketable securities with less than twelve months remaining term to maturity.
5% DISCOUNT	Other bills and certificates of deposit with less than six months remaining term to maturity. Other Government, Government guaranteed and local authority marketable securities with less than five years remaining term to maturity or at variable rates.
10% DISCOUNT	Other bills, certificates of deposit and FRNs with less than five years remaining term to maturity. Other Government, Government guaranteed and local authority marketable debt with more than five years remaining term to maturity.
DISCOUNT TO BE DETERMINED	All other marketable assets.

NB The categories of asset used in this annex approximate to those currently employed in UK statistical returns. Comparable foreign currency assets are to be included on a similar discounted basis.

Annex 2

	Sight-8 days	8 days-1 month	1–3 months	3–6 months	6–12 months
Liabilities					
Deposits					
Commitments					
Less *Assets*					
Marketable					
Non-marketable					
Standby facilities available					
= Net position					
+/– Carried forward					
= Net cumulative position					

BSD/1983/1
(April 1983)

NOTICE TO RECOGNISED BANKS AND LICENSED DEPOSIT-TAKERS

Banking Supervision Division
BANKING ACT 1979

The implementation of the Banking Act 1979 resulted in the recognition of about 300 banks and the licensing of another 300 deposit-taking institutions; many of the latter were new deposit-takers and others that have not previously been subject to the voluntary arrangements for supervision introduced by the Bank in 1975. In the course of its supervision the Bank has identified a number of matters which it feels should be drawn to the attention of authorised institutions generally. Though most of the points set out in this notice will concern only a minority of institutions, it is being addressed for information to all institutions authorised under the Banking Act. The Bank is ready to discuss with individual institutions the application of these points of guidance.

1 Connected lending

Assessment of the risks attaching to loans to companies or persons connected with the lending institution, its managers, directors or controllers, may be obscured by subjective considerations. In the Bank's view such lending can be justified only when undertaken for the clear commercial advantage of the lending institution and should be negotiated and agreed on an arm's length basis.

The Bank does not normally expect connected business to form a significant proportion of assets. However it does not think it appropriate to set a single threshold figure, applicable in all circumstances, to the total amount of this type of lending since lending can be 'connected' in many different ways. In the course of its supervision the Bank has therefore to make a judgment about the degree of connection to be attributed to an institution's loans and its acceptability. In order to do so, it requires full information on all matters relevant to each loan which may be of this kind. When connected lending on any scale exists or is contemplated, institutions should discuss and agree with the Bank the extent of such lending appropriate to their particular circumstances.

As stated in the Measurement of Capital paper, paragraph 26(i),[1] lending to subsidiaries and associated companies which has the character of capital is normally deducted from the capital base of the lending institution. Furthermore, there may be occasions when either under the terms of the lending agreement or by virtue of the financial circumstances of the borrower, connected lending is closer to an injection of risk capital then the provision of a loan of certain value. In such cases the Bank may require the amount of this lending to be deducted from the capital base for prudential calculations.

[1] See now BSD/1990/2 and BSD/1990/3.

2 Annual accounts and returns to the Bank of England

The Bank expects to receive copies of the annual report and audited accounts of each supervised institution not later than 6 months after the end of the institution's financial year and preferably within 3 months. The Bank also expects to receive regular returns within the time specified for each return, since the Bank's system of supervision depends in large measure on the information shown in these returns. Failure to submit returns on time, or to file accounts within 6 months of its year-end, may lead the Bank to review whether the institution concerned continues to meet the criteria in Schedule 2 to the Act.

3 Large loans to individual customers

It has become clear that some institutions are not sufficiently aware of the need to keep the size of individual exposures within prudent limits.

An important measure of capital adequacy used by the Bank is the Risk Asset Ratio[1] which calculates the adequacy of capital in relation to the risk of losses which may be incurred. That calculation takes no account of concentration of risk and the Bank in judging the level of the risk asset ratio appropriate for an institution assumes a good spread of assets. However, where it identifies undue concentration of risk, it will expect a higher ratio to be maintained. It follows that an *increase* in concentration will normally lead to a review of a previously indicated risk asset ratio, with a presumption that a higher ratio will be needed.

Experience suggests that exposures (loans, acceptances, guarantees, etc) to one customer or group of customers should not normally exceed around 10% of an institution's capital base.[2] Lending on such a scale should in any case be made only after the most careful credit assessment, against good and sufficient security and if the directors of the lending institution are confident that such exposure can be justified to the Bank. The more an individual exposure exceeds 10% of the capital base, the more rigorous the Bank will be in requiring justification. If loans in excess of 10% of the capital base have been or are to be made, the institution will normally be requested to maintain a level of capital resources significantly higher than that which would otherwise be required.

[1] See paragraphs 29–34 of the Bank's paper, The Measurement of Capital (September 1980). See now BSD/1990/2 and BSD/1990/3.
[2] Adjusted as set out under the heading 'Risk Asset Ratio' in Appendix B of The Measurement of Capital paper.

4 Risk of fraudulent invitations to lend/borrow/intermediate

Institutions appearing on the lists of authorised institutions published by the Bank – particularly smaller institutions in the licensed deposit-taker sector – may find that they are approached by persons unknown to them suggesting participation in very substantial business out of all proportion to their normal scale of activities. These approaches often concern international activities (involving foreign currencies or gold) and are said to be of a confidential nature. Often these approaches are made with the object of committing a fraud. While tactics may vary, the object of the fraud is usually to induce the institution approached either to make payments itself (eg in the form of advance commission or expenses) or to take some action which may lend plausibility to a story to be told to another institution. For this latter purpose any letter using an institution's printed stationery, even a simple letter declining the offer of funds, may be turned to advantage by those perpetrating the fraud.

If business of any substance is offered to an institution without a proper introduction from a trusted customer or financial associate, extreme care should be exercised in authenticating the nature and origins of the transaction and the bona fides of the agent introducing the business. The Bank asks to be informed of all offers which are considered dubious so that appropriate warnings may be given to other institutions. In doing so, the Bank will exercise the greatest care to respect any necessary confidences.

5 Floating charges

Deposit-taking institutions are reminded that they should not give floating charges over their assets as security for their own borrowing from banks or other sources. Where a lender seeks security in the form of a charge over assets, that charge must either be applied to specific assets or limited to a certain proportion of specified assets, such as hire purchase agreements, in order to ensure that there would always be sufficient unencumbered assets to meet the claims of depositors in a liquidation of the company.

The Bank expects to be informed in advance of any agreement which would create a charge on an authorised institution's assets.   **[803]**

Bank of England
Banking Supervision Division
April 1983
BSD/1983/1

FOREIGN CURRENCY OPTIONS (APRIL 1984)

A number of banks have shown considerable interest in writing currency options for customers or for other banks, or in dealing in contracts on option exchanges. The Bank's paper 'Foreign Currency Exposure' published in April 1981 does not cover this topic. The purpose of this paper is to explain how the Bank of England will treat banks' option business, particularly in relation to the guidelines agreed individually with banks for monitoring their foreign exchange exposure.

The nature of the risk

An option contract allows the holder to exchange (or equally to choose not to exchange) a specific amount of one currency for another at a predetermined rate (the 'exercise price') during some period in the future. In exchange for this right, the holder pays a premium to the person granting the option. The premium is charged to cover the risk borne by the bank or other institution writing the contract; some of this is absorbed by the transaction costs of the bank in covering the risk.

The main risk, therefore, rests with the institution writing the option. Its exposure to movements in the exchange rate between the two currencies involved may be as great as having an open position of the same size as the value of contracts written; it may of course be less to the extent that options are not exercised. An institution which *holds* an option has no exposure to loss, only the possible opportunity for gain (unless it is treating its expenditure on the premium payment as an investment rather than writing it off. If it treats it as an investment it is exposed to the extent of the book value given to the asset).

A bank which writes currency options for its customers may protect its position to the extent that it is able to purchase a corresponding contract either on an exchange or from another bank; but its position is only fully protected if the terms of the contract purchased are at least as favourable as those of the option written. As the organised options exchanges work to specific delivery dates they can never be used as perfect cover against a contract which is exercisable over a period beyond the delivery date of the exchange contract.

As an alternative to taking cover on the option exchanges, a bank might hedge its position on the cash market. If the bank can find a suitable formula for doing this – see below –, it is then able to write options for customers for non-standard amounts, for non-standard periods, and in any freely traded currency, thereby offering a tailor-made product for its customer's needs. It should be noted that because the risk needs to be monitored continuously the use of cash markets to hedge option contracts is restricted for banks which lack the ability to deal in all time zones.

In assessing the risk which a bank bears in writing currency options it is necessary to assume that its counterparties behave in a rational manner. A customer would not exercise his option to buy a currency from the bank if he could purchase it more cheaply on the spot market; similarly he would not opt to sell a currency to a bank at a rate less favourable than that obtainable on the spot market.

At first sight it would appear that all a bank need do to protect its position is to cover fully those options which currently it would be in the customer's interests to exercise ('in the money' options), and leave uncovered those which it would not ('out of the money' options). This method however fails to account for a bank being at risk not only from the current spot rate in relation to the exercise rate, but also to future changes in the spot rate until the expiry of the option. Such changes might alter the bank's position from being exposed to loss – when the rate favoured the customer's exercising the option – to being exposed to no loss – when it would be to the customer's disadvantage to exercise the option. If the spot rate fluctuated around the exercise price the bank would be involved in considerable costs fully covering and then fully uncovering its position, whilst the option holder delayed exercising his option in the hope of the spot rate moving (further) into the money, so enabling him to make a (larger) profit.

Several banks have developed techniques based on mathematical formulae to determine the premium which should be charged for writing an option contract, and the position which should be taken in the cash market to hedge their option contracts.

The variables on which the formulae depend include: the current spot rate and its relation to the exercise rate; the remaining period of the contract; the volatility of the exchange rate; and interest rates in the two currencies concerned. Thus a contract which is a long way 'out of the money' and which has only a short time to run requires virtually no cash cover; one which still has some time to run, other things being equal, will require more cover, particularly if the exchange rate is volatile. Such formulae have become widely accepted as the basis for both hedging and pricing contracts, although individual banks are developing various refinements which they hope will enhance their hedging techniques.

For accounting purposes banks which are active in the market are proposing to value their option contracts by marking them to market (eg options written are revalued to the price which would have to be paid to buy back the rights which have been extended to the option holder).

Foreign exchange guidelines

For the purposes of monitoring a bank's risk the Bank will expect any exposures arising out of option business to be contained within existing guidelines rather than be additional to them.

The Bank will need to have reported to it the extent of banks' exposures; reporting will take one or two forms. Unless a bank is able to satisfy the Bank that its hedging techniques are sufficiently developed, the Bank will take a 'worst view' approach. The approach will take account of the potential effect of the exercise of option rights held by a bank's customers on its open position in individual currencies, including the possibility that the bank's position in a particular currency may be transformed from a long position to a short (or vice versa). It is recognised that this system fails to take any account of the exercise price relative to the current spot rate (and therefore the likelihood of the option being exercised), nor is any credit given for options taken – on the ground that without knowing the full details of the period and exercise rates of options written and options held there is no way of knowing whether options held are of any value in hedging the risks on options which the bank has written. An example of the reporting form (an annex to the existing s 3 form and instructions) is given at Annex A.

Where a bank has considered the mathematics of options in some detail, the Bank will allow it to use its own formula for measuring the extent of its exposure on currency options, which will be assessed with that on cash markets to determine the overall open position for the purposes of monitoring a bank's foreign exchange exposure against the agreed guidelines.

Before a bank will be permitted to use its own formula for calculating its exposure for guideline purposes, the Bank will need to be satisfied not only with the mathematical basis of the formula and procedures for monitoring its continued validity, but also that the operating systems for conducting the business and controlling the options books (including limits) are adequate. The operation of a bank's own formula will be kept under review and the Bank will expect to discuss options business with these banks on a frequent and regular basis. An example of the reporting form for these banks is given in Annex B.

The arrangements outlined in this note will form the basis on which the Bank assesses banks' foreign currency options for prudential purposes. However the case for separate guidelines for options business will be reviewed by the Bank in the light of market developments and discussions with individual banks.

Annex A

	Net dealing long (short) spot & forward position Col 11	Potential purchases under option rights granted to others Col 12	Potential sales under option rights granted to others Col 13	Dealing exposure to depreciation Col 14	Dealing exposure to appreciation Col 15	Options held to purchase currencies Col 16	Options held to sell currencies Col 17
USA							
BELG							
CANA							
DENM							
WGER							
FRAN							
EIRE							
ITAL							
JAPA							
NETH							
SAUA							
SPAI							
SWED							
SWIT							
GOLD							
Foreign currencies not listed above { long short							
UK							
TOTAL	ZERO						
Aggregate of net short open positions							

Instructions for completion of Annex A to Form S3

Enter in Col 12 (Col 13) total amounts of each currency *including sterling* that a bank might purchase (sell) through the exercise of currency options it has given.

Enter in Col 14 the sum of the entries in Cols 11 and 12, except that if this sum is negative, a nil entry should be made.

Enter in Col 15 the sum of the entries in Cols 11 and 13, except that if this sum is positive, a nil entry should be made.

Note that the entries in the sterling rows of columns 12 and 13 arise from options directly involving sterling and are *not* balancing items as in columns 9 and 11.

For the purposes of monitoring a bank's foreign exchange exposure the entries in columns 14 and 15 will each (separately) be assessed against the guidelines agreed with the Bank of England, Banking Supervision Division.

Enter in Col 16 (Col 17) total amounts of each currency *including sterling* that the bank might purchase (sell) through exercise of currency options it holds. Note that these entries are required only for statistical information about the market and do not form part of a bank's exposure.

Annex B

Currency	Net dealing long (short) spot & forward position Col 11	Gross value of potential purchases under option rights granted Col 12	Gross value of potential sales under option rights granted Col 13	Gross value of potential purchases under options rights held Col 14	Gross value of potential sales under options rights held Col 15	Adjusted options position Col 16	Net dealing position including option contracts (Col 11 + Col 16) Col 17
USA							
BELG							
CANA							
DENM							
WGER							
FRAN							
EIRE							
ITAL							
JAPA							
NETH							
SAUA							
SPAI							
SWED							
SWIT							
GOLD							
Foreign currencies not listed above { long / short }							
UK							
TOTAL	ZERO						
Aggregate of net short open positions							

Instructions for completion of Annex B to Form S3

Enter in Col 12 (Col 13) total amounts of each currency *including sterling* that the bank might purchase (sell) through the exercise of currency options it has given.

Enter in Col 14 (Col 15) total amounts of each currency *including sterling* that the bank might purchase (sell) through the exercise of currency options it holds.

Note

    (a) the entries in the sterling rows of columns 12 to 15 arise from options directly involving sterling and are not balancing items as in Columns 9 and 11;

    (b) the entries in Cols 12 to 15 do not cross cast to the adjusted options position in Col 16. This information is required for statistical purposes and is not directly used to assess a bank's foreign exchange exposure.

Enter in Col 16 the adjusted value of options given and taken; the formula used should be that previously agreed between the bank and the Banking Supervision Division of the Bank of England. Note that any positions hedged in the cash market should be included on the main part of the S3 return.

Column 17 (the sum of Cols 11 & 16) will be used for monitoring a bank's foreign exchange exposure against the existing guidelines agreed with the Bank of England.

BSD/1985/2
(April 1985)

NOTICE TO RECOGNISED BANKS AND LICENSED DEPOSIT-TAKERS

Banking Supervision Division
OFF-BALANCE SHEET RISKS
Note issuance facilities/Revolving underwriting facilities

1 Pressures on banks' capital adequacy ratios in recent years have contributed to a significant growth in off-balance sheet instruments not all of which are currently captured in the prudential measurement of capital and liquidity. This has led not only to a growth in such new instruments but also to banks taking on such obligations on terms which, in the Bank's view, do not properly reflect the risks involved. The Bank, therefore, wishes to set in train a review, in consultation with banks and other institutions, of the range of off-balance sheet risks to which they may be exposed in order to assess those risks more accurately. This review will include the treatment of more traditional and well-established contingent liabilities as well as instruments which have been developed more recently.

2 An area of particular concern arises from the obligations assumed by institutions which act as underwriters of note issuance facilities[1] or revolving underwriting facilities. The Bank considers that these obligations represent a long-term credit risk for an underwriting bank[2], as the bank can be called upon to honour its undertaking to lend at any time during the life of the facility, including circumstances in which the financial position of the borrower has deteriorated and when it might otherwise prefer not to lend. This obligation is different from normal underwriting engagements where, unless the issue has been wrongly priced and is left with the bank, a bank's obligation to the borrower terminates when the issue has been completed.

3 Although many facilities now include a condition involving any material adverse change in the financial position of the borrower, the Bank considers that an underwriting bank could find itself under strong pressure to provide funds, particularly where there is a long-term relationship between the borrower and the bank.

4 The Bank therefore considers that a bank's underwriting obligations under a note issuance facility should be included in the measurement and assessment of its capital adequacy. The Bank will henceforth, as a provisional measure, treat all such obligations as contingent liabilities for capital adequacy purposes and will include them at a weight of 0.5 in the calculation of the risk asset ratio, whether or not the facility has been drawn down by the borrower. Where an institution holds paper issued under a note issuance facility of which it is an underwriter, its holding of the paper will be weighted as a balance sheet item, and the amount of its underwriting obligations reduced accordingly.

5 From discussions which the Bank has had with individual institutions, it is clear that many institutions already include underwriting obligations under note issuance facilities within their existing credit limits for individual borrowers. The Bank believes that this is a prudent practice and that it should be adopted by all banks underwriting these facilities. It is important that an underwriting institution makes a full credit assessment of a borrower under a note issuance facility in the same way as it would if it were making an advance, and that it keeps its exposure under continuous review during the life of the facility.

6 An underwriting institution should also ensure that in managing its liquidity it takes account of the possibility that it may be requested to take up at short notice any unsold notes issued by the borrower.

7 Although the Bank does not apply capital adequacy requirements to UK branches of overseas banks, the Bank nevertheless wishes to monitor branches' activities as underwriters of note issuance facilities and to include these obligations in measuring an institution's large exposures to individual customers. Branches of overseas banks should therefore report their underwriting obligations under these facilities to the Bank. Treatment of these obligations of overseas branches for capital adequacy purposes is of

course a matter for the authorities in the home countries of these banks. The issues raised in this note have been discussed by the Bank with the authorities in the major industrialised countries who are also considering their own arrangements in respect of this business.

8 A statistical notice to all reporting institutions is being issued at the same time as this notice. In future an institution's underwriting obligations under a note issuance facility should be reported separately, as a contingent liability, under item 13.7 on the form Q7 or under item 7.6 on the form B7, as appropriate. These obligations should also be included, where appropriate, under item 20 on the form Q7, or under items 11 and 12 on the form B7.

9 The increasing scale of many banks' obligations under note issuance facilities has prompted the Bank to bring them within the measurement of the risk asset ratio at an early stage. The Bank recognises that some of these facilities may be arranged for a bank borrower. In such cases there will initially be an inconsistency between the weight (0.5) given to all obligations under these facilities and the weight given to market lending to monetary sector institutions (0.2). This matter will, inter alia, be taken up in the broader review of off-balance sheet exposure referred to in paragraph 1.

10 Meanwhile the Bank is willing to discuss the impact of the introduction of this policy with any institution the calculations of whose capital adequacy will be materially affected. **[805]**

Bank of England
April 1985

---

[1] For the purpose of this notice, these facilities are defined as arrangements which enable a borrower to raise funds through the issue of short-term paper, where the availability of funds is in effect guaranteed by a bank or a group of banks underwriting the issue of paper by the borrower. These include facilities arranged for both bank and non-bank borrowers, where the paper is issued in the form of certificates of deposit or promissory notes. They may also include multi-component facilities under which the underwriting institutions may make available alternative funds if the borrower chooses not to make an issue of the notes.

[2] For the purpose of this notice, the term 'bank' includes recognised banks and licensed deposit-taking institutions.

STATISTICAL NOTICE TO MONETARY SECTOR INSTITUTIONS

1 In a notice to recognised banks and licensed deposit-takers issued to-day, the Bank announced that a bank's obligation as an underwriter of a note issuance facility/ revolving underwriting facility will henceforth be treated as a contingent liability and be weighted at 0.5 in the risk asset ratio.

2 For this purpose a note issuance facility has been defined as an arrangement which enables a borrower to raise finance through the issue of short-term paper, where the availability of funds is in effect guaranteed by a bank or group of banks underwriting the issue of paper by the borrower. This includes facilities arranged for both bank and non-bank borrowers, where the paper is issued in the form of certificates of deposit or promissory notes. Note issuance facilities also include multi-component facilities under which the underwriting institutions may make available alternative funds if the borrower chooses not to make an issue of notes.

3 The Bank will in future require an institution's underwriting obligations under a note issuance facility to be reported on the form Q7 or B7, according to whether the reporting institution is incorporated in the UK or is a UK branch of an overseas bank. For Q7 reporters, this requirement will apply to all reporting on or after 15 May 1985, for B7 reporters, it will come into effect for returns completed at end June 1985.

4 The total amount of an institution's underwriting obligations under all note issu-ance facilities should be reported separately as a contingent liability under item 13.7 on the Q7, or as an 'other' contingent liability under item 7.6 on the form B7. The amount of these underwriting commitments should also be included for the purpose of

determining whether an institution's total exposure to a customer should be reported as a large exposure under item 20 on the form Q7 or under items 11 and 12 on the form B7. Where a facility has been drawn down by the borrower and the notes are held by anyone other than the underwriting institution, its underwriting obligation must continue to be reported in full.

5 Where an institution holds paper issued under a note issuance facility of which it also acts as an underwriter, the amount of the holding should be reported as an asset in the normal way and not be included in the institution's underwriting obligation reported as a contingent liability (see paragraph 4 above).

6 The reporting instructions for the forms Q7 and B7 will be amended in due course. For the present, there are no changes in the reporting arrangements for other statistical returns submitted to the Bank, so far as underwriting obligations under note issuance facilities are concerned. **[806]**

Bank of England
April 1985

BSD/1986/1
(February 1986)

NOTICE TO RECOGNISED BANKS AND LICENSED DEPOSIT-TAKERS

Large exposures in relation to mergers and acquisitions[1]

1 A number of proposals for large mergers or acquisitions have recently been launched. It appears to the Bank that there has been a significant change in the scale and nature of banks'[1] traditional involvement in facilitating these transactions. In particular the Bank has noted arrangements or proposals for banks or banking groups:

    (i) to acquire significant strategic shareholdings in companies involved;
    (ii) to buy individual subsidiaries from a group involved.

The Bank wishes to make clear its attitude to these arrangements in the light of its responsibilities under the Banking Act 1979.[2]

2 Until further notice the Bank expects banks and banking groups to give it prior notification of their intention to enter into these types of transactions or any similar transactions.

3 The Bank will not normally regard as prudent such acquisitions of shares in a company which, taken together with existing exposures to that company or group, exceed 25% of the bank's or banking group's capital base.

4 Moreover, the Bank will in certain circumstances treat acquisitions of such shares as though they were investments in subsidiaries and will deduct the value of the investment from the capital base.

5 The Bank will not give special treatment to vehicle companies which do not have the effect of transferring the risk of the exposure from the bank or banking group.

6 Where a bank or banking group is already committed, the Bank will discuss with these banks arrangements to bring their position into line with the Bank's requirements as soon as possible. **[807]**

Bank of England
Banking Supervision Division
February 1986

---

[1] For the purpose of this Notice, references to banks should be taken to include recognised banks and licensed deposit-takers.
[2] Now the Banking Act 1987.

BSD/1986/2
(March 1986)

NOTICE TO RECOGNISED BANKS AND LICENSED DEPOSIT-TAKERS

Subordinated loan capital issued by recognised banks and licensed deposit-takers

1 On 28 November 1984, the Bank issued a consultative note entitled 'Subordinated Loan Capital issued by Recognised Banks and Licensed Deposit-takers'. (For the purpose of this Notice, references to banks should be taken to include recognised banks and licensed deposit-takers.) The note addressed various matters relating to issues of loan capital by banks, and formed the basis for detailed discussions with the banking community about the arrangements applying to bank holdings of debt issued by banks for capital adequacy measurement purposes, the inclusion of perpetual subordinated debt in a bank's capital base and the supervisory treatment of all forms of subordinated debt issued by banks.

2 The Bank has since published the text of two letters[1] addressed to the British Bankers' Association, reporting progress on these matters as discussions with the banks have proceeded. This Notice sets out the Bank's policy on these matters and as such is to be regarded as an addendum to the Bank's paper 'The Measurement of Capital' (September 1980). References in this Notice to 'The Measurement of Capital' are to this paper.[2]

---

[1] 16 May and 8 October 1985.
[2] See now BSD/1990/2 and BSD/1990/3.

Bank holdings of subordinated loan capital issued by other banks

3 The Bank is strongly committed to the principle that, in assessing capital adequacy, any investment made in the capital of another bank, whether in the UK or overseas, should be deducted from the holder's capital base, to ensure that the same capital is not used by more than one institution to support its operations. Deduction applies to any subordinated loan capital issued by a UK bank authorised under the Banking Act 1979,[1] or by a bank overseas. It also embraces holdings of subordinated and unsubordinated loan capital issued by holding companies of such institutions or financing vehicles within banking groups.[2]

4 In recognition of the important role played by a number of banks in making a market for bank capital issues, however, the Bank is prepared to consider applications from primary and/or secondary market-makers for concessions from the principle of deduction.

---

[1] Now the Banking Act 1987.
[2] The principle of deduction applies to equity as well as loan capital, but the concessions explained in this Notice apply only to loan capital. If necessary – and presently banks' holdings of equity are not great – further consideration may need to be given to the treatment of holdings of equity.

Primary market-makers

5 Those banks which can satisfy the Bank that they act as managers or underwriters for new issues of bank capital may qualify to be regarded as primary market-makers. The concession will allow such banks to hold such issues for up to 90 days from the date of issue,[1] after which a full deduction from the capital base will be made (unless the holding is accommodated within a bank's concession as a secondary market-maker). A bank to which a primary market-maker's concession applies will therefore be allowed to trade in issues which it has managed or underwritten during this 90 day period.

---

[1] The date of issue is to be taken as the day on which payment is made by the noteholders (and the first such date in the case of a partly paid issue).

Secondary market-makers

6 Secondary market-makers are those banks which can demonstrate to the Bank that they undertake a committed and regular function as market-makers in banks' capital issues. Banks will be required to identify the particular issues for which they act as secondary market-makers.

7 The amount of the concession will be calculated individually for each market-maker and will normally be set within a range up to a maximum of 20% of the bank's adjusted capital base (as explained in the *Measurement of capital* paper).[1] In setting the concession for a subsidiary of a bank, which subsidiary is authorised under the Banking Act, some account may be taken of group capital. In the case of subsidiaries of overseas banks the amount agreed will, inter alia, be subject to the agreement of the supervisor of the parent bank.

8 The concession will be set as an absolute figure and notified in writing to the bank concerned. It will apply to a bank's net long position in bank debt held at the end of each working day, including any debt sold under repurchase agreements. Further details of the scope of the concession are given in the notes for completion of a new statistical return (see paragraph 11 below).

[1] See now BSD/1990/2 and BSD/1990/3.

Primary and secondary market-makers

9 Any bank debt held under a primary or a secondary market-maker's concession will be weighted in the usual way at 1.0 in the calculation of the risk asset ratio. Other holdings of banks' capital will be deducted from the holder's capital base.

10 A holding of group paper by any entity within the bank group concerned should be maintained only on a restricted basis, which will be agreed with individual banks, and will be subject to full deduction from the capital base when calculating the capital ratios of the group on a consolidated basis.

11 Special reporting arrangements will apply in order that the Bank can monitor positions in banks' capital issues. A new quarterly Form MM is being introduced for this purpose. The Bank also reserves the right to call from time to time for greater detail of the primary or secondary market portfolios held within either concession.

12 The size of holdings of individual issues held within either a primary or secondary market-maker's concession will be subject to the policy being established on the treatment of large exposures. (A separate consultative document 'Large exposures undertaken by institutions authorised under the Banking Act 1979' was issued in July 1985, and a further paper will be issued in due course.)

Primary perpetual subordinated debt

13 Subordinated debt can be structured so as to bring it close to equity in terms of the protection which it offers to depositors. The principal features which give it this quality of 'primary' capital are that it can absorb losses whilst leaving a bank able to continue to trade, that it has no fixed servicing costs (ie that there are circumstances in which the borrower can defer a payment of interest without bringing itself into default) and that the proceeds of the debt issue are made permanently available to the borrower.

14 The following are the conditions which must be satisfied for an issue of perpetual debt by a UK bank to be treated by the Bank as primary capital:

(a) The claims of the lender on the borrowing bank must be fully subordinated to those of all unsubordinated creditors.
(b) The debt agreement must not include any clauses which might trigger repayment of the debt. This will not, however, prejudice any right to petition for the winding-up of the borrower, for example, in the event of non-payment of interest on the debt (other than that which is deferred in accordance with paragraph (d) below).
(c) No repayment of the debt may be made without the prior consent of the Bank (see also paragraph 24 below).

(d) The debt agreement must provide for the bank to have the option to defer an interest payment on the debt (eg if the bank has not paid or declared a dividend payment in a preceding period.)

(e) The documents governing the issue of the debt (hereafter referred to as the debt agreement) must provide for the debt and unpaid interest to be able to absorb losses, whilst leaving a bank able to continue trading. This can be achieved by providing for automatic conversion of the perpetual debt, and unpaid interest, into share capital should reserves become negative and where a capital reconstruction has not been undertaken. In such a case the bank will be required to maintain a sufficient margin of authorised but unissued share capital in order to allow a conversion of the debt into equity to be made at any time. Alternatively, instead of providing for automatic conversion, the debt agreement can expressly provide for the principal and interest on the debt to absorb losses, where the bank would not otherwise be solvent, and for the noteholders to be treated as if they were holders of a specified class of share capital in any liquidation of the bank. In this case the debt agreement will provide for the debt to be treated as if it had been converted into share capital either on the day immediately preceding the presentation of a petition for the commencement of a winding-up of the borrowing institution or on the date of the creditors' or shareholders' meeting at which the relevant resolution for a winding-up was passed. The debt agreement must contain an explicit warning to noteholders that the debt can be treated in this way.

Inclusion of primary perpetual subordinated debt in the capital base

15 The amount of perpetual subordinated debt treated as primary capital will be limited to one half of a bank's capital base as defined in the Measurement of Capital paper, excluding all loan capital[1] and after deducting goodwill and other intangible assets. (For example, where the capital base excluding all loan caital and intangible assets is 100, the maximum amount of perpetual subordinated debt which could be treated as primary capital is 50.)

16 The amount of all subordinated debt[1] which can be included in a bank's total capital base will be subject to an upper limit equal to the capital base excluding all loan capital[1] and after deducting goodwill and other intangible assets. (Continuing the example given in paragraph 15 above, the maximum amount of all subordinated debt[1] which could be included in a bank's capital base is 100 – for example, 50 of primary perpetual subordinated debt and 50 of term subordinated debt.)

17 Term subordinated debt, and perpetual subordinated debt exceeding that allowed as primary capital under paragraph 15 above, will remain restricted to a maximum of one third of the total capital base after deducting goodwill and other intangible assets. (Taking the figure of 100 mentioned in paragraph 15 above and assuming an issue of primary perpetual subordinated debt of 20, term subordinated debt of up to 60 could be included in the capital base – on the basis that the term debt of 60 does not exceed one-third of the total capital base of 180.)

18 Any subordinated debt which does not qualify to be included in a bank's capital base, within the limits described in paragraphs 15–17 above, will be treated in the normal way as part of a bank's long term funding.

19 The Bank expects shortly to issue a further Notice to all institutions authorised under the Banking Act, clarifying its treatment of a number of items in the calculation of banks' capital ratios. the Notice will, inter alia, cover the treatment of redeemable shares in a bank's capital base, and this in turn will affect the amount of perpetual subordinated debt which can count as primary capital for banks which have such shares in issue.

---

[1] Primary perpetual and all other subordinated debt.

Supervisory treatment of all subordinated debt

20 The Measurement of Capital[1] paper states that subordinated loan capital which is to be included in a bank's capital base (as defined in paragraph 11 of that paper) must, inter

alia, have a minimum initial term to maturity of five years. However, the Deposit Protection Scheme offers protection to deposits which have an original term to maturity of not more than five years, so giving rise to the possibility of a loan stock with a term to maturity of exactly five years qualifying both as part of the capital base and for protection under the Deposit Protection Scheme. In order to remove this inconsistency, the Bank has for some time required subordinated debt which is to form part of a bank's capital base to have, inter alia, a minimum initial term to maturity of five years and one day. This requirement does not affect loan capital already in issue.

21 The Measurement of Capital[1] paper also states that in order to qualify for inclusion in a bank's capital base, the terms of a loan stock must not contain any restrictive covenants which might trigger immediate repayment.

22 The Bank reaffirms that there should be no clauses in the loan agreement which can trigger early repayment of the debt. This includes cross-default clauses and negative pledges. Issues made before 28 November 1984[2] which contain such clauses will, however, continue to be included in banks' capital bases (although such clauses will not be allowed in respect of any extension of the redemption date or increase in the amount issued).

23 As a further condition, the debt agreement must normally be subject to English law. Where an overseas operating subsidiary is issuing capital in its local market, the Bank will accept foreign law, although the subordination clause contained in the debt agreement or supporting guarantee must still generally be subject to English law. In certain circumstances, however, the Bank will accept foreign law throughout if this is necessary for the success of the issue in the local market. In all cases, however, the Bank must give its prior consent where foreign law is to apply.

24 The Bank requires that no early repayment of any subordinated loan capital may be made without its prior consent: such repayment will be permitted only where the Bank is satisfied that the bank's capital is adequate after repayment. A letter to the Bank, giving effect to this condition and undertaking to seek the Bank's prior consent to any material variation in the terms and conditions of an issue, will be required from the bank concerned. The Bank considers it essential that noteholders should be made aware of the restriction on early repayment, either via the loan agreement or in the offer documents or through other information sources commonly used in the markets.

25 Where it is proposed to make an issue of loan capital which is designed to be included in a bank's capital base, the Bank requires that it should be given prior notice of the issue and sufficient opportunity to consider and agree the loan documentation in advance. However, in order to facilitate the timing of issues, the Bank will accept 'shelf documentation' so that only changes from this documentation need be discussed with the Bank before an issue.   **[808]**

---

[1] See now BSD/1990/2 and BSD/1990/3.
[2] This is the date of the Bank's consultative note referred to in paragraph 1 of this Notice, when the Bank formally clarified its policy towards clauses which can trigger early repayment of debt.

STATISTICAL NOTICE TO MONETARY SECTOR INSTITUTIONS

The measurement of capital

1 In a notice to recognised banks and licensed deposit-takers (BSD/1986/4) issued today, the Bank announced certain modifications of its system of measuring capital adequacy. As a consequence, there are some minor changes in statistical reporting affecting the form Q7. There are no changes in the reporting arrangements for other statistical returns submitted to the Bank associated with the modifications mentioned above.

Leasing business

2 In future, for a lessee bank[1] under a *finance lease*, or a hirer under a hire purchase contract, a full deduction of the value of the asset will be made from its capital base.

Such assets will continue to be reported in item 20.2 of the form BS (or 13 of the form QBS) and in item 12.2 of the form Q7. As a consequence, the reporting instruction for item 12.2 of the form Q7 now reads as follows:

"*Plant and equipment* Include any plant and equipment owned or recorded as such by the reporting institution and used in connection with its own business. Equipment leased out to customers under operating leases should be included in item 12.9 of the form Q7. Equipment leased out under finance leases should be included either in item 17 of the form BS or in item 11 of form QBS."

This revised reporting instruction for item 12.2 of the form Q7 takes account of the new treatment of assets leased out under operating leases (see paragraph 7 below).

3 Assets leased in by a bank lessee under an *operating lease* are not deducted from the capital base and no weight is given to them in the calculation of the risk asset ratio. Accordingly, such assets will continue not to be reported on the form BS or the form Q7.

4 For a lessor bank under a finance lease or an operating lease, a risk asset weight for the asset will be applied according to the status of the lessee. A weight of 0.2 will be applied to assets leased out under such leases to members of the UK monetary sector, UK local authorities, UK public corporations and UK building societies, and a weight of 1.0 to all other leases.

5 All assets leased out under finance leases are currently reported in item 17 of the form BS (or item 11 of the forms QBS) and all assets leased out under operating leases are included in item 20.2 of the form BS (or item 13 of the form QBS). These arrangements will continue.

6 However, in order that the Bank can identify the status of lessees for risk asset weighting purposes, additional information will be required on the form Q7. Assets leased out under *finance leases* and reported in item 17 of the form BS (or item 11 of the form QBS) should also be shown at the bottom of the third page of the form Q7, ie below item 12.9, in the following manner.

	Sterling	*Other currencies*
Assets leased out under finance leases	——	——
		(BS17 or QBS 11)
UK monetary sector, UK local authorities, UK public corporations and UK building societies	– – – –	– – – – – – – –
All other leases	– – – –	– – – – – – – –

7 Assets leased out under *operating leases* should be reported in item 12.9 of the form Q7. Such assets should therefore in future be *excluded* from item 12.2 of the form Q7.

8 Form Q7 will be reprinted in due course to incorporate these amendments.

---

[1] For the purpose of this Notice, references to banks should be taken to include recognised banks and licensed deposit-takers.

Bills

9 The Bank has clarified its treatment of holdings of bills in the calculation of the risk asset ratio (paragraph 14 of the Notice BSD/1986/4). However, this has not involved any change in the statistical reporting instructions for bills.

Lending to UK building societies

10 All lending to UK building societies is now weighted at 0.2 (except for holdings of FRNs or other paper with an original maturity of one year or more, which will attract a weighting of 1.0 or 1.5) in the calculation of the risk asset ratio. Lending to building societies will continue to be reported on forms BS in items 12.10 and 16.5 (or on form QBS in item 10.2), as appropriate. However, in order that the Bank can separately identify the amount of lending to building societies which is included in item 16.5 of the form BS and item 10.2 of the QBS (these items embrace lending to all "Other UK

residents"), any lending to building societies reported as part of these items should in future also be shown *in item 10.9 of the form Q7.*

11 Accordingly, for reporting institutions which complete the form BS, the amount of any lending reported in items 10.4–10.8 of the form Q7 should be reduced by the amount now shown in Q7 item 10.9, so that the sum of items 10.1–10.9 equals BS items 16.5 and 16.6. For reporting institutions which complete the form QBS, item 10.9 of the form Q7 should in future be reserved for lending to building societies and not be used to give a sector classification of advances. **[809]**

Banking Supervision Division
Bank of England
19 June 1986

BSD/1987/3
(October 1987)

NOTICE TO INSTITUTIONS AUTHORISED UNDER THE BANKING ACT 1987

GUIDANCE NOTE ON REPORTING ACCOUNTANTS' REPORTS ON BANK OF ENGLAND RETURNS USED FOR PRUDENTIAL PURPOSES

1 Introduction

1.1 The Bank attaches great importance to the information contained in the returns submitted to it by authorised institutions and believes that the degree of confidence and reliance it places on that information will be maintained and improved by the exercise of its powers to ask for returns to be examined and reported on by independent accountants. These powers are derived from section 39 of the Banking Act 1987.[1]

1.2 The purpose of this Notice is to provide guidance to institutions and to reporting accountants' appointed under section 39 of the Act on the scope of the reporting accountants' examinations of returns and to specify the form of their report.

1.3 The reporting requirements outlined in this Notice relate to those returns which are submitted to Banking Supervision Division and to those other returns which provide the Bank with statistical and other information and which are also used for prudential purposes to enable or assist it to exercise its duties and functions under the Act.

1.4 The management of authorised institutions and reporting accountants should be aware of section 94 of the Act regarding the knowing or reckless provision to the Bank of information which is false or misleading in a material particular. This section is particularly relevant in underlining management's responsibility for the preparation and submission of returns and confirms the importance which the Bank expects management to attach to their preparation.

[1] References in this Notice to 'the Act' are to the Banking Act 1987.

2 Reporting accountants' examinations

2.1 Reporting accountants should have a proper understanding and a working knowledge of:

(a) the returns submitted by an authorised institution as well as the Bank's current reporting instructions (including notes and definitions) and any further rulings that have been agreed in writing between the Bank and an individual institution to reflect its particular circumstances;

(b) the policy notices published by the Bank which relate to the returns; for example, those on subordinated loan capital, and on the measurement of capital;

(c) the Bank's Guidance Note on accounting and other records and internal control systems and reporting accountants' reports thereon (BSD/1987/2) issued in September 1987; and

(d) the Bank's consultative paper on its relationship with auditors and reporting accountants issued in July 1987.

2.2 The Bank will make available to reporting accountants, on their appointment, the current reporting instructions, the specific rulings, policy notices, Guidance Note and the consultative paper referred to above. In addition, it will ensure that reporting accountants are informed of additions and changes to those documents and that they receive replacement or superseding documents as and when they are issued.

2.3 Reporting accountants are required to report whether, in their opinion, in all material respects (see paragraphs 3.1 and 3.2 below) the information contained in the returns examined by them:

(a) is complete in so far as all the relevant information contained in the accounting and other records at the reporting date has been extracted there-from and recorded in the returns;

(b) is accurate in so far as it reflects correctly information contained in, and extracted from, the accounting and other records at the reporting date;

(c) is prepared in accordance with the Bank's current reporting instructions (including notes and definitions) and any further written rulings that apply specifically to the particular institution; and

(d) is prepared, in the case of a UK-incorporated institution, using the same accounting policies as those applied in its most recent statutory accounts.

2.4 The Bank does not require reporting accountants appointed to report in accordance with paragraph 2.3 above to form an opinion on the quality of the information contained in the accounting and other records at the reporting date of the returns examined by them. Nor does it require them to report on the systems and controls maintained to provide and ensure the quality of the information for those returns. However, in undertaking their examinations reporting accountants should be aware of the requirement for authorised institutions to maintain adequate accounting and other records and adequate internal control systems and of the most recent reporting accountants' report on those records and systems. The Bank recognises that in reporting on a return reporting accountants may wish to refer in their report to a qualified opinion in the most recent report on records and systems. Such a reference need not constitute a qualified opinion on the information contained in that return. The Bank recognises that an examination of a return is not an audit and that an opinion on the information in a return is not a statutory audit opinion.

2.5 Reporting accountants may consider that the Bank's reporting instructions (including notes and definitions) do not fully and unambiguously cater for the circumstances and nature of a particular material transaction or series of material transactions. In such circumstances regardless of whether a report contains an unqualified, an exception or an adverse opinion the treatment in the returns of the material transaction or series of material transactions should be described in the report or in an appendix thereto.

2.6 The Bank will ensure that all relevant types of returns are examined over a period of time. This period will, at the discretion of the Bank, vary from one institution to another. In determining the frequency and timing of the examination of a return the Bank will take into account, amongst other factors, the cost to the institution in terms of both management time and reporting accountants' fees.

2.7 While undertaking their work as reporting accountants a firm of accountants may examine a return submitted to the Bank and conclude that it contains material errors or omissions which have not been subsequently discovered by management or reported by them to the Bank. In such an event the firm of accountants should invite management to bring the matter to the attention of the Bank and if management declines, or fails to do so within a specified period of time, they should bring the matter to the attention of the Bank themselves. Section 47 of the Act relating to the disclosure of information to the Bank, and the Bank's guidance on ad-hoc reporting, should be noted in this respect.

2.8 In the case of returns which contain information prepared on a consolidated basis the Bank expects reporting accountants to extend their examination of this consolidated information, as they see fit, to the accounting and other records of any group company from which that information has been extracted. The Bank recognises that where such a company is not an authorised institution the Act's requirement for authorised institutions to maintain adequate accounting and other records and adequate internal control systems does not apply to it. To the extent that information in a return examined by them has been extracted from accounting and other records, and is subject to internal control systems, which have not been examined and reported on by them reporting accountants may wish to refer to this fact in their report on that return.

2.9 Where the Bank has agreed with a particular instititution to accept prudential information in addition to, or instead of, the information contained in standard returns, such information will fall within the scope of the reporting requirements of this Notice.

2.10 Where information contained in the accounting and other records of an overseas branch of a UK-incorporated institution is required for the completion of a return either the reporting instructions for that particular return will make this clear or the Bank will issue a further specific ruling to the institution. Reporting accountants are thus required to satisfy themselves that the requirements of paragraph 2.3 above have been met in respect of the information extracted from the accounting and other records of the overseas branch.

3 The required report

3.1 After consultation with each institution and after its submission the Bank will specify in writing the particular return or range of returns that it wishes to have examined and reported on by reporting accountants and also the level of materiality that they should take into account in reporting. A letter of instruction from the institution to the reporting accountants (or a letter of engagement from the reporting accountants duly acknowledged by the institution) should then be sent. A copy should also be sent to the Bank.

3.2 The Bank does not expect a qualified opinion to be given where an error in the information contained in the returns is immaterial; the level of materiality will vary from institution to institution and from one return to another and will be specified in the letter of instruction from the Bank to each institution (see paragraph 3.1 above). The materiality level will be set to ensure that the Bank is informed of all matters that are likely to affect its supervisory judgment.

3.3 Reporting accountants should give their opinion on the matters set out in paragraph 2.3 above. In the case of the requirement contained in paragraph 2.3(d) where the information in a return is prepared by a UK-incorporated institution using accounting policies different to those applied in its most recent statutory accounts reporting accountants should report the fact and circumstances, and where practicable, provide a quantification of the effect of their application. The Bank recognises that there may be valid reasons for accounting policies to differ, but nevertheless in discharging its functions under the Act it wishes to be advised of any differences so that, where they are material, it can assess their effect. It will not consider a report to be 'qualified' solely because it contains a statement of the application of different accounting policies.

3.4 The reporting accountants' report should be addressed to the directors in the case of a UK-incorporated authorised institution and to the senior manager in the case of UK branch of an overseas-incorporated institution. The report should be completed, dated and submitted to the institution not more than three months after the date of the Bank's letter of instruction (see paragraph 3.1 above). The institution should then submit the report to the Bank, with such comments as management sees fit to make, not more than one month after the date of the report.

3.5 If the reporting accountants conclude, after discussing the matter with their client, that they will give an adverse opinion (as opposed to one qualified by exceptions) or that the issue of a report will be delayed they must immediately inform the Bank in writing giving their reasons. They should send the authorised institution a copy of their letter. Similarly, if the institution is unable to submit a report to the Bank within the required period it should inform the Bank in writing of the reasons for the delay.

3.6 It will be for the Bank to judge in the light of the contents of a report and other information about the institution which is available to it whether the requirements of the Act are satisfied.

3.7 The Auditing Practices Committee of the Consultative Committee of Accountancy Bodies is preparing an Auditing Guideline on the audit of banks which will address the work of reporting accountants in relation to their examinations of and reports on the returns submitted by an institution. Reporting accountants are expected to carry out their examination in accordance with this bank auditing guideline.

3.8 The required report (see below) is prepared on the basis that it will be made by a UK firm of accountants. The Bank's consultative paper 'Reports to supervisors: Requirements for branches of overseas banks' discussed the Bank's approach for branches, indicating preference for a UK firm to be appointed. If, exceptionally, a report from the home country auditors or home country supervisors is accepted by the Bank this would be made on the same terms as the required report below.

Bank of England
Banking Supervision Division
October 1987
BSD/1987/3

REPORTING ACCOUNTANTS' REPORT ON BANK OF ENGLAND RETURNS USED FOR PRUDENTIAL PURPOSES

The Directors, XYZ Bank Limited
The Senior Manager, ABC Branch

Dear Sir(s)

In accordance with your letter of instruction dated [   ], a copy of which is attached, we have examined those returns referred to which you have submitted to the Bank of England. We attach a copy of the returns which we have initialled for the purposes of identification.

Our examination has been carried out having regard to the Bank of England's Guidance Note BSD/1987/3 dated October 1987 and in accordance with the Auditing Guideline-Banks issued by the Auditing Practices Committee of the Consultative Committee of Accountancy Bodies.

In our opinion, in all material respects, the information contained in the returns examined by us

EITHER has been completely and accurately extracted from the accounting and other records and has been prepared and presented in accordance with the current reporting instructions (and specific written rulings) issued by the Bank of England and using the same accounting policies as those applied in the most recent statutory accounts (with the exception of the matters set out in the appendix attached to this report).

OR has not been completely and accurately extracted from the accounting and other records and has not been prepared and presented in accordance with the current reporting instructions (and specific written rulings) issued by the Bank of England and using the same accounting policies as those applied in the most recent statutory accounts for the reasons set out in the appendix attached to this report.

Yours faithfully

A Reporting Accountant
Chartered Accountants **[810]**

BSD/1988/1
(April 1988)

ADVERTISING FOR DEPOSITS

This notice draws attention to recent developments relating to advertisements for deposits. It replaces BSD/1985/1 (February 1985).

Advertisements Regulations

1 The Banking Act 1987 (Advertisements) Regulations 1988 (SI 1988 No 645) have been laid before Parliament and will come into effect on 29 April 1988. These regulations will revoke the Banking Act 1979 (Advertisements) Regulations 1985 and the Banking Act 1979 (Advertisements) (Amendment) Regulations 1987. They have been made by HM Treasury, after consultation with the Bank of England and the Building Societies Commission, under section 32 of the Banking Act 1987. Copies of the Regulations are available from HMSO.

2 Regulations will continue to apply, broadly, to any advertisement issued in the United Kingdom which invites the making of deposits with the deposit-taker's offices outside the United Kingdom[1] or another member State of the European Community. The one change of substance from the previous Regulations is that the new Regulations exclude advertisements for deposits which invite only deposits which are incidental to investment business and which are regulated by rules made in the context of the Financial Services Act 1986.

3 The Regulations require the inclusion in advertisements of specified particulars about the deposit-taker, and control references to the deposit-taker's assets and liabilities, deposit protection arrangements, interest on deposits, and the currency in which the deposits will be made.

4 It is, of course, for those issuing advertisements to which the Regulations apply to ensure that they comply fully with the relevant provisions. While the Bank of England does not give legal advice, it will be prepared, in individual cases, to offer guidance on its interpretation of the Regulations. Enquiries should be addressed to Banking Supervision Division (telephone 0171–601 5020). It must be noted, however, that the Bank's understanding cannot be regarded as definitive: in particular, it may change in the light of subsequent developments, including any decisions of the courts.

---

[1] The Channel Islands and the Isle of Man are not part of the United Kingdom. Advertisements for deposits to be made with the offices of the deposit-taker in the Channel Islands and the Isle of Man are therefore not subject to the Regulations.

Advertising Code of Conduct

5 Since the application in April 1985 of the composite tax arrangements to institutions authorised under the Banking Act, it has been necessary to distinguish between rates of interest which relate to 'relevant deposits' (ie deposits subject to the composite rate tax arrangements) and those which do not. To avoid confusion to depositors, the British Bankers' Association, the Finance Houses Association and the Building Societies Association issued in 1985 a code of conduct recommending the quotation of various types of rate and terminology for referring to such rates. Rates paid on relevant deposits should be shown as **net** rates, and on other deposits as **gross** rates. The code envisages that institutions will wish to quote notional rates which show the value to a depositor of the net rate when account is taken of the discharge of liability to basic rate tax. Such a rate should be called a *gross equivalent rate*.

6 The Bank continues to expect authorised institutions to adhere to the provisions of the code and will keep the standard of advertisements under review. In the event of any queries regarding the provisions of the code or its application in individual cases, institutions which are members of the BBA or FHA should first approach these bodies. In the case of institutions which are not members of these bodies, enquiries may be addressed to Banking Supervision Division (telephone 0171–601 5064).

Other matters relating to advertising

7 In addition to the matters outlined in sections I and II above, it may be helpful to repeat here guidance on two further points relating to advertising which has previously been given.

(1) The Bank has indicated that institutions which wish to draw attention to their authorisation under the Banking Act may do so using the term '(an) authorised (institution) under the Banking Act 1987'. There should, however, be no reference to the Bank of England. Thus, forms of words such as 'authorised/supervised by the Bank of England' are not acceptable.

(2) The Bank has approved a standard form of words which may be used when referring to the protection provided by the Deposit Protection Scheme:
'Each depositor's sterling deposits (with United Kingdom offices) up to a maximum of £20,000 are covered under the Deposit Protection Scheme as to 75% of those deposits, subject to the conditions set out in the Banking Act 1987.' **[811]**

Bank of England
Banking Supervision Division
April 1988
BSD/1988/1

BSD/1988/2
(October 1988)

NOTICE TO INSTITUTIONS AUTHORISED UNDER THE BANKING ACT 1987

BANK OF ENGLAND
Banking Supervision Division

SUPERVISORY TREATMENT OF ECU TREASURY BILLS

1 In a Statistical Notice (1988/07) issued today by the Financial Statistics Division of the Bank of England, certain modifications to statistical reporting are announced consequent to the programme for the issue of UK Treasury bills denominated in ECUs.

2 In measuring capital adequacy, the Banking Supervision Division will apply the same treatment to Treasury bills denominated in ECUs as to those denominated in sterling. All bills reported under item 14.1 on Form BS will therefore be weighted at 0.1.
[812]

Bank of England
October 1988

LETTER TO AUTHORISED INSTITUTIONS CONCERNING MONEY-LAUNDERING (JANUARY 1989)

COMMITTEE ON BANKING REGULATIONS AND SUPERVISORY PRACTICES
PREVENTION OF CRIMINAL USE OF THE BANKING SYSTEM FOR THE PURPOSE OF MONEY-LAUNDERING

Preamble

1 Banks and other financial institutions may be unwittingly used as intermediaries for the transfer or deposit of funds derived from criminal activity. Criminals and their associates use the financial system to make payments and transfers of funds from one account to another; to hide the source and beneficial ownership of money; and to

provide storage for bank-notes through a safe-deposit facility. These activities are commonly referred to as money-laundering.

2 Efforts undertaken hitherto with the objective of preventing the banking system from being used in this way have largely been undertaken by judicial and regulatory agencies at national level. However, the increasing international dimension of organised criminal activity, notably in relation to the narcotics trade, has prompted collaborative initiatives at the international level. One of the earliest such initiatives was undertaken by the Committee of Ministers of the Council of Europe in June 1980. In its report[1] the Committee of Ministers concluded that '. . . the banking system can play a highly effective preventive role while the co-operation of the banks also assists in the repression of such criminal acts by the judicial authorities and the police'. In recent years the issue of how to prevent criminals laundering the proceeds of crime through the financial system has attracted increasing attention from legislative authorities, law enforcement agencies and banking supervisors in a number of countries.

3 The various national banking supervisory authorities represented on the Basle Committee on Banking Regulations and Supervisory Practices[2] do not have the same roles and responsibilities in relation to the suppression of money-laundering. In some countries supervisors have a specific responsibility in this field; in others they may have no direct responsibility. This reflects the role of banking supervision, the primary function of which is to maintain the overall financial stability and soundness of banks rather than to ensure that individual transactions conducted by bank customers are legitimate. Nevertheless, despite the limits in some countries on their specific responsibility, all members of the Committee firmly believe that supervisors cannot be indifferent to the use made of banks by criminals.

4 Public confidence in banks, and hence their stability, can be undermined by adverse publicity as a result of inadvertent association by banks with criminals. In addition, banks may lay themselves open to direct losses from fraud, either through negligence in screening undesirable customers or where the integrity of their own officers has been undermined through association with criminals. For these reasons the members of the Basle Committee consider that banking supervisors have a general role to encourage ethical standards of professional conduct among banks and other financial institutions.

5 The Committee believes that one way to promote this objective, consistent with differences in national supervisory practice, is to obtain international agreement to a Statement of Principles to which financial institutions should be expected to adhere.

6 The attached Statement is a general statement of ethical principles which encourages banks' management to put in place effective procedures to ensure that all persons conducting business with their institutions are properly identified; that transactions that do not appear legitimate are discouraged; and that co-operation with law enforcement agencies is achieved. The Statement is not a legal document and its implementation will depend on national practice and law. In particular, it should be noted that in some countries banks may be subject to additional more stringent legal regulations in this field and the Statement is not intended to replace or diminish those requirements. Whatever the legal position in different countries, the Committee considers that the first and most important safeguard against money-laundering is the integrity of banks' own managements and their vigilant determination to prevent their institutions becoming associated with criminals or being used as a channel for money-laundering. The Statement is intended to reinforce those standards of conduct.

7 The supervisory authorities represented on the Committee support the principles set out in the Statement. To the extent that these matters fall within the competence of supervisory authorities in different member countries, the authorities will recommend and encourage all banks to adopt policies and practices consistent with the Statement. With a view to its acceptance worldwide, the Committee would also commend the Statement to supervisory authorities in other countries.

Basle, December 1988

---

[1] Measures against the transfer and safeguarding of funds of criminal origin. Recommendation No R(80)10 adopted by the Committee of Ministers of the Council of Europe on 27th June 1980.
[2] The Committee comprises representatives of the central banks and supervisory authorities of

the Group of Ten countries (Belgium, Canada, France, Germany, Italy, Japan, Netherlands, Sweden, Switzerland, United Kingdom, United States) and Luxembourg.

Statement of principles

I Purpose

Banks and other financial institutions may unwittingly be used as intermediaries for the transfer or deposit of money derived from criminal activity. The intention behind such transactions is often to hide the beneficial ownership of funds. The use of the financial system in this way is of direct concern to police and other law enforcement agencies; it is also a matter of concern to banking supervisors and banks' managements, since public confidence in banks may be undermined through their association with criminals.

This Statement of Principles is intended to outline some basic policies and procedures that banks' managements should ensure are in place within their institutions with a view to assisting in the suppression of money-laundering through the banking system, national and international. The Statement thus sets out to reinforce existing best practices among banks and, specifically, to encourage vigilance against criminal use of the payments system, implementation by banks of effective preventive safeguards, and co-operation with law enforcement agencies.

II Customer identification

With a view to ensuring that the financial system is not used as a channel for criminal funds, banks should make reasonable efforts to determine the true identity of all customers requesting the institution's services. Particular care should be taken to identify the ownership of all accounts and those using safe-custody facilities. All banks should institute effective procedures for obtaining identification from new customers. It should be an explicit policy that significant business transactions will not be conducted with customers who fail to provide evidence of their identity.

III Compliance with laws

Banks' management should ensure that business is conducted in conformity with high ethical standards and that laws and regulations pertaining to financial transactions are adhered to. As regards transactions executed on behalf of customers, it is accepted that banks may have no means of knowing whether the transaction stems from or forms part of criminal activity. Similarly, in an international context it may be difficult to ensure that cross-border transactions on behalf of customers are in compliance with the regulations of another country. Nevertheless, banks should not set out to offer services or provide active assistance in transactions which they have good reason to suppose are associated with money-laundering activities.

IV Co-operation with law enforcement authorities

Banks should co-operate fully with national law enforcement authorities to the extent permitted by specific local regulations relating to customer confidentiality. Care should be taken to avoid providing support or assistance to customers seeking to deceive law enforcement agencies through the provision of altered, incomplete or misleading information. Where banks become aware of facts which lead to the reasonable presumption that money held on deposit derives from criminal activity or that transactions entered into are themselves criminal in purpose, appropriate measures, consistent with the law, should be taken, for example, to deny assistance, sever relations with the customer and close or freeze accounts.

V Adherence to the Statement

All banks should formally adopt policies consistent with the principles set out in this Statement and should ensure that all members of their staff concerned, wherever located, are informed of the bank's policy in this regard. Attention should be given to staff training in matters covered by the Statement. To promote adherence to these principles, banks should implement specific procedures for customer identification and for retaining internal records of transactions. Arrangements for internal audit may need to be extended in order to establish an effective means of testing for general compliance with the Statement. **[813]**

BSD/1989/1
(February 1989)

LOAN TRANSFERS AND SECURITISATION

Introduction

1 This notice sets out the Bank's supervisory policy on the treatment of loan transfers involving banks. It draws on the legal analysis contained in the consultative paper 'Loan Transfers and Securitisation' published by the Bank of England in December 1987, which is reproduced as an annex to this notice.

Coverage

2 The notice covers both the sale of single loans and the packaging, securitisation and sale of loan pools. It also covers the transfer of risk under sub-participation agreements. Although most references in the notice are to sales of loans, the policy in principle also applies to sales of other forms of assets, and to the transfer of risks under contingent items such as letters of credit and acceptance credits. It also covers the transfer of undrawn commitments.

Implementation

3 The policy set out in this notice has immediate effect, but will not be applied to past sales or packaging schemes which are 'grandfathered'.

Aims of the policy

4 The Bank's principal policy objectives are to ensure that:

(i) loan sales and packaging achieve their intended effect of passing rights and obligations from the seller to the buyer;

(ii) all the parties to the transaction fully understand the responsibilities and risks they have assumed or retained; and

(iii) any material risks to buyers or sellers are properly treated in the Bank's supervision of banks[1].

---

[1] In BSD/1992/3, the following was noted in relation to this para 4:

'II TRANSFERS OF RECEIVABLES ARISING FROM THE FINANCE OF EQUIPMENT OR CONSUMER GOODS

[a] In establishing its policy on loan transfers, the Bank aimed to ensure that all parties to an asset transfer fully understood the responsibilities and risks which they assumed or retained, and that any material risks to buyers or sellers were properly treated in the supervision of banks (see paragraph 4 of the Notice). In the light of this objective, the Bank has been examining the appropriate treatment of certain risks attached to the financing of the purchase of equipment or consumer goods (including hire-purchase). This type of lending can involve lenders in continuing liabilities, for instance for the 'merchantability' of goods or equipment, which it will be difficult legally to transfer to a buyer of the receivables.

[b] Lenders against whom claims are made as a result of their liability for the quality of goods or equipment will usually have recourse to the manufacturer, which, provided the manufacturer has appropriate liability insurance, may limit the risk to the lender. In addition, the Bank has been given to understand that the loss experience of lenders under such claims is historically very small. Nevertheless, the Bank does not view the risk retained by the seller as unimportant. In particular, if defective goods were to cause personal injury, very substantial costs could arise. **The Bank believes that for assets to be viewed as off-balance sheet, sellers should either receive an indemnity from the buyer to cover any liability, or otherwise take steps to minimise the risk of loss (such as taking out insurance to cover the risk).**

[c] In addition to liabilities for the quality of equipment, institutions involved in the finance of equipment hire or leasing may have contractual obligations towards the borrower – for instance to arrange for the servicing of taxation of vehicles. Again, it will be difficult legally to transfer these obligations to the buyer along with the benefits of the asset (unless the transfer is done through novation). In situations where the seller is left with responsibilities of this kind,

the Bank has some concern over the position of the buyer (if the buyer is a bank). There is a clear possibility that the borrower will exercise a right to reduce or withhold payments on the loan to reflect his costs – for instance, the cost of repairing the vehicle – if the original lender fails to meet his obligations under the loan agreement. **The Bank reminds buying banks that risks of this nature need careful evaluation. Buyers should satisfy themselves of the seller's competence to fulfil its obligations towards the borrower in a timely manner.**

Implementation
Regarding liabilities arising from consumer finance (paragraphs [a] and [b] above) the Bank has already required banks transferring automobile receivables to securitisation vehicles to cover themselves against this risk, and takes the view that the same policy should apply to all transfers. However, comments on this aspect of the Bank's amendments are invited, to be received by 31 July.'

Methods of transfer

5 The Bank considers that the method of transfer of a loan can have an important bearing on the risks assumed by buyer and seller. An assessment of the implications of different methods under English law appears in the annex.

6 The cleanest transfer of risk is achieved by *novation*, where the existing loan is cancelled and a new agreement substituted, which transfers all the seller's rights and obligations to the buyer. A legal or equitable *assignment*, if properly structured, can also achieve an effective transfer of the seller's rights and the remedies available to him to enforce those rights. But the seller retains any outstanding obligations (for example, to advance further funds), while the buyer's rights may be impaired by any rights of set-off that exist between the borrower and the seller. Where the assignment is silent (ie the borrower is not notified), there may be additional risks for both buyer and seller – for the buyer because the absence of notice to the borrower removes some legal protection he would otherwise have; and for the seller, because as lender of record he will remain subject to requests to reschedule or renegotiate. The third most common technique, *sub-participation*, does not transfer any rights, remedies or obligations from seller to buyer, but is an entirely separate non-recourse funding arrangement, under which the buyer places funds with the seller in exchange for acquiring a beneficial interest in the underlying loan, but the loan itself is not transferred. In this case, the buyer assumes an exposure to the borrower, but is also at risk to the seller, because he has lent to him and because he relies on him to pass through funds received from the borrower.

Supervisory treatment

7 The Bank will apply the following treatment to a loan (or a part of a loan) transferred using the above methods, subject to the further conditions specified in paragraphs 8 and 14 below:

(i) a transfer through novation will be regarded as a clean transfer. The loan will therefore be excluded from the seller's risk asset ratio and included in the buyer's.

(ii) a transfer through an assignment duly notified to the borrower will be regarded as a clean transfer, provided that the buyer has taken reasonable precautions to ensure that his rights under the transfer are not impaired by an intervening right; for example, a right of set-off between seller and borrower. A minimum requirement should be a warranty from the seller that no such right of set-off exists.

(iii) a transfer through a silent assignment will usually be regarded as a clean transfer. However the seller must recognise that as he remains the lender of record he will be the focal point for pressure from the borrower to re-schedule or renegotiate the terms of the loan, or advance further funds. The volume of loans to individual borrowers sold on a silent assignment basis needs to be subject to appropriate internal controls. Silent assignments may also pose additional risks for buyers (see paragraph 17 of Annex 1), and these need to be kept under careful review. If it is not satisfied on these points the Bank may disregard a transfer of a loan through a silent assignment in calculating the risk asset ratio of the seller.

(iv) a loan sub-participation, while not transferring in a legal sense the rights of the original lender, aims to have the same economic effect. Where a loan is funded in whole or in part via a sub-participation, the Bank will recognise the transfer of credit risk by excluding it (or the relevant part) from the original lender's risk asset ratio, and including it in the sub-participant's as a claim on the underlying borrower. [. . .]¹

(v) Where banks transfer undrawn commitments to lend (or part of them), the commitment (or part) will be excluded from the selling bank's risk asset ratio only when the transfer is either by novation, or by an assignment accompanied by formal acknowledgement from the borrower of a transfer of obligations from the seller to the buyer. A transfer by means of silent assignment or sub-participation will not lead to the exclusion of the commitment from the selling bank's risk asset ratio. Instead it will be treated as a transfer of the seller's exposure from the potential borrower to the buyer. The buyer's assumption of a commitment (or part) will be included in its risk asset ratio as a claim on the borrower, irrespective of the method of transfer used.

8 The above policy in relation to the method of transfer will be applied provided that the following conditions are satisfied:

A In the case of the transfer of a single loan (or part of a loan)

(i) The transfer does not contravene the terms and conditions of the underlying loan agreement and all the necessary consents have been obtained;

(ii) the seller has no residual beneficial interest in the principal amount of the loan (or that part which has been transferred) and the buyer has no formal recourse to the seller for losses;

(iii) the seller has no obligation² to repurchase the loan³, or any part of it, at any time (although he may retain an option to do so provided the loan remains fully-performing);

(iv) the seller can demonstrate, to the satisfaction of the Bank, that it has given notice to the buyer that it is under no obligation to repurchase the loan³ nor support any losses suffered by the buyer and that the buyer has acknowledged the absence of obligation;

(v) the documented terms of the transfer are such that, if the loan is rescheduled or renegotiated, the buyer and not the seller would be subject to the rescheduled or renegotiated terms;

(vi) where payments are routed through the seller, he is under no obligation to remit funds to the buyer unless and until they are received from the borrower. Payments voluntarily made by the seller to the buyer in anticipation of payments from the borrower must be made on terms under which they can be recovered from the buyer if the borrower fails to perform.

B Packaging schemes⁴

9 The process of packaging loans together and selling them as a block or pool can compound risks which are often negligible when a single loan is transferred. For example a seller – or originator – of a pool of loans is more at risk from his misrepresentation as to their quality than if only one of those loans is involved.

10 Sellers – or orginators – of loans who continue to administer (or 'service') them as a securitised portfolio in order to maintain borrower relationships or to earn fees can also run explicit operational risks. Their continued identification with the loans can mean that their commercial reputation is committed and a completely clean break is not achieved. The Bank is concerned that banks in this position may come under pressure to support losses incurred by the investors/buyers and may be inclined to do so in order to protect their name.

11 These operational and 'moral' risks will be present where a bank originates and/or services a portfolio of loans whether they were ever on its balance sheet or not. They apply both to vehicle and pool participation schemes.

12 In the past the risks associated with loan administration have not warranted special treatment (see the Measurement of Capital paper, paragraphs 30–32)⁵ as the capital required to cover credit risk helps to protect a bank against other risks as well.

This would no longer be the case, however, where functions have been unbundled so that the credit risk lies with a third party.

13 The Bank believes that the risks from close association with a securitisation scheme can assume material proportions. The arrangements controlling the association should be carefully assessed and monitored, and subject to internal audit. These may be included in the scope of the reports on records and systems which reporting accountants will prepare each year for management and the Bank (see policy notice BSD/1987/2). The Bank will take into account any significant operational risks not related to balance sheet items when setting a bank's minimum permissible (or 'trigger') risk asset ratio. In exceptional cases it may wish to apply an explicit capital requirement against this sort of risk.

14 In addition to conditions (i) to (vi) in paragraph 8, the Bank will require the following conditions to be met by a bank acting as servicing agent[6] of loan packaging schemes, in order to ensure that its role is not seen as being more than acting as an agent. [The Bank will also require the following conditions to be met by banks which are originators of assets being transferred under packaging schemes, whether or not they retain the servicing role][7].

(vii) The Bank will expect the servicing agent to have evidence available in its records that its auditors and legal advisers are satisfied that the terms of the scheme protect it from any liability to investors in the scheme, save where it is proved to have been negligent;

(viii) the servicing agent must be able to demonstrate that it has taken all reasonable precautions to ensure that it is not obliged nor will feel impelled to support any losses suffered by the scheme or investors in it. Any offering circular should contain a highly visible, unequivocal statement that the servicing agent does not stand behind the issue or the vehicle and will not make good any losses in the portfolio;

(ix) the servicing agent (or any other group entity covered by the Bank's consolidated supervision of a group of which the servicing agent is a part) may not own any share capital in any company used as a vehicle for the scheme; nor in any other form hold a proprietary interest in or control over that company either directly or indirectly. For this purpose 'Share capital' includes all classes of ordinary and preference share capital.

(x) The Board of a company used as vehicle for a scheme must be independent of the servicing agent, although the latter may have one director representing it.

(xi) The name of a company used as vehicle for a scheme must not include the name of the servicing agent or imply any connection with it.

(xii) The servicing agent must not bear any of the recurring expenses of the scheme. However, the agent may make a one-off contribution to enhance the credit worthiness of a vehicle. It may also lend on a long term subordinated basis to the vehicle provided that the loan is only repayable following winding up of the scheme. Any transactions under these headings must be undertaken at the initiation of the scheme and disclosed in any offering circular. They will be deducted from capital for capital adequacy purposes.

(xiii) The servicing agent may not intentionally bear any losses arising from the effect of interest rate changes on the scheme. However the agent may enter into interest rate swap agreements at market prices with the vehicle. There should be provision for unintended temporary losses arising from normal administrative delays in changing mortgage rates to be recovered by the servicing agent as soon as possible.

(xiv) A servicing agent may not fund a vehicle or scheme (except within the terms of condition (xii) above) and in particular may not provide temporary finance to a scheme to cover cash shortfalls arising from delayed payments or non-performance of loans which it administers.

(xv) A servicing agent may not retain an option to repurchase (or refinance) loans except where the loan portfolio has fallen to less than 10% of its maximum value and the option extends only to fully-performing loans.

15 If any of the above conditions is not satisfied, the assets administered by the servicing agent will be consolidated with its balance sheet for risk asset ratio purposes.

[1] Words deleted pursuant to BSD/1992/3. Explanation given:

'Both the 1987 consultative paper and the 1989 policy notice on loan transfers ("the Notice") stressed the fact that in subparticipations, the buyer of the subparticipation has a risk on the seller as well as on the ultimate borrower. The Notice stated that we expected subparticipants, as a matter of best practice, to acquire a charge over the underlying asset, and that we might require justification where this had not been done. The purpose of a charge is to protect the subparticipant's rights in the event of the seller's insolvency.

Since issuing the Notice, the Bank has recognised that such a requirement is often impractical and indeed, if insisted upon, would interfere with normal market practice respecting sub-participations. **The reference in paragraph 7 (iv) to obtaining charges is therefore withdrawn, with immediate effect.** The banking supervisors will nevertheless continue to expect sub-participant banks to evaluate and control their risks on both sellers and underlying borrowers.'

[2] Except where arising from warranties given in respect of the loan at the time of its transfer, provided that these are not in respect of the future credit-worthiness of the borrower.

[3] Not applicable to sub-participations [or to fund the repayment of a subparticipation]. Words in square brackets added pursuant to BSD/1992/3 which provided:

'Since in a subparticipation the loan is not actually sold, it is not correct to refer to "repurchase". This is the reason for the footnote. It does not mean that an equivalent arrangement to an obligatory repurchase, such as an obligation to repay a subparticipation where the cash has not been received from the borrower, would be acceptable. In order to make the meaning clear, the wording of this footnote is amended [as above].'

[4] Schemes involving the 'packaging' of a single loan or commitment are not covered by this part of the notice.

[5] See now BSD/1990/2 and BSD/1990/3.

[6] The Bank would expect to be consulted when a bank proposes to act jointly with one or more other administrators.

[7] Words in square brackets in para 14 added pursuant to BSD/1992/3. Explanation given:

'This paragraph [14] refers throughout to the "servicing agent", although, as is indicated in the preceding context, the risks which concern the Bank arise also for originators which do not have a servicing role. In order to make clear that the policy includes within its scope originators who are not servicing agents, . . . [the words in square brackets in para 14 above] . . . are added after the first sentence . . .'

Annex   Methods of transfer

1 This annex contains a brief review of the position under English law in relation to the disposal of loan assets. The Bank wishes to stress that:

  (i)   except where indicated, this annex deals only with the position under English law; the position in other jurisdictions may differ;

  (ii) the annex does not consider the tax position of transfers, in particular stamp duty and stamp duty reserve tax;[1]

  (iii) the legal position is complex and reliance should not be placed on this annex; where appropriate, independent legal advice should be taken.

2 The annex does not cover the transfer of any security which may support a transferred loan. It is nevertheless important that buyers should ensure that they acquire the full benefit of any security.

---

[1] Although not considered here, the tax position could be of relevance, for example to the attempt by a buyer to enforce a loan. If the transfer has failed to be stamped when it should have been, the buyer may be unable to enforce the loan in the Courts.

Transfer methods

3 Strictly speaking, loans cannot be 'sold' in the same straightforward way as tangible assets (eg cars, equipment etc); a technical but important point. There are, however, three basic methods of transferring the rights and/or the obligations under a loan – novation, assignment and participation – and, throughout this annex, the shorthand 'seller' and 'buyer' is used: 'seller' referring to a bank which is disposing of an asset, by whatever means; and 'buyer' referring to the new lender, transferee, assignee or participant.

Assignment

4 In general, a lender *may assign his rights* under a loan agreement to a third party; ie his rights to interest and principal.

5 A loan agreement may, however, impose restrictions on assignability and it is likely that, if they were breached, the buyer would gain no direct rights against the borrower and may have difficulty in enforcing the assignment against the seller.

6 It is also uncertain whether a buyer can take an assignment of the benefit of certain typical clauses in a loan agreement; eg a provision for grossing-up or for payment of increased costs. Such obligations of the borrower may be construed as personal to the original lender and, as such, unassignable. Even if this is not the case and the loan agreement extends the relevant clauses to assignees of the original lender, it is arguable that an assignee cannot obtain greater rights than those of the original seller; ie that the buyer cannot claim the benefit of, say, a grossing-up clause or an increased costs clause save in circumstances, and to the extent that, the original lender could have claimed the benefit of such clauses.

7 More significantly in the supervisory context, a lending bank may *not 'assign' its obligations* under a loan (or any other) agreement, since these can be transferred only with the consent of all other parties (including the borrower). In order to get over this, an 'assignee' of obligations (as well as rights) will sometimes undertake to meet the assignor's obligations as a condition of the assignment. But this does not actually release the assignor from those obligations to the borrower (or any other parties to the loan agreement), it merely reduces the risks arising out of them.

8 A seller/assignor therefore remains liable to the borrower in respect of any unper-formed obligations under the original loan agreement. So that, for example, the undrawn part of a facility may not be transferred by assignment. Similarly, assignment can be an imperfect means of selling multi-currency loans, where the primary lender has continuing obligations throughout the term of the loan to switch its currency in certain circumstances.

9 Even where a loan is fully drawn down and the original lender has no outstanding obligations to the borrower, the original lender may still have obligations to other parties (eg in a syndicated loan, to indemnify the agent and/or to share recoveries with the other lenders). These obligations will remain on the original lender notwithstanding an assignment. The buyer may agree to be liable to indemnify the seller in respect of such liabilities and may (although this is less clear) be liable directly to the other parties on the basis that the buyer is not entitled to take the benefit of a contract without the burdens.

10 Subject to any provisions to the contrary, assignments are made (and taken) subject to equities. An assignee's rights may therefore be subject to, for example, any rights of set-off which the borrower may have against the assignor, whether arising out of the loan agreement itself, any associated transactions or any other transactions entered into prior to the borrower receiving notice of the assignment. An assignee's claim on the borrower would be impaired by any such rights of set-off.

Types of assignment

11 Assignments for the purpose of disposing of assets may fall into two basic legal categories:

- statutory (or legal) assignments, transferring both legal and beneficial title
- equitable assignments, transferring 'only' beneficial title.

(a) Statutory assignment

12 A statutory assignment will 'pass and transfer' from the seller to the buyer all the legal rights to principal and interest and, in most circumstances, all the legal remedies available against the borrower to ensure discharge of the debt. That is, the buyer acquires the full *legal and beneficial* interest in the loan and is accordingly able (for instance) to sue the borrower directly without having to join the seller/assignor.

13 In order to be a statutory assignment, a transfer must satisfy the conditions of section 136 of the Law of Property Act 1925 (see the Appendix to this Annex 1 for the relevant part of s 136). In particular, it must:

(i) be *in writing* and signed by the seller
(ii) be absolute – that is, unconditional and not merely by way of security
(iii) cover the *whole* of the loan
(iv) be completed by *notice in writing to the borrower* (and any other obligors, eg a guarantor).

(*b*) Equitable assignment

14 An equitable assignment, by contrast, transfers only beneficial *not* legal rights. In consequence a buyer may not be able to proceed directly against a borrower. Instead, the seller must be joined in any action. This is purely procedural; the seller is not liable for the debt.

15 An 'equitable assignment' includes an assignment which fails to satisfy one of the s 136 conditions. An assignment will therefore be equitable where inter alia:

(i) part only of a loan is assigned – for example, where a loan is split between a group of buyers; or
(ii) it is not in writing; or
(iii) written notice is not given to the borrower (eg for 'commercial reasons').

16 As to (iii), where the borrower is not notified of the transfer, although the assignment is valid as between the seller and the buyer, the seller remains the lender of record, the lender in the mind of the borrower and repayments will be made by the borrower to the seller (who can give a good discharge).

17 Moreover, *notice (written or oral) secures some important protections for the buyer*. For example:

(i) if notice is given, the borrower must make payments to the assignee/buyer (unless directed otherwise); without notice, the assignee/buyer has to give credit to the borrower for any payments to the assignor/seller made in ignorance of the assignment
(ii) notice gives the assignee/buyer some protection against intervening equities (in particular those indpendent of the agreement assigned); without notice, further equities and, in particular, rights of set-off, may arise between the borrower and the assignor/seller: this could happen with major corporates which have an active trading relationship with the selling bank – Bank A assigns to Bank B a loan to Corporate X but without notice; Corporate X subsequently places money with Bank A; Corporate X may be able to set-off the two amounts if Bank A does not repay
(iii) notice prevents the assignor/seller and borrower from varying the underlying contract
(iv) where there are successive assignments of the same loan, the priority of the assignee/buyer can be determined by the order in which *written* notice was given to the borrower; notice may therefore protect a buyer against subsequent (accidental or dishonest) assignments.

18 It would accordingly seem to be good practice to give written notice and, if practicable, to obtain confirmation from the borrower that:

– there is agreement on the amount of the debt;
– the borrower has no notice of any other assignment
– the borrower has no right of set-off against the assignor
– the contract between the borrower and assignor/seller has not been varied (for example by a side letter).

19 It should be noted that an equitable assignment of a legal interest in a loan (ie of a legal chose in action) creates an equitable interest in the debt (or an equitable chose in action). Any on-sale by way of a further equitable assignment is therefore an equitable transfer of an equitable chose in action, and is in consequence subject to different provisions from the original sale (in particular s 53(1)(c) of the Law of Property Act

1925 might apply, in which case the assignment would have to be in writing and signed by the assignor).

Novation

20 The cleanest way of selling a loan and the *only* way of effectively transferring both rights and *obligations* is novation. This entails cancelling the original rights and obligations, and substituting new ones in their place, although the only substantive difference is the identity of the lender. The buyer steps into the shoes of the original lender/seller who ceases to have any *obligations* to the borrower.

21 The technique can be somewhat cumbersome, however, as the consent of *all* the parties to the original loan is needed; ie, the borrower, any other lenders and possibly even the guarantor in the case of a syndicated facility. Steps have been taken to overcome this – see 'Transferable loan facilities' below (paras 31 to 33).

22 Novation avoids the difficulties of assignment in relation to 'transfer' of obligations and whether the buyer can be entitled to greater rights than the original lender/seller. However difficulties may arise in particular in relation to secured loans, priorities, consents and questions as to the value given by the buyer (eg to avoid problems in relation to preferences and invalidation of floating charges under the Insolvency Act 1986).

Sub-participation

23 Unlike 'novation' and 'assignment', the terms 'participation' and 'sub-participation' are not terms of art as a matter of English law. Rather, they are market expressions applied to the 'sale' of a loan by way of a back-to-back non-recourse funding arrangement: the buyer deposits a sum of money (equal to the whole or part of the underlying loan) with the seller on terms under which the moneys are repayable (and interest is payable) if and only if the seller receives payments of principal (and interest) from the underlying borrower, and subject to a maximum of the amount received. (This is sometimes called a funded sub-participation or a sub-loan.)

24 The sub-participation, as customarily documented, is a separate legal agreement from the underlying loan, creating a debtor-creditor relationship between buyer and seller. The buyer does not (or at least is not intended to) acquire any legal or beneficial interest in the underlying loan, nor any contractual relationship with the ultimate borrower. In consequence, in contrast to novations and assignments, the buyer does not have any direct recourse to the borrower and is not able to exercise any of the seller's rights against the borrower. Nor can the buyer benefit from any of the other provisions of the underlying loan contract (such as grossing-up in the event of the imposition of withholding tax). The buyer's rights are against the seller and he can benefit only from the provisions of the sub-participation agreement.

(a) Types of participation agreements

25 Some banks use standard documentation for sub-participations. A *medium term agreement* may be used for individual loans and may be drawn widely so as to cover simple bank loans, syndicated credits, guaranteed loans, multicurrency loans, and loan facilities which are wholly or partly drawn.

A '*short-term master participation agreement*' may be used for a series of short-term loans made under a roll-over facility. Technically, each loan is repaid at the end of each interest period, notwithstanding the fact that a new loan is immediately and (in practice) automatically advanced, often without an actual movement of funds. The commercial effect can be equivalent to interest period stripping – as the buyer purchases the interest earned on a short term loan. Such sub-participation agreements tend to be drafted to cover all participants during the life of the facility.

(b) Double credit risk for buyer

27 An important feature of many sub-loans is the double jeopardy of the buyer; that is, that the buyer has a credit exposure to both the seller and the underlying borrower. Say Bank A makes a loan to Corporate X which it 'sells' to Bank B by way of sub-loan. If Corporate X fails and the liquidator recovers 50p in the £, Bank B gets 50p in the £.

28 If Bank A fails and the liquidator pays out 1p in the £, Bank B has a contingent claim in the liquidation. If the Corporate X loan is repaid in full, Bank B still gets only 1p in the £. If Corporate X also fails and nothing is recovered, Bank B gets nothing.

29 A possible remedy for buying Bank B is for its sub-loan to be secured by way of mortgage or charge over Bank A's loan to Corporate X. But banks appear to be reluctant to grant such charges, perhaps in part because they may need to be registered with the Registrar of Companies.

Risk participations

30 Risk participations are used for the undrawn part of a loan facility. Basically, the participant undertakes to fund any drawings on the facility by way of a non-recourse sub-loan. Risk participation is accordingly a commitment (i) to finance the lending bank and (ii) to take on the credit exposure to the borrower.

Transferable loan facilities

31 Many loans are now structured to ease transfer. Essentially, the borrower (and other parties to the loan) agree in advance that the loan – or parts of a loan – may be transferred freely or subject to conditions. The transfer is generally executed between the buyer and seller but with some registration procedure involving an agent bank. Buyers are able to make subsequent transfers and thus the transferable loan facility ('TLF') should help to increase the liquidity of the underlying asset.

32 There are three basic varieties of TLF: the Transferable Loan Certificate ('TLC'), which is based on *novation*; the Transferable Loan Instrument ('TLI'), which is based on legal assignment and the use of debentures (and thus can only be used where a loan is fully drawn); and the *Transferable Participation Certificate* ('TPC'), which combines TLC 'technology' with sub-participation.

33 The TPC is designed in part to avoid multi-tiered sub-participations: ie a sub-participant 'on-selling' the loan to another sub-participant so that in effect Bank 3 is funding Bank 2 which is funding Bank 1 which holds the underlying loan. The use of the TPC should enable Bank 3 to step cleanly into the shoes of Bank 2 and thus to have a direct contractual relationship with Bank 1.

Other legal issues affecting transfers

34 Whatever the method, transfers are complex legal transactions needing great care and professional advice. For example, as already noted, successive equitable assignments may be subject to slightly different conditions.

(*a*) Local law

35 In addition, it is important that all parties to a sale should recognise that, although the novation, assignment or sub-participation may be made under English law, the effectiveness of the transfer may depend on the laws of other countries. The following can all be relevant:

– the law governing the underlying debt;
– the law of the place of incorporation or residence of the borrower or any guarantor;
– the law to which the buyer or sub-participant is subject;
– the law of the place where the debt is to be paid;
– the law applicable to any other parties to the loan – eg the law of incorporation of the agent bank;
– the law of the place(s) in which any secondary market operates.

36 On the whole, novation and assignment are more likely than sub-participation to be affected by local law considerations.

37 Issues which may arise include:

– *priorities* may be forfeited in some jurisdictions if the transfer is by way of novation;

- *consents and notices* may be necessary to make the transfer fully effective; eg exchange control consents may need replacing if transfer is by novation or assignment;
- *formalities* may need to be observed; this can be particularly important when the borrower is from a civil law country – for example, in France notice of assignment may need to be served by a 'huissier';
- *withholding tax* may arise in relation to the buyer.

(*b*) Bankers' duty of confidentiality

38 The simple issue here is that, if a seller discloses to a buyer information about the borrower which was provided in connection with the loan, the seller may have breached its duty of confidentiality to the borrower unless the borrower has consented (in the loan agreement or otherwise) to such disclosure. In consequence, sellers have to exercise great care. Since this may have the effect of limiting the information available to buyers, it could help to ensure that buyers make their own independent credit assessment, which is very important as a matter of general prudence.

Appendix to the Annex

Law of Property Act 1925

The following is the text of the relevant part of section 136 of the 1925 Act:

'136(1) Any absolute assignment by writing under the hand of the assignor (not purporting to be by way of charge only) of any debt or other legal thing in action, of which express notice in writing has been given to the debtor, trustee or other person from whom the assignor would have been entitled to claim such debt or thing in action, is effectual in law (subject to equities having priority over the right of the assignee) to pass and transfer from the date of such notice:

(a) the legal right to such debt or thing in action;
(b) all legal and other remedies for the same; and
(c) the power to give a good discharge for the same without the concurrence of the assignor.'

New Annex pursuant to BSD/1992/3

Securitisation of revolving credits

[39] The term 'revolving credits' refers to loan facilities which permit borrowers to vary the drawn amount within an agreed limit. Repayment can be at the borrower's discretion, subject in some cases to a minimum amount per payment period, or can be by fixed schedule.

[40] Securitisation of such receivables therefore involves issuing notes of a fixed amount and term against the backing of assets of fluctuating amount and indefinite maturity. Typically, schemes will insulate noteholders from the effects of fluctuating balances by assigning shares in the receivables which are the subject of the securitisation to both the noteholders and the originating bank. The amount of the noteholders' interest in the outstanding balances stays fixed at the amount of their funding (until the notes start to amortise) while the amount assigned to the bank goes up or down as borrowers make net drawings or repayments. Schemes are given a fixed maturity by dividing their life into a 'revolving' (or 'interest-only') period and an 'amortisation' period. During the revolving period, the noteholders receive their share of interest payments, but their share of principal repayments by borrowers is reinvested in the pool. During the amortisation period, the noteholder's share of principal repayments is used to redeem the securities, with the result that at the end of the scheme, the full interest in the outstanding balances has reverted to the originating bank.

[41] The Bank has examined a number of schemes on these lines, and has been concerned about the possibility of increased legal risk and moral pressure arising from the complexity of the arrangements and the shared interest of the bank and investors. We have, however, concluded that if carefully structured, such schemes can result in the originating bank successfully transferring the risk on the share of the pool assigned to the noteholders.

Structures of schemes

[42] Securitisation schemes so far proposed to us involve the transfer of a pool of receivables into a Trust. The Trust directs the flows on the accounts to the originating bank and to a special purpose vehicle according to the proportion of the funding they are providing. The SPV in turn directs the flows to the investors who have bought the securities.

[43] The Bank has judged this an acceptable structure to allow the share of the balances funded by the SPV to be removed from the originating bank's balance sheet **provided that arrangements for sharing of interest, principal, expenses, losses and recoveries are made on a clear and consistent basis.** The Bank will look at schemes individually to ensure that they meet this criterion.

[44] The Bank will look particularly carefully at how the securities are amortised at the end of schemes. Under schemes seen so far, noteholders are repaid out of a fixed share of principal repayments arising from the aggregate gross flows on the accounts, including repayments on new borrowings incurred during the amortisation period. The Bank has certain objections to this arrangement. It implies that the SPV may derive repayment flows to a large extent from those borrowers in the pool who turn over their balances quickly, and may have comparatively little reliance on borrowers who pay only the minimum amount each month. Depending on the composition of the pool, the SPV may be able to make an extremely rapid exit from the scheme; and moreover, the variation in payment rates by borrowers in the pool will mean that individual loans which were once part-funded by the SPV return to the originating bank as soon as the vehicle has been fully paid off.

[45] Borrowers who pay their debts slowly are likely to have different risk characteristics from those who repay and renew credit at a fast rate. **The Bank would prefer a repayment arrangement which meant that the SPV was not fully paid off until each borrower in whose debts the SPV shared during the revolving period had made enough payments to cover the credit balance outstanding from the end of the revolving period – or had been recognised as a defaulter. This would mean disaggregating the payments on the pool and assigning the vehicle a share in each borrower's principal payments.**

[46] Where this is not a feasible procedure, however, the Bank is concerned to limit the amount of debts outstanding from the end of the revolving period of the scheme which return to the originating bank's balance sheet once the vehicle has exited from the scheme. **The Bank will require institutions which propose to transfer revolving credits into a securitisation scheme to demonstrate (either on a theoretical basis or on the basis of historical statistics) that all borrowers in the pool should have made sufficient payments towards their debts to ensure that in aggregate, not more than 10% of the total debt outstanding at the beginning of the planned amortisation period will still be outstanding at the end of that period.** Schemes should adhere to the planned amortisation period in all circumstances, and should not allow the vehicle to receive a more favourable allocation of payments in the event of a deterioration in the behaviour of the pool.

Permitted amount of revolving credit securitisation undertaken by banks

[47] As noted above, where revolving credits are the subject of the securitisation, the receivables are funded by the buyer for a set period only. Once this period is over, the bank has to find the full funding for the amounts drawn by borrowers. The Bank is concerned that under certain circumstances – in particular where a replacement securitisation cannot be successfully arranged – this may place strain on the bank's liquidity and capital adequacy positions. In theory, the terms of revolving credit facilities will generally allow the lender to withdraw or reduce the facility; but in practice, such action is likely to be a last resort.

[48] The Bank's policy on the length of amortisation periods outlined in paragraph 17 above will link amortisation periods to turnover of the pool balance and will help to ensure that schemes unwind in a controlled fashion. **In addition, the Bank will impose a limit for each bank on the amount of outstanding securitised revolving credits taken off its balance sheet. This limit will initially be set at 10% of the bank's solo capital base, but will be reviewed periodically.** The banking supervisors will also, in the normal course of

supervision, examine banks' proposals for securitisation to ensure that schemes will not be unwinding at times and in amounts which would pose difficulties for the originating bank. In evaluating a bank's overall ability to cope with any refinancing difficulties, the supervisors will have regard to the presence of any 'early amortisation triggers'[1] which are incorporated into schemes, and the terms of those triggers.

Implementation

[49] Some banks are anxious to proceed with securitisation of revolving credits, but need guidance as to what form of scheme will be acceptable to the Bank of England. The above paragraphs outline the broad criteria which the Bank will henceforth apply to securitised revolving credits. These criteria are additional to the guidelines already laid down in BSD/1989/1.

[50] The policy represents conclusions reached after discussions with banks which have approached us with proposals to securitise revolving credits. The Bank will however welcome comments from other authorised institutions and interested parties on the approach outlined in this section. It is the Bank's intention to keep its policy under review, both in the light of any comments received and in the light of further developments in securitisation techniques. **[814]**

---

[1] Early amortisation means that the repayment period commences sooner than originally planned. It can be distinguished from 'rapid amortisation' (referred to in paragraph [46]), which actually contracts the amortisation period by allocating the vehicle a bigger share (usually 100%) of the cardholder payments. The triggers are again mainly related to changes in borrower behaviour which reduce the yield on the pool below a certain level.

FURTHER LETTER TO AUTHORISED INSTITUTIONS CONCERNING MONEY LAUNDERING

(November 1989)
Bank of England
Banking Supervision Division

Money laundering

In January of this year the Bank circulated the Basle Statement of Principles on Money Laundering (which has been endorsed by the Governors of the central banks of the Group of Ten countries) to all institutions authorised under the Banking Act.

At that time the Bank stated that it believed that the Statement reflected existing best banking practice in the UK. The Bank also made it clear that it expected that all UK banking institutions would be able to demonstrate that their policies in the area were consistent with the Statement of Principles.

In the light of the increasing international concern about money laundering, and drugs-related laundering in particular, it is timely to remind you of the provisions of the Basle Statement.

The Statement of Principles does not restrict itself to drug-related money laundering but extends to all aspects of laundering through the banking system, ie the deposit, transfer and/or concealment of money derived from illicit activities whether robbery, terrorism, fraud or drugs. It seeks to deny the banking system to those involved in money laundering by the application of the following principles:

(a) *Know your customer* – banks should make reasonable efforts to determine the customer's true identity, and have effective procedures for verifying the bona fides of new customers (whether on the asset or liability side of the balance sheet).

(b) *Compliance with laws* – bank management should ensure that business is conducted in conformity with high ethical standards, laws and regulations being adhered to and ensuring that a service is not provided where there is good reason to suppose that transactions are associated with laundering activities.

(c) *Co-operation with law enforcement agencies* – within any constraints imposed by rules relating to customer confidentiality, banks should co-operate fully with national law enforcement agencies including, where there are reasonable grounds for suspecting money laundering, taking appropriate measures which are consistent with the law.

(d) *Adherence to the Statement* – The full text of this section of the Statement is worth quoting in full:

'All banks should formally adopt policies consistent with the principles set out in this Statement and should ensure that all members of their staff concerned, wherever located, are informed of the bank's policy in this regard. Attention should be given to staff training in matters covered by the Statement. To promote adherence to these principles banks should implement specific procedures for customer identification and for retaining internal records of transactions. Arrangements for internal audit may need to be extended in order to establish an effective means of testing for general compliance with the Statement.'

In written and oral evidence to the Home Affairs Select Committee on Drug Trafficking and Related Serious Crime, the Bank emphasised the need to improve the financial community's awareness of relevant UK statutory provisions relating to the requirement for disclosing suspicions of those seeking to hide funds derived from criminal activities. The National Drugs Intelligence Unit, in its evidence, also highlighted this need and noted that there was still extensive potential for an increase in disclosures made under these provisions.

I am therefore also taking this opportunity to remind authorised institutions of the particular UK statutes which, under specific circumstances, allow (by giving statutory exemption from suit by customers for breach of confidentiality) disclosure of customers' transactions. The following summaries are, of course, just that and do not constitute an interpretation of the sections of the legislation referred to, for which appropriate legal advice should be sought where necessary.

Section 24 of the *Drugs Trafficking Offences Act 1986* [in Scotland, the Criminal Justice (Scotland) Act 1987] provides that anyone who assists another to retain the benefit of funds, knowing or 'suspecting' that they may be related to drug trafficking, is guilty of an offence the penalty for which is a maximum 14 years' imprisonment. It is, however, a defence *either* to prove that it was not known or suspected that drug trafficking was involved *or* to have disclosed that knowledge or suspicion to the authorities. The Act provides protection from suit by customers for breaching confidentiality and allows police/customs to give consent to operate an account after disclosure.

Similar provisions exist under the *Prevention of Terrorism (Temporary Provisions) Act 1989*. Under section 11 an offence is committed by anyone who facilitates retention or control of terrorist funds but it is a defence *either* to prove that it was not known or there was 'no reasonable cause to suspect' that the arrangements related to terrorist funds *or* to have disclosed such knowledge or suspicion to the authorities. Again, [under section 12(1)] there is protection from suit by customers for confidentiality breaches.

While the *Criminal Justice Act 1988* contains no *requirement* to make disclosures, section 98 affords protection from suit where disclosure is made of a suspicion or belief that 'property' derives from or in connection with an indictable offence, other than a drug trafficking offence.

Since March 1989 the National Drugs Intelligence Unit (NDIU) has been designated as the single national reception point for disclosures under the Drug Trafficking Offences Act, Prevention of Terrorism Act and Criminal Justice Act. The NDIU's Financial Advisory Team is based at New Scotland Yard, Broadway, London SW1H 0BG; telephone numbers allocated to receive such approaches are: 0171–230 3010, 0171–230 3418 and (a 24 hours manned service) 0171–230 3150 while the fax number is 0171–230 4056.

As part of the regular reports on banks' accounting records and control systems requested under Section 39 of the Banking Act (reporting accountants' reports), the Bank may include a review of the control systems and accounting records which reflect adherence to the Statement of Principles. Failure to install or maintain adequate systems in the area will be taken into account in the Bank's consideration of whether an institution continues to meet the criteria set out in Schedule 3 to the Banking Act. **[815]**

LETTER TO AUTHORISED INSTITUTIONS CONCERNING ADVERTISING OF INTEREST BEARING ACCOUNTS

(December 1990)

Code of conduct for the advertising of interest bearing accounts

In 1985 the British Bankers Association, Building Societies Association and Finance Houses Association developed a code of conduct for the advertising of savings and deposit accounts which concentrated upon the manner of quoting various types of rates in such deposit advertisements.

At the time the code was issued, and again in the notice BSD/1988/1 (April 1988), the Bank advised all authorised institutions of its expectations that they would adhere to the code's provisions.

Following the decision to abolish composite rate tax, the three associations have been considering revisions to the code – to reflect changes in the tax regime and the wider availability of interest bearing accounts. A revised code was issued earlier this week to members of the above associations and copies of this letter going to non-BBA members contain a copy of the text. *You will note from the BBA's accompanying guidance that the new code comes into effect from 6 April 1991.*

As with the earlier code, the Bank expects authorised institutions to adhere to the code's provisions and will continue to monitor the standard of advertising for deposits.

Authorised institutions which are not members of the BBA or FHA may address queries regarding the code as it applies in individual cases to the Banking Supervision Division (0171–601 5064). Members of the BBA or FHA should first approach their association. **[816]**

See **[818]** for the text of the Code of Conduct.

LETTER TO AUTHORISED INSTITUTIONS CONCERNING GUIDANCE NOTES ISSUED BY THE JOINT MONEY LAUNDERING WORKING GROUP

(December 1990)

Money laundering

On 10 November 1989 the Bank wrote to all institutions authorised under the Banking Act reminding them of their responsibilities to adopt policies consistent with the Basle Statement of Principles on Money Laundering (circulated by the Bank in January 1989) and announcing that a review of control systems and accounting records in money laundering related areas may form part of the reports requested under section 39 of the Act. The letter went on to warn that failure to install and maintain adequate systems would be taken into account in the Bank's consideration of whether an institution continues to meet the criteria set out in Schedule 3 to the Banking Act.

Adherence to the Basle Statement is one test of the adequacy of systems in this area. There are a variety of other initiatives to combat money laundering which may become relevant reference points against which to judge the adequacy of an institution's systems and records.

One such initiative has been that undertaken by a working group chaired by the Bank, containing representatives of the British Bankers Association (BBA), Building Societies Association (BSA) and law enforcement agencies. That group has now finalised a set of money laundering Guidance Notes which has just been issued by the BBA and BSA to their members; a copy is enclosed.

The Guidance Notes seek to expand on the Basle Statement in a number of main-stream areas of banking activity. The Bank will expect all banks to be able to demon-strate that their policies, records and systems at least meet the standards set out in the Guidance Notes.   **[817]**

[*The Guidance Notes are not reproduced.*]

CODE OF CONDUCT FOR THE ADVERTISING OF SAVINGS AND DEPOSIT ACCOUNTS AND MONEY MARKET ACCOUNTS

(December 1990)

Member Bank Circular 90/52, issued on 17 July 1990, advised Member Banks that the above Code would need to be revised as a result of the Government's decision, announced in the Chancellor's Budget Speech, to abolish Composite Rate Tax (CRT). That Circular also sought to clarify the relevant issues for the transitional period before the new tax regime came into effect on 6 April 1991.

Following discussions with the Building Societies Association, the Finance Houses Association and the Bank of England, a revised Code, a copy of which is attached, has now been agreed. This Code will replace the previous Code agreed in 1985, with effect from *6 April 1991*. However, in view of the introduction of TESSAs, Member Banks will wish to take into consideration those aspects of the Code which deal with tax-free provisions with effect from 1 January 1991.

In the meantime, the guidance on the transitional period to 6 April 1991 included in Member Bank Circular 90/52 remains applicable. For convenience the relevant contents of that Circular are repeated at the end of this document.

The Revised Code

The opportunity afforded by the need to revise the Code to reflect the changing tax regime has been taken to provide recognition of, in particular, changes in products and services provided by financial institutions which have taken place during the last five years. To this end, the scope of the Code has been expanded to cover all interest bearing accounts including, for instance, interest bearing current accounts and TESSAs. The title of the Code has therefore been amended to 'Code of Conduct for the Advertising of Interest Bearing Accounts'. It is also expressly stated that the Code applies to all such accounts maintained within the United Kingdom.

As in the case of the previous Code, copies of the revised Code have been lodged with the Office of Fair Trading in accordance with the requirements of the Restrictive Trade Practices Act.

Generally efforts have been made to ensure consistency, as far as possible, between the previous Code and the revised version. Additional points of particular importance which Member Banks will wish to note are:

(i) The 'gross' rate is now defined as the contractual rate (Paragraph 6(a)). Accordingly, the term 'gross equivalent' which was defined in Paragraph 6(c) of the previous Code is redundant and has been deleted from the present Code.

(ii) In referring to the gross rate, Paragraph 6(a) emphasises that an explanatory phrase should be used to qualify the rate used. Except in the case of TESSAs and certain non-resident accounts, interest will normally be paid after the deduction of income tax at the basic rate prevailing at that time. Tax may be reclaimed from the Inland Revenue where the amount deducted exceeds an individual's liability to tax. Interest may be paid without deduction of tax to individuals who are eligible and register that they do not expect to be liable to income tax.

(iii) Paragraph 6(c) introduces the possibility of quoting a 'tax free' rate of interest. This is of particular relevance in the case of TESSAs. However, the term 'tax free' should only be used in very limited circumstances, such as TESSAs and relevant non-resident accounts. Explanatory wording conveying its meaning should be included if the phrase 'tax free' is used.

(iv) Paragraph 6(d) provides for 'tax free' as well as 'gross' or 'net' Compounded Annual Rates (CARs) to be quoted where appropriate.

(v) Paragraph 11 expressly provides a very limited exception to certain of the terms of the Code in the case of general notices to customers displayed in offices on a rate board.

Calculation of compounded annual rates

Member Banks Circular 85/139, dated 27 November 1985, contained agreed rules for the calculation of compounded annual rates (CARs) to be used in conjunction with the Code. These rules and the associated tables have been revised to take account of the deletion from the Code of 'gross equivalent CAR' and the introduction of 'tax free CAR'. Copies of both the revised rules and the associated tables are attached as a supplement to the Code. The formula and tables cover those instances where interest is compounded daily, weekly, monthly, quarterly, half-yearly or annually.

Application of the Code

Members of the BBA, BSA and FHA are being asked to bring their advertising into line with the new Code. As with the previous Code, it is believed that the Bank of England will also be advising all authorised institutions, whether or not they are members of one of the above associations, that it expects them to adhere to the provisions of the Code and that it will be continuing to monitor the standard of advertising to satisfy itself that the arrangements are working satisfactorily.

Transitional arrangements

The following arrangements continue to apply during the period up to 6 April 1991.

(a) For Accounts Where the Next Interest Payment is Before 6 April 1991.
Interest payable before 6 April 1991 is not affected by the abolition of CRT. The interest is deemed to be basic rate tax paid in the hands of recipients, although tax cannot be repaid to individual depositors. The paying institution accounts for CRT (22%). There is therefore no change in the way financial institutions quote rates for interest payments before 6 April 1991.

However, where interest on the same account, and under the same basic contractual terms of deposit, will be payable both before and after 6 April 1991, it will be incumbent on the advertising bank to make sure that appropriate information is given to customers and potential customers about the tax treatment of interest for both periods.

(b) For Accounts Where the Next Interest Period is on or After 6 April 1991.

(i) It should be made clear that, although the gross rate is the contractual rate, for most customers income tax at the rate prevailing at the time interest is paid will be deducted from the gross interest payable. As has been indicated above, tax may be reclaimed from the Inland Revenue where the amount deducted exceeds an individual's liability to tax. Interest may be paid without deduction of tax to individuals who are eligible and register that they do not expect to be liable to income tax.

(ii) During the period up to and including 5 April 1991, there will be a possibility that, having quoted a gross rate on the assumption of a post 5 April 1991 payment date, interest is actually paid early (eg the investor closes his account). Institutions will therefore need to caveat their gross rate quotations by indicating clearly the net rate of interest payable in such circumstances. It should be made clear also that the basic rate tax deemed to be paid under the CRT scheme is not repayable to non-taxpayers.

Code of Conduct for the Advertising of Interest Bearing Accounts

General

1 The terms of this Code apply to the advertising of all interest bearing accounts maintained within the United Kingdom. For the purpose of this Code the term 'advertisement' includes press and broadcast advertisements, direct marketing, window displays, posters, brochures, leaflets, and automated teller machine displays.

2 Advertisements must comply with the spirit and letter of this Code, the British Code of Advertising Practice, the Independent Broadcasting Authority Code and with any relevant legislation.

3 Advertisers of interest bearing accounts must take special care to ensure that members of the general public are fully aware of the nature of any commitment into which they may enter as a result of responding to an advertisement.

4 The registered or business name (and, in the case of press advertisements, direct marketing, brochures and leaflets, the address) of the deposit-taking institution must be clearly stated.

5 In advertisements in which an agent advertises deposit-taking facilities on behalf of a principal or a principal indicates that it will accept deposits through an agent, it must be made clear which body is agent and which is principal.

Interest rates

6 Rates of interest shall not be advertised unless they are described appropriately; the following terms should be used—

    (a) 'W% gross';
    (b) 'X% net';
    (c) 'Y% tax free';
    (d) 'Z% compounded annual rate'

Where—

    (a) is the contractual rate of interest payable not taking account of the deduction of income tax at the basic rate; an explanatory phrase conveying this meaning must be used to qualify the rate quoted.
    (b) is the rate which would be payable after allowing for the deduction of income tax at the current basic rate from the gross rate; an explanatory phrase conveying this meaning must be used to qualify the rate quoted. The net rate may only be quoted where the gross rate is also given.
    (c) is the rate payable where interest is exempt from income tax. An explanatory phrase conveying this meaning must be included if the phrase 'tax free' is used.
    (d) is the rate equivalent to a 'gross', 'net' or 'tax free' rate annualised to take account of the compounding of interest paid other than once a year; an explanatory phrase conveying this meaning must be included if the 'compounded annual rate' is quoted. 'CAR', following a percentage rate, is acceptable as the abbreviation of 'compounded annual rate'. A 'CAR' must not be quoted without the relevant 'gross', 'net' or 'tax free' rate and must show the rate to which it applies, for example 'W% gross', 'Z% gross CAR'. A 'CAR' must not have greater prominence in size of type or otherwise than any other rates quoted. The rules for calculation of compounded annual rates are set out in the supplement to the Code.

7 It follows from paragraph 6 above that all advertisements in which a rate is quoted must include the contractual rate, ie the 'gross' or, if applicable, 'tax free' rate. No rate shall be given greater prominence in size of type or otherwise than the contractual rate provided interest is due at least annually. Where interest is paid less frequently (eg after 5 years) the contractual rate shall be given no greater prominence than the 'compounded annual rate'. Where rates are quoted on the basis of other than a 12 month period, this must clearly be stated.

8 Advertisements quoting a rate of interest must contain a specific statement indicating—

    (a) the term, if any, of the deposit;
    (b) the frequency of payment of interest; and either that
    (c) the rate quoted is fixed for any term specified; or
    (d) interest rates are subject to variation.

9 Advertisements quoting a rate of interest or yield which are intended for media or direct mail with long copy dates must contain a suitable qualification, such as 'rates correct at time of going to press', and may state that time.

10 The explanatory phrases and statements required by this Code must be clearly audible or legible as appropriate.

Notices of rates

11 A general notice to customers of changes in rates (or a simple list of the range of accounts and their rates) displayed in offices on a rate board, primarily to fulfil contractual obligations, need only comply with paragraphs 6 and 7 of the Code. In the case of such notices or lists, the words 'gross', 'net', 'tax free' and 'CAR' as appropriate need not appear after each rate. However, it must be clear from the whole of the notice or list which term applies to which rate, for example, by the use of column headings or footnotes.

Terms and conditions

12 A clear indication of the type of deposit must be given by satisfying the following—

    (a) Advertisements must contain a clear statement of the conditions for withdrawal, including the amount of any charges levied, the period of any notice required and the extent of any interest forfeited.
    (b) Where interest is forfeited on any withdrawal without notice, words such as 'instant access' or 'immediate withdrawals' must not be displayed together with the rate of interest without clear qualification.
    (c) For accounts which do not allow withdrawals, even after notice, without forfeiting interest, the text of the advertisement must include a statement indicating that, if a withdrawal is made, the stated interest rate will not be achieved.
    (d) Where a maximum or minimum amount must be deposited to achieve the stated interest rate, the text of the advertisement must include a clear statement to this effect.

13 Advertisements which invite deposits by immediate coupon responses must—

    (a) include the full terms and conditions or state that they are available on request;
    (b) clearly state in the part of the advertisement to be retained by the consumer a full postal address at which the advertiser can be contacted during normal business hours and the description and details of the advertised product including the information required by this Code.

Supplement to the Code

Rules for calculation of compounded annual rates

General

1 These recommended Rules relate to the Code of Conduct for the advertising of interest bearing accounts issued jointly in December 1990 by the British Bankers' Association, The Building Societies Association and the Finance Houses Association.

2 Paragraphs 6(d) and 7 of the Code refer to the use of compounded annual rate ('CAR') as the rate equivalent to a 'gross', 'net' or 'tax free' rate, annualised to take account of the compounding of interest paid other than once a year.

Use of formula

3 The compounded annual rate ('gross', 'net' or 'tax free' as appropriate) is given by the following formula—

$$\left[\left(1 + \frac{r}{m \times 100} \right)^m - 1 \right] \times 100$$

where r is the nominal annual rate ('gross', 'net' or 'tax free' as appropriate); and m is the number of times interest is paid in a year.

Assumptions for calculations

4 For the purpose of calculation of the compounded annual rate—

    (a) it shall be assumed that there are no other associated costs or benefits arising during the period in which the account is held;

    (b) compounded annual rates shall be quoted to two decimal places, except in cases where the final digit or digits is/are zero(s), in which case it/they may be omitted. The decimals shall be rounded up or down to the nearest 0.01% viz. 12.154% should be rounded down to 12.15%, 12.147% should be rounded up to 12.15%, 12.155% should be rounded up to 12.16%. For the purpose of rounding to two decimal places, the third digit after the decimal only should be taken into consideration and subsequent digits ignored. Where the third and fourth decimal places are 50, the figures should be rounded up. For example, 12.5650% becomes 12.57% but 12.5649% must *not* be rounded to 12.565% and then to 12.57%.

Table

5 The calculation of a 'gross', 'net' or 'tax free' compounded annual rate ('CAR') may be made with reference to the attached table. (In practice, of course, the 'gross' and 'tax free' figure will be the same.) The figures shown in the table apply equally to 'gross', 'net' or 'tax free' rates. Therefore, by reference to the nominal rate ('gross', 'net' or 'tax free') in the lefthand column, the appropriate 'CAR' ('gross', 'net' or 'tax free') can be read off from the relevant righthand interest payment frequency column.

Table to be used for the calculation of the compounded annual rate of a gross, net or tax free rate

NOMINAL RATE P.A.	FREQUENCY OF INTEREST PAYMENT					
Gross, Net or Tax free	Daily	Weekly	Monthly	Quarterly	Half Yearly	Yearly
%	(%)	(%)	(%)	(%)	(%)	(%)
0.000	0.00	0.00	0.00	0.00	0.00	0.00
0.125	0.13	0.13	0.13	0.13	0.13	0.13
0.250	0.25	0.25	0.25	0.25	0.25	0.25
0.375	0.38	0.38	0.38	0.38	0.38	0.38
0.500	0.50	0.50	0.50	0.50	0.50	0.50
0.625	0.63	0.63	0.63	0.63	0.63	0.63
0.750	0.75	0.75	0.75	0.75	0.75	0.75
0.875	0.88	0.88	0.88	0.88	0.88	0.88
1.000	1.01	1.00	1.00	1.00	1.00	1.00
1.125	1.13	1.13	1.13	1.13	1.13	1.13
1.250	1.26	1.26	1.26	1.26	1.25	1.25
1.375	1.38	1.38	1.38	1.38	1.38	1.38
1.500	1.51	1.51	1.51	1.51	1.51	1.50
1.625	1.64	1.64	1.64	1.63	1.63	1.63

NOMINAL RATE P.A.	FREQUENCY OF INTEREST PAYMENT					
Gross, Net or Tax free	Daily	Weekly	Monthly	Quarterly	Half Yearly	Yearly
%	(%)	(%)	(%)	(%)	(%)	(%)
1.750	1.77	1.77	1.76	1.76	1.76	1.75
1.875	1.89	1.89	1.89	1.89	1.88	1.88
2.000	2.02	2.02	2.02	2.02	2.01	2.00
2.125	2.15	2.15	2.15	2.14	2.14	2.13
2.250	2.28	2.28	2.27	2.27	2.26	2.25
2.375	2.40	2.40	2.40	2.40	2.39	2.38
2.500	2.53	2.53	2.53	2.52	2.52	2.50
2.625	2.66	2.66	2.66	2.65	2.64	2.63
2.750	2.79	2.79	2.78	2.78	2.77	2.75
2.875	2.92	2.92	2.91	2.91	2.90	2.88
3.000	3.05	3.04	3.04	3.03	3.02	3.00
3.125	3.17	3.17	3.17	3.16	3.15	3.13
3.250	3.30	3.30	3.30	3.29	3.28	3.25
3.375	3.43	3.43	3.43	3.42	3.40	3.38
3.500	3.56	3.56	3.56	3.55	3.53	3.50
3.625	3.69	3.69	3.69	3.67	3.66	3.63
3.750	3.82	3.82	3.82	3.80	3.79	3.75
3.875	3.95	3.95	3.94	3.93	3.91	3.88
4.000	4.08	4.08	4.07	4.06	4.04	4.00
4.125	4.21	4.21	4.20	4.19	4.17	4.13
4.250	4.34	4.34	4.33	4.32	4.30	4.25
4.375	4.47	4.47	4.46	4.45	4.42	4.38
4.500	4.60	4.60	4.59	4.58	4.55	4.50
4.625	4.73	4.73	4.72	4.71	4.68	4.63
4.750	4.86	4.86	4.85	4.84	4.81	4.75
4.875	5.00	4.99	4.99	4.96	4.93	4.88
5.000	5.13	5.12	5.12	5.09	5.06	5.00
5.125	5.26	5.26	5.25	5.22	5.19	5.13
5.250	5.39	5.39	5.38	5.35	5.32	5.25
5.375	5.52	5.52	5.51	5.48	5.45	5.38
5.500	5.65	5.65	5.64	5.61	5.58	5.50
5.625	5.79	5.78	5.77	5.74	5.70	5.63
5.750	5.92	5.92	5.90	5.88	5.83	5.75
5.875	6.05	6.05	6.04	6.01	5.96	5.88
6.000	6.18	6.18	6.17	6.14	6.09	6.00
6.125	6.32	6.31	6.30	6.27	6.22	6.13
6.250	6.45	6.45	6.43	6.40	6.35	6.25
6.375	6.58	6.58	6.56	6.53	6.48	6.38
6.500	6.72	6.71	6.70	6.66	6.61	6.50
6.625	6.85	6.84	6.83	6.79	6.73	6.63
6.750	6.98	6.98	6.96	6.92	6.86	6.75
6.875	7.12	7.11	7.10	7.05	6.99	6.88
7.000	7.25	7.25	7.23	7.19	7.12	7.00
7.125	7.38	7.38	7.36	7.32	7.25	7.13
7.250	7.52	7.51	7.50	7.45	7.38	7.25
7.375	7.65	7.65	7.63	7.58	7.51	7.38
7.500	7.79	7.78	7.76	7.71	7.64	7.50
7.625	7.92	7.92	7.90	7.85	7.77	7.63
7.750	8.06	8.05	8.03	7.98	7.90	7.75
7.875	8.19	8.19	8.17	8.11	8.03	7.88

NOMINAL RATE P.A.	FREQUENCY OF INTEREST PAYMENT					
Gross, Net or Tax free	Daily	Weekly	Monthly	Quarterly	Half Yearly	Yearly
%	(%)	(%)	(%)	(%)	(%)	(%)
8.000	8.33	8.32	8.30	8.24	8.16	8.00
8.125	8.46	8.46	8.43	8.38	8.29	8.13
8.250	8.60	8.59	8.57	8.51	8.42	8.25
8.375	8.73	8.73	8.70	8.64	8.55	8.38
8.500	8.87	8.86	8.84	8.77	8.68	8.50
8.625	9.01	9.00	8.97	8.91	8.81	8.63
8.750	9.14	9.14	9.11	9.04	8.94	8.75
8.875	9.28	9.27	9.25	9.17	9.07	8.88
9.000	9.42	9.41	9.38	9.31	9.20	9.00
9.125	9.55	9.55	9.52	9.44	9.33	9.13
9.250	9.69	9.68	9.65	9.58	9.46	9.25
9.375	9.83	9.82	9.79	9.71	9.59	9.38
9.500	9.96	9.96	9.92	9.84	9.73	9.50
9.625	10.10	10.09	10.06	9.98	9.86	9.63
9.750	10.24	10.23	10.20	10.11	9.99	9.75
9.875	10.38	10.37	10.33	10.25	10.12	9.88
10.000	10.52	10.51	10.47	10.38	10.25	10.00
10.125	10.65	10.64	10.61	10.52	10.38	10.13
10.250	10.79	10.78	10.75	10.65	10.51	10.25
10.375	10.93	10.92	10.88	10.79	10.64	10.38
10.500	11.07	11.06	11.02	10.92	10.78	10.50
10.625	11.21	11.20	11.16	11.06	10.91	10.63
10.750	11.35	11.34	11.30	11.19	11.04	10.75
10.875	11.49	11.48	11.43	11.33	11.17	10.88
11.000	11.63	11.61	11.57	11.46	11.30	11.00
11.125	11.77	11.75	11.71	11.60	11.43	11.13
11.250	11.91	11.89	11.85	11.73	11.57	11.25
11.375	12.05	12.03	11.99	11.87	11.70	11.38
11.500	12.19	12.17	12.13	12.01	11.83	11.50
11.625	12.33	12.31	12.26	12.14	11.96	11.63
11.750	12.47	12.45	12.40	12.28	12.10	11.75
11.875	12.61	12.59	12.54	12.41	12.23	11.88
12.000	12.75	12.73	12.68	12.55	12.36	12.00
12.125	12.89	12.87	12.82	12.69	12.49	12.13
12.250	13.03	13.02	12.96	12.82	12.63	12.25
12.375	13.17	13.16	13.10	12.96	12.76	12.38
12.500	13.31	13.30	13.24	13.10	12.89	12.50
12.625	13.45	13.44	13.38	13.24	13.02	12.63
12.750	13.60	13.58	13.52	13.37	13.16	12.75
12.875	13.74	13.72	13.66	13.51	13.29	12.88
13.000	13.88	13.86	13.80	13.65	13.42	13.00
13.125	14.02	14.01	13.94	13.79	13.56	13.13
13.250	14.17	14.15	14.09	13.92	13.69	13.25
13.375	14.31	14.29	14.23	14.06	13.82	13.38
13.500	14.45	14.43	14.37	14.20	13.96	13.50
13.625	14.59	14.58	14.51	14.34	14.09	13.63
13.750	14.74	14.72	14.65	14.48	14.22	13.75
13.875	14.88	14.86	14.79	14.61	14.36	13.88
14.000	15.02	15.01	14.93	14.75	14.49	14.00
14.125	15.17	15.15	15.08	14.89	14.62	14.13
14.250	15.31	15.29	15.22	15.03	14.76	14.25

NOMINAL RATE P.A.	FREQUENCY OF INTEREST PAYMENT					
Gross, Net or Tax free	Daily	Weekly	Monthly	Quarterly	Half Yearly	Yearly
%	(%)	(%)	(%)	(%)	(%)	(%)
14.375	15.46	15.44	15.36	15.17	14.89	14.38
14.500	15.60	15.58	15.50	15.31	15.03	14.50
14.625	15.75	15.72	15.65	15.45	15.16	14.63
14.750	15.89	54.87	15.79	15.59	15.29	14.75
14.875	16.03	16.01	15.93	15.73	15.43	14.88
15.000	16.18	16.16	16.08	15.87	15.56	15.00
15.125	16.33	16.30	16.22	16.00	15.70	15.13
15.250	16.47	16.45	16.36	16.14	15.83	15.25
15.375	16.62	16.59	16.51	16.28	15.97	15.38
15.500	16.76	16.74	16.65	16.42	16.10	15.50
15.625	16.91	16.88	16.79	16.56	16.24	15.63
15.750	17.05	17.03	16.94	16.70	16.37	15.75
15.875	17.20	17.18	17.08	16.85	16.51	15.88
16.000	17.35	17.32	17.23	16.99	16.64	16.00
16.125	17.49	17.47	17.37	17.13	16.78	16.13
16.250	17.64	17.62	17.52	17.27	16.91	16.25
16.375	17.79	17.76	17.66	17.41	17.05	16.38
16.500	17.93	17.91	17.81	17.55	17.18	16.50
16.625	18.08	18.06	17.95	17.69	17.32	16.63
16.750	18.23	18.20	18.10	17.83	17.45	16.75
16.875	18.38	18.35	18.24	17.97	17.59	16.88
17.000	18.53	18.50	18.39	18.11	17.72	17.00
17.125	18.67	18.65	18.54	18.26	17.86	17.13
17.250	18.82	18.79	18.68	18.40	17.99	17.25
17.375	18.97	18.94	18.83	18.54	18.13	17.38
17.500	19.12	19.09	18.97	18.68	18.27	17.50
17.625	19.27	19.24	19.12	18.82	18.40	17.63
17.750	19.42	19.39	19.27	18.97	18.54	17.75
17.875	19.57	19.54	19.41	19.11	18.67	17.88
18.000	19.72	19.68	19.56	19.25	18.81	18.00
18.125	19.87	19.83	19.71	19.39	18.95	18.13
18.250	20.02	19.98	19.86	19.54	19.08	18.25
18.375	20.17	20.13	20.00	19.68	19.22	18.38
18.500	20.32	20.28	20.15	19.82	19.36	18.50
18.625	20.47	20.43	20.30	19.97	19.49	18.63
18.750	20.62	20.58	20.45	20.11	19.63	18.75
18.875	20.77	20.73	20.60	20.25	19.77	18.88
19.000	20.92	20.88	20.75	20.40	19.90	19.00
19.125	21.07	21.03	20.89	20.54	20.04	19.13
19.250	21.22	21.18	21.04	20.68	20.18	19.25
19.375	21.37	21.34	21.19	20.83	20.31	19.38
19.500	21.52	21.49	21.34	20.97	20.45	19.50
19.625	21.68	21.64	21.49	21.12	20.59	19.63
19.750	21.83	21.79	21.64	21.26	20.73	19.75
19.875	21.98	21.94	21.79	21.41	20.86	19.88
20.000	22.13	22.09	21.94	21.55	21.00	20.00
20.125	22.29	22.25	22.09	21.70	21.14	20.13
20.250	22.44	22.40	22.24	21.84	21.28	20.25
20.375	22.59	22.55	22.39	21.99	21.41	20.38
20.500	22.75	22.70	22.54	22.13	21.55	20.50
20.625	22.90	22.86	22.69	22.28	21.69	20.63

NOMINAL RATE P.A.	FREQUENCY OF INTEREST PAYMENT					
Gross, Net or Tax free	Daily	Weekly	Monthly	Quarterly	Half Yearly	Yearly
%	(%)	(%)	(%)	(%)	(%)	(%)
20.750	23.05	23.01	22.84	22.42	21.83	20.75
20.875	23.21	23.16	22.99	22.57	21.96	20.88
21.000	23.36	23.32	23.14	22.71	22.10	21.00
21.125	23.51	23.47	23.30	22.86	22.24	21.13
21.250	23.67	23.62	23.45	23.00	22.38	21.25
21.375	23.82	23.78	23.60	23.15	22.52	21.38
21.500	23.98	23.93	23.75	23.30	22.66	21.50
21.625	24.13	24.09	23.90	23.44	22.79	21.63
21.750	24.29	24.24	24.05	23.59	22.93	21.75
21.875	24.44	24.39	24.21	23.74	23.07	21.88
22.000	24.60	24.55	24.36	23.88	23.21	22.00
22.125	24.76	24.70	24.51	24.03	23.35	22.13
22.250	24.91	24.86	24.67	24.18	23.49	22.25
22.375	25.07	25.02	24.82	24.32	23.63	22.38
22.500	25.22	25.17	24.97	24.47	23.77	22.50
22.625	25.38	25.33	25.13	24.62	23.90	22.63
22.750	25.54	25.48	25.28	24.77	24.04	22.75
22.875	25.69	25.64	25.43	24.91	24.18	22.88
23.000	25.85	25.80	25.59	25.06	24.32	23.00
23.125	26.01	25.95	25.74	25.21	24.46	23.13
23.250	26.17	26.11	25.89	25.36	24.60	23.25
23.375	26.32	26.27	26.05	25.50	24.74	23.38
23.500	26.48	26.42	26.20	25.65	24.88	23.50
23.625	26.64	26.58	26.36	25.80	25.02	23.63
23.750	26.80	26.74	26.51	25.95	25.16	23.75
23.875	26.96	26.90	26.67	26.10	25.30	23.88
24.000	27.11	27.05	26.82	26.25	25.44	24.00
24.125	27.27	27.21	26.98	26.40	25.58	24.13
24.250	27.43	27.37	27.14	26.55	25.72	24.25
24.375	27.59	27.53	27.29	26.69	25.86	24.38
24.500	27.75	27.69	27.45	26.84	26.00	24.50
24.625	27.91	27.85	27.60	26.99	26.14	24.63
24.750	28.07	28.01	27.76	27.14	26.28	24.75
24.875	28.23	28.17	27.92	27.29	26.42	24.88

[818]

BSD/1990/2
(December 1990)

NOTICE TO INSTITUTIONS AUTHORISED UNDER THE BANKING ACT 1987

IMPLEMENTATION IN THE UNITED KINGDOM OF THE DIRECTIVE ON OWN FUNDS OF CREDIT INSTITUTIONS

Introduction

1 EC member states are required to implement the provisions of the Directive on Own Funds (89/299/EEC of 17 April 1989) no later than 1 January 1993. The Directive

establishes standard EC definitions of capital for prudential supervision purposes and follows closely the Basle Convergence Agreement on capital standards, which was implemented in the UK from end-1989.[1]

2 This Notice reflects the provisions of the Own Funds Directive for the purpose of supervision of institutions authorised under the Banking Act 1987. Except where otherwise specified, the Notice has immediate effect and replaces the section on capital in BSD/1988/3 which is now withdrawn. **However, there are no immediate changes to present policy.**

[1] See 'Implementation of the Basle Convergence Agreement in the United Kingdom' – BSD/1988/3, issued in October 1988.

Scope and application

3 The Own Funds Directive applies to all credit institutions as defined in Article 1 of the First Banking Co-ordination Directive (77/780/EEC, dated 12 December 1977). This Notice applies to all UK institutions authorised under the Banking Act 1987. However, see the Notice on the Implementation of the Solvency Ratio Directive (BSD/1990/3, paragraph 3) for those institutions for which own funds do not have to be calculated for the purpose of determining a solvency ratio.

4 In line with the Basle Agreement and in conjunction with the requirements of Article 3 of the Solvency Ratio Directive (89/647/EEC), the provisions of the Own Funds Directive will be applied on a consolidated basis in the United Kingdom. The Bank will nevertheless continue to assess capital adequacy on an unconsolidated basis to ensure a reasonable distribution of capital within a group, as also required by Article 3(4).

Tier 1 and 2 capital

5 Although the Directive does not refer to Tier 1 and 2 capital as such, as does the Basle Agreement, limits are imposed in Article 6 on certain items that may be included in total capital which effectively create a tiering of capital. The Bank will therefore continue to refer to Tier 1 and 2 capital.

Other items

6 The 'other items' eligible for inclusion in Tier 2 [Article 3(1)] will be general provisions, subject to the Basle limits of 1.5% of weighted risk assets up to the end of 1992, and 1.25% from 1 January 1993. Unpublished reserves and unpublished current year profits subject to verification by internal audit (see para 9 below) will also be included.

Changes resulting from the own funds directive

Holdings of capital issued by other credit institutions

7 The Bank will continue to deduct from capital all holdings of another credit institution's capital. Market-making concessions, by which banks are able to hold such instruments without their deduction from capital will still apply but will have to be subject to certain limits after 1 January 1993.[1] Banks may however hold the capital instruments of another credit or financial institution without their deduction where they are held temporarily as part of a financial rescue of that institution and where the Bank has given its prior consent to this concession [Article 2(12)].

[1] See Article 2(12) and (13). Holdings of another credit or financial institution's capital instruments which constitute more than 10% of the equity of the institution in which the investment is made will be deducted from the reporting institution's own funds. In addition such holdings which constitute less than 10% of the equity of the institution in which the investment is made but which in aggregate exceed 10% of the own funds of the reporting institution will also be deducted.

Current year profits

PUBLISHED PROFITS

8 The Bank's current policy is to allow the inclusion in Tier 1 capital of the current year's retained earnings (net of foreseeable charges and distributions) where they have

been published in the form of an interim statement, including retained earnings of authorised subsidiaries within banking groups which publish interims even if not separately disclosed. The Own Funds Directive allows interim profits to be included in Tier 1 only if they have been 'verified by persons responsible for the auditing of the accounts and if it is proved to the satisfaction of the competent authorities that the amount thereof has been evaluated in accordance with the principles set out in Directive 86/635/EEC (Bank Accounts Directive) and is net of foreseeable charge or dividend' [Article 2(1)(2)]. This requirement is incorporated into Annex I(c). The Bank will discuss with banks and the accountancy profession the detailed implications of this amended requirement in good time before 1 January 1993. Before this date, the current reporting requirements will continue to apply.

UNPUBLISHED PROFITS

9 Unpublished current year profits are currently included in Tier 2 capital. After 1 January 1993 they will only be included if they have been verified by internal audit [Article 3(1)(c)]. The Bank will discuss with the banks the detailed implications of this amendment in good time before that date. Until then there will be no such requirement.

Revaluation reserves

10 At present, revaluation reserves related to tangible fixed assets are included in Tier 2 capital, and other revaluation reserves including those related to fixed asset investments are included in Tier 1. The Directive requires all revaluation reserves to be included in Tier 2 capital. This change will not come into effect until 1 January 1993.

National discretions

11 Hybrid capital instruments, including perpetual subordinated debt and perpetual cumulative preferred shares will continue to be included in Tier 2, as allowed in Article 3(2).

12 Dated preferred shares and subordinated term loan capital will continue to be included in Tier 2, as allowed in Article 4(3).

13 The non-deduction from a parent company's own funds of its holdings in other credit institutions or financial institutions which are included in the consolidation in calculating the parent's unconsolidated own funds [Article 2(1)] will not be adopted.

Exclusions from capital

14 The following components of capital set out in Article 2(1) are not relevant to the United Kingdom:

   (a) Funds for general banking risks [Article 2(1)(4)];
   (b) Value adjustments permitted in Article 37(2) of Directive 86/635/EEC [Article 2(1)(5)];
   (c) Commitments of the members of credit institutions set up as co-operative societies [Article 2(1)(7)].

Annex

15 The Annex details the components of own funds and supersedes Annex 1 of the Basle Implementation notice (BSD/1988/3). It should be read in conjunction with the Bank's more detailed reporting requirements for the Capital Adequacy Return (Form BSD1). It sets out the framework with immediate effect and does not incorporate those changes to the calculation of own funds which will come into effect on 1 January 1993.

Annex Definition of capital

I Tier 1: Core Capital

   (a) Permanent shareholders' equity:
      (i) Allotted, called up and fully paid share capital/common stock (net of any own shares held, at book value);
      (ii) Perpetual non-cumulative preferred shares,[1] including such shares

redeemable at the option of the issuer and with the Bank's prior consent, and such shares convertible into ordinary shares.

(b) Disclosed reserves in the form of general and other reserves created by appropriations of retained earnings, share premiums and other surplus.[2]

(c) Published interim retained profits.[3]

(d) Minority interests arising on consolidation from interests in permanent share-holders' equity.

less

(e) goodwill and other intangible assets[4]

and

(f) current year's unpublished losses

and

(g) fully paid shareholders' equity issued after 1 January 1992 by the capitalisation of property revaluation reserves.

---

[1] Sometimes referred to as preferred stock.
[2] Including capital gifts and capital redemption reserves.
[3] These must be verified by external auditors with effect from 1 January 1993 – see paragraph 8 of this Notice.
[4] Mortgage servicing rights will continue to be regarded as intangible assets, unless it can be demonstrated there is an active and liquid market in which they can be reliably traded. At present this condition is only met in respect of mortgage servicing rights traded in the US market.

II Tier 2: Supplementary Capital

(a) Undisclosed reserves and unpublished current year's retained profits.[1]

(b) Reserves arising from the revaluation of tangible fixed assets and from 1 January 1993, of fixed asset investments.

(c) General provisions:
Provisions held against possible or latent loss but where these losses have not as yet been identified will be included, subject to a limit [see IV(c)].
Provisions earmarked or held specifically against lower valuations of particular claims or classes of claims will *not* be included in capital. This treatment of general provisions will remain in force pending further agreement in Basle on a more precise definition of unencumbered provisions.

(d) Hybrid capital instruments:
  (i) Perpetual cumulative preferred shares, including shares redeemable at the option of the issuer and with the prior consent of the Bank, and such shares convertible into ordinary shares;
  (ii) Perpetual subordinated debt which meets the conditions for primary perpetual subordinated debt set out in BSD/1986/2[2] including such debt which is convertible into equity.

(e) Subordinated term debt:
  (i) Dated preferred shares (irrespective of original maturity);
  (ii) Convertible subordinated bonds not included in (d)(ii);
  (iii) Subordinated term loan capital with a minimum original term to maturity of over five years and otherwise meeting the conditions set out in BSD/1986/2, subject to a straight-line amortisation during the last five years leaving no more than 20% of the original amount issued outstanding in the final year before redemption.

(f) Minority interests arising on consolidation from interests in Tier 2 capital items.

(g) Fully paid shareholders' equity issued after 1 January 1992 by the capitalisation of property revaluation reserves.

---

[1] Unpublished current year's retained profits must be verified by internal audit from 1 January 1993 – see para 9 of this Notice.
[2] March 1986.

III Deductions from Total Capital (total of Tier 1 and Tier 2)

(a) Investments in unconsolidated subsidiaries and associates;

(b) Connected lending of a capital nature;

(c) All holdings of other banks' and building societies' capital instruments. However, the existing concessions (as set out in BSD/1986/2) that apply to primary and secondary market-makers in such instruments will remain in place but will be subject to amendment after 1 January 1993.[1]

---

[1] See para 7, footnote [1] to this Notice.

IV   Limits and Restrictions

(a) The total Tier 2 supplementary elements (a–g) should not exceed a maximum of 100% of Tier 1 elements;

(b) Subordinated term debt [item II(e)] should not exceed a maximum of 50% of Tier 1 elements;

(c) General provisions [item II(c)] should not exceed 1.5% of weighted risk assets up to the end of 1992 and 1.25% of weighted risk assets from 1 January 1993.] **[819]**

This Annex is substituted by Bank of England Notice, BSD/1992/1.

BSD/1990/3
(December 1990)

NOTICE TO INSTITUTIONS AUTHORISED UNDER THE BANKING ACT 1987

IMPLEMENTATION IN THE UNITED KINGDOM OF THE SOLVENCY RATIO DIRECTIVE

Introduction

1 EC Member States are required to adopt the necessary measures to comply with the Solvency Ratio Directive (89/647/EEC of 18 December 1989) by 1 January 1991 and are required to implement the provisions of the Directive in full by 1 January 1993. The Solvency Ratio Directive follows closely the lines of the 1988 Basle Convergence Agreement on capital standards, which was implemented in the United Kingdom from the end of 1989.[1] Implementation of the former therefore implies minimal change to the existing capital adequacy system in the United Kingdom.

2 This Notice adopts the provisions of the Solvency Ratio Directive. Except where otherwise specified, this Notice has immediate effect and replaces the sections on risk weights in the notice BSD/1988/3 which is now withdrawn. The changes from present policy with immediate effect are noted in paragraphs 6–9, 17, 21–23 and 30; none are substantive.

---

[1] See 'Implementation of the Basle Convergence Agreement in the United Kingdom' – BSD/1988/3, issued in October 1988.

Scope and application

3 The Solvency Ratio Directive applies to credit institutions as defined by Article 1 of the First Banking Co-ordination Directive.[1] Although this definition covers UK branches of non-UK incorporated banks, such branches are not required by the Bank of England to maintain capital in the United Kingdom. As a result this Notice applies only to all UK incorporated institutions authorised under the Banking Act 1987, with the exception of those discount houses which meet the specific criteria set out in Article 1(4) of the Solvency Ratio Directive.[2] This Notice applies on a consolidated basis as required under Article 3(3), as well as on a solo or solo consolidated basis in order to ensure a reasonable distribution of capital within a group; this is consistent with the requirements of Article 3(4). This approach continues the Bank's present policy on capital adequacy. The term 'solvency ratio' is not being adopted; the Bank will continue to refer to the 'risk asset ratio'.

4 The Bank's capital requirements will continue to be specified as target and trigger risk asset ratios. The 8% minimum standard, as required by Article 10(1), remains the base line for the Bank's discretion in setting the requirements at both consolidated and solo (or solo consolidated) levels. It is not intended to alter the principles on which the trigger and target ratios are agreed with each bank, and these ratios will continue to reflect each bank's particular circumstances.

5 The frequency of reporting remains unchanged; the present arrangements, which include the calculation of consolidated capital ratios twice yearly, meet the Directive's requirements as set out in Article 3(7).

[1] Those institutions listed in article 2(2) of the First Banking Co-ordination Directive are exempted. In the United Kingdom the exempt institutions are: the National Savings Bank, The Commonwealth Development Finance Company Ltd, the Agricultural Mortgage Corporation Ltd, the Scottish Agricultural Securities Corporation Ltd, the Crown Agents for Overseas Governments and Administrations, credit unions and municipal banks.
[2] The Bank is establishing procedures to enable it to monitor the continuing adherence of the discount houses to the conditions set out in Article 1(4).

Changes resulting from the Solvency Ratio Directive

6 The Bank will continue to weight *on-balance-sheet* claims in gold and silver bullion on the non-bank market-making members of the LBMA at 20% until 1 January 1993. (Previously all claims, not just on-balance-sheet claims, in gold and silver bullion on such counterparties were weighted at 20%.) After this date, when the provisions of the Directive must come into force, such claims will have to be weighted at 100% as claims on the non-bank private sector, unless the claim is unconditionally, explicitly and irrevocably guaranteed by a Zone A bank.

7 Mortgaged-backed securities (MBS) issued by special purpose mortgage finance vehicles are covered by Article 6(1)(c)(1) of the Directive and are weighted at 50% where the following conditions are met:

    (i)   the notes embody an express promise to repay the bearer;
   (ii) the issue documentation contains provisions which would ultimately enable noteholders to initiate legal proceedings directly against the issuer of the MBS. As an example such provisions would allow noteholders to proceed against the issuer where the trustee, having become bound to take steps and/or to proceed against the issuer, fails to do so within a reasonable time and such failing is continuing;
  (iii) the documentation contains provisions which would ultimately enable noteholders to acquire the legal title to the security (ie the mortgagee's interest in it) and to realise the security in the event of a default by the mortgagor;
  (iv) the MBS issue meets the conditions set out in the reporting instructions to the Bank's Capital Adequacy Return, BSD1;
   (v) the mortgage loans must not be in default at the time at which they are transferred to the vehicle.

MBS issues which do not meet conditions (i)–(iii) above but which meet conditions (iv) and (v) will continue to be weighted at 50% until 1 January 1993 from which date they will be weighted at 100%.

The Bank will also apply the principles underlying the above conditions to loans to special purpose mortgage finance vehicles. In order for such loans to be weighted at 50% weight, the loan documentation must provide lenders with the same rights as required for noteholders in conditions (ii) and (iii) above. In addition, the conditions set out in the reporting instructions to the BSD1 Return and in (v) above must be met.

8 Where, under Article 7(2), the Commission has agreed that a zero weight is justified for claims on the regional governments and local authorities of another member state, the Bank will consider applying a zero weighting on a case by case basis. The current treatment is to weight claims on non-domestic regional governments and local authorities at 20%.

9 A reduced weighting may now be applicable where a bank is a member of a syndicate and cash has been deposited as collateral with, and is held by, the agent bank itself, for the benefit of the syndicate. In this case the claims (or the portion of the claims) of syndicate members which are cash collateralised may attract a 20% weight while the portion of the agent bank's own claims which are cash collateralised may be eligible for a 0% weight. Previously, no reduction in weight for the other members of the syndicate has been allowed by the Bank. This change of policy comes into effect immediately. Other claims collateralised by cash deposits with non-group banks will not lead to a reduced weight.

10 The basis for measuring maturity in the Solvency Ratio Directive differs from that in the guidance notes to the Bank's Capital Adequacy Return in that reference to a given maturity is taken to be the amount of time 'up to and including' that specified maturity. Hence in this Notice the distinction is between maturities of 'one year or less' and 'not exceeding one year'. However, the present basis of reporting should continue until the required changes to reporting definitions and forms have been agreed with the banks.

Para 7 substituted by BSD/1992/6.

Country risk

11 The existing Basle distinction between OECD and non-OECD countries has been retained although this Notice uses different terminology. *Zone A* countries are defined as all countries which are full members of the Organisation for Economic Co-operation and Development (OECD), together with those countries which have concluded special lending arrangements with the International Monetary Fund (IMF) associated with the General Agreement to Borrow (GAB) – see Annex 4. *Zone B* comprises all countries not in Zone A.

Counterparty weights

Central governments and central banks

12 Claims (other than securities) on Zone A central governments and central banks are weighted at 0%; claims on the European Communities are included in this category. Claims (other than securities) on Zone B central governments and central banks are weighted at 0% *only* where those claims are denominated in local currency and funded in that currency.

13 However, as a proxy for interest rate risk, and pending further work, the Bank will continue to apply a 10% weight to nil credit risk weighted holdings of fixed-interest rate paper with a remaining term to maturity of one year or less and floating-rate or index-linked paper of any maturity; and 20% for similar fixed-interest rate paper with a remaining term to maturity of over one year.[1]

[1] In the case of Zone B central governments, all holdings of nil credit risk weighted paper with a residual maturity of over one year will receive a proxy weighting of 20%, regardless of whether such paper is fixed or floating.

Regional governments and local authorities (public sector entities)

14 Claims on Zone A regional governments and local authorities (plus certain non-commercial public sector bodies), otherwise known as public sector entities, are weighted at 20%. A detailed list of UK bodies which are to be included in this category will be circulated by the Bank from time to time. Claims on Zone B public sector entities are weighted at 100%. A description of the broad class of UK public sector entities is contained at Annex 5.

Credit institutions

15 Claims on Zone A credit institutions ('banks') are weighted at 20%. In order to preserve the efficiency and liquidity of the international interbank market there is no differentiation between short-term claims (ie with a residual maturity of up to one year) on credit institutions incorporated in Zone A or Zone B: these are weighted at 20%. Claims of over one year on Zone B-incorporated credit institutions are weighted at 100%.

16 In accordance with Article 8(2), the Bank will continue to apply a 10% weight to loans to discount houses, gilt-edged market makers, those Stock Exchange money brokers which operate in the gilt-edged market and any other institutions with a money-market dealing relationship with the Bank of England, where the loans are secured on UK Treasury bills, eligible local authority and eligible bank bills, gilt-edged stocks or London CDs. Where this condition is not met, the basic risk weighting for discount houses, being UK institutions authorised under the Banking Act 1987, is 20%; that for the other groups of institutions listed above is 100%.

Multilateral development banks (MDBs)

17 Claims on certain MDBs are weighted at 20%. Annex 6 contains a list of institutions which qualify as MDBs for this purpose. The list includes the Nordic Investment Bank which has not previously been treated by the Bank as an MDB but is now so treated forthwith. The European Bank for Reconstruction and Development is also included as a result of a Commission Directive (yet to be published) which amends the list of qualifying multilateral development banks. The Council of Europe Resettlement Fund[1], which is listed in Article 2(1) of the Solvency Ratio Directive, is currently excluded from this list pending further consideration of its status in Basle.

[1] Now known as the Council of Europe Social Development Fund.

Other counterparties

18 Claims on all other counterparties are weighted at 100%, subject to paragraphs 19–22 below.

Collateral and guarantees

19 The only forms of collateral which may reduce a risk weight are cash deposited with the lending institution or another bank consolidated with that institution, CDs (or similar instruments) issued by and lodged with the lending institution itself and securities issued by Zone A central governments and central banks and the multilateral development banks listed as such in this Notice. Claims so collateralised attract the same weighting as given to a direct holding of that collateral. Claims partially collateralised attract the reduced weighting on that part of the claim which is fully collateralised.

20 Claims directly *guaranteed* by Zone A central governments and central banks, Zone A public sector entities, multilateral development banks and banks attract the weighting given to a direct claim on the guarantor. Thus, claims guaranteed by Zone B banks are weighted at 20% only where the residual maturity is one year or less. Claims guaranteed by Zone B central governments and central banks are weighted at 0% only where such claims are denominated and funded in the national currency common to the guarantor and the borrower. Indirect guarantees are not recognised for the purpose of reducing risk weightings.

21 As agreed recently in Basle, *guarantees received from a banking subsidiary* will not be taken into account when determining the appropriate risk weight of an asset of the parent bank. The Bank is, however, adopting the national discretion allowed in Basle of recognising such guarantees where they are collateralised by a cash deposit placed with that subsidiary.

Other items

Loans secured on residential property

22 A 50% weighting is applied to loans to individuals that are fully secured by a first priority charge on residential property that is (or is intended to be) occupied by the borrower, or is rented. Loans to housing associations registered with the Housing Corporation, Scottish Homes or Tai Cymru (Housing for Wales) are also weighted at 50% as long as they are fully secured by a *first priority* charge on residential property under development and fully secured by a charge on the housing association's residential property that is being let, on condition that the development project attracts Housing Association Grant (HAG). If this last condition is not being met, a *first priority* charge

on residential property that is being let is required for a 50% weight. This distinction has immediate effect.

Deferred tax assets

23 Forthwith, gross deferred tax assets will be weighted at 100%. This change of treatment results from a policy review by the Bank.

Foreign exchange risk

24 The Bank will continue to apply a 100% weight to a bank's net short open foreign exchange position.

Documentary credits

25 As under Basle, documentary letters of credit that are not collateralised by the underlying shipment are treated as direct credit substitutes ('full risk') and receive a credit conversion factor (CCF) of 100%. Similarly, letters of credit confirmed and acting as guarantees of financial obligations continue to be treated as direct credit substitutes (100% CCF), notwithstanding their inclusion in the Directive under 'medium risk' (50% CCF). (Annex 1 of the Directive, 'medium risk', first indent.)

Sale and repurchase agreements

26 All asset sales with recourse receive a credit conversion factor of 100% as under Basle. As such all asset sale and repurchase agreements continue to be treated as 'full risk' items (100% CCF), including asset sales where the purchaser has the option to put the asset back to the seller, which are classified as 'medium risk' in the Directive (Annex 1 of the Directive, 'medium risk', third indent).

Prepayments and accrued income

27 The Directive applies a 50% weight to these items where the counterparty cannot be specifically identified [Article 6(1)(c)]. The Bank will, however, continue to apply a 100% weight to such items.

Off-balance-sheet risk

28 As under Basle, the Solvency Ratio Directive measures off-balance-sheet risk by multiplying the notional principal amounts involved by a credit conversion factor of 0%, 20%, 50% or 100% and weighting the resultant figure by the counterparty risk.

29 In the case of interest rate and exchange rate related transactions, a maximum counterparty weight of 50% is applied [see Article 5(3) of the Directive]. The Bank continues to believe that the best way to assess the credit risk on these items is the replacement cost method of marking contracts to market and adding on a factor to reflect potential exposure over the remaining life of the contract. It therefore expects banks to adopt the replacement cost method rather than the original exposure method where they actively trade these instruments or where such instruments form a significant part of their treasury operations.

Commodity related transactions (eg swaps, futures) and equity options

30 Whilst the Solvency Ratio Directive does not address itself to such transactions, the Bank nevertheless considers that in undertaking this type of business banks expose themselves to significant credit risk on counterparties. As such, pending further co-ordination and discussion with the banking community, commodity transactions should forthwith be treated and reported as foreign exchange contracts using the foreign exchange 'add-ons' to derive the future credit exposure.[1]

---

[1] Before 1 January 1993 the Bank will review whether a maximum counterparty weight of 50% is appropriate in the context of commodity transactions.

Netting of off-balance-sheet instruments

31 Further work on netting of swaps and similar products is taking place in Basle. Until this work is completed and the Bank has given further guidance, banks should not report on a net basis.

National discretions

32 The following national discretions are adopted:

 (i) a Solvency ratio is to be calculated for a credit institution in a banking group on a solo or solo consolidated basis, as permitted under Article 3(4);

 (ii) credit institutions meeting the conditions in Article 1(4) will be excluded from the scope of the Directive (see paragraph 3 of this Notice);

 (iii) all holdings of another credit institution's capital will be deducted, whereas Article 6(1)(d)(6) permits a 100% weighting in certain circumstances;

 (iv) a 10% weight will apply to certain counterparties as set out in paragraph 16 of this Notice, as permitted under Article 8(2).

33 The following national discretions are **not** being adopted:

 (i) the provisions of Article 1(3) are not relevant in the United Kingdom;

 (ii) the responsibility for supervising the solvency of UK-incorporated institutions can be delegated to supervisory authorities of parent undertakings, as detailed in Article 3(6). This responsibility will not be delegated by the Bank;

 (iii) a 0% weighting may be applied to claims on UK local authorities under Article 7(1). The Bank will continue to weight such claims at 20%;

 (iv) a 20% weight may be applied to claims collateralised by local authority securities and by cash deposited with other credit institutions under Article 8(1). A reduced weighting will not be applied except for the particular case described in paragraph 9 above;

 (v) a 10% weight for certain bonds defined in Article 22(4) of Council Directive 85/611/EEC, permitted under Article 11(2);

 (vi) a 50% weight for certain property leasing transactions, permitted under Article 11(5).

Annexes

34 Annex 1 summarises the on-balance-sheet risk weight categories and Annex 2 the off-balance-sheet credit conversion factors. Annex 3 details the treatment of interest and foreign exchange related instruments. Annex 4 lists Zone A countries, Annex 5 describes UK public sector entities and Annex 6 lists multilateral development banks. These Annexes should be read in conjunction with the Bank's reporting requirements for the Capital Adequacy Return (Form BSD1) which will be updated as soon as practical to take account of the changes to previous policies detailed in this Notice.

Annex 1 Risk weight categories: on-balance-sheet

A

0%

 (i) Cash and claims collateralised by cash deposits placed with the lending institution (or CDs and similar instruments issued by and lodged with the reporting institution) and meeting the conditions set out in the Bank's reporting requirements for 0%;

 (ii) Gold and other bullion held in own vaults or on an allocated basis;

 (iii) Claims[1] on Zone A[2] central governments and central banks including claims on the European Communities;

 (iv) Claims[1] guaranteed by Zone A central governments and central banks[3];

 (v) Claims[1] on Zone B central governments and central banks denominated in local currency and funded in that currency;

 (vi) Claims[1] guaranteed by Zone B central governments or central banks, where denominated in local currency and funded in that currency[3];

 (vii) Certificates of tax deposit;

 (viii) Items in suspense[4].

¹ Other than securities issued by these bodies.
² A list of countries within this grouping is attached at Annex 4.
³ Including lending under ECGD bank guarantee and equivalent schemes in other Zone A countries, but excluding lending against the security of ECGD insurance cover.
⁴ Where such items do not represent a credit risk but rather position risk as detailed in the guidance notes to the form BSD1.

B
10%

    (i) Holdings of fixed-interest securities issued (or guaranteed) by Zone A central governments with a residual maturity of 1 year or less, and floating-rate and index-linked securities of any maturity issued or guaranteed by Zone A central governments;

    (ii) Claims collateralised by Zone A central government fixed-interest securities with a maturity of 1 year or less, and similar floating-rate securities of any maturity;

    (iii) Holdings of securities issued by Zone B central governments with a residual maturity of 1 year or less and denominated in local currency and funded by liabilities in the same currency;

    (iv) Loans to discount houses, gilt-edged market makers, institutions with a money-market dealing relationship with the Bank of England and those Stock Exchange money brokers which operate in the gilt-edged market, where the loans are secured on gilts, UK Treasury bills, eligible local authority and eligible bank bills, or London CDs.

C
20%

    (i) Holdings of fixed-interest securities issued (or guaranteed) by Zone A central governments with a residual maturity of over 1 year;

    (ii) Claims collateralised by Zone A central government fixed-interest securities with a residual maturity of over 1 year;

    (iii) Holdings of Zone B central government securities with a maturity of over 1 year denominated in local currency and funded by liabilities in the same currency;

    (iv) Claims on multilateral development banks (see Annex 6) and claims guaranteed by or collateralised by the securities issued by these institutions;

    (v) Claims on credit institutions incorporated in the Zone A and claims guaranteed (or accepted or endorsed) by Zone A-incorporated credit institutions;

    (vi) On-balance-sheet claims in gold and other bullion on the non-bank market making members of the London Bullion Market Association;¹

    (vii) Claims on credit institutions incorporated in Zone B with a residual maturity of 1 year or less and claims of the same maturity guaranteed by Zone B credit institutions;

    (viii) Claims secured by cash deposited with and held by an agent bank acting for a syndicate of which the reporting institution is a member;

    (ix) Claims on Zone A public sector entities and claims guaranteed by such entities. In the United Kingdom, these comprise local authorities and certain non-commercial public bodies (see Annex 5);

    (x) Claims on discount houses and claims which are guaranteed (or accepted) by discount houses which are unsecured, or secured on assets other than specified in B(iv) above;

    (xi) Cash items in the process of collection.

¹ Until 1 January 1993, from which time such claims will be weighted at 100%.

D
50%

    (i) Loans to individuals fully secured by a first priority charge on residential property that is (or is to be) occupied by the borrower or is rented;

    (ii) Loans to housing associations registered with the Housing Corporation, Scottish Homes and Tai Cymru that are fully secured by a *first priority* charge on the residential property which is under development and fully secured by a charge on the housing association's residential property that is being let, and where the project attracts HAG. If HAG is not available, such loans must be fully secured by a *first priority* charge on residential property that is being let;

(iii) Mortgage sub-participations, where the risk to the sub-participating bank is fully and specifically secured against residential mortgage loans which would themselves qualify for the 50% weight;

[Mortgaged-backed securities (MBS) issued by special purpose mortgage finance vehicles are covered by Article 6(1)(c)(1) of the Directive and are weighted at 50% where the following conditions are met:

(i) the notes embody an express promise to repay the bearer;

(ii) the issue documentation contains provisions which would ultimately enable noteholders to initiate legal proceedings directly against the issuer of the MBS. As an example such provisions would allow noteholders to proceed against the issuer where the trustee, having become bound to take steps and/or to proceed against the issuer, fails to do so within a reasonable time and such failing is continuing;

(iii) the documentation contains provisions which would ultimately enable noteholders to acquire the legal title to the security (ie the mortgagee's interest in it) and to realise the security in the event of a default by the mortgagor;

(iv) the MBS issue meets the conditions set out in the reporting instructions to the Bank's Capital Adequacy Return, BSD1;

(v) the mortgage loans must not be in default at the time at which they are transferred to the vehicle.

MBS issues which do not meet conditions (i)–(iii) above but which meet conditions (iv) and (v) will continue to be weighted at 50% until 1 January 1993 from which date they will be weighted at 100%.

The Bank will also apply the principles underlying the above conditions to loans to special purpose mortgage finance vehicles. In order for such loans to be weighted at 50% weight, the loan documentation must provide lenders with the same rights as required for noteholders in conditions (ii) and (iii) above. In addition, the conditions set out in the reporting instructions to the BSD1 Return and in (v) above must be met.]

Para D (iv) substituted by words in square brackets by BSD/1992/6.

E
100%

(i) Claims on the non-bank private sector;

(ii) Claims on credit institutions incorporated in Zone B with a residual maturity of over 1 year;

(iii) Claims on Zone B central governments and central banks (unless denominated in the national currency and funded in that currency);

(iv) Claims guaranteed by Zone B central governments or central banks, which are not denominated and funded in the national currency common to the guarantor and borrower;

(v) Claims on commercial companies owned by the public sector;

(vi) Claims on Zone B public sector entities;

(vii) Premises, plant, equipment and other fixed assets;

(viii) Real estate, trade investments[1] and other assets not otherwise specified;

(ix) Aggregate net short open foreign exchange position[2];

(x) Gross deferred tax assets.

[1] Excluding: (i) holdings of capital instruments issued by credit institutions which will be deducted from total capital; and
(ii) holdings of capital instruments of other financial institutions which must be deducted according to Article 2(12) and (13) of the Own Funds Directive.

[2] This is a proxy weight for a bank's foreign exchange risk, and will remain in effect until an international framework for capturing foreign exchange risk is agreed. Include the net short open position in gold, silver, platinum and palladium.

Annex 2 Credit conversion factors for off-balance-sheet risk

Credit conversion factors should be multiplied by the weights applicable to the category of the counterparty for an on-balance-sheet transaction.

Instruments	Credit conversion factor
A Direct credit substitutes, including general guarantees of indebtedness, standby letters of credit serving as financial guarantees, acceptances and endorsements (including *per aval* endorsements);	100%
B Sale and repurchase agreements and asset sales with recourse where the credit risk remains with the bank;[1]	100%
C Forward asset purchases, forward forward deposits placed and the unpaid part of partly-paid shares and securities,[1] and any other commitments with a certain drawdown;	100%
D Transaction-related contingent items not having the character of direct credit substitutes (eg performance bonds, bid bonds, warranties and standby letters of credit related to particular transactions);	50%
E Short-term self-liquidating trade-related contingent items (such as documentary credits collateralised by the underlying shipments);	20%
F Note issuance facilities and revolving underwriting facilities;[2]	50%
G Other commitments (eg formal standby facilities and credit lines) with an original[3] maturity of over 1 year;	50%

Instruments	Credit conversion factor
H Similar commitments with an original[3] maturity of up to 1 year, or which can be unconditionally cancelled at any time;	0%
I Endorsements of bills (including *per aval* endorsements) which have previously been accepted by a bank.	0%

Multi-option facilities and other composite products should be disaggregated into their component parts, eg into a credit commitment, NIF, etc, and each component part converted according to the above classification. However, components carrying the lowest credit conversion factors should be disregarded to the extent necessary to ensure that the total value of all the components does not exceed the value of the facility.

---

[1] These items are to be weighted according to category of the issuer of the security (or the borrower in the underlying loan agreement) and not according to the counterparty with whom the transaction has been entered into. Reverse repos (ie purchase and resale agreements where the bank is the receiver of the asset) are treated as collateralised loans, with the risk being measured as an exposure to the counterparty. Where the security temporarily acquired attracts a preferential risk weighting, this is recognised as collateral and the risk weighting of the loan accordingly reduced (eg a Zone A government security).

[2] To be applied to the total of the institution's underwriting obligations of any maturity. Where the facility has been drawn down by the borrower and the notes are held by anyone other than the reporting institution, its underwriting obligations must continue to be reported as the full nominal amount. (Own holdings of notes underwritten are, however, deducted from the overall value of the commitment, because they are weighted as an on-balance-sheet item.)

[3] Banks may report on the basis of residual maturity until the end of 1992 to assist data collection.

Annex 3 Interest and foreign exchange rate related instruments

Banks are exposed to the potential cost of replacing the cash flow arising from these instruments. This cost depends on the maturity of the contract and on the volatility of the underlying interest or exchange rates. Higher conversion factors are applied to those contracts which are based on exchange rate risk, reflecting the greater volatility of exchange rates. For interest and exchange rate related contracts, a 50% weight is applied to counterparties which would otherwise attract a 100% weight.

A Exchange rate contracts include:[1]

    (i)   cross-currency swaps;
    (ii) cross-currency interest rate swaps;
    (iii) outright forward foreign exchange contracts;
    (iv) currency futures;[2]
    (v)   currency options purchased.[2]

B Interest rate contracts include:

    (i)   single currency interest rate swaps;
    (ii) basis swaps;
    (iii) forward rate agreements, forward forward deposits accepted and products with similar characteristics;
    (iv) interest rate futures;[2]
    (v)   interest rate options purchased.[2]

---

[1] Exchange rate contracts with an original maturity of 14 calendar days or less are excluded. Foreign currencies are to include gold, silver, platinum and palladium.
[2] Instruments traded on exchanges may be excluded where they are subject to daily margining requirements.

Replacement cost method

In order to calculate the credit equivalent amount of these instruments, a bank should add together:

    (a) the total replacement cost (obtained by 'marking to market') of all its contracts with a positive value
    (b) an amount for potential future credit exposure which reflects the residual maturity of the contract, calculated as a percentage of notional principal amount according to the following matrix:

Residual maturity	Interest rate contracts	Exchange rate contracts
One year or less	nil	1.0%
Over one year	0.5%	5.0%

No potential exposure should be calculated for single currency interest rate basis swaps; the credit exposure on these contracts should be evaluated solely on the basis of mark-to-market value.

In the case of interest rate or cross-currency swaps arranged at off-market prices, the Bank requires special treatment for contracts which have been created in order to disguise a credit exposure to the counterparty.

Original exposure method

To obtain the credit equivalent amount using the original exposure method, the notional principal amount should be multiplied by the following conversion factors to obtain the future credit exposure:

Original maturity	Interest rate contracts	Exchange rate contracts
One year and less	0.5%	2.0%
Over one year not exceeding two years	1.0%	5.0%
For each additional year	1.0%	3.0%

Annex 4 Zone A: Members of the OECD and those countries which have concluded special lending arrangements with the IMF associated with the fund's general arrangements to borrow

Australia	Luxembourg
Austria	Netherlands
Belgium	New Zealand
Canada ·	Norway
Denmark	Portugal
Finland	Saudi Arabia
France	Spain
Germany	Sweden
Greece	Switzerland
Iceland	Turkey
Ireland	United Kingdom
Italy	United States
Japan	

Annex 5 UK 'regional governments and local authorities' (public sector entities)

Include the following bodies:

London borough councils, county and district councils in England, Northern Ireland and Wales, and district and regional councils in Scotland, together with their departments (eg gas departments and water service departments but not transport departments); those bodies formed on 1 April 1986 to take over the assets and functions of the former metropolitan councils and the GLC.

The state governments in the Channel Islands and the Isle of Man Government are to be included in this category.

The Bank of England will, from time to time, circulate an up to date list of other UK non-commercial bodies ('other public sector entities') which are deemed eligible to receive the same capital treatment as regional governments and local authorities.

Annex 6 Multilateral development banks

The following institutions shall be considered as multilateral development banks for the purpose of this Notice:

European Investment Bank (EIB)

European Bank for Reconstruction and Development (EBRD)

International Bank for Reconstruction and Development (IBRD), including International Finance Corporation (IFC)

Inter-American Development Bank (IADB)

African Development Bank (AfDB)

Asian Development Bank (AsDB)

Caribbean Development Bank (CDB)

Nordic Investment Bank (NIB)   **[820]**

CAPITAL ADEQUACY RETURN (FORM BSD1)

A Guidance notes

1 The following notes and definitions apply specifically to the Capital Adequacy Return and do not relate to the completion of the forms contained in the (blue) Banking Statistics Definitions folder. There are some common areas, nevertheless, where the definitions in the blue folder apply equally to items reported in the Capital Adequacy Return. Thus, where no specific guidance is contained within these notes and definitions, reporting institutions should be guided by the Banking Statistics Definitions.

2 In particular, this return should include all of the assets, liabilities and off-balance sheet items of the reporting institution (for Coverage see notes 3 & 4 below) and not only those related to its UK offices.

Coverage

3 This return is to be completed as at 31 March, 30 June, 30 September and 31 December each year by UK incorporated institutions authorised under the Banking Act 1987 (or on a solo consolidated basis if agreed with Banking Supervision Division). Different reporting dates may be agreed with Banking Supervision Division (BSD) for those institutions with a financial year end which does not coincide with an end calendar quarter date.

4 In addition, the form is to be completed on a consolidated basis as at 30 June and 31 December each year unless otherwise agreed. The companies to be included in the consolidation will be those agreed between the reporting institution and BSD in accordance with the Bank's Notice on Consolidated Supervision (BSD/1986/3).

Valuation

5 Outstanding liabilities and holdings of assets should normally be reported at the value outstanding in the reporting institution's books (ie book value), in accordance with the reporting institution's usual accounting practices. For off-balance sheet items 340–440 (contingents, guarantees, acceptances, etc) the principal amount should be shown. For valuation of interest and exchange rate contracts see the definitions for items 450 and 460.

Specific provisions

6 All loans, advances, bills and securities are to be included in this return net of any specific or earmarked general provisions made.

Off-balance sheet items should also be reported net of specific provisions. However, the amount of such provisions should be included in item 750.

Accruals

7 In general, the return should be completed on an accruals rather than a cash basis. Such accruals should be shown, where possible, against the relevant category of counterparty for assets or under item 260 for accruals not specifically identified. Accruals on liabilities should be included under item 760.2.

Maturity of assets and off-balance sheet items

8 Certain on- and off-balance sheet items are to be reported according to their maturity. The reporting requirements for this return are in line with requirements for the completion of Forms Q6, QMA and S5 but not the Form BS (see Note 14 on Page 6 of the 'General Notes and Definitions' within the blue Banking Statistics Definitions folder), ie on the basis of a residual maturity of one year or less or more than one year. Reporting institutions with overseas offices may discuss the implications of this requirement with BSD if the reporting of exactly one year maturities are treated differently in the countries in which they are operating.

Original/residual maturity

Off-balance sheet commitments should be reported according to their original maturity.

Analysis of Categories

9 For each category of on- and off-balance sheet item there is a breakdown of the total into different weighting bands, ie 0%, 10%, 20%, 50% or 100%, depending on the risk weight attributed to the counterparties. The following summary list identifies the counterparty weights. It is not a full list of all on- and off-balance sheet items, eg cash is not shown here (see Definitions for a full list of items and for more detail generally):

0%   (i) Claims on, other than holding of bills or securities issued by, Zone A
             central governments and central banks;
         (ii) Claims on, other than holdings of bills or securities issued by, Zone B
             central governments and central banks denominated in local currency and
             funded by liabilities in the same currency.

10%   (i) Loans to discount houses, gilt-edged market makers, institutions with a
             money-market dealing relationship with the Bank of England and those
             Stock Exchange money brokers which operate in the gilt-edged market,
             where the loans are secured on gilts, UK Treasury bills, London CDs, or
             eligible local authority and eligible bank bills;
         (ii) Holdings of Treasury bills and fixed interest securities (including index-
             linked securities) issued by Zone A central governments and central
             banks with a residual maturity of 1 year or less, and floating rate Zone A
             central government and central bank securities of any maturity;
        (iii) Holdings of Zone B central government and central bank securities with a
             residual maturity of 1 year or less denominated in local currency and
             funded by liabilities in the same currency.

20%   (i) Holdings of Zone A central government and central bank fixed interest
             securities (including index-linked securities) of a residual maturity of over
             1 year;
         (ii) Holdings of Zone B central government and central bank securities of a
             residual maturity of over 1 year denominated in local currency and funded
             by liabilities in the same currency;
        (iii) Claims on multilateral development banks (see Note 15);
        (iv) Claims on banks incorporated in Zone A countries (see Notes 12 & 14);
         (v) Claims on banks incorporated in Zone B countries with a residual matur-
             ity of 1 year or less;
        (vi) Claims on Zone A public sector entities (PSEs – see Note 19);
       (vii) Loans to discount houses which are unsecured or secured on assets other
             than specified in 10% (i) above.

50%   (i) Certain loans to Housing Associations meeting the criteria set out in item
             90;
         (ii) Mortgage loans to individuals meeting the criteria set out in item 90;
        (iii) Loans to special purpose mortgage finance vehicles meeting the criteria
             set out in item 150;
        (iv) Mortgage sub-participations, where the risk to the sub-participating bank
             is fully and specifically secured against residential mortgage loans which
             would themselves qualify for the 50% weight;
         (v) Mortgage backed securities meeting the criteria set out in item 150;

100%   (i) Claims on the non-bank private sector;
         (ii) Claims on banks incorporated in Zone B countries with a residual matur-
             ity of over 1 year;
        (iii) Claims on Zone B central governments and central banks (unless denomi-
             nated in the national currency and funded by liabilities in the same
             currency);
        (iv) Claims on commercial entities owned by the public sector;
         (v) Claims on Zone B public sector entities.

  Some on- and off-balance sheet assets will be deducted from total capital (total of tier
1 and tier 2) rather than receive a risk weight:

         (i) Investments in unconsolidated subsidiaries and associates;
         (ii) Connected lending of a capital nature;
        (iii) Holdings of all capital instruments issued by any financial institution or
             other bank in which the reporting institution owns more than 10% of the
             equity capital of the financial institution or bank (other than investments
             already deducted in (i) above);
        (iv) All other holdings of other banks' capital instruments including those held
             in the trading portfolio, except those held under primary and secondary
             market makers' concessions;

    (v) The amount by which holdings of capital instruments issued by financial institutions other than those referred to in (iii) above (ie in which the reporting institution owns less than 10% of the equity of the financial institution) taken together with any holdings of bank capital instruments held under a market making concession exceed 10% of the Total (gross) capital of the reporting institution (ie item S30);

    (vi) Guarantees of a capital nature given on behalf of connected companies;

    (vii) Other off-balance sheet items of a capital nature, eg a forward asset purchase of a bank capital instrument.

10 With the prior written agreement of BSD, certain assets may be entered in the 'unanalysed' boxes at the foot of each of the main categories on the return. This is meant to provide for those situations where the difficulty which certain reporting institutions would face in providing a breakdown by counterparty type would be substantial compared to the benefit received from a weighting lower than 100%, eg where a major institution has a category of assets or an overseas branch(es) which represents an insignicant part of the institution's overall assets.

Investment trusts/Unit trusts/Mutual funds

11 Equity holdings in investment trusts and holdings of 'units' in unit trusts or mutual funds will normally attract the highest risk weighting of 100%. However, when the assets held by the investment institution are legally restricted to assets of a lower weight (eg by articles of association or loan documentation) then a holding will be weighted at that lower weight. If a range of lower weighted assets are included in a fund or trust a holding will be weighted at the highest of these weights. Holdings in entities established to hold capital instruments issued by banks will normally be deducted from capital (see definition of item 170).

Zone A/Zone B

12 The term 'Zone A' covers full members of the OECD and those countries which have concluded special lending arrangements with the IMF associated with the IMF's General Arrangements to Borrow. At present, these countries comprise:

Australia, Austria, Belgium, Canada, Denmark, Finland, France, Germany (including any pre-reunification claims on East Germany), Greece, Iceland, Ireland, Italy, Japan, Luxembourg, Netherlands, New Zealand, Norway, Portugal, Saudi Arabia, Spain, Sweden, Switzerland, Turkey, United Kingdom and United States.

The Channel Islands and the Isle of Man should also be regarded as Zone A countries.

The reporting institution should discuss with BSD the appropriate treatment of particular dependencies of Zone A countries.

Zone B comprises all countries not in Zone A.

For the purpose of determining whether a bank is in Zone A or B, the place of incorporation is the relevant factor to be considered rather than location of branch. For example, a loan made to a branch located in a Zone A country of a Zone B incorporated bank should be classified as a loan to a Zone B bank.

Central banks

13 Central banks are as shown in Appendix B List 8 in the blue Banking Statistics Definitions folder, but should exclude the following Eastern European foreign trade banks (FTBs):

Bulgaria	Bulgarian Foreign Trade Bank
Czechoslovakia	Ceskoslovenska Obchodni Banka
Hungary	Hungarian Foreign Trade Bank
Poland	Bank Handlowy w Warszawie (non-UK offices only)
Romania	Romanian Bank for Foreign Trade
Former Soviet Union	Bank for Foreign Economic Affairs

Reporting institutions may however classify FTBs as Zone B banks if they so wish, and should notify BSD if they do so.

Banks

14 The term 'bank' as used in this return refers to those institutions that are regarded as banks in the countries in which they are incorporated, and supervised by the appropriate banking supervisory or monetary authority as banks. In general, banks will engage in the business of banking and have the power to accept deposits in the regular course of business.

For banks incorporated in countries that are members of the European Economic Community (EEC) classify as banks those credit institutions as defined under the First Banking Co-ordination Directive 1977 and as published in the EC Official Journal from time to time. In relation to the United Kingdom, the term 'banks' therefore covers those institutions authorised under the Banking Act 1987 and, for the purpose of this return, building societies authorised under the Building Societies Act 1986.

All banks incorporated in the Channel Islands and Isle of Man, irrespective of whether or not they are classified as UK banks for the purpose of other Bank of England statistical returns, are regarded as Zone A banks.

In the USA, banks are referred to as depository institutions which include branches of federally-insured banks and depository institutions chartered and headquartered in the 50 states of the United States, the District of Columbia, Puerto Rico, and US territories and possessions. The definition encompasses banks, mutual or stock savings banks, savings or building and loans associations, co-operative banks and credit unions; it excludes bank holding companies (other than those which are themselves banks).

Multilateral Development Banks (MDBs)

15 Only the following institutions are classified as MDBs for the purpose of this return:

International Bank for Reconstruction and Development (IBRD): 'World Bank'
International Finance Corporation (IFC)
Inter-American Development Bank (IADB)
Asian Development Bank (AsDB)
African Development Bank (AfDB)
European Investment Bank (EIB)
Caribbean Development Bank (CDB)
Nordic Investment Bank (NIB)
European Bank for Reconstruction and Development (EBRD)
Council of Europe Resettlement Fund

Financial institutions

16 The definition of financial institution to be used in this return is the same as that which applies in the Second Banking Coordination Directive (89/646/EEC). A financial institution is an undertaking, other than a bank, the principal activity of which is to acquire holdings or to carry on one of the activities listed below.

    (i) Lending including inter alia
         – consumer credit
         – mortgage credit
         – factoring, with or without recourse
         – financing of commercial transactions (including forfaiting)
   (ii) Financial leasing
  (iii) Money transmission services
  (iv) Issuing and administering means of Payment (eg credit cards, travellers' cheques and bankers' drafts)
   (v) Guarantees and commitments
  (vi) Trading for own account or for the account of customers in:
        (a) money market instruments (cheques, bills, CDs etc)
        (b) foreign exchange
        (c) financial futures and options
        (d) exchange and interest rate instruments
        (e) transferable securities
 (vii) Participation in share issues and provision of services related to such issues
(viii) Advice to undertakings on capital structure, industrial strategy and related questions and advice and services relating to mergers and acquisitions

    (ix) Money broking
    (x) Portfolio management and advice
    (xi) Safekeeping and administration of securities

Group companies

17 The definition used in this return of group companies is that set out for 'group under-takings' in section 22 of the Companies Act 1989, together with any associated companies that are consolidated with the institution for reporting purposes, or that would be consolidated but for the fact that they are supervised by another UK supervisory authority.

Connected counterparties

18 Connected counterparties are defined as: other group companies (see Guidance Note 17 above), excluding those companies which are included in the consolidation of this particular return; directors, controllers and their associates (as defined in section 105 of the Banking Act 1987); and non-group companies with which directors and controllers are associated (see also the definition of items 290 and 300).

    A *pension fund or other trust fund* of the group should not necessarily be classified as connected for the purposes of this return. However, it should be treated as a connected counterparty if a director/controller of the reporting institution is both a director of the fund and is involved in decision-making on whether or not an exposure to that fund should be undertaken.

    A director (including an alternate director) or controller of the reporting institution is deemed to be associated with another company, whether registered or resident in the UK or overseas, if he holds the office of a director (or alternate director) with that company (whether in his own right, or as a result of a loan granted to, or financial interest taken in, that company by the reporting institution, or even by virtue of a professional interest unconnected with the reporting institution), or if he and/or his associates together hold 10% or more of the equity share capital of that company. For the purpose of this item, include as a director an employee of the reporting institution who is not a director but who is appointed a director of another company. (This definition should be consistent with that adopted for reporting on Form LE.)

Public Sector Entities (PSEs)

19 *General*

Principally regional governments and local authorities, but bodies which carry out non-commercial functions on behalf of and are responsible to regional governments or local authorities similar to those shown in the UK lists below may also be classified as PSEs. Also include bodies owned by the central or regional government or local authorities which perform regulatory or other non-commercial functions. Commercial entities or companies (other than banks) owned by the public sector, including public utilities, should be classified as 'other' and carry a weighting of 100%.

UK

The following lists show examples of UK public bodies which are classified as PSEs for the purposes of this return and also public bodies which are not classified as PSEs. These lists are not intended to be comprehensive and if doubt exists as to the appropriate classification of an organisation reference should be made to BSD.

(i) UK public bodies eligible for classification as PSEs

(a) LOCAL AUTHORITIES
Include London borough councils, county and district councils in England, Northern Ireland and Wales, and district, island and regional councils in Scotland, together with their departments (eg gas departments, passenger transport departments, water service departments); those bodies formed on 1 April 1986 to take over the assets and functions of the former metropolitan councils and the GLC, eg residuary bodies, joint transport authorities, fire and civil defence authorities, joint police authorities, waste disposal authorities.

    The state governments in the Channel Islands, the Isle of Man Government and the following local bodies are also to be included in this category:

Central Scotland Water Development Board
Fire services
Forth Road Bridge Joint Board
Further education establishments maintained by local authorities
Humber Bridge Board
Magistrates' Courts
Police Forces (including Metropolitan Police)
Probation Service in England and Wales
Scottish River Purification Boards
Tay Bridge Joint Board

(b) NON-COMMERCIAL PUBLIC CORPORATIONS

The Audit Commission
Black Country Development Corporation
Bristol Development Corporation
Cardiff Bay Development Corporation
Central Manchester Development
  Corporation
Covent Garden Market Authority
Development Board for Rural Wales
English Industrial Estates Corporation
HM Stationery Office
Highlands and Islands Enterprise
Land Authority for Wales
Leeds Development Corporation
Letchworth Garden City Corporation
London Docklands Development
  Corporation
New Towns Commission (and new town
  development corporations)
Northern Ireland Housing Executive
Oil and Pipelines Agency
Royal Mint
Scottish Enterprise
Scottish Homes
Sheffield Development Corporation
Teesside Development Corporation
Telford Development Corporation
Trafford Park Development Corporation
Tyne and Wear Development Corporation
United Kingdom Atomic Energy Authority
Urban Development Corporations
Welsh Development Agency
Welsh Fourth Channel Authority

(ii) UK public bodies not eligible for classification as PSEs

British Broadcasting Corporation
British Coal Corporation
British Railways Board
British Technology Group
  (including NEB and NRDC and their
  subsidiaries)
British Waterways Board
Civil Aviation Authority
Crown Agents
Crown Agents Holding and Realisation
  Board
Channel Four Television Company
  Limited
Local Authority Airports
Local Authority Bus Companies
London Regional Transport
NHS Trusts
Northern Ireland Electricity Services
Northern Ireland Transport Holding
  Company
Nuclear Electric plc
Passenger Transport Executives
Post Office Corporation
Scottish Nuclear plc
Scottish Transport Group
Trust Ports in Northern Ireland

(iii) Bodies not in the public sector which should be classified as non-bank private sector include:

Agricultural marketing boards
Polytechnics and higher education institutions funded by the Polytechnics and Funding
  Council
Universities
Scottish Colleges of Education
Trust Ports in Great Britain (excluding Northern Ireland)
The former nationalised industries

G10 and EC countries—Belgium, Canada, Denmark, France, Germany, Greece, Ireland, Italy, Japan, Netherlands, Portugal, Spain, Sweden, Switzerland, United States and Luxembourg

Principally regional governments and local authorities. The reporting institution may include those bodies regarded locally as PSEs where the relevant banking supervisor has published either a list or general guidance.

Other countries

The general definition above should be applied. Where doubt exists as to the appropriate classification of an organisation reference should be made to BSD.

Collateral

20 Where claims on a counterparty are collateralised by cash (see Guidance Note 21) or by securities or bills issued by Zone A central governments, Zone A central banks or multilateral development banks (see Guidance Note 15), a lower risk weight may apply. The risk weight category under which the claim should be reported is determined by the nature of the collateral, as follows:

0% Cash (see Note 21).

10% Zone A central government and central bank treasury bills and fixed interest securities (including index-linked securities) of a residual maturity of 1 year or less, or similar floating rate securities of any maturity.

20% (i) Zone A central government and central bank fixed interest securities (including index-linked securities) of a residual maturity of over 1 year;
(ii) Multilateral development banks' securities.

If the value of the collateral covers less than the book value of the asset, only that part of the asset which is fully covered may receive the appropriate lower weight. Securities used as collateral must be marked to market except where otherwise agreed with BSD. No other forms of collateral may reduce a risk weighting.

For collateralised off-balance sheet exposures (other than interest and exchange rate contracts) the value of the collateral should be set against the nominal value of the exposure before calculating the credit equivalent amount. For an exposure to be fully covered the collateral must at least equal 100% of the nominal value of the exposure (not of any smaller credit equivalent amount). For example where cash collateral covers 75% of a nominal exposure, first the collateral should be applied to the nominal principal leaving an uncovered exposure of 25%. The appropriate credit conversion factor should then be applied to this uncovered portion. The full nominal value of collateralised off-balance sheet exposures should be reported on the BSD1 in the risk weighting bands to reflect collateral.

For interest and exchange rate contracts however the value of collateral should be compared to the credit equivalent amount. Where collateral fully covers this amount the risk weighting may be reduced accordingly, where collateral covers only part of the credit equivalent amount only the part that is fully covered may receive the appropriate lower weight.

Where lower risk weights have been applied to reflect collateral, enter the relevant amounts in BSD1(1).

Cash Collateral

21 Where exposures which do not meet the rules for set-off (see Guidance Note 22) are collateralised by cash, ie balances held with the reporting institution denominated in sterling, foreign currency or gold, or CDs issued by the reporting institution and lodged with it, such exposures should be reported under the relevant item in the 0% band. For these purposes an exposure is collateralised by cash only if the cash is held by the reporting institution for the account of the depositor/customer on express terms such that:

(i) the cash may not be withdrawn for the duration of the exposure; and
(ii) the reporting institution may apply the cash to discharge the exposure if and to the extent that it is not discharged by the borrower/customer in accordance with the terms of the loan etc agreement with the borrower/customer.

In the case of an exposure partially collateralised by cash only that part of the exposure which is fully collateralised should be reported in the 0% weight band.

The adjustments made by the reporting institution to the Capital Adequacy Return in respect of exposures collateralised by cash should be shown in BSD1(1).

To qualify as cash collateral:

(i) The customer(s) and the office(s) of the reporting institution or group company(ies) involved in the transaction(s) must have 'local resident' status, ie they must all be resident in the same country. The definition of residency should be the same as that in Appendix A Part 5 of the blue Banking Statistics Definitions folder, which is reproduced as an Annex to these notes.

(ii) In the case of the reporting institution's *unconsolidated* return:
   (a) the cash must be held with the reporting institution;
   (b) the reporting institution should have a right of set-off over the cash which is legally enforceable in a liquidation of the debtor.

(iii) In the case of a reporting institution's *consolidated* return:
   (a) the cash must be held with the company which has the exposure;
   (b) where the lending institution is a UK office of a UK incorporated company, it should have a right of set-off over the cash which is legally enforceable in a liquidation of the debtor;
   (c) where the lending institution is incorporated overseas or is an overseas branch of a UK incorporated company, it should have a first charge over cash held with itself where this is enforceable in the local legal jurisdiction or other equivalent security interest or a right of set-off over the cash which is legally enforceable in a liquidation of the debtor.

(vi) Where BSD has agreed that the reporting institution meets the criteria set out in paragraph 24(c) of BSD/1986/3 as amended by BSD/1989/2, the above rules apply except that the cash may be held with another bank which is consolidated with the reporting institution for the purpose of calculating the institution's consolidated capital ratio. In case the lending institution should have a first charge over the cash held with the other bank or other equivalent security interest. Where an exposure is reported by the lending bank as collateralised by cash under this provision the cash is not available to the other bank as collateral for reporting purposes, and should not be subject to set-off in the other bank's books.

Where the reporting institution is a member of a syndicate and cash has been deposited with, and is held by, the agent itself for the benefit of the syndicate, the claims (or portion of the claims) of members of the syndicate which are cash collateralised may attract the weight appropriate for claims on the agent. If the agent is a bank its own claims which are cash collateralised may be eligible for a 0% weight.

Netting

22 *On-balance sheet*

Debit balances on accounts with the reporting bank may only be offset against credit balances on other accounts with that bank where all of the following criteria are met:

(a) there is formal agreement with the customer(s) to do so, or where a legal right of set-off exists. Such arrangements should, to the best of the reporting institution's knowledge, be enforceable in a liquidation of the customer(s);

(b) both the debit and credit balances are denominated in the same currency. Thus, for example, a debit balance in sterling may not be offset against a credit balance in another currency;

(c) the debit and credit balances relate to the same customer, or to customers in the same company group, eg a parent company and its subsidiary. For a group facility, the facility should be advised in the form of a net amount and controlled by the reporting institution on that basis. Such an arrangement should be preferably supported by a full cross guarantee structure;

(d) the customer(s) involved in the transaction(s) giving rise to the credit and debit balances has local resident status. Local residents are those customers of the reporting institution which are resident in the same country as the office of the reporting institution in whose books the credit and debit balances appears. No set-off is allowed in respect of balances relating to non-local customers, even if one of the parties is a local resident. Where more than one office of the reporting institution is involved in the transactions, the offices should also be in the same country.

The reporting institution's application of these principles must remain consistent.

Credit balances which cannot be offset against debit balances may be eligible for inclusion as cash collateral (see Guidance Notes 20 and 21).

Off-balance sheet

Pending further consideration, net amounts due in respect of foreign exchange transactions may be reported only if the net amount derived is pursuant to the application of a bilateral agreement (between two counterparties) based upon netting by novation. Netting by novation is where obligations between counterparties to deliver given amounts on a given date are automatically amalgamated with all other obligations to deliver the same currency on the same value date and netted. Such netting should have the effect of legally discharging performance of the original obligation and substituting the single net amount as the sole remaining obligation between the parties for the relevant value date.

Long and short positions in investments

23 In certain circumstances long positions in securities may be offset against short positions for the purposes of calculating the weighted amount. The gross amounts should be recorded under items 120–190 (long positions) and under item 710 (short positions). Additionally, short positions in central government and central bank securities should be reported under item 320 and will attract a risk weight.

The conditions to be satisfied for netting of long and short positions are:

(a) Central governments and central banks
Netting of long and short positions will only be permitted if the following criteria are all met:

  (i) the long and short positions are in securities issued by the same central government or bank;
  (ii) the long and short positions are in securities denominated in the same currency;
  (iii) the long and short positions are in fixed rate securities within the same maturity time band, ie one year or less (10% risk weight) or over one year (20% risk weight). Similarly, index-linked securities may only be offset against each other if they are within the same maturity time band. Floating rate securities of any maturity can be offset against each other but no netting of floating rate securities against fixed rate or index-linked securities will be permitted.
  Both the gross and net long positions in central government and central bank securities should be reported under item 120, with the net long positions attracting the relevant risk weights. Gross short positions should be reported under item 710.1 with the net short positions being reported under item 320.

A simplified reporting example is set out below (the netting criteria are met for securities A and B but not C:

	Long position	Short position	Net
UK government security A	100	—	100
UK government security B	—	(50)	(50)
US government security C	5	(25)	(20)
	105	(75)	

Gross long position (item 120)	= 105 ie sum of individual long positions
Gross short position (item 710)	= (75) ie sum of individual short positions
Net long position (item 120)	= [100 + (50)] = 50 ie sum of net long positions after netting gross positions permitted by (i) to (iii) above (in this case the netting of positions in A and B)
Net short position (item 320)	= (20) ie sum of net short positions after netting of gross positions as permitted by (i) to (iii) above (in this case none)

Certain reporting institutions will have made arrangements with a related Gilt Edged Market Maker (GEMM) that the GEMM will take short positions in central government securities on behalf of that institution, any profit or loss from these transactions accruing to the reporting institution. Such short positions should be reported in the net column of item 120 or in item 320 as appropriate (the gross positions should not be adjusted), and a separate note submitted to BSD summarising the positions.

(b) Other securities

Report gross positions, net only of short positions in the same security issue.
Warrants and convertibles should not be offset against the underlying equity into which they may convert.

Guarantees

24 *(a) Guarantees received*

Claims that have been explicitly, irrevocably and unconditionally guaranteed by those counterparties listed below may be weighted according to the risk weight of the guarantor where the effect is to reduce the weighting; such guarantees should be legally enforceable. Where a claim is partially guaranteed only that part of the claim which is fully guaranteed will be weighted according to the risk weight of the guarantor. Only direct guarantees of a bank's claims are recognised. Guarantees of a counterparty's assets, or general guarantees of its financial position, are insufficient in themselves to merit a reduced risk weighting. The notes in this section apply to the instruments serving as guarantees and insurance/indemnities discussed below as well as to guarantees.

INSTRUMENTS SERVING AS GUARANTEES

Apart from traditional bank guarantees, certain other financial instruments (eg a letter of credit (or standby letter of credit), a purchased put option that may be exercised at any time, and a risk participation) may be regarded as guarantees as long as they provide the same comfort as a guarantee, ie they must provide an explicit, irrevocable and unconditional obligation to pay a third party beneficiary when a customer fails to repay an outstanding loan or to meet a financial obligation (including contingent obligations).

INSURANCE/INDEMNITIES

Where a claim is covered for all risks by an insurance policy, or where an indemnity is explicit, irrevocable and unconditional, reduced weighting may also be appropriate; such claims should be discussed on a case by case basis with BSD.

GUARANTEES RECEIVED FROM SUBSIDIARIES

No account should be taken of a guarantee received by the reporting bank from a subsidiary when determining the risk weight of an asset of the parent bank, unless collateralised by a cash deposit placed with that subsidiary.

RISK WEIGHTING

On- and off-balance sheet items subject to guarantees should still be reported in the same counterparty category rather than that of the guarantor but shown in the weighting band relative to the guarantor. For example, a loan to a non-bank customer which is guaranteed by a Zone A incorporated bank should be reported in item 100.3 instead of 100.4, and not in item 70. The relevant risk weights are as follows:

0%   (i) Zone A central governments and central banks (other than securities guaranteed);
     (ii) Zone B central governments and central banks (other than securities guaranteed), where the claim being guaranteed is denominated in the local currency of the guarantor and borrower and funded in that currency.

10% (i) Fixed rate securities, guaranteed by Zone A central governments and central banks, which have a residual maturity of 1 year or less;
     (ii) Floating rate securities of any maturity guaranteed by Zone A central governments and central banks;

(iii) Any securities, guaranteed by Zone B central governments and central banks, which have a residual maturity of 1 year or less and are denominated in the local currency of the guarantor and issuer and funded in that currency.

20%   (i) Fixed rate securities, guaranteed by Zone A central governments and central banks, which have a residual maturity of over 1 year;

(ii) Any securities, guaranteed by Zone B central governments and central banks, which have a residual maturity of over 1 year and are denominated in the local currency of the guarantor and issuer and funded in that currency;

(iii) Multilateral development banks;

(iv) Banks incorporated in Zone A countries;

(v) Banks incorporated in Zone B countries, where the claim being guaranteed has a residual maturity of 1 year or less;

(vi) Zone A public sector entities.

Holdings of bank capital instruments which carry a central government or central bank guarantee should be deducted from capital in accordance with the definition of item 170 except where a market making concession applies when they should be weighted at 100%.

GUARANTEES OF SWAPS ETC

Guarantees of swaps etc will be acceptable for reducing the risk weighting of an item where they meet the above criteria, where the reporting institution receiving the guarantee calculates daily the mark to market valuation of the asset being guaranteed (using the institution's own mark to market methodology) and where the guarantee is valued at the current mark to market value of the contract plus 'adds-ons' (see definitions to items 450/460).

GUARANTEES OF A CAPITAL NATURE

See the definitions section (item 340) for details.

Where lower risk weights have been applied, enter the relevant amounts in BSD1(1).

(b) Guarantees given

JOINT AND SEVERAL GUARANTEES GIVEN BY THE REPORTING INSTITUTION

Where the reporting institution has guaranteed an exposure jointly and severally with other institutions, its share of the guarantee (as explicitly defined or otherwise equal to the total value of the guarantee divided by the number of guarantors) should be reported as an exposure on the counterparty and the balance of the guarantee as an exposure on the other guarantors.

Sale and Repurchase Agreements ('repos')

25 Repos
Reporting institutions that have sold loans or other assets to other institutions for a finite period with a commitment to repurchase should continue to report the loan or asset on the balance sheet. Where this is not the reporting institution's normal accounting practice, sale and repurchase agreements should be reported in the off-balance sheet section of the return.

Reverse repos

Reporting institutions which have purchased such loans or assets (ie purchase and resale agreements or reverse repos) should for the duration of the agreement report the transaction as a collateralised loan, adopting the normal weight for the counterparty unless the assets are eligible for reduced weight (eg government securities).

NB The reporting treatment of these items is different from that for the Form BS (see the Banking Statistics General Definitions) because the figures collected are used for different purposes.

Stock lending/borrowing as principal

26 When a reporting institution has entered into a stock lending agreement as principal the stock lent should continue to be reported as an asset on its balance sheet. No exposure in respect of the counterparty in the transaction should be reported.

When an institution has entered into a stock borrowing transaction as principal the reporting treatment will depend upon the type of collateral given.

If the collateral given is cash, the exposure should be treated as a collateralised loan to the counterparty.

If the securities borrowed by the reporting institution qualify as eligible collateral then a lower risk weighting may be applied accordingly.

If the collateral given is not cash, then the reporting institution should continue to report the collateral given on its own balance sheet. No exposure to the counterparty should be reported.

'Disguised' credit exposure in interest and exchange rate contracts

27 The arrangement of certain contracts may include an element of 'disguised' credit exposure.

In general, BSD would consider a disguised credit exposure to be present where the contract either starts with a significantly positive mark-to-market value, or, on an assumption of unchanged interest and exchange rates, is designed at some time in its life to have a significantly positive mark-to-market value. (Institutions should discuss with BSD what constitutes such a mark-to-market value).

The reporting institution should contact BSD to agree on suitable reporting where it has such contracts. In general, BSD will require the disguised credit exposure to be reported separately from the swap in a manner fixed at the outset of the contract. For example:

(a) the up-front payment of a swap at off-market rates should be reported as a loan in items 50–110, and amortised over the life of the swap;

(b) a staggered exchange of principal, where the reporting institution has paid away its side and has not yet received the counterparty's side, should be reported as a loan in items 50–110.

Where the disguised credit exposure is reported separately as in the above examples, the mark-to-market value of the swap as reported in Appendix I should exclude the disguised credit exposure reported as above.

Where a reporting institution has a contract that gives rise to a 'disguised' credit exposure on itself for its counterparty (eg receiving interest quarterly and paying interest annually), the reporting institution should report the contract as normal.

Participations/Syndications

28 Where the reporting institution transfer a loan by *novation, assignment* or through a *sub-participation*, that part of the loan transferred should not be reported, subject to the conditions specified in paragraphs 8 and 14 of the Bank's Notice on Loan Transfers and Securitisation (BSD/1989/1). In a *sub-participation*, where the reporting institution acts as a manager or co-manager, deposits received from the other participating institutions (representing their shares of the amounts to be lent) should not be included under deposits, nor should their shares of the loan be included in assets.

Where the reporting institution buys all or part of a loan from another institution, it should report its holding as an advance to the borrower and not as lending to the institution from which it has purchased the loan.

If the reporting institution has transferred undrawn commitments to lend (or part of them), the commitment (or part) should not be reported when the transfer is either by *novation*, or by an *assignment* accompanied by a formal acknowledgement from the borrower. A transfer by means of *silent assignment*, or *sub-participation* should be reported as a commitment in the off-balance section of the return with the counterparty risk assigned to the buyer of the commitment. The buyer of a commitment (or part) should report in the off-balance section under the relevant counterparty weight of the borrower, irrespective of the method of transfer used.

Contact with the Bank

29 In the event of any difficulties in completing this return, please contact the Bank on the telephone numbers below or speak to your normal point of contact within BSD:

0171–601 5694/4154/5997

EXTRACTS FROM APPENDIX A OF THE BANKING STATISTICS DEFINITIONS (Feb 91)

Part 5 Residence

For the purposes of all returns, the United Kingdom comprises Great Britain, Northern Ireland, the Channel Islands, the Isle of Man and that part of the continental shelf which is defined by international conventions as belonging to the United Kingdom.

For the purposes of all returns the following rules determine whether a person or body is a UK resident or an overseas resident. They also determine the country of residence of an overseas resident.

5(a) Individuals

UK residents comprise:

(i)   Individuals permanently resident in the United Kingdom.
(ii) Most temporary residents who have stayed, or who intend to stay, in the United Kingdom for a year or more. However, members of the armed forces of other countries and career and established officials of overseas governments serving in the United Kingdom, together with their dependants, are to be treated as residents of the country whose government they serve.
(iii) Individuals normally resident in the United Kingdom who are temporarily overseas for less than a year.
(iv) Members of the United Kingdom armed forces and career and established officials of HM Government serving overseas, together with their dependants.

Note that residence status is not the same as nationality. Overseas residents comprise all who are not classified as UK residents. Individuals visiting the United Kingdom for less than a year are resident of the country of their permanent residence.

Locally recruited staff of government embassies and other government offices are residents of the country in which they are recruited.

5(b) Businesses

UK residents comprise enterprises which produce goods and services in the United Kingdom, including overseas enterprises' branches and subsidiaries located and operating in the United Kingdom, but excluding branches and subsidiaries of UK businesses located and operating abroad. Enterprises with merely a 'brass-plate' presence in the United Kingdom should not be regarded as UK residents. If an enterprise which operates internationally, eg an air or shipping line, is administered from a head office in the United Kingdom, that office should be treated as a UK resident.

Enterprises (including banks) overseas are residents of the country in which they are located and operate, even when they are branches of subsidiaries of enterprises in a third country. Thus, enterprises in various overseas countries include branches and subsidiaries of businesses (including public corporations) which are themselves UK residents.

For definitions of overseas offices of the reporting institution, see 2(c) of the general definitions.

5(c) Governments, etc

HM Government and other UK public authorities, together with HM Government agencies overseas, are UK residents.

Overseas central, state and local governments, together with their diplomatic and military offices and representatives in the United Kingdom, are residents of the overseas country which they serve.

International organisations, including their branches or representatives in the United Kingdom, are overseas residents. They should be classified as 'international organisations' in returns where country breakdowns are required.

5(d) Charities and private non-profit-making bodies

Charities based in the United Kingdom are UK residents; accounts for public subscription in the name of such charities should be classified as accounts for UK residents.

The charitable operations overseas of a charity based in the United Kingdom (eg hospitals or schools abroad) are residents of the countries in which they are located.

5(e) Agencies, agents, etc

(i) Transactions made through agencies and agents should be treated as though made directly with the principal. Payment of agency fees, however, should be regarded as transactions with residents of the country in which the agency or agent is located.

(ii) UK representative offices of overseas banks should be treated as agencies of their parent banks, and thus as overseas residents. UK branches of overseas banks (including the London branch of the Reserve Bank of Australia) are, as stated in 5(b) above, to be treated as UK residents, and transactions with them are transactions with principals.

(iii) The Kuwait Investment Office in London should be regarded as a resident of Kuwait, and as an overseas central monetary institution.

(iv) Funds placed with reporting institutions by Great Peter Nominees Ltd should be regarded as liabilities to (other) overseas residents, and classified as 'unallocated by country' in returns where the country breakdowns are required.

(v) Executors or administrators of the estates of deceased persons who at the time of their death were residents of another country, and agents acting on inter-vivos settlements where the settler is a resident of another country, should in either case be regarded as residents of that other country.

5(f) Assets and liabilities

When it is necessary to define a company security as issued by a UK or an overseas resident, this should be done on the basis of where the issuing enterprise's registered office is situated. Similarly, for a security issued by a government or public corporation, the allocation is based on the residence of the issuing body. The question of where the security is denominated in sterling or an overseas currency is not relevant to this allocation.

When claims on, and liabilities to, overseas residents are classified by country, the country of residence of the immediate overseas debtor or creditor should be used. Bills should be classified according of the country of residence of the drawer, and notes according to that of the issuer; lending under ECGD guarantee should be allocated to the overseas country in which the debtor is resident; and bills accepted by the reporting institution itself reported as acceptances to the country residence of the enterprise or body on whose behalf the acceptance credit facility has been opened.

B Definitions

Summary Schedule

This section of the return should be completed after compiling the other sections of Form BSD1.

S10 Tier 1: Core Capital

This should equate to the amount in item 550.

S20 Tier 2: Supplementary Capital

This should equate to the amount in item 630.

S30 Total (Gross) Capital

This is the sum of items S10 and S20.

S40 Investments in subsidiaries and associates

This should equate to the amount in item 160.

S50 Investments in the capital of other banks

This should equate to the amounts in item 170.1 and 170.2.

S60 Connected lending of a capital nature

This should equate to the amount in item 280.

S70 Off-balance sheet items of a capital nature

This should equate to the amounts in item 340.6, 370.6, 380.6, 380.6, 390.6, 410.5 and 440.7.

S80 Other deductions

These are to be agreed on a case by case basis with BSD and will probably relate to amounts reported in items 290, 300 and 310.

S90 Total (Net) Capital

This should equal item S30 less any amounts reported in items S40–S80.

S100–S140 Weighted Risk Assets

By weight band, ie 10%, 20%, 50%, 100%, sum the amounts reported in the 'amount' column for items 10–260, 320, 340–440 and 470 (credit converted amounts for off-balance sheet items) and apply the appropriate risk weight. Where a memorandum item has been deducted from total capital, the weighted amount already included in the on- or off-balance sheet section of the return should be deducted from the appropriate weight band, eg any amount reported in items 280.1–280.5 should be deducted from the appropriate weight band.

S160 Total Weighted Risk Assets

This is the sum of items S100–S140 and any amount reported in item S150 (items 450 and 460).

S170 Risk Asset Ratio

Divide S90 by S160 and multiply the result by 100. The ratio should be shown to 2 decimal places (with rounding of 0.005 and above to the next highest digit).

Assets

10 Cash

Notes and coin, including holdings of notes issued by the appropriate authority which are required to be held as backing for the reporting institution's own issue of bank notes. (Gold coin should be reported in item 20 unless there is a difficulty in separately identifying such holdings.)

20 Gold bullion and coin

Physical holdings of gold bullion and gold coin beneficially owned by the reporting institution, including that held on an allocated basis by other institutions. Gold held as custodian for others should not be reported. Short positions in gold should not be reported here but reported with liabilities in this return.

The treatment of other precious metals (silver, platinum and palladium) should be discussed with BSD. (See also item 260).

30 Cash items in the course of collection

The total amount of cheques, etc drawn on and in the course of collection on other banks, and debit items in transit between domestic offices of the reporting institution in each country. Report cheques that have been credited to customers' accounts but are held overnight before being presented or paid into the reporting institution's account with another institution.

40 Items in suspense

All debit balances not in customers' names but relating to customers' funds, eg debit balances awaiting transfer to customers' accounts rather than the reporting institution's own internal funds. Also report funds of the reporting institution lodged with applications for new issues, even if the funds may be returnable, and items in the course of settlement (amounts receivable in respect of transactions not due until a future settlement date, where the asset is to be reported on a contract date basis).

Items in the course of settlement resulting from securities transactions should be treated as follows:

(a) Sales of securities where delivery will only take place against receipt of cash ('cash against documents'):

    (i) amounts receivable where the transactions have not reached settlement date should be reported in the 0% band;

    (ii) amounts receivable where the transactions are up to and including 21 days past due settlement date should be reported in the 0% band;

    (iii) all unsettled transactions more than 21 days past the due settlement date should be weighted according to the counterparty of the transaction (ie the purchaser, not the issuer of the securities).

(b) Sales of securities which may have been delivered but where the cash has not yet been received ('free delivery'):

    (i) amounts receivable up to and including the day following the due settlement date should be reported in the 0% band;

    (ii) all unsettled transactions more than one day past the due settlement date should be weighted according to the counterparty of the transaction.

In the case of rolling settlement dates the due settlement date should be interpreted as the first settlement date, ie the settlement date before the settlement date is rolled over.

50–110 Loans, advances and bills held

Funds lent to or placed with customers/counterparties including also:

(a) the book value of assets leased out under finance lease agreements, but legally owned by the reporting institution;

(b) holdings of certificates of deposit (other than those issued by the reporting institution) and negotiable deposits made on terms identical to those on which a certificate of deposit would have been issued, but for which it has been mutually convenient not to have issued a certificate (these items should be reported on a contract date basis);

(c) loans made under conditional sale agreements and hire purchase contracts;

(d) acceptances discounted;

(e) advances purchased by or assigned to the reporting institution under a transferable loan facility, purchase and resale agreements, factoring, or similar arrangement;

(f) initial margin payments with futures markets. These are effectively exposures to a recognised exchange and will therefore attract a weight of 100%.

Exclude unearned finance charges.

Bills, etc

Enter at book value all bills, promissory notes and other negotiable paper owned (including à forfait paper). These items (including those bills eligible for rediscount at the Bank of England and other central banks) should be reported in the categories below according to the drawee; the weighting for accepted bills, however, should be determined according to the acceptor.

Accruals

Wherever possible, accruals should be reported against the relevant category of counterparty (see Guidance Note 7).

Export credit

Report in the 0% band of the relevant counterparty category all medium and long-term lending (ie with an original maturity of two years and over) covered by an unconditional ECGD bank guarantee (Supplier Credit Finance Facility, Buyer Credit, ECGD guaranteed Lines of Credit and any outstanding lending under the, now discontinued, Specific Bank Guarantee, Comprehensive Extended Terms Bank Guarantee and all lending supported by a FINCOBE endorsement or by an irrevocable letter of credit, confirmed by a bank, which, in turn, has obtained an ECGD guarantee on its confirmation).

Only that part of the loan fully and unconditionally guaranteed by ECGD should be reported in the 0% band (that part of the loan not guaranteed by ECGD should be reported in other weighting bands as appropriate).

The reporting institution should report in the 0% band its own participation in syndicated loans made under ECGD bank guarantee, even if it does not itself hold the guarantee.

The following should *not* be reported in the 0% band:

(a) lending under ECGD bank guarantees where the cover is conditional in that it is restricted to certain political risks (eg confiscation cover or, cover under option 1 or 2 of the Project Financing Scheme);
(b) outstanding lending supported by an ABE endorsement under the, now discontinued, ECGD Comprehensive Extended Terms Guarantee;
(c) loans made against assignments of rights by exporters to the reporting institution under ordinary ECGD policies; and
(d) loans made against the security of ECGD insurance cover.

Lending under equivalent schemes operated by other Zone A countries, and Zone B countries where denominated in local currency and funded in that currency, should be reported in the 0% band to the extent of the cover. Reporting institutions should agree with BSD which schemes may be regarded as 'equivalent' and merit a 0% weighting. *Where lower risk weights have been applied as a result of export credit guarantees, an entry should be made in BSD1(1).*

50 Central governments and central banks

Deposits placed with, and loans made to central governments and central banks, including funds which the reporting institution is required to place on deposit with central banks and monetary authorities. Include in the 10% weighting band Treasury bills and any other bills (by definition with one year or less original maturity) issued by central governments and central banks.

Include similar claims on the European Commission, the European Economic Community (EEC), the European Coal and Steel Community (ECSC) and Euratom.

Do not report balances with international organisations such as the Council of Europe, the United Nations or European Space Agency in this item; they should be reported in item 100 in the 100% band.

60 Lending to group companies

Claims on those group companies which are not required to be consolidated for the purposes of this return should be recorded. Only claims on group companies which meet the conditions referred to in the Bank's Notice BSD/1989/2 should be reported in the 0% band. Those claims which are eligible for inclusion in the 0% band should be agreed with Banking Supervision Division (BSD).

For the unconsolidated return, include lending to companies and associates included in the consolidated RAR and those that would be included were it not for the fact they are supervised by another UK regulator.

70 Banks (including building societies discount houses & MDBs), GEMMs, SEMBs

For the definition of banks and multilateral development banks (MDBs), see Guidance Notes 14 and 15. For a list of discount houses, gilt-edged market makers (GEMMs), institutions with a money-market dealing relationship with the Bank, and Stock Exchange money brokers (SEMBs), see Appendix B of the Banking Statistics Definitions.

80 Public sector entities

For the definition of public sector entities, see Guidance Note 9.

90 Loans secured by mortgage[s] on residential property

Report loans to individuals secured by mortgage on residential properties (both free-hold and leasehold) which are or will be occupied by the borrower, or which are rented, where such loans are fully secured by a first priority charge. If any part of the property is used for non-residential purposes, the mortgage loan should not be reported here but should be reported in item 100. However, mortgage loans secured on property where the occupier works at home but no structural alterations are required to return the property to full residential use may be reported here.

Report mortgage loans to housing associations registered with the Housing Corporation, Scottish Homes and Tai Cymru (Housing for Wales) which are fully secured by a first priority charge on housing association residential property which is rented. Loans to such housing associations for residential property development which do not meet the above conditions should be reported here only if all the following conditions are met:

(a) the development attracts Housing Association Grant (HAG); and
(b) the loans are fully secured by a first priority charge on the development property; and
(c) the loans are fully secured by a charge (but not necessarily a first priority charge) on a housing association's residential property which is rented.

Report loans to the Housing Finance Corporation which are secured by a first priority charge over its assets.

Report mortgage sub-participations which are fully and specifically secured against rseidential mortgage loans which are eligible for a 50% weight.

For the purposes of this item the following definitions apply:

'Fully secured' means that the value of the property must be greater than or equal to the value of the loan (ie a maximum loan to value ratio of 100%). Whilst there is no requirement for reporting institutions to revalue properties on a regular basis, where such valuation has been made and it is found that the loan to value ratio exceeds 100%, such loans should be weighted at 100% (and reported in item 100). (However, if the shortfall in the security value is fully covered by a specific provision, the net amount of the exposure can continue to be weighted at 50%). Conversely, where revaluation indicates that the loan to value ratio has fallen to 100% or less, the loan may be weighted at 50% and reported in item 90.

'First priority charge' means a first fixed (legal or equitable) charge or a first floating charge. In the case of the latter, reporting institutions must ensure (by, for example, including a negative pledge to this effect in the documentation) that no prior ranking charges can be taken over the assets concerned.

The above treatment may *also* be applied to loans to *special purpose mortgage finance vehicles* which include covenants restricting the vehicles' activities to mortgage business and which provide for the loan to be repaid on demand should the covenants be breached and which also meet the criteria to be met by mortgage backed securities qualifying for a 50% risk weighting set out in item 90 (see item 90).

100 Other loans, advances and bills held

Report here exposures to counterparties not already included above.

The Council of Europe, United Nations and its agencies (other than the World Bank and International Finance Corporation—see Guidance Note 15), European Space Agency and Eurofima should be included here rather than under item 50. Report balances with Euroclear in the 20% band and those with Cedel in the 100% band.

Factoring

Report the total amount of debts assigned to the reporting institution under factoring or other similar arrangements as an exposure to the debtor.

Where the debt is assigned to the reporting institution with no recourse the debt should be weighted as a claim on the debtor.

Where the debt is assigned to the reporting institution for no consideration and on a recourse basis the debt should be reported in the 0% bands.

Where the debt is assigned to the reporting institution for a consideration and on a recourse basis the amount of the consideration should be weighted as a claim on the debtor and the remaining portion should be weighted at 0%.

Where a guarantee has been given eg from the assignor's parent, the risk weighting of the gurantor may be applied.

120–190 Investments

Report securities, together with any associated accrued interest, with an original maturity of over one year such as equities, euro-bonds and FRNs (instruments of original maturity of one year or less should be reported in items 50–110). All securities (including British Government stocks) should be reported on a contract day basis, with the payments due or receivable in respect of such transactions to be shown gross in items 760 and 40. Only long positions in securities should be reported in this section of the return (see Guidance Note 23). Where it is not possible to identify separately interest accruals they should be reported in item 260 in the appropriate risk weighting band.

Enter in items 130, 140, 150, 170 and 180 securities guaranteed by central governments or central banks meeting the conditions for guarantees (see Guidance Note 24) at either 10% or 20% depending on whether the residual maturity of the security is one year or less or over one year respectively. If the guarantor is a Zone B central government or central bank, the security must be in the local currency of the issuer and guarantor.

120 Central governments and central banks

Holdings of securities and debt instruments (other than bills—see item 50) issued by central governments and central banks. Include such instruments issued by the European Commission, the European Coal and Steel Community and Euratom.

Only holdings of certificates of tax deposit should be reported in the 0% band together with interest accruals on holdings of securities and debt instruments where the issuer is a Zone A central government or central bank or where the issuer is a Zone B central bank or government and the security is in the local currency of the issuer.

For the determination of the appropriate weight band for other securities held, see Guidance Note 9. Where it is not possible to identify separately interest accruals they should be reported in item 260 in the appropriate risk weighting bands.

Report both the gross long position and net long position (ie the gross long position minus the gross short position—item 120 less item 710) in such securities (see Guidance Note 23). The total (item 120) should be the sum of the gross long positions. If there are no short positions relevant to a particular band, the net long position box must nevertheless be completed showing an amount equal to the gross long position.

See Guidance Note 23 for the treatment of short positions in these securities taken on behalf of the reporting institution by related Gilt Edged Market Makers.

130 Public sector entities

For the definition of public sector entities, see Guidance Note 19.

140 Banks (unsubordinated FRNs etc)

Unsubordinated FRNS and similar types of non-capital debt instruments issued by banks (for definition, see Guidance Note 14) with an original maturity of over one year.

In the case of securities issued by Zone B banks, the weight will be 20% if the residual maturity is one year or less and 100% if over one year.

Holdings of subordinated debt issued by any MDBs attract a risk weighting of 100%.

150 Mortgage backed securities

Only holdings of US GNMA securities with a floating rate, or with a fixed rate if the residual maturity is one year or less, should be reported in item 150.1. Fixed rate GNMA securities with a residual maturity of over one year together with FHLMC and FNMA mortgage backed securities should be reported in item 150.2.

Stripped bonds should be reported in the 100% risk weight category regardless of counterparty.

Report in item 150.3 holdings of securities issued by *special purpose mortgage finance vehicles* which meet the following conditions (also set out in the Bank's notice BSD/1992/6). Holdings of securities which do not meet these conditions should be reported in item 150.4:

  (i) they are fully secured at all times against residential mortgage loans which meet the conditions set out in item 90. The nature of the security may be a first fixed or floating charge, either legal or equitable;
 (ii) the vehicle's activities are restricted by its articles of association to mortgage business. The vehicle may also hold assets qualifying for a risk weighting of less than 50%.
(iii) the mortgage loans must not be in default at the time at which they are transferred to the vehicle;
 (iv) the notes embody an express promise to repay the bearer;
  (v) the issue documentation contains provisions which would ultimately enable the noteholders to initiate legal proceedings directly against the issuer of the mortgage backed security. As an example such provisions would allow noteholders to proceed against the issuer where the trustee, having become bound to take steps and/or to proceed against the issuer, fails to do so within a reasonable time and such failing is continuing;
 (vi) the documentation contains provisions which would ultimately enable noteholders to acquire the legal title to the security (ie the mortgagee's interest in it) and to realise the security in the event of a default by the mortgagor.

Report in item 150.4 notes:

  (i) issued by those companies whose business is not limited as specified above by their articles of association; and, or
 (ii) which absorb more than their pro rata share of losses in the event of arrears or default, eg junior notes; and, or
(iii) where the security agreement does not provide that noteholders remain fully secured at all times; and, or
 (iv) where mortgage loans backing the securities were in default at the time when they were transferred to the vehicle.

160 Investments in subsidiaries and associated companies

The same accounting treatment should be adopted as that used in the preparation of statutory accounts. Do not report investments in subsidiary and associated companies where those companies are required to be included in the consolidation for the purposes of this return.

Also report the value placed on long term life policies written by life assurance companies in the group (the 'embedded' value) where the changes in the embedded value are reported in the profit and loss account.

170 Investments in the capital of other banks and financial institutions

All items reported in this section should be shown at full book value, with no reduction for any amortisation which the issuer may be applying in calculating its own capital base.

Report holdings of equity (including UK building society permanent interest bearing shares (PIBs)) in item 170.1 and capital debt instruments (including hybrid debt instruments and subordinated FRNs) in item 170.2. Also report in item 170.2, holdings of subordinated and unsubordinated loan capital (with an original maturity in excess of five years) issued by bank holding companies, or financing vehicles within banking groups. If doubt exists as to the appropriate treatment of an item refer to BSD. Also include securities issued by special purpose finance companies which have been set up to hold ('repackage') bank capital instruments (unless it has been agreed with BSD that the principal and interest on the securities are fully protected from any risk on the underlying bank capital instruments).

Where a reporting institution has satisfied BSD that it is a primary or secondary market-maker in instruments reported in item 170.2, holdings of such instruments within the primary or secondary market concession should be reported in items 170.3 or 170.4 and not in item 170.2. These figures should match those reported on Form M1 for banks who complete that return (those institutions making a market in other banks' capital instruments). See the Bank's Notice BSD/1986/2.

Any amounts reported in this item should not be reported again in items 140 or 160.

Investments in the capital of other banks should be reported here even where the investment is guaranteed by a central government or public sector body. (See Guidance Note 24.)

Report also holdings of capital instruments issued by financial institutions which are required to be deducted under the terms of the Own Funds Directive (see Guidance Note 9). Report holdings of equity in item 170.1 and of debt instruments in item 170.2.

180 Other investments

Report here investments in counterparties not already included above.

200–260 Other assets

210 Other intangible assets

Only report in item 210.1, mortgage servicing rights where there is an active and liquid market in which they can be traded. At present, this condition is only met in respect of mortgage servicing rights traded in the US market. (Valuation of these items should be discussed with BSD.)

220 and 230 Own premises and other property/real estate

Own premises should include the value in its books of property occupied or being developed for occupation by the reporting institution. Also report in item 220, property which is occupied or is for the purpose of occupation by employees of the reporting institution. Other property and real estate beneficially owned by the reporting institution but not occupied or used in the operation of its business should be reported in item 230.

240 Operating leases

Report equipment owned by the reporting institution which has been leased out under an operating lease. Report any contracted future rental payments (net of future finance charges) weighted according to the lessee; the residual value of the asset should be reported in the 100% weighting band.

250 Plant, equipment and other fixed assets

Plant and equipment owned or recorded as such by the reporting institution and used in connection with its own business. Equipment leased out under operating leases should not be reported here but in item 240. Equipment leased out under finance leases should be reported in items 50–110.

Where the reporting institution is the lessee under a finance lease, or a hirer under a hire purchase contract, the asset should be recorded in the 100% band. If the reporting institution is acting as a broker or agent for a sub-lease or back-to-back lease, the asset should not be reported on the balance sheet provided that there is no recourse to the reporting institution in the event of a default (see BSD/1989/1).

260 Other assets

Report any other assets not reported elsewhere, eg sundry debtors, prepayments and accruals not identified elsewhere (see Guidance Note 7).

Overall net positive mark-to-market valuations of interest rate and foreign exchange related contracts should be weighted at 0% here—see items 450/460. Overall net negative mark-to-market values should be included under item 760.2. Assets relating to premia paid out on interest rate and foreign exchange options contracts bought on exchanges and subject to daily margining requirements should be reported under item 260.1.

Net long positions in physical commodities and LME warrants (including silver, platinum and palladium where not already included under item 20) should be weighted at 100% here; positions in different commodities should not be netted. Net short positions in any commodity should be reported in item 760.2.

Deferred tax assets should be included in item 260.4.

280–330 Memorandum items

280 Connected lending of a capital nature

Report all connected lending of a capital nature and indicate, in the lines provided, in which weight band on the assets section of this return the lending has been reported. Also report both long term subordinated loans and one-off payments by the reporting institution to vehicles established for loan packaging schemes, where the reporting institution is the servicing agent (see BSD/1989/1). For the definition of a connected counterparty see Guidance Note 18.

Do not report loans to subsidiaries and associated companies where the loan has already been reported in item 160.

Any items included here should be excluded from total risk assets in the appropriate risk weight band on the Summary Schedule (see notes to items S100–S140). If doubt exists as to the inclusion of an asset in this item refer to BSD for guidance.

290 Loans to directors, controllers and their associates

Directors, controllers, and their associates are as defined in section 105 of the Banking Act 1987. Indicate, in the lines provided, in which weight band on the assets side of this return the lending has been reported.

If a loan reported here is of a capital nature, it should be included additionally in item 280.

300 Loans to non-group companies with which directors and controllers are associated

A director (including an alternate director) or controller of the reporting institution is deemed to be associated with another company, whether registered or resident in the UK or overseas, if he holds the office of a director (or alternate director) with that company (whether in his own right, or as a result of a loan granted by, or financial interest taken by, the reporting institution to, or in, that company, or even by virtue of a professional interest unconnected with the reporting institution), or if he and/or his associates together hold 10% or more of the equity share capital of that company. For the purpose of this item, include as a director an employee of the reporting institution who is not a director but who is appointed a director of another company.

The definition should be consistent with that adopted for reporting on Form LE.

Indicate, in the lines provided, in which weight band on the assets section of this return the lending has been reported.

If a loan reported here is of a capital nature, it should be included additionally in item 280.

310 Direct credit substitutes given on behalf of connected counterparties

For the definition of connected counterparties see Guidance Note 18. Indicate, in the lines provided, in which weight band within item 340 the direct credit substitute has been reported.

320 Investments in central governments and central banks (net short positions)

Report net short positions in central government and central bank securities. This should equal item 710.1 after allowing for any long positions in the same securities (see Guidance Note 23).

See Guidance Note 23 for the treatment of short positions in these securities taken on behalf of the reporting institution by related Gilt Edged Market Makers.

All positions after weighting shown here should be reported with a positive sign.

330 Encumbered assets

List in these lines any assets not freely available to meet the claims of the generality of creditors in a liquidation of the reporting institution because they are subject to a charge, pledge or other restriction.

Under item 330.1, list the assets and the item number on the return to which they refer, which have been given as security in connection with the reporting institution's participation in a payments/settlements system such as Central Gilts Office or Euroclear. The particular payments/settlements system should be listed with the liabilities being secured at the reporting date recorded under column 1. For the purposes of detailing the total amount of assets securing liabilities, assets pledged in excess of the actual liability to individual systems at the reporting date should not be reported.

Under item 330.2, list the assets and the item number on the return to which they refer, which have been given as security to secure the reporting institution's other liabilities (for example, property which has been mortgaged and hire purchase agreements pledged as collateral). Assets reported should exclude any element of unearned finance charges.

Total liabilities being secured at the reporting date (item 330, column 1) should equal the sum of 330.1 and 330.2 below. Total assets at the reporting date securing liabilities reported in column 1 (item 330, column 2), will not necessarily equal the sum of items 330.1 and 330.2 below as any asset which is securing more than one creditor should not be double counted in the total.

Off-balance sheet

The credit equivalent amount for off-balance sheet items is derived by first multiplying the nominal/principal amount by the given credit conversion factor. The weighted amount column is then derived by multiplying the resultant credit equivalent amount by the appropriate risk weight or by deducting it from the reporting institution's capital base (see Guidance Note 9).

Intra group off-balance sheet items should be reported under the relevant item and weighted according to the terms agreed with BSD under BSD/1986/3 as amended by BSD/1989/2.

Multi-option facilities and other composite products should be disaggregated into their component parts, eg into a credit commitment, NIF, etc, and each component weighted according to the usual classification. However, components carrying the lowest conversion factors should be disregarded to the extent that the total value of all components exceeds the value of the facility.

340 Direct credit substitutes

Direct credit substitutes relate to the financial requirements of a counterparty, where the risk of loss to the reporting institution on the transaction is equivalent to a direct claim on the counterparty, ie the risk of loss depends on the creditworthiness of the counterparty. Report instruments such as:

  (a) acceptances granted and risk participations in bankers' acceptances. Where a reporting institution's own acceptances have been discounted by that institution the nominal value of the bills held should be deducted from the nominal amount of the bills issued under the facility and a corresponding on-balance sheet entry made;

  (b) guarantees given on behalf of customers to stand behind the current obligations of the customer and to carry out these obligations should the customer fail to do so, eg a loan guarantee;

  (c) guarantees of leasing operations;

  (d) guarantees of a capital nature such as undertakings given to a non-bank company authorised under the Financial Services Act which are considered as capital by the appropriate regulator (SRO or SIB). Such guarantees given to a company which is not connected to the reporting institution should be weighted at 100% and those to a connected company should be deducted from the reporting institution's capital base (item 340.6);

(e) letters of credit not eligible for inclusion in item 360;
(f) standby letters of credit, or other irrevocable obligations, serving as financial guarantees where the bank has an irrevocable obligation to pay a third party beneficiary if the customer fails to repay an outstanding commitment, eg letters of credit supporting the issue of commercial paper, delivery of merchandise, or for stock lending (standby letters of credit which are related to non-financial transactions should be reported in item 350 below);
(g) re-insurance or window letters of credit;
(h) acceptances drawn under letters of credit, or similar facilities where the acceptor does not have specific title to an identifiable underlying shipment of goods (eg sales of electricity).

Direct credit substitutes of a capital nature

Any direct credit substitutes which are of a capital nature and connected to the reporting institution or given to another bank should be reported in item 340.6 and will be deducted from capital in the calculation of the risk asset ratio.

Include:

(a) a guarantee which takes the place of capital, eg where a regulatory body allows a company to gear up on such guarantees (but see also 340(d) above);
(b) a guarantee of a bank capital instrument (unless otherwise agreed with BSD, eg do not include here the subordinated guarantee of loan stocks raised by vehicle company subsidiaries of the reporting institution, where the loan stock is treated as subordinated term debt of the reporting institution).

350 Transaction-related contingents

Transaction-related contingents relate to the on-going trading activities of a counterparty where the risk of loss to the reporting institution depends on the likelihood of a future event which is independent of the creditworthiness of the counterparty. They are essentially guarantees which support particular non-financial obligations rather than supporting customers' general financial obligations. Report such items as:

(a) performance bonds, warranties and indemnities (indemnities given for lost share certificates or bills of lading and guarantees of the *validity* of papers rather than of *payment* under certain conditions should not be reported in this return);
(b) bid or tender bonds;
(c) advance payment guarantees;
(d) VAT, customs and excise bonds. The amount recorded for such bonds should be the reporting institution's maximum liability (normally twice the monthly amount being guaranteed);
(e) standby letters of credit relating to a particular contract or to non-financial transactions (including arrangements backing, *inter alia*, subcontractors' and suppliers' performance, labour and materials contracts, and construction bids).

360 Trade-related contingents

Report short-term, self liquidating trade-related items such as documentary letters of credit issued by the reporting institution which are, or are to be, collateralised by the underlying shipment, ie where the credit provides for the reporting institution to retain title to the underlying shipment. Such letters should be weighted according to the counterparty on whose behalf the credit is issued and reported whether or not the terms and conditions of the credit have yet to be complied with.

Letters of credit issued by the reporting institution without provision for the reporting institution to retain title to the underlying shipment or where the title has passed from the reporting institution should be reported under direct credit substitutes (item 340). A memorandum of pledge and a trust receipt are not regarded as giving the reporting institution title, and transactions secured by these should be shown under item 340.

Letters of credit confirmed by the reporting institution should be reported as direct credit substitutes whether or not the terms have yet to be complied with, weighted according to the counterparty issuing the letter.

Letters of credit issue on behalf of a counterparty back-to-back with letters of credit of which the counterparty is a beneficiary ('back-to-back' letters) should be reported in full.

Letters of credit advised by the reporting institution or for which the reporting institution is acting as reimbursement agent should not be reported.

370 Sale and repurchase agreements

See Guidance Note 25.

Report sale and repurchase agreements ('repos'), ie when the reporting institution is the seller of the asset where the asset sold is not reported on the balance sheet. If the asset sold is kept on balance sheet it should not be reported here but in the relevant line in the on-balance sheet section of this return. When the asset does not appear on the balance sheet the weighting category is to be determined by the issuer of the security (or borrower in the case of a loan) and not according to the counterparty with whom the transaction has been entered into.

Repos associated with reverse repos should not be reported in item 370; the liability under such repos should be reported under item 720.

The reporting institution should refer to BSD where it has a repo in item 370 and offsettable short stock positions on balance sheet in item 320 or 710.2 which would meet the general requirements for the netting of stock positions (see Guidance Note 23).

380 Asset sales with recourse

Asset sale with recourse where the credit risk remains with the bank fall into the weighting category determined by the asset and *not* according to the counterparty with whom the transaction has been entered into. Report put options written where the holder of the asset is entitled to put the asset back to the reporting institution, eg if the credit quality deteriorates. Also report put options written by the reporting institution attached to marketable instruments or other physical assets.

390 Forward asset purchases

The weight should be determined by the asset to be purchased, not the counterparty with whom the contract has been entered into. Include commitments for loans and other on-balance sheet items with certain drawdown. Exclude foreign currency spot deposits with value dates one or two working days after trade date.

400 Forward forward deposits placed

Agreements between two parties whereby one will pay, and the other receive an agreed rate of interest on, a deposit to be placed by one with the other at some predetermined date in the future. Exclude foreign currency spot deposits with value dates one or two working days after trade date.

The weight should be determined according to the counterparty with whom the deposit will be placed.

410 Uncalled partly-paid shares and securities

Only report if there is a specific date for the call on the unpaid part of the shares and securities held. If there is no specific date, the unpaid part should be treated as a long-term commitment (see item 440).

420 NIFs and RUFs

Note issuance facilities and revolving underwriting facilities should include the total amounts of the reporting institution's underwriting obligations of any maturity. Where the facility has been drawn down by the borrower and the notes are held by anyone other than the reporting institution, the underwriting obligation should continue to be reported at the full nominal amount.

The reporting institution's own holding of the notes should be reported in items 50–110 and therefore the nominal amount of the notes held should be deducted from the nominal amount of the facility to be shown here.

430 Endorsements of bills

Endorsements of bills (including per aval endorsements) should be reported at the full nominal amount, less any amount for bills which the reporting institution now holds but had previously endorsed.

Where the reporting institution is the first endorser of a bill which has been accepted by a bank other than the reporting bank, such endorsements should be reported in item 430.1. (Where a reporting institution has endorsed its own acceptances no further amount should be reported than the acceptance reported in item 340.) If the reporting institution is not the first endorser of a bill already accepted by a bank, such endorsements need not be reported.

Endorsements of bills which have not been accepted by a bank should be reported in items 430.2–430.4 according to the risk weight category of the issuer; where such a bill has been previously endorsed by a bank, the reporting institution's endorsement will warrant a 20% weight. Endorsements of bills which have been prevously endorsed by two or more banks need not be reported.

440 Other commitments

Report here other undrawn commitments, classified as to whether:

(i) they have an original maturity of one year or less or are unconditionally cancellable at any time (item 440.1); or

(ii) they have an original maturity of over one year (items 440.2–440.7).

The reporting institution is regarded as having a commitment from the date the customer is advised of the facility (eg the date of the letter advising the customer) regardless of whether the commitment is revocable or irrevocable, conditional or unconditional, and in particular whether or not the facility contains a 'material adverse change' clause.

Rolling or undated/open-ended commitments ('evergreens' and including overdrafts) should be included under (i) providing that they are unconditionally cancellable at any time without notice and subject to credit review at least annually. Other rolling or undated commitments should be reported under (ii).

Unused credit card lines should be reported under (i).

Securities underwriting

Securities underwriting commitments should not be reported on this return, with the exception of NIFs and RUFs (item 420).

Commitments to provide capital to connected counterparties (and other banks)

Amounts reported under item 440.7 should be multiplied by the 50% credit conversion factor before entering, so that an appropriately reduced amount is carried through to the summary page (item S70). If, however, the item would normally attract a credit conversion factor of 0% for the reasons above, it should continue to be reported under item 440.1.

Commitments with certain drawdown

Commitments for loans and other on-balance sheet items with certain drawdown should not be reported here but in item 390.

The maturity of a commitment

See Guidance Note 8 for general guidance on maturity.

The maturity of a commitment should be determined in accordance with the following:

(a) *Original and remaining maturity*
The maturity of a commitment should be measured as from the date when the commitment was entered into based on original maturity, ie from the date of firm offer, until the final date by which it must be drawn down in full. (However, see Guidance Note 8).

(b) Renegotiations of the term of a commitment
In the case where the terms of a commitment have been renegotiated the maturity should be measured as from the date of the renegotiation until the end of the period of the renegotiated commitment providing the renegotiation involves a full credit assessment of the customer and the lender's right, without notice, to withdraw the commitment.

Where these conditions are not met the original starting date of the commitment must be used to determine its maturity rather than the date of renegotiation.

(c) A commitment to provide a loan (or purchase an asset) which has a maturity of over one year but which must be drawn down within a period of one year or less.
Such commitments should be treated as having a maturity of one year or less so long as any undrawn portion of the facility is automatically cancelled at the end of the draw-down period.

(d) A commitment to provide a loan (or purchase an asset) to be drawn down in a number of tranches, some one year or less and some over one year.
The whole commitment should be considered as having a maturity of over one year.

(e) Commitments for fluctuating amounts
Where a commitment provides for a customer to have a facility limit which varies during the period of the commitment, eg for seasonal reasons, the amount of the commitment should at all times be taken as the maximum amount that can be drawn under the commitment for the remaining period of the commitment.

(f) Forward commitments
A foward commitment is where the reporting institution is committed to granting a facility at a future date. The original maturity of the commitment is to be measured from the date the commitment is entered into until the final date by which the facility must be drawn in full.

(h) Commitments for off-balance sheet transactions
A distinction is drawn between a commitment to provide an off-balance sheet facility which may or may not be drawn by the customer, and a commitment to provide an off-balance sheet instrument with *certain* draw-down. For example:

(i) a commitment of over one year to provide a trade related contingent *facility* at a future date which may or may not be drawn down should be given a credit conversion factor (ccf) of 50% (the ccf for long-term commitments) multiplied by 20% (the ccf for trade-related contingents), ie an effective ccf of 10%. Report 20% of the principal amount in the relevant section in item 440, depending on the counterparty weight. Similarly, a long-term commitment to provide a guarantee *facility* would receive a ccf of 50% multiplied by 100%, ie an effective ccf of 50%; report 100% of the principal amount in the relevant section of item 440;

(ii) a commitment (short-term or long-term) to provide a trade-related contingent *item*, where it is certain that the draw-down will occur at some point in the future, including a range of dates, a ccf of 20% should be applied, ie without multiplying by the relevant ccf for a commitment. Similarly, a commitment to issue a guarantee with certain draw-down at a particular point in the future should receive a ccf of 100% and be reported under item 340.

APPENDICES I AND II

450 Interest rate related contracts

Report single currency interest rate swaps, basis swaps, forward rate agreements and products with similar characteristics, interest rate futures, interest rate options purchased (including caps, collars and floors purchased as stand-alone contracts) and similar instruments. Bond futures and bond options purchased should also be reported here. Interest rate futures and options should not be reported where the contracts concerned are traded on exchanges subject to daily margining requirements. In such instances, the initial cash margin payment should be reported in item 100 in the 100% weight band.

460 Foreign exchange related contracts

Only exchange rate contracts of over 14 days original maturity (excluding a settlement period of up to 2 days) are to be reported.

Foreign currencies are to include gold, silver, platinum and palladium.

Report cross currency swaps, cross currency interest rate swaps (the exchange of principal on such swaps should be excluded from the on-balance sheet section of this return), outright forward foreign exchange contracts, currency futures, currency options purchased and similar instruments. Equity options purchased and equity futures should also be reported here. Also include futures, swaps and similar instruments involving physical commodities. Such futures and options traded on exchanges subject to daily margining requirements should not be reported. In such instances, the initial cash margin payment should be reported in item 100 in the 100% weight band.

For the reporting of SAFEs (synthetic agreements for forward exchange), ERAs are to be treated as interest rate instruments; FXAs will also qualify for interest rate add-ons unless the notional principal amounts for the first (front-end) and second (back-end) contracts differ by more than 10%, in which event the lower amount will be treated as the notional principal for and interest rate contract and the difference in the contract amounts will attract the exchange rate add-ons.

Swaps attached to loans and bonds

Under certain conditions the risk attached to a floating (or fixed) rate loan/bond and a linked interest rate or currency swap may be equivalent to a fixed (or floating) rate loan. In this case the swap need not be reported providing the following conditions are met:

(i) the swap and loan should have matching obligations (ie identical interest periods);
(ii) the swap and loan should be explicitly linked such that if the counterparty defaults under the loan or swap, or goes into liquidation, all payments under the swap agreement cease and the loan becomes immediately repayable;
(iii) netting of floating (or fixed) rate payments on the loan and the swap must meet all the existing (or future) on-balance sheet netting criteria (see Guidance Note 22).

450–460 Interest rate and exchange rate related contracts

Reporting institutions should complete either Appendix I (Replacement cost method) or Appendix II (Original Exposure Method) to derive the credit equivalent amount of these instruments. In general, where a reporting institution actively trades these instruments or where such instruments form a significant part of its treasury operation, Appendix I should be completed; the method of 'marking to market' contracts with a positive value should be discussed with BSD. Appendix II should be completed only by those institutions that do not actively trade interest rate and foreign exchange related instruments, after agreement with BSD. When reporting on an unconsolidated (or solo-consolidated) basis, an institution will therefore complete only one of the Appendices; a consolidated return may include both Appendix I and II, where agreed.

For the purposes of measuring the counterparty risk inherent in such contracts, a risk weight of 50% should be applied in respect of counterparties which would attract a weight of 100% elsewhere on this return.

The following is offered as guidance for the completion of Appendix I or II:

Notional principal amount (column 1)

The notional principal amount for each contract should be reported in this column, regardless of whether it is matched by another contract or whether it has a positive mark to market value.

For *exchange rate contracts*, the notional principal should be taken as the amount of principal underlying the contract, as regards the currency being received by the reporting institution, translated into sterling at the spot exchange rate on the reporting date.

For an *amortising swap*, ie one based on a steadily declining notional principal, the notional principal should be taken as that which is outstanding at the reporting date.

For a swap based on a *fluctuating level of principal*, the notional principal should be taken as the maximum notional principal outstanding over the remaining life of the swap.

For amortising interest rate swaps with *cash-flow mismatches in payments*, the notional principal may differ between the two sides of the swap—the higher of the two should be used.

For swaps involving *physical commodities*, the notional principal should relate to the total volume over the whole contract (not simply the volume per settlement period), eg for a two-year oil swap involving one million barrels with quarterly settlement, the exposure should be reported as covering the full period of the contract (not just one quarter at a time) and the notional principal would be eight million barrels (not just one million), converted to sterling at the spot rate on the day of the report. (The reported principal in this example would decline as each quarterly settlement is made.)

For *options purchased*, the notional principal should be taken as the underlying principal of the option, using, for currency options, the received currency at the spot rate on the reporting date.

Remaining maturity

The remaining maturity of a swap should be taken as the time until final expiry of the swap. For FRAs and similar products, the remaining maturity should be taken as the time from the reporting date until the end of the period to which the interest rate underlying the contract relates, eg for an FRA with three months until settlement based on a one year rate, the remaining maturity would be 15 months. Where settlement of an FRA takes place at the start of the period to which the interest rate underlying the contract relates, no account should be taken of the FRA following such settlement, ie the FRA should no longer be reported; where settlement takes place at the end of this period, the FRA should continue to be reported until settlement takes place given that, even after the settlement amount is fixed, the contract will continue to have a mark-to-market value which will be subject to fluctuation.

For *interest rate options*, the remaining maturity should be taken as the time from the reporting date until the end of the period to which the interest rate underlying the option relates, ie in a similar way to FRAs.

For *swaps with interim mark-to-market settlements*, the remaining maturity should be taken as the time until final maturity, and not the time until the next interim settlement.

Replacement cost method (Appendix I)

Replacement cost/Mark-to-Market amount (column 2)

Reporting institutions should mark-to-market in a prudent and consistent manner; only contracts with a positive mark-to-market value should be reported under this heading (but all contracts should be reported in column 1). Contracts whose mark-to-market value is reported as an asset in the balance sheet, ie those with a positive mark-to-market value, should also be reported here but that mark-to-market value allocated to the 0% band in the on-balance sheet section (see also item 260).

In general, no readily observable market prices will be available for these instruments. Reporting institutions should develop their own methodology for calculating market values, details of which should be made available to BSD. BSD will monitor the approaches adopted by institutions and will be concerned that such approaches should be broadly comparable across all institutions in line with best market and supervisory practice. The following general guidelines should be observed.

For swaps, forward rate agreements and products with similar characteristics, outright forward foreign exchange contracts and futures (if appropriate), the mark-to-market approach should be based on an estimation of the net present value of the future cash flows of the contract, using interest rates based on current market rates and relevant to periods in which the cash-flows will arise (commonly for example, the rates from a derived yield curve for zero-coupon government bonds).

For options purchased, the mark-to-market approach should be based on a valuation of the option reflecting, inter alia, the amount by which the option is 'in the money' (ie the amount, if any, by which the rate at which the option can be exercised is more favourable than the current market rate when applied to the notional principal underlying the option), the time to expiry of the option, the volatility of the underlying exchange or interest rate, and (for currency options) the interest rate differential between the currencies. Typically such valuations will be based on a mathematically complex formula, and will value the option at an amount above its 'in the money' value. Reporting institutions whose involvement in options is limited and who have not developed suitable methodology may, with the written consent of BSD, value options at their 'in the money' value.

Future credit exposure (Add-ons) (columns 3 and 4)

For the replacement cost method, the notional principal amount of all contracts (column 1 on Appendix I) should be multiplied by the following factors (column 3 on Appendix I) to obtain the future credit exposure:

Residual Maturity	Interest Rate Contracts	Exchange Rate Contracts
One year or less	0%	1.0%
Over one year	0.5%	5.0%

For single currency interest rate basis swaps, there is deemed to be no future credit exposure, ie such contracts are treated in the same way as interest rate contracts with a residual maturity of one year or less.

Original exposure method (Appendix II)

Reporting institutions using Appendix II should aggregate contracts with matching combinations of conversion factor and counterparty weight. Where there are more than ten such combinations, either of interest rate contracts or of foreign exchange contracts, the excess combinations should be aggregated in order that ten lines only are completed. This should be done in such a way as to leave the sum of the weighted amounts unchanged (and thus have no effect on the calculation of the reporting institution's risk asset ratio); amounts reported in columns 1 and 3 should be 'grossed up' as necessary to achieve the correct result.

Credit equivalent (column 3)

To obtain the credit equivalent amount using the original exposure method, the notional principal amount (column 1 on Appendix II) should be multiplied by the following conversion factors (column 2) to obtain the future credit exposure:

Original Maturity	Interest Rate Contracts	Exchange Rate Contracts
One year or less	0.5%	2.0%
Over one year and up to and including two years	1.0%	5.0%
For each additional year	1.0%	3.0%

470 Aggregate net short open foreign currency position

This figure should be reported with a positive sign.

For reporting institutions that complete Form S3, the aggregate of net short open positions in column 9 for the same reporting date should be used. Where options business is undertaken, the following adjustments should be made:

  (i) Annex A reporters: columns 14 and 15 on this return should be recalculated using column 9 instead of column 11; the aggregate net short open foreign currency position should be the larger of the totals of the recalculated 14 and 15.
 (ii) Annex B reporters: column 17 on this return should be recalculated using column 9 instead of column 11, ie add columns 9 and 16; the aggregate net short open foreign currency position should be the recalculated column 17.

In some instances structural adjustments, which have been deducted from the capital base, may also be deducted from column 9. Such cases should be discussed with BSD.

When reporting on a consolidated basis, the reporting institution should follow the above instructions although consolidated Form S3 and Annexes do not need to be submitted.

For institutions which do not complete Form S3, the aggregate net short open foreign currency position will be the difference between foreign currency liabilities and assets, irrespective of whether the difference leads to a positive or negative value.

Liabilities

Core and supplementary capital

TIER I

480 Ordinary shares/common stock

This should be reported at nominal paid-up value; where shares have been issued at a premium, the premium should be reported under reserves (item 500.1). Partly-paid shares should be reported at the amount paid. Do not report the unpaid element of partly-paid shares, or authorised but unissued share capital; also exclude holdings by the reporting institution of its own shares and shares issued after 1 January 1992 by the capitalisation of property revaluation reserves.

490 Perpetual non-cumulative preferred shares/stock

Report perpetual non-cumulative preferred shares/stock and perpetual non-cumulative preferred shares convertible into ordinary shares, including any such shares redeemable at the option of the issuer and with the Bank's prior consent. Only shares which have been issued and paid up should be reported.

500 Reserves

500.1 Share premium account

Report any amount received by the reporting institution in excess of the nominal value of shares reported in items 480 or 490. Any share premium in respect of Tier 2 instruments should be reported indistinguishably with those instruments.

500.2 Disclosed prior year reserves (excluding item 580) disclosed current year's positive movements on reserves and negative movements on reserves

Report the disclosed, undistributed balance on profit and loss account attributable to previous years (ie revenue reserves), reserves arising from exchange rate translation differences and other reserves (eg capital redemption reserves and capital gifts). Do not report reserves arising from the revaluation of fixed assets; such reserves should be shown under item 580. Also exclude undisclosed retained profits that have been taken to reserves (inner reserves—see item 570).

Before publication of full year prior year reserves, include here any prior year's earnings which have been verified by external auditors in accordance with the requirements of the Bank's notice BSD/1992/5.

Report here disclosed (ie published) current year's *positive* movements on reserves (other than those shown under item 580). If current year's movements on reserves are *negative* report these here (whether or not disclosed).

500.3 Current year's retained profit verified by external audit

Report only current year's earnings (net of foreseeable charges and distributions) where they have been verified by external auditors in accordance with the requirements of the Bank's notice BSD/1992/5. Interim retained earnings of subsidiaries within banking groups which have been verified by external auditors may also be reported even if they are not separately disclosed. Current year's profit that has not been verified by external audit should be reported in items 560 or 670. Current year's losses should be reported in item 510.

Pension fund assets arising from either a pension fund surplus or deficiency should be deducted from this item. Pension fund liabilities arising from pension fund surpluses should be added; whereas pension fund liabilities arising from pension fund deficiencies should not be added back but should be added to 760.2.

510 Current year's losses

Report all current year's losses. Unpublished losses from the previous accounting period should also be shown here.

520 Minority interests (in Tier 1 capital)

Where the reporting institution reports on a solo consolidated or consolidated basis, enter the claim by outside interests in Tier 1 capital items (see items 480 and 490) of any partly-owned subsidiary company or minority owned company which is included in this particular return.

530 Total of items 480–520

This should equal the sum of items 480–520, taking account of any negative figures, ie those in brackets.

540 Goodwill and other intangible assets

This should equal the sum of items 200 and 210.2.

550 Total Tier 1 capital

Tier 1 capital equals item 530 less any amounts reported in item 540.

TIER 2

560 Current year's profits verified by internal audit

Report all current year's profits (net of any foreseeable charges and distributions) verified by internal audit in accordance with the requirements of the Bank's notice BSD/1992/5. Unpublished profits from the previous accounting period should also be shown here if they have been verified by internal audit.

570 Undisclosed retained profit taken to reserves (Inner Reserves)/undisclosed current year's positive movements on reserves

Report undisclosed reserves maintained by those institutions having exemptions under section 258 of the Companies Act 1985. This item should no longer arise after the implementation of the Bank Accounts Directive which is effective for accounting periods commencing on or after 23 December 1992.

Report also undisclosed (ie unpublished) current year's positive movements on reserves normally reportable in item 500.2.

580 Fixed asset revaluation reserves

Report reserves relating to the revaluation of fixed assets. Report also shares issued by the capitalisation of property revaluation reserves after 1 January 1992.

590 General provisions

Report general provisions that are held against possible or latent loss but where the losses have not as yet been identified. Provisions earmarked or held specifically against lower valuations of particular claims or classes of claims should not be reported here, but netted against the value of the asset against which they have been made (see Guidance Note 6).

General provisions should not exceed 1.5% of total weighted risk assets (see Summary Schedule) up to the end of 1992 and 1.25% of total weighted risk assets from 1 January 1993. Any general provisions exceeding these amounts should be reported in item 660.

600 Hybrid (debt/equity) capital instruments

Report:
  (i) Perpetual cumulative preferred shares, including such shares redeemable at the option of the issuer with the prior consent of the Bank, and including also share premia on these instruments;
  (ii) Perpetual subordinated debt which meets the conditions for primary perpetual subordinated debt set out in the Bank's Notice BSD/1986/2 (issued in March 1986), including such debt which is convertible into equity, either mandatorily or at the option of either the issuer or lender.

610 Subordinated term debt

See item 790. Report only that part that is eligible for inclusion in Tier 2, ie after amortisation and only if such debt does not exceed 50% of Tier 1 elements (item 550). Subordinated term debt that is not eligible for inclusion here should be reported in item 650.

620 Minority interests in Tier 2 capital

Where the reporting institution reports on a solo consolidated or consolidated basis, enter the claim by outside interests in any partly-owned subsidiary or minority owned company in the form of any Tier 2 capital item.

630 Tier 2 capital

This is the total of items 560–620 provided this sum does not exceed Tier 1 capital (item 550), in which case a figure equalling item 550 should be reported here and any surplus should be reported in item 640.

Other capital

640 Surplus Tier 2 capital

Report any amount that has been excluded from item 630, ie the amount by which Tier 2 capital exceeds Tier 1. Do not include here subordinated term debt or general provisions that are not eligible for inclusion as Tier 2 capital (see items 650 and 660).

650 Subordinated term debt (not eligible for inclusion in item 610)

Report subordinated term debt that qualifies for inclusion as capital but which has not been reported in item 610 because:

  (i) the debt is being amortised over the last four years, ie the diffecence between the nominal amount of the stock and the amortised amount;
  (ii) the amount of such debt which exceeds 50% of Tier 1 capital.

  See also item 790.

For treatment of subordinated term debt that does not qualify for inclusion as capital (under the terms of the Bank's Notice BSD/1986/2), see item 670.

660 General Provisions (not eligible for inclusion in item 590)

Report those general provisions that exceed the maximum amount allowable for inclusion in item 590.

670 Other capital

Report preference shares, perpetual loan stocks and subordinated term debt not accepted by the Bank of England as qualifying for inclusion as capital within the terms of the Bank's Notice BSD/1986/2.

Also report working capital provided by an overseas office of the reporting institution.

Report current year's profits which have not been verified by external or internal audit in accordance with the Bank's notice BSD/1992/5 and also any undisclosed profits relating to the previous year which have not been so verified.

Other non-capital liabilities

680 Own bank notes issued

Bank notes in circulation, ie the reporting institution's issue of notes less any own notes held.

700 Marketable securities issued

700.1 Certificates of deposit

Report all certificates of deposit issued by the reporting institution, whether at fixed or floating rates, and still outstanding. Also report negotiable deposits taken on terms in all respects identical to those on which a certificate of deposit would have been issued, but for which it has been mutually convenient not to have issued certificates. If a reporting institution holds certificates of deposits which it has itself issued, these should not be reported in this return.

700.2 Promissory notes and bills

Report promissory notes, bills and other negotiable paper issued (including commercial paper) by the reporting institution including bills drawn under an acceptance credit facility provided by another institution.

700.3 Unsubordinated FRNs and other long term paper

Report unsubordinated FRNs and other unsubordinated market instruments issued. Subordinated capital market instruments should be reported under item 610, 650, or 630 as appropriate.

710 Investments (short positions)

See Guidance Note 23. Do not use brackets in the weighted amount column.

Report gross short positions in securities issued by central governments and central banks under item 710.1 and gross short positions in other investments under item 710.2.

720 Liabilities in respect of sale and repurchase agreements

See Guidance Note 25.

Where the reporting institution reports assets subject to sale and repurchase agreements on the balance sheet, the liability under such agreements should be reported here.

730 Tax provisions

Deferred tax assets should be reported as an asset in item 260.4.

750 Other provisions

Report provisions made other than those reported above (items 590, 660, 730–740). Specific provisions (see Guidance Note 6) should also be excluded from this item, *except where they have been created in respect of off-balance sheet items.*

760 Other

Report credit items in the course of transmission and items in suspense (including credit items in the course of settlement, to be shown separately in item 760.1).

Also report all internal accounts and other liabilities not reported elsewhere, eg sundry creditors and liabilities under finance leases.

Include net short positions in physical commodities. Positions in different commodities should not be netted.

Include also liabilities arising in respect of pension scheme deficiencies; those arising in respect of a pension fund surplus should be included under item 500.3.

770 Total liabilities

This is the sum of items 530 and 560–760 and should equal item 270.

780–790 Memorandum items

780 Deposits from connected customers

Connected customers are defined as other group companies (excluding those companies which are included in the consolidation of this particular return), directors, controllers and their associates, and non-group companies with which directors and controllers are associated as set down in items 290 and 300 and Guidance Notes 17 and 18.

790 Subordinated term debt

Report here only the amount of subordinated term debt which has been approved by BSD as qualifying for inclusion in the capital base under the terms of the Bank's Notice BSD/1986/2.

Report under item 790.1 only convertible subordinated term bonds which are mandatorily convertible into equity (but see item 600 for treatment of convertible subordinated *perpetual* debt). Subordinated bonds which are convertible into equity at either the issuer's or investors' option (where these bonds are not eligible for inclusion in item 600) should be reported under item 790.2.

Dated preference shares and subordinated, unsecured loan stocks of over 5 years' original maturity issued by the reporting institution should be shown after amortisation in item 790.2. The amount shown in item 790.2 should be further divided between items 790.21 and 790.22 as necessary in the relevant sub-total boxes. The amount of principal outstanding before amortisation should also be entered in the sub-total boxes in the 'amount' column in the currency of repayment, which should be entered in the 'currency' column. The 'sterling equivalent' is then this amount converted to sterling at the current exchange rate for the currency concerned on the day of the report unless, via a swap or some other hedging mechanism that is an integral part of the original preference share or subordinated loan stock agreement, the exchange rate has effectively been fixed—in which case that fixed rate may be used.

Individual stocks which are repayable in full on maturity should be listed in item 790.21 in lines a to e. Where there are more than five stocks issued (ie a to e) annotate the form 'see attached list' in this section and attach a full list of such stocks. The amounts to be reported after amortisation are shown below and relate to the period between the date of the return and maturity date:

Less than 1 year to maturity 20%
1 year but less than 2 years to maturity 40%
2 years but less than 3 years to maturity 60%
3 years but less than 4 years to maturity 80%
4 years or more to maturity 100%

The amount of subordinated, unsecured loan stock should be multiplied by the amortisation values shown above. In the case of optional repayment dates the longest date should be used to determine the final maturity if the exercise of the option lies with the issuer, and the shortest date if with investors.

Report in item 790.22 in lines a to e the original outstanding value of individual stocks which are repayable in instalments. The amortised amount shown should be agreed with BSD.

The amortised amounts in item 790.2 should be added to any figures in item 790.1 and reported in item 610, provided the sum does not exceed 50% of Tier 1 capital (item 550). Any excess should be included in item 650 together with the difference between the nominal amount of dated preferred shares and subordinated, unsecured loan stock and the amortised amount.

Current year's profit & loss account—Form BSD1(2)

This form covers the reporting institution's profit & loss account for the current financial year up to the reporting date. It should be submitted on both a supervised entity (or solo consolidated) and consolidated basis (see Guidance Notes 3 & 4) at the same reporting dates as the Capital Adequacy Return (Form BSD1). For those reporting institutions which have elected to report at dates which do not coincide with their financial year end, this form should be completed as at their last management accounts. In such instances, the specific period covered should be inserted in the space provided.

Income

10 and 20 Interest received and receivable/Interest paid and payable

Include under these headings both interest actually received and paid, and interest receivable and payable which has accrued but has not yet been received or paid. Amounts accrued should be based on the latest date to which these calculations were made; thus for an institution which accrues profits on a daily basis, accruals should include amounts up to and including the reporting date. Also include under this heading income accrued in respect of the amortisation of discounts (and premiums) on the purchase of fixed maturity investments which are not held for dealing (eg Treasury Bills).

30 Net interest income

Show under this heading the net interest received and receivable (ie item 10 less item 20). Where interest paid and payable exceeds interest received and receivable the net figures should be shown in brackets to indicate a negative figure.

40 Profit/(Loss) on foreign exchange dealing

Revaluations of foreign exchange positions and, if identifiable, fees and commissions of foreign exchange business should be included under this heading. If it is not possible to identify fees and commissions derived from this activity separately, they should be included with other fees and commissions in item 70.

A net loss should be shown in brackets to indicate a negative figure.

Where the reporting institution is engaged in deposit swap dealing (also sometimes known as interest arbitrage dealing) and does not distinguish between profits and losses on the foreign exchange element of the transaction and the interest differential, the whole transaction should be shown under items 10 to 30; a deposit swap profit should be treated as income (item 10) and a loss as an expense (item 20).

50 Profit/(Loss) on investments held for dealing

Include all profits or losses (including revaluation profits or losses) other than those arising from the sale of investments in subsidiary or associated companies, trade investments or the amortisation of premiums or discounts on the purchase of fixed maturity investments which are not held for dealing.

70 Income from fees and commissions

Include charges made for services provided by the reporting institution, eg for the provision current account facilities, corporate advice, investment management and trustee services, guarantees and indemnities, commission on the sale of insurance or travellers cheques etc. Only include fees and commissions from customers for the provision of foreign exchange services if they cannot be separately identified and included under item 40.

80 Dividends/share of profits from subsidiary and associated companies

Reporting institutions reporting on an unconsolidated basis should include the dividends from other group companies only, together with the revaluation of any investment in subsidiaries or associates if equity accounting; those reporting on a consolidated basis should include only the share of profits from associated companies according to the normal convention of accounting as currently set out in Statement of Standard Accounting Practice number 1, 'Accounting for the Results of Associated Companies'.

90 Profit/(Loss) on fixed assets (including revaluation)

Include the profit or loss on the sale of non-trading assets of the reporting institution, eg premises, equipment, subsidiary and associated companies and trade investments. In respect of revaluation surpluses/deficits, reporting institutions should follow normal accounting practice: amounts in respect of surpluses/deficits normally taken to the profit and loss account, eg movements in provisions against trade investments, should be included in this item; amounts normally taken direct to reserves should not be included here.

100 Other income

Include under this heading income from any other source (other than extraordinary items which should be included under item 200).

Expenses

Operating expenses

110 Staff

Include salary costs, employer's national insurance contributions, the employer's contribution to any pension scheme, and the costs of staff benefits paid on a per capita basis such as private medical insurance and luncheon vouchers; general staff benefits, such as subsidised restaurants, should be included under 'occupancy' (item 120) or 'other' (item 130) as appropriate.

120 Occupancy

Include rates, rent, insurance of building, lighting, heating, depreciation and maintenance costs.

130 Other

This comprises all other expenditure.

140/150 Net charge/(credit) for provisions

This should equal item 40 on Form BSD1(3) (see relevant definition).

160 Provisions for taxation

For returns covering less than a year, the taxation charge should be estimated by applying a reasonable estimate of the reporting institution's effective tax rate applicable for the year in question.

170 Provisions for dividends

For returns covering less than a year, provision should be made for an appropriate portion of the estimated total dividend to be paid for the year.

200 Extraordinary items

Extraordinary items, as defined by Statement of Standard Accounting Practice number 6, should be reported net of attributable taxation. Where extraordinary charges exceed extraordinary income, the net negative figure should be shown in brackets.

Provisions against bad and doubtful debts and investments—Form BSD1(3)

10 Previous balance

Show the balance outstanding on the specific and general provisions account at the end of the previous accounting year relating to debts considered bad or doubtful. Do not include provisions made against the value of investments. The date to which the balance refers should be shown in the space provided.

20 Adjustments for acquisitions/disposals

Enter any adjustments made as a result of an acquisition or disposal of a subsidiary company the balance sheet of which includes specific or general provisions and is included in the consolidation for this particular return. Where the net adjustment is negative, report the amount in brackets.

30 Adjustments for exchange rate movements

Enter any adjustments made for exchange rate movements in respect of provisions denominated in currencies other than sterling. Where the adjustment is negative, report the amount in brackets.

40 Charge/credit to profit and loss account

Enter the net charge or credit to the profit and loss account in respect of provisions; this should equal items 140 and 150 on Form BSD1(2). A net credit should be shown in brackets. The gross charge for new provisions should be offset by other items including any provisions made in earlier years but now released in the current year's profit and loss account. The charge or credit for specific provisions should include the charge or credit for provisions in respect of suspended interest where it is the practice of the reporting institution to show suspended interest as interest receivable in the profit and loss account.

50 Amounts written off

Enter the gross amount written off (before recoveries which should be reported in item 60).

60 Recoveries of amounts previously written off

Enter the total amount of loans recovered which have previously been written off.

70 Other

Enter any other items, including exceptional provisions and transfers between general and specific provisions.

80 Current balance

The current balance should be the sum of items 10–70.

90–150 Specific provisions against bad and doubtful debts

In the relevant boxes, show the assets (by risk weights) against which specific provisions have been made. Total specific provisions (item 150) should equal column 1 of item 80 and the total of items 90 to 140. Include in column 1 earmarked general provisions which it has been agreed with BSD should be treated as specific provisions.

160 Gross value of loans against which specific provisions have been made

Enter the total gross value, before deduction of provisions, of loans against which specific provisions have been made.

Where specific provisions have been made against credit card lending, the aggregate value of these provisions should be reported here, and BSD informed as to the amount of this item relating to such provisions.

170–230 Provisions against the value of investments other than trading investments

Where the reporting institution carries provisions in its books for the diminution in value of investments other than trading investments they should be shown here, analysed according to the risk weighting of the investment to which they relate. Total provisions (item 230) should equal the total of items 170 to 220.

Analysis of large depositors—Form BSD1(4)

This form gives an analysis of the ten largest depositors with the reporting institution, including deposits and loans received from banks. Working capital in the form of deposits should also be included.

Customer

Where the same depositor/lender has made more than one deposit/loan, these should be aggregated for the purposes of this return. Where deposits/loans have been made by a group of connected depositors, they too should be aggregated and treated on this return as one deposit/loan.

Where the reporting bank acts as agent in its receipt of funds, such items should be excluded from this return. Fiduciary/agency funds received from *another* institution should where possible be reported according to the originator of those deposits.

Maturity date

Where deposits have been received with a variety of maturity dates from a depositor/ group of depositors, reporting institutions need not supply a full list of dates but may write the word 'various' in this column.

Currency

Enter in this column the currency rather than the amount of the deposit taken, eg USD, DM, FFr. A variety of currencies received from a depositor/group of depositors may be denoted by writing the word 'various' in this column.

Amount

Enter the sterling amount (or the sterling equivalent if a deposit is made in a currency other than sterling) of the deposit(s) taken. [821]

STATISTICAL NOTICE TO REPORTING BANKS

CAPITAL ADEQUACY TREATMENT OF DEFERRED TAX ASSETS

1 In a Notice on the Solvency Ratio Directive (BSD/1990/3) issued today, the Bank announced a change to its treatment of deferred tax assets in the measurement of capital adequacy (see paragraph 23). As a result, there is a change in the way in which these items should be reported for those institutions completing the Capital Adequacy Return (Form BSD1). There is no change in the reporting arrangements for other statistical returns submitted to the Bank associated with this modification.

2 With effect from the end-December 1990 returns, gross deferred tax assets should be reported in item 260.4 of Form BSD1 ('other assets', weighted at 100% in the calculation of the risk asset ratio) and no longer in item 730.3 as a negative liability. The amount of the item included within item 260.4 should be notified in a separate letter accompanying the form. Gross deferred tax assets should not include amounts resulting from recurring operational expenses.

3 In the event of any queries, please contact the Bank on the following telephone numbers or speak to your normal point of contact within Banking Supervision Division:

0171–601 5694/5078/5997

Bank of England
Banking Supervision Division
December 1990

[822]

BSD/1992/5
(August 1992)

VERIFICATION OF INTERIM PROFITS IN THE CONTEXT OF THE OWN FUNDS DIRECTIVE

Introduction

1 The Directive on Own Funds (89/299/EEC of 17 April 1989) specifies the items which for prudential supervision purposes may be included in the capital base, one of which is interim profits. The Bank presently allows current year profits of UK incorporated institutions, if published in the form of an interim statement, to be included in Tier 1 capital. The Own Funds Directive, however, does not draw a distinction between published and unpublished profits, and will result in a change in the criteria for inclusion of interim profits in capital.

2 The provisions of the Directive require that from **1 January 1993** current year interim profits will be included:

   (a) in Tier 1 capital if they have been verified by a bank's external auditors;[1]
   (b) in Tier 2 capital if they have been verified by a bank's internal audit department.[2]

3 In the absence of such verification current year interim profits will not be included in capital base.

4 This Notice outlines the scope of the work the Bank will expect external or internal auditors to do in verifying current year interim profits and the terms in which they should report. It only applies where an institution wishes to include these profits in its capital base for solo or consolidated supervision purposes.

5 The analytical review procedures commonly used by auditors in the normal course of their work can be helpful in this regard, and a combination of some of them will provide adequate assurance that reported interim profits are of sufficient quality for inclusion in the capital base, provided that the bank has complied in all material respects

with the valuation principles of the Bank Accounts Directive (86/635/EEC), as implemented in the UK.

6 The particular procedures which the Bank considers appropriate for this purpose are listed below (paras 7 and 9). A full scope audit is not required, but in situations where the scope of work carried out differs materially from that set out in this Notice, the Bank will expect to be informed by the auditor in his report.

---

[1] Article 1(2) of 89/299/EEC.
[2] Article 3(1)(c) of 89/299/EEC.

Interim profits – Eligibility for Tier 1 capital

7 Verification by **external** auditors should in normal circumstances entail at least the following:

    (a) satisfying themselves that the figures forming the basis of the interim profits have been properly extracted from the underlying accounting records;

    (b) reviewing the accounting policies used in calculating the interim profits so as to obtain comfort that they are consistent with those normally adopted by the institution in drawing up its annual financial statements and are in accordance with the principles set out in the Bank Accounts Directive;

    (c) performing analytical procedures on the result to date, including comparisons of actual performance to date with budget and with the results of prior period(s);

    (d) discussing with management the overall performance and financial position of the institution;

    (e) obtaining adequate comfort that the implications of current and prospective litigation, all known claims and commitments, changes in business activities and provisioning for bad and doubtful debts have been properly taken into account in arriving at the interim profits; and

    (f) following up problem areas of which the auditors are already aware in the course of auditing the institution's financial statements.

8 The external auditors must submit an opinion to the institution on whether the interim results are fairly stated. The required report, set out in the annex to this Notice, should be attached to a copy of Form BSD1(2) or, in the case of institutions which report via electronic media, a hardcopy of the results submitted to the Bank, and sent to the relevant contact in BSD.

Interim profits – Eligibility for Tier 2 capital

9 Verification by *internal* auditors should in normal circumstances entail at least the following:

    (a) satisfying himself that the figures forming the basis of the interim profits have been properly extracted from the underlying accounting records;

    (b) reviewing the accounting policies used in the determination of interim profits so as to obtain comfort that they are consistent with those normally adopted by the institution in drawing up its annual financial statements, and are in accordance with the principles set out in the Bank Accounts Directive;

    (c) performing a comparison of current performance against budget and prior periods; and

    (d) enquiring into the adequacy of provisions for bad and doubtful debts.

10 If an institution has no separate internal audit function, its board of directors may, with the Bank's prior consent, appoint a suitably qualified member of management with no day to day responsibility for the accounting records to act as internal auditor for this purpose.

11 The Bank will require the internal auditor to evidence his review of the interim profits by countersigning a copy of Form BSD(2) and sent to the relevant contact in BSD.

Interim losses

12 Interim losses, as reported in other prudential returns already submitted to the Bank, will continue to be deducted immediately from Tier 1 capital.

Annex   External auditors' report on interim profits

The Board of Directors, ABC Bank Limited

Dear Sirs

In accordance with your letter of instruction dated [   ], a copy of which is attached, we have reviewed [name of bank's] current year interim profits for the period [   ] as reported on Form BSD1(2) dated ......, a copy of which is attached for identification. Our review, which did not constitute an audit, has been carried out having regard to the Bank of England's Notice [BSD/1991/-] of [   ].

On the basis of the results of our review, nothing came to our attention to indicate that:

   (a) the interim profits as reported on Form BSD1(2) have not been calculated on the basis of the accounting policies adopted by the bank in preparing its latest statutory accounts for the year to ......;

   (b) those accounting policies differ in any material respects from those required by the [Bank Accounts Directive as implemented in the UK] [except for ......];

   (c) the interim profits amounting to £ ..... as so reported are not reasonably stated.

Yours faithfully

Chartered Accountants   **[823]**

LETTER TO AUTHORISED INSTITUTIONS CONCERNING DEBT PROVISIONING (THE NEW MATRIX)

(February 1993)
Bank of England
Banking Supervision Division

To UK incorporated authorised institutions with exposures to countries experiencing debt servicing and repayment difficulties

Country debt provisioning matrix

In January 1990 the Bank wrote to all UK incorporated institutions authorised under the Banking Act with exposures to countries experiencing debt repayment and servicing difficulties. That letter set out a number of technical changes and a significant increase in the average level of provisions produced by the application of the matrix, which was originally issued in 1987.

The Bank has again reviewed the matrix, this time with the aim of simplifying the scoring process, yet at the same time ensuring that the scores generate provisioning levels which continue to be appropriate. The result of this review is a simplified structure and application of the matrix.

A copy of the revised matrix is attached; the Bank proposes that it should be used in the same manner as the existing framework, that is as a basis for discussion between the Bank and each institution.

I would like to draw your attention to a number of the changes which have been made.

   (i) The recommended provisioning bands are abolished and replaced with a recommended minimum provisioning level. A continuous relationship is introduced between the matrix score and the recommended minimum provisioning level.

(ii) In the 1990 revision of the matrix it was suggested that no provisions were required where the score was less than 10. To increase the confidence when provisions are first recommended it is now suggested that no provisions are required until a score of 30 or more is reached.

(iii) To enable provisions to react more swiftly to changing circumstances, the 5-quarter moving average system has been replaced by the latest score in all situations.

(iv) The number of columns in the matrix have been reduced from 16 to 12 and the significance of the 'C' factors have been increased.

(v) To ensure that arbitrary anniversary changes do not have a disproportionate impact on the overall scores, the scoring of the individual columns has been smoothed as described in the annex to the attached paper.

The revised matrix will be first applied in relation to discussions on provisioning as at 30 June 1993.

The Inland Revenue has today issued draft regulations amending the Treasury matrix used in computing the tax allowable provisions against banks' sovereign debt. The draft regulations take into account the changes now being made to the matrix.

Country debt provisioning

Introduction

1 The Bank considers that, for supervisory purposes, it is desirable to set out a framework within which an appropriate level of provision against sovereign and other country risk exposures can be assessed. The matrix which is attached to this paper has been devised to allow such a view to be formed on a country by country basis.

The Matrix

2 There are three stages in the process of deciding an appropriate level of provision:

(i) to identify countries with current or potential repayment difficulties;

(ii) to identify the nature of those difficulties and the extent of the country's problems; and

(iii) to determine, at this point, what proportion of exposures to that country is unlikely to be repaid in full.

3 A number of factors or criteria can be identified to help make this decision. These factors can be incorporated in a matrix and weighted to reflect their relative significance for determining the appropriate level of provision in respect of an exposure. They fall into three categories, namely:

A Factors   which evidence a borrower's inability or unwillingness to meet its obligations, whether at the due date or thereafter;

B Factors   which show a borrower's current difficulties in meeting its obligations; and

C Factors   which provide evidence of the likelihood of repayment difficulties either persisting or arising in the future.

4 The matrix includes a total of 12 factors under these three categories. They can be applied to any country and to any type of exposure taken either in aggregate or by type of exposure. The aim has been to identify a range of observable factors which point to the likelihood of a partial or total failure to repay. For this reason differing levels of maximum score are attributed to the different factors, reflecting their perceived relative weight in the aggregate assessment of repayment difficulties.

5 The factors and the weights attaching to them are set out in the matrix which is attached to this paper, together with a note of the definitions to be used in completing it. Only one factor (12) is to be weighted within a range according to individual judgment.

6 It is suggested that a minimum score of 30 is required before the appropriateness of provisioning needs to be considered.

Method of scoring

7 The total score for a country is simply the sum of the individual scores for each factor. Changes in the circumstances of individual countries should be taken account of by updating country scores whenever provisioning levels are redetermined.

8 In order to introduce a continuous relationship between matrix scores and recommended minimum provisioning levels it is recommended that the following linear relationship should be adopted.

Recommended minimum provision level = Matrix score −25

Countries which score less than 25 will attract no provisioning requirement. In addition scores of 25 to 29 should also attract zero provisions, so that the first recommended minimum provisioning level will be 5%. The maximum recommended minimum provisioning level regardless of score should be 95%. Therefore all scores greater than 120 will require a recommended minimum provisioning level of 95%.

Scope of application

9 There are two alternatives:

(i) to apply the factors and resulting provisioning percentage against all claims on a country;

(ii) to apply the factors and resulting provision percentage separately to different classes of asset.

The Bank's view is that, for supervisory purposes, the percentage provision should be applied to a bank's total exposure to, including risk transfers to and excluding risk transfers from, a particular country, unless it can be satisfied that a particular claim or class of claims will be repaid in full.

Banking Supervision Division
Bank of England
February 1993

Annex

Country debt provisioning matrix

Notes on column definitions

'A' Factors

(1) RESCHEDULED AT ANY TIME IN THE LAST 5 YEARS, OR IN THE PROCESS OF RESCHEDULING, OR IS REFUSING TO CO-OPERATE IN THE RESCHEDULING PROCESS, OR HAS SIGNIFICANT TRANSFER PROBLEMS AND/OR A LIMIT ON DEBT SERVICING WITHOUT AGREEMENT FROM CREDITORS[1]

Score a country that has rescheduled[2] either commercial or official debt in the last five years. Score 2 for a rescheduling agreement signed more than 54 months and up to, and including 60 months ago; score 4 for more than 48 months and up to, and including 54 months ago; score 6 for more than 42 months and up to, and including 48 months ago; score 8 for more than 36 months and up to, and including 42 months ago; score 10 for more than 30 months and up to, and including 36 months ago; score 12 for more than 24 months and up to, and including 30 months ago; score 14 for more than 18 months and up to, and including 24 months ago; score 16 for more than 12 months and up to, and including 18 months ago; score 18 for more than 6 months and up to, and including 12 months ago. Score 20 for:

(i) an agreement signed up to 6 months ago;

(ii) an agreement in principle to reschedule;

(iii) a country which, exceptionally, is refusing to co-operate in the rescheduling process; or

(iv) a country which has significant transfer problems and/or a limit on debt servicing without agreement from creditors.

(2) SECOND OR MORE RESCHEDULING DURING THE LAST 5 YEARS OF PRINCIPAL AMOUNTS RESCHEDULED SINCE JANUARY 1983, OR NEW MONEY TO CLEAR ARREARS, OR CAPITALISATION

CATEGORY	'A' Factors		'B' Factors		'C' Factors								Total score (Max 150)	Recommended minimum provisioning level
COLUMN	1	2	3	4	5	6	7	8	9	10	11	12		
DEFINITION	Rescheduled at any time in the last 5 years, or in the process of rescheduling, or is refusing to co-operate in the rescheduling process, or has significant transfer problems and/or a link on debt servicing without agreement from creditors.	Second or more rescheduling during the last 5 years of principal amounts rescheduled since Jan 1983, or new money to clear arrears, or capitalisation of interest arrears, or rescheduling of principal arrears, or is refusing to co-operate in the rescheduling process, or has significant transfer problems and/or a limit on debt servicing without agreement from creditors.	Significant arrears of interest or principal to IFIs.	Arrears of interest or principal on original or rescheduled loans from other external creditors; excluding agreed arrears.	Debts/GDP ratio	Debts/exports ratio	Scheduled debt service/exports ratio	Scheduled interest service/exports ratio	Visible import cover	Not meeting IMF targets/ unwilling to go to IMF	Secondary market price	Other Factors		
SCORE RANGE	< = 6 mths = 20 < = 12 mths = 18 < = 18 mths = 16 < = 24 mths = 14 < = 30 mths = 12 < = 36 mths = 10 < = 42 mths = 8 < = 48 mths = 6 < = 54 mths = 4 < = 60 mths = 2	2-20	10	< = 6 mths = 10 < = 12 mths = 15 > 12 mths = 20	> = 30% = 2 > = 50% = 4 > = 70% = 6 > = 90% = 8 > = 110% = 10	> = 165% = 2 > = 275% = 4 > = 385% = 6 > = 495% = 8 > = 605% = 10	> = 18% = 2 > = 30% = 4 > = 42% = 6 > = 54% = 8 > = 66% = 10	> = 12% = 2 > = 20% = 4 > = 28% = 6 > = 36% = 8 > = 44% = 10	< = 4.0 = 2 < = 3.0 = 4 < = 2.0 = 6 < = 1.0 = 8 < = 0.5 = 10	5	< = 95% = 2 < = 85% = 4 < = 75% = 6 < = 65% = 8 < = 55% = 10 < = 45% = 12 < = 35% = 14 < = 25% = 16 < = 15% = 18 < = 5% = 20	-5 to 5		
	2-20	2-20	10	10, 15 OR 20	2-10	2-10	2-10	2-10	2-10	5	2-20	-5 TO 5	TOTAL	
Country														

OF INTEREST ARREARS, OR RESCHEDULING OF PRINCIPAL ARREARS, OR IS REFUSING TO CO-
OPERATE IN THE RESCHEDULING PROCESS, OR HAS SIGNIFICANT TRANSFER PROBLEMS AND/OR A
LIMIT ON DEBT SERVICING WITHOUT AGREEMENT FROM CREDITORS[1]

Score a country that has rescheduled[2] principal amounts already rescheduled since
January 1983, or has received new money to clear arrears, or has capitalised interest
arrears, or has rescheduled principal arrears. Score 2 for an agreement signed more than
54 months and up to, and including 60 months ago; score 4 for more than 48 months and
up to, and including 54 months ago; score 6 for more than 42 months and up to, and
including 48 months ago; score 8 for more than 36 months and up to, and including 42
months ago; score 10 for more than 30 months and up to, and including 36 months ago;
score 12 for more than 24 months and up to, and including 30 months ago; score 14 for
more than 18 months and up to, and including 24 months ago; score 16 for more than 12
months and up to, and including 18 months ago; score 18 for more than 6 months and up
to, and including 12 months ago. Score 20 for:

   (i) an agreement signed up to 6 months ago;
   (ii) an agreement in principle to reschedule, etc;
   (iii) a country which, exceptionally, in the last five years has been refusing to
      co-operate in the rescheduling process, or has significant transfer problems
      and/or a limit on debt servicing without agreement from creditors such that it
      would have had to reschedule at least twice in the last five years and in all
      probability would still have arrears.

---

[1] *Creditor:* It is only intended that problems in respect of a general class of creditors should be
scored. Thus, suspension of payments to an individual creditor or creditor country would not be
scored.
[2] *Rescheduling (columns 1 and 2):* For these purposes, rescheduling is defined broadly to include
restructuring agreements which reduce a country's debt or debt servicing obligations.

'B' Factors

(3) SIGNIFICANT ARREARS OF INTEREST OR PRINCIPAL TO IFI'S

Score a country that is in arrears[1] on either interest or principal to the International
Financial Institutions (IMF, World Bank, Regional Development Banks, etc) over the
threshold to be declared ineligible to draw on the General Resources Account (in the
case of the IMF) or to stop disbursement of all loans (in the case of the World Bank and
Regional Development Banks). Score 10 for a country that is in arrears.

(4) ARREARS OF INTEREST OR PRINCIPAL ON ORIGINAL OR RESCHEDULED LOANS FROM OTHER EXTERNAL CREDITORS; EXCLUDING AGREED ARREARS

Score a country that is in arrears[1] on interest or principal on loans (either original or
rescheduled) from external creditors other than those taken into account in column (3).
Exclude arrears effectively capitalised with the agreement of creditors during negotiation of a financing package. Score 10 for arrears in existence for up to, and including 6
months; score 15 for over 6 months and up to, and including 12 months; score 20 for over
12 months.

---

[1] *Arrears (columns 3 and 4):* Arrears arising out of temporary administrative delay which are
expected to be corrected within a relatively short period of time should not be scored, whereas
generalised and non-correcting arrears should be scored. Arrears by private sector debtors should
not be scored unless they are caused by actions (such as exchange restrictions or payment delays)
taken by public sector authorities in the debtor country.

'C' Factors

(5) DEBT/GDP RATIO

This is defined as total external debt divided by Gross Domestic Product for the latest
available 12 month period, expressed as a percentage rounded to the nearest one tenth
of a percentage point. Score 2 for a ratio between 30.0% and 49.9%; score 4 between
50.0% and 69.9%; score 6 between 70.0% and 89.9%; score 8 between 90% and
109.9%; score 10 for 110.0% or more.

(6) DEBT/EXPORTS RATIO

This is defined as total external debt divided by the value of exports of goods and services (including interest receipts and other factor services) for the latest available 12 month period, expressed as a percentage rounded to the nearest one tenth of a percentage point. Score 2 for a ratio between 165.0% and 274.9%; score 4 between 275.0% and 384.9%; score 6 between 385.0% and 494.9%; score 8 between 495.0% and 604.9%; score 10 for 605.0% or more.

(7) SCHEDULED DEBT SERVICE/EXPORTS RATIO

This is defined as the total of interest and principal[1] payable (including any interest and/or principal due but not paid) during the latest available 12 month period, divided by the value of exports of goods and services (including interest receipts and other factor services) for the latest available 12 month period, expressed as a percentage rounded to the nearest one tenth of a percentage point. Score 2 for a ratio between 18.0% and 29.9%; score 4 between 30.0% and 41.9%; score 6 between 42.0% and 53.9%; score 8 between 54.0% and 65.9%; score 10 for 66.0% or more.

[1] Does not include principal repayments of debt of less than 12 months' maturity.

(8) SCHEDULED INTEREST SERVICE/EXPORTS RATIO

This is defined as interest payable (including any interest due but not paid) during the latest available 12 month period, divided by the value of exports of goods and services (including interest receipts and other factor services) for the latest available 12 month period, expressed as a percentage rounded to the nearest one tenth of a percentage point. Score 2 for a ratio between 12.0% and 19.9%; score 4 between 20.0% and 27.9%; score 6 between 28.0% and 35.9%; score 8 between 36.0% and 43.9%; score 10 for 44.0% or more.

(9) VISIBLE IMPORT COVER

This is defined as the value of imports of goods for the latest available 12 month period, divided by 12 and then divided into the value of reserves at the latest available date, the result rounded to the nearest one tenth of a month. Reserves should include gold valued at 75% of the market price at the relevant date. Score 2 for import cover between 4.0 and 3.1 months; score 4 between 3.0 and 2.1 months; score 6 between 2.0 and 1.1 months; score 8 between 1.0 and 0.6 months; score 10 for 0.5 months or less.

(10) NOT MEETING IMF TARGETS/UNWILLING TO GO TO IMF

Score 5 for a country which is in breach of IMF targets (ie performance criteria for any programme) or is unable or unwilling to go to the IMF.

(11) SECONDARY MARKET PRICE

Score a country whose debt is quoted on the secondary market[1]. Score 2 where the mean of bid and offer prices is between 95.0% and 85.1%; score 4 between 85.0% and 75.1%; score 6 between 75.0% and 65.1%; score 8 between 65.0% and 55.1%; score 10 between 55.0% and 45.1%; score 12 between 45.0% and 35.1%; score 14 between 35.0% and 25.1%; score 16 between 25.0% and 15.1%; score 18 between 15.0% and 5.1%; score 20 for 5.0% or less.

[1] Price quotations should refer wherever possible to floating rate debt which is not collateralised, guaranteed or otherwise enhanced.

(12) OTHER FACTORS

Score any number from −5 to +5, depending on your assessment of other conditions in the country (whether economic or political) which affect its ability to repay indebtedness both now and in the future.   **[824]**

BSD/1993/1
(March 1993)

CONSOLIDATED SUPERVISION OF INSTITUTIONS AUTHORISED UNDER THE BANKING ACT 1987

1 This Notice, which takes immediate effect, applies to all institutions authorised under the Banking Act 1987 which are incorporated in the United Kingdom.[1] It implements the Council Directive on the Supervision of Credit Institutions on a Consolidated Basis (92/30/EEC), which replaces the Council Directive of 13 June 1983 (83/350/EEC). The Bank's Notice BSD/1986/3 implementing the 1983 Directive, and the Notices BSD/1989/2 and BSD/1990/4, which amend the 1986 Notice, are therefore withdrawn. The principle of consolidated supervision itself is already reflected in the Banking Act 1987, but changes to the Bank's information gathering powers, required by the Directive, have been implemented by amendments to the Act made by The Banking Co-ordination (Second Council Directive) Regulations 1992.[2]

[1] The institutions covered by this Notice will be referred to as 'authorised institutions' without further qualification. The discount houses will be notified separately of the arrangements for their consolidated supervision.
[2] SI 1992/3218, available from Her Majesty's Stationery Office.

Introduction

2 The Bank is committed to the principle that the supervision of authorised institutions should be conducted on a consolidated basis, whenever such institutions are members of a wider group. The principles previously governing the Bank's consolidated supervision have been based on the Council Directive on consolidated supervision (83/350/EEC) and the 1983 Basle Concordat, with a broader scope of supervision being applied when the Bank judged this to be appropriate. Following adoption of the Council Directive 92/30/EEC,[1] the Bank has carried out a review of the way in which it conducts consolidated supervision, given the Directive's focus on a wider range of financial services and on a wider scope of supervision than its predecessor. In some cases the Bank has concluded that its existing consolidated supervision already complies with the Directive's requirements, but changes in the nature and scope of the Bank's consolidated supervision will be required in other cases. In these instances the Bank believes that the requisite changes will enhance its ability to monitor the risks to authorised institutions arising from other group companies.

3 'Consolidation' is used in this Notice to mean the preparation of consolidated returns covering a group, or part of a group. The term 'consolidated supervision' is used to mean a qualitative assessment of the overall strength of a group to which an authorised institution belongs, to evaluate the potential impact of other group companies on the authorised institution. This assessment will be based on a number of sources of information, one of which will be the consolidated returns. Consolidated supervision also takes into account the activities of group companies which are not included in the consolidated returns because the nature of their assets is such that their inclusion would not be meaningful, for example industrial or insurance companies. The Bank employs a number of different approaches to assess the potential impact of these companies on the authorised institution, and expects to have regular discussions with those members of the group's management who are familiar with, and have responsibility for, the overall group position.

4 The Bank will take account of the activities of group companies to the extent that they may have a material bearing on the reputation and financial soundness of the authorised institution in the group. It must be emphasised that the focus of the Bank's supervision remains the authorised institution itself. The purpose of consolidated supervision is not to supervise all the companies in a group to which a bank belongs, but to supervise the bank as part of its group.

5 The Bank regards consolidated supervision as a complement to, rather than a substitute for, the solo supervision of the authorised institution. Events elsewhere in the group and the activities of other group companies can pose a threat to the authorised

institution in ways which consolidated supervision cannot detect. For example, intra-group linkages arising from transactions between the bank and other group companies will only be revealed by the solo supervision of the bank. Hence the Bank will continue to set solo capital adequacy ratios and large exposures limits for authorised institutions in addition to those which will apply at the consolidated level.

[1] Referred to as the 'Consolidated Supervision Directive' throughout this Notice.

Capital adequacy and large exposures

6 The Bank will require authorised institutions to submit, at least twice each year, consolidated returns covering capital adequacy and large exposures.

7 To assess capital adequacy (other than for market risks) on a consolidated basis, the Bank will apply the Own Funds Directive and the Solvency Ratio Directive, as implemented by the Bank's relevant policy Notices in force. Authorised institutions will be set a consolidated risk assets ratio, in addition to that set on a solo basis.

8 Capital adequacy in respect of market risks (including foreign exchange and interest rate related risks) incurred both by banks and by other group entities principally exposed to market risk will be assessed by a system based on the forthcoming directive on the capital adequacy of investment firms and credit institutions. Pending implementation of this directive, which is likely to be required by 31 December 1995, the Bank intends to employ, for group companies which are not authorised institutions, the interim system outlined in paragraphs 20–23 of this Notice; the interim arrangements for monitoring the market risks of authorised institutions will continue to employ the proxy risk weightings based on the Solvency Ratio Directive.

9 The measurement on a consolidated basis of the concentration of risk and large exposures to individual borrowers or closely related borrowers will be based on the Large Exposures Directive (the implementation of which is required by 1 January 1994). Pending the implementation of this Directive, the system of measurement for the concentration of risk will remain that set out in the Bank's Notice BSD/1987/1 ('Large Exposures undertaken by institutions authorised under the Banking Act 1987') and amendments.

10 In accordance with article 3.6 of the Consolidated Supervision Directive, the Bank will also require authorised institutions to have adequate internal control mechanisms for the production of any data and information which would be relevant for the purposes of supervision on a consolidated basis. The Bank will, therefore, include within the scope of reports commissioned under section 39 of the Banking Act 1987 examinations of the adequacy of internal control systems to generate this data and information.

Scope of consolidation

11 The Bank regards the principles laid down in the Consolidated Supervision Directive as minimum standards, and it will extend its consolidated supervision beyond the requirements of the directive where it judges that to do so results in a more accurate assessment of risk to the authorised institution.

12 The Bank will require consolidation in the following cases:

(i) When the authorised institution is itself the parent of companies which conduct one or more of the activities listed on the Annex to this Notice; and

(ii) When the authorised institution is not the parent company, but is part of a group or sub-group whose business wholly or mainly comprises the activities listed in the Annex to this Notice, and the parent of which is itself a financial institution. To qualify as a financial institution the exclusive or main business of the parent company must be either to carry out one or more of the activities listed in the Annex, or to acquire holdings in companies undertaking these activities.

13 The Bank will interpret the phrases 'mainly' and 'main business' to mean the balance of business, ie it will generally require consolidation when companies carrying out the listed activities comprise the majority (over 50%) of the group or sub-group

balance sheet. In determining the balance of business the Bank will additionally take account of the off-balance sheet activities of group companies, and of fee-based services provided by group companies. Where such a balance of business test proves inconclusive, the Bank will take into consideration the number of subsidiaries which fall into the financial and non-financial categories. As a general rule, the presumption will be in favour of consolidation.

14 Where consolidation of a group is required it will extend to all financial companies in the group, including the parent company itself, subsidiaries of the parent company, and companies in which the parent company or its subsidiaries have a participation of 20% or more of the voting rights or capital ('participations'). Companies whose business is not covered by the list of activities contained in the Annex will not usually be included in the consolidation; however, the Bank may, at its discretion, require their inclusion. When the Bank agrees that a company is to be excluded from consolidation, the investment of the parent in that company will be deducted from the authorised institution's consolidated capital for the assessment of capital adequacy.

15 In certain cases an authorised institution will already be subject to the consolidated supervision of another EC supervisor. The Bank may, at its discretion, agree to forgo consolidation in that case, following discussion with the other supervisor. In those instances in which an authorised institution is a member of a group with banks in a number of other EC Member States, the Bank will generally take the view that responsibility for consolidated supervision should fall to the EC supervisor within whose jurisdiction the principal bank in the group is incorporated.

16 Consolidation of a group whose parent company is incorporated in a country which is not a member of the EC will not normally be required; in determining the appropriate treatment in these cases the Bank will take into account whether or not the parent company is subject to the consolidated supervision of another supervisor which adheres to the Basle minimum standards for the supervision of international banking groups and their cross-border establishments. However, in those cases in which the Bank determines that a group consolidation would not be appropriate, if the authorised institution has any subsidiaries, sub-consolidation will nonetheless usually be required.

Definition of subsidiary and participation

17 The definition of parent and subsidiary which should be applied in the preparation of consolidated returns to the Bank is that contained in the seventh company law directive (83/349/EC); this concept is implemented in the UK in section 258 of the Companies Act 1985. In addition, the threshold for the consolidation of group companies which are not subsidiaries – 'participations' – is the ownership of 20% or more of the voting rights or capital.

18 Consolidation will also normally be required of companies over which the parent or another group company exercises 'dominant influence'. In determining whether or not dominant influence exists the Bank will generally make use of the definition provided by the contemporary UK accounting standards (at present the Accounting Standards Board's Financial Reporting Standard 2 (FRS 2), 'Accounting for Subsidiary Undertakings').

Technique of consolidation

19 The technique of consolidation which will usually be required will be full consolidation for all majority shareholdings, and normally of participations. The Bank will apply proportionate ('pro rata') consolidation to participations in only exceptional circumstances, where it is satisfied that there are other significant shareholders who have the means and the will to provide as much parental support to the entity as the shareholder subject to consolidated supervision. This criterion is usually most likely to be met by another bank.

Interim arrangements for the treatment of group companies principally exposed to market risk

20 Pending implementation of the forthcoming directive on the capital adequacy of investment firms and credit institutions, the Bank will use an interim system for the

consolidated capital adequacy treatment of group undertakings principally exposed to market risk, under the national discretion provided for by article 9.2 of the Consolidated Supervision Directive. For large exposures purposes, these entities will be included in the consolidated returns according to the approach referred to in paragraph 9 of this Notice.

21 The Bank will ensure that its assessment of capital adequacy on a consolidated basis reflects the risks incurred by group undertakings which are principally exposed to market risks. In the Bank's view, the various capital adequacy regimes applied to companies supervised in connection with the Financial Services Act 1986 (including those of Securities and Investments Board, the Securities and Futures Authority, and the Bank's Wholesale Markets Supervision Division) provide close approximations to the risk measurement framework which will be introduced for these companies by the forthcoming capital adequacy directive. Accordingly, the Bank will institute a system of reports designed to make use of these risk measurement frameworks. These reports, produced by the above mentioned supervisors on the basis of information routinely submitted to them by the companies concerned, will be based on an assessment of the risks in the companies as measured by the appropriate supervisor's system of risk measurement, together with an assessment of the capital cover, also on the basis of the same supervisor's system of measurement. In the event that the Bank is informed of a capital deficiency, the Bank will deduct the deficiency from the group's consolidated capital, in addition to the investment in the group company as shown in the group's statutory accounts, and will notify the authorised institution accordingly. Where the reports show the group company to have adequate capital cover, only the value of the investment will be deducted from the group's consolidated capital.

22 Exposures to group companies which are subject to this treatment will, with the Bank's agreement, attract a nil weighting for the purposes of the calculation of the reporting bank's consolidated capital adequacy, in addition to the concessionary treatment of these exposures for solo capital adequacy outlined in paragraph 27.

23 This system will only be applied to those group companies which are principally exposed to market risks and which are supervised in connection with the Financial Services Act 1986. Group companies which are principally exposed to market risks but which are not so supervised will be included in the reporting institution's consolidated returns according to the system of risk measurement based on the Solvency Ratio Directive.

Exceptions to consolidation

24 In a limited number of cases the Bank may permit the exclusion from a group's consolidated returns of subsidiaries and participations which otherwise meet the criteria for consolidation, as provided for by article 3.3 of the Consolidated Supervision Directive:

  (i)   Where inclusion would be inappropriate or misleading;
  (ii) Where institutions within the overall group to be consolidated have a combined balance sheet total of the lower of less than ECU 10 million or 1% of the balance sheet total of the parent (the 'de minimis' exemption);
  (iii) Where there are legal impediments to the transfer of information. Use of this reason for exclusion other than on a temporary basis is likely to be inconsistent with the Basle Minimum Standards and would therefore have to be considered in this light.

The Bank's prior consent must be sought for all proposals to exclude subsidiaries or participations from consolidation.

Distribution of capital resources within the group

25 The Bank will normally apply the same capital ratio to the group as a whole as it applies to the principal bank in the group. Factors which are taken into account in setting a consolidated ratio which differs from that set for the principal bank on a solo basis include: the location of capital in the group, in particular to ensure that reliance is not being placed on surplus capital which is locked in to particular companies or

countries because of regulatory considerations, exchange controls, or taxation; the degree of risk diversification in the group as a whole compared to that of the bank or banks within it; and any risks which arise on a group basis but which are not reflected in the factors influencing the ratio appropriate for the principal bank in the group.

26 Since consolidated supervision does not replace supervision on a solo basis, but is complementary to it, authorised institutions which are members of groups subject to the Bank's consolidated supervision will be expected to maintain minimum capital ratios in line with those expected of entirely independent banks undertaking the same range and scale of business. However, authorised institutions which meet the criteria set out in paragraph 27 will normally be set a capital ratio which is the same as the capital ratio set for the consolidated group, unless there are particular circumstances which warrant a different ratio.

Concessionary weighting of intra-group exposures

27 To minimise double counting of capital requirements, exposures to another group company will be nil-weighted for the calculation of the reporting institution's solo capital ratio in circumstances agreed by the Bank to meet the following criteria:

(i) the group is managed as an integrated banking business by a United Kingdom bank, which is the principal bank in the group; and

(ii) the other group company is consolidated for the purposes of calculating the group's consolidated capital ratio; and

(iii) capital resources are freely transferable between the other group company and the principal bank in the group.

Solo consolidation

28 In calculating an authorised institution's solo ratio the Bank is prepared to consider the consolidation of certain subsidiaries, specifically where all the following conditions apply:

(i) the subsidiary is at least 75% owned by the reporting institution;

(ii) either the subsidiary is wholly funded by its parent bank or all of its exposure to risk is wholly in respect of its parent bank;

(iii) the management is under the effective direction of the parent bank;

(iv) it is clear that there are no potential obstacles to the payment of surplus capital up to the parent bank, in particular taking account of overseas exchange controls, potential legal and regulatory problems and taxation; and

(v) there is sufficient capital in the bank's own balance sheet to fund its investments in those subsidiaries which are to be solo consolidated (ie if the investments were to be deducted rather than solo consolidated, the parent should be left with positive net worth).

Groups not subject to consolidation

29 In those cases in which an authorised institution belongs to a group for which the Bank determines consolidation would be inappropriate (for example in cases where the preponderance of the group's business comprises industrial or insurance business), the Bank will require the parent institution and its other subsidiaries to supply it with any data or information which it considers relevant to the purpose of supervising the authorised institution. The Bank may also, from time to time, seek to have the information with which it is supplied verified by the authorised institution's reporting accountants.

30 When the parent of an authorised institution is an insurance company the Bank will not normally require consolidation, pending further harmonisation of the basis of accounting for banks and insurance companies. However, the Bank will wish to liaise with the supervisors of the insurance company parent.

Annex   Financial activities to be consolidated

Companies undertaking one or more of these activities are classified as 'financial' for the purposes of this Notice.

1 Ancillary Banking Services (defined as: 'an undertaking the principal activity of which consists in owning and managing property, managing data processing services, or any other similar activity which is ancillary to the principal activity of one or more credit institutions').

2 Lending (including, inter alia, consumer credit, mortgage credit, factoring with or without recourse, financing of commercial transactions (including forfaiting)).

3 Financial leasing.

4 Money transmission services.

5 Issuing and administering means of payment (eg credit cards, travellers' cheques and bankers' drafts).

6 Guarantees and commitments.

7 Trading for own account or account of customers in:

(a) money market instruments (cheques, bills, CDs etc);
(b) foreign exchange;
(c) financial futures and options;
(d) exchange and interest rate instruments;
(e) transferable securities.

8 Participation in securities issues and the provision of services relating to such issues.

9 Advice to undertakings on capital structure, industrial strategy and related questions and advice and services relating to mergers and the purchase of undertakings.

10 Money broking.

11 Portfolio management and advice.

12 Safekeeping and administration of securities.   **[825]**

STATEMENTS OF PRINCIPLES BANKING ACT 1987 BANKING COORDINATION (SECOND COUNCIL DIRECTIVE) REGULATIONS 1992

(May 1993)

BANKING ACT 1987, SECTION 16

1 Introduction

1.1 This statement applies generally to all institutions authorised by the Bank under the Banking Act 1987 ('the Act').[1] In a number of instances however different provisions of the Act apply to institutions which are not credit institutions incorporated under the law of the UK (see specific references). The statement is made pursuant to section 16 of the Banking Act which requires the Bank to publish a statement of the principles in accordance with which it is acting or proposing to act:

'(a) in interpreting the criteria specified in Schedule 3 to this Act and the grounds for revocation specified in section 11 . . .; and
(b) in exercising its power to grant, revoke or restrict an authorisation.'

1.2 These principles are, however, not only relevant to the Bank's decisions on whether to authorise an institution or revoke or restrict an authorisation. The Bank's interpretation of the Schedule 3 criteria and of the section 11 grounds for revocation, together with the principles underlying the exercise of its powers to grant, revoke or restrict authorisation, encapsulate the main standards and considerations to which the Bank has regard in conducting its supervision of all authorised institutions. The functions of banking supervision therefore include monitoring the compliance of authorised institutions with these standards and identifying any threats to the interests of depositors and potential depositors. If there are concerns, the Bank will consider what action should be taken to ensure compliance with these standards and to protect depositors and potential depositors. Where appropriate it will seek remedial action by persuasion and encouragement. However, if its legal powers are exercisable and the Bank judges that it is necessary to exercise them in order to ensure compliance with the standards or to protect the interests of depositors and potential depositors it will move to revoke or restrict authorisation.

1.3 The Act requires institutions and their officers and controllers to meet high standards in terms of their conduct. The maintenance of those standards benefits not only depositors and potential depositors but also the interests of the institution's other customers. Nevertheless the Bank's powers under the Act focus primarily on the interests of depositors.

1.4 The statement includes references to various papers published by the Bank which set out its detailed approach to a number of matters relevant to the principles, and the principles should be interpreted accordingly. Copies are available from Banking Supervision Division, Bank of England, Threadneedle Street, London EC2R 8AH (tel: 0171–601 5082).[2]

1.5 Part 2 of the statement considers the interpretation of each of the minimum authorisation criteria in Schedule 3. Part 3 considers some issues which relate only to authorised institutions which are discount houses. Part 4 sets out the considerations relevant to the Bank's exercise of its discretion to grant authorisation. It includes some paragraphs on the authorisation of overseas institutions. Part 5 considers the interpretation of the various grounds for revocation in section 11 of the Act. Part 6 sets out the principles underlying the exercise of the Bank's discretion to revoke or restrict an authorisation.

---

[1] As amended by The Banking Coordination (Second Council Directive) Regulations 1992.

[2] The Bank's policy notices are intended to inform authorised institutions of the approach it generally adopts in relation to particular supervisory issues. The Bank's application of a particular policy in an individual case will, however, need to take into account all the facts of the particular situation and should therefore be interpreted accordingly.

2 Schedule 3: minimum criteria for authorisation

2.1 Before an institution may be granted authorisation the Bank has to be satisfied that all the criteria in Schedule 3 to the Act are fulfilled with respect to it. This part of the statement sets out the Bank's interpretation of these criteria. It considers first the prudent conduct criterion in paragraph 4 of the Schedule as this sets the standards of most obvious relevance to the interests of depositors, actual and potential, and to assessing whether an institution's directors, controllers and managers are fit and proper persons to hold their positions. It then considers the other criteria in Schedule 3, concluding with the fit and proper person criterion.

2.2 Where the applicant institution is a foreign bank whose principal place of business is outside the UK, in assessing whether or not certain of the criteria are met by the institution the Bank has in certain circumstances a discretion to rely on assurances from the supervisor of the institution in that place that the supervisor is satisfied with respect to the prudential management and overall financial soundness of the institution (see Part 4 below).

Schedule 3, paragraph 4: requirement for a bank to conduct its business in a prudent manner

GENERAL

2.3 Paragraph 4(1) of the Schedule requires an institution to conduct its business in a prudent manner.

2.4 Sub-paragraphs (2)–(8) specify various detailed requirements, *each* of which must be fulfilled before an institution may be regarded as conducting its business in a prudent manner in terms of paragraph 4(1). But, as sub-paragraph (9) makes clear, this list of detailed requirements is not exhaustive. There are other considerations relevant to whether the business is being conducted prudently. These considerations, which are sometimes summarised under the heading of the 'general prudent conduct' requirement, are described in more detail below (paragraph 2.31).

SCHEDULE 3, PARAGRAPH 4(2) AND 4(3): REQUIREMENT FOR A BANK TO HAVE ADEQUATE CAPITAL

2.5 The Bank's general approach to the assessment of capital adequacy is set out in the following papers:[1]

Title	Date of issue
Implementation in the United Kingdom of the directive on the own funds of credit institutions[2] (BSD/1990/2)	December 1990
Implementation in the United Kingdom of the solvency ratio directive[3] (BSD/1990/3)	December 1990

These papers were amended by the following:

Title	Date of issue
Implementation in the United Kingdom of the directive on the own funds of credit institutions (BSD/1992/1)	January 1992
Verifications of interim profits in the context of the Own Funds Directive (BSD/1992/5)	August 1992
Amendment to the Bank's notice Implementation in the United Kingdom of the solvency ratio directive	November 1992

The adoption of the method of assessing capital adequacy set out in these papers implements the two EC banking directives which provide agreed minimum standards for the capital adequacy of banks throughout the EC and mirror the Basle Accord, *International Convergence of Capital Measurement and Capital Standards* agreed in 1988 by member countries of the Basle Committee on Banking Supervision[4] including the UK. The Bank applies this method to assess the capital adequacy of all banks incorporated in the UK.

2.6 A number of other papers are also relevant to this subject—

Title	Date of issue
Foreign currency exposure	April 1981
Foreign currency options	April 1984
Note issuance facilities/revolving underwriting facilities (BSD/1985/2)	April 1985
Large exposures in relation to mergers and acquisitions (BSD/1986/1)	February 1986
Subordinated loan capital (BSD/1986/2)	March 1986
Large exposures (BSD/1987/1)[5]	September 1987
Large underwriting exposures (BSD/1987/1.1)	February 1988
Loan transfers and securitisation (BSD/1989/1)[6]	February 1989
Implementation in the United Kingdom of the Directive on the Consolidated Supervision of Credit Institutions (BSD/1993/1)	February 1993
Country debt provisioning matrix	February 1993

2.7 Capital is defined for the purposes of paragraph 4(2) as own funds[7] (as laid down in the Own Funds Directive) and consists of Tier 1 and Tier 2 items. These are defined in the Bank's notice *Implementation in the United Kingdom of the directive on own funds of credit institutions*, as are the limits on how much certain items of Tier 2 capital may contribute to the total of own funds for supervisory purposes. Certain assets items, such as goodwill, are deducted in calculating own funds.

2.8 In order for capital to be sufficient for the purposes of the sub-paragraph it must be of an amount which is commensurate with the nature and scale of the institution's operations; and of an amount and nature sufficient to safeguard the interests of its depositors and potential depositors, having regard to the factors mentioned in paragraph 4(3) and to any other factors which appear to the Bank to be relevant. Paragraph 4(3)(a) refers to the nature and scale of the institution's operations; and paragraph 4(3)(b) to the risks inherent in those operations and in the operations of any other undertaking[8] in the same group in so far as they are capable of affecting the institution.

2.9 In addition, in the case of UK incorporated credit institutions, in order for capital to be sufficient for the purposes of paragraph 4(3A), the institution must maintain own funds which amount to not less than ECU 5mn (or an amount of equal value denominated wholly or partly in another unit of account). However, such institutions which were authorised under the Act immediately before the commencement of the regulations implementing the Second Council Directive are required to maintain own funds of an amount not less than ECU 5mn or the highest level the institution attained at any time after 22 December 1989 (whichever is the lower).[9]

2.10 A key purpose of capital is to provide a stable resource to absorb any losses incurred by an institution, and thus protect the interest of its depositors and potential depositors. Capital must therefore have two main qualities to achieve this purpose fully – a capacity to absorb losses and permanence. All types of capital recognised by the Bank in Tier 1 have these characteristics. Tier 1 capital will not be of an appropriate nature if there are concerns that it may be paid away to the detriment of depositors' interests. Thus, for example, the Bank will only permit distributable reserves to be included in the capital base if the likelihood of such reserves being paid away is remote.

2.11 The Bank recognises that some other types of capital also provide protection to depositors on an on-going basis. In particular, certain other types of capital, while not meeting the two criteria of ability to absorb losses while allowing an institution to continue to trade and permanence, can provide protection to depositors. Some subordinated term debt is therefore eligible to be included in own funds subject to the conditions and limits set out in the paper *Implementation in the United Kingdom of the directive on the own funds of credit institutions* (as amended). It is an essential feature of such capital that it must be fully subordinated to the interests of depositors to give them a measure of protection against loss in a liquidation.

2.12 The Bank would not expect any element of capital regarded as permanent to be repaid except as part of a capital reconstruction it had approved. The Bank would normally only give its consent to the early repayment of capital where it was being replaced by capital of higher quality (for example, replacing term subordinated debt with perpetual debt or equity) or where the institution's need for capital was reduced for the foreseeable future.

2.13 Central to the Bank's approach to the assessment of capital adequacy is the framework of measurement set out in the paper *Implementation in the United Kingdom of the solvency ratio directive* (as amended). The measurement framework focuses primarily on the credit risk to which a bank is subject, ie the risk of counterparty default whether arising from on-balance-sheet or off-balance-sheet business. The Solvency Ratio Directive imposes a minimum standard for risk asset ratios for bank groups of 8%. (Similarly the Basle Accord established a minimum standard for the capital ratio of internationally active banks of 8%.) Although the Solvency Ratio Directive generally applies only on a consolidated basis, the Bank continues to require all UK incorporated banks to maintain a minimum risk asset ratio on a solo basis as well.

2.14 However there are other factors which are not directly addressed within this framework which the Bank takes into account in the assessment of the capital adequacy of an authorised institution. This is achieved in part by requiring institutions to hold capital against certain additional items not specified in the Solvency Ratio Directive; and in part by varying the minimum risk asset ratio applied (known as the 'trigger' ratio). The Bank sets trigger ratios for individual banks according to an overall assessment of the risks that they face and the quality of their risk management. A bank is required to meet its trigger ratio at all times. In order to lessen the risk that the trigger ratio might be breached, the Bank generally expects each institution to conduct its business so as to maintain a higher ratio (the 'target' ratio).

2.15 Part of the risk assessment for capital adequacy assessment purposes is an analysis of the quality of the loan book, for example of its concentration with regard to particular economic sectors or counterparties or geographical concentration. In order to enable the Bank to monitor concentrated positions vis-à-vis individual counterparties or groups of connected counterparties there are special reporting requirements for large exposures.[10] But other risks too are taken into account in this assessment. These include, for example, the market risks which a bank faces, in particular foreign exchange and interest rate risk, and how those risks are managed. The operational risks to which an institution is exposed, that is risks arising from negligence or incompetence in the management of either the institution's own assets and exposures or those of third parties, are covered. Risks arising from holding companies, subsidiaries, associates and other connected companies which might expose an institution to direct financial costs or general loss of confidence by association (contagion risk) are also taken into account.

2.16 The judgment formed about the risks and the institution's ability to manage those risks is largely qualitative, based on the Bank's contact with management and information provided as part of the regular returns or an ad hoc basis. Factors taken into account by the Bank in assessing an institution's risk management capabilities include the expertise, experience and track record of its management, its internal control systems and accounting systems.

2.17 The magnitude of foreign exchange position risk is assessed quantitatively on the basis of a formal measurement system set out in *Foreign currency exposure* (April 1981) and *Foreign currency options* (April 1984).

2.18 In the case of UK incorporated banks, risk analysis is undertaken both on a consolidated basis, in order to capture exposures arising in subsidiaries and other connected companies, as well as the authorised institution, and on an unconsolidated basis, in order to assess whether there is an appropriate distribution of capital within a group. The second EC Directive on the supervision of credit institutions on a consolidated basis was implemented in 1993 by the Bank's notice *Implementation in the United Kingdom of the Directive on the Consolidated Supervision of Credit Institutions* (BSD/1993/1). This requires that consolidated supervision covers capital adequacy and large exposures, and extends to banks' parents and the financial subsidiaries of parents where the majority of the group's activities are financial in nature. For the purposes of the consolidated supervision of capital adequacy, the assets of financial companies in the group are risk weighted and added to the total of risk weighted assets, while their capital liabilities may be included in own funds, provided they meet the conditions set out in the Bank's relevant notices. (Group companies which are principally exposed to market risk are subject to a slightly different treatment, which is described in the Bank's Notice BSD/1993/1.) For the purposes of large exposures monitoring, the exposures incurred by the group companies are aggregated with those of the authorised institution and measured against group capital.

2.19 Consolidated returns covering capital adequacy and large exposures form only one source of information for the Bank's consolidated supervision, which aims to form a qualitative judgment of the strength of the overall group to which a bank belongs in order to evaluate the potential impact of the other group companies on the bank. Thus, for example, where a banking group fails to meet the trigger risk asset ratio set for it, the Bank would consider that this posed a threat to the bank so requiring it to consider whether to take action in respect of the institution.

---

[1] This approach does not however extend to the discount houses, which are authorised under the Banking Act and are supervised not by the Bank's Banking Supervision Division but by its Wholesale Markets Supervision Division (see Part 3 below).

[2] 89/647/EEC.

[3] 89/299/EEC.

[4] Members of the G10 and Luxembourg.

[5] As amended by two subsequent notices, BSD/1990/1 and BSD/1992/2.

[6] As amended by a subsequent notice, BSD/1992/3.

[7] This definition applies in respect of UK incorporated credit institutions only. In respect of other institutions the requirement is expressed in terms of net assets—that is, in relation to a body corporate, paid-up capital and reserves—together with other financial resources available to the institution of such nature and amount as are considered appropriate by the Bank. Such 'other financial resources' are in practice constituted by subordinated loan stock issued by the institutions subject to the conditions set out in the Bank's notice, BSD/1986/2.

[8] 'Body corporate' in the case of an institution which is not a UK incorporated credit institution.

[9] Where there has been a change in the parent controller of the institution after 1 January 1993 the requirement is generally ECU 5mn.

[10] From 1 January 1994 this area will also be covered by the EC directive on the monitoring and control of large exposures of credit institutions.

SCHEDULE 3, PARAGRAPHS 4(4) AND 4(5): REQUIREMENT FOR A BANK TO HAVE ADEQUATE
LIQUIDITY[1]

2.20 An institution's ability to meet its obligations when they fall due depends upon a
number of factors. In normal circumstances it depends, in particular, on the institution's ability to renew or replace its deposits and other funding, the extent to which the
profile of future cash flows from maturing assets matches that of its maturing liabilities,
and the amount of high quality liquid assets which it has readily available. Many of the
factors relating to the assessment of capital adequacy are also relevant to judging the
adequacy of liquidity, notably the quality of management of the institution, its internal
control systems, the nature of its activities and its position in the market. Each institution is assessed in the light of its own particular circumstances, including any potential
liquidity problems which could arise in group or other connected companies or other
developments in or affecting those companies which could have implications for the
liquidity of the institution.

2.21 Each institution is expected to formulate a statement of its liquidity management policy, taking into account the factors described above. It must identify any particular strengths and weaknesses and analyse its capacity to survive a crisis. This policy
is the basis for discussions with the Bank, with the objective of agreeing minimum
standards for that institution's liquidity. As part of its liquidity monitoring framework
established with each institution, the institution will normally be required to comply
with guidelines on the liquidity mismatches it may run in the sight-to-eight-day and
sight-to-one-month bands of a maturity 'ladder' comparing its assets to liabilities and
other commitments. This may be supplemented where appropriate by a requirement
to hold a certain quantity of highly liquid assets.

2.22 The Bank's approach is described in greater detail in its paper *Measurement of
Liquidity*, issued in July 1982.

---

[1] See note [1] above.

SCHEDULE 3, PARAGRAPH 4(6): REQUIREMENT FOR A BANK TO HAVE ADEQUATE PROVISIONS

2.23 This mirrors the Companies Act 1985 (as amended) requirement that provision
should be made for depreciation or diminution in the value of an institution's assets,
for liabilities which will or are expected to fall to be discharged and for any losses
which it will or expects to incur. Thus provisions need to be made for, inter alia, bad
and doubtful debts, expected losses on contingent liabilities (for example, connected
with guarantees or other off-balance-sheet exposures) and tax liabilities. The Bank
regards the accurate valuation of assets and the establishment of provisions of fundamental importance. The Bank would expect liabilities and losses (including contingent losses) to be recognised in accordance with accepted accounting standards (as
embodied in the Statements of Standard Accounting Practice and Financial Reporting
Standards).

2.24 In assessing the adequacy of an institution's provisions, the Bank has regard to
its provisioning policy, including the methods and systems for monitoring the recover-
ability of loans (for example, the monitoring of the financial health of counterparties,
their future prospects, the prospects of the markets and geographical areas in which
they operate, arrears patterns and credit scoring techniques), the frequency with
which provisions are reviewed, the policy and practices for the taking and valuation of
security and the extent to which valuation exceeds the balance-sheet value of the
secured loans. In some cases, clear objective indicators will be available to assist in the
determination of the appropriate level of provisions; in others, more subjective judgments will need to be made. The Bank considers that it is essential that provisions be
reviewed regularly.

2.25 The Bank considers that an adequate level of provisions against country debt
should be made. In February 1993 the Bank issued a paper setting out a revised
framework for determining the level of such provisions, which institutions could use in
establishing an adequate level of provisions against country debt.

SCHEDULE 3, PARAGRAPHS 4(7) AND (8): REQUIREMENT FOR A BANK TO MAINTAIN
ADEQUATE ACCOUNTING AND OTHER RECORDS AND ADEQUATE SYSTEMS OF CONTROL OF ITS
BUSINESS AND RECORDS

2.26 The nature and scope of the records and systems which an institution should maintain should be commensurate with its needs and particular circumstances, so that its business can be conducted prudently. In judging whether an institution's records and systems are adequate the Bank has regard to its size, to the nature of its business, to the manner in which the business is structured, organised and managed, and to the nature, volume and complexity of its transactions. The requirement applies to all aspects of an institution's business, whether on or off balance sheet, and whether undertaken as a principal or as an agent. The Bank's detailed interpretation of the paragraph 4(7) requirement is set out in the *Guidance notes on accounting and other records and internal control systems and reporting accountants' reports thereon* (BSD/1987/2 and BSD/1992/4), issued in September 1987 and July 1992 respectively.

2.27 Paragraph 4(8) of the Schedule provides, inter alia, that an institution's records and systems shall not be regarded as adequate unless they are such as to enable the business of the institution to be prudently managed and the institution to comply with the duties imposed on it by or under the Act. In other words, the records and systems must be such that the institution is able to fulfil the various other elements of the prudent conduct criterion (including appropriate systems to combat money laundering), and to identify other threats to the interests of depositors and potential depositors. They should also be sufficient to enable the institution to comply with the notification requirements which apply to it under the Act (for example, sections 36 and 38) and with requirements for the provision of information and documents under section 39 and section 41. Thus delays in providing information, or inaccuracies in the information provided, will call into question the fulfilment of the requirement in the sub-paragraph.

2.28 In assessing the adequacy of an institution's records and systems the Bank takes into account the complexity of the branch structure of the institution, and the nature of the institution's overseas operations. Owing to the difficulties of controlling overseas operations the Bank requires all UK incorporated institutions to notify it before establishing such operations. In such cases the Bank will need to be satisfied that, inter alia, the institution's systems and controls are adequate to ensure the prudent management of its overseas operations. UK incorporated credit institutions which propose to establish a branch in another EC member State in order to carry on activities listed in Schedule 1 of the Regulations[1] are required under those Regulations to give prior notice to the Bank. Under the Regulations the Bank has power to prevent a UK institution from opening such a branch in another EC member State if, having regard to the activities proposed to be carried on, it doubts the adequacy of the administrative structure or the financial situation of the institution.

2.29 Where an authorised institution proposes to establish another operation either in the UK or overseas, the Bank will require the authorised institution to have adequate internal control mechanisms for the production of any data and information which may be relevant for the purposes of supervision on a consolidated basis. This is in accordance with the Bank's notice on the *Implementation in the United Kingdom of the directive on the Consolidated Supervision of Credit Institutions*.

2.30 Paragraph 4(8) also provides that the Bank, in determining whether an institution's systems are adequate, 'shall have regard to the functions and responsibilities in respect of them of any such directors of the institution as are mentioned in paragraph 3 above'. The Bank interprets this provision as referring to the role of non-executive directors of authorised institutions acting in a control capacity. (This is also discussed below in the context of the requirement relating to non-executive directors in paragraph 3 of Schedule 3.)

---

[1]   The Banking Co-ordination (Second Council Directive) Regulations 1992.

SCHEDULE 3, PARAGRAPH 4(9): THE 'GENERAL PRUDENT CONDUCT' REQUIREMENT

2.31 As noted above, the list of specific points in Schedule 3 relevant to prudent conduct is not exhaustive. Examples of other relevant considerations include the institution's management arrangements (such as those for the overall control and direction by the board of directors); the institution's general strategy and objectives; planning arrangements; policies on accounting, lending and other exposures, and bad debt and tax provisions; policies and practices on the taking and valuation of security, on the monitoring of arrears, on following up debtors in arrears, and interest rate matching; and recruitment arrangements and training to ensure that the institution has adequate numbers of experienced and skilled staff in order to carry out its various activities in a prudent manner.

Schedule 3, paragraph 2: requirement for the business of a bank to be effectively directed by at least two individuals

2.32 This criterion – sometimes known as the 'four eyes' requirement – provides that at least two individuals must effectively direct the business of the institution.[1] In the case of a body corporate, the Bank normally expects that the individuals concerned will be either executive directors or persons granted executive powers by, and reporting immediately to, the board; and, in the case of a partnership, the Bank will look for at least two general or active partners.

2.33 Paragraph 2 requires at least two independent minds to be applied to both the formulation and implementation of the policies of the institution. Where there are just two individuals involved the Bank does not regard it as sufficient for one of them to make some, albeit significant, decisions relating only to a few aspects of the business – each must play a part in the decision-making process on all significant decisions. Both must demonstrate the qualities and application to influence strategy, day-to-day policy and their implementation. This does not require their day-to-day involvement in the execution and implementation of policy. It does however require involvement in strategy and general direction, as well as a knowledge of, and influence on, the way in which strategy is being implemented through day-to-day policy. Where there are more than two individuals directing the business, the Bank does not regard it as necessary for all of these individuals to be involved in all decisions relating to the determination of strategy and general direction. However at least two individuals must be involved in all such decisions. Both individuals' judgments must be engaged in order that major errors leading to difficulties for the institution are less likely to occur. Similarly, each individual must have sufficient experience and knowledge of the business and the necessary personal qualities to detect and resist any imprudence, dishonesty or other irregularities by the other individual. Where a single individual, whether a chief executive, managing director or otherwise, is particularly dominant in an authorised institution this will raise doubts about the fulfilment of the criterion.

---

[1] This requirement relates to the institution as a whole. Thus, in the case of an overseas incorporated authorised institution the Bank assesses whether at least two individuals effectively direct the business of the institution (and not just the business of its branch in the United Kingdom). The Bank would also take into account the manner in which management decisions are taken in the UK branch in assessing whether the institution fulfilled the criterion relating to the adequacy of its systems and controls set out in paragraph 4(7) of Schedule 3.

Schedule 3, paragraph 3: composition of board of directors

2.34 This provides that, in the case of an institution incorporated in the United Kingdom, the directors include such number (if any) of non-executive directors as the Bank considers appropriate having regard to the circumstances of the institution and the nature and scale of its operations.

2.35 The Bank considers that non-executive directors can play a valuable role in bringing an outsider's independent perspective to the running of the business and in questioning the approach of the executive directors and other management.[1] The Bank sees non-executive directors as having, in particular, an important role as members of an institution's audit committee or in performing the role which such a committee would otherwise perform.

2.36 The Bank recognises that some small authorised institutions may find it difficult to appoint sufficient suitable non-executive directors for an audit committee to be established. The Bank is nevertheless committed to the principle that UK-incorporated institutions and UK-based banking groups should have an audit committee and that, unless there are sound reasons to the contrary, all authorised institutions should appoint at least one non-executive director to undertake some audit committee functions. The Bank may consider it unnecessary for an authorised institution to have non-executive directors or an audit committee, if, for example, there is an audit committee of non-executive directors of the institution's holding company which undertakes the functions of an audit committee in respect of the authorised institution itself. (The Bank has expressed its views on the role of audit committee and non-executive directors in the consultative paper on the *Role of audit committees in banks* issued in January 1987, and in the Bank's report under the Banking Act for 1987/88.)

¹ See also para 2.30 above concerning the role of non-executive directors.

Schedule 3, paragraph 5: requirement for the business of a bank to be carried on with integrity and skill

2.37 This criterion is, like the prudent conduct criterion, concerned with the manner in which the business of the institution is carried on (which will partly determine its exposure to 'reputational risk') and is distinct from the question of whether its directors, controllers and managers are fit and proper persons. It covers two elements: whether the institution's business is carried on with integrity; and whether it is carried on with the professional skills appropriate to the nature and scale of the activities of the institution concerned.

2.38 The integrity element of the criterion requires the institution to observe high ethical standards in carrying on its business. Criminal offences or other breaches of statute will obviously call into question the fulfilment of this criterion. Particularly relevant are contraventions of any provision made by or under enactments designed to protect members of the public against financial loss due to dishonesty, incompetence or malpractice. (Examples of such enactments are the Theft Acts of 1968 and 1978, the Consumer Credit Act 1974, the Companies Act 1985 (as amended), the Company Securities (Insider Dealing) Act 1985, the Financial Services Act 1986, the Banking Acts of 1979 and 1987 and foreign legislation dealing with similar matters.) Doubts may also be raised if the institution fails to comply with recognised ethical standards of conduct such as those embodied in various codes of conduct. (Examples of such codes would be the London Code of Conduct for the wholesale markets in sterling, foreign exchange and bullion, the guidance notes on money laundering¹ the Code of Banking Practice, and the Take-over Code.) As with breaches of statutes, the Bank would have regard to the seriousness of the breach of the Code, to whether the breach was deliberate or an unintentional and unusual occurrence, and to its relevance to the fulfilment of the Schedule 3 criteria and otherwise to the interests of depositors and potential depositors.

2.39 Professional skills cover the general skills which bankers should have in conducting their business as bankers, for example, in relation to accounting, risk analysis, establishing and operating systems of internal controls, ensuring compliance with legal and supervisory requirements, and in the standard of the various financial services provided to customers. The level of skills required will vary according to the individual case, depending on the nature and scale of the particular institution's activities.

¹ Issued by the Joint Money Laundering Working Group.

Schedule 3, paragraph 6: requirement for a bank to have minimum net assets or minimum initial capital

2.40 This provides that a UK incorporated credit institution must have at the time it is authorised initial capital¹ amounting to not less than ECU 5mn (or an amount of equal value determined wholly or partly in another unit of account).²

2.41 An institution which is not a UK incorporated credit institution must have at the time it is authorised net assets of not less than £1 million (or an amount of equivalent value denominated wholly or partly otherwise than in sterling).³

¹ Initial capital is defined in regulation 2 of the Regulations.
² Such institutions must also continue to fulfil the capital adequacy requirements set out in paragraphs 4(2) and 4(3A) of Schedule 3 (see paragraphs 2.5–2.19 above).
³ Such institutions must also continue to fulfil the capital adequacy requirement set out in paragraph 4(2) of Schedule 3 (see paragraphs 2.5–2.19 above).

Schedule 3, paragraph 1: requirement for directors, controllers and managers to be fit and proper persons

GENERAL

2.42 This provides that every person who is, or is to be, a director, controller or manager of an authorised institution must be a fit and proper person to hold the position which he holds or is to hold.

2.43 In considering whether a person fulfils the criterion, the Bank has regard to a number of general considerations, whilst also taking account of the circumstances of the particular position held and the institution concerned.

DIRECTORS, CHIEF EXECUTIVES, MANAGING DIRECTORS AND MANAGERS

2.44 With regard to a person who is, or is to be, a director, chief executive, managing director or manager (as defined in section 105 of the Act), the relevant considerations include whether he has sufficient skills, knowledge, and soundness of judgment properly to undertake and fulfil his particular duties and responsibilities. The standards required of persons in these respects will vary considerably, depending on the precise position held by the person concerned. Thus a person could be fit and proper for one position but not fit and proper for a position involving different responsibilities and duties. The diligence with which he is fulfilling or is likely to fulfil those duties and responsibilities is also considered, so that the Bank can assess whether the person does or will devote sufficient time and attention to them.

2.45 The probity of the person concerned is very important: it is essential that a person with responsibility for the conduct of a deposit-taking business is of high integrity. In contrast to the other elements of the fitness and properness criterion, the level of probity required will tend to be much the same whatever position is held.

2.46 In assessing whether a person has the relevant competence, soundness of judgment and diligence, the Bank considers whether the person has had experience of similar responsibilities previously, his record in fulfilling them and, where appropriate, whether he has appropriate qualifications and training. As to his soundness of judgment, the Bank looks to, inter alia, the degree of balance, rationality and maturity demonstrated in his conduct and decision-taking.

2.47 More generally, the Bank takes into account the person's reputation and character. It considers, inter alia, whether the person has a criminal record[1] – convictions for fraud or other dishonesty are obviously relevant to probity. The Bank gives particular weight to whether the person has contravened any provision of banking, insurance, investment or other legislation designed to protect members of the public against financial loss due to dishonesty, incompetence or malpractice. (Examples of such legislation include the Theft Acts of 1968 and 1978, the Consumer Credit Act 1974, the Companies Act 1985 (as amended), the Company Securities (Insider Dealing) Act 1985, the Financial Services Act 1986, the Banking Acts of 1979 and 1987 and foreign legislation dealing with similar matters.) In addition, it considers whether the person has been involved in any business practices appearing to the Bank to be deceitful or oppressive or otherwise improper or which otherwise reflect discredit on his method of conducting business. Some of the relevant considerations here are dealt with by the legislation referred to above. However, not all are spelt out in statute. In this connection, the Bank has regard to the person's record of compliance with various non-statutory codes, such as the Take-over Code, the guidance notes on money laundering,[2] the Code of Banking Practice and London Code of Conduct for the wholesale markets in sterling, foreign exchange and bullion, in so far as they are relevant to the fulfilment of the Schedule 3 criteria and otherwise to the interests of depositors and potential depositors.

2.48 The standards required are particularly high for those persons with the main responsibility for the conduct of an institution's affairs, although they will depend in part on the nature and scale of the business concerned.

2.49 Once an institution is authorised, the Bank has continuing regard to the performance of the person in the exercise of his duties. Imprudence in the conduct of an institution's business, or actions which have threatened (without necessarily having damaged) the interests of depositors or potential depositors will reflect adversely on the competence and soundness of judgment of those responsible. Similarly, failure by an institution to conduct its business with integrity and professional skills will reflect adversely on the probity and/or competence and/or soundness of judgment of those responsible. This applies whether the matters of concern have arisen from the way the persons responsible have acted or from their failure to act in an appropriate manner. The Bank takes a cumulative approach in assessing the significance of such actions or omissions – that is, it may determine that a person does not fulfil the criterion on the basis of several instances of such conduct which, if taken individually, may not lead to that conclusion.

[1] The Bank is permitted by s 95 of the Act to have regard to certain spent convictions under the Rehabilitation of Offenders Act 1974.
[2] Issued by the Joint Money Laundering Working Group.

SHAREHOLDER AND INDIRECT CONTROLLERS[1]

2.50 Shareholder controllers and indirect controllers (as defined in section 105 of the Act) may hold a wide variety of positions in relation to an authorised institution, and the application of the fit and proper criterion must take account of this.[2] A key consideration is the likely or actual impact on the interests of depositors and potential depositors of a person holding his particular position as controller. This is viewed in the context of the circumstances of the individual case, and of the particular position held. The general presumption is that the greater the influence on the authorised institution the higher the standard will be for the controller to fulfil the criterion. Thus, for example, higher standards will generally be required of shareholders who hold 20–33 per cent of its shares than those shareholders who hold only 10–20 per cent. However, in certain instances, a 10 per cent shareholder controller would exert more influence than would normally be implied by a shareholding of this size and such a shareholder would be subject to a higher standard of assessment.

2.51 In considering the application of the criterion to shareholder controllers (and, in the case of UK incorporated credit institutions, parent controllers)[3] or persons proposing to become such controllers, the Bank has particular regard to two main factors. These are relevant whether the person is a shareholder controller or a parent controller by virtue of a shareholding in the authorised institution or by virtue of a shareholding in another institution of which the institution is a subsidiary or subsidiary undertaking.

2.52 First, it considers what influence the person has or is likely to have on the conduct of the affairs of the institution. If the person does, or is likely to, exercise a close control over the business, the Bank would look for evidence that he has soundness of judgment and relevant knowledge and skills for running an authorised institution. The Bank would look therefore for the same range of qualities and experience that it would expect of the executive directors of an authorised institution. On the other hand, if the shareholder does not, and is not likely to, influence the directors and management of the authorised institution in relation to the detailed conduct of the business, it would not be necessary to require such a level of relevant qualities and experience. In general, 10 per cent shareholder controllers are not likely to exercise much, if any, influence or control in relation to the conduct of an authorised institution's business. Accordingly, in general the standards of competence, soundness of judgment and diligence required of such controllers will be lower than that for 20 per cent shareholder controllers and for other controllers which hold a higher percentage of the shares of an authorised institution and to parent controllers. As regards probity, the Bank will give similar consideration to shareholder controllers as it would to managing directors, chief executives, directors or managers. The Bank also has regard in this context to whether there could be conflicts of interest arising from the influence of the shareholder on the authorised institution—this could, in particular, arise from too close an association with another company, the business or affairs of which could have a bearing on the institution's position.

2.53 Second, it considers whether the financial position, reputation or conduct of the parent controller or shareholder controller or prospective controller has damaged or is likely to damage the authorised institution through 'contagion' which undermines confidence in it. For example, if the holding company, or a major shareholder, or a company connected to that shareholder were to suffer financial problems it could lead to a run on the authorised institution, difficulties in obtaining deposits and other funds, or difficulties in raising new equity from other shareholders or potential shareholders. Generally, the higher the shareholding the greater the risk of 'contagion' if the shareholder encounters financial difficulties. The risk of contagion is not confined to financial weakness: publicity about illegal or unethical conduct by the holding company or another member of the group or a company connected to the institution in some other way may also damage confidence in the authorised institution.

2.54 In the case of shareholder controllers holding 10 per cent or more of the non-voting shares[4] in an authorised institution or an institution of which it is a subsidiary institution the Bank takes into account the degree of influence they exert or may be able to exert. In general, because the shares are non-voting, these persons are not likely to exert much influence on authorised institutions and, therefore, the standard which they are required to meet is lower than for voting shareholders. However, situations may arise where non-voting shareholders can exert a material influence over the institution, whether by suasion or any other means, and these persons will be considered in the light of the nature of the influence which they are able to exert then.

2.55 The fitness and properness of minority shareholder controllers of UK incorporated credit institutions are also subject to assessment by the Bank. Minority shareholder controllers are persons who hold less than 10 per cent of the shares and are entitled to exercise or control the exercise of less than 10 per cent of the voting power (whether directly or indirectly) of the institution and, by virtue of their holding, are able to exercise a significant influence over the management of the institution or of the institution's parent company. The Bank's consideration of these persons will take into account the nature of the influence which they are able to exert—issues similar to those taken into account in the assessment of other categories of shareholder controller will be considered.

2.56 In considering the fitness and properness of indirect controllers it is also necessary to have regard to the precise position held.

2.57 In the case of an indirect controller who 'directs' or 'instructs' a shareholder controller, in terms of section 105(3)(d), similar considerations apply as those relevant to assessing the fulfilment of the criterion in relation to shareholder controllers. In other words, the standards which an indirect controller will need to satisfy are likely to be at the minimum the standards also required of the person who is indirectly controlled.

2.58 Where a person is an indirect controller by virtue of 'directing' or 'instructing' the board of an authorised institution, in terms of section 105(3)(d), the standards required will be high. The indirect controller would have to have the probity and relevant knowledge, experience, skills and diligence for running an authorised institution. The qualities required would be those which are also appropriate for the board of directors of an authorised institution.

2.59 The Bank expects both authorised institutions and the controllers themselves to inform it of any material developments which may cast doubt on the continued fitness and properness of the controllers or which otherwise indicate a possible threat to the interests of depositors and potential depositors.

---

[1] The definitions of a shareholder controller applying to institutions under the Banking Act depend upon whether the institution is or is not a UK incorporated credit institution. The considerations the Bank takes into account in considering the fitness and properness of a controller, however, apply equally to both categories of institution.

[2] For UK incorporated credit institutions, the thresholds of shareholding at which the fitness and properness of shareholder controllers must be assessed are 10 per cent, 20 per cent, 33 per cent, 50 per cent and 75 per cent, together with shareholdings of less than 10 per cent where the person is a minority shareholder, as defined in section 105(4)(a) of the Act. For other authorised institutions, the thresholds are 15 per cent, 50 per cent and 75 per cent.

[3] That is a parent undertaking as defined in regulation 2(2) of the Regulations.

[4] Applies to shares in UK incorporated credit institutions only.

3 The discount houses

3.1 The discount houses are counterparties of the Bank in its operations in the sterling money market. They are authorised under the Banking Act, and are supervised by the Wholesale Markets Supervision Division of the Bank. While this statement generally applies to the discount houses, as well as to other institutions authorised under the Banking Act, the sections on capital adequacy and liquidity do not. This is because of the distinct nature of the business they conduct and the risks to which this gives rise. The Bank's arrangements for the supervision of the discount houses are those described in its 1988 paper, *Bank of England operations in the sterling money market* (the 'Red Paper'), although minor refinements have been made from time to time. The most significant of these have been the introduction of a revised treatment of certain off-balance-sheet instruments for the purposes of capital adequacy, and the formalisation of the Bank's policy on the types of business which it believes are appropriate for discount houses to undertake.

3.2 The EC directives relating to banking and the completion of the internal market have consequences for the Bank's supervision of the discount houses. Implementation of the Second Banking Coordination Directive and of the Consolidated Supervision Directive with respect to the discount houses has been largely in line with that for authorised institutions generally. The Bank continues to monitor the compliance of the discount houses with the terms of their exemption from the full provisions of the Solvency Ratio Directive. Because of the availability of this exemption, the discount houses are included by the Bank in the consolidation which is required by the Consolidated Supervision Directive on the basis of the solvency test set out in the Red Paper. The Bank is considering the implications of the Large Exposures Directive and the Capital Adequacy Directive for the discount houses.

4 Principles relating to the grant of authorisation

General

4.1 In order to be able to grant authorisation the Bank must be satisfied that all the minimum authorisation criteria in Schedule 3 are fulfilled with respect to the applicant. It cannot be so satisfied if the applicant institution and other relevant parties have not provided all the information and documents which the Bank has requested in connection with the application. Where the Bank is satisfied that the criteria are fulfilled, it can then decide whether to grant authorisation. It will not do so if it considers for any reason that there are any significant threats to the interests of the depositors and potential depositors, notwithstanding that the criteria are fulfilled.

4.2 The Bank also considers, in exercising its discretion to grant authorisation, whether it is likely that it will receive adequate flows of information from the institution and relevant connected parties in order to monitor the fulfilment of the criteria and to identify and assess any threats to the interest of depositors and potential depositors. In assessing this issue, the Bank requires to be satisfied that the institution and the group to which it may belong will be subject to consolidated supervision in accordance with the Basle Minimum Standards.[1] The Bank will take account of any factors which might inhibit effective supervision, including in particular whether the structure and geographical spread of the bank, the group to which it may belong and other connected companies might hinder the provision of adequate and reliable flows of information to the supervisors. In particular, such flows can be hindered where there are branches or other connected companies in poorly supervised centres or centres with very restrictive secrecy laws. The Bank may also have concerns about the reliability of information if the institution's head office is located in a different country from its registered office or if different group companies have different financial years and accounting dates (thus making it difficult to assess with confidence the overall position of a group at any particular time). In addition, the Bank would have regard to whether the companies in the same group shared common auditors. The Bank's ability to assess a banking institution's exposure to risks elsewhere in the same group may be assisted where there are common auditors and, as with the case where different group companies have different financial years, the Bank would need to be persuaded that there are good reasons for this arrangement not to be adopted and that it would not in the circumstances of the particular case hinder effective supervision.

4.3 The Bank's experience has been that newly-formed institutions which are not directly associated with an established and proven deposit-taking institution can be susceptible to early difficulties. These difficulties on the whole have tended to arise from lack of relevant expertise and judgment, particularly in lending, or from ill-constructed and insufficiently-tested business strategies. The Bank has therefore found it difficult to be satisfied that an applicant institution which is not supported by an established deposit-taking institution will carry on a deposit-taking business in a prudent manner, unless the applicant institution has already for some time been carrying on successfully a business similar to that planned (even if on a lesser scale) but financed either by bank borrowing or from other sources not involving the acceptance of deposits as defined in the Act.

Overseas institutions

4.4 In the case of an institution whose principal place of business[2] is in a country or territory outside the United Kingdom, the Bank, under the terms of section 9(3), may regard itself as satisfied that the criteria relating to fit and proper persons, prudent conduct, and integrity and professional skill (see paragraphs 1, 4 and 5 of Schedule 3) are fulfilled if:

(a) the banking supervisory authority in that country or territory informs the Bank that it is satisfied with respect to the prudent management and overall financial soundness of the applicant; and

(b) the Bank is satisfied as to the nature and scope of the supervision exercised by that authority.

4.5 The Bank has to form its own view directly on whether the 'four eyes' and minimum net assets criteria (paragraphs 2 and 6 of Schedule 3) are fulfilled with respect to the applicant.

4.6 The principal place of business of an institution will normally be where the mind and management, its central direction, resides.

4.7 Despite the reliance that the Bank may place on assurances from overseas supervisory authorities with respect to certain criteria, the Bank must make its own judgment on an institution's suitability for authorisation. In this connection, the Bank examines the planned business of the proposed UK branch of the applicant, its business plan, its liquidity policies, its internal controls, its accounting and other records, and staffing and management arrangements. If there are any concerns, the Bank will discuss these with the applicant and, where necessary, with the overseas supervisory authority. Unless suitable assurances are received, or remedial action taken, the Bank may decide that it cannot be satisfied that all the criteria are fulfilled, and that therefore authorisation should not be granted.

4.8 Once such an institution is authorised, on-going supervision is conducted in accordance with the principles governing the Bank's approach to the supervision of authorised institutions generally. This is adapted as appropriate to take account of the position of the UK branch in the context of the institution as a whole and with regard to the role and approach of other relevant supervisory authorities in relation to the institution and its activities. In practice, the Bank would normally expect on-going supervision to be a matter of collaboration between the Bank and the relevant supervisory authorities in other jurisdictions, following where appropriate the principles governing the supervision of overseas institutions set out in the Basle Concordat(s)[3] and the Basle Minimum Standards.[4]

---

[1] *The minimum standards for the supervision of international banking groups and their cross-border establishments*, issued in June 1992.
[2] See paragraph 5.13.
[3] *Principles for the supervision of banks' foreign establishments*, issued in May 1983 (as amended).
[4] See footnote [1].

5 Section 11: grounds for the revocation of authorisation

5.1 Section 11 sets out the grounds on which the Bank's powers to revoke authorisation or restrict an authorisation become exercisable. Whether such a ground exists generally depends on the Bank's judgment of the circumstances relating to the authorised institution concerned and of the application of provisions of the Act to those circumstances. The following focuses on the Bank's interpretation of the section 11 grounds.

5.2 Although there are other circumstances in which the Bank's powers may be exercisable, as a general matter, the Bank is able to exercise its powers when the interests of depositors and potential depositors are threatened. The threat may be relatively slight or remote, or it may be both immediate and serious. The Act recognises that the immediacy and severity of such threats may vary by, as a general rule, giving the Bank discretion to decide whether to revoke, impose restrictions or take some other action. The main principles underlying the exercise of this discretion are set out in Part 6 below.

Section 11(1)(a)

5.3 This provides that the Bank's powers become exercisable if it appears to the Bank that any of the criteria in Schedule 3 is not or has not been fulfilled, or may not be or may not have been fulfilled. This represents quite a low threshold. The Bank would consider that a criterion 'may not be . . . fulfilled' in circumstances where it had evidence that a criterion may not be or may not have been fulfilled, albeit that the evidence was not sufficient to enable it to satisfy itself that the criterion is not or has not been fulfilled. In other words, where the evidence available raised a material doubt about whether the criterion was or had been in fact fulfilled.

Section 11(1)(b)

5.4 Under this, the Bank's powers become exercisable if the institution fails to comply with any requirement imposed by the Act: for example, if it fails to notify a change of director under section 36. The Bank's powers also become exercisable if the institution fails to comply with any requirement imposed by secondary legislation under the Act (for example, advertisement regulations) or imposed by the Bank using its powers under the Act (for example, a condition imposed under section 12 or a requirement for information under section 39).

Section 11(1)(d)

5.5 This provides that the Bank's powers become exercisable if it is provided with false, misleading or inaccurate information by or on behalf of the institution. The mere provision of inaccurate information will render the power exercisable. In practice, however, the Bank is likely not to contemplate exercising its powers just because of a minor inaccuracy. There would generally have to be a wider prudential concern, of which the inaccuracy may be a symptom.

5.6 The Bank's powers also become exercisable under this paragraph if false, misleading or inaccurate information has been provided, in connection with an application for authorisation, by or on behalf of a person who is, or is to be, a director, controller or manager of the institution.

Section 11(1)(e)

5.7 Although the Schedule 3 authorisation criteria and the other circumstances specified in sections 11(1)(b)–(d) and 11(1A) (below) cover most of the range of circumstances which could pose a threat to the interests of depositors and potential depositors, they do not cover all – for example, a sudden external threat, unconnected with the institution's conduct, such as a natural catastrophe or the imposition by a government of a debt moratorium. Paragraph (e) ensures that the Bank may act by using its revocation or restriction powers in all circumstances where the interests of depositors and potential depositors are in any other way threatened, whether by the manner in which the institution is conducting or proposes to conduct its affairs or for any other reason.

Section 11(2)

5.8 This enables the Bank to revoke in certain circumstances if an institution has failed to make use of its authorisation. Authorisation under the Act is intended to enable a person to accept deposits in the United Kingdom in the course of carrying on a deposit-taking business. Provided that deposits are accepted in the United Kingdom, it is irrelevant where the institution carries on a deposit-taking business.

5.9 Section 5 of the Banking Act defines the meaning of 'deposit'. An institution which accepts deposits as there defined will carry on a deposit-taking business as defined in section 6 of the Act if it (a) lends money received by way of deposit to others; or (b) finances any other activity of the business to any material extent out of the capital of or the interest on money received by way of deposit. However, an institution which utilises deposit money in these ways will not carry on a deposit-taking business if it does not hold itself out as accepting deposits on a day-to-day basis and if any deposits which are accepted are accepted only on particular occasions.

Section 11: subsections (1)(c), (3), (4), (6), (7), (8) and (9)

5.10 These subsections set out circumstances in which the Bank's powers become exercisable because of certain specified events occurring. These include withdrawal of authorisation (in respect of an overseas institution) by the banking supervisory authority of the country or territory in which the institution has its principal place of business; revocation of authorisation under the Financial Services Act 1986 or a licence under the Consumer Credit Act 1974; and the commencement of certain formal insolvency procedures in relation to an authorised institution, such as the making of a winding-up order or the passing of a resolution for voluntary winding-up or the making of an administration order.

5.11 There are two circumstances in which revocation is mandatory rather than discretionary. First, in the case of an authorised institution which is not a credit institution and which has its principal place of business in another Member State of the European Community and the banking supervisory authority there withdraws the institution's authorisation. Second, where a winding-up order has been made against the institution in the United Kingdom or a resolution for its voluntary winding up in the United Kingdom has been passed or where analogous proceedings have occurred in other jurisdictions.

Section 11(1A)

5.12 Section 11(1A) sets out additional grounds on which the Bank's powers to revoke or restrict the authorisation of a credit institution incorporated in the UK become exercisable.

Section 11(1A)(a)

5.13 This provides that the Bank's powers become exercisable if it appears to the Bank that the institution's principal place of business is or may be outside the UK.[1]

Section 11(1A)(b)

5.14 This provides that the Bank's powers become exercisable if it appears to the Bank that the institution has carried on in the United Kingdom or elsewhere a listed activity (ie an activity listed in Schedule 1 of the Regulations) other than the acceptance of deposits from the public, without having given prior notice to the Bank of its intention to do so.

Section 11(1A)(c)

5.15 This provides that the Bank's powers become exercisable where it is informed by The Securities and Investments Board or certain other UK regulatory authorities that the institution has contravened any provision of the Financial Services Act 1986 or any rules or regulations made under it, or certain other related provisions set out in the section.[2]

Section 11(1A)(d)

5.16 This provides that the Bank's powers become exercisable where it is informed by the Director General of Fair Trading that the institution or certain other persons connected to the institution has done any of the things specified in paragraphs (a) to (d) of the section 25(2) of the Consumer Credit Act 1974.

Section 11(1A)(e)

5.17 This provides that the Bank's powers are exercisable where it appears to the Bank that the institution has failed to comply with any obligation imposed on it by The Banking Coordination (Second Council Directive) Regulations 1992.

Section 11(1A)(f)

5.18 This provides that the Bank's powers are exercisable where it is informed by a supervisory authority in another member State that the institution has failed to comply with any obligation imposed on it by or under any rule of law in force in that State for purposes connected with the implementation of the Second Council Directive (ie the Second Banking Coordination Directive).

---

[1] The Bank will expect an institution's mind and management, its central direction, to remain in the United Kingdom.
[2] In the case of an institution which is a member of a self-regulatory organisation, the reference to rules and prohibitions includes the rules of any recognised organisation of which the institution is a member and any prohibition imposed by virtue of those rules.

---

6 Principles relating to the revocation of authorisation and to the restriction of authorisation

6.1 As noted above, the Bank's powers to revoke or restrict an authorisation may become exercisable in a wide range of circumstances.

6.2 The wide diversity of grounds in the Act for the exercise of the Bank's powers enables the Bank to exercise its powers before the threat to the interests of depositors or potential depositors becomes very great or immediate. The Bank can, therefore, where necessary, intervene before the deterioration in the institution's condition is such that there is a serious likelihood that depositors will suffer a loss.

6.3 In view of the need for flexibility in dealing with problem cases, the Act gives the Bank discretion – except in the case of mandatory revocation referred to in paragraph 5.11 above – to decide whether to revoke or restrict the authorisation or seek remedial action by some other means, through persuasion and encouragement. Where the Bank considers that adequate and speedy remedial steps are likely to be taken by an authorised institution (or its shareholders, for example by injecting new capital or appointing new directors) it would generally be reluctant to revoke or restrict the authorisation.

6.4 The Bank would generally consider revocation, however, where there was no reasonable prospect of speedy and comprehensive remedial action, even though the situation did not raise matters of immediate concern, for example where the threat to the interests of depositors is not immediate, because the institution currently had adequate capital and liquidity. In so far as this is consistent with the interests of depositors, actual and potential, the Bank will explore fully the prospects of remedial action; if, however, the financial position of the institution is weak or is deteriorating rapidly, the scope for such inquiries will be limited. The Bank has to balance the interests of existing depositors, for whom it may be desirable to continue the authorisation in order to allow more time for the scope for remedial action to be explored, and the interests of potential depositors who could be exposed to a risk of loss.

6.5 The circumstances in which a restricted authorisation rather than revocation is likely to be appropriate are where the Bank considers that the imposition of conditions is necessary to underpin the institution's efforts to improve matters, and that there is a reasonable prospect that all the relevant criteria for authorisation will be fulfilled again within a reasonable period. Such a restricted authorisation would normally be without time limit but the Bank's intention would be that the conditions would be removed once the remedial action was taken. The Bank would thus look for a sound and viable programme for swift remedial action.

6.6 Alternatively, the Bank may impose a restricted authorisation with a limited life. The Bank may impose such a time limit for a maximum of three years; it may also extend the life of a time-limited authorisation, but only provided the total duration is not more than three years. The Bank would generally impose a time-limited authorisation in order to facilitate an orderly repayment of deposits by avoiding liquidity pressures which could arise from a sudden loss of authorisation.

6.7 On occasion, when concerns arise, it may also be desirable to restrict the authorisation as a holding measure to protect depositors and potential depositors while further information is sought.

6.8 Where the Bank considered that a Schedule 3 criterion may not be fulfilled and therefore that its powers were exercisable, its response would depend on the overall circumstances of the case, and, in particular, on its assessment of the actual or potential threats to the interests of depositors. The Bank would also have regard to any perceived deficiencies in the information available to it. Where further information was required in order to determine whether or not the criterion was in fact fulfilled, the Bank would generally not exercise its revocation or restriction powers where it was satisfied that there was no substantial threat to depositors. (An example would be the case where there was a doubt about the fitness and properness of a manager but otherwise the Bank was satisfied that all the Schedule 3 criteria were met.) In other cases, the Bank would be inclined to use its restriction powers in order to protect depositors and potential depositors pending clarification of whether or not there was in fact a material threat to depositors, unless it was satisfied that adequate protective measures had been put in place.

6.9 In the case of a UK incorporated credit institution which fails to meet the requirement in paragraph 4(3A) of Schedule 3 to maintain own funds which amount to not less than ECU 5mn the Bank will exercise its discretion to take action on this ground consistent with article 10(5) of the Second Banking Coordination Directive which, where the circumstances justify it, allow an institution which fails to meet the requirement a limited period in which to do so or to cease its activities. Where an institution fails to meet the ECU 5mn requirement the Bank requires the institution to produce a viable plan to restore the capital requirement within a limited period.

6.10 The Bank will always review the fulfilment of the Schedule 3 criteria whenever a UK-incorporated bank is considering establishing, for example, an overseas branch in a particular country for the first time or another group company or a substantial expansion or change in its business. It will be particularly concerned to be satisfied that the staffing and management arrangements as well as the proposed systems and controls are adequate for the new business so that there would be, for example, adequate flows of information both to the bank's head office and, where appropriate, to the supervisors. If the arrangements seemed inadequate, the Bank would be likely to conclude that at least one of the Schedule 3 criteria is not met. In which case it is likely to decide to exercise its powers to prevent the establishment of the branch or whatever other new business was envisaged. (See also paragraph 2.28 above.)

7 Conclusion

The principles set out in this statement are of general application, and take account of the wide diversity of institutions authorised under the Act and differing circumstances. Nevertheless, there is likely to be a need for the principles to be developed over time. Section 16(2) of the Act requires the Bank to record in its annual reports under section 1(3) of the Act if it makes a material change in the principles in accordance with which it is acting or proposing to act. This will complement the more detailed papers the Bank publishes on particular aspects of its supervisory requirements. In addition, the Bank will issue revised versions of the statement of principles when there have been significant developments in its approach. **[826]**

The Banking Coordination (Second Council Directive) Regulations 1992:
Schedule 3 (paragraph 5)

1 Introduction

1.1 This statement is made pursuant to Schedule 3 (paragraph 5) of The Banking Co-ordination (Second Council Directive) Regulations 1992 (the 'Regulations'). This requires the Bank to publish a statement of the principles in accordance with which it is acting or proposing to act in exercising its power to impose a prohibition on or to restrict the listed activities of a European institution.[1]

1.2 This statement of the principles the Bank has adopted for determining when, and, if so, in what way, to exercise its powers to impose a prohibition and/or a restriction on a European institution, encapsulate the main standards and considerations to which the Bank has regard in exercising its supervisory responsibilities in respect of European institutions consistent with the allocation of supervisory responsibilities set out in the Second Banking Coordination Directive (the Directive). The principles are likely to require development over time in the light of, inter alia, the Bank's experience in cooperating with EC home State authorities within the framework of the memoranda of understanding which are being agreed with those authorities, and any further clarification of the interpretation of the Directive by the EC or the Courts. The Bank will publish revised versions of this statement should there be significant developments in its approach.

1.3 Part 2 of this statement sets out the general principles underlying the exercise of the Bank's discretion to impose a prohibition and/or to restrict the listed activities of a European institution. Part 3 considers the various grounds in regulations 9 and 10 of the Regulations for imposing a prohibition and/or a restriction on a European institution and expands upon the principles set out in Part 2.

---

[1] 'European institutions' consist of 'European authorised institutions' and 'European subsidiaries'. These are defined in regulation 3 of the Regulations.

---

2 General Principles relating to the imposition of a prohibition and/or a restriction on a European institution

2.1 The Bank uses its discretion to exercise its powers under the Regulations consistent with the provisions of the Directive. The Bank's powers in relation to European institutions are limited as under the Directive the competent authority in the home State has primary responsibility for the supervision of credit institutions incorporated in that State and certain of their subsidiaries (the 'Article 18.2 subsidiaries'). The host State authority, however, has a specific responsibility to cooperate with the home State authority in ensuring that branches of European credit institutions from that State maintain adequate liquidity in the host State. If also has responsibility to collaborate with the home State authority in ensuring that the credit institutions and their Article 18.2 subsidiaries carrying on listed activities in the host State take sufficient steps to cover risks arising from their open positions on financial markets in the host State.

2.2 As set out below the Bank's powers to impose a prohibition and/or a restriction may become exercisable in a wide range of circumstances. In view of the need for flexibility with problem cases, the Regulations give the Bank discretion whether or not to exercise them or to seek remedial action by some other means, for example, through persuasion and encouragement. Where the Bank considers that adequate and speedy remedial steps are likely to be taken by a European institution, it would generally not find it necessary to impose a prohibition or a restriction in relation to the home-regulated activities which the institution carries on in the United Kingdom.

2.3 Consistent with the allocation of supervisory responsibility in the Directive, the Bank will usually only exercise its powers after consulting the home State authority, and indeed, in certain circumstances, the Regulations explicitly require the Bank to do this. In most cases, the home State authority will be best placed to take action to ensure that the institution rectifies a situation which might otherwise provide grounds for the Bank to exercise its powers. In many cases too, the information the Bank would have regarding the activities and state of affairs of European institutions will be limited, reflecting the Bank's restricted role in relation to such institutions. Thus for example although the Regulations give the Bank power to impose a prohibition or a restriction in circumstances where it is informed by the supervisory authority in the home State that the institution is failing to take adequate steps to cover market risk in the UK the Bank, consistent with the terms of the Directive, would collaborate with the home State authority to determine the appropriate action to take in such circumstances.

2.4 To assist the home State authority, and in order to ensure that the Bank is better able to determine whether its powers are exercisable and should be exercised, the Bank has signed memoranda of understanding with a number of the other EC authorities (and is currently in the process of agreeing memoranda with the remaining EC authorities). The memoranda, inter alia, express the willingness of the respective authorities to exchange information in order to facilitate the effectiveness of the supervision of EC credit institutions and their Article 18(2) subsidiaries. They also provide for the exchange of information in crisis situations and in cases where the authorities become aware of contraventions of the law by institutions covered by the Directive operating in their territory.

2.5 In considering whether to exercise its powers the Bank would take into account the nature of the contravention in question and the action taken or to be taken by other relevant authorities in the UK. Thus where another UK regulator has taken action to restrict the activities of European institution in the UK and the Bank considers that this action, if complied with, is sufficient to remedy the situation the Bank would be unlikely to take further action itself. The Bank expects this to be normally the case where the institution's activities in the UK are, for example, largely confined to investment business. It would only be necessary to consider whether to impose a prohibition on deposit-taking in such a case where the institution has notified its intention to accept deposits in the UK.

3 Regulations 9 and 10: grounds for the imposition of a prohibition and/or a restriction on a European institution

3.1 Regulation 9 sets out the grounds upon which the Bank's power to impose a prohibition in relation to a European institution becomes exercisable. A prohibition means a prohibition on accepting deposits in the United Kingdom. These grounds also determine whether the Bank's power under regulation 10 to impose a restriction has become exercisable in relation to a European institution. A restriction means a direction that a European institution may not carry on any specified home-regulated activity (other than the acceptance of deposits) in the UK or that the European institution may not carry on a specified home-regulated activity in the UK other than in accordance with specified conditions.[1]

Regulation 9(2)(a)

3.2 This ground applies only in relation to European authorised institutions which have established a branch in the UK.[2] Under this, the Bank's powers become exercisable if it appears to the Bank that the UK branch of a European authorised institution is not or may not be maintaining or, as the case may be, will not or may not maintain adequate liquidity.

3.3 In considering the liquidity of a branch the Bank has regard to the relationship between its liquid assets and its actual and contingent liabilities, to the times at which those liabilities will or may fall due and its assets mature. Each institution is assessed in the light of its own particular circumstances. In considering whether the liquidity of the UK branch of such an institution is adequate it is also necessary for the Bank to have regard to the liquidity of the institution as a whole. This is because the branch may be called upon to use its liquid funds to finance maturing liabilities of the institution's other branches and head office. Conversely it may not be possible to judge the adequacy of the branch's liquidity without knowledge of the extent to which the institution as a whole at any one time is able to meet maturing liabilities in the UK. Therefore, in order to assist the Bank to determine whether this power is exercisable in relation to European authorised institutions, the Bank will seek from each of the relevant home State authorities an undertaking to notify the Bank immediately should there be any changes in the circumstances of European authorised institutions incorporated in that State which might have an impact on the liquidity of their UK branches.

3.4 The Bank also expects to agree with each institution a statement of liquidity policy covering, inter alia, strategy, management, systems and key variables used for monitoring liquidity, the role of a stock of high quality liquid assets and contingency plans in respect of abnormal circumstances. Once an acceptable liquidity policy is in place the Bank would agree individual liquidity mismatch guidelines with each bank, and subsequently monitor adherence to them on a quarterly basis (although the guidelines apply throughout the period on a continual basis). The appropriateness of the guidelines is also kept under review by the Bank. In order to ensure that the guidelines are appropriate to the institution's overall position the Bank will additionally consult the relevant home State authority on a regular basis.

3.5 In cases where the home State authority and the Bank are satisfied that the institution has an adequate global liquidity management programme, the Bank will not find it necessary to set individual liquidity mismatch guidelines. The Bank would expect to agree to such an arrangement where the branch is fully integrated (including its systems) with the head office for liquidity management purposes, where the head office has assured the Bank that liquidity is available to the branch at all times, if needed, and that there are no known constraints on the provision of liquidity by the head office to the branch. In addition the Bank would on a regular basis consult the home State authority and obtain information from the institution relating to the liquidity of its UK branch.

3.6 The Regulations (regulation 11) require the Bank to comply with the following procedure if the situation as respects a European authorised institution is such that the Bank's powers are exercisable by virtue of the circumstances set out in regulation 11(1) (covering the liquidity requirement in regulation 9(2)(a), and a failure to comply with a requirement imposed under section 39 of the Act for statistical purposes.) The Bank should require the institution in writing to remedy the situation. If the institution has failed to remedy the situation within a reasonable time, the Bank should give notice to that effect to the home State authority requesting that authority to take all appropriate measures for the purpose of ensuring that the institution remedies the situation and to inform the Bank of the measures it proposes to take or has taken or the reasons for not taking such measures. The Bank is only empowered to impose a prohibition or a restriction on a European institution if it is satisfied that the home State supervisory authority has failed or refused to take measures for the purpose of ensuring that the institution remedies the situation or if the measures taken by that authority have proved inadequate for that purpose.

3.7 If the Bank considers that a prohibition or restriction covered by regulation 11(1) should be imposed as a matter of urgency, regulation 11(5) permits the Bank to take steps to impose a prohibition or restriction without first making a written request to the institution to take remedial action, notifying the home State authority or waiting until it is satisfied as to whether the home State authority has taken adequate measures. In such a case, the Bank is required to inform the relevant supervisory authority and the European Commission of the steps taken at the earliest opportunity.[3] The Bank only expects to act under regulation 11(5) in extreme cases where, for example, it is impractical or impossible for the home State authority to take sufficient action in time to rectify a sudden liquidity crisis.

Regulation 9(2)(b)

3.8 This provides that the Bank's powers are exercisable where it is informed by the European institution's home State authority that the institution has failed to take any or sufficient steps to cover market risks arising in the UK. The Bank would generally expect to exercise its powers on this ground in circumstances in which the home State authority agrees that the exercise of such powers is necessary in order to assist it in ensuring that the institution takes adequate steps to cover market risks arising from open positions on the financial markets in the UK. In order to assist the home State authorities in carrying out their responsibilities the memoranda of understanding being agreed between them and the Bank provides that the Bank, on request, will provide information on the UK financial markets. They also provide for the Bank to notify home

State authorities of any developments in the UK which might cause major disruption in the UK financial markets as a whole.

Regulation 9(2)(c)

3.9 This provides that the Bank's powers are exercisable where the European institution has failed to comply with any obligation imposed on it by the Regulations or by or under any of the relevant Acts (ie the Banking Act, the Financial Services Act, the Consumer Credit Act and the Insurance Companies Act).[4] The obligations referred to are many and varied. The Bank will assess the circumstances of any failure to comply with such an obligation in order to determine the reasons for the failure and its significance. Any failure to comply with an obligation imposed on a European institution by the Regulations or by or under any of the relevant Acts will render the Bank's powers exercisable. In practice, however, the Bank is not likely to contemplate exercising its powers just because of an isolated failure which did not raise any wider issues of concern. In assessing this, the Bank is likely to take into account the views of the home State supervisor and if the contravention relates to UK legislation other than the Banking Act and the Regulations, the Bank is likely to seek the view of the other relevant UK supervisory authorities.

3.10 If the failure to comply with an obligation is a failure to comply with a requirement imposed under section 39 of the Banking Act (information and production of documents) for statistical purposes the regulation 11 procedure described in paragraph 3.7 (above) applies. In many cases, the Bank is likely to follow a similar procedure before exercising its powers under regulation 9(2)(c) where the institution has contravened any other obligation covered by that regulation.

Regulation 9(2)(d)

3.11 This provides that the Bank's powers are exercisable where it is informed by a supervisory authority in the European institution's home State that the institution has failed to comply with any obligation imposed on it by or under any rule of law in force in that State for purposes connected with the implementation of the Directive. In considering whether to exercise its powers under this regulation and the manner in which they should be exercised the Bank would generally seek the views of the home State authority as to the nature of the contravention, the degree to which it raises any issues of supervisory concern, and the action, if any, which it may be desirable for the Bank to take in relation to the institution.

Regulation 9(2)(e)

3.12 This provides that the Bank's powers are exercisable if it appears to the Bank that it has been provided with false, misleading or inaccurate information by or on behalf of the European institution or by or on behalf of a person who is or is to be a director, controller or manager of the institution. The mere provision of inaccurate information will render the power exercisable. In practice, however, the Bank is unlikely to contemplate exercising its powers just because of a minor inaccuracy. There would generally have to be a wider prudential concern, of which the inaccuracy may be a symptom.

Regulation 9(2)(f)

3.13 This provides that the Bank's powers are exercisable if it appears to the Bank that the situation as respects the European institution is such that, if it were authorised by the Bank under the Banking Act, the Bank could revoke its authorisation. The Bank is not able to exercise its powers under this regulation unless the Bank has first requested the relevant supervisory authority in the institution's home State to take all appropriate measures for the purpose of ensuring that the institution remedies the situation. Before the Bank's powers pursuant to section 9(2)(f) are exercisable it must also be satisfied either that the authority has failed or refused to take measures for that purpose or that the measures taken by that authority have proved inadequate for that purpose.

3.14 The principal circumstances in which this power would be available are those in which the grounds for revocation set out in section 11(1)(a) (a failure to fulfil the Schedule 3 criteria), section 11(6) (winding-up) and by section 11(1)(e) (other threats to the interests of depositors), would apply if the institution were authorised by the Bank under the Act.

3.15 The Bank's powers under this regulation are only exercisable in the exceptional circumstances where the home authority for some reason is unwilling or unable to adopt appropriate measures to ensure that remedial steps are taken by the institution (despite having received a request from the Bank to take such action). In such circumstances the Bank is most likely to exercise its powers when the situation of an institution is such that if it were authorised under the Act it would not be able to meet the Schedule 3 criteria. It is likely that any action taken by the Bank pursuant to regulation 9(2)(f) would be taken in cooperation with the other relevant UK supervisory authorities.

Other grounds for imposing a restriction

3.16 The Bank also has the power to impose a restriction on an institution proposing under the Regulations to establish a branch in the UK. This power is exercisable in the circumstances set out in regulation 8(2) where the Bank considers that its powers under regulation 9(2) are likely to become exercisable in relation to the institution. In this event the Bank may impose such restriction under regulation 10 as appears to it desirable. This power is most likely to be used by the Bank following discussions with the home state authority as to the situation of the institution in that State, and the nature of the institution's proposed activities in the UK.   **[827]**

---

¹ Section 12(4) of the Act (examples of conditions that may be imposed) applies for the purposes of regulation 10.
² The Bank's powers under regulation 9(2)(a) are only exercisable in relation to such institutions. Its powers under regulations 9(2)(b)–(f) are exercisable in respect of all European institutions including those institutions which have not established a branch in the UK.
³ The regulation 11 procedure does not apply in respect of the imposition of restrictions under regulation 8(2) (restriction imposed on an institution proposing to establish a branch in the UK) or in any case where regulation 12 (prohibition or restriction on information from supervisory authority) applies.
⁴ In the case of a European institution which is a member of a self-regulatory organisation, the reference to any obligation imposed by or under the relevant Acts includes a reference to any obligation imposed by the rules of that organisation.

THE BANKING COORDINATION (SECOND COUNCIL DIRECTIVE) REGULATIONS 1992:
SCHEDULE 7 (PARAGRAPH 6)

1 Introduction

1.1 The statement is made pursuant to Schedule 7 (paragraph 6) of The Banking Coordination (Second Council Directive) Regulations 1992 (the 'Regulations'). This requires the Bank to publish a statement of the principles in accordance with which it is acting or proposing to act in exercising its power to restrict the listed activities of a 'UK subsidiary'.¹

1.2 This statement of the principles the Bank has adopted for determining when, and, if so, in what way, to exercise its powers to impose a restriction on a UK subsidiary, encapsulate the main standards and considerations to which the Bank has regard in exercising its supervisory responsibilities in respect of those institutions. The principles are likely to require development over time in the light of, inter alia, the Bank's experience in cooperating with EC home State authorities within the framework of the memoranda of understanding which are being agreed with those authorities, and any further clarification of the interpretation of the Second Banking Coordination Directive by the EC or the Courts. The Bank will publish revised versions of this statement should there be significant developments in its approach.

2 Principles relating to the imposition of a restriction on the listed activities of a UK subsidiary

2.1 Regulation 23 grants the Bank power to impose a restriction in relation to the listed activities² carried on in the UK by UK subsidiaries. The power of the Bank to impose restrictions under regulation 23 is available only in respect of those UK subsidiaries to which regulation 22(1) applies.

2.2 A restriction means a direction that a UK subsidiary to which section 22(1) applies—

(a) may not carry on in the UK any listed activity which is specified in the direction; or

(b) may not carry on in the UK, otherwise than in accordance with such condition or conditions as may be specified in the direction, any such activity which is so specified.

Subsection (4) of section 12 of the Banking Act (examples of conditions that may be imposed) applies for the purposes of this regulation.

2.3 Regulation 23(2) provides that the Bank may impose such restriction as appears to it desirable where it appears that the situation as respects the UK subsidiary is such that, if it were authorised by the Bank under the Banking Act, the Bank could revoke its authorisation on the ground specified in section 11(1)(a) of the Act. Therefore, the Bank's power is exercisable if it appears to the Bank that, if the UK subsidiary were an authorised institution, any of the criteria specified in Schedule 3 to the Act is not or has not been fulfilled, or may not be or may not have been fulfilled in respect of the UK subsidiary. In respect of UK subsidiaries Schedule 3 to the Act has effect as if paragraph 6 (minimum initial capital) were omitted.[3]

2.4 If it appears to the Bank that any of the Schedule 3 criteria is not or has not been fulfilled or may not be or may not have been fulfilled by the UK subsidiary, the Bank's powers under regulation 23 would be exercisable. In view of the need for flexibility in dealing with problem cases, regulation 23 gives the Bank discretion to decide whether to impose a restriction or seek remedial action by some other means, for example, through persuasion and encouragement. Where the Bank considers that adequate and speedy remedial steps are likely to be taken it would generally not find it necessary to impose a restriction. In many cases the Bank would expect the UK subsidiary to undertake such action without the need for the Bank to exercise its formal powers. The Bank would also expect the parent authorised institution to ensure that this was done. The Bank would generally restrict where there was no reasonable prospect of speedy and comprehensive remedial action.

2.5 In deciding whether to restrict activities which are supervised by other UK supervisors, however, the Bank would normally first seek the view of those supervisors. In many cases the matters which bring into question whether the Schedule 3 criteria are fulfilled are also relevant to whether the business of the UK subsidiary is being conducted in conformity with the requirements of those supervisors. Where this is the case it is likely that the Bank would consult with the other supervisors regarding how the situation should be rectified. In cases where the institution is mainly carrying on business which is supervised by another UK supervisor under UK legislation other than the Banking Act 1987 the Bank is likely to consult the relevant supervisor to establish whether the situation would be best regularised by that supervisor taking action under the relevant legislation. Where this can be achieved the Bank might often find that it is not necessary for it to exercise its powers under regulation 23 in relation to the UK subsidiary.

---

[1] These are financial institutions which are 90% subsidiary undertakings of UK authorised institutions which meet the requirements of regulation 20(3) of the Regulations.
[2] As defined in the Regulations.
[3] The Bank's interpretation of the Schedule 3 criteria as they apply in relation to institutions authorised under the Banking Act is set out in the Statement of principles issued under section 16 of that Act.

BSD/1993/2
(October 1993)

NOTICE TO INSTITUTIONS AUTHORISED UNDER THE BANKING ACT 1987

IMPLEMENTATION IN THE UNITED KINGDOM OF THE DIRECTIVE ON THE MONITORING AND CONTROL OF LARGE EXPOSURES OF CREDIT INSTITUTIONS

Introduction

1 The United Kingdom is required to adopt the necessary measures to comply with the 'Council Directive on the monitoring and control of large exposures of credit institutions'[1] (92/121/EEC of 21 December 1992) by 1 January 1994. This notice is being issued to adopt the provisions of that directive but the Bank has also reviewed its policy on large exposures and has taken this opportunity to make certain changes to policy in addition to those arising from the directive. This notice takes effect from 1 January 1994 and the Bank's notice BSD/1987/1[2], which set out previous policy on large exposures, and the notices BSD/1990/1 and BSD/1992/2, which amend the 1987 notice, will be withdrawn from that date. As required by section 38 of the Banking Act 1987 ('the Act') this notice[3] also sets out the principles by which the Bank will determine whether, and the extent to which, an authorised institution other than one whose principal place of business is outside the UK has an exposure which must be notified to the Bank within the terms of that section.

2 The terms of the Large Exposures Directive are broadly comparable to those of the Bank's 1987 notice on large exposures. The implementation of the directive will lead to a shift in emphasis in the Bank's large exposures policy with the introduction of explicit limits on the size of exposures that may be undertaken. These limits will operate in parallel with the notification requirements of the Act.

3 This notice describes the principal features of the Bank's policy on large exposures and Annex 1 contains definitions and details of reporting requirements and the limits structure which will apply. Annex 2 covers underwriting exposures, Annex 3 reproduces section 38 of the Act and Annex 4 covers the use of national discretion under the Large Exposures Directive.

---

[1] Referred to as the 'Large Exposures Directive' throughout this notice.

[2] BSD/1987/1, 'Large exposures undertaken by institutions authorised under the Banking Act 1987', September 1987.

[3] See Annex 3. It should be noted that s 38(9) of the Banking Act 1987 states that an institution which fails to make a report as required by that section shall be guilty of an offence and (s 38(10)) liable on summary conviction to a fine.

Scope and application

4 The provisions of this notice[1] apply to authorised institutions other than discount houses. The policy applying to discount houses is addressed in a separate notice. The Bank's policy towards branches of banks incorporated outside the EC is described in paragraph 43. The monitoring and limiting of large exposures of branches of banks incorporated in other EC Member States is an aspect of prudential supervision, the responsibility for which is reserved for the home State authorities.

---

[1] The Large Exposures Directives applies to credit institutions defined by the First Banking Co-ordination Directive (77/780/EEC, 'First Council directive on the co-ordination of laws, regulations and administrative provisions relating to the taking up and pursuit of the business of credit institutions', 12 December 1977) which have obtained the authorisation referred to in Article 3 of that directive. The statutory notification requirements of s 38 of the Act apply to authorised institutions other than those with their principal place of business outside the United Kingdom.

Consolidation

5 The Bank will apply its policy for the monitoring and control of large exposures at both the consolidated and unconsolidated (solo) level, unless there is a specific

statement made to the contrary, and throughout this notice the requirements which apply to 'banks' should be understood to apply also to consolidated 'banking groups' and vice versa. The limits and reporting requirements of the Large Exposures Directive apply at a consolidated level[1] and the statutory notification requirements of section 38 of the Act apply on an unconsolidated (solo) basis. All references to consolidation in this notice relate to the principles of consolidation contained in the Second Consolidated Supervision Directive[2] which have been implemented by the Bank in its notice BSD/1993/1[3].

6 In assessing a bank's exposures on a consolidated basis the companies to be consolidated with the bank (which may include sister companies, and holding companies, as well as subsidiaries) must be agreed with the Bank in accordance with the principles set out in the Bank's notice on consolidated supervision. Where these principles determine that a sub-group of a banking group should be separately assessed (including a requirement for separate consolidated returns to be provided) a bank's large exposures will also be assessed on that basis.

[1] For institutions which are supervised solely on an unconsolidated/solo-consolidated basis the requirements of the Large Exposures Directive apply at that level.
[2] 92/30 – EEC, 'Council Directive on the supervision of credit institutions on a consolidated basis', 6 April 1992.
[3] BSD/1993/1, 'Implementation in the United Kingdom of the Directive on the consolidated supervision of credit institutions', February 1993.

Market risks

7 The Bank will, until the implementation of the Capital Adequacy Directive[1], treat exposures arising from activities which are principally subject to market risks in the same way as other sorts of exposures. The Bank will make two exceptions to this approach: it will continue to require that exposures arising from underwriting commitments are monitored and controlled on the same basis as that outlined in BSD/1987/1.1 (see Annex 2); and exposures to Zone B central governments and central banks arising from activities which are principally subject to market risks will be exempt from the limits set out below. In recognition of the interim nature of the regime applying to market risk exposures, the Bank will allow banks to make limited use of the option available under Article 4(9) of the Large Exposures Directive which allows for the scaling down of exposures of one to three years' maturity to banks. This option is described in more detail in paragraph 4 of Annex 1.

[1] 93/6/EEC, 'Council Directive on the capital adequacy of investment firms and credit institutions', 15 March 1993.

Banks' policy statements

8 The Bank requires each bank to set out its policy on large exposures, including exposures to individual customers, banks, countries and economic sectors, in a policy statement. In the case of UK incorporated banks, this policy should be formally adopted by the bank's board of directors. The Bank expects banks not to implement significant changes in these policies without prior discussion with the Bank. Significant departures from a bank's stated policy, in particular those involving breaches of agreed levels, will lead the Bank to consider whether the bank continues to meet the statutory minimum criteria for authorisation.

9 Each bank will be expected to justify to the Bank its policy on exposures to individual counterparties, including the maximum size of an exposure contemplated. Relevant factors which the Bank will expect a bank to have taken into account when setting its policy and considering the acceptability of particular exposures include, for example, the standing of the counterparty, the nature of the bank's relationship with the counterparty, the nature and extent of security taken against the exposure, the maturity of the exposure, and the bank's expertise in the particular type of transaction. Exposures to counterparties connected with the bank – for example, subsidiaries or sister companies or companies with common directors – will continue to be particularly closely examined. (Exposures to counterparties connected to the reporting bank are considered in paragraphs 16–18 and 26–32 below.)

10 The necessary control systems to give effect to a bank's policy on large exposures must be clearly specified and monitored by its board. Banks will be required to detail how they intend to monitor the size of capital base to ensure that the limits detailed in this notice are not exceeded.

The measure of exposure

11 The measure of exposure should reflect the maximum loss should a counterparty fail. Consistent with this, an exposure encompasses the amount at risk arising from the reporting bank's:

(i) claims on a counterparty including actual claims, and potential claims which would arise from the drawing down in full of undrawn advised facilities (whether revocable or irrevocable, conditional or unconditional) which the bank has committed itself to provide, and claims which the bank has committed itself to purchase or underwrite; and

(ii) contingent liabilities arising in the normal course of business, and those contingent liabilities which would arise from the drawing down in full of undrawn advised facilities (whether revocable or irrevocable, conditional or unconditional) which the bank has committed itself to provide; and

(iii) assets, and assets which the bank has committed itself to purchase or underwrite, whose value depends wholly or mainly on a counter party performing his obligations, or whose value otherwise depends on that counterparty's financial soundness but which do not represent a claim on the counterparty. A fuller definition of the measure of exposure and the amount at risk is set out in Annex 1. This definition also covers items which are excluded from the measure of exposure.

Identity of counterparty

12 The identity of a counterparty will generally be the borrower (customer), the person guaranteed, the issuer of a security in the case of a security held or the party with whom a contract was made in the case of a derivatives contract. Where a third party has provided an explicit unconditional irrevocable guarantee, banks may however be permitted to report the exposure as being to the guarantor. As a condition for allowing banks to report exposures in this way, the Bank will require banks to include a section on guaranteed exposures in their large exposures policy statement. In particular the Bank would expect a consistent approach to be adopted in the reporting of such exposures. The Bank does not expect banks to report exposures to guarantors unless the banks have first approved the credit risk on the guarantor and the type of the exposure under the bank's normal credit approval procedures.

Limits for large exposures

13 The implementation of the Large Exposures Directive means that there will be absolute limits on the size of exposures that may be undertaken by UK incorporated banks. The limits are set out in paragraphs (1) to (3) of Article 4 of the Large Exposures Directive which then offers national discretion for the exemption of certain types of exposures from these limits. The limits are of two sorts: an overall limit on the aggregate of large exposures that may be undertaken and limits on the size of individual exposures. The limits are set out in paragraphs 14–17 below, and the exposures that are exempt from these limits (but not from reporting requirements) in paragraphs 25–36, with further details in Annex 1. The Bank may in exceptional circumstances agree to a waiver of any or all of these limits at the unconsolidated, solo-consolidated or consolidated sub-group level for institutions subject to further consolidated supervision by the Bank. This will be taken up with individual institutions on a case by case basis.

Aggregate limit on large exposures

14 A banking group[1] may not incur exposures which exceed 10% of capital base, to individual counterparties or groups of closely related counterparties[2] which in aggregate exceed 800% of the group's consolidated capital base.

---

[1] Institutions supervised solely on an unconsolidated basis (and not part of a wider UK banking group) may not incur exposures which exceed in aggregate 800% of capital base.

[2] See definition in Annex 1. The term 'individual counterparty' is used in this notice to include also 'group of closely related counterparties'.

Single exposure limit

15 A banking group may not incur an exposure to an individual counterparty which exceeds 25% of the group's consolidated capital base[1].

[1] A bank which is supervised solely on an unconsolidated (solo) basis (and is not part of a wider UK banking group) may not incur an exposure to a individual counterparty which exceeds 25% of its unconsolidated (solo) capital base.

Limit on exposures to connected counterparties[1]

16 Exposures to companies or persons connected with the lending bank, its managers, directors or controllers require special care to ensure a proper objective credit assessment is undertaken. Such exposures may be justified only when undertaken for the clear commercial advantage of the lending bank, and when they are negotiated and agreed on an arm's length basis.

17 A bank or banking group's exposures to all connected entities outside the scope of consolidated returns, *when* taken together, may not exceed 25% of capital base[2]. (Although Article 4(2) of the Large Exposures Directive specifies a limit of 20% for exposures to a parent undertaking, subsidiary or sister company of the bank, Member States may exempt these exposures from such a limit where specific monitoring by other means is required. The Bank will not be applying this lower limit because it requires banks to provide a detailed breakdown of their exposures to connected counterparties and will subject them to particular scrutiny.)

18 The Bank will examine particularly closely all exposures to companies or persons connected to a lending bank and will deduct them from the bank's capital base if they are of the nature of a capital investment or are made on particularly concessionary terms.

[1] See Annex 1 for a definition of 'connected counterparty'.
[2] For a bank which is supervised solely on an unconsolidated (solo) basis (and is not part of a wider UK banking group) exposures to connected counterparties other than those included in solo supervision must not exceed 25% of unconsolidated (solo) capital base.

Notification of exposures

Pre-notification of exposures exceeding 25% of capital base

19 There are very limited circumstances in which a bank or banking group may enter into exposures which exceed 25% of capital. These include 'exempt exposures' (**see below for definition**), underwriting exposures and exposures at solo, solo-consolidated or consolidated sub-group level where the Bank has agreed to waive the 25% limit. When a bank or banking group proposes to enter into an exposure, which either alone or together with other existing exposures to the same counterparty exceeds 25% of capital, must be notified to the Bank before the bank becomes committed to the exposure. Where the Bank has been pre-notified of, and agreed, a bank's limits for such an exposure, exposures which do not exceed those limits need not be further pre-notified to the Bank.

20 Exposures to overseas countries, and economic sectors, which exceed 25% of the bank's capital are also not covered by the pre-notification requirements. However, where a proposed transaction will result in an exposure which represents a significant departure from the bank's statement of policy on its large exposures agreed with the Bank (see paragraph 6), the Bank will expect the proposed transaction to be pre-notified to and discussed with it.

Post-notification of exposures

21 UK incorporated banks and banking groups are required to report all large exposures on a quarterly basis. The more an individual exposure exceeds 10% the more rigorous the Bank will be in requiring a bank's management to justify that exposure. In

any case banks are expected to adopt policies which will not lead to 10% being exceeded as a matter of course. Although 10% of capital base is the minimum cut-off level that will be applied for reporting purposes, for some banks the Bank will determine it prudent to set a lower percentage.

22 Should any bank find that for reasons outside its control or otherwise (eg two counterparties merging to form a single counterparty) it has an exposure to an individual counterparty (other than an exempt exposure) which results in it exceeding any of the limits set out in paragraphs 14–17 above, this should be reported immediately to the Bank. The Bank will discuss the circumstances of any such exposures to determine the appropriate means and time-frame for the bank to comply with the limits.

23 It may be impractical for some banks to introduce monitoring systems which would enable them to calculate precisely their exposure (in accordance with the definition of an exposure set out in this notice) to individual counterparties at all times. Such banks, which will usually have an extensive branch network or group structure, will typically have adopted a system of limits which are allocated to individual branches or group companies but which ensure that the overall exposure to a counterparty is controlled. For such banks the Bank may agree that, for the purpose of post-notification, the maximum exposure to a counterparty occurring during a reporting period is not required to be reported; but they will be required to report their actual exposure at the reporting date and the control limit for that counterparty if either exceeds 10% of their capital base. The bank must have satisfied the Bank that it can control the size of its exposures through the adoption and allocation of counterparty limits. The Bank will need to be satisfied that the bank's control systems are such that its exposure to a counterparty may reliably be taken as being no higher than its adopted limit for that counterparty.

24 While most banks should already have systems for monitoring credit risk on interest and exchange rate contracts, the Bank accepts that the measurement of exposure may differ from that required by the Directive. Again the Bank will agree with each bank needing to undertake systems development a deadline by which the bank must comply with the terms of this notice. However, the Bank will only be able to accept an alternative method of monitoring if it can be shown that this results in a measure of exposure which is at least as stringent as that required by the Directive.

Exempt exposures

25 Certain types of exposure are exempt from the limits in paragraphs 14–17 above but the Bank's requirements regarding pre- and post-notification as set out in paragraphs 19–24 continue to apply to these exposures. The exemptions fall into the following categories:

- short term interbank exposures;
- exposures to Zone A central governments (and limited exposures to Zone B central governments);
- exposures secured on cash or Zone A central government securities;
- certain connected exposures, in particular those arising from a group Treasury function;
- exposures which are covered by a parental guarantee; and
- underwriting exposures.

These exemptions are made because of the particular nature of the exposures concerned. For example, the treatment of short-term interbank exposures is justified because such lending to banks is normally liquid and is generally likely to involve a lower degree of risk than lending to other borrowers.

Exempt exposures to connected counterparties

26 Exposures to subsidiaries which are regarded within the Bank's policy on consolidated supervision as, in effect, divisions of the parent bank, and are consolidated with the parent bank in the calculation of the bank's capital ratio on a solo basis (ie are subject to 'solo consolidation'), are excluded from the scope of the large exposures policy.

27 In respect of exposures to other group companies the Bank's policy allows a bank to take on a Treasury role (see also paragraph 28 of Annex 1) on behalf of the group[1] as a whole (provided that the group is subject to consolidated supervision by its home supervisor). Appropriate levels for such exposures will be agreed on a case by case basis. It will be for the bank to satisfy the Bank that it should fulfil such a role and has appropriate management and other group control systems in place to ensure that risk-taking in those group companies is properly monitored and controlled.

28 The implementation of the Large Exposures Directive has brought derivative products within the measure of exposure. For this reason, the Bank's policy regarding the taking on of a Treasury role is extended to cover exposures arising from a central risk management function. In certain cases the Bank will be prepared to consider whether the scope of the Treasury concession should be extended to cover exposures of over one year's maturity arising from the operation of central risk management function. In such cases the Bank will have regard to whether this would lead to an overall reduction in the risks to which a group as a whole is exposed.

29 In certain exceptional cases, exposures of more than 25% of capital base to a bank which controls the lending bank may be permitted, even where the lending bank does not perform a Treasury role. The Bank envisages that such lending would be allowed only in a limited number of cases and would consist of short term lending of surplus liquid funds.

30 The inclusion within the connected lending limit of exposures to connected banks which are incorporated within the EC will be generally considered on a case by case basis. These may also fall within a Treasury concession.

31 Exposures to group banks, financial and non-financial companies, not covered by paragraphs 26–30 above will be aggregated and considered as an exposure to an individual non-bank counterparty (ie will be subject to a 25% limit).

32 Other forms of connected exposure (in particular, to companies with which directors are associated) will be considered on a case by case basis. Where the link with the connected company is fairly remote, for example, where a non-executive director of a large bank is a director of the borrowing company, the exposure may be considered as acceptable up to the normal level for that bank. If, however, there is a particularly close connection, the exposure will be aggregated within the 25% limit for connected lending.

---

[1] In this context a group is limited to parent, subsidiaries, and subsidiaries of a parent.

Exposures undertaken by subsidiary[1] banks which are guaranteed by a parent bank

33 Where exposures undertaken by a subsidiary bank are guaranteed by a parent bank the subsidiary bank may be deemed to have an exposure to the parent. Under the terms of the Large Exposures Directive, exposures to a parent bank may be exempt from the limits on large exposures detailed above where the group is subject to consolidated supervision. The Bank may therefore allow such subsidiaries to take on exposures exceeding 25% of their own capital base but only if they are entered into within the terms of a policy agreed by the parent bank and provided that there are guarantees[2] in place (acceptable to the Bank) from the parent bank to protect the subsidiary should the exposure become non-performing or require to be written off. The Bank will require written confirmation from the parent bank that the exposure is retained in the subsidiary's balance sheet at the parent bank's request in order to meet group objectives and will need to be satisfied as to the nature of the exposure concerned. These requirements recognise that it may be the policy in some bank groups to concentrate particular types of lending or other facilities in one subsidiary.

34 In the case of authorised bank subsidiaries of UK banks, in order for an exposure exceeding 25% of capital base to be acceptable in the subsidiary bank, the parent bank must at all times have room to take over the exposure without itself exceeding the limit of 25% of capital base. Also the total exposure of the banking group to the customer must be within 25% of the group's capital base. The Bank will need to be satisfied that adequate control systems are in place to ensure that credit risk taken in the group as a whole is properly monitored and controlled.

35 In the case of authorised banks which are subsidiaries of overseas banks the Bank will wish to agree with the supervisory authority of the parent bank the size of exposures which can be undertaken by the subsidiary within the terms of this policy. It will also require written assurance from the overseas supervisor that he or she is content for the subsidiary to undertake the level of exposure in question. Before agreeing a level for the subsidiary the Bank will take into account the degree and extent of the consolidated supervision of the banking group exercised by the parent supervisory authority.

36 Overseas bank subsidiaries of UK banks will be expected to conform to the regulatory requirements of the country in which they are located.

---

[1] The definition of, 'subsidiary' will normally be that used in the Companies Act 1985.

[2] An acceptable parental 'guarantee' for this purpose should prevent a bank's capital from becoming deficient as a result of experiencing a loss on such an exposure. It may take a number of forms and may where appropriate include for example a formal guarantee or refinancing agreement to cover the whole of the exposure or an undertaking to make up any resultant deficiency in the subsidiary's capital. The arrangement should be legally enforceable by the subsidiary.

Additional capital requirements

37 The Bank may require a UK incorporated bank to maintain higher capital ratios than would otherwise be the case when it considers it to be exposed to particular concentrations of risk. It is the Bank's practice, where a bank has a number of exposures, which are not exempt from the limits, of more than 10% of capital base and, in particular, where the total of those exposures exceeds 100% of capital base, to consider whether such measures are necessary. However in considering the amount of capital to be maintained the Bank would have regard to the acceptability of the exposures when considered in the context of the bank's large exposures policy agreed with the Bank; the particular characteristics of the individual bank, including the nature of its business and the experience of its management; and the number of such exposures, their individual size and nature.

38 In those cases where an exposure (which is not an exempt exposure) exceeds 25%[1] of capital base, the Bank will require additional capital cover which will be significantly higher than would be required for an exposure of less than 25%, and this requirement will generally apply whether or not the Bank agrees that the exposure has been incurred in the most exceptional circumstances. The undertaking of an exposure in excess of 25% other than the most exceptional circumstances will also call into question the bank's continued authorisation.

39 Where a bank is a subsidiary of another UK bank and it has exposures exceeding 25% of its capital base but the parent bank has made arrangements (within the terms of the policy set out in paragraphs 33–36) to protect the subsidiary if problems occur, the additional capital cover, if any, may be held in the parent bank rather than the subsidiary. The additional capital cover will be determined by the size of the exposure (together with other exposures to the same counterparty entered into by the parent bank) in relation to the parent bank's capital base.

---

[1] See paragraph 13 above, regarding the circumstances in which an exposure exceeding 25% of capital may be incurred.

Exposures to countries

40 The Bank does not believe that a common limit should be applied to the aggregate of banks' exposures to counterparties in the same country; nor does it consider it appropriate to publish guideline percentages for the acceptable level of exposure to counterparties in particular countries. Banks will, however, be expected to set limits for country exposures on the basis of their own risk assessments. The nature of the exposure (for example, whether it is trade finance or longer term balance of payments finance) will be relevant in considering an acceptable level of exposure. The Bank will continue to monitor closely banks' country risk exposures, and discuss them with banks' managements.

Exposures to economic sectors

41 The extent to which a bank may be prudently exposed to a particular industrial sector or geographical region will vary considerably depending upon the characteristics

of the bank and the sector or region concerned. Sectors and regions are difficult to define and the definitions for one bank may not be appropriate for another. The Bank will not therefore apply common maximum percentages to banks' sectoral exposures.

42 The Bank will continue to monitor banks' exposures to sectors and regions and will wish to discuss with all banks their internal monitoring systems and the appropriateness of the sectors identified in their management reports. The Bank will wish to ensure that banks have prudent lending policies which take into account the dangers from over-exposure to particular economic sectors both within the United Kingdom and worldwide. The considerations apply to regional concentrations. Such policies will need to be adjusted from time to time in order to take account of changing market conditions and economic trends. The Bank will continue to obtain information on sectoral and regional exposures from banks' internal monitoring systems.

Exposures undertaken by UK branches of banks incorporated outside the EC

43 The Bank's policy towards large exposures in branches of overseas banks incorporated outside the EC takes into account the need for such exposures to be assessed in relation to the capital and exposures of the bank as a whole as well as to the balance sheet of the branch. Knowledge of large exposures in a branch is important for a host supervisor, particularly, but not solely, in order to carry out a full assessment of the branch's liquidity. The Bank therefore wishes to continue to examine and discuss with the management of each branch its largest exposures measured in relation to the balance sheet of the branch and reserves the right to discuss with the home supervisory authority the size of exposures undertaken by the UK branch. The Bank will also give particular consideration to the exposure of branches of overseas banks to the country of incorporation of the bank.

Annex 1 National discretion

The Large Exposures Directive offers scope for the use of national discretion in a number of areas. The Bank's use of these options is summarised in Annex 4 to this Notice. The Bank reserves the right to make further use of national discretion if it considers it appropriate in the future, for example, in the treatment of exposures arising from activities principally subject to market risk. Such activities are the subject of the Capital Adequacy Directive (93/6/EEC) and its implementation in January 1996 is likely to lead to a review of the Bank's large exposures treatment of them.

Definitions

An exposure

1 An exposure is defined in the Large Exposures Directive as the amount at risk arising from the reporting bank's assets and off-balance sheet items referred to in Article 6 of the Solvency Ratio Directive[1] and in Annexes I and III of that directive before the application of risk weightings and credit conversion factors. In the United Kingdom this definition encompasses the assets and off-balance sheet items set out in Annexes 1, 2 and 3 of BSD/1990/3[2].

2 The amount of risk will be taken as the full amount (ie the book value in accordance with the terms of the Bank Accounts Directive[3]) of the reporting bank's claims and contingent liabilities, and potential claims and liabilities in the case of undrawn facilities, unless stated otherwise in the detailed reporting instructions issued by the Bank for the completion of the large exposures returns or as set out below. In general, exposures should be reported on a gross basis, meaning that credit balances should not be offset against debit balances.

3 The amount at risk arising from interest rate contracts (including interest rate swaps, forward rate agreements and interest rate options purchased), foreign exchange rate contracts (including cross currency swaps, forward foreign exchange contracts and foreign exchange options purchased) and other derivative contracts such as commodity and equity derivatives, is not taken to be the nominal amount of a contract but rather a credit equivalent amount. The method for calculating the credit equivalent amount is the same as that used in the calculation of the risk asset ratio (ie the replacement cost or

original exposure method set out in BSD/1990/3) and described in detail in the reporting instructions for the large exposure return.

4 Article 4(9) of the Large Exposures Directive allows for a scaling down of exposures to banks and building societies, with a maturity of more than one but not more than three years, by the application of a 20% weighting before inclusion in the measure of exposure. The Bank will allow limited use of this concessionary treatment for derivative products only (ie items covered by paragraph 3 above). Banks which wish to take up this option should contact the Banking Supervision Division.

5 Similarly the measure of exposure used in the monitoring and controlling of exposures arising through underwriting activities is not the nominal amount of the exposure but a credit equivalent amount. The method of calculation of this amount is discussed in more detail in Annex 2 covering underwriting exposures.

6 The following items will not be included in the measurement of exposure:

   (i) items deducted from capital base (both for the calculation of capital ratios and for large exposures purposes);
   (ii) claims arising in the course of settlement of a foreign exchange transaction on a counterparty where the reporting institution has its side of the transaction but has not received the countervalue, for a period of up to two working days after payment was made. After this period such claims will constitute an exposure;
   (iii) claims arising in the course of settlement of a securities transaction where such claims are outstanding up to a maximum of five working days. Such claims arise where payment has been made or securities delivered but before the countervalue (ie the securities or cash payment respectively) has been received. Where neither counterparty to the transaction has settled there will be no reportable exposure until 21 days after due settlement date (after which the replacement cost of the transaction will be considered to be an exposure).

7 Apart from the types of exposure mentioned above risks arising from the settlement of transactions are not included within the scope of the Large Exposures Directive. However, the control of such exposures needs to be carefully considered by banks since inadequate controls could be a cause of substantial loss for a bank. The Bank will therefore pay particular attention during the course of its supervision to how individual banks control such risks.

8 A bank's exposure arising from securities trading operations is calculated as its net long position in a particular security (**a short position in one security issue may not be offset against a long position in another issue made by the same issuer**).

[1] 89/647/EEC, 'Council Directive on a solvency ratio for credit institutions', 18 December 1989.
[2] BSD/1990/3, 'Implementation in the United Kingdom of the Solvency Ratio Directive', December 1990, as amended by BSD/1992/6.
[3] 86/935/EEC, 'Council Directive on the annual accounts and consolidated accounts of banks and other financial institutions', 8 December 1986.

A large exposure

9 A large exposure is defined as an exposure to a counterparty or group of closely related counterparties which is greater than or equal to 10% of capital base.

Capital base

10 The capital base used as the basis for monitoring and controlling large exposures should be calculated according to the method set out in the Bank's notice BSD/1990/2[1] (ie the same as that used in the calculation of the risk asset ratio). The figure will be agreed by the Bank with the reporting bank on the basis of the bank's audited balance sheet for the latest financial year, and may be reset during the year, in agreement with the Bank, to take account of verified interim profits. The Bank, will, however, adjust this figure for new issues of capital during the course of the year and take account of other significant changes to the capital base, either upwards or downwards. In either

circumstance the amended figure will be agreed with the bank and advised to it in writing.

[1] BSD/1990/2, 'Implementation in the United Kingdom of the Directive on own funds of credit institutions', December 1990, as amended by BSD/1992/1.

An individual counterparty and a group of closely related counterparties

11 Exposures are required to be reported and controlled according to the nature of the counterparty. For example, exposures to bank and non-bank counterparties will be treated differently. Furthermore exposures to a group of closely related counterparties must be aggregated and treated as if they were exposures to a single counterparty.

Individual non-bank counterparty

12 An 'individual non-bank counterparty' comprises natural and legal persons and includes individual trusts, corporations, unincorporated businesses (whether as sole traders or partnerships) and non-profit making bodies.

Closely related counterparties

13 A group of **closely related counterparties** exists where:

> (i) unless it can be shown otherwise, two or more individual counterparties constitute a single risk because one of them has, directly or indirectly, control[1] over the other or others; or
>
> (ii) individual counterparties are connected in such a way that the financial soundness of any of them may affect the financial soundness of the other or others or the same factors may affect the financial soundness of both or all of them.

In such cases the exposure to these individual counterparties should be aggregated and considered as a single exposure to a group of closely related counterparties.

14 Where there is doubt in a particular case whether a number of individual counterparties constitute a group of closely related counterparties or where, notwithstanding that the relationship between a number of counterparties identified in the reporting instructions exist, the counterparties do not share a common risk, the circumstances should be discussed with the Banking Supervision Division to determine how the exposure(s) should be reported.

[1] 'Control' is defined as the relationship between a parent undertaking and a subsidiary, as defined in Article 1 of Directive 83/349/EEC, 'Council Directive on the supervision of credit institutions on a consolidated basis', of 13 June 1983, or a similar relationship between any natural or legal person and an undertaking.

A connected counterparty

15 Parties connected to the reporting bank comprise:

> (i) group undertakings (including subsidiaries) as defined by section 262 of the Companies Act 1985 as amended by the Companies Act 1989 and related companies as defined by section 105 of the Banking Act as amended by The Banking Coordination (Second Council Directive) Regulations 1992;
>
> (ii) associated companies as defined by the Statement of Standard Accounting Practice 1;
>
> (iii) directors, controllers and their associates as defined in section 105 of the Banking Act 1987 as amended by The Banking Coordination (Second Council Directive) Regulations 1992;
>
> (iv) non-group companies with which the reporting bank's directors and controllers are associated.

A director (including an alternate director) and controller of the reporting bank is deemed to be associated with another company, whether registered or domiciled in the UK or overseas, if he holds the office of a director (or alternate director) with that company (whether in his or her own right, or as a result of a loan granted by, or financial interest taken by, the reporting bank to, or in, that company, or even by virtue of a professional interest unconnected with the reporting bank), or if he and/or his associates, as defined above, together hold 10% or more of the equity share capital of that company. For the purposes of the large exposures policy, an employee of the lending bank who is not a director but who is appointed by the lending bank to be a director of another company is also treated as a director of the lending bank.

16 For exposures to connected counterparties other than parent, subsidiary or sister companies, where the lending bank is able to demonstrate to the Bank's satisfaction that, notwithstanding that a connection with a counterparty exists, the bank's relationship with that counterparty is at arm's length, its exposure to that counterparty will not be considered as an exposure to a counterparty connected to the lending bank.

Zone A/Zone B countries

17 Zone A[1] countries are all countries which are full members of the Organisation for Economic Co-operation and Development (OECD), together with those countries which have concluded special lending arrangements with the International Monetary Fund associated with the General Agreement to Borrow. Zone B countries are all countries not in Zone A.

---

[1] These countries comprise: Australia, Austria, Belgium, Canada, Denmark, Finland, France, Germany, Greece, Iceland, Ireland, Italy, Japan, Luxembourg, the Netherlands, New Zealand, Norway, Portugal, Saudi Arabia, Spain, Sweden, Switzerland, Turkey, United Kingdom and United States.

Limits

Single exposure limit

18 An exposure to an individual counterparty (other than an exempt exposure) may not exceed 25% of capital base.

Aggregate limit

19 Aggregate large exposures (other than exempt exposures) may not exceed 800% of capital base.

Connected counterparty limit

20 Aggregate exposure to counterparties connected to the reporting bank (other than exempt exposures) may not exceed 25% of capital base.

Exempt exposures

Exposures to banks and building societies[1] (not connected to the reporting bank) with a residual maturity of one year or less

21 The Bank will review with each bank at least once a year its policy on, and limits for, lending to other banks, including banks overseas. The risks arising from some forms of exposure which may be nominally short-term may, however, be significantly different in degree from the risks involved in traditional short-term interbank lending. The Bank will expect banks to take account of different types of exposure when considering their limits for other banks and, if necessary, to set separate sub-limits.

22 Exposures of over one year maturity to banks will be considered in the same way as exposures to individual non-bank counterparties and are subject to the limits on large exposures. Exposures to banks which are in the form of holdings of capital instruments (ie items eligible for inclusion in the capital base of the issuing bank) will normally be deducted in the calculation of capital base and excluded from the measure of exposure.

In cases where such holdings are not deducted (ie where a bank has a market making concession) they will be subject to the limits on large exposures.

23 For the purpose of its policy on large exposures, the Bank will treat secured[2] exposures to gilt-edged market-makers and StockExchange money brokers in the same way as interbank exposures.

[1] Exposures to building societies which are authorised under the Building Societies Act 1986 will also be treated in the same way as interbank exposures. Throughout this notice the term 'bank' should be understood to include building societies.
[2] Secured on gilts, UK Treasury bills, eligible local authority and eligible bank bills, or London CDs.

Exposures to Zone A central governments or central banks (which for the purpose of this notice includes the European Communities[1])

24 An exposure guaranteed by a central government or central bank may be treated as an exposure to that central government or central bank. Where, however, an exposure is covered by an ECGD[2] bank guarantee, the Bank will require to be fully satisfied that the reporting bank has sufficient expertise and systems in place to ensure that its obligations under the guarantee are met fully. Unless the Bank has notified the reporting bank that it is fully satisfied in this respect such exposures are not expected to exceed 25%.

[1] The EEC, the European Coal and Steel Community, and Euratom.
[2] Or an equivalent government department/agency in another Zone A country.

Exposures to Zone B central governments and central banks which are denominated and funded (if necessary) in the national currency of the borrower

25 Exposures to Zone B central governments or central banks which are denominated and funded (if necessary) in the national currency of the borrower are exempt from the limits set out above. Until such time as the Capital Adequacy Directive is implemented in the UK, exposures to Zone B central governments **arising from activities** which are principally subject to market risk will, with the prior agreement of the Bank, be exempt from the 25% and 800% limits. Other exposures to Zone B central governments are subject to the large exposures limits.

Secured exposures

26 While the Bank will take security into account when considering the acceptability of a bank's exposure up to 25% of its capital base, the presence of security taken on its own account will generally not be considered by the Bank to be an acceptable reason for an exposure to exceed 25%. However, where the security fully covers all exposures to a given counterparty and is in the form of Zone A central government or central bank securities or cash deposits (which in this context includes CDs issued by the lending bank) held with the lender, the existence of that security will be considered sufficient justification for an exposure to exceed 25% of the bank's capital base and such exposures are exempt from the limits set out above. In the case of:

(i) an exposure secured by Zone A central government or central bank securities, the lender's legal title to the security should be fully protected[1]. An appropriate margin over the amount of the exposure should be maintained to cover fluctuations in the market value of the securities. The margin should, inter alia, take account of the maturity of the exposure, in the case where the security is denominated in a different currency from the exposure, fluctuations in the exchange rate, and the arrangements for marking to market the security and for ensuring that any resultant deficiency in the margin is made up;

(ii) an exposure secured by a cash deposit, the lender's legal title to the deposit should be fully protected. The deposit should have identical or longer maturity than the exposure. Where the cash deposit is in a different currency from the exposure, an appropriate margin over the amount of the exposure should be maintained to cover fluctuations in the relevant exchange rates. The margin should take account of the nature of the arrangements for ensuring that any resultant deficiency in the margin following an exchange rate change is made up.

27 Where the total exposure to a given counterparty consists of a number of discrete transactions and collateral of the form specified above covers one or more of those transactions, but does not cover all exposures to the counterparty, then the Bank will wish to discuss on a case by case basis whether this will be accepted as justification for exposures of over 25%. Such discussions will include, inter alia, consideration of the form of transactions, the nature of the counterparty, and the method by which overall exposure will be controlled. In no case will the uncollateralised transactions be permitted to total more than 25% of capital. A similar treatment may be applied in the case of certain exposures which are partially guaranteed (eg by ECGD) provided that the portion accounts for at least 75% of the complete exposure.

[1] Banks should take legal advice, generally from their external legal advisors, to confirm that their legal title to the deposit is valid in all legal jurisdictions which the transaction may encompass. Banks should discuss with the Banking Supervision Division the circumstances in which internal legal advice will be satisfactory for this purpose.

Exposures to counterparties connected to the reporting bank

28 Exposures to solo consolidated subsidiaries are excluded from the scope of the large exposures policy.

29 Exposures to connected banks incorporated within the EC (other than one which controls, directly or indirectly, the lending bank) will be considered on a case by case basis.

30 Where it is considered appropriate for a bank to undertake a group Treasury role, exposures of an original maturity of one year or less to:

   (i) group non-bank financial[1] companies[2] included in the bank's (or its parent's) consolidated supervisory returns;
   (ii) a bank which controls directly or indirectly the lending bank; and
   (iii) other connected overseas banks;

will be reviewed with the bank's management.

[1] The definition of 'financial company' is that set out in the Bank's notice BSD/1993/1 and the annex to that notice. The definition embraces activities listed in the annex but other activities may be considered as qualifying if appropriate.
[2] Which in this context comprise subsidiaries of the reporting bank and subsidiaries of the parent of the reporting bank.

Exposures covered by a parental guarantee

31 Exposures which meet the terms of paragraphs 33–36 of the main notice will also be exempt from the limits.

Underwriting exposures

32 Exposures arising from underwriting activities which are being monitored and controlled according to the methods set out in Annex 1.

Reporting requirements

33 All large exposures must be reported to the Bank on a quarterly basis. Any breach of the limits set out above (single, aggregate or to connected counterparties) must be reported to the Bank immediately.

34 Any exposure being contemplated which will lead to an overall exposure which exceeds 25% of capital base must be notified to the Bank before a commitment is made. For exposures to banks with a maturity of one year or less, exposures to Zone A central governments and central banks and exempt exposures to Zone B central governments and central banks, the requirement for pre-notification can be addressed by agreement with the Bank in advance of limits to particular counterparties.

Access to information

35 The Bank recognises that it may be difficult to obtain information on large exposures from some overseas branches or overseas companies within a group and that in certain

cases there may be legal obstacles to branches and companies providing the information. The Bank will wish to discuss such difficulties with individual banking groups.

Transitional arrangements

36 While the Large Exposure Directive provides for a concessionary transitional regime, the Bank is of the view that such a regime is not necessary in the UK because, for most UK banks, implementation of the Directive implies only limited change to the system of monitoring and reporting large exposures. The Bank recognises however that the Directive introduces some new reporting requirements and will therefore discuss with the banks to which they apply, on an individual basis, appropriate transitional arrangements in the following areas:

    (i) **Quarterly reporting of large exposures on a consolidated basis.** The Bank will agree, with those banks which need to undertake further systems development in order to report on this basis, a deadline by which the bank must comply with the terms of this notice.

    (ii) **Reduction of exposures to individual counterparties which currently exceed the limits of the Directive.** Exposures entered into before and outstanding at the date of publication of the Directive in the Official Journal (5 February 1993) which exceed the limits laid down in the Directive must be brought within those limits. Banks must not take any measures which would cause such exposures exceeding the limits laid down in the Directive to increase above their level on 5 February 1993. However, those exposures to which a bank **is legally bound** may be continued until their maturity. The Bank will discuss the terms of each such exposure with banks individually to determine whether they can be reduced before the agreed maturity date (eg through sub-participation). In addition the Bank may be prepared to agree to a gradual reduction of certain types of exposure (eg where banks have traditionally had large trading lines with major customers for interest rate and foreign exchange rate instruments or limits in excess of 25% for certain Zone B central governments), as long as any such arrangement meets the transitional terms of the Directive.

Annex 2 Large underwriting exposures

1 Paragraph 7 of the main notice explained that the Bank's approach to the monitoring and controlling of exposures incurred through underwriting will continue unchanged from that set out in its earlier notice BSD/1987/1.1. This annex[1] sets out this approach.

---

[1] Which should be read in conjunction with the SIB's Financial Supervision Rules 1990 (Schedule 2 Part II dealing with offerings of securities) or SFA's Financial Rules (Section 3–130 dealing with the Issuing Market) as appropriate according to whether the reporting institution is authorised by the SIB or SFA.

Summary

2 The risks involved in underwriting differ substantially from those involved in lending activities typically undertaken by banks. The likelihood of a bank experiencing a loss from an underwriting commitment is related to the risk of actually having to take up the securities, possibly leading to a subsequent forced sale. Although there is an element of credit risk this is generally low. The former risk is affected by the type of underwriting commitment and forced sale risk by the nature of the security underwritten. For these reasons the amount at risk on an issue is more reasonably measured in the context of a large exposures policy by some proportion of the amount underwritten rather than by the full amount of the issue. In addition, the Bank recognises that more flexibility is warranted in assessing underwriting proposals which must be notified to it before being entered into.

3 The Securities and Investments Board ('SIB'[1]) and the Securities and Futures Authority ('SFA') set capital requirements for underwriting positions which reflect an assessment of the relative risks in different types of underwriting deals and different types of securities. These capital requirements provide a basis for determining the proportion of the amount underwritten to be considered at risk (the 'credit equivalent'

amount) for the purpose of this policy. Where a bank has taken a position by under-writing a securities issue, the credit equivalent amount (which should be calculated intra-day including the first day of issue) will be the SIB/SFA's capital requirement for that position multiplied by ten.

4 Included within the scope of this annex are offerings of discrete issues of securities (new securities or existing securities which are new to the market) only. Commitments of a continuing or revolving nature (eg under Note Issuance Facilities and similar commitments) are not included. Nor are (block) trades in the secondary market.

---

[1] In this annex 'SIB' should be taken as including the SFA. Where a bank is a member of the SFA, any interpretation of detail should be based on SFA financial regulations and definitions.

Notification of exposures

5 Where the credit equivalent amount of an underwriting exceeds 10% of the reporting bank's capital base, the bank is required to report it as an exposure in the same way as for other forms of exposure. Where the credit equivalent amount of a proposed underwriting exceeds 25% of capital base, the exposure is also required to be notified to the Bank before the commitment is entered into. The Bank will seek to minimise the time it takes to assess whether an underwriting exposure which, as measured, exceeds 25% of capital base is prudent by agreeing general guidelines with each bank which undertakes this business.

6 While the notification requirements (including pre-notification in the case of expo-sures in excess of 25%) will be the same for all banks entering into underwriting commitments, in considering whether an exposure is prudent the Bank's policy will distinguish between banks which are not expert underwriters ('non-experts') and those which are ('experts'). Whether or not a bank is considered expert will, *inter alia*, determine the period of notice the Bank will require before it enters into an under-writing exposure in excess of 25%.

Limits

7 Exposures arising through underwriting activities are not included in the scope of the Large Exposures Directive. They may therefore be exempted from the limits on the size of exposures set out in the main notice. However, for **non-experts**, underwriting exposures will generally be treated in a similar way as other forms of exposure; namely, that the credit equivalent amount of an underwriting commitment should not usually exceed 10% of capital and should exceed 25% of capital only in the most exceptional circumstances.

8 For **experts** the Bank will agree individual Guidelines with underwriters considered expert. An expert's Guidelines will set out the levels of underwriting exposure which the Bank agrees it may enter into without seeking prior approval (where such exposures when measured by the credit equivalent amount are over 25% they are, however, still required to be pre-notified). These Guidelines may include underwriting exposures which, when measured by the credit equivalent amount, exceed 25% of a bank's capital. The Guidelines, when measured by the credit equivalent amount, will not however exceed 75% of a bank's capital base. After the issue date, exposures arising from an underwriting commitment are considered in the same way as other types of exposures under the large exposures policy and are no longer exempt from the limits established by the Large Exposures Directive.

9 Banks wishing to be considered 'experts' will need to demonstrate that they have the experience, skills and the systems to ensure that they can properly monitor and control underwriting risks in particular issues. Particular regard will be had to a bank's track record. It is possible that a bank may be an expert in some market segments but not in others. In that case, it will be considered as an expert for only those types of underwriting for which it can demonstrate that expertise.

Underwriting and other forms of exposure to the same counterparty

10 Exposures in the form of underwriting commitments should be aggregated and reported with other forms of exposure to the same counterparty. The latter reduce *pro*

rata the size of an underwriting exposure the Bank will consider to be prudent. Thus, for example, where a bank has a loan equivalent to 12.5% of its capital base to a counter-party and where the Bank would be content for an exposure up to 25% to be advanced, the size of the underwriting exposure allowed in respect of the same counterparty is one-half of that allowed by the policy detailed above.

Measurement of underwriting exposures

11 The measurement system for underwriting exposures is based on the SIB's capital cover requirements for commitments which arise in connection with an offering of securities, which vary according to deal structure and the volatility of the underlying instrument; so that, for example, a domestic rights issue is typically subject to a lower capital cover requirement than a flotation, and an international market bought deal is subject to a higher capital cover requirement than a conventional Euromarket under-writing. An alternative method of measurement of underwriting exposures, available to expert underwriters only, is set out in paragraphs 17–20 below.

12 The SIB capital cover system has been adopted because the risk of stick (ie being left with securities) and the consequences of suffering stick will vary according to, principally, the volatility of the underlying instrument.

13 The exposure from an underwriting commitment should be taken as its 'credit equivalent amount'. The credit equivalent amount is calculated by multiplying the SIB's position risk requirement for a underwriting commitment by 10. The SIB's Financial Supervision Rules (1990) provide for a temporary reduction in the position risk require-ment (PRR) during a prescribed underwriting period. The PRRs are derived by applying the applicable adjusted position risk factor (PRF) (before any allowances for hedging or diversification or any adjustment to reflect concentrated positions) to an institution's underwriting commitment. However:

(i) where there is no capital requirement for an initial period after entering into an underwriting commitment the initial adjusted PRF should be assumed to apply for that period.
(ii) where the SIB's capital requirements do *not* reflect a reduction from its normal PRFs the full amount of the underwriting commitment should be considered as the exposure.
(iii) in the case of domestic offerings (underwriting where securities are already traded) in those cases where the credit equivalent amount is higher than the amount of the commitment valued at the underwriting price the latter should be considered as the exposure.
(iv) where securities are taken up by a bank following the completion of an underwriting commitment the exposure should be valued at their book value.
(v) where the SIB's adjusted PRF to be applied to a underwriting commitment is less than 1.875% an adjusted PRF of 1.875% should be used in calculating the exposure.

14 As regards the SIB capital requirements for offerings, it should be noted that:

(i) underwritings, bought deals and placings of all types of securities for both primary and secondary offerings are covered (nb secondary 'block trades' are not considered as secondary offerings);
(ii) in **most** circumstances, full credit is given for amounts firmly sold or laid off with sub-underwriters[1] (where full credit is not given the SIB's capital requirement is higher, and therefore the measure of an exposure for the purpose of reporting large exposures is also higher);
(iii) the capital requirements are calculated on an intra-day basis.

15 The Bank's reporting requirements apply in all circumstances immediately from the time an underwriter is committed to proceed with an underwriting. The Bank will use the SIB's definition of when such commitments occur, even though the SIB's 'standard' underwriting capital requirements do not always apply immediately[2].

16 Some illustrative calculations are set out below, assuming a £100mn (net) underwriting commitment.

---

¹ 'Sub-underwriters' should be interpreted as including pre-sub-underwriters ie where the lead underwriter has entered into a legally binding sub-underwriting agreement in advance of committing itself to the underwriting.
² In the case of domestic offerings the SIB may apply a nil capital requirement until the end of the day an underwriter enters into a commitment, provided the commitment is within an overall limit.

Domestic offerings

(i) Underwritings where securities are not already traded (eg offers for sale on a flotation).
For such underwritings the SIB applies 30% of the applicable PRF. For a constituent of FT All-Share index (other than a constituent of the FT-SE 100 index) (PRF = 15%), therefore, the credit equivalent amount equals:

$$100 \times \frac{15}{100} \times \frac{30}{100} \times 10 = £45mn$$

(ii) Other (non-underwriting) commitments to purchase new securities or existing securities which are new to the market (eg vendor placings, vendor rights, or direct placing of new shares or loan stocks).
For such 'underwritings' the SIB applies 50% of the applicable PRF. For a constituent of the FT-SE 100 index (PRF = 10.5%) therefore the credit equivalent amount equals:

$$100 \times \frac{10.5}{100} \times \frac{50}{100} \times 10 = £45mn$$

International offerings

(iii) Bought deal
The SIB applies (until the allotment date)
(*a*) 50% of the applicable PRF applied to the total amount of the commitment less:
   (*a*) sales made by the firm, and
   (*b*) the amount of underwriting commitments obtained by the institutions from others, and
(*b*) 20% of the applicable PRF applied to the total amount of underwriting commitments obtained by the firm from others.
For other constituents of the First Section of the Tokyo Stock Exchange, and assuming the underwriter has obtained £100mn of underwriting commitments from other (ie gross commitment £200mn, net commitment £100mn), the credit equivalent amount equals:

$$100 \times \left[\frac{18}{100} \times \frac{50}{100} \times 10\right] + 100 \times \left[\frac{18}{100} \times \frac{20}{100} \times 10\right] = 90 + 36 = £126mn$$

NB Where the net underwriting commitment is nil the exposure is calculated in accordance with the second element in the calculation only (ie 20% of the applicable PRF applied to the total amount of underwriting commitments obtained by the institution from others).

Alternative method of measurement for expert underwriters

17 Those banks which have been assessed by the Bank as 'experts' have the choice of using the original method for calculating the credit equivalent amount of an underwriting commitment set out above, or an alternative simplified method.

18 The alternative method divides securities into five broad categories and imputes a credit conversion factor to each category. These implied conversation factors are then used to derive in terms of the nominal size of the underwriting commitment, the post notification threshold (equivalent to a credit equivalent amount of 10% of capital base) and the pre-notification threshold (equivalent to a credit equivalent amount of 25% of capital base) and the maximum size of the 'expert' guideline for each type of instrument. The actual figures are set out in the matrix below.

19 The appropriate credit conversion factors of each of the categories under the alternative method are as follows:

		Implied conversion factor	Post-notify (10%)(1)	Pre-notify (25%)(2)	Maximum 'expert' guideline (3)
1.	All debt instruments	18.75%	53%	133%	400%
2.	Preference shares, constituents of the FT-SE 100 index, and related convertibles, US S & P 500, Japan Nikkei 225	23%	44%	108%	325%
3.	Constituents of FT All-share Index & related convertibles; other major non-UK equities	30%	34%	83%	250%
4.	Other equities with a normal market size and other second tier non-equities	43%	24%	58%	175%
5.	Other UK and non-UK equities and related convertibles	75%	14%	33%	100%

(1) The nominal amount (expressed as a percentage of capital) which corresponds to the post-notification threshold when converted into credit equivalent terms.
(2) The nominal amount (expressed as a percentage of capital) which corresponds to the pre-notification threshold when converted into credit equivalent terms.
(3) The lower of 400% nominal or three times the pre-notification trigger. (The latter applies in all cases other than debt underwriting).

20 Once a bank has decided to adopt the above method for calculating the size of its exposures and the limits, the Bank is not willing to agree to that bank reverting to the original method. Nor is it willing for the alternative method to be used for some types of underwriting and the original method for others.

Annex 3 Banking Act 1987. Section 38 Reports of large exposures

(1) An authorised institution, other than one whose principal place of business is outside the United Kingdom, shall make a report to the Bank if:

    (a) it has entered into a transaction or transactions relating to any one person as a result of which it is exposed to the risk of incurring losses in excess of 10 per cent of its available capital resources; or

    (b) it proposes to enter into a transaction or transactions relating to any one person which, either alone or together with a previous transaction or previous transactions entered into by it in relation to that person, would result in its being exposed to the risk of incurring losses in excess of 25 per cent of those resources.

(2) Subsection (1) above applies also where the transaction or transactions relate to different persons if they are connected in such a way that the financial soundness of any of them may affect the financial soundness of other or others or the same factors may affect the financial soundness of both or all of them.

(3) If an authorised institution to which subsection (1) above applies has one or more subsidiaries which are not authorised institutions the Bank may by notice in writing to that institution direct that that subsection shall apply to it as if the transactions and available capital resources of the subsidiary or subsidiaries, or such of them as are specified in the notice, were included in those of the institutions.

(4) The reports required to be made by an institution under subsection (1) above shall be made, in a case within paragraph (a) of that subsection, in respect of such period

or periods and, in a case within paragraph (b) of the subsection, at such time before the transaction or transactions are entered into, as may be specified by notice in writing given to the institution by the Bank; and those reports shall be in such form and contain such particulars as the Bank may reasonably require.

(5) For the purposes of this section a transaction entered into by an institution relates to a person if it is:

    (a)   a transaction under which that person incurs an obligation to the institution or as a result of which he may incur such an obligation;

    (b)   a transaction under which the institution will incur, or a result of which it may incur, an obligation in the event of that person defaulting on an obligation to a third party; or

    (c)   a transaction under which the institution acquires or incurs an obligation to acquire, or as result of which it may incur an obligation to acquire, an asset the value of which depends wholly or mainly on that person performing his obligations or otherwise on his financial soundness;

and the risk of loss attributable to a transaction is, in a case within paragraph (a) or (b) above, the risk of the person concerned defaulting on the obligation there mentioned and, in a case within paragraph (c) above, the risk of the person concerned defaulting on the obligations there mentioned or of a deterioration in his financial soundness.

(6) Any question whether an institution is or would be exposed to risk as mentioned in subsection (1) above (or in that subsection as extended by subsection (2) shall be determined in accordance with principles published by the Bank or notified by it to the institution concerned; and those principles may in particular make provision for determining the amount at risk in particular circumstances or the extent to which any such amount is to be taken into account for the purpose of this section.

(7) For the purpose of this section the available capital resources of an institution (or, in a case within subsection (3) above, of an institution and its relevant subsidiary or subsidiaries) and the value of those resources at any time shall be determined by the Bank and notified by it to the institution by notices in writing; and any such determination, which may be varied from time to time, shall be made by the Bank after consultation with the institution concerned and in accordance with principles published by the Bank.

(8) The principles referred to in subsections (6) and (7) above may make different provisions for different cases and those referred to in subsection (6) may, in particular, exclude from consideration either wholly or in part, risks resulting from transactions of a particular description or entered into in particular circumstances or with persons of particular descriptions.

(9) An institution which fails to make a report as required by this section shall be guilty of an offence; but where an institution shows that at the time when the report was required to be made it did not know that the facts were such as to require the making of the report it shall not be guilty of an offence by reason of its failure to make a report at that time but shall be guilty of an offence unless it makes the report within seven days of becoming aware of those facts.

(10) An institution guilty of an offence under this section shall be liable on summary conviction to a fine not exceeding the fifth level on the standard scale.

(11) The Treasury may after consultation with the Bank by order:

    (a)   amend subsection (1) above so as to substitute for either of the percentages for the time being specified in that subsection such other percentage as may be specified in the order;

    (b)   make provision, whether by amending subsection (5) or otherwise, with respect to the transactions and risks to be taken into account for the purposes of this section,

but any such order shall be subject to annulment in pursuance of a resolution of either House of Parliament.

(12) For the avoidance of doubt it is hereby declared that references in the section to 'one person' include references to a partnership.

Annex 4 National discretion

The following national discretions are adopted:

(i) Article 3(2) – all large exposures will be reported at least four times a year (main notice, paragraph 21; Annex 1, paragraph 33).

(ii) Article 4(2) – connected exposures will not be subject to a 20% limit and specific monitoring by other means used (main notice, paragraph 17).

(iii) Article 4(6) – exemption from limits for exposures to group entities included within consolidated supervision (main notice, paragraphs 27, 33; Annex 1, paragraphs 30(i), 31).

(iv) Articles 4(7)(a), (b), (c), (d) – exemption from limits for exposures to Zone A central governments and central banks (main notice, paragraph 25, Annex 1, paragraph 24).

(v) Article 4(7)(e) – exemption from limits for exposures to Zone B central governments and central banks denominated and where applicable funded in national currency of borrower (Annex 1, paragraph 25).

(vi) Article 4(7)(f) – exemptions for exposures secured by Zone A central government or central bank securities (main notice, paragraph 25; Annex 1, paragraph 26).

(vii) Article 4(7)(g) – exemption from limits for exposures secured by cash and CDs issued by the lending bank. The Bank's requirements are more restrictive than detailed in these Articles (main notice, paragraph 25; Annex 1, paragraph 26).

(viii) Articles 4(7)(i) and (j) – exemption from limits for exposures to banks and for secured exposures to GEMMs and SEMBs with a maturity of one year or less (main notice, paragraph 25; Annex 1, paragraph 23).

(ix) Article 4(7)(k) – exemption from limits for bills of trade with a maturity of one year or less bearing the signature of another credit institution (main notice, paragraphs 12, 25; Annex 1, paragraph 23).

(x) Article 4(9) – application of weighing to interbank exposures of over one year maturity (main notice, paragraph 7; Annex 1, paragraph 4).

(xi) Article 4(11) – treatment of an exposure as having been incurred to a third party guarantor rather than to the customer (main notice, paragraph 12).

(xii) Article 5(3) – waiver of limits and reporting requirements of the Directive on an unconsolidated basis where measures are taken to ensure satisfactory allocation of risks within a group (main notice, paragraph 5).

(xiii) Article 6(8) – temporary reduction in frequency of reporting to twice per year. This is to be applied on a case by case basis (Annex 1, paragraph 36(i)).

The following national discretions will not be adopted:

(i) Article 2(b) – exemption from Large Exposures Directive of institutions listed in Article 2(4)(a) of Directive 77/780/EEC.

(ii) Article 3(2) – alternative frequency of reporting.

(iii) Article 3(3) – exemption from reporting of certain types of exposure.

(iv) Articles 4(7)(l), (m), (n), (q), (r), (s) – exemption from limits for exposures in the form of bonds defined in Article 22(4) of Directive 85/611/EEC, holdings in insurance companies, claims on certain types of credit institution, off-balance sheet items of moderate and low risk (as defined by Directive 89/647/EEC) and guarantees provided under mutual guarantee schemes.

(v) Articles 4(7)(p) and (o) – exemption for exposures secured on mortgages and on securities other than central governments securities.

(vi) Article 4(8) – partial exemption from limits for exposures to local authorities.

(vii) Article 4(10) – partial exemption from limits for all interbank exposures.

(viii) Article 4(11) – exposure to be reported as being to the issuer of securities held as collateral.

(ix) Article 5(5) – transfer of responsibility for monitoring compliance with terms of the Directive for banks which are subsidiaries of banks in other Member States.

(x) Article 6(5), (6), (7) – temporary increase in limit to 40% and in definition of large exposure to 15%.
(xi) Article 6(9) – exemption from limits for certain mortgage loans and property leasing transactions.

For information only

Concordance with the directive

Article 1 – Definitions		Main	Annex
1(a)	credit institution	x	
1(b)	competent authorities	x	
1(c)	parent undertaking	x	
1(d)	subsidiary undertaking	33 footnote (1)	
1(e)	financial holding company	x	
1(f)	ancillary banking services undertaking	x	
1(h)	exposures		1
1(i)	Zone A		17
1(j)	Zone B		17
1(k)	Own funds		10
1(l)	control		13 footnote (1)
1(m)	group of connected clients		11

Article 2 – Scope			
2	application of directive	4	

Article 3 – Reporting			
1	exposures ⩾10%	21	9, 33
2	frequency of reporting	21	33
3	exemption from reporting	not adopted	
4	adequacy of administration etc	10	

Article 3 – Limits			
1	⩽25% single limits	15, 31	18
2	⩽20% for connected counterparties	17	20
3	⩽800% aggregate limits	14	19
4	may impose more stringent limits	x	
5	report breaches w/o delay	22	33
6	exemption of exposures within consolidated supervision	26, 33	30(i), 31
7	other exemptions		
7(a)	Zone A central government	25	24
7(b)	EC	25	24
7(c)	guarantees by Zone A central government or EC	25	24
7(d)	other claims on Zone A central government or EC	25	24
7(e)	Zone B central government	25	25
7(f)	secured on Zone A central government or EC securities	25	26
7(g)	cash collateral	25	26
7(h)	CD collateral	25	26
7(i)	credit institutions ⩽1 year	25, 29, 30	21, 29, 30(ii), (iii)
7(j)	secured exposures to SEMBs, GEMMs ⩽1 year	25	23
7(k)	bills endorsed, accepted by banks	not separately implemented	
7(l)	debt securities	not adopted	
7(m)	insurance companies	not adopted	
7(n)	regional govt/credit institutions	not adopted	

Article 3 – Limits – contd		**Main**	**Annex**
7(o)	other forms of security	not adopted	
7(p)	mortgage security	not adopted	
7(q)	50% of medium risk off-bs	not adopted	
7(r)	mutual guarantees	not adopted	
7(s)	low risk off-balance sheet	not adopted	
8	20% of exposures to local authorities	not adopted	
9	partial exemption of claims on banks	not adopted	
10	further partial exemption of claims on banks	not adopted	
11	risk transfer to guarantor	12, 33 – risk transfer to issuer of collateral not adopted	
12	EC to re-examine interbank concession	n/a	

Article 5 – Consolidation			
1	where neither parent nor sub	5	
2	application on consolidated basis	5	
3	waiver of application to sub group	5	
4		not adopted	

Article 6 – Transitional arrangements			
1	exposures to be brought down	24	36(ii)
2	the process of bringing down exposures		36(ii)
3	exposures not to increase above level at publication date		36(ii)
4	exposures to be brought down by 2001 except where legally bound		36(ii)
5	concessionary limits	not adopted	
6	extension of concessionary limits	not adopted	
7	new definition of large exposures	not adopted	
8	reduced frequency of reporting		36(i)
9	special treatment of mortgage loans	not adopted	
10	special treatment for Portugal		

Article 7 – Subsequent amendments

n/a

Article 8 – Final provisions			
1	provisions to be introduced by 1.1.94	1	
2	provisions to communicated to EC	n/a	
3	treatment of exposures principally exposed to market risk	23	**[829]**

BSD/1993/3
(December 1993)

NOTICE TO INSTITUTIONS AUTHORISED UNDER THE BANKING ACT 1987

ON-BALANCE SHEET NETTING AND CASH COLLATERAL

1 This notice supplements the Bank's notice BSD/1990/3 ('Implementation in the United Kingdom of the Solvency Ratio Directive') dated December 1990. It sets out the conditions under which the Bank will be prepared to view on-balance sheet transactions as either net or cash-collateralised for capital adequacy purposes. Certain amendments to the reporting guidelines issued in December 1992 for the BSD1 (capital adequacy) form were notified to banks earlier this year; this notice brings together both these

changes (with some amendments) together with further substantive changes to the existing policy. The timing for the implementation of the new rules is described in the final section of this notice, and revised reporting instructions are attached.

2 Banks are reminded that in reporting on a net basis for capital adequacy purposes (Form BSD1) they must not only observe the criteria outlined in the attached reporting instructions, but must also have regard to accounting guidelines where relevant.

3 The rules for reporting of balances on a net basis on other forms are affected by some, but not all, of the changes made to the capital adequacy reporting guidelines. The Bank's Financial Statistics Division is today issuing a statistical notice 1993/04 setting out the guidelines for reporting on other forms.

General

Legal opinion on set-off arrangements

4 An authorised institution which reports transactions as either net or cash-collateralised should have obtained an opinion from its legal advisers to the effect that the set-off arrangements are legally well-founded in all relevant jurisdictions and would be enforceable in the default, liquidation or bankruptcy of the customer or depositor as well as in the liquidation or bankruptcy of the reporting institution. The Bank expects that such opinions will be provided by an independent, external source of advice of appropriate professional standing. In those cases involving cross-jurisdictional transactions, the Bank will usually require a side-letter from the institution's legal advisers confirming that the requirements of this Notice have been met in all relevant respects. In some cases, the Bank may also wish to see a copy of the legal opinion itself. Authorised institutions should bear in mind that in certain jurisdictions assets may be seized to satisfy the claims of local creditors.

On-balance sheet netting

(i) Cross-guarantee arrangements

5 The 1992 BSD1 reporting instructions stated that group facilities which are reported on a net basis should **preferably** be supported by a full cross-guarantee structure. Banks were notified earlier this year of the Bank's intention to revise this criterion so that a full cross-guarantee structure would in future be an essential pre-condition for reporting of group facilities on a net basis. However, it is not the Bank's intention to require that each member of the group makes itself responsible for all of the debts of the other members, so it would be acceptable for the cross-guarantees to be restricted to the amount of any credit balances held.

6 The cross-guarantee requirement is intended to create mutuality of debts. In the case of accounts which are the joint and several liabilities of all group members, it is not necessary to create mutuality so cross-guarantees are not required.

(ii) Accounts to be managed on a net basis

7 The Bank of England believes that banks' reporting should not only reflect the legal position, but also the economic substance of the relationship. It is therefore not sufficient that the reporting bank has the legal right to set-off credit balances against debit balances; it must also manage the relevant accounts on a net basis. This is also important from a prudential point of view, in that the bank should be in a position to control its true (ie net) exposure. Thus for a group of customers, as set out in the existing reporting instructions, facilities should be advised and controlled on a net basis. In the future, for single customer balances also, the bank should have regard to the overall position of the customer's accounts. This can be demonstrated in a number of ways, but the existence of a formal agreement allowing the bank to net credit balances against debit balances would provide a strong indication that the accounts were being managed in this way. As with its other requirements, the Bank of England may ask reporting accountants to verify the reporting bank's application of this principle.

(iii) Local residency

8 Subject to the reporting institution obtaining the legal opinion referred to in paragraph 4, the 'local residency' requirement contained in the 1992 guidelines is withdrawn. The Bank will no longer require the customer(s) and the office(s) of the reporting bank to have 'local resident' status for debit balances to be offset against credit balances.

(iv) Denomination

9 The requirement for the debit and credit balances to be denominated in the same currency is withdrawn. A debit balance in one currency may in future be offset against a credit balance in another.

Cash collateral

Local residency

10 Provided the conditions specified in paragraph 4 have been met, the 'local residency' requirement is also withdrawn in respect of cash-collateralised transactions.

Timing

11 All changes to the existing requirements described in this notice come into force at 31 December 1993, with the following exceptions:

banks have until 30 June 1994 to observe the requirement regarding management of accounts in reporting of single customer balances on a net basis – see (ii) above. (This requirement is already in force in the case of group facilities.)

banks may move to take advantage of the liberalisations on local residency and currency denomination as soon as they are able to do so. However, in the case of netting, banks' ability to take advantage of these changes is conditional on their net reporting fully conforming to the requirements set out in (ii) above.

Revised BSD1 Guidance Notes

Cash collateral

21 Where exposures which do not meet the rules for set-off (see Guidance Note 22) are collateralised by cash, ie balances held with the reporting institution denominated in sterling, foreign currency or gold, or CDs issued by the reporting institution and lodged with it, such exposures should be reported under the relevant item in the 0% band. For these purposes an exposure is collateralised by cash only if the cash is held by the reporting institution for the account of the depositor/customer on express terms such that:

(i) the cash may not be withdrawn for the duration of the exposure; and
(ii) the reporting institution may apply the cash to discharge the exposure if and to the extent that it is not discharged by the borrower/customer in accordance with the terms of the loan etc agreement with the borrower/customer.

In the case of an exposure partially collateralised by cash only that part of the exposure which is fully collateralised should be reported in the 0% weight band.

The adjustments made by the reporting institution to the Capital Adequacy Return in respect of exposures collateralised by cash should be shown in BSD1(1).

To qualify as cash collateral:

(i) The reporting institution must obtain an opinion from its legal advisers to the effect that the set-off arrangements, charges, or other equivalent security interests referred to below are legally well founded in **all** relevant jurisdictions, and would be enforceable in the default, liquidation or bankruptcy of the customer or depositor, or in the liquidation or bankruptcy of the institution itself.

(ii) In the case of the reporting institution's *unconsolidated* return, the cash must be held with the reporting institution. In the case of a reporting institution's *consolidated* return, the cash must be held with the company which has the exposure.

(iii) Where the cash is held at a UK office of a UK incorporated lending institution, the lending institution should have a legally enforceable right of set-off over the cash. Where the cash is held at an overseas branch of the lending institution, or where the lending institution is incorporated overseas, it should have a first charge over cash held with itself where this is enforceable in the local legal jurisdiction or other equivalent security interest or a legally enforceable right of set-off over the cash.

(iv) Where BSD has agreed that the reporting institution meets the criteria set out in paragraph 27 of BSD/1993/1, the above rules apply except that the cash may be held with another bank which is consolidated with the reporting institution for the purpose of calculating the institution's consolidated capital ratio. In this case the lending institution should have a first charge over the cash held with the other bank or other equivalent security interest. Where an exposure is reported by the lending bank as collateralised by cash under this provision, the cash is not available to the other bank as collateral for reporting purposes, and should not be subject to set-off in the other bank's books.

Where the reporting institution is a member of a syndicate and cash has been deposited with, and is held by, the agent itself for the benefit of the syndicate, the claims (or portion of the claims) of members of the syndicate which are cash collateralised may attract the weight appropriate for claims on the agent. If the agent is a bank its own claims which are cash collateralised may be eligible for a 0% weight.

Netting

On-balance sheet

22 Debit balances on accounts with the reporting bank may be offset against credit balances on other accounts with that bank only where *all* the following criteria have been met:

(a) a legal right of set-off exists, and the reporting institution has obtained an opinion from its legal advisers to the effect that its right to apply set-off is legally well-founded in all relevant jurisdictions and would be enforceable in the default, liquidation or bankruptcy of the customer(s) or in the liquidation or bankruptcy of the institution itself. For a group facility, the arrangement must be supported by a full cross guarantee structure;

(b) the debit and credit balances relate to the same customer, or to customers in the same company group, eg a parent company and its subsidiary. For all customers, the netted accounts should be managed and controlled on a net basis, and in the case of a group facility, the facility should be advised in the form of a net amount.

The reporting institution's application of these principles must remain consistent.

Where this Guidance Note or Guidance Note 21 require a legal opinion to be sought, the Bank expects such opinions to be provided by an independent, external source of advice of appropriate professional standing. In seeking these opinions, the reporting institution will need to bear in mind that in certain jurisdictions assets may be seized to satisfy local creditors. In those cases involving cross-jurisdictional transactions, the Bank will usually require a side-letter from the institution's advisers confirming that the set-off arrangements have a well-founded legal basis in all relevant jurisdictions. In certain cases the Bank may wish to be provided with a copy of the legal opinion.

Credit balances which cannot be off-set against debit balances may be eligible for inclusion as cash collateral (see Guidance Notes 20 and 21). **[830]**

BSD/1994/1
(March 1994)

THE BANK OF ENGLAND'S RELATIONSHIP WITH AUDITORS AND REPORTING ACCOUNTANTS

Introduction

1 The Bank's primary source of information relating to authorised institutions is the authorised institution itself. The normal reporting procedures, including prudential meetings, the reports on accounting records and systems and on returns and trilateral discussions will generally provide the Bank with all the information it needs to carry out its responsibilities under the Act[1]. This will be augmented in exceptional circumstances by reports made by auditors[2] and reporting accountants[3] under The Accountants (Banking Act 1987) Regulations 1994[4] or under the protection of section 47 of the Act as appropriate.

2 The purpose of this Notice which replaces the Bank's Notice BSD/1987/4 is:

   (a) to outline arrangements for trilateral discussions between the Bank, institutions and their auditors and reporting accountants;

   (b) to provide guidance on the circumstances in which the Bank will expect auditors and reporting accountants to report matters to the Bank, in accordance with the Regulations; and

   (c) to provide guidance on the circumstances in which the Bank will expect auditors and reporting accountants to take the initiative in reporting to the Bank under the protection of section 47 of the Act.

3 The Bank wishes to encourage an open and constructive relationship with auditors and with reporting accountants appointed under the Act. The Bank has the powers to commission reports under section 39 of the Act for all authorised institutions and all European authorised institutions (as defined in Regulation 3 of the Banking Coordination (Second Council Directive) Regulations 1992). The Bank does not ordinarily expect to use these powers over European authorised institutions to commission reports on accounting and other records or internal control systems, although the Bank will commission reports on statistical returns. This relationship will be based on and develop from:

   (a) reports by reporting accountants on:

      (i) the accounting and other records and internal control systems;

      (ii) the returns used for prudential purposes; and

      (iii) any other aspect of the institution's business which the Bank may require for the performance of its functions under the Act;

   (b) a trilateral discussion with an institution and its auditors and reporting accountants to discuss:

      (i) the reporting accountants' reports on records and systems and on prudential returns;

      (ii) the statutory accounts, the auditors' report thereon and matters arising from the audit or work of an audit nature where there is no statutory requirement to appoint auditors; and

      (iii) the scope of the reporting accountants' examinations of the institution's records and systems for the following year;

   (c) disclosure of information by the Bank in the circumstances set out in Part 3 of this guidance note;

   (d) reports by auditors and reporting accountants of matters of material significance in accordance with the Regulations, either with or without the institution's knowledge; and

   (e) exceptionally, under the protection of section 47 of the Act, direct reporting and bilateral discussions with the institution's auditors or reporting accountants, with or without the institution's knowledge.

4 A report on accounting and other records and internal control systems may be commissioned annually and its scope will be determined by the Bank after discussion with the institution and the reporting accountants. The Bank will also select the

particular prudential returns to be examined for each institution and choose the frequency with which those returns will be examined. Where an institution has a proven record of high quality prudential return reporting, the Bank may grant a holiday for the examination of prudential returns by the reporting accountants.

[1] References in this Notice to 'the Act' are to the Banking Act 1987 as amended by The Banking Coordination (Second Council Directive) Regulations 1992 (SI 1992/3218).

[2] References in this Notice to 'auditors' are to auditors appointed under the Companies Act for a UK-incorporated institution or the equivalent for an overseas incorporated institution and to persons carrying out work of an audit nature at UK branches. Guidance on how to interpret the term 'auditor', in relation to the statutory duty is given in the APB Practice Note 3, 'The auditors' right and duty to report the Bank of England'.

[3] References in this Notice to 'reporting accountants' are to persons appointed under section 8(5) or 39(1)(b) of the Act.

[4] References in this Notice to 'Regulations' are to The Accountants (Banking Act 1987) Regulations 1994 (SI 1994/524).

Part 1: Trilateral discussions

General procedures

5 Unless agreed otherwise by all parties there will be at least one meeting each year, called by the Bank, between Banking Supervision Division, each authorised institution and its auditors and reporting accountants. The trilateral discussions with reporting accountants will provide an opportunity to discuss the reporting accountants' examinations of, and reports on, the institution's accounting and other records and internal control systems and the returns made to the Bank. The trilateral discussions with auditors will provide an opportunity to discuss significant matters arising from the statutory audit which relate to the Bank's supervisory responsibilities. In cases where the auditors and reporting accountants are the same firm, there will, of course, be a single meeting.

6 The Bank will prepare and circulate in advance an agenda for each trilateral meeting and will include items at the request of the institution and, via the institution, of its auditors and/or reporting accountants. Any matter arising from the audit (including, in respect of branches, the extent of any audit work and whether the statutory duty applies to the work performed), issues from the reporting accountants' examination, suggestions for future scope of reporting accountants' reports, or any other matter of a prudential nature which may arise out of the auditors' or reporting accountants' work may be included on the agenda. Auditors and reporting accountants may request the Bank to include on the agenda items which they consider to be important even if the institution has not agreed to their inclusion.

7 Auditors and reporting accountants should recognise the Bank's responsibilities for the protection of the interests of depositors and they are expected to participate fully in trilateral meetings. Accordingly, they are expected to contribute to the discussion of matters arising from the audit and from their work under the Act and, thus, are expected to discuss with the Bank the affairs of the institution including, if necessary, information about its customers obtained in the course of that work. The Bank recognises that it would not be appropriate for auditors or reporting accountants to report to the Bank information about the institution or its customers which they have obtained through their professional relationship with another client which is not the institution's subsidiary undertaking, parent undertaking, or fellow group undertaking.

8 The report of Lord Justice Bingham's inquiry into the supervision of the Bank of Credit and Commerce International recommended that a full scope review should be required in respect of smaller and more vulnerable institutions[1]. In all but exceptional cases, the Bank will require an annual full scope review of smaller institutions, as well as those institutions which the Bank considers to be vulnerable. Rolling programmes will be preserved for larger institutions, where the situation merits such an approach. The scope of the following year's reporting accountants' examinations of records and systems (including, where appropriate, a rolling programme of work spread over a number of years) will be discussed and agreed at the trilateral meeting. This provides an opportunity for:

(a) reporting accountants to make suggestions on the areas which could be covered by the following year's scope;

(b) reporting accountants to ask the Bank for clarification on any aspect of its Guidance Notes on records and systems, on prudential returns and on any other matters relevant to their examinations and to their reports;

(c) the Bank to inform the reporting accountants and the institution of matters which it considers relevant to the work to be carried out by the reporting accountants;

(d) the institution to inform its reporting accountants and the Bank of any matters relevant to the examinations and to the reports; and

(e) the institution, by virtue of its size and the complexity of its operations, to obtain the Bank's agreement to a rolling programme of examinations of records and systems spread over a number of years and to the scope of the examinations for the current year.

9 Any party may request an additional trilateral meeting at any time and in the circumstances as outlined in paragraph 20 auditors and reporting accountants may communicate direct with the Bank. The discussions with auditors and reporting accountants referred to in this section may be held at separate meetings when

(a) the timing of receipt of the statutory accounts and auditors' report and of reporting accountants' reports differs; or

(b) different firms are appointed as auditors and as reporting accountants.

10 Following a trilateral meeting the Bank will prepare minutes which will be agreed with the institution and the auditors and reporting accountants before being finalised and circulated to all parties.

[1] Inquiry into the Supervision of the Bank of Credit and Commerce International, HMSO 22.10.92, para 3.53.

Discussions with Reporting Accountants

11 A trilateral discussion with an institution and its reporting accountants will usually be held after the required reports on accounting and other records and internal control systems and on returns used for prudential purposes have been sent to the Bank, accompanied by the comments of management.

12 Reporting accountants should ensure that their records bring to the Bank's attention any matter arising from their work, in accordance with the scope set, of which they believe the Bank should be aware, and the report should be in the format specified in the Bank's notice BSD/1994/2. The reporting accountants' work should be performed with regard to the Auditing Guideline 'Banks in the United Kingdom'[1], Statement of Auditing Standards 620[2] and Practice Note 3[3]. The Bank needs to be informed of matters relevant to the carrying out of its responsibility to form a judgement about whether the criteria for authorisation relating to records and systems are met. The trilateral discussion will assist the Bank in forming this judgement. The specific items to be covered will be identified on the agenda, which can be expected to cover the following areas:

(a) matters which arise from the reporting accountants' examinations and those to which their reports refer;

(b) management's comments on the reports;

(c) the extent of and the reporting accountants' approach to, the work under section 39;

(d) reporting accountants' explanations for a change in a previously reported intention to give a negative opinion in the report, or the reason for and nature of a qualified report;

(e) any other matter which the Bank considers relevant to its judgement;

(f) any step or course of action which may be necessary in the light of the reports; for example, the commissioning of a more detailed report on a particular aspect of the institution's records and systems; and

(g)   an outline agreement to the scope, or a change to the previously agreed
       scope, of the next period's examination of records and systems thereby
       avoiding the need for a separate planning meeting.

[1] Auditing Guideline 'Banks in the United Kingdom' issued in March 1989 by the Auditing
Practices Committee, the predecessor body to the Auditing Practices Board.
[2] Statement of Auditing Standards 620 'The auditors' right and duty to report to regulators in the
financial sector' issued in March 1994 by the Auditing Practices Board.
[3] Practice Note 'The auditor's right and duty to report to the Bank of England' issued in March
1994 by the Auditing Practices Board.

Discussions with Auditors

13 A trilateral discussion with an institution and its auditors will normally be held after
the auditors have issued their audit report on the institution's financial statements,
although where the auditors are also the reporting accountants the trilateral discussion
may be held before the audit report is issued. The work undertaken by accountants is
governed by the standards and guidelines issued by their professional bodies; they
should however, have particular regard to Statement of Auditing Standards 620 and the
Practice Note when conducting their work. In the circumstances outlined in Part 2
below, however, auditors may request a meeting before signing their report. The
trilateral discussion may be expected to cover the following areas, although the specific
items to be covered will be contained on the agenda:

(a)   issues arising from the audit, including discussions with the audit committee
       where appropriate;
(b)   presentation and content of the institution's accounts;
(c)   matters raised by the Bank, or those which the institution or its auditors
       have drawn to its attention, during the year at either routine prudential or
       non-routine meetings, including how such matters have been resolved to the
       satisfaction of the auditors or have been reflected or treated in the accounts;
       and
(d)   matters brought to the Bank's attention in a written notice in accordance
       with section 46 of the Act or the institution's or its auditors' intention to give
       such written notice.

Part 2: Communication to the Bank

The Regulations

14 Where an auditor or reporting accountant has reasonable cause to believe that 'any
of the criteria specified in Schedule 3 to the Act is not or has not been fulfilled, or may
not be or may not have been fulfilled' in respect of the client authorised institution,
paragraph 3 of the Regulations places a duty on them to communicate such matters to
the Bank. The Regulations do not specify how the matter should be reported, and the
Bank believes that this may be either orally or in writing. Where a matter is reported
orally it should be confirmed in writing at the earliest opportunity. The matters to be
reported, however, should only be those which 'are likely to be of material significance
for the exercise, in relation to such an authorised institution, of the Bank's functions
under the Act or under the [Banking Coordination (Second Council Directive)] Regulations [1992]'[1]. The matters to be reported include those in the circumstances referred to
in paragraphs 18 and 20 below.

15 The Bank recognises that auditors and reporting accountants cannot be expected
to be aware of all circumstances which, had they known of them, would have led them to
report under the statutory duty imposed by the Regulations. The auditors and reporting
accountants should perform their work with regard to Statement of Auditing Standards
620 and the Practice Note. The Bank believes that both the Regulations and the Act do
not require auditors to change the scope of their audit work, nor the frequency or timing
of their audit visits, nor do they require the reporting accountants to vary the scope and
timing of their examinations. Neither auditors nor reporting accountants have an
obligation to seek out grounds for making a report under the statutory provisions, nor
do the provisions place an obligation on them to conduct their work in such a way that
there is reasonable certainty that they will discover a breach of the Schedule 3 criteria. It

is only when auditors become aware in the ordinary course of their audit work, or reporting accountants become aware during their examinations, of such an occurrence that they should make detailed enquiries with the statutory provisions specifically in mind.

16 Where the auditors or reporting accountants become aware of a matter to be reported under the Regulations the duty is on the auditors or the reporting accountants to communicate the matter to the Bank. The Bank expects that, normally, the auditors and reporting accountants will discuss with their client any report or matter which they wish to raise at a meeting with the Bank, before the report is issued, or the meeting held. Indeed, discussions between the auditors or reporting accountants and an institution's management are an integral part of the process of deciding whether a matter is reportable. The Bank recognises that circumstances may arise where auditors or reporting accountants consider that it would not be appropriate for the institution to be aware of their direct communication with the Bank, or where they disagree with the institution about matters to be communicated to the Bank. In such circumstances they may wish to take legal or other professional advice. However, in taking such a step they should consider whether any resultant delay or failure to report would put them in breach of the statutory duty to notify the Bank and whether the interests of depositors might be harmed by a delay in bringing important matters to the Bank's attention.

17 The Bank has given an indication of the way in which it interprets the criteria specified in Schedule 3, in its Statement of Principles which was first issued in May 1988 and revised in May 1993. The Bank will expect auditors and reporting accountants to have regard to the Statement of Principles when considering whether a matter represents a breach, or potential breach, of the Schedule 3 criteria. The Schedule 3 criteria are summarised in Appendix 1 to this Notice.

18 The Bank recognises that it is important for auditors or reporting accountants to act in a manner that will preserve their professional relationship with their client. Auditors and reporting accountants may therefore ask the institution to draw matters which they believe should be reported to the attention of the Bank without delay. Auditors and reporting accountants should, nevertheless, normally report matters direct to the Bank. The Bank recognises, however, that where the auditors and reporting accountants are satisfied that the matter has already been fully reported to the Bank there is no need for the auditors and reporting accountants also to report the matter. Examples of circumstances in which the criteria specified in Schedule 3 have been breached and should be reported via the institution, are when the auditors or reporting accountants have reasonable cause to believe that:

(a) the institution has breached, is currently in breach of, or is likely to breach the trigger capital ratio set by the Bank;

(b) the institution has breached by a material amount and especially if for a significant period, or has frequently breached by any amount the liquidity mismatch guidelines (where such a guideline has been set) for the institution as laid down by the Bank;

(c) the institution fails to hold adequate provisions for bad and doubtful debts, expected losses on contingents and tax liabilities, in accordance with accepted accounting standards;

(d) the accounting and other records and systems of control of the institution are not commensurate with the size and nature of business, or the way in which the business is structured, organised and managed. A weakness does not necessarily fall within this category just because it would normally be reported as an exception in a section 39 systems report. The matter should be reported if, were the weakness allowed to continue, the institution would be unable to monitor or control a significant risk and therefore be in danger of sustaining uncontrolled losses;

(e) the business, or a significant component of the business, is effectively being directed, or may be directed for any period of time, by only one individual;

(f) the institution has failed to meet, or is likely to breach, the minimum own funds requirements set out in Schedule 3;

(g) there has been a change in the composition of the board of directors which the institution has not notified to the Bank; and

(h)   there is evidence which calls into question the appropriateness of actions or decisions undertaken by management which are significant for prudential purposes.

19 The Bank recognises that auditors and reporting accountants have no obligation to search for breaches of the Schedule 3 criteria, nor to monitor an institution's compliance with the Schedule 3 criteria throughout the period under review. However, the Bank expects that the auditors and reporting accountants will conduct their work as described in paragraph 15 above, and when they become aware of a breach in the Schedule 3 criteria, including the examples given above, they will report the matter to the Bank, as detailed in paragraph 16.

20 Where, exceptionally, it is in the interests of protecting depositors that the management of the institution should not be informed in advance, auditors or reporting accountants should report the matter immediately to the Bank. Examples of these circumstances in which this approach should be adopted are:

(a)   where there has been an occurrence which causes auditors or reporting accountants no longer to have confidence in the integrity of the directors or senior management, for example, where they believe that a fraud or other misappropriation has been committed by the directors or senior management of the institution, or they have evidence of the intention of directors or senior management to commit such fraud or misappropriation; or

(b)   where there has been an occurrence which causes auditors or reporting accountants no longer to have confidence in the competence of directors or senior management to conduct the business of the institution in a prudent manner so as to protect the interests of depositors, for example, where they have discovered that the directors or senior management are acting in an irresponsible or reckless manner with respect to the institution's affairs, or they have evidence of an intention so to act; or

(c)   where the institution will not itself inform the Bank of a matter, having been advised to do so by its auditors or reporting accountants, or where it has not done so within the specified period of time, or where there is inadequate evidence that the institution has properly reported the matters in question.

---

[1] Paragraph 3 of The Accountants (Banking Act 1987) Regulations 1994, SI 1994/524.

The Act

21 Section 47 of the Act provides that no duty to which an auditor of an authorised institution or a reporting accountant shall be subject will be contravened 'by reason of his communicating in good faith to the Bank, whether or not in response to a request made by it, any information or opinion on a matter to which this section applies and which is relevant to any function of the Bank under this Act'. Sub-sections 47(2) and 47(3) of the Act state that section 47 applies to any matter of which auditors or reporting accountants become aware in their respective capacities and which relates to the business or affairs of their client institution or any associated body. The matters covered by section 47 include those which are relevant to the reports made by reporting accountants, to the regular discussions with the Bank and to those exceptional circumstances which are referred to in paragraph 22 below.

22 Auditors and reporting accountants should take the initiative in reporting directly to the Bank, in addition to their statutory duty under the Regulations and other regular reporting responsibilities, when they consider it expedient to do so in order to protect the interests of depositors because there has been a material loss or there exists a significant risk of material loss.

23 In setting out when it would be appropriate for auditors or reporting accountants to take the initiative in bringing matters to its attention the Bank emphasises that it is primarily the institution's responsibility to report such matters and that there are regular prudential meetings and reporting procedures designed to help them to meet this obligation. Moreover, the Bank expects an institution to bring an event or circumstance to its attention as soon as it has reason to believe that it could have a material adverse effect on the institution or on the interests of depositors because there has been a material loss or there exists a significant risk of material loss.

24 In addition, the Bank reviews prudential returns and other reports to ensure that the interests of depositors are not at risk because of adverse changes in the financial position or in the management or other resources of an institution. The reporting arrangements relating to prudential returns are intended to reassure the Bank about the quality and reliability of the information it receives from an institution. In this regard institutions will be aware of section 94(3) of the Act relating to the knowing or reckless provision of false or misleading information. The Banking Supervision Guide provides guidance on the Bank's interpretation of that section. In particular, institutions should note that section 94(3) makes it an offence for an authorised (or former authorised) institution to withhold information from the Bank knowing or having reasonable cause to believe that it is materially relevant to the Bank's prudential supervision.

25 Accordingly, once auditors or reporting accountants form the view that they should report under the protection of section 47 of the Act concerning a matter which does not give rise to a statutory duty under the Regulations, they should first obtain evidence, normally from the institution, as to whether the matter has been brought to the Bank's attention in a prudential return, at a prudential meeting or in any other way. If the matter has not been brought to the Bank's attention, auditors or reporting accountants should ask the institution to do so and only if it declines, or fails to do so within a specified period of time, will they need to contact the Bank direct to inform it of the matter. The Bank will acknowledge receipt of the information and will advise the auditors or reporting accountants, in general terms, of how it proposes to proceed where such action would not be counter-prudential.

Discussion

26 The Bank believes that a firm of auditors or of reporting accountants which complies with the new duty to communicate a matter to the Bank will not be liable if it thereby contravenes any duty (for example, of confidentiality) owed to its client. This immunity is set out in section 47 of the Act. This protection will apply regardless of the source of that information provided the firm of auditors or of reporting accountants became aware of the matter in its capacity as auditors or reporting accountants of that client.

27 The protection under section 47 of the Act also applies to information disclosed, where the matter relates to the business or affairs of the institution or any associated body. A firm of auditors or of reporting accountants may be exposed to the risk of criminal liability and/or professional disciplinary proceedings arising from a failure to comply with the statutory duty. The Bank would therefore expect the firm to take written legal advice where they are uncertain whether to report the matter to the Bank.

28 It will be for each firm to decide whether it should establish inter-departmental lines of communication so that matters relating to the institution are brought to the attention of the appropriate auditors or reporting accountants in the firm. The Bank recognises that the duty to report relates only to matters which are relevant to the business or affairs of the authorised institution and of which the auditors or reporting accountants become aware in their capacity as its auditors or reporting accountants. However, the Bank will expect institutions to advise their firm of auditors or reporting accountants when they appoint a third party (including another department of the same firm) to review, investigate or report on any aspect of their records and systems. The Bank will expect institutions to provide their auditors and reporting accountants with reports by a third party on any aspect of their records and systems promptly after their receipt.

29 In the exceptional circumstances referred to in paragraph 20 above, auditors and reporting accountants may wish to consider whether the matter should be reported at an appropriate senior level in the institution and whether an appropriate senior representative of the institution should be invited to attend the meeting with the Bank. They may also consider that the audit committee may have a role to play in this respect. A decision following this consideration will have to be made in the light of the circumstances of each case.

30 Speed of reporting will be important to ensure that the auditors or reporting accountants comply with the Regulations, as well as for the protection of depositors as mentioned in paragraph 16 above, and in all cases the Bank will expect a minimum of

delay between auditors and reporting accountants deciding that a report is necessary and their informing the Bank.

31 The other sections of the Act which relate to the Bank's relationship with auditors and reporting accountants are listed in Appendix 2. In addition, the nature of that relationship, as outlined in paragraph 3 above, and the relevant sections of the Act are shown in Appendix 3. In particular, auditors should be aware of their statutory obligations under section 46(2) of the Act.

Part 3: Communication by the Bank

32 Information which is confidential and has been obtained under, or for the purpose of, the Act may only be disclosed by the Bank in the circumstances permitted under the Act. Where a gateway exists under the Act which would enable the Bank to disclose information to third parties, the Bank may disclose this information where:

(a) disclosure enables or assists the Bank to perform its functions under the Act; or

(b) it is otherwise in the interests of depositors for the information to be disclosed.

33 Section 83(1) permits the Bank to disclose information in the circumstances set out in paragraph 32(a) above, and this could, in appropriate circumstances, allow the Bank to disclose information to auditors or reporting accountants. Section 83(2), however, specifically permits disclosure of information by the Bank to the auditor of an authorised institution or former authorised institution where the conditions in paragraph 32 are complied with. Section 85(1)(b) of the Act specifically provides a gateway for the disclosure of information to reporting accountants to enable the accountants to fulfil their duties under section 8(5) or 39(1)(b). The Bank expects that a meeting would normally be required in these circumstances and that it would be appropriate for this to be held on a trilateral basis.

34 Section 83(3) allows the Bank to disclose information to professionally qualified persons for the purpose of seeking advice to enable or assist it properly to discharge its functions under the Act. Disclosure of the information under this subsection may only be made where it is necessary to ensure that the professional person is properly informed with respect to the matters on which his advice is sought.

35 It should be noted that, although the Bank may disclose confidential information to auditors or to reporting accountants, this information will be subject to the restrictions on disclosure contained in the Act. Auditors and reporting accountants are not generally free to pass that information to others, such as their client institution, except in compliance with the Act.

36 The Bank will take the initiative in bringing a matter to the attention of an institution and its auditors or reporting accountants:

(a) when it believes that it is of such significance that the auditors' or reporting accountants' knowledge of it could significantly affect the form of their audit or other report or the way in which they carry out their audit or other reporting responsibility; and

(b) when the disclosure is for the purpose of enabling or assisting the Bank to discharge its functions under the Banking Act or will otherwise be in the interests of depositors.

Appendix 1 The Bank of England's relationship with auditors and reporting accountants

Summary of the Schedule 3 criteria

In outline, the Schedule 3 criteria are as follows:

(c) directors, controllers and managers of the institution are fit and proper persons to hold their particular positions;

(d) at least two individuals effectively direct the business of the institution;

(e) for UK-incorporated institutions there should be as many non-executive directors as the circumstances and scale of the business require;

(f) the business should be conducted in a prudent manner;
(g) the business should be carried on with integrity and professional skills appropriate to the nature and scale of its activities; and
(h) the institution complies with the minimum net assets requirements.

Appendix 2 The Bank of England's relationship with auditors and reporting accountants

Sections of the Banking Act 1987 relevant to auditors and reporting accountants

Number	Title
8	Applications for authorisation
39	Power to obtain information and require production of documents
41	Investigations on behalf of the Bank
45	Audited accounts to be open to inspection
46	Notification in respect of auditors
47	Communication by auditor etc, with the Bank
82	Restricted information
83	Disclosure for facilitating discharge of functions by the Bank
85	Other permitted disclosures
94	False and misleading information
Schedule 3	Minimum criteria for authorisation

Appendix 3 The Bank of England's relationship with auditors and reporting accountants

The relationship and the relevant sections of the Banking Act 1987

Nature of relationship		Section number
(a)	Reports on accounting and other records and on internal control systems	39(1)(b), 39(2), 85(1)(b) [see also Schedule 3 paragraph 3(7)]
(b)	Reports on returns used for prudential purposes	39(1)(b), 39(2), 85(1)(b)
(c)	Incidental reports pursuant to applications for authorisation	8(5)
(d)	Reports pursuant to investigations on behalf of the Bank	41(1)
(e)	Auditors' co-operation with person appointed under clause 41(1)	41(5)
(f)	Notification to Bank of auditors' resignation, decision not to seek re-appointment and decision to qualify the audit report	46(2)
(g)	Auditors' and reporting accountants' communication to the Bank in good faith	47
(h)	Disclosure of information by the Bank to auditors and reporting accountants	83

[831]

BSD/1994/2
(March 1994)

GUIDANCE NOTE ON REPORTING ACCOUNTANTS' REPORTS ON ACCOUNTING AND OTHER RECORDS AND INTERNAL CONTROL SYSTEMS

Part 1: Introduction

1 The maintenance of adequate records and systems is one of the statutory criteria for authorisation under the Act[1]. Schedule 3 of the Act states that 'an institution shall not be

regarded as conducting its business in a prudent manner unless it maintains or, as the case may be, will maintain adequate accounting and other records of its business and adequate systems of control of its business and records'[2]. It further states that 'those records and systems shall not be regarded as adequate unless they are such as to enable the business of the institution to be prudently managed and the institution to comply with the duties imposed on it by or under this Act'[3].

2 In addition, authorised institutions[4] should maintain adequate accounting and other records and internal control systems:

(a) to enable the directors of an institution incorporated under the Companies Act 1985 (or the parallel legislation in Northern Ireland) to fulfil their statutory duties relating to the preparation of accounts;

(b) to provide the management of a UK branch of an overseas-incorporated institution with financial information to enable it to comply with the provisions of the Companies Act relating to the preparation and delivery of its accounts; and

(c) to ensure that directors and management have complete, accurate and timely information to enable them to make returns to the Bank in a proper and prompt fashion; and to enable them to furnish the Bank with any other information which it might reasonably require.

3 The Bank has the powers to commission reports under section 39 of the Act for all authorised institutions and all European authorised institutions (as defined in Regulation 3 of the Banking Coordination (Second Council Directive) Regulations 1992). The Bank does not expect, other than in exceptional circumstances, to use these powers over European authorised institutions to commission reports on accounting and other records or internal control systems; the Bank will, however, periodically commission from European authorised institutions[5] reports on statistical returns.

4 The purpose of this Notice which replaces the Bank's Notices BSD/1987/2 and BSD/1992/4, is to provide guidance on the Bank's interpretation of the Act's requirements in relation to records and systems, to assist authorised institutions to assess whether they meet those requirements and in particular to assist reporting accountants appointed under section 39 of the Act to report on the records and systems of institutions. The guidance is intended to be:

(a) sufficiently comprehensive to encompass the wide range of activities undertaken by both UK-incorporated and overseas-incorporated authorised institutions; and

(b) relevant to the circumstances of both large and small institutions which undertake transactions of varying degrees of volume and complexity.

5 It is the responsibility of an institution's directors and management to ensure that adequate records and systems are maintained and the responsibility of the Bank to judge whether the criterion for authorisation relating to those records and systems is satisfied.

6 The Bank will rarely find it appropriate to prescribe in detail the manner in which a particular institution should maintain its accounting and other records and internal control systems. Rather, this Notice emphasises the scope and nature of the financial information which the accounting and other records must be designed to capture, contain and provide for management and emphasises the scope and nature of the internal control systems and the purposes for which they are established by management.

7 The Act's requirements for adequate accounting and other records and internal control systems to be maintained applies only to authorised institutions; it does not apply to subsidiary or associated companies of an authorised institution which are not themselves authorised. Nevertheless, in accordance with article 3.6 of the Consolidated Supervision Directive (92/30/EEC), the Bank expects authorised institutions to have adequate internal control mechanisms for the production of any data and information which would be relevant for the purposes of supervision on a consolidated basis.

8 The Bank's guidance on the interpretation of the Act's requirements contained in this Notice is intended to encompass all aspects of an institution's business whether on or

off-balance sheet, whether undertaken as principal or as agent and regardless of whether any part of the business is supervised by another regulator.

[1] References in this Notice to 'the Act' are to the Banking Act 1987 as amended by The Banking Coordination (Second Council Directive) Regulations 1992 (SI 1992/3218).
[2] Schedule 3, paragraph 4(7).
[3] Schedule 3, paragraph 4(8).
[4] An authorised institution is an institution directly authorised by the Bank under section 9 of the Act.
[5] A European authorised institution is defined in section 3 of The Banking Coordination (Second Council Directive) Regulations 1992 (SI 1992/3218).

Part 2: Accounting and other records

Introduction

9 The scope and nature of the accounting and other records which are required for the business to be conducted in a prudent manner should be commensurate with an institution's needs and particular circumstances and should have regard to the manner in which the business is structured, organised and managed, to its size and the nature, volume and complexity of its transactions and commitments. The accounting and other records should be located where they will best assist management to conduct the business of the institution in a prudent manner on a day-to-day basis. If the accounting and other records of a UK branch of an overseas-incorporated institution are kept outside the United Kingdom there should be arrangements which allow local management to have immediate access to them.

General requirements

10 It is not appropriate to prepare a comprehensive list of the accounting and other records which an institution should maintain. However, the accounting and other records should meet the following general requirements:

(a) capture and record on a timely basis and in an orderly fashion every transaction and commitment which the institution enters into with sufficient information to explain:
  (i) its nature and purpose;
  (ii) any asset and/or liability, actual and contingent, which respectively arises or may arise from it; and
  (iii) any income and/or expenditure, current and/or deferred, which arises from it;
(b) provide details, as appropriate, for each transaction and commitment, showing:
  (i) the parties including, in the case of a loan, advance or other credit exposure, whether and if so to whom it is sub-participated;
  (ii) the amount and currency;
  (iii) the contract, rollover, value and settlement or repayment dates;
  (iv) the contracted interest rates of an interest rate transaction or commitment;
  (v) the contracted exchange rate of a foreign exchange transaction or commitment;
  (vi) the contracted commission or fee payable or receivable together with any other related payment or receipt;
  (vii) the nature and current estimated value of any security for a loan or other exposure; the physical location and documentary evidence of such security; and
  (viii) in the case of any borrowing, whether it is subordinated and, if secured, the nature and book value of any asset upon which it is secured;
(c) be maintained in such a manner that financial and business information can be extracted promptly to enable management to:
  (i) monitor the quality of and safeguard the institution's assets, including those held as custodian;

    (ii) identify, quantify, control and manage its exposures by related counterparties across all products;

    (iii) identify, quantify, control and manage its exposures to liquidity risk and foreign exchange and other market risks across all products;

    (iv) monitor the performance of all aspects of its business on an up-to-date basis; and

    (v) make timely and informed decisions;

(d) contain details of exposure limits authorised by management which are appropriate to the type, nature and volume of business undertaken. These limits should, where relevant, include counterparty, industry sector, country, settlement, liquidity, interest rate mismatch and securities position limits as well as limits on the level of intra-day and overnight trading positions in foreign exchange, futures, options, future (or forward) rate agreements (FRAs) and swaps; provide information which can be summarised in such a way as to enable actual exposures to be readily, accurately and regularly measured against these limits;

(e) contain details of the factors considered, the analysis undertaken and the authorisation or rejection by management of a loan, advance or other credit exposure; and

(f) provide on a memorandum basis details of every transaction entered into in the name of or on behalf of another party on an agency or fiduciary (trustee) basis where it is agreed that the institution itself is not legally or contractually bound by the transaction.

Information for management

11 Every institution should prepare information for directors and management so that they can monitor, assess and control the performance of its business, the state of its affairs and the risk to which it is exposed. This information should be prepared on an individual company and, where appropriate, on a consolidated basis. The frequency with which information is prepared, its level of detail and the amount of narrative analysis and explanation will depend upon the level of management to which it is addressed. Some types of information will be needed on a more frequent basis than others and it may be appropriate for some to be presented on a basis of breaches from agreed limits by way of exception reports.

12 It is the responsibility of directors and management to decide what information is required and to decide who should receive it. Appropriate management information should be provided to:

(a) persons responsible for exercising managerial functions or for maintaining accounting and other records;

(b) executives who, either alone or jointly, are responsible under the immediate authority of the directors for the conduct of the business of the institution; and

(c) the directors of the institution.

13 This information should be prepared:

(a) to show the state of affairs of the institution;

(b) to show the operational results of the business both on a cumulative basis and by discrete period and to give a comparison with budgets and previous periods;

(c) to provide an analysis of assets and liabilities showing how they have been valued;

(d) to provide an analysis of its off-balance sheet positions showing how they have been valued;

(e) to provide an analysis of income and expenditure showing how it relates to different categories of asset and liability and off-balance sheet positions; and

(f) to show the institution's exposure to each type of risk, compared to the relevant limits set by management.

Part 3: Internal control systems

Introduction

14 The scope and nature of effective control systems should take account of the size of the business, the diversity of operations, the volume and size of transactions, the degree of risk associated with each area of operation, the amount of control by senior management over day-to-day operations, the degree of centralisation and the extent of reliance on information technology. A system of internal control must be designed to provide reasonable assurance that all the institution's revenues accrue to its benefit, all expenditure is properly authorised and disbursed, all assets are adequately safeguarded, all liabilities are recorded, all statutory requirements relating to the provision of accounts are complied with and all prudential reporting conditions are adhered to.

General requirements

15 It is not appropriate to prepare a comprehensive list of internal control procedures which would then be applicable to any authorised institution nor is it possible to prepare a detailed list of particular procedures which should be undertaken, where appropriate, by all authorised institutions. Nonetheless, internal control systems should provide reasonable assurance that:

    (a)   the business is planned and conducted in an orderly and prudent manner in adherence to established policies;

    (b)   transactions and commitments are entered into in accordance with management's general or specific authority;

    (c)   management is able to safeguard the assets and control the liabilities of the business; there are measures to minimise the risk of loss from irregularities, fraud and error, and promptly and readily to identify them when they occur;

    (d)   the accounting and other records of the business provide complete, accurate and timely information;

    (e)   management is able to monitor on a regular and timely basis, inter alia, the adequacy of the institution's capital, liquidity, profitability and the quality of its assets;

    (f)   management is able to identify, regularly assess and, where appropriate, quantify the risk of loss in the conduct of the business so that:

        (i)   the risks can be monitored and controlled on a regular and timely basis; and

        (ii) appropriate provisions can be made for bad and doubtful debts, and for any other exposures both on and off-balance sheet; and

    (g)   management is able to prepare returns made to the Bank completely and accurately and in accordance with the Bank's reporting instructions and to submit them on a timely basis.

16 In seeking to secure reasonable assurance that their internal control objectives are achieved, management must exercise judgment in determining the scope and nature of the control procedures to be adopted. They should also have regard to the cost of establishing and maintaining a control procedure in relation to the benefits, financial or otherwise, that it is expected to provide.

17 It is a responsibility of directors and management to review, monitor and test its systems of internal control on a regular basis in order to assure their effectiveness on a day-to-day basis and their continuing relevance to the business. In many institutions an internal audit function will assist management by providing an independent review of such systems. Such a review should be designed to monitor the effectiveness and operation of the systems and to test compliance with daily procedures and controls (see paragraphs 30–34 below).

Detailed control objectives

18 The scope and nature of the specific control objectives which are required for the business to be conducted in a prudent manner should be commensurate with an institution's needs and particular circumstances and should have regard to the manner in which the business is structured, organised and managed, to its size and the nature, volume and complexity of its transactions and commitments.

19 It is not appropriate for the Bank to provide an exhaustive and prescriptive list of detailed control requirements which should apply to all institutions. However, the Bank considers that each institution should address the following control objectives:

(a) organisational structure;
(b) monitoring procedures;
(c) segregation of duties;
(d) authorisation and approval;
(e) completeness and accuracy;
(f) safeguarding assets; and
(g) personnel.

Organisational structure

20 Institutions should have documented the high level controls in their organisation, defining and allocating responsibilities, identifying lines of reporting for all aspects of the enterprise's operations, including the key controls and giving outline job descriptions for key personnel. The delegation of authority and responsibility should be clearly specified.

Monitoring procedures

21 An institution should have procedures in place to ensure that relevant and accurate management information covering the financial state and performance of the institution and the exposures which the institution has entered into are provided to appropriate levels of management on a regular and timely basis. Procedures should also be in place to ensure compliance with the institution's policies and practices including any limits on delegated authority referred to in paragraph 20, statutory, supervisory and regulatory requirements.

Segregation of duties

22 A prime means of control is the separation of those responsibilities or duties which would, if combined, enable one individual to record and process a complete transaction. Segregation of duties reduces the risk of intentional manipulation or error and increases the element of checking. Functions which should be separated include those of authorisation, execution, valuation, reconciliation, custody and recording. In the case of a computer-based accounting system, systems development and daily operations should be separated.

Authorisation and approval

23 All transactions should require authorisation or approval by an appropriate person and the levels of responsibility should be recorded as prescribed by paragraph 20.

Completeness and accuracy

24 Institutions should have controls to ensure that all transactions to be recorded and processed have been authorised, are correctly recorded and are accurately processed. Such controls include checking the arithmetical accuracy of the records, checking valuations, the maintenance and checking of totals, reconciliations, control accounts and trial balances, and accounting for documents.

Safeguarding assets

25 An institution should have controls designed to ensure that access to assets or information is limited to authorised personnel. This includes both direct access and indirect access via documentation to the underlying assets. These controls are of particular importance in the case of valuable, portable or exchangeable assets and assets held as custodian.

Personnel

26 There should be procedures to ensure that personnel have capabilities commensurate with their responsibilities. The proper functioning of any system depends on the

competence and integrity of those operating it. The qualifications, recruitment and training as well as the innate personal characteristics of the personnel involved are important features to be considered in setting up any control system.

Controls in an information technology environment

27 The information held in electronic form within an institution's information systems is a valuable asset that needs to be protected against unauthorised access and disclosure. The control objectives described above apply equally to operations undertaken in both manual and electronic environments although there are additional risks associated with electronic environments. It is the responsibility of management to understand the extent to which an institution relies upon electronic information to assess the value of that information and to establish an appropriate system of controls. The Bank recognises that this will usually be achieved by a combination of manual and automated controls, the balance of which will vary between institutions, reflecting the need for each to address its particular risks cost effectively.

28 The types of risk most often associated with the use of information technology in financial systems may be classified as follows:

    (a) *Fraud and Theft:* Access to information and systems can create opportunities for the manipulation of data in order to create or conceal significant financial loss. Additionally, information can be stolen, even without its physical removal or awareness of the fact, which may lead to loss of competitive advantage. Such unauthorised activity can be committed by persons with or without legitimate access rights.

    (b) *Errors:* Although they most frequently occur during the manual inputting of data and the development or amendment of software, errors can be introduced at every stage in the life cycle of an information system.

    (c) *Interruption:* The components of electronic systems are vulnerable to interruption and failure; without adequate contingency arrangements this can lead to serious operational difficulty and/or financial loss.

    (d) *Misinformation:* Problems may emerge in systems that have been poorly specified or inaccurately developed. These might become immediately evident, but can also pass undetected for a period during which they could undermine the veracity of supposedly sound information. This is a particular risk in systems where audit trails are poor and the processing of individual transactions difficult to follow.

29 Management should be aware of its responsibility to promote and maintain a climate of security awareness and vigilance throughout the organisation. In particular, it should give consideration to:

    (i) IT security education and training, designed to make all relevant staff aware of the need for, and their role in supporting, good IT security practice and the importance of protecting company assets;

    (ii) IT security policy, standards, procedures and responsibilities, designed to ensure that arrangements are adequate and appropriate.

Internal audit

30 Internal audit is an integral part of the systems of internal control established and maintained by management and may provide independent assurance over the integrity and effectiveness of these systems.

31 The existence, scope and objectives of internal audit are dependent upon the judgement of management as to its own needs and duties, the size and structure of the institution and the risks inherent in its business. Important considerations in assessing the effectiveness of internal audit include the scope of its terms of reference, its independence from operational management, its reporting regime and the quality of its staff (see paragraphs 33 and 34 below).

32 While the Bank does not consider it appropriate at the present time to prescribe that all authorised institutions have an internal audit function, it nevertheless encourages institutions to establish such a function, to facilitate an independent assessment and

monitoring of the effectiveness of internal controls. The following control functions could be undertaken by internal audit:

(a) review of accounting and other records and the internal control environment;
(b) review of the appropriateness, scope, efficiency and effectiveness of internal control systems;
(c) detailed testing of transactions and balances and the operation of individual internal controls to ensure that specific control objectives have been met;
(d) review of the implementation of management policies; and
(e) special investigations for management.

33 It is important to ensure that the internal audit function is appropriately structured and resourced to enable it to provide the independent appraisal of internal controls. There should be clearly defined terms of reference and its independence should be assured by an obligation to report regularly to the audit committee, or in its absence an executive specified by the Board, with the right of access to the audit committee, where one is established. Normally internal audit should not have authority or responsibility for the activities it audits.

34 Internal audit should have unrestricted access to all of an institution's activities, records, property and personnel to the extent necessary for the effective completion of its work. The internal audit function should be staffed with individuals who are appropriately qualified for the function either by holding professional qualifications or by having the requisite experience. Internal auditors should have regard to the Auditing Guideline 'Guidance for internal auditors' issued in June 1990 by the Auditing Practices Committee.

Part 4: Audit committee

35 Although not part of the control environment, the Bank believes that UK-incorporated institutions should have an audit committee and that, unless there are sound reasons to the contrary, which may include the size of the institution, all authorised institutions should appoint at least one non-executive director to undertake some audit committee functions. If the holding company of the institution has an audit committee it may not be necessary for the institution to have a separate audit committee where the audit committee of the holding company undertakes the function for the authorised institution as well.

36 The Bank believes that for an audit committee to be effective the following recommendations of the Committee on the Financial Aspects of Corporate Governance[1], which apply to companies listed on the Stock Exchange should be adopted:

(a) the audit committee should have a formal constitution and terms of reference;
(b) there should be a minimum of three members all of whom should be non-executive and a majority of whom should be independent of the company;
(c) meetings should normally be attended by the external auditors, the head of internal audit and the finance director;
(d) there should be at least one meeting with the external auditors each year, without executive board members present; and
(e) the audit committee should have explicit authority to investigate matters within its terms of reference and access to information and external advice.

37 The Bank recognises that smaller institutions will find it difficult to comply with the requirements in paragraph 35 above. The structure of the audit committee should therefore be commensurate with an institution's needs and particular circumstances, and should have regard to its size and the volume and complexity of its transactions and commitments.

---

[1] The Financial Aspects of Corporate Governance, published on 1 December 1992, by the Committee on the Financial Aspects of Corporate Governance, chaired by Sir Adrian Cadbury.

Part 5: Reporting accountants' examinations and reports

Introduction

38 The examination of accounting records and systems and controls will normally cover a twelve-month period, or possibly a shorter period for instance in the case of a newly authorised institution, and will arise from an annual letter of instruction from the institution to the reporting accountants (or a letter of engagement from the reporting accountants duly acknowledged by the institution), a copy of which should then be sent to the Bank. This letter of instruction or engagement, which will in turn arise from a notice from the Bank under section 39 of the Act requiring the institution to provide it with the required report, will set out in detail the scope of the reporting accountants' examination.

39 The Auditing Practices Committee issued an Auditing Guideline[1] which addressed the work of the reporting accountants in relation to their examinations of and reports on accounting and other records and internal control systems. Reporting accountants are expected to carry out their examination in accordance with this bank auditing guideline. They should also have regard to the Statement of Auditing Standards 620[2], Practice Note 3[3] and BSD/1994/1[4] which give guidance on the circumstances in which the reporting accountants should report matters to the Bank under both the statutory duty[5] on auditors and reporting accountants and under the protection of section 47 of the Act.

40 Reporting accountants appointed by an institution and approved by the Bank will be required to form an opinion on whether the institution's accounting and other records and internal control systems have been maintained by management during the period examined in accordance with the Bank's interpretation of the requirements of the Act. In forming this opinion they will be expected to have regard to the nature and scale of the business undertaken by the institution.

41 The Bank does not expect that reporting accountants will be able to give an unqualified opinion on the records and systems in every institution but that almost invariably they will prefer to draw the Bank's attention in their report to a number of matters which have come to their attention during the course of their work. Where during the course of their work, the reporting accountants believe one of the criteria specified in Schedule 3 to the Act is not or has not been fulfilled, or may not be or may not have been fulfilled and the matter is likely to be of material significance for the exercise of the Bank's supervisory functions the matter should be reported to the Bank without undue delay. Where the reporting accountants believe that a matter should be reported under either the statutory duty or under the protection of section 47 of the Act they should not wait for their report, commissioned under section 39 of the Act, to be submitted to the Bank. Guidance on this particular issue is provided in BSD/1994/1. The information provided in such a report will assist the Bank to make its judgement on the adequacy of an institution's records and systems and on whether the institution's business is conducted in a prudent manner on a day-to-day basis. Reporting accountants are not required to make this judgement.

42 The circumstances giving rise to an opinion qualified by exceptions include those where:

(a) certain records and systems do not exist and the reporting accountants consider that they should exist in order to assist management to conduct the business of the institution in a prudent manner on a day-to-day basis;

(b) there is, or has been, a significant weakness in, or failure of, certain records or systems during the period examined; or

(c) the reporting accountants are unable to form an opinion on a particular aspect of the records and systems and therefore wish to bring details of the matter to the attention of the Bank to place it in a better position to judge whether the criteria for authorisation was satisfied.

43 The Bank does not require reporting accountants to report all omissions, weaknesses and failures however minor in the existence, nature, scope and effectiveness of records and systems. Rather, it requires them to report those which individually or

collectively in their opinion do not enable them to give reasonable assurance that the requirements set out in this Notice are satisfied. The Bank does not expect reporting accountants to examine, assess or report on management's banking judgements and decisions. The assessment of the quality of management and of their banking decisions is a supervisory judgement for the Bank to make.

44 It will be for the Bank to judge in the light of the contents of a report and other information about the institution which is available to it whether the requirements of the Act relating to the records and systems are satisfied.

45 A larger institution may, in consultation with its reporting accountants and with the agreement of the Bank, commission a limited scope examination in one year as part of a rolling programme of examinations spread over a number of years as an alternative to a comprehensive or 'full scope' examination each year.

[1] Auditing Guideline 'Banks in the United Kingdom' issued by the Auditing Practices Committee of the Consultative Committee of Accountancy Bodies (the predecessor of the Auditing Practices Board) in March 1989.
[2] Statement of Auditing Standards 620 'The auditors' right and duty to report to regulators in the financial sector' issued by the Auditing Practices Board in March 1994.
[3] Practice Note 3 'The auditors' right and duty to report to the Bank of England' issued by the Auditing Practices Board in March 1994.
[4] BSD/1994/1 'The Bank of England's relationship with auditors and reporting accountants'.
[5] The Accountants (Banking Act 1987) Regulations 1994, SI 1994/524.

Full scope review

46 When the Bank commissions a full scope review it expects the reporting accountants to consider the adequacy of the accounting and other records and internal control systems, including the internal audit function, throughout the institution. In addition the reporting accountants should consider whether the institution's procedures are adequate to prevent, detect and report suspicions of money laundering[1].

[1] Money laundering Guidance notes for banks and building societies issued by the Joint Money Laundering Steering Group in October 1993.

The required report

47 The reporting accountants' report should be addressed to the directors in the case of a UK-incorporated authorised institution or to the senior manager in the case of a UK branch of an overseas-incorporated institution and should take the form of the proforma report set out in Part 6 of this Notice. The Bank requires the reporting accountants to give an overall assessment of the control environment for each business area which they have been asked to examine. The reporting accountants, unless exempted in the scope letter, should give limited background information on the business area including an organisational structure, nature and approximate volume of transactions (where appropriate), the key risks faced by the institution and the key controls in operation. Additional guidance on the information which the Bank requires will be given in the commissioning letter issued by the Bank to the institution, and where appropriate the information required may be provided by the institution itself.

48 Where the report is qualified by exceptions, the report should clearly set out the risks which the institution runs by not correcting the weakness, with an indication of the severity of the weakness should it not be corrected. The actual time frame for complying with each recommendation is a matter to be decided between the institution and the Bank, although this should be discussed at the trilateral meeting.

49 The report should be completed, dated and submitted with such comments as the institution's management see fit to make and submitted to the Bank by the authorised institution within the timescale laid down by the Bank, but not except in exceptional circumstances, more than three months after the end of the period examined. The comments of the institution's management should be copied to the reporting accountants at the same time as these comments are submitted to the Bank. If the reporting accountants conclude, after discussing the matter with the institution, that they will give a negative opinion (as opposed to one qualified by exceptions) they must

immediately inform the Bank in writing giving their reasons. They should also send the institution a copy of their letter. If the institution, for whatever reason, is unable to submit a report to the Bank within the required period, it should inform the Bank in writing of the reasons for the delay, as soon as the institution becomes aware that the deadline will not be met.

50 The required report (see Part 6) is prepared on the basis that it will be made by a UK firm of accountants. If, exceptionally, a report from the home country auditors or home country supervisors is accepted by the Bank this would be made on the same terms as the required report in Part 6 of this notice.

Part 6: Reporting accountants' report on accounting and other records and internal control systems

The Directors, XYZ Bank Limited

The Senior Manager, ABC Branch

Dear Sir(s)

In accordance with your letter of instruction dated [   ], a copy of which is attached, we have examined the accounting and other records and internal control systems of XYZ Bank Limited (ABC Branch) which were in existence during the year ended [   ].

As directors (senior manager) of XYZ Bank Limited (ABC Branch) you are responsible for establishing and maintaining adequate accounting and other records and internal control systems. In fulfilling that responsibility estimates and judgements must be made to assess the expected benefits and relative costs of management information and of control procedures. The objective is to provide reasonable, but not absolute, assurance that assets are safeguarded against loss from unauthorised use or disposition, that banking risks are properly monitored and evaluated, that transactions are executed in accordance with established authorisation procedures and are recorded properly, and to enable you to conduct the business in a prudent manner.

Because of inherent limitations in any accounting and internal control system errors or irregularities may nevertheless occur and not be detected. Also, projection of any evaluation of the systems to future periods is subject to the risk that management information and control procedures may become inadequate because of changes in conditions or that the degree of compliance with those procedures may deteriorate.

Our examination has been carried out having regard to the Bank of England's Guidance Note BSD/1994/2 dated March 1994 and to the Auditing Guideline 'Banks in the United Kingdom', issued by the Auditing Practices Committee of the Consultative Committee of Accountancy Bodies. Appendix 1 to this report summarises the key risks faced by the institution, the key controls in place and our overall assessment of the control environment which the institution relies on for each business area which we were required to examine in accordance with your letter of instruction dated [   ]. Appendix 2 gives an outline of the organisational structure of the institution together with a brief description of the nature and approximate volume of transactions entered into by the institution in the areas examined.

In our opinion, having regard to the nature and scale of its business, during the year ended [   ].

EITHER the accounting and other records and internal control systems examined by us were established and maintained in accordance with the requirements of the Guidance Note (with the exception of the matters set out in Appendix 3 attached to this report).

OR the accounting and other records and internal control systems examined by us were not established and maintained in accordance with the requirements of the Guidance Note for the reasons set out in Appendix 3 attached to this report.

Yours faithfully

A Reporting Accountant
Chartered Accountants

BSD/1994/3
(May 1994)

SUBORDINATED LOAN CAPITAL ISSUED BY UK INCORPORATED AUTHORISED INSTITUTIONS

Introduction

1 This Notice sets out the Bank's policy in respect of subordinated loan capital issued[1] by UK-incorporated authorised institutions. The terms of the Notice will apply to loan capital issued after the date of its publication, and have immediate effect.

2 The Bank's earlier notice BSD/1986/2 remains in force for loan capital issued before the date of this notice, and is not therefore being withdrawn.

3 The Notice BSD/1990/2 (as amended by BSD/1992/1), 'Implementation in the United Kingdom of the Directive on Own Funds of Credit Institutions', issued in December 1990, identifies two types of subordinated debt which are eligible for inclusion in capital base. These are:

   (i) **Hybrid capital instruments** ('Upper Tier 2')
     – Qualifying perpetual subordinated debt, including such debt which is convertible into equity.
   (ii) **Term subordinated debt** ('Lower Tier 2')
     – Perpetual subordinated debt which does not qualify as a hybrid capital instrument;
     – Subordinated term debt with a minimum original term to maturity of over five years.

This Notice sets out the general conditions that all subordinated debt must meet in order to qualify as capital. These conditions apply to subordinated debt issued by UK institutions directly, and issued by their domestic and overseas subsidiaries for inclusion in the institution's consolidated capital base. The Notice further identifies the special conditions that must be satisfied in order for the debt to qualify as either a hybrid capital instrument or as term subordinated debt eligible for inclusion in the capital base. The references in the Notices BSD/1990/2 and BSD/1992/1 to BSD/1986/2 should now also be understood to be references to BSD/1994/3 for issues made after 23 May 1994.

---

[1] There is a range of terminology that can be used depending on the form of loan capital (eg loan, bond or note, public or private issue). This notice refers to loan capital or subordinated debt, borrower (rather than issuer), lenders or subordinated creditors (rather than noteholders). However, the notice applies to all loan capital irrespective of its description.

General conditions

Subordination

4 The terms of any agreement governing the raising of subordinated loan capital ('the debt agreement') must ensure that **the claims of the lender are fully subordinated to those of all unsubordinated creditors.**

5 The Bank is more concerned that subordination provisions should be effective than that they should follow a particular form. Subordination provisions should therefore ensure that:

   (a) in a liquidation of, or other insolvency proceeding relating to, the institution the subordinated creditor(s) would not be entitled to receive and retain from the institution any amounts in respect of the subordinated debt until all unsubordinated creditors of the institution have been paid the amounts owing to them in full or these amounts have been fully provided for. The Bank would regard any set-off of amounts outstanding between the subordinated creditor(s) and the institution as a payment for these purposes. As a term of the debt agreement, the subordinated creditor should, to the fullest extent possible, waive any rights which it may have to set off amounts it owes to the institution against amounts owed to it by the institution under the debt agreement, or to institute proceedings in respect of such amounts[1];

(b)   the remedies available to the subordinated creditor in the event of default in respect of the subordinated debt should normally be limited to:

   (i)   petitioning for the winding up of the institution (and the borrower where this is not the same, ie in circumstances where the borrower is a subsidiary of the institution or some other related company but the institution is acting as guarantor of the debt)[2]; and

   (ii)   proving for its debt and claiming in the liquidation of the institution (and the borrower where this is not the same);

(c)   the only events of default[3] should be:

   (i)   non-payment of any amount due and payable under the debt agreement (or guarantee); and

   (ii)   the winding-up of the institution (or borrower where this is not the same);

(d)   the Bank recognises that in some jurisdictions it may be legally impossible to limit the remedies available to lenders in the way described in sub-paragraph (b) above[4]; in such jurisdictions, the lender may have a right to sue for unpaid principal which is due and payable under the debt agreement **provided** the institution has an option to defer repayment for at least six months after the contractual repayment date.

---

[1]   The Bank is aware that is not possible to contract out of the statutory right of set-off in Rule 4.90 of the Insolvency Rules 1986.

[2]   This requirement may be relaxed where the issuing company is a single purpose vehicle which meets the criteria for solo-consolidation set out in paragraph 28 of BSD/1993/1.

[3]   The occurrence of an event of default does not imply acceleration of the debt. See also paragraph 7.

[4]   For example, where issues are regulated by the US Trust Indenture Act.

Trigger clauses

6   The debt agreement must not include any clauses which might trigger early repayment of the debt. This will not, however, prejudice any right to petition for the winding-up of the borrower; for example, in the event of non-payment of interest on the debt (other than that which is deferred in accordance with paragraph 9 below).

Repayment

7   No early repayment of the debt, including purchases of capital notes by the institution or its subsidiaries for cancellation, may be made without the prior written consent of the Bank. Consent will depend on the Bank being satisfied that the institution's capital is adequate and is likely to remain so.

English law

8   The debt agreement must normally be subject to English law. However, the Bank will accept law other than English law throughout, or in parts of, a debt agreement provided it is satisfied that an equivalent degree of subordination can be achieved as under English law, meeting the requirements set out in paragraphs 4–5 above. In all cases the Bank must give its prior consent where law other than English law is to apply.

Hybrid capital instruments

9   Perpetual subordinated debt can be structured so as to bring it close to equity in terms of the protection that it offers depositors. The principal features which give it this quality are that it can absorb losses and leave an institution able to continue to trade, that it has no fixed servicing costs (ie that there are circumstances in which the borrower can defer a payment of interest without bringing itself into default) and that the proceeds of the loan are made permanently available to the borrower. In order to qualify as a hybrid capital instrument, a perpetual subordinated loan must satisfy the following conditions, in addition to those set out above in paragraphs 4–5:

(a)   it is undated;

(b) no repayment may be made without the prior consent of the Bank. The Bank would not normally expect to give such consent within five years and one day from the date of draw-down, and only when the Bank is satisfied that the institution's capital is likely to remain adequate after repayment;

(c) the debt agreement must provide for the institution to have the option to defer an interest payment on the debt (eg if it has not paid or declared a dividend in a preceding period);

(d) the debt agreement must provide for the debt and unpaid interest to be able to absorb losses, whilst leaving an institution able to continue trading. This can be achieved by providing for automatic conversion of the perpetual debt, and unpaid interest, into share capital should reserves become negative and where a capital reconstruction has not been undertaken. In such a case the institution will be required to maintain a sufficient margin of authorised but unissued share capital in order to allow a conversion of the debt into equity to be made at any time. Alternatively, instead of providing for automatic conversion, the debt agreement can expressly provide for the principal and interest on the debt to absorb losses where the institution would not otherwise be solvent, and for the subordinated creditors to be treated as if they were holders of a specified class of share capital in any liquidation of the institution. In this case, the debt agreement will provide for the debt to be treated as if it had been converted into share capital either on the day immediately preceding the presentation of a petition for the commencement of a winding-up of the institution or on the date of the creditors' or shareholders' meeting at which the relevant resolution for a winding-up was passed. **The debt agreement must contain an explicit warning to lenders that the debt can be treated in this way**.

Term subordinated loan capital

10 In order to qualify to be treated as capital, term subordinated debt must meet the conditions set out in paragraphs 4–8. In addition, the debt must have a minimum original maturity of five years and one day from draw-down. Where the debt agreement provides for the loan to be drawn down in a series of tranches, the minimum original maturity of each tranche must be five years and one day from the date of its draw-down.

11 Where a debt agreement provides for the lender to have the right to demand repayment, the Bank will regard the first possible repayment date as the maturity date of the loan. Consequently this repayment date must be more than five years and one day from the date of draw-down if the loan is to be eligible for inclusion in the institution's capital base.

Inclusion of subordinated debt in an institution's capital base

12 The details of the limits on the amount of subordinated debt that can be included in an institution's capital base are set out in the Bank's Notice, BSD/1990/2. Any subordinated loan capital which does not qualify for inclusion will be treated in the normal way as part of an institution's long term funding.

Amortisation

13 The amount of term subordinated loan capital included in the capital base will be subject to a straight line amortisation during its last five years to repayment. In the case of loans which are repayable in separate tranches (eg in five tranches in line with the amortisation schedule), the Bank will amortise each tranche individually, as if it were a separate loan. However, where the institution only has the option (as opposed to the obligation) to repay in separate tranches, the Bank will not amortise the tranches individually provided its limits on 'step ups' (see paragraph 14 below) are not exceeded.

14 Where a bank has an option to repay early (as described in paragraph 7 above), the Bank will not normally assume early repayment for amortisation purposes. However, where the decision not to exercise the option leads to an unacceptably large increase in the interest rate paid on the loan (a 'step up'), the loan will be amortised over the five years preceding the exercise date of the option. Institutions should discuss

proposed 'step ups' with the Bank to establish whether they are acceptable in this context. Loans should not contain 'steps ups' within five years and one day from the date of draw-down.

Procedures and requirements for raising loan capital

15 In view of the complex nature of subordination provisions, the Bank will in future require borrowing institutions to confirm to it in writing that they have obtained legal advice that the subordination provisions in the debt agreement will be effective and specifically that they address the issues raised in paragraphs 4–5 above. This advice should be obtained from independent legal advisers with sufficient expertise and experience in this area of the law. In the case of loans which are subject to law other than English law, the opinion must be obtained from lawyers with sufficient expertise and experience in this area of the law in the country whose law has been selected as governing law.

16 No early repayment of any subordinated loan capital may be made without the Bank's prior consent. Consent will only be given where the Bank is satisfied that the institution's capital will be adequate after repayment. A letter to the Bank, giving effect to this condition and undertaking to seek the Bank's prior consent to any material variation in the terms and conditions of a loan, will be required from the institution concerned. The Bank considers it essential that lenders should be made fully aware of the restriction on early repayment. Notice of the restriction should be given either in the loan agreement or in the offer documents or through other information sources commonly used in the markets.

Prior submission of documentation

17 In view of the change to existing arrangements set out in paragraph 15 above, the Bank will no longer require to be given the opportunity to consider and agree the **legal** aspects of loan documentation in advance; it will instead require to be sent a confirmation in the form referred to in paragraph 15 and copies of the executed loan documentation. However, in order to avoid any misunderstanding of the Bank's policy requirements, institutions may approach the Bank with drafts of the documentation prior to the completion of a transaction. In addition, where an issue involves novel commercial aspects (eg relating to interest rate structures etc), institutions are strongly advised to consult the Bank in good time in order to discuss any policy implications. **[833]**

BSD/1994/4
(November 1994)

TREATMENT OF REPURCHASE AGREEMENTS AND STOCK LENDING AND BORROWING FOR CAPITAL ADEQUACY AND LARGE EXPOSURES PURPOSES

Introduction

This Notice supplements the Bank's notice BSD/1990/3 ('Implementation in the United Kingdom of the Solvency Ratio Directive') dated December 1990. It sets out the treatment of sale and repurchase agreements and stock borrowing and lending transactions for capital adequacy and large exposures purposes.

The changes have been adopted to reflect more accurately the risks involved with repurchase agreements and stock lending transactions.

The Notice amends paragraphs 25 and 26 of the guidance notes to the BSD1 return and adds a paragraph to the reporting instructions for the form LE. Compliance officers are requested to ensure that they amend both sets of notes for future reference.

The new rules will apply only to transactions in OECD government securities; transactions involving other types of security should be reported as before.

To report using the new rules, banks will have to meet the minimum requirements set out in paragraph 26 below. If they do not they should report using the rules in paragraph 25.

Where banks make use of the rules in paragraph 26 for reporting reverse repo transactions, they will be obliged to report repos in OECD government securities under the rules in paragraph 26 and any counterparty exposures arising on the form LE. For consolidated returns, however, where banks can meet the minimum requirements in some group companies but not others, use of the rules in paragraph 26 on a selective basis may be agreed. Institutions should discuss this with their line supervisors.

Revised BSD1 guidance notes

Sale and repurchase agreements

25 The following requirements apply to all arrangements where a reporting institution has sold (or lent) securities to a counterparty subject to a buy back (or return clause) including arrangements where the reporting institution has lent a third party's securities at its own risk. Thus, the requirements apply to repos, reverse repos, stock borrowing and lending. (For the remainder of this Notice, repo will be understood to cover also stock lending; reverse repos will cover also stock borrowing.)

Repos

Reporting institutions that have sold loans or other assets to other institutions for an agreed period with a commitment to repurchase should continue to report the loan or asset on the balance sheet. Where this is not the reporting institution's normal accounting practice, sale and repurchase agreements should be reported in the off-balance sheet section of the return.

Reverse repos

Reporting institutions which have purchased such loans or assets (ie purchase and resale agreements or reverse repos) should for the duration of the agreement report the transaction as a collateralised loan, adopting the normal weight for the counterparty unless the assets are eligible for a reduced weight (eg government securities).

If the collateral given is not cash, then the reporting institution should continue to report the collateral given on its own balance sheet. No exposure to the counterparty should be reported.

Repos in OECD government securities

26 For repos and reverse repos in OECD government securities where collateral provided is in the form of cash or other OECD government securities, the following requirements will apply:

Repos

Reporting institutions that have sold OECD government securities to other institutions for a limited period with a commitment to repurchase should continue to report the securities on the balance sheet.

In addition, the reporting institution should report the counterparty risk on the transaction. This is calculated as the difference between the mark to market value of the security sold and the mark to market value of collateral taken plus an add-on to cover potential future exposure. If this difference is zero or negative, the institution should report only the add-on as an exposure.

Add-ons should be calculated in the same way as for interest rate related contracts; to determine the appropriate conversion factor, the residual maturity of the underlying security, and not of the repo itself, should be used. For the purposes of the calculation, the mark to market value of the security repoed should be used for the notional principal amount of the contract.

The counterparty risk should be reported on Appendix I of the return in the same way as counterparty exposures on interest rate related contracts.

Reverse repo

The reporting institution should not report issuer risk in relation to the government security bought. If, however, the reverse repo is taken to cover a short position in the security, that short position should continue to be reported and weighted.

The reporting institution should report counterparty risk arising under the reverse repo (whether the transaction is to cover a short position or not). This is calculated as the difference between the cash given (or mark to market value if a security) and the mark to market value of the security bought plus an add-on for potential future exposure. If this difference is zero or negative, the institution should report only the add-on as an exposure.

The add-on should be calculated in the same way as for repo transactions but using the conversion factor corresponding to the residual maturity of the security bought. The mark to market value of the collateral given should be used for the notional principal amount of the contract in a reverse repo.

Minimum requirements

In order to report on this basis, reporting institutions must first meet the following minimum requirements:

- the transactions must be subject to a written legal agreement (whether under a master agreement, or documentation used on specific occasions) that provides for the claims of the institution to be against the claims of the counterparty in the event of the latter's default;'
- the securities and collateral involved in the transaction must be marked to market daily taking account of any interest accruals;
- collateral is adjusted on a regular basis to take account of material changes in market values.

---

[1] For amendment to para 26 see Bank of England letter dated 16 November 1994.

REVISED INSTRUCTIONS TO THE FORM LE

New paragraph following LE/P4 SECURITIES

LE/94 Repo and reverse repo transactions in OECD government securities

The following requirements apply to all arrangements where a reporting institution has sold (or lent) OECD securities to a counterparty subject to a buy back (or return clause) including arrangements where the reporting institution has lent a third party's securities at its own risk. Thus, the requirements apply to repos, reverse repos, stock borrowing and lending.

Counterparty exposures arising from repo and reverse repo transactions in OECD government securities (ie reported on the basis of paragraph 26 of the BSD1 Guidance Notes) should be aggregated with other exposures to the same counterparty or group of closely related counterparties. The counterparty exposures should be calculated as follows:

Repos

The difference between the mark to market value of securities lent and the collateral taken plus an add-on for potential future exposure.

Reverse repos

The difference between the cash given (or mark to market value if a security) and the security bought plus an add-on for potential future exposure.

Add-ons should be calculated in the same way as for interest rate related contracts (see section on Replacement Costs, LE/P5). The residual maturity of the security underlying the repo or reverse repo should be used to determine the conversion factor that should be used to calculate the add-on. In the calculation, the mark to market value of the security sold in a repo or the collateral provided in a reverse repo should be used for the notional principal amount. **[834]**

LETTER TO UK INCORPORATED AUTHORISED INSTITUTIONS

(16 November 1994)

Bank of England
Banking Supervision Division

Treatment of repurchase agreements and stock lending and borrowing for capital adequacy and large exposures purposes

Following my letter of 11 November 1994, we have given further thought to the arrangements set out in BSD 1994/4 for repos in OECD government securities and, on the basis of representations made to us, have concluded that the following addition should be made to paragraph 26 of the revised BSD1 guidance notes:

"Where repos and reverse repos are subject to daily adjustment of collateral, the conversion factor used for the calculation of add-ons should be reduced by 50%."

I would like to take the opportunity to add that buy/sell transactions in OECD government securities which meet the minimum requirements may be reported using the methodology set out in paragraph 26.

I would be grateful if you could bring this letter to the attention of all relevant staff within your organisation and apologise for any inconvience caused by making this amendment so soon after publication of the notice.   **[835]**

S&S/1995/1
(March 1995)

NOTICE TO INSTITUTIONS AUTHORISED UNDER THE BANKING ACT 1987

AMENDMENT TO THE BANK'S NOTICE ON THE IMPLEMENTATION IN THE UNITED KINGDOM OF THE SOLVENCY RATIO DIRECTIVE (BSD/1990/3)

Revised definition of Zone A

1 Following the amendment to the 1988 Basle Accord agreed in Basle in July last year, the Bank is changing the definitions of Zone A and Zone B in paragraph 11 of its notice 'Implementation in the United Kingdom of the Solvency Ratio Directive' (BSD/1990/3).

   2 Zone A countries are now defined as all countries which are full members of the Organisation for Economic Co-operation and Development (OECD), together with those countries which have concluded special lending arrangements with the International Monetary Fund associated with the General Arrangements to Borrow (GAB), provided they have not rescheduled their external debt, whether to official or private sector creditors, in the previous five years. This group of countries will henceforward be extended automatically to include any new countries which join the OECD, provided they meet the rescheduling criterion, from the date of their admission. All countries not included in Zone A remain Zone B, including any OECD countries which are judged to have rescheduled, which will be separately identified as necessary.

   3 The Bank has also reviewed the status of Gibraltar and Bermuda in the light of this revised definition. The inclusion of these territories within the UK's membership of the OECD was clarified in 1990. Consequently, a claim on the governments of Gibraltar or Bermuda should henceforward be reported as a claim on a Zone A public sector entity (20% weighted) and a claim on a bank incorporated in Gibraltar or Bermuda should be reported as a claim on a Zone A bank (20% weighted).

4 This notice comes into effect from the date of publication. Revised guidance notes for the form BSD1 are also attached.

Revised guidance notes 12, 14 and 19(i)(a) for Form BSD1

Zone A/Zone B

12 The term 'Zone A' covers full members of the OECD and those countries which have concluded special lending arrangments with the IMF associated with the IMF's General Arrangements to Borrow, provided they have not rescheduled their external sovereign debt to official or commercial bank creditors in the previous five years. At present, these countries comprise:

> Australia, Austria, Belgium, Canada, Denmark, Finland, France, Germany (including any pre-reunification claims on East Germany), Greece, Iceland, Ireland, Italy, Japan, Luxembourg, Mexico, Netherlands, New Zealand, Norway, Portugal, Saudi Arabia, Spain, Sweden, Switzerland, Turkey, United Kingdom and United States.

The Channel Islands, Gibraltar, Bermuda and Isle of Man should also be regarded as being within Zone A.

The reporting institution should discuss with S&S the appropriate treatment of particular dependencies of Zone A countries.

Zone B comprises all countries not in Zone A.

For the purpose of determining whether a bank is in Zone A or B, the place of incorporation is the relevant factor to be considered rather than the location of the branch. For example, a loan made to a branch located in a Zone A country of a Zone B incorporated bank should be classified as a loan to a Zone B bank.

Banks

14 The term 'bank' as used in this return refers to those institutions that are regarded as banks in the countries in which they are incorporated, and supervised by the appropriate banking supervisory or monetary authority as banks. In general, banks will engage in the business of banking and have the power to accept deposits in the regular course of business.

For banks incorporated in countries that are members of the European Economic Area (EEA), classify as banks those credit institutions as defined under the First Banking Co-ordination Directive 1977 and as published in the EC Official Journal from time to time. In relation to the United Kingdom, the term 'banks' covers those institutions authorised under the Banking Act 1987 and, for the purpose of this return, building societies authorised under the Building Societies Act 1986.

All banks incorporated in the Channel Islands, Gibraltar, Bermuda and Isle of Man, irrespective of whether they are classified as UK banks for the purpose of other Bank of England statistical returns, are regarded as Zone A banks.

In the USA, banks are referred to as depository institutions which include branches of federally-insured banks and depository institutions chartered and headquartered in the 50 states of the United States, the District of Columbia, Puerto Rico, and US territories and possessions. The definition encompasses banks, mutual or stock savings banks, savings (or building) and loans associations (S&Ls), co-operative banks and credit unions; it excludes bank holding companies (other than those which are themselves banks).

19 *(i) UK public bodies eligible for classification as PSEs*

(a) Local Authorities

Include London borough councils, county and district councils in England, Northern Ireland and Wales, and district, island and regional councils in Scotland, together with their departments (eg gas departments, passenger transport departments, water service departments); those bodies formed on 1 April 1986 to take over the assets and functions of the former metropolitan councils and the GLC, eg residuary bodies, joint transport authorities, fire and civil defence authorities, joint police authorities and waste disposal authorities.

The state governments in the Channel Islands, the Isle of Man Government, the government of Gibraltar, the government of Bermuda and the following local bodies are also to be included in this category:

Central Scotland Water Development Board
Fire Services
Forth Road Bridge Joint Board
Further education establishments maintained by local authorities
Humber Bridge Board
Magistrates' Courts
Police Forces (including Metropolitan Police)
Probation Service in England and Wales
Scottish River Purification Boards
Tay Bridge Joint Board [836]

S&S/1995/2
(April 1995)

NOTICE TO INSTITUTIONS AUTHORISED UNDER THE BANKING ACT 1987

IMPLEMENTATION IN THE UNITED KINGDOM OF THE CAPITAL ADEQUACY DIRECTIVE

Preface

Introduction

1 This document describes the capital requirements which banks must meet from 1 January 1996, the eligible forms of capital, and the way in which banks will be assessed against the standards set by the Bank of England.

2 After a general introduction, this preface discusses aspects of each chapter, indicating what constitutes new policy and what is a continuation of the existing supervisory regime. As far as possible, new policy has been shown in bold type within each chapter: these sections constitute the Bank of England's formal implementation of the European Capital Adequacy Directive (Council Directive 93/6/EEC dated 15 March 1993) and supersede existing policy notices where relevant. In other respects the Bank's policy remains unchanged, and the existing notices remain in force: existing notices should be regarded as the prime source for determining policy in matters not related to the Capital Adequacy Directive.

3 The Capital Adequacy Directive (CAD) sets out the minimum capital requirements for credit institutions and investment firms for the market and other risks associated with their trading activities. In some cases the Bank is proposing more stringent standards than the Directive, in general reflecting either existing policies (such as those for counterparty risk and large exposures), or the experience of other supervisors domestically and internationally. While the CAD applies to credit institutions and investment firms throughout EU/EEA Member States, this text applies only to UK Incorporated Authorised Institutions. In order to simplify the text, the term 'banks' has been used throughout to describe credit institutions.

4 Substantive changes to the current supervisory regime are described in the following chapters:

    (a) The Trading Book;
    (b) Counterparty Risk;
    (c) Foreign Currency Risk;
    (d) Interest Rate Position Risk;
    (e) Equity Position Risk;

(f) Underwriting; and
(g) The Model Review Process;

Implications of the Directive for facets of existing policy are described in the following chapters:

(h) Consolidation;
(i) Own Funds; and
(j) Large Exposures.

5 The Bank may eventually re-issue this document, and perhaps other policy notices, in loose leaf format, to allow updates with a minimum of disruption.

Chapter 1—The Trading Book

6 The CAD prescribes minimum capital requirements for the trading book, encompassing not only market-related risks but also credit risk in the trading book. The trading book is defined according to three broad criteria:

(i) Is the instrument a 'financial instrument'? and
(ii) Is the 'financial instrument' held for trading purposes? or
(iii) Is the position hedging an exposure in the trading book?

The definition of a financial instrument is derived from the Investment Services Directive (ISD), which also becomes operational from 1 January 1996.

7 By default, everything that is not in the trading book is in the banking book and subject to the current credit risk based regime; some amendments have, however, been made to the risk weightings of certain exposures (see Chapter 2—Counterparty Risk). More detailed lists of positions that may form part of the trading book are given in Chapter 2—Counterparty Risk, Chapter 5—Interest Rate Position Risk, and Chapter 6—Equity Position Risk.

8 The segregation of positions between the trading and banking books may not correspond exactly with the way in which banks internally manage their exposures. The chapter sets out the circumstances under which non-financial instruments may be included in the trading book and financial instruments transferred out of the trading book to the banking book.

9 If a bank's trading book is below a certain size on a solo and consolidated basis then the bank will be exempt from the CAD regime.

10 Banks may choose to use a simplified system for calculating capital requirements, which is set out in the relevant chapters. They should be aware, however, that the simplified system may deliver a much higher capital charge for certain portfolios than the standard system. The simplified system might be of interest to those banks which have trading activities marginally above the prescribed cut-off point for CAD exemption, or banks wanting to avoid some of the compliance costs of the standard CAD methods.

Chapter 2—Counterparty Risk

11 This chapter sets out the capital requirements for counterparty risk in the trading book. For the most part, these are unchanged from the present regime, but an important amendment is to treat exposures to the following institutions in the same way as exposures to banks:

(a) investment firms subject to the CAD or a similar regime; and
(b) recognised exchanges and clearing houses.

The chapter also includes details of capital requirements for repos and reverse repos, unsettled transactions, and forward purchases and sales in the trading book.

With the exception of changes mentioned in this chapter, banks should refer to existing policy notices for counterparty (or credit) risk weights in the banking book.

Chapter 3—Large Exposures

12 Most of this chapter is taken from the Bank's existing policy notice and reporting instructions. The CAD does, however, introduce a new feature for large exposures in

the trading book, the so-called 'soft limits'. Additionally, investment firms subject to the CAD, or a similar regime, recognised exchanges and clearing houses receive similar treatment to banks for large exposures purposes. The implementation of the Large Exposures Directive is otherwise unchanged.

13 Soft limits permit large exposures attributable to positions in securities held in the trading book to exceed 25% of the capital base, but if they do so, they will generate extra capital requirements. The Bank is, in general, restricting soft limits to excesses that are caused by positions in securities; by contrast, counterparty exposures in the trading book will normally be subject to the 25% overall 'hard' limit, except in cases where the supervisor of a subsidiary company has allowed a soft limit for counterparty exposure in the trading book, in which case this will be allowed on consolidation.

14 Large exposures arising from underwriting positions must be notified from the day of initial commitment, ie, the existing notification requirement remains. They do not, however, count towards large exposure limits until a point in the underwriting timetable defined by the CAD as Working Day Zero. Starting from Working Day 0, underwriting exposures are progressively added to the recorded large exposure, until by Working Day 5 they are recorded in full.

Chapter 4—Foreign Currency Risk

15 The CAD treatment for foreign currency risk applies to the whole bank irrespective of whether exposures are generated by trading or banking book positions. This chapter describes two techniques for determining the capital requirement, which may be used independently or jointly.

16 The first technique, the 'standard method', is much the same as currently used by the Bank of England, except that it now includes the possibility of recognising binding intergovernmental agreements on exchange rate parities.

17 The second technique is likely to be used more extensively, and is based on historic data: a portfolio of currency positions, including some or all of the bank's net open positions, is assessed against a database of past exchange rates. The database contains the 10-day holding period returns, calculated daily, for the past 3 or 5 years. The capital requirement is based on the 'loss' indicated by a 99% or 95% confidence interval for the past 3 or 5 years, respectively.

18 The chapter also details the treatment of currency option positions to be used by banks which do not have their own models recognised for supervisory purposes; this is an amendment to the existing approach.

Chapter 5—Interest Rate Position Risk

19 Capital requirements for interest rate risk in the trading book are a major component of the CAD. They are set in two components; specific risk and general market risk. Specific and general market risk requirements are calculated on a currency by currency basis, and no offsetting is allowed between positions in different currencies.

20 The chapter outlines two standard techniques for arriving at capital requirements, one approach using maturity bands and the other duration zones. It is possible for the interest rate exposure from swaps and some other derivatives to be pre-processed before application of either of these two methods (see Chapter 8—The Model Review Process). A treatment is provided for those banks which have option positions, but which do not have their own models recognised for supervisory purposes.

21 Specific risk capital requirements are based, inter alia, on the perceived credit quality of the issuer, and they fall into three categories: Zone A government debt instruments; qualifying items; and non-qualifying items. Credit ratings are among the criteria used to determine if an item is qualifying.

22 For general market risk, if the maturity method is used, exposures are allocated to maturity bands in each currency, and weights are applied to each band. A series of offsets are then allowed between the weighted long and short positions in each maturity band and also along the yield curve. If the duration method is used, the calculation is similar, but instead of allocating positions to maturity bands, the modified duration of

each instrument is calculated, and weights are applied based on assumed changes in interest rates. Neither method for generating the general market risk requirement recognises offsetting positions between the yield curves of different currencies.

23 An alternative, simplified, method for calculating the capital requirement for interest rate exposures is also set out, for those banks which do not wish to incur the compliance costs of using either of the two standard methods. This method may deliver a much higher capital charge for certain portfolios than the standard methods.

Chapter 6—Equity Position Risk

24 This chapter sets out capital requirements for equity exposures arising in the trading book. As with interest rate risk, there are two broad requirements, specific and general market risk. These are calculated on a country by country basis.

25 The capital requirement for general market risk is designed to cover the risk of loss due to general movements in equity prices in individual markets, as characterised by changes in stock market indices. A limited amount of netting of general market risk requirements between countries is, however, permitted where a bank has a particularly well diversified international portfolio.

26 The specific risk requirement is designed to cover differences between general market index movements and those of particular equity portfolios; it therefore covers a variety of factors, including perceived credit quality of issuers; liquidity of individual stocks; and diversification within country portfolios. Specific risk requirements are set according to a number of tests for liquidity and diversity which, for the sake of simplicity, rely mainly on lists of equity markets and equity indices.

27 The chapter includes two alternative methods for calculating the requirements. The first is a simplified method, for those banks which do not wish to incur the compliance costs of using the standard method; it will deliver a much higher capital charge for certain portfolios than the standard method. The second is a method currently available under The Securities and Futures Authority rules, based on Sharpe methodology.

28 The chapter includes a treatment for equity option positions for banks which do not have their own model recognised for supervisory purposes. It also includes a treatment for equity derivatives which have embedded interest rate exposure.

Chapter 7—Underwriting

29 The chapter sets out capital requirements for position risk on exposures resulting from underwriting securities. Large exposure requirements for underwriting exposures are covered in Chapter 3. The CAD defines a certain point in the underwriting cycle as 'Working Day 0', and capital requirements are set in terms of those applying before Working Day 0, and those applying thereafter. Allowance is made for position risk to be reduced through sub-underwriting and hedging.

30 Position risk capital requirements apply to underwriting positions from initial commitment day, though at a much reduced scale until Working Day 0. Between Working Day 0 and Working Day 5, the requirements rise progressively to the full normal general and specific risk requirements for the positions. Allowances are made for hedging and amounts sold down, and these and the discounts set from normal requirements vary between bonds and equities.

Chapter 8—The Model Review Process

31 The CAD permits the Bank to recognise the output of certain internal bank models in the calculation of capital requirements for market risk. The use of such models will generally result in lower capital requirements than the standard methods. Models that are eligible for recognition include interest rate sensitivity models (excluding most categories of bonds), risk aggregation models, including option pricing models and foreign exchange back-testing models, and VAR models.

32 Interest rate sensitivity models take cashflows and subject them to predetermined changes in yield to calculate net sensitivities; these are then used in the duration method

calculation (see Chapter 5—Interest Rate Position Risk). These calculations must be carried out on a currency by currency basis.

33 Option pricing models used two broad techniques: buffers and scenarios. The buffer approach generates capital requirements for each of the major classes of option risk (delta, gamma, vega etc). The scenario approach involves revaluing the option for a series of given changes in parameters.

34 Banks which have Value at Risk (VAR) models may be permitted to use these for determining their daily capital requirement, using the standard CAD method for periodic benchmarking purposes. This method will, however, be subject to strictly applied conditions.

35 Before recognising such models, the Bank will review not only the model algorithm but also its operating environment. Unlike the previous chapters, Chapter 8 does not prescribe the detailed capital requirements since these will be dependent on the actual model and the systems used by the individual banks.

Chapter 9—Own Funds

36 The own funds (regulatory capital) of authorised institutions can be composed of Tiers 1, 2 and 3 capital. The definition of Tiers 1 and 2 remains largely unchanged from existing policy. Tier 3 capital comprises subordinated debt with a minimum original maturity of two years or more, and daily net trading book profits. Tier 3 capital may only be used to meet market (as opposed to counterparty) risks. Furthermore, Tier 3 subordinated debt is repayable only with the consent of the supervisor, and – unlike Tier 2 debt – is not amortised for supervisory purposes as it nears maturity.

37 In order to enable uniform comparisons to be made, capital ratios for publication purposes will be calculated according to an internationally agreed process which produces a single ratio for each bank. For supervisory purposes the Bank of England proposes setting separate target and trigger ratios for the trading and banking books; excess capital would be expressed as a percentage over the supervisory minimum.

Chapter 10—Consolidation

38 The consolidated supervision of banks is a continuing requirement under the CAD. Consolidation for banking books remains unchanged from the existing methodology and is carried out on a line-by-line basis. Line-by-line consolidation is also allowed in the trading book, and this would allow banks to offset long and short positions in different companies in the calculation of consolidated capital requirements for market risk.

39 For the trading book, requirements of the CAD have made it necessary to expand the range of consolidation techniques available. As an alternative to line-by-line consolidation, banks may use a new technique described as 'aggregation plus'. Essentially, aggregation plus is the summation of trading book capital requirements for individual companies within a group without any allowance for offsetting between companies. Capital adequacy is then assessed by comparing the consolidated group capital with the capital requirement for group companies: the latter is measured as the sum of the banking book capital requirement of group companies consolidated on a line-by-line basis and the trading book requirements of individual companies.

Chapter 11—Lists

40 This chapter contains lists which are referred to in other chapters. They are collected in a single chapter to facilitate periodic updates.

Chapter 1—The Trading Book

Explanation

1 The capital requirement calculation that banks must meet with effect from 1 January 1996 is based upon the allocation of positions between the trading book and the non-trading, or banking, book. Only certain types of instrument can be included in the

trading book. Although a single instrument cannot simultaneously be in both books it is possible for some types of instrument to be in either the trading or the banking book, for example depending whether it is held for short-term gain, or whether it is held for the purposes of hedging exposures in the banking book. In addition it is possible in certain circumstances to transfer some of the general market risk exposure between the trading book and banking book where a bank has used part of its overall exposure in the trading book to hedge exposures in the banking book. In order to qualify for this treatment, the risk transfers must be documented and subject to audit verification.

2 The capital requirement for positions in the banking book is unchanged from the implementation of the Solvency Ratio Directive apart from:

(a) the extension of the 20% weighted risk asset band to investment firms, recognised exchanges and clearing houses; and
(b) changes to the capital requirements for unsettled and deferred settlement transactions.

These changes apply to all banks irrespective of whether they have a trading book for CAD purposes or not. The counterparty exposure calculations for the trading book may be similar to the banking book, but there are some areas where the differences are substantial.

3 The capital requirements for foreign exchange positions are contained in Chapter 4—Foreign [Currency] Risk and supersede previous requirements. These are applicable irrespective of whether the exposures are incurred in the trading or banking book.

4 This chapter describes the procedures by which banks should allocate positions between the trading and banking books. Subject to satisfying certain criteria, a bank may be deemed not to have a trading book for the purposes of these capital requirements with the result that all its positions are subject to the Solvency Ratio Directive.

5 The contents of this chapter constitute new policy. There are no existing Bank Policy Notices relevant to the concept of a trading book.

6 This chapter covers the following sections of the Capital Adequacy Directive:

— Article 2.6, Article 4.1, Article 9.

Trading Book and Related Definitions

7 The Capital Adequacy Directive (93/6/EEC) Article 2.6 provides the trading book definition, which is reproduced below.

'The trading book of an institution shall consist of:

(a) its proprietary positions in financial instruments which are held for resale and/or which are taken on by the institution with the intention of benefiting in the short term from actual and/or expected differences between their buying and selling prices, or from other price or interest rate variations, and positions in financial instruments arising from matched principal broking, or positions taken in order to hedge other elements of the trading book;
(b) the exposures due to the unsettled transactions, free deliveries and over-the-counter (OTC) derivative instruments referred to in paragraphs 1, 2, 3 and 5 of Annex II (of the CAD),
    — the exposures due to repurchase agreements and securities lending which are based on securities included in the trading book as defined in (a) referred to in paragraph 4 of Annex II (of the CAD),
    — those exposures due to reverse repurchase agreements and securities borrowing transactions described in the same paragraph, provided the competent authorities so approve, which meet either the conditions (i), (ii), (iii) and (v) or conditions (iv) and (v) as follows:
        (i) the exposures are marked to market daily following the procedures laid down in Annex II (of the CAD);
        (ii) the collateral is adjusted in order to take account of material changes in the value of the securities involved in the agreement or transaction in question, according to a rule acceptable to the competent authorities;
        (iii) the agreement or transaction provides for the claims of the institution to

be automatically and immediately offset against the claims of its
counter-party in the event of the latter's defaulting;
(iv) the agreement or transaction in question is an interprofessional one;
(v) such agreements and transactions are confined to their accepted and
appropriate use and artificial transactions, especially those not of a
short term nature, are excluded; and
(c) those exposures in the form of fees, commission, interest, dividends, and
margin on exchange-traded derivatives which are directly related to the items
included in the trading book referred to in paragraph 6 of Annex II (of the
CAD).

Particular items shall be included in or excluded from the trading book in accordance
with objective procedures including, where appropriate, accounting standards in the
institution concerned, such procedures and their consistent implementation being subject
to review by the competent authorities.'

8 The financial instruments referred to in paragraph 7(a) above are defined in Section
B of the Annex to the Investment Services Directive (93/22/EEC). These are:

'(1) (a) Transferable securities;
(b) Units in collective investment undertakings.
(2) Money-market instruments[1].
(3) Financial-futures contracts, including equivalent cash settled instruments.
(4) Forward interest rate agreements (FRAs).
(5) Interest-rate, currency and equity swaps.
(6) Options to acquire or dispose of any instruments falling within this section of
the annex including equivalent cash-settled instruments. This category
includes in particular options on currency and on interest rates.'

More detailed lists of instruments that may be included in the trading book in their own
right can be found in the opening section of the Equity and Interest Rate Position Risk
chapters below. In limited circumstances non-financial instruments may be included in
the trading book, see paragraphs 15 to 18 (Hedging Exposures).

9 The Bank of England is a competent authority for the purposes of the Capital
Adequacy Directive.

10 Positions and exposures which are not in the trading book are deemed to be in the
banking book. Positions and exposures in the banking book will be subject to the risk
weighting capital requirements based on the Solvency Ratio Directive. In addition to
capital requirements for position risk, trading book positions may also give rise to
counterparty risk requirements. (See Chapter 2—Counterparty Risk.)

---

[1] This does *not* include deposits and loans.

Trading Book Requirements

11 A consistent approach must be adopted in relation to those positions in financial
instruments which are capable of being included in the trading book in accordance with
the definition contained in paragraphs 15 to 18. For this purpose positions may be
considered as held with a trading intent if:

(a) they are marked-to-market on a daily basis as a part of the internal risk
management processes;
(b) the position takers have autonomy in entering into transactions within predetermined limits; or
(c) they satisfy any other criteria which the bank applies to the composition of its
trading book on a consistent basis.

Each bank should agree a policy statement with their supervisor about which activities
are normally considered trading and constitute part of the trading book.

12 All positions held in the trading book must be marked-to-market daily, including
the recognition of accruing interest, dividends or other benefits as appropriate. (Some
positions may be marked-to-market for internal purposes or to meet the requirements of
statutory accounts, but nevertheless fail to meet the trading book criteria.) Where a

market determined price is not available then the bank may generate its own mark-to-market valuation. Banks are required to have, and discuss with their line supervisor, a policy statement on the subject of valuing positions, which in particular should address the valuation process for those items where market prices are not readily available. This policy statement should be devised in conjunction with the bank's internal auditors or another qualified independent group and, if necessary, external experts such as reporting accountants. Having arrived at a valuation mechanism for a single position or group of similar positions then the valuation approach must be applied consistently. However, it should be noted that the mark-to-market valuations do not have to meet the requirements for statutory accounts, possibly due to the difference between historic cost accounting and the techniques associated with the mark-to-market requirement of the CAD.

13   A bank must value its positions on a prudent and consistent basis; the applied policy must reflect the points noted below.

   (a) A bank may mark-to-market positions using either a close out valuation based on two way prices (a long position shall be valued at its current bid price and a short position at its current offer price) or alternatively using a mid-market price but making a provision for the spread between bid and offer prices for different instruments. The bank must have due regard to the liquidity of the position concerned and any special factors which may adversely affect the closure of the position.
   (b) Where a bank has been permitted to use a risk assessment model in the calculation of its capital requirements for options, it may value its options using the values derived from the model.
   (c) Where a bank does not use a model and the prices are not published for its options positions, a bank must determine the market value as:
      (i) for purchased options, the mark-to-market value must be the product of:
         – the in the money amount; and
         – the quantity underlying the option;
      (ii) for written options, the mark-to-market value must be the initial premium received for the option plus the product of:
         – the amount by which the current in the money amount exceeds either the in the money amount at the time the contract was written, or zero if the contract was out of the money at the time that it was written; and
         – the quantity underlying the option.
   (d) A bank must calculate the value of a swap contract, or an FRA, having regard to the net present value of the future cashflows of the contract, using current interest rates relevant to the periods in which the cashflows will arise. In the case of interest rate swaps, currency swaps and FRAs, a bank may apply to the Bank to use the valuation under (a) above limited to its net position.
   (The Bank does not consider it appropriate to stipulate a precise formula for calculating the value of swaps and FRAs. However, it will expect a firm to employ a valuation formula which accords with generally accepted market practice.)
   (e) Where a bank is a market maker in the instruments then the valuation should be the bank's own bid or offer price which should reflect the bank's exposure to the market as a whole and its views on future prices. However, where the bank is the sole market maker in a particular instrument it should take care to ensure that the valuation used is prudent in all circumstances.
   (f) In the event that a bank is only able to access indicative prices then, having regard to the fact that they are a guide only, such prices may have to be adjusted to some degree in order to arrive at a prudent valuation.
   (g) In the event that the bank is only able to access mid-market or single values it should have regard to the fact that these prices will have to be adjusted to some degree in order to arrive at a prudent valuation.
   (h) Where a bank has a long (short) position and a short (or long) position in an exactly offsetting instrument, as in the case of a security and an American Depository Receipt representing the same security, they may both be valued on a mid-market basis subject to the following conditions:
      (i) the strategy should have been entered into as a specific arbitrage opportunity and should have the certainty of a locked-in profit (or loss) representing a worst case outcome;

    (ii) the profit (or loss) must be realisable instantly, subject to a reasonably short conversion period, and at any time. Thus at no time should there be restrictions on the ability to convert;

    (iii) positions which are not part of the arbitrage should be valued at their respective bid or offer prices as appropriate;

    (iv) the underlying positions should be of reasonable liquidity and held in quantities which are not so large that they would affect their marketability; and

    (v) any conversion costs and foreign exchange costs should be provided for at the appropriate time and should be separately monitored over the life of the arbitrage.

14 For a repurchase, or equivalent, transaction to be considered to be part of the trading book the securities being repurchased, lent, or contributing collateral for such a transaction, must be in the trading book, (see Chapter 2—Counterparty Risk). The treatment of fees and other sources of counterparty risk generated by trading book positions is also covered in that chapter.

Hedging Exposures

15 A trading book exposure may be hedged, completely or partially, by an instrument that in its own right is not normally considered to be eligible to be part of the trading book, ie instruments other than those listed in paragraph 8 above. Any such trading book position, whether of financial or non-financial instruments, must be subject to the daily mark-to-market discipline, described in paragraph 11 and following. The trading book positions of non-financial instruments will attract both *counterparty risk requirements* (as may be adjusted for use in the trading book), and general market risk requirements on the mark-to-market valuation, but not specific risk requirements.

16 Where a financial instrument which would normally qualify as part of the trading book is being used to hedge an exposure in the banking book, it should be carved out of the trading book for the period of the hedge, and included in the banking book.

17 In addition general market risk arising from the trading book may hedge positions in the banking book without reference to individual financial instruments. In such circumstances, there must nevertheless be underlying positions in the trading book. The positions in the banking book which are being hedged must remain in the banking book, although the general market risk exposure associated with them should be incorporated within the calculation of general market risk capital requirements for the trading book (ie the general market risk element on the banking book side of the hedge should be added to the trading book calculation, rather than that on the trading book side of the hedge be deducted from it). As no individual financial instruments are designated there is no resultant specific risk requirement in the trading book and the risk weighted assets in the banking book will not be reduced. This arrangement for the transfer of risk must be subject to a policy statement agreed with the Bank of England.

18 The allocation or transfer of a final instrument or the transfer of general market risk should be subject to appropriate documentation to ensure that it can be established through audit verification that the item is being treated correctly for the purposes of capital requirements. The documentation should cover, as appropriate:

    (a) The pricing of the transfer, which must be done at arms-length prices;

    (b) Whether the financial instrument or the general market risk elements of a position is hedging a designated banking book exposure;

    (c) Whether the intent (see paragraph 7(a)) for having the position in the financial instrument has changed from short term gains to some other rationale;

    (d) The designated trading book exposure being hedged by the non-financial instrument in the trading book.

Positions in Instruments Issued by Institutions

19 Institutions are defined in the Capital Adequacy Directive as being credit institutions and investment firms as defined by other directives.

(a) Credit Institution
(First Banking Directive 77/780/EEC—Article 1)
A Credit Institution means an undertaking whose business is to receive deposits or other repayable funds from the public and to grant credits for its own account.

(b) Investment Firm
(Investment Services Directive 93/22/EEC—Article 1)
An Investment Firm shall mean any legal or natural person the regular occupation or business of which is the provision of investment services for third parties on a professional basis.
An investment service shall mean any of the services listed in Section A of the Annex to the Investment Services Directive relating to any of the instruments listed in Section B of that same Annex that are provided for a third party.

20 Double gearing of capital in the financial system may occur through the presence in bank portfolios of instruments issued by institutions that contribute to the issuer's capital base—for example, in the case of a UK bank the instruments that are eligible for inclusion in Tier 1, 2 or 3 capital, (see Chapter 9—The Own Funds of Authorised Institutions). Individual positions in capital raising instruments issued by institutions and positions generated via holdings of, or exposures to, broad based equity indices are to be treated as follows:

(i) Physical long positions of capital raising instruments (including those issued by the bank itself or by other group companies) will be deducted from a bank's capital base, but only after the recognition of any hedging benefits against other market exposures as might be generated by index arbitrage positions. In other words such holdings can be used to reduce risk elsewhere, but will nevertheless be treated as a deduction from capital.

(ii) However, in the event that there are no hedging benefits, or only partial hedging benefits, then that position without an offsetting exposure will be deducted from a bank's capital without generating any market related capital requirements. In other words, the total charge on the position can in no circumstances exceed the 100% deduction from capital.

Note: A long stock position, even if hedged with a short futures position, will generally generate a capital deduction. However, long futures positions will not generate a capital deduction, whether or not it is hedged as it does not create a physical holding in the capital raising instrument: it may, of course, attract a market risk requirement. Options positions should be treated in the same way as futures; ie they do not generate a capital deduction.

It should be noted that for firms making markets in these instruments deduction may not be required, although such concessions are subject to limits set out under the Own Funds Directive (89/299/EEC) Article 2.1(12) and (13).

21 Banks may raise funds by the issue of financial instruments, such as CDs or Commercial Paper. Such 'short' positions may be considered to be part of the trading book if the instrument meets the trading book definition and other requirements, see paragraph 8. The treatment of these instruments must be applied consistently. (The treatment of capital raising instruments is covered in paragraph 20.) These fund raising financial instruments will only attract capital requirements for general market risk.

Exemptions from the Trading Book Requirements

22 A bank may be exempted from the trading book capital requirements if its trading book activity is considered to be minimal. *Even if a bank does not have a trading book the capital requirements for foreign exchange exposures are applicable, see Chapter 4—Foreign Currency Risk.*

23 The benchmarks that the supervisors will use to determine if a bank will be subject to the trading book capital requirements are given below. If in doubt banks should check with their supervisor to see whether they have to comply with the trading book treatment. The criteria used by the supervisors to indicate the appropriateness of applying the trading book capital requirements from the CAD Article 4.6 will be:

The trading book business of the bank on a solo or consolidated basis does not normally exceed 5% of its combined on- and off-balance sheet positions and its total 'trading book' positions do not normally exceed ECU 15 Million.

Further:

The trading book business of the bank on a solo or consolidated basis should never exceed 6% of its combined on- and off-balance sheet positions and its total 'trading book' positions should never exceed ECU 20 Million.

Where a banking group is above the threshold at a consolidated level, but has subsidiaries below the threshold it may apply to its supervisor to exclude such subsidiaries from the Capital Adequacy Directive regime. In order to calculate the proportion that trading book business bears in relation to total business the Bank will refer to the size of the combined on- and off-balance sheet business. For these purposes debt instruments shall be valued at their market prices or principal values, equities at their market prices and derivatives according to the nominal or market values of the instruments underlying them. Long and short positions will be summed regardless of their signs. Forward foreign exchange contracts should (for these purposes only) be treated as if they were banking book business, although foreign exchange futures and options unless hedging the banking book are to be treated as trading book items.

24 In the event that a bank subject to an exemption from the trading book requirements exceeds the trading book benchmark it must discuss the situation with the supervisors as soon as possible. Unless the breach is regarded by the supervisors as being likely to exist for a short period, the bank will in such circumstances be required to comply with the trading book capital requirements.

Chapter 2—Counterparty Risk

Explanation

1 Authorised institutions are required to allocate positions, securities, derivatives, assets and liabilities either to the trading book or the banking book. The basis of this allocation is described in Chapter 1—The Trading Book. There are two changes that apply to banking book assets: the counterparty risk weight applicable to investment firms and to exchanges and clearing houses is altered in cases where they are 'recognised' by the Bank; and the treatment of unsettled transactions is amended to bring it into line with the trading book treatment. With these exceptions, the counterparty weights to be used for claims in the banking book are unchanged and remain as stated in BSD/1990/3. These same (amended) weights will also apply when there is counterparty risk in the trading book, although in this case the weighted amount is converted directly into a capital charge (called a haircut).

2 In general, counterparty risk will only be present in the trading book on deals that are not finally settled (ie including OTC derivative contracts), and this will be incurred with respect to the trading counterparty rather than the issuer of the security. (Issuer risk on securities in the trading book is captured by the specific risk requirements set out in Chapters 5 and 6.)

3 The current Bank Policy Notices governing counterparty risk are:

BSD/1990/3 Implementation in the United Kingdom of the Solvency Ratio Directive;
BSD/1992/6 Amendment to BSD/1990/3;
BSD/1993/3 On-Balance Sheet Netting & Cash Collateral;
BSD/1994/4 Treatment of repurchase agreements and stock lending and borrowing for capital adequacy and large exposures purposes.

The last of these notices will be withdrawn on 1 January 1996.

A Policy Notice on Off-Balance Sheet Netting will be issued later in 1995. The contents of this Chapter will be amended by that notice when it is issued.

4 This chapter covers the following parts of the Capital Adequacy Directive:

– Article 2 paragraphs 6, 9, 10
– Annex II.

Scope

BANKING BOOK

5 The counterparty risk weights to be used by banks in calculating their banking book capital requirements are those laid down in the Bank of England's policy notice on the implementation of the Solvency Ratio Directive in the United Kingdom. **The only changes made by this notice relate to investment firms and recognised clearing houses and exchanges. The treatment of unsettled transactions is being amended to bring the treatment in the banking book into line with that being introduced in the trading book.**

TRADING BOOK

6 This chapter also covers counterparty exposures arising from positions reported in the trading book. In general capital must be assigned to counterparty risk on any trade that is not yet due for final settlement (eg OTC derivative exposures, margins and fees payable), and on trades where settlement is actually overdue. By comparison, a bank owning a security is exposed to specific risk—this is covered in Chapters 5 and 6. The following examples illustrate the type of situation in which counterparty risk attracts capital in the trading book from Bank B's perspective and also how counterparty risk differs from specific risk:

(i) Bank A sells shares issued by Company C to Bank B, which places them in its trading book. Once the transaction has settled, Bank B has specific risk on Company C and no counterparty risk on Bank A.

(ii) The above example is repeated, but Bank A fails to settle on time. After five days, Bank B is required to hold capital (for counterparty risk) against Bank A in addition to specific risk on Company C, as if the price moves in Bank B's favour, its profit can only be realised once Bank A has delivered the instruments it has failed to deliver to Bank B on time.

(iii) Bank A enters into a forward contract to sell shares in Company C to Bank B. Bank B acquires specific risk on Company C, but also acquires counterparty risk on Bank A, as there is a risk that Bank A does not perform on its side of the transaction at the future delivery date.

(iv) Bank A enters into a simple interest rate swap with Bank B. As there is no underlying instrument, there is no specific risk, but Bank B acquires counterparty risk on Bank A for the duration of the swap.

Policy Applicable to both Banking and Trading Books

Counterparty Weights

INVESTMENT FIRMS

7 Claims on investment firms, but not their unregulated affiliates, that are subject to the CAD or a regulatory regime that is considered to be at least as stringent as the CAD should be weighted at 20%. Regulatory regimes that meet this standard are listed in Chapter 11—Lists.

8 Claims which are directly, explicitly, unconditionally, and irrevocably *guaranteed* by investment firms falling under the above paragraph will attract the weighting given to a direct non-tradable security claim on the guarantor. Indirect guarantees are not recognised for the purpose of reduced risk weights.

9 Exposures to discount houses, gilt-edged market makers, those Stock Exchange Money Brokers which operate in the gilt-edged market and any other institutions with a money-market dealing relationship with the Bank of England are weighted at 20%. However, where the counterparty exposures to these firms are secured on UK Treasury Bills, eligible local authority and eligible bank bills, gilt-edged stocks or London CDs they are weighted at 10%.

RECOGNISED CLEARING HOUSES AND EXCHANGES

10 Claims on recognised clearing houses and exchanges are weighted at 20%. Such claims should include initial cash margins and surplus variation margin at futures exchanges or clearing houses. Recognised clearing houses and exchanges which qualify for this weighting are listed in Chapter 11—Lists.

11 Claims which are directly, explicitly, unconditionally, and irrevocably *guaranteed* by those recognised clearing houses and exchanges falling under the above paragraph will attract the weighting given to a direct non-tradable security claim on the guarantor. Indirect guarantees are not recognised for the purpose of reduced risk weights.

Netting of Off-Balance Sheet Instruments

12 Further work on netting of swaps and similar products is taking place in the EU. Once this work has been completed the Bank will issue further guidance on this question (expected to be later in 1995).

Settlement/Delivery Risk

UNSETTLED TRANSACTIONS

13 For transactions (excluding repurchase and reverse repurchase agreements and stock borrowing and lending) where delivery of the instrument takes place against receipt of cash, but which remain unsettled five business days after their due date, the difference between the amount due and the current market value of the instrument, which could involve a loss for the bank, will be considered to be a claim on the counterparty. The capital requirement will be this *potential loss* multiplied by the factor in Column 1 of the table below.

14 With the explicit approval of its supervisors a bank may calculate the capital requirement for the counterparty risk on trading book transactions which are past their due date using Column 2 of the table below. The capital requirement will be the *agreed settlement price* multiplied by the factor in Column 2 below. Unless a bank accounts for such positions in this way in its own accounts and management information, the Bank would expect the approach in paragraph 13 above to be adopted.

Number of Working Days after due Settlement Date	Column 1	Column 2
0–4	Nil	Nil
5–15	8%	0.5%
16–30	50%	4.0%
31–45	75%	9.0%
46 or more	100%	100% of Potential Loss (as per Column 1)

FREE DELIVERIES

15 If a transaction in a tradable security involves the delivery of the securities (cash), but the cash (securities) is not received at the same time, this is termed a 'free delivery'. When the securities (cash) have been delivered this will be considered to be a claim on the counterparty equivalent to the current market value of the tradable security for the provider of the cash or the cash for the provider of the securities, whichever is outstanding. The resultant capital requirement in the Trading Book is the counterparty claim multiplied by the counterparty risk weight by 8%. In the Banking Book the risk weighted amount is the counterparty claim multiplied by the counterparty risk weight.

16 If settlement of the transaction is effected across a national border, the capital requirement will only be triggered one business day after the securities (cash) have been delivered without the cash (securities) being received in return.

Policy Applying just to the Banking Book

Repos/Reverse Repos

17 With effect from 1 January 1996, Policy Notice BSD/1994/4 will be withdrawn. Repos and reverse repos in the Banking Book will be treated as in BSD/1990/3.

Policy Applying just to the Trading Book

Counterparty Risk on OTC Derivatives

18 As all trading book exposures must be marked-to-market, all banks are expected to adopt the replacement cost method (as opposed to the original exposure method) for calculating the credit exposure on OTC derivative contracts in the trading book (for details of this method see BSD/1990/3).

Counterparty Risk on Forward Transactions

19 This section covers all forward sales and purchases of financial instruments (ie excluding foreign exchange forwards), where these are defined as transactions that settle on a date beyond the market norm for that instrument. This includes the forward leg of repo/reverse repo (or stock-borrowing/stock-lending or sell-buy/buy-sell) where such an arrangement fails to meet the documentation and margining requirements specified in paragraph 27 below. However, tradable securities which meet the conditions for new issues (see Chapter 7—Underwriting) are excluded.

20 In the trading book, forward transactions are deemed to give rise to counterparty exposure. Furthermore the measure used takes account of both the current replacement cost of the contract, and its potential value. The latter is incorporated through use of risk cushion factors (RCF) which reflect the likely volatility of security prices. These are set out in Annex I to this Chapter.

21 It is important to note that, in addition to the counterparty risk requirements set out in this Chapter, transactions covered by this section attract capital charges for market risk (see Chapter 5—Interest Rate Position Risk and Chapter 6—Equity Position Risk).

22 Where the bank is receiving securities in exchange for cash (or collateral), the counterparty risk requirement will be:

> {replacement cost of forward + potential future credit exposure} × counter-party risk weight × 8%
> where
> replacement cost
> = higher of zero and the difference between market value of securities to be received and contracted value for forward delivery (in the case of forward purchases) or market value of collateral (in the case of repos);
> potential future credit exposure
> = the risk cushion factor applicable to the securities (or collateral if it is higher) multiplied by the contracted value for forward delivery;

Note: Counterparty risk weights are those applying to OTC derivative exposures.

23 Where the bank is receiving cash (or collateral) in exchange for securities, the counterparty risk requirement will be:

> {replacement cost of forward + potential future credit exposure} × counter-party risk weight × 8%
> where
> replacement cost
> = higher of zero and the difference between the contracted value for forward delivery (in the case of forward sales) or market value of collateral (in the case of reverse repos) and the market value of the securities to be delivered;
> potential future credit exposure
> = the risk cushion factor applicable to the securities (or collateral if it is higher) multiplied by the contracted value for forward delivery;

Note: Counterparty risk weights are those applying to OTC derivative exposures.

24 Securities, and if appropriate collateral, must be marked-to-market at least once a day. The amounts to be received or given need to include all cashflows related to the securities and the transactions—manufactured dividends, interest, fees. Thus the amount to be received would include payments which the counterparty should have made to the bank but which have not yet been received, and the amount to be given would include payments which should have been made to the counterparty but which have not yet been paid. Receivables need not be included on the day when they are due, but they must be included if not received the following business day.

25 Collateral received may be in the form of a guarantee, letter of credit, or similar instrument provided by a Zone A bank, but only if that bank would not be considered to be a connected lender if it was making a loan to the recipient of the securities. In the event that the guarantor is not a Zone A bank or is a connected bank, the capital requirement for the securities lender will be:

Market Value of Securities lent × Counterparty Risk Weight × 8%

26 Forward transactions also occur in situations where compensation is due to be paid in the future in exchange for a contract. Option premia to be paid on contingent premia options (ie where the option writer receives the premium upon exercise of the option) are an example of this type of deferred settlement. In such cases, the counterparty risk requirement will be:

Current market value of the payment due × counterparty risk weight × 8%

Counterparty Risk on Documented Repos/Reverse Repos

27 This section covers all arrangements where:

    (i) a bank has sold/bought (or lent/borrowed) trading book securities to/from a counterparty subject to buy back (or a return clause), and

    (ii) the documentation forming the written agreement (whether a master agreement, or documentation used on specific occasions) provides for the claims of the bank to be automatically and immediately set off against the claims of the counterparty in the event of the latter's default, *and* the bank has the right to call for variation margin daily when there is a material adverse market move against it.

As long as arrangements meet these requirements, the capital charge for counterparty risk may be calculated in the manner set out below regardless of the terminology used – ie the arrangements may be called repo/reverse repo or stock-lending/stock-borrowing or sell-buy/buy-sell. Arrangements where the bank has lent a third party's securities at its own risk are also included.

28 It is important to note that, in addition to the counterparty risk requirements set out in this Chapter, transactions covered by this section attract capital charges for market risk (see Chapter 5—Interest Rate Position Risk and Chapter 6—Equity Position Risk).

29 For repos, the capital charge for counterparty risk will be the higher of zero and:

    {Market value of securities sold or lent − Market value of collateral taken} × counterparty risk weight × 8%

Note: Counterparty risk weights are those applying to OTC derivative exposures.

30 For reverse repos, the capital charge for counterparty risk will be the higher of zero and:

    {Market value of collateral given – Market value of securities bought or borrowed} × counterparty risk weight × 8%

Note: Counterparty risk weights are those applying to OTC derivative exposures.

31 If it seems to the Bank that the nature of a bank's repo/reverse repo business is such that the risks are significant (eg in terms of the volume or nature of activity), the Bank may insist that all such transactions are treated as forwards (in the manner set out in paragraphs 19–23 above).

32 Where there is a series of transactions with a single counterparty, the counterparty risk requirements may be calculated on a portfolio basis. (For an example, see Annex II.)

33 Securities, and if appropriate collateral, must be marked-to-market at least once a day. The amounts to be received or given need to include all cashflows related to the securities and the transactions—manufactured dividends, interest, fees. Thus the amount to be received would include payments which the counterparty should have made to the bank but which have not yet been received, and the amount to be given would include payments which should have been made to the counterparty but which have not yet been paid. Receivables need not be included on the day when they are due, but they must be included if not received the following business day.

34 Collateral received may be in the form of a guarantee, letter of credit, or similar instrument provided by a Zone A bank, but only if that bank would not be considered to be a connected lender if it was making a loan to the recipient of the securities. In the event that the guarantor is not a Zone A bank or is a connected bank, the capital requirement for the securities lender will be:

Market Value of Securities lent × Counterparty Risk Weight × 8%

Collateralising Counterparty Exposures

35 Collateral that may reduce the risk weight applicable to a counterparty exposure is as defined in BSD/1990/3.

36 The counterparty risk weight applicable to collateralised exposures in the trading book will (in the case of collateral in the form of securities) equal the specific risk weight applicable to the collateral instrument. However, the collateral must be marked-to-market daily and an add-on (equal to the market value of the collateral multiplied by the relevant risk cushion factor) deducted. The risk cushion factors are set out in Annex·I.

Annex I: Risk Cushion Factors

The table below gives risk cushion factors. They are derived from the matrix of add-ons used to calculate the capital requirements for potential future exposures on off-balance sheet contracts. In determining the size of the risk cushion factor, reference is made to the maturity of the securities and of the collateral, rather than to the maturity of the transaction.
Interest rate products
(residual maturity)
– less than one year   0.25%
– to five years   0.50%
– five years or over   1.50%
Equities   6.00%

Where one side of a transaction is denominated in a currency other than that of the other side, and circumstances are such that a risk cushion factor applies, the risk cushion factors are each increased by 1%.

Notes:

(a) Where the collateral is in the form of Short Term Talisman Certificates (STCs) then they will have a risk cushion factor equivalent to equities.
(b) Where the collateral is provided in the form of cash, a guarantee, a letter of credit, or an instrument performing a similar function issued by a Zone A bank, a risk cushion factor of 0% applies.

Annex II: Example Calculations for Repos/Reverse Repos in the Trading Book

Case 1: Properly documented transaction

A lends £100 cash to B, and receives a 5 year bond (current mark-to-market value: £102) from B; A and B each have 20% counterparty risk weight.

Counterparty Risk Requirement
A = max { 0 , {£100 − £102} × 20% × 8% }
  = Nil

$$B = \max \{ 0 , \{£102 - £100\} \times 20\% \times 8\% \}$$
$$= 0.032$$

Case 2: Properly documented transactions calculated on portfolio basis

A lends 5 year bonds (current mark-to-market value: £100) and US equities (current mark-to-market value: £100) to B, and receives UK equities (current mark-to-market value: £97) and 2 year bonds (current mark-to-market value: £105) from B; A and B each have 20% counterparty risk weight.

Counterparty Risk Requirement
A Securities & Collateral paid away
£100 + £100   = £200.00
  Securities & Collateral received
£97 + £105   = £202.00
  Received > Paid Away
  Therefore, no counterparty risk requirement applies
B Securities & Collateral paid away
£97 + £105   = £202.00
  Securities & Collateral received
£100 + £100   = £200.00
  Received < Paid Away
  A counterparty risk requirement therefore applies
$$= (£202 - £200) \times 20\% \times 8\%$$ = £0.032

Case 3: Inadequate documentation (or business of a type or volume which leads Bank to insist on this treatment even for documented transactions)

A lends a 5 year bond (current mark-to-market value: £102) to B, and receives £100 cash from B; A and B each have 20% counterparty risk weight.
Risk Cushion Factors
for bond = 1.5%
for cash = 0%
Contracted value for forward delivery £100
Counterparty Risk Requirement
A Replacement cost: $\max \{0, (£102 - £100)\}$
  Potential future exposure £100 × 1.5%
  Capital charge $= \{£2 + £1.50\} \times 20\% \times 8\% = £0.056$
B Replacement cost: $\max \{ 0 , (£100 - £102)\}$
  Potential future exposure £100 × 1.5%
  Capital charge $= £1.50 \times 20\% \times 8\% = £0.024$

Case 4: As Case 3 except collateral and securities in differing currencies

A lends a 5 year US government bond (current mark-to-market value: £102) to B, and receives £100 cash from B;
A and B each have 20% counterparty risk weight.
Risk Cushion Factors
for bond = 2.5%
for cash = 1.0%
Contracted value for forward delivery £100
Counterparty Risk Requirement
A Replacement cost: $\max \{ 0 , (£102 - £100)\}$
  Potential future exposure £100 × 2.5%
  Capital charge $= £2 + £2.50\} \times 20\% \times 8\% = £0.072$
B Replacement cost: $\max \{ 0 , (£100 - £102)\}$
  Potential future exposure £100 × 2.5%
  Capital charge $= £2.50 \times 20\% \times 8\% = £0.04$

Chapter 3—Large Exposures

Explanation

1 Authorised institutions are required to adopt the necessary measures to comply with the Large Exposures Directive in both the banking and trading books and the treatment

of Large Exposures under the Capital Adequacy Directive in the trading book. The requirements in this chapter apply to the banking and trading books on a consolidated and unconsolidated (solo) level. The limits and reporting requirements apply at a consolidated level and where institutions are supervised solely on an unconsolidated/solo-consolidated level the requirements in this chapter will be applied at that level. The statutory notification requirements of section 38 of the Banking Act (1987) apply on an unconsolidated (solo) basis. For details on consolidation aspects see Chapter 10—Consolidation.

2 A large exposure is defined as an exposure to a counterparty or group of closely related counterparties which is greater than or equal to 10% of capital base. The large exposure limit for a counterparty or group of closely related counterparties is set at 25% of capital base (see paragraph 31). In the case of traded securities, these limits in relation to capital may be exceeded, but if so, an additional capital requirement (see paragraph 60) is incurred.

3 This chapter details the way in which banks must monitor their Large Exposures, the reporting requirements associated with these exposures and the application of increased capital requirements in some circumstances when Large Exposure limits are breached.

4 The current Bank Policy Notices governing Large Exposures are:

BSD/1993/2 Implementation in the United Kingdom of the Directive on the Monitoring and control of Large Exposures of Credit Institutions.
BSD/1994/4 Treatment of Repurchase Agreements and Stock Lending and Borrowing Agreements for Capital Adequacy and Large Exposures Purposes.

Note: BSD/1994/4 will be withdrawn with effect from 1 January 1996.

5 This chapter covers the following sections of the Capital Adequacy Directive:

– Article 5, annex VI.

Scope

6 The Bank will apply its policy for the monitoring and control of large exposures at both the consolidated and unconsolidated (solo) level, unless there is a specific statement made to the contrary, and throughout this chapter the requirements which apply to 'banks' should be understood to apply also to consolidated 'banking groups' and vice versa. The limits and reporting requirements of the Large Exposures Directive apply at a consolidated level and the statutory notification requirements of section 38 of the Banking Act (1987) apply on an unconsolidated (solo) basis (see Annex). However, for banks which are supervised solely on an unconsolidated/solo-consolidated basis then the requirements of this chapter apply at that level.

7 In assessing a bank's exposures on a consolidated basis the companies to be consolidated with the bank (which may include sister companies and holding companies, as well as subsidiaries) will be agreed by the Bank in accordance with the principles set out in the chapter on consolidated supervision. Where these principles determine that a sub-group of a banking group should be separately assessed (including a requirement for separate consolidated returns to be provided) a bank's large exposures will also be assessed on that basis.

Policy Statements

8 The Bank requires each bank to set out its policy on large exposures, including exposures to individual customers, banks, countries and economic sectors, in a policy statement. In the case of UK incorporated banks, this policy should be formally adopted by the bank's board of directors. The Bank expects banks not to implement significant changes in these policies without prior discussion with the Bank. Significant departures from a bank's stated policy, in particular those involving breaches of agreed levels, will lead the Bank to consider whether the bank continues to meet the statutory minimum criteria for authorisation.

9 Each bank will be expected to justify to the Bank its policy on exposures to individual counterparties, including the maximum size of an exposure contemplated. Relevant factors which the Bank will expect a bank to have taken into account when setting its policy and considering the acceptability of particular exposures include, for example, the standing of the counterparty, the nature of the bank's relationship with the counterparty, the nature and extent of security taken against the exposure, the maturity of the exposure, and the bank's expertise in the particular type of transaction. Exposures to counterparties connected with the bank—for example, subsidiaries or sister companies or companies with common directors—will continue to be particularly closely examined. (Exposures to counterparties connected to the reporting bank are considered in paragraphs 25, 32 and 47 below.)

10 The necessary control systems to give effect to a bank's policy on large exposures must be clearly specified and monitored by its board. Banks will be required to detail how they intend to monitor the size of capital base to ensure that the limits detailed in this notice are not exceeded. **Banks will also have to show that in the special circumstances where they exceed the limits and incremental capital is required that they have sufficient capital to cover the incremental charge.**

Measurement of Exposure

11 The measure of exposure should reflect the maximum loss should a counterparty fail **or the loss that may be experienced due to the realisation of assets or off-balance sheet positions.** Consistent with this, an exposure encompasses the amount at risk arising from the reporting bank's:

(i) Claims on a counterparty including actual claims, and potential claims which would arise from the drawing down in full of undrawn advised facilities (whether revocable or irrevocable, conditional or unconditional) which the bank has committed itself to provide, and claims which the bank has committed itself to purchase or underwrite; and

(ii) Contingent liabilities arising in the normal course of business, and those contingent liabilities which would arise from the drawing down in full of undrawn advised facilities (whether revocable or irrevocable, conditional or unconditional) which the bank has committed itself to provide; and

(iii) Assets, and assets which the bank has committed itself to purchase or underwrite, whose value depends wholly or mainly on a counterparty performing his obligations, or whose value otherwise depends on that counterparty's financial soundness but which do not represent a claim on the counterparty.

12 In reporting large exposures for on-balance sheet positions credit balances should not be offset against debit balances. However, debit balances on accounts may be offset against credit balances on other accounts with the bank where *all* the following criteria have been met:

(a) A legal right of set-off exists, and the reporting institution has obtained an opinion from its legal advisers to the effect that its right to apply set-off is legally well-founded in all of the relevant jurisdictions and would be enforceable in the default, liquidation or bankruptcy of the customer(s) or in the liquidation of the institution itself. For a group facility the arrangement must be supported by a full cross guarantee structure.

(b) The debit and credit balances relate to the same customer, or to customers in the same company group, eg a parent company and its subsidiary. For all customers, the netted accounts should be managed and controlled on a net basis, and in the case of a group facility, the facility should be advised in the form of a net amount.

The bank's application of these principles must remain consistent.

13 **Large exposures are calculated using the sum of the nominal amounts** *before the application of risk weightings and credit conversion factors* **for the following categories:**

(a) **On-balance sheet claims whether in the trading or banking books;**
(b) **Guarantees and other contingent claims in the banking book;**

(c) Potential claims and liabilities in the case of undrawn facilities in the banking book. (For note issuance facilities, etc in the trading book see paragraph 14(b) below.)

ISSUER RISK ON SECURITIES

14 Issuer risk on securities should be calculated as follows:

(a) The exposure is calculated as the excess, where positive, of the current market value of all long positions over all short positions for each instrument issued by the counterparty;

(b) Contingent liabilities in the trading book which arise from a commitment by a bank to an issuer under a note issuance facility to purchase at the request of the issuer securities which are unsold on the issue date are to be *added* to the long position in paragraph (a) above. Note issuance facilities include revolving underwriting facilities, euronote facilities and similar such arrangements;

(c) Commitments to buy securities at a future date should be included in the calculation of exposure to the issuer of the security. Forward sales should be regarded as short positions in the relevant security;

(d) Options positions should be included in the calculation of issuer risk on the following basis: written puts should be included as a long position, purchased puts as a short position in the underlying security, purchased puts as a short position (in both cases using the notional principal valued at the strike price). Other options (written and purchased calls) should not be included in the calculation of issuer risk;

(e) Positions should not be netted between the banking book and trading book (unless the conditions in Chapter 1 for hedges between books are met).

COUNTERPARTY RISK ON DERIVATIVES

15 The counterparty risk arising from interest rate contracts (including interest rate swaps, forward rate agreements and interest rate options purchased), foreign exchange contracts (including cross currency swaps, forward foreign exchange contracts and foreign exchange options purchased) and other derivative contracts such as those based on commodities and equities is not taken to be the nominal amount of a contract but rather a credit equivalent amount. For the banking book, the method for calculating the credit equivalent amount is the replacement cost or original exposure methods which are used in generating the counterparty risk requirement. **For the trading book the replacement cost method must be used (see Chapter 2—Counterparty Risk).**

16 The Bank will allow limited use of a concessionary treatment for derivative products only (ie items covered by paragraph 15 above). Counterparty exposures to banks and building societies in these products, with a residual maturity of more than one, but not more than three years, may be scaled down by the application of a 20% weighting (ie a discount of 80%) before inclusion in the measure of exposure. **This provision will be extended to include counterparty exposures to investment firms that are subject to the CAD, or are subject to a regime that the Bank deems to be equivalent to the CAD, (see Chapter 11—Lists for a list of recognised regimes).**

REPOS AND REVERSE REPOS

17 For repos in the banking book, banks should continue to report the issuer risk on the security for the period of the transaction. No exposure is reportable for reverse repos (either issuer risk **or counterparty risk, although where business is significant line supervisors may decide to apply risk concentration limits).**

18 **For both repos and reverse repos in the trading book, issuer risk should be reported on the bank's asset in the transaction (in a repo the security sold, in a reverse repo the collateral provided, if a security). In addition, counterparty exposure should be reported on both repos and reverse repos (exposures are calculated using the rules set out in Chapter 2 before application of the counterparty weights).**

EXCLUSIONS

19 The following items will not be included in the measurement of exposure:

    (i) Items deducted from capital base (both for the calculation of capital ratios and for large exposures purposes);

    (ii) Claims arising in the course of settlement of a foreign exchange transaction on a counterparty where the reporting institution has settled its side of the transaction but has not received the countervalue, for a period of up to two working days after payment was made. After this period such claims will constitute an exposure;

    (iii) Claims arising in the course of settlement of a securities transaction (see Chapter 2—Counterparty Risk).

20 Apart from the types of exposure mentioned above risks arising from the settlement of transactions are not captured as large exposures. However, the control of such exposures needs to be carefully considered by banks since inadequate controls could be a cause of substantial loss for a bank. Banks should therefore pay particular attention as to how they control such risks.

UNDERWRITING

21 For positions that are acquired as part of an underwriting process the measure of exposure shall run from the time of initial commitment and shall be based upon the gross commitment for any net sales and sub-underwriting agreements.

22 Positions in securities that are acquired as part of an underwriting process and *are* part of the trading book will contribute to the large exposure for the issuer commencing Working Day 0 (as defined in Chapter 7—Underwriting). The exposure is based upon the net underwriting position which may be further reduced to form the net position exposure by the application of the following discount factors:

Working Day 0	**100%**
Working Day 1	**90%**
Working Day 2	**75%**
Working Day 3	**75%**
Working Day 4	**50%**
Working Day 5	**25%**
after Working Day 5	**0%**

Net Underwriting Position = Gross Underwriting Commitment
**   + Purchases − Sales − Sub-Underwriting**
Net Exposure   = Net Underwriting Position* (100% − Discount Factor)

The net exposure, being the net underwriting position adjusted for the discount factors, is then aggregated with other securities exposures for the same issuer generated in the trading book, paragraph 14(a). Although the threshold for incremental capital and related calculations (see paragraph 62) apply to these securities from Working Day 0 the bank must have systems to enable it to monitor the gross exposure, which is subject to the notification requirements (see paragraph 35), from the acquisition of the initial commitment.

Identity of Counterparty

23 The identity of a counterparty will generally be the borrower (customer), the person guaranteed, the issuer of a security in the case of a security held or the party with whom a contract was made in the case of a derivatives contract. Where a third party has provided an explicit unconditional irrevocable guarantee, banks may however be permitted to report the exposure as being to the guarantor. As a condition for allowing banks to report exposures in this way, the Bank will require banks to include a section on guaranteed exposures in their large exposures policy statement. In particular the Bank would expect a consistent approach to be adopted in the reporting of such exposures. The Bank does not expect banks to report exposures to guarantors unless the banks have first approved the credit risk on the guarantor and the type of the exposure under the bank's normal credit approval procedures.

24 An individual counterparty comprises natural and legal persons and includes individual trusts, corporations, unincorporated business (whether as sole traders or partnerships) and non-profit making bodies.

25 A group of closely related counterparties exists where:

(i) Unless it can be shown otherwise, two or more individual counterparties constitute a single risk because one of them has, directly or indirectly, control[1] over the other or others; or

(ii) Individual counterparties are connected in such a way that the financial soundness of any of them may affect the financial soundness of the other or others or the same factors may affect the financial soundness of both or all of them.

In such cases the exposure to these individual counterparties should be aggregated and considered as a single exposure to a group of closely related counterparties.

26 Where there is doubt in a particular case whether a number of individual counterparties constitute a group of closely related counterparties or where, notwithstanding that the relationship between a number of counterparties identified in the reporting instructions exist, the counterparties do not share a common risk, the circumstances should be discussed with the Bank of England to determine how the exposure(s) should be reported.

27 Parties connected to the reporting bank comprise:

(i) Group undertakings (including subsidiaries) as defined by section 262 of the Companies Act 1985 as amended by the Companies Act 1989 and related companies as defined by section 105 of the Banking Act as amended by The Banking Co-ordination (Second Council Directive) Regulations 1992;

(ii) Associated companies as defined by the Statement of Standard Accounting Practice 1;

(iii) Directors, controllers and their associates as defined in section 105 of the Banking Act 1987 as amended by The Banking Co-ordination (Second Council Directive) Regulations 1992;

(iv) Non-group companies with which the reporting bank's directors and controllers are associated.

A director (including an alternate director) and controller of the reporting bank is deemed to be associated with another company, whether registered or domiciled in the UK or overseas, if he holds the office of a director (or alternate director) with that company (whether in his own right, or as a result of a loan granted by, or financial interest taken by, the reporting bank to, or in, that company, or even by virtue of a professional interest unconnected with the reporting bank), or if he and/or his associates, as defined above, together hold 10% or more of the equity share capital of that company. For the purposes of the large exposures policy, an employee of the lending bank who is not a director but who is appointed by the lending bank to be a director of another company is also treated as a director of the lending bank.

28 For exposures to connected counterparties other than parent, subsidiary or sister companies, where the lending bank is able to demonstrate to the Bank's satisfaction that, notwithstanding that a connection with a counterparty exists, the bank's relationship with that counterparty is at arm's length, its exposure to that counterparty will not be considered as an exposure to a counterparty connected to the lending bank.

---

[1] Control is defined as the relationship between a parent undertaking and a subsidiary, as defined in Article 1 of Directive 83/349/EEC, 'Council Directive on the supervision of credit institutions on a consolidated basis' of 13 June 1983, or a similar relationship between any natural or legal person and an undertaking.

Limits for Large Exposures

29 There will be absolute limits on the size of exposures that may be undertaken by banks that generate counterparty risk requirements in either the banking book or the trading book, although certain exposures are exempt from these limits (see paragraph 40). The limits are of two sorts: an overall limit on the aggregate of large exposures and limits on the size of exposures to individuals or connected groups of counterparty. The Bank may in exceptional circumstances agree to a waiver of any or all of these limits at the unconsolidated, solo-consolidated or consolidated sub-group level for institutions

subject to further consolidated supervision by the Bank. **Risk exposures arising from traded securities (ie non-counterparty risk) in excess of this limit may occur in the trading book and exposures in excess of this trigger point (see paragraph 62) will generate incremental capital requirements.**

AGGREGATE LIMIT ON LARGE EXPOSURES

30 A banking group may not incur exposures which exceed 10% of capital base, to individual counterparties or groups of closely related counterparties, the aggregate of which exceeds 800% of the group's consolidated capital base **and this applies whether the exposures arise in the banking or trading books.** Banks supervised solely on an unconsolidated basis (and not part of a wider UK banking group) may also not incur aggregate large exposures which exceed 800% of capital base. **Separate limits apply to exposures arising from traded securities in the trading book, see paragraph 63.**

SINGLE EXPOSURE LIMIT

31 In general, a banking group may not incur a non-exempt exposure to an individual counterparty which exceeds the 25% large exposure limit of the group's consolidated capital base, **except where this limit is breached due *only* to holdings of securities in the trading book or, if specific supervisory consent has been given, where the exposures relate to short-term counterparty exposures in the trading book of a subsidiary. This latter concession will not be given to banks at the unconsolidated (solo) level, as it is designed to accommodate the large exposure regimes of other supervisors. If the excesses breach the trigger point then an incremental capital requirement will be generated.**

LIMITS ON EXPOSURES TO CONNECTED COUNTERPARTIES

32 Exposures to companies or persons connected with the lending bank, its managers, directors or controllers require special care to ensure a proper objective credit assessment is undertaken. Such exposures may be justified only when undertaken for the clear commercial advantage of the lending bank, and when they are negotiated and agreed on an arm's length basis.

33 A bank or banking group's non-exempt exposures to all connected entities outside the scope of consolidated returns, *when* taken together, may not exceed 25% of capital base.

34 The Bank will examine particularly closely all exposures to companies or persons connected to a lending bank and will deduct them from the bank's capital base if they are of the nature of a capital investment or are made on particularly concessionary terms.

Notification of Exposures

PRE-NOTIFICATION OF EXPOSURES EXCEEDING 25% OF CAPITAL BASE

35 There are very limited circumstances in which a bank or banking group may enter into exposures which exceed 25% of capital. These include 'exempt exposures' (see below for definition), **exposures due to securities in the trading book (including underwriting exposures)** and exposures at solo, solo-consolidated or consolidated sub-group level where the Bank has agreed to waive the 25% limit. When a bank or banking group proposes to enter into an exposure, including exposures exempt from the large exposures limit, which either alone or together with other existing exposures to the same counterparty exceeds 25% of capital, the fact must be notified to the Bank before the bank becomes committed to the exposure. Where the Bank has been pre-notified of, and agreed, a bank's limits for such an exposure, exposures which do not exceed those limits need not be further pre-notified to the Bank.

36 Exposures to overseas countries, and economic sectors, which exceed 25% of the bank's capital are also not covered by the pre-notification requirements. However, where a proposed transaction will result in an exposure which represents a significant departure from the bank's statement of policy on its large exposures agreed with the Bank (see paragraph 8), the Bank will expect the proposed transaction to be pre-notified to and discussed with it.

POST-NOTIFICATION OF EXPOSURES

37 UK incorporated banks and banking groups are required to report all large exposures on a quarterly basis. The more an individual exposure exceeds 10% the more rigorous the Bank will be in requiring a bank's management to justify that exposure. In any case banks are expected to adopt policies which will not lead to 10% being exceeded as a matter of course. Although 10% of capital base is the minimum cut-off level that will be applied for reporting purposes, for some banks the Bank will determine it prudent to set a lower percentage.

38 Should any bank find that for reasons outside its control or otherwise (eg two counterparties merging to form a single counterparty) it has an exposure to an individual counterparty (other than an exempt exposure) which results in it exceeding any of the limits described above this should be reported immediately to the Bank. The Bank will discuss the circumstances of any such exposures to determine the appropriate means and time-frame for the bank to comply with the limits.

39 It may be impractical for some banks to introduce monitoring systems which would enable them to calculate precisely their exposure (in accordance with the definition of an exposure set out in this notice) to individual counterparties at all times. Such banks, which will usually have an extensive branch network or group structure, will typically have adopted a system of internal limits which are allocated to individual branches or group companies but which ensure that the overall exposure to a counterparty is controlled. For such banks the Bank may agree that, for the purpose of post-notification, the maximum exposure to a counterparty occurring during a reporting period is not required to be reported; but they will be required to report their actual exposure at the reporting date and the control limit for that. counterparty if either exceeds 10% of their capital base. The bank must have satisfied the Bank that it can control the size of its exposures through the adoption and allocation of counterparty limits. The Bank will need to be satisfied that the bank's control systems are such that its exposure to a counterparty may reliably be taken as being no higher than its adopted limit for that counterparty.

Exempt Exposures

40 Certain types of exposure are exempt from the limits set above *but the Bank's requirements regarding pre- and post-notification as set out in paragraphs 35–39 continue to apply to these exposures.* The exemptions fall into the following categories:

- exposures of one year or less to banks, **investment firms subject to the CAD or an analogous regime, recognised exchanges and clearing houses;**
- exposures to Zone A central governments (and limited exposures to Zone B central governments);
- exposures secured on cash or Zone A central government securities;
- certain connected exposures, in particular those arising from a group Treasury function; and
- exposures which are covered by a parental guarantee.

These exemptions are made because of the particular nature of the exposures concerned.

EXPOSURES TO BANKS, INVESTMENT FIRMS, RECOGNISED EXCHANGES AND CLEARING HOUSES

41 The Bank will review with each bank at least once a year its policy on, and limits for, lending to other banks, **investment firms, recognised exchanges and clearing houses including those overseas.** The risks arising from some forms of exposure may, however, be significantly different in degree from the risks involved in traditional short-term interbank lending. The Bank will expect banks to take account of these different types of exposure when **setting their limits to individual institutions.**

42 Exposures of over one year maturity to banks **and investment firms** will be considered in the same way as exposures to individual non-bank counterparties and are subject to the large exposures limits. Exposures to banks **and investment firms** which are in the form of holdings of capital instruments (ie items eligible for inclusion in the capital base of the issuing bank) will normally be deducted in the calculation of capital base and

excluded from the measure of exposure. In cases where such holdings are not deducted (ie where a bank has a market making concession) they will be subject to the limits on large exposures **and where these securities are held in the trading book incremental capital requirements will be generated in the event of positions breaching the trigger point.**

EXPOSURES TO ZONE A CENTRAL GOVERNMENTS OR CENTRAL BANKS (WHICH FOR THE PURPOSE OF THIS CHAPTER INCLUDES THE EUROPEAN COMMUNITIES)[1]

43 An exposure guaranteed by a central government or central bank may be treated as an exposure to that central government or central bank. Where, however, an exposure is covered by an ECGD bank guarantee (or an equivalent government department/ agency in another Zone A country), the Bank will require to be fully satisfied that the reporting bank has sufficient expertise and systems in place to ensure that its obligations under the guarantee are met fully. Unless the Bank has notified the reporting bank that it is fully satisfied in this respect such exposures are not expected to exceed the 25% large exposures limit.

---

[1] For the purposes of large exposures calculations the EU, EEC, the European Coal and Steel Community and Euratom are exempt from the large exposures limit. Zone B countries are all countries not in Zone A.

EXPOSURES TO ZONE B CENTRAL GOVERNMENTS OR CENTRAL BANKS

44 Exposures to Zone B central governments or central banks which are denominated and funded (if necessary) in the national currency of the borrower are exempt from the large exposure limits set out above irrespective of maturity.

SECURED EXPOSURES

45 While the Bank will take security into account when considering the acceptability of a bank's exposure up to 25% of its capital base, the presence of security on its own will generally not be considered by the Bank to be an acceptable reason for an exposure to exceed 25%. However, where the security fully covers all exposures to a given counterparty and is in the form of Zone A central government or central bank securities or cash deposits (which in this context includes CDs issued by the lending bank) held with the lender, the existence of that security will be considered sufficient justification for an exposure to exceed 25% of the bank's capital base and such exposures are exempt from the limits set out above. In the case of:

  (i) an exposure secured by Zone A central government or central bank securities, the lender's legal title to the security should be fully protected[1]. An appropriate margin over the amount of the exposure should be maintained to cover fluctuations in the market value of the securities. The margin should, inter alia, take account of the maturity of the exposure, in the case where the security is denominated in a different currency from the exposure, fluctuations in the exchange rate, and the arrangements for marking to market the security and for ensuring that any resultant deficiency in the margin is made up;

  (ii) an exposure secured by a cash deposit, the lender's legal title to the deposit should be fully protected. The deposit should have identical or longer maturity than the exposure. Where the cash deposit is in a different currency from the exposure, an appropriate margin over the amount of the exposure should be maintained to cover fluctuations in the relevant exchange rates. The margin should take account of the nature of the arrangements for ensuring that any resultant deficiency in the margin following an exchange rate change is made up.

46 Where the total exposure to a given counterparty consists of a number of discrete transactions and collateral of the form specified above (paragraph 45(i) and (ii)) covers one or more of those transactions, but does not cover all exposures to the counterparty, then the Bank will wish to discuss on a case by case basis whether this will be accepted as justification for exposures in excess of the large exposures limit of 25% of capital. Such discussions will include, inter alia, consideration of the form of transactions, the nature

of the counterparty, and the method by which overall exposure will be controlled. Partial collateralisation of individual transactions may be recognised by the Bank where market rates or prices are used in determining the counterparty exposure, for example in the mark-to-market valuation of off-balance sheet products, see Chapter 2—Counterparty Risk. In no case will the uncollateralised transactions be permitted to total more than 25% of capital. A similar treatment may be applied in the case of certain exposures which are partially guaranteed (eg by ECGD) provided that the portion guaranteed accounts for at least 75% of the complete exposure.

[1] Banks should take legal advice, generally from their external legal advisors, to confirm that their legal title to the deposit is valid in all legal jurisdictions which the transaction may encompass. Banks should discuss with the Bank the circumstances in which internal legal advice will be satisfactory for this purpose.

EXEMPT EXPOSURES TO COUNTERPARTIES CONNECTED TO THE REPORTING BANK

47 Exposures to subsidiaries which are regarded within the Bank's policy on consolidated supervision as, in effect, divisions of the parent bank, and are consolidated with the parent bank in the calculation of the bank's capital ratio on a solo basis (ie are subject to 'solo consolidation'), are excluded from the scope of the large exposures policy.

48 In respect of exposures to other group companies the Bank's policy allows a bank to take on a Treasury role on behalf of the group (parent, subsidiaries and subsidiaries of the parent) as a whole (provided that the group is subject to consolidated supervision by its home supervisor). Appropriate levels for such exposures will be agreed on a case by case basis. It will be for the bank to satisfy the Bank that it should fulfil such a role and has appropriate management and other group control systems in place to ensure that risk-taking in those group companies is properly monitored and controlled.

49 The Bank's policy regarding the taking on of a Treasury role is extended to cover exposures arising from a central risk management function, in particular in managing the exposures derived from derivative contracts. In certain cases the Bank will be prepared to consider whether the scope of the Treasury concession should be extended to cover exposures of over one year's maturity arising from the operation of a central risk management function. In such cases the Bank will have regard to whether this would lead to an overall reduction in the risks to which a group as a whole is exposed.

50 In certain exceptional cases, exposures of more than 25% of capital to a bank which controls the lending bank may be permitted, even where the lending bank does not perform a Treasury role. The Bank envisages that such lending would be allowed only in a limited number of cases and would consist of short term lending of surplus liquid funds.

51 The inclusion within the connected lending limit of exposures to connected banks which are incorporated within the EU will be generally considered on a case by case basis. These may also fall within a Treasury concession.

52 Exposures to group banks, financial and non-financial companies, not covered by paragraphs 47–51 above, will be aggregated and considered as an exposure to an individual non-bank counterparty (ie will be subject to a 25% large exposures limit).

53 Other forms of connected exposure (in particular, to companies with which directors are associated) will be considered on a case by case basis. Where the link with the connected company is fairly remote, for example, where a non-executive director of a large bank is a director of the borrowing company, the exposure may be considered as acceptable up to the normal level for that bank. If, however, there is a particularly close connection, the exposure will be aggregated within the 25% large exposures limit for connected lending.

EXPOSURES UNDERTAKEN BY SUBSIDIARY[1] BANKS WHICH ARE GUARANTEED BY A PARENT BANK

54 Where exposures in a subsidiary (as used in the Companies Act 1985) bank are guaranteed by a parent bank the subsidiary bank may be deemed to have an exposure to the parent. Under the terms of the Large Exposures Directive, exposures to a parent

bank may be exempt from the limits on large exposures detailed above where the group is subject to consolidated supervision. The Bank may therefore allow such subsidiaries to take on exposures exceeding 25% of their own capital base but only if they are entered into within the terms of a policy agreed by the parent bank and provided that there are guarantees in place (acceptable to the Bank) from the parent bank to protect the subsidiary should the exposure become non-performing or require to be written off. The guarantee, which may take a number of forms and should be legally enforceable by the subsidiary, should prevent a bank's capital from becoming deficient as a result of experiencing a loss on such an exposure. The Bank will require written confirmation from the parent bank that the exposure is retained in the subsidiary's balance sheet at the parent bank's request in order to meet group objectives and will need to be satisfied as to the nature of the exposure concerned. These requirements recognise that it may be the policy in some bank groups to concentrate particular types of lending or other facilities in one subsidiary.

55 In the case of authorised bank subsidiaries of UK banks, in order for an exposure exceeding 25% of capital base to be acceptable in the subsidiary bank, the parent bank must at all times have room to take over the exposure without itself exceeding the large exposures limit of 25% of capital base. Also the total counterparty exposure of the banking group to the customer must be within 25% of the group's capital base. The Bank will need to be satisfied that adequate control systems are in place to ensure that credit risk taken in the group as a whole is properly monitored and controlled.

56 In the case of authorised banks which are subsidiaries of overseas banks the Bank will wish to agree with the supervisory authority of the parent bank the size of exposures which can be undertaken by the subsidiary within the terms of this policy. It will also require written assurance from the overseas supervisor that they are content for the subsidiary to undertake the level of exposure in question. Before agreeing a level for the subsidiary the Bank will take into account the degree and extent of the consolidated supervision of the banking group exercised by the parent supervisory authority.

57 Overseas bank subsidiaries of UK banks will be expected to conform to the regulatory requirements of the country in which they are located.

---

[1] The definition of 'subsidiary' will normally be that used in the Companies Act 1985.

CAPITAL BASE

58 The capital base used as the basis for monitoring and controlling large exposures should be calculated according to the methods set out in Chapter 9–The Own Funds of Authorised Institutions (ie the same as that used in the calculation of the risk asset ratio), **unless any breach of the 25% large exposures limit occurs due to holdings of securities in the trading book; in such cases an amended capital base is used (see paragraph 62).** The figure will be agreed by the Bank with the reporting bank on the basis of the bank's audited balance sheet for the latest financial year, and may be reset during the year, in agreement with the Bank, to take account of audited interim profits. The Bank, will, however, adjust this figure for new issues of capital during the course of the year and take account of other significant changes to the capital base, either upwards or downwards. In either circumstance the amended figure will be agreed with the bank and advised to it in writing.

ADDITIONAL CAPITAL REQUIREMENTS

59 The Bank may require a UK incorporated bank to maintain higher capital ratios than would otherwise be the case when it considers it to be exposed to particular concentrations of risk. It is the Bank's practice, where a bank has a number of exposures, which are not exempt from the limits, of more than 10% of capital base and, in particular, where the aggregate total of those exposures exceeds 100% of capital base, to consider whether such measures are necessary. However, in considering the amount of capital to be maintained the Bank would have regard to the acceptability of the exposures when considered in the context of the bank's large exposures policy agreed with the Bank; the particular characteristics of the individual bank, including the nature of its business and the experience of its management; and the number of such exposures, their individual size and nature.

60 In those cases where a counterparty exposure (which is not an exempt exposure) breaches the large exposures limit of 25% of capital base (see paragraph 31) the Bank will require additional capital cover which will be significantly higher than would be required for an exposure of less than 25%, and this requirement will generally apply whether or not the Bank agrees that the exposure has been incurred in the most exceptional circumstances. Unless due to exempt exposures **or non-counterparty risk in the trading book,** the undertaking of an exposure in excess of 25% other than in the most exceptional circumstances will also call into question whether the bank's authorisation should be revoked. **However, special arrangements may apply to exposures in the trading book which at a consolidated level exceed 25% of a bank's capital base—see paragraphs 31 and 63.**

61 Where a bank is a subsidiary of another UK bank and it has exposures exceeding the 25% large exposures limit but the parent bank has made arrangements (within the terms of the policy set out above) to protect the subsidiary if problems occur, the additional capital cover, if any, may be held in the parent bank rather than the subsidiary. The additional capital cover will be determined by the size of the exposure (together with other exposures to the same counterparty entered into by the parent bank) in relation to the parent bank's capital base.

62 Where a non-exempt exposure to a single counterparty exceeds the 25% large exposure limit but this is only as a result of long securities positions in the trading book, then an amended capital base is used to measure the exposure. In such circumstances the capital base may be amended to include any tier 3 capital eligible for inclusion in the capital base available to support the trading book. If the exposure exceeds the trigger point of 25% of the amended capital base, incremental capital is required as set out below.

63 The calculation for determining the incremental capital requirement involves the following sequential steps:

- **(a) Net any short securities positions against long securities positions, netting the short items against the highest long specific risk weighted items (Note: the specific risk weights of netted items need not be identical).**
- **(b) Rank the remaining net long securities positions in order according to specific risk weighting factors (ie lowest weighted items first, highest weighted items last).**
- **(c) Taking the lowest weighted items first, apply these exposures to the difference between the non securities exposure to the counterparty and 25% of the amended capital base (ie the 'headroom' up to 25% of the amended capital base is employed to cover the lowest weighted exposures).**
- **(d) Incremental capital is required for remaining net long securities exposures as follows:**
  - **(i) if the excess exposure has been extant for 10 days or less, the specific risk weighting for exposures ranked in excess of 25% of the amended capital are multiplied by 200%.**
  - **(ii) if the excess exposure has been extant for more than 10 days, the specific risk weightings for exposures ranked in excess of 25% of the amended capital base are multiplied by the following factors.**

Excess exposure over 25% of amended capital base (acb)	Factor applied to specific risk weighting
Up to 40% of acb	200%
From 40% to 60% of acb	300%
From 60% to 80% of acb	400%
From 80% to 100% of acb	500%
From 100% to 250% of acb	600%
Over 250% of acb	900%

Note: The system set out in paragraphs 62 and 63 should be used to cover short term counterparty exposure in the trading book of certain subsidiaries where specific supervisory consent has been given for them to be treated thus at the consolidated level (see also paragraph 31).

64 Where the trading book excess exposure has been extant for 10 days or less the trading book exposure to the counterparty must not exceed 500% of the amended capital base.

65 Any trading book excess exposures which have persisted for more than 10 days must not, in aggregate, exceed 600% of the bank's amended capital base.

Exposures to Countries

66 The Bank does not believe that a common limit should be applied to the aggregate of banks' exposures to counterparties in the same country; nor does it consider it appropriate to publish guideline percentages for the acceptable level of exposure to counterparties in particular countries. Banks will, however, be expected to set limits for country exposures on the basis of their own risk assessments. The nature of the exposure (for example, whether it is trade finance or longer term balance of payments finance) will be relevant in considering an acceptable level of exposure. The Bank will continue to monitor closely banks' country risk exposures, and discuss them with banks' managements.

Exposures to Economic Sectors

67 The extent to which a bank may be prudently exposed to a particular industrial sector or geographical region will vary considerably depending upon the characteristics of the bank and the sector or region concerned. Sectors and regions are difficult to define and the definitions for one bank may not be appropriate for another. The Bank will not therefore apply common maximum percentages to banks' sectoral exposures.

68 The Bank will continue to monitor banks' exposures to sectors and regions and will wish to discuss with all banks their internal monitoring systems and the appropriateness of the sectors identified in their management reports. The Bank will wish to ensure that banks have prudent lending policies which take into account the dangers from over-exposure to particular economic sectors both within the United Kingdom and worldwide. The same considerations apply to regional concentrations. Such policies will need to be adjusted from time to time in order to take account of changing market conditions and economic trends. The Bank will continue to obtain information on sectoral and regional exposures from banks' internal monitoring systems.

Annex 1: Banking Act 1987. Section 38 Reports of Large Exposures

SECTION 38

(1) An authorised institution, other than one whose principal place of business is outside the United Kingdom, shall take a report to the Bank if:

(a) it has entered into a transaction or transactions relating to any one person as a result of which it is exposed to the risk of incurring losses in excess of 10% of its available capital resources; or

(b) it proposes to enter into a transaction or transactions relating to any one person which, either alone or together with a previous transaction or previous transactions entered into by it in relation to that person, would result in its being exposed to the risk of incurring losses in excess of 25% of those resources.

(2) Subsection (1) above applies also where the transaction or transactions relate to different persons if they are connected in such a way that the financial soundness of any of them may affect the financial soundness of the other or others or the same factors may affect the financial soundness of both or all of them.

(3) If an authorised institution to which subsection (1) above applies has one or more subsidiaries which are not authorised institutions the Bank may by notice in writing to that institution direct that that subsection shall apply to it as if the transactions and available capital resources of the subsidiary or subsidiaries, or such of them as are specified in the notice, were included in those of the institutions.

(4) The reports required to be made by an institution under subsection (1) above shall be made, in a case within paragraph (a) of that subsection, in respect of such period or periods and, in a case within paragraph (b) of that subsection, at such time before the transaction or transactions are entered into, as may be specified by notice in writing given to the institution by the Bank; and those reports shall be in such form and contain such particulars as the Bank may reasonably require.

(5) For the purposes of this section a transaction entered into by an institution relates to a person if it is:

(a) a transaction under which that person incurs an obligation to the institution or as a result of which he may incur such an obligation;

(b) a transaction under which the institution will incur, or as a result of which it may incur, an obligation in the event of that person defaulting on an obligation to a third party; or

(c) a transaction under which the institution acquires or incurs an obligation to acquire, or as a result of which it may incur an obligation to acquire, an asset the value of which depends wholly or mainly on that person performing his obligations or otherwise on his financial soundness;

and the risk of loss attributable to a transaction is, in a case within paragraph (a) or (b) above, the risk of the person concerned defaulting on the obligation there mentioned and, in a case within paragraph (c) above, the risk of the person concerned defaulting on the obligations there mentioned or of a deterioration in his financial soundness.

(6) Any question whether an institution is or would be exposed to risk as mentioned in subsection (1) above (or in that subsection as extended by subsection (2)) shall be determined in accordance with principles published by the Bank or notified by it to the institution concerned; and those principles may in particular make provision for determining the amount at risk in particular circumstances or the extent to which any such amount is to be taken into account for the purpose of this section.

(7) For the purpose of this section the available capital resources of an institution (or, in a case within subsection (3) above, of an institution and its relevant subsidiary or subsidiaries) and the value of those resources at any time shall be determined by the Bank and notified by it to the institution by notice in writing; and any such determination, which may be varied from time to time, shall be made by the Bank after consultation with the institution concerned and in accordance with principles published by the Bank.

(8) The principles referred to in subsections (6) and (7) above may make different provisions for different cases and those referred to in subsection (6) may, in particular, exclude from consideration either wholly or in part, risks resulting from transactions of a particular description or entered into in particular circumstances or with persons of particular descriptions.

(9) An institution which fails to make a report as required by this section shall be guilty of an offence; but where an institution shows that at the time when the report was required to be made it did not know that the facts were such as to require the making of the report it shall not be guilty of an offence by reason of its failure to make a report at that time but shall be guilty of an offence unless it makes the report within seven days of becoming aware of those facts.

(10) An institution guilty of an offence under this section shall be liable on summary conviction to a fine not exceeding the fifth level on the standard scale.

(11) The Treasury may after consultation with the Bank by order:

(a) amend subsection (1) above so as to substitute for either of the percentages for the time being specified in that subsection such other percentage as may be specified in the order;

(b) make provision, whether by amending subsection (5) or otherwise, with respect to the transactions and risks to be taken into account for the purposes of this section,

but any such order shall be subject to annulment in pursuance of a resolution of either House of Parliament.

(12) For the avoidance of doubt it is hereby declared that references in this section to 'one person' include references to a partnership.

Annex II: Examples

Calculation of Incremental Trading Book Capital Requirements for Excess Large Exposures, see paragraph 63.

THE CAPITAL BASE OF THE INSTITUTION COMPRISES:

	£
Capital base (tier 1 and tier 2)	1000
Eligible tier 3 capital	100
Amended capital base	1100

THE COMPONENTS OF THE LARGE EXPOSURE COMPRISE:

	% Specific risk weight	£
Counterparty exposure		200
Mark-to-market value of trading book securities		
Short: Qualifying bond	1.00	(20)
Long: Qualifying commercial paper	0.25	100
Long: Equity	4.00	150
Long: Qualifying convertible	1.60	30
Total Net large exposures position		460
o/w Net long securities position		260

Steps in calculation

PARAGRAPH 63(a)

The short position in qualifying bond is offset against the highest specific risk weight items—in this case equities:

	£
Net long equity position (£150–£20)	130

PARAGRAPH 63(b)

Rank remaining items according to specific risk weight.

% Specific Risk	£
0.25 Qualifying commercial paper	100
1.60 Qualifying convertible	30
4.00 Equity (net)	130

PARAGRAPH 63(c)

Calculate 'headroom' between non securities exposures and 25% of amended capital base.

	£
25% of amended capital base (1100)	275
Non securities exposures	200
Headroom	75

PARAGRAPH 63(d)

Applying securities positions in ascending order of specific risk weight.
£75 of the £100 qualifying commercial paper may be counted before 25% of the amended capital base is reached.
The remaining £25 qualifying commercial paper, along with £30 qualifying convertible and £130 equity (net) are traded securities exposures in excess of the limit and require incremental capital.

PARAGRAPH 63(d)(i)

If the excess exposure has been extant for 10 days or less, the specific risk weights are doubled.

Qualifying Commercial paper   £
£25 × 0.25 × 200% =   0.125

Qualifying convertible
£30 × 1.60% × 200% =   0.96

Equity
£130 × 4% × 200% =   10.40

Additional capital requirement   11.485

PARAGRAPH 63(d)(ii)

If the excess exposure has been extant for more than 10 days.

[£200 Counterparty exposure   ]
[£75 Securities exposures (within limit)   ]

Excess exposures

Up to 40% of amended capital base at 200%
(40% of £1100 = £440)   £

£25 × 0.25% × 200% =   0.125
£30 × 1.60% × 200% =   0.96
£110 × 4.00% × 200% =   8.80

Excess exposure 40%–60% of amended capital base at 300%
£20 × 4.00% × 300% =   2.40

Additional capital requirement   12.285

[£460 Total net large exposures position   ]

Chapter 4—Foreign Currency Risk

Explanation

1 A firm which holds net open positions (whether long or short) in foreign currencies either because of FX trading positions or because of exposures caused by its overall assets and liabilities is exposed to the risk that exchange rates may move against it. The FX requirements set out below reflect the fact that movements in various currencies against sterling are likely to be partially correlated and therefore some allowance is made for offsetting long or short positions in different currencies. In particular, firms have the option of adopting a backtesting approach to the generation of the capital requirements which takes the correlation between currencies into account.

2 This chapter describes the way to calculate an institution's open foreign currency position, and the capital required against this position. The position will be calculated with reference to the entire business (ie banking and trading books combined). The chapter replaces existing Bank Policy Notices on foreign exchange risk [Foreign Exchange Exposure (1981); Foreign Exchange Options (1984)], in as much as they cover the manner in which a bank's foreign exchange exposure must be measured for capital adequacy purposes.

3 Unlike interest rate and equity position risk (Chapters 5 and 6 respectively), there is no 'simple approach' (ie an approach with simpler rules but a higher capital charge) for the calculation of foreign exchange risk. This is because the methodology adopted in the Directive for the calculation of foreign exchange risk is very similar to that already used for banks in the UK, and the necessary extra system costs following implementation of the Directive are therefore expected to be small.

4 This chapter covers the following parts of the Capital Adequacy Directive:

– Article 4, paragraph 1(ii)
– Annex III.

Calculating the Net Open Positions

5 The net open position in each currency (including gold[1], but excluding sterling[2]) should be calculated using the method set out in Annex I subject to the following:

(a) *Coverage* All on and off balance sheet positions including irrevocable guarantees. With the agreement of the Bank, net future income/expenses not yet entered in accounting records, but already fully hedged by forward foreign exchange, may be included where it is part of the bank's written policy and is done on a consistent basis.

(b) *Valuation* All assets/liabilities (whether on or off balance sheet) should be included at closing spot rates, and for mark to market items this should be calculated on the basis of the current market value of the positions. Where a bank wishes to show certain assets and liabilities at net present value, they should obtain the prior agreement of the Bank.

(c) *Composite Currencies* Net positions in composite currencies may either be broken down into the component currencies according to the quotas in force and included in the net open position calculations for individual currencies, or treated as a separate currency. However, the mechanism for treating composite currencies must be applied consistently.

(d) *Swaps* Currency swaps should be treated as a combination of a long position in one currency and a short position in the second currency.

(e) *Options* **A number of approaches are possible. First, options (and their associated hedges) can be entirely omitted from the net open position, and capital charges calculated using either the simple carve out approach (set out in Annex II) or a model based on the scenario matrix approach to option risk. In the latter case, the Bank must review and recognise the model prior to its use. Second, the option delta value can be incorporated into the net open position, and capital charges for other option risks calculated separately using a model based on the buffer approach to option risk. Such a model will also need to be reviewed and recognised by the Bank prior to use. Third, where a bank has chosen to use the backtesting method to measure overall foreign exchange exposure (see paragraph 7(b) below), the model used may include several option risks. Where it is not only delta that is incorporated, the model must be reviewed and recognised by the Bank. Extra capital charges will apply for those option risks that the model does not capture.**

Note that, subject to Bank approval, netting of back-to-back option positions is permitted.

(f) *Structural Positions* Certain positions of a structural, or non-banking nature, as set out below, may be excluded, with the prior approval of the Bank, from the calculation of the net open position[3]:

  (i) positions taken deliberately to hedge against the effects of exchange rate movements on the capital adequacy of an institution

  (ii) investments in overseas subsidiaries which are fully deducted from an institution's capital for capital adequacy purposes.

---

[1] Positions in silver, platinum and palladium should also be reported as positions in foreign currency.

[2] Occasionally, and with the prior approval of the Bank, it may be appropriate for a bank to use a 'base currency' other than sterling for assessment of foreign exchange risk.

[3] The structural positions referred to here are those that apply when calculating net open positions for the purposes of determining capital requirements. Other types of structural positions may be deducted in order to arrive at the position to be monitored against a bank's foreign exchange guideline.

Calculating the Overall Net Foreign Exchange Position

6 The institution should then convert each net long or short position into sterling at the prevailing spot rates. For foreign currencies, the total of the net long positions and the total of the net short positions should be calculated. The higher of these two totals is the institution's overall net foreign exchange position. (Gold should be treated separately—see paragraph 8 below.)

Calculating the Capital Requirement

7 The possible methods of calculating the capital requirement on the overall foreign exchange position are set out below. Annex III summarises the manner in which institutions will arrive at their total capital requirement.

(a) *Basic Method*: The overall net foreign exchange position, calculated after excluding positions covered by method (b) and (c) below, carries a requirement of 8%.

(b) *Backtesting Method*: With the agreement of the Bank a backtesting method can be used to calculate the capital requirements for either all or a subset of the currencies comprising an institution's foreign exchange position. The currencies to be included in the backtesting method should be agreed in advance with the Bank and, where option risks other than delta are included in the backtesting model, it will require prior recognition by the Bank. (Occasionally, it will be appropriate for the position in one pre-determined currency to be split, with only a proportion of it included in the backtesting method. Such a treatment should be agreed in advance with the Bank.)

The capital requirement produced by the backtesting method for the portfolio is determined as follows:

(i) Losses, which would have occurred in at least 95% of ten-working-day periods rolled on a daily basis over the preceding five years, are calculated. The 95% loss quantile will, where the observation period covers 1,300 valuations, correspond to the 65th largest loss.

or

Losses, which would have occurred in at least 99% of ten-working-day periods rolled on a daily basis over the preceding three years, are calculated. The 99% quantile will, where the observations cover 780 valuations, correspond to the 8th largest loss.
[The losses must be calculated by assuming that the current portfolio of net open positions in the designated currencies was held at the start of each rolling period.]

(ii) The requirement is the higher of the losses calculated above, 7(b)(i), and 2% of the overall net foreign exchange position as calculated by applying the basic method to the net open positions in the portfolio of designated currencies.

(c) *Currency Pairs Subject to Binding Inter-Governmental Agreements*: Banks may apply a separate treatment to those currencies that are subject to binding inter-governmental agreements. The capital requirements for such currency pairs will be 50% of the maximum movement stipulated by the inter-governmental agreement on the matched net open positions of the individual currencies. At present, the only recognised binding inter-governmental agreement is that applying to the Belgian and Luxembourg francs. These currencies will be treated as one and incorporated in such a manner into either the basic or the backtesting method.

(d) *Additional capital charges for options*: As set out in paragraph 5(e) above, additional capital charges will apply where the bank is using:
– the simple carve out method (Annex II);
– a scenario or buffer based recognised model (see Chapter 8);
– a backtesting model that incorporates some but not all option risks (see Chapter 8).

8 Gold (and other precious metals) should be treated separately. Under the basic method, the capital charge is 8% of the net open position (whether long or short). If the backtesting method is used, the capital charge for gold must be calculated independently of the charge for foreign currencies.

Note

9 In addition to foreign exchange risk, certain foreign exchange positions may be subject to interest rate risk and/or counterparty risk requirements and should be treated under the relevant sections. For the treatment of interest rate risk on foreign exchange positions see Chapter 5—Interest Rate Position Risk. For the treatment of counterparty risk on foreign exchange positions see Chapter 2—Counterparty Risk. (In calculating charges for interest rate and counterparty risk, all foreign exchange positions are deemed to be part of the trading book.)

Annex I: Calculating the Net Open Position

Local Currency
Value

    Net spot position: all assets (gross of provisions for bad and doubtful debts) less all liabilities, including accrued interest, in the currency in question;

+ *Net forward position:* all amounts to be received less all amounts to be paid under forward exchange transactions, including currency futures and the principal on currency swaps not included in the spot position;

+ Irrevocable guarantees (and similar instruments) which are certain to be called;

+ Net future income/expenses not yet accrued but already fully hedged;

+ Profits (net value of income and expense accounts) held in the currency in question;

+ Specific provisions held in the currency in question where the underlying asset is in a different currency;

− Assets held in currency in question where a specific provision is held in a different currency;

+ The net delta (or delta-based) equivalent of options book, if this is the approach taken to measurement of option risk;

= **Net open position**

Annex II: Simple Method for Options (Carve Out)

Where a bank uses this approach, the table below must be used to calculate the capital requirements for market risk on options plus any related hedges. These figures may only be used for options with a residual maturity of less than six months. Advice must be sought for options with a residual maturity of over six months. (Banks that have models which have been recognised by the Bank of England may *not* use the method prescribed below for those option models that have been recognised.)

	Option Position	In the Money by more than P%	In the Money by less than P%	Out of the Money
Naked	**Long Call**	NL	NL	NL
	Long Put	NL	NL	NL
	Short Call	NSI	NSI	NSO
	Short Put	NSI	NSI	NSO
Long in	**Long Put**	0%	LPI	HO
Underlying	**Short Call**	0%	SHI	HO
Short in	**Long Call**	0%	LCI	HO
Underlying	**Short Put**	0%	SHI	HO

Definitions
In the Money means in relation to call options and warrants, that the exercise price is less than the current mark-to-market value of the underlying instrument and, in relation to put options, that the current mark-to-market value is less than the exercise price.
Out of the Money means those options and warrants that are not In the Money.
P% is 8%.
The capital requirements are:

NL   The lesser of:
      (a) the market value of the underlying instrument multiplied by P% and
      (b) the current value of the option on the bank's books.
NSI   The market value of the underlying position multiplied by P%.
NSO   The market value of the underlying position multiplied by P%
      minus
      0.5 multiplied by the amount by which the option is Out of the Money (subject to a
      maximum reduction to zero).
LPI   The market value of the underlying position
      minus
      (1–P%) multiplied by underlying position valued at the exercise price.
HO   The market value of the underlying position multiplied by P%.
SHI   The market value of the underlying position multiplied by P%
      minus
      the mark-to-market value of the option
      (subject to a maximum reduction to zero).
LCI   (1 + P%) multiplied by underlying position valued at the exercise price
      minus
      the market value of the underlying position
      (subject to a maximum reduction to zero).

An option will be deemed to be 'hedged' for the purposes of these calculations when the
size of the offsetting underlying position matches the amounts into which the option is
exercisable. Where the amount underlying the option is larger than the offsetting position
the residual options will be treated as Naked Option Positions.

Annex III: Calculation of the Capital Requirement for Foreign Exchange

Calculate the net open position in each currency, excluding sterling.
Convert into sterling at spot rates.

FOR FOREIGN CURRENCIES SUBJECT TO THE BASIC METHOD:

The sum of all the net short positions (each converted into the reporting currency)	W
The sum of all the net long positions (each converted into the reporting currency)	X
The overall net foreign exchange position	= Y
	= the larger of W and X
Capital charge	= Y × 8% = Z

FOR CURRENCIES SUBJECT TO THE BACKTESTING METHOD:

The capital charge sufficient to cover losses that might have been incurred over the relevant past period (subject to a floor)	= A
+Any extra capital charges incurred if backtesting does not take account of all option risks	= B

EXTRA CAPITAL CHARGES FOR OPTIONS:

Options treated using the carve-out	= C
Options treated using a recognised model	= D

FOR GOLD (AND OTHER PRECIOUS METALS):

Net open position (long or short)	= g
Capital charge under basic method	= g × 8% = G
Capital charge under backtesting method (subject to a floor)	= G*

TOTAL CAPITAL REQUIREMENT: = Z + A + B + C + D
                                                          + (G or G*)

Chapter 5—Interest Rate Position Risk

Explanation

1 Any bank has some degree of interest rate exposure in its trading book. This chapter determines the way in which capital requirements for this type of exposure are calculated. The interest rate exposure captured includes exposures arising from interest-bearing and discounted financial instruments, derivatives based on the movement of interest rates, foreign exchange forwards, and interest rate exposures embedded in derivatives based on non-interest related derivatives. In all cases where positions give rise to interest rate risk there is general market interest rate risk. This may be accompanied by specific interest rate risk, or counterparty risk, or equity or foreign exchange risk, depending on the nature of the position. Banks should consider carefully which risks are generated by each individual source of exposure.

2 The specific risk capital requirement recognises that individual instruments may change in value for reasons other than movements in the yield curve of a given currency. The general risk capital requirement reflects the price change of these products caused by parallel and non-parallel shifts in the yield curve, as well as the difficulty of constructing perfect hedges.

3 Annex II to this chapter outlines a simplified method, which banks may choose to adopt, for the calculation of trading book capital requirements for interest rate risk. The capital requirement generated by application of the simplified method will be higher than that which would result from applying the normal methods. If banks choose to apply this method they should seek permission from their line supervisor and, in most circumstances, they would be expected to adopt the simplified method for both interest rate and equity position risk (see Chapter 6—Equity Position Risk).

4 This chapter describes the way in which a bank will calculate its capital requirements for interest rate positions held in the trading book. The contents of the chapter are all new. There are no existing Bank Policy Notices covering interest rate position risk.

5 The following sections of the CAD are covered by this chapter:

– Annex I Position Risk Introduction section
– Annex I Position Risk Traded Debt Instruments section.

Scope

6 This chapter will apply to trading book positions and exposures of the following instruments whether or not they carry coupons:

  (a) bonds, loan stocks, debentures etc;
  (b) non-convertible preference securities;
  (c) convertible securities such as preference shares and bonds and bonds with embedded options; (see paragraph 17)
  (d) mortgage backed securities and other securitised assets;
  (e) certificates of deposit;
  (f) treasury bills, bank bills (bankers acceptances), local authority bills;
  (g) commercial paper;
  (h) euronotes, medium term notes, etc;
  (i) floating rate notes, FRCDs etc;
  (j) foreign exchange forward positions;
  (k) derivatives based upon the above instruments and interest rates;
  (l) interest rate exposure embedded in other financial instruments.

  This list may be amended periodically.

  For instruments that deviate from the above structures, or could be considered complex, each bank should agree a policy statement with their supervisor about the intended treatment. In some circumstances the treatment of an instrument may be uncertain, for example bonds whose coupon payments are linked to equity indices. Where possible the position risk of such instruments should be broken down into its components and allocated appropriately between the equity, interest rate and foreign

exchange risks categories. Advice must be sought from supervisors in cases of doubt, and when a bank is trading an instrument for the first time.

7 Where a trading book position results from underwriting activities the capital requirement should be considered in accordance with the parameters described in Chapter 7—Underwriting.

8 In addition to interest rate position risk certain debt instruments and related derivates may also be subject to foreign exchange and/or counterparty risk and the exposures should be treated as required in relevant chapters (Chapter 4—Foreign Currency Risk and Chapter 2—Counterparty Risk).

Individual Net Positions

9 A bank may net, by value, long and short positions in the same debt instrument to generate the individual net position in that instrument. Instruments will be considered to be the same where the issuer is the same, they have the equivalent ranking in a liquidation, and the currency, the coupon, and the maturity are the same. When a bank does not have a relevant recognised model (see Chapter 8—The Model Review Process), positions in derivatives, and all positions in repos, reverse repos and similar products should be decomposed into their components within each time band (see paragraphs 27 to 31) prior to calculating individual net positions for general market risk.

10 A bank may net by value a long or short position in one tranche of a debt instrument against another tranche only where the relevant tranches:

(a) rank pari passu in all respects; *and*
(b) become fungible within 180 days and thereafter the debt instruments of one tranche can be delivered in settlement of the other tranche.

Calculation of Capital Requirements

11 Banks should calculate the general market risk arising from interest rate risk and the specific risk arising from debt instruments. The aggregate capital requirement for interest rate risk will be the sum of the general market risk capital requirements across currencies and the specific risk capital requirements.

Specific Risk Calculation

12 In determining its specific risk capital requirement for positions in debt instruments a bank must weight the current market value of each of its individual net positions, whether long or short, according to its allocation amongst the following categories:

	Weighting
(a) Certain Central Government debt instruments	0.00%
(b) Qualifying Items up to 6 months residual maturity	0.25%
(c) Qualifying Items over 6 and up to 24 months residual maturity	1.00%
(d) Qualifying Items over 24 months residual maturity	1.60%
(e) Non-Qualifying Items	8.00%

13 Debt instruments will be given a 0% specific risk weighting if:

(a) they are issued by, fully guaranteed by, or fully collateralised by securities issued by Zone A central governments and central banks, including the European Communities; or
(b) they are issued by, or fully guaranteed by, Zone B central governments and central banks with a residual maturity of 1 year or less and are denominated in local currency and funded by liabilities in the same currency.

14 A list of Zone A countries was originally provided in policy notice BSD/1990/3 (Implementation in the United Kingdom of the Solvency Ratio Directive) and updated by policy notice S&S/1995/1. All other countries not included in Zone A are in Zone B.

15 Debt instruments will be treated as qualifying if any of the following conditions apply:

(a) they are issued by, or fully guaranteed by, Zone B central governments and central banks with a residual maturity of over 1 year and are denominated in local currency and funded by liabilities in the same currency;

(b) they are securities issued by, or fully collateralised by claims on, a multilateral development bank listed in the Solvency Ratio Directive. (See Chapter 11—Lists for a list of these institutions.) The European Commission may amend this list periodically;

(c) they are issued, guaranteed, endorsed, or accepted, by a credit institution incorporated in a Zone A country;

(d) they are issued, or guaranteed, endorsed, or accepted, by a credit institution incorporated in a Zone B country and have a residual maturity of 1 year or less;

(e) they are issued, or guaranteed, by an investment firm that is subject to the Capital Adequacy Directive, or a regime that the Bank deems to be as stringent;

(f) they are issued by, or guaranteed by, Zone A public sector entities;

(g) they are issued by, or guaranteed by, a company whose equity is eligible for 2% equity specific risk weighting (see Chapter 6—Equity Position Risk).

16 Debt items issued by entities not covered by the descriptions in the preceding paragraph *may still* be treated as qualifying if the issue, or an issue of equivalent ranking in a liquidation, or an issue of equivalent ranking in a liquidation of the guarantor, is rated investment grade (or its equivalent for money market obligations), or above and provided that the reporting bank is unaware of any sub-investment grade rating issued by any relevant credit rating agency. When the reporting bank is aware of an announcement that the issue may be downgraded to below investment grade, by at least one relevant credit rating agency[1], that debt will cease to be qualifying unless it meets the criteria of the preceding paragraphs.

17 Convertible securities, such as bonds and preference shares, that are treated as debt instruments will be given a specific risk weighting identical to other debt items for the same issuer as described in the preceding paragraphs. Convertible securities must be treated as equities (see Chapter 6—Equity Position Risk) when:

(a) the first date at which conversion may take place is less than three months ahead, or the next such date (where the first has passed) is less than a year ahead; *and*

(b) the convertible is trading at a premium of less than 10%, where the premium is defined as the current mark-to-market value of the convertible less the mark-to-market value of the underlying equity, expressed as a percentage of the mark-to-market value of the underlying equity.

18 Debt instruments where the issuer does not meet the requirements established above (paragraphs 13 to 16 inclusive) are deemed to be non-qualifying.

19 Derivatives positions will attract specific risk only when they are based upon an underlying instrument or security. For instance, where the underlying exposure is an interest rate exposure, as in a swap based upon interbank rates, there will be no specific risk, just counterparty risk. However, for a swap based upon a bond yield, the underlying bond will generate a specific risk requirement. For options the specific risk will be based upon the delta weighted value, calculated via an approved model. Future cash flows derived from positions in derivatives will generate counterparty risk requirements related to the counterparty in the trade in addition to position risk requirements related to the issuer of the underlying security.

---

[1] See Chapter 11—Lists for a list of agencies and investment grade ratings.

General Risk Calculation

20 A separate general market interest rate risk calculation is calculated for each currency irrespective of where the individual instruments are physically traded or listed. The resultant capital requirements must be converted into the reporting currency by applying the prevailing foreign exchange spot rates. These capital requirements are summed arithmetically to give the total general market risk requirement.

21 The Bank does not intend to distinguish explicitly between the level of general market risk capital requirement for different currencies. However, it recognises that yield curves in some currencies are more volatile and that their markets are less liquid with fewer hedging mechanisms available. When a bank has a portfolio with interest risk in such currencies, this will be taken fully into account when setting the target and trigger capital ratios (see Chapter 9—Own Funds).

General Risk Calculation—Interest Rate Exposure Method 1

22 The capital requirements for general market risk are intended to recognise the risk of parallel and non-parallel shifts in the yield curve. The steps in calculating the general risk requirement for interest rate positions under method 1 are set out below. A worked example is given in Table 5.2.

    (a) Individual net positions (see paragraphs 9 and 10) will be allocated to one of the maturity bands in Table 5.1, on the following basis:
        (i) Fixed-rate instruments will be allotted their maturity bands based upon the residual time to maturity—irrespective of embedded puts and calls – and whether their coupon is below 3%.
        (ii) Floating rate instruments will be allocated to maturity bands based upon the time remaining to the re-determination of the coupon.
        (iii) Advice must be sought from supervisors on the treatment of instruments that deviate from these structures, or may be considered complex.
    Note that the bands are grouped into zones.
    (b) Multiply the market value of the individual long and short net positions (as defined in paragraphs 9 and 10) in each maturity band by the weighting factors given in Table 5.1.
    (c) To calculate matched and unmatched positions per maturity band: where a maturity band has both weighted long and short positions, the extent to which the one offsets the other is called the matched weighted position. The remainder (ie the excess of the weighted long positions over the weighted short positions, or vice versa, within a band) is called the unmatched weighted position for that band.
    (d) To calculate matched and unmatched positions per zone: where a zone has both unmatched weighted long and short positions for various bands, the extent to which the one offsets the other is called the matched weighted position for that zone. The remainder (ie the excess of the weighted long positions over the weighted short positions, or vice versa, within a zone) is called the unmatched weighted position for that zone.
    (e) Unmatched weighted positions for a zone may be offset against positions in other zones as follows:
        (i) The unmatched weighted long (short) position in zone 1 may offset the unmatched weighted position short (long) in zone 2. The extent to which the unmatched weighted positions in zones 1 and 2 are offsetting is described as the matched weighted position between zones 1 and 2.
        (ii) After (i), any residual unmatched weighted long (short) positions in zone 2 may then be matched by offsetting unmatched weighted short (long) positions in zone 3. The extent to which the unmatched positions in zones 2 and 3 are offsetting is described as the matched weighted position between zones 2 and 3.
    The calculations in (i) and (ii) may be carried out in reverse order (ie zones 2 and 3 followed by zones 1 and 2).
        (iii) After (i) and (ii) any residual unmatched weighted long (short) positions in zone 1 may then be matched by offsetting unmatched weighted short (long) positions in zone 3. The extent to which the unmatched positions in zones 1 and 3 are offsetting is described as the matched weighted positions between zones 1 and 3.
    (f) Any residual unmatched weighted positions following the matching within a band, within a zone, and between zones will be summed.

23 The general interest rate risk capital requirements will be the sum of:

(a) Matched Weighted Positions in all Maturity Bands	× 10%
(b) Matched Weighted Positions in Zone 1	× 40%
(c) Matched Weighted Positions in Zone 2	× 30%
(d) Matched Weighted Positions in Zone 3	× 30%
(e) Matched Weighted Positions between Zones 1 & 2	× 40%
(f) Matched Weighted Positions between Zones 2 & 3	× 40%
(g) Matched Weighted Positions between Zones 1 & 3	× 150%
(h) Residual Unmatched Weighted Positions	× 100%

General Risk Calculation—Interest Rate Exposure Method 2

24 This approach to measuring the exposure to parallel and non-parallel shifts of the yield curves recognises the use of duration as an indicator of the sensitivity of individual positions to changes in market yields. As a result banks may use a duration based system for determining their general interest rate risk capital requirements for traded debt instruments and other sources of interest rate exposures including derivatives. It is likely that certain instruments may not be suitable for the duration method and advice must be sought for complex instrument types which must be subjected to the maturity method, and possibly additional capital requirements.

25 Banks should notify their supervisor of the circumstances in which they intend to adopt this method. Once chosen, it must be applied consistently to categories of instruments within trading units. Banks may elect to use a different method in, for instance, an overseas branch to the method adopted in their Head Office. This could result in a bank applying both methods 1 and 2 to a single currency but the capital requirements generated by the two methods must be added arithmetically together. The steps in calculating the general risk requirement for interest rate positions under method 2 are set out below. A worked example is given in Table 5.4.

    (a) The bank will take the market value, for each individual net position (see paragraphs 9 and 10) of each fixed rate instrument—whether or not it is coupon bearing—and determine its Yield-To-Maturity (Redemption Yield).
For each individual net position (see paragraphs 9 and 10) in floating rate instruments the bank will take the market value and treat as its final maturity the date on which the coupon is next re-determined. The bank will then derive a Yield-To-Maturity.

    (b) For each debt instrument the bank will calculate the modified duration of each instrument on the basis of the following formula according to the deemed maturity in (a) above[1]:

$$\text{modified duration} = \frac{\text{duration}(D)}{(1 + r)}$$

$$D = \frac{\sum_{t=1}^{m} \dfrac{t \cdot C_t}{(1 + r)^t}}{\sum_{t=1}^{m} \dfrac{C_t}{(1 + r)^t}}$$

    r = Yield-To-Maturity %pa expressed as a decimal
    C = Cashflow at time t
    t = time at which cashflows occur in years
    m = time to maturity in years

    (c) Individual net positions, at current market value, will be allocated to one of the three zones described in Table 5.4, below, based upon the modified duration.

    (d) The bank will then calculate the modified duration-weighted position for each individual net position by multiplying its current market value by the modified duration and the assumed change in rates to form the weighted positions.

    (e) To calculate the matched and unmatched positions per zone: where a zone has both weighted long and short positions, the extent to which the one offsets the other is called the matched weighted position for that zone. The remainder (ie the excess of the weighted long positions over the weighted short positions, or vice versa) is called the unmatched weighted position for that zone.

    (f) Unmatched weighted positions for a zone may be offset against positions in other zones as follows:

        (i) The unmatched weighted long (short) position for zone 1 may offset the unmatched weighted short (long) position in zone 2. The extent to which the unmatched weighted positions in zones 1 and 2 are offsetting is described as the matched weighted position between zones 1 and 2.

    (ii) After (i), any residual unmatched weighted long (short) positions in zone 2 may then be matched by the unmatched weighted short (long) positions in zone 3. The extent to which the unmatched positions in zones 2 and 3 are offsetting is described as the matched weighted position between zones 2 and 3.

The calculations in (i) and (ii) may be carried out in reverse order (ie zones 2 and 3 followed by zones 1 and 2).

    (iii) After (i) and (ii) any residual unmatched weighted long (short) positions in zone 1 may then be matched by offsetting unmatched weighted short (long) positions in zone 3. The extent to which the unmatched positions in zones 1 and 3 are offsetting is described as the matched weighted position between zones 1 and 3.

(g) Any residual unmatched weighted positions following the matching within a zone and between zones will be summed.

26 The general interest rate risk capital requirements will be the sum of:

(a) Matched Weighted Positions in all Zones	× 2%
(b) Matched Weighted Positions between Zones 1 & 2	× 40%
(c) Matched Weighted Positions between Zones 2 & 3	× 40%
(d) Matched Weighted Positions between Zones 1 & 3	× 150%
(e) Residual Unmatched Weighted Positions	× 100%

---

[1] This formula does not contain provisions for any embedded options. As a result the final maturity must be used for fixed rate instruments in all cases.

Derivatives

27 Many banks will seek approval to use individual models to assess the interest rate risk inherent in derivatives. The output of recognised interest rate sensitivity models will be fed into Interest Rate Exposure Method 2 above. Banks may also seek approval of risk management models for options. If the buffer approach is adopted for options, the delta will be incorporated in Interest Rate Exposure Method 2 above and there will be add-ons for the other 'greek' risks. The scenario method for options will give rise to a single figure for interest rate risk, that will not be fed into the maturity ladders. For more detail on the recognition of models see Chapter 8—The Model Review Process. Where a bank does not propose to use models, it must use the techniques described below for exchange or OTC traded derivatives (including the simple method for options). Model review is intended for large, dynamically managed portfolios; rather than one-off deals. The business to which the model pertains should be a significant component of the bank's activities. Where a bank has express written approval for the use of non-interest rate derivatives models then the embedded interest rate exposures may also be incorporated into the treatments described below.

FX FORWARDS

28 FX Forwards are captured by this chapter and the position is decomposed into legs representing the paying and receiving currencies.

(a) Each of these legs will be treated as if they were zero coupon bonds with zero specific risk in their respective currencies.

(b) If the forward positions are not consistently revalued using discounting or present value techniques then the present value of the payment is inserted into the maturity band approach, Interest Rate Exposure Method 1.

(c) If the forward positions are consistently revalued using discounting or present value techniques then they may be inserted into the duration band approach, Interest Rate Exposure Method 2.

(d) For FX forward positions subject to the duration approach, Interest Rate Exposure Method 2, pre-calculation netting will be permitted (see paragraph 35).

DEPOSIT FUTURES AND FRAS

29 Deposit futures, FRAs (Forward Rate Agreements) and other instruments where the underlying is a money market exposure will be split into two legs.

    (a) The first leg will represent the time to the expiry of the futures contract or the settlement date of the FRA.

    (b) The second leg will represent the time to the expiry of the underlying instrument.

    (c) Each leg will be treated as a zero coupon bond with zero specific risk for the maturity bands, Interest Rate Exposure Method 1, with a size that represents the notional underlying amount.

    (d) For Interest Rate Exposure Method 2 the present values of the notional zero coupon bonds must be used.

For example under Interest Rate Exposure Method 1 a single 3 month Euro$ deposit futures contract expiring in 8 months time will have one leg of $1,000,000 representing the 8 months to contract expiry and another leg of $1,000,000 in the 11 months time band representing the time to expiry of the deposit underlying the futures contract.

Given the way in which futures contracts are traded care should be taken in deciding upon the long and short legs. These positions may benefit from the application of netting (see paragraph 35).

BOND FUTURES AND FORWARD BOND TRANSACTIONS

30 Bond futures, forward bond transactions and the forward leg of repos, reverse repos and other similar transactions (see Chapter 2—Counterparty Risk for detail on what constitutes a similar transaction), will use the two-legged approach. A forward bond transaction is one where settlement is for a period other than the prevailing norm for the market and this may attract counterparty exposure requirements, see Chapter 2—Counterparty Risk. This is distinct from a bond position that may arise from the exercise of a bond option where the holder of the bond option would in any event have a counterparty exposure requirement against the option writer.

    (a) The first leg represents the time to expiry of the futures or forward contract.

    (b) The second leg represents the time to maturity of the underlying bond for fixed rate bonds or the time to the next reset for floating rate bonds.

    (c) For bond forward transactions the underlying bond and amount is used at the present spot price.

    (d) For bond futures the principal amounts in each of these two legs may be generated by one of two processes:

        (i) It may be treated as the notional underlying bond upon which the contract is based using the future price times the notional underlying amount; or

        (ii) Subject to (e) and (f) below it may be one of the deliverable bonds for that contract using the futures price and the conversion factors.

    (e) Under the terms of the futures contract where the 'short' has a choice of deliverable bonds then the 'long' may use one of the deliverable bonds, or the notional bond on which the contract is based, as the underlying instrument, *but* this notional long leg may not be offset against a short cash position in the same bond.

    (f) Under the terms of the futures contract where the 'short' has a choice of deliverable bonds then the 'short' may treat the notional underlying bond as if it were one of the deliverable bonds which may be netted against a long cash position in the same bond.

Care must be taken in the use of conversion factors to transform the bond futures into equivalent cash positions.

SWAPS

31 Swaps will be decomposed into two legs and each of the legs may benefit from the application of netting (see paragraph 35).

(a) For Currency swaps the two parts of the transaction will be split into FX forward contracts and treated accordingly. Alternatively such swaps may be treated as having a fixed/floating leg in each currency.

(b) Interest Rate swaps will also be split into two legs. Each leg will be allocated to the maturity band equating to the time remaining to refixing. However, for complex swaps involving the use of constant maturity bonds for example, then advice must be sought.

For example a $10 Million 5 year fixed/floating swap against 3 month LIBOR would have notional positions of $10 Million in the 5 year maturity band and $10 Million in the 3 month band. The 5 year leg will be weighted according to whether its notional coupon is over or under 3%.

Where a swap has a deferred start it may also be subject to the two leg treatment. A swap will be considered to have a deferred start when the commencement of the interest rate calculation periods is more than two business days from the transaction date and one or both legs have been fixed at the time of commitment. When one or more legs has been fixed then that leg will be sub-divided into the time to the commencement of the leg and the actual swap leg fixed or floating rate. Where the swap has a deferred start and neither leg has been set then there is no interest rate exposure, but there will be counterparty exposure. When a rate has yet to be set, the swap will be treated as having a zero add on and by definition, the mark-to-market must be zero. The treatment in this paragraph is distinct from a swap that arises from the exercise of a Swaption.

Where a swap has a different structure such as multiplier or constant maturity based cashflows, then it may be necessary to adjust the underlying notional principal amount, or the notional maturity of one or both legs of the transaction.

OPTIONS

32 Subject to Bank approval, netting of back-to-back options positions may be permitted.

33 Banks which do not have an approved model for options should apply the simple method (carve out) for options. Details of this method are in Annex I to this Chapter. The specific risk arising from bond options will be based on the delta weighted amount of the underlying debt instrument.

INDEX LINKED GILTS

34 Index linked gilts will be subject to a special treatment for general market risk. The capital requirement must be calculated as if they were a separate currency of issue and different weights will apply to each of the matched and unmatched positions. This treatment is identical to that proposed by the Bank's Wholesale Markets Supervision Division. Banks wishing for more details on how to calculate the capital requirement on such gilts should contact their line supervisor.

Netting of General Market Risk Positions

35 If banks wish to net general market risk positions prior to the general market risk calculations, they may choose to do so on an aggregate basis within and between the following sources of exposures:

(a) Foreign Currency Forwards;
(b) Deposit Futures, and FRAs;
(c) Swaps; *and*
(d) Interest Rate Exposures arising from other derivatives.

For netting to be recognised the positions must be:

(i) in the same currency; *and*
(ii) their coupons, if any, must be within 15 basis points; *and*
(iii) the next interest fixing date, or residual maturity corresponds with the following limits:
  – less than one month hence: same day
  – between one month and one year hence: within seven days
  – over one year hence: within 30 days.

Annex I: Simple Method for Options (Carve Out)

1 The table below should be used to calculate the market risk requirements for options or warrants on the following: bonds; interest rates and their futures; and swaps; their variants; plus any related hedges. These figures may only be used for options with a residual maturity of less than six months; for longer maturity options advice must be sought. (Banks that have models which have been recognised by the Bank of England should not use the method prescribed below for those option models that have been recognised.)

	Option Position	In the Money by more than P% or Q%	In the Money by less than P% or Q%	Out of the Money
Naked	Long Call	NL	NL	NL
	Long Put	NL	NL	NL
	Short Call	NSI	NSI	NSO
	Short Put	NSI	NSI	NSO
Long in	Long Put	0%	LPI	HO
Underlying	Short Call	0%	SHI	HO
Short in	Long Call	0%	LCI	HO
Underlying	Short Put	0%	SHI	HO

In the Money means that the exercise level of a call option or warrant is less than the current mark-to-market value of the underlying instrument and, for put options or warrants that the current mark-to-market value of the underlying is less than the exercise level of the put option or warrant.

Out of the Money means those options and warrants that are not In the Money.

For bond options (where the strike is based upon a price) P% is the sum of the specific and general market risk, under Method 1, for that underlying instrument as if it was the only component in a portfolio.

For options where the strike is based on a yield we determine Q%, the 'assumed interest rate change' from Table 2 in Annex 1 of the CAD (see Annex 1 to Chapter 8—The Model Review Process) based upon the life of the instrument underlying the option. Y% is then Q% multiplied by the period of the underlying. Thus, for example, a two year option on a three month rate would have $Q = 1.00\%$ and $Y = 0.25\%$. A three month option on a two year swap would have $Q = 0.90\%$ and $Y = 1.80\%$.

The capital requirements for *price* based options and their associated hedges are:
NL   The lesser of:
     (a) the market value of the underlying instrument multiplied by P%; *and*
     (b) the current value of the option on the bank's books
NSI The market value of the underlying position multiplied by P%
NSO The market value of the underlying position multiplied by P% minus 0.5 multiplied by the amount by which the option is Out of Money (subject to a maximum reduction to zero)
LPI The market value of the underlying position minus $(1 - P\%)$ multiplied by the underlying position valued at the exercise price
HO   The market value of the underlying position multiplied by P%
SHI The market value of the underlying position multiplied by P% minus the mark-to-market value of the option (subject to a maximum reduction to zero)
LCI $(1 + P\%)$ multiplied by the underlying position valued at the exercise price minus the market value of the underlying position
The capital requirements for *yield* based options and their associated hedges are:
NL   The lesser of:
     (a) the notional amount of the underlying instrument multiplied by Y%; *and*
     (b) the current value of the option on the bank's books

NSI The notional amount of the underlying position multiplied by Y%
NSO The notional amount of the underlying position multiplied by Y% minus 0.5 multiplied by the amount by which the option is Out of the Money (subject to a maximum reduction to zero)
LPI As for SHI below
HO The notional amount of the underlying position multiplied by Y%
SHI The notional amount of the underlying position multiplied by Y% minus the mark-to-market value of the option (subject to a maximum reduction to zero)
LCI As for SHI above

If a bank is unable to determine whether an option is in or out of the money, then the capital charge is the notional amount of underlying multiplied by Y%.

EXAMPLE OF CARVE-OUT APPROACH

2 Consider the example of a £1mn notional cap at 7.00% with four remaining semi-annual caplets and three months to exercise the first of these. Treating these four caplets in the standard way as individual options on FRAs we get:

	Option	Underlying	Q%	Y%
Caplet 1	3 months	6 months	100bp	50bp
Caplet 2	9 months	6 months	100bp	50bp
Caplet 3	15 months	6 months	100bp	50bp
Caplet 4	21 months	6 months	100bp	50bp

3 Now consider, for example, that the current 6 month rate 9 months forward is 7.50%. The second caplet is 'in the money' by 50bp, but thus by less than Q%, which is 100bp. The capital charge for each caplet can thus be determined from the forward rates and definitions above.

4 Alternatively, an institution might treat the cap as a single item, where in this case Q = 100bp still (since the underlying is a six month rate) and Y = 2% (the combined period of the string of FRAs). The 'at the money level' is now the single cap level at which owning all four of the FRAs has neither positive nor negative net present value (often referred to as the par rate for a cap).

5 The Bank of England is aware that these calculations are only approximate, and tend to overstate the market risk of options. Institutions whose option positions are large so that this overstatement puts them at a significant disadvantage are encouraged to apply for model recognition as described in Chapter 8—The Model Review Process.

Annex II: Simplified Method for Calculation of Capital Requirement

1 As the figure for the capital requirement generated by this simplified method is less precise than that generated by the above methods, it will generate a higher capital requirement. Banks which intend to adopt this method should discuss their intention with their line supervisor.

2 One general market risk calculation is required for each currency irrespective of where the individual instruments are physically traded or listed. Specific risk requirements are determined on an instrument by instrument basis. The resulting capital requirements must be converted into the reporting currency by applying the prevailing foreign exchange spot rates. For a list of the positions, instruments and exposures captured in this section see the main introduction to this chapter. The main body of the chapter should be referred to for detail on the treatment of derivative instruments.

INDIVIDUAL NET POSITIONS

3 A bank may net, by value, long and short positions in the same debt instrument to generate the individual net position in that instrument. Instruments will be considered to be the same where the issuer is the same, and the equivalent ranking in a liquidation, and the currency, the coupon, and the maturity are the same.

4 A bank may net by value a long or short position in one tranche of a debt instrument against another tranche only where the relevant tranches:

    (a) rank pari passu in all respects; *and*

    (b) become fungible within 180 days and thereafter the debt instruments of one tranche can be delivered in settlement of the other tranche.

SPECIFIC RISK CALCULATION

5 In determining its specific risk capital requirement for positions in debt instruments a bank must calculate the sum of the weighted current market value of each of its individual net positions, whether long or short, according to the following weights:

		Weighting
(a)	Certain Central Government debt instruments	0.00%
(b)	Qualifying Items up to 6 months residual maturity	0.25%
(c)	Qualifying Items over 6 months residual maturity	1.60%
(d)	Non-Qualifying Items	8.00%

6 Debt instruments will be given a 0% specific risk weighting if:

    (a) they are issued by, fully guaranteed by, or fully collateralised by securities issued by Zone A central governments and central banks, including the European Communities; or

    (b) they are issued by, or fully guaranteed by, Zone B central governments and central banks with a residual maturity of 1 year or less and are denominated in local currency and funded by liabilities in the same currency.

7 A list of Zone A countries was originally provided in policy notice BSD/1990/3 (Implementation in the United Kingdom of the Solvency Ratio Directive) and updated by policy notice S&S/1995/1. All other countries not included in Zone A are in Zone B.

8 Debt instruments will be treated as qualifying if any of the following conditions apply:

    (a) they are issued by, or fully guaranteed by, Zone B central governments and central banks with a residual maturity of over 1 year and are denominated in local currency and funded by liabilities in the same currency;

    (b) they are securities issued by, or fully collateralised by claims on, a multilateral development bank listed in the Solvency Ratio Directive. (See Chapter 11— Lists for a list of these institutions.) The European Commission may amend this list periodically;

    (c) they are issued, guaranteed, endorsed, or accepted, by a credit institution incorporated in a Zone A country;

    (d) they are issued, or guaranteed, endorsed, or accepted, by a credit institution incorporated in a Zone B country and have a residual maturity of 1 year or less;

    (e) they are issued, or guaranteed, by an investment firm that is subject to the Capital Adequacy Directive, or a regime that the Bank deems to be as stringent;

    (f) they are issued by, or guaranteed by, Zone A public sector entities;

    (g) they are issued by, or guaranteed by, a company whose equity is eligible for 2% equity specific risk weighting (see Chapter 6—Equity Position Risk).

9 Debt items issued by entities not covered by the descriptions in the preceding paragraph *may still* be treated as qualifying if the issue, or an issue of equivalent ranking in a liquidation, or an issue of equivalent ranking in a liquidation of the guarantor, is rated investment grade (or its equivalent for money market obligations), or above and provided that the reporting bank is unaware of any sub-investment grade rating issued by any relevant credit rating agency. When the reporting bank is aware of an announcement that the issue may be downgraded to below investment grade, by at least one relevant credit rating agency[1], that debt will cease to be qualifying unless it meets the criteria of the preceding paragraphs.

10 Debt instruments where the issuer does not meet the requirements established above (paragraphs 6 to 9 inclusive) are deemed to be non-qualifying.

---

[1] See Chapter 11—Lists for a list of agencies and investment grade ratings.

GENERAL MARKET RISK CALCULATION[1]

11 A separate general market interest rate risk calculation is calculated for each currency irrespective of where the individual instruments are physically traded or listed. The resultant capital requirements must be converted into the reporting currency by applying the prevailing foreign exchange spot rates. These capital requirements are summed arithmetically to give the total general market risk requirement.

12 The Bank does not intend to distinguish explicitly between the level of general market risk capital requirement for different currencies. However, it recognises that yield curves in some currencies are more volatile and that their markets are less liquid with fewer hedging mechanisms available. When a bank has a portfolio with interest risk in such currencies, this will be taken fully into account when setting the target and trigger capital ratios (see Chapter 9—Own Funds).

13 The capital requirements for general market risk are intended to recognise the risk of parallel and non-parallel shifts in the yield curve. The bank must allocate individual net positions to one of the maturity bands in Table 5.3 below, on the following basis:

    (i) Fixed-rate instruments will be allotted their maturity bands based upon the residual time to maturity—irrespective of embedded puts and calls—and whether their coupon is below 3%.

    (ii) Floating rate instruments will be allocated to maturity bands based upon the time remaining to the re-determination of the coupon.

14 The bank must then sum the market value of its individual net positions within each band irrespective of whether they are long or short positions to produce a gross position figure. This figure should then be multiplied by the weighting factor for the relevant maturity band. These weighted figures should then be summed to give the capital requirement for general market risk.

---

[1] Table 5.5 illustrates this method. Table 5.6 gives an example.

Table 5.1 – Interest Rate General Risk Method 1 – Maturity Bands, Risk Weights

Zone	Band — Coupon of 3% or more	Band — Coupon of under 3%	Individual Net Positions Long	Individual Net Positions Short	Weighting Factors	Weighted Net Positions Long	Weighted Net Positions Short	By Band Matched	By Band Unmatched	By Zone Matched	By Zone Unmatched	Between Zones Matched	Between Zones Matched
1	1 month & under	1 month & under			0.00%								
	1 to 3 months	1 to 3 months			0.20%					B			
	3 to 6 months	3 to 6 months			0.40%								
	6 to 12 months	6 to 12 months			0.70%							Zones 1 & 2	Zones 1 & 3
2	1 to 2 years	1 to 1.9 years			1.25%							E	
	2 to 3 years	1.9 to 2.8 years			1.75%					C			H
	3 to 4 years	2.8 to 3.6 years			2.25%								
3	4 to 5 years	3.6 to 4.3 years			2.75%							Zones 2 & 3	
	5 to 7 years	4.3 to 5.7 years			3.25%							F	
	7 to 10 years	5.7 to 7.3 years			3.75%								
	10 to 15 years	7.3 to 9.3 years			4.50%					D			
	15 to 20 years	9.3 to 10.6 years			5.25%								
	Over 20 years	10.6 to 12 years			6.00%								
		12 to 20 years			8.00%								
		Over 20 years			12.50%								
Totals of Column								A			G		

Total General Interest Rate Risk Capital Requirement = 10%A + 40%B + 30%(C + D) + 40%(E + F) + 100%G + 150%H =

Note: For instruments the maturity of which is on the boundary of two maturity bands, the instrument should be placed into the earlier maturity band. For example instruments with a maturity of exactly one year are placed into the 6 to 12 months band.

Table 5.2 – Interest Rate General Risk Method 1 – Example

Zone	Band (Coupon of 3% or more)	Band (Coupon of under 3%)	Individual Net Positions Long	Individual Net Positions Short	Weighting Factors	Weighted Net Positions Long	Weighted Net Positions Short	By Band Matched	By Band Unmatched	By Zone Matched	By Zone Unmatched	Between Zones Matched (1&2 / 2&3)	Between Zones Matched (1&3)
1	1 month & under	1 month & under	£100	−£50	0.00%	£0.00	£0.00	£0.00	£0.00				
	1 to 3 months	1 to 3 months	£200	−£100	0.20%	£0.40	−£0.20	£0.20	£0.20	£0.00	£1.30		
	3 to 6 months	3 to 6 months	£300	−£200	0.40%	£1.20	−£0.80	£0.80	£0.40			Zones 1 & 2	
	6 to 12 months	6 to 12 months	£400	−£300	0.70%	£2.80	−£2.10	£2.10	£0.70			£1.30	
2	1 to 2 years	1 to 1.9 years	£100	−£200	1.25%	£1.25	−£2.50	£1.25	−£1.25				
	2 to 3 years	1.9 to 2.8 years	£200	−£300	1.75%	£3.50	−£5.25	£3.50	−£1.75	£0.00	−£5.25		
	3 to 4 years	2.8 to 3.6 years	£300	−£400	2.25%	£6.75	−£9.00	£6.75	−£2.25			Zones 2 & 3	
3	4 to 5 years	3.6 to 4.3 years	£100	−£100	2.75%	£2.75	−£2.75	£2.75	£0.00			£3.95	
	5 to 7 years	4.3 to 5.7 years	£200	−£200	3.25%	£6.50	−£6.50	£6.50	£0.00				Zones 1 & 3
	7 to 10 years	5.7 to 7.3 years	£300	−£100	3.75%	£11.25	−£3.75	£3.75	£7.50	£4.50	£8.25		£0.00
	10 to 15 years	7.3 to 9.3 years	£100	−£200	4.50%	£4.50	−£9.00	£4.50	−£4.50				
	15 to 20 years	9.3 to 10.6 years	£200	−£100	5.25%	£10.50	−£5.25	£5.25	£5.25				
	Over 20 years	10.6 to 12 months	£300	−£300	6.00%	£18.00	−£18.00	£18.00	£0.00				
		12 to 20 years			8.00%								
		Over 20 years			12.50%								

Totals of Columns £2,800 −£2,550 ..... £55.35

General Interest Rate Risk Capital Requirement £5.54 ..... £1.35 £4.30 ..... £2.10 £0.00

Total General Interest Rate Risk Capital Requirement = £13.29

Note: For instruments the maturity of which is on the boundary of two maturity bands, the instrument should be placed into the earlier maturity band. For example instruments with a maturity of exactly one year are placed into the 6 to 12 months band.

Table 5.3 – Interest Rate General Risk Method 2 – Duration Bands, Risk Weights

A Zone	B Modified Duration (yrs)	C Individual Net positions Long	D Short	E Assumed move in rates (%pa)	F Modified Duration (yrs)	G Weighted Individual Net Positions Long	H Short	I By Zone Matched	J Unmatched	K Between Zones Matched	L Between Zones Matched
1	1 Year & Under			1.00%		C × E × F	D × E × F				
				1.00%		C × E × F	D × E × F			Zones 1 & 2	Zones 1 & 3
				1.00%		C × E × F	D × E × F			W	
		X	X		TOTAL	SUM	SUM	T			
2	1 to 3.6 years			0.85%		C × E × F	D × E × F				
				0.85%		C × E × F	D × E × F	U			Z
				0.85%		C × E × F	D × E × F			Zones 2 & 3	
		X	X		TOTAL	SUM	SUM			X	
3	Over 3.6 years			0.70%		C × E × F	D × E × F				
				0.70%		C × E × F	D × E × F	V			
				0.70%		C × E × F	D × E × F				
		X	X		TOTAL	SUM	SUM				
Totals of Columns		£0	£0						Y		

General Interest Rate Capital Requirement = 2%(T + U + V) + 40%(W + X) + 100%Y + 150%Z

Assumption: This example assumes a portfolio that has three positions in each of the zones. This is for illustration only, as banks might have any number of positions per zone.

Note: For instruments the maturity of which is on the boundary of two maturity bands, the instrument should be placed into the earlier maturity band. For example instruments with a maturity of exactly one year are placed into the 1 year and under band.

Table 5.4 – Interest Rate General Risk Method 2 – Example

Zone	Modified Duration (yrs)	Individual Net positions Long	Short	Assumed move in rates (%pa)	Modified Duration (yrs)	Weighted Individual Net Positions Long	Short	By Zone Matched	By Zone Unmatched	Between Zones Matched	Between Zones Matched
1	1 Year & Under	£100	−£50	1.00%	0.00	£0.00	£0.00				
		£200	−£100	1.00%	0.20	£0.40	−£0.20				
		£300	−£200	1.00%	0.40	£1.20	−£0.80	£3.10			
		£400	−£300	1.00%	0.70	£2.80	−£2.10		£1.30		
		X	X		TOTAL	£4.40	−£3.10			Zones 1 & 2	
										£1.30	
2	1 to 3.6 years	£100	−£200	0.85%	1.40	£1.19	−£2.38				
		£200	−£300	0.85%	2.20	£3.74	−£5.61	£12.58	−£5.61		Zones 1 & 3
		£300	−£400	0.85%	3.00	£7.65	−£10.20				£0.00
		X	X		TOTAL	£12.58	−£18.19				
3	Over 3.6 years	£100	−£100	0.70%	3.65	£2.56	−£2.56			Zones 2 & 3	
		£200	−£200	0.70%	4.65	£6.51	−£6.51			£4.31	
		£300	−£100	0.70%	5.80	£12.18	−£4.06	£50.75	£9.00		
		£100	−£200	0.70%	7.50	£5.25	−£10.50				
		£200	−£100	0.70%	8.75	£12.25	−£6.13				
		£300	−£300	0.70%	10.00	£21.00	−£21.00				
		X	X		TOTAL	£59.75	−£50.75		£4.69		

Totals: £2,800 −£2,550

General Interest Rate Capital Requirement = 2%(£3.10 + £12.58 + £50.75) + 40%(£1.30 + £1.30 + £4.31) + 100%£4.69 + 150%£0 =

Total General Interest Rate Risk Capital Requirement = £8.26

Assumption: This example uses the same portfolio as was used in Table 9.1 (maturity based approach). The modified duration values are derived from that example. This example is for illustration only, as banks might have any number of positions in each zone, the modified duration of each being calculated on a case by case basis.

Note: For instruments the maturity of which is on the boundary of two maturity bands, the instrument should be placed into the earlier maturity band. For example instruments with a maturity of exactly one year are placed into the 1 year and under band.

Interest Rate General Risk Simplified Method – Maturity Bands, Risk Weights

Zone	Band		Individual Net Positions		Gross Position	Weighting Factors	Capital Requirement
	Coupon of 3% or more	Coupon of under 3%	Long	Short			
1	1 month & under	1 month & under				0.00%	
	1 to 3 months	1 to 3 months				0.20%	
	3 to 6 months	3 to 6 months				0.40%	
	6 to 12 months	6 to 12 months				0.70%	
2	1 to 2 years	1 to 1.9 years				1.25%	
	2 to 3 years	1.9 to 2.8 years				1.75%	
	3 to 4 years	2.8 to 3.6 years				2.25%	
3	4 to 5 years	3.6 to 4.3 years				2.75%	
	5 to 7 years	4.3 to 5.7 years				3.25%	
	7 to 10 years	5.7 to 7.3 years				3.75%	
	10 to 15 years	7.3 to 9.3 years				4.50%	
	15 to 20 years	9.3 to 10.6 years				5.25%	
	Over 20 years	10.6 to 12 years				6.00%	
		12 to 20 years				8.00%	
		Over 20 years				12.50%	

General Interest Rate Risk Capital Requirement

Total General Interest Rate Risk Capital Requirement =

Note: For instruments the maturity of which is on the boundary of two maturity bands, the instrument should be placed into the earlier maturity band. For example instruments with a maturity of exactly one year are placed into the 6 to 12 months band.

Table 5.6 – Interest Rate General Risk Simplified Method – Example

Zone	Band Coupon of 3% or more	Band Coupon of under 3%	Individual Net Positions Long	Individual Net Positions Short	Gross Position	Weighting Factors	Capital Requirement
1	1 month & under	1 month & under	£100	−£50	£150	0.00%	£0.00
	1 to 3 months	1 to 3 months	£200	−£100	£300	0.20%	£0.60
	3 to 6 months	3 to 6 months	£300	−£200	£500	0.40%	£2.00
	6 to 12 months	6 to 12 months	£400	−£300	£700	0.70%	£4.90
2	1 to 2 years	1 to 1.9 years	£100	−£200	£300	1.25%	£3.75
	2 to 3 years	1.9 to 2.8 years	£200	−£300	£500	1.75%	£8.75
	3 to 4 years	2.8 to 3.6 years	£300	−£400	£700	2.25%	£15.75
3	4 to 5 years	3.6 to 4.3 years	£100	−£100	£200	2.75%	£5.50
	5 to 7 years	4.3 to 5.7 years	£200	−£200	£400	3.25%	£13.00
	7 to 10 years	5.7 to 7.3 years	£300	−£100	£400	3.75%	£15.00
	10 to 15 years	7.3 to 9.3 years	£100	−£200	£300	4.50%	£13.50
	15 to 20 years	9.3 to 10.6 years	£200	−£100	£300	5.25%	£15.75
	Over 20 years	10.6 to 12 years	£300	−£300	£600	6.00%	£36.00
		12 to 20 years				8.00%	
		Over 20 years				12.50%	
			£2,800	−£2,550			

General Interest Rate Risk Capital Requirement   £134.50

Total General Interest Rate Risk Capital Requirement =   £134.50

Note: For instruments the maturity of which is on the boundary of two maturity bands, the instrument should be placed into the earlier maturity band. For example instruments with a maturity of exactly one year are placed into the 6 to 12 months band.

Chapter 6—Equity Position Risk

Explanation

1 A bank which holds equity positions (whether long or short) in the trading book is exposed to the risk that the equity market as a whole may move against it—general risk—and that the value of individual equity positions relative to the market may move against the bank—specific risk. The general risk requirements set out in this chapter recognise offsetting positions within national markets. The specific risk requirements recognise that individual equities are subject to issuer risk and liquidity risk, and that these risks may be reduced by portfolio diversification. The chapter also sets out the treatment for related derivative positions.

2 This chapter describes three methods by which banks may calculate their capital requirements for equity positions held in the trading book: the standard method; a simplified method; and an alternative method. There are no existing Bank of England Policy Notices covering equities; the approaches adopted here are in general similar to those of The Securities and Futures Authority.

3 Paragraph 21 of this chapter outlines a simplified method for the calculation of trading book capital requirements for equity position risk, which banks may choose to adopt. The capital requirement generated by application of the simplified method will usually be higher than that which would result from applying the standard method. If banks choose to apply this method they should seek permission from their line supervisor and, in most circumstances, they would be expected to adopt the simplified method also for interest rate position risk (see Chapter 5—Interest Rate Position Risk).

4 The following section of the Capital Adequacy Directive is covered by this Chapter:

- Annex I, paragraphs 31–38.

Scope

5 This Chapter applies to positions and exposures (including forward positions) in the trading book of the following instruments:

    (a) shares;
    (b) depository receipts (see paragraph 6);
    (c) convertible preference securities (non-convertible preference securities should be treated as bonds);
    (d) convertible debt securities which convert into other instruments in this list and are treated as equities (see paragraph 7); *and*
    (e) derivatives based on the above.

6 Depository receipts should be converted into the underlying shares and allocated to the same country as the underlying shares.

7 Convertibles as defined in paragraph 5(d) *must* be treated as equities where

    (a) the first date at which conversion may take place is less than three months ahead, or the next such date (where the first has passed) is less than a year ahead; *and*
    (b) the convertible is trading at a premium of less than 10%, where the premium is defined as the current mark-to-market value of the convertible less the mark-to-market value of the underlying equity, expressed as a percentage of the mark-to-market value of the underlying equity.

Convertibles other than those defined above may be treated as equity or debt securities (see Chapter 5—Interest Rate Position Risk).

8 For instruments which deviate from the structures listed in pararaphs 5 to 7 above, or which could be considered complex, each bank should agree a policy statement with their supervisor about the intended treatment. The treatment of some instruments may be uncertain, (for example, bonds whose coupon payments are linked to equity indices): where possible the position risk of such instruments should be broken down into its components and allocated appropriately between the equity, interest rate and foreign

exchange risk categories. Advice must be sought from supervisors in cases of doubt, and when a bank is trading an instrument for the first time.

9 Where a trading book position results from underwriting activities, the capital requirement may be reduced in accordance with the parameters described in Chapter 7—Underwriting.

10 Where a bank has physical long equity positions in its trading book composed of capital instruments issued by other institutions, the current market value of these positions must be deducted from its capital base, unless the bank has permission to treat the position under a market-maker's concession. **Recognition will be given, however, for any hedging benefits of such positions against other market exposures in calculating capital requirements for position risk (see Chapter 1— The Trading Book).**

Calculation of Capital Requirements—Standard Method

11 Equity positions, arising either directly or through derivatives, should be allocated to the country in which each equity is listed and the calculations described below applied to each country. Capital requirements should be converted into sterling at the prevailing spot foreign exchange rate. Annex I describes an alternative to the basic method.

NETTING

12 A bank may net long and short positions in the same equity instrument, arising either directly or through derivatives, to generate the individual net position in that instrument. Interest rate exposure arising from derivatives must, however, be treated as set out in paragraphs 28–33 below. For the treatment of equity indices, see paragraphs 26 and 27.

13 A bank may net long and short positions in one tranche of an equity instrument against another tranche only where the relevant tranches:

    (a) rank pari passu in all respects; and
    (b) become fungible within 180 days, and thereafter the equity instruments of one
        tranche can be delivered in settlement of the other tranche.

Specific Risk Calculation

14 For each country, the bank should sum the market value of its individual net positions, as determined in paragraphs 11–13, *irrespective of whether they are long or short positions* to produce the overall gross equity position for that country.

QUALIFYING COUNTRIES

15 Chapter 11 sets out the current list of qualifying countries for equity specific risk. The list may be amended periodically, and information likely to be considered in doing so is given in Chapter 11. The Bank will consider carefully any changes to this list made by The Securities and Futures Authority.

16 For equity instruments that are not listed in one of the qualifying countries, the specific risk capital requirement is 8% of the overall gross equity position. For equity instruments that *are* listed in one of the qualifying countries the specific risk requirement is 4% of the overall gross equity position, unless the conditions in paragraphs 17 and 18 are met.

HIGHLY LIQUID INSTRUMENTS AND DIVERSIFIED PORTFOLIOS

17 For equity instruments listed in a qualifying country which are also deemed to be highly liquid (see paragraph 18), the specific risk capital requirement may be further reduced to 2% of the overall gross position of those highly liquid equities, providing that the following portfolio diversification requirements are met:

    (a) No individual highly liquid equity position shall comprise more than 10% of the
        gross value of the country portfolio; and
    (b) The total value of gross highly liquid equity positions which individually
        comprise between 5% and 10% of the gross value of the country portfolio shall
        not exceed 50% of the gross value of that country portfolio.

If a country portfolio can be split into two sub-portfolios such that one of the sub-portfolios would meet the diversification requirements, the lower specific risk requirement may be applied to the diversified sub-portfolio (individual positions may be sub-divided between sub-portfolios). Portfolios or sub-portfolios which do not meet the above requirements will continue to attract the 4% specific risk weight.

18 Individual equities included in the indices listed in Chapter 11 are considered to be highly liquid. This list of indices may be amended periodically, and the information likely to be used in doing so is set out in Chapter 11. The Bank will consider carefully any changes to this list made by The Securities and Futures Authority.

19 A stock of a UK incorporated company traded on the London Stock Exchange, but not a component of an index listed in Chapter 11, will also be considered to be highly liquid if it has:

    (i) at least 6 registered market makers; *and*
    (ii) has a Normal Market Size (NMS) of at least 5,000 shares.

Equities listed in a qualifying country which are included in the FT-Actuaries World Indices are also considered to be highly liquid.

20 The criteria for defining highly liquid equities in other EU/EEA countries may be reviewed in the light of decisions by supervisors in those countries concerning the definitions they employ for highly liquid equities in their domestic markets when implementing the Capital Adequacy Directive.

Simplified Method for Specific Risk

21 The capital requirement generated by this simplified method is less precise than that generated by the standard method, and it will usually, therefore, result in a higher capital requirement. Banks which intend to adopt this method should discuss their intention with their line supervisor. Under this method banks may choose not to apply the tests in paragraphs 17 and 18 above. Further, they may choose simply to assign a specific risk requirement of 8% to all equity instruments.

General Risk Calculation

22 For the general risk calculation, the bank should sum the market value of its individual net positions for each country, as determined in paragraphs 11–13, *taking into account long and short positions*, to produce the overall net equity position for that country. The general risk capital requirement for each country will be 8% of the overall net position, unless the provisions of paragraphs 23 or 24 apply.

23 Where an individual net position represents more than 20% of the gross equity position of that country (as defined in paragraph 14), the amount of the individual net position in excess of 20% must be added in to the overall net equity position calculation on a gross basis.

24 Subject to certain criteria listed below, inter-market offsets are recognised between country portfolios with indices listed in Chapter 11, such that the total general market risk requirement for these portfolios is calculated as:

$$\sqrt{\omega_i^2 + \omega_j^2 + \omega_k^2 + \omega_m^2}$$

where ω represents the general market risk component from each portfolio.

The criteria which must be met to qualify for the above treatment are:

    (a) The calculation must involve the general market risk requirements of at least 4 country portfolios;
    (b) The sum of the general market risk components in the calculation must equal 0 (ie $\Sigma\omega = 0$), where an overall long position in a country portfolio has a positive sign and an overall short position a negative sign; and
    (c) The general market risk component from each country must not account for more than 30% of the overall gross general market risk in the calculation.

The general market risk requirement for a particular country may be divided, so that one part is used in the above calculation and the remainder is added directly into the general risk sum in paragraph 22.

25 The equity general market risk capital requirement for the trading book is the *sum* of the general market risk requirement calculated in paragraph 24 and the general risk requirements for all countries or parts of countries not included in the calculation in paragraph 24.

EQUITY INDICES

26 The treatments described below apply to positions in equity indices, whether they arise directly or through derivatives. Positions in indices listed in Chapter 11 attract no specific risk requirement. They should be included in the general market risk calculation for the relevant country as a single position based on the sum of current market values of the underlying instruments.

27 Positions in indices not listed in Chapter 11, or positions in notional indices or baskets of stocks may either be decomposed into their component stocks, or they may be treated as a single position based on the sum of current market values of the underlying instruments: if treated as a single position, the specific risk requirement is the highest specific risk charge which would apply to any of its components, as set out in paragraphs 14–20, and the general risk charge is as set out in paragraphs 22–25.

Derivatives

28 Derivative positions, in equity futures, forwards, and swaps, based on individual equities, portfolios of equities or equity indices, must be converted into notional underlying instruments, whether long or short. The resultant notional instruments should be treated under the relevant Chapters (see paragraphs 11–25 above for equity position risk; see Chapter 4—Foreign Exchange Risk; see Chapter 5—Interest Rate Position Risk *subject to paragraph 30 below*). For equity swaps, the equity exposure must be treated separately from the interest rate exposure.

29 Derivative positions may also generate counterparty exposures, for example, to counterparties in OTC trades, through margin payments, through fees payable, or through settlement exposures. Capital is required against such counterparty risk for derivatives, as set out in Chapter 2—Counterparty Risk.

30 For interest rate position risk, the notional underlying instruments should be included as government securities with a coupon below 3% in the currency concerned in the interest rate treatments in Chapter 5, but *only* if the Bank is satisfied, and has given express written agreement, that sufficient controls are in place to monitor this interest rate exposure and to take account of dividend exposures and liquidity risk. If a bank has an interest rate sensitivity model approved (see Chapter 8—The Model Review Process), the interest rate exposure may be incorporated into that model.

31 Without such permission from the Bank, embedded interest rate exposures in equity derivatives will be subject to capital requirements based on the following:

Time to expiration	Percentage
0–3 months	0.20
3–6 months	0.40
6–12 months	0.70
1–2 years	1.25
2–3 years	1.75
3–4 years	2.25
4–5 years	2.75
over 5 years	3.75

Positions with maturity of exactly 3 months, 6 months, etc, should be assigned to the shorter maturity band.

The capital requirement is calculated for each notional position *before* any netting permitted under paragraphs 12 and 13, as the mark-to-market value of the underlying position multiplied by the percentage in column 2. The capital requirement for all notional interest rate positions under this treatment is the sum of the absolute values of the individual capital requirements calculated above.

OPTIONS

32 Capital requirements for options or warrants on equities, plus any related hedging positions, must be calculated using either:

(a) the simple method (carve out) set out in Annex I to this Chapter (for options with residual maturity under six months only); or

(b) one of the option risk management models described in Chapter 8—The Model Review Process.

Advice should be sought from the Bank on options or warrants with residual maturity over six months.

33 Banks which have a recognised option pricing model may, with express written agreement of the Bank, use the delta value of options calculated from this model in the determination of the net positions for individual instruments, as set out in paragraphs 12 and 13. Where these delta values represent stock indices or stock index futures, they should be treated as set out in paragraphs 26 and 27.

Annex I: Simple Method for Options (Carve Out)

1 The table below may be used to calculate the market risk requirements for options or warrants on equities, with residual maturity under six months, plus any related hedging positions.

2 The Bank of England is aware that these calculations are approximate, and tend to overstate the market risk of options. Institutions whose option positions are large, so that this overstatement puts them at a significant disadvantage, are encouraged to apply for model recognition as described in Chapter 8—The Model Review Process.

3 An option will be deemed to be 'hedged' for the purposes of the calculations when the size of the offsetting underlying position matches the amounts into which the option is exercisable. Where the amount underlying the option is larger than the offsetting position, the residual options will be treated as Naked Option Positions. Advice should be sought from the Bank on the treatment of options with residual maturity over six months.

	Option position	In the Money by more than P%	In the Money by less than P%	Out of the Money
Naked	Long Call	NL	NL	NL
	Long Put	NL	NL	NL
	Short Call	NSI	NSI	NSO
	Short Put	NSI	NSI	NSO
Long in	Long Put	0%	LPI	HO
Underlying	Short Call	0%	SHI	HO
Short in	Long Call	0%	LCI	HO
Underlying	Short Put	0%	SHI	HO

In the Money means that the exercise level of a call option or warrant is less than the current mark-to-market value of the underlying instrument, and for put options or warrants that the current mark-to-market value of the underlying is less than the exercise level of the put option or warrant.

Out of the Money means those options and warrants that are not In the Money.

P% is the sum of the specific and general market risk for the underlying equity instrument as if it were the only component in a portfolio.

4 The capital requirements for options and warrants and their associated hedges under this method are as set out overleaf:

NL The lesser of:
    (a) the market value of the underlying instrument multiplied by P%; *and*
    (b) the current value of the option on the bank's books.
NSI The market value of the underlying position multiplied by P%.
NSO The market value of the underlying position multiplied by P% minus 0.5 multiplied by the amount by which the option is Out of Money (subject to a maximum reduction to zero).
LPI The market value of the underlying position minus (1 − P%) multiplied by the underlying position valued at the exercise price.
HO The market value of the underlying position multiplied by P%.
SHI The market value of the underlying position multiplied by P% minus the mark-to-market value of the option (subject to a maximum reduction to zero).
LCI (1 + P%) multiplied by the underlying position valued at the exercise price minus the market value of the underlying position.

Annex II: Alternative Method

1 Where a bank chooses to use this method in preference to the standard method, it must calculate the equity position risk capital requirement as being *the higher of*:

    (a) Calculation 1; *and*
    (b) Calculation 2

    Calculation 1 refers to the following table of factors:

	Category	.1 %	2	3
A	UK & Ireland			
	Constituents of FTSE100 Index	10.5	86	27
	Other Constituents of the FT All Share Index	15.0	86	27
	Other Equities with a normal market size	18.0	86	27
	Other UK & Irish equities	25.0	N/A	
B	Japan			
	Constituents of Nikkei225 Index	10.5	88	26
	Other constituents of the First Section of the Tokyo Stock Exchange	18.0	88	26
	Other Japanese Equities	25.0	N/A	
C	USA			
	Constituents of the S&P500 Index	11.5	94	23
	Other constituents of the NYSE, AMEX and NAS-DAQ NMS	20.0	94	23
	Other US equities	25.0	N/A	
D	Constituents of the FT-Actuaries World Indices			
	Australia	21.0	292	72
	Belgium	12.0	75	43
	Canada	17.0	198	31
	Denmark	16.5	157	45
	France	15.5	161	64
	Germany	12.0	92	69
	Hong Kong	22.0	180	121
	Italy	16.5	137	84
	Netherlands	13.0	116	61
	Norway	17.0	179	102
	Singapore	16.0	123	107
	Spain	17.5	170	120
	Sweden	15.5	149	58
	Switzerland	10.0	60	49
E	Other Equities	30.0	N/A	N/A

Calculation 1

2 Having allocated equity positions according to the categories in the table, calculate the capital requirement for each country portfolio separately, and aggregate the results. The equity capital requirement for a country portfolio is:

    (a) {Aggregate Long Positions + Aggregate Short Positions}* Column 1 in the table *unless* the portfolio is a qualifying country portfolio, as set out below, in which case calculate the capital requirement for that country portfolio as:

    (b) 1/100*$\sqrt{}$ {Basic Risk * Liquidity Adjustment Factor}.

Notwithstanding (a) and (b) above, if a bank has a qualifying country portfolio in at least two out of three of the UK, US and Japan, it may calculate the equity position risk capital requirement for these portfolios as:

    (c) 1/100*$\sqrt{}$ {Modified Basic Risk * Modified Liquidity Adjustment Factor}.

The terms used in calculations (a), (b) and (c) are defined below.

3 A qualifying country portfolio is either:

    (i) a UK, US or Japan country portfolio containing positions only in those categories against which figures appear in columns 2 and 3 of the table, and which contains at least 10 long or 10 short individual net positions; or

    (ii) a portfolio of any other country listed in Part D of the table which comprises constituents of the FT-Actuaries World Indices *and* contains at least 5 long or 5 short individual net positions.

4 The Basic Risk Calculation:

    (i) Calculate the square of the net overall position of the qualifying country portfolio;

    (ii) Multiply the figure generated in (i) by the appropriate figure in column 3 of the table;

    (iii) Calculate the square of the value of each individual net position, excluding positions arising from broad based equity index contracts, and total the squared amounts for each country; and

    (iv) Multiply the total calculated in (iii) by the appropriate figure shown in column 2 of the table.

The basic risk of a qualifying country portfolio is the sum of (ii) and (iv).

5 Liquidity Adjustment Factors: Calculate liquidity adjustment factors for the UK, US and Japan country portfolios as follows:

    (i) calculate the overall gross position (ie long plus short positions) in each category and aggregate these to form the overall gross position for each country portfolio;

    (ii) calculate the following proportions:

        I the constituents of the FTSE100 Index category portfolio as a proportion of the UK country portfolio;

        II the FT-All Share Index category, excluding FTSE100 stocks, as a proportion of the UK country portfolio;

        III the constituents of the Nikkei225 Index category portfolio as a proportion of the Japan country portfolio; and

        IV the constituents of the Standard & Poor's 500 Index category portfolio as a proportion of the US country portfolio.

Liquidity adjustment factors for the Japan and US country portfolios are, respectively:

$$\frac{6}{(\text{proportion III} * 4) + 2} \quad \text{and}$$

$$\frac{6}{(\text{proportion IV} * 4) + 2}$$

Liquidity adjustment factor for the UK country portfolio is:

$$\frac{6}{(\text{proportion 1} * 4) + 2 + \text{proportion II}}$$

The liquidity adjustment factor for other qualifying country portfolios is 1.

6 Modified Basic Risk Calculation:

(i) calculate the basic risk for each qualifying country portfolio as in paragraph 4 and take the sum of these

(ii) calculate the overall net position for each qualifying country portfolio; multiply together the overall net positions for pairs of countries; and then multiply by the factors shown below:

Overall Net Position	Factor
UK & US	17
UK & Japan	11
US & Japan	11

The modified basic risk figure is the sum of (i) and (ii).

7 Modified Liquidity Adjustment Factor: Calculate the modified liquidity adjustment factors for UK, US and Japan country portfolios as follows:

(i) calculate the overall gross position of all qualifying country portfolios and sum these to obtain the aggregate overall gross position;

(ii) calculate the following proportions:
I the overall gross position of the portfolio comprising the FTSE100 Index category portfolio plus the Nikkei225 portfolio plus the Standard & Poor's 500 Index category portfolio, all as a proportion of (i); and
II the overall gross position of the FT All Share Index category portfolio, excluding the FTSE100 stocks, as a proportion of (i).

The modified liquidity adjustment factor is:

$$\frac{6}{(\text{proportion I} * 4) + 2 + \text{proportion II}}$$

Calculation 2

8 Calculate the equity position risk capital requirement on a country by country basis as the aggregate of the specific and general market risk requirements, and sum the results across all countries.

SPECIFIC RISK

9 For each country, the specific risk capital requirement is the overall gross position for that country portfolio multiplied by:

(i) For single stocks 4%; or
(ii) For diversified portfolios of highly liquid stocks 2%; or
(iii) For broad-based equity indices which are not broken down into their constituent stocks 0%.

GENERAL MARKET RISK

10 For each country, the general market risk capital requirement is the overall net position for that country portfolio multiplied by 8%.

Chapter 7—Underwriting

Explanation

1 A bank which is involved in the underwriting of debt, and/or equity, and/or other securities issues may take significant direct exposures, to the issuer and to the market place, which in the normal course of events can be expected to reduce quickly through

sales, or by obtaining underwriting commitments from other firms. Underwriting is therefore to be included within the trading book.

2 The underwriting process, whether of bonds, equities or other securities, has a common set of events:
Announcement Date
Launch Date
Commitment Date
Allotment Date
Subscription Date
Closing Date
Payment Date

These events may occur with different time gaps between them depending upon particular aspects of the underwriting mechanism. For example the gap between the Announcement Date and the Launch Date may be negligible for a bond underwriting, but may be several days for an equity underwriting.

3 Reductions in Large Exposures and position risk capital requirements are not available to banks which make purchases on the grey market, and are neither underwriters, nor members of the syndicate for underwriting or distributing the particular securities. The treatments described below only apply to new instruments and new tranches of existing instruments. Large size secondary market trades of equities or bonds will not benefit from any reductions in Large Exposures or position risk capital requirements.

4 Where an underwriting commitment is for a new tranche of existing securities then it may be netted against offsetting positions according to the rules set out in the Interest Rate Position Risk and Equity Position Risk chapters in the sections on Netting. Such netting will lead to reductions in position risk capital requirements and Large Exposures.

5 This chapter describes the way in which the capital required to support the underwriting commitments should be calculated from the perspective of position risk. Large Exposures treatment is covered in Chapter 3—Large Exposures. Where a bank is underwriting a capital raising issue for another financial institution[1], it will not be able to reduce the deduction from its own capital base from 100% of the net underwriting commitment unless it has express written agreement of the Bank for these types of transactions, see Chapter 9—Own Funds of Authorised Institutions.

6 The following section of the CAD is covered by this chapter:

– Annex I paragraph 39.

---

[1] Institutions are defined in Chapter 1—The Trading Book.

Scope

7 Banks may apply the underwriting treatments below to new securities or securities which are new to the market where the bank has given:

    (a) A commitment to an issuer to purchase, underwrite or distribute those securities; or

    (b) It is a member of the syndicate for the underwriting or distribution of those securities.

Where a bank is permitted, but chooses not, to apply the treatments below then the capital requirements must be applied to the net commitment using techniques detailed in the other chapters.

8 Banks which apply the underwriting method may only apply it to:

    (a) Any commitment to an issuer of securities to purchase or distribute new securities and securities that are new to the market;

    (b) Any sub-underwriting commitment obtained by the bank from others; and

    (c) Any allotment, purchase or sale of the securities in respect of which the bank has given a commitment under (a) or (b).

9 A bank may apply the underwriting treatment to a commitment to purchase existing securities that are exchange traded only with the prior written approval of the Bank.

Note: The Bank will only grant approval to apply the underwriting treatment where it determines that the purchase of existing securities has the characteristics of an offering of new securities which are new to the market, by reference to:

(a) the extent of the publicity;
(b) the method of distribution;
(c) how widely the offering is to be made; *and*
(d) the type of documentation to be used.

For example, the sale to the public of further shares of a partially privatised company would generally qualify for underwriting treatment, but the private placement of shares in a subsidiary company sold off by its parent holding company would not.

Commitment

10 A bank must treat its commitment to the issuer, for Large Exposure monitoring and notification purposes, as commencing on the date that the initial commitment is given, except:

(a) For a bond issue with the pricing terms fixed, the commitment shall be deemed to commence on the opening of business on the third UK business day after the launch date; or
(b) For a bond issue with the pricing terms not fixed, the commitment shall be deemed to commence on the day that the pricing terms are fixed (unless the bank has the right to withdraw the commitment in which case the commitment commences when that right has expired), even if it is subject to formal, legal or other conditions which would reasonably be expected to be satisfied;
(c) Where an agreement constituting a commitment is placed in escrow or held in deposit subject to the fulfilment of conditions, the commitment commences on the day on which the agreement is released from escrow or deposit.

For monitoring and notification purposes, this applies to the gross amount to which a bank is potentially committed. Banks will be required to pre-notify all exposures in excess of 25% of their capital base. Banks which have been given 'expert' underwriting status in accordance with Notice to Authorised Institutions BSD/1993/2 should comply with the terms of that notice.

11 Working Day 0 is defined as the working day on which the bank becomes unconditionally committed to accepting a known quantity of securities at a known price:

(a) For bond issues, and other securities that utilise the same underwriting process, such as international equity and warrant issues Working Day 0 is the later of the Allotment Date or the Payment Date.
(b) For domestic equity issues, and other securities that use the same underwriting process, Working Day 0 is the later of the Subscription Date or the announcement of allocations.
(c) The unconditional commitment only falls to the underwriters of rights issues after the subscription period has ended and as a result is in the form of the securities into which the rights are exercisable.

12 A bank's net commitment will be the amount of the gross commitment adjusted for:

(a) Underwriting, or sub-underwriting, commitments obtained from others;
(b) Purchases and Sales of the securities;
(c) Allocations granted, or received, with regard to the underwriting commitments;

to form the net underwriting position. It is only after Working Day 0 that the net commitment must be taken into account for the Large Exposures calculation. A scaling factor is applicable (see Chapter 3—Large Exposures paragraphs 21ff).

Capital Requirements—Commitment to Working Day 0

13 Capital is required to support the net underwriting commitment from the time of initial commitment. The capital requirement differs between the bond type underwriting

techniques in paragraph 11(a) and those equity type underwriting techniques in paragraph 11(b) and 11(c). For the purposes of generating the capital requirements pre-Working Day 5 rights issues and warrant issues will be converted into the underlying instrument using the current market price of the underlying instrument.

14 For bond type underwriting (including warrants on currencies, bullion and debt instruments) the capital requirement, from the close of business on the date of initial commitment until Working Day 0 will be the general market risk requirement only for that instrument. The general market risk requirements which are to be applied to the entire net commitment in that instrument, are determined by the Interest Rate Position Risk, and (if appropriate) Foreign Exchange Exposure chapters. The net commitment may be incorporated into portfolios of other like instruments so as to benefit from any hedging.

15 For equity type underwriting, and rights and warrant issues on equity instruments, the capital requirement, from the close of business on the date of initial commitment until Working Day 0, will be the specific and general market risk requirement for that instrument applied to the entire net commitment in that instrument reduced by 90%. The specific and general market risk requirements are to be generated as for a portfolio containing only the instrument being underwritten. The net commitments, reduced by 90%, may not be incorporated into portfolios of other like instruments.

Capital Requirements—From Working Day 0

16 From Working Day 0 various scaling factors are applied to the specific and general market risk capital requirements for bond and equity positions.

    (a) For bond type underwritings the specific risk is applied to the net commitment from Working Day 0. The specific risk capital requirements are reduced according to the table. For example on Working Day 2 there is no reduction in the general market risk requirement on the net commitment, but for specific risk the capital requirement is reduced by 75%. For general market risk purposes the net commitment may be incorporated into portfolios of similar positions.

    (b) For equity type underwritings the specific and general market risk requirements are reduced from Working Day 0 according to the table below. For example on Working Day 2 the capital requirement of the net commitment will be reduced by 75% of the specific and general market risk requirements of the net commitment.

For general market risk purposes the net commitment may only be incorporated into portfolios of similar positions on Working Day 5 and after. If a bank wishes to incorporate the position in a portfolio of similar positions prior to Working Day 5, it may do so, but in such circumstances it will not be able to benefit from the reduced capital requirements set out in the table below.

Reduction in capital requirements for underwriting				
Time band	Bond Type Issues		Equity Type Issues	
	Specific risk	General market risk	Specific risk	General market risk
Up to and including Working Day 0	100%	0%	90%	90%
Working Day 1	90%	0%	90%	90%
Working Day 2	75%	0%	75%	75%
Working Day 3	75%	0%	75%	75%
Working Day 4	50%	0%	50%	50%
Working Day 5	25%	0%	25%	25%
After Working Day 5	0%	0%	0%	0%

Chapter 8—The Model Review Process

Introduction

1 This chapter is concerned with the procedure that will be adopted by the Bank in recognising models and the capital requirements which will be generated from such models. Eligible models can cover: options risk and interest rate risk in derivatives in the trading book; and foreign exchange risk in the banking and trading books. For these risks, the CAD sets out two methods for determining capital requirements. There is a standard approach for banks without recognised models and a more complex approach for institutions with recognised models—which will normally result in lower capital requirements for a given quantity of position or foreign exchange risk. The methods for determining capital requirements for banks without recognised models are covered in Chapter 4—Foreign Currency Risk, Chapter 5—Interest Rate Position Risk, and Chapter 6—Equity Position Risk. It should be noted that positions in the trading book may also generate counterparty risk requirements independent of the capital requirement determined by a model; this will be calculated in accordance with Chapter 2—Counterparty Risk.

2 The model review process is likely to focus at least as much on the use of the model in the context of the firm's business as on the mathematics—for instance, whether the revaluation rates fed into the model are independently verified, the part played by senior management in control over the use of models, and whether the model is applied to products which stretch it beyond its capability.

3 As the review will encompass both the model and its operating environment it is not the case that a commercially produced model which has been recognised for one bank will automatically be recognised in another. In the case of banks where there are multiple models for one product, the model that is used for risk management and/or determining profit and loss is the model the Bank will be most interested in, although it may be necessary to look at other front and back office models. It is not our intention to examine subtle modifications to models made by traders for quoting prices.

4 The review process does not restrict the use by banks of mathematical or computer models to price any transaction. Similarly, banks may perform their own internal risk assessment using models, without prior reference to the Bank. *Model review only looks at whether a model can be used for the purposes of capital adequacy calculations.*

Models Eligible for Recognition

5 Models eligible for recognition fall into two categories:

    (a) Pricing models (for complex swaps, vanilla and exotic options), and
    (b) Risk Aggregation models (models which summarise and facilitate management of risk).

6 The types of risk aggregation models which the Bank can recognise for CAD purposes are:

    (a) interest rate sensitivity models;
    (b) option risk management models for equity, interest rate and foreign exchange options; and
    (c) foreign exchange backtesting models (which only require recognition if they include option products), and
    (d) in certain circumstances, other value at risk (VAR) models for the measurement of interest rate risk, equity position risk and foreign exchange risk.

Interest Rate Sensitivity Models for Interest Rate, Equity and Foreign Exchange Derivatives

7 Institutions which mark to market and manage the interest rate risk on derivative instruments on a discounted cashflow basis may use sensitivity models to calculate weighted positions for inclusion in the duration approach.

8 Instruments which qualify for this treatment are the following:

    (a) interest rate futures;
    (b) forward rate agreements;
    (c) forward commitments to buy or sell debt instruments;
    (d) options on interest rates, debt instruments, equities, equity indices, financial futures, swaps and foreign currencies;
    (e) warrants;
    (f) swaps;
    (g) amortising bonds.

    Interest rate risk embedded in the following instruments may also be included in the model:

    (i) equity futures, forwards and options;
    (ii) foreign exchange futures, forwards and options.

    Note that the CAD does not allow non-amortising bonds to be included, and that restrictions may be placed on the inclusion of warrants in the model, in the case where warrants do not behave like options. Interest rate risk in each individual currency must be calculated separately.

    9 The interest rate risk model must generate positions which have the same sensitivity to defined interest rate changes as the underlying net cashflows. Models that could conceivably be modified to be acceptable for CAD purposes include: cashflow bucketing, sensitivity models, scenario matrix analysis, parts of value at risk models, simulation models, backtesting, and what the Securities and Futures Authority call 'swaps models'. In all cases models must include the following essential elements: cashflow generation, discount factors, net present values and changes in net present values in response to shifts in the yield curve.

SCOPE OF THE APPLICABILITY OF THE INTEREST RATE RISK MODEL

10 Where debt positions (which may not be incorporated in the interest rate sensitivity model) are hedged by derivatives and vice versa, banks may be permitted to treat these derivatives and the hedged item on the same basis in the maturity or duration approach, rather than in the interest rate sensitivity model. This means that the same type of derivative in the same bank could sometimes be incorporated in the interest rate sensitivity model and sometimes be placed directly into the maturity or duration methods. However, banks must clearly set out their policies on this issue and the system must be capable of being subject to audit verification.

Pricing Models for Complex Swaps and Options

11 As a part of the review of models that assess interest rate sensitivity and option risks, the Bank will wish to review complex swap pricing models, eg models for different swaps and index amortising swaps and pricing models for vanilla and exotic options. Exotic options models will be reviewed separately, even if the pricing algorithms are simply modified 'vanilla' options models. For these products it is important to examine whether the model is applied to products which stretch it beyond its capability.

12 Model review is intended for large, dynamically hedged portfolios of options, rather than one-off deals. The business to which the model pertains should be a significant component of the bank's trading activities.

Option Risk Management/Risk Aggregation Models

13 The review of option pricing models is part of the process of model recognition for option products, but a much more important part of the process is to assess the models with which option risks are managed. Exotic options will be subject to special scrutiny as some of these may require different risk management systems, and capital requirements for these products may not easily be set on the basis of the option's 'Greek' risk parameters.

Foreign Exchange Backtesting Models

14 For foreign exchange risk, the CAD permits banks to use a backtesting method to calculate the capital requirements for either all of an institution's foreign exchange positions (as a portfolio) or the net open position in designated currencies (as a portfolio). Details of the workings of this type of model are set out in Chapter 4—Foreign Exchange Risk. Use of this type of model for capital adequacy purposes will require the agreement of the Bank (including a list of designated currencies) but it will not be necessary for the Bank to review the model, unless options are included in the calculation.

15 Banks may be permitted to include foreign exchange options in the foreign exchange backtesting model but it will be necessary for the Bank to review the method banks use to do this. Losses due to changes in the underlying exchange rate (delta and gamma) and to changes in the volatility of the option would need to be captured by the model. If all these losses are not captured, additional capital requirements will be determined using the buffer approach (as outlined below).

VAR Models

16 In order to avoid banks which have VAR models for evaluating risk being put to the expense of calculating the standard CAD capital requirements for interest rate risk and equity risk on a daily basis, it may be possible for banks to use their own VAR models subject to agreement with the Bank of England. There will be a number of strict conditions to be met before agreement can be given. The underlying principle will be that a bank should compare at a date randomly chosen by the supervisor a scaled up version of its own VAR model calculation with the CAD requirement. Subject to further conditions, the VAR model can then be used to monitor compliance with the CAD requirement until the next benchmarking date.

17 A bank may apply to use this system for all or part of its trading risks. If it is contemplating doing so it should consult its supervisor urgently in order that the arrangements for the comparative measure between the CAD requirement and its VAR model output can be put in place as soon as possible.

The Model Review Process

18 The model review process will include discussion of the following areas:

    (a) The mathematics of the model and the underlying assumptions;
    (b) Systems and controls;
    (c) Risk management, reporting procedures and limits;
    (d) Staffing issues;
    (e) Reconciliation and valuation procedures;
    (f) The setting of capital requirements.

In these areas certain conditions and standards will have to be met prior to the recognition of a model. These standards will vary depending on the size of the firm, the nature of the business, and the models being used. We recognise that some banks will be using models that go beyond the CAD in terms of sophistication of risk measurement. On model visits, we will wish to look at these models as an important part of the examination of the bank's systems and controls. The model visit will also consider how banks plan to adapt existing models to fit the requirements of the CAD. Where a model currently has a broader purview than the CAD calculation but is subsequently adapted for that purpose, model recognition may be possible, but it will be necessary to confirm that the model, with appropriate adaptation, conforms to CAD requirements. Models which are recognised should be integral to bank internal systems and management.

19 In most cases the model review process is likely to take the form of an on site visit followed by a dialogue about matters (if any) which should be addressed before recognition can be granted. It is expected that the Bank will look at several products in a single visit. Once systems and controls have been examined in some detail in a given bank it should be possible to spend less time reviewing each individual model.

CONSOLIDATION

20 Initially the model review process will be confined to UK Incorporated Authorised Institutions. The treatment of the models of subsidiaries in Europe of UK incorporated banks has not yet been finalised; one relevant factor will be whether the model has been recognised by another EU/EEA supervisor for CAD purposes. In the case of subsidiaries outside Europe, the Bank will discuss how such positions should be reported with the parent bank before coming to any decision as to how far reporting can be done on a model-based system.

LETTER OF MODEL RECOGNITION

21 It is intended that the letter of model recognition will be quite specific. For interest rate sensitivity models, the letter will detail the instruments that can be included in the model. For option pricing and risk management models the letter will set out:

(a) Option style (European/American/Asian/Barrier etc);
(b) Type (exchange traded/OTC);
(c) Underlyings;
(d) Currencies;
(e) Maturity (and for bond options the ratio of the maturity of the option to the maturity of the underlying);
(f) In certain cases, maximum volume of business.

22 The detail of the model recognition letter reflects the focus of model review on assessing whether the model is appropriate to determine capital requirements on each individual product type. In many cases, the letter of recognition will cover several product types. However, for some simple options with different underlyings, individual letters of recognition may be necessary because some underlyings are much more difficult to delta hedge than others eg an equity option on an emerging market is often more difficult to hedge than an equity option on a G10 country market index.

23 For exotic options, the definition of an 'individual product type' is potentially problematic. The Bank will look at the payoff structure, exercise features, expiry conditions, strike price determinations and the underlying in order to make a judgment about whether a product is a separate type and should be reviewed accordingly.

24 The letters of recognition will set out the products covered, the method for calculating capital requirements on the products and the conditions of model recognition. The bank will also be told how the outputs of recognised models will feed into the processing of other interest rate, equity and foreign exchange risk. The conditions of model recognition may include additional reporting requirements. In cases where banks make on-going adjustments to models or apply the model to new but similar products, there will be a requirement for the Bank to be informed of significant changes. In some cases the Bank may be able to give provisional approval for the model to be changed or applied to a new class of products, in others it will be necessary to revisit the bank.

25 Where foreign exchange options models are presently recognised for Annex B treatment on the Bank of England form S3 this information and the background already supplied by the bank concerned will be fully taken into account in the subsequent model approval process. In the case of plain vanilla options (American and European puts and

calls on individual specified currency pairs), where the approval is relatively recent and systems are little changed, the presumption will be that no further review is required. However, the Bank may wish to visit the banks concerned to discuss methods for setting capital requirements on these models.

SYSTEMS AND CONTROLS SURROUNDING THE MODEL

26 The systems and controls surrounding the model are at least as important as the model itself. One reason for supervisors to be particularly interested in systems and controls is that the rules on capital requirements do not attempt to cover all market shocks or extraordinary situations and yet these are just the times when the firm is most at risk. Therefore, the Bank is concerned that the control environment and risk management techniques are sufficiently robust to enable prompt action to be taken in times of stress.

27 The sophistication of the systems and controls that the Bank would expect to see surrounding the model will depend on the size and complexity of the bank's business. A number of standards in this area have been produced by international organisations in the private and public sectors and the Bank would expect to see that banks have these in place or be working towards these standards. The main focus of the examination of systems and controls in the model review visit will be to ensure that the firm has in place adequate controls for the risks that are being taken. In particular, the following areas will be discussed: strategy, staff, risk limits, procedures for dealing with excesses to limits, systems, settlements office, revaluation procedures, dealing manuals, disaster recovery and internal audit checks.

28 The Bank intends to speak to a variety of staff including dealers, financial control, settlements staff, internal audit, financial engineering and risk management staff. However, precisely whom the Bank speaks to will depend on the nature of the business being reviewed, with banks receiving guidance prior to each review.

29 In the assessment of a bank's systems and controls existing information in the form of auditors' reports, Bank of England Review Team Visits and reports under section 39 of the Banking Act will be used and may reduce the time needed to review these aspects. Where there is a report from external auditors on risk management and/or option pricing models and the control environment this will be taken into account and clean reports may facilitate model recognition.

EXAMINATION OF MODEL ALGORITHMS

30 Model testing is likely to comprise a relatively small part of the model review process. As stated above, the basic principle behind options model testing is to ensure that the model is appropriate to determine capital requirements on each individual product type. The following are the types of conditions the Bank would expect to see met: the products and instruments to be treated by the model must be clearly and fully defined, and the model must be appropriate for those products and instruments. The inputs to the model must be in the format required for the model. The bank must have sufficient in-house expertise to understand the technical aspects of the model and its weaknesses or limitations. The Bank may apply a benchmark test to the outputs of models.

31 Option models which generate delta values will be recognised only if these models also address the full range of market risks posed by the use of options, including gamma, and sensitivity to implied volatility, time decay, and interest rates. The model must form part of the day-to-day risk management mechanisms employed by the bank. The bank should have the ability to control and monitor its positions, through a timely risk management system and access to a liquid market in hedging instruments. If this latter condition can not be fulfilled—either in normal or extreme market conditions—the Bank would expect to see this issue adequately addressed in other ways.

32 For all option types, before the model review visit, the Bank will ask for details of: payoff diagrams, analytical formulae, numerical techniques, interest rate and volatility term structures and technical papers used to develop the model. For exotic option models it is particularly important that risk management is appropriate to the product type: eg the Bank would expect to see special treatment of barrier options that are close to the barrier. The Bank would also expect to see banks run 'what if' analyses or simulations on

parameters to which the model is particularly sensitive eg correlation assumptions for relative performance options.

Calculation of Capital Requirements for Recognised Models

33 The parameters to be used for measuring capital requirements on interest rate risk are set out below. The parameters for scenario matrix analysis on options will be based on the specific and general market risk parameters in the CAD and will reflect normal market conditions rather than 'stress situations'. Banks should nevertheless be familiar with the possible consequences of stress situations and we would expect them to have developed contingency plans to deal with such eventualities and to carry out scenario analyses to assess their potential losses in such circumstances.

Interest Rate Sensitivity Models

34 Capital requirements for interest rate risk for banks without recognised models may be calculated using either the maturity or duration approaches, for more detail see Chapter 5—Interest Rate Position Risk. Banks with a recognised interest rate sensitivity model are permitted to use it for pre-processing of derivatives positions (see paragraph 8 for the list of instruments that may be included) but after pre-processing it is still necessary to feed the residual positions into the duration ladders. It is expected that the use of interest rate sensitivity models will result in lower capital requirements for a given quantity of interest rate position risk, because sensitivity models permit a greater degree of netting of long and short positions and there is no capital requirement on positions that have been matched within the sensitivity model.

35 There are several different ways of constructing sensitivity models. The description in paragraphs 34 to 40 sets out one method, but as part of the model review process other variations will be considered. However, all interest rate sensitivity models must generate positions which have the same sensitivity to defined interest rate changes as the underlying cashflows and in all cases the cashflows must initially be allocated to maturity bands. The Bank will try to work with banks' existing systems wherever possible, for example if existing models are based on calculation of the value of a basis point shift, then it may be possible for these sensitivities to be multiplied up by the required rate changes to enable the bank's models to conform to CAD specifications.

36 In an interest rate risk model, individual deals are converted into cashflows. The cashflows are discounted and then allocated into 15 maturity bands as set out in the Annex to this chapter (ie the bands applying in the standard approach where coupon rates are less than three percent). The discount functions are generated using zero coupon rates derived from banks' own yield curves. Then the cashflows (which may be different if they are dependent on the shifted yield curve) are discounted using the banks' own yield curves plus the appropriate interest rate shifts. There are different shifts set out for different points along the yield curve.

37 The PV of each band is calculated twice, once for the original yield curve, secondly for the shifted yield curve. The change in the present value in each band is the difference between the PV arrived at from discounting using the banks' own yield curve minus the PV arrived at from discounting at the shifted yield curve. This change is the sensitivity of the bank's positions to changes in interest rates.

38 The sensitivity figures must then be allocated to the three zones in the duration ladder. Positive and negative amounts in the different maturity bands of the sensitivity calculation net off when these are combined into one of three zones. The zones are: up to 1 year, between 1 year and 3.6 years, and over 3.6 years.

39 At this point, if a bank is also using the duration approach[1] set out in Chapter 5—Interest Rate Position Risk to determine the interest rate risk capital requirement on its bonds and bond hedges, the sensitivity figures (one figure per zone in either the long or short column) will be included with the other positions in the weighted individual net positions column in Table 3 of Chapter 5 in the duration approach. The sensitivity figures form a substitute for the general market risk requirement for these items which have been processed by the model.

40 To the extent that the sensitivity figures represent a figure for gross positions which have to be matched within a maturity zone, there is no capital requirement for the matching process. But when they are subsequently incorporated in the standard duration zones, then they become subject to the normal capital requirements. In other words the model process reduces a portfolio of positions to a single set of net figures for each maturity zone which is then slotted into the standard duration method and subject to the standard capital requirements.

41 The net unmatched position in any zone (after netting off bond, bond hedge and sensitivity positions in the 'weighted individual net positions' column) may only be offset against positions in other zones using the following rules (which are the same as those set out in Chapter 5—Interest Rate Position Risk):

(i) The unmatched weighted long (short) position for zone 1 may offset the unmatched weighted short (long) position in zone 2. The extent to which the unmatched weighted positions in zones 1 and 2 are offsetting is described as the matched weighted position between zones 1 and 2.

(ii) After this process, any residual unmatched weighted long (short) positions in zone 2 may then be matched by the unmatched weighted short (long) positions in zone 3. The extent to which the unmatched positions in zones 2 and 3 are offsetting is described as the matched weighted position between zone 2 and 3.

> The two preceding calculations may be carried out in reverse order ie zones 2 and 3 followed by zones 1 and 2.

> After (i) and (ii) any residual unmatched weighted long (short) positions in zone 1 may then be matched by offsetting unmatched weighted short (long) positions in zone 3. The extent to which the unmatched positions in zones 1 and 3 are offsetting is described as the matched weighted position between zone 1 and 3.

> Any residual unmatched weighted positions following the matching within a zone and between zones will be summed.

42 The general interest rate risk capital requirement will be the sum of:

Matched (sensitivity, bond and bond hedge positions)

Weighted Positions in all Zones	×	2%
Matched Weighted Positions between Zones 1 & 2	×	40%
Matched Weighted Positions between Zones 2 & 3	×	40%
Matched Weighted Positions between Zones 1 & 3	×	150%
Residual Unmatched Weighted Positions	×	100%

---

[1] Banks may also use the maturity approach in combination with the sensitivity method. It will be necessary to discuss the procedure for doing this with the Bank.

Option Risk Management/Risk Aggregation Models

43 There will be three main methods for determining capital requirements on option products:

(a) The buffer approach;
(b) The scenario matrix approach;
(c) For foreign exchange options, the foreign exchange backtesting model.

44 The methods set out in this section should be seen as illustrative. If other sophisticated approaches are used by banks to manage option risk, these may also be considered as a basis for determining capital requirements. Hybrid approaches which combine elements of the buffer and scenario approaches will also be considered. In all cases, the Bank will work with the bank concerned to produce an agreed method which is consistent with the requirements of the CAD. Banks that propose to use a models approach are thus encouraged to discuss their proposed methodology with the Bank at the earliest opportunity.

45 In general, the capital requirements generated by the buffer approach will be more penal than those generated using a scenario matrix approach or the backtesting approach. The latter two approaches are generally regarded as more satisfactory for managing options risk as they assess risk over a range of outcomes rather than focusing on the point estimate of the 'Greek' risk parameters.

THE BUFFER APPROACH

46 Capital charges under the buffer approach are comprised of four components. The delta value of the option is treated with other positions in the same underlying in the maturity or duration approach, the equity market risk calculation or the foreign exchange backtesting or standard approach and the calculations proceed as set out in the appropriate chapters for the relevant risk type. The other three components are the 'add-ons' required for gamma, volatility and interest rate risk. For the purposes of the calculation of delta, each option deal must be considered separately. For the calculation of the buffers for gamma, volatility and interest rate risk, individual equities or indices, individual currency pairs and individual bond options must be treated as the underlying unit for the calculation.

47 In some circumstances it may be necessary for equity, foreign exchange and bond options of different maturities on the same underlying to be treated separately for the calculation of the gamma buffer. However, for all buffer calculations interest rate options may be allocated to three zones: 0–1 year maturity, 1–4 years maturity and over 4 years maturity, according to the maturity of the underlying instrument.

48 Following Annex I of the CAD, interest rate risk arising from options on interest rates, debt instruments, equities, equity indices, financial futures, swaps and foreign currencies may be incorporated into the interest rate maturity or duration approaches. The delta value of each option is calculated as the amount of the underlying instrument to which the option refers, multiplied by the delta calculated by the recognised model. Option positions may be netted off against offsetting positions in the underlying securities or derivatives.

49 To capture *delta risk* on options on equity products, the delta value of these options is fed into the calculation of specific and general market risk requirements on equity position risk, as set out in Chapter 6—Equity Position Risk. To capture delta risks for foreign exchange options, the delta value is included in the calculation of the institution's net open position in each currency. The foreign exchange risk requirements on the net open positions are then calculated using the standard method or the backtesting method, as set out in Chapter 4—Foreign Exchange Risk.

50 There will be additional capital buffers to cover gamma, volatility and interest rate risks. The gamma buffer is calculated for each underlying instrument as:

gamma buffer = 0.5* (absolute value of net negative gamma)*
(current market price of underlying* specific and general market risk)^2

obtained from the Taylor series expansion. The total gamma buffer is the aggregate of the buffers set for each and every underlying instrument which has a net negative gamma; ie the gamma figure obtained after netting off positive and negative gamma for each underlying. In cases where the net gamma for an instrument is positive, the gamma buffer will be zero. Adjustments to the gamma buffer on each underlying may be made in some circumstances to prevent banks reducing their total overall gamma risk while retaining significant gamma risk at different maturities in their books.

51 To provide for *volatility risk* for each underlying, banks will be required to revalue their portfolios for an increase in volatility by a percentage specified by the supervisor. Banks who can do so will be permitted to take account of the term structure of volatility and to shift options maturing at different points along the term structure by different percentages (as set by the supervisor). The volatility buffer is equal to the change in the value of the portfolio for the increase in volatility; the total volatility buffer is the aggregate of the calculations for each underlying.

52 Some limited offset of positive and negative volatility risk may be permissible across some categories of underlying. Similarly, some limited offset of gamma risk across different underlyings may also be permissible.

53 To capture *interest rate risk* on the cost of carry of foreign exchange and equity options, there is an interest rate risk buffer. For interest rate and bond options where the maturity of the underlying falls in a different zone from the maturity date of the option, there is also an interest rate buffer because the cost of carry is sensitive to a different section of the yield curve from the delta of the option. The buffer is calculated by revaluing each option for the relevant increase in interest rates set out in Annex 1, corresponding to the maturity date of the option. The change in value of each option resulting from this interest rate shift is then combined into the interest rate sensitivity model into the appropriate zone in the same way as the other positions, as described in paragraphs 39 and 40.

54 To summarise: Capital Requirements for OTC Options using the Buffer Approach:

   (a) **Counterparty Risk (purchased options only)** *plus*
   (b) **Delta Risk: Captured in the Duration Approach (interest rate options)/Equity Market Risk Calculation (equity options)/Foreign Exchange Backtesting Model or the Foreign Exchange Standard method (foreign exchange options)** *plus*
   (c) **Buffers for Gamma, Volatility and Interest Rate Risk.**

SCENARIO MATRIX APPROACH

55 Banks may be permitted to use a scenario matrix approach for options on the following instruments: bonds, interest rates, other debt instruments, equities, equity indices, financial futures, swaps and foreign currencies and exotics; and associated hedges.

56 In the scenario matrix approach, the standard method is to set up a different matrix for each underlying. That is, a separate matrix for each national market for equities including individual equities, indices and baskets, and a separate matrix for each currency pair for foreign exchange products. For bond options, for each currency there will be three separate matrices; bonds with modified duration of less than 1 year, between 1 and 3.6 years, over 3.6 years. For other interest rate products, for each currency there will also be three separate matrices based on the maturity of the underlying instrument: 0–1 year, 1–4 years and over 4 years maturity.

57 At each cell in the matrix, the portfolio will be revalued in response to movements in the price of the option underlying and movements in volatility. Each cell must contain the net profit or loss of the option and the underlying hedge instruments. The cell containing the largest net loss sets the capital requirement for the portfolio for that underlying. This approach captures directional and volatility risks.

58 The Bank will set the parameters for the amounts by which the price of the underlying instrument and volatility must be shifted to form the rows and columns of the scenario matrix and the parameters will reflect specific and general market risk. Banks may be permitted to use a term structure of volatility in the scenario matrix if they wish. The parameters for the term structure will also be set by the Bank. There may be some offset permitted for general market risk within the scenario matrix approach.

59 Cost of carry interest rate risk will be captured using the approach set out in the buffers section, for foreign exchange and equity options, and interest rate and bond options where the maturity of the underlying falls in a different zone from the maturity date of the option.

60 To summarise: Capital Requirements for OTC Options using the Scenario Matrix Approach:

   (a) **Counterparty Risk (purchased options only)**, *plus*
   (b) **Directional and Volatility Risks: The worst case loss from a given scenario matrix analysis**, *plus*
   (c) **Interest Rate Risk Buffer.**

EXOTIC OPTIONS, WARRANTS AND STRUCTURED DEBT INSTRUMENTS

61 The buffer approach and the scenario approach may be permitted for exotic options. If banks can demonstrate a satisfactory method for doing so they will also be permitted to include such instruments in the foreign exchange backtesting approach.

62 Special methods will be devised to determine capital requirements for the more difficult exotics, (for example to deal with discontinuities in deltas in barrier options) and for structured debt instruments, but the Bank will always work with the bank concerned to produce an agreed method, within the confines of the CAD. If a bank uses scenario matrix analysis, it must be able to demonstrate that no substantially larger loss could fall between the nodes—the more sparse the matrix, the more difficult it will be for the Bank to be satisfied on this point.

63 Warrants which trade like options may be included as part of an options portfolio, but in other cases the Bank will have to decide on an alternative treatment with the bank concerned.

Foreign Exchange Backtesting Models

64 As stated above, banks may be permitted to include foreign exchange options in the foreign exchange backtesting model. Losses due to changes in the volatility of the option, and delta and gamma losses due to changes in exchange rates would need to be captured by the model. If all of these losses are not captured, additional capital requirements will be determined using the buffer approach. Details of the method to determine capital requirements on foreign exchange backtesting models are set out in Chapter 4—Foreign Exchange Risk.

VAR Models

65 Banks wishing to use their own VAR model for calculating capital requirements under the CAD must have their models recognised by the Bank; there are a number of conditions which will be strictly applied for banks choosing this method. No particular type of model is prescribed and banks will be able to use models based on back-testing, variance–covariance matrices, Monte Carlo simulations or simple aggregation of sensitivity numbers. The conditions to be met will be based on those set out in Part B of the Consultative Proposal by the Basle Committee on Banking Supervision entitled Planned Supplement to the Capital Accord to Incorporate Market Risks and dated April 1995. If during the consultative process on the Basle document, modifications are made to these requirements, a further notice will be issued to Banks.

66 In order to use this method banks will be required to calculate the CAD requirement for capital on a randomly chosen date. The date will be chosen by the supervisor and notified to the bank the following day. The bank will then be required to calculate its capital requirement both according to the standard CAD method and according to its own VAR model meeting the criteria set out in the previous paragraph. Banks will be given an agreed time to complete this comparison. Supervisors will require this benchmark test to be recalculated periodically (approximately at six monthly intervals, but at a precise date chosen randomly by the supervisor).

67 Banks using this method will be required to hold capital based on the higher of the CAD capital requirement resulting from the latest benchmark test (scaled by any increase in the bank's current VAR capital requirement compared with the benchmark date) and the VAR capital requirement as set out in the Basle Consultative proposals on market risk issued in April 1995.

Annex 1—Shifts in the Yield Curve

For different coupons at different maturities, the CAD sets different assumed interest rate changes. These are summarised in this table extracted from the CAD, Annex I, table 2 and table 3.

Maturity Band for Coupon of 3% or more	Maturity Band for Coupon of less than 3%	Table 2 Assumed Interest Rate Change (in %)	Table 3 Assumed Interest Rate Change (in %)
1 Month and under	1 Month and under	0.00%	1.00%
1 to 3 Months	1 to 3 Months	1.00%	1.00%
3 to 6 Months	3 to 6 Months	1.00%	1.00%

Maturity Band for Coupon of 3% or more	Maturity Band for Coupon of less than 3%	Table 2 Assumed Interest Rate Change (in %)	Table 3 Assumed Interest Rate Change (in %)
6 to 12 Months	6 to 12 Months	1.00%	1.00%
1 to 2 Years	1.0 to 1.9 Years	0.90%	0.85%
2 to 3 Years	1.9 to 2.8 Years	0.80%	0.85%
3 to 4 Years	2.8 to 3.6 Years	0.75%	0.85%
4 to 5 Years	3.6 to 4.3 Years	0.75%	0.70%
5 to 7 Years	4.3 to 5.7 Years	0.70%	0.70%
7 to 10 Years	5.7 to 7.3 Years	0.65%	0.70%
10 to 15 Years	7.3 to 9.3 Years	0.60%	0.70%
15 to 20 Years	9.3 to 10.6 Years	0.60%	0.70%
> 20.0 Years	10.6 to 12.0 Years	0.60%	0.70%
	12.0 to 20.0 Years	0.60%	0.70%
	> 20.0 Years	0.60%	0.70%

For maturities on the boundary between two bands, the instrument is placed in the earlier band. Thus for example, maturities of exactly one year are placed in the six to twelve months band.

Annex 2—Glossary

Delta	The rate of change of the price of an option with respect to the price of the underlying asset.
Delta Value	The amount of the underlying instrument to which the option refers, multiplied by the delta calculated by the recognised model.
Gamma	The rate of change of the option's delta with respect to the price of the underlying asset.
Interest rate risk buffer	Additional capital charge to cover the cost of carry risk on an option.
Risk Aggregation Model	A model that summarises and is used to facilitate management of risk.

Chapter 9—Own Funds

Explanation

1 Authorised institutions such as banks are required to allocate positions, securities, derivatives, assets and liabilities to either the trading book, or the banking book. For items allocated to the trading book, the level of capital (sometimes referred to as a 'haircut') required to support associated risks is expressed as an absolute figure. For items in the banking book, capital requirements are expressed as a percentage of 'risk weighted assets'. *An authorised institution will need — at all times — to have sufficient capital to satisfy both capital requirements*. This chapter defines the own funds of a bank, sets out the limits on use of particular forms of capital, and explains how the Bank will measure an authorised institution's capital adequacy.

2 The current Bank Policy Notices governing Own Funds are:

BSD/1986/2	Subordinated loan capital issued by recognised banks and licensed deposit-takers;
BSD/1990/2	Implementation in the United Kingdom of the Directive on Own Funds of Credit Institutions;
BSD/1992/1	Amendment to BSD/1990/2;

BSD/1992/5   Verification of Interim Profits in the Context of the Own Funds Directive;
BSD/1994/3   Subordinated loan capital issued by UK incorporated authorised
            institutions.

3 This chapter covers the following sections of the Capital Adequacy Directive:

   – Article 3
   – Annex V.

Application of Capital

4 Banks may use three types of own funds to meet their capital requirements as set out
below:

Tiers 1 and 2 May be used to support any activities.
Tier 3   **May only be used to support trading book activities and foreign currency
               risk, and may not be applied to those trading book capital requirements
               arising out of counterparty and settlement risk. (The latter restriction
               may, with the Bank's prior consent, be waived, but only at a consolidated
               level. This concession is designed to accommodate the Own Funds regimes
               of other supervisors.)**

Definition of Capital

5 The capital held/issued by UK banks directly, or by their domestic and overseas
subsidiaries for inclusion in the institution's consolidated capital base, may be of the
following forms:

TIER 1: CORE CAPITAL

6   (a) Permanent Shareholders' equity:
          (i) Allotted, called up and fully paid share capital/common stock (net of any
              own shares held, at book value);
          (ii) Perpetual non-cumulative preferred shares (sometimes referred to as
              preferred stock), including such shares redeemable at the option of the
              issuer and with the Bank's prior consent, and such shares convertible into
              ordinary shares.
       (b) Disclosed reserves in the form of general and other reserves created by
          appropriations of retained earnings, share premiums, capital gifts, capital
          redemption reserves, and other surplus.
       (c) Interim retained profits which have been verified by external auditors (in
          accordance with the terms of BSD/1992/5).
       (d) Minority interests arising on consolidation from interests in permanent share-
          holders equity.

       Less

       (e) Goodwill and other intangible assets (including mortgage servicing rights,
          unless it can be demonstrated, to the Bank's satisfaction, that there is an
          active and liquid market in which they can be traded).
       (f) Current year's cumulative unpublished net *losses* on the banking and trading
          books.
       (g) Fully paid shareholders' equity issued after 1 January 1992 by the capitali-
          sation of property revaluation reserves.

TIER 2: SUPPLEMENTARY CAPITAL

7
       (a) Reserves arising from the revaluation of tangible fixed assets and fixed asset
          investments.
       (b) General Provisions:
          (i) Provisions held against possible or latent loss, but where these losses
              have not as yet been identified will be included to the extent that they do
              not exceed 1.25% of the sum of risk weighted assets in the banking book
              and notional risk weighted assets in the trading book;
          (ii) Provisions earmarked, or held specifically, against lower valuations of
              particular claims or classes of claims *will not* be included in capital.

(c) Hybrid capital instruments:
   (i) Perpetual cumulative preferred shares, including shares redeemable at the option of the issuer and with the prior consent of the Bank, and such shares convertible into ordinary shares;
   (ii) Perpetual subordinated debt, including such debt which is convertible into equity. Where such debt was issued prior to May 1994, it should meet the conditions for primary perpetual subordinated debt set out in BSD/1986/2. Where it was issued after May 1994, it should meet the conditions for hybrid capital instruments set out in BSD/1994/3.
(d) Subordinated term debt:
   (i) Dated preferred shares (irrespective of original maturity);
   (ii) Subordinated term loan capital with a minimum original maturity of at least five years plus one day. Where such debt was issued prior to May 1994, it should meet the conditions set out in BSD/1986/2, subject to a straight-line amortisation during the last five years leaving no more than 20% of the original amount issued outstanding in the final year before redemption. Where such debt was issued after May 1994, it should meet the conditions for term subordinated debt set out in BSD/1994/3.
(e) Minority interests arising upon consolidation from interests in Tier 2 capital items.
(f) Fully paid shareholders' equity issued after 1 January 1992 by the capitalisation of property revaluation reserves.

DEDUCTIONS FROM TIERS 1 AND 2 CAPITAL

8   (a) Investments in unconsolidated subsidiaries and associates;
    (b) Connected lending of a capital nature;
    (c) All holdings of capital instruments issued by other banks, building societies **and those investment firms that are subject to the CAD or an analogous regime (see Chapter 11).** As currently, concessions to this deduction may be granted to banks making markets in such instruments under limits agreed with the Bank.
    (d) Qualifying holdings in financial and non-financial companies (see Consolidated Supervision of Credit Institutions BSD/1993/1).
    (e) Others to be agreed on a case-by-case basis.

TIER 3: TRADING BOOK ANCILLARY CAPITAL

9   **(a) Short term subordinated debt subject to the following restrictions (and otherwise meeting the conditions for term subordinated debt set out in BSD/1994/3):**
      (i) Minimum original maturity of two years.
      (ii) The terms of the debt must provide that if the bank's allowable capital falls below its target capital requirement *then the Bank must be notified* and the Bank may require that interest and principal payments be deferred on Tier 3 debt. (Where Tier 3 capital is issued by a company within the consolidated group but it is not subject to a lock-in clause that refers to 'target capital', the Bank should be consulted prior to its inclusion in the consolidated capital base.)
      (iii) The Bank would not normally expect to give consent to any repayment within two years from the date of issuance of drawdown. Repayment will only be granted when the Bank is satisfied that the institution's capital will be adequate after repayment and is likely to remain so.
      (iv) The contribution that this subordinated debt can make to the capital base does *not* have to be amortised over its life.
   (b) Daily net trading book *profits* net of any foreseeable charges or dividends, subject to the Bank being satisfied that they have been calculated using appropriate techniques.

Limits on the Use of Different Forms of Capital

10 At both a solo (solo-consolidated) and a consolidated level, an institution must satisfy the following limits:

(i) *Limit regarding Tier 2 Subordinated Term Debt:* Total Tier 2 subordinated term debt cannot exceed 50% of total Tier 1;

(ii) *Limits on capital used to meet Banking Book capital requirements:* Tier 2 capital used to meet the banking book capital requirements cannot exceed 100% of the Tier 1 capital used to meet those requirements;

(iii) *Limits on capital used to meet the Trading Book capital requirements:* Tier 2 capital and Tier 3 subordinated debt used to meet the trading book capital requirements must not—in total—exceed 200% of the Tier 1 capital used to meet those requirements.

11 In addition, at the consolidated level (or the solo level when a bank is not part of a consolidated group), the following *overall limit* applies:

Tier 2 and Tier 3 capital cannot—in total—normally exceed 100% of the bank's Tier 1. This limit cannot be exceeded without the Bank's express permission, which will only normally be granted where a bank's trading book accounts for most of its business.

12 Where a bank has any subordinated debt surplus to the ratios described above, this debt will be disregarded in the calculation of a bank's own funds and treated as part of the long term funding of the bank.

Calculation of Capital Adequacy

13 For comparative purposes, published risk asset ratios need to be calculated on a common basis, as set out in paragraph 16. However, banks will also be required to calculate their capital position for supervisory purposes in a way which incorporates the existing concepts of trigger and target ratios. This is set out in paragraphs 17–19. In each case, the calculation is complicated by the existence of tier 3 capital which, subject to the conditions set out in paragraphs 10–11 above, may contribute to meeting some of the capital requirements of the trading book.

14 In each case, the bank should start by determining its capital haircuts for:

(i) FX Position risk (including options);
(ii) Equity Position risk (including options);
(iii) Interest Rate Position risk (including options);
(iv) Large Exposures; *and*
(v) Trading Book Counterparty and settlement risk (using an 8% ratio).

15 The bank should next calculate its banking book risk-weighted assets.

16 A bank's risk asset ratio (for published or comparative purposes) is then eligible capital as a percentage of the sum of banking book risk weighted assets and trading book notional risk weighted assets, where the latter is obtained by multiplying the total capital haircut (as in paragraph 14) by 12.5.

17 For *supervisory purposes*, however, banks will be subject to separate triggers on their banking and trading books rather than the common 8% implied by the preceding paragraph. The minimum capital requirement on the banking book will be equal to risk weighted assets multiplied by the banking book trigger. The minimum capital requirement on the trading book will be notional risk weighted assets (as defined in paragraph 16 above) multiplied by the trading book trigger. Eligible capital will then be expressed as a percentage of the sum of the minimum banking and trading book capital requirements. A bank having capital adequacy of 100% will be deemed to be meeting its minimum capital requirements for supervisory purposes: in other words, it will be at its trigger.

18 Triggers on *banking books* will vary according to an institution's characteristics. In view of the comprehensive coverage of the CAD for *trading book* risks, however, banks with diversified trading books and good internal risk management systems are likely to have trading book triggers close to 8%. Others will have trading book triggers at higher levels; although in most cases these will not be above 12%, this will depend on the nature of the risks faced by the institution.

19 The Bank will set a target as well as a trigger for each book. The target capital requirement for the banking book will be equal to risk weighted assets multiplied by the banking book target. The target capital requirement for the trading book will be equal to notional risk weighted assets (as defined in paragraph 16 above) multiplied by the trading book target. A bank will be deemed to meet its target capital requirement if it satisfies the target capital requirement for both books taken together.

20 Where either the trading book business or the banking book business of a bank on a solo or consolidated basis does not normally exceed 10% of its combined on and off balance sheet business (as defined in Chapter 1, paragraph 23), only one trigger will be set.

Reporting Requirements

21 Authorised institutions will be required to report their capital adequacy to the Bank on a regular basis to be agreed with their supervisor. However, if capital falls below the target level, the Bank must be notified immediately.

Annex: Calculation of Capital Adequacy for Supervisory Purposes

1 Calculate trading book capital requirements

Trading book trigger = x%

	Haircut	Notional risk weighted assets	Capital required
FX Position Risk	A	$12.5 \times A$	x% of $(12.5 \times A)$
Equity Position Risk	B	$12.5 \times B$	x% of $(12.5 \times B)$
Interest Rate Position Risk	C	$12.5 \times C$	x% of $(12.5 \times C)$
Large Exposures	D	$12.5 \times D$	x% of $(12.5 \times D)$
Trading Book Counterparty and Settlement Risk	E	$12.5 \times E$	x% of $(12.5 \times E)$

2 Calculate banking book capital requirement

Banking book trigger = y%

	Risk weighted assets	Capital required
Credit risk	F	y% of F

3 Calculate maximum Tier III capital that can be employed

Subject to limitations lised in paragraphs 10–11, can use a maximum equal to:

$$x\% \text{ of } 12.5 \times (A + B + C + D)$$

4 Calculate maximum Tier II that can be employed

Must satisfy constraints listed in paragraphs 10–11

5 Calculate capital adequacy

$$\frac{\text{Tier I} + \text{eligible Tier II (from (4) above)} + \text{eligible Tier III (from (3) above)} - \text{deductions}}{x\% \text{ of } 12.5 \times (A + B + C + D + E) + y\% \text{ of } F}$$

Chapter 10—Consolidation

Explanation

1 The Bank is committed to the principle that the supervision of authorised institutions should be conducted on a consolidated basis, whenever such institutions are members of

a wider group. The term 'consolidation' is used to mean the preparation of consolidated returns covering a group, or part of a group. The term 'consolidated supervision' is used to mean a qualitative assessment of the overall strength of a group to which an authorised institution belongs, to evaluate the potential impact of other group companies on the authorised institution. Consolidated supervision also takes into account the activities of group companies which are not included in the consolidated returns because the nature of their assets is such that their inclusion would not be meaningful, for example industrial or insurance companies. In general, the Bank takes account of the activities of group companies to the extent that they may have a material bearing on the reputation and financial soundness of the authorised institution in the group. The purpose of supervision on a consolidated basis is not to supervise all the companies in the group to which the bank belongs, but to supervise the bank as part of the group.

2 The Bank regards consolidated supervision as a complement to, rather than a substitute for, the solo supervision of the authorised institution. Events elsewhere in the group and the activities of other group companies can pose a threat to the authorised institution in ways which consolidated supervision cannot detect. For example, intra-group linkages arising from transactions between the bank and other group companies will only be revealed by the solo supervision of the bank. As a consequence the Bank sets solo capital adequacy ratios and large exposures limits for authorised institutions in addition to those which apply at the consolidated level.

3 The current Bank Policy Notice governing consolidated supervision and the implementation of the Consolidated Supervision Directive is:

BSD/1993/1 Implementation in the United Kingdom of the Directive on the Consolidated Supervision of Credit Institutions.

4 This chapter covers the following sections of the Capital Adequacy Directive:
– Article 7.

Scope of Consolidation

5 The scope of consolidation (including the definition of subsidiary and participation) is as set out in BSD/1993/1, paragraphs 11–18.

Exceptions to Consolidation

6 Exceptions to consolidation are as set out in BSD/1993/1, paragraph 24.

Distribution of Capital Resources within the Group

7 Rules governing the distribution of capital resources within the group (including those for concessionary weighting for intra-group exposures and details of the circumstances in which subsidiaries can be solo-consolidated) are as given in BSD/1993/1, paragraphs 25–28.

Groups Not Subject to Consolidation

8 Requirements for those groups not subject to consolidation are as given in BSD/1993/1, paragraphs 29–30.

Techniques of Consolidation

9 As at present, the technique of consolidation usually required will be the full consolidation for all majority shareholdings, and participations. The Bank will apply proportionate ('pro rata') consolidation to participations in only exceptional circumstances, where it is satisfied that there are other significant shareholders who have the means and the will to provide as much parental support to the entity as the shareholder subject to consolidated supervision. This criterion is usually most likely to be met by another bank.

10 The manner in which full consolidation will be achieved varies depending on the type of subsidiary to be consolidated. The various cases are set out below.

(a) Banks: Banking Books

11 Consolidation for banking books will be carried out on a line-by-line (or accounting)

basis across the group members being consolidated, effectively continuing the present regime.

(b) Banks: Trading Books (including foreign exchange exposure)

12 Trading book exposures (including counterparty exposures) and foreign exchange exposure will usually be consolidated using 'aggregation plus'. The trading book's notional risk weighted assets are separately calculated. These are included in the consolidated risk-asset-ratio, and are converted into a capital charge to be included in the supervisor's measure of capital adequacy. (See Chapter 9 and Annex II.)

13 When using 'aggregation-plus', the trading book's notional risk weighted assets, should be determined using:

    (a) the CAD as implemented by the relevant EU/EEA banking supervisor; or
    (b) the host banking supervisor's rules, where these are deemed to be broadly equivalent to the CAD; or
    (c) the CAD as set out in this policy notice.

14 The trading book capital requirement is then generated by multiplying notional risk weighted assets by the bank's trading book trigger, except in cases where other supervisors' rules are used (when multiplication is by the trigger applied to the subsidiary, typically 8%).

15 At present, no non-EU/EEA banking supervisor has adopted a market risk regime of a kind that generates a measure of notional risk weighted assets for trading activity. However, although it is not possible yet to make use of host supervisory rules when consolidating banking subsidiaries based in countries outside the EU/EEA, once a supervisor has implemented the Basle market risk proposals, it will be deemed to have a regime 'broadly equivalent' to the CAD for the purpose of calculating consolidated capital requirements.

16 When using aggregation plus, an institution may satisfy itself on a daily basis that it meets the Bank's minimum capital requirement (ie its target) with reference to position limits as opposed to actual positions. It may adopt such a procedure only after first satisfying the Bank that its control systems are such that actual positions may reliably be taken as being no higher than the adopted position limits.

17 As an alternative to aggregation-plus, consolidation of a banking subsidiary's trading book may be carried out on a line-by-line (or accounting) basis, if the institution can satisfy the line supervisor that:

    (a) the parent bank calculates or monitors trading book positions in an integrated fashion across the entities using this basis of consolidation; *and*
    (b) the banking subsidiary satisfies its local supervisory requirements on a solo basis; *and*
    (c) the parent bank is able to carry out adequate line-by-line consolidation on a daily basis; *and*
    (d) capital resources are freely transferable between the banking subsidiary and the rest of the group.

18 When consolidating using line-by-line, banks — if they wish — can construct their consolidated capital requirement for general market risk without first calculating the net position in each security on a consolidated basis. However, the method used to measure general market risk must be the same for all entities subject to the line-by-line consolidation.

(c) Investment firms

19 Investment firms will usually be consolidated using 'aggregation plus'. The firm's notional risk weighted assets are separately calculated. These are included in the consolidated risk-asset-ratio, and are converted into a capital requirement to be included in the supervisor's measure of capital adequacy. (See Chapter 9 and Annex II.)

20 When using 'aggregation-plus', the investment firm's notional risk weighted assets, should be determined using:

(a) the CAD as implemented by the relevant EU/EEA securities regulator; or
(b) the host securities regulator's rules, where these are deemed to be broadly equivalent to the CAD; or
(c) the CAD as set out in this policy notice.

21 The investment firm's capital requirement is then generated by multiplying its notional risk weighted assets by the bank's trading book trigger, except in cases where other supervisors' rules are used (when multiplication is by the trigger applied to the subsidiary, typically 8%).

22 For the list of non-EU/EEA securities regulators with regimes deemed to be broadly equivalent to the CAD see Chapter 11.

23 When using aggregation plus, an institution may satisfy itself on a daily basis that it meets the Bank's minimum capital requirement (ie its target) with reference to position limits as opposed to actual positions. It may adopt such a procedure only after first satisfying the Bank that its control systems are such that actual positions may reliably be taken as being no higher than the adopted position limits. (The Bank reserves the right to require consolidation of an investment subsidiary on the basis of the parent's total investment in that company, depending on the quality of the bank's control systems and the ease with which surplus capital can be transferred out of the subsidiary.)

24 The use of aggregation-plus for investment subsidiaries may be constrained by the size of non-trading activity. If this is large, the Bank reserves the right to use line-by-line (or accounting) consolidation for these assets.

25 As an alternative to aggregation-plus, consolidation of an investment firm may be carried out on a line-by-line basis, if the institution can satisfy the line supervisor that:

(a) the parent bank calculates or monitors trading book positions in an integrated fashion across the entities using this basis of consolidation; *and*
(b) the investment subsidiary satisfies its local supervisory requirements (where these apply) on a solo basis; *and*
(c) the parent bank is able to carry out adequate line-by-line consolidation on a daily basis; *and*
(d) capital resources are freely transferable between the investment subsidiary and the rest of the group.

26 When consolidating using line-by-line, banks — if they wish — can construct their consolidated capital requirement for general market risk without first calculating the net position in each security on a consolidated basis. However, the method used to measure general market risk must be the same for all entities subject to the line-by-line consolidation.

(d) Other firms

27 Other financial companies (as defined in the Annex to BSD/1993/1) will usually be consolidated on a line-by-line basis.

Other Issues

RECOGNITION FOR OFFSETTING EXPOSURES AMONGST COMPANIES BEING CONSOLIDATED

28 In determining consolidated group capital requirements, recognition for offsetting exposures can *only* be given where consolidation is done on a line-by-line basis. Banks wishing to offset exposures should consult their supervisor first.

LARGE EXPOSURES

29 The application of large exposure limits (see Chapter 3 — Large Exposures) to counterparty exposures will be based upon either: the sum of all the counterparty exposures to an individual entity or group; *or*, where the Bank's prior approval has been granted, a group may aggregate the sum of its counterparty exposure limits to determine its compliance with the Large Exposure requirements for counterparty exposure. When using the aggregation plus approach to consolidation, any incremental capital requirements generated by large exposures at the solo level need not be included in the capital requirement at the consolidated level.

Annex I: A Consolidation Techniques Schematic

LARGE EXPOSURES

Consolidated on a line-by-line basis irrespective of whether the exposure is in the banking or trading books.

CONSOLIDATION TECHNIQUES FOR UK BANKING GROUPS

EU/EEA Non UK Subsidiary	**Bank Subsidiary**	**Investment Subsidiary**[1]
UK Subsidiary	Banking book Line-by-line Trading book Aggregation plus using Bank of England Rules, or Line-by-line	Aggregation plus using local supervisor's rules, or Line-by-line
EU/EEA Non-UK Subsidiary	Banking book Line-by-line Trading book Aggregation plus using CAD as implemented by local supervisor, or — if preferred — as implemented by the Bank of England or Line-by-line	Aggregation plus using CAD as implemented by host supervisor, or — if preferred — as implemented by the Bank of England (and set out in this notice) or Line-by-line
Non-EU/EEA Subsidiary	Banking book Line-by-line Trading book Aggregation plus using Bank of England rules (until a host supervisor implements the Basle market risk proposals), or Line-by-line	Aggregation plus using host supervisor's rules (if deemed broadly equivalent to CAD) or CAD as implemented by the Bank of England (and set out in this notice) or Line-by-line

[1] Use of aggregation plus for non-trading book exposures only permitted if these are not substantial.

Annex II: Calculation of Consolidated Capital Adequacy

Suppose a consolidated group contains three companies:

- a parent bank
- a banking subsidiary outside the UK
- an investment subsidiary

Suppose also that the following applies:

Consolidated banking book risk weighted assets   B(t)
Trading book notional risk weighted assets

– consolidated using line-by-line   T(t)
– parent bank   T(p)
– banking subsidiary   T(b1) according to Bank rules
                                                   T(b2) according to host supervisor
– investment subsidiary   T(i1) according to Bank rules
                                                   T(i2) according to local supervisor
Banking book trigger   y%
Trading book trigger   x%

Case 1: All trading activity consolidated using line-by-line

Risk Asset Ratio: $\dfrac{\text{Total capital}}{B(t) + T(t)}$

Supervisory capital adequacy $\dfrac{\text{Total capital}}{y\% \text{ of } B(t) + x\% \text{ of } T(t)}$

Case 2: Trading activity consolidated using aggregation-plus but Bank rules

Risk Asset Ratio: $\dfrac{\text{Total capital}}{B(t) + T(p) + T(b1) + T(i1)}$

Supervisory capital adequacy $\dfrac{\text{Total capital}}{y\% \text{ of } B(t) + x\% \text{ of } [T(p) + T(b1) + T(i1)]}$

Case 3: Trading activity consolidated using aggregation-plus and host supervisors' rules

Risk Asset Ratio: $\dfrac{\text{Total capital}}{B(t) + T(p) + T(b2) + T(i2)}$

Supervisory capital adequacy $\dfrac{\text{Total capital}}{y\% \text{ of } B(t) + x\% \text{ of } T(p) + 8\% \text{ of } [T(b2) + T(i2)]}$

Chapter 11 — Lists

Explanation

1 This policy notice makes reference to various lists, the contents of which are expected
to change over time. Such updates might occur, for example, as a result of changes
agreed with the European Commission, or as a result of changes in the Bank of
England's implementation policy. Some of the lists are comparable to those used by The
Securities and Futures Authority in calculating capital requirements, and the Bank will
consider carefully any future changes made by the SFA to their lists. Similarly, changes
might be made in the light of policies adopted by other European supervisors in
implementing the Capital Adequacy Directive.

2 The lists have been brought together in a single Chapter to facilitate circulation of
periodic updates. It is not our intention to reissue this entire policy notice on a regular
basis, but this Chapter will be reissued as necessary.

3 Chapter references are given for each list, and detailed information on how the
lists are to be used in calculating capital requirements is given in the relevant policy
Chapters.

Lists Applicable to Market Risk

CURRENCY PAIRS SUBJECT TO BINDING INTER-GOVERNMENTAL AGREEMENTS

4 When measuring foreign exchange risk (see Chapter 4—Foreign Exchange Risk), banks may apply a separate treatment to those currencies that are subject to binding inter-governmental agreements. The following binding inter-governmental agreement is recognised for this purpose:
Belgian and Luxembourg francs.

MULTILATERAL DEVELOPMENT BANKS

5 In measuring interest rate risk (see Chapter 5—Interest Rate Position Risk), debt instruments issued by the following multilateral development banks are deemed to be 'qualifying':

> African Development Bank (AfDB)
> Asian Development Bank (AsDB)
> Caribbean Development Bank (CDB)
> Council of Europe Resettlement Fund
> European Bank for Reconstruction and Development (EBRD)
> European Investment Bank (EIB)
> Inter-American Development Bank (IADB)
> International Bank for Reconstruction and Development (IBRD)
> International Finance Corporation (IFC)
> Nordic Investment Bank (NIB)

This list may be amended periodically as a result of any amendment of the Solvency Ratio Directive.

RELEVANT CREDIT RATING AGENCIES AND INVESTMENT GRADE RATINGS

6 The determination of qualifying debt instruments for the calculation of specific interest rate risk (see Chapter 5 — Interest Rate Position Risk) can be based upon credit ratings. The ratings agencies used for this purpose and the rating deemed to be investment grade are listed below:

	Minimum Ratings	
	Securities	Money Market Obligations
For all issuers		
Moody's Investors Service	Baa3	P3
Standard & Poor's Corporation	BBB−	A3
IBCA Ltd	BBB−	A3
For all banks, Building Societies and parent companies and subsidiaries of banks		
Thomson Bankwatch	BBB−	A3
For Canadian issuers		
Canadian Bond Rating Service	B++low	A-3
Dominion Bond Rating Service	BBB low	R-2
For Japanese issuers		
Japan Credit Rating Agency, Ltd	BBB−	J-2
Nippon Investor Services, Inc	BBB−	a-3
The Japan Bond Research Institute	BBB−	A-2
Fitch Investors Service, Inc	BBB−	F-3
For United States issuers		
Duff & Phelps, Inc	BBB−	3
Fitch Investors Service, Inc	BBB−	F-3

This list may be amended periodically.

QUALIFYING COUNTRIES FOR EQUITY POSITION RISK

7 Equities listed in the following countries qualify for a 4% specific risk charge (see Chapter 6 — Equity Position Risk).

Australia	France	Japan	Spain
Austria	Germany	Luxembourg	Sweden
Belgium	Greece	Netherlands	Switzerland
Canada	Ireland	Norway	UK
Denmark	Italy	Portugal	USA
Finland			

HIGHLY LIQUID EQUITY INDICES

8 Individual equities included in the following indices are automatically considered to be liquid (see Chapter 6 — Equity Position Risk).

Australia	All Ords	Netherlands	EOE25
Austria	ATX	Spain	IBEX35
Belgium	BEL 20	Sweden	OMX
Canada	TSE35	Switzerland	SMI
France	CAC40	UK	FTSE 100
Germany	DAX	UK	FTSE mid-250
Japan	Nikkei255	USA	S&P 500

NOTE ON LISTS FOR EQUITY POSITION RISK

9 Lists for equity position risk may be amended periodically, in consultation with The Securities and Futures Authority. Applications to add Hong Kong and Singapore to the list of qualifying countries have already been received and are being considered. Information likely to be used in revising equity lists is set out below. The precise data required will be dependent on the particular market and/or index being considered. As a guide, the data set would be likely to include:

(a) The existence of a published national broad-based index;
(b) Details of the market structure;
(c) 3 years of daily price data of the major broad-based index of that country;
(d) 3 years of daily price data of a number representative single stocks contained in that index, spread by sector and market capitalisation, and numbering at least 50% of the total number of stocks which make up the index; and
(e) Details of traded futures and options markets together with data on the daily volumes.

The price data should be accompanied by the prevailing spot exchange rates to sterling for the same period.

Lists Applicable to Counterparty Risk and Consolidation

THIRD COUNTRY EQUIVALENT REGIMES FOR INVESTMENT FIRMS

10 The list of third countries with CAD equivalent regimes for the supervision of investment firms is used in three cases:

(a) Investment firms regulated by these third country securities regulators qualify for a 20% counterparty risk weight (see Chapter 2—Counterparty Risk);
(b) Exposures to investment firms regulated by these third country securities regulators should be treated as exposures to banks for large exposure purposes (see Chapter 3—Large Exposures);
(c) When using aggregation-plus to consolidate investment firms regulated by these third country securities regulators, banks may use host country rules (see Chapter 10—Consolidation).

11 Regulators of investment firms from the following countries are deemed to have CAD equivalent regimes:

Australia
Canada
Hong Kong
Japan
Switzerland
USA

Note: This list is provisional. Banks may apply to have countries added to this list, and the Bank will consider any additions suggested by The Securities and Futures Authority.

RECOGNISED CLEARING HOUSES AND EXCHANGES

12 The list of recognised clearing houses and exchanges is used in two cases:

(a) Claims on recognised clearing houses and exchanges are weighted at 20% (see Chapter 2—Counterparty Risk).
(b) Exposures to recognised clearing houses and exchanges should be treated in the same way as exposures to banks for large exposures purposes (see Chapter 3—Large Exposures).

The Bank is considering whether to adopt the same list as The Securities and Futures Authority, who intend to publish their list by the end of June 1995.

THIRD COUNTRY BANKING SUPERVISORS WITH EQUIVALENT REGIMES

13 When using aggregation-plus to consolidate the trading book of third country banking subsidiaries, banks may use host country rules where the Bank has deemed these rules to be 'broadly equivalent' to the CAD (see Chapter 10—Consolidation).

14 At present, no non-EU/EEA banking supervisor has adopted a market risk regime of a kind that generates a measure of notional risk weighted assets for trading activity. However, although it is not possible yet to make use of host supervisory rules when consolidating banking subsidiaries based in countries outside the EU/EEA, once a supervisor has implemented the Basle market risk proposals, it will be deemed to have a regime 'broadly equivalent' to the CAD for the purpose of calculating consolidated capital requirements. **[837]**

GOOD BANKING – CODE OF PRACTICE TO BE OBSERVED BY BANKS, BUILDING SOCIETIES AND CARD ISSUERS IN THEIR RELATIONS WITH PERSONAL CUSTOMERS
(March 1994)

Preface

This Code sets out the standards of good banking practice to be observed by banks, building societies and card issuers in their relations with personal customers in the United Kingdom. Individual customers will find the Code helpful in understanding how every bank, building society or card issuer subscribing to the Code is expected to behave towards them.

It is a voluntary Code which allows competition and market forces to operate to encourage higher standards for the benefit of customers.

The Code first came into effect on 16 March 1992 and it was stated then that it would be reviewed from time to time. This second edition is issued in the light of the first review. It will be effective from 28 March 1994, except for paragraph 5(3).

All institutions subscribing to the second edition of the Code will ensure that their staff are aware of it. They have also agreed to make copies of the Code available or to inform customers about how to obtain them.

This Code will be reviewed from time to time and another revision will be completed by March 1997.

There is a list of definitions of banking terms after the end of the Code.

Code of Banking Practice

1 Introduction

(1) This second edition of the Code has been prepared by the British Bankers' Association (BBA), The Building Societies Association (BSA), and the Association for Payment Clearing Services (APACS) in the light of a review carried out by an independent committee following the receipt of submissions from Government Departments, consumer and other organisations, the Banking and Building Societies Ombudsmen and members of the public.

(2) The Code has been written to promote good banking practice. Specific services may have their own terms and conditions which will comply with the principles contained in the Code.

(3) The Code is in three parts:

Part A – Governing Principles.

Part B – Customers, their Banks and Building Societies – is addressed to banks and building societies who adopt the Code and offer personal customers ('customers' for short throughout the Code) banking services such as current accounts, deposit and other savings accounts, overdrafts and loans, and various services delivered by the use of plastic cards.

Part C – Customers and their Cards – is addressed to banks, building societies and others who adopt the Code and provide financial services by means of plastic cards. All such providers are called card issuers in the Code.

Part A – Governing Principles

2 Governing principles

(1) The governing principles of the Code are:

    (a) to set out the standards of good banking practice which banks, building societies and card issuers will follow in their dealings with their customers;

    (b) that banks, building societies and card issuers will act fairly and reasonably in all their dealings with their customers;

    (c) that banks, building societies and card issuers will help customers to understand how their accounts operate and will seek to give them a good understanding of banking services;

    (d) to maintain confidence in the security and integrity of banking and card payment systems. Banks, building societies and card issuers must recognise that their systems and technology need to be reliable to protect their customers and themselves.

(2) Banks, building societies and card issuers will comply with all relevant legislation, judicial decisions and codes of conduct or similar documents which are observed by members of the BBA, BSA and APACS.

(3) The Code requires banks, building societies and card issuers to provide certain information to customers. This will usually be at the time when an account is opened. Information will also be available to customers from branches, if any, of the bank, building society or card issuer. Banks, building societies and card issuers will provide additional information and guidance about specific services at any time on request.

Part B – Customers, their Banks and Building Societies

3 Opening an account

(1) Banks and building societies are required by law to satisfy themselves about the identity of a person seeking to open an account to assist in protecting their customers, members of the public and themselves against fraud and other misuse of the banking system.

(2) Banks and building societies will provide to prospective customers details of the identification needed.

4 Terms and conditions

(1) Written terms and conditions of a banking service will be expressed in plain language and will provide a fair and balanced view of the relationship between the customer and bank or building society.

(2) Banks and building societies will tell customers how any variation of the terms and conditions will be notified. Banks and building societies will give customers reasonable notice before any variation takes effect.

(3) Banks and building societies should issue to their customers, if there are sufficient changes in a 12 month period to warrant it, a single document to provide a consolidation of the variations made to their terms and conditions over that period.

(4) Banks and building societies will provide new customers with a written summary or explanation of the key features of the more common services that they provide. This will include an explanation, when accounts are held in the names of more than one customer, of the rights and responsibilities of each customer.

(5) Banks and building societies will not close customers' accounts without first giving reasonable notice.

(6) To help customers manage their accounts and check entries, banks and building societies will provide them with regular statements of account. Except where this would be inappropriate to the nature of the account (eg where passbooks are issued) this should be at no less than 12 monthly intervals but customers will be encouraged to request statements at shorter intervals.

5 Charges and debit interest (payable by customers)

(1) Banks and building societies will provide customers with details of the basis of charges, if any, payable in connection with the operation of their accounts. These will be in the form of published tariffs covering basic account services which will

    — be given or sent to customers:

      (a) when accounts are opened;
      (b) at any time on request;

    — and be available in branches.

Details of any changes will also be given or sent to customers and be available in branches before the changes are implemented.

(2) Charges for services outside the tariff will be advised on request or at the time the service is offered.

(3) Banks and building societies will introduce systems to come into effect by 31 December 1996 to ensure that they will give no less than 14 days' notice of the amount to be deducted from their customers' current and savings accounts in respect of interest and charges for account activity that have accumulated during the charging period.

Banks and building societies which have not introduced such systems will disregard the charges to be applied to customers' accounts for any charging period if those were incurred solely as a result of the application of charges for the previous charging period.

(4) Banks and building societies will tell customers the interest rates applicable to their accounts, the basis on which interest is calculated and when it will be charged to their accounts. These will include the rates applicable when accounts are overdrawn without prior agreement or exceed the agreed borrowing limit. Banks and building societies will explain also the basis on which they may vary interest rates.

(5) When banks and building societies change interest rates with immediate effect they will effectively publicise those changes, for example by notices in their branches, if any, or in the press, or on statements.

6 Credit interest (payable to customers)

(1) Banks and building societies will make information about the rates on interest bearing accounts which they offer (whether or not these are open to new customers) freely available and accessible to customers by one or more effective means, for example:

    (a) notices and/or leaflets in branches;
    (b) press advertisements;
    (c) personal notice;
    (d) a branch/central telephone service.

(2) Banks and buildings societies will tell customers the interest rates applicable to their accounts, the basis on which interest is calculated and when it will be paid to their accounts. Banks and buildings societies will explain also the basis on which they may vary interest rates.

(3) When banks and building societies change interest rates with immediate effect they will effectively publicise those changes, for example by notices in their branches, if any, or in the press, or on statements.

7 Handling customers' complaints

(1) Each bank and building society will have its own internal procedures for handling customers' complaints fairly and expeditiously.

(2) Banks and building societies will inform their customers that they have a complaints procedure. Customers who wish to make a complaint will be told how to do so and what further steps are available if they believe that the complaint has not been dealt with satisfactorily either at branch or more senior level within the bank or building society.

(3) Banks and building societies will ensure that all their staff who deal directly with customers are made aware of their institution's internal complaints procedure and are able to help customers by giving correct information about it.

(4) Banks subscribing to the Code will be expected to belong to one or other of the following:

The Banking Ombudsman Scheme;
The Finance and Leasing Association Conciliation and Arbitration Schemes; or
The Consumer Credit Trade Association Arbitration Scheme.

Building societies have to belong to the Building Societies Ombudsman Scheme or another authorised scheme.

Banks and building societies will provide details of the applicable scheme to customers using such methods as leaflets, notices in branches or in appropriate literature, showing their current addresses and telephone numbers.

8 Confidentiality of customer information

(1) Banks and building societies will observe a strict duty of confidentiality about their customers' (and former customers') affairs and will not disclose details of customers' accounts or their names and addresses to any third party, including other companies in the same group, other than in the four exceptional cases permitted by the law, namely:

    (i) where a bank or building society is legally compelled to do so;
    (ii) where there is a duty to the public to disclose;
    (iii) where the interests of a bank or building society require disclosure;
    (iv) where disclosure is made at the request, or with the consent, of the customer.

(2) Banks and building societies will not use exception (iii) above to justify the disclosure for marketing purposes of details of customers' accounts or their names and addresses to any third party, including other companies within the same group.

(3) Banks and building societies will give customers at least 28 days' notice if they intend to disclose to Credit Reference Agencies information on undisputed personal

debts which are in default and where no satisfactory proposals for repayment have been received following formal demand.

Banks and building societies will inform customers that, where they have acquired the legal right to sell mortgaged or charged property, this information may be disclosed to Credit Reference Agencies.

Any other disclosure to Credit Reference Agencies shall be with the customer's consent.

(4) Banks and building societies will at all times comply with the Data Protection Act when obtaining and processing customers' data.

Banks and building societies will explain to their customers that customers have the right of access, under the Data Protection Act 1984, to their personal records held on computer files.

9 Status enquiries (bankers' references)

(1) Banks and building societies will on request:

    (a) advise customers whether they provide bankers' references or bankers' opinions in reply to status enquiries made about their customers;

    (b) explain how the system of Status Enquires (Bankers' References) works.

10 Marketing of services

(1) Except in response to a customer's specific request, banks and building societies will not pass customers' names and addresses to other companies in the same group for marketing purposes, in the absence of express written consent. Banks and building societies will not make the provision of basic banking services conditional on customers giving such written consent. For this purpose 'basic banking services' include the opening and the maintenance of accounts for money transmission by means of cheques and other debit instruments.

(2) Banks and building societies will give new customers at the time they open their accounts the opportunity to give instructions that they do not wish to receive marketing material.

(3) Banks and building societies will remind customers from time to time, and at least once every three years, of their right to give instructions at any time that they do not wish to receive marketing material.

(4) Banks and building societies will not use direct mail indiscriminately and in particular will exercise restraint and be selective:

    (a) where customers are minors; and

    (b) when marketing loans and overdrafts.

11 Marketing and provision of credit

(1) Banks and building societies in their advertising and promotional material will tell customers and potential customers that all lending will be subject to appraisal of their financial standing by the banks and building societies concerned.

(2) Banks and building societies will act responsibly and prudently in marketing. All advertising will comply with the British Code of Advertising Practice, The British Code of Sales Promotion Practice, and other relevant Codes of Practice of similar standing.

In particular banks and building societies will ensure that all advertising and promotional literature is fair and reasonable, does not contain misleading information and complies with all relevant legislation.

(3) In considering whether or not to lend, banks and building societies will take account of information which may include:

    — prior knowledge of their customers' financial affairs gained from past dealings;

    — information obtained from Credit Reference Agencies;

    — information supplied by applicant;

— credit scoring;
— age of applicants; and
— applicants' ability to repay, with the aim of avoiding over-commitment by an applicant.

(4) Banks and building societies will give due consideration to cases of hardship. They will encourage customers who are in financial difficulty to let them know as soon as possible and will use their best endeavours to give practical information and, subject to normal commercial judgement, will try to help.

12 Availability of funds

(1) Banks and building societies will provide customers with details of how their accounts operate, including information about:

— how and when they may stop a cheque or countermand other types of payments;
— when funds can be withdrawn after a cheque or other payment has been credited to the account;
— out of date cheques.

13 Foreign exchange services and cross-border payments

(1) Banks and building societies will provide customers with details of the exchange rate and the charges which will apply to foreign exchange transactions or, when this is not possible, the basis on which they will be calculated.

(2) Banks and building societies will provide customers wishing to effect cross-border payments with details of the services they offer. In doing so, they will provide, as a minimum:

(a) a basic description of the appropriate services available and the manner in which they can be used;
(b) information as to when money sent abroad on customers' instructions will usually reach its destination or, when an exact date cannot be given, the latest date by which the money might be expected to arrive;
(c) the details of any commission or charges payable by customers to their bank or building society including a warning where agents' charges may also be incurred.

14 Guarantees and other types of third party security

(1) Banks and building societies will advise private individuals proposing to give them a guarantee or other security for another person's liabilities:

(i) that by giving the guarantee or third party security he or she might become liable instead of or as well as that other person;
(ii) whether the guarantee or third party security will be unlimited as to amount or, if this is not the case, what the limit of the liability will be;
(iii) that he or she should seek independent legal advice before entering into the guarantee or third party security.

(2) Guarantees and other third party security documentation will contain clear and prominent notice to the above effect.

Part C – Customers and their Cards

15 Opening an account

(1) Card issuers are required by law to satisfy themselves about the identity of a person seeking to open an account or to obtain a card to assist in protecting their customers, members of the public and themselves against fraud and other misuse of the banking and card processing systems.

(2) Card issuers will provide to prospective customers details of the identification needed.

16 Terms and conditions

(1) The written terms and conditions of a card service will be expressed in plain language and will provide a fair and balanced description of the relationship between the customer and the card issuer.

(2) Card issuers will tell customers how any variation of the terms and conditions will be notified. Card issuers will give customers reasonable notice before any variation takes effect.

(3) Card issuers should issue to their customers, if there are sufficient changes in a 12 month period to warrant it, a single document providing a consolidation of the variations made to their terms and conditions over that period.

(4) Card issuers will publish changes to their credit card interest rates in their branches or in the press or in the statement of account sent to credit card holders, or by all those methods when such changes are made with immediate effect.

(5) Card issuers will tell credit card holders how frequently they will receive a demand for payment and the period within which payment should be made.

17 Issue of cards

(1) Card issuers will issue cards to customers only when they have been requested in writing or to replace or renew cards that have already been issued.

(2) Card issuers will tell customers if a card issued by them has more than one function. Card issuers will comply with requests from customers not to issue Personal Identification Numbers (PINs) where customers do not wish to use the functions operated by a PIN.

18 Security of cards

(1) Card issuers will issue PINs separately from cards and will advise the PIN only to the customer.

(2) Card issuers will tell customers of their responsibility to take care of their cards and PINs in order to prevent fraud. Card issuers will emphasise to customers that:

   (a) they should not allow anyone else to use their card and PIN;
   (b) they should take all reasonable steps to keep the card safe and the PIN secret at all times;
   (c) they should never write the PIN on the card or on anything usually kept with it;
   (d) they should never write the PIN down without making a reasonable attempt to disguise it;
   (e) they should destroy any PIN advice promptly on receipt.

(3) When customers are provided with an opportunity to select their own PIN, card issuers should encourage them to do so to help them remember the PIN.

19 Lost cards

(1) Card issuers will inform customers that they must tell their card issuers as soon as reasonably practicable after they find that:

   (a) their card has been lost or stolen;
   (b) someone else knows their PIN.

(2) Card issuers will tell customers, and will remind them at regular intervals on their statement or by other means, of the place and the telephone number where they can give the details of a lost or stolen card at any time of the day or night. Card issuers will arrange for that telephone number to be included in British Telecom Phone Books.

(3) Card issuers will act on telephone notification but may ask customers also to confirm in writing any details given by telephone.

(4) Card issuers, on request, will inform customers whether they accept notification of loss or theft of a card from card notification organisations.

(5) Card issuers on being advised of a loss, theft or possible misuse of a card or that the PIN has become known to someone else will take action to prevent further use of the card.

20 Liability for loss

(1) Card issuers will bear the full losses incurred:

(a) in the event of misuse when the card has not been received by the customer;
(b) for all transactions not authorised by the customer after the card issuer has been told that the card has been lost or stolen or that someone else knows or may know the PIN (subject to (4) below);
(c) if faults have occurred in the machines, or other systems used, which cause customers to suffer direct loss unless the fault was obvious or advised by a message or notice on display.

(2) Card issuers' liability will be limited to those amounts wrongly charged to customers' accounts and any interest on those amounts.

(3) Customers' liability for transactions not authorised by them will be limited to a maximum of £50 in the event of misuse before the card issuer has been notified that a card has been lost or stolen or that someone else knows the PIN (subject to (4) below).

(4) Customers will be held liable for all losses if they have acted fraudulently. They may be held liable for all losses if they have acted with gross negligence. Gross negligence may be construed as including failures to comply with any of the requirements of paragraph 18(2) if such failures have caused those losses.

(5) In cases of disputed transactions the burden of proving fraud or gross negligence or that a card has been received by a customer will lie with the card issuer. In such cases card issuers will expect customers to co-operate with them in their investigations.

21 Records

(1) To help customers manage their accounts and check entries, card issuers will provide customers with a written record on their statement of account of all payments and withdrawals made.

(2) Card issuers will inform customers that they should tell them as soon as reasonably practicable if they receive a statement of account that includes an item which seems to be wrong.

22 Handling customers' complaints

(1) Each card issuer will have its own internal procedures for handling customers' comlaints fairly and expeditiously.

(2) Card issuers will inform their customers that they have a complaints procedure. Customers who wish to make a complaint will be told how to do so and what further steps are available to them if they believe that the complaint has not been dealt with satisfactorily by the card issuer.

(3) Card issuers will ensure that all their staff who deal directly with customers are made aware of their internal complaints procedures and are able to help customers by giving correct information about them.

(4) Card issuers subscribing to the Code will be expected to belong to one or other of the following:

The Banking Ombudsman Scheme;
The Building Societies Ombudsman Scheme or another authorised scheme;
The Finance and Leasing Association Conciliation and Arbitration Schemes;
The Consumer Credit Trade Association Arbitration Scheme; or
The Retail Credit Group Mediation and Arbitration Schemes.

Card issuers will provide details of the applicable scheme to customers using such methods as leaflets, notices or in appropriate literature, showing their current addresses and telephone numbers.

Definitions

These Definitions explain the meaning of words and terms used in the Code. They are not precise legal or technical definitions.

AVAILABILITY OF FUNDS

Cheques paid into an account are 'uncleared' and they may be returned unpaid by the bank or building society on which they are drawn. Customers may not be permitted to draw against uncleared cheques. Cheques which are not returned unpaid become cleared and form part of a 'cleared balance'.

When returning cheques unpaid (see 'Unpaid Cheques' below), banks and building societies have to abide by very strict time limits. Customers may enquire about the timescale involved to establish which part of their balances are cleared and therefore available for withdrawal.

Cash paid direct into an account at the branch at which it is held forms part of a cleared balance.

CARD NOTIFICATION ORGANISATIONS

Companies which will at the request of a card holder maintain a record of all the cards held by the card holder and notify card issuers of the loss or theft of those cards.

CARDS

A general term for any plastic card which may be used to pay for goods and services or to withdraw cash. Cards which store value on the card, ie pre-payment cards, are excluded from this definition.

Common examples are:

Credit Card – a card which allows customers to buy on credit and to obtain cash advances. Customers receive regular statements and may pay the balance in full, or in part usually subject to a certain minimum. Interest is payable on outstanding balances.

Charge Card – similar to a credit card. It enables customers to pay for purchases, and in some cases to obtain cash advances. When the monthly statement is received the balance must be paid in full.

Debit Card – a card, operating as a substitute for a cheque, that can be used to obtain cash or make a payment at a point of sale. The customer's account is subsequently debited for such a transaction without deferment of payment.

Budget Card – similar to a credit card but customers agree to pay a fixed amount into their card account each month.

Store Card – similar to a budget card or charge card, but issued by particular companies or retail groups for use at their own outlets.

Cash Card – a card used to obtain cash and other services from an ATM (Automated Teller Machine/Cash Machine).

Cheque Guarantee Card – a card issued by a bank or building society which guarantees the payment of a cheque up to the amount shown on the card provided its conditions of use are followed.

Eurocheque Card – a specific cheque guarantee card which can be used either with special eurocheques to pay for goods or services, or by itself to withdraw cash from machines, in the UK and other countries.

COUNTERMAND

A customer's instruction to a bank or building society to cancel or override a previous instruction to make a payment or transfer of funds, eg by 'stopping' a cheque.

CREDIT REFERENCE AGENCIES

Organisations licensed under the Consumer Credit Act 1974 to hold information about individuals. Banks, building societies and card issuers may refer to these agencies to assist with various decisions, eg whether or not to open an account or to provide loans or grant credit.

CREDIT SCORING

A method of assessing risk, based on statistical analysis of previous lending experience and other factors: used, for example, to help in deciding whether a loan should be granted.

CROSS-BORDER PAYMENTS

A payment in sterling or a foreign currency between the UK and another country.

GUARANTEE

An undertaking given by a person (the guarantor) promising to pay the debts of another person if that other person fails to do so.

OMBUDSMAN SCHEMES

Banks and building societies have separate independent Ombudsman Schemes. The Ombudsmen resolve complaints made by customers against a bank or building society when customers have been unable to resolve such complaints themselves with their bank or building society. In addition, the Finance and Leasing Association and the Consumer Credit Trade Association operate arbitration and conciliation procedures. Their current addresses and telephone numbers are:

The Office of the Banking Ombudsman
70 Gray's Inn Road
London WC1X 8NB
Tel: 0171 404 9944

The Office of the Building Societies Ombudsmen
Grosvenor Gardens House
35–37 Grosvenor Gardens
London SW1X 7AW
Tel: 0171 931 0044

Finance and Leasing Association
18 Upper Grosvenor Street
London W1X 9PB
Tel: 0171 491 2783

The Consumer Credit Trade Association
159 Great Portland Street
London W1N 6NR
Tel: 0171 636 7564

PERSONAL CUSTOMERS

A private individual who maintains an account (including a joint account with another private individual or an account held as an executor or trustee, but excluding the accounts of sole traders, clubs and societies) or who takes other services from a bank or building society.

PIN – PERSONAL IDENTIFICATION NUMBER

A confidential number provided on a strictly confidential basis by a card issuer to a card holder. Use of this number by the customer will allow the card to be used either to withdraw cash from an Automated Teller Machine or to authorise payment for goods or services in retail or other outlets, by means of a special terminal.

PUBLISHED TARIFF

A list of prices for basic account services provided by a bank or building society.

SECURITY

A general word used to describe items of value such as title deeds, share certificates, life policies, etc, which represent property. Under a secured loan the lender has the right to sell the security if the loan is not repaid.

STATUS ENQUIRIES (BANKERS' REFERENCES)

An opinion as to a customer's ability to support or undertake a financial transaction or commitment. It is given to the enquirer by a bank or building society on request, subject to the express consent of the customer concerned.

THIRD PARTY SECURITY

Security provided by a person who is not the borrower.

UNPAID CHEQUES

A cheque which is not paid, for one of a number of reasons, the most common of which are:

Refer to drawer – this frequently means that there is not sufficient money in the drawer's account. The recipient of the cheque (the payee) should ask the person issuing the cheque (the drawer) why it has not been paid.

Refer to drawer. Please represent – similar to the above, but used when the bank or building society expects money to be available to pay the cheque in the near future and therefore suggests it is presented again for payment.

Post-dated – the cheque cannot be paid because its date is some time in the future.

Out of date – the cheque has not been paid because its date is too old, normally meaning more than six months ago.

Effects not cleared – there is money in the account of the drawer of the cheque but not available as cleared balances, because it is not yet certain that cheques recently credited to the account will be paid.

Words and figures differ – the amount of the cheque written in words is different from the amount written in numbers.

Orders not to pay – the issuer (drawer) of the cheque has instructed his or her bank or building society not to pay the cheque, ie to stop payment.

Signature differs – the signature on the cheque is different from that recorded by the bank or building society.

WRITTEN TERMS AND CONDITIONS

Those provisions governing a banking service which are produced in written form. They will be expressed in clear and straightforward language but the precise wording of some contracts must, of necessity, be in technical or legal language.   **[838]–[850]**

PART IV
EC DIRECTIVES

FIRST COUNCIL DIRECTIVE
of 12 December 1977

on the co-ordination of laws, regulations and administrative provisions relating to the taking up and pursuit of the business of credit institutions

(77/780/EEC)

NOTES

Date of publication in OJ: OJ L322, 17.12.77, p 30.

THE COUNCIL OF THE EUROPEAN COMMUNITIES,

Having regard to the Treaty establishing the European Economic Community, and in particular article 57 thereof,

Having regard to the proposal from the Commission,

Having regard to the opinion of the European Parliament,[1]

Having regard to the opinion of the Economic and Social Committee,[2]

Whereas, pursuant to the Treaty, any discriminatory treatment with regard to establishment and to the provision of services, based either on nationality or on the fact that an undertaking is not established in the Member States where the services are provided, is prohibited from the end of the transitional period;

Whereas, in order to make it easier to take up and pursue the business of credit institutions, it is necessary to eliminate the most obstructive differences between the laws of the Member States as regards the rules to which these institutions are subject;

Whereas, however, given the extent of these differences, the conditions required for a common market for credit institutions cannot be created by means of a single Directive; whereas it is therefore necessary to proceed by successive stages; whereas the result of this process should be to provide for overall supervision of a credit institution operating in several Member States by the competent authorities in the Member State where it has its head office, in consultation, as appropriate, with the competent authorities of the other Member States concerned;

Whereas measures to co-ordinate credit institutions must, both in order to protect savings and to create equal conditions of competition between these institutions, apply to all of them; whereas due regard must be had, where applicable, to the objective differences in their statutes and their proper aims as laid down by national laws;

Whereas the scope of those measures should therefore be as broad as possible, covering all institutions whose business is to receive repayable funds from the public whether in the form of deposits or in other forms such as the continuing issue of bonds and other comparable securities and to grant credits for their own account; whereas exceptions must be provided for in the case of certain credit institutions to which this Directive cannot apply;

Whereas the provisions of this Directive shall not prejudice the application of national laws which provide for special supplementary authorisations permitting credit institutions to carry on specific activities or undertake specific kinds of operations;

Whereas the same system of supervision cannot always be applied to all types of credit institution; whereas provision should therefore be made for application of this Directive to be deferred in the case of certain groups or types of credit institutions to which its immediate application might cause technical problems; whereas more specific provisions for such institutions may prove necessary in the future; whereas these specific provisions should nonetheless be based on a number of common principles;

Whereas the eventual aim is to introduce uniform authorisation requirements throughout the Community for comparable types of credit institution; whereas at the initial stage it is necessary, however, to specify only certain minimum requirements to be imposed by all Member States;

Whereas this aim can be achieved only if the particular wide discretionary powers which certain supervisory authorities have for authorising credit establishments are progressively reduced; whereas the requirement that a programme of operations must be produced should therefore be seen merely as a factor enabling the competent authorities to decide on the basis of more precise information using objective criteria;

Whereas the purpose of co-ordination is to achieve a system whereby credit institutions having their head office in one of the Member States are exempt from any national authorisation requirement when setting up branches in other Member States;

Whereas a measure of flexibility may nonetheless be possible in the initial stage as regards the requirements on the legal form of credit institutions and protection of banking names;

Whereas equivalent financial requirements for credit institutions will be necessary to ensure similar safeguards for savers and fair conditions of competition between comparable groups of credit institutions; whereas, pending further co-ordination, appropriate structural ratios should be formulated that will make it possible within the framework of co-operation between national authorities to observe, in accordance with standard methods, the position of comparable types of credit institutions; whereas this procedure should help to bring about the gradual approximation of the systems of coefficients established and applied by the Member States; whereas it is necessary, however, to make a distinction between coefficients intended to ensure the sound management of credit institutions and those established for the purposes of economic and monetary policy; whereas, for the purpose of formulating structural ratios and of more general co-operation between supervisory authorities, standardisation of the layout of credit institutions' accounts will have to begin as soon as possible;

Whereas the rules governing branches of credit institutions having their head office outside the Community should be analogous in all Member States; whereas it is important at the present time to provide that such rules may not be more favourable than those for branches of institutions from another Member State; whereas it should be specified that the Community may conclude agreements with third countries providing for the application of rules which accord such branches the same treatment throughout its territory, account being taken of the principle of reciprocity;

Whereas the examination of problems connected with matters covered by Council Directives on the business of credit institutions requires co-operation between the competent authorities and the Commission within an Advisory Committee, particularly when conducted with a view to closer co-ordination;

Whereas the establishment of an Advisory Committee of the competent authorities of the Member States does not rule out other forms of co-operation between authorities which supervise the taking up and pursuit of the business of credit institutions and, in particular, co-operation within the Contact Committee set up between the banking supervisory authorities,

NOTES
¹ O J C 128, 9.6.1975, p 25.
² O J C 263, 17.11.1975, p 25.

HAS ADOPTED THIS DIRECTIVE:

TITLE I

DEFINITIONS AND SCOPE

Article 1

For the purposes of this Directive—

— 'credit institution' means an undertaking whose business is to receive deposits or other repayable funds from the public and to grant credits for its own account,

— 'authorisation' means an instrument issued in any form by the authorities by which the right to carry on the business of a credit institution is granted,

— 'branch' means a place of business which forms a legally dependent part of a credit institution and which conducts directly all or some of the operations inherent in the business of credit institutions; any number of branches set up in the same Member State by a credit institution having its head office in another Member State shall be regarded as a single branch, without prejudice to Article 4(1),

— 'own funds' means the credit institution's own capital, including items which may be treated as capital under national rules.

— ['close links' shall mean a situation in which two or more natural or legal persons are linked by—

(a) 'participation', which shall mean the ownership, direct or by way of control, of 20% or more of the voting rights or capital of an undertaking or

(b) 'control', which shall mean the relationship between a parent undertaking and a subsidiary, in all the cases referred to in Article 1(1) and (2) of Directive 83/349/EEC¹, or a similar relationship between any natural or legal person and an undertaking; any subsidiary undertaking of a subsidiary undertaking shall also be considered a subsidiary of the parent undertaking which is at the head of those undertakings.

A situation in which two or more natural or legal persons are permanently linked to one and the same person by a control relationship shall also be regarded as constituting a close link between such persons.]

[851]

NOTES
¹ OJ L 193, 18.7.1983, p 1. Directive as last amended by Directive 90/605/EEC (OJ No L 317, 16.11.1990, p 60).
   Definition 'close links' added by European Parliament and Council Directive 95/26/EC of 29 June 1995, Art 2.

Article 2

1 This Directive shall apply to the taking up and pursuit of the business of credit institutions.

[**2** It shall not apply to—
— the central banks of Member States;
— post office giro institutions;
— in Belgium, the "Institut de Réescompte et de Garantie – Herdiscontering – en Waarborginstituut", the "sociétés nationale et régionales d'investissement – nationale en gewestelijke investeringsmaatschappijen", the regional development companies ("sociétés développement régionales – gewestelijke ontwikkelingsmaatschappijen"), the "Société Nationale du Logement – Nationale Maatschappij voor de Huisvesting" and its authorised companies and the "Société Nationale Terrienne – Nationale Landmaatschappij" and its authorised companies;
— in Denmark, the "Dansk Eksportfinansieringsfond", "Danmarks Skibskreditfond", "Industriens Realkreditfond" and "Dansk Landbrugs Realkreditfond";
— in Germany, the "Kreditanstalt für Wiederaufbau", undertakings which are recognised under the "Wohnungsgemeinnützigkeitsgesetz" as bodies of State housing policy and are not mainly engaged in banking transactions and undertakings recognised under that law as non-profit housing undertakings;
— in Greece, the "Ελληνική Τράπεζα Βιομηχανικής Αναπτύξεως", the "Ταμείο Παρακαταθηκών και Δανείων", the "Τράπεζα Υποθηκών", the "Ταχυδρομικό Ταμειευτήριο" and the "Ελληνικαί Εξαγωγαί ΑΕ";
— in Spain, the "Instituto de Crédito Oficial", with the exception of its subsidiaries;
— in France, the "Caisse des dépôts et consignations"
— in Ireland, credit unions and the friendly societies;
— in Italy, the "Cassa Depositi et Prestiti";
— in the Netherlands, the "NY Export-Financieringsmaatschappij", the "Nederlandse Financieringsmaatschappij voor Ontwikkelingslanden NV", the "Nederlandse Investeringsbank voor Ontwikkelingslanden NV", the "Financierieringsmaatschappij Industrieel Garantiefonds Amsterdam NV", the "Financieringsmaatschappij Industrieel Garantiefonds 's-Gravenhage NV", the "NV Noordelijke Ontwikkelings maatschappij", the "NV Industriebank Limburgs Instituut voor ont-

wikkeling en financiering" and the "Overijsselse Ontwikkelingsmaat-
schappij NV";
— in Portugal, Caixas Económicas existing on 1 January 1986 which are
not incorporated as limited companies;
— in the United Kingdom, the National Savings Bank, the Commonwealth Development Finance Company Ltd, the Agricultural Mortgage Corporation Ltd, the Scottish Agricultural Securities
Corporation Ltd, the Crown Agents for overseas governments and
administrations, credit unions, and municipal banks.]
[— in Austria: enterprises recognized as building associations for the
public benefit;
— in Finland: Teollisen yhteistyön rahasto Oy/Fonden för industriellt
samarbete Ab, Suomen Vientilutotto Oy/Finlands Exportkredit Ab,
Kera Oy/Kera Ab;
— in Sweden: Svenska Skeppshypotekskassan.]

NOTES
This para substituted by Council Directive 86/524/EEC of 27 October 1986, Art 1.
The words in the second pair of square brackets added by the 1994 Act of Accession of the
Kingdom of Norway, the Republic of Austria, the Republic of Finland and the Kingdom of
Sweden, Annex I(XI)(B)(III)(1), as adjusted by Council Decision 95/1/EC, Annex I(XI)(B)(III)(1).

3 The Council, acting on a proposal from the Commission, which, for this
purpose, shall consult the Committee referred to in Article 11 (hereinafter
referred to as 'the Advisory Committee') shall decide on any amendments to
the list in paragraph 2.

4 (a) Credit institutions existing in the same Member State at the time of
the notification of this Directive and permanently affiliated at that
time to a central body which supervises them and which is established
in that same Member State, may be exempted from the requirements
listed in the first, second and third indents of the first subparagraph of
Article 3(2), the second subparagraph of Article 3(2), Article 3(4) and
Article 6, if, no later than the date when the national authorities take
the measures necessary to translate this Directive into national law,
that law provides that—

— the commitments of the central body and affiliated institutions are
joint and several liabilities or the commitments of its affiliated
institutions are entirely guaranteed by the central body.
— the solvency and liquidity of the central body and of all the
affiliated institutions are monitored as a whole on the basis of
consolidated acounts,
— the management of the central body is empowered to issue instructions to the management of the affiliated institutions.

(b) Credit institutions operating locally which are affiliated, subsequent
to notification of this Directive, to a central body within the meaning
of subparagraph (a) may benefit from the condition laid down in
subparagraph (a) if they constitute normal additions to the network
belonging to that central body.

(c) In the case of credit institutions other than those which are set up on
areas newly reclaimed from the sea or have resulted from scission or
mergers of existing institutions dependent or answerable to the central
body, the Council, acting on a proposal from the Commission, which
shall, for this purpose, consult the Advisory Committee, may lay down
additional rules for the application of subparagraph (b) including the
repeal of exemptions provided for in subparagraph (a), where it is of

the opinion that the affiliation of new institutions benefiting from the arrangements laid down in subparagraph (b) might have an adverse effect on competition. The Council shall decide by a qualified majority.

5 Member States may defer in whole or in part the application of this Directive to certain types or groups of credit institutions where such immediate application would cause technical problems which cannot be overcome in the short-term. The problems may result either from the fact that these institutions are subject to supervision by an authority different from that normally responsible for the supervision of banks, or from the fact that they are subject to a special system of supervision. In any event, such deferment cannot be justified by the public law statutes, by the smallness of size or by the limited scope of activity of the particular institutions concerned.

Deferment can apply only to groups or types of institutions already existing at the time of notification of this Directive.

6 Pursuant to paragraph 5, a Member State may decide to defer application of this Directive for a maximum period of five years from the notification thereof and, after consulting the Advisory Committee may extend deferment once only for a maximum period of three years.

The Member State shall inform the Commission of its decision and the reasons thereof not later than six months following the notification of this Directive. It shall also notify the Commission of any extension or repeal of this decision. The Commission shall publish any decision regarding deferment in the *Official Journal of the European Communities*.

Not later than seven years following the notification of this Directive, the Commission shall, after consulting the Advisory Committee, submit a report to the Council on the situation regarding deferment. Where appropriate, the Commission shall submit to the Council, not later than six months following the submission of its report, proposals for either the inclusion of the institutions in question in the list in paragraph 2 or for the authorisation of a further extension of deferment. The Council shall act on these proposals not later than six months after their submission. [852]

TITLE II

CREDIT INSTITUTIONS HAVING THEIR HEAD OFFICE IN A MEMBER STATE AND THEIR BRANCHES IN OTHER MEMBER STATES

Article 3

1 Member States shall require credit institutions subject to this Directive to obtain authorisation before commencing their activities. They shall lay down the requirements for such authorisation subject to paragraphs 2, 3 and 4 and notify them to both the Commission and the Advisory Committee.

2 Without prejudice to other conditions of general application laid down by national laws, the competent authorities shall grant authorisation only when the following conditions are complied with—

— the credit institution must possess separate own funds,
— the credit institution must possess adequate minimum own funds,
— there shall be at least two persons who effectively direct the business of the credit institution.

Moreover, the authorities concerned shall not grant authorisation if the persons referred to in the third indent of the first subparagraph are not of sufficiently good repute or lack sufficient experience to perform such duties.

[Moreover, where close links exist between the credit institution and other natural or legal persons, the competent authorities shall grant authorisation only if those links do not prevent the effective exercise of their supervisory functions.

The competent authorities shall also refuse authorisation if the laws, regulations or administrative provisions of a non-member country governing one or more natural or legal persons with which the undertaking has close links, or difficulties involved in their enforcement, prevent the effective exercise of their supervisory functions.

The competent authorities shall require credit institutions to provide them with the information they require to monitor compliance with the conditions referred to in this paragraph on a continuous basis.]

[2a Each Member State shall require that—

— any credit institution which is a legal person and which, under its national law, has a registered office have its head office in the same Member State as its registered office,
— any other credit institution have its head office in the Member State which issued its authorisation and in which it actually carries on its business.]

3 (a) The provisions referred to in paragraphs 1 and 2 may not require the application for authoristion to be examined in terms of the economic needs of the market.

(b) Where the laws, regulations or administrative provisions of a Member State provide, at the time of notification of the present Directive, that the economic needs of the market shall be a condition of authorisation and where technical or structural difficulties in its banking system do not allow it to give up the criterion within the period laid down in Article 14(1), the State in question may continue to apply the criterion for a period of seven years from notification.

It shall notify its decision and the reasons thereof to the Commission within six months of notification.

[The Hellenic Republic may continue to apply the criterion of economic need. On a request from the Hellenic Republic, the Commission shall, if appropriate, submit to the Council by 15 June 1989 proposals authorising the Hellenic Republic to continue to apply the criterion of economic need until 15 December 1992.

The Council shall act within six months of the submission of those proposals.]

(c) Within six years of the notification of this Directive the Commission shall submit to the Council, after consulting the Advisory Committee, a report on the application of the criterion of economic need. If appropriate, the Commission shall submit to the Council proposals to terminate the application of that criterion. The period referred to in subparagraph (b) shall be extended for one further period of five years, unless, in the meantime, the Council, acting unanimously on proposals from the Commission, adopts a Decision to terminate the application of that criterion.

(d) The criterion of economic need shall be applied only on the basis of general predetermined criteria, pubished and notified to both the Commission and the Advisory Committee and aimed at promoting—

— security of savings,

— higher productivity in the banking system,
— greater uniformity of competition between the various banking networks,
— a broader range of banking services in relation to population and economic activity

    Specification of the above objectives shall be determined within the Advisory Committee, which shall begin its work as from its initial meetings.

4 Member States shall also require applications for authorisation to be accompanied by a programme of operations setting out inter alia the types of business envisaged and the structural organisation of the institution.

5 The Advisory Committee shall examine the content given by the competent authorities to requirements listed in paragraph 2, any other requirements which the Member States apply and the information which must be included in the programme of operations, and shall, where appropriate, make suggestions to the Commission with a view to a more detailed co-ordination.

6 Reasons shall be given whenever an authorisation is refused and the applicant shall be notified thereof within six months of receipt of the application or, should the latter be incomplete, within six months of the applicant's sending the information required for the decision. A decision shall, in any case, be taken within 12 months of the receipt of the application.

7 Every authorisation shall be notified to the Commission. Each credit institution shall be entered in a list which the Commission shall publish in the *Official Journal of the European Communities* and shall keep up to date. **[853]**

NOTES

Para (2): sub-paras added to the end by European Parliament and Council Directive 95/26/EC of 29 June 1995, Art 2.

Para (2a): inserted by European Parliament and Council Directive 95/26/EC of 29 June 1995, Art 3.

Para (3b): sub-paras added to the end by Council Directive 85/345/EEC of 8 July 1985, Art 1.

Article 4

1 Member States may make the commencement of business in their territory by branches of credit institutions covered by this Directive which have their head office in another Member State subject to authorisation according to the law and procedure applicable to credit institutions established on their territory.

2 However, authorisation may not be refused to a branch of a credit institution on the sole ground that it is established in another Member State in a legal form which is not allowed in the case of a credit institution carrying out similar activities in the host country. This provision shall not apply, however, to credit institutions which possess no separate own funds.

3 The competent authorities shall inform the Commission of any authorisations which they grant to the branches referred to in paragraph 1.

4 This Article shall not affect the rules applied by Member States to branches set up on their territory by credit institutions which have their head office there. Notwithstanding the second part of the third indent of Article 1, the laws of Member States requiring a separate authorisation for each branch of a credit institution having its head office in their territory shall apply equally to the branches of credit institutions the head offices of which are in other Member States. **[854]**

Article 5

For the purpose of exercising their activities, credit institutions to which this Directive applies may, notwithstanding any provisions concerning the use of the words' 'bank', 'saving bank', or other banking names which may exist in the host Member State, use throughout the territory of the Community the same name as they use in the Member States in which their head office is situated. In the event of there being any danger of confusion, the host Member State may, for the purposes of clarification, require that the name be accompanied by certain explanatory particulars.   [855]

Article 6

1 Pending subsequent co-ordination, the competent authorities shall, for the purposes of observation and, if necessary, in addition to such coefficients as may be applied by them, establish ratios between the various assets and/or liabilities of credit institutions with a view to monitoring their solvency and liquidity and the other measures which may serve to ensure that savings are protected.

To this end, the Advisory Committee shall decide on the content of the various factors of the observation ratios referred to in the first subparagraph and lay down the method to be applied in calculating them.

Where appropriate, the Advisory Committee shall be guided by technical consultations between the supervisory authorities of the categories of institutions concerned.

2 The observation ratios established in pursuance of paragraph 1 shall be calculated at least every six months.

3 The Advisory Committee shall examine the results of analyses carried out by the supervisory authorities referred to in the third subparagraph of paragraph 1 on the basis of the calculations referred to in paragraph 2.

4 The Advisory Committee may make suggestions to the Commission with a view to co-ordinating the coefficients applicable in the Member States.   [856]

Article 7

1 The competent authorities of the Member States concerned shall collaborate closely in order to supervise the activities of credit institutions operating, in particular by having established branches there, in one or more Member States other than that in which their head offices are situated. They shall supply one another with all information concerning the management and ownership of such credit institutions that is likely to facilitate their supervision and the examination of the conditions for their authorisation [and all information likely to facilitate the monitoring of such institutions, in particular with regard to liquidity, solvency, deposit guarantees, the limiting of large exposures, administrative and accounting procedures and internal control mechanisms].

2 The competent authorities may also for the purposes and within the meaning of Article 6, lay down ratios applicable to the branches referred to in this Article by the specific situation of the branches in relation to national regulations.   [857]

NOTES

Para (1): words substituted by Council Directive 89/646/EEC of 15 December 1989 Art 14(1).

Article 8

1 The competent authorities may withdraw the authorisation issued to a credit institution subject to this Directive or to a branch authorised under Article 4 only where such an institution or branch—

    (a) does not make use of the authorisation within 12 months, expressly renounces the authorisation or has ceased to engage in business for more than six months, if the Member State concerned has made no provision for the authorisation to lapse in such cases;

    (b) has obtained the authorisation through false statements or any other irregular means;

    (c) no longer fulfils the conditions under which authorisation was granted, with the exception of those in respect of own funds;

    (d) no longer possesses sufficient own funds or can no longer be relied upon to fulfil its obligations towards its creditors, and in particular no longer provides security for the assets entrusted to it;

    (e) falls within one of the other cases where national law provides for withdrawal of authorisation.

2 In addition, the authorisation issued to a branch under Article 4 shall be withdrawn if the competent authority of the country in which the credit institution which established the branch has its head office has withdrawn authorisation from that institution.

3 Member States which grant the authorisations referred to in Article 3(1) and 4(1) only if, economically, the market situation requires it may not invoke the disappearance of such a need as grounds for withdrawing such authorisations.

4 Before withdawal from a branch of an authorisation granted under Article 4, the competent authority of the Member State in which its head office is situated shall be consulted. Where immediate action is called for, notification may take the place of such consultation. The same procedure shall be followed, by analogy, in cases of withdrawal of authorisation from a credit institution which has branches in other Member States.

5 Reasons must be given for any withdrawal of authorisation and those concerned informed thereof; such withdrawal shall be notified to the Commission.   **[858]**

TITLE III

BRANCHES OF CREDIT INSTITUTIONS HAVING THEIR HEAD OFFICES OUTSIDE THE COMMUNITY

Article 9

1 Member States shall not apply to branches of credit institutions having their head office outside the Community, when commencing or carrying on their business, provisions which result in more favourable treatment than that accorded to branches of credit institutions having their head office in the Community.

2 The competent authorities shall notify the Commission and the Advisory Committee of all authorisations for branches granted to credit institutions having their head office outside the Community.

3 Without prejudice to paragraph 1, the Community may, through agreements concluded in accordance with the Treaty with one or more third countries, agree to apply provisions which, on the basis of the principle of reciprocity, accord to branches of a credit institution having its head office outside the Community identical treatment throughout the territory of the Community.   **[859]**

TITLE IV

GENERAL AND TRANSITIONAL PROVISIONS

Article 10

1 Credit institutions subject to this Directive, which took up their business in accordance with the provisions of the Member States in which they have their head offices before the entry into force of the provisions implementing this Directive shall be deemed to be authorised. They shall be subject to the provisions of this Directive concerning the carrying on of the business of credit institutions and to the requirements set out in the first and third indents of the first subparagraph and in the second subparagraph of Article 3(2).

Member States may allow credit institutions which at the time of notification of this Directive do not comply with the requirement laid down in the third indent of the first paragraph of Article 3(2), no more than five years in which to do so.

Member States may decide that undertakings which do not fulfil the requirements set out in the first indent of the first subparagraph of Article 3(2) and which are in existence at the time this Directive enters into force may continue to carry on their business. They may exempt such undertakings from complying with the requirement contained in the third indent of the first subparagraph of Article 3(2).

2 All the credit institutions referred to in paragraph 1 shall be given in the list referred to in Article 3(7).

3 If a credit institution deemed to be authorised under paragraph 1 has not undergone any authorisation procedure prior to commencing business, a prohibition on the carrying on of its business shall take the place of withdrawal of authorisation.

Subject to the first subparagraph, Article 8 shall apply by analogy.

4 By way of derogation from paragraph 1, credit institutions established in a Member State without having undergone an authorisation procedure in that Member State prior to commencing business may be required to obtain authorisation from the competent authorities of the Member State concerned in accordance with the provisions implementing this Directive. Such institutions may be required to comply with the requirement in the second indent of Article 3(2) and with such other conditions of general application as may be laid down by the Member State concerned. **[860]**

Article 11

1 An 'Advisory Committee of the Competent Authorities of the Member States of the European Economic Community' shall be set up alongside the Commission.

2 The tasks of the Advisory Committee shall be to assist the Commission in ensuring the proper implementation of both this Directive and Council Directive 73/183/EEC of 28 June 1973 on the abolition of restrictions on freedom of establishment and freedom to provide services in respect of self-employed activities of banks and other financial institutions[1] in so far as it relates to credit institutions. Further it shall carry out the other tasks prescribed by this Directive and shall assist the Commission in the preparation of new proposals to the Council concerning further co-ordination in the sphere of credit institutions.

3 The Advisory Committee shall not concern itself with concrete problems relating to individual credit institutions.

4 The Advisory Committee shall be composed of not more than three representatives from each Member State and from the Commission. These representatives may be accompanied by advisers from time to time and subject to the prior agreement of the Committee. The Committee may also invite qualified persons and experts to participate in its meetings. The secretariat shall be provided by the Commission.

5 The first meeting of the Advisory Committee shall be convened by the Commission under the chairmanship of one of its representatives. The Advisory Committee shall then adopt its rules of procedure and shall elect a chairman from among the representatives of Member States. Thereafter it shall meet at regular intervals and whenever the situation demands. The Commission may ask the Committee to hold an emergency meeting if it considers that the situation so requires.

6 The Advisory Committee's discussions and the outcome thereof shall be confidential except when the Committee decides otherwise.   **[861]**

NOTES
[1] OJ L 194, 16.7.1973, p 1.

[Article 12

1 The Member States shall provide that all persons working or who have worked for the competent authorities, as well as auditors or experts acting on behalf of the competent authorities, shall be bound by the obligation of professional secrecy. This means that no confidential information which they may receive in the course of their duties may be divulged to any person or authority whatsoever, except in summary or collective form, such that individual institutions cannot be identified, without prejudice to cases covered by criminal law.

Nevertheless, where a credit institution has been declared bankrupt or is being compulsorily wound up, confidential information which does not concern third parties involved in attempts to rescue that credit institution may be divulged in civil or commercial proceedings.

2 Paragraph 1 shall not prevent the competent authorities of the various Member States from exchanging information in accordance with the Directives applicable to credit institutions. That information shall be subject to the conditions of professional secrecy indicated in paragraph 1.

3 Member States may conclude cooperation agreements, providing for exchanges of information, with the competent authorities of third countries only if the information disclosed is subject to guarantees of professional secrecy at least equivalent to those referred to in this Article.

4 Competent authorities receiving confidential information under paragraphs 1 or 2 may use it only in the course of their duties:

— to check that the conditions governing the taking-up of the business of credit institutions are met and to facilitate monitoring, on a nonconsolidated or consolidated basis, of the conduct of such business, especially with regard to the monitoring of liquidity, solvency, large exposures, and administrative and accounting procedures and internal control mechanisms, or
— to impose sanctions, or

— in an administrative appeal against a decision of the competent authority, or
— in court proceedings initiated pursuant to Article 13 or to special provisions provided for in the Directives adopted in the field of credit institutions.

5 Paragraphs 1 and 4 shall not preclude the exchange of information within a Member State, where there are two or more competent authorities in the same Member State, or between Member States, between competent authorities and:

— authorities responsible for the supervision of other financial organisations and insurance companies and the authorities responsible for the supervision of financial markets,
— bodies involved in the liquidation and bankruptcy of credit institutions and in other similar procedures,
— persons responsible for carrying out statutory audits of the accounts of credit institutions and other financial institutions.

in the discharge of their supervisory functions, and the disclosure to bodies which administer deposit-guarantee schemes of information necessary to the exercise of their functions. The information received shall be subject to the conditions of professional secrecy indicated in paragraph 1.

[5a Notwithstanding paragraphs 1 to 4, Member States may authorise exchanges of information between, the competent authorities and—

— the authorities responsible for overseeing the bodies involved in the liquidation and bankruptcy of credit institutions and other similar procedures, or
— the authorities responsible for overseeing persons charged with carrying out statutory audits of the accounts of insurance undertakings, credit institutions, investment firms and other financial institutions.

Member States which have recourse to the option provided for in the first subparagraph shall require at least that the following conditions are met—

— the information shall be for the purpose of performing the task of overseeing referred to in the first subparagraph,
— information received in this context shall be subject to the conditions of professional secrecy imposed in paragraph 1,
— where the information originates in another Member State, it may not be disclosed without the express agreement of the competent authorities which have disclosed it and, where appropriate, solely for the purposes for which those authorities gave their agreement.

Member States shall communicate to the Commission and to the other Member States the names of the authorities which may receive information pursuant to this paragraph.]

[5b Notwithstanding paragraphs 1 to 4, Member States may, with the aim of strengthening the stability, including integrity, of the financial system, authorise the exchange of information between the competent authorities and the authorities or bodies responsible under the law for the detection and investigation of breaches of company law.

Member States which have recourse to the option provided for in the first subparagraph shall require at least that the following conditions are met—

— the information shall be for the purpose of performing the task referred to in the first subparagraph,

— information received in this context shall be subject to the conditions of professional secrecy imposed in paragraph 1,

— where the information originates in another Member State, it may not be disclosed without the express agreement of the competent authorities which have disclosed it and, where appropriate, solely for the purposes for which those authorities gave their agreement.

Where, in a Member State, the authorities or bodies referred to in the first subparagraph perform their task of detection or investigation with the aid, in view of their specific competence, of persons appointed for that purpose and not employed in the public sector, the possibility of exchanging information provided for in the first subparagraph may be extended to such persons under the conditions stipulated in the second subparagraph.

In order to implement the final indent of the second subparagraph, the authorities or bodies referred to in the first subparagraph shall communicate to the competent authorities which have disclosed the information, the names and precise responsibilities of the persons to whom it is to be sent.

Member States shall communicate to the Commission and to the other Member States the names of the authorities or bodies which may receive information pursuant to this paragraph.

Before 31 December 2000, the Commission shall draw up a report on the application of the provisions of this paragraph.]

[**6** This Article shall not prevent a competent authority from transmitting—

— to central banks and other bodies with a similar function in their capacity as monetary authorities,

— where appropriate, to other public authorities responsible for overseeing payment systems,

information intended for the performance of their task, nor shall it prevent such authorities or bodies from communicating to the competent authorities such information as they may need for the purposes of paragraph 4. Information received in this context shall be subject to the conditions of professional secrecy imposed in this Article.]

7 In addition, notwithstanding the provisions referred to in paragraphs 1 and 4, the Member States may, by virtue of provisions laid down by law, authorise the disclosure of certain information to other departments of their central government administrations responsible for legislation on the supervision of credit institutions, financial institutions, investment services and insurance companies and to inspectors acting on behalf of those departments.

However, such disclosures may be made only where necessary for reasons of prudential control.

However, the Member States shall provide that information received under paragraphs 2 and 5 and that obtained by means of the on-the-spot verification referred to in Article 15(1) and (2) of Directive 89/646/EEC^T may never be disclosed in the cases referred to in this paragraph except with the express consent of the competent authorities which dislosed the information or of the competent authorities of the Member State in which on-the-spot verification was carried out.]

[**8** This Article shall not prevent the competent authorities from communicating the information referred to in paragraphs 1 to 4 to a clearing house or other similar body recognised under national law for the provision of clearing or settlement services for one of their Member States' markets if they consider that it is necessary to communicate the information in order to ensure the proper functioning of those bodies in relation to defaults or potential defaults by market participants. The information received in this context shall be subject to the conditions of professional secrecy referred to in paragraph 1. The Member States shall, however, ensure that information received under paragraph 2 may not be disclosed in the circumstances referred to in this paragraph without the express consent of the competent authorities which disclosed it.]

[862]

NOTES
[1] OJ L 386, 30.12.1989, p 1.
Substituted by Council Directive 89/646/EEC of 15 December 1989, Art 16.
Paras (5a), (5b): inserted by European Parliament and Council Directive 95/26/EC of 29 June 1995, Art 4.
Para (6): substituted by ibid.
Para (8): added by ibid.

Article 12a

1 Member States shall provide at least that—

(a) any person authorised within the meaning of Directive 84/253/EEC[1], performing in a financial undertaking the task described in Article 51 of Directive 78/660/EEC[2], Article 37 of Directive 83/349/EEC or Article 31 of Directive 85/611/EEC or any other statutory task, shall have a duty to report promptly to the competent authorities any fact or decision concerning that undertaking of which he has become aware while carrying out that task which is liable to—

— constitute a material breach of the laws, regulations sor administrative provisions which lay down the conditions governing authorisation or which specifically govern pursuit of the activities of credit institutions; or

— affect the continuous functioning of the credit institution; or

— lead to refusal to certify the accounts or to the expression of reservations;

(b) that person shall likewise have a duty to report any facts and decisions of which he becomes aware in the course of carrying out a task as described in (a) in an undertaking having close links resulting from a control relationship with the financial undertaking within whcih he is carrying out the abovementioned task.

2 The disclosure in good faith to the competent authorities, by persons authorised within the meaning of Directive 84/253/EEC, of any fact or decision referred to in paragraph 1 shall not constitute a breach of any restriction on disclosure of information imposed by contract or by any legislative, regulatory or administrative provision and shall not involve such persons in liability of any kind.]

[862A]

NOTES
[1] OJ L 126, 12.5.1984, p 20.
[2] OJ L 222, 14.8.1978, p 11. Directive as last amended by Directive 90/60/EEC (OJ L 317, 16.11.1990, p 60).
Inserted by European Parliament and Council Directive 95/26/EC of 29 June 1995, Art 4.

Article 13

Member States shall ensure that decisions taken in respect of a credit institution in pursuance of laws, regulations and administrative provisions adopted in accordance with this Directive may be subject to the right to apply to the courts. The same shall apply where no decision is taken within six months of its submission in respect of an application for authorisation which contains all the information required under the provisions in force.   **[863]**

TITLE V

FINAL PROVISIONS

Article 14

1 Member States shall bring into force the measures necessary to comply with this Directive within 24 months of its notification and shall forthwith inform the Commission thereof.

2 As from the notification of this Directive, Member States shall communicate to the Commission the texts of the main laws, regulations and administrative provisions which they adopt in the field covered by this Directive. **[864]**

Article 15

This Directive is addressed to the Member States.   **[865]**

Done at Brussels, 12 December 1977.

COUNCIL DIRECTIVE
of 8 December 1986

on the annual accounts and consolidated accounts of banks and other financial institutions

(86/635/EEC)

NOTES
Date of publication in OJ: OJ L 372, 31.12.1986, p 1.

THE COUNCIL OF THE EUROPEAN COMMUNITIES,

Having regard to the Treaty establishing the European Community, and in particular article 53(4)(g) thereof,
Having regard to the proposal from the Commission,[1]
Having regard to the opinion of the European Parliament,[2]
Having regard to the opinion of the Economic and Social Committee,[3]
Whereas Council Directive 78/660/EEC of 25 July 1978, based on Article 54(3)(g) of the Treaty, on the annual accounts of certain types of companies,[4] as last amended by Directive 84/569/EEC,[5] need not be applied to banks and other financial institutions, hereafter referred to as 'credit institutions', pending subsequent coordination; whereas in view of the central importance of these undertakings in the Community, such coordination is necessary;
Whereas Council Directive 83/349/EEC of 13 June 1983, based on Article 54(3)(g) of the Treaty, on consolidated accounts,[6] provides for derogations for credit institutions only until expiry of the deadline imposed for the application of this Directive; whereas this Directive must therefore also include provisions specific to credit institutions in respect of considated accounts;
Whereas such coordination has also become urgent because more and more credit institutions are operating across national borders; whereas for creditors, debtors and members and for the general public improved comparability of the annual accounts and consolidated accounts of these institutions is of crucial importance;
Whereas in virtually all the Member States of the Community credit institutions within the meaning of Council Directive 77/780/EEC of 12 December 1977 on the coordination of laws, regulations and administrative provisions relating to the taking up and pursuit of the business of

credit institutions,[7] having many different legal forms are in competition with one another in the banking sector; whereas it therefore seems advisable not to confine coordination in respect of these credit institutions to the legal forms covered by Directive 78/660/EEC but rather to opt for a scope which includes all companies and firms as defined in the second paragraph of Article 58 of the Treaty;

Whereas as far as financial institutions are concerned the scope of this Directive should however be confined to those financial institutions taking one of the legal forms referred to in Directive 78/660/EEC; whereas financial institutions which are not subject to that Directive must automatically come under this Directive;

Whereas a link with coordination in respect of credit institutions is necessary because aspects of the provisions governing annual accounts and consolidated accounts will have an impact on other areas of that coordination, such as authorisation requirements and the indicators used for supervisory purposes;

Whereas although, in view of the specific characteristics of credit institutions, it would appear appropriate to adopt a separate Directive on the annual accounts and consolidated accounts of such institutions, this does not imply a new set of rules separate from those under Directives 78/660/EEC and 83/349/EEC; whereas such separate rules would be neither appropriate nor consistent with the principles underlying the coordination of company law since, given the important role which they play in the Community economy, credit institutions cannot be excluded from a framework of rules devised for undertakings generally; whereas, for this reason, only the particular characteristics of credit institutions have been taken into account and this Directive deals only with exceptions to the rules contained in Directives 78/660/EEC and 83/349/EEC;

Whereas the structure and content of the balance sheets of credit institutions differ in each Member State; whereas this Directive must therefore prescribe the same layout, nomenclature and terminology for the balance sheets of all credit institutions in the Community; whereas derogations should be allowed if necessitated by the legal form of an institution or by the special nature of its business;

Whereas, if the annual accounts and consolidated accounts are to be comparable, a number of basic questions regarding the disclosure of various transactions in the balance sheet and off the balance sheet must be settled;

Whereas, in the interests of greater comparability, it is also necessary that the content of the various balance sheet and off-balance sheet items be determined precisely;

Whereas the same applies to the layout and definition of the items in the profit and loss account;

Whereas the comparability of figures in the balance sheet and profit and loss account also depends crucially on the values at which assets and liabilities are entered in the balance sheet;

Whereas, in view of the particular risks associated with banking and of the need to maintain confidence, provision should be made for the possibility of introducing a liabilities item in the balance sheet entitled 'Fund for general banking risks'; whereas it would appear advisable for the same reasons that the Member States be permitted, pending subsequent coordination, to allow credit institutions some discretion, especially in the valuation of loans and advances and of certain securities; whereas, however, in this last case the Member States should allow these same credit institutions to create the 'Fund for general banking risks' mentioned above; whereas it would also appear appropriate to permit the Member States to allow credit institutions to set off certain charges and income in the profit and loss account;

Whereas, in view of the special nature of credit institutions, certain changes are also necessary with regard to the notes on the accounts;

Whereas, in the desire to place on the same footing as many credit institutions as possible, as was the case with Directive 77/780/EEC, the relief under Directive 78/660/EEC is not provided for in the case of small and medium-sized credit institutions; whereas, nevertheless, if in the light of experience such relief were to prove necessary it would be possible to provide for it in subsequent coordination; whereas for the same reasons the scope allowed the Member States under Directive 83/349/EEC to exempt parent undertakings from the consolidation requirement if the undertakings to be consolidated do not together exceed a certain size has not been extended to credit institutions;

Whereas the application of the provisions on consolidated accounts to credit institutions requires certain adjustments to some of the rules applicable to all industrial and commercial companies; whereas explicit rules have been provided for in the case of mixed groups and exemption from subconsolidation may be made subject to additional conditions;

Whereas, given the scale on which banking networks extend beyond national borders and their constant development, the annual accounts and consolidated accounts of a credit institution having its head office in one Member State should be published in all the Member States in which it is established;

Whereas the examination of problems which arise in connection with the subject matter of this Directive, notably concerning its application, requires the cooperation of representatives of the Member States and the Commission in a contact committee; whereas, in order to avoid the proliferation of such committees, it is desirable that such cooperation take place in the Committee provided for in Article 52 of Directive 78/660/EEC; whereas, nevertheless, when examining problems concerning credit institutions, the Committee will have to be appropriately constituted;

Whereas, in view of the complexity of the matter, the credit institutions covered by this Directive must be allowed a longer period than usual to implement its provisions;

Whereas provision should be made for the review of certain provisions of this Directive after five years' experience of its application, in the light of the aims of greater transparency and harmonisation,

NOTES
[1] OJ C 130, 1.6.1981, p 1, OJ C 83, 24.3.1984, p 6 and OJ C 351, 31.12.1985, p 24.
[2] OJ C 242, 12.9.1983, p 33 and OJ C 163, 10.7.1978, p 60.
[3] OJ C 112, 3.5.1982, p 60.
[4] OJ L 222, 14.8.1978, p 11.
[5] OJ L 314, 4.12.1984, p 28.
[6] OJ L 193, 18.7.1983, p 1.
[7] OJ L 322, 17.12.1977, p 30.

HAS ADOPTED THIS DIRECTIVE:

SECTION 1

PRELIMINARY PROVISIONS AND SCOPE

Article 1

1 Articles 2, 3, 4(1), (3) to (5), 6, 7, 13, 14, 15(3) and (4), 16 to 21, 29 to 35, 37 to 41, 42 first sentence, 45(1), 46, 48 to 50, 51(1), 54, 56 to 59 and 61 of Directive 78/660/EEC shall apply to the institutions mentioned in Article 2 of this Directive, except where this Directive provides otherwise.

2 Where reference is made in Directives 78/660/EEC and 83/349/EEC to Articles 9 and 10 (balance sheet) or to Articles 23 to 26 (profit and loss account) of Directive 78/660/EEC, such references shall be deemed to be references to Articles 4 (balance sheet) or to Articles 27 and 28 (profit and loss account) of this Directive.

3 References in Directives 78/660/EEC and 83/349/EEC to Articles 31 to 42 of Directive 78/660/EEC shall be deemed to be references to those Articles, taking account of Articles 35 to 39 of this Directive.

4 Where reference is made in the aforementioned provisions of Directive 78/660/EEC to balance sheet items for which this Directive makes no equivalent provision, such references shall be deemed to be references to the items in Article 4 of this Directive which include the assets and liabilities in question.   **[866]**

Article 2

The coordination measures prescribed by this Directive shall apply to

    (a) credit institutions within the meaning of the first indent of Article 1 of Directive 77/780/EEC which are companies or firms as defined in the second paragraph of Article 58 of the Treaty;

    (b) financial institutions having one of the legal forms referred to in Article 1(1) of Directive 78/660/EEC which, on the basis of paragraph 2 of that Article, are not subject to that Directive.

For the purposes of this Directive 'credit institutions' shall also include financial institutions unless the context requires otherwise.

2 The Member States need not apply this Directive to—

    (a) the credit insitutions listed in Article 2(2) of Directive 77/780/EEC;

(b) institutions of the same Member State which, as defined in Article 2(4)(a) of Directive 77/780/EEC, are affiliated to a central body in that Member State. In that case, without prejudice to the application of this Directive to the central body, the whole constituted by the central body and its affiliated institutions must be the subject of consolidated accounts including an annual report which shall be drawn up, audited and published in accordance with this Directive;

(c) the following credit institutions—
   — in Greece: ETEBA (National Investment Bank for Industrial Development) and Τράπεζα Επενδύσεων (Investment Bank),
   — in Ireland: Industrial and Provident Societies,
   — in the United Kingdom: Friendly Societies and Industrial and Provident Societies.

4 Without prejudice to Article 2(3) of Directive 78/660/EEC and pending subsequent coordination, the Member States may—

(a) in the case of the credit institutions referred to in Article 2(1)(a) of this Directive which are not companies of any of the types listed in Article 1(1) of Directive 78/660/EEC, lay down rules derogating from this Directive where derogating rules are necessary because of such institutions' legal form;

(b) In the case of specialised credit institutions, lay down rules derogating from this Directive where derogating rules are necessary because of the special nature of such institutions' business.

Such derogating rules may provide only for adaptations to the layout, nomenclature, terminology and content of items in the balance sheet and the profit and loss account; they may not have the effect of permitting the institutions to which they apply to provide less information in their annual accounts than other institutions subject to this Directive.

The Member States shall inform the Commission of those credit institutions, possibly by category, within six months of the end of the period stipulated in Article 47(2). They shall inform the Commission of the derogations laid down to that end.

These derogations shall be reviewed within 10 years of the notification of this Directive. The Commission shall, if appropriate, submit suitable proposals. It shall also submit an interim report within five years of the notification of this Directive. **[867]**

SECTION 2

GENERAL PROVISIONS CONCERNING THE BALANCE SHEET AND THE PROFIT AND LOSS ACCOUNT

Article 3

In the case of credit institutions the possibility of combining items pursuant to Article 4(3)(a) of (b) of Directive 78/660/EEC shall be restricted to balance sheet and profit and loss account sub-items preceded by lower-case letters and shall be authorised only under the rules laid down by the Member States to that end. **[868]**

SECTION 3
LAYOUT OF THE BALANCE SHEET

Article 4

The Member States shall prescribe the following layout for the balance sheet.

Assets

1 Cash in hand, balances with central banks and post office banks

  2 Treasury bills and other bills eligible for refinancing with central banks—

    (a) Treasury bills and similar securities
    (b) Other bills eligible for refinancing with central banks (unless national law prescribes that such bills be shown under Assets items 3 and 4)

  3 Loans and advances to credit institutions—

    (a) repayable on demand
    (b) other loans and advances

  4 Loans and advances to customers

  5 Debt securities including fixed-income securities—

    (a) issued by public bodies
    (b) issued by other borrowers, showing separately—
    — own-debt securities (unless national law requires their deduction from liabilities).

  6 Shares and other variable-yield securities

  7 Participating interests, showing separately—

    — participating interests in credit institutions (unless national law requires their disclosure in the notes on the accounts)

  8 Shares in affiliated undertakings, showing separately—

    — shares in credit institutions (unless national law requires their disclosure in the notes on the accounts)

  9 Intangible assets as described under Assets headings B and C.I of Article 9 of Directive 78/660/EEC, showing separately—

    — formation expenses, as defined by national law and in so far as national law permits their being shown as an asset (unless national law requires their disclosure in the notes on the accounts)
    — goodwill, to the extent that it was acquired for valuable consideration (unless national law requires its disclosure in the notes on the accounts)

  10 Tangible assets as described under assets heading C.II of Article 9 of Directive 78/660/EEC, showing separately—

    — land and buildings occupied by a credit institution for its own activities (unless national law requires their disclosure in the notes on the accounts)

  11 Subscribed capital unpaid, showing separately—

    — called-up capital (unless national law provides for called-up capital to be included under liabilities, in which case capital called but not yet paid must be included either in this Assets item or in Assets item 14)

12 Own shares (with an indication of their nominal value or, in the absence of a nominal value, their accounting par value to the extent that national law permits their being shown in the balance sheet)

13 Other assets

14 Subscribed capital called but not paid (unless national law requires that called-up capital be shown under Assets item 11)

15 Prepayments and accrued income

16 Loss for the financial year (unless national law provides for its inclusion under Liabilities item 14)

Total assets

Liabilities

1 Amounts owed to credit institutions—

    (a) repayable on demand
    (b) with agreed maturity dates or periods of notice

2 Amounts owed to customers:

    (a) savings deposits, showing separately—

        — those repayable on demand and those with agreed maturity dates or periods of notice where national law provides for such a breakdown (unless national law provides for such information to be given in the notes on the accounts)

    (b) other debts
        (ba) repayable on demand
        (bb) with agreed maturity dates or periods of notice

3 Debts evidenced by certificates—

    (a) debt securities in issue
    (b) others

4 Other liabilities

5 Accruals and deferred income

6 Provisions for liabilities and charges—

    (a) provisions for pensions and similar obligations
    (b) provisions for taxation
    (c) other provisions

7 Profit for the financial year (unless national law provides for its inclusion under Liabilities item 14)

8 Subordinated liabilities

9 Subscribed capital (unless national law provides for called-up capital to be shown under this item. In that case, the amounts of subscribed capital and paid-up capital must be shown separately)

10 Share premium account

11 Reserves

12 Revaluation reserve

13 Profit or loss brought forward

14 Profit or loss for the financial year (unless national law requires that this item be shown under Assets item 16 or Liabilities item 7)

Total liabilities

OFF-BALANCE SHEET ITEMS

1 Contingent liabilities, showing separately—
— acceptances and endorsements
— guarantees and assets pledged as collateral security

2 Commitments, showing separately—
— commitments arising out of sale and repurchase transactions

[869]

Article 5

The following must be shown separately as sub-items of the items in question—
— claims, whether or not evidenced by certificates, on affiliated undertakings and included in Assets items 2 to 5,
— claims, whether or not evidenced by certificates, on undertakings with which a credit institution is linked by virtue of a participating interest and included in Assets items 2 to 5,
— liabilities, whether or not evidenced by certificates, to affiliated undertakings and included in Liabilities items 1, 2, 3 and 8.
— liabilities, whether or not evidenced by certificates to undertakings with which a credit institution is linked by virtue of a participating interest and included in Liabilities items, 1, 2, 3 and 8. **[870]**

Article 6

1 Subordinated assets shall be shown separately as sub-items of the items of the layout and the sub-items created in accordance with Article 5.

2 Assets, whether or not evidenced by certificates, are subordinated if, in the event of winding up or bankruptcy, they are to be repaid only after the claims of other creditors have been met. **[871]**

Article 7

The Member States may permit the disclosure of the information referred to in Articles 5 and 6, duly broken down into the various relevant items, in the notes on the accounts. **[872]**

Article 8

1 Assets shall be shown under the relevant balance sheet headings even where the credit institution drawing up the balance sheet has pledged them as security for its own liabilities or for those of third parties or has otherwise assigned them as security to third parties.

2 A credit institution shall not include in its balance sheet assets pledged or otherwise assigned to it as security unless such assets are in the form of cash in the hands of that credit institution. **[873]**

Article 9

1 Where a loan has been granted by a syndicate consisting of a number of credit institutions, each credit institution participating in the syndicate shall disclose only that part of the total loan which it has itself funded.

2 If in the case of a syndicated loan such as described in paragraph 1 the amount of funds guaranteed by a credit institution exceeds the amount which it has made available, any additional guarantee portion shall be shown as a contingent liability (in Off-balance sheet item 1, second indent).   **[874]**

Article 10

1 Funds which a credit institution administers in its own name but on behalf of third parties must be shown in the balance sheet if the credit institution acquires legal title to the assets concerned. The total amount of such assets and liabilities shall be shown separately or in the notes on the accounts, broken down according to the various Assets and Liabilities items. However, the Member States may permit the disclosure of such funds off the balance sheet provided there are special rules whereby such funds can be excluded from the assets available for distribution in the event of the winding-up of a credit institution (or similar proceedings).

2 Assets acquired in the name of and on behalf of third parties must not be shown in the balance sheet.   **[875]**

Article 11

Only those amounts which can at any time be withdrawn without notice or for which a maturity or period of notice of 24 hours or one working day has been agreed shall be regarded as repayable on demand.   **[876]**

Article 12

1 Sale and repurchase transactions shall mean transactions which involve the transfer by a credit institution or customer (the 'transferor') to another credit institution or customer (the 'transferee') of assets, for example, bills, debts or transferable securities, subject to an agreement that the same assets will subsequently be transferred back to the transferor at a specified price.

2 If the transferee undertakes to return the assets on a date specified or to be specified by the transferor, the transaction in question shall be deemed to be a genuine sale and repurchase transaction.

3 If, however, the transferee is merely entitled to return the assets at the purchase price or for a different amount agreed in advance on a date specified or to be specified, the transaction in question shall be deemed to be a sale with an option to repurchase,

4 In the case of the sale and repurchase transactions referred to in paragraph 2, the assets transferred shall continue to appear in the transferor's balance sheet; the purchase price received by the transferor shall be shown as an amount owed to the transferee. In addition, the value of the assets transferred shall be disclosed in a note in the transferor's accounts. The transferee shall not be entitled to show the assets transferred in his balance sheet; the purchase price paid by the transferee shall be shown as an amount owed by the transferor.

5 In the case of the sale and repurchase transactions referred to in paragraph 3, however, the transferor shall not be entitled to show in his balance sheet the assets transferred; those items shall be shown as assets in the transferee's balance sheet. The transferor shall enter under Off-balance sheet item 2 an amount equal to the price agreed in the event of repurchase.

6 No forward exchange transactions, options, transactions involving the issue of debt securities with a commitment to repurchase all or part of the issue before maturity of any similar transactions shall be regarded as sale and repurchase transactions within the meaning of this Article.   **[877]**

SECTION 4
SPECIAL PROVISIONS RELATING TO CERTAIN BALANCE SHEET ITEMS

Article 13

Assets: Item 1—Cash in hand, balances with central banks and post office banks

1 Cash in hand shall comprise legal tender including foreign notes and coins.

2 This item may include only balances with the central banks and post office banks of the country or countries in which a credit institution is established. Such balances must be readily available at all times. Other claims on such bodies must be shown as loans and advances to credit institutions (Assets item 3) or as loans and advances to customers (Assets item 4).   **[878]**

Article 14

Assets: Item 2—Treasury bills and other bills eligible for refinancing with central banks

1 This item shall comprise, under (a), treasury bills and similar securities, ie treasury bills, treasury certificates and similar debt instruments issued by public bodies which are eligible for refinancing with the central banks of the country or countries in which a credit institution is established. Those debt instruments issued by public bodies which fail to meet the above condition shall be shown under Assets sub-item 5(a).

2 This item shall comprise, under (b), bills eligible for refinancing with central banks, ie all bills held in portfolio that were purchased from credit institutions or from customers to the extent that they are eligible, under national law, for refinancing with the central banks of the country or countries in which a credit institution is established.   **[879]**

Article 15

Assets: Item 3—Loans and advances to credit institutions

1 Loans and advances to credit institutions shall comprise all loans and advances arising out of banking transactions to domestic or foreign credit institutions by the credit institution drawing up the balance sheet, regardless of their actual designations.

The only exception shall be loans and advances represented by debt securities or any other security, which must be shown under Assets item 5.

2 For the purposes of this Article credit institutions shall comprise all undertakings on the list published in the *Official Journal of the European Communities* pursuant to Article 3(7) of Directive 77/780/EEC, as well as central banks and official domestic and international banking organisations and all private and public undertakings which are not established in the Community but which satisfy the definition in Article 1 of Directive 77/780/EEC.

Loans and advances to undertakings which do not satisfy the above conditions shall be shown under Assets item 4. **[880]**

Article 16

Assets: Item 4—Loans and advances to customers

Loans and advances to customers shall comprise all types of assets in the form of claims on domestic and foreign customers other than credit institutions, regardless of their actual designations.

The only exception shall be loans and advances represented by debt securities or any other security, which must be shown under Assets item 5. **[881]**

Article 17

Assets: Item 5—Debt securities including fixed-income securities

1 This item shall comprise negotiable debt securities including fixed-income securities issued by credit institutions, by other undertakings or by public bodies; such securities issued by the latter, however, shall be included only if they are not to be shown under Assets item 2.

2 Securities bearing interest rates that vary in accordance with specific factors, for example the interest rate on the inter-bank market or on the Euromarket, shall also be regarded as debt securities including fixed-income securities.

3 Only repurchased and negotiable own-debt securities may be included in sub-item 5(b). **[882]**

Article 18

Liabilities: Item 1—Amounts owed to credit institutions

1 Amounts owed to credit institutions shall include all amounts arising out of banking transactions owed to other domestic or foreign credit institutions by the credit institution drawing up the balance sheet, regardless of their actual designations.

The only exception shall be liabilities represented by debt securities or by any other security, which must be shown under Liabilities item 3.

2 For the purposes of this Article credit institutions shall comprise all undertakings on the list published in the *Official Journal of the European Communities* pursuant to Article 3(7) of Directive 77/780/EEC, as well as central banks and official domestic and international banking organisations and all private and public undertakings which are not established in the Community but which satisfy the definition in Article 1 of Directive 77/780/EEC. **[883]**

Article 19

Liabilities: Item 2—Amounts owed to customers

1 Amounts owed to customers shall include all amounts owed to creditors that are not credit institutions within the meaning of Article 18, regardless of their actual designations.

The only exception shall be liabilities represented by debt securities or by any other security, which must be shown under Liabilities item 3.

2 Only deposits which satisfy the conditions laid down in national law shall be treated as savings deposits.

3 Savings bonds shall be shown under the corresponding sub-item only if they are not represented by negotiable certificates.   **[884]**

Article 20

Liabilities: Item 30—Debts evidenced by certificates

1 This item shall include both debt securities and debts for which negotiable certificates have been issued, in particular deposit receipts, '*bons de caisse*' and liabilities arising out of own acceptances and promissory notes.

2 Only acceptances which a credit institution has issued for its own refinancing and in respect of which it is the first party liable ('drawee') shall be treated as own acceptances.   **[885]**

Article 21

Liabilities: Item 8—Subordinated liabilities

Where it has been contractually agreed that, in the event of winding up or of bankruptcy, liabilities, whether or not evidenced by certificates, are to be repaid, only after the claims of all other creditors have been met, the liabilities in question shall be shown under this item.   **[886]**

Article 22

Liabilities: Item 9—Subscribed capital

This item shall comprise all amounts, regardless of their actual designations, which, in accordance with the legal structure of the institution concerned, are regarded under national law as equity capital subscribed by the shareholders or other proprietors.   **[887]**

Article 23

Liabilities: Item 11—Reserves

This item shall comprise all the types of reserves listed in Article 9 of Directive 78/660/EEC under Liabilities item A.IV, as defined therein. The Member States may also prescribe other types of reserves if necessary for credit institutions the legal structures of which are not covered by Directive 78/660/EEC.

The types of reserve referred to in the first paragraph shall be shown separately, as sub-items of Liabilities item 11, in the balance sheets of the credit institutions concerned, with the exception of the revaluation reserve which shall be shown under item 12.   **[888]**

Article 24

Off-balance sheet: Item 1—Contingent liabilites

This item shall comprise all transactions whereby an institution has under written the obligations of a third party.

Notes on accounts shall state the nature and amount of any type of contingent liability which is material in relation to an institution's activities.

Liabilities arising out of the endorsement of rediscounted bills shall be included in this item only if national law does not require otherwise. The same shall apply to acceptances other than own acceptances.

Sureties and assets pledged as collateral security shall include all guarantee obligations incurred and assets pledged as collateral security on behalf of third parties, particularly in respect of sureties and irrevocable letters of credit. **[889]**

Article 25

Off-balance sheet: Item 2—Commitments

This item shall include every irrevocable commitment which could give rise to a risk.

Notes on accounts shall state the nature and amount of any type of commitment which is material in relation to an institution's activities. **[890]**

Commitments arising out of sale and repurchase transactions shall include commitments entered into by a credit institution in the context of sale and repurchase transactions (on the basis of firm agreements to sell with options to repurchase) within the meaning of Article 12(3). **[891]**

SECTION 5
LAYOUT OF THE PROFIT AND LOSS ACCOUNT

Article 26

For the presentation of the profit and loss account, the Member States shall prescribe one or both of the layouts provided for in Articles 27 and 28. If a Member State prescribes both layouts it may allow undertakings to choose between them. **[892]**

Article 27

Vertical layout

1 Interest receivable and similar income, showing separately that arising from fixed-income securities

  2 Interest payable and similar charges

  3 Income from securities—

    (a) Income from shares and other variable-yield securities
    (b) Income from participating interests
    (c) Income from shares in affiliated undertakings

  4 Commissions receivable

  5 Commissions payable

  6 Net profit or net loss on financial operations

  7 Other operating income

  8 General administrative expenses—

    (a) Staff costs, showing separately—
      — wages and salaries
      — social security costs, with a separate indication of those relating to pensions
    (b) Other administrative expenses

9 Value adjustments in respect of Assets items 9 and 10

10 Other operating charges

11 Value adjustments in respect of loans and advances and provisions for contingent liabilities and for commitments

12 Value re-adjustments in respect of loans and advances and provisions for contingent liabilities and for commitments

13 Value adjustments in respect of transferable securities held as financial fixed assets, participating interests and shares in affiliated undertakings

14 Value re-adjustments in respect of transferable securities held as financial fixed assets, participating interests and shares in affiliated undertakings

15 Tax on profit or loss on ordinary activities

16 Profit or loss on ordinary activities after tax

17 Extraordinary income

18 Extraordinary charges

19 Extraordinary profit or loss

20 Tax on extraordinary profit or loss

21 Extraordinary profit or loss after tax

22 Other taxes not shown under the preceding items

23 Profit or loss for the financial year   [893]

Article 28

Horizontal layout

A CHARGES

1 Interest payable and similar charges

2 Commissions payable

3 Net loss on financial operations

4 General administrative expenses—

   (a) Staff costs, showing separately—
   — wages and salaries
   — social security costs, with a separate indication of those relating to pensions
   (b) Other administrative expenses

5 Value adjustments in respect of Assets items 9 and 10

6 Other operating charges

7 Value adjustments in respect of loans and advances and provisions for contingent liabilities and for commitments

8 Value adjustments in respect of transferable securities held as financial fixed assets, participating interests and shares in affiliated undertakings

9 Tax on profit or loss on ordinary activities

10 Profit or loss on ordinary activities after tax

11 Extraordinary charges

12 Tax on extraordinary profit or loss

13 Extraordinary loss after tax

14 Other taxes not shown under the preceding items

15 Profit for the financial year

B INCOME

1 Interest receivable and similar income, showing separately that arising from fixed-income securities

2 Income from securities:

(a) Income from shares and other variable-yield securities
(b) Income from participating interests
(c) Income from shares in affiliated undertakings

3 Commissions receivable

4 Net profit on financial operations

5 Value re-adjustments in respect of loans and advances and provisions for contingent liabilities and for commitments

6 Value re-adjustments in respect of transferable securities held as financial fixed assets, participating interests and shares in affiliated undertakings

7 Other operating income

8 Profit or loss on ordinary activities after tax

9 Extraordinary income

10 Extraordinary profit after tax

11 Loss for the financial year   **[894]**

SECTION 6

SPECIAL PROVISIONS RELATING TO CERTAIN ITEMS IN THE
PROFIT AND LOSS ACCOUNT

Article 29

Article 27, items 1 and 2 (vertical layout)

Article 28, items A1 and B1 (horizontal layout)

Interest receivable and similar income and interest payable and similar charges

These items shall include all profits and losses arising out of banking activities, including—

1 all income from assets entered under Assets items 1 to 5 in the balance sheet, however calculated. Such income shall also include income arising from the spreading on a time basis of the discount on assets acquired at an amount below, and liabilities contracted at an amount above, the sum payable at maturity;

2 all charges arising out of liabilities entered under Liabilities items 1, 2, 3 and 8, however calculated. Such charges shall also include charges arising from the spreading on a time basis of the premium on assets acquired at an amount above, and liabilities contracted at an amount below, the sum payable at maturity;

3 income and charges resulting from covered forward contracts, spread over the actual duration of the contract and similar in nature to interest;

4 fees and commission similar in nature to interest and calculated on a time basis or by reference to the amount of the claim or liability.   **[895]**

Article 30

Article 27, item 3 (vertical layout)

   Article 28, item B2 (horizontal layout)

Income from shares and other variable-yield securities, from participating interests, and from shares in affiliated undertakings

This item shall comprise all dividends and other income from variable-yield securities, from participating interests and from shares in affiliated undertakings. Income from shares in investment companies shall also be included under this item.   **[896]**

Article 31

Article 27, items 4 and 5 (vertical layout)

   Article 28, items A2 and B3 (horizontal layout)

Commissions receivable and commissions payable

Without prejudice to Article 29, commissions receivable shall include income in respect of all services supplied to third parties, and commissions payable shall include charges for services rendered by third parties, in particular

— commissions for guarantees, loans administration on behalf of other lenders and securities transactions on behalf of third parties,
— commissions and other charges and income in respect of payment transactions, account administration charges and commissions for the safe custody and administration of securities,
— commissions for foreign currency transactions and for the sale and purchase of coin and precious metals on behalf of third parties,
— commissions charged for brokerage services in connection with savings and insurance contracts and loans.   **[897]**

Article 32

Article 27, item 6 (vertical layout)

   Article 28, item A3 or item B4 (horizontal layout)

Net profit or net loss on financial operations.

This item covers—

1 the net profit or loss on transactions in securities which are not held as financial fixed assets together with value adjustments and value re-adjustments on such securities, taking into account, where Article 36(2) has been applied, the difference resulting from application of that article; however, in those Member States which exercise the option provided for in Article 37, these net profits or losses and value adjustments and value re-adjustments shall be included only in so far as they relate to securities included in a trading portfolio;

2 the net profit or loss on exchange activities, without prejudice to Article 9, point 3;

3 the net profits and losses on other buying and selling operations involving financial instruments, including precious metals. **[898]**

Article 33

Article 27, items 11 and 12 (vertical layout)

Article 28, items A7 and B5 (horizontal layout)

Value adjustments in respect of loans and advances and provisions for contingent liabilities and for commitments

Valve re-adjustments in respect of loans and advances and provisions for contingent liabilities and for commitments

1 These items shall include, on the one hand, charges for value adjustments in respect of loans and advances to be shown under Assets items 3 and 4 and provisions for contingent liabilities and for commitments to be shown under Off-balance sheet items 1 and 2 and, on the other hand, credits from the recovery of written-off loans and advances and amounts written back following earlier value adjustments and provisions.

2 In those Member States which exercise the option provided for in Article 37, this item shall also include the net profit or loss on transactions in securities included in Assets items 5 and 6 which are neither held as financial fixed assets as defined in Article 35(2) nor included in a trading portfolio, together with value adjustments and value re-adjustments on such securities taking into account, where Article 36(2) has been applied, the difference resulting from application of that article. The nomenclature of this item shall be adapted accordingly.

3 The Member States may permit the charges and income covered by these items to be set off against each other, so that only a net item (income or charge) is shown.

4 Value adjustments in respect of loans and advances to credit institutions, to customers, to undertakings with which a credit institution is linked by virtue of participating interests and to affiliated undertakings shall be shown separately in the notes on the accounts were they are material. This provision need not be applied if a Member State permits setting-off pursuant to paragraph 3.
[899]

Article 34

Article 27, items 13 and 14 (vertical layout)

Article 28, items A8 and B5 (horizontal layout)

Value adjustments in respect of transferable securities held as financial fixed assets, participating interests and shares in affiliated undertakings

Value re-adjustments in respect of transferable securities held as financial fixed assets, participating interests and shares in affiliated undertakings

1 These items shall include, on the one hand, charges for value adjustments in respect of assets shown in Assets items 5 to 8 and, on the other hand, all the amounts written back following earlier value adjustments, in so far as the charges and income relate to transferable securities held as financial fixed assets as defined in Article 35(2), participating interests and shares in affiliated undertakings.

2 The Member States may permit the charges and income covered by these items to be set off against each other, so that only a net item (income or charge) is shown.

3 Value adjustments in respect of these transferable securities, participating interests and shares in affiliated undertakings shall be shown separately in the notes on the accounts where they are material. This provision need not be applied if a Member State permits setting off pursuant to paragraph 2. **[900]**

SECTION 7
VALUATION RULES

Article 35

1 Assets items 9 and 10 must always be valued as fixed assets. The assets included in other balance sheet items shall be valued as fixed assets where they are intended for use on a continuing basis in the normal course of an undertaking's activities.

2 Where reference is made to financial fixed assets in Section 7 of Directive 78/660/EEC, this term shall in the case of credit institutions be taken to mean participating interests, shares in affiliated undertakings and securities intended for use on a continuing basis in the normal course of an undertaking's activities.

3 (a) Debt securities including fixed-income securities held as financial fixed assets shall be shown in the balance sheet at purchase price. The Member States may, however, require or permit such debt securities to be shown in the balance sheet at the amount repayable at maturity.

(b) Where the purchase price of such debt securities exceeds the amount repayable at maturity the amount of the difference must be charged to the profit and loss account. The Member States may, however, require or permit the amount of the difference to be written off in instalments so that it is completely written off by the time when the debt securities are repaid. The difference must be shown separately in the balance sheet or in the notes on the accounts.

(c) Where the purchase price of such debt securities is less than the amount repayable at maturity, the Member States may require or permit the amount of the difference to be released to income in instalments over the period remaining until repayment. The difference must be shown separately in the balance sheet or in the notes on the accounts. **[901]**

Article 36

1 Where transferable securities which are not held as financial fixed assets are shown in the balance sheet at purchase price, credit institutions shall disclose in the notes on their accounts the difference between the purchase price and the higher market value of the balance sheet date.

2 The Member States may, however, require or permit those transferable securities to be shown in the balance sheet at the higher market value at the balance sheet date. The difference between the purchase price and the higher market value shall be disclosed in the notes on the accounts. **[902]**

Article 37

1 Article 39 of Directive 78/660/EEC shall apply to the valuation of credit institutions' loans and advances, debt securities, shares and other variable-yield securities which are not held as financial fixed assets.

2 Pending subsequent coordination, however, the Member States may permit—

(a) loans and advances to credit institutions and customers (Assets items 3 and 4) and debt securities, shares and other variable yield securities included in Assets items 5 and 6 which are neither held as financial fixed assets as defined in Article 35(2) nor included in a trading portfolio to be shown at a value lower than that which would result from the application of Article 39(1) of Directive 78/660/EEC, where that is required by the prudence dictated by the particular risks associated with banking. Nevertheless the difference between the two values must not be more than 4% of the total amount of the assets mentioned above after application of the aforementioned Article 39;

(b) that the lower value resulting from the application of subparagraph (a) be maintained until the credit institution decides to adjust it;

(c) where a Member State exercises the option provided for in subparagraph (a), neither Article 36(1) of this Directive nor Article 40(2) of Directive 78/660/EEC shall apply. **[903]**

Article 38

1 Pending subsequent coordination, those Member States which exercise the option provided for in Article 37 must permit and those Member States which do not exercise that option may permit the introduction of a Liabilities item 6A entitled 'Fund for general banking risks'. That item shall include those amounts which a credit institution decides to put aside to cover such risks where that is required by the particular risks associated with banking.

2 The net balance of the increases and decreases of the 'Fund for general banking risks' must be shown separately to the profit and loss account. **[904]**

Article 39

1 Assets and liabilities denominated in foreign currency shall be translated at the spot rate of exchange ruling on the balance sheet date. The Member States may, however, require or permit assets held as financial fixed assets and tangible and intangible assets, not covered or not specifically covered in either the spot or forward markets, to be translated at the rates ruling on the dates of their acquisition.

2 Uncompleted forward and spot exchange transactions shall be translated at the spot rates of exchange ruling on the balance sheet date.

The Member States may, however, require forward transactions to be translated at the forward rate ruling on the balance sheet date.

3 Without prejudice to Article 29(3), the differences between the book values of the assets, liabilities and forward transactions and the amounts produced by translation in accordance with paragraphs 1 and 2 shall be shown in the profit and loss account. The Member States may, however, require or permit differences produced by translation in accordance with paragraphs 1 and 2 to be included, in whole or in part, in reserves not available for distribution, where they arise on assets held as financial fixed assets, on tangible and intangible assets and on any transactions undertaken to cover those assets.

4 The Member States may provide that positive translation differences arising out of forward transactions, assets or liabilities not covered or not specifically covered by other forward transactions, or by assets or liabilities shall not be shown in the profit and loss account.

5 If a method specified in Article 59 of Directive 78/660/EEC is used, the Member States may provide that any translation differences shall be transferred, in whole or in part, directly to reserves. Positive and negative translation differences transferred to reserves shall be shown separately in the balance sheet or in the notes on the accounts.

6 The Member States may require or permit translation differences arising on consolidation out of the retranslation of an affiliated undertaking's capital and reserves or the share of a participating interest's capital and reserves at the beginning of the accounting period to be included, in whole or in part, in consolidated reserves, together with the translation differences arising on the translation of any transactions undertaken to cover that capital and those reserves.

7 The Member States may require or permit the income and expenditure of affiliated undertakings and participating interests to be translated on consolidation at the average rates of exchange ruling during the accounting period.

[905]

SECTION 8

CONTENTS OF THE NOTES ON THE ACCOUNTS

Article 40

1 Article 43(1) of Directive 78/660/EEC shall apply, subject to Article 37 of this Directive and to the following provisions.

2 In addition to the information required under Article 43(1)(5) of Directive 78/660/EEC, credit institutions shall disclose the following information relating to Liabilities item 8 (Subordinated liabilities)—

(a) in respect of each borrowing which exceeds 10% of the total amount of the subordinated liabilities:
  (i) the amount of the borrowing, the currency in which it is denominated, the rate of interest and the maturity date or the fact that it is a perpetual issue;
  (ii) whether there are any circumstances in which early repayment is required;
  (iii) the terms of the subordination, the existence of any provisions to convert the subordinated liability into capital or some other form of liability and the terms of any such provisions,

(b) an overall indication of the rules governing other borrowings.

3 (a) In place of the information required under Article 43(1)(6) of Directive 78/660/EEC, credit institutions shall in the notes on their accounts state separately for each of the Assets items 3(b) and 4 and the Liabilities items 1(b), 2(a), 2(b)(bb) and 3(b) the amounts of those loans and advances and liabilities on the basis of their remaining maturity as follows—

— not more than three months,
— more than three months but not more than one year,
— more than one year but not more than five years,
— more than five years.

For Assets item 4, loans and advances on call and at short notice must also be shown.

If loans and advances or liabilities involve payment by instalments, the remaining maturity shall be the period between the balance sheet date and the date on which each instalment falls due.

However, for five years after the date referred to in Article 47(2) the Member States may require or permit the listing by maturity of the assets and liabilities referred to in this Article to be based on the originally agreed maturity or period of notice. In that event, where a credit institution has acquired an existing loan not evidenced by a certificate, the Member States shall require classification of that loan to be based on the remaining maturity as at the date on which it was acquired. For the purposes of this subparagraph, the originally agreed maturity for loans shall be the period between the date of first drawing and the date of repayment; the period of notice shall be deemed to be the period between the date on which notice is given and the date on which repayment is to be made; if loans and advances or liabilities are redeemable by instalments, the agreed maturity shall be the period between the date on which such loans and advances or liabilities arose and the date, on which the last instalment falls due. Credit institutions shall also indicate for the balance sheet items referred to in this subparagraph what proportion of those assets and liabilities will become due within one year of the balance sheet date.

(b) Credit institutions shall, in respect of Assets item 5 (Debt securities including fixed-income securities) and Liabilities item 3(a) (Debt securities in issue), indicate what proportion of assets and liabilities will become due within one year of the balance sheet date.
(c) The Member States may require the information referred to in subparagraphs (a) and (b) to be given in the balance sheet.
(d) Credit institutions shall give particulars of the assets which they have pledged as security for their own liabilities or for those of third parties (including contingent liabilities); the particulars should be in sufficient detail to indicate for each Liabilities item and for each Off-balance sheet item the total amount of the assets pledged as security. **[906]**

4 Where credit institutions have to provide the information referred to in Article 43(1)(7) of Directive 78/660/EEC in Off-balance sheet items, such information need not be repeated in the notes on the accounts.

5 In place of the information required under Article 43(1)(8) of Directive 78/660/EEC, a credit institution shall indicate in the notes on its accounts the proportion of its income relating to items 1, 3, 4, 6 and 7 of Article 27 or to items B1, B2, B3, B4 and B7 of Article 28 by geographical markets, in so far as, taking account of the manner in which the credit institution is organised, those markets differ substantially from one another. Article 45(1)(b) of Directive 78/660/EEC shall apply.

6 The reference in Article 43(1)(9) of Directive 78/660/EEC to Article 23(6) of that Directive shall be deemed to be a reference to Article 27(8) or Article 28(A4) of this Directive.

7 By way of derogation from Article 43(1)(13) of Directive 78/660/EEC, credit institutions need disclose only the amounts of advances and credits granted to the members of their administrative, managerial and supervisory bodies, and the commitments entered into on their behalf by way of guarantees of any kind. That information must be given in the form of a total for each category. **[907]**

Article 41

1 The information prescribed in Article 15(3) of Directive 78/660/EEC must be given in respect of assets held as fixed assets as defined in Article 35 of this Directive. The obligation to show value adjustments separately shall not, however, apply where a Member State has permitted set-offs between value adjustments pursuant to Article 34(2) of this Directive. In that event value adjustments may be combined with other items.

2 The Member States shall require credit institutions to give the following information as well as in the notes on their accounts—

(a) a breakdown of the transferable securities shown under Assets items 5 to 8 into listed and unlisted securities;

(b) a breakdown of the transferable securities shown under Assets items 5 and 6 into securities which, pursuant to Article 35, are or are not held as financial fixed assets and the criterion used to distinguish between the two categories of transferable securities;

(c) the value of leasing transactions, apportioned between the relevant balance sheet items;

(d) a breakdown of Assets item 13, Liabilities item 4, items 10 and 18 in the vertical layout or A6 and A11 in the horizontal layout and items 7 and 17 in the vertical layout or B7 and B9 in the horizontal lay-out in the profit and loss account into their main component amounts, where such amounts are important for the purpose of assessing the annual accounts, as well as explanations of their nature and amount;

(e) the charges paid on account of subordinated liabilities by a credit institution in the year under review;

(f) the fact that an institution provides management and agency services to third parties where the scale of business of that kind is material in relation to the institution's activities as a whole;

(g) the aggregate amounts of assets and of liabilities denominated in foreign currencies, translated into the currency in which the annual accounts are drawn up;

(h) a statement of the types of unmatured forward transactions outstanding at the balance sheet date indicating, in particular, for each type of transaction, whether they are made to a material extent for the purpose of hedging the effects of fluctuations in interest rates, exchange rates and market prices, and whether they are made to a material extent for dealing purposes. These types of transaction shall include all those in connection with which the income or expenditure is to be included in Article 27, item 6, Article 28, items A3 or B4 or Article 29(3), for example, foreign currencies, precious metals, transferable securities, certificates of deposit and other assets. **[908]**

SECTION 9

PROVISIONS RELATING TO CONSOLIDATED ACCOUNTS

Article 42

1 Credit institutions shall draw up consolidated accounts and consolidated annual reports in accordance with Directive 83/349/EEC, in so far as this section does not provide otherwise.

2 Insofar as a Member State does not have recourse to Article 5 of Directive 83/349/EEC, paragraph 1 of this Article shall also apply to parent undertakings the sole object of which is to acquire holdings in subsidiary undertakings and to manage such holdings and turn them to profit, where those subsidiary undertakings are either exclusively or mainly credit institutions.   **[909]**

Article 43

1 Directive 83/349/EEC shall apply, subject to Article 1 of this Directive and paragraph 2 of this Article.

2 (a) Articles 4, 6, 15 and 40 of Directive 83/349/EEC shall not apply.

   (b) The Member States may make application of Article 7 of Directive 83/349/EEC subject to the following additional conditions—

   — the parent undertaking must have declared that it guarantees the commitments entered into by the exempted undertaking; the existence of that declaration shall be disclosed in the accounts of the exempted undertaking;
   — the parent undertaking must be a credit institution within the meaning of Article 2(1)(a) of this Directive,

   (c) The information referred to in the first two indents of Article 9(2) of Directive 83/349/EEC, namely—

   — the amount of the fixed assets and
   — the net turnover

   shall be replaced by—

   — the sum of items 1, 3, 4, 6 and 7 in Article 27 or B1, B2, B3, B4 and B7 in Article 28 of this Directive,

   (d) Where, as a result of applying Article 13(3)(c) of Directive 83/349/ EEC, a subsidiary undertaking which is a credit institution is not included in consolidated accounts but where the shares of that undertaking are temporarily held as a result of a financial assistance operation with a view to the reorganisation or rescue of the undertaking in question, the annual accounts of that undertaking shall be attached to the consolidated accounts and additional information shall be given in the notes on the accounts concerning the nature and terms of the financial assistance operation.

   (e) A Member State may also apply Article 12 of Directive 83/349/EEC to two or more credit institutions which are not connected as described in Article 1(1) or (2) of that Directive but are managed on a unified basis other than pursuant to a contract or provisions in the memorandum or articles of association.

   (f) Article 14 of Directive 83/349/EEC, with the exception of paragraph 2, shall apply subject to the following provision.
   Where a parent undertaking is a credit institution and where one or more subsidiary undertakings to be consolidated do not have that status, those subsidiary undertakings shall be included in the consolidation if their activities are a direct extension of banking or concern services ancillary to banking, such as leasing, factoring, the management of unit trusts, the management of dataprocessing services or any other similar activity.

   (g) For the purposes of the layout of consolidated accounts—

   — Articles 3, 5 to 26 and 29 to 34 of this Directive shall apply;
   — the reference in Article 17 of Directive 83/349/EEC to Article 15(3) of Directive 78/660/EEC shall apply to the assets deemed to be fixed assets pursuant to Article 35 of this Directive.

(h) Article 34 of Directive 83/349/EEC shall apply in respect of the contents of the notes on consolidated accounts, subject to Articles 40 and 41 of this Directive.   **[910]**

SECTION 10
PUBLICATION

Article 44

1 The duly approved annual accounts of credit institutions, together with the annual reports and the reports by the persons responsible for auditing the accounts shall be published as laid down by national law in accordance with Article 3 of Directive 68/151/EEC.[1]

National law may, however, permit the annual report not to be published as stipulated above. In that case, it shall be made available to the public at the company's registered office in the Member State concerned. It must be possible to obtain a copy of all or part of any such report on request. The price of such a copy must not exceed its administrative cost.

2 Paragraph 1 shall also apply to the duly approved consolidated accounts, the consolidated annual reports and the reports by the persons responsible for auditing the accounts.

3 However, where a credit institution which has drawn up annual accounts or consolidated accounts is not established as one of the types of company listed in Article 1(1) of Directive 78/660/EEC and is not required by its national law to publish the documents referred to in paragraphs 1 and 2 of this Article as prescribed in Article 3 of Directive 68/151/EEC, it must at least make them available to the public at its registered office or, in the absence of a registered office, at its principal place of business. It must be possible to obtain copies of such documents on request. The prices of such copies must not exceed their administrative cost.

4 The annual accounts and consolidated accounts of a credit institution must be published in every Member State in which that credit institution has branches within the meaning of the third indent of Article 1 of Directive 77/780/EEC. Such Member States may require that those documents be published in their official languages.

5 The Member States shall provide for appropriate sanctions for failure to comply with the publication rule referred to in this Article.

NOTES
[1] OJ No L 65, 14.3.1968, p 8.

SECTION 11
AUDITING

Article 45

A Member State need not apply Article 2(1)(b)(iii) of Directive 84/253/EEC[1] to public savings banks where the statutory auditing of the documents of those undertakings referred to in Article 1(1) of that Directive is reserved to an existing supervisory body for those savings banks at the time of the entry into force of this Directive and where the person responsible complies at least with the conditions laid down in Articles 3 to 9 of Directive 84/253/EEC.   **[911]**

NOTES
[1] OJ No L 126, 12.5.1984, p 20.

SECTION 12
FINAL PROVISIONS

Article 46

The Contact Committee established in accordance with Article 52 of Directive 78/660/EEC shall, when meeting as constituted appropriately, also have the following functions.

    (a) to facilitate, without prejudice to Articles 169 and 170 of the Treaty, harmonised application of this Directive through regular meetings dealing in particular with practical problems arising in connection with its application;

    (b) to advise the Commission, if necessary, on additions or amendments to this Directive. **[912]**

Article 47

1 The Member States shall bring into force the laws, regulations and administrative provisions necessary for them to comply with this Directive by 31 December 1990. They shall forthwith inform the Commission thereof.

2 A Member State may provide that the provisions referred to in paragraph 1 shall first apply to annual accounts and consolidated accounts for financial years beginning on 1 January 1993 or during the calendar year 1993.

3 The Member States shall communicate to the Commission the texts of the main provisions of national law which they adopt in the field governed by this Directive. **[913]**

Article 48

Five years after the date referred to in Article 47(2), the Council, acting on a proposal from the Commission, shall examine and if need be revise all those provisions of this Directive which provide for Member State options, together with Articles 2(1), 27, 28 and 41, in the light of the experience acquired in applying this Directive and in particular of the aims of greater transparency and harmonisation of the provisions referred to by this Directive. **[914]**

Article 49

This Directive is addressed to the Member States. **[915]**

Done at Brussels, 8 December 1986.

COUNCIL DIRECTIVE
of 13 February 1989

on the obligations of branches established in a Member State of credit institutions and financial institutions having their head offices outside that Member State regarding the publication of annual accounting documents

(89/117/EEC)

NOTES

Date of publication in OJ: OJ L 44, 16.2.1989, p 40.

THE COUNCIL OF THE EUROPEAN COMMUNITIES,

Having regard to the Treaty establishing the European Economic Community, and in particular Article 54 thereof,

Having regard to the proposal from the Commission[1],

In cooperation with the European Parliament[2],

Having regard to the opinion of the Economic and Social Committee[3]

Whereas the establishment of a European internal market presupposes that the branches of credit institutions and financial institutions having their head offices in other Member States should be treated in the same way as branches of credit institutions and financial institutions having their head offices in the same Member State; whereas this means that, with regard to the publication of annual accounting documents, it is sufficient for the branches of such institutions having their head offices in other Member States to publish the annual accounting documents of their institution as a whole;

Whereas, as part of a further instrument of coordination of the disclosure requirements in respect of branches, provision is made for certain documents and particulars relating to branches established in a Member State which certain types of companies governed by the law of another Member State, including banks and other financial institutions, have to publish; whereas, as regards disclosure of accounting documents, reference is made to specific provisions to be laid down for banks and other financial institutions;

Whereas the present practice of some Member States of requiring the branches of credit institutions and financial institutions having their head offices outside these Member States to publish annual accounts relating to their own activities is no longer justified following the adoption of Council Directive 86/635/EEC of 8 December 1986 on the annual accounts and consolidated accounts of banks and other financial institutions[4]; whereas the publication of annual branch accounts cannot in any case provide the public, and in particular creditors, with an adequate view of the financial situation of the undertaking, since part of a whole cannot be viewed in isolation;

Whereas, on the other hand, in view of the present level of integration, the need for certain information on the activities of branches established in a Member State by credit institutions and financial institutions having their head offices outside that Member State cannot be disregarded; whereas, nevertheless, the extent of such information should be limited so as to prevent distortions of competition;

Whereas, however, this Directive affects only disclosure requirements concerning annual accounts, and does not in any way affect the obligations of branches of credit institutions and financial institutions to provide information pursuant to other requirements, deriving, for example, from social legislation, with regard to employees' rights to information, host countries' rights of supervision over credit institutions or financial institutions and fiscal legislation and also for statistical purposes;

Whereas equality of competition means, with regard to the branches of credit institutions and financial institutions having their head offices in non-member countries, that such branches must, on the one hand, in publishing annual accounting documents, adhere to a standard which is the same as, or equivalent to, that of the Community, but, on the other hand, that such branches should not have to publish annual accounts relating to their own activities if they fulfil the abovementioned condition;

Whereas the equivalence, required under this Directive, of annual accounting documents of credit institutions and financial institutions having their head offices in non-member countries may lead to problems of assessment; whereas it is therefore necessary for this and other problems in the area covered by the Directive, and in particular in its implementation, to be dealt with by representatives of the Member States and of the Commission jointly in a Contact Committee; whereas, in order to keep the number of such committees within limits, such cooperation should be carried out within the framework of the Committee set up under Article 52 of Council Directive 78/660/EEC of 25 July 1978 on the annual accounts of certain types of companies[5], as last amended by Directive 84/569/EEC[6]; whereas, however, where problems relating to credit institutions are to be dealt with, the Committee should be appropriately constituted,

NOTES
[1] OJ C 230, 11.9.1986, p. 4.
[2] OJ C 319, 30.11.1987, p. 64 and OJ C 290, 14.11.1988, p. 66.
[3] OJ C 345, 21.12.1987, p. 73.
[4] OJ L 372, 31.12.1986, p. 1.
[5] OJ L 222, 14.8.1978, p. 11.
[6] OJ L 314, 4.12.1984, p. 28.

HAS ADOPTED THIS DIRECTIVE:

Article 1

Scope

1 The coordination measures prescribed by this Directive shall apply to branches established in a Member State by credit institutions and financial institutions within the meaning of Article 2(1)(a) and (b) of Directive 86/635/ EEC having their head offices outside that Member State. Where a credit institution or financial institution has its head office in a non-member country, this Directive shall apply in so far as the credit institution or financial institution has a legal form which is comparable to the legal forms specified in the abovementioned Article 2(1)(a) and (b).

2 The third indent of Article 1 of Directive 77/780/EEC[1] shall apply *mutatis mutandis* to branches of credit institutions and financial institutions covered by this Directive. **[916]**

NOTES
[1] OJ No L 322, 17.12.1977, p 30.

Article 2

Provisions relating to branches of credit institutions and financial institutions having their head offices in other Member States

1 Member States shall require branches of credit institutions and financial institutions having their head offices in other Member States to publish, in accordance with Article 44 of Directive 86/635/EEC, the credit institution or financial institution documents referred to therein (annual accounts, consolidated accounts, annual report, consolidated annual report, opinions of the person responsible for auditing the annual accounts and consolidated accounts).

2 Such documents must be drawn up and audited in the manner required by the law of the Member State in which the credit institution or financial institutions has its head office in accordance with Directive 86/635/EEC.

3 Branches may not be required to publish annual accounts relating to their own activities.

4 Member States may, pending further coordination, require branches to publish the following additional information—

— the income and costs of the branch deriving from items, 1, 3, 4, 6, 7, 8 and 15 of Article 27 or from items A.4, A.9, B.1 to B.4 and B.7 of Article 28 of Directive 86/635/EEC,
— the average number of staff employed by the branch,
— the total claims and liabilities attributable to the branch, broken down into those in respect of credit institutions and those in respect of customers, together with the overall amount of such claims and liabilities expressed in the currency of the Member State in which the branch is established,
— the total assets and the amounts corresponding to items 2, 3, 4, 5 and 6 of the assets, 1, 2 and 3 of the liabilities and 1 and 2 of the off-balance sheet items defined in Article 4 and parallel Articles of Directive 86/635/EEC, and, in the case of items 2, 5 and 6 of the assets, a breakdown of securities according to whether they have or have not been regarded as financial fixed assets pursuant to Article 35 of Directive 86/635/EEC.

Where such information is required, its accuracy and its accordance with the annual accounts must be checked by one or more persons authorised to audit accounts under the law of the Member State in which the branch is established. **[917]**

Article 3

Provisions relating to branches of credit institutions and financial institutions having their head offices in non-members countries

1 Member States shall require branches of credit institutions and financial institutions having their head offices in non-member countries to publish the documents specified in Article 2(1), drawn up and audited in the manner required by the law of the country of the head office, in accordance with the provisions set out therein.

2 Where such documents are in conformity with, or equivalent to, documents drawn up in accordance with Directive 86/635/EEC and the condition of reciprocity, for Community credit institutions and financial institutions, is fulfilled in the non-member country in which the head office is situated, Article 2(3) shall apply.

3 In cases other than those referred to in paragraph 2, Member States may require the branches to publish annual accounts relating to their own activities.

4 In the cases specified in paragraph 2 and 3, Member States may require branches to publish the information referred to in Article 2(4) and the amount of the endowment capital.

5 Article 9(1) and (3) of Directive 77/780/EEC shall apply by anology to branches of credit institutions and financial institutions covered by this Directive. **[918]**

Article 4

Language of publication

Member States may require that the documents provided for in this Directive be published in their official national language or languages and that translations thereof be certified. **[919]**

Article 5

Work of the Contact Committee

The Contact Committee set up pursuant to Article 52 of Directive 78/660/EEC shall, when constituted appropriately, also—

(a) facilitate, without prejudice to Article 169 and 170 of the Treaty, harmonised application of this Directive through regular meetings dealing, in particular, with practical problems arising in connection with its application, such as assessment of equivalence of documents, and facilitate decisions concerning the comparability and equivalence of the legal forms referred to in Article 1(1);

(b) advise the Commission, if necessary, on additions or amendments to this Directive. **[920]**

Final provisions

Article 6

1 Member States shall bring into force the laws, regulations and administrative provisions necessary to comply with this Directive not later than 1 January 1991. They shall forthwith inform the Commission thereof.

2 A Member State may provide that the provisions referred to in paragraph 1 shall apply for the first time to annual accounts for the financial year beginning on 1 January 1993 or during the calendar year 1993.

3 Member States shall communicate to the Commission the texts of the main provisions of national law which they adopt in the field covered by this Directive. **[921]**

Article 7

Five years after the date referred to in Article 6(2), the Council, acting on a proposal from the Commission, shall examine and, upon a Commission proposal and in cooperation with the European Parliament, if need be, revise Article 2(4), in the light of the experience acquired in applying this Directive and of the aim of eliminating the additional information referred to in Article 2(4), taking account of the progress made in striving towards the harmonisation of the accounts of banks and other financial institutions. **[922]**

Article 8

This Directive is addressed to the Member States. **[923]**

Done at Brussels, 13 February 1989.

COUNCIL DIRECTIVE
of 17 April 1989

on the own funds of credit institutions

(89/299/EEC)

NOTES

Date of publication in OJ: OJ L 124, 5.5.1989, p 16.

THE COUNCIL OF THE EUROPEAN COMMUNITIES,

Having regard to the Treaty establishing the European Economic Community, and in particular the first and third sentences of Article 57(2) thereof,

Having regard to the proposal from the Commission,[1]

In cooperation with the European Parliament,[2]

Having regard to the opinion of the Economic and Social Committee,[3]

Whereas common basic standards for the own funds of credit institutions are a key factor in the creation of an internal market in the banking sector since own funds serve to ensure the continuity of credit institutions and to protect savings; whereas such harmonisation will strengthen the supervision of credit institutions and contribute to further coordination in the banking sector, in particular the supervision of major risks and solvency ratios;

Whereas such standards must apply to all credit institutions authorised in the Community;

Whereas the own funds of a credit institution can serve to absorb losses which are not matched by a sufficient volume of profits; whereas the own funds also serve as an important yardstick for the competent authorities, in particular for the assessment of the solvency of credit institutions and for other prudential purposes;

Whereas credit institutions in a common banking market engage in direct competition with each other, and the definitions and standards pertaining to own funds must therefore be equivalent; whereas, to that end, the criteria for determining the composition of own funds must not be left solely to Member States; whereas the adoption of common basic standards will be in the best interests of the Community in that it will prevent distortions of competition and will strengthen the Community banking system;

Whereas the definition laid down in this Directive provides for a maximum of items and qualifying amounts, leaving it to the discretion of each Member State to use all or some of such items or to adopt lower ceilings for the qualifying amounts;

Whereas this Directive specifies the qualifying criteria for certain own funds items, and the Member States remain free to apply more stringent provisions;

Whereas at the initial stage common basic standards are defined in broad terms in order to encompass all the items making up own funds in the different Member States;

Whereas, according to the nature of the items making up own funds, this Directive distinguishes between on the one hand, items constituting original own funds and, on the other, those constituting additional own funds;

Whereas it is recognised that due to the special nature of the fund for general banking risks, this item is to be included provisionally in own funds without limit; whereas, however, a decision on its final treatment will have to be taken as soon as possible after the implementation of the Directive; whereas that decision will have to take into account the results of discussions in international fora;

Whereas, to reflect the fact that items constituting additional own funds are not of the same nature as those constituting original own funds, the amount of the former included in own funds must not exceed the original own funds; whereas, moreover, the amount of certain items of additional own funds included must not exceed one-half of the original own funds;

Whereas, in order to avoid distortions of competition, public credit institutions must not include in their own funds guarantees granted them by the Member States or local authorities; whereas, however, the Kingdom of Belgium should be granted a transitional period up to 31 December 1994 in order to permit the institutions concerned to adjust to the new conditions by reforming their statutes;

Whereas whenever in the course of supervision it is necessary to determine the amount of the consolidated own funds of a group of credit institutions, that calculation shall be effected in accordance with Council Directive 83/350/EEC of 13 June 1983 on the supervision of credit institutions on a consolidated basis;[4] whereas that Directive leaves the Member States scope to interpret the technical details of its application, and that scope should be in keeping with the spirit of this Directive; whereas the former Directive is currently being revised to achieve greater harmonisation;

Whereas the precise accounting technique to be used for the calculation of own funds must take account of the provisions of Council Directive 86/635/EEC of 8 December 1986 on the annual accounts and consolidated accounts of banks and other financial institutions,[5] which incorporates certain adaptations of the provisions of Council Directive 83/349/EEC of 13 June 1983 based on Article 54(3)(g) of the Treaty on consolidated accounts;[6] whereas pending transposition of the provisions of the abovementioned Directives into the national laws of the Member States, the use of a specific accounting technique for the calculation of own funds should be left to the discretion of the Member States;

Whereas this Directive forms part of the wider international effort to bring about approximation of the rules in force in major countries regarding the adequacy of own funds;

Whereas measures to comply with the definitions in this Directive must be adopted no later than the date of entry into force of the measures implementing the future directive harmonising solvency ratios;

Whereas the Commission will draw up a report and periodically examine this Directive with the aim of tightening its provisions and thus achieving greater convergence on a common definition of own funds; whereas such convergence will allow the alignment of Community credit institutions' own funds;

Whereas it will probably be necessary to make certain technical and terminological adjustments to the directive to take account of the rapid development of financial markets; whereas pending submission by the Commission of a proposal which takes account of the special characteristics of the banking sector and which permits the introduction of a more suitable procedure for the implementation of this Directive, the Council reserves the right to take such measures.

NOTES
¹ OJ C 243, 27.9.1986, p 4 and OJ C 32, 5.2.1988, p 2.
² OJ C 246, 14.9.1987, p 72 and OJ C 96, 17.4.1989.
³ OJ C 180, 8.7.1987, p 51.
⁴ OJ L 193, 18.7.1983, p 18.
⁵ OJ L 372, 31.12.1986, p 1.
⁶ OJ L 193, 18.7.1983, p 1.

HAS ADOPTED THIS DIRECTIVE:

Article 1

Scope

1 Wherever a Member State lays down by law, regulation or administrative action a provision in implementation of Community legislation concerning the prudential supervision of an operative credit institution which uses the term or refers to the concept of own funds, it shall bring this term or concept into line with the definition given in the following Articles.

2 For the purposes of this Directive, 'credit institutions' shall mean the institutions to which Directive 77/780/EEC,[1] as last amended by Directive 86/254/EEC,[2] applies. **[924]**

NOTES
[1] OJ L 322, 17.12.1977, p 30.
[2] OJ L 309, 4.11.1986, p 15.

Article 2

General principles

1 Subject to the limits imposed in Article 6, the unconsolidated own funds of credit institutions shall consist of the following items—

  (1) capital within the meaning of Article 22 of Directive 86/635/EEC, in so far as it has been paid up, plus share premium accounts but excluding cumulative preferential shares;
  (2) reserves within the meaning of Article 23 of Directive 86/635/EEC and profits and losses brought forward as a result of the application of the final profit or loss. The Member States may permit inclusion of interim profits before a formal decision has been taken only if these profits have been verified by persons responsible for the auditing of the accounts and if it is proved to the satisfaction of the competent authorities that the amount thereof has been evaluated in accordance with the principles set out in Directive 86/635/EEC and is net of any foreseeable charge or dividend;
  (3) revaluation reserves within the meaning of Article 33 of Council Directive 78/660/EEC of 25 July 1978 based on Article 54(3)(g) of the Treaty on the annual accounts of certain types of companies,[1] as last amended by Directive 84/569/EEC;[2]
  (4) funds for general banking risks within the meaning of Article 38 of Directive 86/635/EEC;
  (5) value adjustments within the meaning of Article 37(2) of Directive 86/635/EEC;
  (6) other items within the meaning of Article 3;
  (7) the commitments of the members of credit institutions set up as cooperative societies and the joint and several commitments of the borrowers of certain institutions organised as funds, as referred to in Article 4(1);
  (8) fixed-term cumulative preferential shares and subordinated loan capital as referred to in Article 4(3).

The following terms shall be deducted in accordance with Article 6—

  (9) own shares at book value held by a credit institution;
  (10) intangible assets within the meaning of Article 4(9) ('assets') of Directive 86/635/EEC;
  (11) material losses of the current financial year;
  (12) holdings in other credit and financial institutions amounting to more than 10% of their capital, subordinated claims and the instruments referred to in Article 3 which a credit institution holds in respect of credit and financial institutions in which it has holdings exceeding 10% of the capital in each case.
       Where shares in another credit or financial institution are held temporarily for the purposes of a financial assistance operation designed to reorganise and save that institution, the supervisory authority may waive this provision;

(13) holdings in other credit and financial institutions of up to 10% of their capital, the subordinated claims and the instruments referred to in Article 3 which a credit institution holds in respect of credit and financial institutions other than those referred to in point 12 in respect of the amount of the total of such holdings, subordinated claims and instruments which exceed 10% of that credit institution's own funds calculated before the deduction of items 12 and 13.

Pending subsequent coordination of the provisions on consolidation, Member States may provide that, for the calculation of unconsolidated own funds, parent companies subject to supervision on a consolidated basis need not deduct their holdings in other credit institutions or financial institutions which are included in the consolidation. This provision shall apply to all the prudential rules harmonised by Community acts.

2 The concept of own funds as defined in points 1 to 8 of paragraph 1 embodies a maximum number of items and amounts. The use of those items and the fixing of lower ceilings, and the deduction of items other than those listed in items 9 to 13 of paragraph 1 shall be left to the discretion of the Member States. Member States shall nevertheless be obliged to consider increased convergence with a view to a common definition of own funds.

To that end, the Commission shall, not more than three years after the date referred to in Article 9(1), submit a report to the European Parliament and to the Council on the application of this Directive, accompanied, where appropriate, by such proposals for amendment as it shall deem necessary. Within five years of the date referred to in Article 9(1), the Council shall, acting by qualified majority on a proposal from the Commission, in cooperation with the European Parliament and after consultation of the Economic and Social Committee, examine the definition of own funds with a view to the uniform application of the common definition.

3 The items listed in points 1 to 5 must be available to a credit institution for unrestricted and immediate use to cover risks or losses as soon as these occur. The amount must be net of any foreseeable tax charge at the moment of its calculation or be suitably adjusted in so far as such tax charges reduce the amount up to which these items may be applied to cover risks or losses. **[925]**

NOTES
[1] OJ L 222, 14.8.1978, p 11.
[2] OJ L 314, 4.12.1984, p 28.

Article 3

Other items referred to in Article 2(1)(6)

1 The concept of own funds used by a Member State may include other items provided that, whatever their legal or accounting designations might be, they have the following characteristics—

(a) they are freely available to the credit institution to cover normal banking risks where revenue or capital losses have not yet been identified;
(b) their existence is disclosed in internal accounting records;
(c) their amount is determined by the management of the credit institution, verified by independent auditors, made known to the competent authorities and placed under the supervision of the latter. With regard to verification, internal auditing may be considered as provisionally meeting the aforementioned requirements until such

time as the Community provisions making external auditing mandatory have been implemented.

2 Securities of indeterminate duration and other instruments that fulfil the following conditions may also be accepted as other items:

(a) they may not be reimbursed on the bearer's initiative or without the prior agreement of the supervisory authority;

(b) the debt agreement must provide for the credit institution to have the option of deferring the payment of interest on the debt;

(c) the lender's claims on the credit institution must be wholly subordinated to those of all non-subordinated creditors;

(d) the documents governing the issue of the securities must provide for debt and unpaid interest to be such as to absorb losses, whilst leaving the credit institution in a position to continue trading;

(e) only fully paid-up amounts shall be taken into account.

To these may be added cumulative preferential shares other than those referred to in Article 2(1)(8).   **[926]**

Article 4

1 The commitments of the members of credit institutions set up as cooperative societies referred to in Article 2(1)(7), shall comprise those societies' uncalled capital, together with the legal commitments of the members of those cooperative societies to make additional non-refundable payments should the credit institution incur a loss, in which case it must be possible to demand those payments without delay.

The joint and several commitments of borrowers in the case of credit institutions organised as funds shall be treated in the same way as the preceding items.

All such items may be included in own funds in so far as they are counted as the own funds of institutions of this category under national law.

2 Member States shall not include in the own funds of public credit institutions guarantees which they or their local authorities extend to such entities.

However, the Kingdom of Belgium shall be exempt from this obligation until 31 December 1994.

3 Member States or the competent authorities may include fixed-term cumulative preferential shares referred to in Article 2(1)(8) and subordinated loan capital referred to in that provision in own funds, if binding agreements exist under which, in the event of the bankruptcy or liquidation of the credit institution, they rank after the claims of all other creditors and are not to be repaid until all other debts outstanding at the time have been settled.

Subordinated loan capital must also fulfil the following criteria—

(a) only full paid-up funds may be taken into account;

(b) the loans involved must have an original maturity of at least five years, after which they may be repaid; if the maturity of the debt is not fixed, they shall be repayable only subject to five years' notice unless the loans are no longer considered as own funds or unless the prior consent of the competent authorities is specifically required for early repayment. The competent authorities may grant permission for the early repayment of such loans provided the request is made at the initiative of the issuer and the solvency of the credit institution in question is not affected;

(c) the extent to which they may rank as own funds must be gradually reduced during at least the last five years before the repayment date;

(d) the loan agreement must not include any clause providing that in specified circumstances, other than the winding up of the credit institution, the debt will become repayable before the agreed repayment date.   **[927]**

[*Article 4a*

Denmark may allow its mortgage credit institutions organised as cooperative societies or funds before 1 January 1990 and converted into public limited liability companies to continue to include joint and several commitments of members, or of borrowers as referred to in Article 4(1) claims on whom are treated in the same way as such joint and several commitments, in their own funds, subject to the following limits—

(a) the basis for calculation of the part of joint and several commitments of borrowers shall be the total of the items referred to in Article 2(1), points 1 and 2, minus those referred to in Article 2(1), points 9, 10 and 11;

(b) the basis for calculation on 1 January 1991 or, if converted at a later date, on the date of conversion, shall be the maximum basis for calculation. The basis for calculation may never exceed the maximum basis for calculation;

(c) the maximum basis for calculation shall, from 1 January 1997, be reduced by half of the proceeds from any issue of new capital, as defined in Article 2(1), point 1, made after that date; and

(d) the maximum amount of joint and several commitments of borrowers to be included as own funds must never exceed—

50% in 1991 and 1992,
45% in 1993 and 1994,
40% in 1995 and 1996,
35% in 1997,
30% in 1998,
20% in 1999,
10% in 2000, and
0% after 1 January 2001,
of the basis for calculation;]   **[928]**

NOTE
Inserted by Council Directive 92/16/EEC of 16 March 1992, Art 1.

Article 5

Until further coordination of the provisions on consolidation, the following rules shall apply.

1 Where the calculation is to be made on a consolidated basis, the consolidated amounts relating to the items listed under Article 2(1) shall be used in accordance with the rules laid down in [Directive 92/350/EEC]. Moreover, the following may, when they are credit ('negative') items, be regarded as consolidated reserves for the calculation of own funds:

— any minority interests within the meaning of Article 21 of Directive 83/349/EEC, where the global integration method is used,

— the first consolidation difference within the meaning of Articles 19, 30 and 31 of Directive 83/349/EEC,

— the translation differences included in consolidated reserves in accordance with Article 39(6) of Directive 86/635/EEC,

— any difference resulting from the inclusion of certain participating interests in accordance with the method prescribed in Article 33 of Directive 83/349/EEC.

2 Where the above are debit ('positive') items, they must be deducted in the calculation of consolidated own funds. **[929]**

NOTES

Para (1): words substituted by Council Directive 92/30/EEC of 6 April 1992, Art 10.

Article 6

Deductions and limits

[**1** The items referred to in Article 2(1), points 3 and 5 to 8, shall be subject to the following limits—

(a) the total of items 3 and 5 to 8 may not exceed a maximum of 100% of items 1 plus 2 and 4 minus 9, 10 and 11;

(b) the total of items 7 and 8 may not exceed a maximum of 50% of items 1 plus 2 and 4 minus 9, 10 and 11;

(c) the total of items 12 and 13 shall be deducted from the total of all items.]

2 . . .

3 The limits referred to in paragraph 1 must be complied with as from the date of the entry into force of the implementing measures for the Council Directive on a solvency ratio for credit institutions and by 1 January 1993 at the latest.

Credit institutions exceeding those limits must gradually reduce the extent to which the items referred to in Article 2(1), points 3 and 5 to 8, are taken into account so that they comply with those limits before the aforementioned date.

4 The competent authorities may authorise credit institutions to exceed the limit laid down in paragraph 1 in temporary and exceptional circumstances. **[930]**

NOTES

Para (1): substituted and para (2) repealed by Council Directive 91/633/EEC of 3 December 1991, Art 1.

Article 7

Compliance with the conditions laid down in Article 2 to 6 must be proved to the satisfaction of the competent authorities. **[931]**

[*Article 8*

1 Without prejudice to the report referred to in the second subparagraph of Article 2(2), technical adaptations to be made to this Directive in the following areas shall be adopted in accordance with the procedure laid down in paragraph 2—

— clarification of the definitions to ensure uniform application of this Directive throughout the Community,

— clarification of the definitions in order to take account in the implementation of this Directive of developments on financial markets, and

— the alignment of terminology on, and the framing of definitions in accordance with, subsequent acts on credit institutions and related matters.

2 The Commission shall be assisted by a committee composed of representatives of the Member States and chaired by a representative of the Commission.

The Commission representative shall submit to the committee a draft of the measures to be taken. The committee shall deliver its opinion on the draft within a time limit which the chairman may lay down according to the urgency of the matter. The opinion shall be delivered by the majority laid down in Article 148(2) of the Treaty in the case of decisions which the Council is required to adopt on a proposal from the Commission. The votes of the representatives of the Member States in the committee shall be weighted in the manner set out in that Article. The chairman shall not vote.

The Commission shall adopt the measures envisaged if they are in accordance with the opinion of the committee.

If the measures envisaged are not in accordance with the opinion of the committee, or if no opinion is delivered, the Commission shall, without delay, submit to the Council a proposal concerning the measures to be taken. The Council shall act by a qualified majority.

If, on the expiry of a period of three months from the date of referral to the Council, the Council has not acted, the proposed measures shall be adopted by the Commission, save where the Council has decided against the said measures by a simple majority.] **[932]**

NOTES
Substituted by Council Directive 92/16/EEC of 16 March 1992, Art 1.

Article 9

1 Member States shall bring into force the laws, regulations and administrative provisions necessary for them to comply with this Directive no later than the date laid down for the entry into force of the implementing measures of the Council Directive on a solvency ratio for credit institutions, and by 1 January 1993 at the latest. They shall forthwith inform the Commission thereof.

2 Member States shall communicate to the Commission the texts of the main provisions of national law which they adopt in the field governed by this Directive.

3 The communication referred to in paragraph 2 must also include a statement, accompanied by an explanatory text, notifying the Commission of the specific provisions adopted and the items selected by the Member States' respective competent authorities as comprising own funds. **[933]**

Article 10

This Directive is addressed to the Member States. **[934]**

Done at Luxembourg, 17 April 1989.

COUNCIL DIRECTIVE
of 13 November 1989

coordinating regulations on insider dealing

(89/592/EEC)

NOTES
Date of publication in OJ: OJ L334, 18.11.1989, p 30.

THE COUNCIL OF THE EUROPEAN COMMUNITIES,

Having regard to the Treaty establishing the European Economic Community, and in particular Article 100a thereof,

Having regard to the proposal from the Commission,[1]

In cooperation with the European Parliament,[2]

Having regard to the opinion of the Economic and Social Committee,[3]

Whereas Article 100a (1) of the Treaty states that the Council shall adopt the measures for the approximation of the provisions laid down by law, regulation or administrative action in Member States which have as their object the establishment and functioning of the internal market;

Whereas the secondary market in transferable securities plays an important role in the financing of economic agents;

Whereas, for that market to be able to play its role effectively, every measure should be taken to ensure that market operates smoothly;

Whereas the smooth operation of that market depends to a large extent on the confidence it inspires in investors;

Whereas the factors on which such confidence depends include the assurance afforded to investors that they are placed on an equal footing and that they will be protected against the improper use of inside information;

Whereas, by benefiting certain investors as compared with others, insider dealing is likely to undermine that confidence and may therefore prejudice the smooth operation of the market;

Whereas the necessary measures should therefore be taken to combat insider dealing;

Whereas in some Member States there are no rules or regulations prohibiting insider dealing and whereas the rules or regulations that do exist differ considerably from one Member State to another;

Whereas it is therefore advisable to adopt coordinated rules at a Community level in this field;

Whereas such coordinated rules also have the advantage of making it possible, through cooperation by the competent authorities, to combat transfrontier insider dealing more effectively;

Whereas, since the acquisitions or disposal of transferable securities necessarily involves a prior decision to acquire or to dispose taken by the person who undertakes one or other of these operations, the carrying-out of this acquisition or disposal does not constitute in itself the use of inside information;

Whereas insider dealing involves taking advantage of inside information; whereas the mere fact that market-makers, bodies authorised to act as *contrepartie*, or stockbrokers with inside information confine themselves, in the first two cases, to pursuing their normal business of buying or selling securities or, in the last, to carrying out an order should not in itself be deemed to constitute use of such inside information; whereas likewise the fact of carrying out transactions with the aim of stabilising the price of new issues or secondary offers of transferable securities should not in itself be deemed to constitute use of inside information;

Whereas estimates developed from publicly available data cannot be regarded as inside information and whereas, therefore, any transaction carried out on the basis of such estimates does not constitute insider dealing within the meaning of this Directive;

Whereas communication of inside information to an authority, in order to enable it to ensure that the provisions of this Directive or other provisions in force are respected, obviously cannot be covered by the prohibitions laid down by this Directive,

NOTES
[1] OJ C 153, 11.6.1987, p 8 and OJ C 277, 27.10.1988, p 13.
[2] OJ C 187, 18.7.1987, p 93 and Decision of 11 October 1989 (not yet published in the Official Journal).
[3] OJ C 35, 8.2.1989, p 22.

HAS ADOPTED THIS DIRECTIVE:

Article 1

For the purposes of this Directive—

1 'inside information' shall mean information which has not been made public of a precise nature relating to one or several issuers of transferable securities or to one or several transferable securities, which, if it were made public, would be likely to have a significant effect on the price of the transferable security or securities in question;

2 'transferable securities' shall mean—
   (a) shares and debt securities, as well as securities equivalent to shares and debt securities;
   (b) contracts or rights to subscribe for, acquire or dispose of securities referred to in (a);
   (c) futures contracts, options and financial futures in respect of securities referred to in (a);
   (d) index contracts in respect of securities referred to in (a),

when admitted to trading on a market which is regulated and supervised by authorities recognised by public bodies, operates regularly and is accessible directly to the public. **[935]**

Article 2

1 Each Member State shall prohibit any person who:

— by virtue of his membership of the administrative, management or supervisory bodies of the issuer,
— by virtue of his holding in the capital of the issuer, or
— because he has access to such information by virtue of the exercise of his employment, profession or duties,

possesses inside information from taking advantage of that information with full knowledge of the facts by acquiring or disposing of for his own account or for the account of a third party, either directly or indirectly, transferable securities of the issuer or issuers to which that information relates.

2 Where the person referred to in paragraph 1 is a company or other type of legal person, the prohibition laid down in that paragraph shall apply to the natural persons who take part in the decision to carry out the transaction for the account of the legal person concerned.

3 The prohibition laid down in paragraph 1 shall apply to any acquisition or disposal of transferable securities effected through a professional intermediary.

Each Member State may provide that this prohibition shall not apply to acquisitions or disposals of transferable securities effected without the involvement of a professional intermediary outside a market as defined in Article 1(2) *in fine*.

4 This Directive shall not apply to transactions carried out in pursuit of monetary, exchange-rate or public debt-management policies by a sovereign State, by its central bank or any other body designated to that effect by the State, or by any person acting on their behalf. Member States may extend this exemption to their federated States or similar local authorities in respect of the management of their public debt. **[936]**

Article 3

Each Member State shall prohibit any person subject to the prohibition laid down in Article 2 who possesses inside information from—

(a) disclosing that inside information to any third party unless such disclosure is made in the normal course of the exercise of his employment, profession or duties;

(b) recommending or procuring a third party, on the basis of that inside information, to acquire or dispose of transferable securities admitted to trading on its securities markets as referred to in Article 1(2) *in fine*.
[937]

Article 4

Each Member State shall also impose the prohibition provided for in Article 2 on any person other than those referred to in that Article who with full knowledge of the facts possesses inside information, the direct or indirect source of which could not be other than a person referred to in Article 2. **[938]**

Article 5

Each Member State shall apply the prohibitions provided for in Articles 2, 3 and 4, at least to actions undertaken within its territory to the extent that the transferable securities concerned are admitted to trading on a market of a Member State. In any event, each Member State shall regard a transaction as carried out within its territory if it is carried out on a market, as defined in Article 1(2) *in fine*, situated or operating within that territory. **[939]**

Article 6

Each Member State may adopt provisions more stringent than those laid down by this Directive or additional provisions, provided that such provisions are applied generally. In particular it may extend the scope of the prohibition laid down in Article 2 and impose on persons referred to in Article 4 the prohibitions laid down in Article 3. **[940]**

Article 7

The provisions of Schedule C.5 (a) of the Annex to Directive 79/279/EEC[1] shall also apply to companies and undertakings the transferable securities of which, whatever their nature, are admitted to trading on a market as referred to in Article 1(2) *in fine* of this Directive. **[941]**

NOTES
[1] OJ L 6, 16.3.1979, p 21.

Article 8

1 Each Member State shall designate the administrative authority or authorities competent, if necessary in collaboration with other authorities to ensure that the provisions adopted pursuant to this Directive are applied. It shall so inform the Commission which shall transmit that information to all Member States.

2 The competent authorities must be given all supervisory and investigatory powers that are necessary for the exercise of their functions, where appropriate in collaboration with other authorities. **[942]**

Article 9

Each Member State shall provide that all persons employed or formerly employed by the competent authorities referred to in Article 8 shall be bound by professional secrecy. Information covered by professional secrecy may not be divulged to any person or authority except by virtue of provisions laid down by law.   [943]

Article 10

1   The competent authorities in the Member States shall cooperate with each other whenever necessary for the purpose of carrying out their duties, making use of the powers mentioned in Article 8(2). To this end, and notwithstanding Article 9, they shall exchange any information required for that purpose, including information relating to actions prohibited, under the options given to Member States by Article 5 and by the second sentence of Article 6, only by the Member State requesting cooperation. Information thus exchanged shall be covered by the obligation of professional secrecy to which the persons employed or formerly employed by the competent authorities receiving the information are subject.

2   The competent authorities may refuse to act on a request for information—

(a) where communication of the information might adversely affect the sovereignty, security or public policy of the State addressed;

(b) where judicial proceedings have already been initiated in respect of the same actions and against the same persons before the authorities of the State addressed or where final judgment has already been passed on such persons for the same actions by the competent authorities of the State addressed.

3   Without prejudice to the obligations to which they are subject in judicial proceedings under criminal law, the authorities which receive information pursuant to paragraph 1 may use it only for the exercise of their functions within the meaning of Article 8(1) and in the context of administrative or judicial proceedings specifically relating to the exercise of those functions. However, where the competent authority communicating information consents thereto, the authority receiving the information may use it for other purposes or forward it to other States' competent authorities.   [944]

Article 11

The Community may, in conformity with the Treaty, conclude agreements with non-member countries on the matters governed by this Directive. [945]

Article 12

The Contact Committee set up by Article 20 of Directive 79/279/EEC shall also have as its function—

(a) to permit regular consultation on any practical problems which arise from the application of this Directive and on which exchanges of view are deemed useful;

(b) to advise the Commission, if necessary, on any additions or amendments to be made to this Directive.   [946]

Article 13

Each Member State shall determine the penalties to be applied for infringement of the measures taken pursuant to this Directive. The penalties shall be sufficient to promote compliance with those measures. **[947]**

Article 14

1 Member States shall take the measures necessary to comply with this Directive before 1 June 1992. They shall forthwith inform the Commission thereof. **[948]**

2 Member States shall communicate to the Commission the provisions of national law which they adopt in the field governed by this Directive. **[949]**

Article 15

This Directive is addressed to the Member States.

Done at Brussels, 13 November 1989.

SECOND COUNCIL DIRECTIVE
of 15 December 1989

on the coordination of laws, regulations and administrative provisions relating to the taking up and pursuit of the business of credit institutions and amending Directive 77/780/EEC

(89/646/EEC)

NOTES
Date of publication in OJ: OJ L386, 30.11.1989, p 1.

THE COUNCIL OF THE EUROPEAN COMMUNITIES,

Having regard to the Treaty establishing the European Economic Community, and in particular the first and third sentences of Article 57(2) thereof,

Having regard to the proposal from the Commission,[1]

In cooperation with the European Parliament,[2]

Having regard to the opinion of the Economic and Social Committee,[3]

Whereas this Directive is to constitute the essential instrument for the achievement of the internal market, a course determined by the Single European Act and set out in timetable form in the Commission's White Paper, from the point of view of both the freedom of establishment and the freedom to provide financial services, in the field of credit institutions;

Whereas this Directive will join the body of Community legislation already enacted, in particular the first Council Directive 77/780/EEC of 12 December 1977 on the coordination of laws, regulations and administrative provisions relating to the taking up and pursuit of the business of credit institutions,[4] as last amended by Directive 86/524/EEC,[5] Council Directive 83/350/EEC of 13 June 1983 on the supervision of credit institutions on a consolidated basis,[6] Council Directive 86/635/EEC of 8 December 1986 on the annual and consolidated accounts of banks and other financial institutions[7] and Council Directive 89/299/EEC of 17 April 1989 on the own funds of credit institutions;[8]

Whereas the Commission has adopted recommendations 87/62/EEC on large exposures of credit institutions[9] and 87/63/EEC concerning the introduction of deposit-guarantee schemes;[10]

Whereas the approach which has been adopted is to achieve only the essential harmonisation necessary and sufficient to secure the mutual recognition of authorisation and of prudential supervision systems, making possible the granting of a single licence recognised through the Community and the application of the principle of home Member State prudential supervision;

Whereas, in this context, this Directive can be implemented only simultaneously with specific Community legislation dealing with the additional harmonisation of technical matters relating to own funds and solvency ratios;

Whereas, moreover, the harmonisation of the conditions relating to the reorganisation and winding-up of credit institutions is also proceeding;

Whereas the arrangements necessary for the supervision of the liquidity, market, interest-rate and foreign-exchange risks run by credit institutions will also have to be harmonised;

Whereas the principles of mutual recognition and of home Member State control require the competent authorities of each Member State not to grant authorisation or to withdraw it where factors such as the activities programme, the geographical distribution or the activities actually carried on make it quite clear that a credit institution has opted for the legal system of one Member State for the purpose of evading the stricter standards in force in another Member State in which it intends to carry on or carries on the greater part of its activities; whereas, for the purposes of this Directive, a credit institution shall be deemed to be situated in the Member State in which it has its registered office; whereas the Member States must require that the head office be situated in the same Member State as the registered office;

Whereas the home Member State may also establish rules stricter than those laid down in Articles 4, 5, 11, 12 and 16 for institutions authorised by its competent authorities;

Whereas responsibility for supervising the financial soundness of a credit institution, and in particular its solvency, will rest with the competent authorities of its home Member State; whereas the host Member State's competent authorities will retain responsibility for the supervision of liquidity and monetary policy; whereas the supervision of market risk must be the subject of close cooperation between the competent authorities of the home and host Member States;

Whereas the harmonisation of certain financial and investment services will be effected, where the need exists, by specific Community instruments, with the intention, in particular, of protecting consumers and investors; whereas the Commission has proposed measures for the harmonisation of mortgage credit in order, *inter alia*, to allow mutual recognition of the financial techniques peculiar to that sphere;

Whereas, by virtue of mutual recognition, the approach chosen permits credit institutions authorised in their home Member States to carry on, throughout the Community, any or all of the activities listed in the Annex by establishing branches or by providing services;

Whereas the carrying-on of activities not listed in the Annex shall enjoy the right of establishment and the freedom to provide services under the general provisions of the Treaty;

Whereas it is appropriate, however, to extend mutual recognition to the activities listed in the Annex when they are carried on by financial institutions which are subsidiaries of credit institutions, provided that such subsidiaries are covered by the consolidated supervision of their parent undertakings and meet certain strict conditions;

Whereas the host Member State may, in connection with the exercise of the right of establishment and the freedom to provide services, require compliance with specific provisions of its own national laws or regulations on the part of institutions not authorised as credit institutions in their home Member States and with regard to activities not listed in the Annex provided that, on the one hand, such provisions are compatible with Community law and are intended to protect the general good and that, on the other hand, such institutions or such activities are not subject to equivalent rules under the legislation or regulations of their home Member States;

Whereas the Member States must ensure that there are no obstacles to carrying on activities receiving mutual recognition in the same manner as in the home Member State, as long as the latter do not conflict with legal provisions protecting the general good in the host Member State;

Whereas the abolition of the authorisation requirement with respect to the branches of Community credit institutions once the harmonisation in progress has been completed necessitates the abolition of endowment capital; whereas Article 6(2) constitutes a first transitional step in this direction, but does not, however, affect the Kingdom of Spain or the Portuguese Republic, as provided for in the Act concerning the conditions of those States' accession to the Community;

Whereas there is a necessary link between the objective of this Directive and the liberalisation of capital movements being brought about by other Community legislation; whereas in any case the measures regarding the liberalisation of banking services must be in harmony with the measures liberalising capital movements; whereas where the Member States may, by virtue of Council Directive 88/361/EEC of 24 June 1988 for the implementation of Article 67 of the Treaty,[11] invoked safeguard clauses in respect of capital movements, they may suspend the provision of banking services to the extent necessary for the implementation of the abovementioned safeguard clauses;

Whereas the procedures established in Directive 77/780/EEC, in particular with regard to the authorisation of branches of credit institutions authorised in third countries, will continue to apply to such institutions; whereas those branches will not enjoy the freedom to provide services under the second paragraph of Article 59 of the Treaty or the freedom of establishment in Member States other than those in which they are established; whereas, however, requests for the authorisation of subsidiaries or of the acquisition of holdings made by undertakings governed by the laws of third countries are subject to a procedure intended to ensure that Community credit institutions receive reciprocal treatment in the third countries in question;

Whereas the authorisations granted to credit institutions by the competent national authorities pursuant to this Directive will have Community-wide, and no longer merely nationwide, application, and whereas existing reciprocity clauses will henceforth have no effect; whereas a flexible procedure is therefore needed to make it possible to assess reciprocity on a Community basis; whereas the aim of this procedure is not to close the Community's financial markets but rather, as the Community intends to keep its financial markets open to the rest of the world, to improve the liberalisation of the global financial markets in other third countries; whereas, to that end, this Directive provides for procedures for negotiating with third countries and, as a last resort, for the possibility of taking measures involving the suspension of new applications for authorisation or the restriction of new authorisations;

Whereas the smooth operation of the internal banking market will require not only legal rules but also close and regular cooperation between the competent authorities of the Member States; whereas for the consideration of problems concerning individual credit institutions the Contract Committee set up between the banking supervisory authorities, referred to in the final recital of Directive 77/780/EEC, remains the most appropriate forum; whereas that Committee is a suitable body for the mutual exchange of information provided for in Article 7 of that Directive;

Whereas that mutual information procedure will not in any case replace the bilateral collaboration established by Article 7 of Directive 77/780/EEC; whereas the competent host Member State authorities can, without prejudice to their powers of control proper, continue either, in an emergency, on their own initiative or following the initiative of the competent home Member State authorities to verify that the activities of a credit institution established within their territories comply with the relevant laws and with the principles of sound administrative and accounting procedures and adequate internal control;

Whereas technical modifications to the detailed rules laid down in this Directive may from time to time be necessary to take account of new developments in the banking sector; whereas the Commission shall accordingly make such modifications as are necessary, after consulting the Banking Advisory Committee, within the limits of the implementing powers conferred on the Commission by the Treaty; whereas that Committee shall act as a 'Regulatory' Committee, according to the rules of procedure laid down in Article 2, procedure III, variant (b), of Council Decision 87/373/EEC of 13 July 1987 laying down the procedures for the exercise of implementing powers conferred on the Commission,[12]

HAS ADOPTED THIS DIRECTIVE:

NOTES
[1] OJ C84, 31.3.1988, p 1.
[2] OJ C96, 17.4.1989, p 33 and Decision of 22 November 1989 (not yet published in the Official Journal).
[3] OJ C318, 17.12.1988, p 42.
[4] OJ L322, 17.12.1977, p 30.'
[5] OJ L193, 4.11.1986, p 15.
[6] OJ L193, 18.7.1983, p 18.
[7] OJ L372, 31.12.1986, p 1.
[8] OJ L124, 5.5.1989, p 16.
[9] OJ L33, 4.2.1987, p 10.
[10] OJ L33, 4.2.1987, p 16.
[11] OJ L178, 8.7.1988, p 5.
[12] OJ L197, 18.7.1987, p 33.

TITLE I

DEFINITIONS AND SCOPE

Article 1

For the purpose of this Directive—

1 'credit institution' shall mean a credit institution as defined in the first indent of Article 1 of Directive 77/780/EEC;

2 'authorisation' shall mean authorisation as defined in the second indent of Article 1 of Directive 77/780/EEC;

3 'branch' shall mean a place of business which forms a legally dependent part of a credit institution and which carries out directly all or some of the transactions inherent in the business of credit institutions; any number of places of business set up in the same Member State by a credit institution with headquarters in another Member State shall be regarded as a single branch;

4 'own funds' shall mean own funds as defined in Directive 89/299/EEC;

5 [the national authorities which are empowered by law or regulation to supervise credit institutions;]

6 'financial institution' shall mean an undertaking other than a credit institution the principal activity of which is to acquire holdings or to carry on one or more of the activities listed in points 2 to 12 in the Annex;

7 'home Member State' shall mean the Member State in which a credit institution has been authorised in accordance with Article 3 of Directive 77/780/EEC;

8 'host Member State' shall mean the Member State in which a credit institution has a branch or in which it provides services;

9 'control' shall mean the relationship between a parent undertaking and a subsidiary, as defined in Article 1 of Directive 83/349/EEC,[1] or a similar relationship between any natural or legal person and an undertaking;

10 'qualifying holding' shall mean a direct or indirect holding in an undertaking which represents 10% or more of the capital or of the voting rights or which makes it possible to exercise a significant influence over the management of the undertaking in which a holding subsists.

For the purposes of this definition, in the context of Articles 5 and 11 and of the other levels of holding referred to in Article 11, the voting rights referred to in Article 7 of Directive 88/627/EEC[2] shall be taken into consideration;

11 'initial capital' shall mean capital as defined in Article 2(1)(1) and (2) of Directive 89/299/EEC;

12 'parent undertaking' shall mean a parent undertaking as defined in Articles 1 and 2 of Directive 83/349/EEC;

13 'subsidiary' shall mean a subsidiary undertaking as defined in Articles 1 and 2 of Directive 83/349/EEC; any subsidiary of a subsidiary undertaking shall also be regarded as a subsidiary of the parent undertaking which is at the head of those undertakings;

14 'solvency ratio' shall mean the solvency coefficient of credit institutions calculated in accordance with Directive 89/647/EEC.[3]   **[950]**

NOTES
[1] OJ L 193, 18.7.1983, p 1.
[2] OJ L 348, 17.12.1988, p 62.
[3] See **[973]–[987]**.
Para (5): substituted by Council Directive 92/30/EEC of 6 April 1992, Art 10.

Article 2

1 This Directive shall apply to all credit institutions.

2 It shall not apply to the institutions referred to in Article 2(2) of Directive 77/780/EEC.

3 A credit institution which, as defined in Article 2(4)(a) of Directive 77/780/EEC, is affiliated to a central body in the same Member State may be exempted from the provisions of Articles 4, 10 and 12 of this Directive provided that, without prejudice to the application of those provisions to the central body, the whole as constituted by the central body together with its affiliated institutions is subject to the abovementioned provisions on a consolidated basis.

In cases of exemption, Articles 6 and 18 to 21 shall apply to the whole as constituted by the central body together with its affiliated institutions. **[950A]**

Article 3

The Member States shall prohibit persons or undertakings that are not credit institutions from carrying on the business of taking deposits or other repayable funds from the public. This prohibition shall not apply to the taking of deposits or other funds repayable by a Member State or by a Member State's regional or local authorities or by public international bodies of which one or more Member States are members or to cases expressly covered by national or Community legislation, provided that those activities are subject to regulations and controls intended to protect depositors and investors and applicable to those cases. **[951]**

TITLE II

HARMONISATION OF AUTHORISATION CONDITIONS

Article 4

1 The competent authorities shall not grant authorisation in cases where initial capital is less than ECU 5 million.

2 The Member States shall, however, have the option of granting authorisation to particular categories of credit institutions the initial capital of which is less than that prescribed in paragraph 1. In such cases—

    (a) the initial capital shall not be less than ECU 1 million;
    (b) the Member States concerned must notify the Commission of their reasons for making use of the option provided for in this paragraph;
    (c) when the list referred to in Article 3(7) of Directive 77/780/EC is published, the name of each credit institution that does not have the minimum capital prescribed in paragraph 1 shall be annotated to that effect;
    (d) within five years of the date referred to in Article 24(1), the Commission shall draw up a report on the application of this paragraph in the Member States, for the attention of the Banking Advisory Committee referred to in Article 11 of Directive 77/780/EEC. **[952]**

Article 5

The competent authorities shall not grant authorisation for the taking-up of the business of credit institutions before they have been informed of the identities of the shareholders or members, whether direct or indirect, natural or legal persons, that have qualifying holdings, and of the amounts of those holdings.

The competent authorities shall refuse authorisation if, taking into account the need to ensure the sound and prudent management of a credit institution, they are not satisfied as to the suitability of the above mentioned shareholders or members. **[953]**

Article 6

1 Host Member States may no longer require authorisation, as provided for in Article 4 of Directive 77/780/EEC, or endowment capital for branches of credit institutions authorised in other Member States. The establishment and supervision of such branches shall be effected as prescribed in Articles 13, 19 and 21 of this Directive.

2 Until the entry into force of the provisions implementing paragraph 1, host Member States may not, as a condition of the authorisation of branches of credit institutions, authorised in other Member States, require initial endowment capital exceeding 50% of the initial capital required by national rules for the authorisation of credit institutions of the same nature.

3 Credit institutions shall be entitled to the free use of the funds no longer required pursuant to paragraphs 1 and 2.   **[954]**

Article 7
There must be prior consultation with the competent authorities of the other Member State involved on the authorisation of a credit institution which is—

— a subsidiary of a credit institution authorised in another Member State, or
— a subsidiary of the parent undertaking of a credit institution authorised in another Member State, or
— controlled by the same persons, whether natural or legal, as control a credit institution authorised in another Member State.   **[955]**

TITLE III

RELATIONS WITH THIRD COUNTRIES

Article 8
The competent authorities of the Member States shall inform the Commission:

(a) of any authorisation of a direct or indirect subsidiary one or more parent undertakings of which are governed by the laws of a third country. The Commission shall inform the Banking Advisory Committee accordingly;
(b) whenever such a parent undertaking acquires a holding in a Community credit institution such that the latter would become its subsidiary. The Commission shall inform the Banking Advisory Committee accordingly.

When authorisation is granted to the direct or indirect subsidiary of one or more parent undertakings governed by the law of third countries, the structure of the group shall be specified in the notification which the competent authorities shall address to the Commission in accordance with Article 3(7) of Directive 77/780/EEC.   **[956]**

Article 9

1 The Member States shall inform the Commission of any general difficulties encountered by their credit institutions in establishing themselves or carrying on banking activities in a third country.

2 Initially no later than six months before the application of this Directive and thereafter periodically, the Commission shall draw up a report examining the treatment accorded to Community credit institutions in third countries, in the terms referred to in paragraphs 3 and 4, as regards establishment and the carrying-on of banking activities, and the acquisition of holdings in third-country credit institutions. The Commission shall submit those reports to the Council, together with any appropriate proposals.

3 Whenever it appears to the Commission, either on the basis of the reports referred to in paragraph 2 or on the basis of other information, that a third country is not granting Community credit institutions effective market access comparable to that granted by the Community to credit institutions from that third country, the Commission may submit proposals to the Council for the appropriate mandate for negotiation with a view to obtaining comparable competitive opportunities for Community credit institutions. The Council shall decide by a qualified majority.

4 Whenever it appears to the Commission, either on the basis of the reports referred to in paragraph 2 or on the basis of other information that Community credit institutions in a third country do not receive national treatment offering the same competitive opportunities as are available to domestic credit institutions and the conditions of effective market access are not fulfilled, the Commission may initiate negotiations in order to remedy the situation.

In the circumstances described in the first subparagraph, it may also be decided at any time, and in addition to initiating negotiations, in accordance with the procedure laid down in Article 22(2), that the competent authorities of the Member States must limit or suspend their decisions regarding requests pending at the moment of the decision or future requests for authorisations and the acquisitions of holdings by direct or indirect parent undertakings governed by the laws of the third country in question. The duration of the measures referred to may not exceed three months.

Before the end of that three-month period, and in the light of the results of the negotiations, the Council may, acting on a proposal from the Commission, decide by a qualified majority whether the measures shall be continued.

Such limitations or suspension may not apply to the setting up of subsidiaries by credit institutions or their subsidiaries duly authorised in the Community, or to the acquisition of holdings in Community credit institutions by such institutions or subsidiaries.

5 Whenever it appears to the Commission that one of the situations described in paragraphs 3 and 4 obtains, the Member States shall inform it at its request—

(a) of any request for the authorisation of a direct or indirect subsidiary one or more parent undertakings of which are governed by the laws of the third country in question;

(b) whenever they are informed in accordance with Article 11 that such an undertaking proposes to acquire a holding in a Community credit institution such that the latter would become its subsidiary.

This obligation to provide information shall lapse whenever an agreement is reached with the third country referred to in paragraph 3 or 4 or when the measures referred to in the second and third subparagraphs of paragraph 4 ceases to apply.

6 Measures taken pursuant to this Article shall comply with the Community's obligations under any international agreements, bilateral or multilateral, governing the taking-up and pursuit of the business of credit institutions.   **[957]**

TITLE IV
HARMONISATION OF THE CONDITIONS GOVERNING PURSUIT OF THE BUSINESS OF CREDIT INSTITUTIONS

Article 10

1 A credit institution's own funds may not fall below the amount of initial capital required pursuant to Article 4 at the time of its authorisation.

2 The Member States may decide that credit institutions already in existence when the Directive is implemented, the own funds of which do not attain the levels prescribed for initial capital in Article 4, may continue to carry on their activities. In that event, their own funds may not fall below the highest level reached after the date of the notification of this Directive.

3 If control of a credit institution falling within the category referred to in paragraph 2 is taken by a natural or legal person other than the person who controlled the institution previously, the own funds of that institution must attain at least the level prescribed for initial capital in Article 4.

4 However, in certain specific circumstances and with the consent of the two competent authorities, where there is a merger of two or more credit institutions falling within the category referred to in paragraph 2, the own funds of the institution resulting from the merger may not fall below the total own funds of the merged institutions at the time of the merger, as long as the appropriate levels pursuant to Article 4 have not been attained.

5 However, if, in the cases referred to in paragraphs 1, 2 and 4, the own funds should be reduced, the competent authorities may, where the circumstances justify it, allow an institution a limited period in which to rectify its situation or cease its activities.   **[958]**

Article 11

1 The Member States shall require any natural or legal person who proposes to acquire, directly or indirectly a qualifying holding in a credit institution first to inform the competent authorities, telling them of the size of the intended holding. Such a person must likewise inform the competent authorities if he proposes to increase his qualifying holding so that the proportion of the voting rights or of the capital held by him would reach or exceed 20%, 33% or 50% or so that the credit institution would become his subsidiary.

Without prejudice to the provisions of paragraph 2 the competent authorities shall have a maximum of three months from the date of the notification provided for in the first subparagraph to oppose such a plan if, in view of the need to ensure sound and prudent management of the credit institution, they are not satisfied as to the suitability of the person referred to in the first subparagraph. If they do not oppose the plan referred to in the first subparagraph, they may fix a maximum period for its implementation.

2 If the acquirer of the holdings referred to in paragraph 1 is a credit institution authorised in another Member State or the parent undertaking of a credit institution authorised in another Member State or a natural or legal person controlling a credit institution authorised in another Member State and if, as a result of that acquisition, the institution in which the acquirer proposes to acquire a holding would become a subsidiary or subject to the control of the acquirer, the assessment of the acquisition must be the subject of the prior consultation referred to in Article 7.

3 The Member States shall require any natural or legal person who proposes to dispose, directly or indirectly, of a qualifying holding in a credit institution first to inform the competent authorities, telling them of the size of his intended holding. Such a person must likewise inform the competent authorities if he proposes to reduce his qualifying holding so that the proportion of the voting rights or of the capital held by him would fall below 20%, 33% or 50% or so that the credit institution would cease to be his subsidiary.

4 On becoming aware of them, credit institutions shall inform the competent authorities of any acquisitions or disposals of holdings in their capital that cause holdings to exceed or fall below one of the thresholds referred to in paragraphs 1 and 3.

They shall also, at least once a year, inform them of the names of shareholders and members possessing qualifying holdings and the sizes of such holdings as shown, for example, by the information received at the annual general meetings of shareholders and members or as a result of compliance with the regulations relating to companies listed on stock exchanges.

5 The Member States shall require that, where the influence exercised by the persons referred to in paragraph 1 is likely to operate to the detriment of the prudent and sound management of the institution, the competent authorities shall take appropriate measures to put an end to that situation. Such measures may consist for example in injunctions, sanctions against directors and managers, or the suspension of the exercise of the voting rights attaching to the shares held by the shareholders or members in question.

Similar measures shall apply to natural or legal persons failing to comply with the obligation to provide prior information, as laid down in paragraph 1. If a holding is acquired despite the opposition of the competent authorities, the Member States shall, regardless of any other sanctions to be adopted, provide either for exercise of the corresponding voting rights to be suspended, or for the nullity of votes cast or for the possibility of their annulment.   **[959]**

Article 12

1 No credit institution may have a qualifying holding the amount of which exceeds 15% of its own funds in an undertaking which is neither a credit institution, nor a financial institution, nor an undertaking carrying on an activity referred to in the second subparagraph of Article 43(2)(f) of Directive 86/635/EEC.

2 The total amount of a credit institution's qualifying holdings in undertakings other than credit institutions, financial institutions or undertakings carrying on activities referred to in the second subparagraph of Article 43(2)(f) of Directive 86/635/EEC may not exceed 60% of its own funds.

3 The Member States need not apply the limits laid down in paragraphs 1 and 2 to holdings in insurance companies as defined in Directive 73/239/EEC,[1] as last amended by Directive 88/357/EEC,[2] and Directive 79/267/EEC,[3] as last amended by the Act of Accession of 1985.

4 Shares held temporarily during a financial reconstruction or rescue operation or during the normal course of underwriting or in an institution's own name on behalf of others shall not be counted as qualifying holdings for the purpose of calculating the limits laid down in paragraphs 1 and 2. Shares which are not financial fixed assets as defined in Article 35(2) of Directive 86/635/EEC, shall not be included.

5 The limits laid down in paragraphs 1 and 2 may be exceeded only in exceptional circumstances. In such cases, however, the competent authorities shall require a credit institution either to increase its own funds or to take other equivalent measures.

6 Compliance with the limits laid down in paragraphs 1 and 2 shall be ensured by means of supervision and monitoring on a consolidated basis in accordance with [Directive 92/30/EEC].

7 Credit institutions which, on the date of entry into force of the provisions implementing this Directive, exceed the limits laid down in paragraphs 1 and 2 shall have a period of 10 years from that date in which to comply with them.

8 The Member States may provide that the competent authorities shall not apply the limits laid down in paragraph 1 and 2 if they provide that 100% of the amounts by which a credit institution's qualifying holdings exceed those limits must be covered by own funds and that the latter shall not be included in the calculation of the solvency ratio. If both the limits laid down in paragraphs 1 and 2 are exceeded, the amounts to be covered by own funds shall be the greater of the excess amounts. [960]

NOTES
[1] OJ L 228, 16.8.1973, p 3.
[2] OJ L 172, 4.7.1988, p 1.
[3] OJ L 63, 13.3.1979, p 1.
Para (6): words substituted by Council Directive 92/30/EEC of 6 April 1992, Art 10.

Article 13

1 The prudential supervision of a credit institution, including that of the activities it carries on in accordance with Article 18, shall be the responsibility of the competent authorities of the home Member State, without prejudice to those provisions of this Directive which give responsibility to the authorities of the host Member State.

2 Home Member State competent authorities shall require that every credit institution have sound administrative and accounting procedures and adequate internal control mechanisms.

3 Paragraphs 1 and 2 shall not prevent supervision on a consolidated basis pursuant to [Directive 92/30/EEC]. [961]

NOTES
Para (3): words substituted by Council Directive 92/30/EEC of 6 April 1992, Art 10.

Article 14

1 In Article 7(1) of Directive 77/780/EEC, the end of the second sentence is hereby replaced by the following: 'and all information likely to facilitate the monitoring of such institutions, in particular with regard to liquidity, solvency, deposit guarantees, the limiting of large exposures, administrative and accounting procedures and internal control mechanisms'.

2 Host Member States shall retain responsibility in cooperation with the competent authorities of the home Member State for the supervision of the liquidity of the branches of credit institutions pending further coordination. Without prejudice to the measures necessary for the reinforcement of the European Monetary System, host Member States shall retain complete responsibility for the measures resulting from the implementation of their monetary policies. Such measures may not provide for discriminatory or restrictive treatment based on the fact that a credit institution is authorised in another Member State.

3 Without prejudice to further coordination of the measures designed to supervise the risks arising out of open positions on markets, where such risks result from transactions carried out on the financial markets of other Member States, the competent authorities of the latter shall collaborate with the competent authorities of the home Member State to ensure that the institutions concerned take steps to cover those risks. [962]

Article 15

1 Host Member States shall provide that, where a credit institution authorised in another Member State carries on its activities through a branch, the competent authorities of the home Member State may, after having first informed the competent authorities of the host Member State, carry out themselves or through the intermediary of persons they appoint for that purpose on-the-spot verification of the information referred to in Article 7(1) of Directive 77/780/EEC.

2 The competent authorities of the home Member State may also, for purposes of the verification of branches, have recourse to one of the other procedures laid down in [Article 7(7) of Directive 92/30/EEC].

3 This Article shall not affect the right of the competent authorities of the host Member State to carry out, in the discharge of their responsibilities under this Directive, on-the-spot verifications of branches established within their territory.   **[963]**

NOTES
Para (2): words substituted by Council Directive 92/30/EEC of 6 April 1992, Art 10.

Article 16 (Substitutes Council Directive 77/780/EEC, Art 12.)

Article 17

Without prejudice to the procedures for the withdrawal of authorisations and the provisions of criminal law, the Member States shall provide that their respective competent authorities may, as against credit institutions or those who effectively control the business of credit institutions which breach laws, regulations or administrative provisions concerning the supervision or pursuit of their activities, adopt or impose in respect of them penalties or measures aimed specifically at ending observed breaches or the causes of such breaches.
                                                                                                        [964]

TITLE V

PROVISIONS RELATING TO THE FREEDOM OF ESTABLISHMENT AND THE FREEDOM TO PROVIDE SERVICES

Article 18

1 The Member States shall provide that the activities listed in the Annex may be carried on within their territories, in accordance with Articles 19 to 21, either by the establishment of a branch or by way of the provision of services, by any credit institution authorised and supervised by the competent authorities of another Member State, in accordance with this Directive, provided that such activities are covered by the authorisation.

2 The Member States shall also provide that the activities listed in the Annex may be carried on within their territories, in accordance with Articles 19 to 21, either by the establishment of a branch or by way of the provision of services, by any financial institution from another Member State, whether a subsidiary of a credit institution or the jointly-owned subsidiary of two or more credit institutions, the memorandum and articles of association of which permit the carrying on of those activities and which fulfils each of the following conditions—

— the parent undertaking or undertakings must be authorised as credit institutions in the Member State by the law of which the subsidiary is governed,

— the activities in question must actually be carried on within the territory of the same Member State,

— the parent undertaking or undertakings must hold 90% or more of the voting rights attaching to shares in the capital of the subsidiary,

— the parent undertaking or undertakings must satisfy the competent authorities regarding the prudent management of the subsidiary and must have declared, with the consent of the relevant home Member State competent authorities, that they jointly and severally guarantee the commitments entered into by the subsidiary,

— the subsidiary must be effectively included, for the activities in question in particular, in the consolidated supervision of the parent undertaking, or of each of the parent undertakings, in accordance with [Directive 92/30/EEC], in particular for the calculation of the solvency ratio, for the control of large exposures and for purposes of the limitation of holdings provided for in Article 12 of this Directive.

Compliance with these conditions must be verified by the competent authorities of the home Member State and the latter must supply the subsidiary with a certificate of compliance which must form part of the notification referred to in Articles 19 and 20.

The competent authorities of the home Member State shall ensure the supervision of the subsidiary in accordance with Articles 10(1), 11, 13, 14(1), 15 and 17 of this Directive and Articles 7(1) and 12 of Directive 77/780/EEC.

The provisions mentioned in this paragraph shall be applicable to subsidiaries, subject to the necessary modifications. In particular, the words 'credit institution' should be read as 'financial institution fulfilling the conditions laid down in Article 18(2)' and the word 'authorisation' as 'memorandum and articles of association'.

The second subparagraph of Article 19(3) shall read—

'The home Member State competent authorities shall also communicate the amount of own funds of the subsidiary financial institution and the consolidated solvency ratio of the credit institution which is its parent undertaking.'

If a financial institution eligible under this paragraph should cease to fulfil any of the conditions imposed, the home Member State shall notify the competent authorities of the host Member State and the activities carried on by that institution in the host Member State shall become subject to the legislation of the host Member State.   **[965]**

NOTES

Para (2): words substituted by Council Directive 92/30/EEC of 6 April 1992, Art 10.

Article 19

1 A credit institution wishing to establish a branch within the territory of another Member State shall notify the competent authorities of its home Member State.

2 The Member State shall require every credit institution wishing to establish a branch in another Member State to provide the following information when effecting the notification referred to in paragraph 1—

   (a) the Member State within the territory of which it plans to establish a branch;

(b) a programme of operations setting out *inter alia* the types of business envisaged and the structural organisation of the branch;

(c) the address in the host Member State from which documents may be obtained;

(d) the names of those responsible for the management of the branch.

3 Unless the competent authorities of the home Member State have reason to doubt the adequacy of the administrative structure or the financial situation of the credit institution, taking into account the activities envisaged, they shall within three months of receipt of the information referred to in paragraph 2 communicate that information to the competent authorites of the host Member State and shall inform the institution concerned accordingly.

The home Member State competent authorities shall also communicate the amount of own funds and the solvency ratio of the credit institution and, pending subsequent coordination, details of any deposit-guarantee scheme which is intended to ensure the protection of depositors in the branch.

Where the competent authorities of the home Member State refuse to communicate the information referred to in paragraph 2 to the competent authorities of the host Member State, they shall give reasons for their refusal to the institution concerned within three months of receipt of all the information. That refusal or failure to reply shall be subject to a right to apply to the courts in the home Member State.

4 Before the branch of a credit institution commences its activities the competent authorities of the host Member State shall, within two months of receiving the information mentioned in paragraph 3, prepare for the supervision of the credit institution in accordance with Article 21 and if necessary indicate the conditions under which, in the interest of the general good, those activities must be carried on in the host Member State.

5 On receipt of a communication from the competent authorities of the host Member State, or in the event of the expiry of the period provided for in paragraph 4 without receipt of any communication from the latter, the branch may be established and commence its activities.

6 In the event of a change in any of the particulars communicated pursuant to paragraph 2(b), (c) or (d) or in the deposit-guarantee scheme referred to in paragraph 3 a credit institution shall give written notice of the change in question to the competent authorities of the home and host Member States at least one month before making the change so as to enable the competent authorities of the home Member State to take a decision pursuant to paragraph 3 and the competent authorities of the host Member State to take a decision on the change pursuant to paragraph 4. **[966]**

NOTES

For a modification of the second sub-para of para (3), see Article 18(2).

Article 20

1 Any credit institution wishing to exercise the freedom to provide services by carrying on its activities within the territory of another Member State for the first time shall notify the competent authorities of the home Member State of the activities on the list in the Annex which it intends to carry on.

2 The competent authorities of the home Member State shall, within one month of receipt of the notification mentioned in paragraph 1, send that notification to the competent authorities of the host Member State. **[967]**

Article 21

1 Host Member State may, for statistical purposes, require that all credit institutions having branches within their territories shall report periodically on their activities in those host Member States to the competent authorities of those host Member States.

In discharging the responsibilities imposed on them in Article 14(2) and (3), host Member States may require that branches of credit institutions from other Member States provide the same information as they require from national credit institutions for that purpose.

2 Where the competent authorities of a host Member State ascertain that an institution having a branch or providing services within its territory is not complying with the legal provisions adopted in that State pursuant to the provisions of this Directive involving powers of the host Member State competent authorities, those authorities shall require the institution concerned to put an end to that irregular situation.

3 If the institution concerned fails to take the necessary steps, the competent authorities of the host Member State shall inform the competent authorites of the home Member State accordingly. The competent authorities of the home Member State shall, at the earliest opportunity, take all appropriate measures to ensure that the institution concerned puts an end to that irregular situation. The nature of those measures shall be communicated to the competent authorities of the host Member State.

4 If, despite the measures taken by the home Member State or because such measures prove inadequate or are not available in the Member State in question, the institution persists in violating the legal rules referred to in paragraph 2 in force in the host Member State, the latter State may, after informing the competent authorities of the home Member State, take appropriate measures to prevent or to publish further irregularities and, insofar as is necessary, to prevent that institution from initiating further transactions within its territory. The Member States shall ensure that within their territories it is possible to serve the legal documents necessary for these measures on credit institutions.

5 The foregoing provisions shall not affect the power of host Member States to take appropriate measures to prevent or to punish irregularities committed within their territories which are contrary to the legal rules they have adopted in the interest of the general good. This shall include the possibility of preventing offending institutions from initiating any further transactions within their territories.

6 Any measure adopted pursuant to paragraphs 3, 4 and 5 involving penalties or restrictions on the exercise of the freedom to provide services must be properly justified and communicated to the institution concerned. Every such measure shall be subject to a right of appeal to the courts in the Member State the authorities of which adopted it.

7 Before following the procedure provided for in paragraphs 2 to 4, the competent authorities of the host Member State may, in emergencies, take any precautionary measures necessary to protect the interests of depositors, investors and others to whom services are provided. The Commission and the competent authorities of the other Member States concerned must be informed of such measures at the earliest opportunity.

The Commission may, after consulting the competent authorities of the Member States concerned, decide that the Member State in question must amend or abolish those measures.

8 Host Member States may exercise the powers conferred on them under this Directive by taking appropriate measures to prevent or to publish irregularities committed within their territories. This shall include the possibility of preventing institutions from initiating further transactions within their territories.

9 In the event of the withdrawal of authorisation the competent authorities of the host Member State shall be informed and shall take appropriate measures to prevent the institution concerned from initiating further transactions within its territory and to safeguard the interests of depositors. Every two years the Commission shall submit a report on such cases to the Banking Advisory Comittee.

10 The Member States shall inform the Commission of the number and type of cases in which there has been a refusal pursuant to Article 19 or in which measures have been taken in accordance with paragraph 4. Every two years the Commission shall submit a report on such cases to the Banking Advisory Committee.

11 Nothing in this Article shall prevent credit institutions with head offices in other Member States from advertising their services through all available means of communication in the host Member State, subject to any rules governing the form and the content of such advertising adopted in the interest of the general good.   **[968]**

TITLE VI

FINAL PROVISIONS

Article 22

1 The technical adaptations to be made to this Directive in the following areas shall be adopted in accordance with the procedure laid down in paragraph 2—

— expansion of the content of the list referred to in Article 18 and set out in the Annex or adaptation of the terminology used in that list to take account of developments on financial markets,
— alteration of the amount of initial capital prescribed in Article 4 to take account of developments in the economic and monetary field,
— the areas in which the competent authorities must exchange information as listed in Article 7(1) of Directive 77/780/EEC,
— clarification of the definitions in order to ensure uniform application of this Directive throughout the Community,
— clarification of the definitions in order to take account in the implementation of this Directive of developments on financial markets,
— the alignment of terminology on and the framing of definitions in accordance with subsequent acts on credit institutions and related matters.

2 The Commission shall be assisted by a committee composed of representatives of the Member States and chaired by a representative of the Commission.

The Commission representative shall submit to the committee a draft of the measures to be taken. The committee shall deliver its opinion on the draft within a time limit which the chairman may lay down according to the urgency of the matter. The opinion shall be delivered by the majority laid down in Article 148(2) of the Treaty in the case of decisions which the Council is required to adopt on a proposal from the Commission. The votes of the representatives of the Member States in the committee shall be weighted in the manner set out in that Article. The chairman shall not vote.

The Commission shall adopt the measures envisaged if they are in accordance with the opinion of the committee.

If the measures envisaged are not in accordance with the opinion of the committee, or if no opinion is delivered, the Commission shall, without delay, submit to the Council a proposal concerning the measures to be taken. The Council shall act by a qualified majority.

If the Council does not act within three months of the referral to it the Commission shall adopt the measures proposed, unless the Council has decided against those measures by a simple majority.   **[969]**

Article 23

1 Branches which have commenced their activities, in accordance with the provisions in force in their host Member States, before the entry into force of the provisions adopted in implementation of the Directive shall be presumed to have been subject to the procedure laid down in Article 19(1) to (5). They shall be governed, from the date of that entry into force, by Articles 5, 18, 19(6) and 21. They shall benefit pursuant to Article 6(3).

2 Article 20 shall not affect rights acquired by credit institutions providing services before the entry into force of the provisions adopted in implementation of this Directive.   **[970]**

Article 24

1 Subject to paragraph 2, the Member States shall bring into force the laws, regulations and administrative provisions necessary for them to comply with this Directive by the later of the two dates laid down for the adoption of measures to comply with Directives 89/299/EEC and 89/647/EEC and at the latest by 1 January 1993. They shall forthwith inform the Commission thereof.

2 The Member States shall adopt the measures necessary for them to comply with Article 6(2) by 1 January 1990.

3 The Member States shall communicate to the Commission the texts of the main provisions of national law which they adopt in the field covered by this Directive.   **[971]**

Article 24

This Directive is addressed to the Member States.

Done at Brussels, 15 December 1989.

ANNEX

LIST OF ACTIVITIES SUBJECT TO MUTUAL RECOGNITION

1 Acceptance of deposits and other repayable funds from the public.

2 Lending.[1]

3 Financial leasing.

4 Money transmission services.

5 Issuing and administering means of payment (e.g. credit cards, travellers' cheques and bankers' drafts).

6 Guarantees and commitments.

7 Trading for own account or for account of customers in—

(a) money market instruments (cheques, bills, CDs, etc.);
(b) foreign exchange;
(c) financial futures and options;
(d) exchange and interest rate instruments;
(e) transferable securities.

8 Participation in share issues and the provision of services related to such issues.

9 Advice to undertakings on capital structure, industrial strategy and related questions and advice and services relating to mergers and the purchase of undertakings.

10 Money broking.

11 Portfolio management and advice.

12 Safekeeping and administration of securities.

13 Credit reference services.

14 Safe custody services.

[972]

NOTES
[1] Including *inter alia*—
— consumer credit,
— mortgage credit,
— factoring, with or without recourse,
— financing of commercial transactions (including forfaiting).

COUNCIL DIRECTIVE
of 18 December 1989

on a solvency ratio for credit institutions

(89/647/EEC)

NOTES
Date of publication in OJ: OJ L 386, 30.12.1989, p 14.

THE COUNCIL OF THE EUROPEAN COMMUNITIES,

Having regard to the Treaty establishing the European Economic Community, and in particular the first and third sentences of Article 57(2) thereof,
Having regard to the proposal from the Commission,[1]
In cooperation with the European Parliament,[2]
Having regard to the opinion of the Economic and Social Committee,[3]
Whereas this Directive is the outcome of work carried out by the Banking Advisory Committee, which, pursuant to Article 6(4) of Council Directive 77/780/EEC of 12 December 1977 on the coordination of laws, regulations and administrative provisions relating to the taking up and

pursuit of the business of credit institutions,[4] as last amended by Directive 89/646/EEC,[5] is responsible for making suggestions to the Commission with a view to coordinating the coefficients applicable in the Member States;

Whereas the establishment of an appropriate solvency ratio plays a central role in the supervision of credit institutions;

Whereas a ratio which weights assets and off-balance-sheet items according to the degree of credit risk is a particularly useful measure of solvency;

Whereas the development of common standards for own funds in relation to assets and off-balance-sheet items exposed to credit risk is, accordingly, an essential aspect of the harmonisation necessary for the achievement of the mutual recognition of supervision techniques and thus the completion of the internal banking market;

Whereas, in that respect, this Directive must be considered in conjunction with other specific instruments also harmonising the fundamental techniques of the supervision of credit institutions;

Whereas this Directive must also be seen as complementary to Directive 89/646/EEC, which lays out the broader framework of which this Directive is an integral part;

Whereas, in a common banking market, institutions are required to enter into direct competition with one another and whereas the adoption of common solvency standards in the form of a minimum ratio will prevent distortions of competition and strengthen the Community banking system;

Whereas this Directive provides for different weightings to be given to guarantees issued by different financial institutions; whereas the Commission accordingly undertakes to examine whether the Directive taken as a whole significantly distorts competition between credit institutions and insurance companies and, in the light of that examination, to consider whether any remedial measures are justified;

Whereas the minimum ratio provided for in this Directive reinforces the capital of credit institutions in the Community; whereas a level of 8% has been adopted following a statistical survey of capital requirements in force at the beginning of 1988;

Whereas measurement of and allowance for interest-rate, foreign-exchange and other market risks are also of great importance in the supervision of credit institutions; whereas the Commission will accordingly, in cooperation with the competent authorities of the Member States and all other bodies working towards similar ends, continue to study the techniques available; whereas it will then make appropriate proposals for the further harmonisation of supervision rules relating to those risks; whereas in so doing it will keep a special watch on the possible interaction between the various banking risks and consequently pay particular attention to the consistency of the various proposals;

Whereas, in making proposals for rules for the supervision of investment services and the adequacy of the capital of entities operating in that area, the Commission will ensure that equivalent requirements are applied in respect of the level of own funds, if the same type of business is transacted and identical risks are assumed;

Whereas the specific accounting technique to be used for the calculation of solvency ratios must take account of the provisions of Council Directive 86/635/EEC of 8 December 1986 on the annual accounts and consolidated accounts of banks and other financial institutions,[6] which incorporates certain adaptations of the provisions of Council Directive 83/349/EEC,[7] as amended by the Act of Accession of Spain and Portugal; whereas, pending transposition of the provisions of those Directives into the national laws of the Member States, the use of a specific accounting technique for the calculation of solvency ratios should be left to the discretion of the Member States;

Whereas the application of a 20% weighting to credit institutions' holdings of mortgage bonds may unsettle a national financial market on which such instruments play a preponderant role; whereas, in this case, provisional measures are taken to apply a 10% risk weighting;

Whereas technical modifications to the detailed rules laid down in this Directive may from time to time be necessary to take account of new developments in the banking sector; whereas the Commission will accordingly make such modifications as are necessary, after consulting the Banking Advisory Committee, within the limits of the implementing powers conferred on the Commission by the provisions of the Treaty; whereas that Committee will act as a 'Regulatory' Committee, according to the rules of procedure laid down in Article 2, procedure III, variant (b), of Council Decision 87/373/EEC of 13 July 1987 laying down the procedures for the exercise of implementing powers conferred on the Commission,[8]

NOTES
[1] OJ C 135, 25.5.1988, p 2.
[2] OJ C 96, 17.4.1984, p 86 and OJ C 304, 4.12.1985.
[3] OJ C 337, 31.12.1988, p 8.
[4] OJ L 322, 17.12.1977, p 30.
[5] See **[950]**.
[6] OJ L 372, 31.12.1986, p 1.
[7] OJ L 193, 18.7.1983, p 18.
[8] OJ L 197, 18.7.1987, p 33.

HAS ADOPTED THIS DIRECTIVE:

SCOPE AND DEFINITIONS

Article 1

1 This Directive shall apply to credit institutions as defined in the first indent of Article 1 of Directive 77/780/EEC.

2 Notwithstanding paragraph 1, the Member States need not apply this Directive to credit institutions listed in Article 2(2) of Directive 77/780/EEC.

3 A credit institution which, as defined in Article 2(4)(a) of Directive 77/780/EEC, is affiliated to a central body in the same Member State, may be exempted from the provisions of this Directive, provided that all such affiliated credit institutions and their central bodies are included in consolidated solvency ratios in accordance with this Directive.

4 Exceptionally, and pending further harmonisation of the prudential roles relating to credit, interest-rate and market risks, the Member States may exclude from the scope of this Directive any credit institution specialising in the inter-bank and public-debt markets and fulfilling, together with the central bank, the institutional function of banking-system liquidity regulator, provided that—

— the sum of its asset and off-balance-sheet items included in the 50% and 100% weightings, calculated in accordance with Article 6, must not normally exceed 10% of total assets and off-balance-sheet items and shall not in any event exceed 15% before application of the weightings,
— its main activity consists of acting as intermediary between the central bank of its Member State and the banking system,
— the competent authority applies adequate systems of supervision and control of its credit, interest-rate and market risks.

The Member States shall inform the Commission of the exemptions granted, in order to ensure that they do not result in distortions of competition. Within three years of the adoption of this Directive, the Commission shall submit to the Council a report together, where necessary, with any proposals it may consider appropriate.   [973]

Article 2

1 For the purposes of this Directive—

— [the national authorities which are empowered by law or regulation to supervise credit institutions];
— 'Zone A' shall comprise all the Member States and all other countries which are full members of the Organisation for Economic Cooperation and Development (OECD) and those countries which have concluded special lending arrangements with the International Monetary Fund (IMF) associated with the Fund's General Arrangements to Borrow (GAB),
— 'Zone B' shall comprise all counties not in Zone A,
— 'Zone A credit institutions' shall mean all credit institutions authorised in the Member States, in accordance with Article 3 of Directive 77/780/EEC, including their branches in third countries, and all private and public undertakings covered by the definition in the first indent of Article 1 of Directive 77/780/EEC and authorised in other Zone A countries, including their branches,

— 'Zone B credit institutions' shall mean all private and public undertakings authorised outside Zone A covered by the definition in the first indent of Article 1 of Directive 77/780/EEC, including their branches within the Community,
— 'non-bank sector' shall mean all borrowers other than credit institutions as defined in the fourth and fifth indents, central governments and central banks, regional governments and local authorities, the European Communities, the European Investment Bank and multilateral development banks as defined in the seventh indent,
— 'multilateral development banks' shall mean the International Bank for Reconstruction and Development, the International Finance Corporation, the Inter-American Development Bank, the Asian Development Bank, the African Development Bank, the Council of Europe Resettlement Fund, the Nordic Investment Bank and the Caribbean Development Bank,
— 'full-risk', 'medium-risk', 'medium/low-risk' and 'low-risk' off-balance-sheet items shall mean the items described in Article 6(2) and listed in Annex I.

2 For the purposes of Article 6(1)(b), the competent authorities may include within the concept of regional governments and local authorities non-commercial administrative bodies responsible to regional governments or local authorities, and those non-commercial undertakings owned by central governments, regional governments, local authorities or authorities which, in the view of the competent authorities, exercise the same responsibilities as regional and local authorities. [974]

NOTES
Words in the first indent substituted by Council Directive 92/30/EEC of 6 April 1992, Art 10.
The definition of 'multilateral development banks' in the seventh indent of Article 2(1) includes the European Bank for Reconstruction and Development; see Commission Directive 91/31/EEC, Art 1. For adaptations to para (1), see Commission Directive 94/7/EC of 15 March 1994, Art 1 at **[1045]** and Commission Directive 95/15/EC of 31 May 1995, Art 1 at **[1063]**.

Article 3

General principles

1 The solvency ratio referred to in paragraphs 2 to 7 expresses own funds, as defined in Article 4, as a proportion of total assets and off-balance-sheet items, risk-adjusted in accordance with Article 5.

2 The solvency ratios of credit institutions which are neither parent undertakings as defined in Article 1 of Directive 83/349/EEC nor subsidiaries of such undertakings shall be calculated on an individual basis.

3 The solvency ratios of credit institutions which are parent undertakings shall be calculated on a consolidated basis in accordance with the methods laid down in this Directive and in [Directives 92/30/EEC] and 86/635/EEC.[1]

4 The competent authorities responsible for authorising and supervising a parent undertaking which is a credit institution may also require the calculation of a subconsolidated or unconsolidated ratio in respect of that parent undertaking and of any of its subsidiaries which are subject to authorisation and supervision by them. Where such monitoring of the satisfactory allocation of capital within a banking group is not carried out, other measures must be taken to attain that end.

5 Where the subsidiary of a parent undertaking has been authorised and is situated in another Member State, the competent authorities which granted that authorisation shall require the calculation of a subconsolidated or unconsolidated ratio.

6 Notwithstanding paragraph 5, the competent authorities responsible for authorising the subsidiary of a parent undertaking situated in another Member State may, by way of a bilateral agreement, delegate their responsibility for supervising solvency to the competent authorities which have authorised and which supervise the parent undertaking so that they assume responsbility for supervising the subsidiary in accordance with this Directive. The Commission shall be kept informed of the existence and content of such agreements. It shall forward such information to the other authorities and to the Banking Advisory Committee.

7 Without prejudice to credit institutions' compliance with the requirements of paragraphs 2 to 6, the competent authorities shall ensure that ratios are calculated not less than twice each year, either by credit institutions themselves, which shall communicate the results and any component data required to the competent authorities, or by the competent authorities, using data supplied by the credit institutions.

8 The valuation of assets and off-balance-sheet items shall be effected in accordance with Directive 86/635/EEC. Pending implementation of the provisions of that Directive, valuation shall be left to the discretion of the Member States. **[975]**

NOTES
[1] OJ L 372, 31.12.1986, p 1.
Para (3): words substituted by Council Directive 92/30/EEC of 6 April 1992, Art 10.

Article 4

The numerator: own funds

Own funds as defined in Directive 89/299/EEC[1] shall form the numerator of the solvency ratio. **[976]**

NOTES
[1] OJ No L 124, 5.5.1989, p 16.

Article 5

The denominator: risk adjusted assets and off-balance-sheet items

1 Degrees of credit risk, expressed as percentage weightings, shall be assigned to asset items in accordance with Articles 6 and 7, and exceptionally Articles 8 and 11. The balance-sheet value of each asset shall then be multiplied by the relevant weighting to produce a risk-adjusted value.

2 In the case of the off-balance-sheet items listed in Annex I, a two-stage calculation as prescribed in Article 6(2) shall be used.

3 In the case of the interest-rate- and foreign-exchange-related off-balance-sheet items referred to in Article 6(3), the potential costs of replacing contracts in the event of counterparty default shall be calculated by means of one of the two methods set out in Annex II. Those costs shall be multiplied by the relevant counterparty weightings in Article 6(1), except that the 100% weightings as provided for there shall be replaced by 50% weightings to produce risk-adjusted values.

4 The total of the risk-adjusted values of the assets and off-balance-sheet items mentioned in paragraphs 2 and 3 shall be the denominator of the solvency ratio. **[977]**

Article 6
Risk weightings

1 The following weightings shall be applied to the various categories of asset items, although the competent authorities may fix higher weightings as they see fit:

(a) *Zero weightings*
1   cash in hand and equivalent items;
2   asset items constituting claims on Zone A central governments and central banks;
3   asset items constituting claims on the European Communities;
4   asset items constituting claims carrying the explicit guarantees of Zone A central governments and central banks;
5   asset items constituting claims on Zone B central governments and central banks, denominated and funded in the national currencies of the borrowers;
6   asset items constituting claims carrying the explicit guarantees of Zone B central governments and central banks, denominated and funded in the national currency common to the guarantor and the borrower;
7   asset items secured, to the satisfaction of the competent authorities, by collateral in the form of Zone A central government or central bank securities, or securities issued by the European Communities, or by cash deposits placed with the lending institution or by certificates of deposit or similar instruments issued by and lodged with the latter;

(b) *20% weighting*
1   asset items constituting claims on the European Investment Bank (EIB);
2   asset items constituting claims on multilateral development banks;
3   asset items constituting claims carrying the explicit guarantee of the European Investment Bank (EIB);
4   asset items constituting claims carrying the explicit guarantees of multilateral development banks;
5   asset items constituting claims on Zone A regional governments or local authorities, subject to Article 7;
6   asset items constituting claims carrying the explicit guarantees of Zone A regional governments or local authorities, subject to Article 7;
7   asset items constituting claims on Zone A credit institutions but not constituting such institutions' own funds as defined in Directive 89/299/EEC;
8   asset items constituting claims, with a maturity of one year or less, on Zone B credit institutions, other than securities issued by such institutions which are recognised as components of their own funds;
9   asset items carrying the explicit guarantees of Zone A credit institutions;
10   asset items constituting claims with a maturity of one year or less, carrying the explicit guarantees of Zone B credit institutions;
11   asset items secured, to the satisfaction of the competent authorities, by collateral in the form of securities issued by the EIB or by multilateral development banks;

12 cash items in the process of collection;

(c) 50% weighting
1 loans fully and completely secured, to the satisfaction of the competent authorities, by mortgages on residential property which is or will be occupied or let by the borrower [and loans fully and completely secured, to the satisfaction of the competent authorities, by shares in Finnish residential housing companies, operating in accordance with the Finnish Housing Company Act of 1991 or subsequent equivalent legislation, in respect of residential property which is or will be occupied or let by the borrower];
2 prepayments and accrued income: these assets shall be subject to the weighting corresponding to the counterparty where a credit institution is able to determine it in accordance with Directive 86/635/EEC. Otherwise, where it is unable to determine the contraparty, it shall apply a flat-rate weighting of 50%;

(d) 100% weighting
1 asset items constituting claims on Zone B central governments and central banks except where denominated and funded in the national currency of the borrower;
2 asset items constituting claims on Zone B regional governments or local authorities;
3 asset items constituting claims with a maturity of more than one year on Zone B credit institutions;
4 asset items constituting claims on the Zone A or Zone B non-bank sectors;
5 tangible assets within the meaning of assets as listed in Article 4(10) of Directive 86/635/EEC;
6 holdings of shares, participations and other components of the own funds of other credit institutions which are not deducted from the own funds of the lending institutions;
7 all other assets except where deducted from own funds.

2 The following treatment shall apply to off-balance-sheet items other than those covered in paragraph 3. They shall first be grouped according to the risk groupings set out in Annex I. The full value of the full-risk items shall be taken into account, 50% of the value of the medium-risk items and 20% of the medium/low-risk items, while the value of low-risk items shall be set at zero. The second stage shall be to multiply the off-balance-sheet values, adjusted as described above, by the weightings attributable to the relevant counterparties, in accordance with the treatment of asset items prescribed in paragraph 1 and Article 7. In the case of asset sale and repurchase agreements and outright forward purchases, the weightings shall be those attaching to the assets in question and not to the counterparties to the transactions.

3 The methods set out in Annex II shall be applied to the interest-rate and foreign-exchange risks listed in Annex III.

4 Where off-balance-sheet items carry explicit guarantees, they shall be weighted as if they had been incurred on behalf of the guarantor rather than the counterparty. Where the potential exposure arising from off-balance-sheet transactions is fully and completely secured, to the satisfaction of the competent authorities, by any of the asset items recognised as collateral in paragraph 1(a)(7) or (b)(11), weightings of 0% or 20% shall apply, depending on the collateral in question.

5 Where asset and off-balance-sheet items are given a lower weighting because of the existence of explicit guarantees or collateral acceptable to the

competent authorities, the lower weighting shall apply only to that part which is guaranteed or which is fully recovered by the collateral. **[978]**

NOTES
Para (6): the words in square brackets in para (1)(c)(1) added by the 1994 Act of Accession of Kingdom of Norway, the Republic of Austria, the Republic of Finland and the Kingdom of Sweden, Annex I(XI)(B)(III)(2)(a), as adjusted by Council Decision 95/1/EC, Annex I(XI)(B)(III)(2)(a).
For an adaptation to para (1)(a), see Commission Directive 95/15/EC of 31 May 1995 at **[1064]**.

Article 7

1 Notwithstanding the requirements of Article 6(1)(b), the Member States may fix a weighting of 0% for their own regional governments and local authorities if there is no difference in risk between claims on the latter and claims on their central governments because of the revenue-raising powers of the regional governments and local authorities and the existence of specific institutional arrangements the effect of which is to reduce the chances of default by the latter. A zero weighting fixed in accordance with these criteria shall apply to claims on and off-balance-sheet items incurred on behalf of the regional governments and local authorities in question and claims on others and off-balance-sheet items incurred on behalf of others and guaranteed by those regional governments and local authorities.

2 The Member States shall notify the Commission if they believe a zero weighting to be justified according to the criteria laid down in paragraph 1. The Commission shall circulate that information. Other Member States may offer the credit institutions under the supervision of their competent authorities the possibility of applying a zero weighting where they undertake business with the regional governments or local authorities in question or where they hold claims guaranteed by the latter. **[979]**

Article 8

1 The Member States may apply a weighting of 20% to asset items which are secured, to the satisfaction of the competent authorities concerned, by collateral in the form of securities issued by Zone A regional governments or local authorities, by deposits placed with Zone A credit institutions other than the lending institution, or by certificates of deposit of similar instruments issued by those credit institutions.

2 The Member States may apply a weighting of 10% to claims on institutions specialising in the inter-bank and public-debt markets in their home Member States and subject to close supervision by the competent authorities where those asset items are fully and completely secured, to the satisfaction of the competent authorities of the home Member States, by a combination of asset items mentioned in Article 6(1)(a) and (b) recognised by the latter as constituting adequate collateral.

3 The Member States shall notify the Commission of any provisions adopted pursuant to paragraphs 1 and 2 and of the grounds for such provisions. The Commission shall forward that information to the Member States. The Commission shall periodically examine the implications of those provisions in order to ensure that they do not result in any distortions of competition. Within three years of the adoption of this Directive, the Commission shall submit to the Council a report together, where necessary, with any proposals it may consider appropriate. **[980]**

Article 9

1 The technical adaptations to be made to this Directive in the following areas shall be adopted in accordance with the procedure laid down in paragraph 2—

— a temporary reduction in the minimum ratio prescribed in Article 10 or the weightings prescribed in Article 6 in order to take account of specific circumstances,
— the definition of 'Zone A' in Article 2,
— the definition of 'multilateral development banks' in Article 2,
— amendment of the definitions of the assets listed in Article 6 in order to take account of developments on financial markets,
— the lists and classification of off-balance-sheet items in Annexes I and II and their treatment in the calculation of the ratio as described in Articles 5, 6 and 7 and Annex II,
— clarification of the definitions in order to ensure uniform application of this Directive throughout the Community,
— clarification of the definitions in order to take account in the implementation of this Directive of developments on financial markets,
— the alignment of terminology on and the framing of definitions in accordance with subsequent acts on credit institutions and related matters.

2 The Commission shall be assisted by a committee composed of representatives of the Member States and chaired by a representative of the Commission.

The Commission representative shall submit to the committee a draft of the measures to be taken. The committee shall deliver its opinion on the draft within a time limit which the chairman may lay down according to the urgency of the matter. The opinion shall be delivered by the majority laid down in Article 148(2) of the Treaty in the case of decisions which the Council is required to adopt on a proposal from the Commission. The votes of the representatives of the Member States in the committee shall be weighted in the manner set out in that Article. The chairman shall not vote.

The Commission shall adopt the measures envisaged if they are in accordance with the opinion of the committee.

If the measures envisaged are not in accordance with the opinion of the committee, or if no opinion is delivered, the Commission shall, without delay, submit to the Council a proposal concerning the measures to be taken. The Council shall act by a qualified majority.

If the Council does not act within three months of the referral to it the Commission shall adopt the measures proposed, unless the Council has decided against those measures by a simple majority.   **[981]**

Article 10

1 With effect from 1 January 1993 credit institutions shall be required permanently to maintain the ratio defined in Article 3 at a level of at least 8%.

2 Notwithstanding paragraph 1, the competent authorities may prescribe higher minimum ratios as they consider appropriate.

3 If the ratio falls below 8% of the competent authorities shall ensure that the credit institution in question takes appropriate measures to restore the ratio to the agreed minimum as quickly as possible.   **[982]**

Article 11

1 A credit institution the minimum ratio of which has not reached the 8% prescribed in Article 10(1) by the date prescribed in Article 12(1) must gradually approach that level by successive stages. It may not allow the ratio to fall below the level reached before that objective has been attained. Any fluctuation should be temporary and the competent authorities should be apprised of the reasons for it.

2 For not more than five years after the date prescribed in Article 10(1) the Member States may fix a weighting of 10% for the bonds defined in Article 22(4) of Council Directive 85/611/EEC on the coordination of laws, regulations and administrative provisions relating to undertakings for collective investment in transferable securities (UCITS),[1] as amended by Directive 88/220/EEC,[2] and maintain it for credit institutions when and if they consider it necessary, to avoid grave disturbances in the operation of their markets. Such exceptions shall be reported to the Commission.

3 For not more than seven years after 1 January 1993, Article 10(1) shall not apply to the Agricultural Bank of Greece. However, the latter must approach the level prescribed in Article 10(1) by successive stages according to the method described in paragraph 1.

4 By derogation from Article 6(1)(c)(1), until 1 January 1996 [Germany, Denmark, Greece and Austria] may apply a weighting of 50% to assets which are entirely and completely secured to the satisfaction of the competent authorities concerned, by mortgages on completed residential property, on offices or on multi-purpose commercial premises, situated within the territories of those three Member States provided that the sum borrowed does not exceed 60% of the value of the property in question, calculated on the basis of rigorous assessment criteria laid down in statutory or regulatory provisions.

5 Member States may apply a 50% weighting to property leasing transactions concluded within ten years of the date laid down in Article 12(1) and concerning assets for business use situated in the country of the head office and governed by statutory provisions whereby the lessor retains full ownership of the rented asset until the tenant exercises his option to purchase.   **[983]**

NOTES
[1] OJ L 375, 31.12.1985, p 3.
[2] OJ L 100, 19.4.1988, p 31.
   Para (4): words in square brackets substituted by the 1994 Act of Accession of the Kingdom of Norway, the Republic of Austria, the Republic of Finland and the Kingdom of Sweden, Annex I(XI)(B)(III)(2)(b), as adjusted by Council Decision 95/1/EC, Annex I(XI)(B)(III)(2)(b).

Article 12

1 The Member States shall adopt the measures necessary for them to comply with the provisions of this Directive by 1 January 1991 at the latest.

2 The Member States shall communicate to the Commission the texts of the main laws, regulations and administrative provisions which they adopt in the field covered by this Directive.   **[984]**

Article 13

This Directive is addressed to the Member States.   **[985]**

Done at Brussels, 18 December 1989.

ANNEX I

CLASSIFICATION OF OFF-BALANCE-SHEET ITEMS

Full risk

   — Guarantees having the character of credit substitutes,
   — Acceptances,

— Endorsements on bills not bearing the name of another credit institution,
— Transactions with recourse,
— Irrevocable standby letters of credit having the character of credit substitutes,
— Asset sale and repurchase agreements as defined in Articles 12(1) and (2) of Directive 86/635/EEC, if these agreements are treated as off-balance-sheet items pending application of Directive 86/635/EEC,
— Assets purchased under outright forward purchase agreements,
— Forward forward deposits,
— The unpaid portion of partly-paid shares and securities,
— Other items also carrying full risk.

Medium risk

— Documentary credits issued and confirmed (see also medium/low risk),
— Warranties and indemnities (including tender, performance, customs and tax bonds) and guarantees not having the character of credit substitutes,
— Asset sale and repurchase agreements as defined in Article 12(3) and (5) of Directive 86/635/EEC,
— Irrevocable standby letters of credit not having the character of credit substitutes,
— Undrawn credit facilities (agreements to lend, purchase securities, provide guarantees or acceptance facilities) with an original maturity of more than one year,
— Note issuance facilities (NIFs) and revolving underwriting facilities (RUFs),
— Other items also carrying medium risk.

Medium/low risk

— Documentary credits in which underlying shipment acts as collateral and other self-liquidating transactions,
— Other items also carrying medium/low risk.

Low risk

— Undrawn credit facilities (agreements to lend, purchase securities, provide guarantees or acceptance facilities) with an original maturity of up to and including one year or which may be cancelled unconditionally at any time without notice,
— Other items also carrying low risk.

The Member States undertake to inform the Commission as soon as they have agreed to include a new off-balance-sheet item in any of the last indents under each category of risk. Such items will be definitively classified at Community level once the procedure laid down in Article 9 has been completed. **[986]**

ANNEX II

THE TREATMENT OF OFF-BALANCE-SHEET ITEMS CONCERNING INTEREST AND FOREIGN-EXCHANGE RATES

Subject to the consent of their supervisory authorities, credit institutions may choose one of the methods set out below to measure the risks associated with the transactions listed in Annex III. Interest rate and foreign-exchange contracts traded on recognised exchanges where they are subject to daily margin requirements and foreign-exchange contracts with an original maturity of 14 calendar days or less are excluded.

Where there is a separate bilateral contract for novation, recognised by the national supervisory authorites, between a credit institution and its counterparty under which any obligation to each other to deliver payments in their common currency on a given date are automatically amalgamated with other similar obligations due on the same date, the single net amount fixed by such novation is weighted, rather than the gross amounts involved.

Method 1: the 'marking to market' approach

Step (a): by attaching current market values to contracts (marking to market) the current replacement cost of all contracts with positive values is obtained.

Step (b): to obtain a figure for potential future credit exposure,[1] the notional principal amounts or values underlying an institution's aggregate books are multiplied by the following percentages:

Residual maturity	Interest-rate contracts	Foreign-exchange contracts
One year or less	0 %	1%
More than one year	0,5%	5%

Step (c): the sum of current replacement cost and potential future credit exposure is multiplied by the risk weightings allocated to the relevant counterparties in Article 6.

Method 2: the 'original exposure' approach

Step (a): the notional principal amount of each instrument is multiplied by the percentages given below:

Original maturity[1]	Interest-rate contracts	Foreign-exchange contracts
One year or less	0,5%	2%
More than one year but not exceeding two years	1 %	5%
Additional allowance for each additional year	1 %	3%

[1] In the case of interest-rate contracts, credit institutions may, subject to the consent of their supervisory authorities, choose either original or residual maturity.

Step (b): the original exposure thus obtained is multiplied by the risk weightings allocated to the relevant counterparties in Article 6.   [986A]

[1] Except in the case of single-currency 'floating/floating interest rate swaps' in which only the current replacement cost will be calculated.

ANNEX III

TYPES OF OFF-BALANCE-SHEET ITEMS CONCERNING INTEREST RATES AND FOREIGN EXCHANGE

Interest-rate contracts

— Single-currency interest rate swaps,
— Basis swaps,
— Forward-rate agreements,
— Interest-rate futures,
— Interest-rate options purchased,
— Other contracts of a similar nature.

Foreign-exchange contracts

— Cross-currency interest-rate swaps,
— Forward foreign-exchange contracts,
— Currency futures,
— Currency options purchased,
— Other contracts of a similar nature.

[987]

COUNCIL DIRECTIVE
of 10 June 1991

on prevention of the use of the financial system for the purpose of money laundering

(91/308/EEC)

NOTES

Date of publication in OJ: OJ L166, 28.6.1991, p 77.

THE COUNCIL OF THE EUROPEAN COMMUNITIES,

Having regard to the Treaty establishing the European Economic Community, and in particular Article 57(2), first and third sentences, and Article 100a thereof,

Having regard to the proposal from the Commission[1],

In cooperation with the European Parliament[2],

Having regard to the opinion of the Economic and Social Committee[3],

Whereas when credit and financial institutions are used to launder proceeds from criminal activities (hereinafter referred to as 'money laundering'), the soundness and stability of the institution concerned and confidence in the financial system as a whole could be seriously jeopardised, thereby losing the trust of the public;

Whereas lack of Community action against money laundering could lead Member States, for the purpose of protecting their financial systems, to adopt measures which could be inconsistent with completion of the single market; whereas, in order to facilitate their criminal activities, launderers could try to take advantage of the freedom of capital movement and freedom to supply financial services which the integrated financial areas involves, if certain coordinating measures are not adopted at Community level;

Whereas money laundering has an evident influence on the rise of organised crime in general and drug trafficking in particular; whereas there is more and more awareness that combating money laundering is one of the most effective means of opposing this form of criminal activity, which constitutes a particular threat to Member States' societies;

Whereas money laundering must be combated mainly by penal means and within the framework of international cooperation among judicial and law enforcement authorities, as has been undertaken, in the field of drugs, by the United Nations Convention Against Illicit Traffic in Narcotic Drugs and Psychotropic Substances, adopted on 19 December 1988 in Vienna (hereinafter referred to as the 'Vienna Convention') and more generally in relation to all criminal activites, by the Council of Europe Convention on laundering, tracing, seizure and confiscation of proceeds of crime, opened for signature on 8 November 1990 in Strasbourg;

Whereas a penal approach should, however, not be the only way to combat money laundering, since the financial system can play a highly effective role; whereas reference must be made in this context to the recommendation of the Council of Europe of 27 June 1980 and to the declaration of principles adopted in December 1988 in Basle by the banking supervisory authorities of the Group of Ten, both of which constitute major steps towards preventing the use of the financial system for money laundering;

Whereas money laundering is usually carried out in an international context so that the criminal origin of the funds can be better disguised; whereas measures exclusively adopted at a national level, without taking account of international coordination and cooperation, would have very limited effects;

Whereas any measures adopted by the Community in this field should be consistent with other action undertaken in other international fora; whereas in this respect any Community action should take particular account of the recommendations adopted by the financial action task force on money laundering, set up in July 1989 by the Paris summit of the seven most developed countries;

Whereas the European Parliament has requested, in several resolutions, the establishment of a global Community programme to combat drug trafficking, including provisions on prevention of money laundering;

Whereas for the purposes of this Directive the definition of money laundering is taken from that adopted in the Vienna Convention; whereas, however, since money laundering occurs not only in relation to the proceeds of drug-related offences but also in relation to the proceeds of other criminal activities (such as organised crime and terrorism), the Member States should, within the meaning of their legislation, extend the effects of the Directive to include the proceeds of such activities, to the extent that they are likely to result in laundering operations justifying sanctions on that basis;

Whereas prohibition of money laundering in Member States' legislation backed by appropriate measures and penalties is a necessary condition for combating this phenomenon;

Whereas ensuring that credit and financial institutions require identification of their customers when entering into business relations or conducting transactions, exceeding certain thresholds, are necessary to avoid launderers' taking advantage of anonymity to carry out their criminal activities; whereas such provisions must also be extended, as far as possible, to any beneficial owners;

Whereas credit and financial institutions must keep for at least five years copies or references of the identification documents required as well as supporting evidence and records consisting of documents relating to transactions or copies thereof similarly admissible in court proceedings under the applicable national legislation for use as evidence in any investigation into money laundering;

Whereas ensuring that credit and financial institutions examine with special attention any transaction which they regard as particularly likely, by its nature, to be related to money laundering is necessary in order to preserve the soundness and integrity of the financial system as well as to contribute to combating this phenomenon; whereas to this end they should pay special attention to transactions with third countries which do not apply comparable standards against money laundering to those established by the Community or to other equivalent standards set out by international fora and endorsed by the Community;

Whereas, for those purposes, Member States may ask credit and financial institutions to record in writing the results of the examination they are required to carry out and to ensure that those results are available to the authorities responsible for efforts to eliminate money laundering;

Whereas preventing the financial system from being used for money laundering is a task which cannot be carried out by the authorities responsible for combating this phenomenon without the cooperation of credit and financial institutions and their supervisory authorities; whereas banking secrecy must be lifted in such cases; whereas a mandatory system of reporting suspicious transactions which ensures that information is transmitted to the abovementioned authorities without alerting the customers concerned, is the most effective way to accomplish such cooperation; whereas a special protection clause is necessary to exempt credit and financial institutions, their employees and their directors from responsibility for breaching restrictions on disclosure of information;

Whereas the information received by the authorities pursuant to this Directive may be used only in connection with combating money laundering; whereas Member States may nevertheless provide that this information may be used for other purposes;

Whereas establishment by credit and financial institutions of procedures of internal control and training programmes in this field are complementary provisions without which the other measures contained in this Directive could become ineffective;

Whereas, since money laundering can be carried out not only through credit and financial institutions but also through other types of professions and categories of undertakings, Member States must extend the provisions of this Directive in whole or in part, to include those professions and undertakings whose activities are particularly likely to be used for money laundering purposes;

Whereas it is important that the Member States should take particular care to ensure that coordinated action is taken in the Community where there are strong grounds for believing that professions or activities the conditions governing the pursuit of which have been harmonised at Community level are being used for laundering money;

Whereas the effectiveness of efforts to eliminate money laundering is particularly dependent on the close coordination and harmonisation of national implementing measures; whereas such coordination and harmonisation which is being carried out in various international bodies requires, in the Community context, cooperation between Member States and the Commission in the framework of a contact committee;

Whereas it is for each Member State to adopt appropriate measures and to penalise infringement of such measures in an appropriate manner to ensure full application of this Directive,

HAS ADOPTED THIS DIRECTIVE:

[1] OJ C 106, 24.4.1990, p 6; and OJ C 319, 19.12.1990, p 9.
[2] OJ C 324, 24.12.1990, p 264; and OJ C 129, 20.5.1991.
[3] OJ C 332, 31.12.1990, p 86.

Article 1

For the purpose of this Directive—

— 'credit institution' means a credit institution, as defined as in the first indent of Article 1 of Directive 77/780/EEC[1], as last amended by Directive 89/646/EEC[2], and includes branches within the meaning of the third indent of that Article and located in the Community, of credit institutions having their head offices outside the Community,

— 'financial institution' means an undertaking other than a credit institution whose principal activity is to carry out one or more of the operations included in numbers 2 to 12 and number 14 of the list annexed to Directive 89/646/EEC, or an insurance company duly authorised in accordance with Directive 79/267/EEC[3], as last amended by Directive 90/619/EEC[4], in so far as it carries out activities covered by that Directive; this definition includes branches located in the Community of financial institutions whose head offices are outside the Community,

— 'money laundering' means the following conduct when committed intentionally:

  — the conversion or transfer of property, knowing that such property is derived from criminal activity or from an act of participation in such activity, for the purpose of concealing or disguising the illicit origin of the property or of assisting any person who is involved in the commission of such activity to evade the legal consequences of his action,

  — the concealment or disguise of the true nature, source, location, disposition, movement, rights with respect to, or ownership of property, knowing that such property is derived from criminal activity or from an act of participation in such activity,

  — the acquisition, possession or use of property, knowing, at the time of receipt, that such property was derived from criminal activity or from an act of participation in such activity,

  — participating in, association to commit, attempts to commit and aiding, abetting, facilitating and counselling the commission of any of the actions mentioned in the foregoing paragraphs.

Knowledge, intent or purpose required as an element of the above-mentioned activities may be inferred from objective factual circumstances.

Money laundering shall be regarded as such even where the activities which generated the property to be laundered were perpetrated in the territory of another Member State or in that of a third country.

— 'Property' means assets of every kind, whether corporeal or incorporeal, movable or immovable, tangible or intangible, and legal documents or instruments evidencing title to or interests in such assets.

— 'Criminal activity' means a crime specified in Article 3(1)(a) of the Vienna Convention and any other criminal activity designated as such for the purposes of this Directive by each Member State.

— 'Competent authorities' means the national authorities empowered by law or regulation to supervise credit or financial institutions. **[988]**

NOTES
[1] OJ L 322, 17.12.1977, p 30.
[2] OJ L 386, 30.12.1989, p 1.
[3] OJ L 63, 13.3.1979, p 1.
[4] OJ L 330, 29.11.1990, p 50.

Article 2

Member States shall ensure that money laundering as defined in this Directive is prohibited. **[989]**

Article 3

1 Member States shall ensure that credit and financial institutions require identification of their customers by means of supporting evidence when entering into business relations, particularly when opening an account or savings accounts, or when offering safe custody facilities.

2 The identification requirement shall also apply for any transaction with customers other than those referred to in paragraph 1, involving a sum amounting to ECU 15,000 or more, whether the transaction is carried out in a single operation or in several operations which seem to be linked. Where the sum is not known at the time when the transaction is undertaken, the institution concerned shall proceed with identification as soon as it is apprised of the sum and establishes that the threshold has been reached.

3 By way of derogation from paragraphs 1 and 2, the identification requirements with regard to insurance policies written by insurance undertakings within the meaning of Directive 79/267/EEC, where they perform activities which fall within the scope of that Directive shall not be required where the periodic premium amount or amounts to be paid in any given year does or do not exceed ECU 1,000 or where a single premium is paid amounting to ECU 2,500 or less. If the periodic premium amount or amounts to be paid in any given year is or are increased so as to exceed the ECU 1,000 threshold, identification shall be required.

4 Member States may provide that the identification requirement is not compulsory for insurance policies in respect of pension schemes taken out by virtue of a contract of employment or the insured's occupation, provided that such policies contain no surrender clause and may not be used as collateral for a loan.

5 In the event of doubt as to whether the customers referred to in the above paragraphs are acting on their own behalf, or where it is certain that they are not acting on their own behalf, the credit and financial institutions shall take reasonable measures to obtain information as to the real identity of the person on whose behalf those customers are acting.

6 Credit and financial institutions shall carry out such identification, even where the amount of the transaction is lower than the threshold laid down, wherever there is suspicion of money laundering.

7 Credit and financial institutions shall not be subject to the identification requirements provided for in this Article where the customer is also a credit or financial institutions covered by this Directive.

8 Member States may provide that the identification requirements regarding transactions referred to in paragraphs 3 and 4 are fulfilled when it is established that the payment for the transaction is to be debited from an account opened in the customer's name and a credit institution subject to this Directive according to the requirements of paragraph 1. **[990]**

Article 4

Member States shall ensure that credit and financial institutions keep the following for use as evidence in any investigation into money laundering:

— in the case of identification, a copy or the references of the evidence required, for a period of at least five years after the relationship with their customer has ended,

— in the case of transactions, the supporting evidence and records, consisting of the original documents or copies admissible in court proceedings under the applicable national legislation for a period of at least five years following execution of the transactions. **[991]**

Article 5

Member States shall ensure that credit and financial institutions examine with special attention any transaction which they regard as particularly likely, by its nature, to be related to money laundering. **[992]**

Article 6

Member States shall ensure that credit and financial institutions and their directors and employees cooperate fully with the authorities responsible for combating money laundering—

— by informing those authorities, on their own initiative, of any fact which might be an indication of money laundering,
— by furnishing those authorities, at their request, with all necessary information, in accordance with the procedures established by the applicable legislation.

The information referred to in the first paragraph shall be forwarded to the authorities responsible for combating money laundering of the Member State in whose territory the institution forwarding the information is situated. The person or persons designated by the credit and financial institutions in accordance with the procedures provided for in Article 11(1) shall normally forward the information.

Information supplied to the authorities in accordance with the first paragraph may be used only in connection with the combating of money laundering. However, Member States may provide that such information may also be used for other purposes. **[993]**

Article 7

Member States shall ensure that credit and financial institutions refrain from carrying out transactions which they know or suspect to be related to money laundering until they have apprised the authorities referred to in Article 6. Those authorities may, under conditions determined by their national legislation, give instructions not to execute the operation. Where such a transaction is suspected of giving rise to money laundering and where to refrain in such manner is impossible or is likely to frustrate efforts to pursue the beneficiaries of a suspected money-laundering operation, the institutions concerned shall apprise the authorities immediately afterwards. **[994]**

Article 8

Credit and financial institutions and their directors and employees shall not disclose to the customer concerned nor to other third persons that information has been transmitted to the authorities in accordance with Articles 6 and 7 or that a money laundering investigation is being carried out. **[995]**

Article 9

The disclosure in good faith to the authorities responsible for combating money laundering by an employee or director of a credit or financial institution of the information referred to in Articles 6 and 7 shall not constitute a breach of any restriction on disclosure of information imposed by contract or by any legislative, regulatory or administrative provision, and shall not involve the credit or financial institution, its directors or employees in liability of any kind. **[996]**

Article 10

Member States shall ensure that if, in the course of inspections carried out in credit or financial institutions by the competent authorities, or in any other way, those authorities discover facts that could constitute evidence of money laundering, they inform the authorities responsible for combating money laundering. **[997]**

Article 11

Member States shall ensure that credit and financial institutions—

1　establish adequate procedures of internal control and communication in order to forestall and prevent operations related to money laundering,

2　take appropriate measures so that their employees are aware of the provisions contained in this Directive. These measures shall include participation of their relevant employees in special training programmes to help them recognize operations which may be related to money laundering as well as to instruct them as to how to proceed in such cases. **[998]**

Article 12

Member States shall ensure that the provisions of this Directive are extended in whole or in part to professions and to categories of undertakings, other than the credit and financial institutions referred to in Article 1, which engage in activities which are particularly likely to be used for money-laundering purposes. **[999]**

Article 13

1 A contact committee (hereinafter referred to as 'the Committee') shall be set up under the aegis of the Commission. Its function shall be—

(a) without prejudice to Articles 169 and 170 of the Treaty, to facilitate harmonised implementation of this Directive through regular consultation on any practical problems arising from its application and on which exchanges of view are deemed useful;

(b) to facilitate consultation between the Member States on the more stringent or additional conditions and obligations which they may lay down at national level;

(c) to advise the Commission, if necessary, on any supplements or amendments to be made to this Directive or on any adjustments deemed necessary, in particular to harmonise the effects of Article 12;

(d) to examine whether a profession or a category of undertaking should be included in the scope of Article 12 where it has been established that such profession or category of undertaking has been used in a Member State for money laundering.

2 It shall not be the function of the Committee to appraise the merits of decisions taken by the competent authorities in individual cases.

3 The Committee shall be composed of persons appointed by the Member States and of representatives of the Commission. The secretariat shall be provided by the Commission. The chairman shall be a representative of the Commission. It shall be convened by its chairman, either on his own initiative or at the request of the delegation of a Member State. **[1000]**

Article 14

Each Member State shall take appropriate measures to ensure full application of all the provisions of this Directive and shall in particular determine the penalties to be applied for infringement of the measures adopted pursuant to this Directive. **[1001]**

Article 15

The Member States may adopt or retain in force stricter provisions in the field covered by this Directive to prevent money laundering. **[1002]**

Article 16

1 Member States shall bring into force the laws, regulations and administrative decisions necessary to comply with this Directive before 1 January 1993 at the latest.

2 Where Member States adopt these measures, they shall contain a reference to this Directive or shall be accompanied by such reference on the occasion of their official publication. The methods of making such a reference shall be laid down by the Member States.

3 Member States shall communicate to the Commission the text of the main provisions of national law which they adopt in the field governed by this Directive. **[1003]**

Article 17

One year after 1 January 1993, whenever necessary and at least at three yearly intervals thereafter, the Commission shall draw up a report on the implementation of this Directive and submit it to the European Parliament and the Council. **[1004]**

Article 18

This Directive is addressed to the Member States.

Done at Luxembourg, 10 June 1991.

STATEMENT BY THE REPRESENTATIVES OF THE GOVERNMENTS OF THE MEMBER STATES MEETING WITHIN THE COUNCIL

The representatives of the Governments of the Member States, meeting within the Council,

Recalling that the Member States signed the United Nations Convention against illicit traffic in narcotic drugs and psychotropic substances, adopted on 19 December 1988 in Vienna;

Recalling also that most Member States have already signed the Council of Europe Convention on laundering, tracing, seizure and confiscation of proceeds of crime on 8 November 1990 in Strasbourg;

Conscious of the fact that the descriptions of money laundering contained in Article 1 of Council Directive 91/308/EEC[1] derives its wording from the relevant provisions of the aforementioned Conventions;

Hereby undertake to take all necessary steps by 31 December 1992 at the latest to enact criminal legislation enabling them to comply with their obligations under the aforementioned instruments. **[1004A]**

NOTES
[1] OJ L 166, 28.6.1991, p 77.

COUNCIL DIRECTIVE
of 6 April 1992

on the supervision of credit institutions on a consolidated basis

(92/30/EEC)

NOTES

Date of publication in OJ: OJ L110, 28.4.1992, p 52.

THE COUNCIL OF THE EUROPEAN COMMUNITIES,

Having regard to the Treaty establishing the European Economic Community, and in particular the first and third sentences of Article 57(2) thereof,

Having regard to the proposal from the Commission,

In cooperation with the European Parliament[1],

Having regard to the opinion of the Economic and Social Committee[2],

Whereas Council Directive 83/350/EEC of 13 June 1983 on the supervision of credit institutions on a consolidated basis[3] established the necessary framework for the introduction of supervision of credit institutions on a consolidated basis; whereas, following the transposition of that Directive into the national law of the Member States, the principle of supervision on a consolidated basis is now applied throughout the Community;

Whereas, in order to be effective, supervision on a consolidated basis must be applied to all banking groups, including those the parent undertakings of which are not credit institutions; whereas the competent authorities must hold the necessary legal instruments to be able to exercise such supervision;

Whereas, in the case of groups with diversified activities the parent undertakings of which control at least one credit institution subsidiary, the competent authorities must be able to assess the financial situation of a credit institution in such a group; whereas, pending subsequent coordination, the Member States may lay down appropriate methods of consolidation for the achievement of the objective of this Directive; whereas the competent authorities must at least have the means of obtaining from all undertakings within a group the information necessary for the performance of their function; whereas cooperation between the authorities responsible for the supervision of different financial sectors must be established in the case of groups of undertakings carrying on a range of financial activities;

Whereas rules limiting the risks taken by a credit institution on the mixed activity holding company of which it is a subsidiary, as well as those taken on the other subsidiaries of the same mixed-activity holding company, can be particularly useful; whereas it would, however, appear to be preferable to settle this question in a more systematic manner in the framework of a future Directive on the limitation of large exposures;

Whereas the Member States can, furthermore, refuse or withdraw banking authorisation in the case of certain group structures considered inappropriate for carrying on banking activities, in particular because such structures could not be supervised effectively; whereas in this respect the competent authorities have the powers mentioned in Article 8(1)(c) of the First Council Directive (77/780/EEC) of 12 December 1977 on the coordination of the laws, regulations and administrative provisions relating to the taking up and pursuit of the business of credit institutions[4] and in Articles 5 and 11 of the Second Council Directive (89/646/EEC) of 15 December 1989 on the coordination of laws, regulations and administrative provisions relating to the taking up and pursuit of the business of credit institutions[5], in order to ensure the sound and prudent management of credit institutions;

Whereas the Member States can equally apply appropriate supervision techniques to groups with structures not covered by this Directive; whereas, if such structures become common, this Directive should be extended to cover them;

Whereas supervision on a consolidated basis must take in all activities defined in the Annex to Directive 89/646/EEC; whereas all undertakings principally engaged in such activities must therefore be included in supervision on a consolidated basis; whereas, as a result, the definition of a financial institutions given in Directive 83/350/EEC must be widened to cover such activities;

Whereas, regarding the consolidation of financial institutions involved in activities principally subject to market risks and subject to particular rules of supervision, the coordination of the methods for the consolidated supervision of market risks is possible in the framework of Community harmonisation of capital adequacy of investment firms and credit institutions, for which the Commission has introduced a proposal for a Directive; whereas such harmonisation concerns, *inter alia*, the conditions which must be applied when offsetting opposing positions in the group and the case where these financial institutions are subject to specific supervisory rules regarding their financial stability; whereas this implies that, until the future Directive on capital adequacy to cover market risks is brought into effect, the competent authorities shall include in consolidated supervision financial institutions which are principally exposed to market risks, in accordance with methods determined by those authorities in the light of the particular nature of the risks involved;

Whereas, following the adoption of Council Directive 86/635/EEC of 8 December 1986 on the annual accounts and consolidated accounts of banks and other financial institutions[6], which, together with the Seventh Council Directive (83/349/EEC) of 13 June 1983 on consolidated accounts[7], established the rules of consolidation applicable to consolidated accounts published by credit institutions, it is now possible to define more precisely the methods to be used in prudential supervision exercised on a consolidated basis;

Whereas this Directive is fully in keeping with the objectives defined in the Single European Act; whereas it will, in particular, ensure the homogeneous application throughout the Community of prudential rules established by other Community legislation, which must be observed on a consolidated basis; whereas this Directive is, in particular, necessary for the correct application of Council Directive 89/299/EEC of 17 April 1989 on the own funds of credit institutions[8];

Whereas supervision of credit institutions on a consolidated basis must be aimed at, in particular, protecting the interests of the depositors of the said institutions and at ensuring the stability of the financial system;

Whereas it is desirable that agreement should be reached, on the basis of reciprocity, between the Community and third countries with a view to allowing the practical exercise of consolidated supervision over the largest possible geographical area;

Whereas the amendments to be made to Directive 83/350/EEC are so considerable that it is preferable that it by wholly replaced by this Directive.

NOTES
[1] OJ C 326, 16.12.1991, p 106, and OJ C 94, 13.4.1992.
[2] OJ C 102, 18.4.1991, p 19.
[3] OJ L 193, 18.7.1983, p 18.
[4] OJ L 322, 17.12.1977, p 30. Directive as last amended by Directive 89/646/EEC (OJ L 386, 30.12.1989, p 1).
[5] OJ L 386, 30.12.1989, p 1.
[6] OJ L 372, 31.12.1986, p 1.
[7] OJ L 193, 18.7.1983, p 1. Directive as last amended by Directive 90/605/EEC (OJ L 317, 16.11.1990, p 60).
[8] OJ L 124, 5.5.1989, p 16.

HAS ADOPTED THIS DIRECTIVE:

Article 1

Definitions

For the purposes of this Directive—

— *credit institution* shall mean a credit institution within the meaning of the first indent of Article 1 of Directive 77/780/EEC, or any private or public undertaking which corresponds to the definition in the first indent of Article 1 of Directive 77/780/EEC and has been authorised in a third county,

— *financial institution* shall mean an undertaking, other than a credit institution, the principal activity of which is to acquire holdings or to carry on one or more of the activities referred to in numbers 2 to 12 of the list appearing in the Annex to Directive 89/646/EEC,

— *financial holding company* shall mean a financial institution the subsidiary undertakings of which are either exclusively or mainly credit institutions or financial institutions, one at least of such subsidiaries being a credit institution,

— *mixed-activity holding company* shall mean a parent undertaking, other than a financial holding company or a credit institution, the subsidiaries of which include at least one credit institution,

— *ancillary banking services* undertaking shall mean an undertaking the principal activity of which consists in owning or managing property, managing data-processing services, or any other similar activity which is ancillary to the principal activity of one or more credit institution,

— *participation* shall mean the ownership, direct or indirect, of 20% or more of the voting rights or capital of an undertaking,

— *parent undertaking* shall mean a parent undertaking within the meaning of Article 1(1) of the Directive 83/349/EEC and any undertaking which, in the opinion of the competent authorities, effectively exercises a dominant influence over another undertaking,

— *subsidiary* shall mean a subsidiary undertaking within the meaning of Article 1(1) of Directive 83/349/EEC and any undertaking over which, in the opinion of the competent authorities, a parent undertaking effectively exercises a dominant influence. All subsidiaries of subsidiary undertakings shall also be considered subsidiaries of the undertaking that is their original parent,

— *competent authorities* shall mean the national authorities which are empowered by law or regulation to supervise credit institutions.

[1005]

Article 2

Scope

This Directive shall apply to credit institutions that have obtained the authorisation referred to in Article 3 of Directive 77/780/EEC, financial holding companies and mixed-activity holding companies which have their head offices in the Community.

The institutions permanently excluded by Article 2 of Directive 77/780/EEC, with the exception, however, of the Member States' central banks, shall be treated as financial institutions for the purposes of this Directive. **[1006]**

Article 3

Supervision on a consolidated basis of credit institutions

1 Every credit institution which has a credit institution or a financial institution as a subsidiary or which holds a participation in such institutions shall be subject, to the extent and in the manner prescribed in Article 5, to supervision on the basis of its consolidated financial situation. Such supervision shall be exercised at least in the areas referred to in paragraphs 5 and 6.

2 Every credit institution the parent undertaking of which is a financial holding company shall be subject, to the extent and in the manner prescribed in Article 5, to supervision on the basis of the consolidated financial situation of that financial holding company. Such supervision shall be exercised at least in the areas referred to in paragraphs 5 and 6. The consolidation of the financial situation of the financial holding company shall not in any way imply that the competent authorities are required to play a supervisory role in relation to the financial holding company standing alone.

3 The Member States or the competent authorities responsible for exercising supervision on a consolidated basis pursuant to Article 4 may decide in the cases listed below that a credit institution, financial institution or auxiliary banking services undertaking which is a subsidiary or in which a participation is held need not be included in the consolidation—

— if the undertaking that should be included is situated in a third country where there are legal impediments to the transfer of the necessary information,

— if, in the opinion of the competent authorities, the undertaking that should be included is of negligible interest only with respect to the objectives of monitoring credit institutions and in all cases if the balance sheet total of the undertaking that should be included is less than the smaller of the following two amounts: ECU 10 million or 1% of the balance sheet total of the parent undertaking or the undertaking that holds the participation. If several undertakings meet the above criteria, they must nevertheless be included in the consolidation where collectively they are of non-negligible interest with respect to the aforementioned objectives, or

— if, in the opinion of the competent authorities responsible for exercising supervision on a consolidated basis, the consolidation of the financial situation of the undertaking that should be included would be inappropriate or misleading as far as the objectives of the supervision of credit institutions are concerned.

4 When the competent authorites of a Member State do not include a credit institution subsidiary in supervision on a consolidated basis under one of the cases provided for in the second and third indents of paragraph 3, the competent authorities of the Member State in which that credit institution subsidiary is situated may ask the parent undertaking for information which may facilitate their supervision of that credit institution.

5 Supervision of solvency, and of the adequacy of own funds to cover market risks and control of large exposures, as governed by the relevant Community acts in force, shall be exercised on a consolidated basis in accordance with this Directive. Member States shall adopt any measures necessary, where appropriate, to include financial holding companies in consolidated supervision, in accordance with paragraph 2.

Compliance with the limits set in Article 12(1) and (2) of Directive 89/646/EEC shall be supervised and controlled on the basis of the consolidated or sub-consolidated financial situation of the credit institution.

6 The competent authorities shall ensure that, in all the undertakings included in the scope of the supervision on a consolidated basis that is exercised over a credit institution in implementation of paragraphs 1 and 2, there are adequate internal control mechanisms for the production of any data and information which would be relevant for the purposes of supervision on a consolidated basis.

7 Without prejudice to specific provisions contained in other Directives, Member States may waive application, on an individual or sub-consolidated basis, of the rules laid down in paragraph 5 to a credit institution that, as a parent undertaking, is subject to supervision on a consolidated basis, and to any subsidiary of such a credit institution which is subject to their authorisation and supervision and is included in the supervision on a consolidated basis of the credit institution which is the parent company. The same exemption option shall be allowed where the parent undertaking is a financial holding company which has its head office in the same Member State as the credit institution, provided that it is subject to the same supervision as that exercised over credit institutions, and in particular the standards laid down in paragraph 5.

In both cases, steps must be taken to ensure that capital is distributed adequately within the banking group.

If the competent authorities do apply those rules individually to such credit institutions, they may, for the purpose of calculating own funds, make use of the provision in the last subparagraph of Article 2(1) of Directive 89/299/EEC.

8 Where a credit institution the parent of which is a credit institution has been authorised and is situated in another Member State, the competent authorities which granted that authorisation shall apply the rules laid down in paragraph 5 to that institution on an individual or, when appropriate, a sub-consolidated basis.

9 Notwithstanding the requirements of paragraph 8, the competent authorities responsible for authorising the subsidiary of a parent undertaking which is a credit institution may, by bilateral agreement, delegate their responsibility for supervision to the competent authorities which authorised and supervise the parent undertaking. The Commission must be kept informed of the existence and content of such agreements. It shall forward such information to the competent authorities of the other Member States and to the Banking Advisory Committee.

10 Member States shall provide that their competent authorities responsible for exercising supervision on a consolidated basis may ask the subsidiaries of a credit institution or a financial holding company which are not included within the scope of supervision on a consolidated basis for the information referred to in Article 6. In such a case, the procedures for transmitting and verifying the information laid down in that Article shall apply. **[1007]**

Article 4

Competent authorities responsible for exercising supervision on a consolidated basis

1 Where a parent undertaking is a credit institution, supervision on a consolidated basis shall be exercised by the competent authorities that authorised it under Article 3 of Directive 77/780/EEC.

2 Where the parent of a credit institution is a financial holding company, supervision on a consolidated basis shall be exercised by the competent authorities which authorised that credit institution under Article 3 of Directive 77/780/EEC.

However, where credit institutions authorised in two or more Member States have as their parent the same financial holding company, supervision on a consolidated basis shall be exercised by the competent authorities of the credit institution authorised in the Member State in which the financial holding company was set up.

If no credit institution subsidiary has been authorised in the Member State in which the financial holding company was set up, the competent authorities of the Member States concerned (including those of the Member State in which the financial holding company was set up) shall seek to reach agreement as to who amongst them will exercise supervision on a consolidated basis. In the absence of such agreement, supervision on a consolidated basis shall be exercised by the competent authorities that authorised the credit institution with the greatest balance sheet total; if that figure is the same, supervision on a consolidated basis shall be exercised by the competent authorities which first gave the authorisation referred to in Article 3 of Directive 77/780/EEC.

3 The competent authorities concerned may by common agreement waive the rules laid down in the first and second subparagraphs of paragraph 2.

4 The agreements referred to in the third subparagraph of paragraph 2 and in paragraph 3 shall provide for procedures for cooperation and for the transmission of information such that the objectives of this Directive may be achieved.

5 Where Member States have more than one competent authority for the prudential supervision of credit institutions and financial institutions, Member

States shall take the requisite measures to organise coordination between such authorities.   **[1008]**

Article 5

Form and extent of consolidation

1 The competent authorities responsible for exercising supervision on a consolidated basis must, for the purposes of supervision, require full consolidation of all the credit institutions and financial institutions which are subsidiaries of a parent undertaking.

However, proportional consolidation may be prescribed where, in the opinion of the competent authorities, the liability of a parent undertaking holding a share of the capital is limited to that share of the capital because of the liability of the other shareholders or members whose solvency is satisfactory. The liability of the other shareholders and members must be clearly established, if necessary by means of formal, signed commitments.

2 The competent authorities responsible for carrying out supervision on a consolidated basis must, in order to do so, require the proportional consolidation of participations in credit institutions and financial institutions managed by an undertaking included in the consolidation together with one or more undertakings not included in the consolidation, where those undertakings' liability is limited to the share of the capital they hold.

3 In the case of participations or capital ties other than those referred to in paragraphs 1 and 2, the competent authorities shall determine whether and how consolidation is to be carried out. In particular, they may permit or require use of the equity method. That method shall not, however, constitute inclusion of the undertakings concerned in supervision on a consolidated basis.

4 Without prejudice to paragraphs 1, 2 and 3, the competent authorities shall determine whether and how consolidation is to be carried out in the following cases—

— where, in the opinion of the competent authorities, a credit institution exercises a significant influence over one or more credit institutions or financial institutions, but without holding a participation or other capital ties in these institutions,
— where two or more credit institutions or financial institutions are placed under single management other than pursuant to a contract or clauses of their memoranda or articles of association,
— where two or more credit institutions or financial institutions have administrative, management or supervisory bodies with the same persons constituting a majority.

In particular, the competent authorities may permit, or require use of, the method provided for in Article 12 of Directive 83/349/EEC. That method shall not, however, constitute inclusion of the undertakings concerned in consolidated supervision.

5 Where consolidated supervision is required pursuant to Article 3(1) and (2), ancillary banking services undertakings shall be included in consolidations in the cases, and in accordance with the methods, laid down in paragraphs 1 to 4, of this Article.   **[1009]**

Article 6

Information to be supplied by mixed-activity holding companies and their subsidiaries

1 Pending further coordination of consolidation methods, Member States shall provide that, where the parent undertaking of one or more credit institutions is a mixed-activity holding company, the competent authorities responsible for the authorisation and supervision of those credit institutions shall, by approaching the mixed-activity holding company and its subsidiaries either directly or via credit institution subsidiaries, require them to supply any information which would be relevant for the purposes of supervising the credit institution subsidiaries.

2 Member States shall provide that their competent authorities may carry out, or have carried out by external inspectors, on-the-spot inspections to verify information received from mixed-activity holding companies and their subsidiaries. If the mixed-activity holding company or one of its subsidiaries is an insurance undertaking, the procedure laid down in Article 7(4) may also be used. If a mixed-activity holding company or one of its subsidiaries is situated in a Member State other than that in which the credit institution subsidiary is situated, on-the-spot verification of information shall be carried out in accordance with the procedure laid down in Article 7(7).   **[1010]**

Article 7

Measures to facilitate the application of this Directive

1 Member States shall take the necessary steps to ensure that there are no legal impediments preventing the undertakings included within the scope of supervision on a consolidated basis, mixed-activity holding companies and their subsidiaries, or subsidiaries of the kind covered in Article 3(10), from exchanging amongst themselves any information which would be relevant for the purposes of supervision in accordance with this Directive.

2 Where a parent undertaking and any of its subsidiaries that are credit institutions are situated in different Member States, the competent authorities of each Member State shall communicate to each other all relevant information which may allow or aid the exercise of supervision on a consolidated basis.

Where the competent authorities of the Member State in which a parent undertaking is situated do not themselves exercise supervision on a consolidated basis pursuant to Article 4, they may be invited by the competent authorities responsible for exercising such supervision to ask the parent undertaking for any information which would be relevant for the purposes of supervision on a consolidated basis and to transmit it to these authorities.

3 Member States shall authorise the exchange between their competent authorities of the information referred to in paragraph 2, on the understanding that, in the case of financial holding companies, financial institutions or ancillary banking services undertakings, the collection or possession of information shall not in any way imply that the competent authorities are required to play a supervisory role in relation to those institutions or undertakings standing alone.

Similarly, Member States shall authorise their competent authorities to exchange the information referred to in Article 6 on the understanding that the collection or possession of information does not in any way imply that the competent authorities play a supervisory role in relation to the mixed-activity holding company and those of its subsidiaries which are not credit institutions, or to subsidiaries of the kind covered in Article 3(10).

4 Where a credit institution, financial holding company or a mixed-activity holding company controls one or more subsidiaries which are insurance companies or other undertakings providing investment services which are subject to authorisation, the competent authorities and the authorities entrusted with the public task of supervising insurance undertakings or those other undertakings providing investment services shall cooperate closely. Without prejudice to their respective responsibilities, those authorities shall provide one another with any information likely to simplify their task and to allow supervision of the activity and overall financial situation of the undertakings they supervise.

5 Information received pursuant to this Directive and in particular any exchange of information between competent authorities which is provided for in this Directive shall be subject to the obligation of professional secrecy defined in Article 12 of Directive 77/780/EEC.

6 The competent authorities responsible for supervision on a consolidated basis shall establish lists of the financial holding companies referred to in Article 3(2). Those lists shall be communicated to the competent authorities of the other Member States and to the Commission.

7 Where, in applying this Directive, the competent authorities of one Member State wish in specific cases to verify the information concerning a credit institution, a financial holding company, a financial institution, an ancillary banking services undertaking, a mixed-activity holding company, a subsidiary of the kind covered in Article 6 or a subsidiary of the kind covered in Article 3(10), situated in another Member State, they must ask the competent authorities of that other Member State to have that verification carried out. The authorites which receive such a request must, within the framework of their competence, act upon it either by carrying out the verification themselves, by allowing the authorities who made the request to carry it out, or by allowing an auditor or expert to carry it out.

8 Without prejudice to their provisions of criminal law, Member States shall ensure that penalties or measures aimed at ending observed breaches or the causes of such breaches may be imposed on financial holding companies and mixed-activity holding companies, or their effective managers, that infringe laws regulations or administrative provisions enacted to implement this Directive. In certain cases, such measures may require the intervention of the courts. The competent authorities shall cooperate closely to ensure that the abovementioned penalties or measures produce the desired results, especially when the central administration or main establishment of a financial holding company or of a mixed-activity holding company is not located at its head office. **[1011]**

Article 8

Third countries

1 The Commission may submit proposals to the Council, either at the request of a Member State or on its own initiative, for the negotiation of agreements with one or more third countries regarding the means of exercising supervision on a consolidated basis over—

— credit institutions the parent undertakings of which have their head offices situated in a third country, and
— credit institutions situated in third countries the parent undertakings of which, whether credit institutions or financial holding companies, have their head offices in the Community.

2 The agreements referred to in paragraph 1 shall in particular seek to ensure both—

— that the competent authorities of the Member States are able to obtain the information necessary for the supervision, on the basis of their consolidated financial situations, of credit institutions or financial holding companies situated in the Community and which have as subsidiaries credit institutions or financial institutions situated outside the Community, or which hold participations in such institutions,

— that the competent authorities of third countries are able to obtain the information necessary for the supervision of parent undertakings the head offices of which are situated within their territories and which have as subsidiaries credit institutions or financial institutions situated in one or more Member States, or which hold participations in such institutions.

3 The Commission and the Advisory Committee set up under Article 11 of Directive 77/780/EEC shall examine the outcome of the negotiations referred to in paragraph 1 and the resulting situation.   **[1012]**

Article 9

Final provisions

1 Member States shall being into force the laws, regulations and administrative provisions necessary to comply with this Directive before 1 January 1993. They shall forthwith inform the Commission thereof.

When Member States adopt the abovementioned measures, the measures shall contain a reference to this Directive or be accompanied by such reference on the occasion of their official publication. The methods of making such a reference shall be laid down by the Member States.

2 Notwithstanding the provisions of Article 3(5) and until the future Directive on capital adequacy to cover market risks is brought into effect, the competent authorities shall include in consolidated supervision financial institutions which are principally exposed to market risks in accordance with methods to be determined by those authorities in the light of the particular nature of the risks involved.

3 Member States shall communicate to the Commission the texts of the main provisions of internal law which they adopt in the field governed by this Directive.   **[1013]**

Article 10

1 Directive 83/350/EEC is hereby repealed with effect from 1 January 1993.

2 In the following provisions, the words 'Directive 83/350/EEC' shall be replaced by 'Directive 92/350/EEC'—

— Article 5 of Directive 89/229/EEC,
— Article 12(5), 13(3) and 15(2) and the fifth indent of the first subparagraph of Article 18(2) of Directive 89/646/EEC,
— Article 3(3) of Directive 89/647/EEC.

3 In Article 1, point 5, of Directive 89/646/EEC and the first indent of Article 2(1) of Directive 89/647/EEC, the definition of competent authorities shall be replaced by the following:

'the national authorities which are empowered by law or regulation to supervise credit institutions'.   **[1014]**

Article 11

This Directive is addressed to the Member States.

Done at Luxembourg, 6 April 1992.

COUNCIL DIRECTIVE
of 21 December 1992

on the monitoring and control of large exposures of credit institutions

(92/121/EEC)

NOTES

Date of publication in OJ: OJ L 29, 5.2.1993, p 1.

THE COUNCIL OF THE EUROPEAN COMMUNITIES,

Having regard to the Treaty establishing the European Economic Community, and in particular the first and third sentences of Article 57(2) thereof,

Having regard to the proposal from the Commission[1],

In cooperation with the European Parliament[2],

Having regard to the opinion of the Economic and Social Committee[3],

Whereas this Directive comes within the framework of the aims set out in the Commission's White Paper on completing the internal market;

Whereas the essential rules for monitoring large exposures of credit institutions should be harmonised; whereas Member States should still be able to adopt provisions more stringent than those provided for by this Directive;

Whereas this Directive has been the subject of consultation with the Banking Advisory Committee, which, under Article 6(4) of Council Directive 77/780/EEC of 12 December 1977 on the coordination of laws, regulations and administrative provisions relating to the taking-up and pursuit of the business of credit institutions[4], is responsible for making suggestions to the Commission with a view to coordinating the coefficients applicable in the Member States;

Whereas the monitoring and control of a credit institution's exposures is an integral part of its supervision; whereas an excessive concentration of exposures to a single client or group of connected clients may result in an acceptable risk of loss; whereas such a situation may be considered prejudicial to the solvency of a credit institution;

Whereas common guidelines for monitoring and controlling credit institutions' large exposures were initially introduced by Commission recommendation 87/62/EEC[5]; whereas that instrument was chosen because it permitted the gradual adjustment of existing systems and the establishment of new systems without dislocating the Community's banking system; whereas, now that that first phase is over, a binding instrument applicable to all Community credit institutions should be adopted;

Whereas in a unified banking market credit institutions are engaged in direct competition with one another and monitoring requirements throughout the Community should therefore be equivalent; whereas, to that end, the criteria applied to determining the concentration of exposures must be the subject of legally binding rules at Community level and cannot be left entirely to the discretion of the Member States; whereas the adoption of common rules will therefore best serve the Community's interests, since it will prevent differences in the conditions of competition, while strengthening the Community's banking system;

Whereas, for the precise accounting technique to be used for the assessment of exposures reference is made to Council Directive 86/635/EEC of 8 December 1986 on the annual accounts and consolidated accounts of banks and other financial institutions[6];

Whereas Council Directive 89/647/EEC of 18 December 1989 on a solvency ratio for credit institutions[7] includes a list of credit risks which may be incurred by credit institutions; whereas that list should therefore be used for the definition of exposures for the purposes of this Directive; whereas it is not, however, appropriate to refer on principle to the weightings or degress of risk laid down in that Directive; wheres those weightings and degrees of risk were devised for the purpose of establishing a general solvency requirement to cover the credit risk of credit institutions; whereas, in the context of the regulation of large exposures, the aim is to limit the maximum loss that a credit institution may incur through any single client or group of connected clients; whereas it is therefore appropriate to adopt a prudent approach in which, as a general rule, account is taken of the nominal value of exposures, but no weightings or degrees of risk are applied;

Whereas, when a credit institution incurs an exposure to its own parent undertaking or to other subsidiaries of its parent undertaking, particular prudence is necessary; whereas the management of exposures incurred by credit institutions must be carried out in a fully autonomous manner, in accordance with the principles of sound banking management, without regard to any considerations other than those principles; whereas the Second Council Directive 89/646/EEC of 15 December 1989 on the coordination of laws, regulations and administrative provisions relating to the taking up and pursuit of the business of credit institutions[8] requires that where the influence exercised by persons directly or indirectly holding a qualifying participation in a credit institution is likely to operate to the detriment of the sound and prudent management of that institution, the competent authorities shall take appropriate measures to put an end to that situation; whereas, in the field of large exposures, specific standards should also be laid down for exposures incurred by a credit institution to its own group and in such cases more stringent restrictions are justified than for other exposures; whereas more stringent restrictions need not, however, be applied where the parent undertaking is a financial holding company or a credit institution or where the other subsidiaries are either credit or financial institutions or undertakings offering ancillary banking services, provided that all such undertakings are covered by the supervision of the credit institution on a consolidated basis; whereas in such cases the consolidated monitoring of the group of undertakings allows for an adequate level of supervision, and does not require the imposition of more stringent limits on exposure; whereas under this approach banking groups will also be encouraged to organise their structures in such a way as to allow consolidated monitoring, which is desirable because a more comprehensive level of monitoring is possible;

Whereas, in order to ensure harmonious application of this Directive, Member States should be allowed to provide for the two-stage application of the new limits; whereas, for smaller credit institutions, a longer transitional period may be warranted inasmuch as too rapid an application of the 25% rule could reduce their lending activity too abruptly;

Whereas implementing powers of the same type as those which the Council reserved for itself in Directive 89/299/EEC on the own funds of credit institutions[9] were granted to the Commission in Directive 89/646/EEC;

Whereas, taking account of the specific characteristics of the sector in question, it is appropriate to give the Committee set up by Article 22 of Directive 89/646/EEC the role of assisting the Commission in exercising the powers conferred on it under the procedure laid down in Article 2 (Procedure III, Variant (b)) of Council Decision 87/373/EEC of 13 July 1987 laying down the procedures for the exercise of implementing powers conferred on the Commission [10];

Wheres, with regard to the monitoring of large exposures concerning activities which are principally exposed to market risks, the necessary coordination of monitoring methods can be ensured under a Community act on the capital adequacy of investments firms and credit institutions; whereas that implies that until Community legislation on the aforementioned large exposures is adopted the monitoring of large exposures relating to activities which are principally exposed to market risks, such as the trading portfolio, underwriting commitments for the issue of securities and claims related to the settlement of securities transactions may be left to the competent authorities of each Member State,

HAS ADOPTED THIS DIRECTIVE:

NOTES

[1] OJ No C 123, 9.5.1991, p 18 and OJ No C 175, 11.7.1992, p 4.
[2] OJ No C 150, 15.6.1992, p 74 and OJ No C 337, 21.12.1992.
[3] OJ No C 339, 31.12.1991, p 35.
[4] OJ No L 322, 17.12.1977, p 30. Directive last amended by Directive 89/646/EEC (OJ No L 386, 30.12.1989, p 1).
[5] OJ No L 33, 4.2.1987, p 10.
[6] OJ No L 372, 31.12.1986, p 1.
[7] OJ No L 386, 30.12.1989, p 14.
[8] OJ No L 386, 30.12.1989, p 1. Directive amended by Directive 92/30/EEC (OJ No L 110, 28.4.1992, p 52).
[9] OJ No L 124, 5.5.1989, p 16.
[10] OJ No L 197, 18.7.1987, p 33.

Article 1

Definitions

For the purposes of this Directive:

(a) *credit institution* shall mean a credit institution as defined in the first indent of Article 1 of Directive 77/780/EEC, including such a credit institution's branches in third countries, and any private or public undertaking, including its branches, which satisfies the definition in the first indent of Article 1 of Directive 77/780/EEC and which has been authorised in a third country;

(b) *competent authorities* shall mean the competent authorities as defined in the ninth indent of Article 1 of Council Directive 92/30/EEC of 6 April 1992 on the supervision of credit institutions on a consolidated basis[1];

(c) *parent undertaking* shall mean a parent undertaking as defined in the seventh indent of Article 1 of Directive 92/30/EEC;

(d) *subsidiary undertaking* shall mean a subsidiary undertaking as defined in the eighth indent of Article 1 of Directive 92/30/EEC.;

(e) *financial holding company* shall mean a financial holding company as defined in the third indent of Article 1 of Directive 92/30/EEC;

(f) *financial institution* shall mean a financial institution as defined in the second indent of Article 1 of Directive 92/30/EEC;

(g) *ancillary banking-services undertaking* shall mean an undertaking as defined in the fifth indent of Article 1 of Directive 92/30/EEC;

(h) *exposures* shall mean the assets and off-balance-sheet items referred to in Article 6 of Directive 89/647/EEC and in Annexes I and III thereto, without application of the weightings or degrees of risk there provided for; the risks referred to in the aforementioned Annex III must be calculated in accordance with one of the methods set out in Annex II to that Directive, without application of the weightings for counter-party risk; all elements entirely covered by own funds may, with the agreement of the competent authorities, be excluded from the definition of exposures provided that such own funds are not included in the calculation of the solvency ratio or of other monitoring ratios provided for in Community acts; exposures shall not include:
— in the case of foreign exchange transactions, exposures incurred in the ordinary course of settlement during the 48 hours following payment, or
— in the case of transactions for the purchase or sale of securities, exposures incurred in the ordinary course of settlement during the five working days following payment or delivery of the securities, whichever is the earlier;

(i) *Zone A* shall mean the zone referred to in the second indent of Article 2(1) of Directive 89/647/EEC;

(j) *Zone B* shall mean the zone referred to in the third indent of Article 2(1) of Directive 89/647/EEC;

(k) *own funds* shall mean the own funds of a credit institution as defined in Directive 89/299/EEC;

(l) *control* shall mean the relationship between a parent undertaking and a subsidiary, as defined in Article 1 of Directive 83/349/EEC, or a similar relationship between any natural or legal person and an undertaking;

(m) *group of connected clients* shall mean:
— two or more natural or legal persons who, unless it is shown otherwise, constitute a single risk because one of them, directly or indirectly, has control over the other or others, or
— two or more natural or legal persons between whom there is no relationship of control as defined in the first indent but who are to be regarded as constituting a single risk because they are so interconnected that, if one of them were to experience financial problems, the other or all of the others would be likely to encounter repayment difficulties. **[1015]**

NOTES
[1] OJ No L 110, 28.4.1992, p 52.

Article 2

Scope

This Directive shall apply to credit institutions which have obtained the authorisation referred to in Article 3 of Directive 77/780/EEC.

Member States need not, however, apply this Directive to:

  (a) the institutions listed in Article 2(2) of Directive 77/780/EEC, or

  (b) the institutions in the same Member State which, as defined in
     Article 2(4)(a) of Directive 77/780/EEC, are affiliated to a central
     body established in that Member State, provided that, without pre-
     judice to the application of this Directive to the central body, the
     whole as constituted by the central body and its affiliated institutions
     is subject to global monitoring.   **[1016]**

Article 3

Reporting of large exposures

1 A credit institution's exposure to a client or group of connected clients shall be considered a large exposure where its value is equal to or exceeds 10% of its own funds.

2 A credit institution shall report every large exposure within the meaning of paragraph 1 to the competent authorities. Member States shall provide that that reporting is to be carried out, at their discretion, in accordance with one of the following two methods:

  — reporting of all large exposures at least once a year, combined with
    reporting during the year of all new large exposures and any increases
    in existing large exposures of at least 20% with respect to the previous
    communication,
  — reporting of all large exposures at least four times a year.

3 Exposures exempted under Article 4(7)(a), (b), (c), (d), (f), (g) and (h) need not, however, be reported as laid down in paragraph 2. The reporting frequency laid down in the second indent of paragraph 2 may be reduced to twice a year for the exposures referred to in Article 4(7)(e) and (i) to (s), (8), (9) and (10).

4 The competent authorities shall require that every credit institution have sound administrative and accounting procedures and adequate internal control mechanisms for the purpose of identifying and recording all large exposures and subsequent changes to them, as defined and required by this Directive, and for that of monitoring those exposures in the light of each credit institution's own exposure policies.

Where a credit institution invokes paragraph 3, it shall keep a record of the grounds advanced for at least one year after the event giving rise to the dispensation, so that the competent authorities may establish whether it is justified.   **[1017]**

Article 4

Limits on large exposures

1 A credit institution may not incur an exposure to a client or group of connected clients the value of which exceeds 25% of its own funds.

2 Where that client or group of connected clients is the parent undertaking or subsidiary of the credit institution and/or one or more subsidiaries of that parent undertaking, the percentage laid down in paragraph 1 shall be reduced to 20%. Member States may, however, exempt the exposures incurred to such clients from the 20% limit if they provide for specific monitoring of such exposures by other measures or procedures. They shall inform the Commission and the Banking Advisory Committee of the content of such measures or procedures.

3 A credit institution may not incur large exposures which in total exceed 800% of its own funds.

4 Member States may impose limits more stringent than those laid down in paragraphs 1, 2 and 3.

5 A credit institution shall at all times comply with the limits laid down in paragraphs 1, 2 and 3 in respect of its exposures. If in an exceptional case exposures exceed those limits, that fact must be reported without delay to the competent authorities which may, where the circumstances warrant it, allow the credit institution a limited period of time in which to comply with the limits.

6 Member States may fully or partially exempt from the application of paragraphs 1, 2 and 3 exposures incurred by a credit institution to its parent undertaking, to other subsidiaries of that parent undertaking or to its own subsidiaries, in so far as those undertakings are covered by the supervision on a consolidated basis to which the credit institution itself is subject, in accordance with Directive 92/30/EEC or with equivalent standards in force in a third country.

7 Member States may fully or partially exempt the following exposures from the application of paragraphs 1, 2 and 3:

    (a) asset items constituting claims on Zone A central governments or central banks;

    (b) asset items constituting claims on the European Communities;

    (c) asset items constituting claims carrying the explicit guarantees of Zone A central governments or central banks or of the European Communities;

    (d) other exposures attributable to, or guaranteed by, Zone A central governments or central banks or the European Communities;

    (e) asset items constituting claims on and other exposures to Zone B central governments or central banks which are denominated and, where applicable, funded in the national currencies of the borrowers;

    (f) asset items and other exposures secured, to the satisfaction of the competent authorities, by collateral in the form of Zone A central government or central bank securities, or securities issued by the European Communities or by Member State regional or local authorities for which Article 7 of Directive 89/647/EEC lays down a zero weighting for solvency purposes;

    (g) asset items and other exposures secured, to the satisfaction of the competent authorities, by collateral in the form of cash deposits placed with the lending institution or with a credit institution which is the parent undertaking or a subsidiary of the lending institution;

    (h) asset items and other exposures secured, to the satisfaction of the competent authorities, by collateral in the form of certificates of deposit issued by the lending institution or by a credit institution which is the parent undertaking or a subsidiary of the lending institution and lodged with either of them;

    (i) asset items constituting claims on and other exposures to credit institutions, with a maturity of one year or less, but not constituting such institutions' own funds as defined in Directive 89/229/EEC;

(j) asset items constituting claims on and other exposures to those institutions which are not credit institutions but which fulfil the conditions referred to in Article 8(2) of Directive 89/647/EEC, with a maturity of one year or less, and secured in accordance with the same paragraph;

(k) bills of trade and other similar bills, with a maturity of one year or less, bearing the signatures of other credit institutions;

(l) debt securities as defined in Article 22(4) of Directive 85/611/EEC[1];

(m) pending subsequent coordination, holdings in the insurance companies referred to in Article 12(3) of Directive 89/646/EEC up to 40% of the own funds of the credit institution acquiring such a holding;

(n) asset items constituting claims on regional or central credit institutions with which the lending institution is associated in a network in accordance with legal or statutory provisions and which are responsible, under those provisions, for cash-clearing operations within the network;

(o) exposures secured, to the satisfaction of the competent authorities, by collateral in the form of securities other than those referred to in (f) provided that those securities are not issued by the credit institution itself, its parent company or one of their subsidiaries, or by the client or group of connected clients in question. The securities used a collateral must be valued at market price, have a value that exceeds the exposures guaranteed and be either traded on a stock exchange or effectively negotiable and regularly quoted on a market operated under the auspices of recognised professional operators and allowing, to the satisfaction of the competent authorities of the Member State of origin of the credit institution, for the establishment of an objective price such that the excess value of the securities may be verified at any time. The excess value required shall be 100%; it shall, however, be 150% in the case of shares and 50% in the case of debt securities issued by credit institutions, Member State regional or local authorities other than those referred to in Article 7 of Directive 89/647/EEC, and in the case of debt securities issued by the European Investment Bank and multilateral development banks as defined in Article 2 of Directive 89/647/EEC. Securities used as collateral may not constitute credit institutions' own funds as defined in Directive 89/229/EEC;

[(p) loans secured, to the satisfaction of the competent authorities, by mortgages on residential property or by shares in Finnish residential housing companies, operating in accordance with the Finnish Housing Company Act of 1991 or subsequent equivalent legislation and leasing transactions under which the lessor retains full ownership of the residential property leased for as long as the lessee has not exercised his option to purchase, in all cases up to 50% of the value of the residential property concerned.] The value of the property shall be calculated, to the satisfaction of the competent authorities, on the basis of strict valuation standards laid down by law, regulation or administrative provisions. Valuation shall be carried out at least once a year. For the purposes of this subparagraph residential property shall mean a residence to be occupied or let by the borrower;

(q) 50% of the medium/low-risk off-balance-sheet items referred to in Annex I to Directive 89/647/EEC;

(r) subject to the competent authorities' agreement, guarantees other than loan guarantees which have a legal or regulatory basis and are given for their members by mutual guarantee schemes possessing the status of credit institutions as defined in Article 1(a), subject to a weighting of 20% of their amount.

Member States shall inform the Commission of the use they make of this option in order to ensure that it does not result in distortions of competition. Within five years of the adoption of this Directive, the Commission shall submit to the Council a report accompanied, if necessary, by appropriate proposals;

(s) the low-risk off-balance-sheet items referred to in Annex I to Directive 89/647/EEC, to the extent that an agreement has been concluded with the client or group of connected clients under which the exposure may be incurred only if it has been ascertained that it will not cause the limits applicable under paragraphs 1, 2 and 3 to be exceeded.

8 For the purposes of paragraphs 1, 2 and 3, Member States may apply a weighting of 20% to asset items constituting claims on Member State regional and local authorities and to other exposures to or guaranteed by such authorities; subject to the conditions laid down in Article 7 of Directive 89/647/EEC, however, Member States may reduce that rate to 0%.

9 For the purposes of paragraphs 1, 2 and 3, Member States may apply a weighting of 20% to asset items constituting claims on and other exposures to credit institutions with a maturity of more than one but not more than three years and a weighting of 50% to asset items constituting claims on credit institutions with a maturity of more than three years, provided that the latter are represented by debt instruments that were issued by a credit institution and that those debt instruments are, in the opinion of the competent authorities, effectively negotiable on a market made up of professional operators and are subject to daily quotation on that market, or the issue of which was authorised by the competent authorities of the Member State of origin of the issuing credit institution. In no case may any of these items constitute own funds within the meaning of Directive 89/299/EEC.

10 By way of derogation from paragraph 7(i) and 9, Member States may apply a weighting of 20% to asset items constituting claims on and other exposures to credit institutions, regardless of their maturity.

11 Where an exposure to a client is guaranteed by a third party, or by collateral in the form of securities issued by a third party under the condition laid down in paragraph 7(o), Member States may:
— treat the exposure as having been incurred to the third party rather than to the client, if the exposure is directly and unconditionally guaranteed by that third party, to the satisfaction of the competent authorities,
— treat the exposure as having been incurred to the third party rather than to the client, if the exposure defined in paragraph 7(o) is guaranteed by collateral under the conditions there laid down.

12 Within five years of the date referred to in Article 8(1), the Council shall, on the basis of a report from the Commission, examine the treatment of interbank exposures provided for in paragraphs 7(i), 9 and 10. The Council shall decide on any changes to be made on a proposal from the Commission.

[1018]

NOTES
[1] OJ No L 375, 31.12.1985, p 3. Directive as amended by Directive 88/220/EEC (OJ No L 100, 19.4.1988, p 31).
    Para (7): the words in square brackets in sub-para (p) substituted by the 1994 Act of Accession of the Kingdom of Norway, the Republic of Austria, the Republic of Finland and the Kingdom of Sweden, Annex I(XI)(B)(III)(3)(a), as adjusted by Council Decision 95/1/EC, Annex I(XI)(B)(III)(3)(a).

Article 5

Supervision on a consolidated or unconsolidated basis

1 If the credit institution is neither a parent undertaking nor a subsidiary, compliance with the obligations imposed in Articles 3 and 4 or in any other Community provision applicable to this area shall be monitored on an unconsolidated basis.

2 In the other cases, compliance with the obligations imposed in Articles 3 and 4 or in any other Community provision applicable to this area shall be monitored on a consolidated basis in accordance with Directive 92/30/EEC.

3 Member States may waive monitoring on an individual or subconsolidated basis of compliance with the obligations imposed in Articles 3 and 4 or in any other Community provision applicable to this area by a credit institution which, as a parent undertaking, is subject to monitoring on a consolidated basis and by any subsidiary of such a credit institution which is subject to their authorisation and supervision and is covered by monitoring on a consolidated basis.

Member States may also waive such monitoring where the parent undertaking is a financial holding company established in the same Member State as the credit institution, provided that the company is subject to the same monitoring as credit institutions.

In the cases referred to in the first and second subparagraphs measures must be taken to ensure the satisfactory allocation of risks within the group.

4 Where a credit institution the parent undertaking of which is a credit institution has been authorised and has its registered office in another Member State, the competent authorities which granted the authorisation shall require compliance with the obligations imposed in Articles 3 and 4 or in any other Community provision applicable to this area on an individual basis or, when appropriate, a subconsolidated basis.

5 Notwithstanding paragraph 4, the competent authorities responsible for authorising the subsidiary of a parent undertaking which is a credit institution which has been authorised by and has its registered office in another Member State may, by way of bilateral agreement transfer responsibility for monitoring compliance with the obligations imposed in Articles 3 and 4 or in any other Community provision applicable to this area to the competent authorities which have authorised and which monitor the parent undertaking. The Commission and the Banking Advisory Committee shall be kept informed of the existence and content of such agreements. **[1019]**

Article 6

Transitional provisions relating to exposures in excess of the limits

1 If, when this Directive is published in the *Official Journal of the European Communities*, a credit institution has already incurred an exposure or exposures exceeding either the large exposure limit or the aggregate large exposure limit laid down in this Directive, the competent authorities shall require the credit institution concerned to take steps to have that exposure or those exposures brought within the limits laid down in this Directive.

2 The process of having such an exposure or exposures brought within authorised limits shall be devised, adopted, implemented and completed within the period which the competent authorities consider consistent with the principle of sound administration and fair competition. The competent authorities shall inform the Commission and the Banking Advisory Committee of the schedule for the general process adopted.

3 A credit institution may not take any measure which would cause the exposures referred to in paragraph 1 to exceed their level on the date of the publication of this Directive in the *Official Journal of the European Communities*.

4 The period applicable under paragraph 2 shall expire no later than 31 December 2001. Exposures with a longer maturity, for which the lending institution is bound to observe the contractual terms, may be continued until their maturity.

5 Until 31 December 1998, Member States may increase the limit laid down in Article 4(1) to 40% and the limit laid down in Article 4(2) to 30%. In such cases and subject to paragraphs 1 to 4, the time limit for bringing the exposures existing at the end of this period within the limits laid down in Article 4 shall expire on 31 December 2001.

6 In the case of credit institutions the own funds of which, as defined in Article 2(1) of Directive 89/299/EEC, do not exceed ECU 7 million, and only in the case of such institutions, Member States may extend the time limits laid down in paragraph 5 by five years. Members States that avail themselves of the option provided for in this paragraph shall take steps to prevent distortions of competition and shall inform the Commission and the Banking Advisory Committee thereof.

7 In the cases referred to in paragraphs 5 and 6, an exposure may be considered a large exposure if its value is equal to or exceeds 15% of own funds.

8 Until 31 December 2001 Member States may substitute a frequency of at least twice a year for the frequency of notification of large exposures referred to in the second indent of Article 3(2).

9 Member States may fully or partially exempt from the application of Article 4(1), (2) and (3) exposures incurred by a credit institution consisting of mortgage loans as defined in Article 11(4) of Directive 89/647/EEC concluded within eight years of the date laid down in Article 8(1) of this Directive, as well as property leasing transactions as defined in Article 11(5) of Directive 89/647/ EEC concluded within eight years of the date laid down in Article 8(1) of this Directive, in both cases up to 50% of the value of the property concerned.

[The same treatment applies to loans secured, to the satisfaction of the competent authorities, by shares in Finnish residential housing companies, operating in accordance with the Finnish Housing Company Act of 1991 or subsequent equivalent legislation which are similar to the mortgage loans referred to in the previous subparagraph.]

10 Without prejudice to paragraph 4, Portugal may, until 31 December 1998, fully or partially exempt from the application of Article 4(1) and (3) exposures incurred by a credit institution to Electricidade de Portugal (EDP) and Petrogal. **[1020]**

NOTES

Para (9): the words in square brackets added by the 1994 Act of Accession of the Kingdom of Norway, the Republic of Austria, the Republic of Finland and the Kingdom of Sweden, Annex I(XI)(B)(III)(3)(b), as adjusted by Council Decision 95/1/EC, Annex I(XI)(B)(III)(3)(b).

Article 7

Subsequent amendments

1 Technical amendments to the following points shall be adopted in accordance with the procedure laid down in paragraph 2:

— the clarification of definitions to take account of developments on financial markets,
— the clarification of definitions to ensure the uniform application of this Directive,
— the alignment of the terminology and of the wording of the definitions on those in subsequent instruments concerning credit institutions and related matters,
— the clarification of the exemptions provided for in Article 4(5) to (10).

2 The Commission shall be assisted by the committee provided for in the first subparagraph of Article 22(2) of Directive 89/646/EEC.

The Commission representative shall submit to the committee a draft of the measures to be taken. The committee shall deliver its opinion on that draft within a time limit which the chairman may lay down according to the urgency of the matter. The opinion shall be delivered by the majority laid down in Article 148(2) of the Treaty in the case of decisions which the Council is required to adopt on a proposal from the Commission. The votes of the Member States' representatives on the committee shall be weighted as laid down in that Article. The chairman shall not vote.

The Commission shall adopt the measures envisaged if they are in accordance with the committee's opinion.

If the measures envisaged are not in accordance with the committee's opinion, or if no opinion is delivered, the Commission shall, without delay, submit to the Council a proposal concerning the measures to be taken. The Council shall act by a qualified majority.

If the Council does not act within three weeks months of the referral to it the Commission shall adopt the measures proposed unless the Council has decided against those measures by a simple majority.   **[1021]**

Article 8

Final provisions

1 Member States shall bring into force the laws, regulations and administrative provisions necessary to comply with this Directive by 1 January 1994. They shall forthwith inform the Commission thereof.

When Member States adopt these measures, they shall include a reference to this Directive or be accompanied by such a reference on the occasion of their official publication. The manner in which such a reference is to be made shall be laid down by the Member States.

2 Member States shall communicate to the Commission the texts of the main provisions of national law which they adopt in the field governed by this Directive.

3 Pending Community legislation on the monitoring on a consolidated or non-consolidated basis of large exposures concerning activities which are principally exposed to market risks the Member States shall deal with such large exposures in accordance with methods which they shall determine, having regard to the particular nature of the risks involved.   **[1022]**

Article 9

This Directive is addressed to the Member States.

Done at Brussels, 21 December 1992.

COUNCIL DIRECTIVE
of 15 March 1993

on the capital adequacy of investment firms and credit institutions

(93/6/EEC)

NOTES

Date of publication in OJ: OJ L141, 11.6.1993, p 1.

THE COUNCIL OF THE EUROPEAN COMMUNITIES

Having regard to the Treaty establishing the European Economic Community, and in particular the first and third sentences of Article 57(2) thereof,

Having regard to the proposal from the Commission[1],

In cooperation with the European Parliament[2],

Having regard to the opinion of the Economic and Social Committee[3],

Whereas the main objective of Council Directive 93/22/EEC of 10 May 1993 on investment services in the securities field[4] is to allow investment firms authorised by the competent authorities of their home Member States and supervised by the same authorities to establish branches and provide services freely in other Member States; whereas that Directive accordingly provides for the coordination of the rules governing the authorisation and pursuit of the business of investment firms;

Whereas that Directive does not, however, establish common standards for the own funds of investment firms nor indeed does it establish the amounts of the initial capital of such firms; whereas it does not establish a common framework for monitoring the risks incurred by the same firms; whereas it refers, in several of its provisions, to another Community initiative, the objective of which would be precisely to adopt coordinated measures in those fields;

Whereas the approach that has been adopted is to effect only the essential harmonisation that is necessary and sufficient to secure the mutual recognition of authorisation and of prudential supervision systems; whereas the adoption of measures to coordinate the definition of the own funds of investment firms, the establishment of the amounts of their initial capital and the establishment of a common framework for monitoring the risks incurred by investment firms are essential aspects of the harmonisation necessary for the achievement of mutual recognition within the framework of the internal financial market;

Whereas it is appropriate to establish different amounts of initial capital depending on the range of activities that investment firms are authorised to undertake;

Whereas existing investment firms should be permitted, under certain conditions, to continue their business even if they do not comply with the minimum amount of initial capital fixed for new firms;

Whereas the Member States may also establish rules stricter than those provided for in this Directive;

Whereas this Directive forms part of the wider international effort to bring about approximation of the rules in force regarding the supervision of investment firms and credit institutions (hereinafter referred to collectively as 'institutions');

Whereas common basic standards for the own funds of institutions are a key feature in an internal market in the investment services sector, since own funds serve to ensure the continuity of institutions and to protect investors;

Whereas in a common financial market, institutions, whether they are investment firms or credit institutions, engage in direct competition with one another;

Whereas it is therefore desirable to achieve equality in the treatment of credit institutions and investment firms;

Whereas, as regards credit institutions, common standards are already established for the supervision and monitoring of credit risks in Council Directive 89/647/EEC of 18 December 1989 on a solvency ratio for credit institutions[5];

Whereas it is necessary to develop common standards for market risks incurred by credit institutions and provide a complementary framework for the supervision of the risks incurred by institutions, in particular market risks, and more especially position risks, counterparty/settlement risks and foreign-exchange risks;

Whereas it is necessary to introduce the concept of a 'trading book' comprising positions in securities and other financial instruments which are held for trading purposes and are subject mainly to market risks and exposures relating to certain financial services provided to customers;

Whereas it is desirable that institutions with negligible trading-book business, in both absolute and relative terms, should be able to apply Directive 89/647/EEC, rather than the requirements imposed in Annexes I and II to this Directive;

Whereas it is important that monitoring of settlement/delivery risks should take account of the existence of systems offering adequate protection that reduces that risk;

Whereas, in any case, institutions must comply with this Directive as regards the coverage of the foreign-exchange risks on their overall business; whereas lower capital requirements should be imposed for positions in closely correlated currencies, whether statistically confirmed or arising out of binding intergovernmental agreements, with a view in particular to the creation of the European Monetary Union;

Whereas the existence, in all institutions, of internal systems for monitoring and controlling interest-rate risks on all of their business is a particularly important way of minimising such risks; whereas, consequently, such systems must be subject to overview by the competent authorities;

Whereas Council Directive 92/121/EEC of 21 December 1992 on the monitoring and control of large exposures of credit institutions[6] is not aimed at establishing common rules for monitoring large exposures in activities which are principally subject to market risks; whereas that Directive makes reference to another Community initiative intended to adopt the requisite coordination of methods in that field;

Whereas it is necessary to adopt common rules for the monitoring and control of large exposures incurred by investment firms;

Whereas the own funds of credit institutions have already been defined in Council Directive 89/299/EEC of 17 April 1989 on the own funds of credit institutions[7];

Whereas the basis for the definition of the own funds of institutions should be that definition;

Whereas, however, there are reasons why for the purposes of this Directive the definition of the own funds of institutions may differ from that in the aforementioned Directive in order to take account of the particular characteristics of the activities carried on by those institutions which mainly involve market risks;

Whereas Council Directive 92/30/EEC of 6 April 1992 on the supervision of credit institutions on a consolidated basis[8] states the principle of consolidation; whereas it does not establish common rules for the consolidation of financial institutions which are involved in activities principally subject to market risks; whereas that Directive makes reference to another Community initiative intended to adopt coordinated measures in that field;

Whereas Directive 92/30/EEC does not apply to groups which include one or more investment firms but no credit institutions; whereas it was, however, felt desirable to provide a common framework for the introduction of the supervision of investment firms on a consolidated basis;

Whereas technical adaptations to the detailed rules laid down in this Directive may from time to time be necessary to take account of new developments in the investment services field; whereas the Commission will accordingly propose such adaptations as are necessary;

Whereas the Council should, at a later stage, adopt provision for the adaptation of this Directive to technical progress in accordance with Council Decision 87/373/EEC of 13 July 1987 laying down the procedures for the exercise of implementing powers conferred on the Commission; whereas meanwhile the Council itself, on a proposal from the Commission, should carry out such adaptations;

Whereas provision should be made for the review of this Directive within three years of the date of its application in the light of experience, developments on financial markets and work in international fora of regulatory authorities; whereas that review should also include the possible review of the list of areas that may be subject to technical adjustment;

Whereas this Directive and Directive 93/22/EEC on investment services in the securities field are so closely interrelated that their entry into force on different dates could lead to the distortion of competition,

NOTES
[1] OJ C 152, 21.6.1990, p 6 and OJ C 50, 25.2.1992, p 5.
[2] OJ C 326, 16.12.1991, p 89 and OJ C 337, 21.12.1992, p 114.
[3] OJ C 69, 18.3.1991, p 1.
[4] See OJ L 141, 11.6.1993, p 27.
[5] OJ L 386, 30.12.1989, p 14. Directive as amended by Directive (92/30/EEC) OJ L 110, 28.4.1992, p 52.
[6] OJ L 29, 5.2.1993, p 1.
[7] OJ L 124, 5.5.1989, p 16. Directive as last amended by Directive (92/30/EEC) OJ L 110, 24.9.1992, p 52.
[8] OJ L 110, 28.4.1992, p 52.
[9] OJ L 197, 18.7.1987, p 33.

HAS ADOPTED THIS DIRECTIVE:

Article 1

1 Member States shall apply the requirements of this Directive to investment firms and credit institutions as defined in Article 2.

2 A Member State may impose additional or more stringent requirements on the investment firms and credit institutions that it has authorised. **[1023]**

DEFINITIONS

Article 2

For the purposes of this Directive:

1 *credit institutions* shall mean all institutions that satisfy the definition in the first indent of Article 1 of the First Council Directive (77/780/EEC) of 12 December 1977 on the coordination of laws, regulations and administrative provisions relating to the taking up and pursuit of the business of credit institutions[1] which are subject to the requirements imposed by Directive 89/647/EEC;

2 *investment firms* shall mean all institutions that satisfy the definition in point 2 of Article 1 of Directive 93/22/EEC, which are subject to the requirements imposed by the same Directive, excluding:

— credit institutions,
— local firms as defined in 20, and
— firms which only receive and transmit orders from investors without holding money or securities belonging to their clients and which for that reason may not at any time place themselves in debit with their clients;

3 *institutions* shall mean credit institutions and investment firms;

4 *recognised third-country investment firms* shall mean firms which, if they were established within the Community, would be covered by the definition of investment firm in 2, which are authorised in a third country and which are subject to and comply with prudential rules considered by the competent authorities as at least as stringent as those laid down in this Directive;

5 *financial instruments* shall mean the instruments listed in Section B of the Annex to Directive 93/22/EEC;

6 the *trading book* of an institution shall consist of—

    (a)   its proprietary positions in financial instruments which are held for resale and/or which are taken on by the institution with the intention of benefiting in the short term from actual and/or expected differences between their buying and selling prices, or from other price or interest-rate variations, and positions in financial instruments arising from matched principal broking, or positions taken in order to hedge other elements of the trading book;

    (b)   the exposures due to the unsettled transactions, free deliveries and over-the-counter (OTC) derivative instruments referred to in paragraphs 1, 2, 3 and 5 of Annex II, the exposures due to repurchase agreements and securities lending which are based on securities included in the trading book as defined in (a) referred to in paragraph 4 of Annex II, those exposures due to reverse repurchase agreements and securities-borrowing transactions described in the same paragraph, provided the competent authorities so approve, which meet either the conditions (i), (ii), (iii) and (v) or conditions (iv) and (v) as follows:

        (i)   the exposures are marked to market daily following the procedures laid down in Annex II;

      (ii) the collateral is adjusted in order to take account of material changes in the value of the securities involved in the agreement or transaction in question, according to a rule acceptable to the competent authorities;

     (iii) the agreement or transaction provides for the claims of the institution to be automatically and immediately offset against the claims of its counter-party in the event of the latter's defaulting;

     (iv) the agreement or transaction in question is an interprofessional one;

     (v) such agreements and transactions are confined to their accepted and appropriate use and artificial transactions, especially those not of a short-term nature, are excluded; and

  (c) those exposures in the form of fees, commission, interest, dividends and margin on exchange-traded derivatives which are directly related to the items included in the trading book referred to in paragraph 6 of Annex II.

Particular items shall be included in or excluded from the trading book in accordance with objective procedures including, where appropriate, accounting standards in the institution concerned, such procedures and their consistent implementation being subject to review by the competent authorities;

7 *parent undertaking, subsidiary undertaking* and *financial institution* shall be defined in accordance with Article 1 of Directive 92/30/EEC;

8 *financial holding company* shall mean a financial institution the subsidiary undertakings of which are either exclusively or mainly credit institutions, investment firms or other financial institutions, one of which at least is a credit institution or an investment firm;

9 *risk weightings* shall mean the degrees of credit risk applicable to the relevant counter-parties under Directive 89/647/EEC. However, assets constituting claims on and other exposures to investment firms or recognised third-country investment firms and exposures incurred to recognised clearing houses and exchanges shall be assigned the same weighting as that assigned where the relevant counterparty is a credit institution;

10 *over-the-counter (OTC) derivative instruments* shall mean the interest-rate and foreign-exchange contracts referred to in Annex II to Directive 89/647/EEC and off-balance-sheet contracts based on equities, provided that no such contracts are traded on recognised exchanges where they are subject to daily margin requirements and, in the case of foreign-exchange contracts, that every such contract has an original maturity of more than 14 calendar days;

11 *regulated market* shall mean a market that satisfies the definition given in Article 1(13) of Directive 93/22/EEC;

12 *qualifying items* shall mean long and short positions in the assets referred to in Article 6(1)(b) of Directive 89/647/EEC and in debt instruments issued by investment firms or by recognised third-country investment firms. It shall also mean long and short positions in debt instruments provided that such instruments meet the following conditions: such instruments must firstly be listed on at least one regulated market in a Member State or on a stock exchange in a third country provided that that exchange is recognised by the competent authorities of the relevant Member State; and secondly both be considered by the institution concerned to be sufficiently liquid and, because of the solvency of the issuer, be subject to a degree of default risk which is comparable to or lower than that of the assets referred to in Article 6(1)(b) of Directive 89/647/EEC; the manner in which the instruments are assessed shall be subject to scrutiny by the competent authorities, which shall overturn the judgment of the institution if they consider that the instruments concerned are subject to too high a degree of default risk to be qualifying items.

Notwithstanding the foregoing and pending further coordination, the competent authorities shall have the discretion to recognise as qualifying items instruments which are sufficiently liquid and which, because of the solvency of the issuer, are subject to a degree of default risk which is comparable to or lower than that of the assets referred to in Article 6(1)(b) of Directive 89/647/EEC. The default risk associated with such instruments must have been evaluated at such a level by at least two credit-rating agencies recognised by the competent authorities or by only one such credit-rating agency so long as they are not rated below such a level by any other credit-rating agency recognised by the competent authorities.

The competent authorities may, however, waive the condition imposed in the preceding sentence if they judge it inappropriate in the light of, for example, the characteristics of the market, the issuer, the issue, or some combination of those characteristics.

Furthermore, the competent authorities shall require the institutions to apply the maximum weighting shown in Table 1 in paragraph 14 of Annex I to instruments which show a particular risk because of the insufficient solvency of the issuer or liquidity.

The competent authorities of each Member State shall regularly provide the Council and the Commission with information concerning the methods used to evaluate the qualifying items, in particular the methods used to assess the degree of liquidity of the issue and the solvency of the issuer;

13 *central government items* shall mean long and short positions in the assets referred to in Article 6(1)(a) of Directive 89/647/EEC and those assigned a weighting of 0% in Article 7 of the same Directive;

14 *convertible* shall mean a security which, at the option of the holder, can be exchanged for another security, usually the equity of the issuer;

15 *warrant* shall mean an instrument which gives the holder the right to purchase a number of shares of common stock or bonds at a stipulated price until the warrant's expiry date. They may be settled by the delivery of the securities themselves or their equivalent in cash;

16 *covered warrant* shall mean an instrument issued by an entity other than the issuer of the underlying instrument which gives the holder the right to purchase a number of shares of common stock or bonds at a stipulated price or a right to secure a profit or avoid a loss by reference to fluctuations in an index relating to any of the financial instruments listed in Section B of the Annex to Directive 93/22/EEC until the warrant's expiry date;

17 *repurchase agreement* and *reverse repurchase agreement* shall mean any agreement in which an institution or its counter-party transfers securities or guaranteed rights relating to title to securities where that guarantee is issued by a recognised exchange which holds the rights to the securities and the agreement does not allow an institution to transfer or pledge a particular security to more than one counter-party at one time, subject to a commitment to repurchase them (or substituted securities of the same description) at a specified price on a future date specified, or to be specified, by the transferor, being a *repurchase agreement* for the institution selling the securities and a *reverse repurchase agreement* for the institution buying them.

A reverse repurchase agreement shall be considered an interprofessional transaction when the counter-party is subject to prudential coordination at Community level or is a Zone A credit institution as defined in Directive 89/647/EEC or is a recognised third-country investment firm or when the agreement is concluded with a recognised clearing house or exchange;

18 *securities lending* and *securities borrowing* shall mean any transaction in which an institution or its counter-party transfers securities against appropriate collateral subject to a commitment that the borrower will return equivalent securities at some future date or when requested to do so by the transferor, being *securities lending* for the institution transferring the securities and *securities borrowing* for the institution to which they are transferred.

Securities borrowing shall be considered an interprofessional transaction when the counterparty is subject to prudential coordination at Community level or is a Zone A credit institution as defined in Directive 89/647/EEC or is a recognised third-country investment firm or when the transaction is concluded with a recognised clearing house or exchange;

19 *clearing member* shall mean a member of the exchange or the clearing house which has a direct contractual relationship with the central counterparty (market guarantor); non-clearing members must have their trades routed through a clearing member;

20 *local firm* shall mean a firm dealing only for its own account on a financial-futures or options exchange or for the accounts of or making a price to other members of the same exchange and guaranteed by a clearing member of the same exchange. Responsibility for ensuring the performance of contracts entered into by such a firm must be assumed by a clearing member of the same exchange, and such contracts must be taken into account in the calculation of the clearing member's overall capital requirements so long as the local firm's positions are entirely separate from those of the clearing member;

21 *delta* shall mean the expected change in an option price as a proportion of a small change in the price of the instrument underlying the option;

22 for the purposes of paragraph 4 of Annex I, *long position* shall mean a position in which an institution has fixed the interest rate it will receive at some time in the future, and *short position* shall mean a position in which it has fixed the interest rate it will pay at some time in the future;

23 *own funds* shall mean own funds as defined in Directive 89/299/EEC. This definition may, however, be amended in the circumstances described in Annex V;

24 *initial capital* shall mean items 1 and 2 of Article 2(1) of Directive 89/299/EEC;

25 *original own funds* shall mean the sum of items 1, 2 and 4, less the sum of items 9, 10 and 11 of Article 2(1) of Directive 89/299/EEC;

26 *capital* shall mean own funds;

27 *modified duration* shall be calculated using the formula set out in paragraph 26 of Annex I.   **[1024]**

NOTES
[1] OJ L 322, 17.12.1977, p 30. Directive as amended by Directive (89/646/EEC) OJ L 386, 30.12.1989, p 1.

INITIAL CAPITAL

Article 3

1 Investment firms which hold clients' money and/or securities and which offer one or more of the following services shall have initial capital of ECU 125 000—

— the reception and transmission of investors' orders for financial instruments,
— the execution of investors' orders for financial instruments,
— the management of individual portfolios of investments in financial instruments,

provided that they do not deal in any financial instruments for their own account or underwrite issues of financial instruments on a firm commitment basis.

The holding of non-trading-book positions in financial instruments in order to invest own funds shall not be considered as dealing for the purposes set out in the first paragraph or for the purposes of paragraph 2.

The competent authorities may, however, allow an investment firm which executes investors' orders for financial instruments to hold such instruments for its own account if—

— such positions arise only as a result of the firm's failure to match investors' orders precisely,
— the total market value of all such positions is subject to a ceiling of 15% of the firm's initial capital,
— the firm meets the requirements imposed in Articles 4 and 5, and
— such positions are incidental and provisional in nature and strictly limited to the time required to carry out the transaction in question.

2 Member States may reduce the amount referred to in paragraph 1 to ECU 50 000 where a firm is not authorised to hold clients' money or securities, to deal for its own account, or to underwrite issues on a firm commitment basis.

3 All other investment firms shall have initial capital of ECU 730 000.

4 The firms referred to in the second and third indents of Article 2(2) shall have initial capital of ECU 50 000 in so far as they benefit from freedom of establishment or provide services under Articles 14 or 15 of Directive 93/22/EEC.

5 Notwithstanding paragraphs 1 to 4, Member States may continue the authorisation of investment firms and firms covered by paragraph 4 in existence before this Directive is applied the own funds of which are less than the initial capital levels specified for them in paragraphs 1 to 4. The own funds of such firms shall not fall below the highest reference level calculated after the date of notification of this Directive. That reference level shall be the average daily level of own funds calculated over a six-month period preceding the date of calculation. It shall be calculated every six months in respect of the corresponding preceding period.

6 If control of a firm covered by paragraph 5 is taken by a natural or legal person other than the person who controlled it previously, the own funds of that firm must attain at least the level specified for it in paragraphs 1 to 4, except in the following situations:

(i) in the case of the first transfer by inheritance after the application of this Directive, subject to the competent authorities' approval, for not more than 10 years after that transfer;

    (ii) in the case of a change in the composition of a partnership, as long as at least one of the partners at the date of the application of this Directive remains in the partnership, for not more than 10 years after the date of the application of this Directive.

7 In certain specific circumstances and with the consent of the competent authorities, however, in the event of a merger of two or more investment firms and/or firms covered by paragraph 4, the own funds of the firm produced by the merger need not attain the level specified in paragraphs 1 to 4. Nevertheless, during any period when the levels specified in paragraphs 1 to 4 have not been attained, the own funds of the new firm may not fall below the merged firms' total own funds at the time of the merger.

8 The own funds of investment firms and firms covered by paragraph 4 may not fall below the level specified in paragraphs 1 to 5 and 7. If they do, however, the competent authorities may, where the circumstances justify it, allow such firms a limited period in which to rectify their situations or cease their activities. **[1025]**

PROVISIONS AGAINST RISKS

Article 4

1 The competent authorities shall require institutions to provide own funds which are always more than or equal to the sum of:

    (i) the capital requirements, calculated in accordance with Annexes I, II and VI, for their trading-book business;

    (ii) the capital requirements, calculated in accordance with Annex III, for all of their business activities;

    (iii) the capital requirements imposed in Directive 89/647/EEC for all of their business activities, excluding both their trading-book business and their illiquid assets if they are deducted from own funds under paragraph 2(d) of Annex V;

    (iv) the capital requirements imposed in paragraph 2.

Irrespective of the amount of the capital requirement referred to in (i) to (iv) the own-funds requirement for investment firms shall never be less than the amount prescribed in Annex IV.

2 The competent authorities shall require institutions to cover the risks arising in connection with business that is outside the scope of both this Directive and Directive 89/647/EEC and considered to be similar to the risks covered by those Directives by adequate own funds.

3 If the own funds held by an institution fall below the amount of the own funds requirement imposed in paragraph 1, the competent authorities shall ensure that the institution in question takes appropriate measures to rectify its situation as quickly as possible.

4 The competent authorities shall require institutions to set up systems to monitor and control the interest-rate risk on all of their business, and those systems shall be subject to overview by the competent authorities.

5 Institutions shall be required to satisfy their competent authorities that they employ systems which can calculate their financial positions with reasonable accuracy at any time.

6 Notwithstanding paragraph 1, the competent authorities may allow institutions to calculate the capital requirements for their trading-book business in accordance with Directive 89/647/EEC rather than in accordance with Annexes I and II to this Directive provided that—

    (i) the trading-book business of such institutions does not normally exceed 5% of their total business;

    (ii) their total trading-book positions do not normally exceed ECU 15 million; and

    (iii) the trading-book business of such institutions never exceeds 6% of their total business and their total trading-book positions never exceed ECU 20 million.

7 In order to calculate the proportion that trading-book business bears to total business as in paragraph 6(i) and (iii), the competent authorities may refer either to the size of the combined on- and off-balance-sheet business, to the profit and loss account or to the own funds of the institutions in question, or to a combination of those measurements. When the size of on- and off-balance-sheet business is assessed, debt instruments shall be valued at their market prices or their principal values, equities at their market prices and derivatives according to the nominal or market values of the instruments underlying them. Long positions and short positions shall be summed regardless of their signs.

8 If an institution should happen for more than a short period to exceed either or both of the limits imposed in paragraph 6(i) and (ii) or to exceed either or both of the limits imposed in paragraph 6(iii), it shall be required to meet the requirements imposed in Article 4(1)(i) rather than those of Directive 89/647/EEC in respect of its trading-book business and to notify the competent authority. **[1026]**

MONITORING AND CONTROL OF LARGE EXPOSURES

Article 5

1 Institutions shall monitor and control their large exposures in accordance with Directive 92/121/EEC.

2 Notwithstanding paragraph 1, those institutions which calculate the capital requirements for their trading-book business in accordance with Annexes I and II shall monitor and control their large exposures in accordance with Directive 92/121/EEC subject to the modifications laid down in Annex VI to this Directive. **[1027]**

VALUATION OF POSITIONS FOR REPORTING PURPOSES

Article 6

1 Institutions shall mark to market their trading books on a daily basis unless they are subject to Article 4(6).

2 In the absence of readily available market prices, for example in the case of dealing in new issues on the primary markets, the competent authorities may waive the requirement imposed in paragraph 1 and require institutions to use alternative methods of valuation provided that those methods are sufficiently prudent and have been approved by competent authorities. **[1028]**

SUPERVISION ON A CONSOLIDATED BASIS

Article 7

General principles

1 The capital requirements imposed in Articles 4 and 5 for institutions which are neither parent undertakings nor subsidiaries of such undertakings shall be applied on a solo basis.

2 The requirements imposed in Articles 4 and 5 for:

— any institution which has a credit institution within the meaning of Directive 92/30/EEC, an investment firm or another financial institution as a subsidiary or which holds a participation in such an entity, and

— any institution the parent undertaking of which is a financial holding company

shall be applied on a consolidated basis in accordance with the methods laid down in the above-mentioned Directive and in paragraphs 7 to 14 of this Article.

3 When a group covered by paragraph 2 does not include a credit institution, Directive 92/30/EEC shall apply, subject to the following adaptations:

— *financial holding company* shall mean a financial institution the subsidiary undertakings of which are either exclusively or mainly investment firms or other financial institutions one at least of which is an investment firm,

— *mixed-activity holding company* shall mean a parent undertaking, other than a financial holding company or an investment firm, the subsidiaries of which include at least one investment firm,

— *competent authorities* shall mean the national authorities which are empowered by law or regulation to supervise investment firms,

— every reference to *credit institutions* shall be replaced by a reference to *investment firms*,

— the second subparagraph of Article 3(5) of Directive 92/30/EEC shall not apply,

— in Articles 4(1) and (2) and 7(5) of Directive 92/30/EEC each reference to Directive 77/780/EEC shall be replaced by a reference to Directive 93/22/EEC,

— for the purposes of Articles 3(9) and 8(3) of Directive 92/30/EEC the references to the *Banking Advisory Committee* shall be substituted by references to the Council and the Commission,

— the first sentence of Article 7(4) of Directive 92/30/EEC shall be replaced by the following:

'Where an investment firm, a financial holding company or a mixed-activity holding company controls one or more subsidiaries which are insurance companies, the competent authorities and the authorities entrusted with the public task of supervising insurance undertakings shall cooperate closely'.

4 The competent authorities required or mandated to exercise supervision of groups covered by paragraph 3 on a consolidated basis may, pending further coordination on the supervision of such groups on a consolidated basis and where the circumstances justify it, waive that obligation provided that each investment firm in such a group—

(i) uses the definition of own funds given in paragraph 9 of Annex V;
(ii) meets the requirements imposed in Articles 4 and 5 on a solo basis;
(iii) sets up systems to monitor and control the sources of capital and funding of all other financial institutions within the group.

5 The competent authorities shall require investment firms in a group which has been granted the waiver provided for in paragraph 4 to notify them of those risks, including those associated with the composition and sources of their capital and funding, which could undermine their financial positions. If the competent authorities then consider that the financial positions of those investment firms is not adequately protected, they shall require them to take measures including, if necessary, limitations on the transfer of capital from such firms to group entities.

6 Where the competent authorities waive the obligation of supervision on a consolidated basis provided for in paragraph 4 they shall take other appropriate measures to monitor the risks, namely large exposures, of the whole group, including any undertakings not located in a Member State.

7 Member States may waive the application of the requirements imposed in Articles 4 and 5, on an individual or subconsolidated basis, to an institution which, as a parent undertaking, is subject to supervision on a consolidated basis, and to any subsidiary of such an institution which is subject to their authorisation and supervision and is included in the supervision on a consolidated basis of the institution which is its parent company.

The same right of waiver shall be granted where the parent undertaking is a financial holding company which has its head office in the same Member State as the institution, provided that it is subject to the same supervision as that exercised over credit institutions or investment firms, and in particular the requirements imposed in Articles 4 and 5.

In both cases, if the right of waiver is exercised measures must be taken to ensure the satisfactory allocation of own funds within the group.

8 Where an institution the parent undertaking of which is an institution has been authorised and is situated in another Member State, the competent authorities which granted that authorisation shall apply the rules laid down in Articles 4 and 5 to that institution on an individual or, where appropriate, a subconsolidated basis.

9 Notwithstanding paragraph 8, the competent authorities responsible for authorising the subsidiary of a parent undertaking which is an institution may, by a bilateral agreement, delegate their responsibility for supervising the subsidiary's capital adequacy and large exposures to the competent authorities which authorised and supervise the parent undertaking. The Commission must be kept informed of the existence and content of such agreements. It shall forward such information to the competent authorities of the other Member States and to the Banking Advisory Committee and to the Council, except in the case of groups covered by paragraph 3.

Calculating the consolidated requirements

10 Where the rights of waiver provided for in paragraphs 7 and 9 are not exercised, the competent authorities may, for the purpose of calculating the capital requirements set out in Annex I and the exposures to clients set out in Annex VI on a consolidated basis, permit net positions in the trading book of one institution to offset positions in the trading book of another institution according to the rules set out in Annexes I and VI respectively.

In addition, they may allow foreign-exchange positions subject to Annex III in one institution to offset foreign-exchange positions subject to Annex III in another institution in accordance with the rules set out in Annex III.

11 The competent authorities may also permit offsetting of the trading book and of the foreign-exchange positions of undertakings located in third countries, subject to the simultaneous fulfilment of the following conditions:

   (i) those undertakings have been authorised in a third country and either satisfy the definition of credit institution given in the first indent of Article 1 of Directive 77/780/EEC or are recognised third-country investment firms;

  (ii) such undertakings comply, on a solo basis, with capital adequacy rules equivalent to those laid down in this Directive;

 (iii) no regulations exist in the countries in question which might significantly affect the transfer of funds within the group.

12 The competent authorities may also allow the offsetting provided for in paragraph 10 between institutions within a group that have been authorised in the Member State in question, provided that:

   (i) there is a satisfactory allocation of capital within the group;

  (ii) the regulatory, legal or contractual framework in which the institutions operate is such as to guarantee mutual financial support within the group.

13 Furthermore, the competent authorities may allow the offsetting provided for in paragraph 10 between institutions within a group that fulfil the conditions imposed in paragraph 12 and any institution included in the same group which has been authorised in another Member State provided that that institution is obliged to fulfil the capital requirements imposed in Articles 4 and 5 on a solo basis.

Definition of consolidated own funds

14 In the calculation of own funds on a consolidated basis Article 5 of Directive 89/299/EEC shall apply.

15 The competent authorities responsible for exercising supervision on a consolidated basis may recognise the validity of the specific own-funds definitions applicable to the institutions concerned under Annex V in the calculation of their consolidated own funds.   **[1029]**

REPORTING REQUIREMENTS

Article 8

1 Member States shall require that investment firms and credit institutions provide the competent authorities of their home Member States with all the information necessary for the assessment of their compliance with the rules adopted in accordance with this Directive. Member States shall also ensure that institutions' internal control mechanisms and administrative and accounting procedures permit the verification of their compliance with such rules at all times.

2 Investment firms shall be obliged to report to the competent authorities in the manner specified by the latter at least once every month in the case of firms covered by Article 3(3), at least once every three months in the case of firms covered by Article 3(1) and at least once every six months in the case of firms covered by Article 3(2).

3 Notwithstanding paragraph 2, investment firms covered by Article 3(1) and (3) shall be required to provide the information on a consolidated or subconsolidated basis only once every six months.

4 Credit institutions shall be obliged to report in the manner specified by the competent authorities as often as they are obliged to report under Directive 89/647/EEC.

5 The competent authorities shall oblige institutions to report to them immediately any case in which their counterparties in repurchase and reverse repurchase agreements or securities-lending and securities-borrowing transactions default on their obligations. The Commission shall report to the Council on such cases and their implications for the treatment of such agreements and transactions in this Directive not more than three years after the date referred to in Article 12. Such reports shall also describe the way that institutions meet those of conditions (i) to (v) in Article 2(6)(*b*) that apply to them, in particular that referred to in condition (v). Furthermore it shall give details of any changes in the relative volume of institutions' traditional lending and their lending through reverse repurchase agreements and securities-borrowing transactions. If the Commission concludes on the basis of this report and other information that further safeguards are needed to prevent abuse it shall make appropriate proposals. **[1030]**

COMPETENT AUTHORITIES

Article 9

1 Member States shall designate the authorities which are to carry out the duties provided for in this Directive. They shall inform the Commission thereof, indicating any division of duties.

2 The authorities referred to in paragraph 1 must be public authorities or bodies officially recognised by national law or by public authorities as part of the supervisory system in operation in the Member State concerned.

3 The authorities concerned must be granted all the powers necessary for the performance of their tasks, and in particular that of overseeing the constitution of trading books.

4 The competent authorities of the various Member States shall collaborate closely in the performance of the duties provided for in this Directive, particularly when investment services are provided on a services basis or through the establishment of branches in one or more Member States. They shall on request supply one another with all information likely to facilitate the supervision of the capital adequacy of investment firms and credit institutions, in particular the verification of their compliance with the rules laid down in this Directive. Any exchange of information between competent authorities which is provided for in this Directive in respect of investment firms shall be subject to the obligation of professional secrecy imposed in Article 25 of Directive 93/22/EEC and, as regards credit institutions, to the obligation imposed in Article 12 of Directive 77/780/EEC, as amended by Directive 89/646/EEC.
[1031]

Article 10

Pending adoption of a further Directive laying down provisions for adapting this Directive to technical progress in the areas specified below, the Council shall, acting by qualified majority on a proposal from the Commission, in accordance with Decision 87/373/EEC, adopt those adaptations which may be necessary, as follows:

— clarification of the definitions in Article 2 in order to ensure uniform application of this Directive throughout the Community,
— clarification of the definitions in Article 2 to take account of developments on financial markets,

— alteration of the amounts of initial capital prescribed in Article 3 and the amount referred to in Article 4(6) to take account of developments in the economic and monetary field,
— the alignment of terminology on and the framing of definitions in accordance with subsequent acts on institutions and related matters.

[1032]

TRANSITIONAL PROVISIONS

Article 11

1 Member States may authorise investment firms subject to Article 30(1) of Directive 93/22/EEC the own funds of which are on the day of the application of this Directive lower than the levels specified in Article 3(1) to (3) of this Directive. Thereafter, however, the own funds of such investment firms must fulfil the conditions laid down in Article 3(5) to (8) of this Directive.

2 Notwithstanding paragraph 14 of Annex I, Member States may set a specific-risk requirement for any bonds assigned a weighting of 10% under Article 11(2) of Directive 89/647/EEC equal to half the specific-risk requirement for a qualifying item with the same residual maturity as such a bond.

[1033]

FINAL PROVISIONS

Article 12

1 Member States shall bring into force the laws, regulations and administrative provisions necessary for them to comply with this Directive by the date fixed in the second paragraph of Article 31 of Directive 93/22/EEC. They shall forthwith inform the Commission thereof.

When Member States adopt these provisions they shall include a reference to this Directive or add such a reference on the occasion of their official publication. The manner in which such references are to be made shall be laid down by the Member States.

2 Member States shall communicate to the Commission the main provisions of national law which they adopt in the field covered by this Directive. **[1034]**

Article 13

The Commission shall as soon as possible submit to the Council proposals for capital requirements in respect of commodities trading, commodity derivatives and units of collective-investment undertakings.

The Council shall decide on the Commission's proposals no later than six months before the date of application of this Directive. **[1035]**

REVIEW CLAUSE

Article 14

Within three years of the date referred to in Article 12, acting on a proposal from the Commission, the Council shall examine and, if necessary, revise this Directive in the light of the experience acquired in applying it, taking into account market innovation and, in particular, developments in international fora of regulatory authorities. **[1036]**

Article 15

This Directive is addressed to the Member States.

Done at Brussels, 15 March 1993.

ANNEX I
POSITION RISK

INTRODUCTION

Netting

1 The excess of an institution's long (short) positions over its short (long) positions in the same equity, debt and convertible issues and identical financial futures, options, warrants and covered warrants shall be its net position in each of those different instruments. In calculating the net position the competent authorities shall allow positions in derivative instruments to be treated, as laid down in paragraphs 4 to 7, as positions in the underlying (or notional) security or securities. Institutions' holdings of their own debt instruments shall be disregarded in calculating specific risk under paragraph 14.

2 No netting shall be allowed between a convertible and an offsetting position in the instrument underlying it, unless the competent authorities adopt an approach under which the likelihood of a particular convertible's being converted is taken into account or have a capital requirement to cover any loss which conversion might entail.

3 All net positions, irrespective of their signs, must be converted on a daily basis into the institution's reporting currency at the prevailing spot exchange rate before their aggregation.

Particular instruments

4 Interest-rate futures, forward-rate agreements (FRAs) and forward commitments to buy or sell debt instruments shall be treated as combinations of long and short positions. Thus a long interest-rate futures position shall be treated as a combination of a borrowing maturing on the delivery date of the futures contract and a holding of an asset with maturity date equal to that of the instrument or notional position underlying the futures contract in question. Similarly a sold FRA will be treated as a long position with a maturity date equal to the settlement date plus the contract period, and a short position with maturity equal to the settlement date. Both the borrowing and the asset holding shall be included in the Central government column of Table 1 in paragraph 14 in order to calculate the capital required against specific risk for interest-rate futures and FRAs. A forward commitment to buy a debt instrument shall be treated as a combination of a borrowing maturing on the delivery date and a long (spot) position in the debt instrument itself. The borrowing shall be included in the Central government column of Table 1 for purposes of specific risk, and the debt instrument under whichever column is appropriate for it in the same table. The competent authorities may allow the capital requirement for an exchange-traded future to be equal to the margin required by the exchange if they are fully satisfied that it provides an accurate measure of the risk associated with the future and that the method used to calculate the margin is equivalent to the method of calculation set out in the remainder of this Annex.

5 Options on interest rates, debt instruments, equities, equity indices, financial futures, swaps and foreign currencies shall be treated as if they were positions equal in value to the amount of the underlying instrument to which the option refers, multiplied by its delta for the purposes of this Annex. The latter positions may be netted off against any offsetting positions in the identical underlying securities or derivatives. The delta used shall be that of the exchange concerned, that calculated by the competent authorities or, where that is not available or for OTC options, that calculated by the institution itself, subject to the competent authorities' being satisfied that the model used by the institution is reasonable.

However, the competent authorities may also prescribe that institutions calculate their deltas using a methodology specified by the competent authorities.

The competent authorities shall require that the other risks, apart from the dealt risk, associated with options are safeguarded against. The competent authorities may allow the requirement against a written exchange-traded option to be equal to the margin required by the exchange if they are fully satisfied that it provides an accurate measure of the risk associated with the option and that the method used to calculate the margin is equivalent to the method of calculation set out in the remainder of this Annex for such options. In addition they may allow the requirement on a bought exchange-traded or OTC option to be the same as that for the instrument underlying it, subject to the constraint that the resulting requirement does not exceed the market value of the option. The requirement against a written OTC option shall be set in relation to the instrument underlying it.

6 Warrants and covered warrants shall be treated in the same way as options under paragraph 5.

7 Swaps shall be treated for interest-rate risk purposes on the same basis as on-balance-sheet instruments. Thus an interest-rate swap under which an institution receives floating-rate interest and pays fixed-rate interest shall be treated as equivalent to a long position in a floating-rate instrument of maturity equivalent to the period until the next interest fixing and a short position in a fixed-rate instrument with the same maturity as the swap itself.

8 However, institutions which mark to market and manage the interest-rate risk on the derivative instruments covered in paragraphs 4 to 7 on a discounted-cash-flow basis may use sensitivity models to calculate the positions referred to above and may use them for any bond which is amortised over its residual life rather than via one final repayment of principal. Both the model and its use by the institution must be approved by the competent authorities. These models should generate positions which have the same sensitivity to interest-rate changes as the underlying cash flows. This sensitivity must be assessed with reference to independent movements in sample rates across the yield curve, with at least one sensitivity point in each of the maturity bands set out in Table 2 of paragraph 18. The positions shall be included in the calculation of capital requirements according to the provisions laid down in paragraphs 15 to 30.

9 Institutions which do not use models under paragraph 8 may instead, with the approval of the competent authorities, treat as fully offsetting any positions in derivative instruments covered in paragraphs 4 to 7 which meet the following conditions at least:

  (i) the positions are of the same value and denominated in the same currency;
 (ii) the reference rate (for floating-rate positions) or coupon (for fixed-rate positions) is closely matched;
(iii) the next interest-fixing date or, for fixed coupon positions, residual maturity corresponds with the following limits:

 — less than one month hence: same day,
 — between one month and one year hence: within seven days,
 — over one year hence: within 30 days.

10 The transferor of securities or guaranteed rights relating to title to securities in a repurchase agreement and the lender of securities in a securities lending shall include these securities in the calculation of its capital requirement under this Annex provided that such securities meet the criteria laid down in Article 2(6)(a).

11 Positions in units of collective-investment undertakings shall be subject to the capital requirements of Directive 89/647/EEC rather than to position-risk requirements under this Annex.

Specific and general risks

12 The position risk on a traded debt instrument or equity (or debt or equity derivative) shall be divided into two components in order to calculate the capital required against it. The first shall be its specific-risk component – this is the risk of a price change in the instrument concerned due to factors related to its issuer or, in the case of a derivative, the issuer of the underlying instrument. The second component shall cover its general risk – this is the risk of a price change in the instrument due (in the case of a traded debt instrument or debt derivative) to a change in the level of interest rates or (in the case of an equity or equity derivative) to a broad equity-market movement unrelated to any specific attributes of individual securities.

TRADED DEBT INSTRUMENTS

13 The institution shall classify its net positions according to the currency in which they are denominated and shall calculate the capital requirement for general and specific risk in each individual currency separately.

Specific risk

14 The institution shall assign its net positions, as calculated in accordance with paragraph 1, to the appropriate categories in Table 1 on the basis of their residual maturities and then multiply them by the weightings shown. It shall sum its weighted positions (regardless of whether they are long or short) in order to calculate its capital requirement against specific risk.

Table 1

Central government items	Qualifying items			Other items
	Up to 6 months	Over 6 and up to 24 months	Over 24 months	
0,00%	0,25%	1,00%	1,60%	8,00%

General risk

(a) Maturity-based

15 The procedure for calculating capital requirements against general risk involves two basic steps. First, all positions shall be weighted according to maturity (as explained in paragraph 16), in order to compute the amount of capital required against them. Second, allowance shall be made for this requirement to be reduced when a weighted position is held alongside an opposite weighted position within the same maturity band. A reduction in the requirement shall also be allowed when the opposite weighted positions fall into different maturity bands, with the size of this reduction depending both on whether the two positions fall into the same zone, or not, and on the particular zones they fall into. There are three zones (groups of maturity bands) altogether.

16 The institution shall assign its net positions to the appropriate maturity bands in column 2 or 3, as appropriate, in Table 2 appearing in paragraph 18. It shall do so on the basis of residual maturity in the case of fixed-rate instruments and on the basis of the period until the interest rate is next set in the case of instruments on which the interest rate is variable before final maturity. It shall also distinguish between debt instruments with a coupon of 3% or more and those with a coupon of less than 3% and thus allocate them to column 2 or column 3 in Table 2. It shall then multiply each of them by the weighting for the maturity band in question in column 4 in Table 2.

17 It shall then work out the sum of the weighted long positions and the sum of the weighted short positions in each maturity band. The amount of the former which are matched by the latter in a given maturity band shall be the matched weighted position in that band, while the residual long or short position shall be the unmatched weighted position for the same band. The total of the matched weighted positions in all bands shall then be calculated.

18 The institution shall compute the totals of the unmatched weighted long positions for the bands included in each of the zones in Table 2 in order to derive the unmatched weighted long position for each zone. Similarly the sum of the unmatched weighted short positions for each band in a particular zone shall be summed to compute the unmatched weighted short position for that zone. That part of the unmatched weighted long position for a given zone that is matched by the unmatched weighted short position for the same zone shall be the matched weighted position for that zone. That part of the unmatched weighted long or unmatched weighted short position for a zone that cannot be thus matched shall be the unmatched weighted position for that zone.

Table 2

Zone	Maturity band		Weighting (in %)	Assumed interest rate change (in %)
	Coupon of 3% or more	Coupon of less than 3%		
(1)	(2)	(3)	(4)	(5)
One	$0 \leq 1$ month	≤ 1 month	0,00	—
	$> 1 \leq 3$ months	$> 1 \leq 3$ months	0,20	1,00
	$> 3 \leq 6$ months	$> 3 \leq 6$ months	0,40	1,00
	$> 6 \leq 12$ months	$> 6 \leq 12$ months	0,70	1,00
Two	$> 1 \leq 2$ years	$> 1,0 \leq 1,9$ years	1,25	0,90
	$> 2 \leq 3$ years	$> 1,9 \leq 2,8$ years	1,75	0,80
	$> 3 \leq 4$ years	$> 2,8 \leq 3,6$ years	2,25	0,75
Three	$> 4 \leq 5$ years	$> 3,6 \leq 4,3$ years	2,75	0,75
	$> 5 \leq 7$ years	$> 4,3 \leq 5,7$ years	3,25	0,70
	$> 7 \leq 10$ years	$> 5,7 \leq 7,3$ years	3,75	0,65
	$> 10 \leq 15$ years	$> 7,3 \leq 9,3$ years	4,50	0,60
	$> 15 \leq 20$ years	$> 9,3 \leq 10,6$ years	5,25	0,60
	> 20 years	$> 10,6 \leq 12,0$ years	6,00	0,60
		$> 12,0 \leq 20,0$ years	8,00	0,60
		$> 20,0$ years	12,50	0,60

19 The amount of the unmatched weighted long (short) position in zone one which is matched by the unmatched weighted short (long) position in zone two shall then be computed. This shall be referred to in paragraph 23 as the matched weighted position between zones one and two. The same calculation shall then be undertaken with regard to that part of the unmatched weighted position in zone two which is left over and the unmatched weighted position in zone three in order to calculate the matched weighted position between zones two and three.

20 The institution may, if it wishes, reverse the order in paragraph 19 so as to calculate the matched weighted position between zones two and three before working out that between zones one and two.

21 The remainder of the unmatched weighted position in zone one shall then be matched with what remains of that for zone three after the latter's matching with zone two in order to derive the matched weighted position between zones one and three.

22 Residual positions, following the three separate matching calculations in paragraphs 19, 20 and 21, shall be summed.

23 The institution's capital requirement shall be calculated as the sum of:

(a) 10% of the sum of the matched weighted positions in all maturity bands;
(b) 40% of the matched weighted position in zone one;
(c) 30% of the matched weighted position in zone two;
(d) 30% of the matched weighted position in zone three;
(e) 40% of the matched weighted position between zones one and two and between zones two and three (see paragraph 19);
(f) 150% of the matched weighted position between zones one and three;
(g) 100% of the residual unmatched weighted positions.

(b) Duration-based

24 The competent authorities in a Member State may allow institutions in general or on an individual basis to use a system for calculating the capital requirement for the general risk on traded debt instruments which reflects duration instead of the system set out in paragraphs 15 to 23, provided that the institution does so on a consistent basis.

25 Under such a system the institution shall take the market value of each fixed-rate debt instrument and thence calculate its yield to maturity, which is implied discount rate for that instrument. In the case of floating-rate instruments, the institution shall take the market value of each instrument and thence calculate its yield on the assumption that the principal is due when the interest rate can next be changed.

26 The institution shall then calculate the modified duration of each debt instrument on the basis of the following formula:

$$\text{modified duration} = \frac{\text{duration (D)}}{(1 + r)}, \text{ where:}$$

$$D = \frac{\displaystyle\sum_{t=1}^{m} \frac{t\,C_t}{(1 + r)^t}}{\displaystyle\sum_{t=1}^{m} \frac{C_t}{(1 + r)^t}}$$

where—
r = yield to maturity (see paragraph 25),
C_t = cash payment in time t,
m = total maturity (see paragraph 25).

27 The institution shall then allocate each debt instrument to the appropriate zone in Table 3. It shall do so on the basis of the modified duration of each instrument.

Table 3

Zone	Modified duration (in years)	Assumed interest (change in %)
(1)	(2)	(3)
One	$> 0 \leq 1{,}0$	1,0
Two	$> 1{,}0 \leq 3{,}6$	0,85
Three	$> 3{,}6$	0,7

28 The institution shall then calculate the duration-weighted position for each instrument by multiplying its market price by its modified duration and by the assumed interest-rate change for an instrument with that particular modified duration (see column 3 in Table 3).

29 The institution shall work out its duration-weighted long and its duration-weighted short positions within each zone. The amount of the former which are matched by the latter within each zone shall be the matched duration-weighted position for that zone.

The institution shall then calculate the unmatched duration-weighted positions for each zone. It shall then follow the procedures laid down for unmatched weighted positions in paragraphs 19 to 22.

30 The institution's capital requirement shall then be calculated as the sum of:

    (a)   2% of the matched duration-weighted position for each zone;
    (b)   40% of the matched duration-weighted positions between zones one and two and between zones two and three;
    (c)   150% of the matched duration-weighted position between zones one and three;
    (d)   100% of the residual unmatched duration-weighted positions.

EQUITIES

31 The institution shall sum all its net long positions and all its net short positions in accordance with paragraph 1. The sum of the two figures shall be its overall gross position. The difference between them shall be its overall net position.

Specific risk

32 It shall multiply its overall gross position by 4% in order to calculate its capital requirement against specific risk.

33 Notwithstanding paragraph 32, the competent authorities may allow the capital requirement against specific risk to be 2% rather than 4% for those portfolios of equities that an institution holds which meet the following conditions:

    (i)   the equities shall not be those of issuers which have issued traded debt instruments that currently attract an 8% requirement in Table 1 appearing in paragraph 14;
    (ii)   the equities must be adjudged highly liquid by the competent authorities according to objective criteria;
    (iii)   no individual position shall comprise more than 5% of the value of the institution's whole equity portfolio. However, the competent authorities may authorise individual positions of up to 10% provided that the total of such positions does not exceed 50% of the portfolio.

General risk

34 Its capital requirement against general risk shall be its overall net position multiplied by 8%.

Stock-index futures

35 Stock-index futures, the delta-weighted equivalents of options in stock-index futures and stock indices collectively referred to hereafter as 'stock-index futures', may be broken down into positions in each of their constituent equities. These positions may be treated as underlying positions in the equities in question; therefore, subject to the approval of the competent authorities, they may be netted against opposite positions in the underlying equities themselves.

36 The competent authorities shall ensure that any institution which has netted off its positions in one or more of the equities constituting a stock-index future against one or more positions in the stock-index future itself has adequate capital to cover the risk of loss caused by the future's values not moving fully in line with that of its constituent equities; they shall also do this when an institution holds opposite positions in stock-index futures which are not identical in respect of either their maturity or their composition or both.

37 Notwithstanding paragraphs 35 and 36, stock-index futures which are exchange traded and – in the opinion of the competent authorities – represent broadly diversified indices shall attract a capital requirement against general risk of 8%, but no capital requirement against specific risk. Such stock-index futures shall be included in the calculation of the overall net position in paragraph 31, but disregarded in the calculation of the overall gross position in the same paragraph.

38 If a stock-index future is not broken down into its underlying positions, it shall be treated as if it were an individual equity. However, the specific risk on this individual equity can be ignored if the stock-index future in question is exchange traded and, in the opinion of the competent authorities, represents a broadly diversified index.

UNDERWRITING

39 In the case of the underwriting of debt and equity instruments, the competent authorities may allow an institution to use the following procedure in calculating its capital requirements. Firstly, it shall calculate the net positions by deducting the underwriting positions which are subscribed or sub-underwritten by third parties on the basis of formal agreements; secondly, it shall reduce the net positions by the following reduction factors:

— working day 0:	100%
— working day 1:	90%
— working days 2 to 3:	75%
— working day 4:	50%
— working day 5:	25%
— after working day 5:	0%

Working day zero shall be the working day on which the institution becomes unconditionally committed to accepting a known quantity of securities at an agreed price.

Thirdly, it shall calculate its capital requirements using the reduced underwriting positions. The competent authorities shall ensure that the institution holds sufficient capital against the risk of loss which exists between the time of the initial commitment and working day 1. **[1037]**

ANNEX II

SETTLEMENT AND COUNTER-PARTY RISK

SETTLEMENT/DELIVERY RISK

1 In the case of transactions in which debt instruments and equities (excluding repurchase and reverse repurchase agreements and securities lending and securities borrowing) are unsettled after their due delivery dates, an institution must calculate the price difference to which it is exposed. This is the difference between the agreed settlement price for the debt instrument or equity in question and its current market value, where the difference could involve a loss for the institution. It must multiply this difference by the appropriate factor in column A of the table appearing in paragraph 2 in order to calculate its capital requirement.

2 Notwithstanding paragraph 1, an institution may, at the discretion of its competent authorities, calculate its capital requirements by multiplying the agreed settlement price of every transaction which is unsettled between 5 and 45 working days after its due date by the appropriate factor in column B of the table below. As from 46 working days after the due date it shall take the requirement to be 100% of the price difference to which it is exposed as in column A.

Number of working days after due settlement date	*Column A (%)*	*Column B (%)*
5–15	8	0,5
16–30	50	4,0
31–45	75	9,0
46 or more	100	see paragraph 2

COUNTER-PARTY RISK

Free deliveries

3.1 An institution shall be required to hold capital against counter-party risk if—

    (i) it has paid for securities before receiving them or it has delivered securities before receiving payment for them; and

    (ii) in the case of cross-border transactions, one day or more has elapsed since it made that payment or delivery.

3.2 The capital requirement shall be 8% of the value of the securities or cash owed to the institution multiplied by the risk weighting applicable to the relevant counter-party.

Repurchase and reverse repurchase agreements and securities lending and borrowing

4.1 In the case of repurchase agreements and securities lending based on securities included in the trading book the institution shall calculate the difference between the market value of the securities and the amount borrowed by the institution or the market value of the collateral, where that difference is positive. In the case of reverse repurchase agreements and securities borrowing the institution shall calculate the difference between the amount the institution has lent or the market value of the collateral and the market value of the securities it has received, where that difference is positive.

The competent authorities shall take measures to ensure that the excess collateral given is acceptable.

Furthermore, the competent authorities may allow institutions not to include the amount of excess collateral in the calculations described in the first two sentences of this paragraph if the amount of excess collateral is guaranteed in such a way that the transferor is always assured that the excess collateral will be returned to it in the event of defaults of its counter-party. Accrued interest shall be included in calculating the market value of amounts lent or borrowed and collateral.

4.2 The capital requirement shall be 8% of the figure produced in accordance with paragraph 4.1, multiplied by the risk weighting applicable to the relevant counter-party.

OTC derivative instruments

5 In order to calculate the capital requirement on their OTC derivative instruments, institutions shall apply Annex II to Directive 89/647/EEC in the case of interest-rate and exchange-rate contracts; bought OTC equity options and covered warrants shall be subject to the treatment accorded to exchange-rate contracts in Annex II to Directive 89/647/EEC.

The risk weightings to be applied to the relevant counter-parties shall be determined in accordance with Article 2(9) of this Directive.

OTHER

6 The capital requirements of Directive 89/647/EEC shall apply to those exposures in the form of fees, commission, interest, dividends and margin in exchange-traded futures or options contracts which are neither covered in this Annex or Annex I nor deducted from own funds under paragraph 2(d) of Annex V and which are directly related to the items included in the trading book.

The risk weightings to be applied to the relevant counter-parties shall be determined in accordance with Article 2(9) of this Directive.   **[1038]**

ANNEX III

FOREIGN-EXCHANGE RISK

1 If an institution's overall net foreign-exchange position, calculated in accordance with the procedure set out below, exceeds 2% of its total own funds, it shall multiply the excess by 8% in order to calculate its own-funds requirement against foreign-exchange risk.

2 A two-stage calculation shall be used.

3.1 Firstly, the institution's net open position in each currency (including the reporting currency) shall be calculated. This position shall consist of the sum of the following elements (positive or negative)—

— the net spot position (ie all asset items less all liability items, including accrued interest, in the currency in question),
— the net forward position (ie all amounts to be received less all amounts to be paid under forward exchange transactions, including currency futures and the principal on currency swaps not included in the spot position),
— irrevocable guarantees (and similar instruments) that are certain to be called,
— net future income/expenses not yet accrued but already fully hedged (at the discretion of the reporting institution and with the prior consent of the competent authorities, net future income/expenses not yet entered in accounting records but already fully hedged by forward foreign-exchange transactions may be included here). Such discretion must be exercised on a consistent basis,
— the net delta (or delta-based) equivalent of the total book of foreign-currency options,
— the market value of other (ie non-foreign-currency) options,
— any positions which an institution has deliberately taken in order to hedge against the adverse effect of the exchange rate on its capital ratio may be excluded from the calculation of net open currency positions. Such positions should be of a non-trading or structural nature and their exclusion, and any variation of the terms of their exclusion, shall require the consent of the competent authorities. The same treatment subject to the same conditions as above may be applied to positions which an institution has which relate to items that are already deducted in the calculation of own funds.

3.2 The competent authorities shall have the discretion to allow institutions to use the net present value when calculating the net open position in each currency.

4 Secondly, net short and long positions in each currency other than the reporting currency shall be converted at spot rates into the reporting currency. They shall then be summed separately to form the total of the net short positions and the total of the net long positions respectively. The higher of these two totals shall be the institution's overall net foreign-exchange position.

5 Notwithstanding paragraphs 1 to 4 and pending further coordination, the competent authorities may prescribe or allow institutions to use alternative procedures for the purposes of this Annex.

6 Firstly, the competent authorities may allow institutions to provide lower capital requirements against positions in closely correlated currencies than those which would result from applying paragraphs 1 to 4 to them. The competent authorities may deem a pair of currencies to be closely correlated only if the likelihood of a loss – calculated on the basis of daily exchange-rate data for the preceding three or five years – occurring on equal and opposite positions in such currencies over the following 10 working days, which is 4% or less of the value of the matched position in question (valued in terms of the reporting currency) has a probability of at least 99%, when an observation period of three years is used, or 95%, when an observation period of five years is used. The own-funds requirement on the matched position in two closely correlated currencies shall be 4% multiplied by the value of the matched position. The capital requirement on unmatched positions in closely correlated currencies, and all positions in other currencies, shall be 8%, multiplied by the higher of the sum of the net short or the net long positions in those currencies after the removal of matched positions in closely correlated currencies.

7 Secondly, the competent authorities may allow institutions to apply an alternative method to those outlined in paragraphs 1 to 6 for the purposes of this Annex. The capital requirement produced by this method must be sufficient—

    (i) to exceed the losses, if any, that would have occurred in at least 95% of the rolling 10-working-day periods over the preceding five years, or, alternatively, in at least 99% of the rolling 10-working-day periods over the preceding three years, had the institution begun each such period with its current positions;

    (ii) on the basis of an analysis of exchange-rate movements during all the rolling 10-working-day periods over the preceding five years, to exceed the likely loss over the following 10-working-day holding period 95% or more of the time, or, alternatively, to exceed the likely loss 99% or more of the time where the analysis of exchange-rate movements covers only the preceding three years; or

    (iii) irrespective of the size of (i) or (ii) to exceed 2% of the net open position as measured in paragraph 4.

8 Thirdly, the competent authorities may allow institutions to remove positions in any currency which is subject to a legally binding intergovernmental agreement to limit its variation relative to other currencies covered by the same agreement from whichever of the methods described in paragraphs 1 to 7 that they apply. Institutions shall calculate their matched positions in such currencies and subject them to a capital requirement no lower than half of the maximum permissible variation laid down in the intergovernmental agreement in question in respect of the currencies concerned. Unmatched positions in those currencies shall be treated in the same way as other currencies.

Notwithstanding the first paragraph, the competent authorities may allow the capital requirement on the matched positions in currencies of Member States participating in the second stage of the European monetary union to be 1,6%, multiplied by the value of such matched positions.

9 The competent authorities shall notify the Council and Commission of the methods, if any, that they are prescribing or allowing in respect of paragraphs 6 to 8.

10 The Commission shall report to the Council on the methods referred to in paragraph 9 and, where necessary and with due regard to international developments, shall propose a more harmonised treatment of foreign-exchange risk.

11 Net positions in composite currencies may be broken down into the component currencies according to the quotas in force. **[1038]**

ANNEX IV

OTHER RISKS

Investment firms shall be required to hold own funds equivalent to one quarter of their preceding year's fixed overheads. The competent authorities may adjust that requirement in the event of a material change in a firm's business since the preceding year. Where a firm has not completed a year's business, including the day it starts up, the requirement shall be a quarter of the fixed overheads figure projected in its business plan unless an adjustment to that plan is required by the authorities. **[1039]**

ANNEX V

OWN FUNDS

1 The own funds of investment firms and credit institutions shall be defined in accordance with Directive 89/299/EEC.

For the purposes of this Directive, however, investment firms which do not have one of the legal forms referred to in Article 1(1) of the Fourth Council Directive 78/660/EEC of 25 July 1978 based on Article 54(3)(g) of the Treaty on the annual accounts of certain types of companies[1] shall nevertheless be deemed to fall within the scope of Council Directive 86/635/EEC of 8 December 1986 on the annual accounts and consolidated accounts of banks and other financial institutions[2].

2 Notwithstanding paragraph 1, the competent authorities may permit those institutions which are obliged to meet the own-funds requirements laid down in Annexes I, II, III, IV and VI to use an alternative definition when meeting those requirements. No part of the own funds thus provided may be used simultaneously to meet other own-funds requirements. This alternative definition shall include the following items (a), (b) and (c) less item (d), the deduction of that item being left to the discretion of the competent authorities—

(a) own funds as defined in Directive 89/299/EEC excluding only items (12) and (13) of Article 2(1) of the same Directive for those investment firms which are required to deduct item (d) of this paragraph from the total of items (a), (b) and (c) of this paragraph;

(b) an institution's net trading-book profits net of any foreseeable charges or dividends, less net losses on its other business provided that none of those amounts has already been included in item (a) of this paragraph under item 2 or 11 of Article 2(1) of Directive 89/299/EEC;

(c) subordinated loan capital and/or the items referred to in paragraph 5, subject to the conditions set out in paragraphs 3 to 7;

(d) illiquid assets as defined in paragraph 8.

3 The subordinated loan capital referred to in paragraph 2(c) shall have an initial maturity of at least two years. It shall be fully paid up and the loan agreement shall not include any clause providing that in specified circumstances other than the winding up of the institution the debt will become repayable before the agreed repayment date, unless the competent authorities approve the repayment. Neither the principal nor the interest on such subordinated loan capital may be repaid if such repayment would mean that the own funds of the institution in question would then amount to less than 100% of the institution's overall requirements.

In addition, an institution shall notify the competent authorities of all repayments on such subordinated loan capital as soon as its own funds fall below 120% of its overall requirements.

4 The subordinated loan capital referred to in paragraph 2(c) may not exceed a maximum of 150% of the original own funds left to meet the requirements laid down in Annexes I, II, III, IV and VI and may approach that maximum only in particular circumstances acceptable to the relevant authorities.

5 The competent authorities may permit institutions to replace the subordinated loan capital referred to in paragraphs 3 and 4 with items 3 and 5 to 8 of Article 2(1) of Directive 89/299/EEC.

6 The competent authorities may permit investment firms to exceed the ceiling for subordinated loan capital prescribed in paragraph 4 if they judge it prudentially adequate and provided that the total of such subordinated loan capital and the items referred to in paragraph 5 does not exceed 200% of the original own funds left to meet the requirements imposed in Annexes I, II, III, IV and VI, or 250% of the same amount where investment firms deduct item 2(d) referred to in paragraph 2 when calculating own funds.

7 The competent authorities may permit the ceiling for subordinated loan capital prescribed in paragraph 4 to be exceeded by a credit institution if they judge it prudentially adequate and provided that the total of such subordinated loan capital and the items referred to in paragraph 5 does not exceed 250% of the original own funds left to meet the requirements imposed in Annexes I, II, III and VI.

8 Illiquid assets include:

— tangible fixed assets (except to the extent that land and buildings may be allowed to count against the loans which they are securing),

— holdings in, including subordinated claims on, credit or financial institutions which may be included in the own funds of such institutions, unless they have been deducted under items 12 and 13 of Article 2(1) of Directive 89/299/EEC or under paragraph 9(iv) of this Annex.

Where shares in a credit or financial institution are held temporarily for the purpose of a financial assistance operation designed to reorganise and save that institution, the competent authorities may waive this provision. They may also waive it in respect of those shares which are included in the investment firm's trading book,

— holdings and other investments, in undertakings other than credit institutions and other financial institutions, which are not readily marketable,

— deficiencies in subsidiaries,

— deposits made, other than those which are available for repayment within 90 days, and also excluding payments in connection with margined futures or options contracts,

— loans and other amounts due, other than those due to be repaid within 90 days,
— physical stocks, unless they are subject to the capital requirements imposed in Article 4(2) and provided that such requirements are not less stringent than those imposed in Article 4(1)(iii).

9 Those investment firms included in a group subject to the waiver described in Article 7(4) shall calculate their own funds in accordance with paragraphs 1 to 8 subject to the following modifications—

(i) the illiquid assets referred to in paragraph 2(d) shall be deducted;
(ii) the exclusion referred to in paragraph 2(a) shall not cover those components of items 12 and 13 of Article 2(1) of Directive 89/299/EEC which an investment firm holds in respect of undertakings included in the scope of consolidation as defined in Article 7(2) of this Directive;
(iii) the limits referred to in Article 6(1)(a) and (b) of Directive 89/299/EEC shall be calculated with reference to the original own funds less those components of items 12 and 13 of Article 2(1) of Directive 89/299/EEC described in (ii) which are elements of the original own funds of the undertakings in question;
(iv) those components of items 12 and 13 of Article 2(1) of Directive 89/299/EEC referred to in (iii) shall be deducted from the original own funds rather than from the total of all items as prescribed in Article 6(1)(c) of the same Directive for the purposes, in particular, of paragraphs 4 to 7 of this Annex. **[1040]**

NOTES
[1] OJ L 222, 14.8.1978, p 11. Directive as last amended by Directive (90/605/EEC) OJ L 317, 16.11.1990, p 60.
[2] OJ L 372, 31.12.86, p 1.

ANNEX VI

LARGE EXPOSURES

1 Institutions referred to in Article 5(2) shall monitor and control their exposures to individual clients and groups of connected clients as defined in Directive 92/121/EEC, subject to the following modifications.

2 The exposures to individual clients which arise on the trading book shall be calculated by summing the following items (i), (ii) and (iii):

(i) the excess – where positive – of an institution's long positions over its short positions in all the financial instruments issued by the client in question (the net position in each of the different instruments being calculated according to the methods laid down in Annex I);
(ii) in the case of the underwriting of a debt or an equity instrument, the institution's exposure shall be its net exposure (which is calculated by deducting those underwriting positions which are subscribed or sub-underwritten by third parties on the basis of a formal agreement) reduced by the factors set out in paragraph 39 of Annex I.
Pending further coordination, the competent authorities shall require institutions to set up systems to monitor and control their underwriting exposures between the time of the initial commitment and working day one in the light of the nature of the risks incurred in the markets in question;
(iii) the exposures due to the transactions, agreements and contracts referred to in Annex II with the client in question, such exposures being calculated in the manner laid down in that Annex, without application of the weightings for counter-party risk.

3 Thereafter, the exposures to groups of connected clients on the trading book shall be calculated by summing the exposures to individual clients in a group, as calculated in paragraph 2.

4 The overall exposures to individual clients or groups of connected clients shall be calculated by summing the exposures which arise on the trading book and the exposures which arise on the non-trading book, taking into account Article 4(6) to (12) of Directive 92/121/EEC. In order to calculate the exposure on the non-trading book, institutions shall take the exposure arising from assets which are deducted from their own funds by virtue of paragraph 2(d) of Annex V to be zero.

5 Institutions' overall exposures to individual clients and groups of connected clients calculated in accordance with paragraph 4 shall be reported in accordance with Article 3 of Directive 92/121/EEC.

6 That sum of the exposures to an individual client or group of connected clients shall be limited in accordance with Article 4 of Directive 92/121/EEC subject to the transitional provisions of Article 6 of the same Directive.

7 Notwithstanding paragraph 6 the competent authorities may allow assets constituting claims and other exposures on investment firms, on recognised third-country investment firms and recognised clearing houses and exchanges in financial instruments to be subject to the same treatment accorded to those on credit institutions in Article 4(7)(i), (9) and (10) of Directive 92/121/EEC.

8 The competent authorities may authorise the limits laid down in Article 4 of Directive 92/121/EEC to be exceeded subject to the following conditions being met simultaneously—

    1 the exposure on the non-trading book to the client or group of clients in question does not exceed the limits laid down in Directive 92/121/EEC, calculated with reference to own funds as defined in Directive 89/299/EEC, so that the excess arises entirely on the trading book;

    2 the firm meets an additional capital requirement on the excess in respect of the limits laid down in Article 4(1) and (2) of Directive 92/121/EEC. This shall be calculated by selecting those components of the total trading exposure to the client or group of clients in question which attract the highest specific-risk requirements in Annex I and/or requirements in Annex II, the sum of which equals the amount of the excess referred to in 1; where the excess has not persisted for more than 10 days, the additional capital requirement shall be 200% of the requirements referred to in the previous sentence, on these components.

      As from 10 days after the excess has occurred, the components of the excess, selected in accordance with the above criteria, shall be allocated to the appropriate line in column 1 of the table below in ascending order of specific-risk requirements in Annex I and/or requirements in Annex II. The institution shall then meet an additional capital requirement equal to the sum of the specific-risk requirements in Annex I and/or the Annex II requirements on these components multiplied by the corresponding factor in column 2;

Table

Excess over the limits (on the basis of a percentage of own funds)	Factors
(1)	(2)
Up to 40%	200%
From 40% to 60%	300%
From 60% to 80%	400%
From 80% to 100%	500%
From 100% to 250%	600%
Over 250%	900%

    3 where 10 days or less has elapsed since the excess occurred, the trading-book exposure to the client or group of connected clients in question must not exceed 500% of the institution's own funds;

    4 any excesses which have persisted for more than 10 days must not, in aggregate, exceed 600% of the institution's own funds;

    5 institutions must report to the competent authorities every three months all cases where the limits laid down in Article 4(1) and (2) of Directive 92/121/EEC have been exceeded during the preceding three months. In each case in which the limits have been exceeded the amount of the excess and the name of the client concerned must be reported.

9 The competent authorities shall establish procedures, of which they shall notify the Council and the Commission, to prevent institutions from deliberately avoiding the additional capital requirements that they would otherwise incur on exposures exceeding the limits laid down in Article 4(1) and (2) of Directive 92/121/EEC once those exposures have been maintained for more than 10 days, by means of temporarily transferring the exposures in question to another company, whether within the same group or not, and/or by undertaking artificial transactions to close out the exposure during the 10-day period and create a new exposure. Institutions shall maintain systems which ensure that any transfer which has this effect is immediately reported to the competent authorities.

10 The competent authorities may permit those institutions which are allowed to use the alternative definition of own funds under paragraph 2 of Annex V to use that definition for the purposes of paragraphs 5, 6 and 8 of this Annex provided that the institutions concerned are required, in addition, to meet all of the obligations set out in Articles 3 and 4 of Directive 92/121/EEC, in respect of the exposures which arise outside their trading books by using own funds as defined in Directive 89/299/EEC.

COMMISSION DIRECTIVE
of 15 March 1994

adapting Council Directive 89/647/EEC on a solvency ratio for credit institutions as regards the technical definition of 'multilateral development banks'

(94/7/EC)

NOTES
Date of publication in OJ: OJ L89, 6.4.1994, p 17.

THE COMMISSION OF THE EUROPEAN COMMUNITIES

Having regard to the Treaty establishing the European Community,

Having regard to Council Directive 89/647/EEC of 18 December 1989 on a solvency ratio for credit institutions[1], as amended by Directive 92/30/EEC[2], and in particular Article 9 thereof,

Whereas the Commission has submitted to the Council a proposal for amending the Protocol on the Statute of the European Investment Bank (EIB) empowering the Board of Governors of the EIB to establish a European Investment Fund (EIF);

Whereas the seventh indent of Article 2(1) of Directive 89/647/EEC defines 'multilateral development banks' in an enumerate manner;

Whereas the European Investment Fund embodies the same main characteristics as the said multilateral development banks; whereas this new multilateral financial institution is European in its basic character and in its membership; whereas it constitutes a new and unique structure of cooperation in Europe in order to contribute to the strengthening of the internal market, the promotion of economic recovery in Europe, and the furthering of economic and social cohesion; whereas for these reasons, the European Investment Fund should be included in the definition of multilateral development banks in Directive 89/647/EEC;

Whereas the provisions of this Directive are in accordance with the opinion of the Banking Advisory Committee acting as the committee which is to assist the Commission in accordance with the procedure laid down in Article 9(2) of Directive 89/647/EEC;

Whereas this Directive is relevant for the European Economic Area (EEA) and the procedure laid down in Article 99 of the Agreement on the European Economic Area has been followed.

NOTES
[1] OJ L 386, 30.12.1989, p 14.
[2] OJ L 110, 28.4.1992, p 52.

HAS ADOPTED THIS DIRECTIVE:

Article 1

The definition of 'multilateral development banks' in the seventh indent of Article 2(1) of Directive 89/647/EEC shall include the European Investment Fund.   **[1042]**

Article 2

1 Member States shall adopt the measures necessary for them to comply with the provisions of this Directive within six months of the date of the decision of the Board of Governors of the European Investment Bank establishing the European Investment Fund.

When Member States adopt these measures, these shall contain a reference to this Directive or shall be accompanied by such reference at the time of their official publication. The procedure for such reference shall be adopted by Member States.

2 Member States shall communicate to the Commission the texts of the main laws, regulations and administrative provisions which they adopt in the field covered by this Directive. **[1043]**

Article 3

This Directive shall enter into force on the 20th day following its publication in the *Official Journal of the European Communities*. **[1044]**

Done at Brussels, 15 March 1994.

COUNCIL AND EUROPEAN PARLIAMENT DIRECTIVE
of 30 May 1994

on deposit-guarantee schemes

(94/19/EC)

NOTES
Date of publication in OJ: OJ L135, 31.5.1994, p 5.

THE EUROPEAN PARLIAMENT AND THE COUNCIL OF THE EUROPEAN UNION,

Having regard to the Treaty establishing the European Community, and in particular the first and third sentences of Article 57(2) thereof,

Having regard to the proposal from the Commission[1],

Having regard to the opinion of the Economic and Social Committee[2],

Acting in accordance with the procedure referred to in Article 189b of the Treaty[3],

Whereas, in accordance with the objectives of the Treaty, the harmonious development of the activities of credit institutions throughout the Community should be promoted through the elimination of all restrictions on the right of establishment and the freedom to provide services, while increasing the stability of the banking system and protection for savers;

Whereas, when restrictions on the activities of credit institutions are eliminated, consideration should be given to the situation which might arise if deposits in a credit institution that has branches in other Member States become unavailable; whereas it is indispensable to ensure a harmonised minimum level of deposit protection wherever deposits are located in the Community; whereas such deposit protection is as essential as the prudential rules for the completion of the single banking market;

Whereas in the event of the closure of an insolvent credit institution the depositors at any branches situated in a Member State other than that in which the credit institution has its head office must be protected by the same guarantee scheme as the institution's other depositors;

Whereas the cost to credit institutions of participating in a guarantee scheme bears no relation to the cost that would result from a massive withdrawal of bank deposits not only from a credit institution in difficulties but also from healthy institutions following a loss of depositor confidence in the soundness of the banking system;

Whereas the action the Member States have taken in response to Commission recommendation 87/63/EEC of 22 December 1986 concerning the introduction of deposit-guarantee schemes in the Community[4] has not fully achieved the desired result; whereas that situation may prove prejudicial to the proper functioning of the internal market;

Whereas the Second Council Directive 89/646/EEC of 15 December 1989 on the coordination of laws, regulations and administrative provisions relating to the taking up and pursuit of the business of credit institutions and amending Directive 77/780/EEC[5], provides for a system for the single authorisation of each credit institution and its supervision by the authorities of its home Member State, which entered into force on 1 January 1993;

Whereas a branch no longer requires authorisation in any host Member State, because the single authorisation is valid throughout the Community, and its solvency will be monitored by the competent authorities of its home Member State; whereas that situation justifies covering all the branches of the same credit institution set up in the Community by means of a single guarantee scheme; whereas that scheme can only be that which exists for that category of institution in the State in which that institution's head office is situated, in particular because of the link which exists between the supervision of a branch's solvency and its membership of a deposit-guarantee scheme;

Whereas harmonisation must be confined to the main elements of deposit-guarantee schemes and, within a very short period, ensure payments under a guarantee calculated on the basis of a harmonised minimum level;

Whereas deposit-guarantee schemes must intervene as soon as deposits become unavailable;

Whereas it is appropriate to exclude from cover, in particular, the deposits made by credit institutions on their own behalf and for own account; whereas that should not prejudice the right of a guarantee scheme to take any measures necessary for the rescue of a credit institution that finds itself in difficulties;

Whereas the harmonisation of deposit-guarantee schemes within the Community does not of itself call into question the existence of systems in operation designed to protect credit institutions, in particular by ensuring their solvency and liquidity, so that deposits with such credit institutions, including their branches established in other Member States, will not become unavailable; whereas such alternative systems serving a different protective purpose may, subject to certain conditions, be deemed by the competent authorities to satisfy the objectives of this Directive; whereas it will be for those competent authorities to verify compliance with those conditions;

Whereas several Member States have deposit-protection schemes under the responsibility of professional organisations, other Member States have schemes set up and regulated on a statutory basis and some schemes, although set up on a contractual basis, are partly regulated by statute; whereas that variety of status poses a problem only with regard to compulsory membership of and exclusion from schemes; whereas it is therefore necessary to take steps to limit the powers of schemes in this area;

Whereas the retention in the Community of schemes providing cover for deposits which is higher than the harmonised minimum may, within the same territory, lead to disparities in compensation and unequal conditions of competition between national institutions and branches of institutions from other Member States; whereas, in order to counteract those disadvantages, branches should be authorised to join their host countries' schemes so that they can offer their depositors the same guarantees as are offered by the schemes of the countries in which they are located; whereas it is appropriate that after a number of years the Commission should report on the extent to which branches have made use of this option and on the difficulties which they or the guarantee schemes may have encountered in implementing these provisions; whereas it is not ruled out that home Member State schemes should themselves offer such complementary cover, subject to the conditions such schemes may lay down;

Whereas market disturbances could be caused by branches of credit institutions which offer levels of cover higher than those offered by credit institutions authorised in their host Member States; whereas it is not appropriate that the level of scope of cover offered by guarantee schemes should become an instrument of competition; whereas it is therefore necessary, at least during an initial period, to stipulate that the level and scope of cover offered by a home Member State scheme to depositors at branches located in another Member State should not exceed the maximum level and scope offered by the corresponding scheme in the host Member State; whereas possible market disturbances should be reviewed after a number of years, on the basis of the experience acquired and in the light of developments in the banking sector;

Whereas in principle this Directive requires every credit institution to join a deposit-guarantee scheme; whereas the Directives governing the admission of any credit institution which has its head office in a non-member country, and in particular the First Council Directive (77/780/EEC) of 12 December 1977 on the coordination of the laws, regulations and administrative provisions relating to the taking up and pursuit of the business of credit institutions[6] allow Member States to decide whether and subject to what conditions to permit the branches of such credit institutions to operate within their territories; whereas such branches will not enjoy the freedom to provide services under the second paragraph of Article 59 of the Treaty, nor the right of establishment in Member States other than those in which they are established; whereas, accordingly, a Member State admitting such branches should decide how to apply the principles of this Directive to such branches in accordance with Article 9(1) of Directive 77/780/EEC and with the need to protect depositors and maintain the integrity of the financial system; whereas it is essential that depositors at such branches should be fully aware of the guarantee arrangements which affect them;

Whereas, on the one hand, the minimum guarantee level prescribed in this Directive should not leave too great a proportion of deposits without protection in the interest both of consumer protection and of the stability of the financial system; whereas, on the other hand, it would not be appropriate to impose throughout the Community a level of protection which might in certain cases have the effect of encouraging the unsound management of credit institutions; whereas the cost of funding schemes should be taken into account; whereas it would appear reasonable to set the harmonised minimum guarantee level at ECU 20 000; whereas limited transitional arrangements might be necessary to enable schemes to comply with that figure;

Whereas some Member States offer depositors cover for their deposits which is higher than the harmonised minimum guarantee level provided for in this Directive; whereas it does not seem appropriate to require that such schemes, certain of which have been introduced only recently pursuant to recommendation 87/63/EEC, be amended on this point;

Whereas a Member State must be able to exclude certain categories of specifically listed deposits or depositors, if it does not consider that they need special protection, from the guarantee afforded by deposit-guarantee schemes;

Whereas in certain Member States, in order to encourage depositors to look carefully at the quality of credit institutions, unavailable deposits are not fully reimbursed; whereas such practices should be limited in respect of deposits falling below the minimum harmonised level;

Whereas the principle of a harmonised minimum limit per depositor rather than per deposit has been retained; whereas it is therefore appropriate to take into consideration the deposits made by depositors who either are not mentioned as holders of an account or are not the sole holders; whereas the limit must therefore be applied to each identifiable depositor; whereas that should not apply to collective investment undertakings subject to special protection rules which do not apply to the aforementioned deposits;

Whereas information is an essential element in depositor protection and must therefore also be the subject of a minimum number of binding provisions; whereas, however, the unregulated use in advertising of references to the amount and scope of a deposit-guarantee scheme could affect the stability of the banking system or depositor confidence; whereas Member States should therefore lay down rules to limit such references;

Whereas, in specific cases, in certain Member States in which there are no deposit-guarantee schemes for certain classes of credit institutions which take only an extremely small proportion of deposits, the introduction of such a system may in some cases take longer than the time laid down for the transposition of this Directive; whereas in such cases a transitional derogation from the requirement to belong to a deposit-guarantee scheme may be justified; whereas, however, should such credit institutions operate abroad, a Member State would be entitled to require their participation in a deposit-guarantee scheme which it had set up;

Whereas it is not indispensable, in this Directive, to harmonise the methods of financing schemes guaranteeing deposits or credit institutions themselves, given, on the one hand, that the cost of financing such schemes must be borne, in principle, by credit institutions themselves and, on the other hand, that the financing capacity of such schemes must be in proportion to their liabilities; whereas this must not, however, jeopardise the stability of the banking system of the Member State concerned;

Whereas this Directive may not result in the Member States' or their competent authorities' being made liable in respect of depositors if they have ensured that one or more schemes guaranteeing deposits or credit institutions themselves and ensuring the compensation or protection of depositors under the conditions prescribed in this Directive have been introduced and officially recognised;

Whereas deposit protection is an essential element in the completion of the internal market and an indispensable supplement to the system of supervision of credit institutions on account of the solidarity it creates amongst all the institutions in a given financial market in the event of the failure of any of them,

NOTES

[1] OJ C 163, 30.6.1992, p 6 and OJ C 178, 30.6.1993, p 14.
[2] OJ C 332, 16.12.1992, p 13.
[3] OJ C 115, 26.4.1993, p 96 and Decision of the European Parliament of 9 March 1994 (OJ C 91, 28.3.1994).
[4] OJ L 33, 4.2.1987, p 16.
[5] OJ L 386, 30.12.1989, p 1. Directive as amended by Directive 92/30/EEC (OJ L 110, 28.4.1992, p 52).
[6] OJ L 322, 17.12.1977, p 30. Directive as last amended by Directive 89/646/EEC (OJ L 386, 30.12.1989, p 1).

HAS ADOPTED THIS DIRECTIVE:

Article 1

For the purposes of this Directive:

1 *'deposit'* shall mean any credit balance which results from funds left in an account or from temporary situations deriving from normal banking transactions and which a credit institution must repay under the legal and contractual conditions applicable, and any debt evidenced by a certificate issued by a credit institution.

Shares in United Kingdom and Irish building societies apart from those of a capital nature covered in Article 2 shall be treated as deposits.

Bonds which satisfy the conditions prescribed in Article 22(4) of Council Directive 85/611/EEC of 20 December 1985 on the co-ordination of laws, regulations and administrative provisions relating to undertakings for collective investment in transferable securities (Ucits)[1] shall not be considered deposits.

For the purpose of calculating a credit balance, Member States shall apply the rules and regulations relating to set-off and counterclaims according to the legal and contractual conditions applicable to a deposit;

2 *'joint account'* shall mean an account opened in the names of two or more persons or over which two or more persons have rights that may operate against the signature of one or more of those persons;

3 *'unavailable deposit'* shall mean a deposit that is due and payable but has not been paid by a credit institution under the legal and contractual conditions applicable thereto, where either:

> (i) the relevant competent authorities have determined that in their view the credit institution concerned appears to be unable for the time being, for reasons which are directly related to its financial circumstances, to repay the deposit and to have no current prospect of being able to do so.
>
> > The competent authorities shall make that determination as soon as possible and at the latest 21 days after first becoming satisfied that a credit institution has failed to repay deposits which are due and payable; or
>
> (ii) a judicial authority has made a ruling for reasons which are directly related to the credit institution's financial circumstances which has the effect of suspending depositors' ability to make claims against it, should that occur before the aforementioned determination has been made;

4 *'credit institution'* shall mean an undertaking the business of which is to receive deposits or other repayable funds from the public and to grant credits for its own account;

5 *'branch'* shall mean a place of business which forms a legally dependent part of a credit institution and which conducts directly all or some of the operations inherent in the business of credit institutions; any number of branches set up in the same Member State by a credit institution which has its head office in another Member State shall be regarded as a single branch.   **[1045]**

NOTES
[1] OJ L 375, 31.12.1985, p 3. Directive as last amended by Directive 88/220/EEC (OJ L 100, 19.4.1988, p 31).

Article 2

The following shall be excluded from any repayment by guarantee schemes—

— subject to Article 8(3), deposits made by other credit institutions on their own behalf and for their own account,

— all instruments which would fall within the definition of 'own funds' in Article 2 of Council Directive 89/299/EEC of 17 April 1989 on the own funds of credit institutions[1],

— deposits arising out of transactions in connection with which there has been a criminal conviction for money laundering as defined in Article 1 of Council Directive 91/308/EEC of 10 June 1991 on prevention of the use of the financial system for the purpose of money laundering[2].

[1046]

NOTES
[1] OJ L 124, 5.5.1989, p 16. Directive is last amended by Directive 92/16/EEC (OJ L 75, 21.3.1992, p 48).
[2] OJ No L 166, 28.6.1991, p 77.

Article 3

1 Each Member State shall ensure that within its territory one or more deposit-guarantee schemes are introduced and officially recognised. Except in the circumstances envisaged in the second subparagraph and in paragraph 4, no credit institution authorised in that Member State pursuant to Article 3 of Directive 77/780/EEC may take deposits unless it is a member of such a scheme.

A Member State may, however, exempt a credit institution from the obligation to belong to a deposit-guarantee scheme where that credit institution belongs to a system which protects the credit institution itself and in particular ensures its liquidity and solvency, thus guaranteeing protection for depositors at least equivalent to that provided by a deposit-guarantee scheme, and which, in the opinion of the competent authorities, fulfils the following conditions:

— the system must be in existence and have been officially recognised when this Directive is adopted,
— the system must be designed to prevent deposits with credit institutions belonging to the system from becoming unavailable and have the resources necessary for that purpose at its disposal,
— the system must not consist of a guarantee granted to a credit institution by a Member State itself or by any of its local or regional authorities,
— the system must ensure that depositors are informed in accordance with the terms and conditions laid down in Article 9.

Those Member States which make use of this option shall inform the Commission accordingly; in particular, they shall notify the Commission of the characteristics of any such protective systems and the credit institutions covered by them and of any subsequent changes in the information supplied. The Commission shall inform the Banking Advisory Committee thereof.

2 If a credit institution does not comply with the obligations incumbent on it as a member of a deposit-guarantee scheme, the competent authorities which issued its authorisation shall be notified and, in collaboration with the guarantee scheme, shall take all appropriate measures including the imposition of sanctions to ensure that the credit institution complies with its obligations.

3 If those measures fail to secure compliance on the part of the credit institution, the scheme may, where national law permits the exclusion of a member, with the express consent of the competent authorities, give not less than 12 months' notice of its intention of excluding the credit institution from membership of the scheme. Deposits made before the expiry of the notice period shall continue to be fully covered by the scheme. If, on the expiry of the notice period, the credit institution has not complied with its obligations, the guarantee scheme may, again having obtained the express consent of the competent authorities, proceed to exclusion.

4 Where national law permits, and with the express consent of the competent authorities which issued its authorisation, a credit institution excluded from a deposit-guarantee scheme may continue to take deposits if, before its exclusion, it has made alternative guarantee arrangements which ensure that depositors will enjoy a level and scope of protection at least equivalent to that offered by the officially recognised scheme.

5 If a credit institution the exclusion of which is proposed under paragraph 3 is unable to make alternative arrangements which comply with the conditions prescribed in paragraph 4, then the competent authorities which issued its authorisation shall revoke it forthwith.   **[1047]**

Article 4

1 Deposit-guarantee schemes introduced and officially recognised in a Member State in accordance with Article 3(1) shall cover the depositors at branches set up by credit institutions in other Member States.

Until 31 December 1999 neither the level nor the scope, including the percentage, of cover provided shall exceed the maximum level or scope of cover offered by the corresponding guarantee scheme within the territory of the host Member State.

Before that date, the Commission shall draw up a report on the basis of the experience acquired in applying the second subparagraph and shall consider the need to continue those arrangements. If appropriate, the Commission shall submit a proposal for a Directive to the European Parliament and the Council, with a view to the extension of their validity.

2 Where the level and/or scope, including the percentage, of cover offered by the host Member State guarantee scheme exceeds the level and/or scope of cover provided in the Member State in which a credit institution is authorised, the host Member State shall ensure that there is an officially recognised deposit-guarantee scheme within its territory which a branch may join voluntarily in order to supplement the guarantee which its depositors already enjoy by virtue of its membership of its home Member State scheme.

The scheme to be joined by the branch shall cover the category of institution to which it belongs or most closely corresponds in the host Member State.

3 Member States shall ensure that objective and generally applied conditions are established for branches' membership of a host Member State's scheme in accordance with paragraph 2. Admission shall be conditional on fulfilment of the relevant obligations of membership, including in particular payment of any contributions and other charges. Member States shall follow the guiding principles set out in Annex II in implementing this paragraph.

4 If a branch granted voluntary membership under paragraph 2 does not comply with the obligations incumbent on it as a member of a deposit-guarantee scheme, the competent authorities which issued the authorisation shall be notified and, in collaboration with the guarantee scheme, shall take all appropriate measures to ensure that the aforementioned obligations are complied with.

If those measures fail to secure the branch's compliance with the aforementioned obligations, after an appropriate period of notice of not less than 12 months the guarantee scheme may, with the consent of the competent authorities which issued the authorisation, exclude the branch. Deposits made before the date of exclusion shall continue to be covered by the voluntary scheme until the dates on which they fall due. Depositors shall be informed of the withdrawal of the supplementary cover.

5 The Commission shall report on the operation of paragraphs 2, 3 and 4 no later than 31 December 1999 and shall, if appropriate, propose amendments thereto.   **[1048]**

Article 5

Deposits held when the authorisation of a credit institution authorised pursuant to Article 3 of Directive 77/780/EEC is withdrawn shall continue to be covered by the guarantee scheme.   **[1049]**

Article 6

1 Member States shall check that branches established by a credit institution which has its head office outwith the Community have cover equivalent to that prescribed in this Directive.

Failing that, Member States may, subject to Article 9(1) of Directive 77/780/EEC, stipulate that branches established by a credit institution which has its head office outwith the Community must join deposit-guarantee schemes in operation within their territories.

2 Actual and intending depositors at branches established by a credit institution which has its head office outwith the Community shall be provided by the credit institution with all relevant information concerning the guarantee arrangements which cover their deposits.

3 The information referred to in paragraph 2 shall be made available in the official language or languages of the Member State in which a branch is established in the manner prescribed by national law and shall be drafted in a clear and comprehensible form.   **[1050]**

Article 7

1 Deposit-guarantee schemes shall stipulate that the aggregate deposits of each depositor must be covered up to ECU 20,000 in the event of deposits' being unavailable.

Until 31 December 1999 Member States in which, when this Directive is adopted, deposits are not covered up to ECU 20,000 may retain the maximum amount laid down in their guarantee schemes, provided that this amount is not less than ECU 15,000.

2 Member States may provide that certain depositors or deposits shall be excluded from guarantee or shall be granted a lower level of guarantee. Those exclusions are listed in Annex I.

3 This Article shall not preclude the retention or adoption of provisions which offer a higher or more comprehensive cover for deposits. In particular, deposit-guarantee schemes may, on social considerations, cover certain kinds of deposits in full.

4 Member States may limit the guarantee provided for in paragraph 1 or that referred to in paragraph 3 to a specified percentage of deposits. The percentage guaranteed must, however, be equal to or exceed 90% of aggregate deposits until the amount to be paid under the guarantee reaches the amount referred to in paragraph 1.

5 The amount referred to in paragraph 1 shall be reviewed periodically by the Commission at least once every five years. If appropriate, the Commission shall submit to the European Parliament and to the Council a proposal for a Directive to adjust the amount referred to in paragraph 1, taking account in particular of developments in the banking sector and the economic and monetary situation in the Community. The first review shall not take place until five years after the end of the period referred to in Article 7(1), second subparagraph.

6 Member States shall ensure that the depositor's rights to compensation may be the subject of an action by the depositor against the deposit-guarantee scheme.   **[1051]**

Article 8

1 The limits referred to in Article 7(1), (3) and (4) shall apply to the aggregate deposits placed with the same credit institution irrespective of the number of deposits, the currency and the location within the Community.

2 The share of each depositor in a joint account shall be taken into account in calculating the limits provided for in Article 7(1), (3) and (4).

In the absence of special provisions, such an account shall be divided equally amongst the depositors.

Member States may provide that deposits in an account to which two or more persons are entitled as members of a business partnership, association or grouping of a similar nature, without legal personality, may be aggregated and treated as if made by a single depositor for the purpose of calculating the limits provided for in Article 7(1), (3) and (4).

3 Where the depositor is not absolutely entitled to the sums held in an account, the person who is absolutely entitled shall be covered by the guarantee, provided that that person has been identified or is identifiable before the date on which the competent authorities make the determination described in Article 1(3)(i) or the judicial authority makes the ruling described in Article 1(3)(ii). If there are several persons who are absolutely entitled, the share of each under the arrangements subject to which the sums are managed shall be taken into account when the limits provided for in Article 7(1), (3) and (4) are calculated.

This provision shall not apply to collective investment undertakings. **[1052]**

Article 9

1 Member States shall ensure that credit institutions make available to actual and intending depositors the information necessary for the identification of the deposit-guarantee scheme of which the institution and its branches are members within the Community or any alternative arrangement provided for in Article 3(1), second subparagraph, or Article 3(4). The depositors shall be informed of the provisions of the deposit-guarantee scheme or any alternative arrangement applicable, including the amount and scope of the cover offered by the guarantee scheme. That information shall be made available in a readily comprehensible manner.

Information shall also be given on request on the conditions for compensation and the formalities which must be completed to obtain compensation.

2 The information provided for in paragraph 1 shall be made available in the manner prescribed by national law in the official language or languages of the Member State in which the branch is established.

3 Member States shall establish rules limiting the use in advertising of the information referred to in paragraph 1 in order to prevent such use from affecting the stability of the banking system or depositor confidence. In particular, Member States may restrict such advertising to a factual reference to the scheme to which a credit institution belongs.   **[1053]**

Article 10

1 Deposit-guarantee schemes shall be in a position to pay duly verified claims by depositors in respect of unavailable deposits within three months of the date on which the competent authorities make the determination described in Article 1(3)(i) or the judicial authority makes the ruling described in Article 1(3)(ii).

2 In wholly exceptional circumstances and in special cases a guarantee scheme may apply to the competent authorities for an extension of the time limit. No such extension shall exceed three months. The competent authorities may, at the request of the guarantee scheme, grant no more than two further extensions, neither of which shall exceed three months.

3 The time limit laid down in paragraphs 1 and 2 may not be invoked by a guarantee scheme in order to deny the benefit of guarantee to any depositor who has been unable to assert his claim to payment under a guarantee in time.

4 The documents relating to the conditions to be fulfilled and the formalities to be completed to be eligible for a payment under the guarantee referred to in paragraph 1 shall be drawn up in detail in the manner prescribed by national law in the official language or languages of the Member State in which the guaranteed deposit is located.

5 Notwithstanding the time limit laid down in paragraphs 1 and 2, where a depositor or any person entitled to or interested in sums held in an account has been charged with an offence arising out of or in relation to money laundering as defined in Article 1 of Directive 91/308/EEC, the guarantee scheme may suspend any payment pending the judgment of the court.　　　　　　**[1054]**

Article 11

Without prejudice to any other rights which they may have under national law, schemes which make payments under guarantee shall have the right of subrogation to the rights of depositors in liquidation proceedings for an amount equal to their payments.　　　　　　**[1055]**

Article 12

Notwithstanding Article 3, those institutions authorised in Spain or in Greece and listed in Annex III shall be exempt from the requirement to belong to a deposit-guarantee scheme until 31 December 1999. Such credit institutions shall expressly alert their actual and intending depositors to the fact that they are not members of any deposit-guarantee scheme.

During that time, should any such credit institution establish or have established a branch in another Member State, that Member State may require that branch to belong to a deposit-guarantee scheme set up within its territory under conditions consonant with those prescribed in Article 4(2), (3) and (4).　**[1056]**

Article 13

In the list of authorised credit institutions which it is required to draw up pursuant to Article 3(7) of Directive 77/780/EEC the Commission shall indicate the status of each credit institution with regard to this Directive.　　**[1057]**

Article 14

1 The Member States shall bring into force the laws, regulations and administrative provisions necessary for them to comply with this Directive by 1 July 1995. They shall forthwith inform the Commission thereof.

When the Member States adopt these measures they shall contain a reference to this Directive or shall be accompanied by such reference on the occasion of their official publication. The methods of making such reference shall be laid down by the Member States.

2 The Member States shall communicate to the Commission the texts of the main provisions of national law which they adopt in the field governed by this Directive.   **[1058]**

Article 15

This Directive shall enter into force on the day of its publication in the *Official Journal of the European Communities*.   **[1059]**

Article 16

This Directive is addressed to the Member States.

Done at Brussels, 30 May 1994.

Annex I

List of exclusions referred to in Article 7(2)

(1) Deposits by financial institutions as defined in Article 1(6) of Directive 89/646/EEC.

(2) Deposits by insurance undertakings.

(3) Deposits by government and central administrative authorities.

(4) Deposits by provincial, regional, local and municipal authorities.

(5) Deposits by collective investment undertakings.

(6) Deposits by pension and retirement funds.

(7) Deposits by a credit institution's own directors, managers, members personally liable, holders of at least 5% of the credit institution's capital, persons responsible for carrying out the statutory audits of the credit institution's accounting documents and depositors of similar status in other companies in the same group.

(8) Deposits by close relatives and third parties acting on behalf of the depositors referred to in 7.

(9) Deposits by other companies in the same group.

(10) Non-nominative deposits.

(11) Deposits for which the depositor has, on an individual basis, obtained from the same credit institution rates and financial concessions which have helped to aggravate its financial situation.

(12) Debt securities issued by the same institution and liabilities arising out of own acceptances and promissory notes.

(13) Deposits in currencies other than:
— those of the Member States,
— ecus.

(14) Deposits by companies which are of such a size that they are not permitted to draw up abridged balance sheets pursuant to Article 11 of the Fourth Council Directive (78/660/EEC) of 25 July 1978 based on Article 54(3)(g) of the Treaty on the annual accounts of certain types of companies[1].   **[1060]**

NOTES
[1] OJ L 222, 14.8.1978, p 11. Directive as last amended by Directive 90/605/EEC (OJ L 317, 16.11.1990, p 60).

Annex II

Guiding principles

Where a branch applies to join a host Member State scheme for supplementary cover, the host Member State scheme will bilaterally establish with the home Member State scheme appropriate rules and procedures for paying compensation to depositors at that branch. The following principles shall apply both to the drawing up of those procedures and in the framing of the membership conditions applicable to such a branch (as referred to in Article 4(2))—

(a) the host Member State scheme will retain full rights to impose its objective and generally applied rules on participating credit institutions; it will be able to require the provision of relevant information and have the right to verify such information with the home Member State's competent authorities;

(b) the host Member State scheme will meet claims for supplementary compensation upon a declaration from the home Member State's competent authorities that deposits are unavailable. The host Member State scheme will retain full rights to verify a depositor's entitlement according to its own standards and procedures before paying supplementary compensation;

(c) home Member State and host Member State schemes will cooperate fully with each other to ensure that depositors receive compensation promptly and in the correct amounts. In particular, they will agree on how the existence of a counterclaim which may give rise to set-off under either scheme will affect the compensation paid to the depositor by each scheme;

(d) host Member State schemes will be entitled to charge branches for supplementary cover on an appropriate basis which takes into account the guarantee funded by the home Member State scheme. To facilitate charging, the host Member State scheme will be entitled to assume that its liability will in all circumstances be limited to the excess of the guarantee it has offered over the guarantee offered by the home Member State regardless of whether the home Member State actually pays any compensation in respect of deposits held within the host Member State's territory.   **[1061]**

Annex III

List of credit institutions mentioned in Article 12

(a) Specialised classes of Spanish institutions, the legal status of which is currently undergoing reform, authorised as:
  — Entidades de Financiación o Factoring,
  — Sociedades de Arrendamiento Financiero,
  — Sociedades de Crédito Hipotecario.

(b) The following Spanish state institutions:
  — Banco de Crédito Agrícola, SA,
  — Banco Hipotecario de España, SA,
  — Banco de Crédito Local, SA.

(c) The following Greek credit cooperatives:
  — Lamia Credit Cooperative,
  — Ioannina Credit Cooperative,
  — Xylocastron Credit Cooperative,]

as well as those of the credit cooperatives of a similar nature listed below which are authorised or in the process of being authorised on the date of the adoption of this Directive:

— Chania Credit Cooperative,
— Iraklion Credit Cooperative,
— Magnissia Credit Cooperative,
— Larissa Credit Cooperative,
— Patras Credit Cooperative,
— Thessaloniki Credit Cooperative.   **[1062]**

COMMISSION DIRECTIVE
of 31 May 1995

adapting Council Directive 89/647/EEC on a solvency ratio for credit institutions, as regards the technical definition of 'Zone A' and in respect of the weighting of asset items constituting claims carrying the explicit guarantee of the European Communities

(Text with EEA relevance)

(95/15/EC)

NOTES
Date of publication in OJ: OJ L125, 8.6.1995, p 23.

THE COMMISSION OF THE EUROPEAN COMMUNITIES

Having regard to the Treaty establishing the European Community,

Having regard to Council Directive 89/647/EEC of 18 December 1989 on a solvency ratio for credit institutions[1], as amended by Directive 92/30/EEC[2], and in particular Article 9 thereof,

Whereas the second indent of Article 2(1) of Directive 89/647/EEC defines 'Zone A' as comprising 'all the Member States and all other countries which are full members of the Organisation for Economic Cooperation and Development (OECD) as well as those countries having concluded special lending arrangements with the International Monetary Fund (IMF) associated with the Fund's General Arrangements to Borrow (GAB)';

Whereas the full membership of the OECD has been considered for the time being as the most appropriate criterion to distinguish the credit risk between countries with regard to the weighting of asset items constituting claims on or carrying the explicit guarantee of these countries;

Whereas an enlargement of the number of full members of the OECD is taking place as a consequence of a higher level of development reached by other countries together with democratic and economic freedom in line with the general principles for membership of the OECD;

Whereas it is important from a prudential supervisory point of view to maintain the creditworthiness of all countries in the 'Zone A' category; whereas for this reason an additional criterion should be included in the definition of 'Zone A'; whereas this criterion should imply that any country which rescheduled its external sovereign debt should be precluded from the 'Zone A' category for a period of five years; whereas the same additional criterion has been introduced in the Basle Capital Accord and consistency with this Accord is desirable;

Whereas the second indent of Article 9(1) of Directive 89/647/EEC provides that technical adaptations as regards amendment of the definition of 'Zone A' in Article 2 are to be adopted in accordance with the procedure laid down in Article 9(2);

Whereas, when Directive 89/647/EEC was adopted, the possibility that loans might carry the explicit guarantee of the European Communities was not foreseen; whereas, for that reason, the Directive did not expressly provide for a reduced weighting and, as a result, such assets guaranteed by the European Communities are currently assigned a weighting of 100%;

Whereas, however, points 3 and 7 of Article 6(1)(a) of Directive 89/647/EEC apply a zero weighting to asset items constituting claims on the European Communities and to asset items secured to the satisfaction of the competent authorities by collateral in the form of securities issued by the European Communities;

Whereas it is appropriate to apply a 100% weighting to asset items carrying the explicit guarantee of the European Communities and whereas a zero weighting should be applied in order to ensure consistency with points 3 and 7 of Article 6(1)(a);

Whereas the fourth indent of Article 9(1) of Directive 89/647/EEC provides that technical adaptations as regards amendment of the definitions of the assets listed in Article 6 in order to take account of developments on financial markets are to be adopted in accordance with the procedure laid down in Article 9(2);

Whereas this Directive is relevant for the European Economic Area (EEA) and the procedure laid down in Article 99 of the Agreement on the European Economic Area has been followed;

Whereas the measures provided for in this Directive are in accordance with the opinion of the Banking Advisory Committee,

NOTES
[1] OJ L386, 30.12.1989, p 14.
[2] OJ L110, 28.4.1992, p 52.

HAS ADOPTED THIS DIRECTIVE:

Article 1

In Article 2(1) of the Directive 89/647/EEC, the following sentence is added to the second indent—

> 'Any country which reschedules its external sovereign debt is, however, precluded from Zone A for a period of 5 years.'　　　　**[1063]**

Article 2

In point (a) of Article 6(1) of Directive 89/647/EEC, point 4 is replaced by the following—

'4 asset items constituting claims carrying the explicit guarantees of Zone A central governments and central banks or of the European Communities;'.   **[1064]**

Article 3

1 Member States shall bring into force the laws, regulations and administrative provisions necessary to comply with Article 1 of this Directive by 30 September 1995. They shall forthwith inform the Commission thereof.

When Member States adopt these provisions, these shall contain a reference to this Directive or shall be accompanied by such reference at the time of their official publication. The procedure for such reference shall be adopted by Member States.

2 Member States shall immediately inform the Commission of the measures taken pursuant to Article 2 of this Directive.   **[1064A]**

Article 4

This Directive shall enter into force on the 20th day following its publication in the *Official Journal of the European Communities*.

Article 5

This Directive is addressed to the Member States.

APPENDIX
EC PROPOSALS

Proposal for a European Parliament and Council Directive amending [Council Directives 89/647/EEC and 93/6/EEC] with respect to the supervisory recognition of contracts for novation and netting agreements ('contractual netting')

(94/C 142/10)

(Text with EEA relevance)

COM(94) 105 final – 94/0099(COD)

(Submitted by the Commission on 28 April 1994)

THE EUROPEAN PARLIAMENT AND THE COUNCIL OF THE EUROPEAN UNION)

Having regard to the Treaty establishing the European Community, and in particular Article 57 (2) thereof,

Having regard to the proposal from the Commission,

Having regard to the opinion of the Economic and Social Committee,

Whereas Annex II to Council Directive 89/647/EEC of 18 December 1989 on a solvency ratio for credit institutions[1], as amended by Directive 92/30/EEC[2] lays down the treatment of off-balance-sheet items concerning interest and foreign exchange rates in the framework of the calculation of capital requirements for credit institutions;

Whereas this Directive is in accordance with the work of another international forum of banking supervisors on the supervisory recognition of bilateral netting, notably the possibility of calculating the own funds requirements for certain transactions on the basis of a net instead of a gross amount provided that legally binding agreements exist which ensure that the credit risk is confined to the net amount;

Whereas the rules envisaged for the supervisory recognition of netting at the wider international level will lead to the possibility of reducing the capital requirements for internationally active credit institutions and groups of credit institutions in a wide range of countries whose credit institutions compete with Community credit institutions;

[Whereas the effect of the rules envisaged for the recognition of netting will be to reduce the level of credit institutions' compulsory cover through their own funds;]

Whereas[, however,] for credit institutions incorporated in the Member States, only an amendment of Directive 89/647/EEC can open a similar possibility for the supervisory recognition of bilateral netting and thereby provide them with equal conditions of competition; whereas the rules are both well balanced and suited to further reinforce the application of prudential supervisory measures to the sector of credit institutions;

Whereas, having regard to this situation, this Directive is in line with the principle of subsidiarity, since the aim of this Directive is achievable only by a harmonised amendment of existing Community legislation,

[Whereas Member States in which the validity of 'contractual netting' is not yet legally recognised should introduce the provisions needed to ensure such recognition as soon as possible;]

NOTES
[1] OJ L 386, 30. 12. 1989, p 14.
[2] OJ L 110, 28. 4. 1992, p 52, as rectified in OJ L 280, 24. 9. 1992, p 59.

Words in square brackets inserted or substituted by the Amended proposal for a European Parliament and Council Directive amending Council Directives 89/647/EEC and 93/6/EEC with respect to the supervisory recognition of contracts for novation and netting agreements ('contractual netting'), OJ C 142, 25. 5. 1994, p 8.

HAVE ADOPTED THIS DIRECTIVE:

Article 1

Annex II to Directive 89/647/EEC is replaced by the Annex hereto.

[To Annex II, point 5, first subparagraph of Directive 93/6/EEC1 the following sentence shall be added:

'Competent authorities shall mean the national authorities which are empowered by law or regulation to supervise investment firms.']   **[1065]**

NOTES
 ¹ OJ L 141, 11. 6. 1993, p 1.

Words in square brackets inserted by the Amended proposal for a European Parliament and Council Directive amending Council Directives 89/647/EEC and 93/6/EEC with respect to the supervisory recognition of contracts for novation and netting agreements ('contractual netting'), OJ C 142, 25. 5. 1994, p 8.

Article 2

Article 1 leaves without prejudice the supervisory recognition of bilateral contracts for novation which have been concluded before the entry into force of the laws, regulations and administrative provisions necessary for the implementation of this Directive. **[1066]**

Article 3

1 Member States shall bring into force the laws, regulations and administrative provisions necessary to comply with this Directive by 31 December [1995] at the latest. [They shall forthwith inform the Commission of the fact of the enactment of these provisions.]

When Member States adopt these measures, these shall contain a reference to this Directive or shall be accompanied by such reference at the time of their official publication. The procedure for such reference shall be adopted by Member States.

2 Member States shall communicate to the Commission the text of the main provisions of national law which they adopt in the field covered by this Directive.   **[1067]**

NOTE
  Words in square brackets inserted or substituted by the Amended proposal for a European Parliament and Council Directive amending Council Directives 89/647/EEC and 93/6/EEC with respect to the supervisory recognition of contracts for novation and netting agreements ('contractual netting'), OJ C 142, 25. 5. 1994, p 8.

Article 4

This Directive shall enter into force on the 20th day following that of its publication in the *Official Journal of the European Communities*.   **[1068]**

Article 5

This Directive is addressed to the Member States.

ANNEX

ANNEX II

THE TREATMENT OF OFF-BALANCE-SHEET ITEMS CONCERNING INTEREST AND FOREIGN EXCHANGE/RATES

1   SCOPE AND CHOICE OF THE METHOD

Subject to the consent of their [competent] authorities, credit institutions may choose one of the methods set out below to measure the risks associated with the transactions listed in Annex III. Interest-rate and foreign-exchange contracts traded on recognised exchanges where they are subject to daily margin requirements and foreign-exchange contracts with an original maturity of 14 calendar days or less are excluded.

2 METHODS

Method 1: the 'marking to market' approach

Step (a): by attaching current market values to contracts (marking to market) the current replacement cost of all contracts with positive values is obtained.

Step (b): to obtain a figure for potential future credit exposures[1], the notional principal amounts or values underlying an institution's aggregate books are multiplied by the following percentages:

NOTES
[1] Except in the case of single-currency 'floating/floating interest rate swaps' in which only the current replacement cost will be calculated.

Words in square brackets substituted by the Amended proposal for a European Parliament and Council Directive amending Council Directives 89/647/EEC and 93/6/EEC with respect to the supervisory recognition of contracts for novation and netting agreements ('contractual netting'), OJ C 142, 25. 5. 1994, p 8.

Table 1

Residual maturity	Interest-rate contracts	Foreign-exchange contracts
One year or less	0%	1%
More than one year	0,5%	5%

Step (c): the sum of current replacement cost and potential future credit exposure is multiplied by the risk weightings allocated to the relevant counterparties in Article 6.

Method 2: the 'original exposure' approach

Step (a): the notional principal amount of each instrument is multiplied by the percentages given below:

Table 2

Original maturity[1]	Interest-rate contracts	Foreign-exchange contracts
One year or less	0,5%	2%
More than one year but not exceeding two years	1%	5%
Additional allowance for each additional year	1%	3%

NOTES
[1] In the case of interest-rate contracts, credit institutions may, subject to the consent of their [competent] authorities, choose either original or residual maturity.

Words in square brackets in footnote above substituted by the Amended proposal for a European Parliament and Council Directive amending Council Directives 89/647/EEC and 93/6/EEC with respect to the supervisory recognition of contracts for novation and netting agreements ('contractual netting'), OJ C 142, 25. 5. 1994, p 8.

Step (b): the original exposure thus obtained is multiplied by the risk weightings allocated to the relevant counterparties in Article 6.

3 CONTRACTS FOR NOVATION AND NETTING AGREEMENTS ('CONTRACTUAL NETTING')

(a) Supervisory acknowledgeable types of netting

The [competent] authorities may recognise as risk reducing the following types of contracts for novation and netting agreements—

    (i) bilateral contracts for novation between a credit institution and its counter-party under which mutual claims and obligations are automatically amalgamated in such a way that this novation fixes one single net amount and thus creates a legally binding, single new contract extinguishing the former contracts;

    (ii) other bilateral netting agreements between the credit institution and its counterparty.

['Counter party' shall mean any entity (including natural persons) having the power to conclude a contractual netting agreement.]

    (b) Conditions for the recognition

The [competent] authorities may recognise as risk reducing a contract for novation or a netting agreement under the following conditions only—

    (i) the credit institution has a contract for novation or a netting agreement with its counterparty which creates a single legal obligation, covering all included transactions, such that, in the event of a counterparty's failure to perform due to default, bankruptcy or liquidation, the credit institution would have a claim or obligation, respectively, to receive or pay only the net value of the sum of unrealised gains and losses on included transactions;

    (ii) the credit institution has [arranged to show clearly and precisely to the competent authority the list of written and reasoned legal opinions available to the authority that, in the event of a legal challenge,] the relevant Courts and administrative authorities would find that in the cases described under (i) the claims and obligations of the credit institution to be confined to the net value as described in (b)(i) above under—

      —the law of the jurisdiction in which the counterparty is incorporated and if a foreign branch of an undertaking is involved, then also under the law of the jurisdiction in which the branch is located,

      —the law that governs the individual transactions included, and

      —the law that governs any contract or agreement necessary to effect the contract for novation or the netting agreement;

    (iii) the credit institution has procedures in place to ensure that the legal validity of contracts for novation and netting agreements are kept under review in the light of possible changes in relevant laws.

      [The competent authorities may accept reasoned legal opinions drawn up by group or types of contractual netting.]

      The [competent] authorities, after consultation when necessary with other relevant supervisory authorities, must be satisfied that the contractual netting is legally valid under the law of each of the relevant jurisdictions. If one of these supervisory authorities is not convinced of the legal validity of the contractual netting under the law of its country the relevant contract for novation or the relevant netting agreement may not be recognised as risk reducing for either of the counterparties.

      Contracts containing a walkaway clause shall not be recognised as risk reducing

      With respect to a smooth functioning of the single market, Member States are obliged to strive for a uniform assessment of the agreements for contractual netting by their competent authorities. [Such action by the competent authorities must not be responsible for distorting competition.]

(c)   Effects of the recognition

(i)   Contracts for novation:

The single net amount fixed by contracts for novation may be weighted, rather than the gross amounts involved. Thus, in application of method 1 for;

—Step (a): the current replacement cost,
—Step (b): the notional principal amounts or values underlying an institution's aggregate books,

may be obtained taking account of the contract for novation. In application of method 2 for step (a) the notional principal amount may be calculated taking account of the contract for novation; the percentages of table 2 apply.

(ii)   Other netting agreements

In application of method 1 for step (a) the current replacement cost for the contracts included in a netting agreement may be obtained by taking account of the actual hypothetical net replacement cost which result from the agreement. For step (b): the netting agreement may only be taken into account for foreign-exchange contracts and other similar contracts, in which notional principal is equivalent to cash flows, in cases where the amounts to be claimed or delivered fall due on the same value date and in the same currency.

In application of method 2 for step (a)

—or foreign-exchange contracts and other similar contracts, in which notional principal is equivalent to cash flows, in cases where the amounts to be claimed or delivered fall due on the same value date and in the same currency, the notional principal amount may be calculated taking account of the netting agreement; to all these contracts table 2 applies,

—or all other contracts included in a netting agreement, the applicable percentages may be reduced as indicated in table 3:

Table 3

Original maturity[1]	Interest-rate contracts	Foreign-exchange contracts
One year or less	0,35%	1,50%
More than one year but not exceeding two years	0,75%	3,75%
Additional allowance for each additional year	0,75%	2,25%

NOTES
[1] In the case of interest-rate contracts, credit institutions may, subject to the consent of their supervisory authorities, choose either original or residual maturity.'

Words in square brackets inserted or substituted by the Amended proposal for a European Parliament and Council Directive amending Council Directives 89/647/EEC and 93/6/EEC with respect to the supervisory recognition of contracts for novation and netting agreements ('contractual netting'), OJ C 142, 25. 5. 1994, p 8.   **[1069]**

MODIFIED PROPOSAL FOR A EUROPEAN PARLIAMENT AND COUNCIL DIRECTIVE ON [EU] CREDIT TRANSFERS

(94/C 360/11)

(Text with EEA relevance)

COM(94) 436 final – 94/0242(COD)

(Submitted by the Commission on 18 November 1994)

THE EUROPEAN PARLIAMENT AND THE COUNCIL OF THE EUROPEAN UNION,

Having regard to the Treaty establishing the European Community, and in particular Article 100a thereof,
Having regard to the proposal from the Commission,
Having regard to the opinion of the Economic and Social Committee,
Having regard to the opinion of the European Monetary Institute,
In accordance with the procedure laid down in Article 189b of the Treaty,
Whereas the volume of remote cross-border payments is growing steadily as the completion of the internal market and the progressive move towards full economic and monetary union lead to greater trade flows and movement of people throughout the Community; whereas [EU] credit transfers account for a substantial part of the volume and the value of remote cross-border payments;
Whereas it is of paramount importance for individuals and businesses to be able to make credit transfers rapidly, reliably, and cheaply from one part of the Community to another; whereas a market in which there is competition for [EU] credit transfers should lead to improved services and reduced prices;
Whereas this Directive intends to follow up the progress towards the liberalisation of capital movements reached during stages 1 [and 2] of Economic and Monetary Union; whereas it takes account of the purpose of facilitating the use of the ecu . . .; whereas it is conceived as a step towards the progressive implementation of Economic and Monetary Union; whereas its provisions should apply to credit transfers in [the currencies of the Member States and the ecu];
Whereas this Directive is intended to implement one aspect of the programme of work drawn up by the Commission following its Green Paper 'Making payments in the internal market';
Whereas the Commission has recommended to the Member States that the threshold below which crossborder payments should not have to be reported should be fixed at not less than ecu 10 000;
Whereas the Committee of Governors of the central banks of the Member States recommended that payment systems in all Member States should have a sound legal basis; whereas the Commission has set up a working group on the legal framework for cross-border payments, which consists of legal experts of governments and of the EMI; whereas this group has advised the Commission that the issues covered by this Directive may be dealt with separately from the systemic issues which remain under consideration; whereas it may be necessary to make a further proposal to cover these systemic issues, principally settlement finality;
Whereas the purpose of this Directive is to improve [EU] credit transfer services and thus assist the EMI in its task of promoting the efficiency of cross-border payments with a view to the preparation of the third stage of economic and monetary union;
Whereas, having regard to the third paragraph of Article 3b of the Treaty, this Directive lays down the minimum requirements needed to ensure an adequate level of customer information; whereas greater transparency is ultimately dependent on institutions' adherence to minimum performance requirements; whereas this Directive lays down the minimum performance requirements which institutions offering [EU] credit transfer services should adhere to; whereas this Directive fulfils the . . . principles set out in Commission recommendation 90/109/EEC[1]; whereas it is without prejudice to Council Directive 91/308/EEC of 10 June 1991 on prevention of the use of the financial system for the purpose of money laundering[2];
Whereas the nature of [EU] credit transfers, being a series of operations involving institutions in different Member States, is such that a coordinated approach at Community level is appropriate and necessary; whereas a self-regulatory approach has been attempted by the Commission by its recommendation 90/109/EEC; whereas this voluntary approach has not achieved the desired results; whereas a binding measure is therefore appropriate;

Whereas this Directive should apply to [EU] credit transfers for any amount; whereas institutions should be under an obligation to refund in the case of a non-completed transfer;

[Whereas an independent complaints and redress procedure relating to the areas covered by the present directive should be available to afford the customer better protection; whereas such procedure should be established at Member State level, with the minimum cost, using existing procedures where available;]

Whereas the European Parliament, in its resolution of 12 February 1993, called for a Council Directive to lay down rules in the area of transparency and performance of cross-border payments;

Whereas the Economic and Social Committee, in its opinion of 6 July 1994, stated a preference for a code of good conduct; whereas the Commission has previously pursued this approach; whereas the Economic and Social Committee advised that, if a directive were to be proposed, it should be limited to setting out a general framework; whereas this Directive follows this model, by allowing a large measure of freedom of contract,

NOTES
[1] OJ L 67, 15. 3. 1990, p 39.
[2] OJ L 166, 28. 6. 1991, p 77.

Words in square brackets substituted or inserted, and words omitted repealed, by the Amended proposal for a European Parliament and Council Directive on EU Credit Transfers.

HAVE ADOPTED THIS DIRECTIVE:

SECTION I

Scope and definitions

Article 1

Scope

1 Member States shall apply the requirements of this Directive to credit institutions and to other institutions which supply [EU] credit transfer services to the public as part of their business.

2 This Directive shall apply to [EU] credit transfers in [the currencies of the Member States and] the ecu, and for any amount. **[1070]**

NOTE
Words in square brackets substituted or inserted by the Amended proposal for a European Parliament and Council Directive on EU Credit Transfers.

Article 2

Definitions

For the purpose of this Directive:

(a) 'credit institution' shall mean an institution as defined in Article 1 of Council Directive 77/780/EEC[3]; for the purposes of this Directive, branches of credit institutions in different Member States are deemed to be separate institutions;

(b) 'other institution' shall mean any legal person, other than a credit institution, that supplies to the public, by way of business, [EU] credit transfer services;

(c) 'institution' shall mean a credit institution or other institution;

(d) 'person' shall mean either a legal or a natural person, as the context may require;

(e) 'payment' shall mean the transfer by an originator of a monetary claim on a party acceptable to the beneficiary, including cases where the originator and the beneficiary are the same person;

(f) 'cross-border payment' shall mean a payment by an originator whose account, from which the payment is made, is held by an institution or its branch in one Member State, to be made available to a beneficiary at an institution or its branch in another Member State;

(g) 'originator' shall mean a person that authorises the making of a [EU] credit transfer to a beneficiary;

(h) 'beneficiary' shall mean the final recipient of a [EU] credit transfer;

(i) 'customer' shall mean the originator or the beneficiary, as the context may require, and may be one and the same person;

(j) 'payment order' shall mean an instruction in any form, given direct to an institution, to place at the disposal of a beneficiary a fixed or determinable amount of money.

(k) '[EU] credit transfer' shall mean a cross-border payment, consisting of a series of operations beginning with the originator's payment order. The term includes any payment order issued by the originator's institution or any intermediary institution intended to carry out the originator's payment order;

(l) *'force majeure'* [shall mean unusual and unforeseeable circumstances beyond the control of the party by whom it is pleaded, the consequences of which could not have been avoided even if all due care has been exercised (indent (ii) of the second subparagraph of Article 4 (6) of Council Directive 90/314/EEC[4])]

(m) 'interest' [shall mean the rate which the institution would apply to its customer's account, for the relevant period, if that customer's account were then overdrawn];

(n) 'value date' shall mean the date on which the customer's account is debited (for originators) or credited (for beneficiaries) such date being that applied by the institution of the customer for the purpose of calculating interest (if any) on the account or assessing the availability of funds, where interest is not an appropriate criterion;

(o) 'acceptance' shall mean the acceptance by an institution of a payment order, upon fulfilment of the institution's conditions as to the availability of financial cover and the identification of the parties named in the payment order and any other pre-conditions agreed by the parties;

(p) 'completion' of a [EU] credit transfer shall mean acceptance by the beneficiary's institution;

(q) 'intermediary institution' shall mean an institution which is neither that of the originator nor that of the beneficiary [and which participates in the execution of an EU credit transfer];

(r) 'business day' in relation to any particular institution shall mean a day, or part of a day, on which that institution is open for the processing of [EU] credit transfers.

NOTES
[3] OJ L 322, 17. 12. 1977, p 30.
[4] OJ L 158, 23. 6. 1990, p 59.

Words in square brackets substituted or inserted by the Amended proposal for a European Parliament and Council Directive on EU Credit Transfers.

SECTION II

Transparency of conditions for [EU] credit transfers

Article 3

Information prior to a [EU] credit transfer (made or received)

The institution shall supply its customers with clear [and readily comprehensible] written information [including, where appropriate by electronic means,] about the services it provides to effect or receive [EU] credit transfers. This information shall [at least] include:

—an indication of the time needed for the funds to be credited to the account of the beneficiary's institution or to the beneficiary, as appropriate,

—the basis of the calculation[, including the rates,] of any commission [fees] and charges payable by the customer to the institution, [including any taxes applied,]

[—an indication of the exchange rate references used,]

—the value date, if any, applicable by the institution,

—a reference to the redress [and complaints] procedures available to the customer and the method of gaining access to them.   **[1072]**

NOTES
   Words in square brackets substituted or inserted by the Amended proposal for a European Parliament and Council Directive on EU Credit Transfers.

Article 4

Information subsequent to a [EU] credit transfer (made or received)

The institution shall supply its customers with clear [and readily comprehensible] written information[, including, where appropriate, by electronic means,] subsequent to their making or receiving a [EU] credit transfer. This information shall at least include:

—a reference enabling its customer to identify the payment,

—the [commission fees and] charges payable by its customer. Where the originator has authorised a deduction from the amount of a [EU] credit transfer, this fact and the original amount of the [EU] credit transfer should be stated by the beneficiary's bank to the beneficiary,

—the value date, if any, applied by the institution.   **[1073]**

NOTES
   Words in square brackets substituted or inserted by the Amended proposal for a European Parliament and Council Directive on EU Credit Transfers.

SECTION III

Minimum obligations of institutions in respect of [EU] credit transfers

Article 5

Obligation to execute in good time

1 Each institution having accepted a payment order shall execute the related [EU] credit transfer within the time scale agreed with the customer (or institution) making the payment order. In the absence of a specific agreement, [each institution shall act as fast as possible and, in that event,] the following obligations shall apply:

—the institution of the originator shall be responsible to the originator for ensuring that the [EU] credit transfer is completed no later than the end of the fifth business day following acceptance by it of the payment order from the originator, and

—the institution of the beneficiary shall be obliged to place the amount of the [EU] credit transfer at the disposal of the beneficiary, at the latest by the end of the business day following completion of the [EU] credit transfer.

2 The originator's institution shall compensate the originator by the payment of interest on the amount of the [EU] credit transfer where it is completed late, but shall not be liable for consequential losses under this Directive. [Where the originator's institution is not responsible for the delay, it may claim from the institution that caused the delay the amount it was required to pay out as interest.] No compensation shall be payable where the originator's bank can establish that the delay was attributable to the originator.

3 In addition to the obligation of execution in paragraph 1, the beneficiary's institution shall compensate the beneficiary by the payment of interest on the amount of the [EU] credit transfer where it is late in [placing such amount] at the beneficiary's disposal.

[1074]

NOTES

Words in square brackets substituted or inserted by the Amended proposal for a European Parliament and Council Directive on EU Credit Transfers.

Article 6

Obligation to execute in accordance with the instructions contained in the payment order

1 The originator's institution, any intermediary institution and the beneficiary's institution, once they have accepted the payment order, shall each be obliged to execute the related [EU] credit transfer for the full amount thereof unless authorised [by the originator] to make a deduction therefrom. Without prejudice to the duty not to deduct, the beneficiary's institution may, where appropriate, levy an additional charge on the beneficiary relating to the administration of his account. However, any such additional administrative charge shall not exceed the charge that would be made for a domestic credit transfer.

2 Where a breach of the duty to execute in accordance with the payment order as described in paragraph 1 has been caused by any institution other than the beneficiary's institution, and without prejudice to any other claim which might be made, the institution of the originator shall be liable to credit to the [beneficiary] any sum wrongly deducted by any institution, at its own cost. Alternatively, if [requested] to do so by the originator it shall transfer such amount to [his credit], free of all deductions, at its own cost. Any intermediary institution making a deduction in breach of the duty in paragraph 1 shall be liable to credit the sum so deducted to the institution of the [beneficiary]. Alternatively, if [requested] by the institution of the originator, it shall transfer such amount, free of all deductions, to the [originator's institution], at its own cost.

3 Where a breach of the duty to execute in accordance with the payment order has been caused by the beneficiary's institution, and without prejudice to any other claim which may be made, the beneficiary's institution shall be liable to credit to the beneficiary, at its own cost, any sum wrongly deducted.

[1075]

NOTES

Words in square brackets substituted or inserted by the Amended proposal for a European Parliament and Council Directive on EU Credit Transfers.

Article 7

Obligation of institutions to refund in case of non-completed [EU] credit transfers

1 If, after a payment order has been accepted by the originator's institution, the related [EU] credit transfer is not . . . completed, and without prejudice to any other claim which may be made, the originator is entitled to have his account credited [at his request] with the full amount of the [EU] credit transfer [up to ecu 10 000] plus interest and the amount of the charges for the non-completed [EU] credit transfer, [15 business days after such request. This request may not be introduced before the expiry of the timescale set out in article 5, paragraph 1.] Each intermediary institution which has accepted the payment order likewise owes an obligation to refund at its own cost the amount of the [EU] credit transfer to the institution which instructed it.

2 If the non-completion of the [EU] credit transfer was caused by defective instructions given by the originator to his institution, the originator's institution and the other institutions involved shall use their best endeavours to make the refund referred to in paragraph 1. [The institutions are not obliged in this case to refund the interest accruing.]

[**3** Paragraph 1 is without prejudice to the possibility for Member States to provide for an obligation to refund non-completed EU credit transfers, for amounts exceeding ecu 10 000.] **[1076]**

NOTES
  Words in square brackets substituted or inserted, words omitted repealed, and para 3 substituted, by the Amended proposal for a European Parliament and Council Directive on EU Credit Transfers.

[Article 7a

Institutions may be exempt from the provisions of the present Directive to the extent that they can invoke reasons of *force majeure* pertinent to such provisions.] **[1077]**

NOTES
  Inserted by the Amended proposal for a European Parliament and Council Directive on EU Credit Transfers.

[Article 7b

1 Any institution involved in a EU credit transfer shall take a decision without delay on complaints by customers.

2 If a complaint has not been remedied or a decision has not been taken on it within four weeks, complainants may approach one of the independent complaints offices to be set up for this purpose by the Member States.

3 A list of addresses of such offices shall be available at all institutions carrying out EU credit transfers.] **[1078]**

NOTES
  Inserted by the Amended proposal for a European Parliament and Council Directive on EU Credit Transfers.

SECTION IV

Final provisions

Article 8

Implementation

1 Member States shall bring into force the laws, regulations and administrative provisions necessary to comply with this Directive before 31 December 1996 at the latest. They shall forthwith inform the Commission thereof.

When Member States adopt these provisions, these shall contain a reference to this Directive or shall be accompanied by such reference at the time of their official publication. The procedure for such reference shall be adopted by Member States.

2 Member States shall communicate to the Commission the text of the main provisions of national law which they adopt in the field governed by this Directive. In this Communication Member States shall provide a table of correspondence showing the national provisions which exist or are introduced in respect of each Article of this Directive.

[1079]

Article 9

Report to the European Parliament and the Council

No later than 31 December 1999, the Commission shall present a report to the European Parliament and the Council on the application of this Directive, accompanied where appropriate by proposals for its revision. **[1080]**

Article 10

Entry into force

This Directive shall enter into force on the 20th day following its publication in the Official Journal of the European Communities. **[1081]**

Article 11

Addresses

This Directive is addressed to the Member States. **[1082]**

INDEX

Bank of England—*continued*
accounts, authorised institution,
  requirements, [68], [655C], [803],
  [810], [831], [832]
  see also **Accountant; Accounts**
acquisitions—
  large exposures, notice, [807]
advertisement by authorised institution for
  deposit—
  direction, [52]
auditor, accounts, authorised institution—
  relationship with, [655C], [831]
  report, matters on which required,
    [655C], [831]
  see also **Advertisement**
authorised institution, powers re, generally
  see **Authorised Institution**
bad faith—
  damages, liability, extent, [18]
bankers' books, production to court—
  bank not party to proceedings—
    not compellable witness, [6]
Board of Banking Supervision—
  duty to establish, [19]
  see also **Board of Banking**
    Supervision
connected lending, notice, [803]
consent to Banking Act 1987 proceedings,
  [114]
consolidated supervision, credit institution,
  notice, [825]
country debt provisioning (the new
  matrix)—
  banking Supervision Division letter,
    [824]
Court of Directors, [18]
damages, liability, extent, [18]
definition, Banking Act 1987, [9], [122]–
  [124]
Deposit Protection Fund, investment *see*
  Deposit Protection Fund
Director—
  Board of Banking Supervision,
    membership, [19]
disclosure, powers to require, [60], [103]–
  [108]
  see also **Disclosure**
documents, production to, [60], [694]
  see also **Documents**
duties, generally, [18]
entry to premises to obtain document/
  information—
  right, [61]
  warrant—
    constable, when suspected
      contravention, [64]
European authorised institution—
  powers re—
    documents, production, [693]
    information, to obtain, [693]
    investigation, [693]

Bank of England—*continued*
European authorised institution—*continued*
  powers re—*continued*
    non-urgent case—
      notice of prohibition/restriction,
        [690]
    prohibitions, [690]
    restrictions, [690]
    statement of principles, [690], [826]–
      [828]
    urgent case—
      notice of prohibitions/restrictions,
        [690]
  recognition—
    duty to prepare for supervision, [672]
    information from supervisory
      authority—
      prohibition/restriction, [676]
    limitation, powers, [675]
    obligation.institution ceasing to be
      European institution, [677]
    prohibition, acceptance, deposit,
      power, [673]
    restriction, listed activities, power,
      [674]
false and misleading information to,
  offence, [112]
foreign currency exposures, notice, [801]
foreign currency options, notice, [804]
functions, [18]
information required to be given to,
  [55]–[59], [694]
injunction application—
  Banking Act 1987 contravention,
    likelihood, [111]
internal control systems, authorised
  institution, notice, [832]
investigative powers—
  deposits with authorised institution—
    appointment, investigator, [62]
    contraventions, suspected, [64]
    entry, powers—
      contravention, suspected, [64]
    obstruction, offence, [65]
liquidity, measurement, notice, [802]
loan transfers and securitisation, notice,
  [814]
mergers—
  large exposures, notice, [807]
money laundering—
  Banking Supervision Division letter,
    [815]
    see also **Money Laundering**
note issuance facilities, paper, [805]
notices, [55]–[59], [801]–[838]
off-balance-sheet risks, notice, [805]
own funds, credit institution, notice—
  implementation, EC directive, [819]
reasonable grounds for suspicion—
  contravention, deposit-taking regulation,
    investigation, [63]

Minor—*continued*
contract, party—
  generally, [333]–[336]
  inapplicable legislation, [333]
  unenforceable—
    restitution, other party, [335]
guarantee by—
  unenforceable, [334]
meaning, [333]
Misrepresentation
damages—
  misrepresentation not fraudulent, [308]
exclusion of liability—
  avoidance, contractual term purporting, [309]
generally, [307]–[311]
innocent—
  rescission of contract—
    removal, bars, [307]
Money Laundering
accounting records, authorised institutions—
  reports, [817]
Bank of England Banking Supervision Division—
  letter to authorised institutions, [815]
Basle Statement of Principles, [813], [817], [1004A]
Committee on Banking Regulation and Supervisory Practices—
  letter to authorised institutions, [813], [815]
control systems, reports, [815], [817]
Conventions, relevant, to which EC member states signatory, [817]
deposit protection regulations—
  exemption from protection, deposit in course of money laundering, [81]
drug trafficking, association, [813], [815], [817]
EC directive—
  criminal sanctions, [817]
  generally, [988]–[1004]
Joint Money Laundering Working Group—
  letter to authorised institutions, [817]
meaning, [81]
terrorist funds, [813]
transaction, meaning, [81]
Money Market Accounts
advertisement, Code of Conduct, [818]
Moratorium
country debt provisioning, [824]
Mortgage
aircraft—
  bankruptcy, unaffected by, [725]
  discharge, [720]
  generally, [712]–[729]
  priority, [725]
  register—
    amendment, [719]
    copies of entries, [722]

Mortgage—*continued*
aircraft—*continued*
  register—*continued*
    inspection, [722]
    notice of facts appearing, as, [724]
    rectification, [719]
    registration, [715]–[719]
    UK nationality register—
      removal from, [723]
mortgagee *see* **Mortgagee**
priority—
  merchant ship, [408]–[413]
ship, merchant—
  discharge—
    entry in register, [408]–[413], [729G]
  form, [729B]
  generally, [406]–[413]
  priority, [408]–[413], [729D]
  registration, [408]–[413], [729C]
  termination, registration, effect, [729H]
  transfer, [408]–[413]
  transmission, interest, [408]–[413], [729E]
Mortgagee
merchant ship or share—
  intending—
    notices, [729D]
  registered—
    power of sale, [408]–[413]
    protection, [403]–[413]
Multilateral Development Banks
solvency ratio, credit institution and adaptation, definition, [1042]–[1044]
Multilateral Investment Guarantee Agency
arbitration—
  documents, production, [452]
  enforcement, award, [450]
  generally, [455]
  registration, award, [450], [451]
  witnesses, attendance, [452]
archives, inviolability, [455]
assets, [455]
capital, subscribed, [455]
description as bank, [90]
disputes procedure—
  Agency and members, [455]
establishment, [447], [455]
generally, [447]–[455]
immunities, [449]
legal process, [455]
meaning, [121], [124]
payments from/to, [448]
privileges, [449]
Sponsorship Trust Fund, [455]
status, [449], [455]
structure, [455]
taxation etc, immunity, [455]
waiver—
  immunities and privileges, [455]